Hall
ANF

HUMAN RESOURCE MANAGEMENT

Fourth Edition

R. WAYNE MONDY, SPHR
McNeese State University

ROBERT M. NOE, SPHR
East Texas State University

In Collaboration With

SHANE R. PREMEAUX, PHR
McNeese State University

ARTHUR SHARPLIN
McNeese State University

HARRY N. MILLS, JR., SPHR
East Texas State University

ALLYN AND BACON
Boston • London • Sydney • Toronto

To My Daughters:
Alyson Lynn and Marianne Elizabeth
RWM

To
Judy Lynne Noe
RMN

Series Editor *Jack Peters*
Editorial-Production Service *York Production Services*
In-house Production Coordinator *Peter Petraitis*
Cover Coordinator *Linda Dickinson*
Manufacturing Buyer *Bill Alberti*

Copyright © 1990, 1987, 1984, 1981 by Allyn and Bacon, A Division of Simon & Schuster, Inc., 160 Gould Street, Needham Heights, Massachusetts 02194. All rights reserved. No part of the material protected by this copyright notice may be reproduced or utilized in any form or by any means, electronic or mechanical, including photocopying, recording, or by any information storage and retrieval system, without written permission from the copyright owner.

Library of Congress Cataloging-in-Publication Data

Mondy, R. Wayne, 1940–
    Human resource management / R. Wayne Mondy, Robert M. Noe, in collaboration with Shane R. Premeaux, Arthur Sharplin, Harry N. Mills, Jr. — 4th ed.
      p.   cm.
    Rev. ed. of: Personnel, the management of human resources. 3rd ed. ©1987.

    Includes bibliographical references.
    ISBN 0-205-12121-7
    1. Personnel management—United States. 2. Personnel management. I. Noe, Robert M. II. Mondy, R. Wayne, 1940– Personnel, the management of human resources. III. Title.
HF5549.2.U5M66   1990
658.3—dc20   89-17686
                                                                 CIP

Printed in the United States of America

10 9 8 7 6 5 4 3 2 1   95 94 93 92 91 90

CONTENTS

Preface ix

P·A·R·T O·N·E

INTRODUCTION 1

CHAPTER 1
Human Resource Management: An Overview 2

Human Resource Management and the Human Resource Manager 4
Executive Insights: Kathryn D. McKee 6
Human Resource Management Functions 8
The Evolution of Human Resource Management 12
The Changing World of the Chief Human Resource Officer 13
Human Resource Executives, Generalists, and Specialists 15
HRM In Action 16
The Human Resource Function in Organizations of Various Sizes 17
Professionalization of Human Resource Management 17
Ethics and Human Resource Management 23
Scope of This Book 25
Summary 27
Questions for Review 28
Terms for Review 28
Incident 1: A Day to Remember 29
Incident 2: Learn What They Really Want 30
Experiencing Human Resource Management 31
References 31
Appendix: Professional Accreditation 33

CHAPTER 2
The Environment of Human Resource Management 38

Environmental Factors Affecting Human Resource Management 40
The External Environment 41
Executive Insights: Robert L. Berra 42
The Internal Environment 54
HRM In Action 56
Environmental Factors Affecting Multinational Corporations 57
Summary 63
Questions for Review 65
Terms for Review 65
Incident 1: A Japanese View of the Trade Imbalance 66
Incident 2: Getting By? 67
Experiencing Human Resource Management 68
References 69

CHAPTER 3
Equal Employment Opportunity and Affirmative Action 72

Equal Employment Opportunity: An Overview 74
Laws Affecting Equal Employment Opportunity 74
Executive Insights: Gayla S. Godfrey 76
Executive Order 11246, as Amended by EO 11375 79
Significant U.S. Supreme Court Decisions 80
HRM In Action 81
Equal Employment Opportunity Commission 86

iii

Uniform Guidelines for Employee Selection
Procedures 88
Additional Guidelines 90
Affirmative Action Programs 93
Implications for Multinational Corporations 99
Summary 100
Questions for Review 102
Terms for Review 102
Incident 1: So, What's Affirmative Action? 102
Incident 2: Retire? 103
Experiencing Human Resource Management 104
References 105

CHAPTER 4
Job Analysis 106

Job Analysis: A Basic Human Resource Tool 108
Reasons for Conducting Job Analysis 109
Types of Job Analysis Information 111
Job Analysis Methods 111
Executive Insights: Walter W. Tornow 112
Conducting Job Analysis 118
Job Description 118
HRM In Action 121
Other Job Analysis Methods 121
Job Specification 120
Job Analysis and the Law 130
Job Design 131
Summary 133
Questions for Review 134
Terms for Review 134
Incident 1: Who Needs Job Descriptions? 135
Incident 2: A Job Well Done 136
Experiencing Human Resource Management 137
References 138

Part One Case—Parma Cycle Company: An Overview 139

P·A·R·T T·W·O

HUMAN RESOURCE PLANNING, RECRUITMENT, AND SELECTION 143

CHAPTER 5
Human Resource Planning 144

The Human Resource Planning Process 146

Executive Insights: James G. Parkel 147
Terminology of Forecasting 149
Human Resource Forecasting Techniques 150
HRM In Action 151
Forecasting Human Resource Requirements 153
Forecasting Human Resource Availability 154
Surplus of Employees 158
Human Resource Planning: An Example 159
Human Resource Information Systems 162
Summary 166
Questions for Review 167
Terms for Review 167
Incident 1: A Degree for Meter Readers? 168
Incident 2: A Busy Day 169
Experiencing Human Resource Management 170
References 171

CHAPTER 6
Recruitment 172

The Recruitment Process 174
Alternatives to Recruitment 175
External Environment of Recruitment 178
Internal Environment of Recruitment 179
Methods Used in Internal Recruitment 180
External Sources of Recruitment 181
External Methods of Recruitment 185
Executive Insights: Susan J. Marks 188
Tailoring Recruitment Methods to Sources 194
HRM In Action 196
Recruitment Under the Law 196
Summary 199
Questions for Review 200
Terms for Review 201
Incident 1: Right Idea, Wrong Song 201
Incident 2: Time to Do Something 202
Experiencing Human Resource Management 203
References 204

CHAPTER 7
Selection 206

The Selection Process 208
Environmental Factors Affecting the Selection Process 209
Executive Insights: Charles E. Brown 216
Preliminary Interview 218
Review of Application for Employment 219

CONTENTS

Administration of Selection Tests 222
Types of Validation Studies 227
Cut-Off Scores 228
Types of Psychological Tests 228
The Employment Interview 231
Methods of Interviewing 236
Reference Checks 240
Background Investigation 241
Polygraph Tests 241
The Selection Decision 241
Physical Examination 242
HRM In Action 243
Acceptance of Job Applicants 243
Rejection of Job Applicants 243
Selection and Utility Analysis 244
Staffing in the Multinational Environment 245
Summary 247
Questions for Review 249
Terms for Review 249
Incident 1: Business First! 250
Incident 2: Should We Test? 251
Experiencing Human Resource Management 252
References 253
Appendix: Potential Interviewing Problems 254

Part Two Case—Parma Cycle Company: Workers for the New Plant 259

P·A·R·T T·H·R·E·E

HUMAN RESOURCE DEVELOPMENT

CHAPTER 8
Organization Change and Human Resource Development 262

Organization Change 263
Executive Insights: Robert E. Edwards 268
Human Resource Development: Definition and Scope 270
The Human Resource Development Process 271
Factors Influencing Human Resource Development 273
Determining Human Resource Development Needs 276
Establishing Human Resource Development Objectives 278

Selecting Human Resource Development Methods 279
Management Development 279
Management Development Programs at IBM 285
Supervisory Management Training Programs: An Illustration 286
Training Methods for Entry-Level Professional Employees 290
Training Methods for Operative Employees 290
HRM In Action 291
Effectiveness of Various Human Resource Development Methods 293
Selecting Human Resource Development Media 294
Implementing Human Resource Development Programs 296
Evaluating Human Resource Development 298
Orientation 300
Summary 305
Questions for Review 306
Terms for Review 307
Incident 1: What to Do? 307
Incident 2: Management Support of HRD? 308
Experiencing Human Resource Management 309
References 310

CHAPTER 9
Corporate Culture and Organization Development 312

Corporate Culture Defined 313
Factors That Determine Corporate Culture 315
Executive Insights: Drew M. Young 316
Types of Cultures 321
The Participative Culture 322
Organization Development 323
HRM In Action 333
Organizational Development: An Example 341
Use of Consultants 342
Organization Development Program Evaluation 343
Summary 344
Questions for Review 345
Terms for Review 345
Incident 1: Implementing MBO 346
Incident 2: Close to the Vest 347
Experiencing Human Resource Management 348
References 349

CHAPTER 10
Career Planning and Development 350

Career Planning and Development Defined 352
Factors Affecting Career Planning 352
Executive Insights: Ronald C. Pilenzo 354
Career Planning 356
HRM In Action 361
Career Paths 362
Plateauing 365
Career Development 367
Methods of Organization Career Planning and Development 368
Beginning a Career in Human Resources 369
Summary 374
Questions for Review 375
Terms for Review 375
Incident 1: In the Dark 376
Incident 2: Decisions, Decisions 377
Experiencing Human Resource Management 378
References 379

CHAPTER 11
Performance Appraisal 380

Performance Appraisal Defined 382
Uses of Performance Appraisal 382
Executive Insights: Joyce Lawson 384
The Performance Appraisal Process 387
Responsibility for Appraisal 388
The Appraisal Period 391
Performance Appraisal Methods 392
Problems in Performance Appraisal 404
Characteristics of an Effective Appraisal System 408
HRM In Action 409
Legal Implications 412
The Appraisal Interview 413
Assessment Centers 416
Human Resource Development in Multinational Corporations 417
Summary 420
Questions for Review 421
Terms for Review 422
Incident 1: Objectives? 422
Incident 2: Performance Appraisal? 423
Experiencing Human Resource Management 424
References 425

Part Three Case—Parma Cycle Company: Training the Workforce 426

P·A·R·T F·O·U·R
COMPENSATION AND BENEFITS

CHAPTER 12
Financial Compensation 430

Compensation: An Overview 432
Compensation Equity 432
Executive Insights: Richard G. Jamison 434
Determinants of Individual Financial Compensation 436
The Organization as a Determinant of Financial Compensation 436
The Labor Market as a Determinant of Financial Compensation 438
The Job as a Determinant of Financial Compensation 444
The Employee as a Determinant of Financial Compensation 454
Job Pricing 457
HRM In Action 460
Other Compensation Issues 462
Summary 466
Questions for Review 467
Terms for Review 468
Incident 1: It's Just Not Fair! 468
Incident 2: Job Evaluation: Who or What? 469
Experiencing Human Resource Management 470
References 471

CHAPTER 13
Benefits and Other Compensation Issues 472

Benefits (Indirect Financial Compensation) 474
Executive Insights: Beverly J. Mason 476
Incentive Compensation 486
HRM In Action 492
Compensation for Managers 494
Compensation for Professionals 496
Sales Compensation 497
Nonfinancial Compensation 498
Compensation in Multinational Corporations 506
Summary 507
Questions for Review 509

CONTENTS

Terms for Review 509
Incident 1: A Double-Edged Sword 510
Incident 2: A Benefits Package Designed for Whom? 511
Experiencing Human Resource Management 512
References 513

Part Four Case—Parma Cycle Company: The Pay Plan 514

P·A·R·T F·I·V·E

SAFETY AND HEALTH

CHAPTER 14
A Safe and Healthy Work Environment 518

The Occupational Safety and Health Act 520
Safety 522
Health and Wellness Programs 529
Executive Insights: Nina E. Woodard 530
Stress Management 532
Burnout 534
Physical Fitness Programs 541
Alcohol Abuse Programs 543
Drug Abuse Programs 544
Employee Assistance Programs 545
HRM In Action 547
AIDS in the Workplace 548
Summary 550
Questions for Review 551
Terms for Review 551
Incident 1: To Test or Not to Test 552
Incident 2: A Star Is Falling 552
Experiencing Human Resource Management 553
References 554

Part Five Case—Parma Cycle Company: Safety and Health at the New Plant 556

P·A·R·T S·I·X

EMPLOYEE AND LABOR RELATIONS

CHAPTER 15
The Labor Union 558

The Labor Movement Before 1930 560
Executive Insights: Art Hobbs 562
The Labor Movement After 1930 564
The Public Sector 569
Union Objectives 572
Why Employees Join Unions 574
Union Structure 578
Establishing the Collective Bargaining Relationship 581
Signs of a Troubled Labor Movement 585
HRM In Action 586
The Growing Legalistic Approach 586
The Future of Unionism and Collective Bargaining in a Global Economy 588
Summary 589
Questions for Review 590
Terms for Review 591
Incident 1: Work Rules 591
Incident 2: Union Appeal 592
Experiencing Human Resource Management 593
References 593

CHAPTER 16
Collective Bargaining 596

The Collective Bargaining Process 598
Executive Insights: Marsha Slaughter 600
The Human Resource Manager's Role 603
Psychological Aspects of Collective Bargaining 604
Preparing for Negotiations 605
Bargaining Issues 608
Negotiating the Agreement 612
Breakdowns in Negotiations 614
Ratifying the Agreement 618
Administering the Agreement 619
HRM In Action 621
The Future of Collective Bargaining 621
Technology and Productivity 623
Summary 625
Questions for Review 627
Terms for Review 627
Incident 1: Maybe I Will, Maybe I Won't 627

Incident 2: What's Causing the Turnover? 628
Experiencing Human Resource Management 629
References 630

CHAPTER 17
Union-Free Organizations 632

Why Employees Avoid Joining Unions 634
Executive Insights: R. H. Heil 636
Costs and Benefits of Unionization 638
Strategies and Tactics for Remaining
Union-Free 640
HRM In Action 644
Union Decertification 649
The Role of the Human Resource Manager 652
Summary 653
Questions for Review 654
Terms for Review 654
Incident 1: Being Fair 655
Incident 2: Open the Door! 655
Experiencing Human Resource Management 656
References 657

CHAPTER 18
Internal Employee Relations 660

Internal Employee Relations Defined 662
Disciplinary Action 662
The Disciplinary Action Process 663
Executive Insights: Barbara Sullivan 664
Approaches to Disciplinary Action 667
Administration of Disciplinary Action 670
Grievance Handling Under a Collective Bargaining
Agreement 672
HRM In Action 673
Grievance Handling in Union-free
Organizations 678
Termination 679
Employment at Will 681
Resignation 682
Demotion as an Alternative to Termination 685
Layoff 685
Transfer 686
Promotion 687
Retirement 688
Legal Implications of Internal Employee
Relations 689
Internal Employee Relations in Multinational
Corporations 690

Summary 691
Questions for Review 692
Terms for Review 692
Incident 1: Step Over the Line 693
Incident 2: Something Is Not Right 694
Experiencing Human Resource Management 695
References 695

Part Six Case: Parma Cycle Company—The Union
Organizing Attempt 697

P·A·R·T S·E·V·E·N

HUMAN RESOURCE RESEARCH

CHAPTER 19
Human Resource Research 700

The Productivity Challenge 702
Benefits of Human Resource Research 702
Executive Insights: Paul A. Banas 704
Methods of Inquiry in Human Resource
Research 709
The Research Process 713
Recognize the Problem 714
HRM In Action 714
Quantitative Methods in Human Resource
Research 716
Discriminant Analysis 718
Human Resource Research: An Illustration 719
Evaluating the Human Resource Management
Function 723
Technological Advances Affecting Human Resource
Management 724
Summary 729
Questions for Review 730
Terms for Review 730
Incident 1: Best Not to Know 731
Incident 2: So What's the Problem? 731
Experiencing Human Resource Management 732
References 733

Part Seven Case: Parma Cycle Company—Looking
Ahead 734

Glossary G-1

Index I-1

PREFACE

The fourth edition of *Human Resource Management* continues to offer a practical and realistic approach to the study of human resource management. Essentially pragmatic, the book is balanced throughout by current human resource management concepts. A common theme—the interrelationships among the various human resource management functions—runs throughout the book. Each function is described in terms of its relation to the total scope of human resource management. The book is written primarily for students who are being exposed to human resource management for the first time. It puts the student in touch with the real world through the use of numerous illustrations and company-provided material that show how human resource management is practiced in today's organizations.

The Challenge

Effective human resource management is more vital today than ever. Never before have domestic business and industry faced the intense competition now presented by foreign and multinational corporations. Never before have our public agencies faced the current degree of conflict resulting from increased demands for service and limited resources. As one human resource director stated, "The survival of business in a free economy will be determined by the influence and use of human resources...." All managers are vitally concerned with human resources. However, it is the human resource manager and his or her professional staff who are the leaders in providing policies and programs for maximizing human potential in the workplace. This potential relates both to productivity and quality of work life. Tapping it requires fully utilizing all groups of people within our society and keeping private and public organizations on the leading edge of change. Our society possesses all the ingredients to fulfill this potential.

Features of the Book

We included the following features to promote the understanding of important human resource management concepts:

- A model (see Figure 2-1) that provides a vehicle for relating all human resource management topics. We believe that this overview will serve as an excellent teaching device.
- A short case study involving human resource management at the beginning of each chapter. We use these anecdotes to set the stage for discussing the topics in the chapter.
- A brief exercise called "HRM in Action." Included in the body of each chapter, these exercises are designed to permit students to make decisions regarding situations that could occur in the real world. Possible responses are provided for the instructor in the *Instructor's Manual*.
- A comprehensive exercise called "Experiencing Human Resource Management." These exercises at the end of each chapter provide for considerable class participation and group involvement. A comprehensive explanation of each exercise is provided for the instructor in the *Instructor's Manual*.
- Actual company material to illustrate how concepts are actually applied in the real world. Organizations described in the text include:

A. B. Volvo
Alumax, Inc.
American Airlines
American Coil Spring Company
American General Life Insurance Company
American Society for Personnel Administration
ARCO Oil and Gas Company
Bell Telephone Company
Bendix Corporation
Bristol-Myers Company
Cessna Aircraft
Champion International Corporation
Chevron Corporation
Conoco, Inc.
Control Data Corporation
Delta Air Lines, Inc.
Denny's, Inc.
Detroit Edison Company
Dr Pepper Company
Drake Beam Morin, Inc.
DynaCor, Inc.
E-Systems, Inc.
First Interstate Bancorp.
FL Industries, Inc.
Ford Motor Company
Fotomat Corporation
GAF Corporation
Gates Learjet
General Cable Technologies
General Electric Company
General Mills
General Telephone Company of the Southwest
Georgia-Pacific Corporation

Gerber Products Company
Grumman Corporation
Hartmarx
Honeywell, Inc.
Information Science Incorporated
International Business Machines Corporation
International Paper Company
Kemper Group
Kennecott Corporation
Kimberly-Clark Corporation
Korn/Ferry International
Lincoln Electric Company
Lone Star Industries
Manville Corporation
Massachusetts Mutual Life Insurance Company
Midland-Ross
Monsanto Company
Montgomery Ward
Motorola, Inc.
Nabisco Brands, Inc.
New York Telephone
New York Times Company
Pan American World Airways
ProStaff
Quest Personnel Services
RCA Corporation
Rockwell International Corporation
St. Paul Property and Liability Insurance Company
Shell Oil Company
Southland Corporation
Southwestern Bell Telephone Company

PREFACE

Southwestern Life Insurance Company	The Upjohn Company
	Trans World Airlines
Squibb Corporation	TRW, Inc.
Stokely-Van Camp, Inc.	United States Tobacco Company
Teledyne, Inc.	USX
Texas Instruments	Walt Disney Productions
The Singer Company	Xerox Corporation

- Career profiles of human resource professionals. The profile in each chapter demonstrates the interesting and challenging work that human resource professionals do and conveys each person's perception of human resource management.
- Two incidents at the end of each chapter. These short case studies highlight material covered in the chapter.
- A comprehensive continuing case at the end of each part. This long case study ties all of the human resource functions together.
- Objectives at the beginning of each chapter. They highlight the general purpose and key concepts of the chapter.
- Review questions at the end of each chapter. These questions test the student's understanding of the material covered in the chapter.
- Key terms which are presented in bold print the first time they are defined or described in the chapter, listed at the end of each chapter, and compiled in a glossary at the end of the book.
- A list of references at the end of each chapter. These suggested readings permit additional indepth study of selected topics.

Improvements Over Previous Editions

The first, second, and third editions of this book enjoyed considerable success, and many of our adopters gave us valuable suggestions for improvements.

We added an experiential base to the book in the form of "HRM in Action" and "Experiencing Human Resource Management." The HRM in Action exercises provided in each chapter are designed literally to put students on the spot to see how they would react in a human resource management situation. Experiencing Human Resource Management exercises are provided at the end of each chapter. Each exercise is tied to the respective chapter and encourages considerable class participation and group involvement.

We gave greater recognition to the impact of multinational corporations on human resource management. We interspersed liberally throughout the book—in Chapters 2, 3, 7, 11, 13, 15, 16, and 18—descriptions of human resource management functions as they apply to multinational corporations.

We added a major new section to Chapter 2 describing the new workforce. In it we describe the effects of more working women, single parents, and older persons; the use of part-time workers, often for shared jobs; the use of temporary and "leased" employees; inclusion of handicapped employees in increasing numbers; and the flood of immigrants from developing areas, especially Southeast Asia and Latin America.

We cover the implications of new laws affecting HRM that have been passed since the previous edition. We discuss the Consolidated Omnibus Budget Reconciliation Act, the Immigration Reform and Control Act, the Plant Closing/Layoff Act, and the Employee Polygraph Protection Act in appropriate chapters. Also, significant new court decisions are presented in Chapter 3.

We added to Chapter 1 a new section entitled "Ethical Aspects of Human Resource Management." With the professionalization of human resource management, a need arises for the development of a uniform code of ethics.

We substantially rewrote Chapters 15, 16, and 17 to reflect the latest trends in employee and labor relations. The decade of the 1980s has seen many changes impacting employee and labor relations and these chapters reflect the present and future relationships existing in employee and labor relations.

We also added two new sections to Chapter 19 entitled "Evaluating the Human Resource Function" and "Technological Advances Affecting Human Resource Management." As the human resource function receives ever more attention from top level managers throughout the organization, there must be means developed to evaluate this important function. Also technological advances have the potential to affect the workforce of the future and the actual manner in which human resource managers perform their tasks.

All these features are intended to stimulate student interest. We sincerely hope that students of human resource management derive as much pleasure from reading the book as we did from writing it.

Acknowledgements

The assistance and encouragement of many people is required in the writing of any book. This was especially true of *Human Resource Management*, fourth edition. Although it would be virtually impossible to list each person who assisted in this project, we feel that certain people must be acknowledged because of the magnitude of their contributions.

We express our sincere appreciation to the many members of the faculty and staff at McNeese State University and East Texas State University. Special notes of thanks go to Art Bethke of Northeast Louisiana University and Donald Caruth of East Texas State University, both of whom provided valuable suggestions, advice, and encouragement through the project. As with the previous editions, the support and encouragement of many practicing HRM professionals has made this book possible. Some of these people are Richard Walter, Kean College of New Jersey; Chalmer Labig, Oklahoma State University; Stephen Owens, Western Carolina University; Marvin Levine, Orange County Community College; Peter Repolge, Orange County Community College; Razelle Frankl, Wynnewood, PA; Arthur Bethke, Northeast Louisiana University; Don Caruth, East Texas State University; and Debra Nelson, Oklahoma State University.

P·A·R·T O·N·E

INTRODUCTION

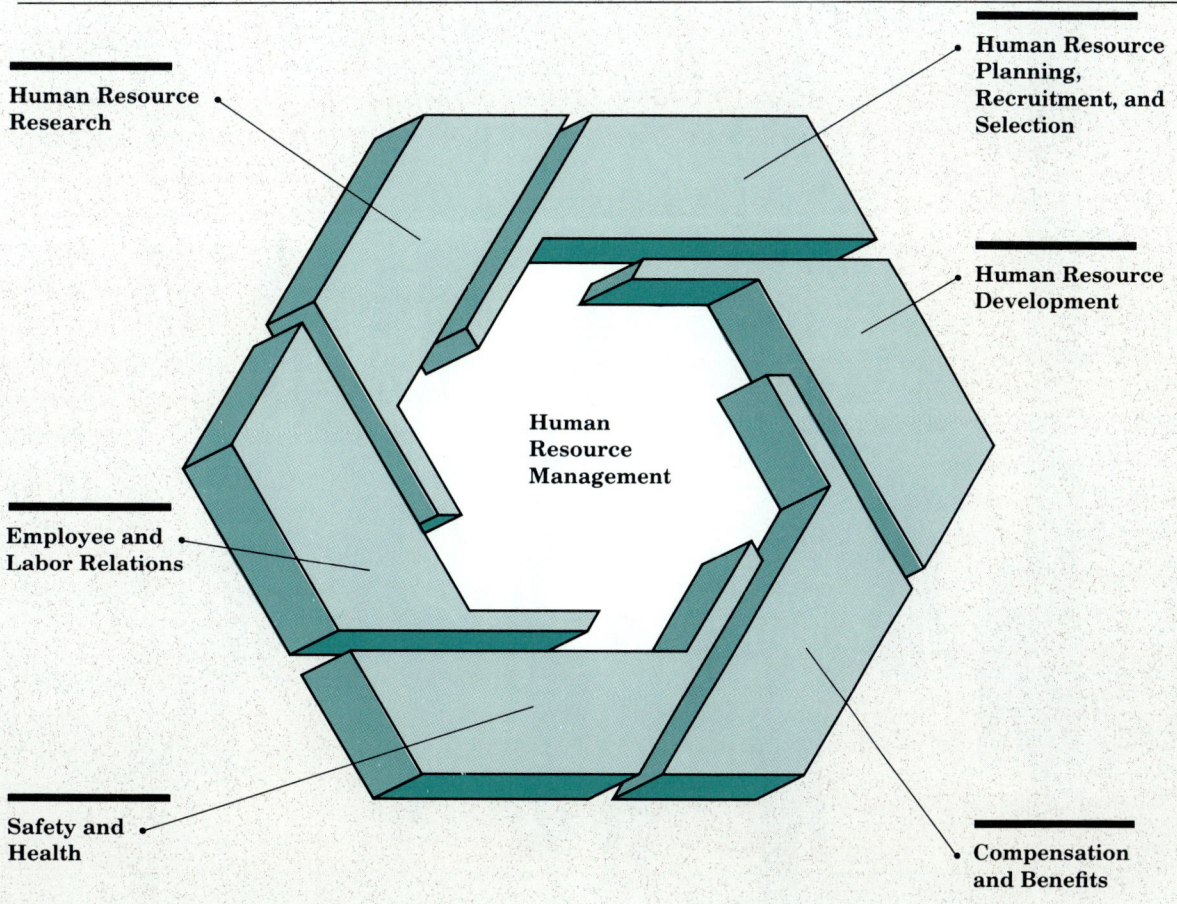

CHAPTER 1

HUMAN RESOURCE MANAGEMENT: AN OVERVIEW

CHAPTER OBJECTIVES

1. Distinguish between human resource management and the human resource manager. Describe the functions of human resource management.
2. Describe the changes that have taken place in the human resource field in recent years. Define human resource executive, specialist, and generalist. Describe the changes that occur in the human resource function as a firm grows larger and more complex.
3. Express the nature of professionalization of human resources and the direction it has taken. Define ethics and relate ethics to human resource management.

■ As David Curtis, vice-president of human resources for Nelson Enterprises, headquartered in New York City, rose to leave the executive meeting, he realized that his job would be even busier than usual during the next six months. Nelson Enterprises produces high-tech components for both government and private industry, and greater production capacity is needed to meet industry demands. A decision had been made at the meeting to open a new plant in Mobile, Alabama. David and other members of the council had analyzed numerous other sites and had determined that Mobile most closely met their needs. When the plant is completed in a year, 500 new employees must be available and trained. In addition, 75 employees at the New York facility will be transferred to Mobile. It is David's responsibility to ensure that qualified new workers are hired and trained, and that the transferred workers are effectively integrated into the work force.

■ Carl Edwards is the supervisor of ten Baby Giant convenience stores in Sacramento, California. As the Baby Giant chain is relatively small (only 40 stores), it has no human resource department. Each supervisor is in charge of all employment activities for his or her store. Carl must ensure that only the best people are recruited for positions as store managers and then must properly train these individuals. If one of the managers fails to report for an assigned shift and Carl cannot find a replacement, he is expected to work the shift. It is Friday afternoon and Carl is hurriedly attempting to locate a replacement because one store manager just quit without giving notice.

■ Judy Lynley is the industrial relations manager for Axton Pneumotives, a small manufacturer of pumps located in Bangor, Maine. The 65 machine operators in the firm are unionized. Judy has been

continued on next page

> *continued from previous page*
>
> negotiating with union leaders for five weeks with little success. The union members have threatened to walk off the job if the contract is not resolved by midnight. However, if Judy's firm agrees to all the union's demands, it will no longer be competitive in the industry because of the higher wage level.

David, Carl, and Judy all have one thing in common: they are deeply involved with some of the challenges and problems related to human resource management. Managers of human resources must constantly deal with the often volatile and unpredictable human element that makes working in this field very challenging. Managing people in organizations is becoming more complex than ever because of rapidly changing and increasingly complicated work environments.

In the first part of this chapter, we distinguish between human resource management and the human resource manager. Next, we review the human resource management functions. We then present topics related to the revolution in human resource management and the changing world of the chief human resource officer. We make a distinction among human resource executives, generalists, and specialists, and discuss the human resource function in organizations of different size. Finally, we discuss professionalism and ethics in this dynamic discipline.

■ HUMAN RESOURCE MANAGEMENT AND THE HUMAN RESOURCE MANAGER

The field of human resource management changed dramatically during the 1980s, in ways that created a greatly expanded role for the human resource manager. In order to understand this development, we must make a distinction between human resource management and the human resource manager.

Human resource management (HRM) is the utilization of human resources to achieve organizational objectives. Consequently, managers at all levels must concern themselves with human resource management at least to some extent. Basically managers get things done through the efforts of others, which requires effective human resource management. In a manufacturing firm, for instance, the production manager meshes physical and human resources to produce goods in sufficient numbers and quality; the marketing manager works through sales representatives to sell the firm's products; and the finance manager obtains capital and manages investments to ensure sufficient operating funds. These individuals are called "line" managers because they have formal authority and responsibility for achieving their firm's primary objectives. Although involved in human resource management, they are not human resource managers. They are responsible primarily for specific functional areas of the business. Carl Edwards, the convenience store supervisor in Sacramento, fully understands the challenges that a line manager faces with human resources because he will have to work Friday night if he cannot find a replacement.

A **human resource manager** is an individual who normally acts in an advisory, or "staff," capacity, working with other managers to help them deal with human resource matters. In the first three editions of this book, the term "personnel manager" denoted the individual who performed staff functions similar to those now performed by the human resource manager. This evolving change in terminology reflects the expanded role of HRM and an increasing awareness that human resources are the key to a successful organization. Although only cosmetic in some instances, this change has been substantive in most cases. Thus it reflects a new and continually expanding role for the human resource manager.[1] The current functions of many chief human resource managers is illustrated by Kathryn McKee, senior vice-president, human resources, for First Interstate Bank, Ltd. As she states in Executive Insights, "I am now a strategic partner with line management and participate in business decisions which bring human resources perspectives to the general management of the company."

The human resource manager is primarily responsible for coordinating the management of human resources to help the organization achieve its goals. Jane Kay, formerly vice-president of employee relations for Detroit Edison Company, states, "The human resource manager acts more in an advisory capacity, but should be a catalyst in proposing human relations policies to be implemented by line managers." William B. Pardue, senior vice-president for American General Life Insurance Company, says, "The real human resource management game is played by the line manager. The human resource manager's role is to develop policies and programs—the rules of the game—and to function as a catalyst and energizer of the relationship between line management and employees." The distinction between human resource management and the human resource manager is clearly illustrated by the following account:

> Bill Brown, the production supervisor for Ajax Manufacturing, has just learned that one of his machine operators quit. He immediately calls Sandra Williams, the human resource manager, and says, "Sandra, I just had a Class A machine operator quit down here. Can you find some qualified people for me to interview?" "Sure Bill," Sandra replies. "I'll send two or three down to you within the week, and you can select the one that best fits your needs."

In this instance, both Bill and Sandra are concerned with accomplishing organizational goals, but from different perspectives. Sandra, as a human resource manager, identifies applicants who meet the criteria specified by Bill. Yet, Bill will make the final decision as to who is hired because he is responsible for the machine operator's performance. His primary responsibility is production. Hers is human resources. As a human resource manager, Sandra must constantly deal with the many problems related to human resources Bill and the other managers face. Her job is to help them meet

---

[1] James L. Harvey, "Nine Major Trends in HRM," *Personnel Administrator*, 31 (November 1986), p. 102.

EXECUTIVE INSIGHTS

Kathryn D. McKee, SPHR, CCP
Senior Vice-President,
Human Resources,
First Interstate Bank, Ltd.

Kathryn D. McKee, former president of the International Association for Personnel Women, says, "The field of human resources is on the cutting edge of major social change. In today's highly complex environment, I believe that the programs developed and the decisions made by human resources can profoundly impact a business firm's profits."

McKee's extensive background in human resources includes experience with several organizations. After she graduated from college, her first assignment was as an employment clerk for a major aerospace firm in southern California. She later obtained a position as employment security officer with the State of California, and, as she puts it, she was "out from behind the typewriter at last!" At this job she received a solid foundation for her career in human resources management. She obtained invaluable experience in job classification, employment interviewing, unemployment claims determination, and vocational counseling.

McKee next joined Mattel, Inc., as an employment interviewer. She progressed rapidly to salary analyst and later to corporate compensation manager. While at Mattel, she demonstrated that raising a family and being a business executive are not mutually exclusive—her employment with Mattel was interrupted briefly for two maternity leaves.

The next phase of McKee's career began when the president of a small firm sought her out to serve as director of industrial relations. Three weeks into her job, she was faced with a Teamsters' effort to organize the office employees. "Ironically they picked the day we were to implement the new salary administration plan for all nonunion employees to pass out the signature cards, almost as if they knew we were starting to create programs. After a few harried hours of panic and some counsel from our labor attorney, we proceeded to implement our programs and face down the union. Anyone who has been through that experience will attest to the exhilaration and the anxiety it creates. There are so many things employers can't do in such situations. The episode came to a head when, on advice of counsel, we held an open meeting for all nonunion employees and the new president in effect said, 'We're new and we're here to make this company run better. Give us six months to make improvements. If, after that time, you feel you need a union to make it better, then do what you want, but at least give us a chance.' The upshot of that was, acting upon a request from an employee, top management held a series of small-group, open meetings to air problems and respond with what we could do to solve them. The problems ranged from 'The carpet is dirty' to 'We have lousy benefits,' both of which were true at that time. After three months, we had resolved all the issues, the Teamsters had no show of interest, and the organizing attempt was moot."

When Twentieth Century Fox needed to fill the position of corporate compensation manager, they selected Kathryn McKee. After a year of developing, organizing, and implementing a compensation program, she embarked on still another major project, which encompassed designing the company's corporate equal opportunity program. Later she moved from compensation to establish a management development program.

McKee's next career opportunity came when First Interstate Bancorp recruited her as vice-president of compensation and benefits. In this position, she was responsible for designing and implementing benefit programs that affected over 35,000 employees. She also guided development of corporate compensation policies and administrative tools, such as a state of the art quantitative job evaluation plan used to analyze and evaluate work in the financial services industry positions.

She is now senior vice-president and chief human resources officer for First Interstate Bank, Ltd., where she is a member of the managing committee and is responsible for all aspects of the bank's human resources worldwide. "I am now a strategic partner with line management and participate in business decisions which bring human resources perspectives to the general management of the company."

the human resource needs of the entire organization. In some firms her function is also referred to as personnel, employee relations, or industrial relations.

■ HUMAN RESOURCE MANAGEMENT FUNCTIONS

Today's human resource problems are enormous and appear to be ever expanding. The human resource manager faces a multitude of problems, ranging from motivating a constantly changing work force to coping with the ever-present scores of government regulations.[2] Because of the critical nature of human resource problems, they are receiving increased attention from upper management. Therefore, the human resource executive who is able to deal effectively with those problems often becomes one of the firm's top managers.[3]

Human resource managers develop and work through a human resource management system. As Figure 1-1 shows, six functional areas are associated with effective human resource management. A major study conducted for the Personnel Accreditation Institute in 1988 confirmed that these areas reveal the way human resource positions are structured regarding knowledge requirements.[4] Sound management practices are required for successful performance in each area. We discuss these functions next.

Human Resource Planning, Recruitment, and Selection

An organization must have qualified individuals in specific jobs at specific places and times in order to accomplish its goals. Obtaining such people involves human resource planning, recruitment, and selection.

Human resource planning (HRP) is the process of systematically reviewing human resource requirements to ensure that the required numbers of employees, with the required skills, are available when they are needed. Recruitment is the process of attracting such individuals in sufficient numbers and encouraging them to apply for jobs with the organization. Selection is the process through which the organization chooses, from a group of applicants, those individuals best suited both for open positions, and for the company. Successful accomplishment of these three tasks is vital if the plant is to become operational and accomplish its mission.

Human Resource Development

Human resource development (HRD) assists individuals, groups, and the entire organization in becoming more effective. Human resource develop-

---

[2] *Ibid.*, p. 28.

[3] James D. Portwood and Robert W. Eichinger, "The Challenge of Human Resource Management: Adding Value," *Human Resource Planning*, 8 (December 1985), p. 209.

[4] Walter W. Tornow, Janis S. Houston, and Walter C. Borman, "An Evaluation of the Body-of-Knowledge," *Personnel Administrator*, 34 (June 1989), p. 140.

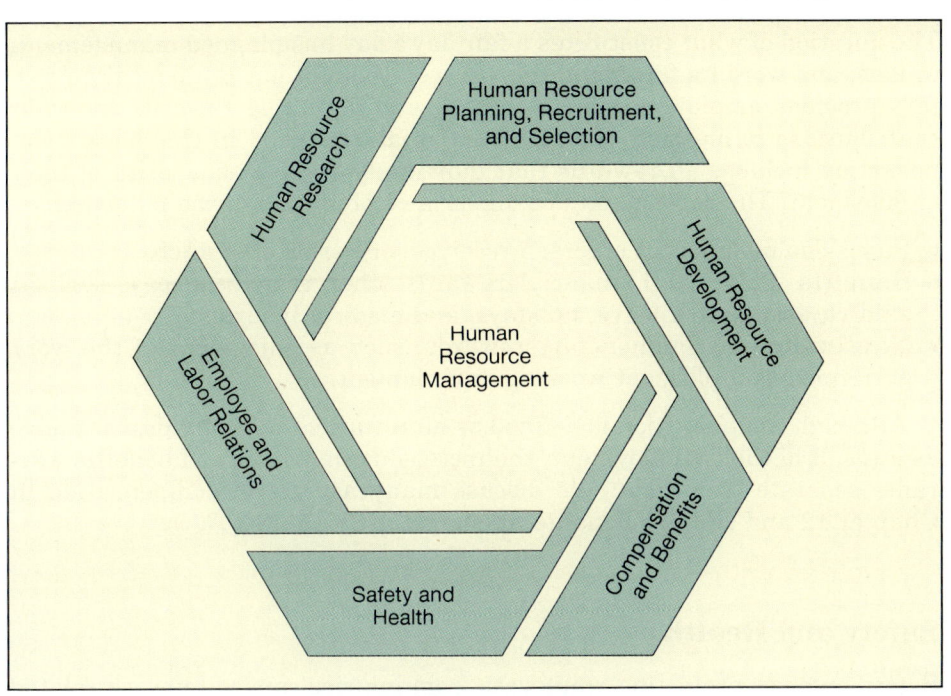

FIGURE 1-1 | The Human Resource Management System

ment is needed because people, jobs, and organizations are always changing. The development process should begin when individuals join the firm and continue throughout their careers. Large-scale HRD programs are referred to as organization development (OD). The purpose of OD is to alter the environment within the firm to help employees perform more productively.

Other aspects of HRD include career planning and performance appraisal. Career planning is a process of setting human resource goals and establishing the means to achieve them. Individual careers and organizational needs are not separate and distinct. Organizations should assist employees in career planning so that the needs of both can be satisfied. Through performance appraisal, employees are evaluated to determine how well they are performing their assigned tasks. Performance appraisal affords employees the opportunity to capitalize on their strengths and overcome identified deficiencies, thereby becoming more satisfied and productive employees.

Throughout this text, but especially in the HRD chapters, we use the term "operative" workers or employees. **Operative employees** are all workers in an organization except managers and professionals such as engineers or accountants. Steel workers, secretaries, truck drivers, and waiters are examples of operative employees.

Compensation and Benefits

The question of what constitutes a fair day's pay has plagued management, unions, and workers for a long time. A well thought out compensation system provides employees with adequate and equitable rewards for their contributions to meeting organizational goals. As used in this book, compensation includes all rewards that individuals receive as a result of their employment. The reward may be one or a combination of the following:

- **Pay** The money that a person receives for performing a job.
- **Benefits** Additional financial rewards other than base pay, such as paid vacations, sick leave, holidays, and medical insurance.
- **Nonfinancial** Nonmonetary rewards, such as enjoyment of the work performed or a pleasant working environment.

Although compensation is defined as all rewards that individuals receive as a result of their employment, the increasing importance of benefits warrants separate treatment. We discuss many aspects of compensation in Chapter 12 and address benefits in Chapter 13.

Safety and Health

Safety involves protecting employees from injuries caused by work-related accidents. Health refers to the employees' freedom from illness and their general physical and mental well-being. These aspects of the job are important because employees who work in a safe environment and enjoy good health are more likely to be productive and yield long-term benefits to the organization. For this reason, progressive managers have long advocated and put in place adequate safety and health programs. Today, because of federal and state legislation, which reflect societal concerns, most organizations have become attentive to their employees' safety and health.[5]

Employee and Labor Relations

In 1987, unions represented 17 percent of all nonfarm workers.[6] By the year 2000, unions will likely represent only 13 percent of all nonfarm workers.[7] Even so, a business firm is required by law to recognize a union and bargain with it in good faith, if the firm's employees want the union to represent them. In the past, this relationship was an accepted way of life for many employers. But according to a recent Conference Board survey of labor-management relations, preventing the spread of unionism and devel-

---

[5] The key law in the area of health and safety is the Occupational Safety and Health Act of 1970. We will discuss the effect of the act later in this book.

[6] Larry T. Adams, "Union Membership of Wage and Salary Employees in 1987," *Current Wage Developments*. (Washington, D.C.: U.S. Department of Labor Bureau of Labor Statistics, February 1988), p. 4.

[7] "Beyond Unions: A Revolution in Employee Relations Is in the Making," *Business Week* (July 8, 1985), p. 72.

oping effective employee relations systems are now more important to *some* managers than achieving sound collective bargaining results.[8]

As Judy Lynley, industrial relations manager for Axton Pneumotives, discovered, dealing with a union often presents difficult problems. During the stressful bargaining process, Judy may have tended to agree with the Conference Board survey conclusion. The union placed her in a difficult position: if the workers walk off the job, production stops; agreeing to all the union's demands may result in pricing the firm's products out of the market. Judy must be a skilled negotiator to solve these problems. When a labor union represents a firm's employees, the human resource activity is often referred to as industrial relations.

Human resource managers in union-free organizations are often quite knowledgeable about union goals and activities. Such organizations typically strive to satisfy all reasonable employee work-related needs. Employees often conclude that a union isn't necessary for them to achieve their personal goals. Remaining union free requires a strong commitment by management and a freely communicative and open environment. In many ways, the commitment necessary to maintain a union-free environment is more demanding on the human resources department than is working in a unionized environment. Organizations that do not make and maintain that commitment are vulnerable to union organizing efforts. The old maxim is still true: "Unions don't organize employees, managers do"—through mistakes, neglect, and, unfortunately, plain greed.[9] The human resource manager, therefore, must create and manage an employee relations system that treats employees positively. The system should allow each individual worker to maintain his or her self-esteem and grow individually within the organization.

Human Resource Research

Every human resource management function needs effective research. For instance, research may be conducted to determine the type of workers who will be most successful.[10] Or it may be aimed at determining the causes of certain work-related accidents. As you will see in Chapter 19, numerous quantitative methods are used in human resource research. This function will become increasingly important because, as the work environment becomes more complex, the value of timely and accurate information increases dramatically.

The Interrelationships of HRM Functions

The functional areas of HRM are not separate and distinct; they are highly interrelated. Management must recognize that decisions in one area will

---

[8] Alexander B. Trowbridge, "A Management Look at Labor Relations," *Unions in Transition* (San Francisco: ICS Press, 1988), p. 414.

[9] *Ibid.*, p. 417.

[10] R. Wayne Mondy and Frank N. Edens, "An Empirical Test of the Decision to Participate Model," *Journal of Management*, 2 (Fall 1976), pp. 11–16.

have impacts on other areas—and what those impacts are likely to be. For instance, a firm that emphasizes recruiting and training of a sales force while neglecting to provide adequate compensation is wasting time, effort, and money. In addition, if management is truly concerned about employee welfare, it must ensure a safe and healthy work environment. An added benefit may be keeping the firm union free. The interrelationships among the six HRM functional areas will become more obvious to you as we address each topic in greater detail.

■ THE EVOLUTION OF HUMAN RESOURCE MANAGEMENT

One of the major changes in business in recent years has been the increased respect and responsibility afforded human resource professionals.[11] These individuals are now expected to provide the direction necessary to meet the many human resources problems and challenges of the future. For example, within the next decade, the content of more than half of all existing jobs is likely to change, and 30 percent of all existing jobs will be eliminated by technological advances.[12] Human resource professionals will have to respond positively to these trends, while keeping an alert eye on the organization's overall goals.[13]

Not many decades ago, people engaged in human resource work had titles such as "welfare secretary" and "employment clerk." Their duties were rather restrictive and often dealt only with such items as workers' wages, minor medical problems, recreation, and housing.[14] Personnel, as human resources was most commonly called, as a profession was generally held in low esteem, and its organizational position was typically near the bottom of the hierarchy. "In the past," says John L. Quigley, vice-president of human resources, Dr Pepper Company, "the personnel executive was the 'glad hander' or 'back slapper' who kept morale up in a company by running the company picnic, handling the United Fund drive, and making sure the recreation program went off well." Those days are over in most organizations. The human resource manager's position is no longer a "retirement" position given managers who cannot perform adequately anywhere else in the organization. Firms have now learned that the human resource department can have a major impact on the organization's overall effectiveness and profitability.

According to the 1988 ASPA/Mercer-Meidinger-Hansen survey of some 20,000 human resource professionals in 1,400 organizations of varying size, top human resource executives are generally being paid in line with other

---

[11] Trowbridge, p. 414.

[12] Eric G. Flamholtz, Yvonne Randle, and Sonja Sackmann, "Personnel Management: The Tenor of Today," *Personnel Journal*, 66 (June 1987), p. 64.

[13] Jack F. Gow, "Human Resources Managers Must Remember the Bottom Line," *Personnel Journal*, 64 (April 1985), p. 30.

[14] Henry Eibirt, "The Development of Personnel Management in the United States," *Business History Review*, 33 (August 1969), pp. 348–349.

upper level managers. As might be expected, salaries of corporate human resource executives depend largely on the size of the organization. For firms with annual sales of over $1.5 billion, the average salary was $140,800, but increased to $179,100 when bonuses were added. The average salary of human resource executives in firms with annual sales of under $100 million was $63,800, but increased to $72,900 when bonuses were added. For all top corporate human resource executives the average salary was $75,220, or $85,000 including bonuses.[15]

The same survey identified the human resource specialists who had received the most and least amount of salary increase. Human resource professionals with specialist job functions such as executive compensation manager, international compensation manager, employee relations executive, and equal employment opportunity manager had the highest salary growth between 1983 and 1988. Those who performed job functions such as training/organizational development manager, training specialist, and management development manager had the lowest salary growth during the same period.[16]

Many human resource professionals now report directly to the CEOs of their company.[17] Some human resource executives have even become top managers with their firms. These achievements clearly reflect the recently gained respect from chief executive officers and other senior executives for the human resource professional. The increased status of the human resource field is not limited to the United States. In his research on Japanese industry, William Ouchi found that "ordinarily, the most senior and the most respected managing director is in charge of human resources."[18]

■ THE CHANGING WORLD OF THE CHIEF HUMAN RESOURCE OFFICER

The work of the chief human resource executive is affected greatly by top management's human resource priorities and the major changes occurring in management responsibilities and organizational relationships. Fifty top chief human resource officers were asked, "What are the principal human resource areas attracting top management attention?" The results, shown in Figure 1-2, indicate that compensation was the number one concern, with succession planning (planning for the replacement of key employees) a close second.[19] However, each of the areas mentioned by those interviewed are vitally important and are covered in this book.

---

[15] John D. McMillan and Claire O. Walters, "Dominating the Dollars," *Personnel Administrator*, 33 (August 1988), pp. 26–28.
[16] *Ibid.*, p. 28.
[17] "Anatomy of a Human Resource Executive," *Training*, 22 (May 1985), p. 146.
[18] William G. Ouchi, *Theory Z* (Reading, Mass.: Addison-Wesley, 1981), p. 30.
[19] John S. Hellman (ed.), "The Changing World of the CPO," Spencer Stewart & Associates special report, 1984, pp. 3–4.

14   PART ONE   Introduction

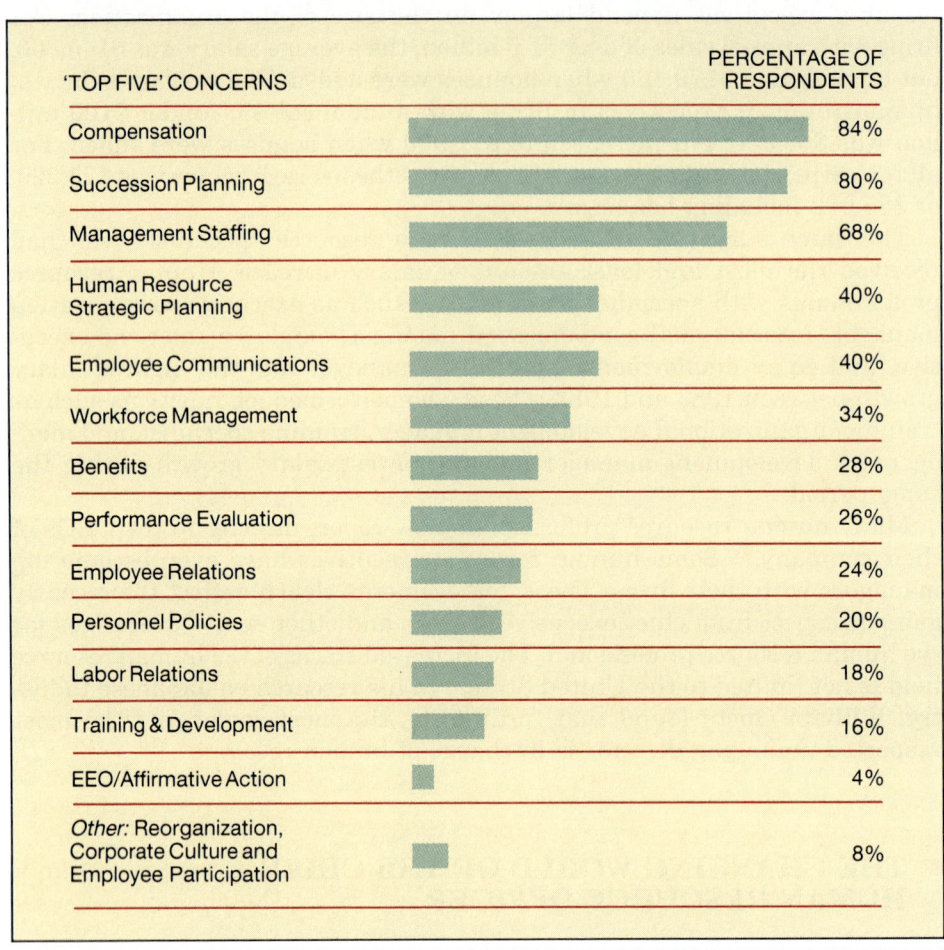

FIGURE 1-2 | Principal Human Resource Areas Attracting Top Management Attention

Source: John S. Hellman (ed.), "The Changing World of the CPO," A Spencer Stewart & Associates special report, 1984, p. 6. Used with permission.

The same executives were also asked to identify the major changes occurring in their management responsibilities and organizational relationships.[20] Their responses are summarized as follows:

1. *Greater emphasis and more time spent on human resource strategic planning and management succession planning.* Integrating human resource strategic planning into the corporate strategic planning process is apparently taking on greater importance.
2. *More involvement in all aspects of the business.* Just as the production and finance departments are important to the success of the organiza-

---
[20] *Ibid.*, p. 13.

tion, so too is the human resource department. As a result, it is achieving similar respect. Today's human resource managers must know more than just "personnel." They must have a firm grasp of finance, marketing, operations, and the nature of their firm's business. They must be as profit oriented as any other executive. Merely "liking people" is not enough for the successful human resource manager of the 1990s.

3. *A significant member of the management team.* Top-level managers have begun to realize the vital contributions of effective human resource management.
4. *Key role as consultant to the CEO on organization and succession planning.* Chief human resource officers have become key advisors and counselors to the CEO.
5. *More emphasis on cost-related issues and cost control.* The emphasis here is on workforce management. Chief human resource officers are taking on greater responsibility, facing tougher challenges, and working harder and smarter. But, as one executive stated, the job today is "a lot more fun,"[21] and undoubtedly, a lot more challenging.

■ HUMAN RESOURCE EXECUTIVES, GENERALISTS, AND SPECIALISTS

Within the human resource profession are various classifications that you need to recognize and understand. Among them are human resource executives, generalists, and specialists. An **executive** is a top-level manager who reports directly to the corporation's chief executive officer (CEO) or to the head of a major division. A **generalist** (who often is an executive) performs tasks in various human resource-related areas. The generalist often is involved in several, or all, of the six human resource management functions. A **specialist** may be a human resource executive, manager, or nonmanager who is typically concerned with only one of the six functional areas of human resource management. Figure 1-3 helps clarify these distinctions.

The vice-president of industrial relations shown in Figure 1-3 specializes primarily in union-related matters. This person is both an executive and a specialist. The human resource vice-president is both a generalist and an executive, having responsibility for a wide variety of functions. The manager of compensation and benefits is a specialist, as is the benefits analyst. Whereas an executive may be identified by position level in the organization, generalists and specialists are distinguished by their positions' breadth of responsibility.

The distinction between generalists and specialists should be even clearer from the Monsanto example in Figure 1-4. It lists the type of general work assignments at various levels in the organization for both generalists and specialists. Also interesting are the "two bits of advice" that Monsanto gives with regard to career development for both generalists and specialists. Although the assignments of both generalists and specialists at the

---
[21] *Ibid.*

16   PART ONE   Introduction

HRM In Action

Scotty, I know that you are the human resource manager, and I really appreciate your concern for my career, but the position you are offering me as assistant human resource director is, in my opinion, a deadend job. Recruiters just find employees to fill vacant positions. They don't get involved in other areas of the company, so my achievements could easily go unnoticed and I'd be stuck there forever. Another thing, I have heard that top management really only cares about marketing, production, and finance—not human resources. I appreciate the thought, Scotty, but don't put me in a deadend job.

How should Scotty respond?

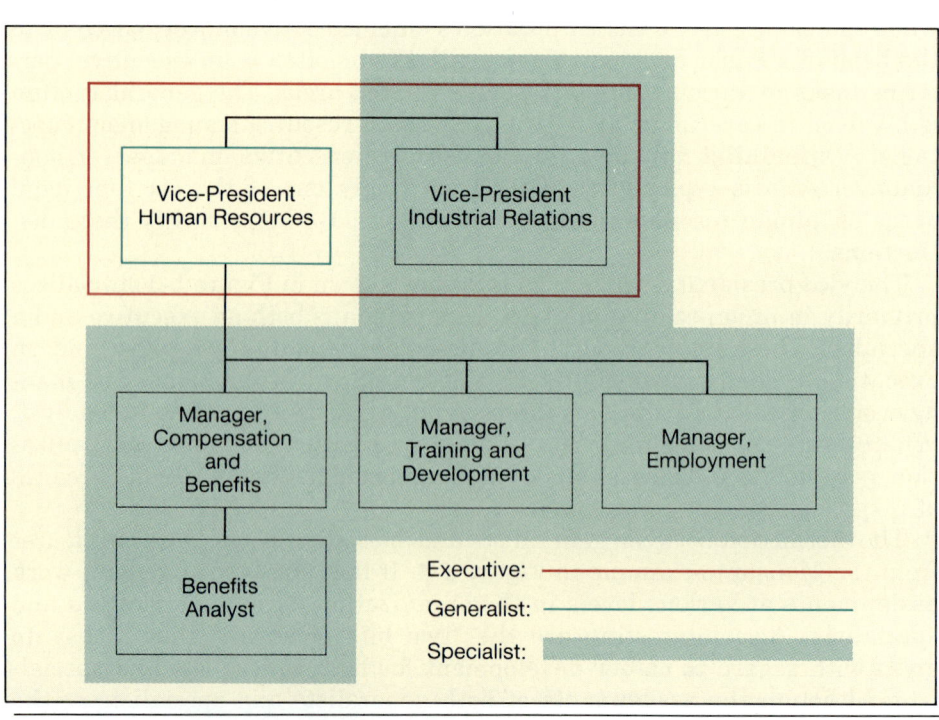

FIGURE 1-3 | Human Resource Executives, Generalists, and Specialists

CHAPTER 1 Human Resource Management: An Overview 17

departmental and corporate levels vary considerably, the lines between these assignments blur at times, and the career path for both may not always be "up."

■ THE HUMAN RESOURCE FUNCTION IN ORGANIZATIONS OF VARIOUS SIZES

The human resource function tends to change as firms grow and become more complex—and as the function achieves greater importance. Although the basic purpose of human resource management remains the same, the approach followed in accomplishing its objectives often changes.

Small businesses seldom have a formal human resource unit and HRM specialists, as Figure 1-5 shows. Rather, other managers handle human resource functions. The focus of these activities is generally on hiring and retaining capable employees.

Some aspects of the human resource function may actually be more significant in small firms than in large organizations. For instance, if the owner of a small business hires her first and only full-time salesperson—and this individual promptly alienates the firm's customers—the business might actually fail. In a larger firm, such an error would likely be much less devastating.

As a firm grows, a separate staff function may be required to coordinate human resource activities. In a larger firm, the person chosen to do so will be expected to handle most of the human resource activities, as Figure 1-6 implies. For this size of firm there is little specialization. A secretary may be available to handle correspondence, but the human resource manager is essentially the entire department.

When the organization's human resource function becomes too much for one person to handle, separate sections often are created and placed under a human resource manager. These sections will typically perform tasks involving human resource development, compensation and benefits, employment, safety and health, and labor relations, as depicted in Figure 1-7.

In still larger firms, the human resource function takes on even more responsibility, requiring even greater specialization. Figure 1-8, organization chart for Champion International Corporation, illustrates this condition. The unit responsible for compensation, for example, will most likely include some specialists who concentrate on hourly wages and others who devote their time to salary administration. The employee relations vice-president works closely with top management in formulating corporate policy. Table 1-1 outlines the duties and responsibilities of Champion's employee relations executive. As you can see, the scope of such a position is quite broad, ranging from the coordination, recommendation, and implementation of plans to auditing performance.

■ PROFESSIONALIZATION OF HUMAN RESOURCE MANAGEMENT

A **profession** is characterized by the existence of a common body of knowledge and a procedure for certifying members of the profession. Performance

Starting Assignment	
Specialist	Generalist
Work for a supervisor in an area like labor relations, employment, training and benefits. This would be at a larger location, where the function is broken down into areas of specialty.	Work for a supervisor or superintendent in several areas. You might be responsible for training, communications, employment, benefits, safety. This would be at a smaller location with two or three personnel professionals on the staff.

Later Assignments	
Specialist	Generalist
Manage one or two areas of responsibility, such as labor relations, training and development, a combination of employment and benefits. Again, this would be at a larger location.	Manage the total human resource function: ■ For a sub-unit within the location (such as for the maintenance department, or for a geographic area within the location), ■ For a smaller Monsanto location, ■ For a larger location.

Operating Company/Staff Department	
Specialist	Generalist
Manage one or two functions such as human resource planning, compensation, recruiting, or an entire company or staff department.	Manage the total human resource function for a sub-unit within a company (e.g., a division) or for the entire company or staff department.

Corporate	
Specialist	Generalist
Work in or manage an entire area of expertise for the corporation, such as labor relations, equal employment opportunity, development, benefits.	Manage the total corporate human resource function.

Two bits of advice:
- Don't get hung up on whether you begin your career as a specialist or generalist. The lines between generalist and specialist are not as neat as the chart would indicate. For example, as an employment "specialist," you would daily become involved with questions of labor relations, compensation, human resource planning and equal employment policy—and much more! Or as a small-plant "generalist," you would have to learn the basics of several specialties. Also, the overwhelming odds are that you will get both types of exposure—specialist and generalist—in your career.
- Career development will not always be "up." It's to the professional's advantage to get as much experience and exposure as possible—and many times, this will mean lateral moves into different areas of specialty.

FIGURE 1-4 | Career Development at Monsanto

Source: Used with the permission of the Monsanto Company.

CHAPTER 1   Human Resource Management: An Overview   19

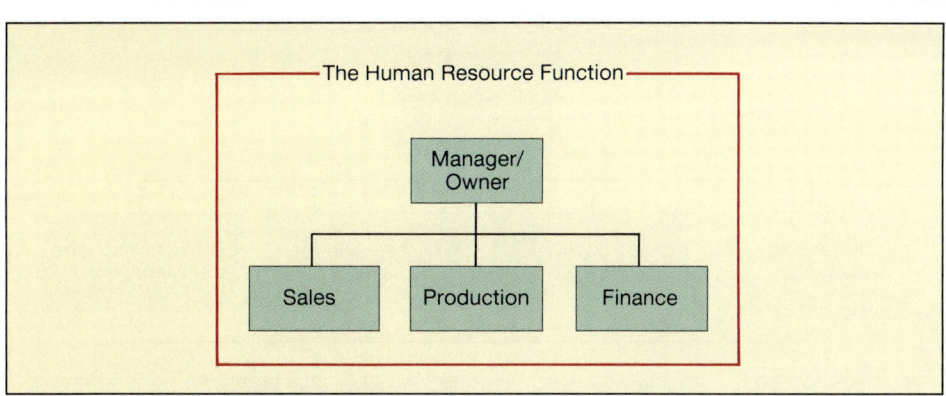

FIGURE 1-5 | The Human Resource Function in a Small Business

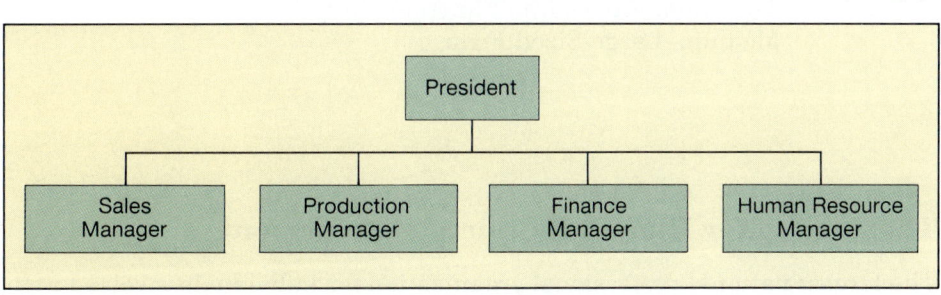

FIGURE 1-6 | The Human Resource Function in a Medium-Sized Firm

standards are established by members of the profession (self-regulation) rather than by outsiders. Most professions also have effective representative organizations that permit members to exchange ideas of mutual concern. These characteristics apply to the field of human resources, and several well-known organizations serve the profession.[22] Among the more prominent are the Society for Human Resource Management, the Personnel Accreditation Institute, the American Society for Training and Development, the American Compensation Association, the International Association for Personnel Women, and the International Personnel Management Association.

---

[22] Cheryl Haigley, "Professionalism in Personnel," *Personnel Administrator*, 29 (June 1984), p. 103.

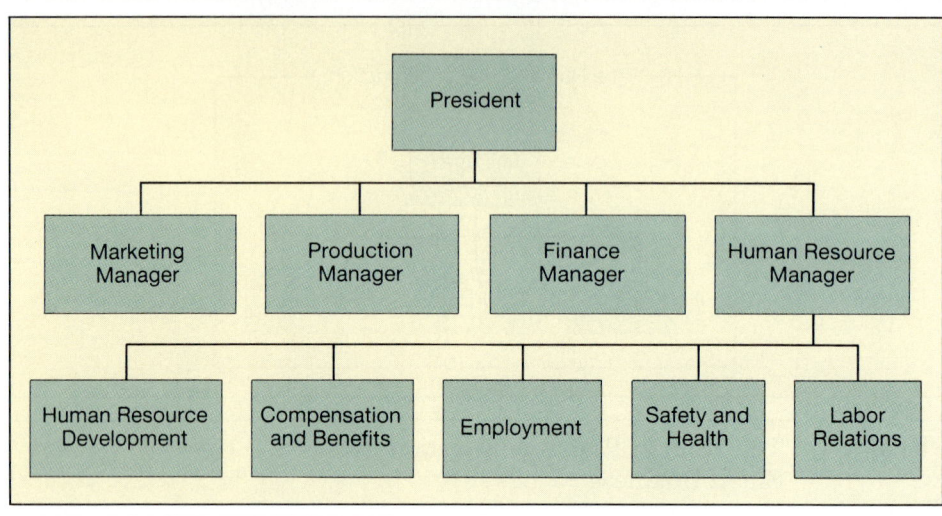

FIGURE 1-7 | The Human Resource Functions in a Medium–Large-Sized Firm

The Society for Human Resource Management

The largest national professional organization for individuals involved with human resource management is the Society for Human Resource Management (SHRM). Formerly called the American Society for Personnel Administration (ASPA), the name change became official in 1990. The name change reflects the increasingly important role that human resource management plays in the overall bottom line of organizations. The basic goals of the society include defining, maintaining, and improving standards of excellence in the practice of human resource management. Membership consists of 34,500 individuals and there are currently more than 400 local chapters, and numerous student chapters on university campuses across the country.[23] The *Personnel Administrator* is published monthly by the society as a means of disseminating human resource information.

Personnel Accreditation Institute

One of the more significant developments in the field of HRM has been the establishment of the Personnel Accreditation Institute (PAI), a subsidiary

---

[23] Katherine Gruber (ed.), *Encyclopedia of Associations*, 20th ed., vol. 1: National Organizations of the United States, part 1 (Detroit: Gale Research Company, 1985), p. 259.

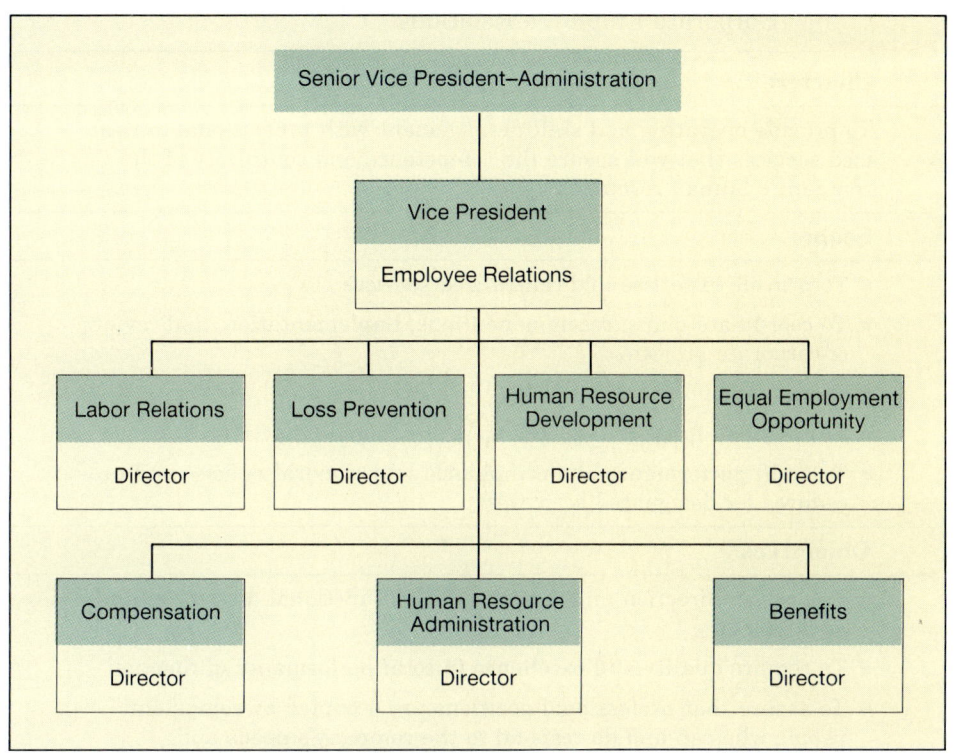

FIGURE 1-8 | The Employee Relations Organization—
Champion International Corporation

Source: Used with the permission of Champion International Corporation.

of SHRM.[24] Founded in 1976, PAI's goal is to recognize human resource professionals through an accreditation program.[25] This program encourages human resource professionals to continuously update their knowledge and skills. Accreditation indicates that they have mastered a validated common body of knowledge. The advantages of human resource accreditation were outlined a number of years ago by a former national president of ASPA, Wiley Beavers, who wrote:

> First, we would benefit at the college and university level. The development of the body of knowledge required for successful practice in the various areas of personnel would provide invaluable assistance in curricula design. The breakdown of the field into its specialties would also allow students to focus on career directions earlier in their education.

---

[24] Juanita F. Parry, "Accredited Professionals Are Better Prepared," *Personnel Administrator*, 30 (December 1985), p. 48.

[25] Details of the PAI are shown in the Appendix to this Chapter.

TABLE 1-1 | Champion International Corporation Corporate Employee Relations

Charter:
To provide operating and staff management with professional centralized services that will assure the competence and continuity of the company's human resources
Scope:
▪ To provide expertise and centralized services ▪ To coordinate plans, recommendations, implementation, and review of corporate projects ▪ To recommend general policies ▪ To establish functional procedures for designated activities ▪ To audit performance and compliance with general policies and procedures for designated activities
Objectives:
▪ To provide direction and support to each functional director and his department ▪ To require quality and excellence in total performance of function ▪ To assure that professional positions are occupied by competent people who can and do respond to the company's needs and requirements

Source: Used with permission of Champion International Corporation.

Second, young practitioners would have sound guidelines and information covering areas in which they should be boning up and could avoid the mistakes many of us older types make.

Third, senior practitioners would be encouraged to update their knowledge. (Don't know how many of them will be interested in accreditation. There will be an appreciable reaction along the lines of: "I don't need to take tests to prove I know what I'm doing. I have already proven it by the job I'm doing." And they will be right in about 50 percent of the cases.)[26]

American Society for Training and Development

Founded in 1944, the American Society for Training and Development (ASTD) has grown to become the largest specialized professional organiza-

---

[26] Wiley Beavers, "Accreditation: What Do We Need That For?" *Personnel Administrator*, 18 (November 1975), pp. 39-41.

tion in human resources. Its membership exceeds 23,000, and it has over 147 local groups.[27] The membership is comprised of individuals who are concerned specifically with training and development. The society publishes the *Training and Development Journal* monthly to encourage its members to remain current in the field.

American Compensation Association

The American Compensation Association (ACA) was founded in 1954 and currently has a membership that exceeds 10,000.[28] The ACA is comprised of managerial and human resource professionals who are responsible for the establishment, execution, administration, or application of compensation practices and policies in their organizations. The ACA's journal, which contains information related to compensation issues, is the *Compensation Review*.

International Association for Personnel Women

Founded in 1950, the International Association for Personnel Women (IAPW) was established to expand and improve the professionalism of women in human resource management. Its membership consists of human resource executives in business, industry, education, and government. The IAPW has approximately 1,900 members.[29] IAPW's journal, *Human Resources: Journal of the International Association for Personnel Women*, is published quarterly to disseminate information of interest to its members.

International Personnel Management Association

The International Personnel Management Association (IPMA) was founded in 1973 and currently has more than 5,400 members. This organization seeks to improve human resource practices by providing testing services, an advisory service, conferences, professional development programs, research, and publications. It sponsors seminars and workshops on various phases of public human resource administration. The organization's journal, *Public Personnel Management*, is published quarterly for those involved in public-agency human resource administration.[30]

■ ETHICS AND HUMAN RESOURCE MANAGEMENT

Professionalization of human resource management created the need for a uniform code of ethics. The discipline dealing with what is good and bad or

---

[27] *Ibid.*, p. 129.
[28] *Ibid.*, p. 259.
[29] *Ibid.*
[30] *Ibid.*, p. 260.

right and wrong or with moral duty and obligation is **ethics**. Every day, individuals working in human resources must make decisions that have ethical implications. Ethical dilemmas, such as whether a manager should recommend against a women applicant for employment strictly because she will be working exclusively with men, occur frequently and must be correctly addressed. These issues must be dealt with on the basis of what is ethically correct, not just from the standpoint of what will benefit the organization most.

There are many kinds of ethical codes, and most professions have their own. An example is SHRM's Code of Ethics, shown in Figure 1-9. Some firms also have formally stated ethical codes to guide employee behavior. And individual employees have their own personal codes of behavior. Of the numerous codes that exist in our society, few conflict in principle. They

---

Each member of the Society shall acknowledge his or her personal responsibility to strive for growth in the field of human resources management, and will pledge to carry out the following Society objectives, to the best of his or her ability.

- Support the goals and objectives of the Society in order to reflect the highest standards of the human resource management profession.
- Support the personal and professional development programs of the Society in Personnel Administration and Industrial Relations to help create an environment of recognition and support of human values in the workplace.
- Support the self-enforcement provisions in the codes of other associations to achieve the overall goal of development of each person to his/her full human potential.
- Display a unity of spirit and cohesiveness of purpose in bringing fair and equitable treatment of all people to the forefront of employers' thought; transmit that cohesiveness to academia by actively cooperating to instill the PAIR ethic into the curricula of accredited institutions.
- Practice respect and regard for each other as a paramount personal commitment to a lifestyle exemplary in its motivation toward making business profitable in both human and monetary values.
- Express in the workplace through corporate codes the basic rules governing moral conduct of the members of the organization in order to provide employees and the public with a sense of confidence about the conduct and intentions of management.
- Personally refrain from using their official positions (regular or volunteer) to secure special privilege, gain or benefit for themselves, their employers or the Society.

FIGURE 1-9 | **SHRM Code of Ethics**

Source: Reprinted from *Who's Who in ASPA 1988 Directory*. p. 49, copyright 1988, The American Society for Personnel Administration, Alexandria, VA.

vary primarily in their extent and application to particular circumstances. It is vitally important for the human resource manager to understand those practices that are unacceptable and to make every attempt to act ethically in dealing with others.

■ SCOPE OF THIS BOOK

Effective human resource management is crucial to every organization's success. In order to be effective, managers must understand and competently practice human resource management. We designed this human resource management book to give you:

- An insight into the role of human resource management in today's organizations.
- An understanding of human resource planning, recruitment, and selection.
- An awareness of the importance of human resource development.
- An appreciation of how compensation and benefits programs are formulated and administered.
- An understanding of safety and health factors as they impact a firm's profitability.
- An opportunity to view employee and labor relations from both unionized and union-free standpoints.
- An understanding of the role of research in human resource management.
- An appreciation of the multinational dimension of human resource management.

Students often question whether the content of a book corresponds to the realities of the business world. In writing and revising this book we have drawn heavily on the comments, observations, and experiences of human resource practitioners—and our own extensive research efforts. We cite human resource practices of leading business organizations to illustrate how theory can be applied in the real world. Our intent is to enable you to experience human resource management in action.

This book is organized under seven parts, as shown in Figure 1-10. Combined, they provide a comprehensive view of human resource management. As you read this book, we hope you will be stimulated to increase your knowledge in this rapidly changing, expanding, and challenging field.

I. Introduction

Chapter 1: Human Resource Management: An Overview
Chapter 2: The Environment of Human Resource Management
Chapter 3: Equal Employment Opportunity and Affirmative Action
Chapter 4: Job Analysis

II. Human Resource Planning, Recruitment, and Selection

Chapter 5: Human Resource Planning
Chapter 6: Recruitment
Chapter 7: Selection

III. Human Resource Development

Chapter 8: Organization Change and Training and Development
Chapter 9: Corporate Culture and Organization Development
Chapter 10: Career Planning and Development
Chapter 11: Performance Appraisal

IV. Compensation and Benefits

Chapter 12: Financial Compensation
Chapter 13: Benefits and Other Compensation Issues

V. Safety and Health

Chapter 14: A Safe and Healthy Work Environment

VI. Employee and Labor Relations

Chapter 15: The Labor Union
Chapter 16: Collective Bargaining
Chapter 17: Union-Free Organizations
Chapter 18: Internal Employee Relations

VII. Human Resource Research

Chapter 19: Human Resource Research and Evaluation

FIGURE 1-10 | Organization of This Book

SUMMARY

Human resource management (HRM) is the utilization of the firm's human resources to achieve organizational goals. Human resource managers normally act in an advisory (staff) capacity, working with other managers regarding human resource matters. Human resource managers have the primary responsibility of coordinating the firm's human resource actions through a well-conceived human resource management system. That system embraces six functional areas of effective human resource management.

An organization must have qualified individuals available at specific places and times to accomplish its goals. Among the tasks involved in accomplishing this objective are human resource planning, recruitment, and selection.

Human resource development (HRD) is designed to assist individuals, groups, and the entire organization in becoming more effective. Such programs are needed because people, jobs, and organizations are always changing. Development should begin when individuals join the firm and continue throughout their careers. Large-scale HRD programs are referred to as organizational development (OD). Other aspects of HRD are career planning and development and performance appraisal.

The question of what constitutes a fair day's pay has plagued managers for decades. An effective compensation and benefits system rewards employees adequately and equitably for their contributions to the organization. As used in this book, the term compensation includes all rewards that individuals receive as a result of their employment.

Safety involves protecting employees from injuries caused by work-related accidents. Health refers to the employees' freedom from illness, and their general physical and mental well-being. A safe and healthy work environment is important not only to employees but also to the organization. Employees who enjoy these conditions are more likely to be productive and provide long-term benefits to the organization.

A business firm is required by law to recognize a union, and bargain with it in good faith, if the firm's employees want the union to represent them. However, union-free firms typically strive to satisfy their employees' work-related needs in order to make union representation unnecessary for individuals to achieve their personal goals.

Every human resource management function needs effective research. This need is particularly strong today because of the rapid changes taking place in the HRM field.

In recent years, human resource professionals have been afforded increased respect and responsibility. They are now expected to provide the direction necessary to meet the many HRM problems and challenges of the future.

Within the human resource profession are executives, generalists, and specialists. Executives are top-level managers who report directly to the corporation's CEO or to the head of a major division. A generalist (who often is an executive) performs tasks in many human resource-related areas. A specialist may be an executive, a manager, or a nonmanager who is typically concerned with only one of the six functional areas of HRM.

Human resource functions tend to change as firms grow and become more complex—as HRM becomes more important. Although the basic purpose of human resource management remains the same, the approach followed in accomplishing its objectives often changes.

A profession is characterized by the existence of a common body of knowledge and a procedure for certifying members of the profession. Performance standards are established by members of the profession itself (self-regulation). Professional organizations offer their members the chance to exchange ideas and grow. Among the more prominent professional organizations in the field of human resources are the Society for Human Resource Management (formerly the American Society for Personnel Administration), the Personnel Accreditation Institute, the American Society for Training and Development, the American Compensation Association, the International Association for Personnel Women, and the International Personnel Management Association.

Professionalization of human resource management created a need for a uniform code of ethics. Individuals working in human resources must constantly make decisions that have ethical implications. Most professions, organizations, and individuals subscribe to ethical codes of one type or another.

Questions for Review

1. Justify the statement, "All managers are involved in human resource management."
2. Distinguish between human resource management and the human resource manager.
3. What human resource management functions must be performed regardless of the organization's size?
4. By definition and example distinguish among human resource executives, generalists, and specialists.
5. How does the human resource function change as a firm grows? Briefly describe each stage of the development.
6. Define *profession*. Do you believe that the field of human resource management is a profession? Explain your answer.
7. Define *ethics*. Why is ethics important to the field of human resource management?

Terms for Review

Human resource management (HRM)
Human resource manager
Operative employees
Executive
Generalist
Specialist
Profession
Ethics

INCIDENT 1 — A Day to Remember

The day was one of the happiest in Ed Beaver's life. He had been told that he was being promoted to corporate vice-president for human resources from his present position as human resource manager for his firm's large New York plant. As he leaned back in his office chair, he felt a deep sense of accomplishment. He thought back to the day fifteen years earlier when, fresh out of college, he had joined Duncan Foods as an assistant compensation specialist. He had always wanted to be in human resources, but he got his degree in business management because the university didn't have a human resource curriculum. Ed remembered how tense he was when he arrived at work that first day. College graduates were rarely given the opportunity to start work directly in human resources in those days, and he was the youngest employee in the department.

Ed learned his job well and the older workers quickly accepted him. Three years later he was promoted to the position of compensation manager. Immediately after the promotion he was given the task of designing a new pay system for operative employees. As he remembers, "Designing the system wasn't difficult. Convincing the employees that the new system was better than the old one was the real chore." But he overcame that obstacle.

A few years later Ed moved up again. He was chosen to become the new human resource manager for a small Duncan plant outside Chicago. The move required a major adjustment for his family. At the time Ed's wife had remarked, "I sure hated to move in the middle of the school year. And we'd just begun to enjoy our new house." Ed was able to find another house that the family came to like just as well, and the children adjusted quickly. The job was certainly no bed of roses. Six months after Ed arrived, he led negotiations for a new union contract. He worked night and day for months to develop a contract that would be acceptable to both the company and the union. Successful signing of the new agreement was one of his most satisfying experiences.

Four years later, Ed was asked to accept the position of human resource manager for the large New York plant. This plant employed five times as many workers as the Chicago plant and had many different types of problems. After a family discussion, the Beavers were off to new adventures in the Big Apple.

At that moment, Ed's nostalgia came to a halt. The challenge of the new job suddenly came home to him. As vice-president of human resources for Duncan Foods he would be responsible for the human resource management activities for fifty plants and warehouses employing 13,000 people. What an overwhelming responsibility he faced! Human resource management had changed greatly during the previous fifteen years and the rate of change seemed to be accelerating. Ed wondered about these problems and the role he would play in solving them as the new vice-president for human resources.

Questions

1. Trace Ed's progression to vice-president of human resources. Do you believe that this progression qualifies him for this job?
2. What problems do you imagine that Ed will face in his new role that he didn't have to deal with as plant human resource manager?
3. What future challenges do you think Ed will confront in the field of human resources?

INCIDENT 2 — Learn What They Really Want

Marsha Smith was exceptionally happy the day she received word of her appointment as assistant human resource director at Nelson Electronics in Boise, Idaho. Marsha had joined the company as a recruiter three years earlier. Her degree from the University of Missouri was in human resource administration and she had four years' experience as a human resource specialist with Nelson Electronics.

As she walked to her office, she thought about how much she had learned while working as a recruiter. The first year with Nelson, she went on a recruiting trip to Southern Idaho College, only to find its placement director extremely angry with her company. She was visibly upset when the placement director said, "If you expect to recruit any of our students, you people at Nelson had better get your act together." Questioning of the placement director revealed that a previous recruiter had failed to show up for a full afternoon of scheduled interviews with Southern's students. Marsha's trip ended amicably, though, and she eventually recruited a number of excellent employees from the college.

Another important lesson began when the production manager asked for some help. "I need you to find an experienced quality control inspector," he said. "I want to make sure that the person has a degree in statistics. Beyond that, you decide on the qualifications." Marsha advertised the position and checked through dozens of résumés in search of the right person. She sent each promising applicant to the production manager. This went on for six months with the production manager giving various obscure reasons for not hiring any of the applicants. Finally, the production manager called Marsha and said, "I just hired a QC person. He has a degree in history, but he seems eager. Besides, he was willing to work for only a thousand dollars a month."

Marsh learned more with each passing day. She felt that one of her greatest accomplishments was improving the firm's minority recruiting program. Her ability to do this was based on something of a coincidence. One of her close friends in school had become a leader in the Black Chamber of Commerce. With his advice she was able to develop a recruiting program that attracted blacks to Nelson Electronics.

As Marsha began to clean out her desk, she suddenly realized that the learning process was really just beginning. As assistant human resource director, she would be responsible not only for matters related to recruiting, but for all aspects of human resource management. It was a little scary, but she felt ready.

Questions

1. What are the lessons that can be learned from each of the three situations described?
2. How will the problems Marsha faces as an assistant human resource director differ from those she handled as a recruiter?

EXPERIENCING HUMAN RESOURCE MANAGEMENT

In every organization, human resource professionals work with many individuals and groups. Cooperation is a must if the tasks involved in human resource management are to be accomplished effectively. The Blue-Green exercise provides an excellent experience in the value of cooperation. This exercise is a good "ice-breaker" and discussion-stimulator. Specifically, this exercise provides students with the opportunity to experience some of the interrelationships that occur in a structured setting, such as an organization or work group.

The Blue-Green exercise is one of the best exercises to use with a relatively large group. In fact, it is not recommended for groups of less than 12. It has been successfully used in groups as large as 40. This exercise works equally well with groups of people who have been working together for some time and with heterogeneous groups who barely know one another. Its impact, however, is probably greater when dealing with people who are *supposed* to work together. The language used by the person in charge of conducting the exercise is extremely important, so participants should listen carefully to the rules.

This exercise is usually quite enlightening to those who participate, and has therefore been repeated many times over the years. The total group will be divided into four sub-groups of as nearly equal size as possible. These sub-groups will be called "teams" and designated as Team A-1, Team A-2, Team B-1, and Team B-2. Your instructor will provide the participants with additional information necessary to participate. Enjoy the classic Blue-Green exercise, and experience the first of the experiential exercises provided to expand your educational horizons.

REFERENCES

Andrews, Janet R. "Where Doubts About the Personnel Role Begin." *Personnel Journal*, 66 (June 1987), pp. 84–89.

Bellman, Geoffrey M. "Doing More with Less." *Personnel Administrator*, 31 (July 1986), pp. 47–52.

Dunsing, Richard J. "Macho Management: What HR Professionals Should Watch For." *Personnel*, 64 (July 1987), pp. 62–66.

Gow, Jack F. "Human Resources Managers Must Remember the Bottom Line." *Personnel Journal*, 64 (April 1985), pp. 30–33.

Haigley, Cheryl. "Professionalism in Personnel." *Personnel Administrator*, 29 (June 1984), pp. 103–106.

Harvey, L. James. "Nine Major Trends in HRM." *Personnel Administrator*, 31 (November 1986), pp. 102–109.

Holman, Gil. "In Search of Excellence in Personnel Management." *Personnel Management*, 17 (November 1985), pp. 28–31.

Kiechel, Walter. "Living with Human Resources: Believe It or Not, Managers Can Profit by Working with What Used to Be Called the Personnel Department." *Fortune*, 114 (August 18, 1986), pp. 99–101.

Layton, William G., and Eric J. Johnson. "Break the Mold: Strategies for Productivity." *Personnel Journal*, 66 (May 1987), pp. 74–78.

Mondy, R. Wayne, Robert M. Noe, and Robert E. Edwards. "What the Staffing Function Entails." *Personnel*, 63 (April 1986), pp. 55–58.

Mondy, R. Wayne, Shane R. Premeaux, and Larry Worley. "People Problems: Substance Use and Abuse."

Management Solutions, 32 (February 1987), pp. 22–25.

Parry, Juanita F. "Accredited Professionals Are Better Prepared." *Personnel Administrator*, 30 (December 1985), pp. 48–52.

Portwood, James D., and Robert W. Eichinger. "The Challenge of Human Resource Management: Adding Value." *Human Resource Planning*, 8 (December 1985), pp. 209–228.

Premeaux, Shane R., R. Wayne Mondy, and Art Bethke. "Decertification: Fulfilling Unions' Destiny?" *Personnel Journal*, 66 (June 1987), pp. 144–148.

Vicere, Albert A. "Break the Mold: Strategies for Leadership." *Personnel Journal*, 66 (May 1987), pp. 67–74.

APPENDIX

PROFESSIONAL ACCREDITATION

The Personnel Accreditation Institute (PAI) is a subsidiary of the Society for Human Resource Management. Since its inception in 1976, the PAI has granted accreditation to more than 6,000 individuals. The number of accredited individuals will likely increase substantially as the benefits of accreditation become more apparent.

The Personnel Accreditation Institute's program provides for two levels of accreditation: operational and policy level. These two levels recognize degrees of expertise and responsibility.

Operational: Requires an examination and some experience. The examination covers the general body of knowledge.

Policy: Requires an examination and senior level experience. Practitioners must also have policy-developing responsibilities.

Specialist: A practitioner, consultant, educator or researcher who characteristically provides in-depth expertise or management in a segment of the field.

Generalist: A senior practitioner or consultant whose responsibilities span the field and whose knowledge is broad-based rather than specialized.

■ OPERATIONAL LEVEL ACCREDITATION, PROFESSIONAL IN HUMAN RESOURCES (PHR)

Specific Requirements

Practitioners. Four years of professional experience in the field in the last six years. A B.B.A., B.S., or B.A. degree in personnel/human resource management or social sciences may be substituted for experience, allowing two years for a bachelor's degree and three years for a master's degree. The minimum experience requirement is one year of recent full-time professional practice in the field.

Educators. Three academic years of full-time teaching at the undergraduate level or two years at the graduate level at an accredited college or university. Two current years of teaching in the personnel or human resources field.

Consultants or Researchers (Academe, Business, Government, etc.). Four years of consulting or significant and recorded research related to the field of personnel or human resources. Minimum of one current full-time year of consulting or research in the field.

Combination. Practical experience, teaching, research and/or consulting may be combined. A minimum of one year of recent experience or two recent academic years of teaching in the field of personnel and human resources.

Examination

Successful completion of the operational level examination of the body of knowledge in the field of personnel and human resources.

■ POLICY LEVEL ACCREDITATION, SENIOR PROFESSIONAL IN HUMAN RESOURCES (SPHR)—SPECIALIST

Functional Areas

1. Employment, placement and personnel planning
2. Training and development
3. Compensation and benefits
4. Health, safety, and security
5. Employee and labor relations
6. Personnel research

Specific Requirements

Practitioners. Eight years of experience in the field. College degrees may be substituted for experience. Minimum experience is five years. Recent three years must include policy-developing responsibility. Recent position must encompass the full scope of the functional area in which accreditation is sought.

Educators, Researchers, or Consultants. Eight years of experience equivalent to that specified for practitioners.

Combination. Eight years of combined practical experience, teaching, research, and/or consulting. Minimum of five years of experience in the functional area in which accreditation is sought. Recent position must encompass the full scope of senior responsibilities in the functional area in which accreditation is sought.

Examination

Successful completion of an examination at the policy level in one, or possibly two, functional areas. The examination also includes some items from the basic body of knowledge across the personnel and human resources field.

■ POLICY LEVEL ACCREDITATION, SENIOR PROFESSIONAL IN HUMAN RESOURCES (SPHR)—GENERALIST

Policy level senior experience in four of the six functional areas plus an examination covering all functional areas and management practices. Generalists are typically practitioners, although some consultants and educators may qualify.

Specific Requirements

Eight years of experience in the field. College degrees may be substituted for experience. Minimum of five years of experience in the field. Three years of recent experience with policy-developing responsibility spanning at least four functional areas. Candidates with specialist and generalist policy-influencing experience may qualify with at least two years in each of four functional areas in the last six years.

Examination

Successful completion of an examination at the senior level demonstrating broad-based knowledge across the personnel and human resources field.

Accreditation and reaccreditation, together, sum up human resources professionalism. Accreditation is earned by individuals who demonstrate their mastery of the defined body of knowledge. The human resources field, however, is not static. Rapid changes require new and more sophisticated knowledge and behaviors by personnel professionals who wish to grow and develop. Reaccreditation is a method for accredited individuals to demonstrate their accomplishments in keeping abreast of changes and to update their knowledge in the field.

Reaccreditation is required within three years of accreditation. The actual expiration date is June 30 or December 31, whichever date occurs first, following the three-year anniversary of the accreditation. Each reaccreditation period is also for three years. Senior Professionals in Human Resources who are reaccredited twice are not required to become reaccredited again. There are two ways to become reaccredited. One method is by testing. The other method is through a variety of specified activities.

Accreditation examinations are given on the first Saturday of each May and December at designated test sites. Applications must be submitted to the Institute at least six weeks in advance of the examination date. For additional accreditation information, contact the Personnel Accreditation Institute, 606 North Washington Street, Alexandria, VA 22314.

CHAPTER 2

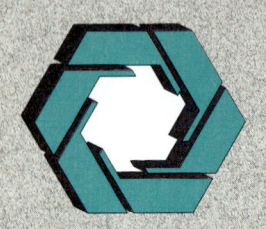

THE ENVIRONMENT OF HUMAN RESOURCE MANAGEMENT

CHAPTER OBJECTIVES

1. Identify and describe the external environmental factors that affect human resource management.
2. Identify and describe the internal environmental factors that affect human resource management.
3. Identify and describe external environmental factors that uniquely affect human resource management for multinational corporations.

■ As Wayne Simmons, vice-president of human resources for Lone Star Manufacturing, returned to his office from the weekly executive staff meeting, he was visibly disturbed. Lone Star, a producer of high-quality telecommunications equipment, is headquartered in Longview, Texas, and has manufacturing plants throughout Texas, Louisiana, and Oklahoma. Wayne had just heard a rumor that the firm's major competitor had developed a new manufacturing process—one that has the potential to cut costs substantially. Should this report prove true, customers might well switch to the cheaper product. The three plants in the Longline Division, which produce similar products, would then be in serious trouble. The Longline Division had been expanding rapidly, but Wayne knew that demand for Lone Star's product was far from automatic. He also knew that if the new technology was really superior, Lone Star might have to cut back production severely or even close the three plants in the Longline Division. These plants are located in areas that are already experiencing high unemployment because of the depressed price of crude oil. Plant closings would have a devastating effect on the economies of their respective communities. A few workers could be transferred to other locations, but most would have to be laid off. Thus Wayne is now keenly aware of ways in which the external environment can have an impact on Lone Star Manufacturing's operations.

In this chapter, we first identify the environmental factors affecting human resource management. Then we describe the means by which specific external environmental factors can influence human resource management. Next, we discuss some of the major internal environmental factors that can affect human resource management. Because of the continuing growth of multinational organizations, we devote the final section to describing major external environmental factors that multinational firms confront.

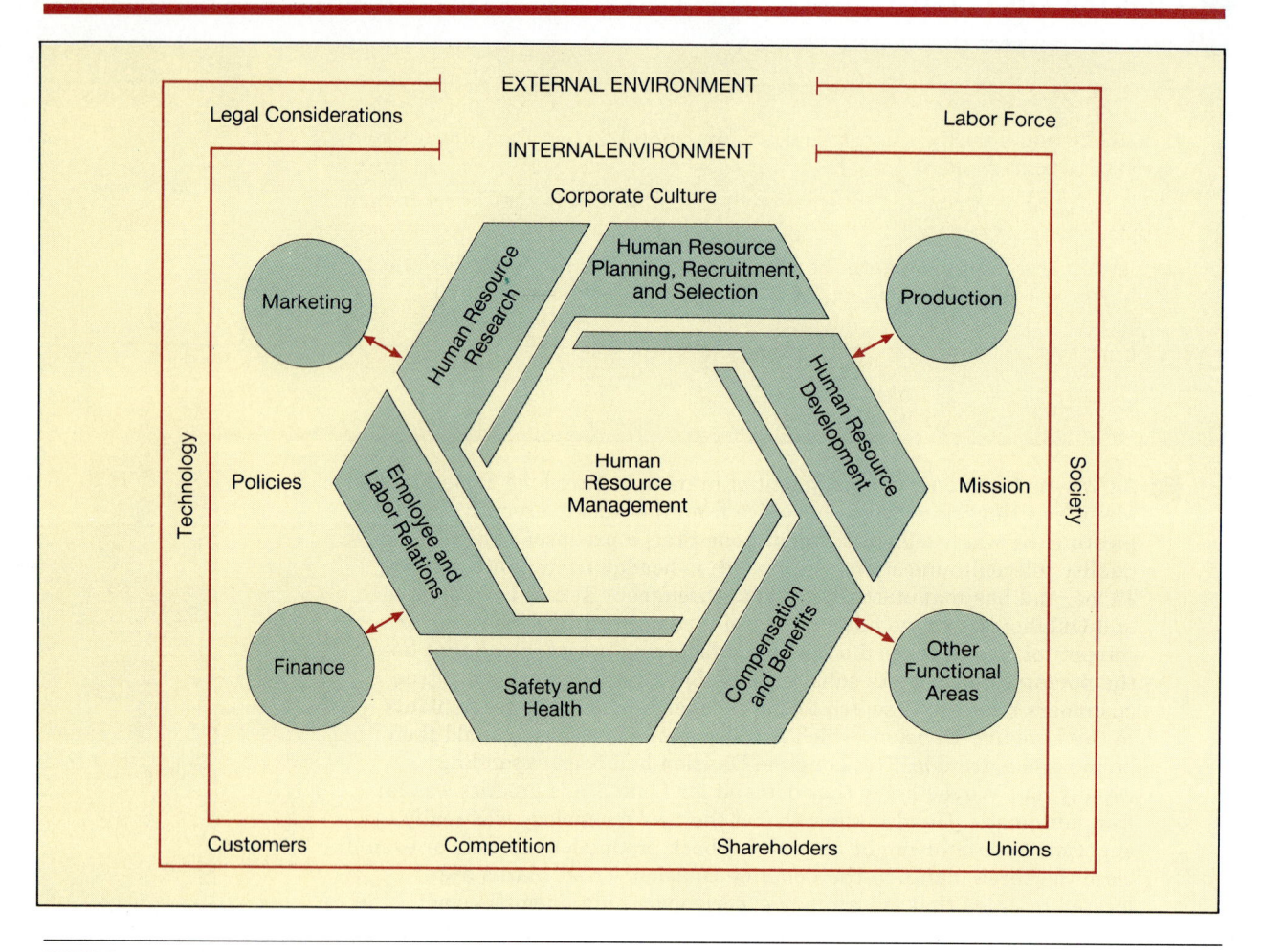

FIGURE 2-1 | The Environments of Human Resource Management

■ ENVIRONMENTAL FACTORS AFFECTING HUMAN RESOURCE MANAGEMENT

Many interrelated factors affect human resource management. Such factors are part of either the firm's external environment or its internal environment (see Figure 2-1). The firm often has little, if any, control over how the external environment affects management of its human resources. These factors impinge on the organization from outside its boundaries. Moreover, important factors within the firm itself also have an impact on how the firm manages its human resources.

Certain interrelationships tend to complicate the management of human resources. For instance, human resource professionals constantly work with people who represent all organizational levels and functional areas. Therefore, they must recognize the different perspectives that these individuals bring to HRM in order to perform their own human resource tasks properly. This point is made in Executive Insights by Robert L. Berra who states, "Today, the human resource executive wears many hats: manager, member of top management, advisor, employee representative, corporate officer, and professional."

Understanding the many interrelationships implied in Figure 2-1 is essential in order for the human resource professional to help other managers resolve issues and problems. For instance, a production manager may want to give a substantial pay raise to a particular employee. The human resource manager may know that this employee does an exceptional job but should also be aware that granting the raise may affect pay practices in the production department *and* set a precedent for the entire firm. The human resource manager may have to explain to the production manager that such an action isn't an isolated decision. They may have to consider alternative means of rewarding the employee for superior performance, without upsetting the organization's reward system. Perhaps the human resource manager can point to a higher paying position that the employee is qualified to fill.

Whatever the case, the implications of a particular act must be considered in light of its potential impact on a department and the entire organization. Human resource managers must realize the overwhelming importance of the big picture, rather than concentrating on a narrow phase of the company's operation. The basic HRM tasks remain essentially the same regardless of the source of the impact. However, the manner in which those tasks are accomplished may be altered substantially by factors in the external environment.

■ THE EXTERNAL ENVIRONMENT

Those factors that affect a firm's human resources from outside its boundaries comprise the **external environment**. As illustrated in Figure 2-1, external factors include: the labor force, legal considerations, society, unions, shareholders, competition, customers, and technology. Each—either separately or in combination with others—can place constraints on the human resource manager's job. Thus the HR manager must always try to identify and consider the impact of such factors.

The Labor Force

The capabilities of its employees determine in a large part how well an organization can perform its mission. The labor force is a pool of individuals external to the firm, from which the organization obtains its workers. To some degree, as the labor force changes so will the composition of the work force within the organization. And today's labor force is far different from that of the past.

The projected size of the U.S. labor force in 1995 is some 129 million. This projection represents an increase of about 14 percent from the 1984

Executive Insights

Robert L. Berra
Senior Vice-President,
Administration,
Monsanto Company

Bob Berra never had any doubts about what profession he would pursue as a career. "Personnel played to my strengths as I perceived them," he says. "I felt I had strong communication skills and an ability to sense the meaning behind complex relationships—in other words, being able to cut through to what people really say and mean."

Berra received a B.S. degree in commerce and finance from St. Louis University in 1947 and an M.B.A. degree from Harvard Graduate School of Business Administration that same year. "I took all the courses in personnel administration that Harvard offered at the time—both of them," he notes. He has also done graduate work in psychology at Washington University in St. Louis. He joined Monsanto in 1951 as assistant training manager for the company's Springfield, Massachusetts, plant and subsequently served there as employee relations manager, director of sales training, and director of sales administration. In 1959 he was appointed director of personnel for the Plastic Products and Resins Division. He was appointed director of administration for the division in 1966 and was named assistant director of the corporate personnel department in 1967.

From 1970 to 1974, Berra was employed by McKesson, Inc., as corporate vice-president of personnel and public relations. He rejoined Monsanto in 1974 as vice-president of personnel and was named senior vice-president, administration, in 1980. As the "chief morale officer," as he describes it, for an organization of 60,000 employees world-wide, Berra is ultimately responsible for all human resource policies and programs, executive services, and the corporate public affairs department. He is a prolific author of articles on management and motivation and has served as guest lecturer at numerous universities.

He is past president of the Industrial Relations Association of Greater St. Louis and a past president and member of the executive committee of the American Society for Personnel Administration. "Monsanto gets first call on my time, but you have to feel strongly enough about your profession to take the time to contribute to it," he says. Berra also serves on the board of directors of Fisher Controls International, Inc., on the advisory council of St. John's Mercy Medical Center in St. Louis, as an adjunct faculty member of Washington University, and with other civic organizations.

Berra has witnessed and participated in the evolution of the human resource function from specialty area to profession and senior management responsibility. "Today," he says, "the human resource executive wears many hats: manager, member of top management, advisor, employee representative, corporate officer, and professional. The successful human resources executive must be intelligent, sensitive, and healthy enough to handle the pressures. He has to be willing to stand up and be counted when the chips are on the line. Above all, he has to exercise good judgment and then make things happen." An essential element of good judgment, he says, is to seek "in-depth exposure to all parts of the organization to assure properly balanced decisions."

Robert Berra stresses the importance of getting the right experience at the right time—forcing the issue, if necessary. "In most careers, it's necessary to do this only once or twice; but when the need is obvious, don't delay."

level of 114 million. Figure 2-2 shows actual and expected labor-force growth rates from 1945 through 1995. But size alone doesn't tell the entire story. The labor force now includes more working women and older persons. Companies increasingly hire part-time workers, use temporary and "leased employees," and include handicapped people in their workforces. Many new immigrants from developing areas, especially Southeast Asia and Latin America, are also joining the labor force. The breakdown of new entrants in the labor force from 1985 to 2000 are expected to be U.S. born white males, 15 percent; U.S. born white females, 42 percent; U.S. born nonwhite males, 7 percent; U.S. born nonwhite females, 13 percent; immigrant males, 13 percent; and immigrant females, 10 percent.[1]

Women in the Labor Force. Through the mid-1990s, the chief cause of labor-force growth will be the continued, though slower, rise in the number of women seeking jobs. Women are expected to account for more than three fifths of the labor-force growth between 1984 and 1995 (see Figure 2-3). As the number of women entering the labor force continues to increase, their problems are becoming of greater concern to human resource managers. In spite of progress made in adapting the workplace to working mothers, most of them must still personally resolve the problems that their working creates.

Finding good care for children, for example, is a major problem—although by no means the only problem—faced by working mothers. Many companies provide child-care services for their employees. Others, such as IBM, provide day-care referral services. There is an increasing tendency to provide maternity and parenting leave, sometimes even for men. Hewlett-Packard Company and Lotus Development Corporation expanded their maternity leave programs in 1988. Most firms give their employees time off to take their children to a doctor, allowing the employee to charge this time against sick leave or personal leave. When their children are ill, working parents often experience stress, which may affect their job performance. They should, therefore, receive special consideration if for no other reason than to maintain their on-the-job effectiveness.

Older Workers. The U.S. population grew older through the 1980s, a trend which will continue at least through the year 2000. The reason is that the baby-boom generation—born from the end of World War II through 1964—has had only half as many children as their parents did. And life expectancy continues to increase. The trend toward earlier retirement reversed itself in the mid 1980s. Today, many older persons don't want to retire or even to slow down. Some desire semiretirement, preferring part-time work or a less demanding full-time job.

Older workers offer real dividends to the creative human resource manager. Firms such as Marriott Corporation and McDonald's have already engaged in much-publicized efforts to recruit them. Companies such as these claim that older workers make nearly ideal employees. Advantages

---

[1] Bruce Nussbaum, "Needed: Human Capital," *Business Week* (September 19, 1988), p. 103.

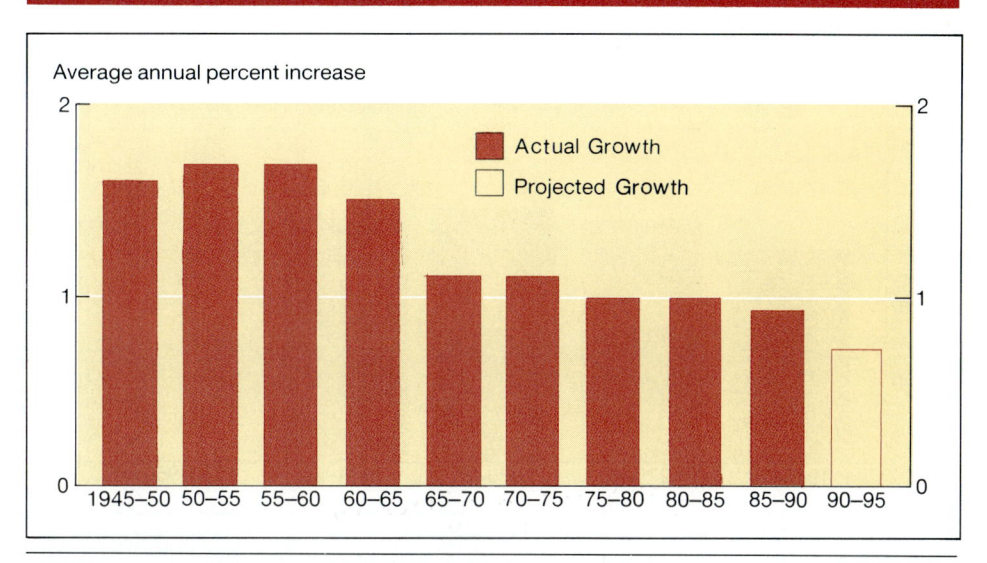

CHAPTER 2　　The Environment of Human Resource Management

FIGURE 2-2 | Labor Force Growth Rate

Source: U.S. Bureau of the Census

cited include reliability, honesty, good people skills, and availability on short notice or for part-time work. A major 1986 study indicated that older workers generally have the following advantages over younger workers: greater job stability, fewer accidents, fewer absences, greater loyalty to the organization, more pride in craftsmanship, and greater adherence to the work ethic.[2] Older persons often have other sources of income and medical care, and do not demand fringe benefits as a condition of employment.

The idea that performance generally deteriorates with age has been shown to be a myth. Still, older workers may require retraining or reassignment as their job preferences and physical abilities change. Human resource managers should be alert to such opportunities to enhance productivity. For example, a telephone operator may decide that it's time to pull back from the constant pressure of that job and ask to be retrained as a receptionist. Or a machinist whose eyesight deteriorates may be shifted to a machine with less sophisticated, though no less vital, operations. At times, like young people, older employees simply want a change in their job or job environment. Human resource managers should be alert to opportunities to retrain or help educate older workers for alternative positions.

Part-Time Workers. More and more organizations employ part-time workers. In fact, it has been estimated that part-time workers were the fastest

---

[2] Fabius D. O'Brien, Jerold F. Robinson, and G. Stephen Taylor, "The Effects of Supervisor Sex and Work Environment on Attitudes Toward Older Workers," *Public Personnel Management*, 15 (Summer 1986), p. 121.

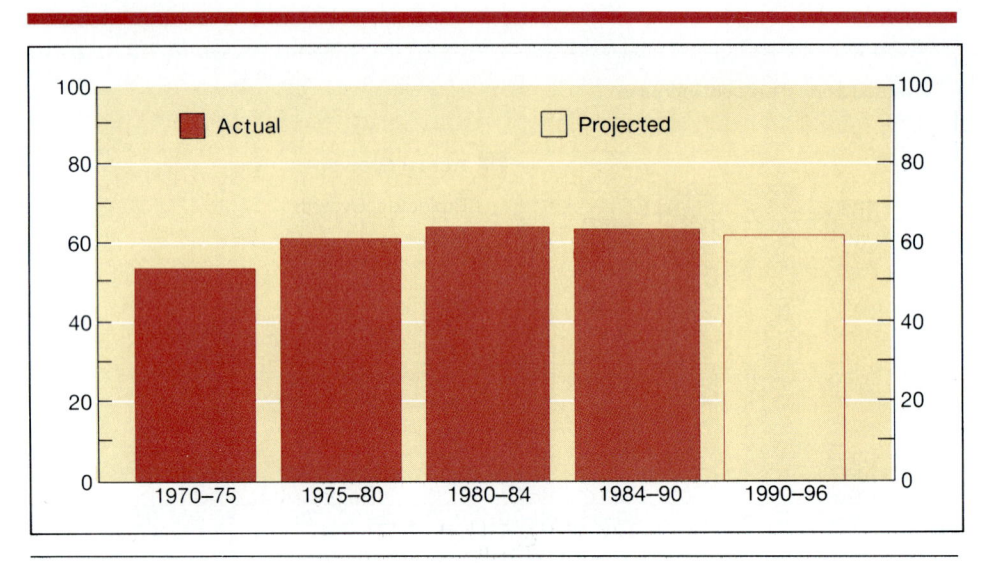

FIGURE 2-3 | Women as a Percentage of Labor Force Growth

Source: U.S. Bureau of Labor Statistics

growing segment of the workforce after 1970.[3] The use of part-time workers offers a number of advantages. First, it allows access to employees who are available only during certain hours or for a limited number of hours per week. For example, women with small children sometimes work part-time when their children are young. Students may schedule work around their class hours. Second, a company's less than full-time need for a skilled person may be filled, saving on both salary and benefits. Third, part-time workers often are not provided benefits, such as medical insurance and pension programs, thereby saving the company money. However, this advantage has eroded somewhat in recent years. Fourth, part-time workers usually think of their jobs as temporary, so they can be easily hired or laid off as work volume fluctuates. Fifth, if employers restrict employees with demanding family situations to full-time jobs only, the results might include absenteeism, personal business conducted on company time, or loss of good workers.

Although utilizing part-time workers has many advantages, it often presents unique problems for human resource managers. For example, part-time workers require more employee training and orientation, which is both costly and time consuming. Also, they often are not as loyal as full-time employees, sometimes becoming disgruntled as they work alongside full-timers who receive full company benefits. Further, managers must confront the personal problems and complications of a larger work group. Employing part-time workers requires managers to relate to and commu-

---

[3] Harry Bacas, "Desperately Seeking Workers," *Nation's Business* February 1988, p. 20.

nicate with different people performing the same job, thus increasing the complexity of the situation. Company policy can lessen some of these problems by giving part-time workers first chance at full-time jobs when they become open. Treating part-time and full-time workers as equally as possible is vitally important in order to tap the part-timers' sense of responsibility and need to feel worthwhile. Overcoming these disadvantages requires that human resource managers exercise extraordinary leadership.

A special case in the use of part-time workers is known as job sharing. **Job sharing** involves filling a job with two or more part-time employees, each working part of a regular work week and sharing the benefits of one full-time worker. Companies such as Walgreen's Drugs, New York Life Insurance Company, and Fireman's Fund Insurance Company offer job-sharing arrangements.

Temporary and "Leased" Employees. The need for traditional temporary employees increased after the mid 1980s, in part because more women, and a few men, were taking maternity and parenting leave. Also, the corporate takeover fever late in the decade caused many firms to cut work forces to bare minimums. They often filled gaps with temporaries.

A special case of temporary workers is leased employees. **Leased employees** are individuals provided by an outside firm at a fixed hourly rate, similar to a rental fee, often for extended periods. Employee leasing goes beyond the use of short-term "temps" furnished by such agencies as Kelly Services, Inc., and Manpower, Inc., to help companies through vacation periods and so forth.

Managers of temporary or leased workers generally find them to be well qualified and eager to please, though less tied to their employers than are traditional employees. Major temporary help and employee leasing firms have tight reporting systems to ensure that an employee can fit in and do the job intended. Such employees are usually very productive and extremely beneficial to the organization utilizing them.

Persons with Disabilities. According to one estimation, there are approximately 36 million disabled employees in the United States, not including mentally handicapped persons.[4] A handicap, or disability, is a disadvantage that limits the amount or kind of work a person can do or makes its achievement unusually difficult.

Laws relating to handicapped workers generally define handicap or disability quite broadly. More common disabilities include limited hearing or sight, limited mobility, mental or emotional deficiencies, and various nerve disorders. Recent studies indicate that handicapped workers do as well as the unimpaired in terms of productivity, attendance, and average tenure.[5] In fact, in certain high-turnover occupations, handicapped workers had lower turnover rates.

---

[4] Susan Goff Condon, "Hiring the Handicapped Confronts Cultural Uneasiness," *Personnel Journal*, 66 (April 1987), p. 28.

[5] *Ibid*.

Research suggests that disabled persons can be as productive as the unimpaired in many jobs. A blind person, for example, may be a perfectly competent PBX operator; paraplegics have no disability with regard to most desk jobs. Even when the disabling condition directly affects performance, the handicapped person often compensates for it through extra effort.

Immigrants from Developing Areas. Large numbers of immigrants from developing areas, particularly Southeast Asia and Latin America have settled in many parts of the United States. These immigrants bring with them the attitudes, values, and mores peculiar to their home-country cultures.

Vietnamese settled along the Mississippi, Louisiana, and Texas Gulf coast in the 1970s and 1980s, after the end of hostilities in Vietnam. Thousands of Thais fleeing the upheaval in Thailand came to the Boston area to work and live. New York's Puerto Rican community has long been an economic and political force there. Cubans who fled Castro's regime congregated in southern Florida, especially Miami. A flood of Mexicans and other Hispanics continues across the southern border of the United States. The Irish, the Poles, the Italians and others who came here in past decades have long since assimilated into—and indeed have become—the culture. Newer immigrants require time to adapt. Meanwhile, they generally take low-paying and menial jobs, live in substandard housing, and form enclaves where they cling to some semblance of the cultures they left.

Wherever they settle, these nationalistic groups soon begin to become part of the regular work force, no longer isolated in certain occupations. They begin to adopt American language and customs. They begin to learn new skills and to adapt old skills to their new country. Human resource managers can place these individuals in jobs appropriate to their skills, with excellent results for the organization.

Young Persons with Limited Education or Skills. Especially during holiday buying seasons, businesses hire thousands of young, unskilled workers. In general, they have limited education—high school or less. Some who have high school diplomas find that their education hardly fits the work they are expected to do. For example, most lack familiarity with computers. Many of these young adults and teenagers have poor work habits. They tend to be tardy or absent more often than experienced or better educated workers. Interviews with supervisors of such workers at J. C. Penney Company and other firms, both large and small, revealed the following recurrent problems with young workers: they do not pay attention to instructions; they will concentrate on the job only for short periods of time; they tend to think that the paycheck is their due for being at the workplace and is unrelated to how much they contribute; they often have transportation problems, such as missed buses or cars that break down frequently; they do not respect their supervisors, often gossiping or speaking openly to other workers; they lack company loyalty; and, to make matters worse, they change jobs frequently.

On the positive side, human resource managers cite these advantages of hiring young, unskilled persons: they work for low wages and few benefits; they are willing to work part-time and during short periods; they can easily be fired if they do not perform; they are exciting, vivacious, and interesting; they generally have high levels of strength, endurance, and energy, which needs to be directed to productive purposes; they thrive on competition; they readily respond to praise; they also respond to monetary incentives, especially piece rates; many are physically attractive and make good impressions on customers; and they often have a sincere desire to overcome their shortcomings, especially to get additional education or to gain management experience.

Regardless of whether the positive attributes of such workers outweigh the negative, more workers will be needed in the future, including younger workers with limited skills and education. Because a chronic shortage of qualified workers has been predicted for the future, human resource managers need to view each young worker as a potential long-term employee and carefully avoid stereotyping. Young, unskilled workers can serve as a rich source of permanent employees, even junior managers, and can contribute productively.

Legal Considerations

Another significant external force affecting human resource management relates to federal, state, and local legislation and the many court decisions interpreting this legislation. In addition, many presidential executive orders have had a major impact on human resource management. These legal considerations affect virtually the entire spectrum of human resource policies. We highlight in Chapter 3 the most significant of these considerations that affect equal employment opportunity. Laws, court decisions, and executive orders affecting other human resource management activities will be described in the appropriate chapters.

Society

Society may also exert pressure on human resource management. The public is no longer content to accept, without question, the actions of business. Individuals and special interest groups have found that they can effect change through their voices, votes, and other actions. The influence of activists is obvious by the large number of regulatory laws that have been passed since the early 1960s. To remain acceptable to the general public, a firm must accomplish its purpose while complying with societal norms.

A major point that management must consider is that society includes the firm's employees. For instance, if an organization has 10,000 employees, these individuals will influence a larger number of people who are not connected with the firm, including friends and members of an employee's family. Therefore, it behooves a firm to maintain clear and honest communications with its employees so that they understand and appreciate the firm's position.

The general public's attitude and beliefs can affect the firm's behavior, because those attitudes and beliefs often directly affect profitability. When a corporation behaves as if it has a conscience, it is said to be socially responsible. **Social responsibility** is the implied, enforced, or felt obligation of managers, acting in their official capacities, to serve or protect the interests of groups other than themselves.[6] Many companies develop patterns of concern for moral and social issues. They do so through policy statements, practices, and the leadership of morally strong employees and managers over time. Open-door policies, grievance procedures, and employee benefit programs often stem as much from a desire to do what is right as from a concern for productivity and avoidance of strife.[7]

You may well ask, "Why should a business be concerned with the welfare of society? Its goal is to make a profit and grow." Obviously, a business must make a profit over the long run if it is to survive. But you should also remember another basic point: If society's needs are not satisfied, a firm will ultimately cease to exist. A firm operates by public consent to satisfy society's requirements. Although such issues relate to the organization as a whole, you can easily see how human resource managers might be expected to become involved in them. The organization is a member of the community in which it operates. Just as citizens work to improve the quality of life in their community, the organization should also respect and work with the other members of its community. For instance, a high unemployment rate of a certain minority group may exist within the firm's service area. A philosophy of hiring workers who are capable of being trained as opposed to hiring only qualified applicants may help to reduce unemployment for that group. In the long run, this philosophy will certainly enhance the firm's image, and may actually improve profitability.

Unions

Wage levels, benefits, and working conditions for millions of employees now reflect decisions made jointly by unions and management. A **union** is a group of employees who have joined together for the purpose of dealing with their employer. Unions are treated as an environmental factor because, essentially, they become a third party when dealing with the company. In a unionized organization, the union rather than the individual employee negotiates an agreement with management.

Although unions remain a powerful force, union membership as a percentage of the nonagricultural workforce slipped from 33 percent in 1955 to about 17 percent in 1987.[8] As we mentioned in Chapter 1, between 1980 and 1984 alone, organized labor lost 2.7 million members.[9] This trend is

---

[6] R. Wayne Mondy, Arthur Sharplin, and Edwin B. Flippo, *Management: Concepts and Practices*, 4th ed. (Boston: Allyn & Bacon, 1988), p. 632.

[7] Kenneth E. Goodpaster and John B. Matthews, Jr., "Can a Corporation Have a Conscience?" *Harvard Business Review*, 60 (January–February 1982), pp. 132–141.

[8] Larry T. Adams, "Union Membership of Wage and Salary Employees in 1987," *Current Wage Developments*. (Washington, D.C.: U.S. Department of Labor Bureau of Labor Statistics, February 1988), p. 4.

[9] Shane R. Premeaux, R. Wayne Mondy, and Art Bethke, "Decertification: Fulfilling Unions' Destiny?" *Personnel Journal*, 66 (June 1987), p. 144.

likely to continue for a number of reasons, which we discuss in greater detail in Chapter 17. However, as the power and influence of unions continues to decline, the emphasis will likely shift to a human resource system that deals directly with the individual worker and his or her needs.

Shareholders

The owners of a corporation are called **shareholders**. Because shareholders have invested money in the firm, they may at times challenge programs considered by management to be beneficial to the organization. Managers may be forced to justify the merits of a particular program in terms of how it will affect future projects, costs, revenues, and profits. For instance, $50,000 spent on implementing a management development program may require more justification than saying, "Managers should become more open and adaptive to the needs of employees." Shareholders are concerned with how such expenditure decisions will increase revenues or decrease costs. Thus management must be prepared to explain the merits of a particular program in terms of its economic costs and benefits.

Another way in which shareholders can influence a company is through shareholder activism. Such activism was virtually unheard of in the 1960s, but now management has become extremely sensitive to its public image. The last thing most corporations want is criticism of the firm's performance on the front page of a major newspaper or on the TV evening news. Therefore, corporations have become increasingly sensitive to shareholder pressure.[10]

Competition

Unless an organization is in the unusual position of monopolizing the market it serves, other firms will be producing similar products or services. For a firm to succeed, grow, and prosper, it must maintain a supply of competent employees. But other organizations are also striving for that same objective. A firm's major task is to ensure that it obtains and retains a sufficient number of employees in various career fields to allow the firm to compete effectively. A bidding war often results when competitors attempt to fill certain critical positions in their firms. Because of the strategic nature of their needs, firms are sometimes forced to resort to unusual means to recruit and retain such employees. The poster shown in Figure 2-4 illustrates the extreme approaches that some organizations have used to recruit qualified workers.

Moreover, because of the competitive nature of many businesses, managers may feel considerable pressure to improve their company's compensation system. In order to meet this challenge, many firms not only are improving salaries but also are emphasizing other forms of rewards. Thus

---

[10] David Vogel, "Ralph Nader's All Over the Place: Citizens vs. the Corporation," *Across the Board*, 1 (April 1979), pp. 26–31.

WANTED

- $1,000 in cash,* less taxes, for the referral and subsequent hire of all exempt engineers and any technically related positions of non-exempt Grade 9 or above; i.e., technical writers, draftspersons, etc.

- New employee must be employed 180 days before "bounty" is paid.

- In order to qualify, the person referred must indicate the Ampex employee's name on the Ampex employment application under the column headed "Referred By," and Ampex must be free of any obligation to pay an agency or any other fee upon employment of the person.

- Non-eligible persons for this "bounty" are Department Managers, exempt Personnel Department employees, and managers directly involved in the selection of the person for the opening to be filled.

$1000 REWARD

* Redwood City and Sunnyvale employees only

FIGURE 2-4 | A Recruitment Poster

the firm's total financial compensation program has to be considered as part of the overall working environment.

Customers

The people who actually use a firm's goods and services also are part of its external environment. Because sales are crucial to the firm's survival, management has the task of ensuring that its employment practices do not antagonize the customers it serves. For example, consumer boycotts have been triggered by organizations that limited the number of minorities they employ. If a certain minority or ethnic group purchases a large share of the firm's products, the organization should look closely at including a representative proportion of this group in its workforce.

Customers constantly demand high-quality products and after-purchase service. Therefore, a firm's workforce should be capable of providing quality goods and services. Sales are often lost or gained because of variances in product quality and follow-up service. These conditions relate directly to the skills, qualifications, and motivations of the organization's employees.

Technology

The rate of technological change is accelerating, and as a result, few firms operate today as they did even a decade ago. Of major concern to those in HRM is the effect that technological changes have had, and will have on businesses. Frederick W. Bahl, director of human resource administration for Alumax, Inc., believes that "during the next decade, the most challenging area in human resource management will be training employees to stay up with rapidly advancing technology." Products that were not envisioned only a few years ago are now being mass produced, substantially enlarging the tasks of all managers, including human resource managers. New skills are continually needed to meet new technological demands. These skills are typically not in large supply, and recruiting qualified individuals in these areas is often difficult.

As technological changes occur, certain skills also are no longer required. This situation necessitates some retraining of the current workforce. As we mentioned in Chapter 1, within the next decade, more than half of all existing jobs are expected to change and another 30 percent to be eliminated as a result of technological advances.[11] For instance, the traditional role of the secretary has changed substantially since the advent of word processing. Rather than writing or dictating a letter to give to the secretary, some managers are even entering their own letters in word processors and then printing them out.

Partly because of technological change, the industries that will need new employees through 1995 will likely be different from those of today. Figure 2-5 shows that employment in service-producing industries has increased faster than employment in goods-producing industries since 1959—and is expected to continue to do so through 1995. As incomes and living standards have risen, largely because of technological change, people's desires for services have grown more rapidly than their desires for goods. In fact, service-producing industries are likely to account for about nine out of ten new jobs between 1984 and 1995. Employment in these industries is expected to increase by 18 percent, from 77.2 million in 1984 to 91.3 million in 1995.

---

[11] Eric G. Flanholtz, Yvonne Randle, and Sonja Sackmann, "Personnel Management: The Tenor of Today," *Personnel Journal*, 66 (June 1987), p. 64.

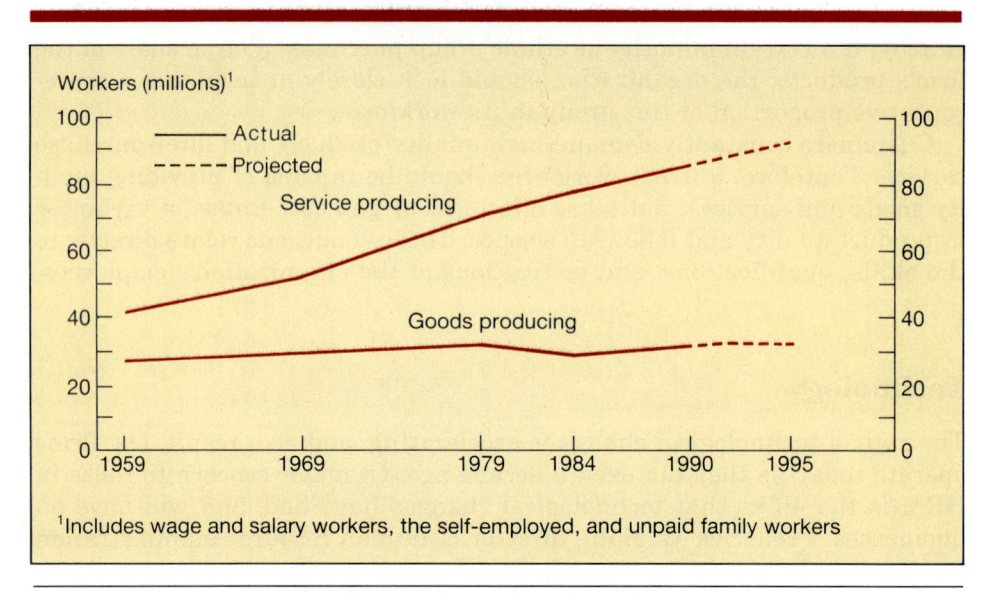

FIGURE 2-5 | Projected Growth of Service-Producing versus Goods-Producing Industries

Source: U.S. Bureau of Labor Statistics

■ THE INTERNAL ENVIRONMENT

The internal environment also exerts considerable pressure on human resource management. Those factors that affect a firm's human resources from inside its boundaries comprise the **internal environment**. As indicated in Figure 2-1, the primary internal factors include the firm's mission, policies, and corporate culture. These factors have a major impact in determining the interaction between HRM and other departments within the organization. This interaction has a major effect on overall organizational productivity, so it is vital that the interaction be positive and supportive of the firm's mission.

Mission

Mission is the organization's continuing purpose or reason for being. Each management level should operate with a clear understanding of the firm's mission. In fact, each organizational unit (division, plant, department) should have clearly understood objectives that coincide with that mission.

The specific company mission must be regarded as a major internal factor that affects the tasks of human resource management. Consider two companies, each having a broadly based mission and envision how certain tasks might differ from one firm to the other. Company A's goal is to be an industry leader in technological advances. Its growth occurs through the pioneering of new products and processes. Company B's goal is one of conservative growth, with little risk taking. Only after another company's product or process has proven itself in the marketplace will Company B commit itself.

Company A needs a creative environment to encourage new ideas. Highly skilled workers must be recruited to foster technological advancement. Constant attention to the workforce training and development is essential. A compensation program designed to retain and motivate the most productive employees is especially important.

The basic tasks of human resource management are the same for Company B, but the mission dictates that they be altered somewhat. A different kind of workforce will likely be needed. Highly creative individuals may not want to work for Company B. Perhaps because the mission encourages little risk taking, most of the major decisions will be made at higher levels in the organization. Thus management development at lower levels in the organization may receive less emphasis. The compensation program may reflect the different requirements of this particular workforce. As this comparison indicates, a human resource manager must clearly understand the company's mission.

Policies

A **policy** is a predetermined guide established to provide direction in decision making. As guides, rather than hard and fast rules, policies are somewhat flexible, requiring interpretation and judgment in their use. They can exert significant influence on how managers accomplish their jobs. For instance, many firms have an "open door" policy, which permits an employee to take a problem to the next higher level in the organization if it can't be solved by the immediate supervisor. Knowing that their subordinates can take problems to a higher echelon tends to encourage supervisors to try harder to resolve problems at their level.

Many larger firms have policies related to every major operational area. Although policies are established for marketing, production, and finance, the largest number of policies often relate to human resource management. Some potential policy statements that affect human resource management are:

- To provide employees with a safe place to work.
- To encourage all employees to achieve as much of their human potential as possible.
- To provide compensation that will encourage a high level of productivity in both quality and quantity.
- To ensure that current employees are considered first for any vacant position for which they may be qualified.

Because policies have a degree of flexibility, the manager is not necessarily required to adhere strictly to the policy statement. Often the tone of a policy guides managers as much as the actual words. Consider, for instance, the policy to ensure that "all members of the labor force have equal opportunity for employment." This policy implies more than merely adhering to

HRM In Action

Barbara Williams, the financial vice-president for Bendon Corporation, is speaking with Steve Allen, the vice-president of human resources. "Steve," says Barbara, "The accounting manager has just retired and his replacement must be selected. I would like to promote from within, but there are also qualified applicants from outside the firm. My alternatives are numerous and complicated. If I hire from within, the best qualified person may not be selected. On the other hand, if I hire from outside the firm, the current employees may not accept the new manager."

How would you respond?

---

certain laws and government regulations. Confronted with this policy, the human resource manager will likely do more than merely conform to the law. Perhaps the manager will initiate a training program to permit hiring of minorities or women who are not totally qualified to perform available jobs. Rather than just seek qualified applicants, a firm that actively implements this policy goes beyond the minimum required by law.

Corporate Culture

As an internal environmental factor affecting human resource management, corporate culture refers to the firm's social and psychological climate. **Corporate culture** is defined as the system of shared values, beliefs, and habits within an organization that interacts with the formal structure to produce behavioral norms.[12] An infinite variety of cultures could exist, so we probably should view them as a continuum.

A closed and threatening culture is at one extreme. In this type of culture, decisions tend to be made at higher levels in the organization; management and subordinates lack trust and confidence in each other; secrecy abounds; and workers aren't encouraged to be creative and solve problems. At the other extreme is an open culture in which decisions tend to be made at lower levels in the organization; a high degree of trust and confidence exists between management and subordinates; communication is open; and workers are encouraged to be creative and to solve problems. In all likelihood, the exact nature of any particular corporate culture falls somewhere between these extremes. Regardless of its nature, identification of the corporate culture in a firm is important. It affects job performance throughout

---

[12] Arthur Sharplin, *Strategic Management* (New York: McGraw-Hill, 1985), p. 102.

the organization and consequently affects profitability. We discuss corporate culture in considerable detail in Chapter 9.

■ ENVIRONMENTAL FACTORS AFFECTING MULTINATIONAL CORPORATIONS

As recently as the 1960s, management did not fully appreciate the need to adapt business practices to different national environments. However, global competition, air travel, satellite communication technology, and wage differentials have made doing business abroad both necessary and feasible. Companies have responded by establishing more and more operations overseas. Unfortunately, American managers have tended to fall back on their own limited experiences, treating an assignment in Hong Kong, Sydney, or Paris much like a stint in Dallas or Atlanta.[13] Some managers thought that international businesses could simply force foreign countries to conform to the companies' usual ways of operating.[14] Today, managers commonly recognize that this way of doing business is unacceptable and that, in fact, the challenge of multinational operations is not easily met. This is especially true with regard to the challenges of human resource management.

Earlier in this chapter our discussion focused primarily on environmental factors affecting organizations located and doing business only in the United States. The external environment confronting multinational enterprises is even more diverse and complex than that confronting domestic firms. A **multinational corporation** (MNC) conducts a large part of its business outside the country in which it is headquartered and has a significant percentage of its physical facilities and employees in other countries. Thus, as illustrated in Figure 2-6, multinational operations add another environmental layer to human resource management. Although the basic HRM tasks remain essentially the same, the manner in which they are accomplished may be altered substantially by the multinational's external environment.

Legal Considerations

Not only must the multinational corporation adhere to the federal, state, and local legislation of its parent country, it must also obey the laws of the host country. However, there is no comprehensive system of international law or courts requiring that the MNC understand in detail the laws of each host country. The United States, United Kingdom, Canada, Australia, and New Zealand have developed their legal systems from English common law. Under it, judges are extremely important, for they are guided by principles declared in previous cases. In most of Europe, Asia, and Africa, the

---

[13] Phillip R. Harris, "Employees Abroad: Maintain the Corporate Connection," *Personnel Journal*, 65 (August 1986), p. 108.

[14] Geert Hofstede, "The Cultural Relativity of Organizational Practices and Theories," *Journal of International Business Studies*, 24 (Fall 1983), p. 75.

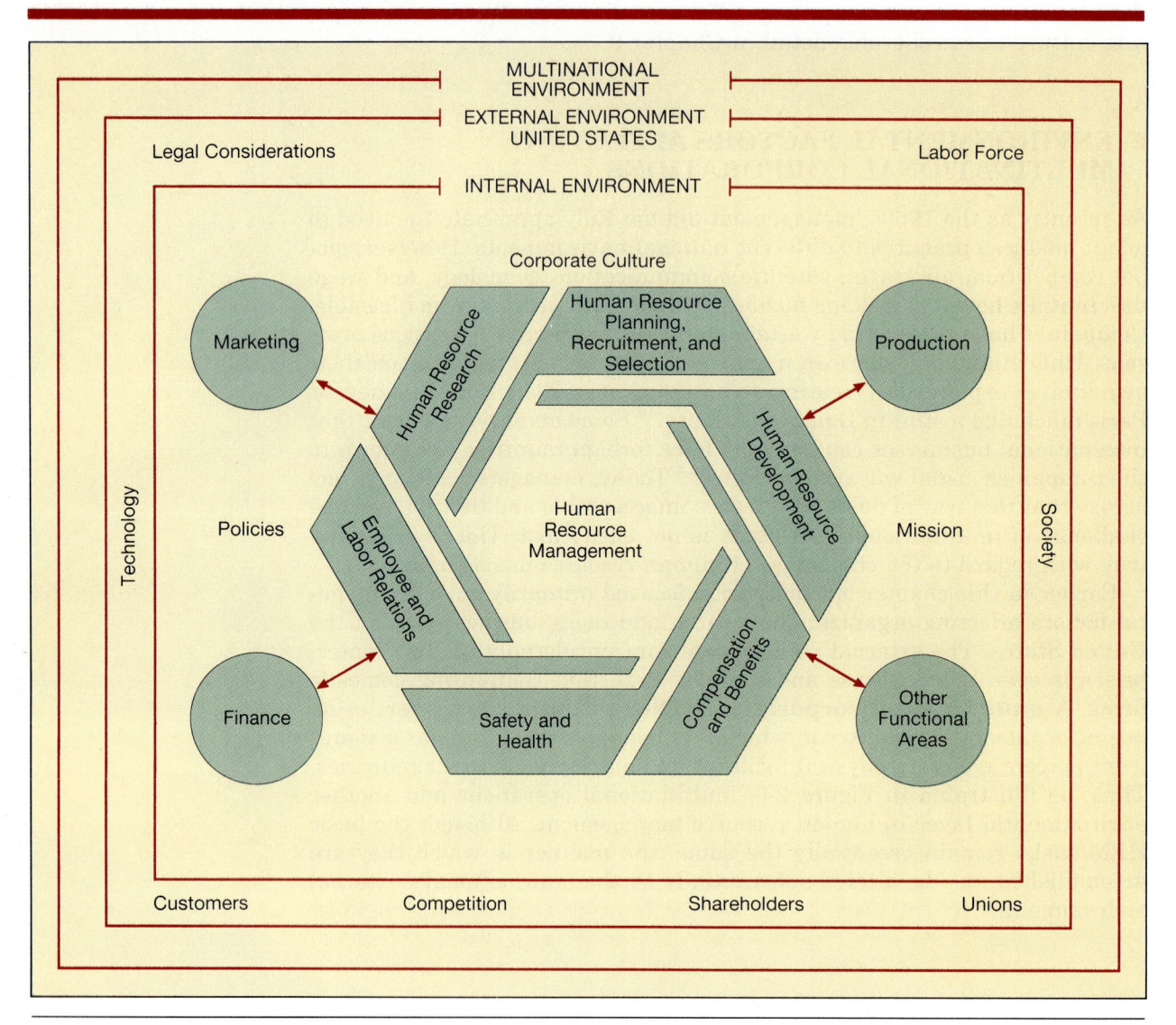

FIGURE 2-6 | Human Resource Management in the Multinational Environment

legal systems are based on civil law, and judges play a lesser role because the legal requirements are codified. The civil servant has greater power under civil law than under the common law.

Although the United States is a highly legalistic country and American MNCs tend to carry U.S. law with them, those involved in human resource management must realize that the legal systems of other countries can differ considerably. For example, the Japanese dislike laws, lawyers, and litigation. In France, lawyers are prohibited from serving on boards of directors by codes of the legal profession. The vastness and sheer complexity of varying legal systems throughout the world demonstrates clearly the intricate and demanding legal environment in which the MNCs operate. In order to function in a manner consistent with the host country, those involved in human resource management should become familiar with the legal requirements of the host country that relate to human resources.

Labor Force

In filling key managerial, technical, or professional positions abroad, multinational corporations can choose from among three basic types of employees: (1) parent country nationals (PCNs), (2) host country nationals (HCNs), and (3) third country nationals (TCNs). Until the 1950s, MNCs routinely filled key foreign posts with trusted and experienced employees from PCNs. Recently, stronger nationalistic feelings have led companies to alter their policies and employ more people from the HCNs. Additionally, some firms have used TCNs. For example, one U.S. based firm received a contract to build highways in Saudi Arabia using workers from Turkey and Italy. Still, many companies attempt to keep parent country employees in at least half the identified key positions, particularly in the financial area.

Using workers from the parent nation of the MNC ensures a greater degree of consistency and control in the firm's operations around the world. However, this approach is not without its costs, because PCNs may have great difficulty understanding cultural differences and adapting to life in the host country. In an attitude survey of workers in forty-nine multinationals, HCNs contended that parent country workers tended not to question orders from headquarters even when they should have done so.[15] Unquestioning attitudes and actions enabled these individuals to advance their own long-term interests in the firm by getting better evaluations from headquarters and easing repatriation at the end of their tours of duty. In addition, the common practice to rotate key employees frequently intensified the problem of understanding and adapting to local cultures. However, using PCNs facilitates communications with headquarters because both parties are of the same culture.

Utilizing workers from the host country in key positions usually improves the MNC's relations with the government of the host country. It also fosters quicker and more accurate adaptation to the requirements of the host country. Disadvantages include a lessened degree of centralized control and increased communication problems with headquarters. In addition, if the HCNs perceive that the opportunity for higher level positions is blocked for ethnic reasons, they will use the MNC to gain experience and then move to a higher position with a host country national firm. Properly balancing the type of key employees stationed in the host country is often a complex and difficult human resource task but one that is crucial to the success of an MNC.

---

[15] Yoram Zeira, "Overlooked Personnel Problems of Multinational Corporations," *Columbia Journal of World Business*, 10 (Summer 1975), pp. 96–103.

Society

The significant societal norms—customs, beliefs, values, attitudes, and habits—of one nation differ at least to some extent from those of other countries. If the multinational corporation is to operate in many nations, it will necessarily have to adapt some of its managerial practices to the specific and unique expectations and situations of each nation. Attitudes concerning work, risk taking, change introduction, line authority, and material gain will differ. Those in human resource management should never assume that the attitudes within the parent country will be similar to those in various host countries.

Lack of cultural sensitivity has limited the transfer of successful U.S. management practices to European countries. The same is true for some foreign MNCs doing business in the United States. For example, when Renault built plants in the United States, it had to adapt to the U.S. work ethic. Primarily, U.S. workers tend to prefer less direct supervision than do the French, so Renault adapted its management style to better accommodate U.S. employees.

In certain societies, authority is viewed as a natural right and is not questioned by subordinates. In other cultures, authority must be earned and is granted to those who have demonstrated their ability to lead. In some cultures, work is good and moral; in others it is to be avoided. Accumulating wealth in some nations is proper behavior; in others, riches are to be avoided. David McClelland discovered that basic attitudes toward achievement correspond somewhat to rates of economic development. If a nation's citizens are willing to commit themselves to the accomplishment of tasks deemed worthwhile and difficult, a country tends to benefit economically. McClelland contends that a person's perceived ability to influence the future has a definite impact on the behavior of a country's workforce.[16] If the basic belief is one of fatalism—what will be, will be—the importance of planning and organizing for the future is downgraded.

Interclass mobility and sources of status also vary. If people have little hope of moving up socially and economically in a society, fatalism and an absence of a drive for achievement are likely results. In many instances, the MNC will have to adapt and conform to the societal norms of the host country in order to operate successfully. Obviously, human resource management is directly affected by societal concerns and, therefore, such concerns must be carefully considered by MNC managers.

Unions

The prospect for future unionism throughout the world is not bright. Factors such as the decline in union membership in the United States since the 1950s, the lack of government support for employee organizations in countries that do not have free-market economies, and the troubled labor

---

[16] Peter Wright, David Townsend, Jerry Kinard, and Joe Iverstine, "The Developing World to 1990: Trends and Implications for Multinational Business," *Long Range Planning*, 15 (May 1982), p. 122.

movements in other industrialized free nations, dims the prospects for worldwide unionism.[17] During the past decade, many Western democracies have moved politically toward conservatism and against unionism. Conservative legislation and administration of this legislation may also limit the growth of union organizing efforts.[18]

Unions in industrialized nations with free-market economies seem to be yielding to management demands for enhanced productivity, often without the benefit of increased compensation. In most such countries, union demands for higher wages are gradually taking a backseat to concerns for retraining, improved working conditions, and job security. The Federal Republic of Germany is a perfect example of an industrialized nation in which many employees are quitting unions because of the unions' lack of flexibility in dealing with management.[19]

The pressures of a global economy are creating the need for greater productivity at reduced or capped wage levels, which greatly limits a union's attractiveness to employees. The state of unionism worldwide can have a dramatic impact on the competitiveness of MNCs. Therefore, MNC managers must consider the impact of unionism throughout the world when making many HRM decisions.

Shareholders

At first glance, MNC goals may not appear much different from those of domestic businesses. The typical goals of survival, profit, and growth are indeed similar. Shareholders must be satisfied with their return on investment, or they will seek other investment opportunities. An MNC seeks to produce and distribute products throughout the world in return for a satisfactory return on its invested capital. It survives, grows, and remains attractive to shareholders by maintaining its technological advantages and minimizing risk.

However, the MNC differs from the domestic firm because of the potential clash of its goals with those of the economic and political systems of the various countries within which it operates. Some may coincide; some may not. Because most countries want improved standards of living for their people, goals such as a trained labor force, full employment, reasonable price stability, a favorable balance of payments, and steady economic growth are fairly common.

In achieving some of these goals, the interests of the MNC and those of the host country overlap. For example, a new MNC in a country will usually create new jobs, thereby contributing to a higher level of employment, increased income, and economic growth. Thus an MNC may provide an out for political leaders accused of having contributed to unemployment in their

---

[17] Joseph Krislov, "Unions in the Next Century: An Exploratory Essay," *Journal of Labor Research*, 7 (Spring 1986), pp. 165–166.

[18] *Ibid.* p. 169.

[19] Gail Schares, "Are Labor Leaders Asking for the Moon?" *Business Week* (September 19, 1988), p. 50.

countries.[20] Although the MNC usually contributes to the accomplishment of such goals, it may not do so at the rate expected by the host country, which can create problems. In the final analysis, the interests of shareholders must be protected, regardless of whether the firm is a domestic or multinational corporation.

Competition

Competition in a multinational environment typically comes from many directions. In the past, U.S. firms had the luxury of viewing competition as primarily American. This is no longer true, however. These same firms now find themselves competing with corporations in many countries. Furthermore, MNCs may find themselves competing with other multinationals and host country firms for the same personnel. This situation further compounds the HRM tasks and emphasizes the importance of HRM in multinational corporations.

Customers

In this new global environment, potential customers may exist in any country in the world. Cultivating them often requires new, and sometimes innovative, HRM approaches. For example, fundamental selling skills transcend cultural barriers. However, the perception of the salesperson differs from country to country, and the manner in which the sale is culminated often differs.[21] Consequently, sales force preparation could mean the difference between success and failure. Therefore, HRM professionals must make every attempt to ensure that key personnel who directly influence customers are properly prepared to represent the MNC.

Technology

Although the host country has power as a result of national sovereignty, MNCs are not helpless. Their power lies primarily in the ability to grant or withhold needed economic resources and technological knowledge. Other MNCs will observe the treatment accorded by the host country, which will affect their decisions to invest in that country. Should the host country have enterprises with investments in the parent country, retaliation can be threatened. If the parent country provides foreign economic aid, it can also be used as leverage in promoting equitable treatment for the MNC.

Transfer of technological expertise is the primary advantage of multinational enterprises. Many MNCs operate in high-technology industries such

---

[20] J. O. Enitame, "Do Multinationals Create Wealth?" *International Management*, 37 (January 1983), p. 48.

[21] Brian H. Flynn, "The Challenge of Multinational Sales Training," *Training and Development Journal*, 41 (November 1987), p. 54.

as petroleum, pharmaceuticals, tires, electronics, and motor vehicles. There are fewer MNCs in such fields as cotton, textiles, and cement. The technological gap that exists in some nations provides a unique opportunity for the MNC to transfer high technology from the parent country. The reverse can also be true. The existing situation in a country will dictate the nature of the technology required to accomplish its goals. Obviously, the vast range of environments, goals, and technologies precludes any significant generalizations for multinationals. However, we can say that the strength of most MNCs lies in their ability to operate highly complex technologies.

Of course, transferring technologies profitably requires specially designed strategies. Among the factors that must be considered are host country laws, the stability of the region, and financial incentives.[22] Obviously, the technological nature of the operation will have a direct bearing on certain aspects of human resource management. Basically, human resource managers must maintain the personnel needed to support the level of technology employed by the MNC, and provide assistance to those who must adapt to a high-tech work environment.

SUMMARY

Many interrelated factors affect human resource management. Effective HRM requires careful consideration of all environmental variables. The external environment affects a firm's human resources from outside the organization. The internal environment affects the firm's human resources from inside. In addition, certain interrelationships complicate the management of human resources.

Factors in the external environment include: the labor force, legal considerations, society, unions, shareholders, competition, customers, and technology, Each, separately or in combination with others, can impose constraints on the human resource manager's job.

The capabilities of a firm's employees determines largely how well an organization can perform its mission. The organization obtains its workers from a labor pool external to the firm. To some degree, as the labor force changes so will the composition of the organization's workforce. The labor force with which today's human resource managers have to deal is far different from that of the past.

The size of the labor force alone does not tell the entire employment story. The labor force now includes more working women, single parents, and older persons. Many companies hire part-time workers, often for shared jobs. The use of temporary and "leased" employees is also increasing. Handicapped employees are being included in the work force in increasing numbers. Many new immigrants from developing areas, especially Southeast Asia and Latin America, continue to swell the U.S. labor force.

---

[22] Wright et al., p. 119.

Another significant external force affecting human resource management relates to federal, state, and local legislation and court decisions interpreting this legislation. In addition, many presidential executive orders have had a major impact on human resource management. These legal considerations affect virtually the entire spectrum of human resource policies and practices.

Society may also exert pressure on human resource management. The public is no longer content to accept, without question, the actions of business. Firms must increasingly accomplish their purposes while meeting societal norms. Social responsibility is the implied, enforced, or felt obligation of managers, acting in their official capacities, to serve or protect the interests of groups other than themselves.

Wage levels, benefits, and working conditions for millions of employees now reflect decisions made jointly by unions and management. A union is a group of employees who have joined together for the purpose of dealing with their employer. Unions are external factors because, essentially, they become a third party when dealing with the company. In a unionized organization, the union rather than the individual employee negotiates an agreement with the firm.

The owners of a corporation are called shareholders. Because shareholders have invested in the firm, they may challenge programs considered by management to be beneficial to the organization. Managers may be forced to justify the merits of a particular program in terms of how it will affect future projects, costs, revenues, and profits.

Unless an organization is in the unusual position of monopolizing the market it serves, other firms will be producing similar goods or services. For a firm to succeed, grow, and prosper, it must be able to maintain a supply of competent employees.

Customers are those who actually use a firm's products and also are part of the external environment. Because sales are crucial to the firm's survival, management must ensure that its employment practices and employees do not antagonize its customers.

Change is occurring at an ever-increasing rate, and few firms operate today as they did even a decade ago. Of major concern to those in HRM is the effect that technological changes have had and will have on businesses.

The internal environment also exerts considerable pressure on human resource management. Internal factors include the firm's mission, policies, and corporate culture. Mission is the organization's continuing purpose or reason for being. A policy is a predetermined guide established to provide direction in decision making. Corporate culture is defined as the system of shared values, beliefs, and habits within an organization that interacts with the formal structure to produce behavioral norms.

A multinational corporation (MNC) conducts a large part of its business outside the country in which it is headquartered and has a significant percentage of its physical facilities and employees in other countries. Another layer is added to the environment affecting human resource management in a multinational climate. Although the basic HRM tasks remain essentially the same, the manner in which the tasks are accomplished may be altered substantially by the multinational's external environment.

Questions for Review

1. What is meant by the statement, "The human resource manager's job is not accomplished in a vacuum"?
2. What factors comprise the external environment of human resource management? Briefly describe each.
3. How is the composition of the U.S. labor force expected to change during the next decade?
4. What internal environment considerations exert pressure on the human resource manager?
5. How could changes in an organizational policy affect the human resource professional's work? Give an example.
6. Define corporate culture. What effect could it have on human resource management?
7. Describe how the external environmental factors for a multinational corporation affect human resource management.

Terms for Review

External environment
Job sharing
Leased employees
Social responsibility
Union
Shareholders

Internal environment
Mission
Policy
Corporate culture
Multinational corporation (MNC)

INCIDENT 1 — A Japanese View of the Trade Imbalance

Throughout the mid-1980s the U.S. trade deficit with Japan grew worse. The Japanese share of American markets steadily increased, especially in automobiles and electronics. But very few products or services flowed the other way. The steadily growing stock of U.S. dollars in Japanese hands was used to buy up increasing shares of U.S. companies. Labor unions and politicians complained about the loss of American jobs. Citizens expressed fear that the Japanese would come to own too much of American industry. Corporations complained that they were shut out of a potentially profitable foreign market.

The United States accused the Japanese of "dumping" products (that is, selling items inthe United States for less than the cost of production). Another frequent complaint was that the Japanese government erected every conceivable trade barrier to keep American products out of Japan, while American markets were essentially open to Japanese products.

But George Tanaka, senior vice-president of Toyonoka Electronics, said that the problems were the Americans' own fault. Tanaka described what he saw as the "real" source of U.S. trade balance problems:

"In a nutshell, in Japan we treat customers as God and you only say, 'The customer is king.' Let me explain. Toyonoka sells microwave ovens in the United States. I have been trying for over a year to find an American company to make some of the parts we need. We want to have the parts shipped to Japan for installation in United States bound ovens. That would improve your trade balance. It would also allow us to take advantage of present favorable exchange rates."

"But I cannot find anyone who will produce the quality we need to stay competitive. American managers tell me, 'This is as good as we can do. You will have to change your operation to make the parts work.' In Japan, of course, suppliers value contracts like this and do all they can to meet our specifications. I am under a great deal of pressure to buy American. But American firms just do not seem to care about our needs."

"The same kind of attitude surfaces when I ask about shipping schedules. In our factories, we practice 'just-in-time' inventory control. Japanese suppliers deliver the parts we need just when we need them—and in small quantities. I know United States companies have to ship long distances. So we are willing to accept larger shipments and be somewhat flexible about delivery dates. But no American firm I have talked to will guarantee even the week of delivery. They say there are too many variables involved—strikes, raw materials shortages, shipping problems. In Japan, a supplier would not ask me to worry about those things. I am the customer."

"The language also presents a problem. United States firms will not bother to use Japanese. They refuse to even print installation instructions and invoices in any language but English. So the only way we can use parts made in America is to teach our people English. This is especially grating since we take the time to learn even the American dialect of English. Can any American imagine buying a Toyonoka stereo or a Mazda automobile with the owner's manual written in Japanese. We take care of those problems because Americans are our valued customers."

Mr. Tanaka went on to reemphasize that American companies could sell as much in Japan as Japan sells in the United States if they gave Japanese customers proper regard.

Questions

1. Does Mr. Tanaka's "ugly American" argument have some validity?
2. What are the external environmental factors that both Japanese and U.S. companies encounter?

INCIDENT 2 ■ Getting By? ■

As the human resource director for KBH Stores in St. Louis, Missouri, Virginia Stutes knew that she had her work cut out for her. Company management was moving forward on a goal of opening ten new stores in twelve months. KBH already employed 480 people in 35 stores, in addition to the headquarters staff of 31. Virginia knew that staffing the 10 new stores would require hiring and training about 150 people. She felt that her own small office was inadequately funded and staffed to handle this task. She sat at her desk, mulling over how to present a recommendation for her own staffing needs.

One of her concerns was broaching the subject with her boss, because she had not officially been told of the expansion plans. Virginia had learned about them through the office grapevine. While she did not like being kept in the dark, she was not surprised that she hadn't been told. Glenn Sullivan, the president of KBH, was noted for his autocratic leadership style. Virginia had been warned early on that Glenn told subordinates only what he wanted them to know and that he expected everyone who worked for him to follow orders without question. He was not an unkind person, though, and Virginia had always gotten along with him well enough. She had never confronted Mr. Sullivan about anything, so it was with some concern that she approached him in his office later that day.

"Mr. Sullivan," she began, "I hear that we are going to be opening ten new stores next year."

"That's right, Virginia," said Mr. Sullivan. "We've already arranged the credit lines and picked out several of the sites."

"What about staffing?" asked Virginia.

"Well, I assume you will take care of that, Virginia, when we get to that point."

"What about my own staff?" asked Virginia, "I think I am going to need at least three or four more people. And we are already crowded for space. So I hope you plan to expand the human resource office."

"Not really," said Mr. Sullivan, "The new demands on the human resource staff will be a temporary situation. It wouldn't be cost effective to hire and train additions to your staff that will only be cut the next year. I am counting on you to plan the expansion staffing within our current proposed budget allowances for the human resource office. It may require some reallocation, but I am sure you can handle that."

Questions

1. What should Virginia do? Explain.
2. Describe the elements of the internal environment which the case highlights. How does each affect Virginia?

Experiencing Human Resource Management

This is an exercise involving Jesse Heard, the human resource manager at Parma Cycle Company; Gene Wilson, the corporate planner; and Edmont Fitzgerald, the controller. Parma Cycle Company is one of only three companies in the United States that actually manufactures complete bicycles. Most of Parma's competitors import parts from other countries and simply assemble bicycles here. Parma Cycle currently employs about 800 workers at wages well above the average wage levels in the area. Most of these workers are machine operators and assemblers. Parma Cycle Company is experiencing severe difficulties competing with lower cost bicycles, and the time had come for Parma to lower costs.

Jesse Heard, the human resource manager, is faced with a dilemma. He feels obligated to find the best quality labor at the best available price, but he is also concerned about the workers, some of whom have been with Parma Cycle for many years. Even though the highly favorable labor market allows replacement of many of them with lower paid workers, he hesitates to do so. Yesterday Jesse received an angry call from the president, Mr. Burgess, who told him to meet with the corporate planner and the controller to come up with a unified recommendation for taking advantage of the improved labor market.

Gene Wilson never really had much power at Parma Cycle, although his title sounds impressive enough. Primarily, he maintains a chart room and keeps track of various trends. He basically agrees that Parma Cycle Company is headed downhill because of depressed markets and an inability on the part of company managers to decrease unit costs. In his opinion, the most important asset that Pama Cycle has is a trained and loyal workforce. While many of the workers could be replaced with lower paid workers, he is afraid that this would destroy the team spirit that now exists at Parma Cycle. He believes that workers are more likely than ever to respond to financial incentives, such as some kind of piece-rate program or bonus system.

Edmont Fitzgerald, an Ohio State University graduate in finance, believes that, above all, the corporation is an economic entity. He believes that market forces will take care of those workers who really wish to contribute to the economy. He believes in purchasing all resources, including labor, at the lowest possible price. He views the current situation as an opportunity to decrease costs radically. The union is weak, jobs are scarce, and there is a surplus of skilled workers in the Cleveland area.

Three students will serve as the Parma Cycle management: one as Jesse Heard, the human resource manager; one as Edmont Fitzgerald, the controller; and one as Gene Wilson, the corporate planner. All students not playing roles in the exercise should carefully observe the behavior of all participants. Your instructor will provide the participants with necessary additional information that they will need.

REFERENCES

Adler, Nancy J. "Women in Management Worldwide." *International Studies of Management & Organization*, 16 (Fall–Winter 1986), pp. 3–33.

Bartlett, Christopher A., and Sumantra Ghoshal. "Managing Across Borders: New Organizational Responses." *Sloan Management Review*, 29 (Fall 1987), pp. 43–54.

Bellman, Geoffrey M. "The Quest for Staff Leadership." *Training and Development Journal*, 10 (January 1986), pp. 36–41.

Calvo, Guillermo A. "The Inefficiency of Unemployment: The Supervision Perspective." *Quarterly Journal of Business and Economics*, 100 (May 1985), pp. 373–387.

Conway, Michael A. "Reducing Expatriate Failure Rates: Developing a Unified Selection-Orientation-Repatriation System." *Personnel Administrator*, 29 (July 1984), pp. 31–35.

Dugan, Terry M. "Helping Disabled Older People Find Jobs." *Aging* (July 1985), pp. 31–32.

Dymont, John J. "Strategies and Management Controls for Global Corporations." *Journal of Business Strategy*, 7 (Spring 1987), pp. 20–27.

Gajek, Marion, and Monica M. Sabo. "The Bottom Line: What HR Managers Need to Know About the New Expatriate Regulations." *Personnel Administrator*, 31 (February 1986), pp. 87–92.

Glassman, Edward. "Leadership Style's Effect on the Creativity of Employees." *Management Solutions*, 31 (November 1986), pp. 18–25.

Greene, Walter E., and Gary D. Walls. "Human Resources: Hiring Internationally." *Personnel Administrator*, 29 (July 1984), pp. 61–66.

Guptara, Prabhu. "Searching the Organization for the Cross-Cultural Operators." *International Management*, 29 (July 1986), pp. 40–43.

Harris, Phillip R. "Employees Abroad: Maintain the Corporate Connection." *Personnel Journal*, 65 (August 1986), pp. 107–110.

Herzberg, Frederick. "Overcoming the Betrayals of the '80s." *Industry Week*, 231 (July 13, 1987), p. 72.

Hixon, Allen L. "Why Corporations Make Haphazard Overseas Staffing Decisions." *Personnel Administrator*, 31 (March 1986), pp. 91–94.

Jelinek, Mariann, and Nancy J. Adler. "Women: World-Class Managers for Global Competition." *The Academy of Management Executive*, 2 (February 1988), pp. 11–19.

Kleinman, Dan. "What to Look for in Tomorrow's Employee." *Personnel Journal*, 66 (October 1987), pp. 192–206.

Krupp, Neil B. "Managing Benefits in Multinational Organizations." *Personnel*, 63 (August 1986), pp. 76–79.

Lewis, John C. "Issues Concerning High Technology Managers from Multiple Cultural Backgrounds." *Journal of Management Development*, 6 (Fall 1987), pp. 73–86.

Kleinschrod, Walter A. "Where Have All the Workers Gone?" *Administrative Management*, 48 (February 1987), p. 45.

Mondy, R. Wayne, et al. "Supervising Employees with Job Insecurities." *Management Solutions*, 32 (June 1987), pp. 28–30.

Nardone, Thomas. "Decline in Youth Population Does Not Lead to Lower Jobless Rates." *Monthly Labor Review*, 110 (June 1987), pp. 37–42.

Nelson-Horchler, Joani. "Still No Way to the Top?" *Industry Week*, 231 (July 13, 1987), pp. 57–58.

Norwood, Janet L. "The Labor Force of the Future." *Business Economics*, 22 (July 1987), pp. 9–14.

Osterman, Paul. "Choice of Employment Systems in Internal Labor Markets." *Industrial Relations*, 26 (Winter 1987), pp. 46–66.

Premeaux, Shane R., et al. "Supervising Employees with Marital Difficulties." *Management Solutions*, 32 (December 1987), pp. 27–31.

Rigby, J. Malcolm. "The Challenge of Multinational Team Development." *Journal of Management Development*, 6 (Fall 1987), pp. 65–73.

Saad, Henry N. "AIDS Discrimination in the Workplace." *Small Business Report*, 12 (March 1987), p. 79.

Scelsi, Paul. "Middle Manager Woes?" *Management World*, 16 (April–May 1987), pp. 20–21.

Schoenberger, Barbara A. "Managing Multiple Personalities." *Management World*, 16 (February–March 1987), pp. 10–11.

Schroeder, Edward A. IV, et al. "A Long-Term Profit-Sharing Plan to Stimulate Motivation and Innovation Among R&D Personnel." *Personnel Review*, 16 (Summer 1987), pp. 31–35.

Shenkar, Oded, and Yoram Zcira. "Human Resources Management in International Joint Ventures: Directions for Research." *Academy of Management Review*, 12 (July 1987), pp. 549–561.

Silver, P. G., and Craig Jurgenson. "The Disabled Employee: A Supervisory Challenge." *Thrust: Journal for Employment & Training Professionals*, 7 (Fall–Winter 1986), pp. 65–70.

Smith, Harold Ivan. "Singles in the Workplace." *Personnel Administrator*, 33 (February 1988), pp. 76–81.

Smith, Linda. "Coping with a Staff Shortage in a Hiring Freeze." *Management Solutions*, 31 (October 1986), pp. 25–26.

Solomon, Jeffrey R. "How to Work with the Rehabilitated Mentally Ill." *Supervisory Management*, 31 (January 1986), p. 32.

Standing, Guy. "Unemployment and the Recomposition of Labor Reserves." *Annals of the American Academy of Political and Social Science*, 492 (July 1987), pp. 80–96.

Steers, Richard M., and Edwin L. Miller. "Management in the 1990s: The International Challenge." *The Academy of Management Executive*, 2 (February 1988), pp. 21–22.

Tabatabai, Cheryl. "Staff Productivity: The Other Side of Cost Cutting." *Healthcare Financial Management*, 11 (May 1987), 12–14.

Taylor, Alex, Jr. "Why Women Managers Are Bailing Out." *Fortune* (August 18, 1986), pp. 16–23.

Turbett, Peggy. "To Balance a Job and Motherhood." *American Banker* (February 6, 1987), pp. 16–17.

Wheelock, Keith. "A Tough Job Market Ahead, Especially for Working Mothers." *Personnel Administrator*, 31 (April 1986), pp. 119–128.

White, B. Joseph. "The Internationalization of Business: One Company's Experience." *The Academy of Management Executive*, 2 (February 1988), pp. 29–32.

Willis, H. L. "Selection for Employment in Developing Countries: Gaging the Difference Between 'Can Do' and 'Will Do'." *Personnel Administrator*, 29 (July 1984), pp. 53–57.

Yamaguchi, Tamotsu. "The Challenge of Internationalization: Japan's Kokusaika." *The Academy of Management Executive*, 2 (February 1988), pp. 33–36.

CHAPTER 3

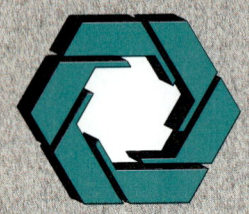

EQUAL EMPLOYMENT OPPORTUNITY AND AFFIRMATIVE ACTION

CHAPTER OBJECTIVES

1. Explain the major laws affecting equal employment opportunity.
2. Explain Presidential Executive Orders 11246 and 11375.
3. Identify and briefly describe some of the major Supreme Court decisions that have had an impact on equal employment opportunity.
4. Explain the purpose of the Equal Employment Opportunity Commission.
5. Describe the Uniform Guidelines on Employee Selection Procedures and the additional guidelines that have been adopted.
6. Explain adverse impact.
7. Describe affirmative action programs.

■ "I agree with you Phyllis," said Art Kurth, supervisor of the maintenance division of Allied Chemical. "Mary Martin is by far the best qualified to fill that vacant position in my department. She has done similar work at Olin for seven years and comes highly recommended. I really want to hire her, but do you think a woman could survive with that crew? They might not work with her, and you know how important cooperation is in that job. Remember what happened when we hired that woman a couple of years ago. She lasted a week before she walked out crying and didn't return."

■ Phyllis Jordon, human resource manager of Allied, was visibly upset when she heard Art's comments. Ten years ago when she joined Allied, she might have expected something like that, but not now. Allied has an aggressive nondiscrimination policy. "Listen, Art," she said, "I still recommend that you hire her. I know that you can find a way to see that she fits in. From all I can gather, she is a top notch worker, and Allied is lucky to have an applicant of that quality. I'll help you make this work."

The difficulty that Phyllis now confronts has new meaning since the Civil Rights Act of 1964. However, since then, many laws, court decisions, and Executive Orders have been handed down affecting HRM. Virtually all managers must now be aware of and work within these constraints.

In this chapter, we provide an overview of the major equal employment opportunity legislation that has had an impact on human resource management. We first discuss the significant equal employment opportunity laws affecting human resource management. Then we describe the importance of Presidential Executive Orders 11246 and 11375. Next, we review significant Supreme Court decisions and describe the Equal Employment Opportunity Commission. Then we discuss the *Uniform*

Guidelines and address the issue of adverse impact. We devote the remainder of the chapter to affirmative action programs and the legal aspects of human resource management in the multinational environment.

■ EQUAL EMPLOYMENT OPPORTUNITY: AN OVERVIEW

The concept of equal employment opportunity has undergone much modification and fine-tuning since the passage of the Civil Rights Act of 1964. Congress has passed numerous amendments to that act and has passed other acts, as voids in the initial act surfaced. Major Supreme Court decisions have also been handed down, interpreting the provisions of the act. Executive Orders were signed into law which further strengthened equal employment opportunity. Now over two decades have passed, and equal employment opportunity has become embedded in the workplace. Most likely, Gayla Godfrey, featured in the Executive Insight, would not have been employed as a personnel specialist/EEO coordinator in 1981 if it had not been for the equal employment opportunity movement.

Although continuing efforts are required, equal employment opportunity has come a long way since the early 1960s. Today, the majority of businesses do attempt to make employment decisions based on who is the best qualified, as opposed to whether an individual is of a certain gender, race, religion, color, national origin, or age. By and large, the laws, the Supreme Court decisions, and the Executive Orders have provided organizations—both public and private—the opportunity to tap the abilities of a work force that was largely underutilized in the early 1960s and before.

■ LAWS AFFECTING EQUAL EMPLOYMENT OPPORTUNITY

Numerous national laws have been passed that have had an impact on equal employment opportunity. Their passage signified a societal attitude that changes should be made to give everyone an equal opportunity for employment. We briefly describe the most significant of these laws in the following sections.

Civil Rights Acts of 1866 and 1871

The 1866 Civil Rights Act is based on the Thirteenth Amendment to the Constitution and prohibits racial discrimination in the making and enforcement of contracts which could include hiring and promotion decisions. Private employers, unions, and employment agencies are all covered under this act. The 1871 act is based on the Fourteenth Amendment and prohibits deprivation of equal employment rights under coverage of state laws. State and local governments are included. There is virtually no effective statute of limitation on filing charges under these acts.[1] However, on June 15, 1989, the Supreme Court ruled that the 1866 act does not apply to cases by an employer after a person is hired.[2]

Title VII of the Civil Rights Act of 1964— Amended 1972

One law that has greatly influenced human resource management is Title VII of the 1964 Civil Rights Act, as amended by the Equal Employment Opportunity Act of 1972. This legislation prohibits discrimination based on race, color, sex, religion, or national origin. Title VII covers employers engaged in an industry affecting interstate commerce with fifteen or more employees for at least twenty calendar weeks in the year in which a charge is filed, or the year preceding the filing of a charge. Included in the definition of employers are state and local governments, schools, colleges, unions, and employment agencies. The act created the Equal Employment Opportunity Commission (EEOC), which is responsible for its enforcement.

Age Discrimination in Employment Act of 1967— Amended in 1978 and 1986

As originally enacted, the Age Discrimination in Employment Act (ADEA) prohibited employers from discriminating against individuals who were from forty to sixty-five years of age. The 1978 amendment provided protection for individuals who were at least forty, but less than seventy years old. A 1986 amendment made employer discrimination against anyone over 40 years of age illegal. The latest amendment not only gives older employees the option to continue working past age 70, but the health care provision of the amendment also provides them with an additional incentive to continue to do so.[3] The act pertains to employers with twenty or more employees for twenty or more calendar weeks (either in the current or preceding calendar year), unions of twenty-five or more members, employment agencies, and federal, state, and local government subunits. Administration of the Act was transferred from the U.S. Department of Labor to the EEOC in 1979.

Enforcement begins when a charge is filed, but the EEOC can review compliance even if no charge is filed. The Age Discrimination Act differs from Title VII of the Civil Rights Act in that it provides for trial by jury and carries a possible criminal penalty. The trial-by-jury provision is important because juries may have great sympathy for older people who may have been discriminated against. The criminal penalty provision means that a

---

[1] Howard C. Lockwook, "Equal Employment Opportunities," in Dale Yoder and Herbert G. Heneman (eds.). *Staffing Policies and Strategies* (Washington, D.C.: Bureau of National Affairs, Inc., 1979), pp. 4–252.

[2] See Patterson v. McLean Credit Union discussed later in the chapter.

[3] Michael R. Carrell and Frank E. Kuzmits, "Amended ADEA's Effects on HR Strategies Remain Dubious," *Personnel Journal*, 66 (May 1987), p. 112.

Executive Insights

Gayla S. Godfrey, SPHR
Human Resources Manager,
Pneumotive Division,
Thomas Industries, Inc.

When Gayla S. Godfrey first entered college in 1966, she jokingly referred to her major as "fun." Godfrey says, "It was several years before I recognized the true value of a formal education and returned to earn a degree from Northeast Louisiana University." Because the human resource field is dynamic, she believes that professionals working in this area must keep abreast of expanding knowledge and current laws through a continuing process of career growth and development. In view of this, she has attended and completed more than eighty human resource-related courses and seminars. She is accredited by the Personnel Accreditation Institute as a Senior Professional in Human Resources (SPHR).

Godfrey has a varied work history that includes experience in government, private industry, service organizations, and direct selling. Oddly enough, her first job was in personnel. She was fresh out of college (the first time) and went to an employment agency, which could not place her because of lack of work experience—so they hired her. Later, she worked in several secretarial positions in the banking industry. Being highly motivated by the challenge and reward of sales, she joined Home Interiors & Gifts, Inc., and rose to the top 1 percent of 16,000 saleswomen nationwide for three consecutive years. "Mary Crowley, founder of Home Interiors, inspired me with her famous quotation, 'Be somebody. God doesn't have time to make a nobody.'"

Godfrey goes on to say, "I've been extremely fortunate to have worked for people who expressed confidence in me and who gave me the opportunity to grow professionally. I set my goals high and was promoted through the ranks to the position of personnel director for the Ouachita Parish Police Jury (local government)." In that position, she directed all activities of the personnel department, including planning, organizing, developing, and coordinating the functions of recruitment, selection, evaluation, classification, administration of compensation and benefits, EEO compliance, grievances, and training and development. She also developed the human resource management system for the Ouachita Parish Public Libraries, which included conducting job analysis; writing job descriptions, the policy manual, and the employee handbook; and developing the classification and compensation plan. Next, as personnel director for G. B. Cooley Hospital, Godfrey met the challenge of developing the first human resource department for the hospital.

In 1981, she accepted an opportunity to join ITT Pneumotive, a unit of ITT Corporation, as personnel specialist/EEO coordinator. She said, "During my first interview with ITT, I was asked if I considered this position a step backward in my career from my current position as director. I told my future boss it's difficult to consider working for one of the world's largest corporations as anything but a step forward, and besides, my intentions were to do such an outstanding job that he would be promoted and I would be in line for his position." Three years later this goal was achieved and she was promoted to personnel/industrial relations manager. Since that time, the company has gone through two acquisitions and is currently a subsidiary of Thomas Industries, Inc. Providing a smooth transition for all employees has presented Godfrey with her greatest career challenge yet.

Today, as human resources manager, she is responsible for employee relations policies and practices, as well as for the functional areas of human resource services, union negotiations and labor relations, and safety and security.

Godfrey believes that the human resource professional must be active in professional, civic, and community organizations. She is past president of the local chapter of the American Society for Personnel Administration (ASPA), served on the Intergovernmental Personnel Advisory Board to the Governor of Louisiana, and is active in the Chamber of Commerce and United Way.

person may receive more than lost wages if discrimination is proved. The 1978 amendment also makes class action suits possible.

Rehabilitation Act of 1973

The Rehabilitation Act covers certain government contractors and subcontractors and organizations that receive federal grants in excess of $2500. Individuals are considered handicapped if they have a physical or mental impairment that substantially limits one or more major life activities or have a record of such impairment. The Office of Federal Contract Compliance Programs (OFCCP) administers the act. If a contract or subcontract exceeds $50,000, or if the contractor has fifty or more employees, an affirmative action program must be prepared. In it, the contractor must specify reasonable steps that are being taken to hire and promote handicapped persons.

This act is expected to have even more impact in the future because the definition of "handicapped" has not been thoroughly tested by the courts. As more and more cases go to court, additional ailments will probably be labeled as handicapping conditions. For example, the Vickers v. Veterans Administration case determined that a person who is hypersensitive to tobacco smoke is handicapped.[4] It is also possible that AIDS victims will be included under the Act in the future.

Pregnancy Discrimination Act of 1978

Passed as an amendment to Title VII of the Civil Rights Act, the Pregnancy Discrimination Act prohibits discrimination in employment based on pregnancy, childbirth, or related medical conditions. The basic principle of the act is that women affected by pregnancy, and related conditions, must be treated the same as other applicants and employees on the basis of their ability or inability to work. A woman is therefore protected against such practices as being fired, or refused a job or promotion, merely because she is pregnant or has had an abortion. She usually cannot be forced to take a leave of absence so long as she can work. If other employees on disability leave are entitled to return to their jobs when they are able to work again, so too are women who have been unable to work because of pregnancy.

The same principle applies in the benefits area, including disability benefits, sick leave, and health insurance. A woman unable to work for pregnancy-related reasons is entitled to disability benefits or sick leave on the same basis as employees unable to work for medical reasons. Also, any health insurance provided must cover expenses for pregnancy-related conditions on the same basis as expenses for other medical conditions. However, health insurance for expenses arising from an abortion is not required except where the life of the mother would be endangered if the fetus

---

[4] George E. Stevens, "Exploding the Myths About Hiring the Handicapped," *Personnel*, 63 (December 1986), p. 57.

were carried to term or where medical complications have arisen from an abortion.

Immigration Reform and Control Act of 1986

The Immigration Reform and Control Act (IRCA) established criminal and civil sanctions against employers who knowingly hire an unauthorized alien. The act further makes hiring anyone without verifying employment authorization and identity unlawful. Employers who unlawfully hire an illegal alien will be subject to fines of $250–$2,000 per worker for the first offense; $2,000–$5,000 for the second offense; and $3,000–$10,000 for the third offense. In addition, employers who fail to comply with the record keeping provisions of the law are subject to a penalty of $100–$1,000 for each individual they fail to document, even if the individual is legally entitled to be employed. Moreover, when dealing with the national origin provision of the Civil Rights Act, IRCA reduces the threshold coverage from fifteen to four employees. The effect of this extension of the 1964 law will be to curtail hiring actions of some businesses. They may choose to hire only U.S. citizens and thereby avoid any potential violation of IRCA. However, many foreign nationals are in this country legally (many who are legal immigrants awaiting citizenship) and refusing to hire them would violate their civil rights.[5]

State and Local Laws

Numerous state and local laws also affect equal employment opportunity. A number of states and some cities have passed fair employment practice laws prohibiting discrimination on the basis of race, color, religion, gender, or national origin. Even prior to federal legislation, several states had antidiscrimination legislation relating to age and gender. For instance, New York protected individuals between the ages of 18 and 65 prior to the 1978 and 1986 ADEA amendments, and California had no upper limit on protected age. However, when EEOC regulations conflict with state or local civil rights regulations, the legislation more favorable to women and minorities applies.

■ EXECUTIVE ORDER 11246, AS AMENDED BY EO 11375

An **Executive Order (EO)** is a directive issued by the president and has the force and effect of laws enacted by Congress. On September 24, 1965, President Lyndon B. Johnson signed EO 11246. This EO made it the policy of the government of the United States to provide equal opportunity in

---

[5] Art L. Bethke, "The IRCA: What's an Employer to Do?" *Wisconsin Small Business Forum*, 6 (Fall 1987), p. 26.

federal employment for all qualified persons. It prohibits discrimination in employment because of race, creed, color, or national origin. The EO also requires promoting the full realization of equal employment opportunity through a positive, continuing program in each executive department and agency. The policy of equal opportunity applies to every aspect of federal employment policy and practice.

A major provision of EO 11246 requires adherence to a policy of nondiscrimination in employment as a condition for the approval of a grant, contract, loan, insurance, or guarantee. Every executive department and agency that administers a program involving federal financial assistance must include such language in their contracts. Contractors must agree not to discriminate in employment because of race, creed, color, or national origin during performance of a contract.

Affirmative action, stipulated by EO 11246, requires employers to take positive steps to ensure employment of applicants and treatment of employees during employment without regard to race, creed, color, or national origin. Human resource practices covered relate to employment, upgrading, demotion, transfer, recruitment or recruitment advertising, layoffs or termination, rates of pay or other forms of compensation, and selection for training, including apprenticeships. Employers are required to post notices to this effect in conspicuous places in the workplace. In the event of contractor noncompliance, contracts can be canceled, terminated, or suspended in whole, or in part, and the contractor may be declared ineligible for future government contracts. In 1968, EO 11246 was amended by EO 11375, which changed the word creed to religion and added sex discrimination to the other prohibited items. These EOs are enforced by the Department of Labor through the Office of Federal Contract Compliance Programs (OFCCP).

■ SIGNIFICANT U.S. SUPREME COURT DECISIONS

Knowledge of the law is obviously important for human resource managers. However, they must be aware of and understand much more than the words in the law itself. The manner in which the courts interpret the law is also vitally important. And interpretation continuously changes, even though the law itself may not have been amended. Some of the more significant U.S. Supreme Court decisions affecting equal employment opportunity follow.

Griggs v. Duke Power Company

A major decision affecting the field of human resource management was rendered on March 8, 1971. A group of black employees at Duke Power Company had charged job discrimination under Title VII of the Civil Rights Act of 1964. Prior to Title VII, Duke Power Company had two workforces, separated by race. After passage of the act, the company required applicants to have a high school diploma and pass a paper-and-pencil test to

CHAPTER 3   Equal Employment Opportunity and Affirmative Action

HRM In Action

Jack Johnson, human resource manager for Zoomer Electronics, was speaking to the production manager, Philip Lewis, regarding who should be hired to fill a newly created position. Jack started the conversation by saying, "Of all the applicants, Betty Jones scored highest on the tests. Her previous work experience is right in line with our needs, and her references check out great. What do you think, Philip?"

Philip replied, "I don't know. We've never had a woman in that position, and I don't know if she could handle the job. Besides, she is only 25 years old and recently married. I'll bet she wants to have kids."

How should Jack respond?

---

qualify for certain jobs. The plaintiff was able to demonstrate that, in the relevant labor market, 34 percent of the white males but only 12 percent of the black males had a high school education. The plaintiff was also able to show that people already in those jobs were performing successfully even though they did not have a high school diploma. No business necessity could be shown for this educational requirement.

In an 8–0 vote, the Supreme Court ruled against Duke Power Company and stated, "If an employment practice which operates to exclude Negroes cannot be shown to be related to job performance, the practice is prohibited." A major implication of the decision is that when human resource management practices eliminate substantial numbers of minority or women applicants, the burden of proof is on the employer to show that the practice is job related. This court decision significantly affected the human resource practices of many firms.

Albermarle Paper Company v. Moody

In August 1966, a class action suit was brought against Albermarle Paper Company and the plant employees' labor union. A permanent injunction was requested against any policy, practice, custom, or usage at the plant that violated Title VII. In 1975, the Supreme Court reaffirmed the idea that any test used in the selection process, or in promotion decisions, must be validated if it is found that its use has had an adverse impact on women and minorities. The employer has the burden of proof for showing that the test is valid. Subsequently, the employer must show that any selection or promotion device actually measures what it is supposed to measure.

Washington v. Davis

In 1970, two Washington, D.C., black police officers filed suit alleging that the promotion policies of their department were racially discriminatory. To be accepted by the department and to enter an intensive seventeen-week training program, the police recruit was required to satisfy certain physical and character standards, to be a high school graduate or its equivalent, and to receive a grade of at least 40 on Test 21. Test 21 was an examination that was used generally throughout the federal service and had been developed by the Civil Service Commission. The examination was designed to test verbal ability, vocabulary, reading, and comprehension.

The validity of Test 21 was in question. The test was based on the level of material that the applicants would learn in the training program. Also, a positive relationship existed between success in the training program and success on the job. However, blacks and women failed the test at a much higher rate than white males, which provided the basis for the discrimination charge. The Federal District Court noted that, since August 1969, 44 percent of new police force recruits had been black. That figure represented the proportion of blacks on the total force and was roughly equivalent to the proportion of 20–29-year-old blacks in the 50-mile recruiting radius. The District Court rejected the assertion that Test 21 was culturally slanted to favor whites. The court was satisfied that indisputable facts proved the test to be reasonable, directly related to the requirements of the police recruit training program, and neither so designed nor operated to discriminate against blacks.

Phillips v. Martin Marietta Corporation

In this 1971 case, the Court ruled that the company had discriminated against a woman because she had young children. The company had a rule of not hiring women with school-age children. The company argued that it did not preclude all women from job consideration; only those women with school-age children were not considered. Martin Marietta contended that this was a business requirement. The argument was obviously based on stereotypes and was rejected. A major implication of this decision is that a firm cannot impose standards for employment only on women. For example, a firm cannot reject divorced women if it does not also reject divorced men. Neither application forms nor interviewers should contain questions for women that do not also apply to men.

Weber v. Kaiser Aluminum and Chemical Corporation

In 1974, the United Steelworkers of America and Kaiser Aluminum and Chemical Corporation entered into a master collective bargaining agreement covering terms and conditions of employment at fifteen Kaiser plants. The agreement contained an affirmative action plan designed to eliminate conspicuous racial imbalances in Kaiser's then almost exclusively white craft work force. Black craft hiring goals equal to the percentage of blacks in the respective local labor forces were set for each Kaiser plant. To enable plants to meet these goals, on-the-job training programs were established to teach unskilled production workers—black and white—the skills necessary to become craft workers. The plan reserved 50 percent of the openings in these newly created in-plant training programs for black employees.

In 1974, only 1.83 percent (five out of 273) of the skilled craft workers at the Gramercy, Louisiana, plant were black, even though the labor force in the Gramercy area was approximately 39 percent black. Thirteen craft trainees, of which seven were black and six were white, were selected from Gramercy's production work force. The most junior black selected for the program had less seniority than several white production workers whose bids for admission were rejected. Brian Weber subsequently instituted a class action suit alleging that the action by Kaiser and USWA discriminated against him and other similarly situated white employees in violation of Title VII. Although the lower courts ruled that Kaiser's actions were illegal because they fostered reverse discrimination, the Supreme Court reversed the decision, stating that Title VII does not prohibit race-conscious affirmative action plans. Since the affirmative action plan was voluntarily agreed to by the company and the union, it did not violate Title VII.

Dothard v. Rawlingson

At the time Rawlingson applied for a position as correctional counselor trainee, she was a 22-year-old college graduate whose major course of study had been correctional psychology. She was refused employment because she failed to meet the minimum height and weight requirements. In this 1977 case, the Supreme Court upheld the Federal District Court's decision that Alabama's statutory minimum height requirement of five feet two inches and minimum weight requirement of 120 pounds for the position of correctional counselor had a discriminatory impact on women applicants. The contention was that minimum height and weight requirements for the position of correctional counselor were job related. However, the Court stated that this argument does not rebut *prima facie* evidence showing that these requirements have a discriminatory impact on women, whereas no evidence was produced correlating these requirements with a requisite amount of strength thought essential to good performance. The impact of the decision is that height and weight requirements must be job related.

University of California Regents v. Bakke

This Supreme Court decision involved the first major test involving reverse discrimination. The University of California had reserved sixteen places in each beginning medical school class for minority persons. Allen Bakke, a white man, was denied admission even though he scored higher on the admission criteria than some minority applicants who were admitted. The

Supreme Court ruled 5–4 in Bakke's favor. As a result, Bakke was admitted to the university and later received his degree. But, at the same time, the Court reaffirmed that race may be taken into account in admission decisions.

American Tobacco Company v. Patterson

This 1982 Supreme Court decision allows seniority and promotion systems established since Title VII to stand, although they unintentionally hurt minority workers. Under *Griggs* v. *Duke Power Company*, a *prima facie* violation of Title VII may be established by policies or practices that are neutral on their face and in intent, but that nonetheless discriminate against a particular group. A seniority system would fall under the Griggs rationale if it were not for Section 703 (h) of the Civil Rights Act. That section provides:

> Notwithstanding any other provision of this subchapter, it shall not be an unlawful employment practice for an employer to apply different standards of compensation, or different terms, conditions, or privileges of employment pursuant to a bona fide seniority or merit system, . . . provided that such differences are not the result of an intention to discriminate because of race, color, religion, sex, or national origin, nor shall it be an unlawful employment practice for an employer to give and to act upon the results of any professionally developed ability test provided that such test, its administration or action upon the results is not designed, intended or used to discriminate because of race, color, religion, sex, or national origin. . . ."

Thus the court ruled that a seniority system adopted after Title VII may stand, even though it has an unintended discriminatory impact.

Firefighters Local Union #1984 v. Carl W. Stotts

The U.S. Supreme Court ruled on June 12, 1984, on the relationship between affirmative action and last-hired, first-fired seniority. Essentially, when seniority systems are involved, only individuals who can prove that they are victims of discrimination by an employer may benefit from affirmative action. In May 1981, the City of Memphis, Tennessee, had a budget deficit and had to lay off some employees. The city decided that the fairest policy was to use the last-hired, first-fired seniority system. Stotts appealed to the U.S. District Court for an order forbidding a layoff of any black employee. Both the District Court and the Appeals Court ruled in favor of Stotts, but the Supreme Court overturned the ruling.

Meritor v. Savings Bank v. Vinsion

The first sexual harassment case to reach the U.S. Supreme Court was the June 1986 case involving *Meritor* v. *Savings Bank* v. *Vinson*. In ruling for the plaintiff, one of the outcomes from the case was that Title VII is not limited to discrimination having only economic or tangible effects. In this case, the plaintiff had obtained two promotions based on merit, even though sexual harassment was involved. The Court also ruled on whether an employee's voluntary participation in sexual acts with a manager constitutes a valid defense for an employer to a Title VII complaint. Here they said that the appropriate test is whether the sexual activity was "unwelcomed," not whether the employee voluntarily engaged in sexual activity with her manager.[6]

City of Richmond v. J. A. Croson Co.

The City of Richmond adopted a Minority Business Utilization Plan requiring prime contractors awarded city construction contracts to subcontract at least 30% of the dollar amount of each contract to one or more "Minority Business Enterprises" (MBEs), which the Plan defined to include a business from anywhere in the country at least 51% of which is owned and controlled by black, Spanish-speaking, Oriental, Indian, Eskimo, or Aleut citizens. After J. A. Croson Co. was denied a waiver and lost its contract it brought suit alleging that the Plan was unconstitutional under the Fourteenth Amendment's Equal Protection Clause. On January 23, 1989, the Supreme Court affirmed a Court of Appeals ruling that the city's plan was not justified by a compelling governmental interest, since the record revealed no prior discrimination by the city itself in awarding contracts, and the 30% set-aside was not narrowly tailored to accomplish a remedial purpose. The decision forced 36 states and many cities and counties to review their programs.

Wards Cove Packing Co., Inc. v. Atonio

Jobs at petitioners' Alaskan salmon canneries are of two general types: unskilled "cannery jobs" on the cannery lines, which are filled predominantly by nonwhites; and "noncannery jobs," most of which are classified as skilled positions and filled predominantly with white workers, and virtually all of which pay more than cannery positions. The nonwhite cannery workers filed suit under Title VII of the Civil Rights of 1964, that the company's hiring/promotion practices were responsible for the work force's racial stratification and had denied them employment as noncannery workers on the basis of race. The District Court rejected these claims, finding, among other things, that nonwhite workers were overrepresented in cannery jobs because many of those jobs were filled under a hiring hall agreement with a predominantly nonwhite union. The Court of Appeals ultimately reversed holding that respondents had made out a prima facie case of disparate impact in hiring for both skilled and unskilled noncannery jobs, relying

---

[6] Frederick L. Sullivan, "Sexual Harassment: The Supreme Court's Ruling," *Personnel*, 63 (December 1986), pp. 37–38.

solely on respondents statistics showing a high percentage of nonwhite workers in cannery jobs and a low percentage of such workers in noncannery positions. On June 5, 1989, the Supreme Court ruled that the Court of Appeals erred in ruling that a comparison of the percentage of cannery workers who are nonwhite and the percentage of noncannery workers who are nonwhite makes out a prima facie disparate-impact case. This ruling made it more difficult for minorities and women to win cases based on statistics.

Martin v. Wilks

On June 12, 1989, the Supreme Court ruled that a voluntary settlement in the form of a consent decree between one group of employes and their employer cannot possibly "settle," voluntarily or otherwise, the conflicting claims of another group of employees who do not join the agreement. This 5-4 decision said that court-approved affirmative action settlements can be reopened when white male employees allege reverse discrimination. Black individuals and a branch of the NAACP brought actions in Federal District Court against the City of Birmingham, Alabama, and the Jefferson County Personnel Board, alleging that the defendants had engaged in racially discriminatory hiring and promotion practices in violation of Title VII of the Civil Rights Act of 1964 and other federal law. Consent decrees were eventually entered that included goals for hiring blacks as firefighters and for promoting them. Respondent white firefighters subsequently brought suit in the District Court against the City and the Board, alleging that, because of their race, they were being denied promotions in favor of less qualified blacks in violation of federal law.

Patterson v. McLean Credit Union

Patterson, a black woman, was employed by McLean Credit Union as a teller and file coordinator for 10 years until she was laid off. Thereafter, she brought suit under the Civil Rights Act of 1866 alleging that McLean had harassed her, failed to promote her to accounting clerk and then discharged her, all because of her race. The Court ruled that since the 1866 Act is restrictive in its scope to forbidding racial discrimination in the "make[ing] and enforce[ment]" of contracts, it cannot be construed as a general prescription of discrimination in all aspects of contracts relations. Thus, Patterson's racial harassment claim is not actionable with the possible exception of her claim that McLean's refusal to promote her was discriminatory. The 1866 Act was not overturned, but was made more restrictive.

■ EQUAL EMPLOYMENT OPPORTUNITY COMMISSION

As we mentioned previously, Title VII of the Civil Rights Act, as amended, created the Equal Employment Opportunity Commission. Under Title VII, filing a discrimination charge initiates EEOC action. Charges may be filed by one of the presidentially appointed EEOC commissioners, by any aggrieved person, or by anyone acting on behalf of an aggrieved person. Charges must be filed within 180 days of the alleged act. However, the time is extended to 300 days if a state or local agency is involved in the case.

As you can see in Figure 3-1, when a charge is filed, the EEOC typically proceeds in the following manner. First, an attempt at no-fault settlement is made. Essentially, the organization charged with the violation is invited to settle the case with no admission of guilt. Most charges are settled at this stage.

Failing settlement, the EEOC investigates the charges. Once the employer is notified that an investigation will take place, no records relating to the charge may be destroyed. During the investigative process, the employer is permitted to present a position statement. After the investigation has been

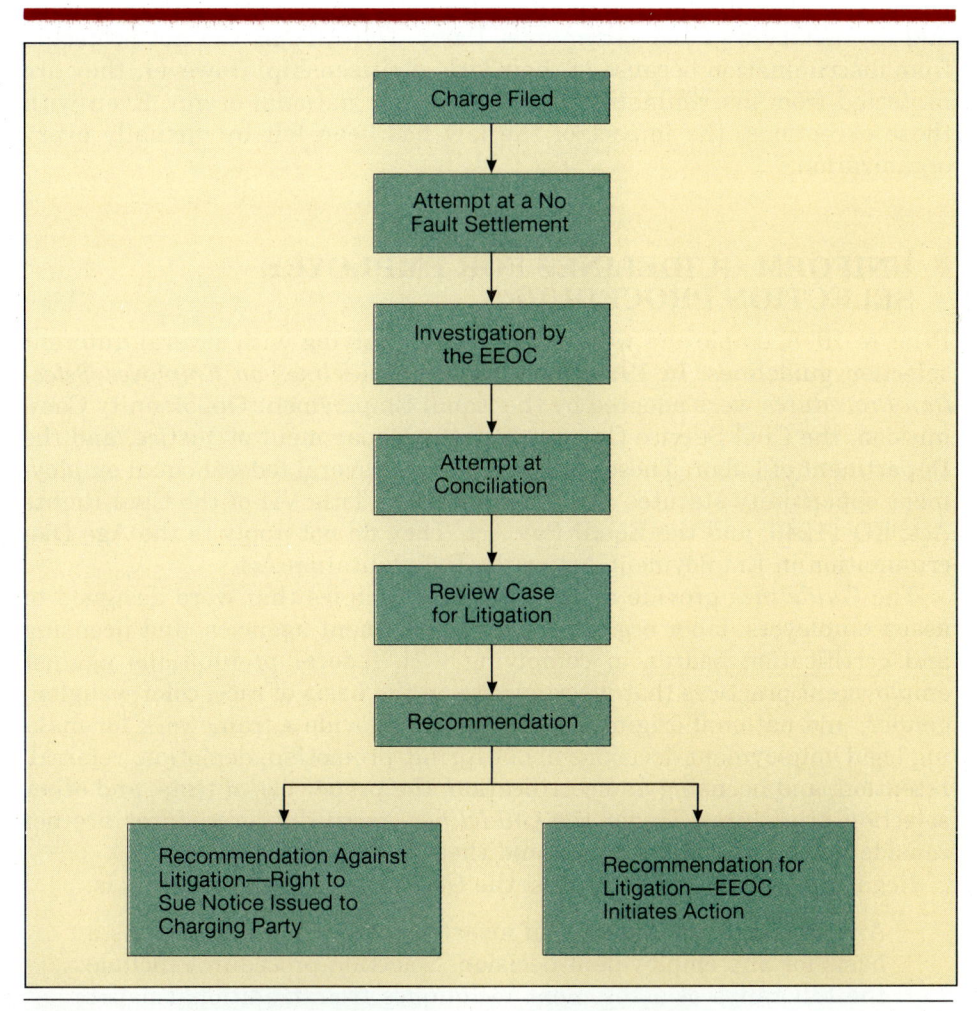

FIGURE 3-1 | **EEOC Procedure Once a Charge Is Filed**

completed, the district director of the EEOC will issue a "probable cause" or "no probable cause" statement.

The next step involves attempted conciliation. In the event this effort fails, the case will be reviewed for litigation potential. Some of the factors that determine whether the EEOC will pursue litigation are: (1) the number of people affected by the alleged practice; (2) the amount of money involved in the charge; (3) other charges against the employer; and (4) the type of charge. Recommendations for litigation are then passed on to the general counsel of the EEOC. If the recommendation is against litigation, a right to sue notice will be issued to the charging party.

It is important to note that the Civil Rights Act prohibits retaliation against employees who have opposed an illegal employment practice. The act also protects those who have testified, assisted, or participated in an investigation of discrimination.

There are certain exceptions to the coverage of Title VII. These exceptions include: (1) religious institutions, with respect to the employment of persons of a specific religion in any of the institution's activities; (2) aliens; and (3) members of the Communist Party. Noncitizens are not protected from discrimination because of their lack of citizenship. However, they are protected from discrimination because of their national origin. Even with these exceptions, the impact of the law has been felt by virtually every organization.

■ UNIFORM GUIDELINES FOR EMPLOYEE SELECTION PROCEDURES

Prior to 1978, employers were faced with complying with several different selection guidelines. In 1978, the *Uniform Guidelines on Employee Selection Procedures* were adopted by the Equal Employment Opportunity Commission, the Civil Service Commission, the Department of Justice, and the Department of Labor. These *Guidelines* cover several federal equal employment opportunity statutes and EOs, including Title VII of the Civil Rights Act, EO 11246, and the Equal Pay Act. They do not apply to the Age Discrimination in Employment Act or the Rehabilitation Act.

The *Guidelines* provide a single set of principles that were designed to assist employers, labor organizations, employment agencies, and licensing and certification boards in complying with federal prohibitions against employment practices that discriminate on the basis of race, color, religion, gender, and national origin. The *Guidelines* provide a framework for making legal employment decisions about hiring, promotion, demotion, referral, retention, and licensing and certification, the proper use of tests, and other selection procedures. Under the *Guidelines*, recruiting procedures are not considered selection procedures, and therefore are not covered.

Regarding selection procedures, the *Guidelines* state that a test is:

> Any measure, combination of measures, or procedures used as a basis for any employment decision. Selection procedures include the full range of assessment techniques from traditional paper and pencil tests, performance tests, testing programs or proba-

tionary periods and physical, education, and work experience requirement through informal or casual interviews and unscored application forms.

Using this definition, virtually any instrument or procedure used in the selection decision is considered a test.

The Concept of Adverse Impact

Prior to the issuance of the *Uniform Guidelines on Employee Selection Procedures* in 1978, the only way to prove job relatedness was to validate each test. The *Guidelines* do not require validation in all cases. It is essentially required only in instances where the test or other selection device produces an adverse impact on a minority group. Under the new *Guidelines*, adverse impact has been defined in terms of selection rates, the selection rate being the number of applicants hired or promoted, divided by the total number of applicants.[7] **Adverse impact**, a concept established by the *Uniform Guidelines*, occurs if women and minorities are not hired at the rate of at least 80 percent of the best-achieving group. This has also been called the four-fifths rule, which is actually a guideline subject to interpretation by the EEOC. The groups identified for analysis under the guidelines are (1) blacks, (2) American Indians (including Alaskan natives), (3) Asians, (4) Hispanics, (5) women, and (6) men.

The following formula is used to compute adverse impact for hiring:

$$\frac{\text{Success rate for women and minorities applicants}}{\text{Success rate for best-achieving group applicants}} = \text{Determination of adverse impact.}$$

The success rate for women and minorities applicants is determined by dividing the number of members of a specific group *employed* in a period by the number of women and minority *applicants* in a period. The success rate for best-achieving group applicants is determined by dividing the number of people in the best-achieving group *employed* by the number of the best-achieving group *applicants* in a period.

Using the formula, let's determine whether there has been an adverse impact in the following case. During 1989, 400 people were hired for a particular job. Of the total, 300 were white and 100 were black. There were 1500 applicants for these jobs, of whom 1000 were white and 500 were black. Using the adverse impact formula, we have:

$$\frac{100/500}{300/1000} = \frac{0.2}{0.3} = 66.67\%$$

We conclude that adverse impact exists.

Evidence of adverse impact involves more than the total number of minority workers *employed*. Also considered are the total number of qualified *applicants*. For instance, assume that 300 blacks and 300 whites were

---

[7] David E. Robertson, "New Directions in EEO Guidelines," *Personnel Journal*, 57 (July 1978), p. 361.

hired. But there were 1500 black applicants and 1000 applicants. Putting these figures into the adverse impact formula, we conclude that adverse impact still exists:

$$\frac{300/1500}{300/1000} = \frac{.2}{.3} = 66.67\%$$

Thus it is clear that firms must monitor their recruitment efforts very carefully. Obviously, firms should attempt to recruit qualified individuals only because once in the applicant pool, they will be used in computing adverse impact.

Assuming that adverse impact is shown, employers have two avenues available to them if they still desire to use a particular standard. First, the employer may validate a selection device to show that it is indeed a predictor of success. When the device has proved to be a predictor of job performance, business necessity has been shown. If the firm's selection device has not been validated, business necessity may be demonstrated in another manner: the employer can show a strong relationship between the selection device and job performance and that, without using this procedure, the firm's training costs would become prohibitive.

The second avenue available to employers should adverse impact be shown is the bona fide occupational qualification (BFOQ) defense. The BFOQ defense means that only one group is capable of performing the job successfully. As you might expect, the BFOQ defense has been narrowly interpreted by the courts because it almost always relates to sex discrimination cases. For instance, courts have rejected the concept that because most women cannot lift fifty pounds that all women would be eliminated from consideration for a job requiring heavy lifting.

Creators of the *Guidelines* adopted the bottom-line approach in assessing whether a firm's employment practices are discriminatory. For example, if a number of separate procedures are used in making a selection decision, the enforcement agencies will focus on the end result of these procedures to determine whether adverse impact has occurred. Essentially, the EEOC is concerned more with what is occurring than how it occurred. They admit that discriminatory employment practices that cannot be validated may exist. However, the net effect, or the *bottom line*, of the selection procedures is the focus of their attention.

■ ADDITIONAL GUIDELINES

Since the *Uniform Guidelines* were published in 1978, they have been modified several times. Some of these changes reflect Supreme Court decisions; others clarify implementation procedures. Three major changes—Interpretative Guidelines on Sexual Harassment, Guidelines on Discrimination Because of National Origin, and Guidelines on Discrimination Because of Religion—merit additional discussion.

Interpretative Guidelines on Sexual Harassment

During the 1980s, one of the most fervently pursued civil rights issues related to sexual harassment. As we previously mentioned, Title VII of the Civil Rights Act generally prohibits discrimination on the basis of gender in employment. In 1980, the EEOC issued interpretative guidelines, which state that employers have an affirmative duty to maintain a work place free from sexual harassment. The OFCCP issued similar guidelines in 1981. Managers in both for-profit and not-for-profit organizations should be particularly alert to the issue of sexual harassment. The EEOC issued the *Guidelines* because of the belief that sexual harassment continued to be a widespread problem. In one study 59 percent of the women employees interviewed reported experiencing one or more incidents of sexual harassment on the job.[8] Table 3-1 contains the EEOC's definition of sexual harassment.

According to these guidelines, employers are totally liable for the acts of their supervisors regardless of whether the employer is aware of the sexual harassment act. Where co-workers are concerned, the employer is responsible for such acts if the employer knew, or should have known, about them. The employer is not responsible when it can show that it took immediate and appropriate corrective action upon learning of the problem.

Another important aspect of these guidelines is that employers may be liable for acts committed by nonemployees in the workplace if the employer knew, or should have known, of the conduct and failed to take appropriate action. Firms are responsible for developing programs to prevent sexual harassment in the workplace. They must also investigate all formal and

TABLE 3-1 | EEOC Definition of Sexual Harassment

Unwelcome sexual advances, requests for sexual favors, and other verbal or physical conduct of a sexual nature that occur under any of the following situations:

1. When submission to such contact is made either explicitly or implicitly a term or condition of an individual's employment.
2. When submission to or rejection of such conduct by an individual is used as the basis for employment decisions affecting such individual.
3. When such conduct has the purpose or effect of unreasonably interfering with an individual's work performance or creating an intimidating, hostile, or offensive working environment.

---

[8] Michelle Hoyman and Ronda Robinson, "Interpreting the New Sexual Harassment Guidelines," *Personnel Journal*, 59 (December 1980), p. 996.

informal complaints alleging sexual harassment. After investigating, a firm must take immediate and appropriate action to correct the situation. Failure to do so constitutes a violation of Title VII, as interpreted by the EEOC.

There have been numerous sexual harassment court cases. In *Miller* v. *Bank of America*, a U.S. Circuit Court of Appeals held an employer liable for the sexually harassing acts of its supervisors, even though the company had a policy prohibiting such conduct and even though the victim did not formally notify the employer of the problem. Another U.S. Circuit Court of Appeals ruled that sexual harassment, in and of itself, is a violation of Title VII. The court ruled that the law does not require the victim to prove that she resisted harassment and was penalized for that resistance. As we previously mentioned, the first sexual harassment case to reach the U.S. Supreme Court was the June 1986 case of *Meritor* v. *Savings Bank* v. *Vinson*.

Guidelines on Discrimination Because of National Origin

The EEOC broadly defined discrimination on the basis of national origin as the denial of equal employment opportunity because of an individual's ancestors or place of birth; or because an individual has the physical, cultural, or linguistic characteristics of a national origin group. Because height or weight requirements tend to exclude individuals on the basis of national origin, firms are expected to evaluate their selection procedures for adverse impact, regardless of whether the total selection process has an adverse impact based on national origin. Height and weight requirements are, therefore, exceptions to the bottom-line concept. As Table 3-2 shows, the EEOC has identified certain selection procedures that may be discriminatory.

Harassment on the basis of national origin is a violation of Title VII. Employers have an affirmative duty to maintain a working environment free from such harassment. Ethnic slurs and other verbal or physical con-

TABLE 3-2 | Selection Procedures That May Be Discriminatory Regarding National Origin

1. Fluency-in-English requirements: One questionable practice involves denying employment opportunities because of an individual's foreign accent or inability to communicate well in English. When this practice is continually followed, the Commission will presume that such a rule violates Title VII and will closely study it. However, a firm may require that employees speak only in English at certain times if business necessity can be shown.
2. Training or education requirements: Denying employment opportunities to an individual because of his or her foreign training or education; or practices that require an individual to be foreign trained or educated may be discriminatory.

duct relating to an individual's national origin constitute harassment when this conduct: (1) has the purpose or effect of creating an intimidating, hostile, or offensive working environment; (2) has the purpose or effect of unreasonably interfering with an individual's work performance; or (3) otherwise adversely affects an individual's employment opportunity.

Guidelines on Discrimination Because of Religion

Employers have an obligation to accommodate religious practices unless they can demonstrate a resulting undue hardship. In determining whether an accommodation would constitute undue hardship, consideration is given to identifiable costs in relation to the size and operating costs of the employer and the number of individuals who actually need the accommodation. These guidelines recognize that regular payment of premium wages constitute undue hardship, whereas these payments on an infrequent or temporary basis do not. Undue hardship would also exist if an accommodation required a firm to vary from its bona fide seniority system.

These guidelines identify several means of accommodating religious practices that prohibit working on certain days. Some of the methods suggested include voluntary substitutes, flexible scheduling, lateral transfer, and change of job assignments. Some collective bargaining agreements include a provision that each employee must join the union or pay the union a sum equivalent to dues. When an employee's religious beliefs prevent compliance, the union should accommodate the employee by permitting that person to make an equivalent donation to a charitable organization.

■ AFFIRMATIVE ACTION PROGRAMS

An **affirmative action program (AAP)** is an approach that certain organizations with government contracts develop to demonstrate that workers are employed in proportion to their representation in the firm's relevant labor market. The need for affirmative action programs was created by EO 11246, as amended by 11375, and placed enforcement with the OFCCP. An affirmative action program may be voluntarily implemented by an organization. In such an event, goals are established and action is taken to hire and move minorities and women upward in the organization. In other situations, an AAP may be mandated by the OFCCP. The degree of control the OFCCP will impose depends on the size of the contract. Contracts of $10,000 or less are not covered. The first level of control involves contracts that exceed $10,000 but are less than $50,000. These contractors are governed by the equal opportunity clause, as shown in Table 3-3.

The second level of control occurs if the contractor has (1) 50 or more employees; (2) a contract of $50,000 or more; (3) contracts which, in any twelve month period total $50,000 or more, or reasonably may be expected to total $50,000 or more; or (4) is a financial institution that serves as a depository for government funds in any amount, acts as an issuing or redeeming agent for U.S. savings bonds and savings notes in any amount, or sub-

TABLE 3-3 | **Equal Opportunity Clause—Government Contracts**

1. The contractor will not discriminate against any employee or applicant for employment because of race, color, religion, sex, or national origin. The contractors will take affirmative action to ensure that applicants are employed, and that employees are treated during employment, without regard to their race, color, religion, sex, or national origin. Such action shall include, but not be limited to the following: Employment, upgrading, demotions, or transfer; recruitment or recruitment advertising, layoff or termination; rates of pay or other forms of compensation; and selection for training, including apprenticeship. The contractor agrees to post in conspicuous places, available to employees and applicants for employment, notices to be provided by the contracting officer setting forth the provisions for this nondiscrimination clause.

2. The contractor will in all solicitations or advertisements for employees placed by or on behalf of the contractor, state that all qualified applicants will receive consideration for employment without regard to race, color, religion, sex, or national origin.

3. The contractor will send to each labor union or representative of workers with which he has a collective bargaining agreement or other contract or understanding, a notice to be provided by the agency contracting officer, advising the labor union or workers' representative of the contractor's commitments under section 202 of Executive Order 11246 of September 24, 1965, and shall post copies of the notice in conspicuous places available to employees and applicants for employment.

4. The contractor will comply with all provisions of Executive Order 11246 of September 24, 1965, and of the rules, regulations, and relevant orders of the Secretary of Labor.

5. The contractor will furnish all information and reports required by Executive Order 11246 of September 24, 1965, and by the rules, regulations, and orders of the Secretary of Labor, or pursuant thereto, and will permit access to his books, records, and accounts by the contracting agency and the Secretary of Labor for purposes of investigation to ascertain compliance with such rules, regulations, and orders.

6. In the event of the contractor's noncompliance with the nondiscrimination clauses of this contract or with any of such rules, regulations, or orders, this contract may be canceled, terminated or suspended in whole or in part and the contractor may be declared ineligible for further Government contracts in accordance with procedures authorized in Executive Order 11246 of September 24, 1965, or by rule, regulation, or order of the Secretary of State, or as otherwise provided by law.

7. The contractor will include the provisions of paragraphs (1) through (7) in every subcontract or purchase order unless exempted by rules, regulations, or orders of the Secretary of Labor issued pursuant to section 204 of Executive Order 11246 of September 24, 1965, so that such provisions will be binding upon each subcontractor or vendor. The contractor will take such action with respect to any subcontract or purchase order as may be directed by the Secretary of Labor as a means of enforcing such provisions including sanctions for noncompliance: *Provided, however,* that in the event the contractor becomes involved in, or is threatened with litigation with a subcontractor or vendor as a result of such direction, the contractor may request the United States to enter into such litigation to protect the interests of the United States.

Source: *Federal Register*, Vol. 45, No. 251, Tuesday, December 30, 1980, p. 86230.

scribes to federal deposit or share insurance. Contractors meeting these criteria must develop a written affirmative action program for each of its establishments and file an annual EEO-1 report (see Figure 3-2). The affirmative action program is the major focus of EO 11246. It requires specific steps to guarantee equal employment opportunity. Prerequisite to development of a satisfactory AAP is identification and analysis of problem areas inherent in employment of minorities and women and an evaluation of opportunities for utilizing minority and women employees.

The third level of control on contractors is when contracts exceed $1 million. All previously stated requirements must be met, and in addition, the OFCCP is authorized to conduct preaward compliance reviews. The purpose of a compliance review is to determine whether the contractor is maintaining nondiscriminatory hiring and employment practices. The review also ensures that the contractor is taking affirmative action to guarantee that applicants are employed, placed, trained, upgraded, promoted, terminated, and otherwise treated during employment without regard to race, color, religion, gender, national origin, veteran status, or handicap. In determining whether to conduct a preaward review, the OFCCP may consider, for example, the items presented in Table 3-4.

If an investigation indicates a violation, the OFCCP first tries to secure compliance through persuasion. If persuasion fails to resolve the issue, the OFCCP serves a notice to show cause or a notice of violation. A show cause notice contains a list of the violations, a statement of how the OFCCP proposes that corrections be made, a request for a written response to the findings, and a suggested date for a conciliation conference. The firm usually has thirty days to respond. Successful conciliation results in a written contract between the OFCCP and the contractor. In a conciliation agreement the contractor agrees to take specific steps to remedy noncompliance with the EO. Firms that do not correct violations can be passed over in the awarding of future contracts.

The procedures for developing affirmative action plans were published in the *Federal Register* of December 4, 1974. These regulations are referred to

TABLE 3-4 | Factors That the OFCCP May Consider in Conducting a Preaward Review

1. The past EEO performance of the contractor, including its current EEO profile and indications of underutilization.
2. The volume and nature of complaints filed by employees or applicants against the contractor.
3. Whether the contractor is in a growth industry.
4. The level of employment or promotional opportunities resulting from the expansion of, or turnover in, the contractor's workforce.
5. The employment opportunities likely to result from the contract in issue.
6. Whether resources are available to conduct the review.

Joint Reporting Committee

- Equal Employment Opportunity Commission
- Office of Federal Contract Compliance Programs (Labor)

EQUAL EMPLOYMENT OPPORTUNITY

EMPLOYER INFORMATION REPORT EEO–1

Standard Form 100 (Rev. 5–84)
O.M.B. No. 3046–0007
EXPIRES 3/31/85
100–211

Section A—TYPE OF REPORT
Refer to instructions for number and types of reports to be filed.

1. Indicate by marking in the appropriate box the type of reporting unit for which this copy of the form is submitted (MARK ONLY ONE BOX).

   (1) ☐ Single-establishment Employer Report

   Multi-establishment Employer:
   (2) ☐ Consolidated Report (Required)
   (3) ☐ Headquarters Unit Report (Required)
   (4) ☐ Individual Establishment Report (submit one for each establishment with 50 or more employees)
   (5) ☐ Special Report

2. Total number of reports being filed by this Company (Answer on Consolidated Report only) _____

Section B—COMPANY IDENTIFICATION (To be answered by all employers)

1. Parent Company
   a. Name of parent company (owns or controls establishment in item 2) omit if same as label

   Name of receiving office | Address (Number and street)
   City or town | County | State | ZIP code | b. Employer Identification No.

2. Establishment for which this report is filed. (Omit if same as label)
   a. Name of establishment

   Address (Number and street) | City or Town | County | State | ZIP code
   b. Employer Identification No. | (Omit if same as label)

Section C—EMPLOYERS WHO ARE REQUIRED TO FILE (To be answered by all employers)

☐ Yes ☐ No 1. Does the entire company have at least 100 employees in the payroll period for which you are reporting?

☐ Yes ☐ No 2. Is your company affiliated through common ownership and/or centralized management with other entities in an enterprise with a total employment of 100 or more?

☐ Yes ☐ No 3. Does the company or any of its establishments (a) have 50 or more employees AND (b) is not exempt as provided by 41 CFR 60-1.5, AND either (1) is a prime government contractor or first-tier subcontractor, and has a contract, subcontract, or purchase order amounting to $50,000 or more, or (2) serves as a depository of Government funds in any amount or is a financial institution which is an issuing and paying agent for U.S. Savings Bonds and Savings Notes?

→ If the response to question C-3 is yes, please enter your Dun and Bradstreet identification number (if you have one): _____

☐ Yes ☐ No 4. Does the company receive financial assistance from the Small Business Administration (SBA)?

NOTE: If the answer is yes to questions 1, 2, or 3, complete the entire form, otherwise skip to Section G.

NSN 7540-00-180-6384

FIGURE 3-2 | Equal Employment Opportunity Employer Information Report (EEO-1)

CHAPTER 3 Equal Employment Opportunity and Affirmative Action

SF 100 Page 2

Section D—EMPLOYMENT DATA

Employment at this establishment—Report all permanent full-time or part-time employees including apprentices and on-the-job trainees unless specifically excluded as set forth in the instructions. Enter the appropriate figures on all lines and in all columns. Blank spaces will be considered as zeros.

NUMBER OF EMPLOYEES

JOB CATEGORIES		OVERALL TOTALS (SUM OF COL. B THRU K) A	MALE					FEMALE				
			WHITE (NOT OF HISPANIC ORIGIN) B	BLACK (NOT OF HISPANIC ORIGIN) C	HISPANIC D	ASIAN OR PACIFIC ISLANDER E	AMERICAN INDIAN OR ALASKAN NATIVE F	WHITE (NOT OF HISPANIC ORIGIN) G	BLACK (NOT OF HISPANIC ORIGIN) H	HISPANIC I	ASIAN OR PACIFIC ISLANDER J	AMERICAN INDIAN OR ALASKAN NATIVE K
Officials and Managers	1											
Professionals	2											
Technicians	3											
Sales Workers	4											
Office and Clerical	5											
Craft Workers (Skilled)	6											
Operatives (Semi-Skilled)	7											
Laborers (Unskilled)	8											
Service Workers	9											
TOTAL	10											
Total employment reported in previous EEO-1 report	11											

(The trainees below should also be included in the figures for the appropriate occupational categories above)

| Formal On-the-job trainees | White collar | 12 | | | | | | | | | | | |
| | Production | 13 | | | | | | | | | | | |

NOTE: Omit questions 1 and 2 on the Consolidated Report.
1. Date(s) of payroll period used: 2. Does this establishment employ apprentices?
                                                      1 ☐ Yes   2 ☐ No

Section E—ESTABLISHMENT INFORMATION *(Omit on the Consolidated Report)*

1. Is the location of the establishment the same as that reported last year?
   1 ☐ Yes   2 ☐ No   3 ☐ No report last year

2. Is the major business activity at this establishment the same as that reported last year?
   1 ☐ Yes   2 ☐ No   3 ☐ No report last year

OFFICE USE ONLY

3. What is the major activity of this establishment? (Be specific, i.e., manufacturing steel castings, retail grocer, wholesale plumbing supplies, title insurance, etc. Include the specific type of product or type of service provided, as well as the principal business or industrial activity.)

Section F—REMARKS

Use this item to give any identification data appearing on last report which differs from that given above, explain major changes in composition or reporting units and other pertinent information.

Section G—CERTIFICATION *(See Instructions G)*

Check one
1 ☐ All reports are accurate and were prepared in accordance with the instructions (check on consolidated only)
2 ☐ This report is accurate and was prepared in accordance with the instructions.

Name of Certifying Official	Title	Signature	Date
Name of person to contact regarding this report (Type or print)	Address (Number and street)		
Title	City and State	ZIP code	Telephone Area Code	Number	Extension

All reports and information obtained from individual reports will be kept confidential as required by Section 709(e) of Title VII
WILLFULLY FALSE STATEMENTS ON THIS REPORT ARE PUNISHABLE BY LAW, U.S. CODE, TITLE 18, SECTION 1001

as Revised Order No. 4. The OFCCP guide for compliance officers, outlining what to cover in a compliance review, is known as Order No. 14.

The OFCCP is very specific about what should be included in an affirmative action program. A policy statement has to be developed that reflects the CEO's attitude regarding equal employment opportunity, assigns overall responsibility for preparing and implementing the affirmative action program, and provides for reporting and monitoring procedures. The policy should state that the firm intends to recruit, hire, train, and promote persons in all job titles without regard to race, color, religion, gender, or national origin, except where gender is a bona fide occupational qualification (BFOQ). The policy should guarantee that all human resource actions involving such areas as compensation, benefits, transfers, layoffs, returns from layoff, company sponsored training, education, tuition assistance, and social and recreational programs will be administered without regard to race, color, religion, gender, or national origin.

Revised Order No. 4 is quite specific with regard to dissemination of a firm's EEO policy, both internally and externally. An executive should be appointed to manage the firm's equal employment opportunity program. This person should be given the necessary support by top management to accomplish the assignment. Revised Order No. 4 specifies the minimum level of responsibility associated with the task of EEO manager.

An acceptable AAP must include an analysis of deficiencies in the utilization of minority groups and women. The first step in conducting a utilization analysis is to make a workforce analysis.

The second step involves an analysis of all major job groups. An explanation of the situation is required if minorities or women are currently being underutilized. A job group is defined as one or more jobs having similar content, wage rates, and opportunities. Underutilization is defined as having fewer minorities or women in a particular job group than would reasonably be expected by their availability. The utilization analysis is important because the calculations determine whether underutilization exists. For example, if the utilization analysis shows that the availability of blacks for a certain job group is 30 percent, the organization should have at least 30 percent black employment in that group. If actual employment is less than 30 percent, underutilization exists, and the firm should set a goal of 30 percent black employment for that job group.

The primary focus of any affirmative action program is on goals and timetables: how many, by when. Goals and timetables developed by the firm should cover its entire affirmative action program, including correction of deficiencies. These goals and timetables should be attainable; that is, they should be based on results that the firm, making good-faith efforts, could reasonably expect to achieve.

Both human resource managers and line managers should be involved in the goal-setting process. Goals should be significant and measurable, as well as attainable. Two goals must be established regarding underutilization: annual and ultimate. The annual goal is to move toward elimination of underutilization, whereas the ultimate goal is to correct all underutilization. Goals should be specific in terms of planned results with timetables for completion. However, goals should not establish inflexible quotas that must be met. Rather, they should be targets that are reasonably attainable.

Employers should also conduct a detailed analysis of job descriptions to ensure that they accurately reflect job content. In addition, job specifications should be validated, with special attention given to academic, experience, and skills requirements. If a job specification screens out a disproportionate number of minorities or women, the requirements must be professionally validated in relation to job performance. Thus a comprehensive job analysis program is required.

When an opening occurs, everyone involved in human resource recruiting, screening, selection, and promotion should be aware of the opening. In addition, the firm should evaluate the entire selection process to ensure freedom from bias. And individuals involved in the process should be carefully selected and trained in order to minimize bias in all human resource actions.

Firms should observe the requirements of the *Uniform Guidelines*. Selection techniques other than tests can also be used improperly and thus discriminate against minorities and women. Such techniques include unscored interviews, unscored or casual application forms, use of arrest records and credit checks, and consideration of marital status, dependency, and minor children. Where data suggest that discrimination or unfair exclusion of minorities and women exists, the firm should analyze its unscored procedures and eliminate them if they are not objective and valid. Some techniques that can be used to improve recruitment and increase the flow of minority and women applicants are shown in Table 3-5.

■ IMPLICATIONS FOR MULTINATIONAL CORPORATIONS

Domestic firms obviously are greatly affected by statutes, executive orders, and court decisions—and must abide by them or face legal consequences. However, multinational corporations headquartered in the United States must obey the laws of the host country. When operating in the multinational environment, U.S.-based firms often find their human resource policies to be in conflict with the laws and accepted norms of the host country. For instance, the influence of Title VII of the Civil Rights Act of 1964, as amended, has been felt by virtually all firms operating in the United States. But most countries in the world do not have such laws prohibiting discrimination. In fact, some countries practice overt discrimination against certain groups, which would be protected if they were employed in the United States. In certain Middle East countries, women are subordinate to men. A U.S. firm desiring to conduct business in those countries would have a difficult time gaining acceptance of a woman manager. Therefore, even if these firms have a strong affirmative action program at home, the decision not to place women managers in certain countries may not only be expedient—but necessary. With regard to the law and customs, multinational corporations may have to abide by the old expression, "When in Rome, do as the Romans."

TABLE 3-5 | Techniques to Improve Recruitment of Minorities and Women

- Identify referral organizations for minorities and women.
- Hold formal briefing sessions with representatives of referral organizations.
- Encourage minority and women employees to refer applicants to the firm.
- Include minorities and women on the Personnel Relations staff.
- Permit minorities and women to participate in Career Days, Youth Motivation Programs and related activities in their community.
- Actively participate in job fairs and give company representatives the authority to make on-the-spot commitments.
- Actively recruit at schools having predominant minority or female enrollments.
- Recruiting efforts at all schools should use special efforts to reach minorities and women.
- Special employment programs should be undertaken whenever possible for women and minorities. These might include technical and nontechnical co-op programs, "after school" and/or work-study jobs, summer jobs for underprivileged, summer work—study programs, and motivation, training and employment programs for the hardcore unemployed.
- Pictorially present minorities and women in recruiting brochures.
- Help wanted advertising should be expanded to include the minority news media and women's interest media.

Source: *Federal Register*, vol. 45, no. 251, Tuesday, December 30, 1980, p. 86243.

SUMMARY

The concept of equal employment opportunity has evolved considerably since passage of the Civil Rights Act of 1964. Numerous amendments, and even other acts, have been passed when voids were found in the initial act. Major Supreme Court decisions have interpreted the provisions of these statutes. Presidential Executive Orders further strengthened the quest for equal employment opportunity.

The 1866 and 1871 Civil Rights Acts, based on the Thirteenth and Fourteenth Amendments to the Constitution, represented early efforts to outlaw discrimination in the workplace. Title VII of the 1964 Civil Rights Act, as amended by the Equal Employment Opportunity Act of 1972, has had a major impact on HRM. These laws prohibit discrimination based on race, color, sex, religion, or national origin. The Age Discrimination in Employment Act (ADEA), as amended, prohibits employers from discriminating against individuals because of age. The Rehabilitation Act covers certain government contractors and subcontractors, and organizations that receive federal grants in excess of $2500. Passed as an amendment to Title VII of the Civil Rights Act, the Pregnancy Discrimination Act prohibits discrimination in employment based on pregnancy, childbirth, or related medical conditions. The Immigration Reform and Control Act of 1986 established criminal and civil sanctions against employers who knowingly hire an illegal immigrant, and made it unlawful to hire anyone without verifying employment authorization and identity.

Presidential Executive Orders (EOs) apply to governmental agencies and have the force and effect of laws enacted by Congress. In 1965, EO 11246 made it federal policy to provide equal opportunity in federal employment for all qualified persons. It not only prohibits discrimination in employment, but it also requires promoting the full realization of equal employment opportunity through a positive, continuing program in each executive department and agency.

The manner in which the courts interpret the law is vitally important. Important Supreme Court decisions related to equal employment opportunity and affirmative action include: *Albermarle Paper Company v. Moody, Washington v. Davis, Griggs v. Duke Power Company, Phillips v. Martin Marietta Corporation, Espinoza v. Farah Manufacturing Company, Weber v. Kaiser Aluminum and Chemical Corporation, Dothard v. Rawlingson, University of California v. Bakke, American Tobacco Company v. Patterson, Firefighters Local Union #1984 v. Carl W. Stotts, Meritor v. Savings Bank v. Vinson, City of Richmond v. J. A. Croson Co., Wards Cove Packing Co., Inc., v. Atonio, Martin v. Wilks,* and *Patterson v. McLean Credit Union.*

Title VII of the Civil Rights Act, as amended, created the Equal Employment Opportunity Commission. Under Title VII, filing a discrimination charge initiates EEOC action. Charges may be filed by one of the appointed EEOC commissioners, by any aggrieved person, or by anyone acting on behalf of an aggrieved person.

In 1978, the *Uniform Guidelines on Employee Selection Procedures* were adopted by the EEOC, the Civil Service Commission, the Department of Justice, and the Department of Labor. The guidelines provide a single set of principles designed to assist employers, labor organizations, employment agencies, and licensing and certification boards in complying with federal prohibitions against discriminatory employment practices. The fundamental principle underlying the guidelines is that employer policies or practices that have an adverse impact on the employment opportunities of any protected race, gender, or ethnic group are illegal under Title VII and/or EO 11246 unless justified by business necessity. Adverse impact occurs when members of protected groups receive unequal consideration for employment. Specifically, adverse impact occurs if women and minorities are not hired at the rate of at least 80 percent of the best-achieving group. This has also been called the four-fifths rule. Three major changes in the *Uniform Guidelines* were the Interpretative Guidelines on Sexual Harassment, Guidelines on Discrimination Because of National Origin, and Guidelines on Discrimination Because of Religion.

An affirmative action program (AAP) is developed by an organization to demonstrate that women and minorities are employed in proportion to their representation in the firm's labor market. The need for affirmative action programs was created by the signing of Executive Order 11246, as amended by 11375, and placed enforcement with the OFCCP.

Firms in the United States are greatly affected by statutes, executive orders, and court decisions. But, when an organization headquartered in the United States goes multinational, the laws of the host country must be obeyed. Firms operating in the multinational environment often find their human resource policies to be in conflict with the laws and accepted norms of the host country and must adapt to them.

Questions for Review

1. Briefly describe the following laws:
    a. Title VII of the Civil Rights Act of 1964, as amended in 1972.
    b. Age Discrimination in Employment Act of 1976, as amended in 1978 and 1986.
    c. Rehabilitation Act of 1973.
    d. Pregnancy Discrimination Act of 1978.
    e. Immigration Reform and Control Act of 1986.
2. What is a Presidential Executive Order? Describe the major provisions of EO 11246, as amended by EO 11375.
3. What is the purpose of the Office of Federal Contract Compliance Programs?
4. Discuss the significant U.S. Supreme Court decisions that have had an impact on equal employment opportunity.
5. What is the purpose of the *Uniform Guidelines on Employee Selection Procedures?*
6. Distinguish between adverse impact and affirmative action programs.
7. How does the EEOC define sexual harassment?

Terms for Review

Executive Order (EO)
Adverse impact

Affirmative action
Affirmative action program (AAP)

INCIDENT 1 ▪ So, What's Affirmative Action? ▪

Supreme Construction Company began as a small commercial builder located in Baytown, Texas. Until the 1980s, Alex Boyd, Supreme's founder, concentrated his efforts on small, free-standing shops and offices. Up to that time Alex never employed more than fifteen people.

In 1982 Alex's son, Michael, graduated from college with a degree in construction and immediately joined the company full-time. Mike had worked on a variety of Supreme jobs while in school and Alex felt his son was really cut out for the construction business. Mike was given increasing responsibility and the company continued its success, although with a few more projects—and a few more employees—than before. In 1986 Mike approached his father with a proposition: "Let's get into some of the bigger projects now. We have the capital to expand and I really believe we can do it." Alex approved and Supreme began doing small shopping centers and multi-story office buildings in addition to its traditional specialization. Soon, employment had grown to 75.

In 1989, NASA released construction specifications for two aircraft hangars to be built southeast of Houston. Although Supreme had never done any construction work for the government, Mike and Alex considered the job within their capabilities. Michael worked up the $582,000 bid and submitted it to the NASA procurement office.

Several weeks later the bids were opened. Supreme had the low bid. However, the acceptance letter was contingent on submission of a satisfactory affirmative action program.

Questions

1. Explain why Supreme must submit an affirmative action program.
2. Generally, what should the program be designed to accomplish?

INCIDENT 2 ■ Retire? ■

Les Partain, human resource development manager for Gazelle Corporation, was sixty-four years old in 1989 and had been with the firm for over 30 years. He had been in his current job twelve years. During those years he had received excellent performance reports.

Six months before Les's sixty-fifth birthday, he and Bennie Helton, the human resource director, were enjoying a cup of coffee together. "Les," said Bennie, "I'll bet you and the missus are looking forward to retirement. You can certainly look back on a fine career at Gazelle."

"Gee, Bennie, I really appreciate the good words, but I've never felt better in my life. I figure that I have at least five more good years. There are many other things I would like to do for the department before I retire. I have some excellent employees and we can get a lot done in the next five years."

Bennie was surprised, to say the least. He had assumed that Les would retire, since his longevity would give him maximum retirement benefits. Later that day he discussed the matter with Jim Altic, the company president and a long-time friend. He told Jim, "My gosh, I had no idea that Les intended to hang on. We really need a younger, more aggressive person in that job. The human resource development department is more important than ever and Les's old ideas just won't cut it anymore."

Questions

1. What should Bennie do about this situation? Discuss.
2. What actions should Bennie have taken in the past to avoid his current predicament?

Experiencing Human Resource Management

Many laws have been passed and court decisions rendered that affect the everyday actions of human resource managers. Past decisions may no longer apply. Human resource managers have a responsibility to ensure that actions affecting human resource management adhere to both the letter and intent of the law. Unfortunately, not everyone may share this view, which is when problems occur. In this situation, the human resource manager and a dock foreman for New York-based Hoffa Loading and Storage Company are having a disagreement on the necessity of hiring women dock workers.

The human resource manager must talk to the dock foreman concerning future hiring practices. The dock foreman is aware that the firm follows the policy of affirmative action; but, he rejects virtually every woman that is sent over to the docks. On the rare occasion that he does hire a woman, she does not last very long. The human resource manager realizes that this hiring practice puts the dock foreman in a somewhat precarious position, but this is the way things have to be.

The dock foreman is quite disgruntled about the company's directive to hire women on the dock. The human resource manager, and the bosses upstairs, do not understand that on the dock, men are needed, red-blooded American men. The foreman believes that his men are the best dock workers on the pier and wants to keep the situation as it is. They have always exceeded the tonnage moved by any other group and they work so well together. Everybody pulls their own weight. He also believes that women are just going to mess things up and the wives of his male dock workers do not want their husbands working with women.

Certainly, a potential for conflict exists in this situation. Two individuals will participate in this exercise: one to serve as the human resource manager and the other to play the role of dock foreman. All students not playing a role should carefully observe the behavior of both participants. Your instructor will provide the participants with necessary additional information that they will need.

REFERENCES

Bradshaw, David S. "Sexual Harassment: Confronting the Troublesome Issues." *Personnel Administrator*, 32 (January 1987), pp. 51–53.

Buonocore, Anthony J., and Dallas R. Crable. "Equal Opportunity: An Incomplete Evolution." *Personnel Journal*, 65 (August 1986), pp. 32–35.

Carrell, Michael R., and Frank E. Kuzmits. "Amended ADEA's Effects on HR Strategies Remain Dubious." *Personnel Journal*, 66 (May 1987), pp. 111–119.

Caudill, Donald W. "Is Your Climate Ripe for Sexual Harassment?" *Management World*, 111 (July–August 1986), pp. 26–27.

D'Amico, Thomas F. "The Economics of Discrimination Thirty Years Later." *The American Economic Review*, 77 (May 1987), pp. 310–315.

Greenlaw, Paul S. "Affirmative Action or Reverse Discrimination?" *Personnel Journal*, 64 (September 1985), pp. 84–87.

Grider, Doug, and Mike Shurden. "The Gathering Storm of Comparable Worth." *Business Horizons*, 30 (July–August 1987), pp. 81–86.

Heller, Philip S. "EEOC Standards: What Makes for a Good Test?" *Personnel Journal*, 65 (July 1986), pp. 102–105.

Kohl, John P., and David B. Stephens. "Expanding the Legal Rights of Working Women." *Personnel*, 64 (May 1987), pp. 46–51.

Koral, Alan M. "Social Invitations, Strict Liability, and Sexual Harassment," *Employment Relations Journal*, 13 (Spring 1986), pp. 13–19.

Martin, Bob, and Stephanie Lawrence. "Personnel Executives Respond to Reaffirmation of Affirmative Action." *Personnel Journal*, 66 (May 1987), pp. 9–15.

Mulcahy, Robert W., and Jon E. Anderson. "The Bargaining Battleground Called Comparable Worth." *Public Personnel Management*, 15 (Fall 1986), pp. 233–245.

Poole, Jeanne C., and E. Theodore Kantz. "An EEO–AA Program That Exceeds Quotas—It Targets Biases." *Personnel Journal*, 66 (January 1987), pp. 103–105.

Romberg, Roberta V. "Performance Appraisal, 1: Risks and Rewards." *Personnel*, 63 (August 1986), pp. 20–26.

Ruben, George. "Supreme Court Hears Sexual Harassment Case." *Monthly Labor Review*, 109 (September 1986), p. 39.

Stevens, George E. "Exploding the Myths About Hiring the Handicapped." *Personnel*, 63 (December 1986), pp. 57–60.

Strayer, Jacqueline F., and Sandra E. Rapoport. "Sexual Harassment, 2: Limiting Corporate Liability." *Personnel*, 63 (April 1986), pp. 26–32.

Sullivan, Frederick L. "Sexual Harassment: The Supreme Court's Ruling." *Personnel*, 63 (December 1986), pp. 37–44.

Sutton, Charlotte D., and Kris K. Moore. "Attitudes Toward Executive Women: Do They Differ Geographically?" *Personnel Administrator*, 31 (May 1986), pp. 75–88.

Thornton, Terry. "Sexual Harassment, 1: Discouraging It in the Work Place." *Personnel*, 63 (August 1986), pp. 18–26.

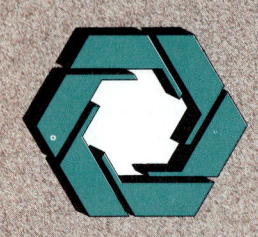

CHAPTER 4   JOB ANALYSIS

Chapter Objectives

1. Define job analysis and explain the reasons for conducting job analysis.
2. State the types of information required for job analysis, describe the various job analysis methods, and explain the components of a well-designed job description and job specification.
3. Describe the newer methods available for conducting job analysis and describe how job analysis helps to satisfy various legal requirements.
4. Explain job design, job enrichment, and job enlargement.

> ■ "Mary, I'm having trouble figuring out what kind of machine operators you need," said John Anderson, the human resource director at Gulf Machineries. "I've sent four people for you to interview who seemed to meet the requirements outlined in the job description. You rejected all of them."
>
> "To heck with the job description," replied Mary. "What I'm concerned with is finding someone who can do the job. And, the people you sent me couldn't do the job. Besides, I've never even seen the job description."
>
> John took a copy of the job description to Mary and went over it point by point. They discovered that either the job description never fit the job, or the job had changed a great deal since it was written. For example, the job description specified experience on an older model drill press while the one in use is a new digital machine. Workers had to be more mathematically oriented to effectively use the new machine.
>
> After hearing Mary describe the qualifications needed for the machine operators' job, and explaining the duties they perform, John said, "I think that we can now write an accurate description of the job and, using it as a guide, find the right kind of people. Let's work more closely so this kind of situation won't happen again."

The situation just described reflects a very common problem in human resource management; the job description did not adequately define the duties and skills needed to perform the job. Therefore, it became virtually impossible for John Anderson, the human resource director, to locate people with the required skills. Job analysis was critically needed to resolve the problem. As we stress throughout the remainder of this book, job analysis is the most basic function of human resource management.

We begin the chapter by defining job analysis and describing its importance to all human resource functions. Next, we discuss job analysis methods and the types of data gathered in the process. We then explain the use of job analysis data in preparing job descriptions and job specifications. We describe newer methods for conducting job analysis and conclude the chapter by reviewing the legal implications of job analysis.

■ JOB ANALYSIS: A BASIC HUMAN RESOURCE TOOL

A **job** consists of a group of tasks that must be performed for an organization to achieve its goals. A job may require the services of one person, such as that of president, or the services of seventy-five, as might be the case with data entry operators in a large firm.

In a work group consisting of a supervisor, two senior clerks, and four stenographers, there are three jobs and seven positions. A **position** is the collection of tasks and responsibilities performed by one person; there is a position for every individual in an organization. For instance, a small company might have 25 jobs for its 75 employees, whereas in a large company 2,000 jobs may exist for 50,000 employees. In some firms, as few as 10 jobs constitute 90 percent of a work force.[1]

Job analysis is the systematic process of determining the skills, duties, and knowledge required for performing jobs in an organization.[2] It is an essential and pervasive human resource technique. As you will note in the Executive Insight of Walter Tornow of Control Data Corporation, it was one of the first duties he performed when he began his career in human resources. The purpose of job analysis is to obtain answers to six important questions:

1. What physical and mental tasks does the worker accomplish?
2. When is the job to be completed?
3. Where is the job to be accomplished?
4. How does the worker do the job?
5. Why is the job done?
6. What qualifications are needed to perform the job?

Job analysis provides a summary of a job's duties and responsibilities, its relationship to other jobs, the knowledge and skills required, and working conditions under which it is performed. Job facts are gathered, analyzed, and recorded as the job exists, not as the job should exist.[3] The latter function is most often assigned to industrial engineers, methods analysts, or others. Job analysis is conducted after the job has been designed, the worker has been trained, and the job is being performed.

---

[1] Donald W. Myers, "The Impact of a Selected Provision in the Federal Guidelines on Job Analysis and Training," *Personnel Administrator*, 26 (July 1981), p. 45.

[2] R. Wayne Mondy, Robert M. Noe, and Robert E. Edwards, "What the Staffing Function Entails," *Personnel*, 63 (April 1986), p. 55.

[3] John C. Crystal and Richard S. Deems, "Redesigning Jobs," *Training and Development Journal*, 37 (February 1983), p. 45.

CHAPTER 4   Job Analysis

Job analysis is performed on three occasions. First, it is done when the organization is founded and a job analysis program is initiated for the first time. Second, it is performed when new jobs are created. Third, it is used when jobs are changed significantly as a result of new technology, methods, procedures, or systems. The majority of job analyses are performed because of changes in the nature of jobs. Job analysis information is used to prepare both job descriptions and job specifications.

The **job description** is a document that provides information regarding the tasks, duties, and responsibilities of the job. The minimum acceptable qualifications that a person should possess to perform a particular job are contained in the **job specification**. We discuss both types of documents in greater detail later in the chapter.

■ REASONS FOR CONDUCTING JOB ANALYSIS

As Figure 4-1 shows, data derived from job analysis have an impact on virtually every aspect of human resource management. A major use of job analysis data is in the area of human resource planning. Merely knowing that the firm will need 1,000 new employees to produce goods or services to satisfy sales demand is insufficient. Each job requires different knowledge, skills, and ability levels. Obviously, effective human resource planning must take these job requirements into consideration.

Employee recruitment and selection would be haphazard if the recruiter didn't know the qualifications needed to perform the job. Lacking up-to-date job descriptions and specifications, employees would have to be recruited and selected for a job without clear guidelines, and this practice could have disastrous consequences. Such a practice is virtually unheard of when firms procure raw materials, supplies, or equipment. For example, even when ordering a copying machine, the purchasing department normally develops precise specifications. Surely, the same logic should apply when searching for a firm's most valuable asset!

Also, job specification information often proves beneficial in identifying human resource development needs. If the specification suggests that the job requires a particular knowledge, skill, or ability—and the person filling the position does not possess all the qualifications required—training and/or development is probably in order. It should be directed at assisting workers in performing duties specified in their present job descriptions or preparing them for promotion to higher level jobs. With regard to performance appraisal, employees should be evaluated in terms of how well they accomplish the duties specified in their job descriptions. A manager who evaluates an employee on factors not included in the job description is left wide open to allegations of discrimination.

In the area of compensation, the relative value of a particular job to the company must be known before a dollar value can be placed on it. The more significant its duties and responsibilities, the more the job is worth relatively. Jobs that require greater knowledge, skills, and abilities should be worth more to the firm. For example, the relative value of a job that calls for a master's degree normally would be higher than that of a job that requires only a high school diploma.

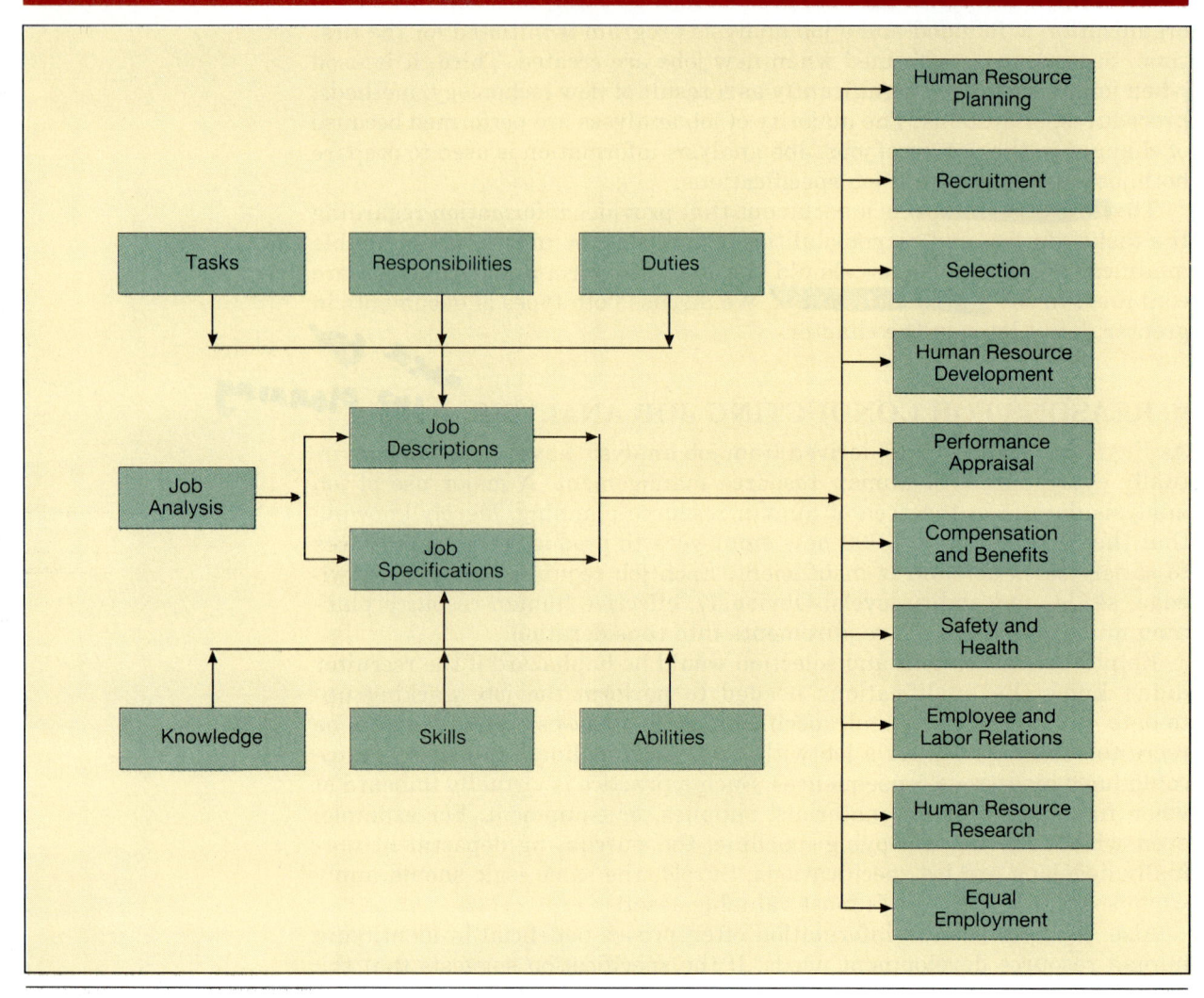

FIGURE 4-1 | Job Analysis: The Most Basic Human Resource Management Tool

Information derived from job analysis is also valuable in identifying safety and health considerations. For example, employers are required to state whether a job is hazardous. The job description/specification should respond to this requirement. In addition, in certain hazardous jobs, workers may need specific information about the hazards in order to perform the jobs safely.

Job analysis information is also important to employee and labor relations. When employees are considered for promotion, transfer, or demotion, the job description provides a standard for comparison of talent. Regardless of whether the firm is unionized, information obtained through job analysis can often lead to more objective human resource decisions.

When human resource research is undertaken, job analysis information provides the researcher with a starting point. For example, if the human resource manager is trying to identify factors that distinguish successful from less successful employees, the researcher needs to study only those employees who have similar job descriptions/specifications.

Finally, having properly accomplished job analysis is particularly important for supporting the legality of employment practices. Job analysis data are needed to defend, for example, decisions involving promotion, transfers, and demotions.

Thus far, we have described job analysis as it pertains to specific HRM functions. However, in practice these functions are interrelated. In fact, job analysis provides the basis for tying the functional areas together and the foundation for developing a sound human resource program.

■ TYPES OF JOB ANALYSIS INFORMATION

Considerable information is needed for successful accomplishment of job analysis. The job analyst identifies the job's actual duties and responsibilities and gathers the other types of data shown in Table 4-1. Note that work activities, worker-oriented activities, and the types of machines, tools, equipment, and work aids used in the job are important. This information is used later to help determine the job skills needed. In addition, the job analyst looks at job-related tangibles and intangibles, such as the knowledge needed, the materials processed, and the goods made or services performed.

Some job analysis systems identify job standards. Work measurement studies may be needed to determine, for example, how long it takes to perform a task. With regard to job content, the analyst studies the work schedule, financial and nonfinancial incentives, and physical working conditions. Since jobs are often performed in conjunction with others, organizational and social contexts are also noted. And, finally, specific education, training, and work experience pertinent to the job are identified.

■ JOB ANALYSIS METHODS

Job analysis has traditionally been conducted in a number of different ways because organizational needs and resources for conducting job analysis differ.[4] Selection of a specific method should be based on the ways in which the information is to be used (job evaluation, pay increases, development, and so on) and the approach that is most feasible for a particular organization. We describe the most common methods of job analysis in the following sections.

---

[4] Ronald A. Ash and Edward L. Levine, "A Framework for Evaluating Job Analysis Methods," *Personnel*, 57 (November–December 1980), pp. 53–54.

EXECUTIVE INSIGHTS

Walter W. Tornow, SPHR
Vice-President and Executive Consultant, Control Data Corporation

Walter Tornow's first jobs included being a "bag boy" at a supermarket, an inventory clerk at a sports shop, and an orderly at a cancer hospital. It even included being a Santa's helper at a department store—a job he regretted was very seasonal.

In his undergraduate training, Tornow's academic interests ranged from premed, philosophy, the humanities, and economics to psychology. In graduate school he continued his interest in philosophy but became more and more attracted to industrial and organizational psychology. It was in courses such as differential psychology and social psychology that he learned to appreciate individual differences and interpersonal dynamics, and their importance to the workplace. He received his Ph.D. in industrial-organizational psychology in 1970 from the University of Minnesota, with a minor in statistics and industrial relations.

While finishing his degree, Tornow directed employee survey programs for the Industrial Relations Center and also worked part time at Control Data Corporation. Upon graduation in 1970, he received a full-time offer from Control Data. Since then he has enjoyed a challenging career with the company, which has cast him in varied roles having many different responsibilities and areas of concentration.

He started as an associate personnel administrator in human resource research, then advanced through the ranks of staff specialist, personnel consultant, senior personnel consultant, manager of personnel research, and director of personnel research to vice-president and executive consultant, human resources research. His duties have included job analysis, selection and validation research, job classification and evaluation, performance appraisal, program evaluation, employee surveys and survey research, training needs analysis and training evaluation, productivity improvement, health habit assessment, organization culture change, and integrated tool development for key human resource functions.

His work also has included developing an inmate behavior description system for evaluating prisoners at a large midwestern prison, directing the development of a computer-based system for diagnosing and treating learning disabled children, evaluating the impact of alcoholism and treatment on employee productivity and health care utilization, developing a "quality of service" index for evaluating psychological staff services at a midwestern clinic, and directing the development of the employee case against unwanted company takeovers.

As a major proponent of the practical value of human resource research, Tornow defines human resource research in three ways—as an activity, a responsibility, and an organizational unit. As an activity, human resource research involves asking strategic questions concerning HR tools and programs, collecting and analyzing appropriate information, and then providing answers that are valuable, that is, answers that can be applied by practitioners toward more effective employee utilization and relations.

As a responsibility, human resource research is really conducted, however, informally, by all human resource and line managers. Thus it is done continuously as an integral and necessary part of sound human resource management.

As an organizational unit, human resource research can represent a basic and multipurpose resource to other functions in the organization by providing research, development, and evaluation support.

In his role as head of human resource research at Control Data, Tornow supported the training of many graduate students and their thesis research. He holds the rank of clinical associate professor from the University of Minnesota in recognition of the contribution he and his company have made to the training and experience of graduate students.

In his current role, Tornow heads human resource research and planning for the corporation. This function involves responsibility for employee surveys and consulting on performance management, selection, assessment, evaluation and culture change, as well as HR planning and audit.

Finally, Tornow has been active in professional affairs. He is a licensed consulting psychologist and is an accredited senior professional in human resources (SPHR). He is national chairperson of the Personnel Accreditation Institute's functional standards committee on personnel research. Also, he has been an active member of the American Psychological Association's Society for Industrial-Organizational Psychology. For PAI, Tornow has directed a major professional effort aimed at codifying body-of-knowledge standards for the human resource profession.

TABLE 4-1 | Types of Data Normally Gathered in Job Analysis

Summary of Types of Data Collected Through Job Analysis*

1. **Work activities**
    a. Work activities and processes.
    b. Activity records (in film form, for example).
    c. Procedures used.
    d. Personal responsibility.

2. **Worker-oriented activities**
    a. Human behaviors, such as physical actions and communicating on the job.
    b. Elemental motions for methods analysis.
    c. Personal job demands, such as energy expenditure.

3. **Machines, tools, equipment, and work aids used**

4. **Job-related tangibles and intangibles**
    a. Knowledge dealt with or applied (as in accounting).
    b. Materials processed.
    c. Products made or services performed.

5. **Work performance**[†]
    a. Error analysis.
    b. Work standards.
    c. Work measurements, such as time taken for a task.

6. **Job context**
    a. Work schedule.
    b. Financial and nonfinancial incentives.
    c. Physical working conditions.
    d. Organizational and social contexts.

7. **Personal requirements for the job.**
    a. Personal attributes such as personality, interests.
    b. Education and training required.
    c. Work experience.

---

*This information can be in the form of qualitative, verbal, narrative descriptions or quantitative measurements of each item, such as error rates per unit of time or noise level.

[†]All job analysis systems do not develop the work performance aspects.

Source: E. J. McCormick, "Job and Task Analysis," in Marvin D. Dunnette (ed.), *Handbook of Industrial and Organizational Psychology*. New York: John Wiley & Sons. Copyright © 1976. Reprinted by permission of John Wiley & Sons, Inc.

Questionnaires

Questionnaires are typically quick and economical to use. The job analyst may administer a structured questionnaire to employees, who identify the tasks they perform. However, in some cases employees may lack verbal skills, which makes this method less useful. Also, some employees may tend to exaggerate the significance of their tasks, suggesting more responsibility than actually exists.

A portion of a job analysis questionnaire used by First Interstate Bancorp is presented in Figure 4-2. Although the entire questionnaire consists of six sections, only Section III, Position Skills and Knowledge required, is shown.

Observation

When using the observation method, the job analyst usually watches the worker perform job tasks and records his or her observations. This method is used primarily to gather information on jobs emphasizing manual skills, such as those of a machine operator. It can also help the analyst identify interrelationships between physical and mental tasks. However, observation alone is usually an insufficient means of conducting job analysis, particularly when mental skills are dominant in a job. Observing a financial analyst at work for even a short period of time makes this point clearly.

Interview

An understanding of the job may also be gained through interviewing both the employee and the supervisor. Usually the analyst interviews the employee first, helping the worker describe the duties performed. Then the analyst normally contacts the supervisor for additional information, to check the accuracy of the information obtained from the worker, and to clarify certain points.

Employee Recording

In some instances, job analysis information is gathered by having the employees describe their daily work activities in a diary or log. Again, the problem of employees exaggerating job importance may have to be overcome. However, valuable understanding of highly specialized jobs, such as a financial analyst, may be obtained in this way.

Combination of Methods

Usually, an analyst does not use one job analysis method exclusively. A combination of methods is often more appropriate. For instance, in analyzing clerical and administrative jobs, the analyst might use questionnaires supported by interviews and limited observation. In studying production jobs, interviews supplemented by extensive work observation may provide the needed data. Basically, the analyst should employ the combination of techniques needed to conduct an effective job analysis.

Job Analysis Questionnaire

First Interstate Bancorp

Name _____
Position Title _____
Affiliate _____
Division/Group/Unit _____
City and State _____
Immediate Manager _____

General Instructions

This questionnaire is designed to provide information about your current position. It is *not* intended to measure your performance or productivity. It is a tool for analyzing and describing your job.

The questionnaire consists of six sections.
- **Section I** deals with the tasks and activities that comprise your job.
- **Section II** asks you to compare various job dimensions, which are groupings of similar tasks.
- **Section III** covers the skills and knowledge required to perform the tasks and activities of your position.
- **Section IV** identifies specific scope measures of your position.
- **Section V** focuses on individual factors that you bring to your job.
- **Section VI** includes additional factors which may have an impact on your position.

Because this questionnaire covers a broad range of affiliates and jobs, a number of the questions may not apply to your position. However, *if you perform tasks that are not covered by the questionnaire, space has been provided for you to write them in*. Whether you perform a large number of tasks or only a few is not important. What is essential is that you respond to *all* of the questions (for example, you may perform certain financial management tasks, although you are in a marketing function), and in a manner which best describes your position as it is typically performed by you.

In responding to the questions, please use the following definitions:
- **affiliate** refers to an individual bank (e.g., First Interstate Bank of Arizona) or a nonbank subsidiary (e.g., First Interstate Services Company).
- **customer** means any individual or group, inside or outside the company, with which you deal on a client or customer basis. For example, an affiliate bank can be a customer for the data processing unit, a small business can be a customer for the venture capital group, and an individual or a corporation can be a customer for a bank.
- **unit** is the organizational group in which you report or for which you have responsibility. This could be a functional group, a department, or a division of a company. For example, for a Cashier position, the unit might be the Cashier's Department; for a VP Operations, the unit might be the Operations Department; for a VP Administration, the unit might be the Administration Division; or for a Chief Executive Officer, the unit would be the entire bank.

The questionnaires will be returned directly to Towers, Perrin, Forster & Crosby (TPF&C), so all responses on this form will remain confidential. However, to ensure that the information about your position is accurate and consistent, you and your immediate manager will review the results of TPF&C's analysis of the questionnaire.

Please follow the specific instructions at the beginning of each section. Read each section in full before attempting to complete it so that you can respond as accurately as possible.

Thank you for your efforts in participating in this study.

FIGURE 4-2 | A Job Analysis Questionnaire

Source: Used with the permission of First Interstate Bancorp.

CHAPTER 4   Job Analysis   117

Section III: Position Skills and Knowledge

This section focuses on the type and depth of skills and knowledge that are 1) required to perform your job, and 2) that you may possess.

For each of the skills listed, you are asked to rate two items: the *level required* and the *level you possess*. In the appropriate boxes, write the number that best describes the skill or knowledge level, according to the following scale:

0 = Job neither requires nor do I possess skill/knowledge.
1 = Familiarity with skill/knowledge
2 = General working skill/knowledge
3 = Advanced skill/knowledge
4 = Unique expertise in skill/knowledge

In the first column of boxes, identify the *level of skill/knowledge required* to successfully perform your present job.

In the second column of boxes, identify the *level of skill/knowledge* that *you possess*, regardless of whether the job requires it.

The third column identifies sources of skills and knowledge. To indicate where you acquired each skill or knowledge that is required for the performance of your current position, identify up to, but no more than, two sources. Mark 1 in the column that represents the primary source. Mark 2 in the column that represents the secondary source.

A. Planning, Policies, Procedures

1. Organization design
2. Short-term planning (setting budgets, goals, etc.)
3. Strategic planning
4. Pricing fee structuring

B. Business Development/Marketing

5. Market research (identifying markets, competitive analyses and evaluation)
6. Market analysis (client needs, trends, strategies, etc.)
7. Marketing tools (advertising, promotional campaigns, etc.)
8. Products services (bank unit services, systems, etc.)
9. Marketing sales

C. Customer Relations

10. Customer counsel (objectives, economics, trends, etc.)
11. Customer counsel/problem solving
12. Account management
13. Profit analysis

For every statement:
- If a task is not part of your job, mark X in the first box
- If a task is a part of your job, rate:

Relative Time Spent   Relative Importance
1 = Very small amount   A Unimportant
2 = Small amount   B Minor importance
3 = Moderate amount   C Important
4 = Large amount   D Very important
5 = Very large amount   E Crucial

A. Planning

1. Develops business planning activities
2. Directs business planning activities
3. Develops annual unit goals and objectives
4. Approves annual unit goals and objectives
5. Develops longer-range strategic goals
6. Approves longer-range strategic goals
7. Develops specific strategy and action plans for unit
8. Approves specific strategy and action plans for unit
9. Reviews approves and monitors business plans
10. Prepares profit plans and updates
11. Approves profit plans and updates
12. Prepares operating budgets
13. Approves operating budgets
14. Approves requests for nonbudgeted items
15. Develops plans to improve administrative efficiency
16. Approves plans to improve administrative efficiency
17. Integrates the plans of other organizational units
18. Coordinates with other units to meet predetermined schedules
19. Proposes new or customized programs
20. Approves new or customized programs, services, products and research
21. Identifies impact of external conditions on unit
22. Coordinates units in the development of plans and programs
23. Monitors progress of specific projects
24. Recommends revisions to the unit organizational structure
25. Approves revisions to the unit organizational structure
26. Evaluates and recommends approval of affiliate facility projects
27. Recommends potential mergers, acquisitions or relocations
28. Approves potential mergers, acquisitions or relocations
29. Other: please list task(s) and check boxes

a. _____
b. _____
c. _____

From the above list of Planning tasks, please mark the numbers of the three most important tasks in rank order

1. _____
2. _____
3. _____

B. Policies and Procedures

30. Formulates and recommends policies or procedures for others to follow
31. Approves policies or procedures for others to follow
32. Reviews agreements or documentation for compliance with appropriate policies and standards
33. Directs the establishment of review or control procedures
34. Evaluates operating policies or procedures against desired objectives
35. Develops or maintains standards for service
36. Develops quality control programs and procedures
37. Approves quality control programs and procedures
38. Formulates or recommends pricing policies
39. Approves pricing policies
40. Develops methods and procedures to evaluate business strategies
41. Establishes planning guidelines and procedures
42. Directs creation, handling and disposition of official records
43. Directs safeguarding of records and documents
44. Approves procedures for automating existing manual systems
45. Other: please list task(s) and check boxes

a. _____
b. _____
c. _____

From the above list of Policies and Procedures tasks, please mark the numbers of the three most important tasks in rank order

1. _____
2. _____
3. _____

FIGURE 4-2 | *Continued*

■ CONDUCTING JOB ANALYSIS

The person who conducts job analysis is interested in gathering data on what is involved in performing a particular job. The people who participate in job analysis should include, at a minimum, the employee and the employee's immediate supervisor. Large organizations may have one or more job analysts but in small organizations line supervisors may be responsible for job analysis. Organizations that lack the technical expertise often use outside consultants to perform job analysis.

Before conducting job analysis, the analyst learns as much as possible about the job by reviewing organizational charts and talking with individuals acquainted with the jobs to be studied. Before beginning, the supervisor should introduce the analyst to the employees and explain the purpose of the job analysis. Although employee attitudes about the job are beyond the job analyst's control, the analyst must attempt to develop mutual trust and confidence with those whose jobs are being analyzed. Failure in this area will detract from an otherwise technically sound job analysis. Upon completion of job analysis, two basic human resource documents—job descriptions and job specifications—can be prepared.

■ JOB DESCRIPTION

Information obtained through job analysis is crucial to the development of job descriptions. Recall that we previously defined the job description as a document that states the tasks, duties, and responsibilities of the job. Job descriptions are accurate, concise statements of what employees are expected to do on the job. They should indicate what employees do, how they do it, and the conditions under which the duties are performed.[5]

Among the items frequently included in a job description are:

- Major duties performed.
- Percentage of time devoted to each duty.
- Performance standards to be achieved.
- Working conditions and possible hazards.
- Number of employees performing the job and who they report to.
- The machines and equipment used on the job.

The contents of the job description vary somewhat with the purpose for which it will be used. Let's consider the sections most commonly included in a job description.

Job Identification

The job identification section includes the job title, department, reporting relationship, and a job number or code. A good title will closely approxi-

---

[5] Hubert S. Feild and Robert D. Gatewood, "Matching Talent with the Task: To Find the Right People, First Define the Jobs You Want Them to Do," *Personnel Administrator*, 32 (April 1987), p. 113.

mate the nature of the work content and will distinguish that job from others. Unfortunately, job titles are often misleading.[6] An "executive secretary" in one organization may be little more than a highly paid clerk, whereas a person with the same title in another firm may practically run the company. For instance, one former student's first job after graduation was with a major tire and rubber company as an "assistant district service manager." Because the primary duties of the job were to unload tires from trucks, check the tread wear, and stack the tires in boxcars, a more appropriate title would probably have been "tire checker and stacker."

One information source that assists in standardizing job titles is the *Dictionary of Occupational Titles* (DOT).[7] The DOT includes standardized and comprehensive descriptions of job duties and related information for over 200,000 occupations. Such standardization permits employers in different industries and parts of the country to match job requirements with worker skills better.

An example of a DOT definition—for a "branch manager," occupational code 183.137-010—is provided in Figure 4-3. The first digit of the code identifies one of the following major occupations:

0/1 Professional, technical, and managerial
2 Clerical and sales
3 Service
4 Farming, fishing, forestry, and related
5 Processing
6 Machine trade
7 Bench work
8 Structural work
9 Miscellaneous

For the branch manager, the major classification would be "managerial" occupations.

The next two digits represent breakdowns of the general occupation category.

Digits four through six describe the job's relationship to data, people, and things. For the "branch manager," a code "1" for data would be "coordinating," a code "3" for people would be "supervising," and a code "7" for things would be "handling."

The final three digits indicate the alphabetical order of titles within the six-digit code group. These codes assist in distinguishing a specific occupation from other similar ones. The alphabetical order for "branch manager" is indicated by the digits 010.

---

[6] James N. Baron and William T. Bilby, "The Proliferation of Job Titles in Organizations," *Administrative Science Quarterly*, 31 (December 1986), p. 561.

[7] U.S. Department of Labor, *Dictionary of Occupational Titles*, 4th ed. (Washington, D.C.: U.S. Government Printing Office, 1977).

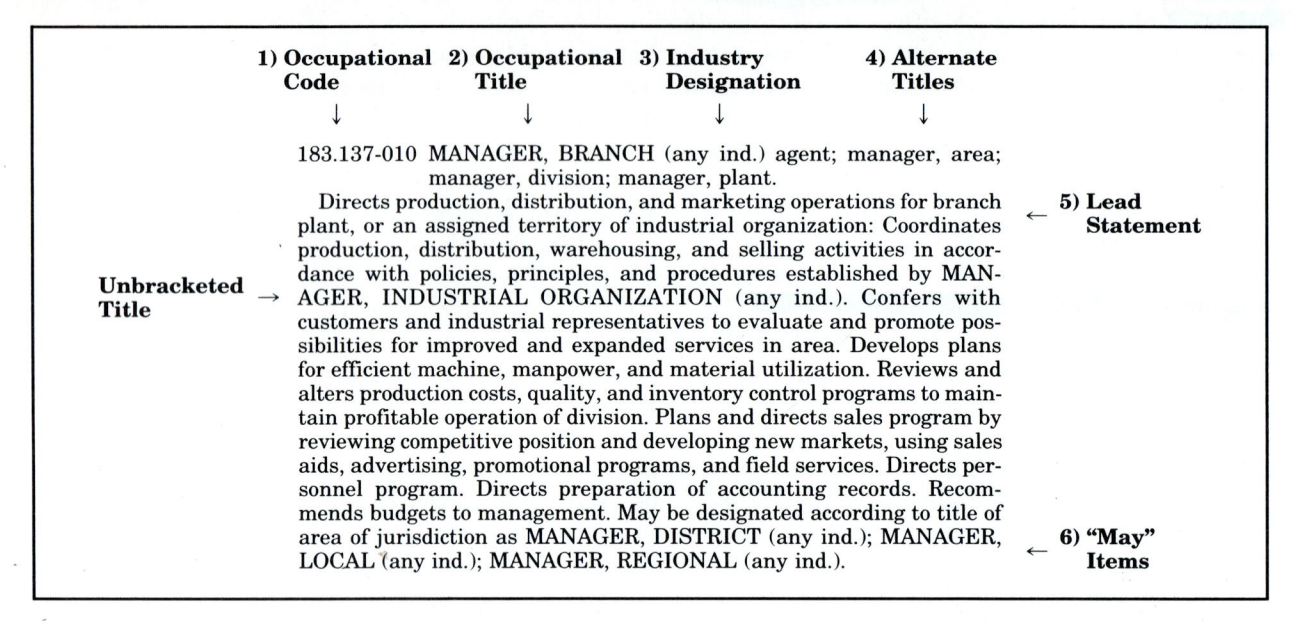

```
┌─────────────────────────────────────────────────────────────────────────────┐
│         1) Occupational  2) Occupational  3) Industry      4) Alternate     │
│            Code             Title            Designation      Titles        │
│              ↓                ↓                 ↓               ↓           │
│         183.137-010 MANAGER, BRANCH (any ind.) agent; manager, area;        │
│                     manager, division; manager, plant.                      │
│           Directs production, distribution, and marketing operations for branch │
│           plant, or an assigned territory of industrial organization: Coordi- │    5) Lead
│           nates production, distribution, warehousing, and selling activities ← Statement
│           in accordance with policies, principles, and procedures established │
│ Unbracketed → by MANAGER, INDUSTRIAL ORGANIZATION (any ind.). Confers with   │
│ Title        customers and industrial representatives to evaluate and promote │
│           possibilities for improved and expanded services in area. Develops │
│           plans for efficient machine, manpower, and material utilization.   │
│           Reviews and alters production costs, quality, and inventory control │
│           programs to maintain profitable operation of division. Plans and   │
│           directs sales program by reviewing competitive position and devel- │
│           oping new markets, using sales aids, advertising, promotional      │
│           programs, and field services. Directs personnel program. Directs   │
│           preparation of accounting records. Recommends budgets to manage-   │
│           ment. May be designated according to title of area of jurisdiction │    6) "May"
│           as MANAGER, DISTRICT (any ind.); MANAGER, LOCAL (any ind.);      ← Items
│           MANAGER, REGIONAL (any ind.).                                      │
└─────────────────────────────────────────────────────────────────────────────┘
```

FIGURE 4-3 | The Parts of a Dictionary of Occupational Titles Definition

Source: U.S. Department of Labor, *Dictionary of Occupational Titles*.

Date of the Job Analysis

The job analysis date is placed on the job description to aid in identifying job changes that would make the description obsolete. Some firms have found it useful to place an expiration date on the document. This practice ensures periodic review of job content and minimizes the number of obsolete job descriptions.

Job Summary

The job summary provides a concise overview of the job. It is generally a short paragraph that states job content.

Duties Performed

The body of the job description delineates the major duties to be performed. Usually one sentence beginning with an action verb such as receives, performs, establishes, or assembles, adequately explains each duty.

■ JOB SPECIFICATION

Recall that we defined job specification as a document containing the minimum acceptable qualifications that a person should possess to perform a

CHAPTER 4   Job Analysis

HRM In Action

I can't determine what kind of computer programmer you need, Alex," said Bob Sanders, the human resource director. "Every applicant I sent down was proficient in FORTRAN, just like the job description stated."

"Get real, Bob," replied Alex. "We haven't required FORTRAN in ten years. The person I need has to be up-to-date on the latest software. None of those people you sent me were qualified."

How would you respond?

---

particular job. Items typically included in the job specification are educational requirements, experience, personality traits, and physical abilities. In practice, job specifications are often included as a major section of job descriptions. Figure 4-4 is an actual job description provided by General Mills, Inc. As you can see, the qualifications needed for the job of "Secretary II" include typing at least sixty words per minute and demonstrated proficiency in English grammar, punctuation, spelling, and proper word usage. This type of information is extremely valuable in the recruiting and selection process.

After jobs have been analyzed and the descriptions written, the results should be reviewed with the supervisor and the worker to ensure that they are accurate, clear, and understandable. The courtesy of reviewing results with employees also helps to gain their acceptance. Because the job description and job specification are often combined into one form, we use the term *job description* in this book to include both documents.

■ OTHER JOB ANALYSIS METHODS

Over the years, attempts have been made to provide more systematic methods of conducting job analysis. We describe several of these approaches next.

Department of Labor Job Analysis Schedule

The U.S. Department of Labor established a method of systematically studying jobs and occupations called the **job analysis schedule (JAS).** Its basic content is shown in Figure 4-5. When the JAS method is used, information is gathered by a trained analyst.

A major component of the JAS is the work performed ratings. Here, what workers do in performing a job with regard to data, people, and things

POSITION TITLE			POSITION NUMBER
SECRETARY II			217
			APPROVAL
			RHS

DIVISION OR STAFF DEPARTMENT	LOCATION	REPORTS TO		EFFECTIVE DATE
All	All			May 1989
DEPARTMENT OR ACTIVITY	**SECTION**	**POINTS**	**GRADE**	**REVISES**
		165	6	

JOB SUMMARY
Performs clerical and administrative duties for a manager and often one or more staff members of a major function.

NATURE OF WORK
Performs a wide variety of office duties including most of the following:
a. Typing correspondence, reports, manuscripts, graphs, charts, etc., from notes, dictating machine, and/or hand written drafts proficiently and with minimum direction and instructions.
b. Receiving telephone calls and visitors skillfully and handling incoming mail efficiently.
c. Originating routine correspondence and handling inquiries, and routing non-routine inquiries and correspondence to proper persons.
d. Establishing and maintaining department files and records.
e. Assuming responsibility for arranging appointments and meetings, screening calls, and handling personal and confidential matters for superior.
f. Assembling, organizing, processing, and evaluating data and reports; operating office machines needed for accomplishing this.
g. Performing administrative duties and special projects as directed, such as collecting and compiling general reference materials and information pertaining to company, division, or department practices and procedures.

Works independently, receiving a minimum of supervision and guidance on established office procedures. Relieves supervisor of minor administrative details. May have some light work direction over others in department. Structure is light and most work is not checked.

QUALIFICATIONS
High school education or its equivalent plus three years of clerical experience, including one year with the Company, and a typing skill of at least 60 WPM. Demonstrated proficiency in English grammar, punctuation, spelling, and proper word usage. Must be able to anticipate problems and use sound judgment and tact in handling confidential matters, screening telephone calls and visitors, and scheduling superior's time. Must have the ability to acquire a thorough knowledge of the organization's policies, procedures, and personnel in order to relieve superior of specified administrative duties. A basic figure aptitude and/or a working knowledge of certain business machines may be necessary depending on the specific job.

FIGURE 4-4 | A Job Description

Source: Used with the permission of General Mills, Inc.

CHAPTER 4 Job Analysis

JOB ANALYSIS SCHEDULE

1. Estab. Job Title   DOUGH MIXER
2. Ind. Assign.   (bake. prod.)
3. SIC Code(s) and Title(s)   2051 Bread and other bakery products

Code 520.782   Oper. Control p. 435   WTA Group   DOT Title   Ind. Desig.

4. JOB SUMMARY:
Operates mixing machine to mix ingredients for straight and sponge (yeast) doughs according to established formulas, directs other workers in fermentation of dough, and cuts dough into pieces with hand cutter.

5. WORK PERFORMED RATINGS:

	D	P	(T)
Worker Functions	Data	People	Things
	5	6	2

Work Field   148 - Cooking, Food Preparing

M.P.S.M.S.   384 - Bakery Products

6. WORKER TRAITS RATINGS:

GED   1 (2) 3 4 5 6
SVP   1 2 3 (4) 5 6 7 8 9
Aptitudes   G 3 V 3 N 3 S 3 P 3 Q 4 K 3 F 3 M 3 E 4 C 4
Temperaments   D F I J (M) P R S (T) V
Interests   (1a) 1b 2a 2b 3a 3b 4a (4b) 5a (5b)
Phys. Demands S L M (H) V 2 (3) (4) 5 (6)
Environ. Cond. (I) O B 2 3 4 (5) 6 7

7. General Education

   a. Elementary   6   High School _____ Courses _____
   b. College   None   Courses _____

8. Vocational Preparation

   a. College   None   Courses _____

   b. Vocational Education   None   Courses _____

   c. Apprenticeship   None _____

FIGURE 4-5 | A Department of Labor Job Analysis Schedule (Figure continued on next two pages)

Source: U.S. Department of Labor, Manpower Administration, *Handbook for Analyzing Jobs*. Washington, D.C.: U.S. Government Printing Office, 1972, pp. 42–45.

> d. Inplant Training _None_
>
> e. On-the-Job Training _Six Months_
>
> f. Performance on Other Jobs _DOUGH-MIXER HELPER - One Year_
>
> **9.** Experience _One Year as DOUGH-MIXER HELPER_
>
> **10.** Orientation _Four Hours_
>
> **11.** Licenses, etc. _Food Handlers Certificate Issued by the Health Department_
>
> **12.** Relation to Other Jobs and Workers
>
> Promotion: From _DOUGH-MIXER HELPER_ To _BAKER_
>
> Transfers: From _None_ To _None_
>
> Supervision Received _By BAKER_
>
> Supervision Given _DOUGH-MIXER HELPER_
>
> **13.** Machines, Tools, Equipment, and Work Aids - Dough-mixing machine; balance scales; hand scoops; measuring vessels; portable dough troughs.
>
> **14.** Materials and Products
>
> Bread dough
>
> **15.** Description of Tasks:
>
> 1. Dumps ingredients into mixing machine: Examines production schedule to determine type of bread to be produced, such as rye, whole wheat, or white. Refers to formula card for quantities and types of ingredients required, such as flour, water, milk, vitamin solutions, and shortening. Weighs out, measures, and dumps ingredients into mixing machine. (20%)

FIGURE 4-5 | *Continued*

is evaluated. Subdivisions of these three categories are shown in Table 4-2. Each is viewed as a hierarchy of functions, with those higher in the category being more difficult. The codes in the worker functions section represent the highest level of involvement in each of the three categories.

The JAS component worker traits ratings relates primarily to job requirement data. Topics such as general education (GED), specific vocational preparation (SVP), aptitudes, temperaments, interests, physical demands, and environmental conditions are included. The description of tasks section provides a specific description of the work performed. Both routine tasks and occasionally performed tasks are included.

Functional Job Analysis

Functional job analysis (FJA) is a comprehensive job analysis approach that concentrates on the interactions among the work, the worker, and the

> 2. Operates mixing machine: Turns valves and other hand controls to set mixing time according to type of dough being mixed. Presses button to start agitator blades in machine. Observes gauges and dials on equipment continuously to verify temperature of dough and mixing time. Feels dough for desired consistency. Adds water or flour to mix measuring vessels and adjusts mixing time and controls to obtain desired elasticity in mix. (55%)
>
> 3. Directs other workers in fermentation of dough: Prepares fermentation schedule according to type of dough being raised. Sprays portable dough *Trough* with lubricant to prevent adherence of mixed dough to trough. Directs DOUGH-MIXER HELPER in positioning trough beneath door of mixer to catch dough when mixing cycle is complete. Pushes or directs other workers to push troughs of dough into fermentation room. (10%)
>
> 4. Cuts dough: Dumps fermentated dough onto worktable. Manually kneads dough to eliminate gases formed by yeast. Cuts dough into pieces with hand cutter. Places cut dough on proofing rack and covers with cloth. (10%)
>
> 5. Performs miscellaneous duties: Records on work sheet number of batches mixed during work shift. Informs BAKE SHOP FOREMAN when repairs or major adjustments are required for machines and equipment. (5%)
>
> **16.** Definition of Terms
> *Trough* - A long, narrow, opened vessel used for kneading or washing ingredients.
>
> **17.** General Comments
> None
>
> **18.** Analyst   Jane Smith   Date 3/21/87   Editor   John Rilley   Date 3/30/87
>
> Reviewed By   Alexandra Purcey   Title, Org.   Foreman, Bake Shop

FIGURE 4-5 | *Continued*

organization. This approach is a modification of the job analysis schedule. It is a worker-oriented method of describing jobs that identify what a person actually does rather than his or her responsibilities.[8] The fundamental elements of FJA are:

1. A major distinction is made between what gets done and what workers do to get things done. It is more important in job analysis to know the latter. For instance, a word processing operator doesn't just keep the system running; a number of tasks must be performed in accomplishing the job.
2. Each job is concerned with data, people, and things.
3. Workers function in unique ways as they relate to data, people and things.
4. Each job requires the worker to relate to data, people, and things in some way.

---

[8] Felix M. Lopez, Gerald A. Kesselman, and Felix E. Lopez, "An Empirical Test of a Trait-Oriented Job Analysis Technique," *Personnel Psychology*, 35 (August 1981), p. 480.

TABLE 4-2 | Worker Function Scale for Job Analysis Schedule

Data (4th digit)	People (5th digit)	Things (6th digit)
0 Synthesizing	0 Monitoring	0 Setting-up
1 Coordinating	1 Negotiating	1 Precision working
2 Analyzing	2 Instructing	2 Operating–controlling
3 Compiling	3 Supervising	3 Driving–operating
4 Computing	4 Diverting	4 Manipulating
5 Copying	5 Persuading	5 Tending
6 Comparing	6 Speaking–signaling	6 Feeding–offbearing
7 No significant relationship	7 Serving	7 Handling
8	8 No significant relationship	8 No significant relationship

5. Only a few definite and identifiable functions are involved with data, people, and things (Refer again to see Table 4-2).
6. These functions proceed from the simple to the complex. The least complex form of data would be comparing, and the most complex would be synthesizing. In addition, the assumption is that, if an upper level function is required, all the lower level functions are also required.
7. The three hierarchies for data, people, and things provide two measures for a job. First, there is a measure of relative complexity in relation to data, people, and things—in essence, the amount of interrelationship among the three functions. Second, there is a measure of proportional involvement for each function. For instance, 50 percent of a person's time may be spent in analyzing, 30 percent in supervising, and 20 percent in operating.[9]

One study determined that FJA was a useful technique for defining the work of heavy-equipment operators. Therefore, the knowledge, skills, and abilities required for the job could be easily communicated to the courts and the public.[10]

---

[9] Ernest J. McCormick, "Job Information: Its Development and Application," in Dale Yoder and Herbert S. Heneman (eds.), *Staffing Policies and Strategies* (Washington, D.C.: The Bureau of National Affairs, 1979), pp. 4–58.

[10] Howard C. Olson, Sidney A. Fine, David C. Myers, and Margarette C. Jennings, "The Use of Functional Job Analysis in Establishing Performance Standards for Heavy Equipment Operators," *Personnel Psychology*, 34 (Summer 1981), p. 351.

Position Analysis Questionnaire

The **position analysis questionnaire (PAQ)** is a structured job analysis questionnaire that uses a checklist approach to identify job elements. Some 194 job descriptors relate to job-oriented or worker-oriented elements. Advocates of the PAQ believe that its ability to identify job elements, behaviors required of job incumbents, and other job characteristics makes procedure applicable to analysis of virtually any type of job. Each job descriptor is evaluated on a specified scale such as extent of use, amount of time, importance of job, possibility of occurrence, and applicability.

With the aid of a computer program, each job being studied is scored relative to the thirty-two job dimensions. The score derived represents a profile of the job, which can be compared with standard profiles to group the job into known job families, that is, jobs of a similar nature. In essence, the PAQ identifies significant job behaviors and classifies jobs. Using the PAQ, job descriptions can be based on the relative importance and emphasis placed on various job elements.

The PAQ is completed by an employee or employees familiar with the job being studied—typically an experienced job incumbent or the immediate supervisor. The profiles and job descriptions are then prepared by a job analyst.[11]

Management Position Description Questionnaire

The **management position description questionnaire (MPDQ)** is a method of job analysis designed for management positions and uses a checklist to analyze jobs. It contains 208 items that are related to the concerns and responsibilities of managers.[12] These 208 items have been reduced to 13 primary job factors:

1. Product, market, and financial planning
2. Coordination of other organizational units and workers
3. Internal business control
4. Products and service responsibility
5. Public and customer relations
6. Advanced consulting
7. Autonomy of action
8. Approval of financial commitment
9. Staff service
10. Supervision
11. Complexity and stress
12. Advanced financial responsibility
13. Broad human resources responsibility

---

[11] Donald L. Caruth, Robert M. Noe III, and R. Wayne Mondy, *Staffing the Contemporary Organization*. (New York: Quorum Books, 1988), p. 100.
[12] W. W. Tornow and P. R. Pinto, "The Development of Management Job Taxonomy: A System for Describing, Classifying and Evaluating Executive Positions," *Journal of Applied Psychology*, 11 (1976), pp. 410–418.

The MPDQ has been used to determine the training needs of individuals who are slated to move into managerial positions. It has also been used to evaluate and set compensation rates for managerial jobs and to assign these jobs to job families.

Guidelines Oriented Job Analysis

The **guidelines oriented job analysis (GOJA)** responds to the growing amount of legislation affecting staffing and involves a step-by-step procedure for describing the work of a particular job classification.[13] It is also used for developing selection tools, such as application forms and for documenting compliance with various legal requirements.

There are three versions of GOJA. The original method, *full* GOJA, is very detailed and requires approximately twenty hours to analyze a job completely. Its use is most appropriate when there is a high probability of discrimination suits. Next, *brief* GOJA was developed after the *Uniform Guidelines* were published in order to reduce the amount of time required to complete a job analysis. To reduce the amount of time required still further, a third version, *simplified* GOJA, was developed. Only about two to four hours are required to complete this job analysis form. The GOJA obtains the following types of information: (1) machines, tools and equipment; (2) supervision; (3) contacts; (4) duties; (5) knowledge, skills, and abilities; (6) physical and other requirements; and (7) differentiating requirements.

Occupational Measurement System[14]

The **occupational measurement system (OMS)** enables organizations to collect, store, and analyze information pertinent to human resources by means of an electronic database. The computer provides fast turnaround and more accurate job analysis, job descriptions, and evaluations. The computer also makes feasible the use of multiple regression statistical techniques that increase objectivity and hence responsiveness to potential discrimination claims.

The OMS is designed to work with task-based information. Task-based job evaluation uses structured job analysis questionnaires covering work performed within the organization as the basic input document. The questionnaires are developed from a number of different sources, including a database of industry job tasks, the organization's job descriptions, and job experts within the firm's workforce. The system includes a booklet with instructions and general information. The questionnaire contains items specifically tailored to the category of positions covered. Responses are given in data entry or optical scanning format. Sample items from a questionnaire are shown in Figure 4-6.

---

[13] Stephen E. Bemis, Ann Holt Belenky, and Dee Ann Soder, *Job Analysis: An Effective Management Tool* (Washington, D.C.: The Bureau of National Affairs, 1983), p. 42.

[14] Information for this section was furnished by First Interstate Bancorp.

CHAPTER 4   Job Analysis

For Every Statement:

- If a task is part of your job, mark X in the first box.

- If you PERFORM and/or SUPERVISE a task, rate it using the adjacent RELATIVE TIME SPENT scale:

1 = An extremely small amount of time.
2 = Between levels 1 and 3.
3 = A small amount of time.
4 = Between levels 3 and 5.
5 = A moderate amount of time.
6 = Between levels 5 and 7.
7 = A large amount of time.
8 = Between levels 7 and 9.
9 = An extremely large amount of time.

Relative time spent SUPERVISING
Relative time spent PERFORMING
Part of job

Relative time spent SUPERVISING
Relative time spent PERFORMING
Part of job

CREDIT ADMINISTRATION

1. Works with officers on national accounts to solve credit problems.

2. Responds to inquiries from branches regarding consumer regulations.

3. Establishes goals for delinquency ratios, charge-offs and recoveries.

4. Maintains annual forecasts for nonaccrual loans and other nonperforming assets.

5. Develops loan policy and procedures.

6. Recommends loan policy and procedures.

7. Maintains annual forecasts of commercial, consumer and real estate loan losses.

8. Prepares reports on branch compliance with consumer regulations.

9. Recommends interest rates for loans.

10. Reviews periodicals for changes to consumer protection laws.

11. Reviews analysis reports and financial statement spreads.

12. Performs commercial credit investigations.

13. Prepares credit memos.

14. Prepares loan write-ups.

15. Assembles and interprets debtor credit information.

16. Surveys collateral status for credit extension on potential and current customers.

17. Contacts credit agencies to secure credit reports and special services.

FIGURE 4-6 | A Job Analysis Questionnaire

Source: Used with the permission of First Interstate Bancorp.

The OMS is used to analyze the information obtained in the job analysis questionnaire. The OMS is an integrated computer software system specifically designed to process, analyze, and display task-based information. The following are a few of the reports generated by OMS:

1. A functional and a detailed task-level job description. The job descriptions contain the functions performed by each employee, job, or job classification, the specific tasks covered by those functions, and the amount of time spent on the functions and tasks.
2. Skill and knowledge levels required to perform a function or job, those possessed by the incumbents, and the differences between the two, if any, along with identified training needs.
3. Costs of production, both in terms of performance and supervision.

■ JOB ANALYSIS AND THE LAW

Effective job analysis is essential to sound human resource management as an organization recruits, selects, and promotes employees. In particular, HRM has focused on job analysis because selection methods need to be clearly job related.[15] Legislation requiring thorough job analysis includes:

Fair Labor Standards Act: Employees are categorized as exempt or nonexempt, and job analysis is basic to this determination. Nonexempt workers must be paid time and a half when they work more than 40 hours per week. Overtime pay is not required for exempt employees.

Equal Pay Act: In the past, and to some extent today, men were often paid higher salaries than women, even though they performed essentially the same job. If jobs are not substantially different, similar pay should be provided. When pay differences exist, job descriptions can be used to show whether jobs are substantially equal in terms of skill, effort, responsibility, or working conditions.

Civil Rights Act: As with the Equal Pay Act, job descriptions may provide the basis for adequate defenses against unfair discrimination charges in initial selection, promotion, and all other areas of human resource administration. When job analysis is not performed, defending certain qualifications established for the job is usually difficult. For instance, stating that a high school diploma is required without having determined its necessity through job analysis leaves the firm open to possible discrimination charges.

Occupational Safety and Health Act: Job descriptions are required to specify "elements of the job that endanger health, or are considered unsatisfactory or distasteful by the majority of the population." Showing the job description to the employee in advance is a good defense.

---

[15] Donald W. Myers, "The Impact of a Selected Provision in the Federal Guidelines on Job Analysis and Training," *Personnel Administrator*, 26 (July 1981), pp. 41–45.

■ JOB DESIGN

Increasingly, the labor force is more highly educated. Workers expect more from the job than having it meet only their financial needs. They also want jobs that allow them to satisfy other needs, such as achievement, growth, recognition, and self-fulfillment. In other words, the challenge is to increase worker productivity by finding ways to "unlock the potential that exists in the overwhelming majority of our workforce."[16]

J. Richard Hackman and Greg R. Oldham contend that the quality of work life can be improved, while at the same time increasing or maximizing worker productivity.[17] They challenge several long-held assumptions, such as:

- The basic nature of work is fixed and cannot be changed.
- Technology and work processes determine job design.
- All that management can do is properly select and train workers.

Accordingly, they believe, job design should focus on enhancing employee productivity and not be constrained by long-held assumptions.

Job design is the process of determining the specific tasks to be performed, the methods used in performing these tasks, and how the job relates to other work in the organization. In their book, *Work Redesign*, Hackman and Oldham assert that if managers want to achieve a high level of motivation, they must give reliable feedback on performance to employees. Workers must also sense that they are accountable for specific results and feel that the job has meaning beyond pay.[18] Many workers get more satisfaction from completing an entire task or an identifiable part of a process than from producing indistinguishable and seemingly unrelated pieces of work. In spite of its bright promise, however, job design alternatives face some realistic constraints.

Technology has an impact on job design. The type of equipment and tools, as well as particular work layout and methods, used in producing goods or services tend to act as constraints. Technology may make job redesign difficult and expensive, but not impossible.

Economic factors also affect job design. If management believes that redesigning jobs can improve output and the level of worker satisfaction, it must also consider the adequacy of the firm's other resources. Although job redesign may be desirable, its cost may be prohibitive. A manager must continually balance the benefits of job design with its costs.

Job design is also affected by laws and government regulations. Management may want to design a job in a way that might increase worker performance, but in doing so would violate labor laws or environmental or safety standards.

If a company has a union, job design can be affected by the philosophy, policies, and strategies of the union. Typically, the contract between the

---

[16] Robert H. Guest, "Review of Work Redesign," *Harvard Business Review*, 24 (January–February 1981), pp. 46–47, 52.

[17] *Ibid.*, p. 46.

[18] J. Richard Hackman and Greg R. Oldham, *Work Redesign*. (Reading, Mass.: Addison-Wesley, 1980).

company and the union specifies and defines the types of jobs and the duties and responsibilities of workers. Unions generally have opposed work redesign experiments. They have perceived them to be attempts by management to squeeze more work out of the worker without increasing wages. Also, unions may view job redesign as a threat to their power and position with the workers. However, in recent years unions have become more flexible in order to maintain job security for their members.

Other important considerations for job design include the abilities, attitudes, and motivation of the firm's employees. Obviously, the design of particular jobs depends on the abilities or training potential of employees. Designing a job that would be far more complex than the ability level of employees available to do it wouldn't make sense unless they are willing to be trained or new employees with the necessary capabilities can be hired.

Finally, management philosophy and organizational goals and strategies may determine the degree to which job redesign is possible. Top management must be committed to the concept of job redesign. Job redesign may give employees greater authority in determining how their jobs are performed and how they are managed. Job enrichment and job enlargement are two ways of enhancing jobs through job design and can result in greater employee productivity.

Job Enrichment

During the past twenty years or so, a great deal of interest has been shown in job enrichment. Strongly advocated by Frederick Herzberg, **job enrichment** refers to basic changes in a job's content and level of responsibility, providing a greater challenge to the worker. In this approach to job design, the employee is given a chance to experience greater achievement, recognition, responsibility, and personal growth.

Many job enrichment programs have improved job performance and employee satisfaction. AT&T, Polaroid, Texas Instruments, Monsanto, Weyerhaeuser, Corning Glass, and many other firms have achieved excellent results with job enrichment programs. In most of these cases, productivity and job satisfaction increased, and employee turnover and absenteeism decreased.[19]

According to Herzberg, job enrichment efforts should be based on the following principles.

1. *Increasing job demands*: Changing the job to increase the levels of difficulty and responsibility of the job.
2. *Increasing a worker's accountability*: Allowing more worker control and authority over the work, while retaining the manager's ultimate accountability.
3. *Providing work scheduling freedom*: Within limits, allowing workers to schedule their own work.

---

[19] See "Case Studies in the Humanization of Work," in *Work in America: Report of Special Task Force to the Secretary of Health, Education, and Welfare* (Cambridge, Mass.: MIT Press, 1973), Appendix, pp. 188–200.

4. *Providing feedback*: Making timely periodic reports on performance directly to the worker.
5. *Providing new learning experiences*: Creating opportunities for new personal experiences and growth.[20]

Job Enlargement

There is a basic distinction between job enrichment and job enlargement. **Job enlargement** changes the scope of a job to provide a greater variety of tasks for the worker to perform; it expands duties horizontally. For example, instead of knowing how to operate only one machine, a worker is taught to operate two or even three with the same level of responsibility. Job enrichment, on the other hand, involves increased responsibility; a vertical extension of duties.

SUMMARY

A job consists of a group of tasks that must be performed for an organization to achieve its goals. The systematic process of determining the duties and skills required for performing the organization's jobs is referred to as job analysis. Job analysis is the most basic human resource management tool. Without a properly conducted job analysis, satisfactorily performing the other human resource functions would be difficult, if not impossible.

Job analysis information is used to prepare both job descriptions and job specifications. A job description specifies the tasks, duties, and responsibilities associated with a job. A job specification states the knowledge, skills, and abilities a person must possess in order to perform the job.

Job analysis may be conducted in several different ways. When using questionnaires, the job analyst has employees identify the tasks they perform in accomplishing the job. The job analyst actually watches the employee work and records observations when using the observation method. The job analyst may also gain an understanding of the job by interviewing both the employee and the supervisor. In some instances, job analysis information is gathered by having employees describe their daily work activities in a diary or log. Finally, the analyst may use a combination of any of these methods. Basically, the person who conducts job analysis is interested in gathering data about what is involved in performing a particular job.

The sections most commonly used in a job description are (1) job identification, (2) date of the job analysis, (3) job summary, and (4) duties performed. Some of the items often included in the job specification section are requirements for education, experience, personality traits, and physical abilities.

---

[20] Frederick Herzberg, "One More Time: How Do You Motivate Employees?" *Harvard Business Review*, 22 (Winter 1979), p. 59.

In recent years, attempts have been made to provide more systematic methods for conducting job analysis. These newer approaches include: (1) U.S. Department of Labor Job Analysis Schedule (JAS); (2) Functional Job Analysis (FJA); (3) Position Analysis Questionnaire (PAQ); (4) Management Position Description Questionnaire (MPDQ); (5) Guidelines Oriented Job Analysis (GOJA); and (6) Occupational Measurement System (OMS). Job analysis has become a focus of HRM because selection methods need to be job related.

Job design is the process of determining the specific tasks to be performed, the methods used in performing these tasks, and how the job relates to other work in the organization. Job enrichment refers to basic changes in the content and level of responsibility of a job to provide a greater challenge to the worker. Job enlargement involves changes in the scope of a job to provide greater variety to the worker.

Questions for Review

1. What is the distinction between a job and a position? Define job analysis.
2. Discuss what is meant by the statement, "Job analysis is the most basic human resource management tool."
3. Describe the traditional methods used to conduct job analysis.
4. List and briefly describe the types of data that are typically gathered when conducting job analysis.
5. What are the basic components of a job description? Briefly describe each.
6. What are the items typically included in a job specification?
7. Briefly describe each of the following: (a) U.S. Department of Labor job analysis schedule (JAS); (b) functional job analysis (FJA); (c) position analysis questionnaire (PAQ); and (d) management position description questionnaire (MPDQ).
8. How can effective job analysis be used to satisfy each of the following statutes: (a) Fair Labor Standards Act; (b) Equal Pay Act; (c) Civil Rights Act; and (d) Occupational Safety and Health Act?
9. Distinguish among job design, job enrichment, and job enlargement.

Terms for Review

Job
Position
Job analysis
Job description
Job specification
Job analysis schedule (JAS)
Functional job analysis (FJA)
Position analysis questionnaire (PAQ)

Management position description questionnaire (MPDQ)
Guidelines oriented job analysis (GOJA)
Occupational measurement system (OMS)
Job design
Job enrichment
Job enlargement

INCIDENT 1 — Who Needs Job Descriptions?

John Case, accounting supervisor, was clearly annoyed as he approached his boss, Gerald Jones. He began, "Gerald, this note you sent me says I have to update descriptions for all ten of the jobs in my department within the next two weeks."

"Well," asked Gerald, "what's the problem with that?"

John explained, "This is a waste of time, especially since I have other deadlines. It will take at least thirty hours. We still have two weeks of work left on the internal audit reviews. You want me to push that back and work on *job descriptions*? No way.

"We have not looked at these job descriptions in years. They will need a great deal of revision. And as soon as they get into the hands of the employees, I will get all kinds of flack."

"Why would you get flack for getting the job descriptions in order?" asked Gerald. John answered, "This whole thing is a bag of worms. Just calling attention to the existence of job descriptions will give some people the idea they don't have to do things that aren't in the description. And if we write what the people in my division really do, some jobs will have to be upgraded and others downgraded, I'll bet. I just can't afford the morale problem and the confusion right now."

Gerald replied, "What do you suggest, John? I have been told just to get it done, and within two weeks." "I don't want to do it at all," said John, "but certainly not during the audit period. Can't you just go back up the line and get it put off until next month?"

Questions

1. What have John and Gerald forgotten to do prior to the creation of job descriptions? Why is that step important?
2. Evaluate John's statement, "Just calling attention to the existence of job descriptions will give some people the idea they don't have to do things that aren't in the description."

INCIDENT 2 ▪ A Job Well Done ▪

As Professor Sharpland toured the Plymouth Tube Corporation plant in Pontiac, New Jersey, he became more and more impressed with his young guide, Jim Murdoch. Jim was the assistant human resource director at Plymouth Tube and was primarily responsible for job analysis. An industrial engineer was assigned full-time to the human resource department to assist Jim in job design. Professor Sharpland had been retained by the human resource director to study Plymouth Tube's job analysis system and to make recommendations for improvements. He had gone through the files of job descriptions in the human resource office with Jim and found them, in general, to be complete and directly related to the jobs to be performed.

One of the first stops on the tour was the office of the weld mill supervisor, a 10-foot by 10-foot room out on the factory floor with glass windows on all sides. As Jim approached, the supervisor, Roger Dishongh, was outside his office. "Hi, Jim," he said. "Hello, Roger," said Jim. "This is Professor Sharpland. Could we look at your job descriptions and chat with you for a moment?" "Sure, Jim," said Roger, opening the door. "Come on in and have a seat and I'll get them out." From their vantage point, the men in the office could see the workers in the weld mill area. As they reviewed each job description it was possible to observe every worker actually performing the work described. Roger Dishongh was familiar with each of the jobs. He was very knowledgeable about the job descriptions themselves, having contributed in preparing or revising each of them. "How are the job descriptions related to the performance evaluations here?" asked Professor Sharpland. "Well," answered Roger, "I only evaluate the workers on the items specified in the job descriptions, which were determined through careful job analysis. Limiting performance evaluations to those items encourages me to correct the job descriptions when something changes and they no longer accurately describe the job. Jim has conducted training sessions for all the supervisors so that we understand the relationships among job analysis, job descriptions, and performance evaluations. I think it's a pretty good system."

Jim and Professor Sharpland went on to several other areas of the plant and found similar situations. Jim seemed to have a good relationship with each of the supervisors as well as with the plant manager and the two or three mid-level managers they visited. As they headed back to the front office, Professor Sharpland was considering the comments that he would soon make to the plant manager.

Questions

1. What desirable attributes of job analysis are evident at Plymouth Tube Company?
2. What kind of report do you think Professor Sharpland should present to the plant manager?
3. Describe the relationship that might exist between the industrial engineer and the assistant human resource director regarding job analysis.

Experiencing Human Resource Management

Developing and updating job descriptions is an integral part of the job of any human resource professional. Without properly designed job descriptions, performing necessary human resource management activities is extremely difficult. This exercise will permit students to gain a better appreciation of what is involved in preparing job descriptions. Job descriptions may vary even when the job analysis information is similar.

As a senior human resource specialist at Pedal Cycle Company, you have been involved in job analysis planning for the new plant in Springfield, Missouri. Most of the job analysis data has been gathered and now it is time to prepare specific job descriptions. You have been given a stack of job analysis information sheets and assigned the task of writing job descriptions based on this information. When the assistant human resource director, Ed Deal, handed you the data sheet, he said, "I'd like for you to do the first one, then bring it to me and we'll go over it together."

The initial job description will be for the position of **Spot Welder**. **Work Activities** primarily involve welding parts together. All parts consist of thin steel pieces weighing less than two pounds. The preformed pieces to be welded together are taken from numbered bins surrounding the spot welder, placed in position on the machine, and welded. **Relationship With Other Workers** is fairly standard for a factory floor worker.

Other machine operators running similar machines are within view, twenty to thirty feet away. The crane operator moves the parts bins to this work station and away as required, placing them wherever specified by the operator. There is little time for social interaction on the job. **Degree of Supervision** involved is fairly standard in this industry. The spot welder supervisor supervises twelve operators, all doing essentially the same job. Operators are expected to do their jobs essentially without supervision, consulting the supervisor infrequently. **Records and Reports** are not generated as part of this job. **Skill and Dexterity Requirements** are marginal. In order to meet the standard times, the worker must be able to take two parts from separate bins, place them together in the correct position and complete the part within 3.2 seconds. **Working Conditions** are not ideal; the work station is relatively crowded, the operator is required to wear safety goggles, ambient temperature varies from 60° F to 80° F in summer. The noise level is about 60 decibels, safe but distracting, and the lighting is excellent.

Each participant will use the **Pedal Cycle Company's Job Description Form** and develop an appropriate job description. Several class members can participate in this exercise. Your instructor will provide the participants with additional information necessary to complete the exercise.

REFERENCES

Baron, James N., and William T. Biolby. "The Proliferation of Job Titles in Organizations," *Administrative Science Quarterly*, 31 (December 1986), pp. 561–586.

Buckham, Robert H. "Applying Role Analysis in the Workplace." *Personnel*, 54 (February 1987), pp. 53–56.

Davidson, Jeffrey P. "What's My Job Again?" *Management World*, 15 (July–August 1986), pp. 24–26.

Feild, Hubert S., and Robert D. Gatewood. "Matching Talent with the Task: To Find the Right People, First Define the Jobs You Want Them to Do." *Personnel Administrator*, 32 (April 1987), pp. 113–123.

Fenton, John. "Let's See Your Job Description." *Accountancy*, 98 (July 1986), pp. 114–115.

Fouracre, Sandra, and Angela Wright. "New Factors in Job Evaluation." *Personnel Management*, 18 (May 1986), pp. 40–44.

Friedman, Lee, and Robert J. Harvey. "Can Raters with Reduced Job Descriptive Information Provide Accurate Position Analysis Questionnaire (PAQ) Ratings?" *Personnel Psychology*, 39 (Winter 1986), pp. 779–790.

Green, Samuel B., and Thomas Stutzman. "An Evaluation of Methods to Select Respondents to Structured Job-Analysis Questionnaires." *Personnel Psychology*, 39 (August 1985), pp. 543–565.

Kennedy, William R. "Train Managers to Write Winning Job Descriptions." *Training and Development Journal*, 41 (April 1987), pp. 52–55.

Markovitz, Jarroid. "Managing the Job Analysis Process." *Training and Development Journal*, 41 (August 1987), pp. 64–67.

Matejka, J. Kenneth, and Richard J. Dunsing. "Great Expectations." *Management World*, 16 (January 1987), pp. 16–18.

Mondy, R. Wayne, Robert M. Noe, and Robert E. Edwards. "What the Staffing Function Entails." *Personnel*, 63 (April 1986), pp. 55–58.

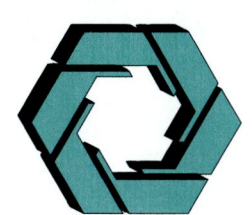

PART ONE

CASE I

Parma Cycle Company: An Overview

According to the National Sporting Goods Association, over 23 million Americans participate in bicycling. This makes it third among sports activities, behind swimming and exercise walking. Sales of bicycles in the United States recently exceeded 12 million a year, up over 50 percent in just a decade. But imports accounted for all of the gain. Domestic sales of U.S.–made bicycles trended downward throughout the 1980s.

Parma Cycle Company of Parma, Ohio, a Cleveland suburb, is one of only three companies that actually manufacture complete bicycles in the United States. Most of Parma's competitors import parts from other countries and simply assemble bicycles here. Even Parma finally began to import many parts, mainly from Italy, Japan, and, more recently, Korea. Parma Cycle employed about 800 workers in the late 1980s, most of them machine operators and assemblers. Cuyahoga County, where Parma is located, suffered from auto industry layoffs in the early 1980s. But conditions steadily improved during the late 1980s, with unemployment falling below the national average of about 5.5 percent. The county population in 1989 exceeded 1.4 million, with Cleveland accounting for about half. Per capita income in Cleveland was near the national average at $8,000 in 1985. But the figure was about 30 percent higher for the county as a whole.

Bicycles are typically classified as eight types, including one-speed, low-priced multispeed, sport, touring, and all-terrain bicycles. Parma Cycle made only one-speed and low-priced multispeed bicycles, leaving the premium types to Schwinn, Panasonic, Peugeot, and a host of other competitors. Parma distributed bicycles under its own name through distributors to small retailers. However, most of the bicycles Parma manufactured were purchased by large national retailers and marketed under those retailers' house names. A few bicycles were exported to Europe and South America, but Parma found it difficult to compete in the international market with Japanese and Italian manufacturers.

Parma Cycle Company, Inc., is a publicly held corporation, although 30 percent of its shares are controlled by a major recreational conglomerate corporation. There have been rumors of a takeover from time to time but none ever materialized. Because of depressed earnings in the late 1980s, Parma's stock declined from $27 per share to $13 per share. Interest rates increased significantly during the same period. The company found it costly, therefore, to raise funds to purchase the new machines that have been developed for bicycle manufacture. A high-performance racing cycle was planned for introduction in the early 1990s. But a research and development program aimed at cutting the cost of producing that bicycle was canceled because of the high cost of financing.

Jesse Heard is the human resource director. He went to work at Parma Cycle in 1966. His first job was as a painter, when painting was done with a hand-held spray gun. He was later promoted to supervisor and worked in several departments at the plant. Because the company paid for college tuition and fees, as well as books, to encourage supervisors to advance their education, Jesse had gone on to college. In 1976, he received his bachelor's degree in personnel administration from Case Western University in Cleveland. Jesse was immediately promoted to a job in the human resource department and three years later became the human resource director.

In May 1987, the Equal Employment Opportunity Commission received a complaint about employment practices at Parma. It was alleged that while the proportion of blacks in the Cleveland area approached 25 percent, only 8 percent of the Parma Cycle workforce was black. There were only two black managers above the level of supervisor. Jesse Heard was advised of the complaint. He felt that the company was doing everything it should with regard to equal opportunity.

The company had an affirmative action program and encouraged managers to employ blacks, other minority group members, and women. In fact, Jesse's efforts to encourage the employment of women and minorities had provoked some managers to complain to the company president, his immediate superior.

In general, the working environment at Parma Cycle was a good one. The company had a relatively flat organizational structure with few managerial levels, as shown in Figure I-1.

Most of Parma's workers are of European stock and are acclimated to working in a factory environment. Beginning in 1978, the company conducted periodic management training seminars in which managers were taught to be sensitive to workers and cooperative with one another. The management philosophy was always one of decentralized authority. Managers, like Jesse Heard, were

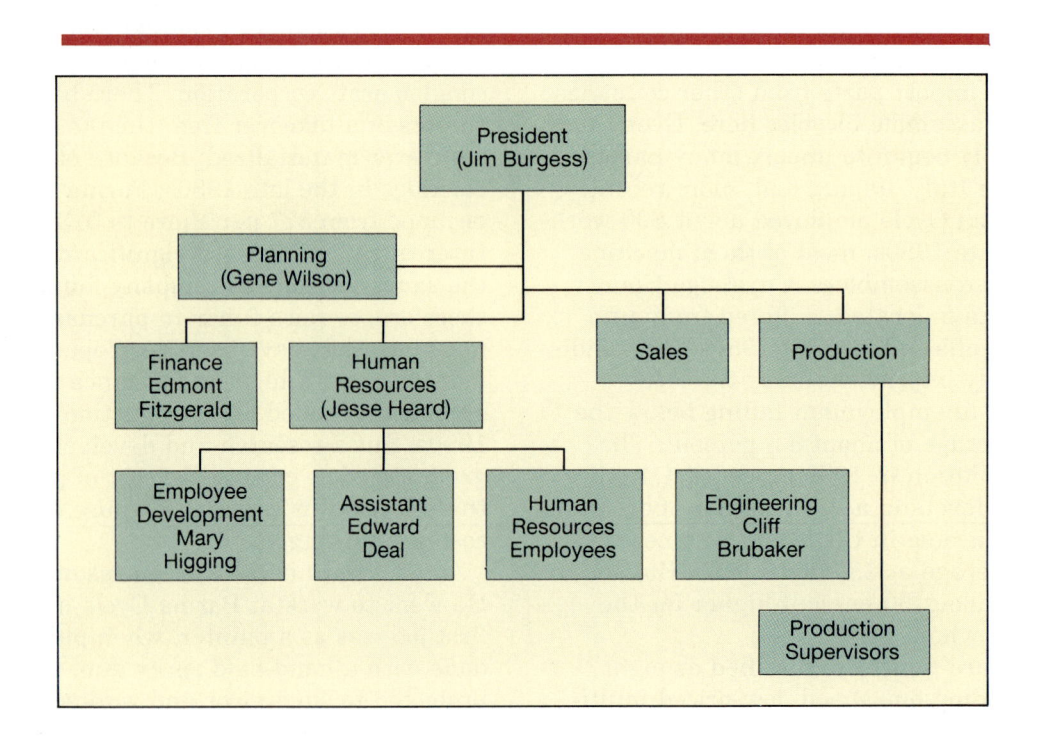

FIGURE I-1 | Parma Cycle Company: Organization Chart

essentially responsible for their own operations.

As a result of an aggressive safety program, there was only one fatal accident at Parma during the 1980s, and work-related injuries remained well below the industry average. Starting in about 1980, the ventilation system in the factory was modernized. The lighting is good, by Cleveland area standards, and the health and safety officer once remarked that the air was cleaner inside the factory than outside. Gene Wilson, the corporate planner, said that he believed the company spent too much money on employee safety and working conditions and that this was a reason for Parma's declining profits. The company's mission had not changed since 1960, when it was stated as: "To enhance the wealth of the common shareholder through efficient production and aggressive marketing of bicycles while contributing to the well-being of our workers and the stability of the Cleveland economy."

Parma's work force was unionized, with the local union being a member of the National Association of Machinists. Employee recruitment was done primarily through referrals from current workers. Selection was based on personal interviews, evaluation of job-related application forms, and, for certain jobs, a basic skills test conducted by the supervisor. The supervisor made the final hiring decision. Workers must join the union before the end of a three-month probationary period. Over the years, the union won wages and benefits that remained about average for the Cleveland area.

The Cleveland factory was laid out, coincidentally, like a bicycle wheel, with component manufacturing departments representing the tire and spoke area and assembly being done in the center of the factory, representing the hub. The factory work was neither especially difficult nor complicated. Technology for the bicycles Parma made changed very little over the years and most of the jobs became standardized. However, growing foreign competition caused an increasing emphasis on productivity and a heightened concern for quality. Consequently, workers were encouraged to put forth additional effort, and production standards were raised to the point where many employees complained of the faster work pace. The productivity improvement program was carried forward with the union's assistance. The union justified its participation on the basis of saving jobs. The last strike at Parma occurred in 1976.

Questions

1. Discuss the external environment of Parma Cycle Company and its impact on human resource management.
2. Is the internal environment at Parma Cycle a good one? Explain.

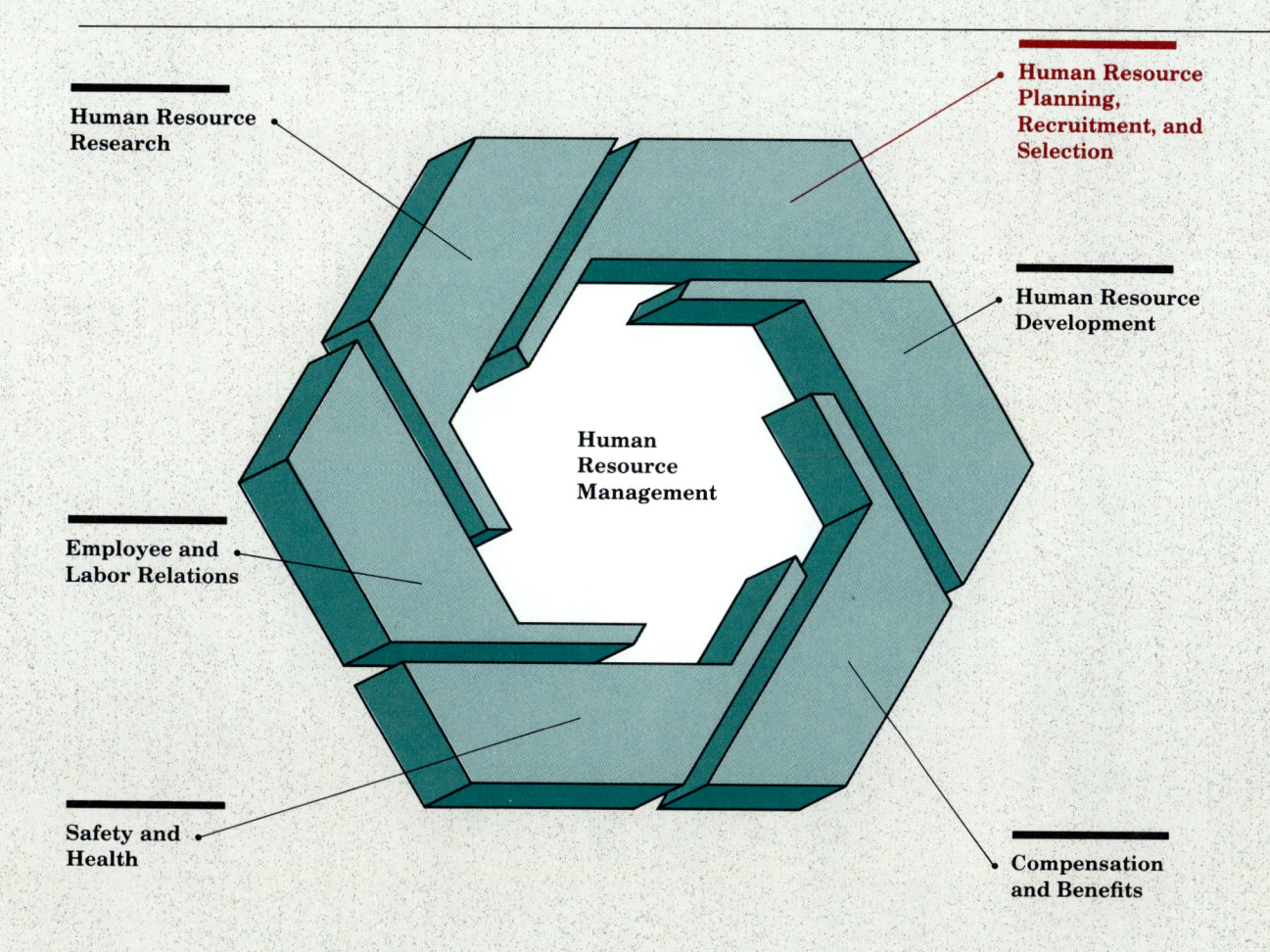

P·A·R·T T·W·O

HUMAN RESOURCE PLANNING, RECRUITMENT, AND SELECTION

- Human Resource Research
- **Human Resource Planning, Recruitment, and Selection**
- Human Resource Development
- Compensation and Benefits
- Safety and Health
- Employee and Labor Relations

Human Resource Management

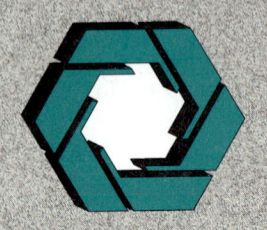

CHAPTER 5   HUMAN RESOURCE PLANNING

CHAPTER OBJECTIVES

1. Explain the human resource planning process and define the basic terms used in forecasting.
2. Describe some human resource forecasting techniques and explain how human resource requirements are forecasted.
3. State what a firm can do when a surplus of workers exists and explain how human resource availability is forecasted.
4. Describe the importance of a human resource information system.

> Mark Swann, the marketing director for Sharpco Manufacturing, commented at the weekly executive directors' meeting, "I have good news. We can get the large contract with Medord Corporation. All we have to do is complete the project in one year instead of two. I told them we could do it."
>
> Linda Cane, vice-president of human resources, brought everyone back to reality by asserting, "As I understand it, our present workers do not have the expertise required to produce the quality that Medord's particular specifications require. Under the two-year project timetable, we planned to retrain our present workers gradually. With this new time schedule, we will have to go into the job market and recruit workers who are already experienced in this process. We may need to analyze this proposal further to see if that is really what we want to do. Human resource costs will rise considerably if we attempt to complete the project in one year instead of two. Sure, Mark, we can do it, but with these constraints, will the project be cost effective?"

While the situation described is not typical, it occurs often enough to prompt one corporate executive to state: "The human resource is perhaps the last great cost that is relatively unmanaged."[1] This may be an overstatement, but it is true that human resource planning traditionally has not received the same attention as other components of business planning. Indeed, people-planning was often considered after the fact. However, neglecting human resources in the planning process can be very disruptive if adequately trained people are not available when needed.[2]

Our overall purpose in this chapter is to explain the role and nature of human resource planning in organizations today. First, we define human resource plan-

---

[1] Charles F. Russ, Jr., "Manpower Planning Systems: Part II," *Personnel Journal*, 61 (February 1982), p. 123.
[2] Douglas B. Gehrman, "Objective Based Human Resources Planning," *Personnel Journal*, 60 (December 1981), p. 942.

ning and describe the human resource planning process. We then review terminology of forecasting and examine some human resource forecasting techniques. Next, we discuss forecasting human resource requirements and availability. We then examine action to be taken when the firm has a surplus of workers and follow up with an example of effective human resource planning. We devote the final sections of the chapter to a discussion of the human resource information system.

■ THE HUMAN RESOURCE PLANNING PROCESS

Human resource planning (HRP) is the process of systematically reviewing human resource requirements to ensure that the required number of employees, with the required skills, are available when they are needed.[3] It is the process of matching the internal and external supply of people with job openings anticipated in the organization over a specified period of time.[4] Although some organizations continue to provide only lip service to human resource planning, HRP is increasingly being recognized as an important activity.

The human resource planning process is illustrated in Figure 5-1. Note that strategic planning—which requires consideration of both the external and internal environment—precedes human resource planning. **Strategic planning** is the determination of overall organizational purposes and goals and how they are to be achieved.[5] Although strategic plans affect every major department, in the past the chief human resource officer was often excluded from strategic planning. This practice has changed in most firms.[6] Top management now realizes the necessity of including human resource managers in the process. In fact, in this decade—and in those to follow—human resource planning will become an even more important aspect of strategic planning.[7] In the Executive Insights, James G. Parkel, director of personnel plans and programs for IBM, states that "human resource management has taken on new power and prestige in the corporate structure." He explains that one reason for this is that human resource issues have become mainstream business issues. This fact reveals the absolute necessity for integrating people-planning into a firm's strategic plans.

After organizational strategic plans have been formulated, human resource planning can be undertaken. Strategic plans are reduced to specific quantitative and qualitative human resource plans. For example, note in Figure 5-1 that human resource planning has two components: requirements and availability. Forecasting human resource requirements involves determining the number and type of employees needed, by skill level and location. These projections will reflect various factors, such as production plans and

---

[3] R. Wayne Mondy, Robert M. Noe, and Robert E. Edwards, "What the Staffing Function Entails," *Personnel*, 63 (April 1986), p. 55–56.

[4] Charles F. Russ, Jr., "Manpower Planning Systems: Part I," *Personnel Journal*, 61 (January 1982), p. 41.

[5] R. Wayne Mondy, Arthur Sharplin, and Edwin B. Flippo, *Management: Concepts and Practices*, 4th ed. (Boston: Allyn & Bacon, 1988), p. 120.

[6] Kendrith M. Rowland and Scott L. Summers, "Human Resource Planning: A Second Look," *Personnel Administrator*, 26 (December 1981), p. 73.

[7] Jeffrey O. Nyweide, "Simply Sophisticated," *Management World*, 16 (April–May 1987), p. 34.

Executive Insights

James G. Parkel, SPHR
Director of Personnel Plans and Programs, International Business Machines Corporation

Jim Parkel is presently IBM director of personnel plans and programs. He has worldwide responsibility for benefits, employee and executive compensation, resources, health and safety, community programs, and equal opportunity.

Parkel began his career at IBM in 1962 as a junior engineer after graduating from the University of Denver with a B.S. degree in electrical engineering. Later, he began his career in personnel and has held various human resource positions. In 1974, Parkel was named corporate director of management development planning. He joined the IBM Americas/Far East Corporation where he held the position of director of personnel from 1977 to 1981. He was then named IBM director of employment and recruiting. In 1982, Parkel was appointed IBM director of personnel programs. He has held his present position since July 1987.

Parkel believes that human resource management has taken on new power and prestige in the corporate structure for at least two major reasons. First, corporate management recognizes the importance of its greatest asset—employees. The labor force is aging and thus competition for those entering the labor force will increase. The human resource professional will be judged more than ever on his or her ability to recruit and help retrain a competent workforce. This workforce may be comprised of full-time regular employees, retirees, part-time employees, and/or supplementals. To retain these employees, innovative, cost-effective benefits and flexible programs must be in place.

Second, human resource issues have become mainstream business issues. The human resource professional is concerned with business management functions, government relations, and international issues. Topics discussed today among human resource professionals are not the topics discussed as recently as five years ago. Factors such as new laws and regulations at all levels of government, increasing technological innovation, and changing demographics all contribute to this change. Parkel feels that human resource professionals must be able to speak not only about human resource programs but also on such issues as quality, competitiveness, state, national, and financial issues, balance of trade, and a whole host of subjects that say we know our profession and how it integrates into the business world.

Currently, Parkel is immediate past chairman of the American Society for Personnel Administration and a board member of the American Graduate School of International Management.

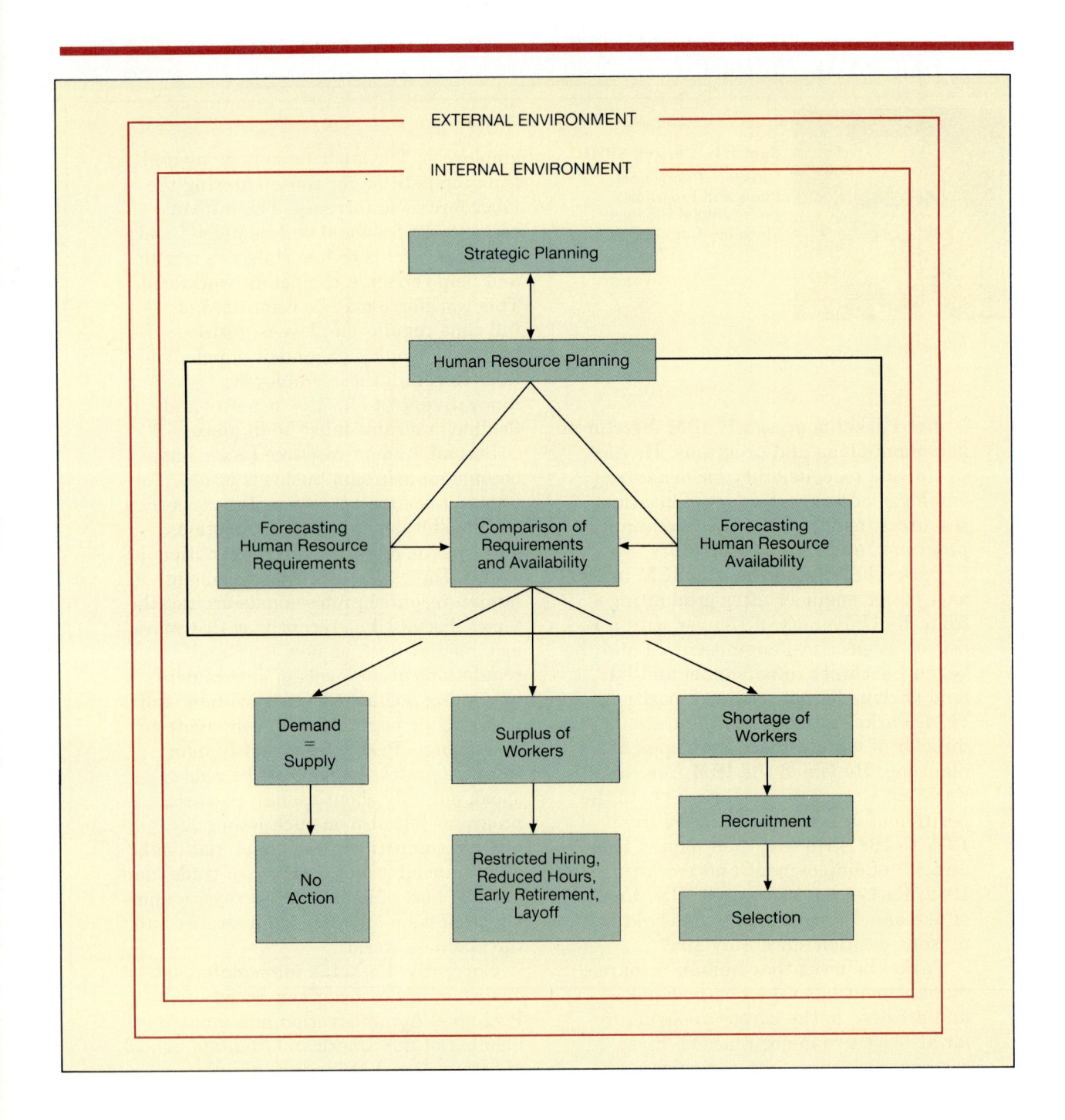

FIGURE 5-1 | The Human Resource Planning Process

changes in productivity.[8] In order to forecast availability, the human resource manager looks to both internal sources (presently employed employees) and external sources (the labor market). When employee requirements and availability have been analyzed, the firm can determine whether it will have a surplus or shortage of employees. Ways must be found to reduce the number of employees if a surplus is projected. Some of these methods include restricted hiring, reduced hours, early retirements, and layoffs. If a shortage is forecast, the firm must obtain the proper quantity and quality of workers outside the organization. External recruitment and selection is required.

Because conditions in the external and internal environments can change quickly, the human resource planning process must be continuous. Changing conditions could affect the entire organizations, thereby requiring extensive modification of forecasts. Planning in general enables managers to anticipate and prepare for changing conditions, and HRP in particular allows flexibility in the area of human resource management. During the past ten years, various factors have caused some organizations to downsize (reduce the size of their workforces).[9] Human resource planning allows workforce reductions with a minimum of disruption.

■ TERMINOLOGY OF FORECASTING

Four basic terms are used in forecasting. First, the **long-term trend** is a projection of demand for a firm's products, typically five years or more into the future. As Figure 5-2 shows, the hypothetical long-term trend is for increased sales: Sales are expected to double during the period shown. Early recognition of such a trend is crucial. A firm may not be able to fill the positions necessary to support such sales levels quickly, if considerable training and development are required. Some employees may need extensive training and development before they are capable of taking on new or added responsibilities. Proper estimation of long-term trends, therefore, is essential for organizational success.

Second, **cyclical variations** are reasonably predictable movements about the trend line that occur over a period of more than a year. Cyclical variations may be caused by war, elections, changes in economic conditions and consumer demand, and societal pressures. These variations typically last between one and five years. Anticipating cyclical demand is important because of the potential for severe peaks and valleys. Extra people may be required to meet high cyclical demand, even though a stable long-term demand has been forecast. Conversely, although the long-term forecast may be upward, conditions such as a short-term recession may require a temporary workforce reduction.

Third, **seasonal variations** are reasonably predictable changes that occur over a period of a year. Seasonal variations follow cyclical variations,

---
[8] Gehrman, p. 944.
[9] Colin P. Silverthorne, "Planning for a Smaller Organization: A Guide for HR Managers," *Personnel*, 64 (March 1987), p. 60.

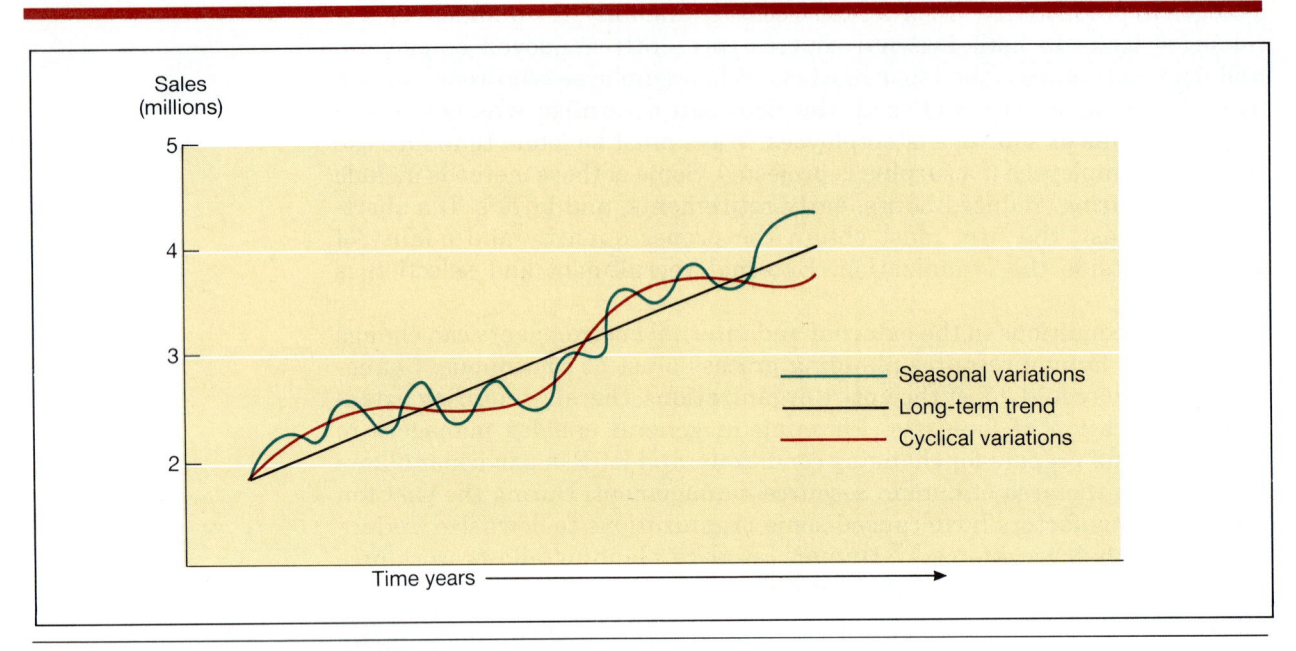

FIGURE 5-2 | Forecasting Terminology Example

but may fluctuate drastically (see Figure 5-2). These variations occur within a twelve-month period and are of most immediate concern to many firms. Electric shavers are sold primarily during the Christmas holiday season, whereas motor boats are sold primarily in the spring. Seasonal demand can have a major impact on a firm as it attempts to stabilize its workforce and still meet production and inventory requirements.

Finally, **random variations** are changes without pattern. Even the most sophisticated forecasting techniques cannot anticipate such changes. Management must therefore anticipate and plan for long-term trends, cyclical variations, and seasonal variations—and be ready to deal with random variations.

■ HUMAN RESOURCE FORECASTING TECHNIQUES

Several techniques of forecasting human resource requirements and availability are currently used by those in the profession. Some of the techniques are qualitative in nature, and others are quantitative. We describe next several of the better known methods.

Zero-Base Forecasting

The **zero-base forecasting** approach uses the organization's current level of employment as the starting point for determining future staffing needs.

HRM In Action

"Cynthia, what do you mean by saying that I'm going to have to justify my need for the typesetter's position? One of my ten employees in this job just quit, and I want a replacement now. We've had ten typesetters in my department for the thirteen years that I've been here. Probably a long time before that. If we've needed them in the past, certainly we will need them in the future." This is the beginning of a conversation between Richard Wiley, a first-line supervisor with Allen Industries, and Cynthia Larger, its human resource manager.

How should Cynthia respond?

Essentially the same procedure is used for human resource planning as for zero-base budgeting, whereby each budget must be rejustified each year.[10] If an employee retires, is fired, or leaves the firm for any other reason, the position is not automatically filled. Instead, an analysis is made to determine whether the firm can justify filling it. Equal concern is shown for creating new positions when they appear to be needed. The key to zero-base forecasting is a thorough analysis of human resource needs.

Bottom-Up Approach

Some firms use what might be called the bottom-up approach to employment forecasting. It is based on the reasoning that the manager in each unit is the most knowledgeable about employment requirements. In the **bottom-up approach**, each successive level in the organization—starting with the lowest—forecasts its requirements, ultimately providing an aggregate forecast of employees needed. Human resource forecasting is often most effective when managers periodically project their human resource needs, comparing their current and anticipated levels, and giving the human resource department adequate lead time to explore internal and external sources.[11] According to one practitioner, the most common approach to human resource forecasting is to rely most heavily on the judgments of unit managers, supplemented with basic statistical analysis.[12]

---

[10] Ernie A. Kurbis, "The Case for Zero-Base Budgeting," *CA Magazine*, 119 (April 1986), p. 104.

[11] John F. DeSanto, "Work Force Planning and Corporate Strategy," *Personnel Administrator*, 28 (October 1983), p. 34.

[12] Richard B. Frantzreb, "Human Resource Planning: Forecasting Manpower Needs," *Personnel Journal*, 60 (November 1981), p. 854.

Use of Predictor Variables

Another means of forecasting human resource requirements is to use past employment levels to predict future requirements. **Predictor variables** are factors known to have had an impact on employment levels. One of the most useful predictors of employment levels is sales volume. The relationship between demand and number of employees needed is a positive one. As you can see in Figure 5-3, a firm's sales volume is depicted on the horizontal axis and the number of employees actually required is shown on the vertical axis. In this illustration, as sales increase, so does the number of employees. Using this method, managers can approximate the number of employees required at different demand levels.

With the increased use of computers and statistical software packages, human resource managers have at their disposal an important forecasting tool: regression analysis. **Regression analysis** is used to predict one item (known as the dependent variable) through knowledge of other items (known as the independent variables). When there is one dependent variable and one independent variable, the process is called simple linear regression. When there is more than one independent variable, the technique is called multiple regression.

Regression is often used because of the direct relationship between demand for a firm's goods and/or services and employment levels. However,

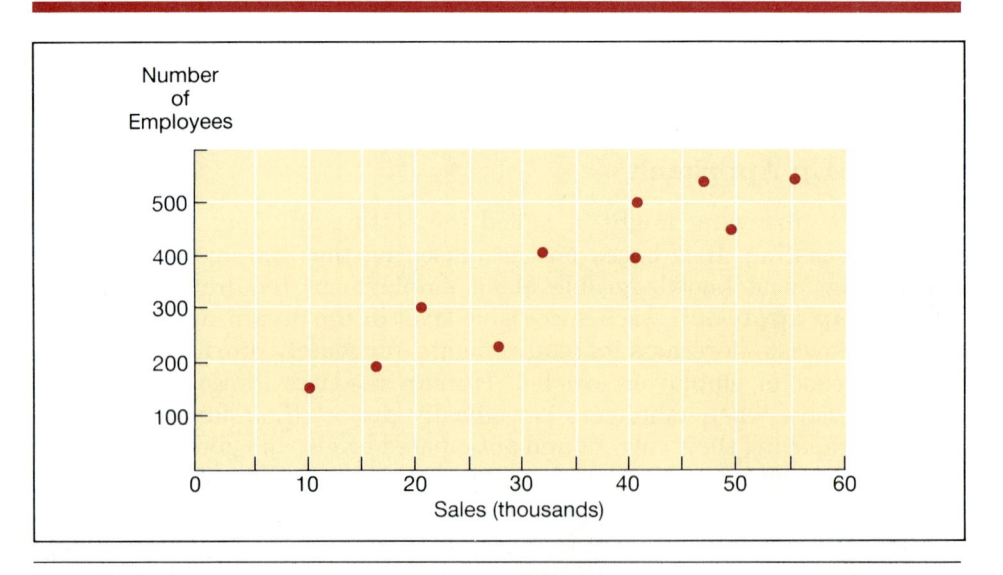

FIGURE 5-3 | The Relationship of Sales Volume to Number of Employees

in most instances, the employment level is determined by several independent variables, and multiple regression is required. Instead of predicting employment levels solely on the basis of sales, an analyst might also use other variables, such as productivity of the workforce. Multiple regression often produces results superior to those obtained from simple linear regression because it recognizes that a variety of factors may influence future employment levels.

Simulation

Simulation is a technique for experimenting with a real-world situation through a mathematical model representing that situation. A model is an abstraction of the real world. Thus a simulation model is an attempt to represent a real-world situation through mathematical logic in order to predict what will occur. Simulation assists the human resource manager by permitting the asking of many "what if . . ." questions without having to make a decision with its real-world consequences.

In human resource management, a simulation model might be developed to represent the interrelationships among employment level and many other variables. The manager could then ask "what if . . ." questions such as:

- What would happen if we put 10 percent of the present workforce on overtime?
- What would happen if the plant utilized two shifts? Three shifts?

The purpose of the model is to permit the human resource manager to gain considerable insight into a particular problem before making an actual decision.

■ FORECASTING HUMAN RESOURCE REQUIREMENTS

A **requirements forecast** is an estimate of the numbers and kinds of employees the organization will need at future dates in order for it to realize its stated goals. Before human resource requirements can be projected, demand for the firm's goods or services must first be forecast. This forecast is then converted into people requirements for the activities that will be required to meet this demand. For a firm that manufactures personal computers, activities might be stated in terms of the number of units to be produced, number of sales calls to be made, number of vouchers to be processed, or a variety of other activities. For example, manufacturing 1,000 personal computers each week might require 10,000 hours of work by assemblers during a 40-hour week. Dividing the 10,000 hours by the 40 hours in the work week gives 250 assembly workers needed. Similar calculations are performed for the other jobs needed to produce and market the personal computers.

■ FORECASTING HUMAN RESOURCE AVAILABILITY

Forecasting requirements provides managers with the means of estimating how many and what types of employees will be required. But there is another side to the coin.

> A large manufacturing firm on the West Coast was preparing to begin operations in a new plant. Analysts had already determined that there was a large long-term demand for the new product. Financing was available and equipment was in place. But production did not begin for two years! Management had made a critical mistake: It had studied the demand side of human resources but not the supply side. There weren't enough qualified workers in the local labor market to operate the new plant. New workers had to receive extensive training before they could move into the newly created jobs.

Determining whether the firm will be able to secure employees with the necessary skills and from what sources is called an **availability forecast**. It helps the human resource manager to determine whether the needed employees may be obtained from within the company, from outside the organization, or from a combination of the two sources.

Internal Sources of Supply

Many of the workers that will be needed for future positions may already work for the firm. If the firm is small, management probably knows all the workers well enough to easily match their skills and aspirations with the company's needs. If, for instance, the firm is creating a new sales position, it may be common knowledge that Mary Garcia, a five-year employee with the company, has both the skills and desire to take over the new job. This unplanned process of matching people and positions may be sufficient for smaller firms. As organizations grow, however, the matching process becomes increasingly difficult. Both management and skills inventories increasingly are being used by human resource professionals and organizations that take human resources seriously.[13]

Management Inventories. Managerial talent is an essential resource in every organization. Thus firms maintain better data on managers than they do on employee skills. A **management inventory** contains detailed

---
[13] John Lawrie, "Skill Inventories: Pack for the Future," *Personnel Journal*, 66 (March 1987), p. 127.

information about each manager and is used to identify individuals who have the potential to move into higher level positions. Essentially, this type of inventory provides information for replacement and promotion decisions. It would likely include data such as:

- Work history and experience
- Educational background
- Assessment of strengths and weaknesses
- Developmental needs
- Promotion potential at present and with further development
- Current job performance
- Field of specialization
- Job preferences
- Geographic preferences
- Career goals and aspirations
- Anticipated retirement date
- Personal history, including psychological assessments

One of the outcomes of a management inventory is a management replacement chart, which can be most useful in human resource planning. Detroit Edison calls its chart a Career Planning Inventory Organization Review Chart. As you can see in Figure 5-4, the chart shows a manager in the top box with immediate subordinates in the lower boxes. Information shown on the chart includes the following.

- *Position Box*: The position title and incumbent's name appear in each box. The symbol * preceding the name identifies incumbents who will retire between 1991 and 1995, indicating that short-range planning is required. The symbol ** preceding the name identifies incumbents who will retire between 1996 and 2002, indicating that long-range planning is required. If the word *Open* appears in the box, the position is unfilled; if *Future* appears, the position is anticipated but does not yet exist.
- *Dev Pgm*: Identifies the particular development program in which the employee participates.
- *Retire*: The month and year of the employee's planned retirement.
- *Est Prom*: Indicates the employee's estimated potential for promotion.
- *Lrp*: Indicates the employee's long-range career potential with the Company.
- *Ppc*: Indicates the incumbent's current organizational level.
- *3 Development Needs*: Describes three priority development needs that have been identified.
- *Potential Positions*: The title of each position to which the incumbent is potentially promotable, along with codes that indicate an estimate of when the employee would be ready.
- *Possible Replacements*: The names of up to ten possible replacements for the incumbent, with codes indicating when the replacements would be ready for promotion to this position.

Skills Inventories. A **skills inventory** is information that is maintained on the availability and preparedness of nonmanagerial employees to move

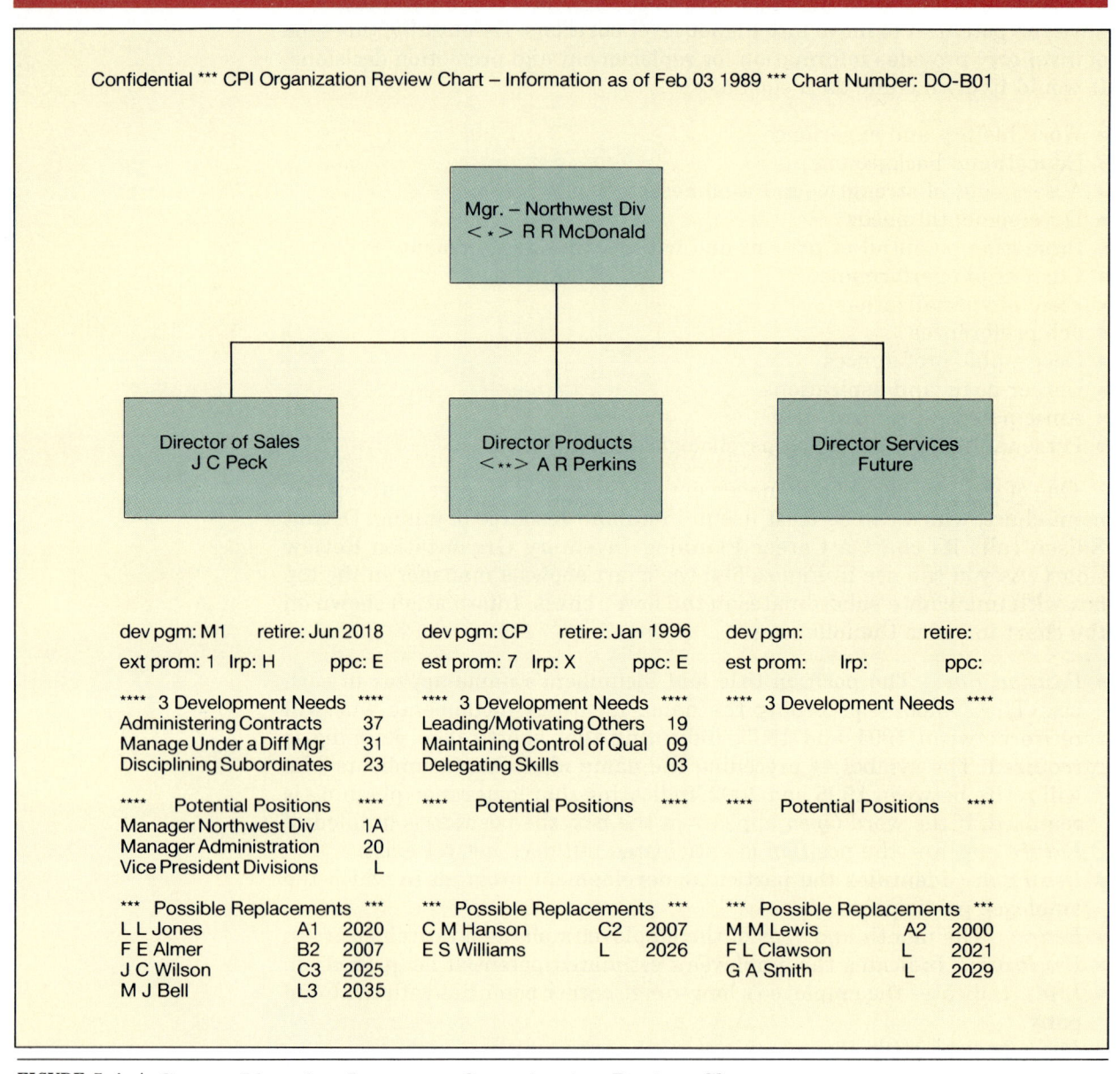

```
Confidential *** CPI Organization Review Chart – Information as of Feb 03 1989 *** Chart Number: DO-B01


                            ┌──────────────────────┐
                            │  Mgr. – Northwest Div │
                            │    < * >  R R McDonald │
                            └──────────┬───────────┘
                                       │
              ┌────────────────────────┼────────────────────────┐
     ┌────────────────┐       ┌────────────────┐       ┌────────────────┐
     │Director of Sales│       │Director Products│       │Director Services│
     │    J C Peck     │       │ < ** > A R Perkins│     │     Future      │
     └────────────────┘       └────────────────┘       └────────────────┘


 dev pgm: M1    retire: Jun 2018     dev pgm: CP    retire: Jan 1996     dev pgm:            retire:
 ext prom: 1   lrp: H      ppc: E    est prom: 7   lrp: X    ppc: E      est prom:   lrp:      ppc:

 ****  3 Development Needs  ****    ****  3 Development Needs  ****    ****  3 Development Needs  ****
 Administering Contracts     37     Leading/Motivating Others   19
 Manage Under a Diff Mgr     31     Maintaining Control of Qual 09
 Disciplining Subordinates   23     Delegating Skills           03

 ****   Potential Positions  ****    ****   Potential Positions  ****    ****   Potential Positions  ****
 Manager Northwest Div       1A
 Manager Administration      20
 Vice President Divisions     L

 ***  Possible Replacements ***     ***  Possible Replacements ***     ***  Possible Replacements ***
 L L Jones          A1   2020       C M Hanson         C2   2007       M M Lewis          A2   2000
 F E Almer          B2   2007       E S Williams        L   2026       F L Clawson         L   2021
 J C Wilson         C3   2025                                          G A Smith           L   2029
 M J Bell           L3   2035
```

FIGURE 5-4 | Career Planning Inventory Organization Review Chart

into higher level positions or laterally in the organization. Although the process and the intent of the skills inventory are essentially the same as for a management inventory, the information differs somewhat. Generally included in a skills inventory are:

- Background and biographical data
- Work experience

- Specific skills and knowledge
- Licenses or certifications held
- In-house training programs completed
- Previous performance appraisal evaluations
- Career goals

A properly designed and updated skills inventory system permits management to readily identify employees with particular skills and match them insofar as possible to the changing needs of the company.

External Supply

Unless a firm is experiencing declining demand, it will have to recruit some employees from outside the organization. However, finding and hiring new employees capable of performing immediately is usually quite difficult. The best source of supply varies by industry, firm, and geographic location. Some organizations find that their best sources of potential employees are colleges and universities. Others get excellent results from vocational schools, competitors, or even unsolicited applications.

If the company has information revealing where its present employees were recruited, it can develop statistics and project the best sources. For instance, a firm may discover that graduates from a particular college or university adapt well to the firm's environment and culture. One large farm-equipment manufacturer has achieved excellent success in recruiting from regional schools located in rural areas. Managers in this firm believe that since many students come from a farming environment, they can adapt more quickly to the firm's method of operation.

Other firms may discover from past records that the majority of their more successful employees lived no more than twenty miles from their place of work. This information may suggest concentrated recruiting efforts in that particular geographic area.

Forecasting can assist not only in identifying where potential employees may be found but also in predicting the type of individuals that will likely succeed in the organization. A regional medical center—located far from any large metropolitan area—reviewed its employment files of registered nurses. It discovered that RNs born and raised in smaller towns adapted better to the medical center's small-town environment than those who grew up in large metropolitan areas. After studying these statistics, management modified its recruiting efforts.[14]

However, forecasting has many pitfalls, and examples of improper forecasting are numerous. Managers of one large convenience store chain were disturbed by their unusually high employee turnover rate. When they analyzed their recruiting efforts, they discovered that the large majority of short-term employees had merely seen a sign in the store window announcing that a position was available. These individuals, often unemployed at

---

[14] Wayne Mondy and Harry N. Mills, "Choice Not Chance in Nurse Selection," *Supervisor Nurse*, 9 (November 1978), pp. 35–39.

the time, were highly transient. The source of supply virtually guaranteed a high turnover rate. When they discovered this fact, the managers found new sources of supply, which significantly reduced turnover.

■ SURPLUS OF EMPLOYEES

When a comparison of requirements and availability indicates a worker surplus, restricted hiring, reduced hours, early retirements, or layoffs may be required to correct the situation.

Restricted Hiring

When a firm implements a restricted hiring policy, it reduces the workforce by not replacing employees who leave. New workers are hired only when overall performance of the organization may be affected. For instance, if a quality control department that consisted of four inspectors lost one to a competitor, this individual probably would not be replaced. However, if the firm lost all its inspectors, it would probably replace at least some of them to ensure continued operation.

Reduced Hours

Reaction to declining demand can also be made by reducing the total number of hours worked. Instead of continuing a forty-hour week, management may decide to cut each employee's time to thirty hours. This cutback normally applies only to hourly employees because management and other professionals typically are salaried, not paid on an hourly basis.

Early Retirement

Early retirement of some present employees is another way to reduce the number of workers. Some employees will be delighted to retire, but others will be somewhat reluctant. The latter may be willing to accept early retirement if the total retirement package is made attractive enough. A key point to remember is that because of the Age Discrimination in Employment Act, as amended, retirement can no longer be mandated by age.

Layoffs

At times, a firm has no choice but to lay off part of its workforce. A layoff is not the same as being fired, but it has the same short-term effect—the worker is no longer employed. When the firm is unionized, layoff procedures are usually stated clearly in the labor–management agreement. Typically, workers with the least seniority are laid off first. If the organization is nonunion, it may base layoff on a combination of factors, such as seniority and productivity level. When managers and other professionals are laid off, the decision is likely to be based on ability, although internal politics may be a factor.

■ HUMAN RESOURCE PLANNING: AN EXAMPLE

The human resource planning model presented in Figure 5-1 is a generalized one. Each firm must tailor human resource planning to fit its specific needs. Figure 5-5 shows the human resource planning process for Honeywell, Inc. We discuss each element of the plan in the following sections.

Organizational Goals

To be relevant, a human resource planning process should be clearly tied to the organization's strategic goals. It must rest on a solid foundation of information about sales forecasts, market trends, technological advances, and major changes in processes and productivity. Considerable effort should be devoted to securing reliable data on business trends and needs—in terms of quantity and quality of labor—as the basic input for human resource planning.

Human Resource Needs Forecast

A second element in the planning process is forecasting human resource needs based on business strategies, production plans, and the various indicators of change in technology and operating methods. Forecasting is usually accomplished by utilizing historical data and reliable ratios (such as indirect/direct labor) and adjusting them for productivity trends. The result of this forecast is a spread sheet of employees in terms of numbers, mix, cost, new skills, and job categories and numbers and levels of managers needed to accomplish the organization's goals. Experience has shown that producing this forecast is the most challenging part of the planning process because it requires creative and highly participative approaches to dealing with business and technical uncertainties several years in the future.

Employee Information

A third element of the planning process is maintaining accurate information concerning the composition, assignments, and capabilities of the current workforce. This information includes job classifications, age, gender, minority status, organization level, rate of pay, and functions. Employee information may also include résumé data, such as skills, education, training received, and career interests. Much of the data needed for human resource planning currently exists in other data systems (such as payroll, talent review, or professional development).

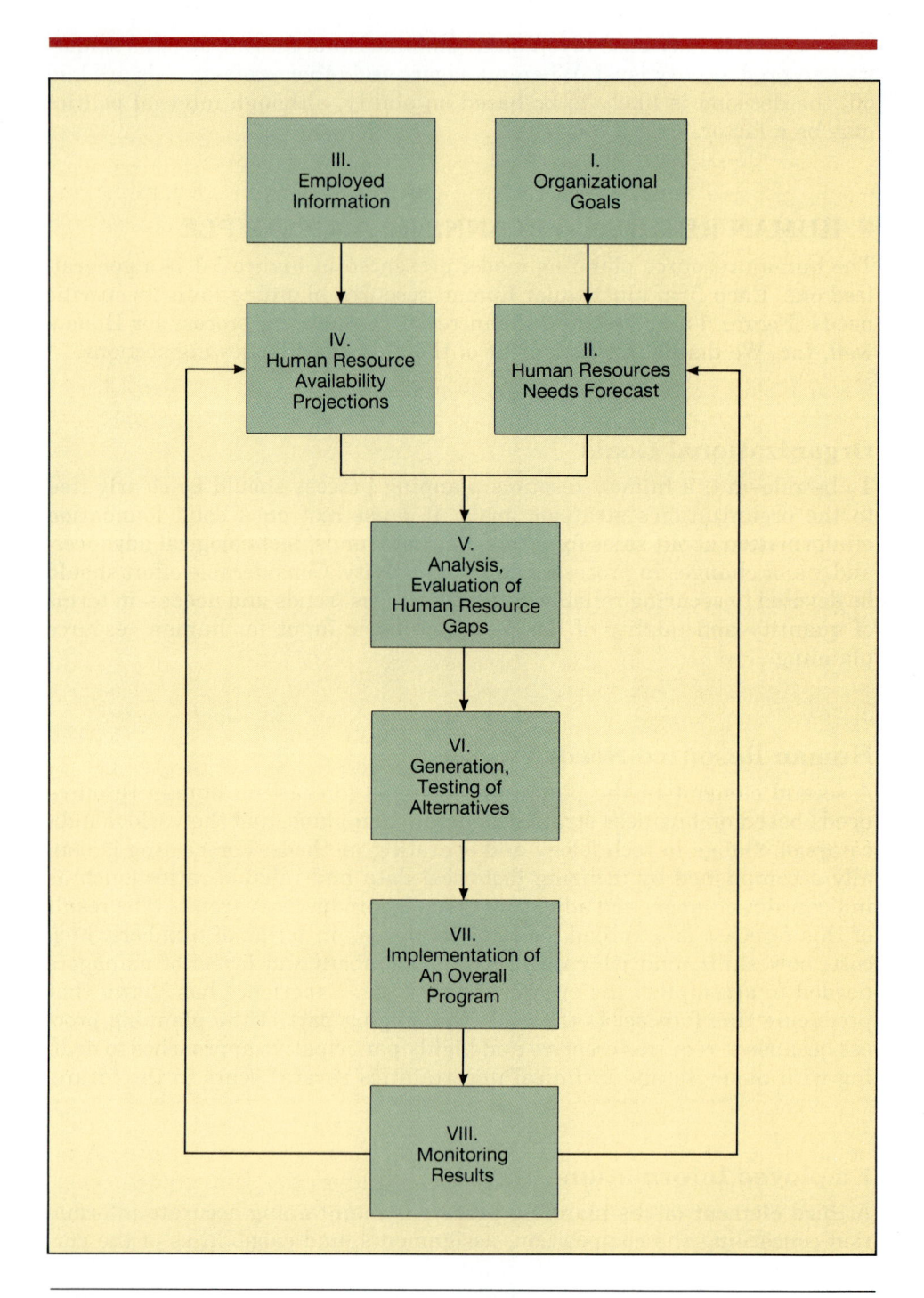

FIGURE 5-5 | Elements of a Human Resource Plan

Source: Used with the permission of Honeywell, Inc.

Human Resource Availability Projections

The fourth element of the planning process is estimating which current employees could or will be available in the future. By projecting past data about the size, organization, and composition of the workforce and about turnover, aging, and hiring, availability at a specific future date can be estimated. The result is a picture of the organization's current human resources and how they can be expected to evolve over time in terms of turnover, retirement, obsolescence, promotability, and other relevant characteristics.

Analyzing and Evaluating Human Resource Gaps

The fifth element of the planning process is comparing what is needed with what is available in terms of numbers, mix, skills, and technologies. This comparison permits the human resource manager to determine gaps and evaluate where the most serious mismatches are likely to be. This type of analysis should help management address issues such as:

- Are imbalances developing between projected human resource needs and availability?
- What is the effect of current productivity trends and pay rates on workforce levels and costs?
- Do turnover problems exist in certain jobs or age levels?
- Are there problems of career blockage and obsolescence?
- Are there sufficient high-potential managers to fulfill future needs?
- Is there a shortage of any critical skills?

Such an analysis permits development of long-range plans for recruiting, hiring, training, transferring, and retraining appropriate numbers and types of employees.

Generating and Testing Alternatives

The analysis of human resources should reveal much about a wide range of policies and practices, such as staffing plans, promotion practices and policies, EEO plans, organization design, training and development programs, salary planning, and career management. This phase of the process explores the implications of the analysis and generates alternatives to current practices and policies. Some of the more comprehensive human resource planning systems utilize modeling to simulate the types and organization of employees that would result from specific changes in employment strategies or policies. Testing of complex alternatives and anticipated consequences is usually performed on a computer model. However, manual systems should be utilized if computers aren't available.

Implementing an Overall Human Resource Program

After the optimal alternative for addressing the organization's human resource issues has been chosen, it is translated into operational programs with specific plans, target dates, schedules, and resource commitments. The analytical steps described—from considering organizational goals to generating and testing alternatives—should shape an organization's staffing plan, EEO plan, human resource development activities, mobility plans, productivity programs, bargaining strategies, and compensation programs.

Monitoring Results

The final element in any human resource planning process is to provide a means for management to monitor results of the overall program. This step should address such questions as:

- How well is the plan working?
- Is it cost effective?
- What is the actual versus planned impact on the workforce?
- Where are the plan's weaknesses?
- What changes will be needed during the next planning cycle?

■ HUMAN RESOURCE INFORMATION SYSTEMS

A **human resource information system (HRIS)** is any organized approach to obtaining relevant and timely information on which to base human resource decisions. An effective HRIS is crucial to sound human resource decision making. Typically, human resource professionals utilize computers and other sophisticated technologies to maintain and process information on a day-to-day basis.

An HRIS should be designed to provide information that is:

- *Timely*—A manager must have access to up-to-date information.
- *Accurate*—A manager must be able to rely on the accuracy of the information provided.
- *Concise*—A manager can absorb only so much information at any one time.
- *Relevant*—A manager should receive only the information needed in a particular situation.
- *Complete*—A manager should receive complete, not partial, information.

The absence of even one of these characteristics reduces the effectiveness of an HRIS and complicates the decision-making process. Conversely, a system possessing all these characteristics enhances the ease and accuracy of the decision-making process. An effective HRIS also produces several important reports and forecasts related to business operations.

Routine Reports. Business data summarized on a scheduled basis are referred to as routine reports. Weekly and monthly employment status reports may be sent to the general manager, whereas quarterly reports may be forwarded to top management.

Exception Reports. Exception reports highlight variations in operations that are serious enough to require management's attention. One type of exception report is the quality-exception report, which is completed when the number of product defects exceeds a predetermined maximum. The human resource manager may be interested in this type of information in order to identify additional training needs.

On-Demand Reports. An on-demand report provides information in response to a specific request. The number of engineers with five years' work experience who speak fluent Spanish is an example of an on-demand report that management could request.

Forecasts. A forecast applies predictive models to specific situations. Managers need forecasts of the number and types of employees required to satisfy projected demand for the firm's product.

Creating the HRIS

Let's consider four steps in designing an HRIS that will provide the types of output just discussed and also conform to the HRIS criteria presented. These steps are not separate and distinct—in fact, they overlap considerably. Development of an HRIS is not merely a matter of properly designing the system. Without a major commitment from top management, creating a smoothly functioning and operational HRIS is virtually impossible. However, following the four steps can result in a HRIS design, which could become quite an effective system if supported strongly by top management.

Study the Present System. In assessing the existing information system, three questions need to be answered: (1) What is the present flow of information? (2) How is the information used? (3) How valuable is this information to decision making? A prime example of a flawed system was encountered by Art Simmons. Art was employed as a consultant to develop a human resource information system for a national forest products firm. In studying the firm's existing system, Art was amazed to discover a large amount of duplication and wasted effort. Some weekly reports were essentially useless for decision making. In addition, two employees had to work a total of eight hours weekly to prepare one particular report. If the report was late, the vice-president's secretary would send a strongly worded reprimand to the delinquent division chief. However, when the information arrived at headquarters, it was neatly filed and was never used. Numerous questions regarding this practice finally revealed that about five years ago this type of information was requested—as a one-time report. Preparation of the report had continued through the administrations of three vice-presidents because no one thought to stop it.

Develop a Priority of Information That Managers Need. Once the current system is thoroughly understood, it is used to develop information priorities. A manager must have certain information in order to make proper decisions. Other information is nice to have but isn't essential to the manager's decision making. The HRIS design must ensure provision of high-priority information. Data having a lower priority should be generated only if the benefits exceed the costs of producing it.

One approach is to have individual managers develop their own priority lists and then integrate them into a list for the entire organization. Certain departments may discover that the information they identify as top priority will be far down the list for the organization as a whole. In such cases the needs of the entire organization may well be the controlling factor.

Develop the New Information System. The organization-wide priority list should govern the design of the HRIS. Information judged not worth the cost would not be included. A system of required reports should be developed and diagrammed. The entire organization is treated as a unit to eliminate duplication of information.

Choose a Computer. Today, it is reasonable to assume that the HRIS of most organizations will be computerized. Because of the increasing reliance on computers, the human resource manager should be computer literate. The presence of computers is far too pervasive and their usefulness far too great for human resource managers to ignore their capabilities.

An Illustrative HRIS

Historically, the accounting information system was the first to be established in a firm, and the human resource information system was often the last. Firms now realize that a properly developed HRIS can provide tremendous benefits to the organization.

Figure 5-6 presents an overview of the human resource information system designed for one organization. Utilizing numerous types of input data, the HRIS makes available many types of output data that have far-reaching human resource planning and operational value. The HRIS ties all human resource information together into a system. Data from various input sources are integrated to provide the needed outputs. Information needed in the firm's human resource decision-making process is readily available when the system is properly designed. For instance, many firms are now studying historical trends to determine the best means of securing qualified applicants. In addition, complying with statutes and government regulations would be extremely difficult were it not for the modern HRIS. As the human component of the firm gains greater importance, use of the HRIS will likely continue to expand in the future.

CHAPTER 5   Human Resource Planning   165

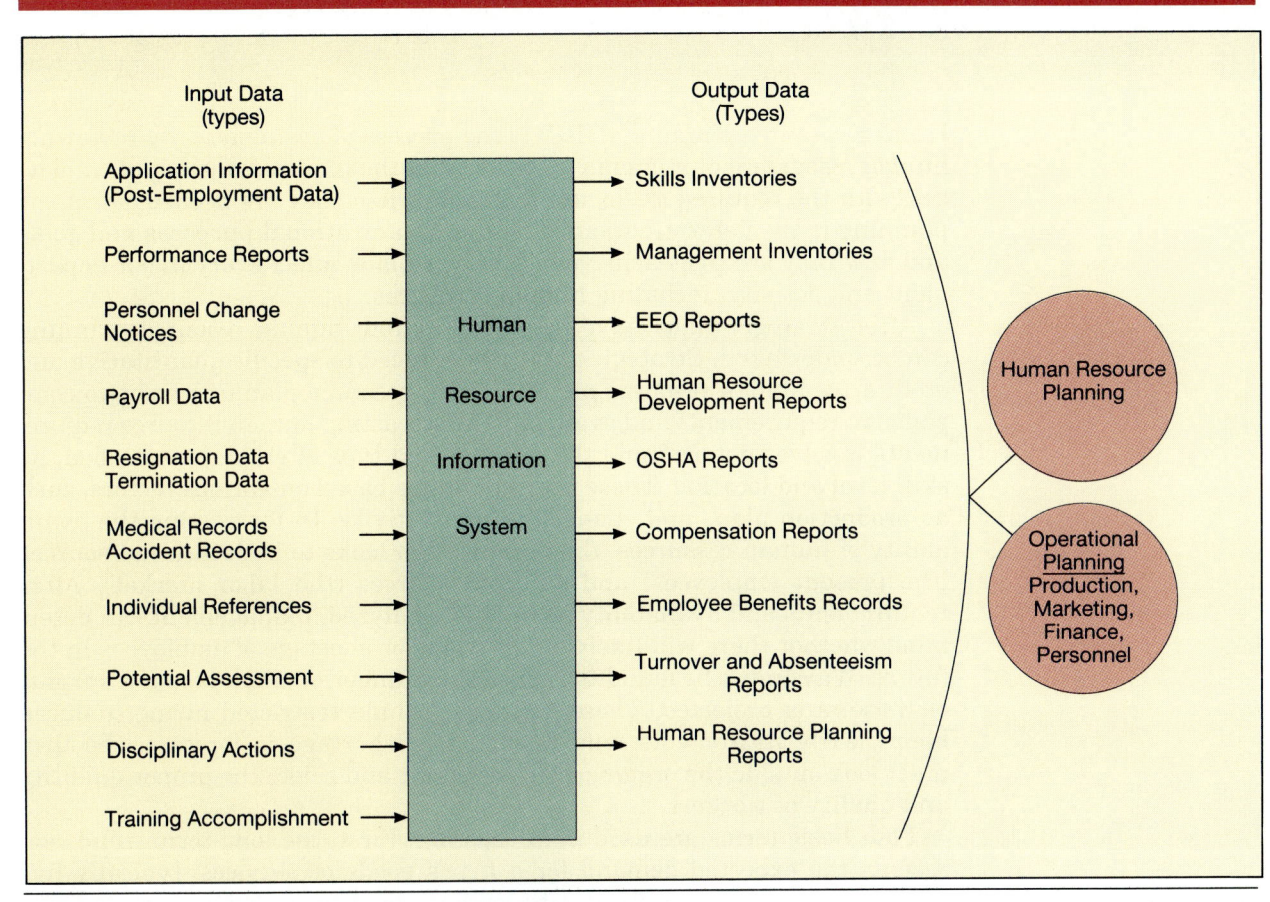

```
Input Data                              Output Data
 (types)                                  (Types)

Application Information          →  Skills Inventories
(Post-Employment Data)

Performance Reports              →  Management Inventories

Personnel Change                 →  EEO Reports
Notices                     Human
                           Resource    Human Resource
Payroll Data                     →  Development Reports
                          Information
Resignation Data                 →  OSHA Reports
Termination Data            System

Medical Records                  →  Compensation Reports
Accident Records

Individual References            →  Employee Benefits Records

Potential Assessment             →  Turnover and Absenteeism
                                     Reports

Disciplinary Actions             →  Human Resource Planning
                                     Reports

Training Accomplishment
```

(Human Resource Planning) — (Operational Planning: Production, Marketing, Finance, Personnel)

FIGURE 5-6 | A Human Resource Information System

One firm that has pioneered the development of human resource information systems is Information Science Incorporated (InSci). Founded in 1965, InSci was the first company to engage in the commercial development of computer-based human resource information systems. InSci's comprehensive concept of human resource management consists of human resource, payroll, pension, health claim, flexible compensation, and decision support systems. Today more than 1,000 organizations, including half of *Fortune*'s top 100 and 45 of the nation's largest banks, rely on InSci systems to help them manage their human resources effectively. One major advantage of the InSci system is its ability to provide management with information in the form required for planning.

SUMMARY

Human resource planning (HRP) is the process of systematically reviewing human resource requirements to ensure that the required number of employees, with the required skills, are available when they are needed. Strategic planning is the determination of overall organizational purposes and goals and how they are to be achieved. Strategic plans affect every major department and activity, including human resources.

After strategic plans have been formulated, human resource planning can be undertaken. Strategic plans are reduced to specific quantitative and qualitative human resource plans. Human resource planning has two components: requirements and availability. Forecasting human resource requirements involves determining the number and type of employees needed, by skill level and location. These projections are based on various factors, such as production plans and changes in productivity. In forecasting the availability of human resources, the organization looks to both internal sources (the present employees) and external sources (the labor market). After requirements and availability have been analyzed, management can determine whether there will likely be a surplus or shortage of employees in the future. Ways must be found to reduce the number of employees if a surplus of workers is projected. These methods include restricted hiring, reduced hours, early retirements, and layoffs. If a shortage is forecast, the firm must look outside the organization to recruit and select the proper quantity and quality of workers.

Four basic terms are used in forecasting. First, the long-term trend represents the expected demand for a firm's goods or services, typically five years or more into the future. Second, cyclical variation is a reasonably predictable movement about the trend line that occurs over a period of more than a year. Third, seasonal variations are reasonably predictable changes that occur over a period of a year. Finally, random variations are changes for which there are no patterns.

Several techniques of forecasting human resource requirements and availability are currently in use by human resource professionals. The zero-base forecasting approach uses the organization's current level of employment as the starting point for determining future staffing needs. The bottom-up approach is a forecasting method that progresses upward from lower organizational units to ultimately provide an aggregate forecast of employment needs for the organization. Another method is to use past employment levels as a predictor of future requirements. Regression analysis is used to predict one item (the dependent variable) through knowledge of other items (the independent variables). Simulation is a technique for testing alternatives on a mathematical model representing a real-world situation.

A management inventory contains information about each manager for use in identifying individuals having the potential to move into higher level positions. A skills inventory is information maintained on the availability and readiness of nonmanagerial employees to move into higher level or lateral positions.

A human resource information system (HRIS) is any organized approach for obtaining relevant and timely information on which to base human resource decisions. An effective HRIS typically employs computers and other sophisticated technologies to maintain and process information reflecting the day-to-day human resource operations. An HRIS organizes data and outputs to facilitate the decision-making process.

Questions for Review

1. Describe the human resource planning process.
2. Identify and define the basic terms used in demand forecasting.
3. Identify and briefly describe the methods used to forecast human resource needs.
4. Distinguish by definition and example between forecasting human resource requirements and availability.
5. What actions could a firm take if it had a worker surplus?
6. Distinguish between a management inventory and a skills inventory. What are the essential components of each?
7. What is the purpose of a human resource information system? What are the basic steps that should be considered in developing an HRIS?

Terms for Review

Human resource planning
Strategic planning
Long-term trend
Cyclical variations
Seasonal variations
Random variations
Zero-base forecasting
Bottom-up approach
Predicator variables

Regression analysis
Simulation
Requirements forecast
Availability forecast
Management inventory
Skills inventory
Human resource information system (HRIS)

INCIDENT 1 ■ A Degree for Meter Readers? ■

Judy Anderson was the personnel recruiter for South Illinois Electric Company (SIE), a small supplier of natural gas and electricity for Cairo, Illinois, and the surrounding area. The company had grown rapidly during the last half of the 1980s, and this growth was expected to continue into the 1990s. In January 1989, SIE purchased the utilities system serving neighboring Mitchell County. The expansion concerned Judy. The company workforce had increased by 30 percent the previous year and Judy had found it a struggle to recruit enough qualified job applicants. She knew that the new expansion will intensify the problem.

Meter readers were of particular concern. The tasks required in meter reading are relatively simple. A person drives to homes served by the company, finds the gas or electric meter, and records its current reading. If the meter has been tampered with, it is reported. Otherwise no decision making of any consequence is associated with the job. The reader performs no calculations. The pay was $8.00 per hour, high for unskilled work in the area. Even so, Judy had been having considerable difficulty keeping the 37 meter reader positions filled.

Judy was thinking about how to attract more job applicants when she received a call from the human resource director, Sam McCord. "Judy," Sam said, "I'm unhappy with the job specification calling for only a high school education for meter readers. In planning for the future we need better educated people in the company. I've decided to change the education requirement for the meter reader job from a high school diploma to a college degree." "But, Mr. McCord," protested Judy, "the company is growing rapidly. If we are to have enough people to fill those jobs we just can't insist on finding college applicants to perform such basic tasks. I don't see how we can meet our future needs for this job with such an unrealistic job qualification." Sam terminated the conversation abruptly by saying, "No, I don't agree. We need to upgrade all the people in our organization. This is just part of a general effort to do that. Anyway, I cleared this with the president before I decided to do it."

Questions

1. Should there be a minimum education requirement for the meter reader job? Discuss.
2. What is your opinion of Sam's effort to upgrade the people in the organization?
3. What legal ramifications, if any, should Sam have considered?

INCIDENT 2 ▪ A Busy Day ▪

David Johnson, human resource manager for Eagle Aircraft, had just returned from a brief vacation in Cozumel, Mexico. Eagle is a Wichita, Kansas, maker of small commercial aircraft. Eagle's workforce in 1989 totaled 236. Dave's friend Carl Edwards, vice-president of marketing, stopped by to ask Dave to lunch, as he often did. In the course of their conversation Carl asked Dave's opinion on the president's announcement concerning expansion. "What announcement?" was Dave's response.

Carl explained that there had been a special meeting of the executive council to announce a major expansion, involving a new plant, to be built near St. Louis, Missouri. He continued, "Everyone at the meeting seemed to be completely behind the president. Joe Davis, the controller, stressed our independent financial position; the production manager had done a complete work-up on the equipment we are going to need, including availability and cost information. And I have been pushing for this expansion for some time. So I was ready. I think it will be good for you too, Dave. The president said he expects employment to double in the next year."

As Carl left, Rex Schearer, a production supervisor, arrived. "Dave," said Rex, "the production manager jumped me Friday because maintenance doesn't have anybody qualified to work on the new digital lathe they are installing." "He's right," Dave replied, "Maintenance sent me a requisition last week. We'd better get hot and see if we can find someone." David knew that it was going to be another busy Monday.

Questions

1. What should David do, if anything, about being kept in the dark about the expansion? Explain.
2. Discuss any additional problems highlighted by the case and tell what should be done to solve them.

Experiencing Human Resource Management

This exercise is designed to give participants experience in dealing with some aspects of planning that a typical human resource manager faces. Students will also be exposed to some of the activities that human resource managers confront on a daily basis. The old axiom, "plan your work and work your plan," will probably have new meaning after this exercise.

You are the human resource manager at a large canning plant. Your plant produces several lines of canned food products that are shipped to wholesale distributors nationwide. You are responsible for the human resource activities at the plant.

It is Monday morning, August 30. You have just returned from a week long corporate executives' meeting at the home office. The meeting was attended by all human resource managers from every one of the company's plants. You returned with notes from the meeting and other materials you were given concerning the company's goals and plans for the next six months. When you arrive at your office (an hour early), you find your "in basket" full of notes, messages, and other correspondence.

The material provided to participants represents your notes and information from the meeting, plus what was in your "in basket." You must go through these and be prepared for the meeting the plant manager has scheduled for 8:00 A.M. It is now 7:30 A.M. Remember, you need to deal with some items immediately, some later today, and some tomorrow or later in the week, or some other time. You will need to sort, prioritize, and set up your plan of activities. Participants will sort the material and information according to some priority in order to sequence handling properly. After sorting, participants can address each item concerning the action they plan to take. The participants will do the following on each item:

1. Note when it is to be handled.
2. Note who is to handle it, if not themselves.
3. Note what is to be done or who is to be informed.
4. If a meeting is to be called, set up an agenda.
5. If a memo or notice is to be sent out, write it out.

Your instructor will provide the participants with additional information necessary to participate.

REFERENCES

Blair, Edward. "Bootstrapping Your HRIS Capabilities." *Personnel Administrator*, 33 (February 1988), pp. 68–72.

Holloway, William W. "Coping with Employee Turnover in the Age of High Technology." *Personnel Administrator*, 30 (May 1985), pp. 108–115.

Kustoff, Marc. "The Role of Human Resources Information Systems in Personnel." *Personnel*, 63 (November 1986), pp. 68–70.

Lawrie, John. "Skill Inventories: Pack for the Future." *Personnel Journal*, 66 (March 1987), pp. 127–130.

Mondy, R. Wayne, Robert M. Noe, and Robert E. Edwards. "What the Staffing Function Entails." *Personnel*, 63 (April 1986), pp. 55–58.

Montana, Patrick J. "Preretirement Planning: How Corporations Help." *Personnel Administrator*, 31 (June 1986), pp. 121–128.

Nkomo, Stella M. "The Theory and Practice of HR Planning: The Gap Still Remains." *Personnel Administrator*, 31 (August 1986), pp. 71–81.

Nyweide, Jeffrey O. "Simply Sophisticated." *Management World*, 16 (April–May 1987), pp. 34–36.

Perry, Stephen G. "The PC-Based HRIS." *Personnel Administrator*, 33 (February 1988), pp. 60–63.

Silverthorne, Colin P. "Planning for a Smaller Organization: A Guide for HR Managers." *Personnel*, 64 (March 1987), pp. 60–66.

Simon, Sidney H. "Accountability and Control of Human Resource Information." *Personnel Administrator,* 30 (July 1985), pp. 24–28.

Snyders, Jan. "A Dynamic Field for Software." *Infosystems*, 32 (August 1985), pp. 42–44.

Straight, Jay T., Jr. "Introducing CHRIS: Chevron's Human Resources Information System." *Personnel Administrator*, 32 (May 1987), pp. 24–27.

Silverhorn, Colin P. "Planning for a Smaller Organization: A Guide for HR Managers." *Personnel*, 64 (March 1987), pp. 60–67.

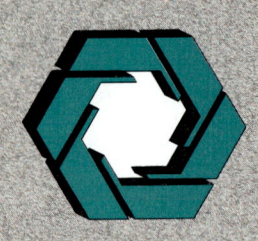

CHAPTER 6 RECRUITMENT

Chapter Objectives

1. Describe the recruitment process, explain why it is so closely related to human resource planning, and identify actions that a firm might consider before resorting to outside recruitment.
2. Describe the external and internal factors that can influence the recruitment process and explain internal recruitment methods.
3. Identify the various sources and methods available to an organization for external recruiting.
4. State what should be done to ensure that recruitment efforts meet legal requirements.

Dorothy Bryant, recruiting supervisor for International Manufacturing Company, had been promoted to her position after several years as a group leader in the production department. One of Dorothy's first assignments was to recruit two software design engineers for International. After considering various recruitment alternatives, Dorothy placed the following ad in a local newspaper with a circulation in excess of 1,000,000:

EMPLOYMENT OPPORTUNITY
FOR SOFTWARE DESIGN ENGINEERS
Progressive firm in growth industry has
2 positions available for software design
engineers with 3 years of computer related experience.
Apply Today! Send your resume, in
confidence, to: D. A. Bryant, International
Manufacturing Co., P.O. Box 1515, Alexandria, VA 22314

More than 300 applications were received in the first week and Dorothy was elated. However, when she reviewed the applicants, it appeared that few people possessed the desired qualifications for the job.

Dorothy has learned the importance of proper recruiting practices. She obviously failed to include important job requirements in her newspaper advertisement. As a result, an excessive number of unqualified persons applied. Determining the proper means to encourage potential future employees to apply for employment is extremely important. Tapping appropriate sources of applicants and utilizing appropriate recruitment methods are essential to maximize recruiting effectiveness.

We begin this chapter by describing the recruitment process and alternatives to recruitment. Next, we describe the external and internal environments of recruitment. Then, we present methods used in internal recruitment, external sources and external methods of recruitment, and how methods should be tailored to sources. We devote the final portion of the chapter to recruiting efforts under the law.

■ THE RECRUITMENT PROCESS

Recruitment is the process of attracting individuals on a timely basis, in sufficient numbers and with appropriate qualifications, and encouraging them to apply for jobs with an organization.[1] Applicants with qualifications most closely related to job specifications may then be selected. However, in practice, recruitment is often very demanding and seldom so straightforward. According to the recruitment director of a leading energy company, "Recruitment today is like marketing breakfast cereals . . . tough and competitive."[2] Unless a sufficient number of qualified prospects apply, a firm cannot have a truly selective employment system.[3]

In most medium-sized and large organizations, the human resource department is responsible for the recruitment process. In small firms, recruitment is likely the responsibility of individual managers. Regardless of who is responsible for the recruitment process, it is an essential function of every firm.

As you can see in Figure 6-1, when human resource planning indicates a need for employees, the firm may evaluate alternative ways to meet this demand. When other alternatives are not appropriate, the recruitment process starts. Frequently, recruitment begins when a manager initiates an employee requisition. The **employee requisition** is a document that specifies job title, department, the date the employee is needed for work, and other details (see Figure 6-2). With this information, the human resource manager can refer to the appropriate job description to determine the qualifications the person to be recruited needs. At times, firms continue to recruit even when they have no vacancies. This practice permits them to maintain recruitment contacts and to identify exceptional candidates for future employment.

The next step in the recruitment process is to determine whether qualified employees are available within the firm (the internal source) or must be recruited from external sources, such as colleges, universities, and other organizations. Because of the high cost of recruiting, organizations need to utilize the most productive recruitment sources and methods available. **Recruitment sources** are where qualified individuals can be found. **Recruitment methods** are the specific means by which potential employees can be attracted to the firm. When the sources of potential employees

---

[1] R. Wayne Mondy, Robert M. Noe, and Robert E. Edwards, "What the Staffing Function Entails," *Personnel*, 63 (April 1986), pp. 54–58.

[2] Murray J. Lubliner, "Developing Recruiting Literature That Pays Off," *Personnel Administrator*, 26 (February 1981), p. 51.

[3] Edwin S. Stanton, "The Sequential Selection System: The Key to Hiring Better People," *Training and Development Journal*, 33 (March 1979), p. 61.

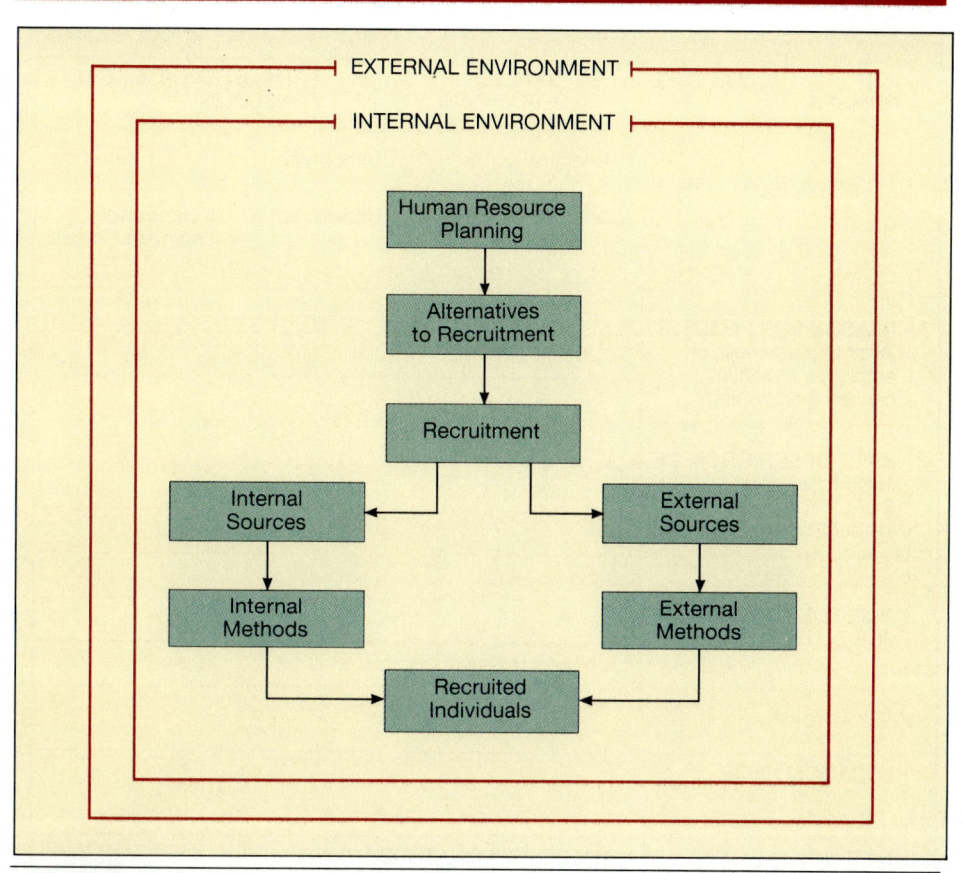

FIGURE 6-1 | The Recruitment Process

have been identified, appropriate methods for either internal or external recruitment are used to accomplish recruitment objectives.

Companies may discover that one recruitment method is superior to another for locating potential executive talent. For instance, one large equipment manufacturer determined that medium-sized, state-supported colleges and universities located in rural areas were good sources of potential managers. Other firms may determine the opposite. Thus in order to maximize recruiting effectiveness, utilizing recruitment sources and methods tailored to each organization's needs is vitally important.

▪ ALTERNATIVES TO RECRUITMENT

Even when human resource planning indicates a need for additional or replacement employees, a firm may decide against jumping immediately into recruitment efforts. Recruitment and selection costs are high. For example, one organization estimates the median cost-per-hire for a new employee

JOB NUMBER	JOB TITLE	DATE OF JOB VACANCY	DATE REPLACEMENT NEEDED

PLEASE CHECK	☐ Permanent	☐ Temporary	☐ Part-Time
	☐ Exempt	☐ Nonexempt	If Nonexempt, Enter Job Class

REASON FOR REQUEST: What management or employee action(s) caused the opening?	
BRIEF DESCRIPTION OF MINIMUM QUALIFICATIONS FOR THE JOB CANDIDATES:	
BRIEF DESCRIPTION OF JOB DUTIES:	

LOCATION NAME	
DATE	MANAGER'S SIGNATURE

FIGURE 6-2 | An Employee Requisition

to be $15,017, with a high-end cost of $27,030.[4] Often included in the calculation are costs of the search process, interviewing, agency fee payment, and relocation and processing of the new employee. Although selection decisions are not irreversible, once employees are placed on the payroll, they may be difficult to remove, even if their performance is marginal. Therefore, a firm should consider its alternatives carefully before engaging in recruitment. Alternatives to recruitment commonly include overtime, subcontracting, temporary employees, and employee leasing.

Overtime

Perhaps the most commonly used method of meeting short-term fluctuations in work volume is through the use of overtime. Overtime may help

---

[4] Margaret Magnus, "Is Your Recruitment All It Can Be?" *Personnel Journal*, 66 (February 1987), pp. 54–63.

both employer and employee. The employer may benefit by avoiding recruitment, selection, and training costs. The employee may benefit from a higher rate of pay.

Along with the obvious advantages of using overtime are potential problems. Many managers believe that when they work employees for unusually long periods of time, the company pays more and receives less in return. Employees may become fatigued and lack the energy to perform at a normal rate, especially when excessive overtime is required.

Two additional potential problems are related to the use of prolonged overtime. Employees may, consciously or not, pace themselves so that overtime will be assured. They may also become accustomed to the added income resulting from overtime pay. Employees may even elevate their standard of living to the level permitted by this additional income. Then, when overtime is no longer required, and the paycheck shrinks, employees may become disgruntled.

Subcontracting

Even though a long-term increase in demand for its goods or services is anticipated, an organization may still decide against further hiring. Rather, the firm may choose to subcontract the work to someone else. This approach has a special appeal when the subcontractor actually has greater expertise in producing certain goods or services. This arrangement often has considerable benefits for both parties.

Temporary Employees

The total cost of a permanent employee is generally estimated at 30 to 40 percent above gross pay. This does not include, among other things, the costs of recruitment. To avoid some of these costs and to maintain flexibility as workloads vary, many organizations utilize temporary employees. During certain periods in the past, as many as nine of ten companies in this country have used temporary-help services.[5] Temporary-help companies assist their clients by handling excess or special workloads. They assign their own employees to their customers and fulfill all the obligations normally associated with an employer.[6] The expenses of recruitment, absenteeism and turnover, and employee benefits are avoided. Suppose that the supervisor of the stenographic pool has an immediate, but short-term, need for six secretaries. Rather than recruit and hire additional employees, the supervisor calls a local organization that supplies temporary workers. This firm immediately sends the employees needed. These secretaries remain on the payroll of the temporary-help organization, which bills the using firm

---

[5] Charles J. Sigrist, "Nine Out of Ten Firms Use Temporary Help," *The Office*, 87 (January 1987), p. 90.

[6] Charles W. L. Deale, "How to Choose a Temporary Help Service: A Guide to Quality Supplemental Staffing," *Personnel Administrator*, 25 (December 1980), p. 56.

for their services. To illustrate the rapidly increasing popularity of firms specializing in providing "temps," one executive of a temporary-help firm stated, "In the last two years, our business has gone from $15 million to $45 million."[7]

Employee Leasing

An alternative to recruitment that has grown in popularity in recent years is employee leasing.[8] In employee leasing, a company obtains certain workers by contracting for the services of another company's employees. Employee leasing differs from temporary help services in that it focuses on placing employees permanently. Since passage of the Tax Equity and Fiscal Responsibility Act of 1982, employers who otherwise might be required to provide pension benefits can avoid this responsibility by leasing. Employee leasing is particularly attractive to small businesses because it avoids the expense and problems of human resource administration.

Another benefit of employee leasing is that it provides a way of avoiding union organizing activities or the requirement to recognize and bargain with an existing union. If the company that leases workers does not qualify as an "employer" under the National Labor Relations Act, employee leasing permits a firm to escape any requirement to recognize a representative of leased workers.[9]

Managers of temporary or leased workers generally find them to be well qualified and eager to please, though less tied to their employers than permanent employees. Major temporary-help and employee leasing firms have tight reporting systems to ensure that an employee fits in and does the job intended. Consequently, these employees are usually very productive and extremely beneficial to the using organization.

■ EXTERNAL ENVIRONMENT OF RECRUITMENT

As with the other human resource functions, the recruitment process doesn't take place in a vacuum. Factors external to the organization can significantly affect the firm's recruitment efforts. Of particular importance is the demand for and supply of specific skills in the labor market. If demand for a particular skill is high relative to supply, an extraordinary recruiting effort may be required. For instance, demand for technical salespeople is likely to be greater than their supply, relative to the demand–supply relationship for nontechnical employees.

When the unemployment rate in its labor market is high, a firm's recruitment process may be simplified. The number of unsolicited applicants is usually greater, and the increased size of the labor pool provides a better

---

[7] Magnus, p. 63.

[8] "Employee Leasing," *Newsweek* (May 14, 1984), p. 55.

[9] John V. Jansonius, "Use and Misuse of Employee Leasing," *Labor Law Journal*, 36 (January 1985), p. 35.

CHAPTER 6 Recruitment

opportunity for attracting qualified applicants. Conversely, as the unemployment rate drops, recruitment efforts must be increased and new sources explored.

Local labor market conditions are of primary importance in recruitment for most nonmanagerial, many supervisory, and even some middle-management positions. However, recruitment for executive and professional positions often extends to the national market. Although the recruiter's day-to-day activities provide a feel for the labor market, accurate employment data—found in professional journals and U.S. Department of Labor reports—is essential.

Legal considerations also play a significant role in recruitment practices in the United States. The individual and the employer first make contact during the recruitment process. Therefore, nondiscriminatory practices at this stage are absolutely essential. We discuss this topic later in this chapter.

The firm's corporate image is another important factor that affects recruitment. If employees believe that their employer deals with them fairly, the positive word-of-mouth support they provide is of great value to the firm. It assists in establishing credibility with prospective employees. Good reputations earned in this manner can result in more and better qualified applicants seeking employment with the firm. Prospective employees are more inclined to respond positively to the organization's recruitment efforts if the firm is praised by employees. The firm with an untarnished public image is one believed to be a "good place to work," and the recruitment efforts of such a firm are greatly enhanced.

■ INTERNAL ENVIRONMENT OF RECRUITMENT

Although the labor market and the government exert powerful external influences, the organization's own practices and policies also affect recruitment. A major internal factor that can greatly aid recruitment is human resource planning. In most cases, a firm cannot attract prospective employees in sufficient numbers and with the required skills overnight. Examining alternative sources of recruits and determining the most productive methods for obtaining them takes time. After identifying the best alternatives, the human resource manager can make appropriate recruitment plans.

An organization's promotion policy can also have a significant impact on recruitment. Basically, an organization can stress a policy of promotion from within its own ranks or a policy of filling positions from outside the organization. Depending on the circumstances, either approach may have merit.

Promotion from within is the policy of filling vacancies above entry-level positions with current employees. When an organization emphasizes promotion from within, its workers have an incentive to strive for advancement. When employees see co-workers being promoted, they become more aware of their own opportunities. Motivation provided by this practice often improves employee morale.

Another advantage of internal recruitment is that the organization is usually well aware of its employees' capabilities. An employee's job performance may not, by itself, be a reliable criterion for promotion. Nevertheless, many of the employee's personal and job-related qualities will be known. The employee has a track record, as opposed to being an "unknown quantity." Also, the company's investment in the individual may yield a higher return. Still another positive factor is the employee's knowledge of the firm, its policies, and its people.

Yet it is unlikely that a firm can or would even desire to adhere rigidly to a practice of promotion from within. The vice-president of human resources for a major automobile manufacturer offers this advice: "A strictly applied 'PFW' policy eventually leads to inbreeding, a lack of cross-fertilization, and a lack of creativity. A good goal, in my opinion, is to fill 80 percent of openings above entry-level positions from within." Frequently, new blood is needed to provide new ideas and innovation that must take place for firms to remain competitive. In such cases, even organizations with promotion from within policies may opt to look outside the organization for new talent. In any event, a promotion policy that first considers insiders is great for employee morale and motivation and is often beneficial to the organization.

Policies related to the employment of relatives may also affect a firm's recruitment efforts. The content of such policies varies greatly, but it is not uncommon for companies to have policies that discourage the employment of close relatives. This is especially true when their assignments would place them in the same department, under the same supervisor, or in supervisor–subordinate roles.

■ METHODS USED IN INTERNAL RECRUITMENT

Management should be able to identify current employees who are capable of filling positions as they become available. Helpful tools used for internal recruitment include management and skills inventories and job posting and bidding procedures. As we mentioned in Chapter 5, management and skills inventories permit organizations to determine whether current employees possess the qualifications for filling open positions. As a recruitment device, these inventories have proved to be extremely valuable to organizations when they are kept up to date. Inventories can be of tremendous value in locating talent internally and supporting the concept of promotion from within.

Job posting is a procedure for informing employees that job openings exist. **Job bidding** is a technique that permits employees who believe that they possess the required qualifications to apply for a posted job. Table 6-1 shows the procedure that a medium-sized firm might use. Larger firms often provide employees with a weekly list of job openings. Any qualified employee is encouraged to apply. Figure 6-3 shows an example of this approach.

The procedure followed by Texas Instruments minimizes the complaint commonly heard in many companies that insiders never hear of a job opening until it has been filled. Implementation of a job posting and bidding system avoids this problem. It reflects an openness that employees gener-

TABLE 6-1 | Job Posting and Bidding Procedure

Responsibility	Action Required
Personnel assistant	1. Upon receiving a *Human Resource Requisition*, write a memo to each appropriate supervisor stating that a job vacancy exists. The memo should include a job title, job number, pay grade, salary range, a summary of the basic duties performed, and the qualifications required for the job (data to be taken from job description/specification). 2. Ensure that a copy of this memo is posted on all company bulletin boards.
Supervisors	3. Make certain that every employee who might qualify for the position is made aware of the job opening.
Interested employee	4. Contact the Human Resource department.

ally value highly. In addition, this system can assist in college recruitment efforts. A firm that offers freedom of choice and encourages career growth has a distinct advantage over those organizations that don't.[10]

However, a job posting and bidding system does have some negative features. An effective system requires the expenditure of considerable time and money. When bidders are unsuccessful, someone must explain to them why they weren't chosen. If care has not been taken to ensure that the most qualified applicant is chosen, the system will lack credibility. Even successful implementation of such a system can't completely eliminate complaints.

■ EXTERNAL SOURCES OF RECRUITMENT

At times, a firm must look beyond itself to find employees, particularly when expanding its workforce. The following circumstances require external recruitment: (1) to fill entry-level jobs; (2) to acquire skills not possessed by current employees; and (3) to obtain employees with different backgrounds to provide new ideas. As Figure 6-4 shows, even when promotions are made internally, entry-level jobs must be filled from the outside. Thus after the president retires, a series of internal promotions are made. Ultimately, however, the firm has to recruit externally to fill the entry-level position of salary analyst. If the president's position had been filled from the outside, the chain-reaction promotions from within would not

---

[10] J. Robert Garcia, "Job Posting for Professional Staff," *Personnel Journal*, 60 (March 1981), p. 192.

1. If you are interested in any of the opportunities listed below, please complete a "Job Opportunity Request" form and submit it to your Job Opportunity Office. Forms may be obtained from your personnel department.
2. Each opportunity will be held open for consideration of TIers for one week. To be considered, your Job Opportunity Request must be received in your site Job Opportunity Office by no later than seven days from the date of this bulletin.
3. To qualify for a job, you must satisfy all requirements of the job and you must list these qualifications on your Job Opportunity Request form. A resume or additional information may be attached if desired but the required qualifications as described in the job posting must be listed on the Job Opportunity Request form.
4. Each opportunity is coded to indicate payment of transfer expenses in accordance with Personnel Procedure PM 2-3-4 (Transfer Expenses of TI Personnel) as follows:
    CR—Candidates urgently needed. Transfer expenses including Home Guarantee Program paid.
    ER—Internal and external candidates are being sought locally and nationally. Transfer expenses paid as listed in PM 2-3-4.
    LR—Adequate local supply of qualified people. TIers in other locations may bid with understanding that no transfer expenses will be paid by TI.
    For details of transfer expenses paid for by each of the above classifications, see your administrator.
5. JOB GRADES—On jobs in locations other than your own, see your personnel administrator for comparison with your grading system.
6. If you do not receive an answer to your Job Opportunity Request by four weeks from the date of this Bulletin, call Job Opportunity at Dallas Expressway 5336. Remember the Job Number in requesting information about your Job Opportunity Request.

NON-EXEMPT ADMINISTRATIVE

EQUIPMENT

CLK, GEN (JPN)01DN2040 (JRC)0922723053
DUTIES: Prmf gen cler tasks; oper IBM PC; oper calcul; some typg; maint logs, files, etc. MIN SKILL REQD: Prfm cler tasks. JG53: 1–3 yrs rel expr. JG55: 3–5 yrs rel expr. SECURITY CLEARANCE REQD Grd 53/55 LR–CC922

CLK, GEN (JPN)01DN2011 (JRC)0988723053
DUTIES: Oper various types of reprod/copy equip. Asst in oper of classified document contrl syst to include registration, transfer, filg % destruction of classified matl Typg ability reqd. Wrk hrs 10:30 a.m. – 7:00 p.m. MIN SKILL REQD: JG53: type 40–50 WPM, 1–5 yrs rel expr. JG55: type 50–60 WPM, 3–5 yrs rel expr. SECURITY CLEARANCE REQD. Grd 53/55 LR–CC988 s/lor Rotg

SECRETARY (JPN)01DN2016 (JRC)0431731053
DUTIES: Sec duties Contract Admin includg hvy data entry typg. filg, handlg classified documents, hvy phone liaison (cust/TI). JG53: over 1 yr dir rel expr. JG55: over 3 yrs dir rel expr MIN SKILL REQD: Typg 50–60 WPM. IBM PC expr helpful. Abil to wrk under pressure & get along well w/others. Dependable, mature. Contracts or purchasing expr helpful. MIN EDUC REQD: Some bus sch &/or coll prefd. SECURITY CLEARANCE REQD. Grd 53/55 LR–CC431

WORD PROCESS OPER (JPN)01DN2032 (JRC)0713723053
DUTIES: Data entry of draft copy, reprod copy & finished copy to meet contract data reqmts. Train on Word Procg Typg syst. Reqs attention to detail & sustained concentration f/long periods of time; abil to follow written, oral & mach-coded instructions. Prfm other rel duties as reqd. MIN SKILL REQD: JG53: 1–3 yrs rel expr & 40–50 WPM data entry. JG55: 3–5 yrs rel expr & 60 WPM typg. SECURITY CLEARANCE REQD. Grd 53/55 LR–CC713

FIGURE 6-3 | An Example of Texas Instruments' Job Posting System

Source: Texas Instruments, Inc.

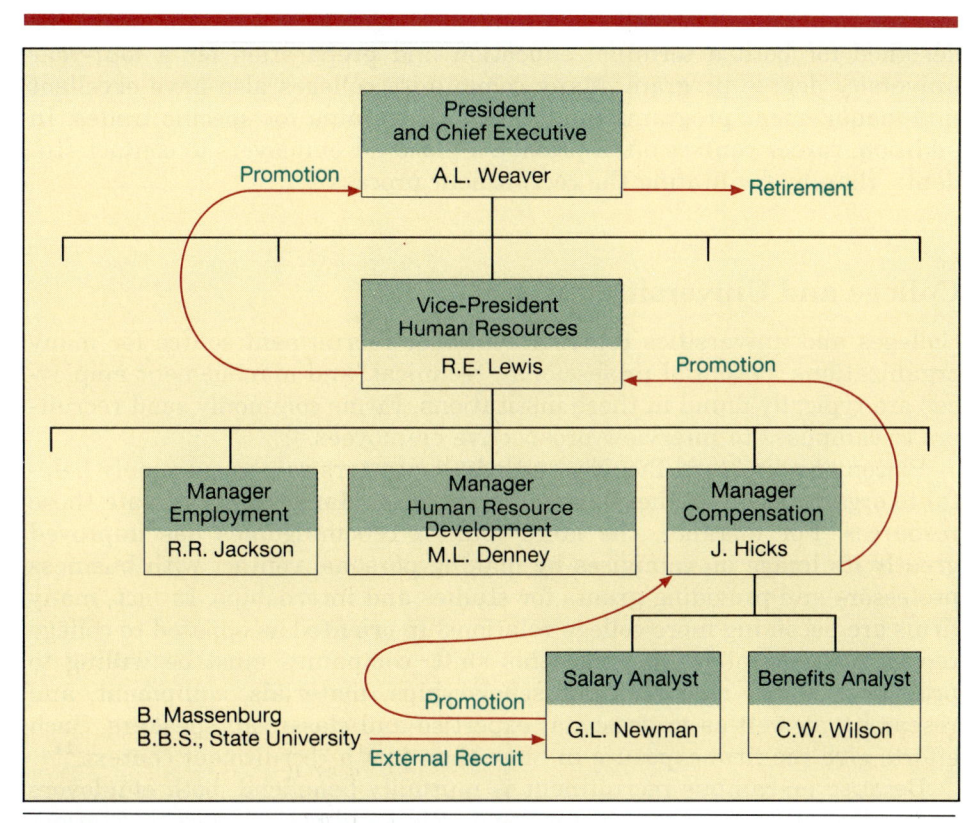

FIGURE 6-4 | Internal Promotion and External Recruitment

have occurred. Depending on the qualifications desired, employees may be attracted from a number of outside sources.

High Schools and Vocational Schools

Organizations concerned with recruiting clerical and other entry-level operative employees often depend heavily on high schools and vocational schools. Many schools have outstanding training programs for specific occupational skills, such as home-appliance repair and small-engine mechanics. Some companies work with schools to ensure a constant supply of trained individuals with specific job skills. In some areas, companies even loan employees to schools to assist in the training programs.

Community Colleges

Many community colleges are sensitive to the specific employment needs in their local labor markets and graduate highly sought after students with marketable skills. Typically, community colleges have two-year programs designed for both a terminal education and preparation for a four-year university degree program. Many community colleges also have excellent mid-management programs combined with training for specific trades. In addition, career centers often provide a place for employers to contact students, thereby facilitating the recruitment process.

College and Universities

Colleges and universities represent a major recruitment source for many organizations. Potential professional, technical, and management employees are typically found in these institutions. Firms commonly send recruiters to campuses to interview prospective employees.

Placement directors, faculty, and administrators can be extremely helpful to organizations in their search for recruits. Many firms cultivate these resources. For instance, the large retailer Bloomingdales has improved greatly its image on campuses by making personal contact with business professors and providing grants for studies and internships. In fact, many firms are becoming more college relationship oriented as opposed to college recruitment oriented. To make this shift, companies must be willing to provide financial resources (for scholarships, materials, equipment, and research), as well as professional expertise and classroom speakers. Such efforts give the firm exposure in more than just a recruitment context.[11]

Because on-campus recruitment is mutually beneficial, both employers and universities should take steps to develop and maintain close relationships. When a company establishes recruitment programs with educational institutions, it should continue those programs year after year to maintain an effective relationship with each school. It is important that the firm knows the school and that the school knows the firm.

Competitors and Other Firms

Competitors and other firms in the geographic area or industry may be the most important source of recruits for positions where recent experience is highly desired. The fact that approximately five percent of the working population, at any one time, is either actively seeking or receptive to change of position emphasizes the importance of these sources. Further, one of every three people—especially managers and professionals—changes jobs every five years.[12]

Even organizations that have strong policies of promotion from within must occasionally look elsewhere (which includes competitors) to fill important positions. When Cessna Aircraft entered the business-jet market, it needed a top sales executive with experience in this field. Cessna was able

---

[11] Magnus, p. 58.

[12] Dan Lionel, "Dow Jones Tests Recruitment Weekly," *Editor and Publisher* (May 24, 1980), p. 29.

to lure a successful executive from Pan American World Airways to run its marketing operations.[13] Other organizations are valuable sources of high-quality talent and raiding often occurs.

Smaller firms, in particular, look for employees who have been trained by larger organizations that have the necessary developmental resources. For instance, one optical firm believes that its own operation is not large enough to provide extensive training and development programs. Thus a person recruited by this firm for a significant management role is likely to have held at least two positions previously with a competitor.

The Unemployed

The unemployed often provide a valuable source of recruits. Qualified applicants join the unemployment rolls every day for various reasons. Companies may go out of business, cut back, or be merged with other firms leaving qualified workers without jobs. Employees are also fired sometimes merely because of personality differences with their bosses. Not infrequently, employees get fed up with their jobs and simply quit.

Self-Employed Workers

Finally, the self-employed worker may also be a good potential recruit. Such individuals may constitute a source of applicants for any number of jobs requiring technical, professional, administrative, or entrepreneurial expertise within a firm.

■ EXTERNAL METHODS OF RECRUITMENT

By examining recruitment sources, a firm determines where potential job applicants are. It then seeks to attract them by specific recruitment methods. Recruitment methods such as advertising, employment agencies, and employee referrals may be effective in attracting individuals with virtually every type of skill. Recruiters, special events, and internships are used primarily to attract students, especially those attending colleges and universities. Also, executive search firms and professional organizations are particularly helpful in the recruitment of managerial and professional employees.

Advertising

Advertising communicates the firm's employment needs to the public through media such as radio, newspaper, television, and industry publica-

---

[13] Richard R. Conarroe, *Executive Search: A Guide For Recruiting Outstanding Executives* (New York: Van Nostrand Reinhold, 1976), p. 8.

tions. In determining the content of an advertising message, a firm must decide on the corporate image it wants to project. Obviously, the firm should give prospective employees a clear and honest picture of the job and the organization. At the same time, the firm should attempt to appeal to the self-interest of prospective employees, emphasizing the unique qualities of the job. The advertisement must tell them why they should be interested in that particular job and organization. The message should also indicate how an applicant is to respond: apply in person, by telephone, or submit a résumé.

The firm's previous experience with various media should suggest the approach to be taken for specific types of jobs. The least expensive form of advertising that provides the broadest coverage is probably the newspaper advertisement. Many firms use help-wanted advertising, and studies indicate that approximately 40 percent of all jobs are filled through recruitment advertising.[14] The greatest problem with its use is the large number of unqualified individuals who respond to such ads.

Although no one bases a decision to change jobs on an advertisement, an ad creates awareness, generates interest, and encourages a prospect to seek more information about the firm and the job opportunities that it provides.[15] Examination of the Sunday edition of any major newspaper reveals the extensive use of advertising in recruiting virtually every type of employee.

Certain media attract audiences that are more homogeneous in terms of employment skills, education, and orientation. Advertisements placed in publications such as the *Wall Street Journal* relate primarily to managerial, professional, and technical positions. The readers generally are individuals who are qualified for many of the positions advertised. Focusing on a specific labor market minimizes the likelihood of receiving marginally qualified or even totally unqualified applicants.

Virtually every professional group publishes a journal that is widely read by its members. Advertising for a human resource executive position in *Personnel Administrator*, for example, would be an excellent choice because it is read almost exclusively by human resource professionals.

Trade journals are widely utilized, but their use presents some problems.[16] For example, regional editions are not offered, so the journals may be useless to the employer who wants to avoid paying relocation expenses. Also, they lack scheduling flexibility. Their deadlines are usually thirty days prior to the issue date, and may be even further in advance for four-color material. Since staffing needs cannot always be anticipated far in advance, the use of trade journals for recruitment obviously is not too helpful at times.

Recruitment advertisers assume that qualified prospects who read job ads in newspapers and professional and trade journals are dissatisfied with

---

[14] James W. Schreier, "Deciphering Messages in Recruitment Ads," *Personnel Administrator*, 28 (March 1983), p. 35.

[15] Rick Stoops, "Recruitment," *Personnel Journal*, 63 (December 1984), p. 60.

[16] Jo Bredwell, "The Use of Broadcast Advertising for Recruitment," *Personnel Administrator*, 26 (February 1981), p. 45.

their present jobs to the extent that they will pursue opportunities advertised. This is not always the case, especially for those qualified individuals who are not actively considering a job change. Therefore, in high-demand situations, the firm needs to consider *all* available media resources.[17]

Other media that can also be used include radio, billboards, and television. These methods are likely to be more expensive than newspapers or journals, but they have been used with success in specific situations. For instance, a regional medical center used billboards successfully to attract registered nurses. One large manufacturing firm achieved considerable success in advertising for production trainees by means of spot advertisements on the radio. A large electronics firm used television to attract experienced engineers when it opened a new facility and needed more engineers immediately. Thus in situations where hiring needs are urgent, television and radio may provide good results although by themselves, they may not be sufficient. Broadcast messages can alert people to the fact that an organization is seeking recruits, but they are limited in their ability to provide much more information than the general type of job available and company address and phone number. For this reason, broadcasting and print media are often used together to attract qualified applicants.[18]

Employment Agencies—Private and Public

An **employment agency** is an organization that helps firms to recruit employees and, at the same time, aids individuals in their attempts to locate jobs. They perform many recruitment and selection functions for the employer. The tasks that employment agencies perform have proven quite beneficial to many organizations.

Private employment agencies are utilized by firms for virtually every type of position. However, they are best known for recruiting white-collar employees. Although some parts of the industry have a bad reputation, a number of highly reputable employment agencies have operated successfully for decades. Difficulties that occasionally occur stem from a lack of industry standards. The quality of a particular agency depends on the professionalism of its management. Even though problems may exist, private employment agencies offer an important service in bringing qualified applicants and open positions together. They should not be overlooked by either the organization or the job applicant. Individuals are often turned off by the fees that agencies charge. However, the fee is frequently paid by the employer. An example of a typical employment agency fee schedule is shown in Table 6-2. Fee percentages are based on gross salary.

The public employment agencies operated by each state receive overall policy direction from the U.S. Employment Service. Public employment agencies are best known for recruiting and placing individuals in operative jobs. But recently they have become increasingly involved in matching peo-

---

[17] Lionel, p. 29.
[18] Margaret M. Nemec, "Recruitment Advertising—It's More Than Just 'Help Wanted,'" *Personnel Administrator*, 26 (February 1981), p. 57.

Executive Insights

Susan J. Marks, SPHR, CPC
President, ProStaff, Milwaukee, Wisconsin

Susan Marks is president of ProStaff, Milwaukee, Wisconsin, a human resource consulting firm providing both permanent and temporary personnel services. She is a past national president of the International Association for Personnel Women (IAPW) and the current treasurer of the Personnel Accreditation Institute (PAI), a subsidiary of the Society for Human Resource Management. With PAI, her challenge is to help distinguish the human resource profession through its credentialing process.

Prior to founding ProStaff, Marks spent four years as manager and principal of a Milwaukee personnel firm. Today, as president of ProStaff, her many responsibilities include management of both client development and service activities, and individual consulting and personnel search and placement in the human resource area.

Founded in 1981, ProStaff has grown to a multiemployee, multispecialty human resource firm, serving several hundred clients in Wisconsin and nationally. Marks has overseen the firm's tremendous growth and expects it to continue.

A graduate of Marquette University in Milwaukee, Marks holds a B.S. degree in business administration, with a major in human resource management. She was awarded the Senior Professional in Human Resources Designation in December 1984 from the Personnel Accreditation Institute and the Certified Personnel Consultants Designation in June 1978 from the National Association of Personnel Consultants.

Her many professional affiliations include the International Association for Personnel Women, of which she was the founder and president of the Milwaukee affiliate in 1980. She served as a conference co-director, secretary/treasurer, and president-elect prior to being named the association's president in 1985.

Marks has also received a service award the past three years from the Personnel Industrial Relations Association of Wisconsin, an organization she has been involved with since 1981. She is also on the board of Future Milwaukee, a community-based leadership development program.

TABLE 6-2 | Typical Employment Agency Fee Schedule

Annual Gross Salary	Fee
$ 0–$9,999	10%
10,000–10,999	11
11,000–11,999	12
12,000–12,999	13
13,000–13,999	14
14,000–14,999	15
15,000–15,999	16
16,000–16,999	17
17,000–17,999	18
18,000–18,999	19
19,000–19,999	20
20,000–20,999	21
21,000–21,999	22
22,000–22,999	23
23,000–23,999	24
24,000–24,999	25
25,000–25,999	26
26,000–26,999	27
27,000–27,999	28
28,000–28,999	29
29,000+	30

ple with technical, professional, and managerial positions. Some public agencies utilize computerized job matching systems to aid in the recruitment process. Public employment agencies provide their services without charge to either the employer or prospective employee.

Recruiters

The most common use of recruiters is with technical and vocational schools, community colleges, colleges, and universities. The key contact for recruiters on college and university campuses is often the director of student placement. This administrator is in an excellent position to arrange interviews with students possessing the qualifications desired by the firm. Placement services help organizations utilize their recruiters efficiently. Qualified candidates are identified, interviews are scheduled, and suitable rooms are provided for interviews.

The company recruiter plays a vital role in attracting applicants. The interviewee often perceives the recruiter's actions as a reflection of the character of the firm. If the recruiter is dull, the interviewee may think the company dull; if the recruiter is apathetic, discourteous, or vulgar, the interviewee may well attribute all these negative characteristics to the firm. Recruiters must always be aware of the image they present at the screening interview because it makes a lasting impression.

Recruiters determine which individuals possess the best qualifications and therefore should be encouraged in their interest in the firm. In making this determination, the recruiter becomes involved with the interviewee in two-way communication about the company, its products, its general organizational structure, its policies, its compensation and benefits program, and the position to be filled. The recruiter will also ask the prospect numerous questions, which may range from "What position do you want to occupy five years from now?" to "How will your employment benefit our firm?" Although such questions may be difficult to answer, the recruiter expects the prospect to respond in some logical manner. Other questions may be more predictable, such as those relating to grades, extracurricular activities, employment while attending school, and hobbies.

Considering the importance of the occasion, the interview is often short—about thirty minutes on average. Recruiters may spend over half this time discussing the student's high school and college education. Information sought and topics that may reveal this information are as follows:[19]

Intelligence and aptitudes	Grades
	Amount of effort to achieve grades
	College board scores
Motivation	Effort spent on academic work
Judgment and maturity	Decisions involving choice of college and major field
Analytical power	Reasons for subject preferences
Leadership and ability to get along with people	Participation in extracurricular activities

An applicant should prepare for the recruitment interview. In order to make a good impression, the prospect must do some homework on the company. The school's placement service often has literature that generally describes the organization and its operations. In addition, library research may yield information about the company's sales volume, number of employees, products, and so on. Prospects armed with facts such as these can confidently engage the recruiter in conversation and ask relevant questions. Other things being equal, an informed prospect has a competitive advantage.

Numerous college placement offices have installed the visual equivalent of a juke box to handle recruiting messages from companies. The proliferation of video-disk equipment suggests that organizations utilize playback machines and disks at campus locations. In the near future, the high cost of travel for screening interviews may be reduced through the use of cable and satellite communications.[20]

---

[19] Richard A. Fear, *The Evaluation Interview*, 3rd ed. (New York: McGraw-Hill, 1984), pp. 74–75.

[20] Roy G. Foltz, "Recruiting Communications," *Personnel Administrator*, 26 (February 1981), p. 14.

Special Events

Holding **special events** is a recruiting method that involves an effort on the part of a single employer, or group of employers, to attract a large number of applicants for interviews. Job fairs, for example, are designed to bring together applicants and representatives of various companies. One convention held exclusively for women attracted 90 firms and about 4,000 prospects from 16 states. The president of the sponsoring organization stated, "Employers want good women but often don't know how to get them. Women want good jobs and don't know how to go about it."[21] From an employer's viewpoint, a primary advantage of job fairs is the opportunity to meet a large number of candidates in a short time—usually one or two days. More than a dozen commercial firms operate job fairs, but they are also frequently sponsored by government agencies, charitable organizations, and business alliances. They provide a recruitment method that offers the potential for a much lower cost per hire than traditional approaches.[22]

Internships

An **internship** is a special form of recruiting that involves placing a student in a temporary job with no obligation either by the company to permanently hire the student or by the student to accept a permanent position with the firm following graduation. An internship typically involves a temporary job for the summer months or a part-time job during the school year. In many instances, students alternate their schedule by working full-time one semester and becoming full-time students the next. During the internship, the student gets to view business practices first hand. At the same time, the intern contributes to the firm by performing needed tasks. Through this relationship, a student can determine whether a company would be a desirable employer. Similarly, the firm can make a sound judgment regarding the candidate's qualifications. Internships provide opportunities for students to bridge the gap from business theory to practice.

Internships have also proved useful in moving minorities into the workforce. Bob Edwards, senior vice-president, Drake Beam Morin, Inc., describes a program he helped implement for a former employer:

> The successful integration of our office workforce after the Civil Rights legislation in 1964 required innovative approaches to selection as well as placement of minorities. The business leaders in the city were not yet confident that an acceptable solution could be found to answer the critics of integration or those advocates who did not want to weaken their companies' performance by active compliance. We elected to deal with this important issue

---

[21] "Career Conventions Open Doors To Jobs," *Nation's Business* (December 1981), p. 86.

[22] Gloria Glickstein and Donald C. Z. Ramer, "The Alternative Employment Marketplace," *Personnel Administrator*, 33 (February 1988), p. 101.

by strengthening our high school internship program. Business-minded students in this program were provided full-time summer jobs in our home office prior to their senior year and were moved to part-time jobs through their final school term.

Our approach provided:

1. Summer employment to a predominantly minority population.
2. Part-time employment, without giving any employment test, to high school students that more accurately reflected the demands of an adult work environment.
3. Maximum discretion for the student, as the company required no commitment beyond the school term.
4. Maximum discretion for the company, as full-time employment could be offered to those students who performed well on the internship jobs.
5. Up-to-date information for high school teachers and administrators on industry needs and hard data to motivate student development.

In summary, we integrated our workforce with performers and minimized management reluctance to enter an unknown and, in some situations, a feared adventure with a population whose background was different from their own. Our success with this approach was evidenced by the size of our employee minority population and their presence at all levels of responsibility.

Local communities also view favorably firms that offer internships. Internships serve as an effective public relations tool that provides visibility for the company name. As one recruiting manager stated, "There should be more internships to give students hands-on exposure. Internships provide an opportunity to give a little and get back a lot, especially in terms of productivity."[23]

Executive Search Firms

Executive search firms may be used by organizations in their recruitment efforts to locate experienced professionals and top level executives when other sources prove inadequate. **Executive search firms** are organizations that seek the most qualified executive available for a specific position and are generally retained by the companies needing specific types of individuals.[24]

In the past ten years, the executive search industry has evolved from a basic recruitment service to a highly sophisticated profession serving a

---

[23] Austin Weber, "Internships Offer Something to Root For," *Data Management*, 24 (May 1986), p. 8.

[24] Richard J. Cronin, "Executive Recruiters: Are They Necessary?" *Personnel Administrator*, 26 (February 1981), p. 32.

greatly expanded role. Search firms now assist organizations in determining their human resource needs, establishing compensation packages, and revising organizational structures.[25]

Most executive search firms differ from employment agencies and job advisory consultants in that they do not work for individuals. Retainer search firms work for corporations and governmental agencies, which pay the fees. These firms normally search in strict confidence for executives to fill upper management positions.[26] For example, Korn/Ferry International, a prominent firm of this type, has thirty-one offices around the world, of which thirteen are in the United States. They concentrate on executives earning in excess of $60,000.[27] Contingency search firms, which grew out of the employment agency industry, focus on lower management positions for which confidentiality is not so important or where multiple openings for a position exist. Unlike retainer search firms, these organizations are paid only when an individual is placed.[28]

An executive search firm's representatives often visit the client's offices and interview the company's management. This enables them to gain a clear understanding of the company's goals and the job qualifications required. After obtaining this information, they contact and interview potential candidates, check references, and refer the best qualified to the client for the selection decision. The search firm's fee is generally a percentage of the individual's compensation for the first year. Expenses, as well as the fee, are paid by the client.

The key problem in executive searches is poor communication between the client and the search firm. Face-to-face meetings are highly desirable in enabling the parties to agree on the specifications for the executive position. Competent executive search firms will be successful in their searches 70 to 80 percent of the time.[29]

The relationship between a client company and a search firm should be based on mutual trust and understanding. In order to be successful, the search firm must understand in detail the nature of the client's operations, the responsibilities of the position being filled, and the client's corporate culture. Similarly, the client must understand the search process, work with the consultant, and provide continuous, honest feedback.[30]

Professional Associations

Finance, marketing, accounting, and human resource professional associations provide recruitment and placement services for their members. The

---

[25] Cronin, p. 32.

[26] Norman E. Van Maldegiam, "Executive Pursuit," *Personnel Administrator*, 33 (September 1988), p. 95.

[27] Interview with J. Alvin Wakefield, senior vice-president and partner, Korn/Ferry International, August 9, 1982.

[28] Van Maldegiam, p. 95.

[29] Thomas A. Byrnes, "Why an Executive Search Fails," *Personnel Journal*, 60 (December 1981), pp. 922–923.

[30] Robert LoPresto, "Ethical Recruiting," *Personnel Administrator*, 31 (November 1986), pp. 90–91.

Society for Human Resource Management, for example, operates a job referral service for members seeking new positions and employers with positions to fill.

Employee Referrals

Many organizations have found that their employees can assist in the recruitment process. Employees often actively solicit applications from their friends and associates. In some organizations, especially where certain skills are scarce, this approach has proven quite effective. For example, one survey found that 27.8 percent of professional hires and 57.2 percent of management hires were from employee referrals.[31]

Unsolicited Applicants

If an organization has the reputation of being a good place to work, it may be able to attract qualified prospects even without extensive recruitment efforts. Acting on their own initiative, well-qualified workers may seek out a specific company to apply for a job. Unsolicited applicants who apply because they are favorably impressed with the firm's reputation often prove to be valuable employees.

Résumé Databases

Résumé database services, which are operated by several independent networks, obtain detailed information on job seekers' professional and educational backgrounds. These data are then fed into a central database, which is accessed by corporate clients using their own terminals. When an individual's background matches an open position, the client may obtain a copy of the potential employee's résumé to review. The use of computer technology greatly facilitates the process of matching candidates with positions and dramatically reduces paperwork costs.[32]

■ TAILORING RECRUITMENT METHODS TO SOURCES

Because each organization is unique in many ways, the types and qualifications of workers needed to fill positions vary greatly. Thus successful recruitment must be tailored to the needs of each firm. In addition, recruitment sources and methods often vary according to the type of position being filled.

---

[31] Magnus, p. 55.
[32] Glickstein and Ramer, p. 102.

CHAPTER 6   Recruitment

Figure 6-5 shows a matrix that depicts methods and sources of recruitment. A human resource professional must first identify the source (where prospective employees are) before choosing the methods (how to get them). Suppose, for example, that a large firm has an immediate need for an accounting manager with a minimum of five-years' experience. Most likely, such an individual is employed by another firm, very possibly a competitor, or is self-employed. The recruiter must then choose the method (or methods) of recruitment that offers the best opportunity for attracting qualified candidates. Perhaps the job can be advertised in the classified section of the *Wall Street Journal*, the *National Employment Weekly*, or *The CPA Journal*. Or an executive search firm may have to be employed to locate a qualified person. In addition, the recruiter may want to attend meetings of professional accounting associations. In all likelihood, other methods would be of little or no value in this case.

Suppose now, for example, that a firm needs twenty entry-level machine operators, which the firm is willing to train. High schools and vocational

	Advertising	Private employment agencies	Public employment agencies	Recruiters	Special events	Internships	Executive search firms	Unsolicited applications	Professional associations	Employee referrals	Unsolicited applicants
High schools											
Vocational schools											
Community colleges											
Colleges and universities											
Competitors and other firms	X	X					X		X		
Unemployed											
Self-employed											

METHODS OF RECRUITING

FIGURE 6-5 | Methods and Sources for Recruitment of a Data Processing Manager

HRM In Action

Mark Smith and Debra Coffee, two executives from competing firms, met at their annual product conference. They were discussing the effect of civil rights legislation on their firm. Mark said "I don't think we will have any difficulty at our company. I'm told that our workforce is composed of 35 percent minorities."

"Sounds good," Debra replied, "How many of your minorities fill middle-management positions?" After thinking a moment, Mark said, "I believe we have one over in maintenance."

As a human resource professional, how would you respond?

---

schools would probably be good recruitment sources. Methods of recruitment might include newspaper advertisements, public employment agencies, sending recruiters to vocational schools, and employee referrals.

The specific recruitment methods used will depend on external environmental factors, including market supply and job requirements. Each organization should maintain employment records and conduct its own research in order to determine which recruitment sources and methods are most appropriate under various circumstances.

■ RECRUITMENT UNDER THE LAW

In spite of equal opportunity laws, some human resource practices that continue to have an unequal impact on women and minorities are deeply embedded in some organizations. Some traditional employment systems, such as employee referrals, perpetuate the effects of past discrimination even after the original practices have been discontinued. The result, though not necessarily conscious, is a continuation of what has been labeled systemic discrimination.[33] Courts have found that some employment practices, regardless of intent, have resulted in discrimination against women and minorities.

Gender stereotypes may contribute to beliefs held by employers that members of one sex either do not prefer, or perform less well in, certain jobs than members of the other sex. To offset the effects of past discrimination in employment, firms may need to use new recruitment approaches. Because of past unequal opportunity, women and minorities may not

---

[33] Gary N. Powell, "The Effects of Sex and Gender on Recruitment," *Academy of Management Review*, 12 (October 1987), p. 732.

respond to traditional recruitment methods or be part of typical recruitment sources. Therefore, a recruitment program that is designed specifically to attract women and minorities should be implemented and carefully monitored for effectiveness.

Analysis of Recruitment Procedures

To ensure that its recruitment program is nondiscriminatory, a firm must analyze its recruitment procedures. For example, it might be wise to stop using employee referral or unsolicited applicants as primary recruitment methods. These actions may perpetuate the composition of the organization's workforce. In cases where minorities and women are not well represented at all levels, the courts have ruled that reliance on these particular practices is discriminatory.

In identifying sources of continuing discrimination, it is helpful to develop a record of applicant flow. In fact, this record may be mandatory if the firm has been found guilty of discrimination or operates under an AAP. An applicant flow record includes personal and job-related data concerning each applicant. It indicates whether a job offer was extended and, if no such offer was made, an explanation of the decision. Such records enable the organization to analyze its recruitment and selection practices related to minority and women candidates and take corrective action when necessary.

Utilization of Minorities and Women

Recruiters should be trained in the use of objective, job-related standards because they occupy a unique position in terms of encouraging or discouraging women and minorities to apply for jobs. Qualified minorities and women may be utilized effectively in key recruitment activities, such as visiting schools and colleges and participating in career days. They also are in an excellent position to provide valuable inputs for recruitment planning and can effectively serve as referral sources. Pictures of minority and women employees in help-wanted advertisements and company brochures give credibility to the message, "We are an equal opportunity employer."

Advertising

With few exceptions, jobs must be open to all individuals. Therefore, gender-segregated advertisements, for example, should not be used unless gender is a bona fide occupational qualification. The BFOQ exception provided in Title VII of the Civil Rights Act requires that qualifications be job related. This definition is narrowly interpreted by EEOC and the courts. The burden of proof is on the employer to establish that the requirements are essential for successful performance of the job.

Other advertising practices designed to provide equal opportunity include:

1. Ensuring that the content of advertisements does not indicate preference for any race, gender, or age or that these factors are a qualification for the job.

2. Utilizing media that are directed toward minorities, such as appropriate radio stations.
3. Emphasizing the intent to recruit both men and women by including the phrase "Equal Opportunity Employer, M/F" where jobs have traditionally been held by either men or women (see Figure 6-6).

Employment Agencies

An organization should emphasize its nondiscriminatory recruitment practices when utilizing employment agencies. Even when private agencies, which are also covered under Title VII, are retained, jobs at all levels should be listed with the state employment service. These agencies can provide valuable assistance to organizations seeking to fulfill affirmative action goals. In addition, agencies and consultant firms that specialize in minority and women applicants should be contacted.

Other Suggested Affirmative Recruitment Approaches

Personal contact should be made with counselors and administrators at high schools, vocational schools, and colleges with large minority and/or women enrollments. Counselors and administrators should be made aware that the organization is actively seeking minorities and women for jobs that they have not traditionally held. Also, they should be familiar with the

---

CORPORATE CONTROLLER

Sureway Development Company offers an outstanding opportunity for an individual with a degree in accounting and a minimum of 4 years experience. Background should include financial analysis and budgeting. Real estate development experience preferred and/or CPA. Please contact Mary Smith 318/255-1656.

Equal Opportunity Employer M/F

FIGURE 6-6 | A Newspaper Ad Stressing Equal Employment Opportunity for Men and Women

types of jobs available and the training and education needed to perform these jobs successfully. The possibilities for developing internships and summer employment for minorities and women should be carefully investigated. Firms should develop contact with minority, women's, and other community organizations. In general, these organizations include: National Association for the Advancement of Colored People, League of United Latin American Citizens, National Urban League, American Association of University Women, Federation of Business and Professional Women's Talent Bank, National Council of Negro Women, and the Veterans Administration. The EEOC's regional offices will assist employers in locating appropriate local agencies.

SUMMARY

Recruitment is the process of attracting individuals on a timely basis, in sufficient numbers and with appropriate qualifications, and encouraging them to apply for jobs with an organization. When human resource planning indicates a need for employees, a firm should first evaluate alternatives to hiring additional workers. Common alternatives to recruitment include overtime, subcontracting, temporary employees, and employee leasing.

When these other alternatives won't meet the demand, the recruitment process starts. Frequently, recruitment begins when a manager initiates an employee requisition. It specifies job title, department, the date the employee is needed for work, and other details. With this information, the human resource manager can refer to the appropriate job description to determine the qualifications needed by the person to be recruited.

The next step is to determine whether qualified employees are available within the firm (the internal source) or must be recruited externally from sources such as colleges, universities, and other organizations. Because of the high cost of recruiting, organizations must be assured that they are utilizing the most productive recruitment sources and methods. Recruitment sources are places where qualified individuals can be found. Recruitment methods are the specific means by which potential employees are attracted to the firm. After identifying the sources of potential employees, the human resource manager chooses the appropriate methods for internal and/or external recruitment.

External factors can significantly affect a firm's recruitment efforts. Of particular importance is the demand for and supply of specific skills in the labor market. If demand for a particular skill is high relative to supply, an extraordinary recruitment effort may be required. When the unemployment rate in the firm's labor market is high, its recruitment process may be simplified. Legal considerations and the firm's corporate image also play significant roles in recruitment practices in the United States.

An organization's promotion policy can also have a significant impact on recruitment. Basically, an organization can utilize two promotion approaches: a policy of promotion from within or a policy of filling positions from outside the organization. Depending on the circumstances, each approach may have merit.

Tools used for internal recruitment include management and skill inventories and job posting and bidding procedures. Management and skills inventories indicate whether current employees possess the qualifications needed for promotion. Job posting informs employees of job openings. Job bidding permits employees who believe that they possess the required qualifications to apply for a posted job.

Candidates for jobs may be attracted from various outside sources. Firms often depend heavily on high schools and vocational schools when recruiting clerical and other entry-level operative employees. Many community colleges are sensitive to specific employment needs in local labor markets and graduate highly sought after students. Colleges and universities represent a major source of recruitment for many organizations. Competitors and other firms in the same geographic area or industry may be the most important source of recruits for positions where recent experience is highly desired. The unemployed and the self-employed may also be good sources of recruits.

Recruitment methods such as advertising, employment agencies, and employee referrals may be effective in attracting individuals with virtually every type of skill. Recruiters, special events, and internships are used primarily to attract college and university students. Also, executive search firms and professional organizations are particularly useful in the recruitment of managerial and professional employees.

In spite of equal opportunity laws, many human resource practices that continue to have an unequal impact on women and minorities are deeply embedded in some organizations. Some traditional recruitment methods, such as employee referrals, perpetuate the effects of past discrimination even after the original practices have been discontinued. The result is a continuation of what has been labeled systemic discrimination.

To ensure that its recruitment program is nondiscriminatory, a firm must analyze its recruitment procedures. Continuing to use employee referral or unsolicited applicants as primary recruitment methods may perpetuate the present composition of the firm's workforce. Where minorities and women are not well represented at all levels, the courts have ruled that reliance on these particular practices is discriminatory.

Questions for Review

1. Describe the basic components of the recruitment process.
2. What are some actions that can be taken prior to engaging in recruitment?
3. List and discuss the various external and internal factors that may affect recruitment.
4. What is meant by the term internal recruitment? Describe the advantages and disadvantages of internal recruitment.
5. Describe the methods commonly used in internal recruitment. Briefly define each.
6. Discuss the reasons for an external recruitment program.

7. Distinguish between sources and methods of external recruitment. Identify various sources and methods of external recruitment.
8. Explain the difference between an executive search firm and an employment agency.
9. How can a firm improve its recruiting efforts under the law?

Terms for Review

Recruitment
Employee requisition
Recruitment sources
Recruitment methods
Promotion from within
Job posting

Job bidding
Advertising
Employment agency
Special events
Internship
Executive search firms

INCIDENT 1 ■ Right Idea, Wrong Song ■

Robert Key was human resource manager at Epler Manufacturing Company in Greenfield, Wisconsin. He was considering the need to recruit qualified blacks for Epler when Betty Alexander walked into his office. "Got a minute?" asked Betty, "I need to talk to you about the recruiting trip to Michigan State next week." "Sure," Robert replied, "but, first I need your advice about something. How can we get more blacks to apply for work here? We're running ads on WBEZ-TV along with the classified ads in the *Tribune*. I think you and John have made recruiting trips to every community college within 200 miles. We've encouraged employee referral, too, and I still think that's the most reliable source of new workers we have. But we just aren't getting any black applicants."

From the president on down, the management at Epler claimed commitment to equal employment opportunity. According to Robert, the commitment went much deeper than posting the usual placards and filing an "affirmative action program" with the federal government. Still, the percentage of black employees at Epler remained at only 5 percent, while the surrounding community was 11 percent black. Epler paid competitive wages and had a good training program.

One need was for machine operator trainees. The machines were not difficult to operate and there was no educational requirement for the job. There were also several clerical and management trainee positions open.

Questions

1. Evaluate the current recruitment effort. How could Robert better the firm's goal of equal employment?

INCIDENT 2 — Time to Do Something?

Five years ago when Bobby Bret joined Crystal Productions as a junior accountant, he felt that he was on his way up. He had just graduated with a B+ average from college, where he was well liked by his peers and by the faculty and had been an officer in several student organizations. Bobby had shown a natural ability to get along with people as well as to get things done. He remembered what Roger Friedman, the controller at Crystal, had told him when he was hired, "I think you will do well here, Bobby. You've come highly recommended. You are the kind of guy that can expect to move right on up the ladder."

Bobby felt that he had done a good job at Crystal and everybody seemed to like him. In addition, his performance appraisals had been excellent. However, after five years he was still a junior accountant. He had applied for two senior accountant positions that had come open, but they were both filled by people hired from outside the firm. When the accounting supervisor's job came open two years ago, Bobby had not applied. He was surprised when his new boss turned out to be a hot shot graduate of State University whose only experience was three years with a "Big Eight" accounting firm. Bobby had hoped that Ron Greene, a senior accountant he particularly respected, would get the job.

On the fifth anniversary of his employment at Crystal, Bobby decided it was time to do something. He made an appointment with the controller. At that meeting Bobby explained to Mr. Friedman that he had worked hard to obtain a promotion and shared his frustration about having been in the same job for so long. "Well," said Mr. Friedman, "you don't think that you were all that much better qualified than the people that we have hired, do you?" "No," said Bobby, "but, I think I could have handled the senior accountant job. Of course, the people you have hired are doing a great job too." The controller responded, "We just look at the qualifications of all of the applicants for each job and, considering everything, try to make a reasonable decision."

Questions

1. Explain the impact of a promotion-from-within policy on outside recruitment.
2. Do you believe that Bobby has a legitimate complaint? Explain.

EXPERIENCING HUMAN RESOURCE MANAGEMENT

Human resource managers have the responsibility for preparing job descriptions. From these job descriptions profiles of the types of individuals needed to fill various positions in the firm can be developed and recruitment efforts can be designed. The human resource manager must determine where the best applicants are located (recruitment sources) and how to entice them to join the organization (recruitment methods). This exercise is designed to provide an understanding of the relationship between recruitment sources and methods.

Each participant will identify both recruitment sources and methods for the job description. The job description is for a **Human Resource Assistant**, who reports to the Manager of Employee Relations and Recruitment, in the human resources department. **Accountability Objective** for the position is fairly standard. This position is accountable for performing employment activities for the off-site claims division in order to staff the organization with proficient, suitable personnel, and provide effective administration of personnel policies and procedures. The successful applicant will have a four-year college degree, preferably in business administration, but needs little or no experience because the candidate selected for the position will be placed in a six-month training program before assuming these duties and functions. Span of control is limited to two people, one clerk, and one secretary.

Primary duties of the incumbent include recruitment and interviewing of applicants for employment, and performing the basic employment function, which includes screening, recruiting, and interviewing candidates (clerical, technical, and professional), devising recruiting ads, performing reference checks, and administering standard skills tests where applicable.

The incumbent will function independently as a counseling source, and is expected to create an atmosphere of impartiality and equity, and will probably choose the appropriate method of communicating information to location personnel. The incumbent may also assess training needs for on-site personnel. In order to make personnel recommendations, the incumbent must be capable of maintaining an updated knowledge of all areas of human resources, a knowledge base of the external environment, and an awareness of the internal climate. Knowledge of the employment marketplace, as well as hiring practices and legal considerations, is required. Excellent interpersonal skills and the ability to establish rapport are also required.

Participants will attempt to determine the most appropriate recruitment sources and methods for the job description that will be given to them. Your instructor will provide the participants with additional information necessary to complete the exercise.

REFERENCES

Baier, L. L. "Job Searching and the Advertising Dilemma." *Personnel Administrator*, 29 (April 1984), pp. 22–24.

Baldwin, Wren. "I Am a Professional Temp . . ." *Personnel Journal*, 64 (October 1985), pp. 32–39.

Britt, Louis P. III. "Affirmative Action: Is There Life After Stotts?" *Personnel Journal*, 29 (September 1984), pp. 96–100.

Byrne, John A. "Punch Me Up a Future." *Forbes* (October 22, 1984), pp. 216–220.

Dennis, Donn L. "Evaluating Corporate Recruitment Efforts." *Personnel Administrator*, 30 (January 1985), pp. 21–26.

"Employee Leasing." *Newsweek* (May 14, 1984), p. 55.

Fader, Shirley Sloan. "Fielding Tough Questions." *Working Woman* (October 1984), pp. 64–68.

Fear, Richard A. *The Evaluation Interview*, 3rd ed. (New York: McGraw-Hill, 1984).

Ferron, Robbi. "Affirmative Action: A Program in Trouble." *Women in Business*, 38 (May–June 1986), pp. 30–31.

Feuer, Dale. "Adverse Impact: Can Your Hiring System Pass the Test?" *Training*, 22 (March 1985), pp. 111–112.

Foxmoon, Loretta D., and Walter L. Polsky. "Recruitment on a Budget." *Personnel Journal*, 64 (September 1985), pp. 26–28.

Gest, Ted. "Why Drive on Job Bias Is Still Going Strong." *U.S. News & World Report* (June 17, 1985), pp. 67–68.

Greenlaw, Paul S. "Affirmative Action or Reverse Discrimination." *Personnel Journal*, 61 (September 1985), p. 81.

Halcrow, Allan. "Anatomy of a Recruitment Ad." *Personnel Journal*, 64 (August 1985), pp. 64–65.

Hallett, Jeffrey J. "Why Does Recruitment Cost So Much?" *Personnel Administrator*, 31 (December 1986), pp. 22–24.

Hansen, Thomas J. "Recruitment." *Personnel Journal*, 64 (June 1985), pp. 114–121.

Hutton, Thomas J. "Recruiting the Entrepreneurial Executive." *Personnel Journal*, 30 (January 1985), pp. 35–41.

Ingber, Dina. "Omigod, I've Hired a Turkey: How to Pick Winners and Avoid Personnel Disasters." *Success* (June 1985), pp. 22–29.

Jansonius, John V. "Use and Misuse of Employee Leasing." *Labor Law Journal* (January 1985), pp. 35–41.

Kelley, Robert E. "The Gold-Collar Worker." *Success* (June 1985), pp. 38–41.

Kenney, Robert M. "The Open House Complements Recruitment Strategies." *Personnel Administrator*, 27 (March 1982), pp. 27–32.

LoPresto, Robert. "Ethical Recruiting." *Personnel Administrator*, 31 (November 1986), p. 90–92.

Lorber, Lawrence Z. "Employers Should Not Take Precipitous Action in Affirmative Action Cases." *Personnel Journal*, 29 (September 1984), pp. 101–102.

Magnus, Margaret. "Is Your Recruitment All It Can Be?" *Personnel Journal*, 66 (February 1987), pp. 54–63.

Magnus, Margaret. "Recruitment Ads at Work." *Personnel Journal*, 64 (August 1985), pp. 42–63.

Magnus, Margaret. "Recruitment Advantages." *Personnel Journal*, 65 (August 1986), pp. 58–79.

McCreary, Charles. "Recruitment: Don't Assume Anything About Executive Search Firms." *Personnel Journal*, 64 (October 1985), pp. 92–94.

McKendrick, J. "The Employee as Entrepreneur." *Management World*, 14 (January 1985), pp. 12–13.

McLaughlin, Mark. "Minority Recruitment Specialist Capitalizes on Racism and Sexism." *New England Business* (November 2, 1987), pp. 81–82.

Mondy, R. Wayne, Robert M. Noe, and Robert E. Edwards. "What the Staffing Function Entails." *Personnel*, 63 (April 1986), pp. 55–58.

Myers, D. C., and S. A. Fine. "Development of a Methodology to Obtain and Assess Applicant Experiences for Employment." *Public Personnel Management*, 14 (Spring 1985), pp. 51–64.

Powell, G. N. "Effects of Job Attributes and Recruiting Practices on Applicant Decisions: A Comparison." *Personnel Psychology*, 37 (Winter 1984), pp. 721–732.

Powell, Gary N. "The Effects of Sex and Gender on Recruitment." *Academy of Management Review*, 12 (October 1987), pp. 731–743.

Rohan, Thomas M. "Loaded Questions . . . Help to Hire the Right People." *Industry Week* (January 21, 1985), pp. 43–44.

Schenkel-Savitt, Susan, and Steven P. Seltzer. "Recruitment as a Successful Means of Affirmative Action." *Employee Relations Law Journal*, 13 (Winter 1987), pp. 165–179.

"Sexual Harassment." *Supervision*, 46 (August 1984), p. 20.

Skeegan, Sam. "Six Steps to Hiring Success." *Management World*, 14 (May 1985), pp. 11–13.

Stacy, Donald R. "A Case Against Extending the Adverse Impact Doctrine to ADEA." *Employee Relations Law Journal*, 10 (Winter 1984–85), pp. 437–455.

"Star Tracks." *Forbes* (October 8, 1984), p. 228.

"Recruitment: The Supply and Demand of College Recruiting." *Personnel Journal*, 64 (April 1985), pp. 84, 86.

Waldo, William S., and Bernadette M. Davison. "Renewed Affirmative Action Enforcement Is Imminent." *Personnel Journal*, 66 (November 1987), pp. 59–62.

Webb, Susan L. "Sexual Harassment: Court Costs Rise for Persistent Problem." *Management Review* (December 1984), pp. 25–28.

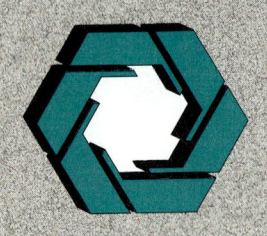

CHAPTER 7 SELECTION

CHAPTER OBJECTIVES

1. Explain how environmental factors affect the selection process.
2. Describe the importance of the preliminary interview and the application for employment in the selection process.
3. State the role of tests and the importance of interviewing in the selection process.
4. State why reference checks and background investigations are conducted, describe the reasons for preemployment physical examinations, and explain the considerations related to acceptance or rejection of job applicants.
5. Explain selection and utility analysis and describe human resource planning, recruitment, and selection in the multinational environment.

■ Bill Jenkins is the printing shop owner/manager of Quality Printing Company. Because of an increase in business, shop employees have been working overtime for almost a month. Last week, Bill put an ad in the newspaper to hire a printer. Three people applied for the job. Bill considered only one of them, Mark Ketchell, to be qualified. When he called Mark's previous employer in Detroit, he responded, "Mark is a diligent, hard-working person. He is as honest as the day is long. He knows his trade, too." Bill also found that Mark had left Detroit after he was divorced a few months ago and that his work had deteriorated slightly prior to the divorce. The next day, Bill asked Mark to operate one of the printing presses. Mark did so competently and Bill immediately decided to hire him.

■ Mary Howard is the shipping supervisor for McCarty-Holman Warehouse, a major food distributor. One of Mary's truck drivers just quit. She spoke to the human resource manager, Tom Sullivan, who said that he would begin the search right away. The next day an advertisement appeared in the local paper for the position. Tom considered three of the fifteen applicants to be qualified and called them in for an initial interview. The next morning Tom called Mary and said, "I have three drivers that look like they fill the bill. When do you want me to set up an interview for you with them? I guess you'll want to give them a driving test at that time." Mary interviewed the three drivers and gave them each a driving test and then called Tom to tell him her choice. The next day the new driver reported to Mary for work.

These incidents provide only a brief look at the all-important selection process. In the first instance, Bill Jenkins, as owner/manager of a small printing shop, handled the entire selection process himself. In the second instance, Tom, the human resource manager, was heavily involved in the selection process but Mary made the actual decision. However, knowledge of the selection process was important in both situations.

We begin the chapter with a discussion of the selection process and the environmental factors that affect it. Then, we describe the preliminary interview and review of the application for employment. Next, we cover administration of selection tests, validity studies, cut-off scores, and psychological testing. In the ensuing sections, we present the employment interview, methods of interviewing, the interviewer, interview planning, and the interview process. We follow those topics with a discussion of reference checks, background investigation, and polygraph tests. We then describe factors related to the selection decision, physical examination, and acceptance or rejection of job applicants. We devote the remainder of the chapter to selection and utility analysis and human resource planning, recruitment, and selection in the multinational environment.

■ THE SELECTION PROCESS

Whereas recruitment encourages individuals to seek employment with a firm, the purpose of the selection process is to identify and employ the best qualified individuals for specific positions. **Selection** is the process of choosing from a group of applicants the individual best suited for a particular position. As you might expect, a firm's recruitment efforts have a significant impact on the efficiency of the selection process. The organization may be forced to employ marginally acceptable workers if recruitment attracts only a few qualified applicants.

Employee selection is perhaps the most significant task that managers perform. The importance of proper selection is emphasized in Executive Insights by Charles Brown, senior staff vice-president at Honeywell, Inc., who said: "Team building starts with the basic task of selection." If mediocre or poor performers are hired, a firm cannot long be successful even if it has perfect plans, a sound organizational structure, and finely tuned control systems. These organizational factors are not self-actuating. Competent people must be available to "make things happen."

Studies suggest that the differences between poor and superior performers significantly affect an organization. For example, the difference in productivity can amount to more than $20,000 per employee per year. Thus we can easily conclude that a firm which selects qualified employees can reap substantial benefits.[1]

The selection process affects, and is also affected by, the other human resource functions. For instance, if the selection process only provides the firm with marginally qualified workers, the organization may have to develop an extensive training program. If the compensation package is inferior to

---

[1] Vandra L. Huber, Margaret A. Neale, and Gregory B. Northcraft, "Decision Bias and Personnel Selection Strategies," *Organizational Behavior and Human Decision Processes*, 40 (August 1987), p. 136.

those provided by the firm's competition, attracting the best qualified applicants may be difficult or impossible.

As we emphasized in Chapter 4, job analysis provides data for preparing job descriptions and specifications, which in turn are essential for making good selection decisions. However, a real problem exists when selection criteria are different from what is actually required by the job.[2] Therefore, human resource managers must continually update job descriptions and specifications to ensure that only properly qualified employees are recruited.

Figure 7-1 shows the selection process in general. It typically begins with the preliminary interview, after which obviously unqualified candidates are rejected. Next, applicants complete the firm's application for employment, then progress through a series of selection tests, the employment interview, and reference and background checks. The successful applicant receives a company physical examination. The individual is employed if the physical examination is satisfactory. Several external and internal factors have an impact on the selection process, and the manager must take them into account in making selection decisions.

■ ENVIRONMENTAL FACTORS AFFECTING THE SELECTION PROCESS

A permanent, standardized screening process could greatly simplify the selection process. However, development of such a process—even if it were possible and desirable—would not eliminate deviations to meet the unique needs of particular situations. As one human resource manager expressed it, "The only thing certain is that exceptions will be made." And exceptions are often made in accordance with the following environmental factors.

Legal Considerations

As we described in Chapter 3, legislation, executive orders, and court decisions have had a major impact on human resource management. However, merely having knowledge of the legal aspects of selection is often insufficient. All human resource managers should also be aware of which selection criteria to avoid, based on the law and court decisions. Table 7-1 identifies selection criteria that obviously should not be used because of their discriminatory potential.

Speed of Decision Making

The time available to make the selection decision can have a major effect on the selection process. Suppose, for instance, that the production foreman for a manufacturing firm comes to the human resource manager's office

---
[2] Joseph D. Levesque, "Selecting and Managing Competent Managers," *Personnel Administrator*, 30 (March 1985), p. 64.

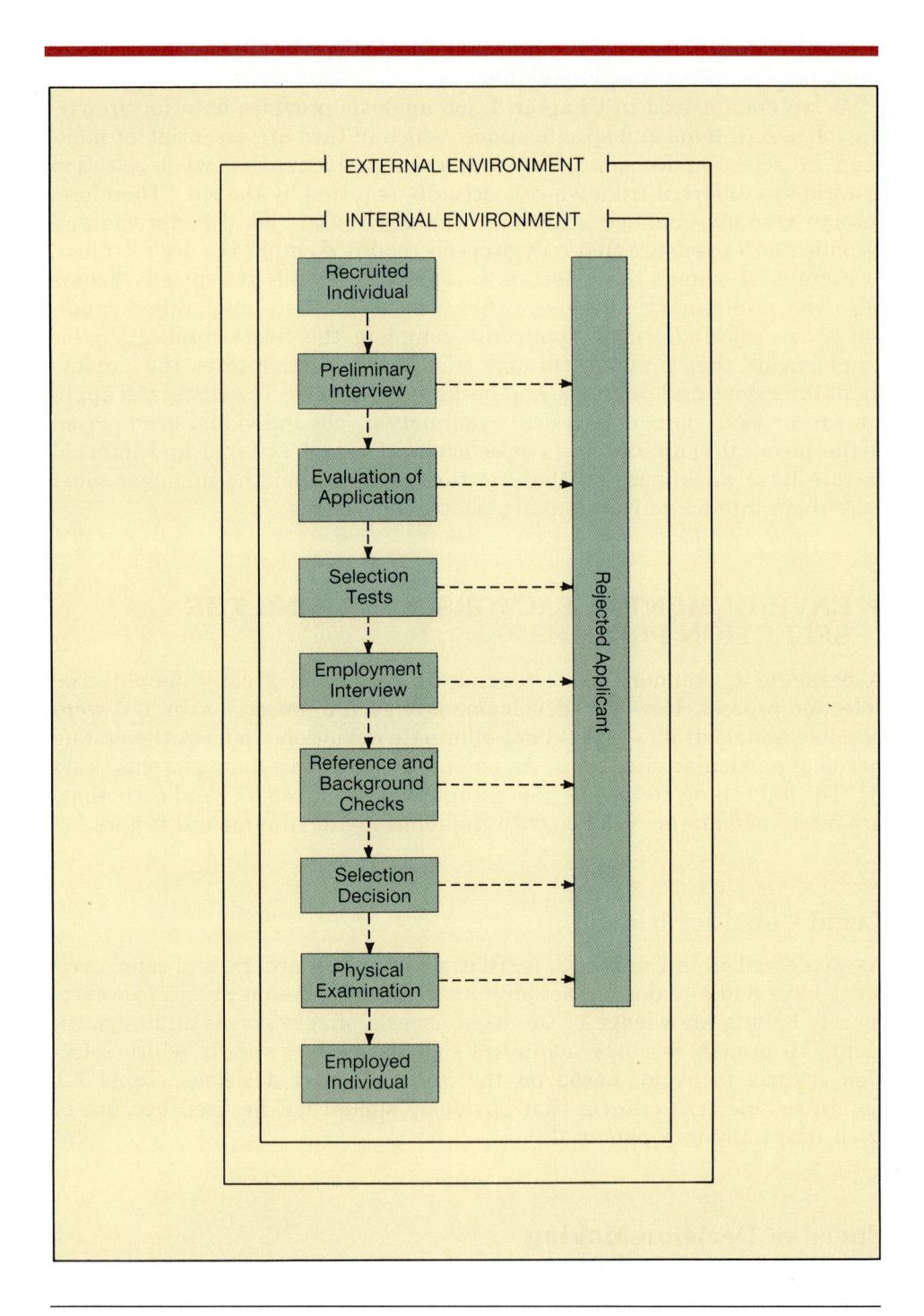

FIGURE 7-1 | The Selection Process

and says, "My only quality control inspectors just had a fight and both resigned. I can't operate until those positions are filled." Speed is crucial in this instance, and two interviews, a few phone calls, and a prayer may comprise the entire selection process. On the other hand, selecting a university dean may take an entire year, with considerable attention being devoted to careful study of résumés, intensive reference checking, and hours of interviews. Regardless of whether the process is casual and hurried or more careful and deliberate, errors will be made.

Organizational Hierarchy

Different approaches to selection are generally used for filling positions at different levels in the organization. For instance, consider the variations in hiring a top-level executive and in hiring a person to fill a clerical position. Extensive background checks and interviewing would be conducted to verify the character and capabilities of the applicant for a high-level position. However, an applicant for a clerical position would most likely take only a word processing test and perhaps have a short employment interview.

Applicant Pool

The number of applicants for a particular job can also affect the selection process. The process can be truly selective only if there are several qualified applicants for a particular position. However, only a few applicants with highly demanded skills may be available. The selection process then becomes a matter of choosing whomever is available. Expansion and contraction of the labor market also exert considerable influence on availability and thus the selection process.

The number of people hired for a particular job compared to the individuals in the applicant pool is often expressed as a **selection ratio**, or

$$\text{Selection ratio} = \frac{\text{Number of persons hired to fill a particular job}}{\text{Number of available applicants}}$$

A selection ratio of 1.00 indicates that there is one applicant for each position. Having an effective selection process is difficult if this situation exists. People who might otherwise be rejected are often hired. The lower the ratio falls below 1.00, the more alternatives the manager has in making a selection decision. For example, a selection ratio of 0.10 indicates that there are ten applicants for each position.

Type of Organization

The sector of the economy for which individuals are to be employed—private, governmental, or not-for-profit—can also affect the selection process. A business in the private sector is heavily profit oriented. Prospective employees are screened with regard to how they can help achieve profit

TABLE 7-1 | Hiring Criteria and Standards to Avoid

Gender

Hiring persons based on whether they are men or women is unlawful. The only exception is where gender is a bona fide occupational qualification (BFOQ). However, the use of BFOQs has been narrowly interpreted by EEOC and the courts. The specification of a man versus a woman must be made in view of whether gender is absolutely job related. For example, if the job in question is for an attendant for a women's restroom, gender can legitimately be specified.

Presuming that a particular job is physically too demanding for a woman to perform is also ill-advised. Instead, women applicants should be given the opportunity to prove that they can perform the job. For example, if a job requires frequent lifting of a fifty-pound object, an employer may require applicants to demonstrate that they—both men and women—can regularly lift the required weight.

National Origin

Information regarding an applicant's national origin should not be sought. In addition, other data that might be used to determine national origin should not be requested. Questions regarding an applicant's place of birth and the place of birth of parents, grandparents, or spouse fall into this category.

Marital Status

This is a difficult selection standard to defend and should be avoided. Although asking marital status is not by itself illegal under federal law, the standard has often been applied differently to women than to men.

Physical Handicap

The key factor in determining whether an applicant's physical handicap should be used in the selection decision is job relatedness. This standard applies to those employers with federal contracts of $2500 or more and in the states that have passed nondiscrimination laws on behalf of the handicapped.

Religion

Discrimination based on religious beliefs is generally unlawful. The only exception is when the employer is a religious corporation, association, educational institution, or society. Questions regarding the applicant's religious denomination, religious affiliation, church, parish, or religious holidays observed are generally ill-advised. Another form of discrimination occurs when individuals' religious beliefs cause them to be away from work before sundown, on Saturdays, or at other times. When this occurs, these practices should be reasonably accommodated unless undue hardships are imposed on the employer.

Race

Race is very rarely a legal employment requirement. Therefore selection decisions should be made without regard to this factor.

Age

Questions asked about an applicant's age or date of birth may be ill-advised in light of the Age Discrimination in Employment Act as amended. However, a firm may ask for age information to comply with the child labor law. For example, the question could be asked, "Are you under the age of 18?" With this exception, an applicant should not be asked his or her age or date of birth. Also, questions about the ages of children, if any, could be potentially discriminatory because a close approximation of the applicant's age often is obtained through knowledge of the ages of the children.

Pregnancy

Discrimination in employment based on pregnancy, childbirth, or complications arising from either is illegal. Questions regarding a woman's family and child-bearing plans should not be asked. Similarly, questions relating to family plans, birth control techniques, and the like may be viewed as discriminatory because they are not also asked of men.

Physical Requirements

Specifications that set a minimum height or weight should be used only when these characteristics are necessary for performing a particular job. Women, Hispanics, Asians, and Pacific Islanders are generally shorter and smaller than others. Therefore nonjob-related physical requirements would tend to reject a disproportionate number of individuals in those groups.

Standards relating to the ability to lift a certain amount of weight also should not be used unless they are clearly job related. At times, it may be feasible for the employer to redesign the job to overcome a weight-lifting requirement.

Credit Record

An individual's poor credit rating has been found to be an improper standard for rejecting applicants where this has a disproportionate negative effect on women and minorities. Members of certain groups are more likely to have credit problems than others. Therefore the standard should not be used unless the employer has a business necessity for obtaining the information. Inquiries about charge accounts, credit references, home, or car ownership should not be made unless they are job related.

TABLE 7-1 | *Continued*

Background of Spouse

Basing employment decisions on the background of a spouse is very difficult, if not impossible, to support. Some employers believe that they need to know what the spouse does for a living in making selection decisions. Merely asking this type of question may be interpreted as sex discrimination. In certain instances, women have been turned down for employment because the employer believed that a woman with a working husband would be denying an unemployed man the opportunity for a job.

Care of Children

Employers have, at times, denied employment to women who have nonschool-age children. If this standard is imposed on women and not on men, it amounts to sex discrimination. While it may be true that some women find it difficult to work and take care of children at the same time, the same can be said for men. A person should be evaluated on his or her ability to perform a particular job. The U.S. Supreme Court has clearly decided this issue.

Arrest Record

In our system of justice, an arrest is not an indication of guilt. Standards related to arrest records have been found to constitute race or national origin discrimination because the arrest rate for minority group members tends to be higher than that for nonminorities. Therefore this selection criterion can rarely be used as a justification for rejecting applicants from certain minority groups.

Conviction Record

Unlike an arrest record, a conviction record is an indication of guilt. Even though some minorities have a greater conviction rate than nonminorities, this standard may be used if it is job related. It would be quite acceptable to reject a job applicant who had been convicted of robbery if the job required handling of large sums of money. On the other hand, it would be difficult to justify rejecting an applicant for a laborer job if that individual had only been convicted for failure to pay alimony.

Work Experience Requirements

Experience requirements should be reviewed to ensure that they are actually job related. Many women and minorities have not been in the labor force long enough to gain extensive work experience. Requiring that a person have, for example, ten-years' work experience may tend to eliminate a large proportion of women and minorities and would be discriminatory if this experience is not actually needed to perform the job.

Garnishment Record

As with arrest and conviction records, members of certain minority groups have had their wages garnisheed more than nonminorities. Therefore, if knowledge of this information cannot be shown to be job related, it should not be used as an employment standard.

Dress and Appearance

Employers have the right to establish standards relating to dress and appearance. This is especially true in situations where the applicant is dealing directly with the public. Requiring hair to be a certain length has been found by the courts to be nondiscriminatory except when standards have varied by gender. Care should be taken when rejecting applicants strictly on their appearance. A person's appearance may be related to a special dress and style typical of a certain group.

Education Requirements

Nonjob-related educational standards should not be used because of their potential for discrimination. For example, the ability to speak English should be required only if it is job related. A disproportionate number of certain minorities have not graduated from high school or college. Stating that a job requires a college degree when it could be accomplished effectively by a high school graduate can potentially be discriminatory.

Any educational standard may be difficult to defend. Therefore it may be advisable to state such a standard in terms like "High school diploma or equivalent required."

Relatives Working for the Company (Antinepotism Rule)

Standards established about an applicant's relatives working for the company may be discriminatory if they result in reducing employment opportunities for members of women and minorities. Some firms have rules that prohibit hiring the spouse of a current employee. On the surface, this rule appears to affect men and women similarly. In reality, because men have normally been in the labor force longer, the rule reduces employment opportunities much more for women. Therefore antinepotism rules should be avoided unless they can be shown to be a business necessity.

---

goals. Consideration of the total individual, including personality factors, is involved in the selection of future employees for this sector.[3]

Government civil service systems typically identify qualified applicants through competitive examinations. Often, a manager is allowed to select only from among the top three applicants for a position. A manager in this

---

[3] Sampo V. Paunonen, Douglas N. Jackson, and Steven M. Oberman, "Personnel Selection Decisions: Effects of Applicant Personality and the Letter of Reference," *Organizational Behavior and Human Decision Processes*, 40 (August 1987), p. 97.

EXECUTIVE INSIGHTS

Charles E. Brown
Senior Staff Vice-President (Retired),
Honeywell, Inc.

Charles E. Brown says, "My career in employee relations came about quite by accident. After serving as a noncommissioned infantry officer in World War II, I was attached to a personnel unit. It was there that I first encountered the 'personnel business.' "

Returning to Indiana, Brown noted that a number of management schools had a personnel emphasis, which he decided to pursue. Many years later, as head of employee relations for Honeywell, he had human resource responsibilities for 100,000 employees in thirty-five countries.

Upon leaving Indiana University in 1949 with B.S. and M.S. degrees in personnel management, he joined the Glidden Company's corporate personnel staff. In 1959 he became director of industrial relations for the Cleveland Pneumatic Tool Company and in 1962 accepted an opportunity to join Honeywell, Inc., as director of industrial relations. This decision proved to be a good one, as he progressed steadily through the ranks to the highest human resource position in Honeywell.

He believes that a business enterprise, or a department of a business enterprise, is very much like a professional athletic team. "We are the managers of our teams, and we have players in various positions. We compete with other teams, winning some games and losing some, and we are highly interested in finding ways to improve our won–loss ratio." He suggests that team building starts with the basic task of selection and placement. "When we have big wins or losses they are normally traceable to a small group of managers who were well suited to the task, or vice versa."

Brown believes that managers should devote more time to the selection of new entrants into the department. He says, "We spend a lot of time examining proposals for new buildings and equipment, but we tend to neglect the process of carefully selecting the best qualified candidate for each opening."

When asked about motivation he replies, "What can you and I as managers do to cause people who work for us to apply their very best efforts? You might say, 'Pay them more than they can earn elsewhere,' and it is true that pay is an important factor. More important, however, is the working climate, which is made up of many ingredients. Among these important ingredients is the attitude employees have toward their job and toward the boss. Is the boss basically fair? Does he or she care about the well-being of employees? Is he or she approachable? Can an employee talk with the boss on issues of real concern, both business and personal matters?"

When asked what he would do differently if he were starting over in his chosen field of human resource management Brown replied, "I would learn more about my company's business—its products, customers, financial requirements, etc. I would establish priorities more carefully, concentrating on those items that are most critical to the success of the business. Finally, I would spend more time developing strong interpersonal relationships among employees at all levels so that I would know the organization more from personal contact than from studying reports."

sector frequently does not have the prerogative to interview other applicants.

Individuals being considered for positions in not-for-profit organizations (such as the Scouts or YMCA or YWCA) confront a different situation. The salary level may not be competitive with private and governmental organizations. Therefore a person who fills one of these positions must not only be qualified but also dedicated to this type of work.

Probationary Period

Many firms use a probationary period, which provides for the evaluation of an employee's ability based on performance. This may be either a substitute for, or a supplement to, the use of tests. The rationale is that if an individual can successfully perform the job during the probationary period, tests may not be needed. However, newly hired employees should be monitored to determine whether the hiring decision was a good one. Employees who voluntarily leave should have an exit interview. The results of this interview should be shared with all managers who are involved in the selection process.[4]

Even though a firm may be unionized, a new employee typically is not protected by the union-management agreement until after a certain probationary period. This period is typically from 60 to 90 days. During that time, an employee may be terminated with little or no justification. When the probationary period is over, terminating a marginal employee may prove to be quite difficult. When a firm is unionized, it becomes especially important for the selection process to identify the most productive workers. Once they come under the union–management agreement, its terms must be followed in changing the status of a worker.

■ PRELIMINARY INTERVIEW

The selection process often begins with an initial screening of applicants to eliminate those who obviously do not meet the position's requirements. At this stage, the interviewer asks a few straightforward questions. For instance, a position may require a degree in petroleum engineering and considerable work experience. If an applicant has no experience and a degree in an unrelated field, any further discussion regarding this particular position will prove useless for both the firm and the applicant.

In addition to eliminating obviously unqualified job applicants quickly, a preliminary interview may produce other positive benefits for the firm. It is likely that the position for which the applicant applied is not the only one available. A skilled interviewer will know about other vacancies in the firm and may be able to steer the prospective employee to another position. A person who does not qualify for one position may be capable of performing well in another. For instance, an applicant may obviously be unqualified to

---

[4] Alan Weiss, "Select, Don't Settle," *Training*, 24 (September 1987), p. 90.

fill the advertised position of senior programming analyst but be well qualified to work as a computer operator. This type of interviewing not only builds goodwill for the firm but also can maximize recruitment and selection effectiveness.

■ REVIEW OF APPLICATION FOR EMPLOYMENT

The next step in the selection process may involve having the prospective employee complete an application for employment. The employer then evaluates it to see whether there is an apparent match between the individual and the position. A well-designed and properly used application form can be a real time saver. It can be used much more effectively than résumés to reduce dozens of applicants to a few bona fide candidates. The application, creatively constructed to reveal a candidate's true qualifications, is making a comeback as a selection tool.[5]

The specific type of information requested on an application for employment may vary from firm to firm, and even by job type within an organization. An application form typically contains sections for name, address, telephone number, physical condition, military service, education, and work history.

An employment application form must reflect not only the firm's informational needs but also EEO requirements. An excellent example of a properly designed application form is provided in Figure 7-2. Potentially discriminatory questions, such as gender, race, age, and number of children living at home, have been eliminated from the form.

The information contained in a completed application for employment is compared to the job description to determine whether a potential match exists between the firm's requirements and the applicant's qualifications. As you might expect, this comparison is often difficult. Applicants frequently attempt to present themselves in a positive, somewhat unrealistic light. Comparing past duties and responsibilities with those needed for the job the applicant is seeking isn't always easy. A person with the title of "manager" in one firm may actually have performed few managerial tasks, whereas a person with the same title in another firm may have had a great deal of managerial responsibility.

Over the years, much effort has been devoted to using employment application data to assist in spotting individuals who will succeed and those who won't. Research results over the past fifty years suggest that the application can be a valuable predictor for certain types of positions. One technique for identifying factors that differentiate successful from less successful employees is the **weighted application blank (WAB)**. The WAB is an approach used to analyze variables such as long- and short-term employees, productive and less productive employees, and satisfied and less satisfied employees. One variable, years on the last job, is shown in Figure 7-3.

---

[5] Bradford D. Smart, "Progressive Approaches for Hiring the Best People," *Training and Development Journal*, 41 (September 1987), p. 49.

220　PART TWO　Human Resource Planning, Recruitment, and Selection

FIGURE 7-2 | **An Application for Employment**

Source: General Electric Company

Employment History

Please read carefully before starting. List all employment starting with **present** or **most recent** employer. Account for all periods, including unemployment and **service with the Armed Forces**. Also include relevant voluntary and/or part-time work experience. Use additional sheet if necessary.

Employer	Dates		Hourly Rate/Salary	
	From	Month / Year	Starting	$ per
Address	To	Month / Year	Final	$ per
Job Title	Describe Major Duties			
Department				
Supervisor	Reason For Leaving			

Employer	Dates		Hourly Rate/Salary	
	From	Month / Year	Starting	$ per
Address	To	Month / Year	Final	$ per
Job Title	Describe Major Duties			
Department				
Supervisor	Reason For Leaving			

Employer	Dates		Hourly Rate/Salary	
	From	Month / Year	Starting	$ per
Address	To	Month / Year	Final	$ per
Job Title	Describe Major Duties			
Department				
Supervisor	Reason For Leaving			

Employer	Dates		Hourly Rate/Salary	
	From	Month / Year	Starting	$ per
Address	To	Month / Year	Final	$ per
Job Title	Describe Major Duties			
Department				
Supervisor	Reason For Leaving			

Interviewer's Comments:

Interviewed By: _____ Date: _____

Continue on Next Page

Affirmative Action

Special Employment Notice To Disabled Veterans, Vietnam Era Veterans And Individuals With Physical Or Mental Handicaps:

Government contractors are subject to Section 402 of the Vietnam Era Veterans Readjustment Act of 1974 which requires that they take affirmative action to employ and advance in employment qualified disabled veterans and veterans of the Vietnam Era (i.e. served more than 180 days between August 5, 1964 and May 7, 1975), and Section 503 of the Rehabilitation Act of 1973, as amended, which requires government contractors to take affirmative action to employ and advance in employment qualified handicapped individuals.

Please Check Below If You Are A:
- ☐ Vietnam Era Veteran
- ☐ Disabled Veteran
- ☐ Handicapped Individual

And wish to be considered under our Affirmative Action Program(s). **Submission of this information is voluntary.**

Please read this carefully before signing:

Employee Release and Privacy Statement

I understand that the General Electric Company requires certain information about me to evaluate my qualifications for employment and to conduct its business if I become an employee. Therefore, I authorize the Company to investigate my past employment, educational credentials and other employment-related activities. I agree to cooperate in such investigations, and release those parties supplying such information to the Company from all liability or responsibility with respect to information supplied.

I agree that the Company may use the information it obtains concerning me in the conduct of its business. I understand that such use may include disclosure outside the Company in those cases where its agents and contractors need such information to perform their functions, where the Company's legal interests and/or obligations are involved, or where there is a medical emergency involving me. I understand, however, that the Company intends to protect the confidentiality of personal information it obtains concerning me. Consequently, personal information in Company recordkeeping systems, other than the fact and location of past or present Company employment, the dates of employment, or the job name or description of general duties, will not otherwise be disclosed outside the Company with a personal identifier without my consent. Further, the Company will require its agents and contractors to safeguard personal information disclosed to them by the Company.

I understand that any employment with the Company would not be for any fixed period of time and that, if employed, I may resign at any time for any reason or the Company may terminate my employment at any time for any reason in the absence of a specific written agreement to the contrary.

I understand that any false answers or statements made by me on this application or any supplement thereto or in connection with the above-mentioned investigations will be sufficient grounds for immediate discharge, if I am employed.

Applicant's Signature: _____ Date: _____

FIGURE 7-2 | *Continued*

	Percentage Responding			
Item	Short-term	Long-term	Difference	Weight
Years on the Last Job				
No response	4	12	+ 8	0
Less than 1	50	0	−50	−5
1–1 1/2	7	35	+28	+2
1 1/2–2 1/2	37	12	−25	−2
2 1/2–3	0	6	+ 6	0
More than 3	2	35	+33	+3

FIGURE 7-3 | An Example of a Weighted Application Blank Question

First, the percentage difference between short- and long-term workers is computed. Then a weight is assigned, based on the percentage difference. After the weights for all variables on the application have been calculated, applicants can be screened on the basis of their point totals. Using the WAB, applicants with the highest point totals are considered to have the greatest potential for success.

At times, the WAB has proved to be quite accurate. In spite of the WAB's ability to determine which factors are important for predicting tenure and job success, the overwhelming majority of U.S. firms continue to use traditional application forms.[6] And, in some instances, the WAB's benefits have been only marginal. Because this approach has produced some unsatisfactory results, many human resource researchers have turned to other quantitative techniques for evaluating employment application data, such as regression analysis and discriminant analysis (discussed in Chapter 19).

■ ADMINISTRATION OF SELECTION TESTS

Selection tests are often used to assist in assessing an applicant's qualifications and potential for success. The popularity of selection tests declined sharply following enactment of the Civil Rights Act and subsequent court decisions. For instance, in *Griggs, et al.* v. *Duke Power Company*, the U.S. Supreme Court ruled that preemployment requirements, including tests, must be related to job performance. In *Albermarle Paper* v. *Moody*, the Supreme Court ruled that any test used in the selection process or in promotion decisions must be validated if its use has had an adverse impact on women or minorities. For a selection test to be considered nondiscriminatory, it must conform to the *Uniform Guidelines*. The general standard is

---

[6] Daniel G. Lawrence, Barbara L. Salsburg, John G. Dawson, and Zachary D. Fashman, "Design and Use of Weighted Application Blanks," *Personnel Administrator*, 27 (March 1982), p. 47.

that if the use of test results has an adverse impact on women or minorities the employer will be required to show that it is job related; that is, the employer must validate the test.

By curtailing test usage, some employers apparently felt that they would be immune from legal requirements for valid instruments. Clearly, however, all the tools used in making selection and other employment decisions are subject to the same validity requirements. Although many individuals distrust tests, they may well be the most valid instrument available. Recognition of this—and increased awareness of the interview's vulnerability—has recently led to a resurgence of test usage in the selection process.[7]

Evidence suggests that the use of tests is more widespread in the public sector than in the private sector and in medium-sized and large companies than in small companies—and that large organizations are likely to have trained specialists to run their testing programs.[8] A survey of companies that use selection tests revealed that more than 80 percent use them for office positions, 20 percent for production positions, and only 10 percent for sales and service positions.[9]

Advantages of Selection Tests

Selection tests help managers make better hiring decisions. One example of the contribution of effective selection tests to productivity is provided by the Philadelphia Police Department. Labor savings in this 5,000-member organization from the use of cognitive ability tests to select officers has been estimated to be $18 million for each year's hires.[10]

In an earlier study, using a computer programming test as an example, it was suggested that if all 18,498 programmers employed by the federal government had been selected by the use of a specific test, the productivity gain would have been $1.2 billion. If use of this procedure were to include all programmers employed in the public and private sectors, the productivity gain would have been $10.78 billion.[11]

Disadvantages of Selection Tests

Job performance is related primarily to an individual's ability and motivation to do the job. Selection tests may accurately predict an applicant's ability to perform the job, but be less successful in indicating the extent to

---

[7] "Employee Selection Tests: Upping the Odds for Success," *Personnel*, 57 (November–December 1980), p. 48.

[8] "Ability Tests: They Can Provide Useful Information about the Probability of an Applicant's Performing Successfully on the Job," *Across the Board*, 19 (July–August 1982), p. 27.

[9] *Ibid.*

[10] John E. Hunter and Frank L. Schmidt, "Ability Tests: Economic Benefits versus the Issue of Fairness," *Industrial Relations*, 21 (Fall 1982), p. 293.

[11] Frank L. Schmidt, John E. Hunter, Robert C. McKenzie, and Tressie W. Muldrow, "Impact of Valid Selection Procedures on Work-Force Productivity," *Journal of Applied Psychology*, 64 (1979), p. 624.

which the individual will want to perform it. For one reason or another, many employees with high potential never seem to reach it. The factors related to success on the job are so numerous and complex that selection may always be more of an art than a science.

Another potential problem, related primarily to personality tests and interest inventories, has to do with applicants' honesty. An applicant may be strongly motivated to respond to questions untruthfully or provide answers that he or she believes the firm expects. To prevent this occurrence, some tests have built-in lie detection scales.

A common problem is test anxiety. Applicants often become quite anxious when confronting yet another hurdle that might eliminate them from consideration. The test administrator's reassuring manner and a well-organized testing operation should serve to reduce this threat. Actually, although a great deal of anxiety is detrimental to test performance, a slight amount is helpful.[12]

The dual problems of hiring unqualified or less qualified candidates and rejecting qualified candidates will continue regardless of the procedures followed. Organizations can minimize such errors through the use of well-developed tests administered by competent professionals. Nevertheless, selection tests rarely, if ever, are perfect predictors. Using even the best test, errors will be made in predicting success. For this reason, tests alone should not be used in the selection process but rather in conjunction with other tools.

Characteristics of Properly Designed Selection Tests

Properly designed selection tests are standardized, objective, based on sound norms, reliable, and—of utmost importance—valid. We discuss the application of these concepts next.

Standardization. **Standardization** refers to the uniformity of the procedures and conditions related to administering tests. In order to compare the performance of several applicants on the same test, it is necessary for all to take the test under conditions that are as close to identical as possible. For example, the content of instructions provided and the time allowed must be the same, and the physical environment must be similar. If one person takes a test in a noisy room and another takes it in a quiet environment, differences in test results are likely. Differences in conditions may affect an applicant's performance. Even though test administration procedures may be specified by a test's developers, test administrators are responsible for ensuring standardized conditions.

Objectivity. **Objectivity** in testing is achieved when everyone scoring a test obtains the same results. Multiple-choice and true–false tests are said to be objective. The person taking the test either chooses the correct answer

---
[12] Anne Anastasi, *Psychological Testing*, 5th ed. (New York: Macmillan, 1982), pp. 36–37.

CHAPTER 7   Selection

or does not. Scoring these tests is a highly mechanical process, which lends itself to machine grading.

Norms. A **norm** provides a frame of reference for comparing an applicant's performance with that of others. Specifically, a norm reflects the distribution of many scores obtained by people similar to the applicant being tested. The scores will tend to be distributed according to the normal probability curve presented in Figure 7-4. Standard deviations measure the amount of dispersion of the data. A normalized test will have approximately 68.3 percent of the scores within ±1 standard deviation from the mean. Individuals scoring in this range would be considered average. Individuals achieving scores outside the range of ±2 standard deviations would probably be highly unsuccessful or highly successful, based on the particular criteria used.

When a sufficient number of employees are performing the same or similar work, employers can standardize their own tests. Typically this is not the case, and national norm for a particular test must be used. A prospective employee takes the test, the score obtained is compared to the norm, and the significance of the test score is determined.

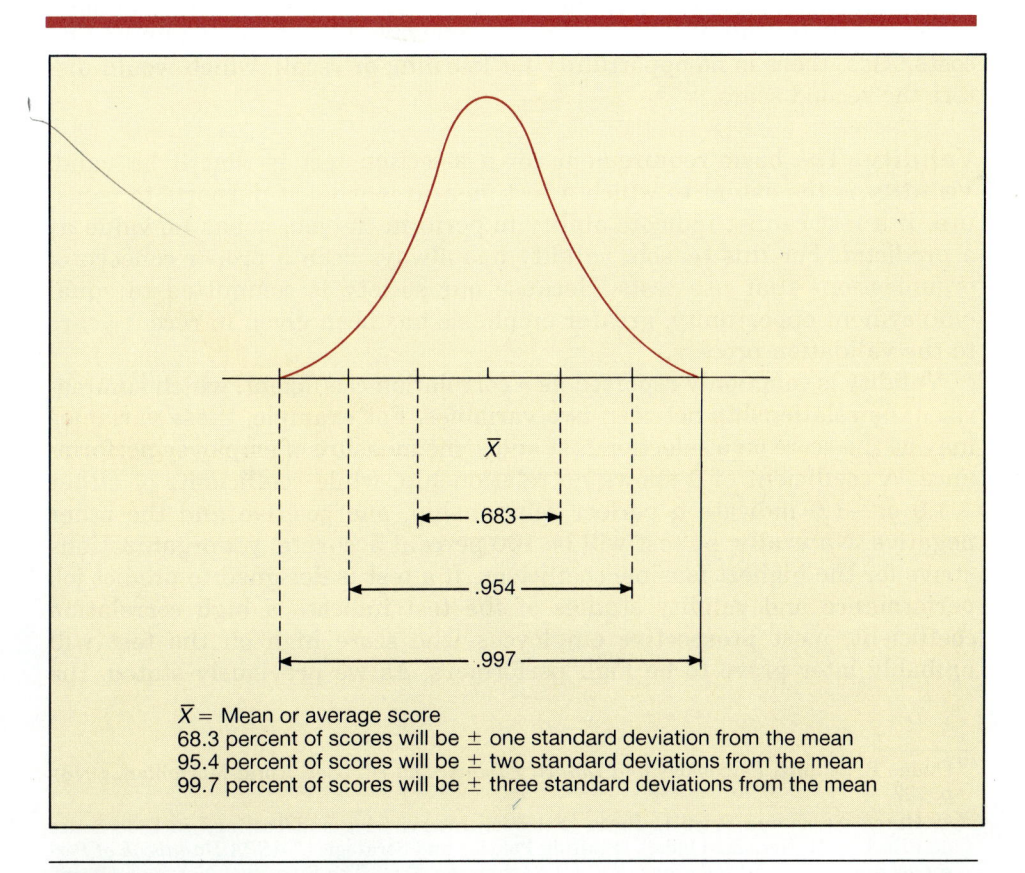

$\overline{X}$ = Mean or average score
68.3 percent of scores will be ± one standard deviation from the mean
95.4 percent of scores will be ± two standard deviations from the mean
99.7 percent of scores will be ± three standard deviations from the mean

FIGURE 7-4 | A Normal Probability Curve

Reliability. **Reliability** is the extent to which a selection test provides consistent results. Reliability data reveal the degree of confidence that can be placed in a test.[13] If a test has low reliability, its validity as a predictor will also be low. But the existence of reliability does not in itself guarantee validity.[14]

To ensure its usefulness, the test's reliability must be verified. The **test–retest method** is a method of determining selection test reliability by giving the test twice to the same group of individuals and correlating the two sets of scores. A perfect positive correlation is +1.00. The closer the reliability coefficient is to perfection, the more consistent the results, and therefore the more reliable the test. Problems with this method for determining reliability include the cost of administering the test twice, employees recalling test questions, and the learning that may take place between tests.

Similar to the test–retest method, the **equivalent forms method** tests reliability by correlating the results of tests that are similar but not identical. This approach overcomes some of the difficulties encountered with the test–retest method, but developing two forms of a test can be expensive. To overcome this weakness somewhat, the split-halves method may be used. The **split-halves method** tests reliability by dividing the results of a test into two parts and then correlating the results of the two parts. The onetime administration of the test has the obvious advantage of minimizing costs. Also, there is no opportunity for learning or recall, which would distort the second score.

Validity. The basic requirement for a selection test is that it be valid. **Validity** is the extent to which a test measures what it purports to measure. If a test cannot indicate ability to perform the job, it has no value as a predictor. For this reason, validity has always been a proper concern of organizations that use tests. Because our society is committed to equal employment opportunity, greater emphasis has been given in recent years to the validation process.

Validity is commonly reported as a correlation coefficient, which summarizes the relationship between two variables. For example, these variables may be the score on a selection test and some measure of employee performance. A coefficient of 0 shows no relationship, while coefficients of either +1.0 or −1.0 indicate a perfect relationship, one positive and the other negative. Naturally, no test will be 100 percent accurate, yet organizations strive for the highest feasible coefficient. If a test is designed to predict job performance and validity studies of the test indicate a high correlation coefficient, most prospective employees who score high on the test will probably later prove to be high performers. As we previously stated, the

---

[13] Duane P. Schultz, *Psychology and Industry Today*, 2nd ed. (New York: Macmillan, 1978), p. 122.

[14] C. Harold Stone and Floyd L. Ruch, "Selection Interviewing and Testing," in Dale Yoder and Herbert G. Heneman (eds.), "Staffing Policies and Strategies," *ASPA Handbook of Personnel and Industrial Relations*, Vol. I. (Washington, D.C., The Bureau of National Affairs, 1979), p. 4-135.

ability to select better qualified individuals will help increase the firm's productivity.

Employers are not required to automatically validate their selection tests. Generally speaking, validation is required only when the selection process as a whole results in an adverse impact on women or minorities.[15] Validation of selection tests is expensive. However, an organization cannot know whether the test is actually measuring the qualities and abilities being sought without validation.

■ TYPES OF VALIDATION STUDIES

The *Uniform Guidelines* established three approaches that may be followed to validate selection tests: criterion-related validity, content validity, and construct validity.[16]

Criterion-Related Validity

Criterion-related validity is determined by comparing the scores on selection tests to some aspect of job performance as determined, for example, by performance appraisal. Performance measures might include quantity and quality of work, turnover, and absenteeism. A close relationship between the score on the test and job performance suggests that the test is valid.

There are two basic forms of criterion-related validity: concurrent and predictive validity. With **concurrent validity**, the test scores and the criterion data are obtained at essentially the same time. For instance, all currently employed telemarketers may be given a test. Company records contain current information about each employee's job performance. If the test is able to identify productive and less productive workers, we say that it is valid. A potential problem in using this validation procedure results from changes that may have occurred within the work group. For example, the less productive may have been fired, and the more productive may have been promoted out of the group.

Predictive validity involves administering a test and later obtaining the criterion information. For instance, a test might be administered to all applicants but test results not used in the selection decision; employees are hired on the basis of other selection criteria. After employee performance has been observed over a period of time, the test results are analyzed to determine whether they differentiate the successful and less successful employees. Predictive validity is considered to be a technically sound procedure. However, because of the time and cost involved, its use is often not feasible.

---

[15] Charles F. Schanie and William L. Holley, "An Interpretive Review of Federal Uniform Guidelines on Employee Selection Procedures," *Personnel Administrator*, 25 (June 1980), p. 45.

[16] Dwight R. Norris and James A. Buford, Jr., "A Content Valid Writing Test: A Case Study," *Personnel Administrator*, 25 (January 1980), p. 40.

Content Validity

Although statistical concepts are not involved, many human resource practitioners believe that content validity provides a sensible approach to validating a selection test. **Content validity** is a test validation method whereby a person performs certain tasks that are actually required by the job or completes a paper-and-pencil test that measures relevant job knowledge. Thorough job analysis and carefully prepared job descriptions are needed when this form of validation is used.

The classic example of the use of content validity is giving a typing test to an applicant whose primary job would be to type. In *Washington* v. *Davis*, the Supreme Court supported content validity and its use will likely grow in the future.

Construct Validity

Construct validity is a test validation method that determines whether a test measures certain traits or qualities that are important in performing the job. For instance, if the job requires a large amount of persistence, such as in some forms of life insurance sales, a test would be used to measure persistence. However, traits or qualities needed on the job must first be carefully identified through job analysis.

■ CUT-OFF SCORES

After a test has been shown to be valid, an appropriate cut-off score must be established. A **cut-off score** is the score below which an applicant will not be selected. Cut-off scores will vary over time because they are directly related to the selection ratio. The more individuals applying for a job, the more selective the firm can be and therefore can establish high cut-off scores. Cut-off scores should normally be set to reflect a reasonable expectation of acceptable proficiency.

An example of what would likely occur when a validated test is administered to prospective employees is shown in Figure 7-5. The firm's experience indicates that individuals who score 40 and above on the test will be successful. Those who score below 40 will be less successful. Note that test results do not precisely predict performance. A small number of individuals who scored below the cut-off score of 40 proved to be good workers. Also, some applicants scoring above 40 proved to be less successful. However, the test appears to be a reasonably good predictor a large portion of the time. It is because of this gray area that test results should serve as only one of several criteria in the selection decision. The setting of a cut-off score to determine who will be screened out may have adverse impact. If so, the *Uniform Guidelines* require an employer to justify the initial cut-off score used.

■ TYPES OF PSYCHOLOGICAL TESTS

Individuals differ in characteristics related to job performance. These differences, which are measurable, relate to cognitive abilities, psychomotor

CHAPTER 7 Selection

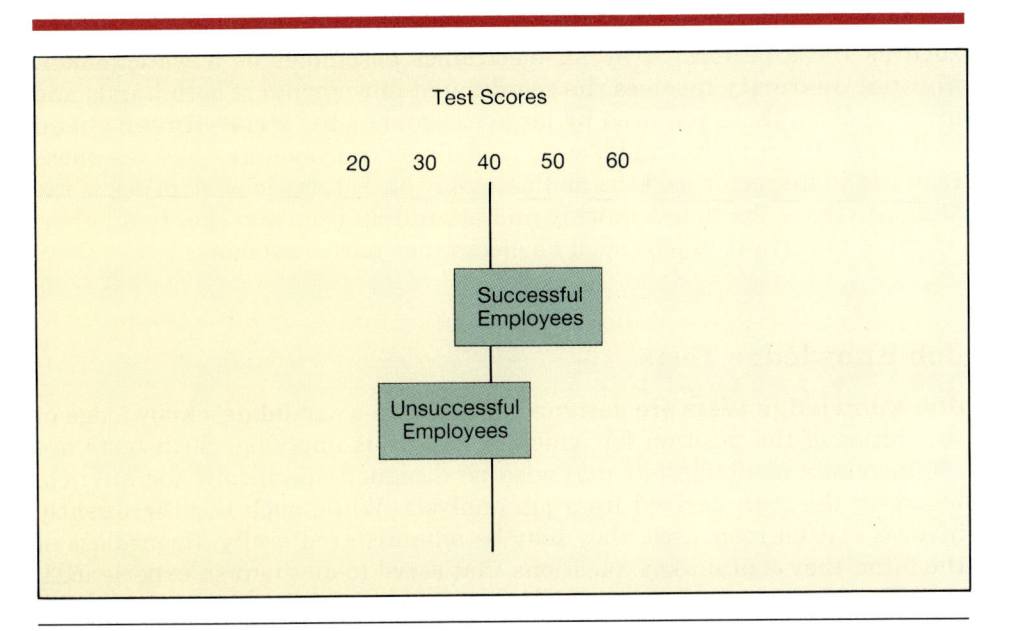

```
                        Test Scores

              20    30    40    50    60
                           |
                           |
                      ┌─────────┐
                      │Successful│
                      │Employees │
                      └─────────┘
                     ┌───────────┐
                     │Unsuccessful│
                     │ Employees │
                     └───────────┘
                           |
                           |
```

FIGURE 7-5 | An Example of Results from a Validated Test

abilities, job knowledge, interests, and personality. We discuss tests to measure these characteristics next.[17]

Cognitive Aptitude Tests

Cognitive aptitude tests measure an individual's ability to learn, as well as to perform a job. This type of test is particularly appropriate for making a selection from a group of inexperienced candidates. Job-related abilities may be classified as verbal, numerical, perceptual speed, spatial, and reasoning.

Psychomotor Abilities Tests

Psychomotor abilities tests measure strength, coordination, and dexterity. The development of tests to determine these abilities has been accelerated by miniaturization in assembly operations. Much of this work is so delicate that magnifying lenses must be used, and the psychomotor abilities required to perform the tasks are critical. While standardized tests are not available to cover all these abilities, it is feasible to measure those that are involved in many routine production jobs and some office jobs. **Finger**

---
[17] Stone and Ruch, pp. 4-138–4-142.

dexterity is the ability to make precise, coordinated finger movements, such as those performed by an electronics assembler or a watchmaker. **Manual dexterity** involves the coordinated movements of both hands and arms, such as those required by large assembly jobs. **Wrist–finger speed** is the ability to make rapid wrist and finger movements, such as those required in inspector-packers and assembly operations jobs. **Aiming** is the ability to move the hands quickly and accurately from one spot to another, which is important in jobs such as electronics parts assembly.

Job Knowledge Tests

Job knowledge tests are designed to measure a candidate's knowledge of the duties of the position for which he or she is applying. Such tests are commercially available but may also be designed specifically for any job, based on the data derived from job analysis. While such tests frequently involve written responses, they may be administered orally. Regardless of the form, they contain key questions that serve to distinguish experienced, skilled workers from those with less experience or skill.

Job knowledge tests, based on job analysis information, must be designed specifically for unique jobs. When in-house specialists are not available, consultants are often utilized to design the tests.

Job knowledge tests are by definition job related, but they do present some problems. For example, heavy equipment may not easily be moved to a testing site, untrained applicants may injure themselves or damage expensive equipment, and the economy of group testing isn't always feasible.

Work-Sample Tests

Work-sample tests require an applicant to perform a task or set of tasks representative of the job.[18] The evidence to date concerning these tests is that they produce high predictive validities, reduce adverse impact, and are more acceptable to applicants.[19]

Vocational Interest Tests

Vocational interest tests indicate the occupation in which a person is most interested and is most likely to receive satisfaction from. These tests compare the individual's interests with those of successful employees in a specific job.

Interests appear to be stable over a long period of time and have been related to success in some fields. However, interests must not be confused

---

[18] I. T. Robertson and R. M. Mindel, "A Study of Trainability Testing," *Journal of Occupational Psychology*, 53 (June 1980), p. 131.

[19] I. T. Robertson and R. S. Kandola, "Work Sample Tests: Validity, Adverse Impact, and Applicant Reaction," *Journal of Occupational Psychology*, 55 (1982), p. 180.

with aptitudes or abilities. Tests for these characteristics should accompany the administration of an interest test. Moreover, answers to interest test questions can easily be faked. Although interest tests may possibly have some application in employee selection, their primary use has been in counseling and vocational guidance.

Personality Tests

As selection tools, personality tests have not been as useful as other types of tests. They are often characterized by low reliability and low validity. Because some personality tests emphasize subjective interpretation, the services of a qualified psychologist are required to administer them. Additional research is needed before personality tests can be used with confidence as a selection tool.

Drug Testing

Overall, about 14 percent of U.S. firms require job applicants to take a drug test before they are employed. In companies with 10,000 employees or more, over 39 percent use drug tests to screen applicants. Drug testing appears to be most common in the public sector and in industries where public and employee safety is critical. Although more than two thirds of all organizations claim to have formal substance abuse policies, only about 25 percent conduct or sponsor substance abuse training programs.[20]

Testing for Acquired Immune Deficiency Syndrome (AIDS)

A recent survey found that only 1.5 percent of the responding firms reported AIDS antibody testing of job applicants. The same study indicated that a slightly larger percentage of small companies (50–99 employees) conduct tests than larger firms. A possible explanation is the prohibitive cost for large firms. Less than one percent of health service companies test for AIDS, whereas over 12 percent of transportation/communications/utilities firms and over 19 percent of public administration organizations do so.[21] We discuss AIDS further in Chapter 14.

■ THE EMPLOYMENT INTERVIEW

The **employment interview** is a goal-oriented conversation in which the interviewer and applicant exchange information. The employment inter-

---

[20] Dale Feuer, "Workplace Issues: Testing, Training and Policy," *Training: The Magazine of Human Resources Development*, 24 (October 1987), p. 67.
[21] *Ibid.*

view, along with letters of recommendation, continues to be the primary method used to evaluate applicants.[22] It is utilized by virtually every company in the United States.[23] The employment interview is especially significant because the applicants who reach this stage are the most promising candidates.[24] They have survived the preliminary interview, scored satisfactorily on selection tests, and fared well in reference and background checks. At this point, the candidates appear to be qualified, at least on paper. Every seasoned manager knows, however, that appearances can be quite misleading. Additional information is needed to indicate whether the individual is willing to work and can adapt to that particular organization.[25]

Legal Implications of Interviewing

For a number of years following the enactment of the Civil Rights Act, many employers stopped using tests and relied even more heavily on the employment interview as a selection tool. This change in practice was based on the false assumption that legal validity requirements applied only to tests.[26] But the definition of a test in the *Uniform Guidelines* included "physical, education and work experience requirements from informal or casual interviews." Since the interview is clearly a test, it is subject to the same validity requirements as any other step in the selection process, should adverse impact be shown. For the interview, this constraint presents special difficulties. To begin with, few firms are willing to pay the cost of validating interviews. They can be validated only by a long-term follow up—a method that requires collecting much data over a long period of time.[27] However, significant evidence indicates that if two managers in a firm interview the same applicant at different times, the outcomes will differ.[28]

The interview is perhaps more vulnerable to charges of discrimination than any other tool used in the selection process. In most cases, there is little or no documentation of the questions asked or the answers received. The interviewer may tend to ask irrelevant questions that would never appear on an application form. Some interviewers are inclined to ask questions that are not job related and that reflect their personal biases. They probably reason that this practice will go uncriticized because there is no

---

[22] Sampo V. Paunonen, Douglas N. Jackson, and Steven M. Oberman, "Personnel Selection Decisions: Effects of Applicant Personality and the Letter of Reference," *Organizational Behavior and Human Decision Processes*, 40 (August 1987), p. 96.

[23] Gary P. Latham, Lise M. Saari, Elliott D. Pursell, and Michael A. Campion, "The Situational Interview," *Journal of Applied Psychology*, 65 (1980), p. 422.

[24] Richard A. Fear and James F. Ross, *Jobs, Dollars—and EEO: How to Hire More Productive Entry-Level Workers* (New York: McGraw-Hill, 1983), p. 113.

[25] Ibid.

[26] James G. Goodale, *The Fine Art of Interviewing* (Englewood Cliffs, N.J.: Prentice-Hall, 1982), p. 41.

[27] Robert L. Decker, "The Employment Interview: Are We Seeing the Demise of Another Management Prerogative?" *Personnel Administrator*, 27 (November 1981), p. 71.

[28] James G. Goodale, "The Neglected Art of Interviewing," *Supervisory Management*, 26 (July 1981), p. 2.

written or verbal record of the interview. Nevertheless, interviewing in this manner is risky and can lead to charges of discrimination. Since an interview is a test, all questions should be job related. In the appendix to this chapter, we discuss further the potential interviewing problems.

Objectives of the Interview

Employment interviews have several basic objectives. It is important that at least the following objectives be successfully achieved.

Obtain Additional Information from the Applicant. The interview is an essential method of obtaining additional information about the applicant to complement the data provided by other selection tools. The interview permits clarification of certain points, the uncovering of additional information, and the elaboration of data needed to make a sound selection decision.

Provide Information Regarding the Firm. General information about the job, company policies, its products, and its services should be communicated to the applicant during the interview. If the interviewee is adequately prepared, this information will not come as a surprise.

Sell the Company. The employment interview provides an excellent opportunity for selling the company to the applicant. The interviewer should do so in a realistic manner, not through rose-colored glasses. Describing the company as a virtual utopia may well result in a disappointed employee or even an ex-employee.

Make New Friends. The applicant should leave the interview with a positive attitude about the company. If treated properly, the interviewee will not change this attitude even if no job offer is made. The interview should never serve to make the applicant feel inadequate.

Content of the Interview

The specific content of employment interviews varies greatly by organization and the level of the job. However, the following general topics appear fairly consistently in employment interviews: technical competence (often revealed through academic achievement and occupational experience), personal qualities (such as interpersonal competence), and potential, which includes the candidate's career orientation.[29]

Academic Achievement. The interviewer should try to discover any underlying factors related to academic performance. For example, a student who

---

[29] Gary T. Hunt and William F. Eadie, *Interviewing: A Communication Approach* (New York: Holt, Rinehart and Winston, 1987), p. 170.

earned only a 2.28/4.0 GPA may turn out to be a very bright individual who, because of financial difficulties, might have worked virtually full time while still participating in a variety of activities. On the other hand, a student who received a 3.8/4.0 GPA may not be a well-rounded individual and may be a weak candidate for the position.

Personal Qualities. Personal qualities normally observed during the interview include physical appearance, speaking ability, vocabulary, poise, and assertiveness. Even though he or she may have personal preferences, the interviewer should make every effort to keep nonjob-related personal biases out of the selection process.

Because of the legal ramifications, permitting the applicant's personal characteristics to influence the selection decision would obviously be unwise, unless they were BFOQs. Physical appearance might very well be an occupational qualification if the job being filled were that of an actress who is to portray the early career of Glenn Close. Speaking ability, vocabulary, and poise may be job-related qualifications if the job is that of a sportscaster. Assertiveness may be required for the successful performance of a credit collector's job.

Occupational Experience. Exploring an individual's occupational experience requires finding out about the applicant's skills, abilities, and willingness to handle responsibility. Job titles in one organization do not necessarily represent the same job content in another. Successful performance in one job does not guarantee success in another. At the same time, past performance does provide some indication of the employee's ability and willingness to work.

Interpersonal Competence. To a degree, an interviewer may observe an applicant's interpersonal competence. However, the interviewer may be witnessing an academy award performance by the candidate displaying an "I like people" nature. For this reason, the interviewer may need to ask questions regarding the applicant's interpersonal relationships with family and friends and how he or she behaves in other social and civic situations. The primary cause of failure in performing jobs is not the lack of technical ability but rather shortcomings in interpersonal competence. Even though an individual may be a highly skilled worker, if he or she cannot work well with other employees, chances for success are less.

Career Orientation. Questions about a candidate's career objectives may help the interviewer to determine whether the applicant's aspirations are realistic. The odds are rather great that a recent college graduate who expects to become a senior vice-president within six months will become quickly dissatisfied.

In addition to determining an applicant's career goals, the interviewer should present an honest and accurate description of career prospects in the organization. Deception may well prove counterproductive if the applicant is hired and later becomes dissatisfied as the truth unfolds. The firm

CHAPTER 7 Selection

may lose a substantial investment in the form of recruitment, selection, and training.

Types of Interviews

Interviews may be classified as highly structured at one extreme and as having virtually no structure at the other. In practice, interviews fall between these extremes. Regardless of structure, interviews should solicit the following types of information from applicants: (1) ability to perform the job; (2) motivation to stay on the job; and (3) adaptability to the job situation.[30]

The Unstructured (Nondirective) Interview. In the **unstructured interview**, the interviewer asks probing, open-ended questions. This type of interview is comprehensive, and the interviewer encourages the applicant to do much of the talking. The nondirective interview is often more time-consuming than more structured interviews, yet some interviewers believe that it has greater effectiveness in obtaining significant information. The nature of the nondirective interview requires a highly trained and skillful interviewer who asks open-ended questions such as:

What do you believe are your primary strengths? Your main weaknesses?

How will our company benefit by having you as an employee?

Where do you want to be in this firm five years from now?

What was your most significant contribution in your last job?

The specific answers may not be as important to the interviewer as how the applicant answers the questions and the thought process leading to the response. The nondirective interview consists of a highly subjective appraisal of the candidate. Research conducted on traditional selection interviews indicates very low reliability and little or no validity.[31] Various types of errors have contributed to this poor performance (see the Appendix to this chapter), and therefore the use of such an approach may not be extremely effective in many interview situations.

The Structured (Directive or Patterned) Interview. The **structured interview** consists of a series of job-related questions that are consistently asked of each applicant for a particular job.[32] Use of structured interviews increases reliability and accuracy by reducing the subjectivity and inconsistency of unstructured (traditional) interviews.

Interviewers should follow a structured, systematic interview procedure in order to obtain the information necessary to evaluate the candidate

---

[30] Barbara Felton and Sue Ries Lamb, "A Model for Systematic Selection Interviewing," *Personnel*, 59 (January–February 1982), p. 43.

[31] Elliott D. Pursell, Michael A. Campion, and Sara R. Gaylord, "Structured Interviewing: Avoiding Selection Problems," *Personnel Journal*, 59 (November 1980), p. 908.

[32] *Ibid.*

fairly and objectively.[33] The advantages of structure are diminished, however, if the interviewer asks each of the questions perfunctorily. This approach could easily result in an overly formal setting and severely impair the candidate's ability or desire to respond.

A structured job interview typically contains four types of questions. **Situational questions** pose a hypothetical job situation to determine what the applicant would do in that situation. **Job knowledge questions** probe the applicant's job-related knowledge. These questions may relate to basic educational skills or complex scientific or managerial skills. **Job-sample simulation questions** involve situations in which an applicant may be required to actually perform a sample task from the job. When this isn't feasible, a simulation of critical job aspects may be utilized. As suggested, answering these types of questions may require physical activity.

The last type of question used in structured interviews deal with worker requirements. **Worker requirements questions** seek to determine the applicant's willingness to conform to the requirements of the job. For example, the interviewer may ask whether the applicant is willing to perform repetitive work or to move to another city. The nature of these questions serves as a realistic job preview and may aid in self-selection.

A properly designed patterned interview will contain only job-related questions. An illustration of a patterned interview guide for discussing work experience is provided in Table 7-2. Note that each question is asked for a specific purpose.

■ METHODS OF INTERVIEWING

Interviews may be conducted in several ways. In a typical employment interview, the applicant meets one-on-one with an interviewer. As the interview may be a highly emotional occasion for the applicant, meeting alone with the interviewer is often less threatening.

Unlike a one-on-one interview, in a **group interview** several applicants interact in the presence of one or more company representatives. This approach, while not mutually exclusive of other interview types, may provide useful insights into the candidates' interpersonal competence as they engage in group discussion. This technique is often used because it saves time for busy professionals and executives.

In a **board interview**, one candidate is interviewed by several representatives of the firm. Although a thorough examination of the applicant is likely, the interviewee's anxiety level is often quite high. L. C. Barry, vice-president of industrial relations for Gates Learjet said, "We use a three-person board to screen each applicant, asking a series of questions designed to ferret out the individual's attitudes toward former employers, jobs, etc. Then, a week later, we bring successful applicants and their spouses in for a family-night meeting with top management and their spouses, where we further screen them while discussing the company and employee benefits." Naturally, the amount of time devoted to a board interview will differ depending on the type and level of job.

---

[33] Weiss, p. 90.

TABLE 7-2 | Portion of a Patterned Interview Guide

Work Experience

Cover:	Look for:
Earliest jobs: part-time, temporary	Relevance of work
Military assignments	Sufficiency of work
Full-time positions	Skill and competence
Ask:	Adaptability
	Productivity
Things done best? Done less well?	Motivation
Things liked best? Liked less well?	Interpersonal relations
Major accomplishments? How achieved?	Leadership
Most difficult problems faced? How handled?	Growth and development
Ways most effective with people?	
Ways less effective?	
Level of earnings?	
Reasons for changing jobs?	
What learned from work experience?	
What looking for in job? In career?	

Source: Reproduced from *The Interviewer's Manual* by special permission. Copyright © 1980, by Drake Beam Morin, Inc. All rights reserved.

Most interview sessions are designed to minimize stress on the part of the candidate. However, the **stress interview** intentionally creates anxiety to determine how an applicant will react in certain types of situations. The stress interview should be used only by highly trained and skilled interviewers. Interviewers for some types of sales jobs subject applicants to stress situations in order to determine how they will react under pressure. For instance, on the first interview, everything might progress smoothly. The applicant is led to believe that all he or she has to do is come back for the second interview and the job offer will be made. However, during the second interview, events progress a bit differently. The individual might have to wait in the outer office for a considerable period of time before the interview begins. This tactic allows the candidate's anxiety to build. Then the interviewer might begin with a statement such as, "Mr. Noles, I appreciate your interest, but we just don't believe there is any need to continue this interview. Your qualifications just don't appear to match our needs." The purpose of this approach is to see how the applicant will react when confronted with an unexpected situation. Individuals who are able to turn this situation around may demonstrate that they can become successful sales representatives, for example.

Another point of view relative to stress interviews relies on evidence indicating that the stress interview is not only inconsiderate but is also ineffective. Proponents of this view feel that information exchange in a stressful environment is often distorted and misinterpreted. These critics maintain that the data obtained is not the type of information upon which to base a selection decision.[34] In any event, it seems clear that the stress interview is not appropriate for the majority of situations.

The Interviewer, Interview Planning, and the Interview Process

The interviewer should possess a pleasant personality, empathy, and the ability to listen and communicate effectively. He or she should respect those who have different personal attributes and backgrounds. Interviewers must be aware of stereotyped views of the capabilities of women and minorities. Everyone has biases, and some are not bad. However, those based on a false value system about people tend to be destructive[35] and consequently have no place in the interview process. Interviewers should also have a solid knowledge of actual job requirements so that they can properly assess the applicant's qualifications.

In addition, interview planning is essential to effective employment interviews. The physical location of the interview should be both pleasant and private, providing for a minimum of interruptions. The interviewer should become familiar with the applicant's record by reviewing the data collected by means of other selection tools.

The interview process should begin with a warm and sincere welcome for the candidate, and rapport should be quickly developed. Because people can often talk most easily about themselves, it is a good practice for the interview to begin in this manner. After this initial ice breaking, the interviewer can proceed to ask relevant, job-related questions. The interviewer should never ask leading questions, such as, "You didn't do too well in statistics, did you?" Rather, questions should be asked in a manner that permits the applicant some flexibility in answering.

When the interviewer has obtained the necessary information and answered the applicant's questions, the interview should be concluded. At this point, the interviewer should tell the applicant that he or she will receive notification of the selection decision shortly. Unfortunately, this promise is often broken, and this may destroy a positive relationship between the applicant and the organization.

---

[34] Susan Gribben, "A Guide to the Hiring Process," *CA Magazine*, 115 (September 1982), p. 85.
[35] Joseph D. Levesque, "Selecting and Managing Competent Managers," *Personnel Administrator*, 30 (March 1985), p. 67.

CHAPTER 7   Selection

Realistic Job Previews[36]

Many applicants have unrealistic expectations about the prospective job and employer. This inaccurate perception, which may have negative consequences, is often encouraged by firms that present themselves in overly attractive terms. To correct this situation, a realistic job preview should be given to applicants early in the selection process and definitely before a job offer is made.

A **realistic job preview (RJP)** conveys job information to the applicant in an unbiased manner, including both positive and negative factors. This approach helps applicants develop a more accurate perception of the job and the firm. Research results suggest that newly hired employees who received RJPs have a greater rate of job survival and higher job satisfaction. At the same time, use of this technique should not reduce the flow of qualified applicants. A comparison of the results of traditional preview procedures and realistic preview procedures is shown in Figure 7-6. Note that traditional procedures result in low job survival and dissatisfaction, whereas RJPs help to overcome these difficulties.

Traditional procedures	Realistic procedures
Set initial job expectations too high ↓	Set job expectations realistically ↓
Job is typically viewed as attractive ↓	Job may or may not be attractive, depending on individual's needs ↓
High rate of job offer acceptance ↓	Some accept, some reject job offer ↓
Work experience disconfirms expectations ↓	Work experience confirms expectations ↓
Dissatisfaction and realization that job not matched to needs ↓	Satisfaction; needs matched to job ↓
Low job survival, dissatisfaction, frequent thoughts of quitting	High job survival, satisfaction, infrequent thoughts of quitting

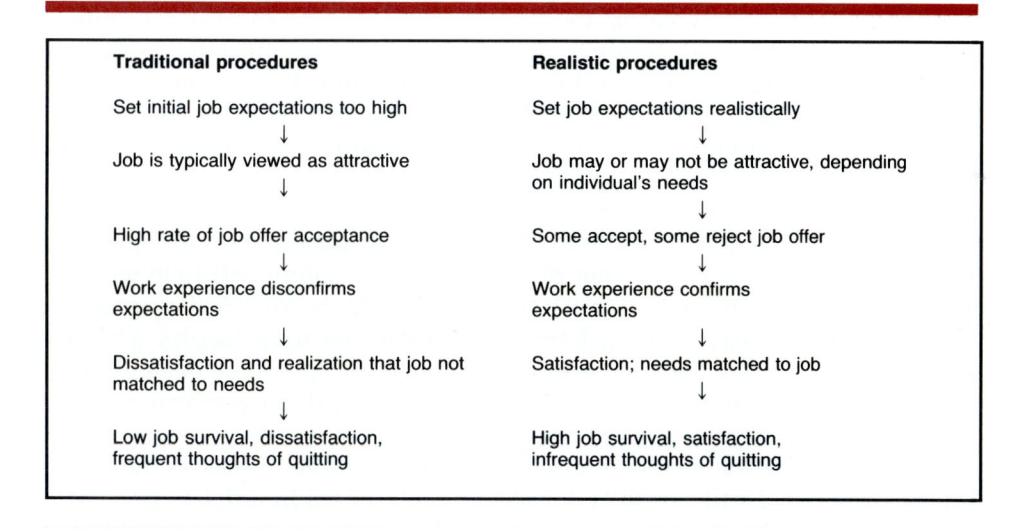

FIGURE 7-6 | Typical Consequences of Job Procedures

Source: Reprinted by permission of the publisher, from "Tell It Like It Is at Realistic Job Previews," by John Wanous, *Personnel*, 52 (July–August 1975), p. 54.

---

[36] John P. Wanous, "Tell It Like It Is at Realistic Job Previews," in Kendrith M. Rowland, Manual London, Gerald R. Ferris, and Jay L. Sherman (eds.), *Current Issues in Personnel Management* (Boston: Allyn & Bacon, 1980), pp. 41–50.

■ REFERENCE CHECKS

Information contained in the completed application for employment is at times incorrect or colored to present the applicant in a favorable light. **Reference checks** provide additional insight into the information furnished by the applicant and allow verification of its accuracy. Most individuals who apply for jobs have to submit several references. References are normally checked by letter, by telephone, or both. When reference letters are used, the writer usually describes the nature of the job for which the applicant is being considered. Information requested from the reference is typically limited to dates of employment, job title, absentee record, promotions and demotions, compensation, and reason for termination.[37] As you might expect, written reference checks raise numerous problems.

The Privacy Act of 1974 has had a major impact on obtaining references. The act was passed to provide certain safeguards for an individual against an invasion of personal privacy but is limited to the federal government and its contractors. It applies to all executive departments, the military, independent regulatory agencies, government corporations, and government-controlled corporations. Any private business that has a contract with any of these agencies is also covered for the duration of the contract. The purpose of the act is to limit the amount and type of information that federal agencies maintain in records about individuals and to control dissemination of that information to other agencies. Individuals must be permitted access to any personal records concerning them and those covered by this act have the legal right to review reference checks that have been made regarding their employment unless the individual waives this right. There have been instances where applicants have sued and won court cases when it was proven that the reference was biased.

Today many organizations refuse to release any information except dates of employment and salary. Even this information is often withheld without the former employee's written authorization. Furthermore, previous employers may "whitewash" a record by emphasizing positive factors and not mentioning negative factors, even when the applicant had been fired.[38] Comments regarding the reason for termination and job performance are often not included in a written response.

Another difficulty is that the applicant provides the names of the references. Applicants will carefully select their references in order to present a positive image. An applicant is not likely to use a person who would give an unfavorable response. Therefore the majority of references are biased in a positive manner.

Perhaps because of the bias associated with written references, many reference checkers use the telephone. They reason that a more objective appraisal will result if there is no documentation of the conversation. Still, they must be careful of the type of questions they ask. However, if the respondent desires to elaborate on a particular topic, the reference checker

---

[37] G. Bruce Knecht, "Screening Out Thieves Before They're Hired," *Dun's Business Month*, 120 (October 1982), p. 70.

[38] Smart, p. 51.

should certainly encourage further discussion. Basically, the reference checker should always remember that comments from a reference can be biased.

■ BACKGROUND INVESTIGATION

Although a reference check often verifies certain statements on the application blank, it frequently does not. Performing a background investigation of the applicant's past employment history may be necessary. This background investigation may be helpful in determining whether past work experience is related to the qualifications needed for the new position. As we previously noted, job titles may not accurately reflect the nature of past work experience.

Another reason for background investigations is that credential fraud has increased in recent years. Some 7–10 percent of job applicants are not what they present themselves to be.[39] Some applicants are not even who they say they are. Although background checks are expensive, properly conducted they can confirm or disprove claims made by job applicants.[40]

■ POLYGRAPH TESTS

Another means used for many years to verify background information has been the polygraph, or lie detector, test. One purpose of the polygraph was to confirm or refute the information contained in the application blank. However, on July 27, 1988 the Employee Polygraph Protection Act was passed and went into effect December 27, 1988. This act severely limited the use of polygraph tests. It made it unlawful for any employer engaged in or affecting commerce or in the production of goods for commerce to use a polygraph test. However, the act does not apply to governmental employers and there are limited exceptions for ongoing investigations and for drug security, drug theft, or drug diversion investigations.

■ THE SELECTION DECISION

After obtaining and evaluating information about the finalists, the manager must take the most critical step of all: making the actual hiring decision. The other stages in the selection process have been used to narrow the number of candidates. The final choice will be made from among those still in the running after reference checks, selection tests, background investigations, and interview information have been evaluated. The individual with the best overall qualifications may not be hired. Rather, the person

---

[39] Scott T. Rickard, "Effective Staff Selection," *Personnel Journal*, 60 (June 1981), p. 477.
[40] Rickard, p. 477.

whose qualifications most closely conform to the requirements of the open position should be selected.[41]

Human resource professionals have been heavily involved in all phases leading up to the final employment decision. However, the person who normally makes the final selection is the manager who will be responsible for the performance of the new employee. In making this decision, the operating manager may or may not ask the advice of the human resource manager. The role of HRM in this process is to provide service and counsel to help the operating manager make the selection decision. The rationale for permitting the supervisor to make the final selection is simple: managers should be allowed to select the individuals for whom they will be responsible.

In certain instances, however, the human resource manager serves in a strong advisory capacity. For example, if the organization is under pressure from the federal government to employ more women and minorities, a recommendation by the human resource manager may carry additional weight.

■ PHYSICAL EXAMINATION

After the decision has been made to extend a job offer, the next phase of the selection process involves a physical examination for the successful applicant. Typically, a job offer is contingent on the applicant's passing of this examination. The purposes of the physical examination are several. Obviously, one reason is to screen out individuals who have a contagious disease. The exam also assists in determining whether an applicant is physically capable of performing the work. For instance, if the work is physically demanding and a heart problem is detected, the individual will likely be rejected. Finally, physical examination information may be used to determine whether certain physical capabilities differentiate successful from less successful employees. A physical examination can also be used to establish a record of preexisting physical conditions for insurance and workers' compensation purposes.

Human resource managers should be aware of the legal liabilities related to physical examinations. The *Uniform Guidelines* state that examinations should be used only to reject applicants when the results show that job performance would be adversely affected.

The Rehabilitation Act of 1973 does not prohibit employers from requiring physical examinations. However, it has encouraged covered employees to consider carefully each job's physical requirements. The act requires employers to take affirmative action to hire qualified handicapped persons who, with reasonable accommodation, can perform the essential components of a job.

---

[41] Hall A. Acuff, "Quality Control in Employee Selection," *Personnel Journal*, 60 (July 1981), p. 563.

CHAPTER 7   Selection   243

HRM In Action

Julie Thompson, the production manager for Ampex Manufacturing, called her friend, Bill Alexander, in human resources, to ask a favor. "Bill, I have a friend I'd like you to consider for the new sales manager's position. I really like the fellow and would appreciate anything you could do."

"Tell me about the person," said Bill.

"Just graduated from State University with a degree in history, I believe. No real work experience, but I am sure he could learn quickly. Parents are real good friends of mine, and I sure would like to help him out."

How would you respond?

■ ACCEPTANCE OF JOB APPLICANTS

Assuming that the physical examination fails to uncover any disqualifying medical problems, the applicant can be employed. The starting date normally is based on the wishes of both the firm and the individual. If currently employed by another firm, the individual customarily gives between two and four weeks notice. Even after this notice, the individual may need some personal time to prepare for the new job. This transition time is particularly important if the new job requires a move to another city. Thus the amount of time before the individual can join the firm is often considerable—but necessary.

The firm may also want the individual to delay the date of employment. If, for example, the new employee's first assignment upon joining the firm is to attend a training school, the organization may request that the individual delay joining the firm until the school begins. This practice, which would be strictly for the benefit of the company, should not be abused, especially if an undue hardship would be placed on the individual.

■ REJECTION OF JOB APPLICANTS

Applicants may be rejected during any phase of the selection process. In this section, we focus on the applicants who for various reasons were not offered employment. When someone applies for a position, that person is essentially saying, "I think I am qualified for the job. Why don't you hire me?" Tension builds as the applicant progresses through the selection process. If the preliminary interview shows that the applicant clearly is not qualified, the ego damage is likely to be slight. The company may even be able to steer the individual to other jobs in the firm that better match his or her qualifications.

For most people, the employment interview is not one of the most enjoyable of experiences. Taking a test that could affect an individual's career often causes hands to become moist and perspiration to break out on the forehead. Suffering through all this only to be told, "There does not appear to be a proper match between your qualifications and our needs" can be a painful experience. Most firms recognize this fact and attempt to let the individual down as easily as possible. But it is often difficult to tell people that they will not be hired.

When considerable time has been spent on the individual in the selection process, a company representative often sits down with the applicant and explains why another person was offered the job. But if there were many applicants, time constraints may force the firm to notify individuals by letter that they were not chosen. However, a rejection letter can still be personalized. A personal touch will often reduce the stigma of rejection and the chance that the applicant will feel negatively about the company. An impersonal letter is likely to cause the opposite reaction. If the selection was made objectively, most individuals can, with time, understand why they were not chosen.

■ SELECTION AND UTILITY ANALYSIS

Determining the ratio of benefits to costs for any selection technique is referred to as **utility analysis**. Each step in the selection process involves a cost. If tests are to be used, they need to be validated. Professionals are required to administer the tests, interpret the results, and explain the results to management. In addition, employment applications that are job related for particular job classes need to be developed. Properly conducted reference checks and background investigations require trained checkers. Even the preliminary interview requires that an individual be trained and time provided to perform the task properly. All these tasks require time, effort, and money.

Even though substantial costs are involved in developing, implementing, and using a job-related selection process, the benefits are likely to outweigh the costs. If individuals are placed in positions for which they are not suited, dissatisfaction is inevitable.[42] Numerous hidden costs are involved. For example, before discovering that the individual was not suited for the job, considerable supervisory effort may have been expended. The quality and quantity of work in the department may suffer. And the new employee may have a negative impact on other workers. If the worker then leaves the firm, the recruitment and selection process must start all over to find a replacement. If training has been provided, it is wasted and must be provided again when a replacement is hired. Turnover costs associated with a poor selection process can be substantial.

---

[42] John C. Hafer and C. C. Hoth, "Selection Characteristics: Your Priorities and How Students Perceive Them," *Personnel Administrator*, 28 (March 1983), p. 25.

Formal utility analysis attempts to assign dollar values to the various selection activities.[43] Managers are first asked to estimate the dollar value of hypothetical performance levels. They are then asked to estimate the performance level they expect to be achieved by the firm's selection activities. Managers seldom do a formal utility analysis but often perform informal utility analysis as they estimate the benefits and costs of employing a particular applicant.[44]

■ STAFFING IN THE MULTINATIONAL ENVIRONMENT

One of the most difficult human resource management problems for the multinational organization is that of selecting suitable people to be sent on foreign assignments. Inappropriate selections are often made, which negatively affect the multinational operation. A National Industrial Conference Board survey has called staffing overseas executive positions the second most serious problem facing multinational corporations.[45] Although specific failure rates vary by country and company, an estimated 25 percent of Americans selected for overseas assignments are obvious failures and return home prematurely. Approximately the same number are hidden failures or marginal performers.[46] Some firms have experienced a 60 to 90 percent failure rate in certain countries.[47]

After being carefully selected for the assignment and briefed on the new job and locale, employees based in the United States do business in familiar surroundings. However, the multinational environment is often unfamiliar and doing business as it's always been done may be ineffective. The tasks of everyday living may also be very different and unnerving.[48] Poor selection, coupled with the stress of living and working overseas, are documented contributors to mental breakdown, alcoholism, and divorce.

There are three primary reasons why U.S. workers sent overseas fail: (1) their families are misjudged, or are not even considered at the time of selection; (2) they are selected because of their domestic track records; or (3) they lack adequate cross-cultural training.[49] To overcome these obstacles human resource managers should plan carefully to ensure that selectees possess certain basic characteristics. Obviously, they must be technically

---

[43] Frank L. Schmidt, John E. Hunter, and Kenneth Pearlman, "Assessing the Economic Impact of Personnel Programs on Workforce Productivity," *Personnel Psychology*, 35 (1982), pp. 333–347.

[44] Kendrith M. Rowland and Gerald R. Ferris, *Personnel Management* (Boston: Allyn & Bacon, 1982); p. 134.

[45] Philip R. Harris, "Employees Abroad: Maintain the Corporate Connection," *Personnel Journal*, 65 (August 1986), pp. 107–108.

[46] Allen L. Hixon, "Why Corporations Make Haphazard Overseas Staffing Decisions," *Personnel Administrator*, 31 (March 1986), p. 91.

[47] Prabhu Guptara, "Searching the Organization for the Cross-Cultural Operators," *International Management* (August 1986), pp. 39–40.

[48] Harris, pp. 107–108.

[49] Hixon, p. 91.

qualified to do the job.[50] Unfortunately, however, U.S. firms seem to focus their selection efforts on the single criterion "technical competence" at the expense of other criteria. For example, few firms administer tests to determine the relational/cross-cultural/interpersonal skills of their selectees. Other contributing factors are also needed:

- A real desire to work in a foreign country.
- Spouses and families who have actively encouraged the person to work overseas.
- Cultural sensitivity and flexibility.
- A sense for politics.

Several surveys of overseas managers have revealed that the spouse's opinion and attitude should be considered the most important screening factor. Cultural sensitivity is also essential to avoid antagonizing host country nationals unnecessarily.

The selection process should measure and evaluate the candidate's expertise broadly. Psychological tests, stress tests, evaluations by the candidate's superiors, subordinates, peers, acquaintances, and professional evaluations from licensed psychologists can all aid in ascertaining the candidate's current level of interpersonal and cross-cultural skills. The candidate's spouse and children should undergo modified versions of the selection process, since the family members confront slightly different challenges overseas than do employees.[51]

In selecting individuals for overseas assignments, management must recognize that no one style of leadership will be equally effective in all countries. People in various countries have widely divergent backgrounds, education, cultures, and religions—and live within a variety of social conditions and economic and political systems. Human resource managers must consider all these factors because they can have a rather dramatic effect on the working environment of the person selected.

An appropriate management approach for the multinational corporation must be based on common sense and informed conjecture. It seems reasonable that a successful international manager should possess the following qualities, among others:

- A basic knowledge of history, particularly in countries of old and homogeneous cultures.
- An understanding of the basic economic and sociological concepts of various countries.
- An interest in the host country and a willingness to learn and use its language.
- A respect for differing philosophical and ethical approaches to living.

---

[50] Gurudutt M. Baliga and James C. Baker, "Multinational Corporate Policies for Expatriate Managers: Selection, Training, Evaluation," *Sam Advanced Management Journal*, 50 (Autumn 1985), p. 32.

[51] Mark E. Mendenhall, Edward Dunbar, and Gary R. Oddou, "Expatriate Selection, Training and Career-Pathing: A Review and Critique," *Human Resource Management*, 26 (Fall 1987), pp. 331–345.

Basically, individuals transferred overseas should have a desire to function, as well as possible, in the host country's environment.

SUMMARY

Selection is the process of choosing from a group of applicants those individuals best suited for a particular position. The selection process often begins with an initial screening of applicants to eliminate those who obviously do not meet the position's requirements. The next step may involve having the prospective employee complete an application for employment. The employer evaluates it to see whether the individual's qualifications match the position's requirements. A well-designed and properly used application form is much more effective than résumés in reducing dozens of applicants to a few bona fide candidates.

Selection tests are often used to help assess an applicant's qualifications and potential for success. Although selection tests may accurately predict an applicant's ability to perform a job, they cannot indicate the extent to which the individual will want to perform it. Another potential problem related primarily to personality tests and interest inventories has to do with the applicant's honesty. There may be a strong motivation for the applicant to respond to questions untruthfully or provide answers that he or she believes the firm expects.

Properly designed selection tests are standardized, objective, based on sound norms, reliable and, of utmost importance, valid. Standardization refers to the uniformity of the procedures and conditions related to administering tests. Objectivity in testing is achieved when all individuals scoring a test obtain the same results. Norms provide a frame of reference for comparing an applicant's performance with that of other similar individuals. Reliability is the extent to which a selection test provides consistent results. Validity is the extent to which a test measures what it purports to measure.

The *Uniform Guidelines* established three approaches to validation: criterion-related validity, content validity, and construct validity. Criterion-related validity is determined by comparing the scores on selection tests to some aspect of job performance as determined, for example, by performance appraisal. There are two basic forms of criterion-related validity: concurrent and predictive. With concurrent validity, the test scores and the criterion data are obtained at essentially the same time. Predictive validity involves administering a test and later obtaining the criterion data. Content validity is a test validation method whereby a person performs certain tasks actually required by the job or completes a paper-and-pencil test that measures relevant job knowledge. Construct validity is a test validation method to determine whether a test measures certain traits or qualities that have been identified as important in performing the job. After a test has been validated, an appropriate cut-off score must be established. An applicant scoring less than the cut-off score will be disqualified. Characteristics related to job performance—and which are measurable—include cognitive aptitudes, psychomotor abilities, job knowledge, interests, and personality.

The employment interview is a goal-oriented conversation in which the interviewer and applicant exchange information. The specific content of employment interviews varies greatly, but the following general topics appear fairly consistently in employment interviews: technical competence, personal qualities, and career potential.

Interviews may be conducted in several ways. In a group interview, several applicants interact with one or more company representatives. In a board interview, one candidate is interviewed by several company representatives. The stress interview intentionally creates anxiety to determine how an applicant will react in certain types of situations. A realistic job preview (RJP) conveys unbiased job information to the applicant.

Reference checks provide additional insight into the applicant and are used to verify the accuracy of the information provided. Often a background investigation of the applicant's past employment history is necessary.

Based on all the information obtained, the manager must take the critical step of making the actual hiring decision. The other stages in the selection process have been used to narrow the number of candidates, and the final decision will choose from among those still in the running.

After the decision has been made to extend a job offer, the successful candidate takes a physical examination. Typically, a job offer is contingent on the candidate's successful passing of the physical examination. Assuming that no disqualifying medical problems are discovered during the physical examination, the applicant can now be employed.

One of the most difficult human resource management problems for the multinational organization is that of selecting the appropriate people for foreign assignments. Inappropriate selections are often made, which have negative impacts on multinational operations. In selecting individuals for overseas assignments, management must recognize that no one style of leadership will be equally effective in all countries. People selected must respect and be comfortable with the backgrounds, education, cultures, religions, social conditions, and economic and political systems of the country in which they will work.

Questions for Review

1. What basic steps are normally followed in the selection process?
2. Identify and describe the various factors outside the control of the human resource manager that could affect the selection process.
3. What would be the selection ratio if there were fifteen applicants to choose from and only one position to fill? Interpret the meaning of this selection ratio.
4. If a firm wants to use selection tests, how should they be used to avoid discriminatory practices?
5. What is the general purpose of the preliminary interview?
6. What types of questions should be asked on an application form?
7. What basic conditions should be met if selection tests are to be used in the screening process? Briefly describe each.
8. Briefly describe the objectives of the employment interview.
9. Define each of the following: (a) nondirective interview; (b) structured interview; (c) group interview; (d) board interview; and (e) stress interview.
10. What is the purpose of reference checks and background investigations?
11. What are the reasons for administering a physical examination?
12. Describe the most important factors in selecting someone for an overseas assignment.

Terms for Review

Selection
Selection ratio
Weighted application blank (WAB)
Standardization
Objectivity
Norms
Reliability
Test–retest method
Equivalent forms method
Split-halves method
Validity
Criterion-related validity
Concurrent validity
Predictive validity
Content validity
Construct validity
Cut-off score
Cognitive aptitude tests
Psychomotor abilities tests

Finger dexterity
Manual dexterity
Wrist–finger speed
Aiming
Job knowledge tests
Work-sample tests
Vocational interest tests
Employment interview
Unstructured interview
Structured interview
Situational questions
Job knowledge questions
Job-sample simulation questions
Worker requirements questions
Group interview
Board interview
Stress interview
Realistic job preview (RJP)
Reference checks
Utility analysis

INCIDENT 1 ▪ Business First!

As production manager for Thompson Manufacturing, Jack Stephens has the final authority to approve the hiring of any new supervisors who work for him. The human resource manager performs the initial screening of all prospective supervisors and then sends the most likely candidates to Jack for interviews.

One day recently, Jack received a call from Pete, the human resource manager. "Jack, I've just spoken to a young man who may be just who you're looking for to fill that final line supervisor position. He has some good work experience and it appears as if his head is screwed on straight. He's here right now and available if you could possibly see him." Jack hesitated a moment before answering, "Gee Pete," he said, "I'm certainly busy today but I'll try to squeeze him in. Send him on down."

A moment later Allen Guthrie, the new applicant, arrived at Jack's office and introduced himself. "Come on in, Allen," said Jack. "I'll be right with you after I make a few phone calls." Fifteen minutes later Jack finished the calls and began talking with Allen. Jack was quite impressed. After a few minutes Jack's door opened and a supervisor yelled, "We have a small problem on line number one and need your help." "Sure," Jack replied, "Excuse me a minute, Allen." Ten minutes later Jack returned and the conversation continued for at least ten more minutes before a series of phone calls again interrupted them.

The same pattern of interruptions continued for the next hour. Finally Allen looked at his watch and said, "I'm sorry, Mr. Stephens, but I have to pick up my wife." "Sure thing, Allen," Jack said as the phone rang again. "Call me later today."

Questions

1. What specific policies should a company follow to avoid interviews like this one?
2. Explain why Jack, not Pete, should make the selection decision.

INCIDENT 2 — Should We Test?

"Mrs. Peacock, I've decided that we should quit using selection tests altogether," said John Barnes, the human resource manager. "I'm not sure there are any that could be defended if we ever got a discrimination complaint." John had just read a report of a court decision finding a large company nearby guilty of discriminatory employment practices. Essentially, the company had been using tests designed to measure general intelligence as a screening device for all categories of employees. The court held that the tests caused certain groups to be eliminated from employment consideration.

The tests that John's firm, Miller Chemical Company, used were aptitude tests, carefully designed for specific jobs. For example, the test for a certain mechanical mixer operator job included questions about the relative weights of various liquids and solids, the ways in which emulsions were formed, and the dangers involved in working with rotating machinery. No study had been done, however, to determine the relationship between performance on the test and success on the job. Most of the managers felt that the interviews and references were more valuable than the tests anyway. Besides, John thought that validation of the tests would be too expensive and time consuming.

As John was thinking about all of this, Nancy Peacock called back. "Mr. Barnes," she said, "I've been thinking about your decision to eliminate our tests. Do we still have enough to go on in making an employment decision?" "Not really," said John, "but I don't know what else we can do to be safe. A discrimination suit could tie us up for months. The tests may not be any more discriminatory than interviews, but I don't think that interviews can get us into trouble. The same thing is true of applications and reference checks. It would just be harder for the EEOC to attack us on those points." "Then I suppose the decision is final?" asked Nancy. "I've thought about it a lot, Mrs. Peacock," said John, "and I suppose it is."

Questions

1. Do you agree with the rationale for John's decision? Explain.
2. Under what circumstances might Miller Chemical have been required to validate the tests?

Experiencing Human Resource Management

Selecting the best person to fill a vacant position is one of the most important tasks of human resource management. As all managers recognize, many factors must be considered in order to ensure proper selection. The selection decision you will be dealing with in this exercise is necessary because George Hendricks has just been promoted, and before he starts his new job, his replacement must be determined. George's firm is an affirmative action employer, and presently there are few women in management. George has some excellent employees to choose from, but there are many factors to consider before a decision can be made. The people upstairs made it perfectly clear that they expect George to select an individual who can perform as well he did over the last six years. The people he worked with on the line made it clear that they want Sam. The women on the line have indicated, to everyone who will listen, that it is time for a female supervisor, in at least one division. But, it is George's decision, and he must select the best person regardless of the heat.

Sam Philips, an employee of the company for the past eleven years, is one possible candidate. He wants this promotion, needs the higher pay, wants the respect and influence to be gained, and the nice office that George has now. Sam is recognized as one of the most technically capable individuals in the division. He is from the old school: we get things done through discipline, we don't put up with people allowing their personal problems to interfere with work.

Fred Rubble, an employee of the company for six years, is another candidate. He believes he should get the promotion primarily because he can do the best job. Fred is very capable, but not quite as familiar with all the technical aspects of the job as is Fredda or Sam. He has an associate degree in liberal arts, but is taking business classes at night. Fred is also actively involved in the community and has held various civic offices.

Fredda Lott, an employee for seven years, is the final candidate for the promotion. She wants the promotion primarily because she can do a good job and represent the women on the line. She was an excellent student in college and believes she can deal effectively with the personal problems of others. She is recognized as technically capable and has an undergraduate degree in management.

Four individuals will have roles in this exercise: one to serve as George Hendricks, the current supervisor, and three to be the candidates for the promotion. Your instructor will provide the participants with additional information necessary to complete the exercise.

REFERENCES

"Adverse Impact: Can Your Hiring System Pass the Test?" *Training*, 22 (March 1985), pp. 111–112.

Ayers, J., and R. E. Heineman. "The Most Cost Effective Part of the Hiring Process (Preemployment Screening)." *Security Management*, 29 (March 1985), pp. 55–56.

Barrett, G. V. et al. "The Concept of Dynamic Criteria: A Critical Reanalysis." *Personnel Psychology*, 38 (Spring 1985), pp. 41–56.

Berger, Raymond M., and Donna H. Tucker. "How to Evaluate a Selection Test." *Personnel Journal*, 66 (February 1987), pp. 88–90.

Bottorf, Dana. "The Velvet Boot." *New England Business*, 9 (October 19, 1987), pp. 21–25.

Briscoe, Dennis R., and Susan Harwood. "Improving the Interview Process." *Personnel*, 61 (September 1987), pp. 18–20.

"Companies Move Cautiously into 1985 with Employment Plans for Marketers." *Marketing News* (January 18, 1985), pp. 1ff.

Davey, B. W. "Personnel Testing and the Search for Alternatives (Selection Procedures)." *Public Personnel Management*, 13 (Winter 1984), pp. 361–374.

Davidson, Jeffrey P. "Checking References." *Supervisory Management*, 31 (January 1986), pp. 29–31.

Dawley, Patricia K. "Interviews By Tape." *ABA Banking Journal*, 79 (November 1987), pp. 101–102.

Driskell, Paul C. "Recruitment: A Manager's Checklist for Labor Leasing." *Personnel Journal*, 65 (October 1986), p. 108.

Fear, Richard A., and James F. Ross. *Jobs, Dollars—and EEO: How to Hire More Productive Entry-Level Workers* (New York: McGraw-Hill, 1983), p. 113.

Garaventa, Eugene. "The Polygraph: A Dubious Preemployment Screening Technique." *Review of Business*, 7 (Spring 1986), pp. 26–28.

Goodale, James G. *The Fine Art of Interviewing* (Englewood Cliffs, N.J.: Prentice-Hall, 1982).

Heller, Philip S. "EEOC Standards: What Makes a Good Test?" *Personnel Journal*, 65 (July 1986), pp. 102–103.

Huber, Vandra L., Margaret A. Neale, and Gregory B. Northcraft. "Decision Bias and Personnel Selection." *Organizational Behavior and Human Decision Processes*, 40 (August 1987), p. 136.

Hunt, Gary T., and William F. Eadie. *Interviewing: A Communication Approach* (New York: Holt, Rinehart and Winston, 1987).

Jenks, James M. "Protecting Privacy Rights." *Personnel Journal*, 66 (September 1987), p. 123.

Lawrence, Daniel G., Barbara L. Salsburg, John G. Dawson, and Zachary D. Fasman. "Design and Use of Weighted Application Blanks." *Personnel Administrator*, 27 (March 1982), pp. 47–53.

Levesque, J. D. "Selecting and Managing Competent Managers." *Personnel Administrator*, 30 (March 1985), pp. 63–64ff.

Matarazzo, James M. "Honesty Is the Best Policy." *Library Journal* (March 15, 1987), pp. 60–62.

McKee, Thomas E., and Paul E. Bayes. "Why Audit Background Investigations?" *Internal Auditor*, 11 (October 1987), p. 53.

Melohn, Thomas. "Screening for the Best Employees." *Inc*, 9 (January 1987), pp. 101–103.

Mercer, Michael W., and John J. Seres. "Using Scorable Interview 'Tests' in Hiring." *Personnel*, 61 (June 1987), p. 57.

Miceli, Marcia P. "Effects of Realistic Job Previews on Newcomer Affect and Behavior." *Journal of Organizational Behavior Management*, 8 (Spring–Summer 1986), pp. 73–88.

Muczyk, Jan P., and Brian P. Heshizer. "Managing in an Era of Substance Abuse." *Personnel Administrator*, 31 (August 1986), pp. 91–96.

Nelson-Horchler, Joani. "The Trouble With Temps." *Industry Week* (December 11, 1987), pp. 53–55.

Newman, M., and G. Marks de Chabris, "Employment and Privacy." *Journal of Business Ethics*, 6 (February 1987), pp. 153–163.

Paunonen, Sampo V., Douglas N. Jackson, and Steven M. Oberman. "Personnel Selection Decisions: Effects of Applicant Personality and the Letter of Reference." *Organizational Behavior and Human Decision Processes*, 40 (August 1987), p. 97.

Perham, J. C. "How Recruiters Get the Low Down (Confidential Information about Executives Is Easy to Obtain)." *Dun's Business Month*, 125 (May 1985), pp. 60–61.

Pratt, Henry J. "Improving Your Interviews." *Records Management Quarterly*, 21 (October 1987), p. 32.

Rehfuso, John. "Management Development and the Selection of Overseas Executives." *Personnel Administrator*, 27 (July 1982), pp. 35–43.

Sacco, Samuel R. "Temporary Help Services: The Choice Is Up to You." *The Office*, 106 (September 1987), pp. 51–52.

Schneider-Jenkins, C., and N. Carr-Ruffino. "Smart Selection: Three Steps to Choosing New Employees." *Management World*, 14 (March 1985), pp. 38–39.

Schultz, C. B. "Saving Millions Through Judicious Selection of Employees (Valid Tests)." *Public Personnel Management*, 13 (Winter 1984), pp. 409–415.

Scott, R. A. et al. "On-Campus Recruiting: The Students Speak Up (CPA Firms)." *Journal of Accounting*, 159 (January 1985), pp. 60–62ff.

Sewell, C. "Be Prepared—The Overriding Concern in Personnel Screening for Data Processing Positions." *Security Management*, 29 (March 1985), pp. 57–59.

Smart, Bradford D. "Progressive Approaches for Hiring the Best People." *Training and Development Journal*, 41 (September 1987), pp. 46–53.

Susser, Peter A. "Update on Polygraphs and Employment." *Personnel Administrator*, 31 (February 1986), pp. 28–29.

Voluck, Philip R. "Recruiting, Interviewing and Hiring: Staying Within the Boundaries." *Personnel Administrator*, 32 (May 1987), pp. 15–19.

Weiss, Alan. "Select, Don't Settle." *Training*, 24 (September 1987); p. 90.

Williams, J. "The Baby Bust Hits the Job Market." *Fortune* (May 27, 1985), pp. 122–126ff.

APPENDIX POTENTIAL INTERVIEWING PROBLEMS

One source alone lists almost a dozen serious problems associated with unstructured interviews.[1] Although each of the following potential interviewing problems can be satisfactorily dealt with, they nevertheless threaten the success of employment interviews.

■ LACK OF GOALS

A management axiom is that clearly stated goals are essential if meaningful activity is to take place. This requirement is no less essential for the interviewing process. Goals for the selection interview are tied to both the job to be filled and the qualifications of the applicant. Unfortunately, individuals are often selected on the basis of whim, with less sufficient consideration for the skills, knowledge, and abilities required to perform the job.

In order to effectively conduct an interview, the interviewer must know the job's content and the human requirements for satisfactorily performing the job. As we previously discussed, this information is obtained from job analysis. Without it, the interviewer cannot set goals, ask pertinent questions, or make rational judgments about candidates.

■ PREMATURE JUDGMENTS (FIRST IMPRESSION BIAS)

Some researchers have established that the first few minutes of personal meetings typically provide the most lasting impressions of ourselves to others. This being the case, an interviewer should consciously resist the temptation to make quick decisions about applicants. When this does occur, the interviewer will likely spend the remaining interview time searching for information to support the decision already made. This practice represents not only wasted time but a foolhardy approach to selection. A more appropriate technique is to objectively gather all needed data, analyze it, and then make an evaluation.

---

[1] Terry W. Mullins and Ronald H. Davis, "A Strategy for Managing the Selection Interview Process," *Personnel Administrator*, 26 (March 1981), pp. 66–67.

■ INTERVIEWER DOMINATION

When interviewers dominate the conversation, collecting job-related information about the candidate is hindered. In successful interviews, relevant information must flow both ways: thus interviewers must develop listening skills. Listening is essential for effective communication, but studies have shown that most of us listen with about 25 percent efficiency.[2] One of the most common errors made by an interviewer is talking too much. The applicant should be permitted to talk about 75 percent of the time during a job interview.[3] People listen in different ways, but all listening methods do not provide satisfactory results. Individuals can engage in marginal listening, giving the speaker only part of their attention. When people do this, they may understand only a part of what is said. But what about the remainder? Often the most essential part of what was said is not heard, in which case it obviously will not be understood.

A second type of listening is referred to as evaluative. In this case, while the speaker is talking, the listener starts formulating his or her response or rebuttal to what is being said. Once again, parts of the speaker's message are not even received, and portions that were received are often misunderstood.

A third type of listening is called empathic. Here, the listener makes an effort to enter the mind of the speaker. The listener attempts to put aside personal biases and his or her own frame of reference. While all transmissions must ultimately be evaluated, the evaluation is not made prematurely. It is delayed until the entire message has been received and a sincere effort has been made to understand what the speaker means. Empathic listening is difficult. Yet, it is this approach that permits understanding, therefore communication, to take place.

From the firm's viewpoint, the objective of the employment interview is to acquire sufficient information for making an informed choice. If the interviewer dominates the conversation, dispenses facts, or merely outlines the parameters of the position, he or she will not succeed. A primary interviewing goal is to gather information. To do so, interviewers must question and listen.

■ INCONSISTENT QUESTIONS

Various applicants may be asked different questions by the same or different interviewers. When this happens, all the applicants are not judged on the same basis and charges of discrimination may result. If interviewers ask applicants essentially the same questions and in the same sequence, a

---

[2] Joel P. Bowman and Bernadine P. Branchaw, *Business Communication* (Chicago: The Dryden Press, 1987), p. 587.

[3] Charles Denova, "The Job Interviewer and the Supervisor," *Supervision*, XLV (September 1983), p. 26.

better foundation is provided for comparing the qualifications of the applicants, and higher reliability should occur.[4]

■ CENTRAL TENDENCY

The central tendency error occurs when an interviewer rates virtually all candidates as average. In this instance, the interviewer refuses to differentiate between strong and weak candidates.

■ HALO ERROR

The type of bias known as halo error occurs when an interviewer is overly impressed with one or more personal characteristics and permits this bias to unduly affect his or her opinion of the applicant. For example, an interviewer who places a high value on neatness or communication skill may automatically favor candidates who rate high on these attributes, without due regard for other abilities that may relate more directly to job requirements.

■ CONTRAST EFFECTS

An error in judgment may occur when, for example, an interviewer meets with several poorly qualified applicants and then confronts a mediocre candidate. By comparison, the last applicant may appear to be better qualified than he or she actually is and, as a result, receive a higher rating than deserved.

■ INTERVIEWER BIAS

All individuals, through their experiences, have acquired certain biases. These biases can totally disrupt the interviewing process, which should be as objective as possible. Thus interviewers must know themselves, acknowledge and understand their own prejudices, and learn to deal with those prejudices. If he or she is unable to do this, the interviewer's attitude—perhaps at the unconscious level—can lead to unfair treatment of candidates. For example, research has indicated that interviewers terminate interviews with physically handicapped applicants sooner than they do with nonhandicapped candidates.[5]

---

[4] Paul S. Greenlaw and John P. Kohl, "Selection Interviewing and the New Uniform Federal Guidelines," *Personnel Administrator*, 25 (August 1980), p.78.

[5] Robert L. Dipboye, "Self-Fulfilling Prophecies in the Selection-Recruitment Interview," *The Academy of Management Review*, 7 (October 1982), p. 52.

CHAPTER 7 Selection

Another example of such bias is stereotyping; where the interviewer has a preconception of the ideal candidate. Some interviewers may not believe that women or blacks, for example, are qualified to handle executive positions because they do not match the interviewers' stereotypes. They may view such individuals as best suited for secretarial, clerical, or more menial jobs. Although actions based on these stereotyped views are illogical and clearly illegal, they do occur and, as a result, qualified candidates may be eliminated from the selection process.

■ LACK OF INTERVIEWER TRAINING

Employment interviews are often conducted by line managers who interview infrequently. Typically, they are not well trained in interviewing techniques. This deficiency is compounded by other pressures of their jobs. As a result, interview goals may not be clearly formulated, and these interviewers may not be prepared to answer questions asked by the candidate.

■ BEHAVIOR SAMPLE

It has been suggested that even if an interviewer spent a week with an applicant, the sample of behavior would be too small to properly assess the candidate's qualifications. Furthermore, not only is the sample of behavior inadequate, the candidate's behavior during an interview is also seldom typical or natural.[6]

■ NONVERBAL COMMUNICATION

Words are the most important symbols used in communication. As a result, employment interviews tend to focus on them. However, facial expressions and body movements can often convey meaning very effectively. An interviewer should be aware of his or her nonverbal behavior, which might transmit unintended signals. For example, the interviewer may glance at the clock to determine how much time is left for the interview. The applicant may interpret this action as meaning "the interview is over." Other actions that often occur during the interview and common interpretations of them by applicants are shown in Table A-1.

Often interviewers are not fully aware of their nonverbal behavior. Actually, they should make a conscious effort to view themselves as applicants do in order to avoid sending inappropriate or unintended signals.

---

[6] Robert L. Decker, "The Employment Interview: Are We Seeing the Demise of Another Management Prerogative?" *Personnel Administrator*, 27 (November 1981), p. 72.

TABLE A-1 | Nonverbal Communication

Behavior	Possible Interpretation
Sitting stiffly behind desk	*This is a very formal meeting. I'd better not reveal too much of myself.*
Reading the application form	*This interviewer doesn't even know who I am.*
Nodding head	*You understand what I'm saying.*
Frequent glancing out the window	*This person would rather be someplace else.*
Receiving telephone calls	*This manager is too busy to see me.*
Frowning	*My answer to that question didn't go over very well.*

■ INTERPRETATION OF BEHAVIOR

An additional problem in assessing an applicant is that of interpreting his or her behavior. Suppose, for example, that during a stress interview, in which the interviewer makes insulting remarks, the candidate simply gets up and walks out or decides to sue. Should this be interpreted as (1) an indication that the candidate is well informed, that is, knows his or her rights; (2) an indication of immaturity and insecurity; or (3) an indication of stupidity, in that the candidate has lost a chance of a job? No one, including the "experts," has satisfactorily solved this problem.[7]

■ INAPPROPRIATE QUESTIONS

A basic requirement in employee selection is that the questions asked be job related. During an interview, it is very easy for an interviewer to innocently ask questions, the answers to which may reveal irrelevant information about women or minorities. Employers must be extremely cautious in asking questions that are generally considered risky from a legal viewpoint.

At this point, litigation has revolved around two basic themes. First, do questions give the impression of a discriminatory attitude? For example, is reference made to "girls" and are women asked about marital status, child care, and so on? Second, does the question have the effect of creating an adverse impact on women or minorities?[8]

---

[7] *Ibid.*

[8] Richard D. Arvey and James E. Campion, "The Employment Interview: A Summary and Review of Recent Research," *Personnel Psychology*, 35 (1982), p. 289.

PART TWO

CASE II

Parma Cycle Company: Workers for the New Plant

Gene Wilson, the corporate planner at Parma Cycle Company, was ecstatic as he talked with the human resource director, Jesse Heard, that Tuesday morning in early 1988. He had just received word that the board of directors had approved the plan for Parma's new southern plant, to be located in Clarksdale, Mississippi. "I really appreciate your help on this, Jesse," Gene said. "Without the research you did on the human resource needs for the new plant, I don't think that it would have been approved." "We still have a long way to go," said Jesse. "There's no doubt that we can construct the building and install the machinery, but getting skilled workers in Clarksdale, Mississippi, may not be so easy." "Well," said Gene, "the results of the labor survey that you did in Clarksdale last year indicate that we'll be able to get by. Anyway, some of the people here at Parma will surely agree to transfer."

Clarksdale, population 25,000, is the county seat of Coahoma County, in the Mississippi River delta below Memphis, Tennessee. Per capita income in the county hovered above $5,000 a year in the late 1980s, far below the national average and less than half the level in the Parma, Ohio, area.

"When is the new plant scheduled to open?" asked Jesse. Gene replied, "The building will be finished in June, the machinery will be in by July, and the goal is to be in production by September." "Gosh," said Jesse, "I'd better get to work."

A few minutes later, back in his office, Jesse considered what the future held at Parma Cycle. The company had been located in Parma, Ohio, a Cleveland suburb, since its founding. It had grown over the years to become the nation's third largest bicycle manufacturer. The decision to open the southern plant had been made in hopes of cutting production costs, through lower wages, and improving quality. Although no one ever came right out and said it, it was assumed that the southern plant would be nonunion. The elimination of union work rules was expected to be a benefit.

The state of Mississippi had offered a ten-year exemption from all property taxes. This was a significant advantage because tax rates for Cleveland area industries were extremely high. Jesse was pleased that he had been involved in the discussions from the time that the new plant had been first suggested. Even with all the advanced preparation he had done, he knew that the coming months would be extremely difficult for him and his staff.

As Jesse was thinking about all this, his assistant, Ed Deal, walked in with a bundle of papers. "Hi, Ed," said Jesse, "I'm glad you're here. The Clarksdale plant is definitely on the way and you and I need to get our act together." "That's great," said Ed. "It's quite a coincidence, too, because I was just going over this stack of job descriptions, identifying which ones might be eliminated as we scale back at this plant." Jesse said, "Remember, Ed, we are not going to cut back very much here. Some jobs will be deleted and others added. But out of the 800 positions here, I'll bet that not more than forty will actually be cut." "So, what you are saying is that we basically have to staff the plant with people we hire from the Clarksdale area?" Ed asked.

Jesse replied, "No, Ed, we will have some people here who are willing to transfer even though their jobs are not being eliminated. We will then replace them with others we hire in the Cleveland area. Most of the workers at Clarksdale, though, will be recruited from that area."

"What about the management team?" asked Ed. "Well," said Jesse, "I think the boss already knows who the main people will be down there. They are managers we currently have on board plus a fellow we located at a defunct three-wheeler plant in Mound Bayou, Mississippi."

"Who will be the human resource director down there?" asked Ed. "Well," replied Jesse, "I don't think I'm talking out of school by telling you that I plan to recommend you for the job." After letting that soak in for a minute, Ed said, "It's no secret I was hoping for that. When will we know for sure?" "There's really not much doubt," said Jesse, "I'm so sure that I've decided to put you in charge of human resources for the whole project. During the next two weeks I'd like you to put together a comprehensive plan. I want a detailed report of the people we will need, including their qualifications. Secondly, we need more information about the labor supply in Clarksdale. Finally, I'd like for you to come up with a general idea of who might be willing to transfer from this plant. They are really going to be the backbone of our work force at Clarksdale." "Okay, Jesse, but I'll need a lot of help," said Ed as he gathered his papers and left. As Jesse watched Ed leave he thought he noticed a certain snappiness about Ed's movements that had not been there before.

Questions

1. What procedures should be followed in determining the human resource needs at the new plant?
2. How might Jesse and Ed go about recruiting workers in Clarksdale? Managers?

P·A·R·T T·H·R·E·E

HUMAN RESOURCE DEVELOPMENT

- Human Resource Research
- Human Resource Planning, Recruitment, and Selection
- **Human Resource Development**
- Employee and Labor Relations
- Compensation and Benefits
- Safety and Health

Human Resource Management

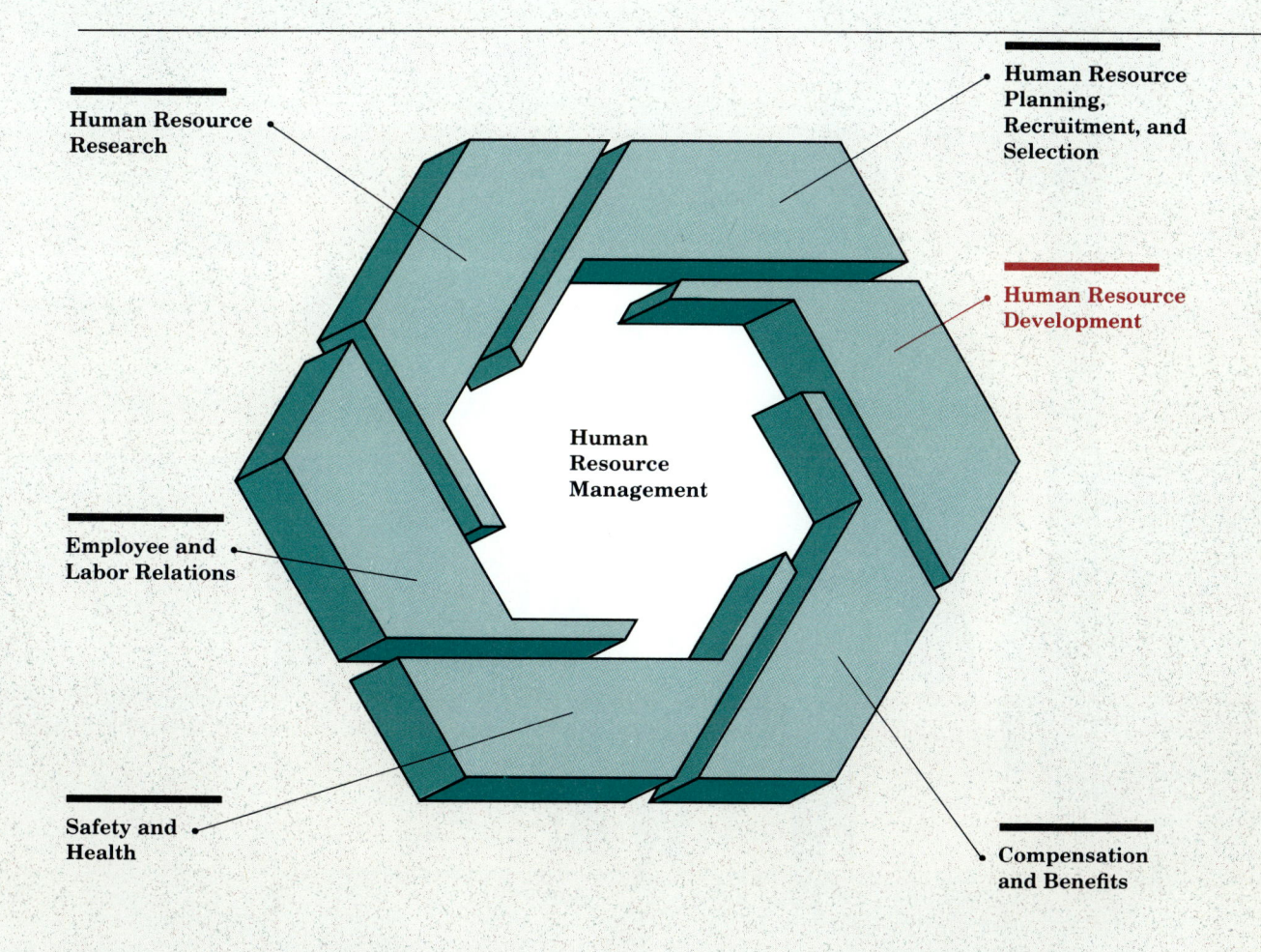

CHAPTER 8

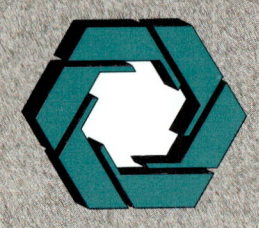

ORGANIZATION CHANGE AND HUMAN RESOURCE DEVELOPMENT

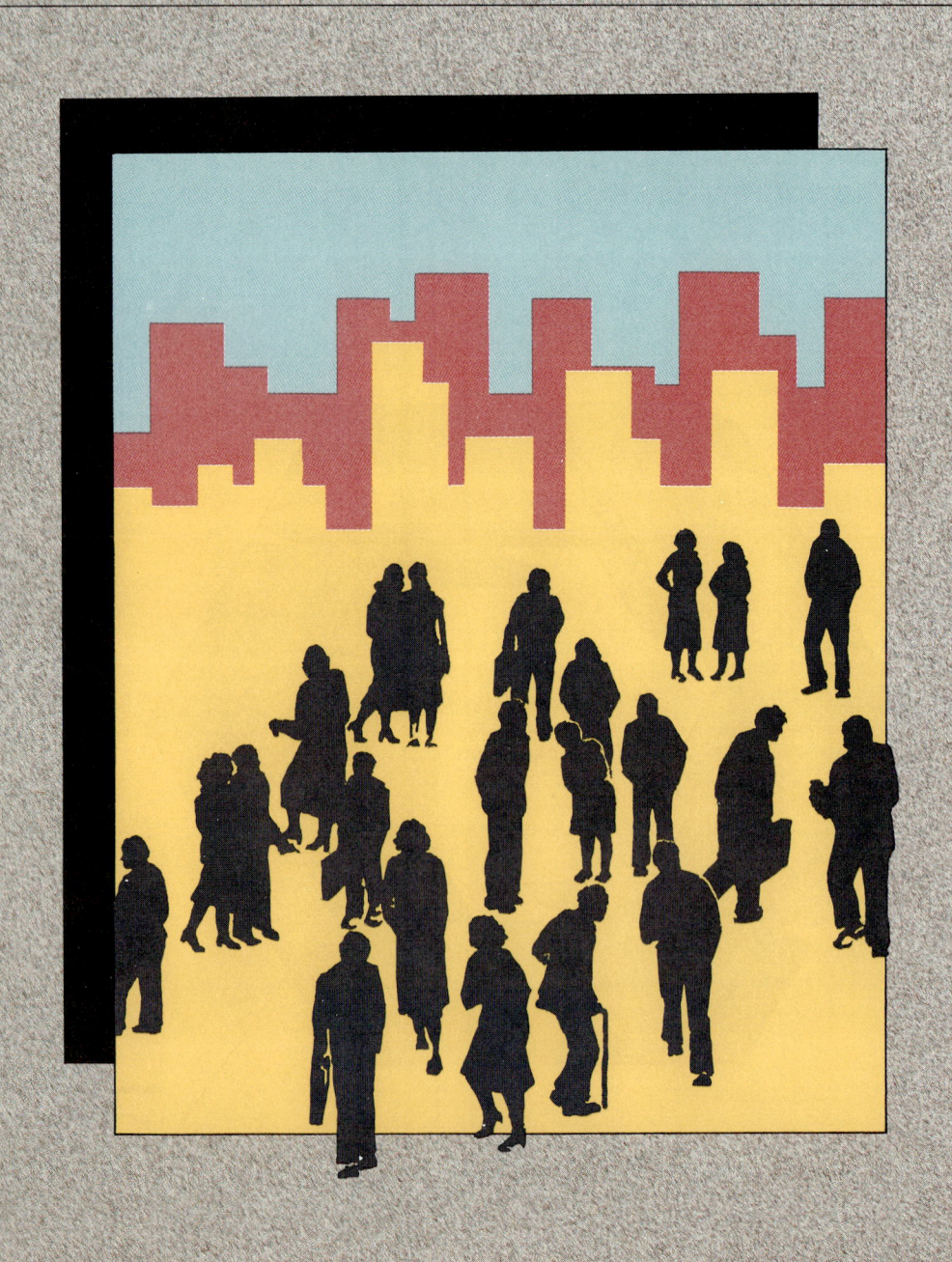

CHAPTER OBJECTIVES

1. Describe the organization change sequence, accompanying difficulties, and ways to reduce resistance to change.
2. Define human resource development (HRD), list the general purposes of HRD, describe factors influencing HRD, and explain the human resource development process.
3. Explain how HRD needs are determined and HRD objectives are established, describe the various management development methods, and explain the HRD methods specifically available for operative employees.
4. Describe problems associated with implementation of HRD programs, explain the importance of HRD evaluation, and describe the significance of employee orientation.

> ■ Marian Lillie, an experienced accountant, competently handled the administrative tasks for an automobile dealership for over ten years. She was familiar with all aspects of the business. Two months ago, the dealership was sold to a young man who had an MBA from a prominent university in the northeast. Soon after he assumed control of the firm, he automated every conceivable administrative function. Marian was not consulted at any point in the process. She was, however, presented with a procedures manual when the project was completed. Later she was overheard telling a co-worker, "I know this new system is not going to work."
>
> Imagining Marian Lillie's opposition to changes that she doesn't understand isn't difficult. Based on her last statement she isn't likely to support the changes, which were made without her consultation.

We devote the first portion of this chapter to a discussion of organization change and to defining human resource development (HRD). Then we describe factors that influence HRD. Next, we address elements of the HRD process, which include determining HRD needs, establishing objectives, selecting methods and media, and implementing and evaluating the HRD program. We devote the final portion of the chapter to employee orientation.

■ ORGANIZATION CHANGE

Change involves moving from one condition to another, and it may affect individuals, groups, or even an entire organization. Therefore, those who want to learn about human resource development must first understand the change sequence, the accompanying difficulties, and ways to reduce resistance to change.

The Change Sequence

Change for the sake of change is seldom justified. Some degree of stability is needed to allow employees to accomplish assigned tasks. Even too many rational changes over a short period of time may leave workers bewildered and confused.[1] Change can also be a source of mental and physical problems, regardless of whether the change has favorable or unfavorable consequences. It is a contributing factor for most mental and physical health problems, as it destroys homeostasis.[2]

Because of the impact of change on the organization and its employees, change should be undertaken only when a real need for it exists. Of course, circumstances in the internal or external environments may make change desirable or even necessary (see Figure 8-1). Basically, the impetus for change comes from a belief that the organization and its human resources can be more productive and successful after change occurs. But if change is to be successfully implemented, it must be approached systematically. Many managers tend to feel that "we have always done it this way, so why argue with success?" However, a firm's past success does not guarantee future prosperity. Once the need for change has been recognized, an HRD method tailored to the particular situation can be selected.

Reducing resistance to change is crucial to success. At times, this may be extremely difficult because it usually requires shifts in attitudes. Although Marian Lillie is not likely to overtly resist a change and risk losing her job, the new owner could have prepared her better to accept the change and work to make it successful. Many times resistance to change is substantial. Consider, for instance, a machine operator who has been using one piece of equipment over a long period of time and has just been told that she will have to learn another skill. In this situation, the machine operator may become quite anxious and vigorously oppose any proposed changes in her work routine.

However, if resistance to it can be reduced, or even eliminated, change can be implemented more effectively. Change may stem from an order or a suggestion, or it may be undertaken voluntarily. The change will be accomplished more satisfactorily if the person involved in it desires the change and believes that it is needed. Bringing about changes in attitude requires trust and respect between the person attempting to implement the change and the individual(s) affected by the changes.

The change sequence does not end when a change is implemented. A new and flexible position capable of dealing with present requirements and adapting to further change must be developed. The final phase of the change sequence involves evaluating the effectiveness of the specific HRD method

---

[1] H. Kent Baker and Stephen R. Holmberg, "Stepping Up to Supervision: Coping with Change," *Supervisory Management*, 27 (March 1982), p. 23.

[2] George S. Everly, Jr., "Managing Change Demands Three Simple, Personal Steps," *Data Management*, 22 (September 1984), p. 21.

CHAPTER 8 Organization Change and Human Resource Development

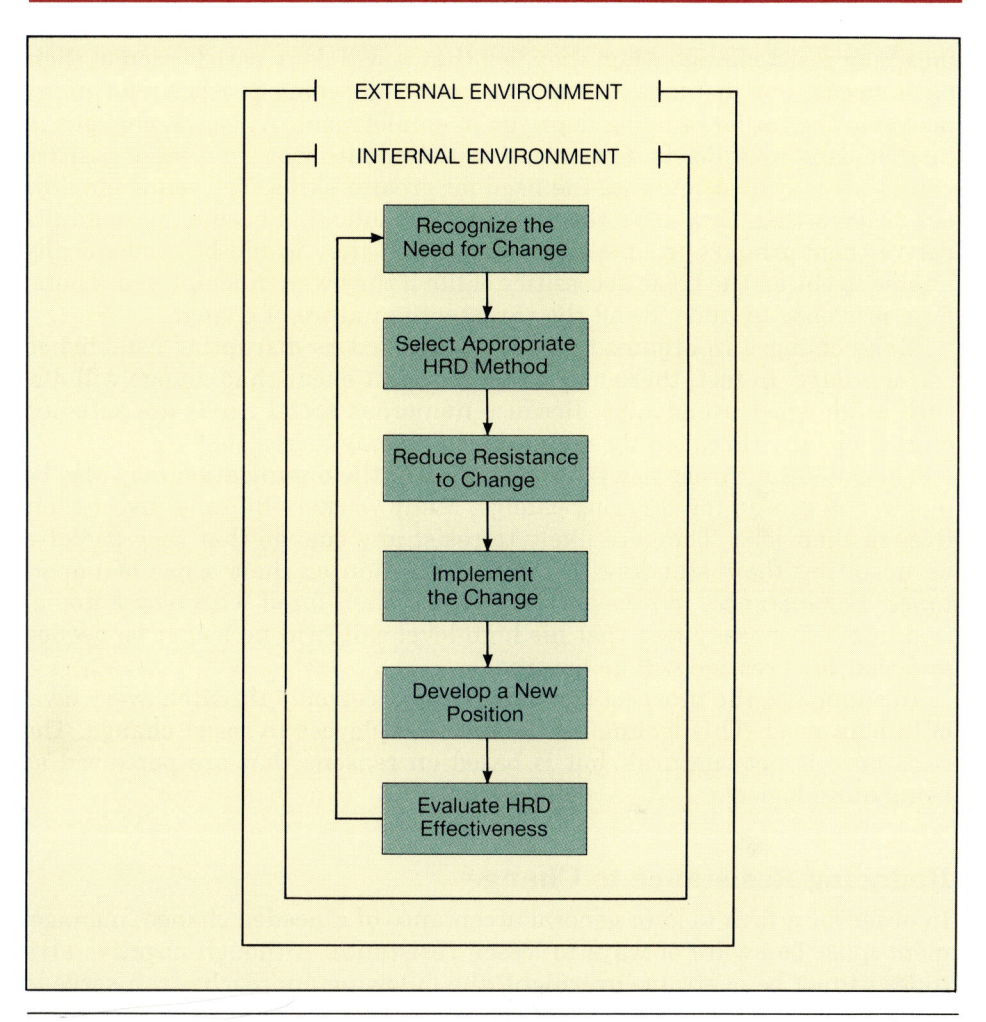

FIGURE 8-1 | The Organization Change Sequence

chosen. As we mentioned previously, one primary measure of effectiveness is how the program affected the firm's "bottom line." Human resource development is an on-going process because both the organization's internal and external environments are dynamic and are always impinging upon the status quo.

Reasons for Resistance to Change

In business circles, employees' "natural" resistance to change has been discussed widely. Although change is often resisted, sometimes quite vigorously,[3] such opposition is not innate. Rather, the resistance may be explained in terms of employee expectations and past experiences. Individuals may resist change when they feel that it will deny satisfaction of their basic needs. For instance, one of the most frightening prospects for many people is the threat of being deprived of employment. At times, changes in methods and systems do downgrade and eliminate jobs. In a more positive vein, they may also generate the need for greater skills. Yet, many employees believe that they lack the flexibility to adjust. Because most adults derive their primary income from their work, they would be economically unable to obtain the basic necessities of life if they were unemployed. Therefore, it is easy to understand the threatening nature of change.

Many changes in organizations are perceived as disrupting established social groups. In fact, there may be an inordinate fear that change will disturb established friendships. Because numerous social needs are satisfied on the job, any threat to these relationships may be resisted.

The potential threat to a person's status in the organization may also be a powerful reason for resisting change. Many workers literally invest their lives in their jobs. They are likely to resist any change that they perceive as upsetting their standing in the organization or their sense of importance. For instance, the master machinist, when faced with new automation in his firm, may fear that his high-level skill will no longer be needed and that his prestige will be lowered.

In summary, the prospect of change can conceivably threaten every level of human need. This feeling often causes employees to resist change. The resistance is not "natural" but is based on reasons that are perceived as being quite logical.

Reducing Resistance to Change

In order for a firm to gain general acceptance of a needed change, management must be aware of ways to lessen resistance. Although negative attitudes cannot be overcome overnight, the following approaches can serve to increase employees' acceptance of change.

Building Trust and Confidence. The degree of employee trust and confidence in management relates directly to their past experiences. If employees have suffered in the past as a result of change, they may reasonably attempt to avoid future changes. When management has misrepresented the effects of change, resistance tends to be even greater. For example, when faced with the prospect of having to reduce the workforce, management may assure employees that layoffs will be based on individual performance. However, if previous layoffs appeared to be determined by seniority or favoritism, employees may not believe that current actions will be any different.

Conversely, management builds trust by dealing with employees in an open and straightforward manner. Workers who are told that they need

---

[3] Rensis Likert and Jane Gibson Likert, *New Ways of Managing Conflict* (New York: McGraw-Hill, 1976), p. 245.

additional training will accept the idea much more readily if they have confidence in management. The desired level of trust cannot be achieved quickly. Rather, it results from a long period of fair dealing by the firm's management.

Developing Open Communication. An estimated 90 percent of "confidential" information in most organizations is not truly confidential. It is withheld from employees because of management's unwillingness to share information.[4] Such managers create a climate that breeds mistrust and fear. Any rumor of planned changes may then become extremely distorted, with the firm's employees programed to fear the worst.

By sharing information with employees, management can take a giant step toward developing open communications. In speaking to this point, Louis Lunborg, former chairman of the board of Bank of America, once stated:

> People want to know several things. They want to know what their own job is all about, why they are doing what we ask them to do, what good it does anybody, and above all, how well they are doing it. And then they want to know what's going on. If they see strange things happening or hear rumors that something new is about to happen, they want to know about it.
>
> If you don't tell them, you're saying, "It's none of your business," and that in turn means, "I just don't think you are important enough." It is the deadliest thing you can do to people.[5]

Managers must recognize that subordinates are human beings and deal with them accordingly. Their informational needs should be recognized and reasonably met, whenever possible.

Employee Participation. People such as Marian Lillie are more inclined to accept changes if they are given the opportunity to participate in the planning. For instance, suppose that management determines that a department's operating budget must be cut by 25 percent. The department's manager may more readily accept this change if permitted to help determine the extent of the cuts and where they should be made. Participation is also more effective when permitted in the early planning stages. For example, an employee might not feel too involved if brought in on a change the day before it is to be implemented.

Through participation, resistance to change can be minimized and in some cases eliminated. In fact, developing a participative climate within which employees aggressively seek change is often possible. In order to achieve such an atmosphere, it is necessary to remove, or at least minimize, the employee fears of being unable to satisfy their personal needs.

---

[4] Justin G. Longnecker, *Principles of Management and Organizational Behavior*, 3rd ed. (Columbus, Ohio: Charles E. Merrill, 1973), p. 479.

[5] Louis B. Lunborg, "Managing for Tomorrow," *Information and Records Management* (April 1971), p. 72. Reprinted by permission.

Executive Insights

Robert E. Edwards, AEP
Senior Vice-President
Drake Beam Morin, Inc.

Bob Edwards is presently a Senior Vice-President in the downtown Dallas office of Drake Beam Morin, Inc. He has full responsibility for the management of the office, development of new business, key account management, and for the development and delivery of consulting services. Prior to accepting employment with his present firm in 1984, Edwards held a key human resource management position in the life insurance operations of Tenneco, Inc. Previous major business affiliations included a national retailer, a bank, and a manufacturer of sports clothing.

Edward's first job was as a caddie at the Ohio State University golf course at age eleven. He then worked at a variety of jobs, such as bundle boy in a textile mill, bank clerk, theater usher, warehouseman, and newspaper route salesman. Because of his father's failing health and the economic hardships of a depressed era, Bob frequently moved with his family to areas that offered better economic opportunities. In order to boost family income and obtain some financial independence, he found jobs in each new location.

He reentered college after serving a four-year military commitment in the U.S. Air Force, where he was trained as an airborne communications specialist and as a fighter pilot. He completed his undergraduate degree while working a part-time job in the credit department of a large retailer, where he became involved with the extension of credit and repossession of unpaid-for goods, which was one of the few tasks he disliked.

His breadth of work experience at an early age had given him an understanding of jobs, people, and organizations. This knowledge proved invaluable as his career progressed.

Edwards joined Southwestern Life Insurance Company in 1957 after graduating from college with a degree in personnel and industrial relations. Subsequently, he earned an M.S. degree in communications and industrial psychology. Although he began his professional career in a general management training program, he soon accepted an opportunity to head up a major staff function. He was transferred to the personnel department in 1962. In 1965, he was promoted to assistant personnel manager and in 1969 to personnel director with responsibility for two life insurance companies, a real estate development company, and a mutual fund company. In 1971, he was promoted to vice president for personnel for Southwestern Life Corporation, with full accountability for contributing to the profitability of the company through human resource leadership.

When asked why he avoided sales work, Edwards replies simply, "I haven't." He also explains, "A good human resource executive must sell—he or she must have all the sales tools to be effective. To reinforce the point, he tells a story about two of his top assistants who left personnel to become Southwestern sales representatives. In their first year, both individuals received their company's top newcomer sales award.

Edwards says, "As an enterprising human resource executive, you have a perspective of the organization as much like the chief executive as any other person. In a top management role, you don't overlook a corner of the business. You are in a unique position to shape the organization because you deal clearly with both its people and structure. This challenge—if met—results in a tremendous amount of intrinsic satisfaction."

He believes that professionals with knowledge gained from continuing academic curiosity and a searching examination of company operations determine the quality of the human resource department's contribution to the success of the company. He suggests that managers should strive for an organizational climate that motivates individuals to perform to the best of their abilities. In explaining how this can be accomplished, he identifies one of the major areas, saying, "Training and development should be on a continuous basis. This permits employees to know that we care about them and that we are vitally concerned about their performance and mobility within that company."

Currently, Edwards is a member of the Society for Human Resource Management, Dallas Personnel Association, and the Life Office Management Association. He is a past executive director of the North Texas Personnel Conference and past president of the Dallas Personnel Association. He has served as chairman of the National Chapter Awards Committee as well as district director of the American Society for Personnel Administration, and as national chairman of the Personnel Accreditation Institute Management Practices Committee. He has also served as a member of the Executive Committee and Secretary of PAI. He has earned the AEP designation and an FMLI (fellowship in the Life Office Management Institute) with a specialization in personnel administration.

Managers must be convinced that their own actions—not the employee's inherent nature—are most often responsible for attitudes toward change. Only then can human resource development programs be effective.

■ HUMAN RESOURCE DEVELOPMENT: DEFINITION AND SCOPE

Human resource development (HRD) is planned, continuous effort by management to improve employee competency levels and organizational performance through training, education, and development programs. The broad scope of the HRD function is reflected in its three components: training, education, and development.[6] **Training** includes those activities that serve to improve an individual's performance on a currently held job or one related to it.[7] Showing a worker how to operate a lathe or a supervisor how to schedule daily production are examples of training. **Education** consists of activities that are conducted to improve the overall competence of an individual in a specific direction and beyond the current job.[8] Seminars designed to develop communication or leadership skills fall into this category. Training and education both focus on either currently held jobs or predetermined different jobs within the organization. **Development** involves learning opportunities aimed at the individual's growth but not restricted to a specific present or future job.[9] It prepares employees to keep pace with the organization as it changes and grows. Developing human resources has become crucial with the rapid advances in technology. "High tech" has made the need for development quite apparent.[10] As jobs grow increasingly complex and impersonal, the need for improved human relations within a firm also becomes increasingly significant. Largely because of this, as Bob Edwards, in his Executive Insight, commented, "Training and development should be on a continuous basis."

The connection between economic survival and productivity has become obvious in the last decade, with the result that increased productivity has become a strategic goal for many firms.[11] In fact, the primary purpose of HRD is to improve worker productivity and the firm's profitability. Most organizations invest in HRD because they believe that higher profits will result—which often happens. Training frequently improves workers' skills and boosts their motivation. This, in turn, leads to higher productivity and

---

[6] Leonard Nadler, "Human Resources Development." In Leonard Nadler (ed.), *The Handbook of Human Resource Development* (New York: John Wiley & Sons, 1984), p. 1.16.

[7] *Ibid.*, p. 1.18.

[8] *Ibid.*, p. 1.19.

[9] *Ibid.*, p. 1.22.

[10] Benjamin B. Tregoe and John W. Zimmerman, "Needed: A Strategy for Human Resource Development," *Training and Development Journal*, 38 (May 1984), p. 78.

[11] George J. McManus, "Team Concept Stressed in Productivity Confab," *Iron Age* (December 7, 1981), p. 47.

increased profitability.[12] "The recognition that people are a company's critical resource—and its greatest storehouse of knowledge—is creating a boom in corporate training and education."[13]

Another major goal of HRD is to prevent obsolescence of skills at all levels in the company. Not only can effective HRD programs play a vital role in achieving this goal, they can also upgrade employees' skills to qualify them for promotion. The organization is responsible for helping employees to upgrade their skills based on employee aptitudes and interests, in addition to meeting the needs of the company. Human resource development costs should be accepted for what they are: an investment in human resources.

■ THE HUMAN RESOURCE DEVELOPMENT PROCESS

Major adjustments in the external and internal environments necessitate corporate change. The general human resource development process that helps facilitate change is shown in Figure 8-2. Once the need for change is recognized, the process of determining training, education, and development needs begins. Essentially two questions must be asked. The first is, "What are our training needs?" The second is, "What do we want to accomplish through our HRD efforts?" The objectives might be quite narrow if limited to the supervisory ability of a manager. Or they might be so broad as to include improving the management skills of all first-line supervisors.

After stating the process's objectives, management can determine the appropriate methods and media for accomplishing them. Various methods and media are available; the selection depends on the nature of HRD goals. Naturally, HRD must be continuously evaluated in order to properly facilitate change and accomplish organizational objectives.

Probably the most common function of an HRD process revolves around training. Increasingly, training departments are being considered as profit centers rather than overhead. The training manager at Hewlett-Packard's Business Computer Sales Center has commented, "We present our contribution to division management, along with the other groups. We are measured on the results we show—more training provided, more skills learned, more quickly." A training department that is evaluated on results achieved *must* think like a profit center.[14] Training, as with all HRD functions, requires continuous reevaluation.

---

[12] Michael Godkewitsch, "The Dollars and Sense of Corporate Training," *Training: The Magazine of Human Resources Development*, 24 (May 1987), pp. 79–81.

[13] John Naisbitt and Patricia Aburdene, *Re-inventing the Corporation* (New York: Warner Books, 1985), p. 165.

[14] Chris Lee, "Training Profiles: The View from Ground Level," *Training: The Magazine of Human Resources Development,* 23 (October 1986), p. 76.

PART THREE   Human Research Development

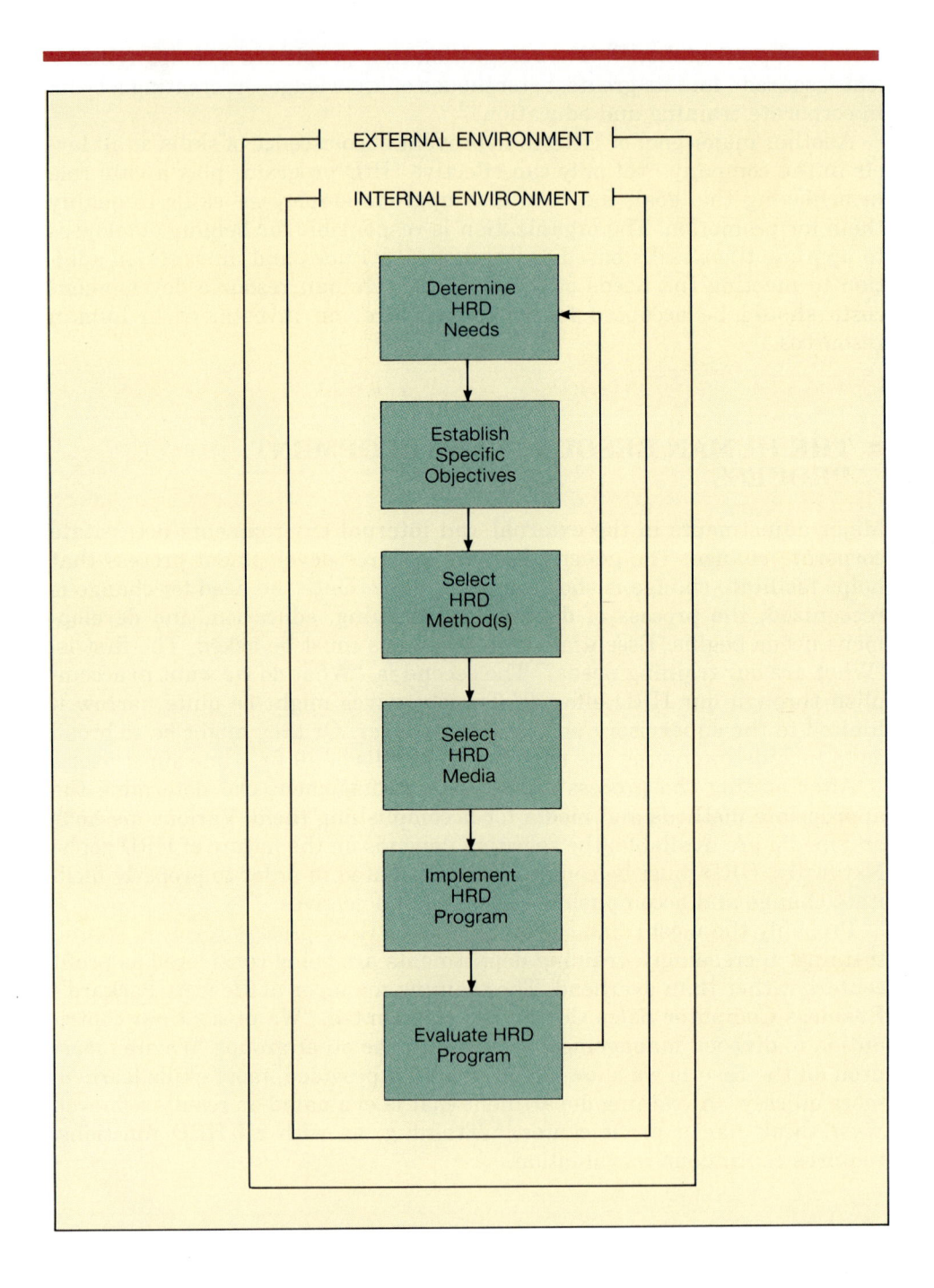

```
                EXTERNAL ENVIRONMENT
                INTERNAL ENVIRONMENT

                    Determine
                      HRD
                     Needs
                        ↓
                    Establish
                     Specific
                    Objectives
                        ↓
                     Select
                      HRD
                    Method(s)
                        ↓
                     Select
                      HRD
                     Media
                        ↓
                   Implement
                      HRD
                    Program
                        ↓
                  Evaluate HRD
                    Program
```

FIGURE 8-2 | The Human Resource Development Process

CHAPTER 8 Organization Change and Human Resource Development

■ FACTORS INFLUENCING HUMAN RESOURCE DEVELOPMENT

Several of the most important factors that influence training and development are shown in Figure 8-3. How these factors are addressed often determines whether a firm achieves its HRD objectives.

First and foremost, training and development programs must have top management's full support. This support must be real—not merely lip service—and it should be communicated to the entire organization. True support becomes evident when executives provide the resources needed for the HRD function. The support is further strengthened when top executives actually take part in the training. These actions tend to convince employees of the true importance of HRD programs.

In addition, other managers, both generalists and HRD specialists, should be committed to and involved in the HRD process. Views of several practitioners concerning the HRD manager's role are presented in Table 8-1. Some important conclusions regarding the HRD manager's responsibilities can be drawn from these comments.

The HRD manager operates essentially in a staff, or advisory, capacity. According to Milton R. Scheiber, director of corporate management development for Lone Star Industries, Inc., "The primary responsibility for training and development lies with line managers, from the president

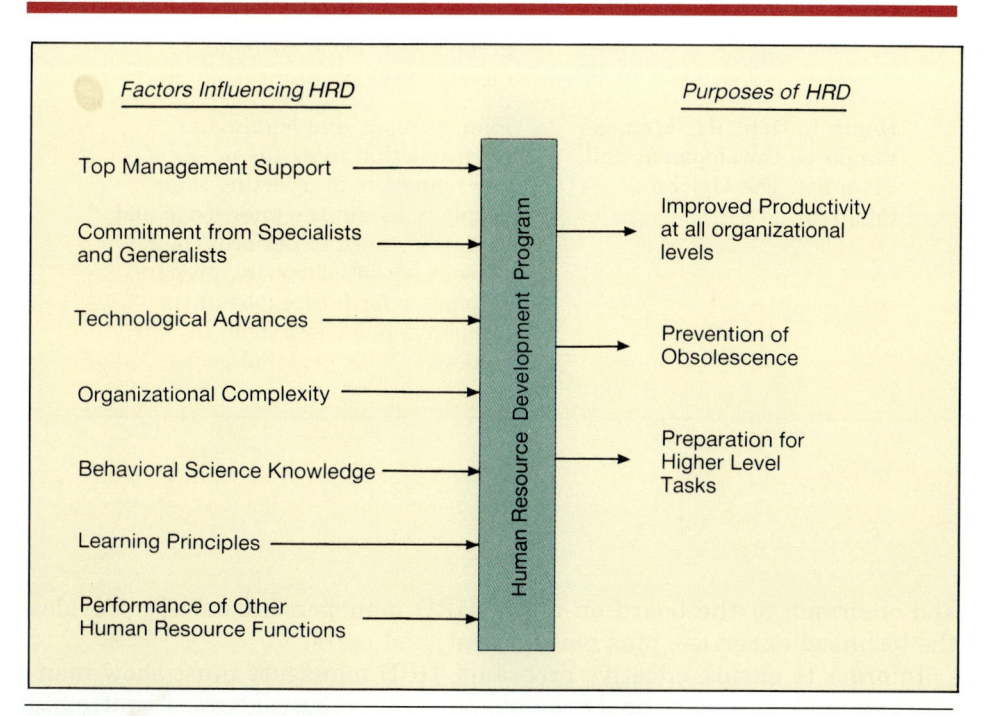

FIGURE 8-3 | Factors Influencing Human Resource Development

Factors Influencing HRD
- Top Management Support
- Commitment from Specialists and Generalists
- Technological Advances
- Organizational Complexity
- Behavioral Science Knowledge
- Learning Principles
- Performance of Other Human Resource Functions

→ Human Resource Development Program →

Purposes of HRD
- Improved Productivity at all organizational levels
- Prevention of Obsolescence
- Preparation for Higher Level Tasks

TABLE 8-1 | Today's Role of the Human Resource Development Manager

Personnel Executive	Comments
Barry N. Lastra, Senior Advisor, Personnel Development, Chevron Corporation	Principal role is to be a consultant to managers to help identify: (1) operating problems or potential problems; (2) scenarios or alternative courses of action to solve these problems or prevent them from occurring; and (3) feedback processes to see that on-job results are consistent with stated management goals.
Raymond Lee, Director of Personnel, Fotomat Corporation	The role varies greatly, depending on the industry and the individual in the job. My perception is that the role is becoming more important and is expanding into nontraditional training and development functions.
T. M. Fabek, District Manager, Training, Ohio Bell Telephone Company	The role of the training/development manager is a staff function that must prove to the line organization and users that the services provided are job relevant, and will improve productivity, lower costs, and increase profits.
Henry L. Dahl, Jr., Manager, Employee Development and Planning, The Upjohn Company	Plan, develop, and administer programs that meet the needs of line managers in assisting their people to obtain the knowledge and skills they need to perform their present job satisfactorily, prepare employees for future jobs in the company, and assist them in achieving their personal goals.

and chairman of the board on down. HRD management merely provides the technical expertise, plus blood, sweat, and tears."

In order to ensure effective programs, HRD managers must show management that there will be a tangible payoff if resources are committed to this effort. One firm, Florida Power Corporation, has a battle cry, "No more training for training's sake." Instead, the company designed a new system, which focuses on specific job objectives and ensures that training is provided—but only when needed.[15]

Some form of cost-benefit analysis should be made prior to implementing any HRD program. The program should be job related, improve productivity, lower costs, and increase profits. The following statement by Chip R. Bell, in his article "Building a Reputation for Training Effectiveness," stresses the importance of accomplishing this task:

> This is the era of "pursuit of excellence," "high performance," and "the right stuff." When quality is returning to popularity, it is important to review, rethink and perhaps reshape the building blocks of our corporate reputation for training effectiveness. It is helpful to examine anew the trail between training effectiveness and our reputation for being/for doing (what we are and what we achieve).[16]

A major role of the HRD manager is to assist people in obtaining the knowledge and skills they need for present and future jobs and to assist them in attaining personal goals. Learning is a self-activity, and all development is self-development. The HRD manager explains the type of training available, shows how it can be accomplished, and provides encouragement to ensure its successful accomplishment.

In recent years, the increasingly rapid changes in products, systems, and methods have had a significant impact on job requirements. Thus employees face the need to constantly upgrade their skills and to develop an attitude that permits them not only to adapt to change, but also to accept and even seek it.

Many organizations have grown to gigantic size in terms of the number of employees, sales volume, and diversity of products. This growth has resulted in extremely complex organizational structures and a high degree of specialization. These conditions necessitate greater operating interdependence. More than ever, people must interact with groups of peers, subordinates, and superiors to perform their jobs successfully.

During the past several decades, a vast amount of new knowledge has emerged from the behavioral sciences. Much of it relates directly to human resource management. Today's managers must be aware of this knowledge and capable of utilizing it. The HRD function faces a substantial task in keeping pace with behavioral science developments and informing others in the organization about them.

Human resource development specialists must know more than the topic to be presented in a training program. He or she must also have some understanding of basic learning principles. The purpose of training is to change employee behavior, and information must be learned if change is to occur. Although much remains to be discovered about the learning process, several generalizations may be helpful in understanding this phenomenon.

---

[15] *Ibid.*

[16] Chip R. Bell, "Building a Reputation for Training Effectiveness," *Training and Development Journal*, 38 (May 1984), p. 50.

Some general concepts—fundamentals related to learning—are shown in Table 8-2.

Most of these concepts relate to the management and development of human resources. For example, behavior that is rewarded (reinforced) is more likely to recur. In applying this thought to managing people, management should strive to ensure that the firm's pay system rewards productivity. In addition, HRD specialists need to praise trainees for their accomplishments. Failure to provide the desired feedback on their performance—according to this concept—would not encourage learning.

From the human resource manager's viewpoint, successful accomplishment of other human resource functions can have a significant impact on HRD. For instance, if recruitment and selection efforts attract only unskilled workers, an extensive HRD program may be needed to train entry-level workers. Training and development efforts may also be influenced by the firm's compensation package. A firm with a competitive program may find it easier to attract qualified workers, which substantially influences the type of training required. Also, a competitive compensation plan may help lower the turnover rate, thereby minimizing the need to train new workers.

A firm's employee relations efforts can also influence the HRD program. Workers want to feel that the company is interested in them. One way to express this interest is through management's support of HRD. The HRD process can also train managers to deal more effectively with employees and their problems. Managers can be taught to treat employees as individuals and not merely as numbers.

The emphasis a firm places on its employees' health and safety can also affect the HRD process. Heavy emphasis in this area can pave the way for extensive training programs throughout the organization. Providing a healthy and safe work environment can benefit all other human resource functions as the firm gains a reputation as a healthful and safe place to work.

■ DETERMINING HUMAN RESOURCE DEVELOPMENT NEEDS

The first step in the HRD process is to determine training, education, and development needs. In today's highly competitive business environment, undertaking programs simply because "other firms are doing it" is asking for trouble. Rather, a systematic approach to addressing bona fide needs must be undertaken.

Three types of analysis are required in order to determine an organization's HRD needs: an organization analysis, a task analysis, and a person analysis.[17] In this context, organizational analysis examines the entire firm to determine where training, education, and development should be conducted. The firm's strategic goals and plans should be studied along with the results of human resource planning.

---

[17] Kenneth Wexley and Gary Latham, "Identifying Training Needs." In Lloyd Baird, Craig Eric Schneir, and Dugan Laird (eds.), *The Training and Development Sourcebook* (Amherst, Mass.: Human Resource Development Press, 1983).

TABLE 8-2 | General Learning Concepts

- Behavior that is rewarded (reinforced) is more likely to recur.
- This reinforcement, to be most effective, must immediately follow the desired behavior and be clearly connected with that behavior.
- Mere repetition, without reinforcement, is an ineffective approach to learning.
- Threats and punishment have variable and uncertain effects on learning. Punishment may disturb the learning process.
- The sense of satisfaction that stems from achievement is the type of reward that has the greatest transfer value to other situations.
- The value of any external reward depends on who dispenses the reward. If the reward giver is highly respected, the extrinsic reward may be of great value; if not, it may be without value.
- Learners progress in an area of learning only as far as they need to in order to achieve their purposes.
- Individuals are more likely to be enthusiastic about a learning situation if they themselves have participated in the planning of the project.
- Autocratic leadership has been found to make members more dependent on the leader and to generate resentment in the group.
- Overstrict discipline tends to be associated with greater conformity, anxiety, shyness, and acquiescence; greater permissiveness is associated with more initiative and creativity.
- Many people experience so much criticism, failure, and discouragement that their self-confidence, level of aspiration, and sense of worth are damaged.
- When people experience too much frustration, their behavior ceases to be integrated, purposeful, and rational.
- People who have met with little success and continual failure are not apt to be in the mood to learn.
- Individuals tend to think whenever they encounter an obstacle or intellectual challenge which is of interest to them.
- The best way to help people form a general concept is to present an idea in numerous and varied situations.
- Learning from reading is aided more by time spent recalling what has been read than by rereading.
- Individuals remember new information that confirms their previous attitudes better than they remember new information that does not confirm their previous attitudes.
- What is learned is more likely to be available for use if it is learned in a situation much like that in which it is to be used, and immediately preceding the time when it is needed.
- The best time to learn is when the learning can be useful. Motivation is then at its strongest peak.

Task analysis relies largely on the results of job analysis. However, if job descriptions are not sufficiently comprehensive, they may have to be expanded by adding job information. In obtaining task analysis data, managers may also refer to job performance standards as they observe workgroup performance. In addition, both managers and operative employees may be interviewed or surveyed to obtain suggestions.

Person analysis, which focuses on the individual employee, deals with two questions: "Who needs to be trained?" and "What kind of training is needed?" A first step in a person analysis is to compare employee performance with established standards. If the person's work is acceptable, training may not be needed. If the employee's performance is below standard, further investigation will be needed to identify the specific knowledge and skills required for satisfactory job performance.[18]

In addition, tests, role playing, and assessment centers may be helpful in conducting person analyses. The results of career planning programs may also prove to be quite revealing.

■ ESTABLISHING HUMAN RESOURCE DEVELOPMENT OBJECTIVES

Clear and concise objectives must be formulated for HRD. Without them, designing meaningful HRD programs wouldn't be possible. Worthwhile evaluation of a program's effectiveness would also be difficult at best. The following statement of purposes and objectives are from a segment of a training program designed by the Chevron Corporation.

Employment Compliance

Purpose. To provide supervisor with:

1. Knowledge and value of consistent human resource practices.
2. The intent of EEO legal requirements.
3. The skills to apply them.

Objectives. Be able to:

1. Cite the supervisory areas affected by EEO laws on discrimination.
2. Identify acceptable and nonacceptable actions, according to EEO laws.
3. State how to get help on EEO and Affirmative Action matters.
4. Describe why we have discipline and grievance procedures.
5. Describe our discipline and grievance procedures, including who is covered.

As you can see, the purpose is clearly established first. Managers would have little difficulty in determining whether this is the type of training a

---

[18] *Ibid.*

subordinate needs. The specific learning objectives leave little doubt of what should be learned from the training. Action words such as *cite*, *identify*, *state*, and *describe* are used to disclose the specific content of the program. With these types of objectives, the HRD specialist may determine whether a person has obtained the necessary knowledge. For instance, a trainee either can or cannot state how to get help on EEO and Affirmative Action matters.

■ SELECTING HUMAN RESOURCE DEVELOPMENT METHODS

When a person is working on a car, some tools are more helpful in doing certain tasks than others. The same logic applies when considering various HRD methods. Note the diverse methods shown in Table 8-3. Some apply strictly to managers and entry-level professionals, others to operative employees, and several can be used in the training and development of both managers and operative employees. We include methods that apply to both management and operative employees under management development.

Again referring to Table 8-3, note that HRD methods are used both on and off the job. Often it is not feasible to learn while doing. Thus, although a large portion of training and development takes place on the job, many HRD programs occur away from the work setting.

■ MANAGEMENT DEVELOPMENT

A firm's future lies primarily in the hands of its management. This group performs certain functions that are essential to the organization's survival and prosperity. Managers must make the right choice in most of the numerous decisions they make. Otherwise, the firm will not grow and may even fail. For these reasons, it is imperative that managers keep up with the latest developments in their respective fields and—at the same time—manage an ever-changing work force operating in a dynamic environment. Thus many organizations emphasize training and development programs for managers. **Management development** consists of all learning experiences provided by an organization to impart and upgrade skills and knowledge required in current and future managerial positions. First-line supervisors, middle managers, and executives may all be expected to participate in management development programs. These programs are offered in-house, by professional organizations, and by colleges and universities. In-house programs are planned and presented by a firm's HRD specialists from the human resource department. Line managers are also frequently utilized to conduct segments of a program.

Professional organizations and universities are additional sources of management development programs. Organizations such as the Society for Human Resource Management and the American Management Association conduct conferences and seminars in a number of specialties. Numerous universities also provide management training and development programs.

TABLE 8-3 | Human Resource Development Methods

Method	Utilized for: Managers and entry-level professionals	Utilized for: Operative employees	Utilized for: Both	Conducted: On the job	Conducted: Off the job
Coaching			X	X	
Business games	X				X
Case study	X				X
Conference/discussion	X				X
Behavior modeling	X				X
In-basket training	X				X
Internships	X			X	
Role playing	X				X
Job rotation			X	X	
Programmed instruction			X		X
Computer-based training			X		X
Classroom lecture			X		X
On-the-job training		X		X	
Apprenticeship training		X		X	
Simulators		X			X
Vestibule training		X			X

At times, colleges and universities possess expertise not available within business organizations. Another possible advantage of such programs is that they may be less expensive than in-house programs. In some cases, academicians and management practitioners can advantageously present HRD programs jointly.

Basically, companies have various management development options. A 1986 survey revealed numerous general types of training used by organizations of varying size. These data are shown in Table 8-4. As you can see, management skills/development was the most popular type of training for all size organizations. The same study also indicated that the types of training most commonly used were new-employee orientation, performance appraisal, new equipment operation, leadership, and time management.[19]

Regardless of whether programs are presented in-house or by an outside source, a number of methods are utilized in imparting knowledge to managers. We discuss these methods next.

---

[19] Jack Gordon, "Where the Training Goes," *Training: The Magazine of Human Resources Development*, 23 (October 1986), p. 63.

CHAPTER 8 Organization Change and Human Resource Development

TABLE 8-4 | General Types of Training by Size of Organization*

	Number of Employees					
Type of Training	50–99	100–499	500–999	1,000–2,499	2,500–9,999	10,000 or more
Management skills/development	69.0	82.4	88.9	91.7	89.7	92.4
Technical skills/knowledge	65.5	73.1	75.2	80.8	82.0	86.1
Supervisory skills	58.4	78.2	82.9	86.1	89.7	88.4
Communication skills	60.7	69.5	76.1	83.1	87.2	85.7
New methods/procedures	56.0	59.9	66.7	64.7	66.4	67.1
Clerical/secretarial skills	56.0	59.4	60.7	67.6	71.8	67.5
Executive development	54.8	58.4	60.7	72.9	74.4	79.1
Computer literacy/basic computer skills	51.2	51.6	58.1	66.6	71.8	78.3
Customer relations/services	44.1	58.2	56.4	60.4	64.1	66.7
Personal growth	47.6	52.1	58.1	61.3	64.1	63.3
Sales skills	41.7	44.8	43.6	43.3	48.7	60.0
Employee/labor relations	36.9	41.6	49.6	56.2	64.1	64.9
Disease prevention/health promotion	35.8	43.0	47.0	53.1	48.7	48.0
Customer education	33.4	27.0	29.1	33.0	35.9	40.2
Remedial basic education	11.9	16.7	19.7	20.7	25.6	28.3

*Percentage of organizations providing these types of training to employees.

Source: Adapted from Jack Gordon, "Where the Training Goes," from the October 1986 issue of *Training: The Magazine of Human Resources Development*. Copyright © 1986, Lakewood Publications, Inc., Minneapolis, Minn. (612) 333-0471. All rights reserved.

Coaching

Coaching is an on-the-job approach to management development in which the manager is given an opportunity to teach on a one-to-one basis. Some firms create "assistant to" positions for this purpose. An individual placed in this type of staff position becomes an understudy to his or her boss. In addition to having the opportunity to observe, the subordinate will also be assigned significant tasks requiring decision-making skills. To be productive, coach-counselor managers must have a thorough knowledge of the job and how it relates to the firm's goals. They should also have a strong desire to share information with the understudy and be willing to take the time—which can be considerable—for this endeavor. The relationship between the supervisor and subordinate must be based on mutual trust and confidence for this approach to be effective.

Business Games

Simulations that represent actual business situations are referred to as **business games**. These simulations attempt to duplicate selected factors in a particular situation, which are then manipulated by the participants. Business games involve two or more hypothetical organizations competing in a given product market. The participants are assigned such roles as president, controller, and marketing vice-president. They make decisions affecting price levels, production volumes, and inventory levels. Their decisions are manipulated by a computer program, with the results simulating those of an actual business situation. Participants are able to see how their decisions affect other groups and vice versa. The best part about this type of learning is that if a decision is made that costs the company $1 million, no one gets fired, and still the business lesson is learned.

Case Study

The **case study** is a training method that utilizes simulated business problems for trainees to solve. The individual is expected to study the information given in the case and make decisions based on the situation. If the student is provided a case involving an actual company, he or she would be expected to research the firm to gain a better appreciation of its financial condition and environment. Typically, the case study method is used in the classroom with an instructor who serves as a facilitator.

Conference Method

The **conference method**, or discussion method, is a widely used instructional approach that brings together individuals with common interests to discuss and attempt to solve problems. Often the leader of the group is the supervisor. The group leader's role is to keep the discussion on course and avoid the tendency of some individuals to get off the subject. As problems are discussed, the leader listens and permits group members to solve their own problems. Individuals engaged in the conference method, although in training, work to solve actual problems that they face in their everyday activities.

Behavior Modeling

Behavior modeling utilizes videotapes prepared specifically to illustrate how managers function in various situations and to develop interpersonal skills.[20] The trainees observe the "model's" actions. For example, a supervisor may act out her role in disciplining an employee who has been consistently late in reporting to work. Since the situations presented are typical of their firm's problems, the participants are able to relate the behavior to their own jobs.

---

[20] Bernard L. Rosenbaum, "Common Misconceptions about Behavior Modeling and Supervisory Skill Training (SST)," *Training and Development Journal*, 33 (August 1979), pp. 40–44.

Although the technique of behavior modeling as a training method is relatively new to industry, the concept is not. For example, most linguists agree that the learning of language is imitative. Learning through modeling occurs continuously. Consider for a moment how most individuals learn to drive a car, shoot a basketball, or mow the grass. Chances are that these behaviors are learned by observing others.[21]

The most important characteristic of high-performance managers is that they set high standards for themselves and others. This is the heart of behavior modeling,[22] which appears to have outstanding potential as an HRD method. In fact, more than 300 companies—including such giants as Exxon, Westinghouse, Union Carbide, and Federal Department Stores—now use this method.

In-Basket Training

In-basket training is a simulation in which the participant is given a number of business papers such as memoranda, reports, and telephone messages that would typically cross a manager's desk. The papers, presented in no particular order, call for actions ranging from urgent to routine handling. The participant is required to act on the information contained in these papers. In this training method, assigning a priority to each particular situation precedes making decisions called for in each situation.

Internships

As we mentioned in Chapter 5, an **internship** program is a recruitment method whereby university students divide their time between attending classes and working for an organization. Internships can also serve as an effective training method.

From the employer's viewpoint, an internship provides an excellent means of viewing a potential permanent employee at work. Internships also provide advantages for students. The experience they obtain through working enables them to integrate theory learned in the classroom with the practice of management. At the same time, the interns' experience will help them determine whether that type of firm and job appeals to them.

Role Playing

In **role playing**, training participants "act out" responses to specific situations without the benefit of either a script or rehearsal. In addition, the outcome is not known in advance. In one type of role playing, the leader

---

[21] Stephen Wehrenberg and Robert Kuhnle, "How Training Through Behavior Modeling Works." In Lloyd Baird, Craig Eric Schneir, and Dugan Laird (eds.), *The Training and Development Sourcebook* (Amherst, Mass.: Human Resource Development Press, 1983), pp. 133–134.

[22] Kenneth H. Blanchard and Alice S. Sargent, "The One Minute Manager Is an Androgynous Manager," *Training and Development Journal*, 38 (May 1984), p. 83.

assigns roles and tells the "actors" how they feel and each attempts to behave according to these feelings.[23] Or participants may choose specific roles in a situation and then act them out. For example, a trainee might play the role of a supervisor who is required to discipline an employee for substandard performance. Another participant would play the role of the employee. The individual in the supervisory role would then proceed to take whatever action is deemed appropriate. This action then provides the basis for discussion and comments by the group. Role reversal—an exchange of roles by the participants—is an effective version of role playing, which provides trainees with a different perspective of the problem. It helps them develop empathy, a quality vitally needed by managers. The Experiencing Human Resource Management section at the end of each chapter is a role playing exercise that demonstrates the benefits of this training approach.

Job Rotation

Job rotation involves moving employees from one job to another to broaden their experience. This breadth of knowledge is often needed for performing higher level tasks. Consider this example:

> Roy Jackson's firm is grooming him to fill the position of plant controller at the company's new branch plant. Roy is expected to assume his new responsibilities within the next six months. In preparing Roy for his new job, the vice-president for finance and the human resource director have decided that he needs additional experience in credit operations and accounts receivable. They have arranged for him to spend three months in each of these departments prior to his move to the new plant.

As you might expect, Roy's temporary assignments will not make him an expert in either area. He will, however, gain an overview of these functions, which will assist him in his new position.

Several potential problems are related to job rotation. Individuals are often not permitted to remain on a job long enough to really learn its essentials. Because these assignments are temporary, individuals may not be very productive during this time. In fact, they may even lower the productivity of the work group. In addition, employees who observe or have to work with an individual rotating through their department may resent the so-called "fair-haired" employee.

Programmed Instruction

A teaching method that provides instruction without the intervention of an instructor is called **programmed instruction (PI)**. In PI, information is

---

[23] John S. Randall, "Methods of Teaching." In Lloyd Baird, Craig Eric Schneir, and Dugan Laird (eds.), *The Training and Development Sourcebook* (Amherst, Mass.: Human Resource Development Press, 1983), p. 128.

broken down into small portions (frames). The learner reads each frame in sequence and responds to questions, receiving immediate feedback on response accuracy. If correct, the learner proceeds to the next frame. If not, the learner repeats the frame. Primary features of this approach are immediate reinforcement and the ability of learners to proceed at their own pace. Programmed instruction material may be presented in a book or by more sophisticated means, such as teaching machines and computers.

Computer-Based Training

Computer-based training takes advantage of the speed, memory, and data manipulation capabilities of the computer for greater flexibility. For example, a student's response may determine the difficulty level of the next frame in a PI session. This information can be selected and displayed almost instantaneously.

The increased speed of presentation and less dependence on an instructor are advantages of this training approach. However, some students object to the absence of a human facilitator. Another primary disadvantage is the cost of software. However, with enough trainees, the cost may quickly reach an acceptable level. Computer-based training appears to be much more than a fad. A recent study indicated that almost half of all firms with 50 or more employees use computers in connection with their training efforts.[24] Although used primarily to teach technical skills, a growing number of firms are using computer-based training for subjects such as management and sales skills.[25]

Classroom Lecture

The classroom lecture is effective for certain types of employee training. The lecturer may convey a great deal of information in a relatively short time. The effectiveness of lectures can be improved when groups are small enough to permit discussion, the lecturer is able to capture the imagination of the class, and audiovisual equipment is used in a timely and appropriate manner.

■ MANAGEMENT DEVELOPMENT PROGRAMS AT IBM

At IBM, formal management development programs are conducted for three groups of individuals: new managers, middle managers, and executives. These groups are described as follows:

> New managers—those appointed to their first level of management responsibility.

---

[24] Gordon, p. 53.
[25] Carlene Reinhart, "How Do You Determine the Use of New Training Technologies?" *Training and Development Journal*, 41 (August 1987), p. 22.

Middle managers—those who are responsible for managing managers.

Executives—those who have reached top-management positions and those who are considered to have potential for such responsibility.

An overview of the programs provided for these management groups is provided in Figure 8-4. In addition to providing training early in the manager's career, IBM emphasizes regular and continuous development. For example, annual training programs have been initiated to ensure that IBM's managers have an opportunity to receive at least one week of formal training each year.[26] More and more organizations are expected to implement management development programs for their employees in the future.

■ SUPERVISORY MANAGEMENT TRAINING PROGRAMS: AN ILLUSTRATION

Many firms conduct supervisory training programs. They consider such training to be necessary for their first-line managers to perform to their maximum potential. An overview of a supervisory training program developed by Chevron Corporation for its first-line managers is shown in Figure 8-5. This program is designed to provide new supervisors with the skills and knowledge they need to manage people effectively. The training program is also available to supervisors with long-term service to update their knowledge. The program has three phases: presession activities; a five-day, live-in session; and postsession activities.

Several weeks prior to the live-in session participants are asked to engage in the following activities which will prepare them for involvement in the program:

1. Identify productive and nonproductive activities.
2. Discuss the basic elements of their jobs with their bosses.
3. Select a major opportunity or problem that both the participant and the boss are committed to deal with (this becomes an action plan).
4. Send a sample of an employee evaluation to the training program coordinator.

The five-day live-in session comprises the heart of the program. It begins on a Sunday night with a social get-together, dinner, and business meeting. Participants are asked to tell briefly about their jobs and discuss their action plans. A top-management representative meets with the group during this initial meeting to discuss the role of the supervisor, the purpose of the program, and expected on-the-job results.

During this main session, a number of support subjects and key course subjects are presented. At the same time, information is provided concerning laws and company policies and practices. Brief descriptions of the purposes of support subjects and key course subjects are presented in Table 8-5. Action plan projects are worked with during the program evaluation phase, and the results are used to measure the program's value.

---

[26] Ken Macher, "The Politics of Organizations," *Personnel Journal*, 65 (February 1986), p. 83.

New Manager School

All individuals appointed to the initial level of management responsibility, after receiving basic orientation to their job by their immediate managers, are enrolled, usually within one month, in a one-week basic training program.

The objectives of this training are:

Developing a deeper awareness of the basic policies and practices by which the company is managed.

Learning the practical application of these policies and practices.

Acquiring the basic management concepts, skills and techniques.

Included in the program are such subjects as A Business and Its Beliefs, Performance Planning, Counseling and Evaluation, and Managing Individuals.

Middle Management Training

Individuals newly appointed to the responsibility of managing managers attend, usually within ninety days, a week-long program.

The objectives of such training are:

Defining the role of the manager of managers.

Learning the organization, delegation, and control skills required of this level of management.

Understanding the interrelationship of the various business functions within the company.

Acquiring a knowledge of, and appreciation for, the issues and challenges of the business environment.

Included in the program are such subjects as Transition to Middle Management, Business Management Issues, People Management, and Leadership Styles.

Executive Development

Managers who have been appointed to executive-level positions, and those identified as having potential to be promoted to such positions, receive formal training at internally conducted programs as well as out-company programs.

The earliest of this series of company-conducted internal programs is scheduled within a year of the individual being included in the executive resource category. These classes, usually of three to four weeks duration, have objectives related to these areas:

The IBM Company: its organization, missions, management system; its policies, practices, and strategies; and its current issues and challenges.

Management Practices: leadership and decision making, general management concepts, functional integration, and management of change.

External Environment: international economic, political, and social changes; the current relationship of business, government, and other institutions.

Included in the programs are such courses as Finance, Marketing, Personnel, Environmental Analysis and Strategic Thinking, Goals and Means of Our Economy, and Business Ethics.

In addition, individuals attend external training programs conducted by colleges, universities, and other institutions. Such programs include concentration on general management, leadership, government relations, and the humanities. Attendance at such internal and external executive development programs is scheduled at intervals to complement on-the-job experiences.

FIGURE 8-4 | IBM's Management Development Programs

Source: Used with the permission of International Business Machines Corporation.

Presession Activities	Five-Day, Live-In Session Activities			Postsession Activities
	Support subjects	Key course subjects	Program evaluation	
Time Analysis	Why We Are Here	Performance Planning and Review	Formulate an Action Plan Project	Approval and Implementation of an Action Plan Project
Work Analysis	Analyzing Performance Problems	Documentation Skills		
Performance Planning Discussion	Training	Employee Ranking	Rank Session's Topics	Possible Performance Planning and Review Discussions
Selecting an Action Plan Project	Special Health Services	Salary Administration	Evaluate Program	Follow-up Questionnaire to Participant and Boss
Writing a Performance Evaluation	Time Management	Employee Development		
Interview with Coordinator	Employment Compliance			
Time:	*Time:*		*Time:*	*Time:*
Completed Prior to Start of Program	1 1/2 days	2 1/2 days	1 day	2–4 months after program

FIGURE 8-5 | An Overview of Chevron Corporation's Supervisory Training Program

Source: Used with the permission of the Chevron Corporation.

TABLE 8-5 | Chevron Corporation's Supervisory Training Program's Purpose for a Five-Day Live-In Session

Support Subjects	Key Course Subjects
Why we are here	**Performance planning and review**
To orient participants with top management views of the role of a supervisor, the purpose of this program, and what on-job results are expected to occur.	To increase supervisory productivity and efficiency by creating better: ▪ Communications ▪ Understanding of the job ▪ Planning and allocation of time ▪ Data for evaluating employees' work performance
Analyzing performance problems	
To provide supervisors with the skills necessary to analyze a performance discrepancy so that they can determine the best solution.	**Documentation skills**
	To improve writing skills of supervisors in order that they may better manage their human resources.
Training	
To provide supervisors with the skill and knowledge to effectively train others.	**Employee ranking**
	To provide supervisors with the skill and knowledge needed to objectively evaluate employee performance on the job.
Special health services	
To provide supervisors with an expanded awareness of their responsibilities in the area of Special Health Services and with information and skills to deal with the troubled employee.	**Salary administration**
	To review the basics of salary administration so that supervisors can provide meaningful inputs to higher management and provide feedback to employees about salary decisions.
Time management	
To provide skills in how to better manage and use time.	**Employee development**
Employment compliance	To assist supervisors in their role of developing employees both within their current jobs and for future jobs as appropriate.
To teach supervisors the value of consistent personnel practices and the skills to apply them, as well as the intent of EEO legal requirements.	

Source: Used with the permission of the Chevron Corporation.

The postsession phase of the program consists of implementing the action plans. Further attempts are also made to relate the program's impact to the supervisor's job performance. At this point, training needs that are not being met are emphasized. Appropriate changes are made to ensure that the training program continues to have practical value to both the employee and the company.

■ TRAINING METHODS FOR ENTRY-LEVEL PROFESSIONAL EMPLOYEES

Firms have a special interest in college-trained employees hired for entry-level professional positions, including management trainees. For example, General Electric conducts programs for new employees in numerous fields. One such program is the information systems manufacturing program (ISMP). This is a two-year program combining rotational work assignments with graduate-level seminars. It prepares employees to design, program, and implement integrated computerized and manual information systems.

General Electric's ISMP emphasizes challenging work assignments in such areas as programming, systems analysis and design, computer center operation, project management, and functional work. The length of these assignments varies, and individual progress is determined by employee performance and demonstrated potential.

A candidate for ISMP must have taken at least two computer science courses in college and have a bachelor's degree in one of the following majors or related fields: computer science, industrial engineering, accounting, mathematics, business administration, industrial management, or management information systems. Selection for the ISMP is based on a careful review of the employee's course curriculum, academic records, leadership in extracurricular activities, and work experience.

Other training programs for college graduates may have more or less structure than GE's ISMP. However, most of them also emphasize training provided on the job. "Hands-on" experience, alone or in combination with other methods, appears to be an essential component of these programs.

■ TRAINING METHODS FOR OPERATIVE EMPLOYEES

Unlike managers, operative employees do not make their contributions to the firm through the efforts of other people. They are, always, the "other people." Their contributions are direct and, collectively, are essential to the production of goods and services. Organizations rely heavily on their executive secretaries, senior clerks, systems analysts, and other operative employees. Every position in an organization is necessary or it would not (or should not) exist. Therefore, training and development for operative employees must also be given high priority.

In this section, we discuss HRD methods that apply to the training of operative employees. However, these are not the only available methods; they are just an overview of methods commonly utilized. Recall the methods listed in Table 8-3 that are applicable to both management and operative employees.

HRM In Action

Marian Lillie, the training and development manager was studying the weekly training schedule when she heard a tap at her door. "Got a minute, Marian?" asked Scotty Needham, production manager.

"Sure, come on in," said Marian. "What've you got?"

"You may know that I recently hired Brit Salvo, a retired Marine officer who wanted to begin his second career with us. Brit's military record was excellent and I was shocked when the grapevine began talking about his high-handed methods. Apparently he still thinks he's in the Marines the way he bosses people around. When I spoke to Brit, he said 'I've been successful for twenty years managing people and using these exact methods.' Marian, something has to be done, do you have any ideas?"

How would you respond?

On-the-Job Training

On-the-job training (OJT) is an informal approach to training that permits an employee to learn job tasks by actually performing them. Although some may not consider OJT to be a bona fide training method, it is the most commonly used approach to HRD. With OJT, there is no problem in later transferring what has been learned to the task. Individuals may also be more highly motivated to learn because they are acquiring the knowledge needed to perform their jobs. At times, however, the emphasis on production may tend to detract from the training process. The trainee may feel pressure to perform to the point where learning is negatively affected.

Both the manager and the trainee must recognize that OJT is a joint effort. In addition, the manager must create a climate of trust and open communication to make OJT effective.

Apprenticeship Training

Another approach, **apprenticeship training**, combines classroom instruction with on-the-job training. Such training is traditionally used in craft jobs, such as those of plumber, barber, carpenter, machinist, and printer. While in training, the employee earns less than the master craftsperson who is the instructor. The training period varies according to the craft, as shown in Table 8-6. For instance, the apprenticeship training period for barbers is two years; for machinists, four years; and for pattern makers, five years.

TABLE 8-6 | Selected Apprenticeable Occupations Classified by Length of Apprenticeship

Two years	Barber Cosmetician	Four years	Boilermaker Carpenter
Two to three years	Brewer Butcher Roofer		Machinist Printing pressman Tailor
Two to four years	Bindery worker	Four to five years	Electrical worker Lithographer Mailer
Three years	Baker Bricklayer Photographer	Four to eight years	Die sinker
Three to four years	Airplane mechanic Leatherworker Operating engineer Sheet-metal worker	Five years	Lead burner Pattern maker
		Five to six years	Electrotyper Photoengraver Stereotyper
Three to five years	Draftsman—designer		

Source: U.S. Department of Labor, *The National Apprenticeship Program* (Washington, D.C.: U.S. Government Printing Office, 1972), pp. 9–27.

Simulators

Simulators are training devices of varying degrees of complexity that model the real world. They range from simple paper mock-ups of mechanical devices to computerized simulations of total environments. Human resource development specialists often simulate sales counters, automobiles, and airplanes.[27] Although simulator training may be less valuable than on-the-job training for some purposes, it has certain advantages. A prime example is the training of airline pilots: simulated training crashes neither take lives nor deplete the firm's fleet of jets.

Vestibule Training

Vestibule training takes place away from the production area on equipment that closely resembles equipment actually used on the job. For example, a group of lathes may be located in a training center where the trainees will be instructed in their use. A primary advantage of vestibule training is that it removes the employee from the pressure of having to produce while learning. The emphasis is on learning the skills required by the job.

---

[27] Dugan Laird, *Approaches to Training and Development* (Reading, Mass.: Addison-Wesley, 1978), pp. 206–207.

Job Training Partnership Act

Administered by the Employment and Training Administration of the Department of Labor, the **Job Training Partnership Act (JTPA)** provides job training and employment services for economically disadvantaged adults and youth, dislocated workers and other persons who face exceptional employment hurdles. The act became operational in 1983 with the goal of moving the unemployed into permanent, unsubsidized, self-sustaining jobs. An overview of selected programs included within the JTPA are shown in Table 8-7.

■ EFFECTIVENESS OF VARIOUS HUMAN RESOURCE DEVELOPMENT METHODS

Selecting an appropriate HRD method is a crucial step in developing any training program. Results of a study of training directors' perceptions provides some insights into the effectiveness of various training methods. These specialists were employed by the 200 U.S. firms identified by *Forbes* as

TABLE 8-7 | Selected Programs Included within the Job Training Partnership Act

Job corps	A federally administered employment and training program for seriously disadvantaged youth between the ages of 16 and 21. The program's goal is to prepare youth for productive employment and entrance into vocational and technical schools, junior colleges, or other institutions for further education and training.
Adult and youth programs	Provides participants (primarily economically disadvantaged youth and adults) with various job-related services including classroom and on-the-job training. This program is administered through a block grant to the states.
Summer youth employment and training programs	Provides disadvantaged youth with jobs, training, and education services during the summer months.
Assistance for dislocated workers	Provides aid to experienced workers who have become unemployed due to economic and technological change. A number of services are provided to the participants including training and job search assistance.
Migrant and seasonal farmworker programs	Job training and supportive services are provided to farmworkers and their families in an attempt to combat chronic unemployment, underemployment, and substandard living conditions.
Native American programs	A variety of employment related services are provided to native Americans who are without jobs.
Pilot and demonstration projects	These projects provide job training, employment opportunities, and other services to people with specific disadvantages.

Source: "Job Training," *Congressional Digest* 67 (February 1988), p. 37.

having the largest number of employees. The results of this study are shown in Table 8-8.

In terms of meeting training objectives, the case study was ranked highest for both problem-solving skills and participant acceptance. The conference (discussion) method topped the list for knowledge acquisition. Programmed instruction was rated best for knowledge retention. Role playing was ranked highest for interpersonal skills and was perceived as being the best overall method. Sensitivity training, although no longer a popular training method, topped the list for changing attitudes. The most-criticized method—lecture—generally did not fare well. However, it was ranked a respectable third for knowledge retention, following only programmed instruction and the conference method for this training objective. The television lecture was rated the poorest overall method. Generally, methods requiring participant involvement were rated higher than those allowing little or no participation.

Another study revealed the frequency of use of instructional methods (see Table 8-9). Comparing the results of the two studies, we find that the lecture method (rated low for most training objectives) is apparently one of the most frequently used instructional methods. Conversely, the highly rated methods of role playing and case study are used much less frequently. (We assumed that role playing is included as part of experiential exercises in Table 8-9.)

■ SELECTING HUMAN RESOURCE DEVELOPMENT MEDIA

Organizations have utilized various media to enhance their training programs. As used in this context, **media** are special methods of communicating ideas and concepts in training and development. These media include videotapes, films, closed-circuit television, slide projectors, overhead and opaque projectors, flip charts, and chalkboards.

Some critics have referred to audiovisual aids as "gadgetry for its own sake." Yet, these devices play an essential role in training and development.[28] In fact, 75 percent of what we learn is learned by sight, whereas about 75 percent of what we hear is forgotten within two days.[29]

Various forms and uses of audiovisual media are described briefly in Table 8-10. Audiovisual aids are valuable supplements to training methods. For example, a lecture might be greatly enhanced by use of an overhead projector or a short film. These media can assist in gaining and maintaining trainee interest and attention. Various applications of audiovisual media are not mutually exclusive. The use of more than one type of audiovisual aid (multimedia) may be appropriate for many training sessions. An example would be a slide–tape presentation.

---

[28] Max H. Forster, "Training and Development Programs, Methods, and Facilities." In Dale Yoder and Herbert G. Heneman, Jr. (eds.), *ASPA Handbook of Personnel and Industrial Relations: Training and Development* (Washington, D.C.: The Bureau of National Affairs, 1977), pp. 5–53.

[29] Martin M. Broadwell, *The Supervisor as an Instructor*, 3rd ed. (Reading, Mass.: Addison-Wesley, 1978), p. 85.

CHAPTER 8 Organization Change and Human Resource Development

TABLE 8-8 | Ratings of Effectiveness of Alternative Training Methods For Various Training Objectives

Training Method	Knowledge Acquisition Mean rank	Changing Attitudes Mean rank	Problem-Solving Skills Mean rank	Interpersonal Skills Mean rank	Participant Acceptance Mean rank	Knowledge Retention Mean rank
Case study	4	5	1	5	1	4
Conference (discussion) method	1	3	5	4	5	2
Lecture (with questions)	8	7	7	8	8	3
Business games	5	4	2	3	2	7
Movie films	6	6	9	6	4	5
Programmed instruction	3	8	6	7	9	1
Role playing	2	2	3	1	3	5
Sensitivity training (T-group)	7	1	4	2	6	9
Television lecture	9	9	8	9	7	8

Note: 1 = highest rank.

Source: Adapted from John W. Newstrom, "Evaluating the Effectiveness of Training Methods," from the January 1980 issue of *Personnel Administrator*, p. 58. Copyright © 1980, The American Society for Personnel Administration, Alexandria, Va.

TABLE 8-9 | Frequency of Use of Instructional Methods

	Number of Using Firms	Percent of Firms in Study
Lectures	99	73
Discussions	98	73
Reading books	39	29
Textbooks	108	80
Films/audio-visual materials	15	11
Cases	54	40
Incidents	36	27
Experiential exercises	46	34
Guest speakers	7	5
Internships/co-op programs	7	5

Source: Adapted from "Newsletter of Personnel/Human Resources Division," *Academy of Management*, 3 (1) (December 1978), p. 3. Reprinted by permission.

IMPLEMENTING HUMAN RESOURCE DEVELOPMENT PROGRAMS

A perfectly conceived training program can fail if management can't convince the participants of its merits. Participants must believe that the program has value and will help them achieve their personal and professional goals. The credibility of HRD specialists may come only after a series of successful programs.

Implementing HRD programs is often difficult. One of the reasons is that many managers are action oriented and frequently feel that they are too busy for HRD. According to one management development executive, "Most busy executives are too involved chopping down the proverbial tree to stop for the purpose of sharpening their axes...." Another difficulty in program implementation is that qualified trainers must be available. In addition to possessing communication skills, the trainers must know the company's philosophy, its objectives, its formal and informal organization, and the training program's goals. Human resource development requires more creativity than perhaps any other human resource specialty.

A new program must be monitored carefully, especially during its initial phases. Training implies change, which employees may resist vigorously. Others may sit back waiting, perhaps even hoping, that the program will

TABLE 8-10 | Audiovisual Media

Films

Films are useful due to their versatility. They combine many elements such as color, motion, action, plot, and musical scoring. Films provide a wide range of topics available for rental at a relatively low cost but are very expensive for an organization to produce.

Slide projectors

Slide projectors are commonly used, with slide–tape presentations becoming more popular. In these programs, the projector may be advanced automatically by an inaudible signal from one stereo channel.

Overhead Projectors

An overhead projector, providing an image on a screen by passing light through a transparency, can be used to provide colorful visual presentations. The trainer can maintain eye contact in an undarkened room and the trainees may take notes.

Audio Tapes

There are several types of audio tape systems on the market, and the running time varies from sixty minutes (thirty minutes per side) to two hours.

Video

The instant-replay capability of video makes it a particularly valuable medium for use in training programs. Most of the advantages of film are inherent in video.

Flip Charts, Chalkboards, and Slap Boards

These relatively inexpensive pieces of equipment can assist the trainer in emphasizing major points. One type of chalkboard permits the use of a colored ink pen, and the ink may be easily erased.

Source: Adapted from Devin O'Sullivan, "Audiovisuals and the Training Process." In Robert L. Craig (ed.), *Training and Development Handbook, A Guide to Human Resource Development*, 2nd ed. (New York: McGraw-Hill, 1976). Reprinted by permission.

fail. Participant feedback is vital at this stage because there will be "bugs" in any new program. The sooner these problems are resolved, the better the chances for success.

The HRD manager often has unique problems in implementing training programs. For example, it may be difficult to schedule the training around present work requirements. Unless the employee is new to the firm, he or she undoubtedly has specific full-time duties to perform. Although it is the line manager's job to have positions covered while an employee is in training, the HRD manager must assist with this problem.

Another difficulty in implementing HRD programs is record keeping. Records should be maintained on all training the employee receives and how well he or she performs during training and on the job. This information is important in terms of measuring program effectiveness and charting the employee's progress in the company.

Training conducted outside the organization requires considerable coordination. Consider the coordination required to get managers from all parts of the country to participate in an HRD program in Storrs, Connecticut. The logistics and costs involved in this type of undertaking can be significant.

In order to deal with these factors, a relatively new approach has been developed. **Teletraining** utilizes teleconferencing (with or without video) to train people in their own locations rather than bringing them together at one place. This approach can complement existing professional development training programs and, in many instances, make it possible economically to reach individuals who would not otherwise have access to training.[30]

■ EVALUATING HUMAN RESOURCE DEVELOPMENT

The credibility of HRD can be greatly enhanced by showing that the organization benefits tangibly from such programs. Thus the HRD department must document its efforts and clearly show that it provides a valuable service. The documentation should be in the form of memoranda to management, written reports of activities, and any other evidence that indicates a quality product.[31]

Organizations have taken several approaches to determining the worth of specific programs. These involve evaluations of (1) the participants' opinion of the program; (2) the extent to which participants have learned the material; (3) the participants' ability to apply the new knowledge; and (4) whether the stated training goals have been achieved.

Participants' Opinions

Evaluating an HRD program by asking the participants' opinion of it is an inexpensive approach that provides an immediate response and suggestions for improvements. The basic problem with this type of evaluation is that it is based on opinion rather than fact. In reality, the trainee may have learned nothing, but perceive that a learning experience occurred.[32] For

---

[30] Mary E. Boone and Susan Schulman, "Teletraining: A High Tech Alternative," *Personnel*, 62 (May 1985), p. 4.

[31] James R. Cook and Carol M. Panza, "ROI: What Should Training Take Credit For?" *Training: The Magazine of Human Resources Development*, 24 (January 1987), p. 64.

[32] John Dopyera and Louise Pitone, "Decision Points in Planning the Evolution of Training," *Training and Development Journal*, 37 (May 1983), p. 67.

example, Tom Dickson has just completed a three-day executive seminar in Honolulu. At the conclusion of the program, Tom was given a brief questionnaire that, in essence, asked him whether the seminar was beneficial. It is difficult to imagine Tom or any of his fellow participants downgrading this training program. Even if it had been conducted in a less exotic location, a brief break from the hectic part of an executive's job can be a welcome relief. Participants' perceptions of the value of such programs may prove useful, but they must be interpreted cautiously.

Extent of Learning

Some organizations administer tests to determine what the participants in an HRD program have learned. The most widely accepted evaluation procedure is referred to as the pretest–posttest, control group design.[33] In this procedure, the same test is used before and after training. It also calls for both a control group (which does not receive the training) and an experimental group (which does). Trainees are randomly assigned to each group. Differences in pretest and posttest results between the groups are then attributed to the training provided.

Behavioral Change

Tests may indicate fairly accurately what has been learned, but they give little insight into desired behavioral changes. For example, it is one thing for a manager to learn about motivational techniques but quite another matter for this person to apply the new knowledge. Consider the situation involving Pat Sittel:

> Pat Sittel sat in the front row at the supervisory training seminar her company sponsored. The primary topic of the program was delegation of authority. As the lecturer made each point regarding effective delegation techniques, Pat would nod her head in agreement. She thoroughly understood what was being said over the three-day period of the seminar. At the end of the program, Pat returned to her department and continued the management style she had followed for ten years—little delegation of authority. Although she had understood the material presented in the seminar, Pat's failure to apply what she had learned did not benefit the organization.

Accomplishment of HRD Objectives

Still another approach to evaluating HRD programs involves determining the extent to which stated objectives have been achieved. For instance, if

---

[33] John H. Zenger and Kenneth Hargis, "Assessing Training Results: It's Time to Take the Plunge!" *Training and Development Journal*, 36 (January 1982), pp. 13–14.

the objective of an accident prevention program is to reduce the number and severity of accidents by 15 percent, comparing accident rates before and after training provides a useful measurement of success. However, many programs dealing with broader topics are more difficult to evaluate. A group of executives may, for example, be sent to a state university for a one-week course in management and leadership development. "Before" and "after" performance appraisals of the participants may be available. Following the course, the managers may actually perform at a higher level, but other variables may distort the picture. For instance, a mild recession may force the layoff of several key employees; a competing firm may be successful in luring away one of the department's top engineers; or the company president could pressure the employment director to hire an incompetent relative. These and many other factors could cause the performance level of the group to decline, even though the managers had benefited from the HRD program.

In evaluating HRD programs, managers should strive for proof that the program is effective. While such proof may be difficult to establish, the effect on performance should at least be estimated to show whether the training achieved its desired purpose.[34] In spite of problems associated with evaluation, the human resource manager must continue to strive for solid evidence of HRD's contributions in achieving organizational goals.

■ ORIENTATION

The initial HRD effort designed for employees is orientation. **Orientation** is the guided adjustment of new employees to the company, the job, and the work group. It is the most prevalent type of formal training in U.S. organizations.[35] Comprehensive orientation makes many of the other tasks associated with human resource management easier.

In an orientation program, requirements for promotion will likely be explained. Rules, the infraction of which may lead to potential disciplinary action, will be stated. The mechanics of promotion, demotion, transfer, resignation, discharge, layoff, and retirement should be spelled out in policy handbooks and given to each new employee. Also, a summary of employee benefits is often provided.

Purposes of Orientation

A new employee's first few days on the job may be spent in orientation. Orientation programs are designed basically for new employees. An estimated 60–80 percent of an organization's current workforce is new not only to the job, but also to the job market. These new workers include a large number of late entries or reentries of women, men and women who were

---

[34] Cook and Panza, p. 64.

[35] Jack Gordon, "Training Magazine's Industry Report 1986," *Training: The Magazine of Human Resources Development*, 23 (October 1986), p. 28.

self-employed, recent graduates, and people who have made radical career changes.[36] Many of these individuals are inexperienced and have anxieties about entering the organization. An effective orientation program can do much to reduce these anxieties. Orientation has three primary purposes, which we discuss next.

Easing the New Employee's Adjustment to the Organization. Orientation helps the new employee adjust to the organization, both formally and informally. Formally, the organization wants the employee to become productive as rapidly as possible. In order to facilitate this process, the employee needs to know specifically what doing the job involves. Explanations concerning the job by the supervisor can do much to speed this process.

Many of the benefits of orientation relate to the informal organization. New employees are not automatically greeted with open arms. There may be a certain amount of hazing and kidding. Older workers may want to make sure that the new employee knows his or her place. A mistake or slowness in accomplishing tasks may encourage joking comments such as, "The last person who messed up like that was fired the next day" or "If you can't produce any more than that, there's no need to stay here." Taking such remarks seriously may make the new employee wonder whether he or she made the proper decision in accepting the job.

In order to reduce the anxiety that new employees experience, attempts should be made to integrate the person into the informal organization. Perhaps a senior employee—not the supervisor—can be assigned the task of showing the new person the "ropes." High turnover is often associated with the failure of workers to informally accept new employees. It is a lonely feeling to be on a job when you feel unwanted by peers.

Members of certain groups may also experience rejection from the informal work group. Women, blacks, and other minorities often have to actively seek acceptance into the work group. Initial job turnover may be highest among these individuals than for those in the more traditional work group.

Providing Information Concerning Tasks and Performance Expectations. Another purpose of orientation is to provide specific information about task and performance expectations. Employees want and need to know precisely what is expected of them. Thus new employees should be informed of the standards that they must meet in order to qualify for pay raises and the criteria for promotion. Rules of the company and of the particular department to which the individual is assigned should also be explained.

Creating a Favorable Impression. A final purpose of orientation is to create a favorable impression on new employees of the organization and its work. Doubts may arise after employees begin their new jobs. The new

---

[36] Mark S. Tauber, "New Employee Orientation: A Comprehensive Systems Approach," *Personnel Administrator*, 26 (January 1981), p. 65.

employee may begin to wonder, "Did I make the right decision?" The orientation process can do much to allay any such fears.

Stages in Effective Orientation

There are essentially three different stages in an effective orientation program.[37] During the first, general information about the organization is provided. Matters that relate to all employees, such as a company overview, review of company policies and procedures, and salary, are presented. A checklist for new employees is often used to ensure that certain information is provided the new hire. One such checklist is shown in Figure 8-6. It is also helpful for the new employee to know how his or her department fits into the overall scheme of the company's operations. Orientation programs should also provide information about how the products or the services of the company benefit society as a whole. Another purpose of this stage is anxiety reduction. New employees are informed of some of the possible hazing games that longer term employees may play. The human resource department may be heavily involved in this stage.

The employee's immediate supervisor usually is responsible for the second stage of orientation. Topics and events covered include an overview of the department, job requirements, safety, a tour of the department, a question and answer session, and introductions to other employees. It is crucial that the supervisor clearly explain performance expectations and specific work rules at this point. It is also important for the supervisor to ease the new hire into social acceptance by the work group as quickly as possible.

The third stage involves evaluation and follow up, which are conducted by the human resource department in conjunction with the immediate supervisor. The new employee does not go through the orientation program simply to be forgotten. During the first week or so, the supervisor works with the new employee to clarify information and make sure of integration into the work group. Human resource professionals assist supervisors to ensure that this vital third step is accomplished.

Training the Supervisor

One of the most vital aspects of an orientation program is training supervisors to conduct orientation properly.[38] Human resource professionals can provide the new hire with organizational information, but it is the supervisor who must successfully integrate the employee into the work setting.

The supervisor should first express confidence that new employees are going to do well on the job. New hires often begin work not fully convinced that they are capable of doing the job. Supervisors need to reassure these individuals that the company would not have hired them if it didn't believe that they could do the job.

---

[37] Diana Reed-Mendenhall and C. W. Millard, "Orientation: A Training and Development Tool," *Personnel Administrator*, 25 (August 1980), pp. 42–44.

[38] Loi Dene Williams, "Off to a Good Beginning," *Supervision*, 44 (October 1982), pp. 4–5.

CHAPTER 8   Organization Change and Human Resource Development   303

NEW EMPLOYEE CHECKLIST

NAME _____ EMPLOYMENT DATE _____

POSITION TITLE _____ DEPARTMENT _____

PAY GRADE _____ APPOINTMENT TYPE: PT ____ FT ____ SUPERVISOR _____

PROBATIONARY PERIOD ENDS _____

FIVE MONTH PERFORMANCE APPRAISAL DUE _____

INFORMATION PROVIDED:

_____ Orientation packet	By: _____	Date _____
_____ I.D. card	By: _____	Date _____
_____ Staff handbook	By: _____	Date _____
_____ Grievance guide	By: _____	Date _____
_____ Retirement information	By: _____	Date _____
_____ Life insurance	By: _____	Date _____
_____ Disability insurance	By: _____	Date _____
_____ Health insurance	By: _____	Date _____

I understand that an exit interview with a Personnel Department representative is required of all terminating employees receiving benefits.

I have received the information checked above, understand my employment status, and have been fully informed about my insurance options and benefits.

I have chosen not to enroll in HEALTH, LIFE, DISABILITY insurance (Circle those you are not enrolling in.)

_____
Employee Signature   Date

_____
Personnel Representative   Date

Effective Date _____

FIGURE 8-6 | Checklist for a New Employee

Second, supervisors need to explain both the good and bad points of the job. During the orientation period, managers often spend most of their time emphasizing the positive aspects of the job, leaving the new employees to learn of the negative features on their own. Studies have verified that good employee understanding of the job lowers turnover rates. Ideally, new employees will have received a realistic job preview, and will not face any unpleasant surprises at this time.

Third, the supervisor should inform the new hire of what he or she likes and dislikes in job performance. Every supervisor has particular preferences—usually small things that they react to favorably or unfavorably. Knowing these preferences, employees can more easily adapt to a particular work situation. For example, a supervisor who is a stickler for neatness should communicate this fact to new hires.

Fourth, the supervisor should describe both the standards set by the company and any unique customs of the employee's particular work group. All company rules, especially those pertaining to the new hire's section, should also be explained.

Finally, the supervisor should introduce the new employee to members of the work group. Any informal group leader should be identified. Here again, an attempt should be made to minimize the number of surprises that the employee will encounter. Starting off on the wrong foot with leaders of the informal organization can hurt the new employee's chances for quick acceptance. In jobs that require considerable interaction among group members, group acceptance is especially important.

Reorientation

While orientation programs are typically conducted for new employees, programs designed for employees who have been on the payroll for a longer period are also needed. Organizations are constantly changing. Different management styles may evolve, communication methods may be altered, and the structure of the organization itself may—and typically does—change frequently. Even the corporate culture may take on a new flavor over time. Changes in any of these conditions warrant reorientation. Without it, employees may find themselves in organizations that they don't even recognize.[39]

---

[39] Margaret Magnus, "Training Futures," *Personnel Journal*, 65 (May 1986), p. 63.

SUMMARY

Change involves moving from one condition to another and affects individuals, groups, and even entire organizations. If change is to be successfully implemented, it must be approached systematically. A crucial aspect of the change process involves reducing resistance to change. Change can be accomplished more readily if those involved want it and believe that it is needed. The most successful approach to changing attitudes is to create trust and confidence between those proposing the change and those affected by it. The change sequence does not end with implementation. A new and flexible position capable of dealing with present requirements and adapting to further change must be developed. The final phase of the change sequence involves evaluating the effectiveness of the change process.

Human resource development (HRD) is planned, continuous effort by management to improve employee competency levels and organizational performance through training, education, and development programs. The purpose of training is to improve an individual's performance on a currently held job or one related to it. The purpose of education is to improve the overall competence of an individual in a specific direction and beyond the current job. The purpose of development is to nurture the individual's growth but not with regard to any specific job.

Following recognition that change is needed, the process of determining training, education, and development needs (objectives) begins. Two questions must be answered: "What are our training needs?" and "What do we want to accomplish through our HRD efforts?"

Several factors can greatly influence a training and development program's effectiveness. First and foremost, training and development must have top management's full support. In addition, the HRD process must have the commitment of other managers, both generalists and HRD specialists. A firm's employee relations efforts and the firm's emphasis on employee health and safety can also influence the HRD process.

Management development provides learning experiences for the purpose of upgrading the skills and knowledge required for managerial positions. Coaching is an on-the-job approach to management development in which the manager is given an opportunity to teach on a one-to-one basis. Simulations that represent actual business situations are referred to as business games. The case study is a training method that utilizes simulated business problems for trainees to solve. The conference, or discussion, method brings together individuals with common interests to discuss and attempt to solve problems. Behavior modeling utilizes videotapes prepared specifically to illustrate how managers function in various situations and to develop interpersonal skills. In-basket training simulates business papers, such as memoranda, reports, and telephone messages that a manager would typically have to deal with. In an internship program, university students divide their time between attending classes and working for an organization. In role playing, participants "act out" responses to specific situations without the benefit of either a script or rehearsal. Job rotation moves employees from one job to another to broaden their experience. A teaching method that provides instruction without the intervention of an instructor is called programmed instruction (PI). Computer-based training takes advantage of the speed, memory, and data manipulation capabilities of the computer for greater flexibility. The classroom lecture is effective for certain types of employee training.

Training of operative employees includes on-the-job training (OJT), in which the person learns job tasks by actually performing them. Apprenticeship training combines classroom instruction with on-the-job training. Simulators are training devices of varying degrees of complexity that model the real world. Vestibule training takes place away from the production area on equipment that closely resembles the equipment actually used on the job.

Many organizations utilize various media to enhance training programs. As used in this context, media are special methods used in training and development to communicate ideas and concepts. These media include videotapes, films, closed-circuit television, slide projectors, overhead projectors, flip charts, and chalkboards.

A perfectly conceived training program can fail if the participants are not convinced that it has merit. They must believe that the program is valuable and can help them achieve their personal and professional goals. The credibility of HRD specialists may depend on a successful series of programs.

Organizations take several approaches to determining the worth of specific HRD programs, including evaluations of (1) the participants' opinions of the program; (2) the extent to which the participants learned the material; (3) the participants' ability to apply the new knowledge; and (4) whether the stated training objectives have been achieved. In evaluating HRD programs, managers should determine whether the programs were effective and document their findings.

The initial HRD effort designed for employees is orientation. Orientation introduces new employees to the company, the job, and the work group. The three primary purposes of orientation are: easing the new employee's adjustment to the organization, providing information concerning tasks and performance expectations, and creating a favorable impression.

Questions for Review

1. What can the manager do to reduce resistance to change?
2. Define and explain the scope of human resource development.
3. What are the general purposes of HRD?
4. Describe the HRD process.
5. Define *management development*. Why is it important?
6. List and describe the primary methods used in management development.
7. What methods are used primarily to train operative employees?
8. Describe the major factors that should be considered in the implementation of human resource development programs.
9. What are some of the means of evaluating HRD programs? Discuss.
10. Define *orientation* and explain the importance of employee orientation to a firm.

CHAPTER 8 Organization Change and Human Resource Development

Terms for Review

Human resource development (HRD)	Internship
Training	Role playing
Education	Job rotation
Development	Programmed instruction (PI)
Management development	Computer-based training
Coaching	On-the-job training (OJT)
Business games	Apprenticeship training
Case study	Simulators
Conference method	Vestibule training
Behavior modeling	Media
In-basket training	Teletraining
	Orientation

INCIDENT 1 ■ What to Do? ■

"I'm a little discouraged," said Susan Matthews to the training officer. "I keep making mistakes running the new printing press. It's a lot more complicated than the one I operated before, and I just can't seem to get the hang of it." "Well, Susan," responded George Duncan, "Maybe you're just not cut out for the job. You know that we sent you to the two-week refresher course in Atlanta to get you more familiar with the new equipment." "Yes," said Susan, "they had modern equipment at the school, but it wasn't anything like this machine." "What about the factory rep," asked George. "Didn't he spend some time with you?" "No, I was on vacation at that time," said Susan. "Have you asked your boss to get him back for a day or two?" "I asked him," said Susan, "but he said training was your responsibility. That's why I'm here." After she was gone, George got a yellow legal pad and began to write a letter to the printing press manufacturer.

Questions

1. What steps in the HRD process has the company neglected?
2. Is George taking the proper action? What would you do?

INCIDENT 2 ■ Management Support of HRD? ■

As the initial training session began, John Robertson, the hospital administrator, spoke of the tremendous benefits he expected from the management development program the hospital was starting. He also complimented Brenda Short, the human resource director, for her efforts in arranging the program. As he finished his five-minute talk, he said, "I'm not sure what Brenda has in store for you, but I know that management development is important, and I'll expect each of you to put forth your best efforts to make it work." Mr. Robertson then excused himself from the meeting and turned the program over to Brenda.

For several years Brenda had been trying to convince Mr. Robertson that the supervisors could benefit from a management development program. She believed that many problems within the hospital were management related. Reluctantly, Mr. Robertson had agreed to authorize funds to employ a consultant. Through employee interviews and a self-administered questionnaire completed by the supervisors, the consultant attempted to identify development needs. The consultant recommended twelve four-hour sessions emphasizing communication, leadership, and motivation. Each session was to be repeated once so that supervisors who missed the first session could attend the second.

Mr. Robertson had signed the memo that Brenda had prepared, directing all supervisors to support the management development program. There was considerable grumbling, but all the supervisors agreed to attend. As Brenda replaced Mr. Robertson at the podium, she could sense the lack of interest in the room.

Questions

1. Have any serious errors been made so far in the management development program? What would you have done differently?
2. What advice do you have for Brenda at this point to help make the program effective?

Experiencing Human Resource Management

Human resource development (HRD) is very important to any organization as it faces change and for the continual development of employees. An integral part of the HRD process, training can often be used to improve employee productivity. However, effective training cannot occur in a vacuum, and therefore, training requires the support and understanding of the entire organization.

This day will be a training day, with the training specialist from the main office attempting to train several unwilling supervisors. The training specialist has almost completed this very difficult task and is looking forward to the last training session. All of the supervisors in this training session have risen through the ranks and have a definite dislike of college graduates. In addition, they all believe that they are experts on training in their areas. The training specialist wants to just get through this last briefing. As with the other supervisors, he'll show this supervisor the basics, and then go back to the main office where people are more receptive. As with the others, if no in-depth questions are asked, he'll provide no additional details. He really doubts if the main office really expects improvement anyway. This operation seems to be going OK as it is. On to the last final briefing.

The last supervisor involved in a training session is really opposed to the training specialist trying to tell the supervisors how to train. It really grinds on this individual's nerves that since the company was bought out, the supervisors must do things their way. This person is scheduled to meet with the training specialist to learn how to train. The rumor mill has it that the training specialist is some 21-year-old college grad. According to this supervisor, "I was training my people before this person was born. All of a sudden, we can't do anything right. I look forward to my private session with that individual, I'm going to re-educate the college grad on training."

Two individuals will play roles in this exercise: one to serve as the training specialist, and the other to play the supervisor. Each participant should carefully follow the roles given them. All students not playing roles should carefully observe the behavior of both participants. Your instructor will provide the participants with additional information necessary to complete the exercise.

REFERENCES

Aptman, Leonard H. "Project Management: A Process to Manage Change." *Management Solutions*, 31 (August 1986), pp. 30–35.

Argyris, Chris. *Management and Organizational Development* (New York: McGraw-Hill, 1971).

Bell, Chip R. "Building a Reputation for Training Effectiveness." *Training and Development Journal*, 38 (May 1984), p. 50.

Bennis, Warren G. *Changing Organizations* (New York: McGraw-Hill, 1966).

Bernstein, Beverly J., and Beverly L. Kaye. "Teacher, Tutor, Colleague, Coach." *Personnel Journal*, 65 (November 1986), pp. 11–17.

Blanchard, Kenneth H., and Paul Hersey. "The Management of Change." *Training and Development Journal*, 34 (June 1980), pp. 80–98.

Blanchard, Kenneth H., and Alice S. Sargent. "The One Minute Manager Is an Androgynous Manager." *Training and Development Journal*, 38 (May 1984), p. 83.

Boone, Mary E., and Susan Schulman. "Teletraining: A High Tech Alternative." *Personnel*, 62 (May 1985), p. 4.

Bove, Robert. "Video Training: The State of the Industry." *Training and Development Journal*, 10 (August 1986), pp. 27–29.

Bownas, D. A. et al. "A Quantitative Approach to Evaluating Training Curriculum Content Sampling Adequacy." *Personnel Psychology*, 38 (Spring 1985), pp. 117–131.

Buzzotta, V. R. "Does 'People-Skills' Training Really Work?" *Training: The Magazine of Human Resources Development*, 23 (August 1986), pp. 59–60.

Caffarella, R. S. "A Checklist for Planning Successful Training Programs." *Training and Development Journal*, 39 (March 1985), pp. 81–83.

Chapados, Deborah Rentfrow, and Louis I. Hochheiser. "Four Principles of Training." *Training and Development Journal*, 11 (December 1987), p. 63.

Cook, James R., and Carol M. Panza. "P.O.I. What Should Training Take Credit For?" *Training: The Magazine of Human Resources Development*, 24 (January 1987), p. 64.

Dickey, John D. "Training with a Focus on the Individual." *Personnel Administrator*, 27 (June 1982), pp. 35–38.

Everly, George S., Jr. "Managing Change Demands Three Simple, Personal Steps." *Data Management*, 22 (September 1984), p. 21.

Fiedler, F. E., and J. E. Garcia. "Comparing Organization Development and Management Training." *Personnel Administrator*, 30 (March 1985), pp. 35–37ff.

"First Ask What You Want Training to Achieve." *Human Resources: Journal of the International Association for Personnel Women*, 2(3) (Summer 1985), pp. 3–5.

Frank, Frederic D., and James R. Preston. "The Validity of the Assessment Center Approach and Related Issues." *Personnel Administrator*, 27 (June 1982), pp. 87–95.

Godkewitsch, Michael. "The Dollars and Sense of Corporate Training." *Training: The Magazine of Human Resources Development*, 24 (May 1987), pp. 79–81.

Goodale, James G. "Employee Involvement Sparks Diagnostic Conference." *Personnel Journal*, 66 (February 1987), p. 79.

Gordon, Jack. "Training Magazine's Industry Report 1986." *Training: The Magazine of Human Resources Development*, 23 (October 1986), p. 28.

Gordon, Jack. "Where the Training Goes." *Training: The Magazine of Human Resources Development*, 23 (October 1986), pp. 49–63.

Hance, Marjorie Mathison, and Sam Campbell. "Management Development: It's More Than Just Training." *Human Resources: Journal of the International Association for Personnel Women*, 2(3) (Summer 1985), pp. 6–7.

Hays, Richard D. "The Myth and Reality of Supervisory Development." *Business Horizons*, 28 (January–February 1985), pp. 75–79.

Huber, V. L. "Training and Developing: Not Always the Best Medicine." *Personnel*, 62 (January 1985), pp. 12–15.

Jamieson, David W. "Developing the Profession and the Professional." *Training and Development Journal*, 36 (May 1982), pp. 118–121.

Kakabadse, Andrew. "Planning for Change." *Management Decision*, 25 (July 1987), pp. 22–27.

Kronenberger, George K., and David L. Banker. "Effective Training and the Elimination of Sexual Harassment." *Personnel Journal*, 60 (November 1981), pp. 879–933.

Kuzmits, Frank E. "Train Your New Managers with CCI." *Personnel*, 62 (April 1985), pp. 69–72.

Lambert, L. L. "Nine Reasons That Most Training Programs Fail." *Personnel Journal*, 64 (January 1985), p. 62ff.

Lawris, John. "How to Establish a Mentoring Program." *Training and Development Journal*, 11 (March 1987), pp. 25–27.

Lee, Chris. "Training Profiles: The View from Ground Level." *Training: The Magazine of Human Resources Development*, 23 (October 1986), pp. 67–83.

Leifer, M. "Things People Never Tell You about Corporate Training." *Personnel Administrator*, 30 (February 1985), p. 19ff.

Macher, Ken. "The Politics of Organizations." *Personnel Journal*, 65 (February 1986), p. 83.

Mangrum, S. L. "On-The-Job versus Classroom Training: Some Deciding Factors." *Training*, 22 (February 1985), pp. 75–77.

McAfee, R. Bruce, and Paul J. Champagne. "Employee Development: Discovering Who Needs What." *Personnel Administrator*, 33 (February 1988), pp. 92–98.

McLagan, Patricia A. "The ASTD Training and Development Competency Study: A Model Building Challenge." *Training and Development Journal*, 36 (May 1982), pp. 18–24.

Milbrath, Mona A. "Professional Accreditation Training Programs: An Overlooked Resource?" *Training: The Magazine of Human Resources Development*, 19 (June 1982), pp. 52–53.

Mirabile, Richard J. "A Model for Competency-Based Career Development." *Personnel*, 62 (April 1985), pp. 30–38.

Monat, Jonathan S. "A Perspective on the Evaluation of Training and Development Programs." *Personnel Administrator*, 26 (July 1981), pp. 47–52.

Muna, Farid A. "Manpower Training and Development: The Qatari Experience." *Journal of Management Development*, 6 (Fall 1987), pp. 55–64.

Niehoff, Marilee S., and M. Jay Romans. "Needs Assessment as Step One Toward Enhancing Productivity." *Personnel Administrator*, 27 (May 1982), pp. 35–39.

O'Leary, Meghan. "In-House Training Becomes Part of the Daily Agenda." *PC Week* (March 10, 1987), pp. 33–34.

Pascarella, Perry. "Resistance to Change: It Can Be a Plus." *Industry Week* (July 27, 1987), pp. 15–17.

Ponthieu, J. F. "Gaining Mutual Independence Through Training." *Supervisory Management*, 27 (April 1982), pp. 16–19.

Randall, John S. "Methods of Teaching." In Lloyd Baird, Craig Eric Schneir, and Dugan Larid (eds.), *The Training and Development Sourcebook* (Amherst, Mass.: Human Resource Development Press, 1983).

Reinhart, Carlene, David Jamisson, and Lynn Baroff. "How Do You Determine the Use of New Training Technologies?" *Training and Development Journal*, 11 (August 1987), pp. 22–26.

Roman, D. "Laughter Leavens Learning." *Computer Decisions* (January 29, 1985), p. 70ff.

Schrader, Albert W. "How Companies Use University-Based Executive Development Programs." *Business Horizons*, 28 (March–April 1985), pp. 53–62.

Stahl, Diana, Terry O'Grady, and Dick Schaaf. "How Trainees Interact with Interactive Video." *Training: The Magazine of Human Resources Development*, 21 (April 1987), pp. 98–99.

Stark, Chris. "Ensuring Skills Transfer: A Sensitive Approach." *Training and Development Journal*, 10 (March 1986), pp. 50–51.

Swierczek, F. W., and L. Carmichael. "The Quantity and Quality of Evaluating Training." *Training and Development Journal*, 39 (January 1985), pp. 95–99.

Torrence, David R. "How Video Can Help: Video Can Be an Integral Part of Your Training Effort." *Training and Development Journal*, 39 (December 1985), pp. 50–51.

Tregoe, Benjamin B., and John W. Zimmerman. "Needed: A Strategy for Human Resource Development." *Training and Development Journal*, 38 (May 1984), p. 78.

Trost, A. "They May Love It But Will They Use It?" *Training and Development Journal*, 39 (January 1985), pp. 78–81.

Truskie, Stanley D. "Getting the Most from Management Development Programs." *Personnel Journal*, 61 (January 1982), pp. 66–68.

Urban, T. F. et al. "Management Training: Justify Costs or Say Good-bye." *Training and Development Journal*, 39 (March 1985), pp. 68–71.

Wexley, Kenneth, and Gary Latham. "Identifying Training Needs." In Lloyd Baird, Craig Eric Schneir, and Dugan Laird (eds.), *The Training and Development Sourcebook* (Amherst, Mass.: Human Resource Development Press, 1983).

Yeomans, William N. "How to Get Top Management Support." *Training and Development Journal*, 36 (June 1982), pp. 38–40.

Zemke, Ron. "Job Competencies: Can They Help You Design Better Training?" *Training: The Magazine of Human Resources Development*, 19 (May 1982), pp. 28–31.

Zenger, John, and Kenneth Hargis. "Assessing Training Results: It's Time to Take the Plunge." Training and Development Journal, 36 (January 1982), pp. 11–16.

CHAPTER 9

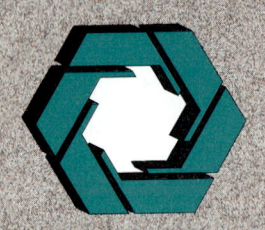

CORPORATE CULTURE AND ORGANIZATION DEVELOPMENT

CHAPTER OBJECTIVES

1. Define corporate culture, describe the factors that interact to affect corporate culture, and explain the various types of cultures.
2. Define organization development and explain the organization development methods of survey feedback, team building, and quality circles.
3. Describe the organization development methods of management by objectives, job enrichment, transactional analysis, quality of work life, and sensitivity training.
4. Explain the use of consultants in organization development and state the ways in which managers can use to evaluate OD programs.

> During the past four years, the profits of International Motor Corporation have declined sharply. Teddy McCoy, International's CEO, is especially concerned about the results of an attitude survey, which revealed that 60 percent of International's employees were dissatisfied with their jobs. Teddy felt certain that this condition was directly related to an excessive number of product recalls and employee turnover. In a recent board meeting he asserted, "With competition from both domestic and foreign corporations increasing, broad changes are needed throughout the firm if International is to survive and prosper. If we maintain the status-quo, we may go under."

In all likelihood, International Motor Corporation requires an organization-wide human resource development program. In this chapter, we first define corporate culture and then present factors that determine corporate culture. Next, we describe types of cultures, and the participative culture. We then discuss organization development methods and illustrate them with an example of organization development. The last two topics that we cover in this chapter are the use of consultants and organization development evaluation.

■ CORPORATE CULTURE DEFINED

When beginning a new job, an employee may soon hear, "This is the way to do things around here." This bit of informal communication refers to something more formally known as corporate culture.[1] **Corporate culture** is the system of shared values, beliefs, and habits within an organization

---
[1] Arthur Sharplin, *Strategic Management* (New York: McGraw-Hill, 1985), p. 102.

that interacts with the formal structure to produce behavioral norms.[2] It stems from the firm's mission, setting, and requirements for success. Important cultural factors include high quality, efficiency, reliable products and customer service, innovation, hard work, and loyalty. The firm's reward systems, policies, and procedures reflect the types of behavior and attitudes that are important for success.[3] According to Howard M. Schwartz, vice-president of Management Analysis Center, Inc., a leader in corporate culture consulting, "Culture gives people a sense of how to behave and what they ought to be doing."[4]

Corporate culture is similar in concept to meteorological climate. Just as the weather is described by variables such as temperature, humidity, and precipitation, corporate culture reflects characteristics such as friendliness, supportiveness, and risk taking. Each individual forms perceptions of the job and organization over a period of time as he or she works under the general guidance of a superior and a set of organizational policies. A firm's culture has an impact on employee job satisfaction, as well as on the level and quality of employee performance. However, each employee may assess the nature of an organization's culture differently. One person may perceive the culture negatively, and another may view it positively. Employees who are quite dissatisfied may even leave an organization in the hope of finding a more compatible culture.

According to Anthony Jay, an eminent researcher in the field of corporate culture, "It has been known for some time that corporations are social institutions with customs and taboos, status groups, and pecking orders. But they are also political institutions, autocratic and democratic, peaceful and warlike, liberal and paternalistic."[5] What Jay was writing about, although the term had not then achieved broad usage, was "corporate culture." In the early 1980s, several best-selling books on corporate culture appeared, including *In Search of Excellence, Theory Z: How American Business Can Meet the Japanese Challenge,* and *Corporate Cultures.*[6] In 1981, Harvard University introduced its first corporate culture course. By the mid 1980s the term was regularly used by those in both the business and academic communities. Corporate culture is an integral part of accomplishing an organization's mission and objectives, and therefore, the factors that determine corporate culture are also crucial to success.

---

[2] Jane C. Linder, "Computers, Corporate Culture and Change," *Personnel Journal,* 64 (September 1985), pp. 49–55.

[3] Ralph H. Kilmann, "Corporate Culture: Managing the Intangible Style of Corporate Life May Be the Key to Avoiding Stagnation," *Psychology Today,* 19 (April 1985), p. 64.

[4] "Corporate Culture: The Hard to Change Values That Spell Success or Failure," *Business Week* (October 27, 1980), pp. 148–160.

[5] Anthony Jay, *Management and Machiavelli* (New York: Holt, Rinehart and Winston, 1967), p. 231.

[6] Thomas J. Peters and Robert H. Waterman, Jr., *In Search of Excellence: Lessons from America's Best Run Companies* (New York: Harper & Row, 1982); William G. Ouchi, *Theory Z: How American Business Can Meet the Japanese Challenge* (New York: Avon Books, 1987); and Terrence E. Deal and Allan A. Kennedy, *Corporate Culture* (Reading, Mass.: Addison-Wesley, 1981).

CHAPTER 9 Corporate Culture and Organization Development 315

■ FACTORS THAT DETERMINE CORPORATE CULTURE

The culture of a corporation evolves from the examples set by top management. It stems largely from what these executives do, not what they say.[7] In addition, other factors can interact to shape the culture of a firm. We emphasize three of them—communication, motivation, and leadership—because of the special impact they have on a firm's psychological environment. Other factors that can interact to determine corporate culture include organizational characteristics, administrative processes, organizational structure, and management style.

Communication

Communication is the transfer of information, ideas, understanding, and feelings between people. All managers must communicate effectively if they are to be successful. Moreover, effective organizational communication has a positive influence on corporate culture. By communicating effectively within the organization, management can accomplish its objectives more readily, helping to ensure the firm's success.

John Kasper, president of Elco Industries realizes the importance of effective communication. According to Kasper, "We have our communication department, with a full-time group working to refine communication with our people. They're going out on the plant floor to ask questions and get opinions."[8] To reinforce successful communication throughout the firm, Elco Industries has created a position of corporate director of communication, which reports directly to the president.

Many other companies recognize that communication can break down in a multitude of ways. Fortunately, the ability to communicate effectively can be learned, and many communication breakdowns can be avoided. Individuals who are willing to make the effort to improve their ability to communicate can benefit both themselves and the organization.

Motivation

Motivation is the willingness to put forth effort in pursuit of organizational goals. Managers do not actually motivate their employees because motivation is internal to each individual. Motivation cannot be viewed directly; as with the wind, only the results are observable. Management's job is to provide an organizational culture that encourages positive employee behaviors.

Management traditionally has relied on the use of rewards—such as increased pay, job security, and good working conditions—or punishments—

---

[7] Peter C. Reynolds, "Imposing a Corporate Culture," *Psychology Today*, 21 (March 1987), pp. 32–38.

[8] Keith W. Bennett, "Communication and Costs Can Alter the Bottom Line," *Iron Age* (June 26, 1978), p. 28.

Executive Insights

Drew M. Young, SPHR
Vice-President, Employee Relations (Retired), ARCO Oil and Gas Company (Division of Atlantic Richfield Company)

When the term human resource professional is used to suggest excellence in the field of human resource management, the name of Drew M. Young must certainly come to mind. Throughout his career, Young has participated in professional and civic activities. He believes that a person should give something back to the profession and community of which he is a part. As a result of practicing this philosophy, he has held numerous leadership positions in professional associations, including the national presidency of the American Society for Personnel Administration, the presidency of the Personnel Accreditation Institute, and a vice-presidency and membership on the board of directors and the executive committee of the American Society for Training and Development.

Young's long and varied career began in the late 1930s after he received a B.A. degree in English and philosophy from Swarthmore College. He added to his education through the years by doing graduate studies in psychology and music at Temple University, graduating from the Executive Program at Columbia University's Graduate School of Business, and participating in numerous seminars, training programs, and workshops in the human resource field. His first position was that of director of music at Henry C. Conrad High School in Richardson Park, Delaware. The pay was higher for band directors than English teachers, and he thoroughly enjoyed what he did.

During five years in the U.S. Army, he taught training management at the Signal Corps Officer Candidate School (Ft. Monmouth, N.J.) and was a training supervisor at the Army Signal Corps School in New Guinea and the Philippines. These positions marked the beginning of his work in the field of training.

Young's transition to the world of business took place during the two years that he was an area training supervisor with the Veterans Administration. He and the training officers reporting to him were responsible for administering training for 12,000 veterans in Philadelphia, Chester, and Delaware Counties, Pennsylvania.

In 1947 he voluntarily took a cut in pay to enter the private sector as a training assistant with The Atlantic Refining Company, one of the predecessors of Atlantic Richfield Company. As a member of the corporate training staff he found it somewhat frustrating to develop training programs for other company units and then not to see the results by not being involved in implementing the programs. Thus, when several years later he was asked to be the training supervisor on the personnel staff of the company's North American Producing Division in Dallas, he jumped at the opportunity. He found it challenging to initiate the division's first supervisory training program and even more challenging to convince the management of the Atlantic Pipe Line Company that it needed such a program for supervisors. One tool used to accomplish this objective was a survey of employee morale. The survey results showed definite needs for improving supervisory skills and changing work procedures. Shortly thereafter management implemented a specially designed supervisory training program.

After six years as supervisor of an ever-growing training function, Young was promoted to the position of personnel supervisor. His responsibilities included all human resource functions except safety and employment. After several years in this position, he accepted the assignment of manager of industrial relations for the Venezuelan Atlantic Refining Company in Caracas, Venezuela. During his almost four years in that position, he was responsible for all human resource functions and the medical department, which operated two hospitals, the schools for employees' children in field locations, and the travel and documentation section. Operating in a different culture with employees whose value systems varied somewhat from those of U.S. employees was a broadening and interesting experience. One thing he had to learn was to be able to say "no" in such a way that the other person could save face. He also found that negotiating collective labor agreements under circumstances where the Ministry of Labor might make the final decisions was a whole new ball game. Young said, "Working overseas provides valuable experience and is enriching in many ways. I would recommend it for anyone who is adaptable and has the opportunity. Many of the lessons that I have learned there stood me in good stead in subsequent years."

Several years after returning to Dallas as general personnel supervisor, he was promoted to the position that he held until he retired in May 1981. In addition to being responsible for all human resource functions, he was involved in many interesting special projects. Several projects that stood out in his mind were: working on a task force to plan the logistics and human resource requirements for ARCO operations on the North Slope of Alaska; chairing a task force to develop organizational and policy recommendations for the corporate medical department; and overseeing the development and implementation of an integrated human resource planning system.

Young believes that human resource professionals should be well prepared to

EXECUTIVE INSIGHTS *Continued*

help their organizations meet three important needs:

- The need for greater, more creative contributions to productivity in the face of rising labor costs, stiffer competition, and economic changes.
- The need for more broadly skilled managers at the top of the company and stable executive succession.
- The need to plan and assimilate changes in status, work, and evolving relationships and expectations of employees.

Since his retirement from ARCO, Young has continued to be active in human resource consulting and in the Personnel Accreditation Institute, of which he is a past president. Over a four-year period, he and his wife Mary conducted preretirement planning workshops attended by more than 600 people. He also continues to actively participate in community activities, serving as chairman of the board of the Visiting Nurse Association and a member of the board of the Southwest Family Institute in Dallas.

---

such as dismissal, demotions, or withholding rewards—to encourage worker motivation. Management in today's environment, however, cannot rely on the manipulation of pay, benefits, or working conditions to motivate workers to perform effectively. Motivation is a much more complicated process.

Managers need to understand the forces that energize workers' behaviors. A manager's major motivational task is to develop and maintain an environment in which workers will want to be productive, contributing members of the organization. Today's human resource management professionals recognize that, in order to achieve a corporate culture that fosters improved productivity, employees' personal needs must be reasonably well satisfied.

Leadership

Leadership is influencing others to do what the leader wants them to do. The manner in which different managers attempt to persuade their employees may vary greatly and can affect the organization's culture in different ways. In the following discussion, we concentrate on the practical aspects of choosing an effective leadership style.

Factors Related to the Manager. Self-knowledge is important to effective leadership. Leaders have different abilities and goals and also have had different experiences. Through such experiences, managers develop basic beliefs about people. Some believe that people must be threatened to make them perform. Others believe in encouraging employees and rewarding them for performance. Although managers should be flexible in the choice of a leadership style, they usually perform better if they use a style consistent with their personal beliefs.

A manager's professional and technical competence also affects leadership style. Not only are competent managers more confident, but workers are also less likely to challenge or question them. This would seem to allow the manager to be more autocratic. In fact, it permits managers more flexibility in establishing an appropriate leadership style.

Factors Related to Employees. When deciding on a leadership style, a manager must also take into account characteristics of subordinates. One important consideration is their work ethic. Some employees feel that work, in and of itself, is satisfying, pleasurable, and fulfilling. Such workers are easy to lead. Others see work merely as an unpleasant way to obtain money. Such workers are more difficult to influence.

Workers' attitudes toward authority must also be considered. Some believe that the job of the manager is to tell them what to do. They don't want to be involved in decision making. Others want to make all the decisions. They resist any exercise of authority by the leader.

The maturity level of subordinates influences the manager's leadership style. Some workers approach their work maturely. They take the initiative not only in doing their jobs but also in self-development. Others may have to be watched quite closely to obtain even minimal performance. However, a worker may handle one aspect of the job adequately but not other aspects of it.

Another factor is the experience level and skills of subordinates. The leadership style used with a trainee may be different from that used with an experienced craftsperson. A more directive style may prove best for the trainee, while the craftsperson may need no direction at all. For some employees an autocratic style works best. This may be particularly true in extremely favorable or extremely unfavorable situations. However, employees generally respond better to a participative approach.

Factors Related to the Situation. The situation that managers confront can also have a significant effect on the type of leadership style that will prove most effective. Many factors in the external and internal environments may cause a leader to alter his or her style. For instance, a firm's policies or pressures to produce may encourage an autocratic managerial style.

Leadership styles may vary within a firm for a number of reasons. An organization's overall leadership approach must of necessity be stated in broad terms. Thus in a firm that generally exhibits autocratic leadership, there may be some managers whose leadership style is highly participative. At the same time, an individual manager's leadership style isn't monolithic; it has various aspects, although there is usually a dominant one. A manager may, for example, normally stress employee participation. However, when the building is on fire, he or she may issue an order, "Get out of here now through exit number 2!" The leader does not consult anyone about this decision, and no committees are formed to study the problem. The situation required that the leader respond quickly and the leader simply reverted to a more autocratic style. In organizations, there are many "fires," that is, situations that require immediate and decisive action. Leaders who develop a high degree of mutual trust and confidence within their work group will be able to adjust their leadership styles to differing situations and have them more readily accepted by everyone involved.

Organizational Characteristics

Organizational characteristics also affect corporate culture. The size and complexity of organizations vary. Large organizations tend to have more specialization and be less personal. Labor unions often find that large firms are easier to organize than small ones because small firms tend to have closer and more informal relationships between employees and management. Complex organizations tend to employ a greater number of professionals and specialists, which alters the general approach to solving problems. The degree to which organizations use written communications and attempt to program behavior through rules, procedures, and regulations varies widely. The degree to which organizations decentralize their decision-making authority also differs, which affects employee autonomy, freedom and responsibility.

Administrative Processes

Administrative processes can also affect corporate culture. Firms that can develop a direct link between performance and rewards tend to create cultures that foster achievement. Communication systems that are open and free-flowing tend to promote participation and creative atmosphere. General attitudes about the handling of risk and the tolerance of conflict will, in turn, have considerable impact on the type and amount of teamwork, organizational innovation, and creativity generated.

Organizational Structure

Organizational structure is the purposeful way in which the human resources of the firm are related or arranged. An organization's structure may be rigid or flexible, depending on managerial style or how rapidly its environment is changing. In some companies, all important decisions are made by top management. In other firms, lower level managers are permitted to make significant decisions. Lincoln Electric Company, a highly successful maker of welding products, is one such company. Richard Sabo, an executive with this firm, says, "Around here we give a high school graduate more authority than some companies give their mid-level managers." Yet another important characteristic of organizational structure is the number of managerial levels—whether the structure is tall (many managerial levels) or flat (few managerial levels). The manager's job is very different in a flexible and flat organization than in an inflexible one which has more managerial levels.

Management Style of Upper Management

The attitudes and preferences of middle and top management constrain first-line managers in somewhat the same way that the attitudes and preferences of shareholders constrain top managers. This is why it is important for organizations to have a consistent policy about the amount of openness and participation to be encouraged.

At times, the managerial style of upper management is different from that of subordinate managers. For example, an executive manager may believe in simply giving orders and having them followed. A middle manager who works for the executive may prefer to involve supervisors and employees in decision making and give them a relatively large amount of freedom. This difference in approach may lead to conflict, especially if the executive believes that the middle manager's approach indicates a lack of toughness or decisiveness. Subordinate managers should attempt to follow their individual management styles, and at the same time, work to limit overt conflicts with the styles of their superiors.

■ TYPES OF CULTURES

At times an organization must alter its culture in order to succeed or influence events just to survive. This was necessary at IBM when the computer industry changed so drastically in the early 1980s. However, alterations made to the corporate culture should be superior to the existing one.

Management must be aware of the types of corporate culture that a firm may wish to emulate—and why one particular culture may prove superior to another. Most behavioralists advocate an open and participative culture. Some go so far as to contend that such a culture is best for all situations. This type of culture is characterized by:

Trust in subordinates
Open communication
Considerate and supportive leadership
Group problem solving
Worker autonomy
Information sharing
High output goals

Many U.S. businesses are culturally permissive and therefore embrace behavioralist principles. They have been guided by a philosophy that organization members who are free to choose among alternatives make the soundest decisions. When employees are asked to give up some of their individuality for the common good, the end result is often reinforcement of the status quo.[9]

The opposite of the open and participative culture is a closed and autocratic one. It, too, may be characterized by high output goals. But such goals are more likely to be declared and imposed on the organization by autocratic and threatening leaders. The greater rigidity in this culture results from strict adherence to a formal chain of command, narrower spans of management, and stricter individual accountability. The emphasis is on the individual rather than on teamwork. Employees often simply go through the motions and do as they are told.

■ THE PARTICIPATIVE CULTURE

The prevailing managerial approach in many organizations is highly structured. Consequently, most attempts to alter organizational culture have been directed toward opening it up and making it more participative. The theme of participation developed by McGregor, Herzberg, and Maslow, among others, relates primarily to self-actualization, consultative and democratic leadership, job enrichment, and management by objectives.

Values of Participation

The value of involving more people in the decision-making process relates primarily to productivity and morale. Increased productivity can result from the stimulation of ideas and encouragement of greater cooperative effort. Psychologically involved employees will often respond to shared problems with innovative suggestions and unusually productive effort.

Open and participative cultures are often used to improve employee morale and satisfaction. Specific benefits to be derived include:

Increased acceptability of management's ideas

Increased cooperation between management and staff

Reduced turnover

Reduced absenteeism

Reduced complaints and grievances

Greater acceptance of changes

Improved attitudes toward the job and the organization

In general, greater employee participation seems to have a direct and immediate effect on employee morale. Employees take more interest in the job and the organization. They tend to accept—and sometimes initiate—change not only because they understand the necessity for it, but also because they are more secure as a result of knowing more about the change. Most experience and research indicates a positive relationship between

---

[9] Richard Pascale, "The Paradox of Corporate Culture: Reconciling Ourselves to Socialization," *California Management Review*, 27 (Winter 1985), p. 28.

employee participation and measures of morale, turnover, and absenteeism. However, little evidence has been presented that suggests a positive relationship between job satisfaction and productivity. Therefore, if productivity is not adversely affected by participation, the supplementary benefits alone may make participation worthwhile. However, if productivity actually fell, management would have to carefully scrutinize its organizational and managerial approach.

Limitations of Participation

Despite its benefits, the participative approach to decision making has certain prerequisites and limitations. The requirements for greater participation in decision making are: (1) sufficient time; (2) adequate ability and interest on the part of the participants; and (3) restrictions generated by the present structure and system.

If immediate decisions are required, time may not be available for group participation. The manager may be forced to decide what to do and issue directives accordingly. Participation calls for some measure of self-discipline instead of leaning on others. In addition, participation requires that the subordinate learn to handle freedom and the supervisor learn to trust the subordinate.

Whether greater involvement in decision making can be developed depends largely on the abilities and interests of the participants, both subordinates and managers. Obviously, if the subordinate knows or cares nothing about a subject, there is little reason to consult that person. As organizations and technology become increasingly complex, and as management becomes more professional, employee participation will likely involve more cooperation seeking or information sharing. However not all employees want to participate in decisions about their work. Managers must face the fact that some workers do not seek and won't accept more job responsibility and involvement.

■ ORGANIZATION DEVELOPMENT

In the preceding discussion, we examined various factors that affect employee behavior on the job. To bring about desired changes in these factors and behaviors, some firms utilize an HRD approach which involves the entire firm. **Organization development (OD)** is an organization-wide application of behavioral science knowledge to the planned development and reinforcement of a firm's strategies, structures, and processes for improving its effectiveness.[10]

Organization development applies to an entire system, such as a company or a plant. Based on behavioral science knowledge, OD emphasizes personal needs. Although it doesn't produce a blueprint for how things

---

[10] Edgar F. Huse and Thomas G. Cummings, *Organization Development and Change*, 3rd ed. (St. Paul, Minn.: West, 1985), p. 2.

should be done, OD does provide an adaptive strategy for planning and implementing change. In addition, OD ensures a long-term reinforcement of change. Organization development involves both changes in the grouping of people (structure) and changes in the methods of communication (process).[11]

In order for the International Motor Corporation (referred to at the beginning of the chapter) to overcome substantial problems, it must alter its corporate culture significantly. A special HRD program here and a management development session there may not be sufficient. In fact, some advocates of OD view traditional management development as an antiquated idea. The essential problem with traditional HRD programs is that they usually address organizational change in an environment away from the job. Individual managers are often provided with a good educational experience, but when the development program ends and they return to their firms, they find it very difficult to apply their new skills and knowledge. To avoid this problem, OD practitioners focus on changing organizational conditions that regulate individual behavior.[12] The best training in the world could be offered and the participants could recite verbatim what they learned. However, if inappropriate behavior is not punished and appropriate behavior rewarded in the workplace, no form or amount of training will yield the desired results.[13]

Some commonly used OD techniques include survey feedback, team building, quality circles, management by objectives, job enrichment, transactional analysis, quality of work life, and sensitivity training. From a practical standpoint, some of these techniques may be combined to provide a strategic approach to organization development.

Survey Feedback

Survey feedback consists of collecting information about the organization and making the data available to employees so that they can diagnose problems and develop action plans to solve them. It is probably the most popular OD method.[14]

Survey feedback involves three essential steps, as Figure 9-1 shows. In the first step, a consultant collects data from employees, normally using questionnaires that the employees answer anonymously. The survey probably should cover only those areas in which management is willing to make changes. Otherwise, the possibility of raising employee expectations but not fulfilling them risks even greater dissatisfaction.[15]

---

[11] *Ibid.*, p. 2.

[12] Harvey A. Hornstein and Fred T. MacKenzie, "Consultraining: Merging Management Education with Organization Development," *Training and Development Journal*, 38 (January 1984), p. 52.

[13] Stephen B. Wehrenberg, "The Vicious Circle of Training and Organizational Development," *Personnel Journal*, 65 (July 1986), p. 98.

[14] Huse and Cummings, p. 129.

[15] Don Hellriegel, John W. Slocum, and Richard W. Woodman, *Organizational Behavior*, 4th ed. (St. Paul, Minn.: West, 1986) p. 610.

CHAPTER 9 Corporate Culture and Organization Development

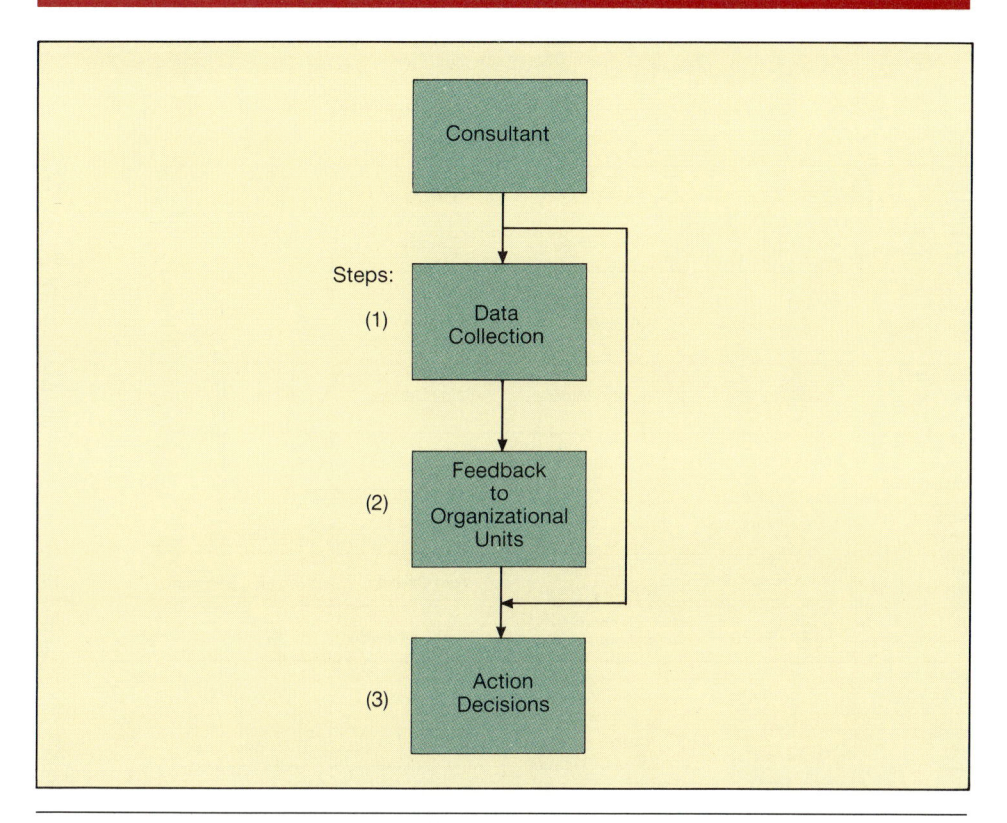

FIGURE 9-1 | The Survey Feedback Method

Source: Reprinted by permission of the publisher, from *Organization Development for Operating Managers* by Michael E. McGill, p. 66. Copyright © 1977 by AMACOM, a division of American Management Associations, New York. All rights reserved.

The second step involves presenting the results of the study in the form of feedback to the participants. In the third step, employees analyze the data, which reveal problem areas, and make action decisions. These decisions are directed at improving relationships in the organization. The consultants act as facilitators to help the employees deal with the problems and make decisions through straightforward discussions.

An example of a management survey feedback instrument is provided in Figure 9-2. This chart is used to analyze management performance in leadership, motivation, communication, decision making, goals, controls, and other critical areas. Employees are asked to check—along a continuum—the point that best describes their organization. They are also asked to indicate their views of a desired state. Averaging the responses and charting them gives an organizational profile. Referring again to Figure 9-2, note that the present state of leadership is perceived as being quite negative. The employees surveyed apparently felt that their company's leadership was condescending. The consensus was that the leader should show "substantial" confidence in subordinates (the desired state).

		Present State		Desired State	
LEADERSHIP	How much confidence is shown in subordinates?	None	Condescending	Substantial	Complete
	How free do they feel to talk to superiors about job?	Not at All	Not Very	Rather	Fully
	Are subordinates' ideas sought and used, if worthy?	Seldom	Sometimes	Usually	Always
MOTIVATION	Is predominant use made of (1) fear, (2) threats, (3) punishment, (4) rewards, (5) involvement?	1, 2, 3 Occasionally 4	4, Some 3	4, Some 3 and 5	5, 4, based on group-set goals
	Where is responsibility felt for achieving organization's goals?	Mostly at Top	Top and Middle	Fairly General	All Levels
COMMUNICATION	How much communication is aimed at achieving organization's objectives?	Very Little	Little	Quite a Bit	A Great Deal
	What is the direction of information flow?	Downward	Mostly Downward	Down and Up	Down, Up and Sideways
	How is downward communication accepted?	With Suspicion	Possibly with Suspicion	With Caution	With an Open Mind
	How accurate is upward communication?	Often Wrong	Censored for the Boss	Limited Accuracy	Accurate
	How well do superiors know problems faced by subordinates?	Know Little	Some Knowledge	Quite Well	Very Well
DECISIONS	At what level are decisions formally made?	Mostly at Top	Policy at Top, Some Delegation	Broad Policy at Top, More Delegation	Throughout but well integrated
	What is the origin of technical and professional knowledge used in decision making?	Top Management	Upper and Middle	To a Certain Extent Throughout	To a Great Extent Throughout
	Are subordinates involved in decisions related to their work?	Not at all	Occasionally Consulted	Generally Consulted	Fully Involved
	What does the decision making process contribute to motivation?	Nothing, Often Weakens it	Relatively Little	Some Contribution	Substantial Contribution
GOALS	How are organizational goals established?	Orders Issued	Orders, Some Comment invited	After Discussion, by Orders	By Group Action (Except in Crisis)
	How much covert resistance to goals is present?	Strong Resistance	Moderate Resistance	Some Resistance at Times	Little or None
CONTROL	How concentrated are review and control functions?	Highly at Top	Relatively Highly at Top	Moderate Delegation to Lower Levels	Quite Widely Shared
	Is there an informal organization resisting the formal one?	Yes	Usually	Sometimes	No—Same Goals as Formal
	Where are cost, productivity and other control data used for?	Policing, Punishment	Reward and Punishment	Reward, Some Self-guidance	Self-guidance Problem Solving

FIGURE 9-2 | An Example of a Survey Feedback Questionnaire

Source: Reprinted by permission of the publisher, from *Organization Development for Operating Managers* by Michael E. McGill. Copyright © 1977 by AMACOM, a division of American Management Associations, New York. All rights reserved.

Team Building

A conscious effort to develop effective work groups throughout the organization is referred to as **team building**. Although some activities may be more efficiently pursued by an individual, many problems are too broad and complex for one person to handle. In these instances, management teams can be more effective. A task-focused approach to team building may be more beneficial than an approach that views harmony and cooperation as end products in themselves. A work unit's attention is given to actual organizational tasks, with harmony and cooperation being by-products of the problem-solving process. This approach has been effectively used by both businesses and government agencies.[16]

Douglas McGregor has identified several characteristics of effective management teams (see Table 9-1). His version of an effective group emphasizes an informal organizational culture that is relatively free from tension. The group's decision-making process involves much discussion and broad participation. Communications are open, with listening to the views of others emphasized. Members feel free to disagree but do so in an atmosphere of acceptance. The effective group works as a team in pursuing goals that its members understand and accept.

Effective work groups focus on solving actual problems while building efficient management teams. The team-building process begins when the team leader defines a problem that requires organizational change (see Figure 9-3). The group diagnoses the problem to determine the underlying causes. These causes may be related to breakdowns in communication, inappropriate leadership styles, or deficiencies in the organizational structure, or other factors. The group then considers alternative solutions and selects the most appropriate one. The result of open and frank discussions is likely to be commitment to the proposed course of action. The interpersonal relations developed by group members improve the chances for implementing the change.[17]

Quality Circles

Another OD approach is the use of quality circles. **Quality circles** are groups of employees who meet regularly with their supervisors to identify production problems and recommend solutions. These recommendations are then presented to higher level management for review, and the approved actions are implemented with employee participation.[18]

---

[16] Jeffrey P. Davidson, "A Task-Focused Approach to Team Building," *Personnel*, 62 (March 1985), p. 16.

[17] Michael A. Hitt, R. Dennis Middlemist, and Robert L. Mathis, *Management: Concepts and Effective Practice* (St. Paul, Minn.: West, 1983), p. 394.

[18] Robert J. Shaw, "From Skepticism to Support: Middle Management's Role in Quality Circles," *Peat Marwick/Management Focus*, 29 (May–June 1982), p. 35.

TABLE 9-1 | Characteristics of Effective Groups

1. The atmosphere, which can be sensed in a few minutes of observation, tends to be informal, comfortable, and relaxed. There are no obvious tensions.
2. There is a lot of discussion in which virtually everyone participates, but it remains pertinent to the task of the group.
3. The task or the objective of the group is well understood and accepted by the members.
4. The members listen to each other! The discussion does not have the quality of jumping from one idea to another unrelated one. Every idea is given a hearing. People are not afraid of seeming foolish by expressing a creative thought even if it seems fairly extreme.
5. There is disagreement. The group is comfortable with this and shows no signs of having to avoid conflict or to keep everything on a plane of sweetness and light. Disagreements are not suppressed or overridden by premature group action. Individuals who disagree do not appear to be trying to dominate the group or to express hostility. Their disagreement is an expression of a genuine difference of opinion, and they expect a hearing in order to find a solution.
6. Most decisions are reached by a kind of consensus in which it is clear that everybody is in general agreement and willing to go along.
7. Criticism is frequent, frank, and relatively comfortable. There is little evidence of personal attack, either open or hidden. The criticism has a constructive flavor in that it is oriented toward removing an obstacle that prevents the group from getting the job done.
8. People freely express their feelings as well as their ideas on both the problem and the group's operation. There is little pussyfooting, there are few hidden agendas. Everybody appears to know quite well how everybody else feels about any matter under discussion.
9. When action is taken, clear assignments are made and accepted.
10. The chairman of the group does not dominate it, or to the contrary, does the group defer unduly to him or her. In fact, the leadership shifts from time to time, depending on the circumstances. At various times different members, because of their knowledge or experience, are in a position to act as "resources" for the group. The members utilize them in this fashion and they occupy leadership roles while they are thus being used. There is little evidence of a struggle for power as the group operates. The issue is not who controls but how to get the job done.
11. The group is conscious of its own operations. Frequently, it will stop to examine how well it is doing or what may be interfering with its operation. The problem may be a matter of procedure, or it may be that an individual's behavior is interfering with the accomplishment of the group's objectives. Whatever the problem, it is openly discussed until a solution is found.

Source: Adapted from Douglas McGregor, *The Human Side of Management* (New York: McGraw-Hill, 1960), pp. 232–235. Reprinted by permission of the McGraw-Hill Book Company.

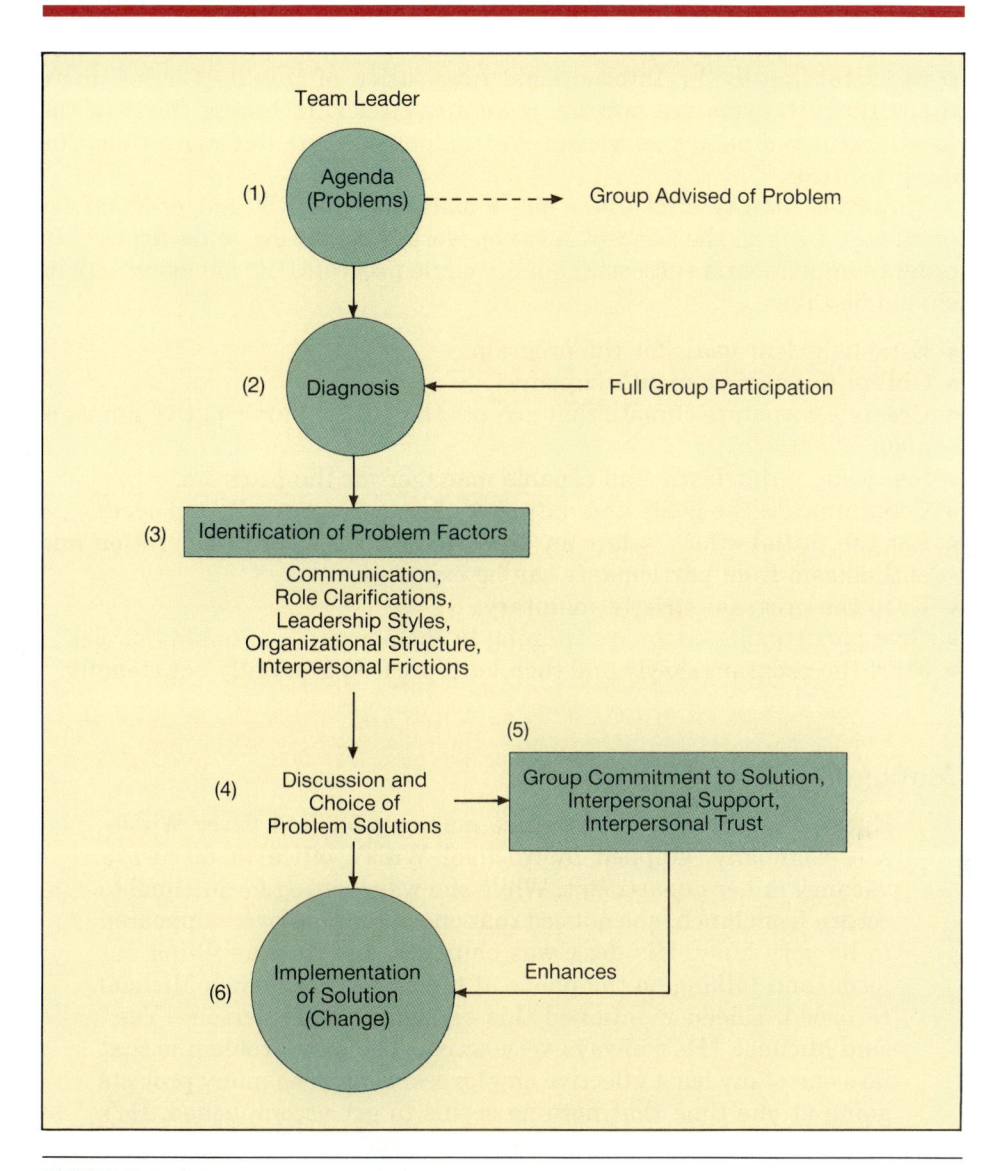

CHAPTER 9 Corporate Culture and Organization Development

FIGURE 9-3 | The Team Building Process

Source: Reproduced by permission from Michael A. Hitt, R. Dennis Middlemist, and Robert L. Mathis, *Management: Concepts and Effective Practice* (St. Paul, Minn.: West, 1983), p. 393. Copyright © 1983 by West Publishing Company. All rights reserved.

In Japan, more than ten million workers participate in quality circles, which results in annual savings of $20–$25 billion.[19] Even though the cor-

---

[19] Sud Ingle, "How to Avoid Quality Circle Failure in Your Company," *Training and Development Journal*, 36 (June 1982), p. 59.

porate culture in the United States is different, an increasing number of firms are adapting the quality circle concept to their operations. To illustrate, according to the International Association of Quality Circles, more than 100 U.S. firms are now using quality circles, including thirty of the fifty largest companies surveyed. Westinghouse alone has more than 700 quality circles.[20]

However, quality circles are not a panacea for HRD and productivity problems. In fact, the concept has not worked at all for some firms.[21] In order to implement a successful quality circle program, the following actions should be taken:

- Establish clear goals for the program.
- Obtain top-management's support.
- Create a corporate climate that accepts the idea of participative management.
- Select an enthusiastic and capable manager for the program.
- Communicate the goals and nature of the program to all employees.
- For the initial effort, select an area of the firm where cooperation and enthusiasm from participants can be expected.
- Keep the program strictly voluntary.
- Give participants adequate training in the operation of quality circles.
- Start the program slowly and then let it proceed gradually but steadily.[22]

Management by Objectives

> Eileen Murphy, human resource manager for Red River Wholesale Company, stopped by Michael Wills's office to discuss a vacancy in her department. While she was waiting for Michael to return from lunch, she noticed that one of his employees appeared to be very busy. His desk was cluttered and he was filling out forms and talking on the phone at the same time. When Michael returned, Eileen mentioned this extremely busy person. "Yes," said Michael, "He's always very active. The only problem is that he's one of my least effective employees. He has so many projects going at one time that nothing seems to get accomplished. He's very active, yes. But highly productive, no!"

Michael Willis is keenly aware that activity is not necessarily a measure of productivity. He also believes that random, ineffective behavior may result from a lack of clearly defined objectives. **Management by objectives (MBO)** is a philosophy of management that emphasizes the setting of agreed-on objectives by superior and subordinate managers and using these objectives as the primary basis for motivation, evaluation, and self-control. As a management approach that encourages managers to anticipate and plan for the future, MBO directs efforts toward attainable goals.

---

[20] Roy G. Folz, "QWL's Effect on Productivity," *Personnel Administrator*, 27 (May 1982), p. 20.
[21] Ingle, p. 54.
[22] *Ibid*. pp. 57–59.

It deemphasizes guessing or making decisions based on hunches. Knowledge of MBO is especially important to the human resource manager as that department is often responsible for overseeing the entire company's MBO program.

Because MBO emphasizes participative management approaches, it has been called a philosophy of management. Within this broader context, MBO becomes an important method of organization development. It focuses on the achievement of individual and organizational goals. The participation of individuals in setting goals and the emphasis on self-control promote not only personal development but also organizational development.

Management by objectives is a dynamic process that must be continuously reviewed, modified, and updated. Top management must both initiate the MBO process by establishing long-range goals (see Figure 9-4) and support the process. For example, the president and vice-president of human resources (superior and subordinate) may jointly establish the firm's HRM long-range goals and intermediate and short-range objectives. At this point, the president and vice-president mutually agree on the subordinate's performance objectives and action plans, which outline how the objectives will be achieved. The subordinate proceeds to work toward his or her goals. At the end of the appraisal period, both parties review the subordinate's performance and determine what can be done to overcome any problems encountered. Goals are then established for the next period and the process is repeated.

From an organization development standpoint, MBO offers numerous potential benefits. It:

- Provides an opportunity for development of managers and employees.
- Increases the firm's ability to change.
- Provides a more objective and tangible basis for performance appraisal and salary decisions.
- Results in better overall management and higher performance levels.
- Provides an effective overall planning system.
- Forces managers to establish priorities and measurable targets or standards of performance.
- Clarifies the specific roles, responsibilities, and authority of employees.
- Encourages the joint participation of employees and managers in establishing objectives.
- Promotes accountability.
- Lets individuals know clearly what is expected of them.
- Improves communication within the organization.
- Helps identify promotable managers and employees.
- Increases employee motivation and commitment.

However, certain problems are associated with MBO. Without the full support of top management, it is bound to fail. This commitment may be difficult to obtain because implementing such a system often takes from three to five years. In addition, goals may be difficult to establish. Another potential weakness is a tendency to concentrate on short term plans. For example, short-term objectives may be achieved at the expense of long-term goals. The system also has the potential to create a seemingly insurmount-

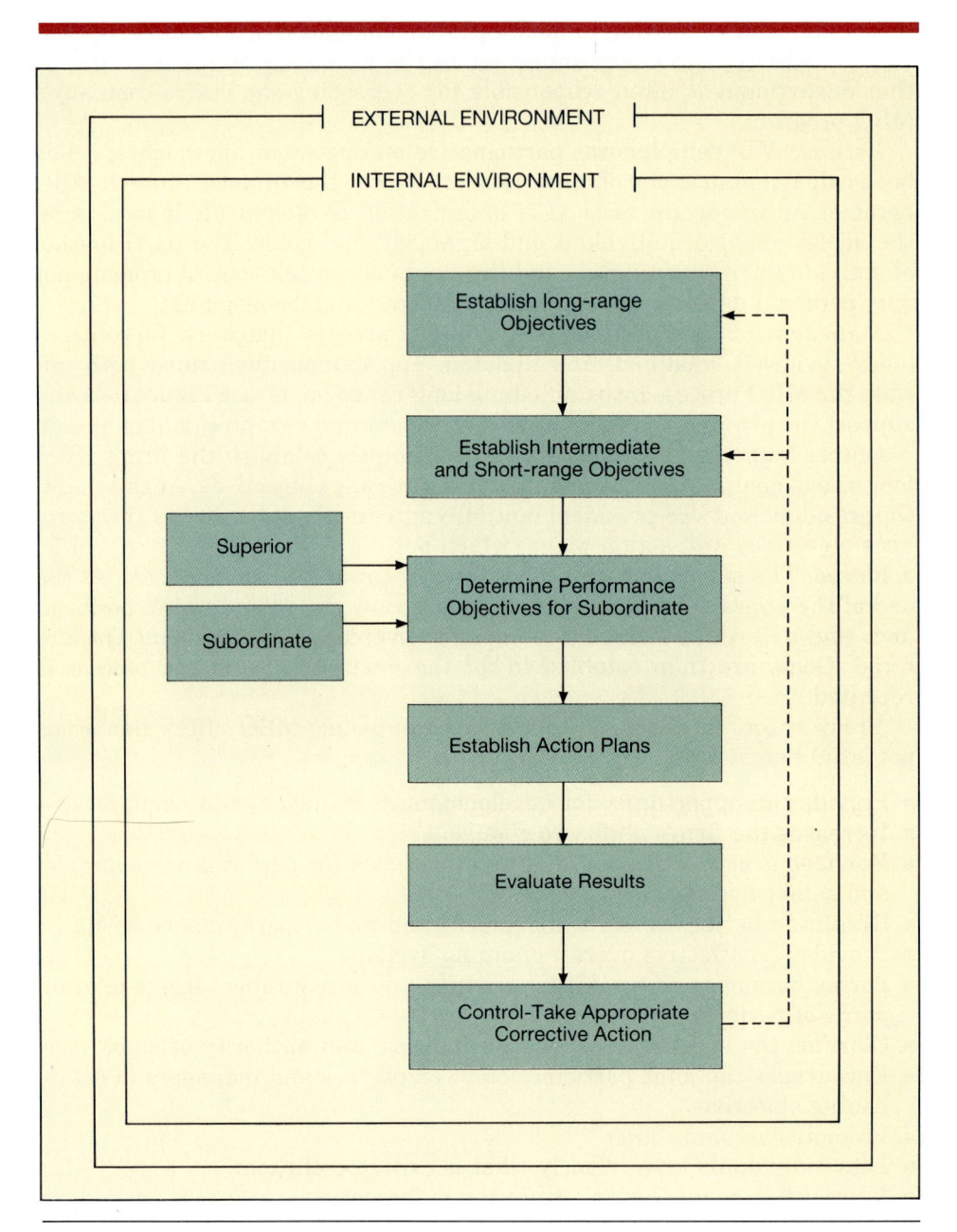

FIGURE 9-4 | The MBO Process

able paper mill if it isn't closely monitored. Finally, some managers believe that MBO is excessively time consuming. The process forces people to think ahead and be capable of seeing how their goals and actions fit into the overall picture. This is not an easy task for some managers, but it is one that can prove quite beneficial.

HRM In Action

"Charlie," said Byran Atrip, president of Sharpco Industries, to Charlie Wallace, the human resource manager, "I've been reading and hearing a lot about management by objectives. Sounds like something that we need to get into. Work up a procedure to get it started at Sharpco. I'll inform the vice-presidents at next month's executive council meeting that this is the thing for us."

How would you respond?

Monsanto's Use of MBO Concepts

Utilizing many MBO concepts, the Monsanto Company has installed a management by results (MBR) program throughout the company. Although the initial direction came from top management, program implementation was decentralized. Management by results is now part of the fabric of Monsanto's management process. Its purpose is to motivate people, assist them in setting unit and personal directions, evaluate performance, provide equitable compensation, and ensure employee development throughout the firm.

Management by results ensures that plans of individuals are properly integrated with those of their reporting unit and that involvement and cooperation are encouraged as the unit seeks to achieve group goals. In addition, Monsanto's system permits flexibility by focusing not on subordinates' specific and immediate activities, but rather on their broader and longer-term progress. By emphasizing results for one year or longer, employees are encouraged to avoid short-term gains at the expense of longer-term results.

One mechanism for achieving these ends is the job results analysis/goals form—the basic document in the direction-setting phase of Monsanto's system. The corporate guidelines for preparing this document are broad and flexible. They emphasize that managers and units should exercise their best judgment when using the form. The first four sections constitute the job results analysis and center on the job's longer-term definition and direction. The last five sections, the goals document, deal with coming-year expectations and performance (see Figure 9-5).

The following briefly describes each section:

1. **General conditions**. In this section, employees state their assumptions about the environment in which they plan to operate for the coming year. For example, a salesperson would consider the growth rate of industries to be served and make projections about the health of the economy. If those assumptions later turn out to be off the mark, supervisor and subordinate are encouraged to review the document for a possible change in overall direction or level of expectation.

| Monsanto | COMPANY CONFIDENTIAL | JOB RESULTS ANALYSIS – GOALS 19 |

Principal Thrust ②
Location _____ Name _____
JRA—Date _____ Goals Date _____ Title _____

General Conditions Premises ①

Results To Be Worked Toward	Major Results	Goals	Joint Account Ability	Range — Basic	Range — Outstanding	Weight
*relates to Principal Thrust ③	④	⑤	⑥	⑦		⑧

JRA Approved By _____
Date _____

Goals Approved By _____
Date _____

Goals represent ⑨ % of total performance

FIGURE 9-5 | Monsanto's Job Results Analysis/Goals Form

2. **Principal thrust**. The most important thing to be done during the next year is stated in this section. It serves as a good check on the goals set later.
3. **Results sought**. Here, employees identify the areas of longer-term accomplishment that are important to the job and the unit.
4. **Major results**. An X is placed in this column to identify the most important results, which helps to establish priorities.
5. **Goals**. Here, the most important accomplishments for the coming year are identified. Goals are considered milestones toward longer-term results. Normally, a Monsanto employee has from three to five goals for the year.
6. **Joint accountability**. The purpose of this section is to identify and gain commitment from those individuals—other than the supervisor or subordinates—who give or receive help in achieving each goal. Employees are encouraged to discuss their goals with others from whom support is required.

7. **Range**. The range of performance for each goal is established and stated in this portion of the form. As an example, suppose that a goal was established "to achieve new customer sales of $1,000,000 (expected)." In this case, $500,000 would be entered in the basic column and perhaps $2,000,000 in the outstanding column.
8. **Weight**. The entries in this column establish goal priorities for the coming year. The weight established indicates priority—not the amount of time to be spent on each goal. To accomplish this ranking process, 100 points may be allocated among the goals or the goals may be numerically ranked.
9. **Goals represent _____% of your performance**. The purpose of this entry is to show the relative importance of the stated goals to the entire job.

Monsanto's MBR program ensures continuous employee training and development. This approach integrates training and development into the overall Monsanto management process.

Job Enrichment

Job enrichment is the deliberate restructuring of a job to make it more challenging, meaningful, and interesting. It emphasizes accomplishing significant tasks so that the employee can feel a sense of achievement. Job enrichment takes an optimistic view of employee capabilities. Its use presumes that individuals have the ability to perform more difficult and responsible tasks than they are currently performing. Further, it assumes that most people will respond favorably if given the opportunity to accomplish challenging tasks and will also be motivated to be more productive. When job enrichment is applied on a broad scale, it becomes an important OD method.

The use of job enrichment is illustrated by a department of the First National Bank of Chicago in which 110 employees worked on a "paperwork assembly line."[23] The primary responsibility of the department was to issue letters of credit. The work consisted of fragmented tasks that prevented employees from fully grasping the overall meaning of their work. The unit's productivity was less than that desired by management.

After a survey indicated an 80 percent dissatisfaction rate, the bank initiated a program whereby employees redesigned their work with the assistance of an OD specialist. Discrete tasks were consolidated into complete jobs that required broadly trained professionals performing in a more responsible, highly paid job classification. As a result, profitability, productivity, customer satisfaction, and staff morale increased sharply.

A less recent, but more highly publicized experience with job enrichment involved Sweden's leading car manufacturer, A. B. Volvo. Pehr Gyllenhammar introduced a drastic alternative to the traditional assembly line soon after assuming the presidency in 1971. Work at the Kalmar plant was arranged so that groups of about twenty employees could assemble com-

---

[23] F. K. Plous, Jr., "Redesigning Work," *Personnel Administrator*, 32 (March 1987), p. 99.

plete car components. This work arrangement permitted them to personally identify with their product. Gyllenhammar wanted his production employees to see a Volvo being driven down the street and say, "I made that car."[24]

When jobs are restructured to increase responsibility and challenge, employees continually develop while performing them. The nature of these jobs actually requires that employees keep their skills up to date.

Transactional Analysis[25]

How widespread the use of transactional analysis is as an OD method isn't clear. However, it has been used for a number of years as a technique for teaching behavioral principles to individuals and small groups in training and development programs. **Transactional analysis (TA)** is an OD method that considers each individual's three ego states, the *Parent*, the *Adult*, and the *Child*, in helping people understand interpersonal relations. It provides a system for forming a mental image of the emotions and thought processes used by people interacting in either a social or business setting. It can be most useful in permitting an employee to understand where a customer or fellow employee "is coming from" and to respond appropriately.[26]

The attitudes, beliefs, and values learned from authority figures early in each person's life are stored in the Parent ego state. Everything seen or heard is recorded, as on tape, and these messages influence current behavior. The Parent ego state may reflect nurturing behavior that is sympathetic, protective, and instructive or critical behavior that is punitive, prejudicial, and judgmental. The boss who comes on as a critical parent tends to find fault excessively and to punish, rather than to guide and develop subordinates.

The Adult ego state, on the other hand, is the objective part of each person. Through the Adult, data are analyzed permitting each person to make independent, logical judgments. The Adult serves as an internal computer, and behavioral changes occur through this ego state.

The emotional side of individual behavior stems from the Child ego state. This state may take on different qualities—the Natural Child, the Little Professor, or the Adaptive Child. When the Natural Child dominates, the individual is expressive, self-centered, impulsive, and curious. The Little Professor centers around being intuitive, manipulative, and creative. The manner in which the Adaptive Child behaves is determined by the parental figures with whom the individual was associated.

The interaction of ego states can have a significant impact on behavior in organizations. If organizational members are able to recognize the ego state affecting a given communication, they may be able to respond appro-

---

[24] "Lessons from the Volvo Experience," *International Management*, 33 (February 1978), p. 42.

[25] The material on transactional analysis in this section is abridged and adapted from Thomas A. Harris, M.D., *"I'm O.K.—You're O.K."* Copyright © 1967, 1968, and 1969 by Thomas A. Harris, M.D. Reprinted by permission of Harper & Row Publishers, Inc.

[26] David J. Lill and John T. Rose, "Transactional Analysis and Personal Selling: A Primer for Banks," *Journal of Commercial Bank Lending*, 70 (February 1988), p. 57.

CHAPTER 9   Corporate Culture and Organization Development

priately. Various situations that a person may confront are presented in Figures 9-6 through 9-8. In Figure 9-6, Frank's three ego states are shown on the left and John's are shown on the right. The two have engaged in an adult-to-adult transaction. It is a complementary transaction because Frank's message gets the expected response. When this occurs, communication remains open and there is no conflict or difficulty between the two.

A different situation is presented in Figure 9-7. Here, Frank speaks from his Parent ego state to John's Child state. This also illustrates a complementary transaction. The lines of communication are open for the present, but condescending behavior of this sort may have negative long-term consequences.

Crossed transactions occur when the message sent gets an unexpected response. Note in Figure 9-8 that Frank delivers a message from his Parent ego state intended for John's Child state, "I never want you to interrupt me again like you did in that meeting yesterday." Instead, John replies from his Parent state, "Who the hell are you to hog the whole conversation?" Frank expected an apologetic response but instead received one that was unexpected. Here, the transaction was crossed. These types of trans-

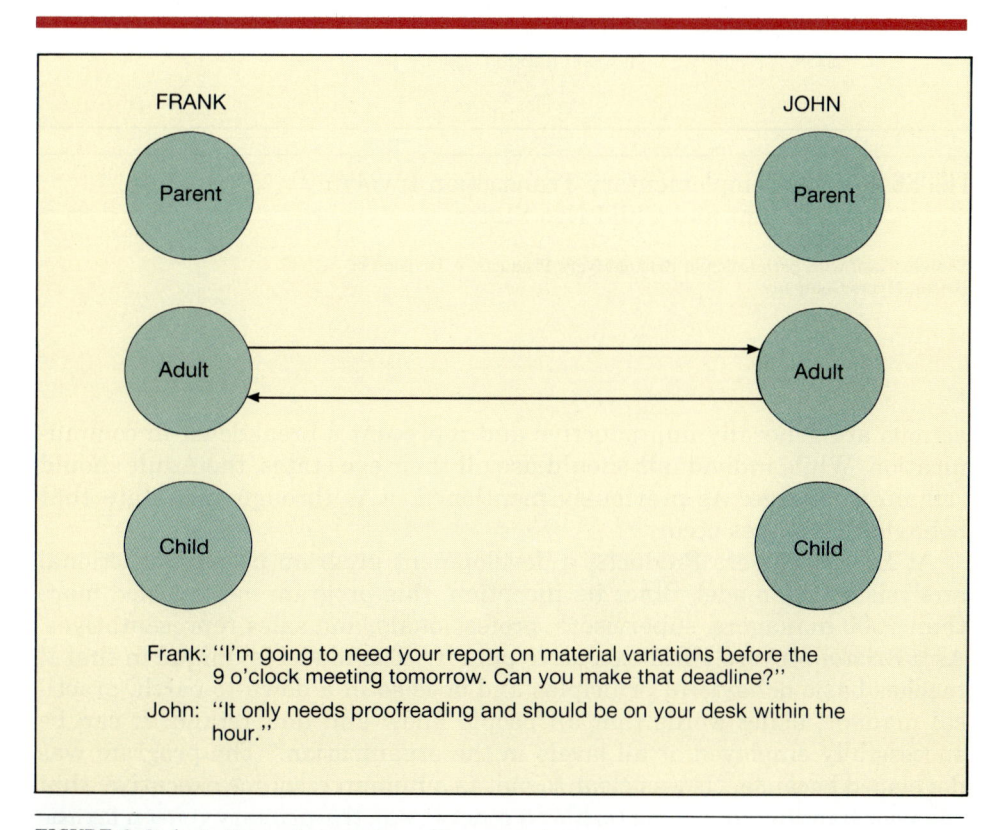

FRANK   JOHN

Parent   Parent

Adult ⟶⟵ Adult

Child   Child

Frank: "I'm going to need your report on material variations before the 9 o'clock meeting tomorrow. Can you make that deadline?"

John: "It only needs proofreading and should be on your desk within the hour."

FIGURE 9-6 | A Complementary Transaction

Source: Used with permission of Bristol-Myers Products, A Division of Bristol-Myers Company.

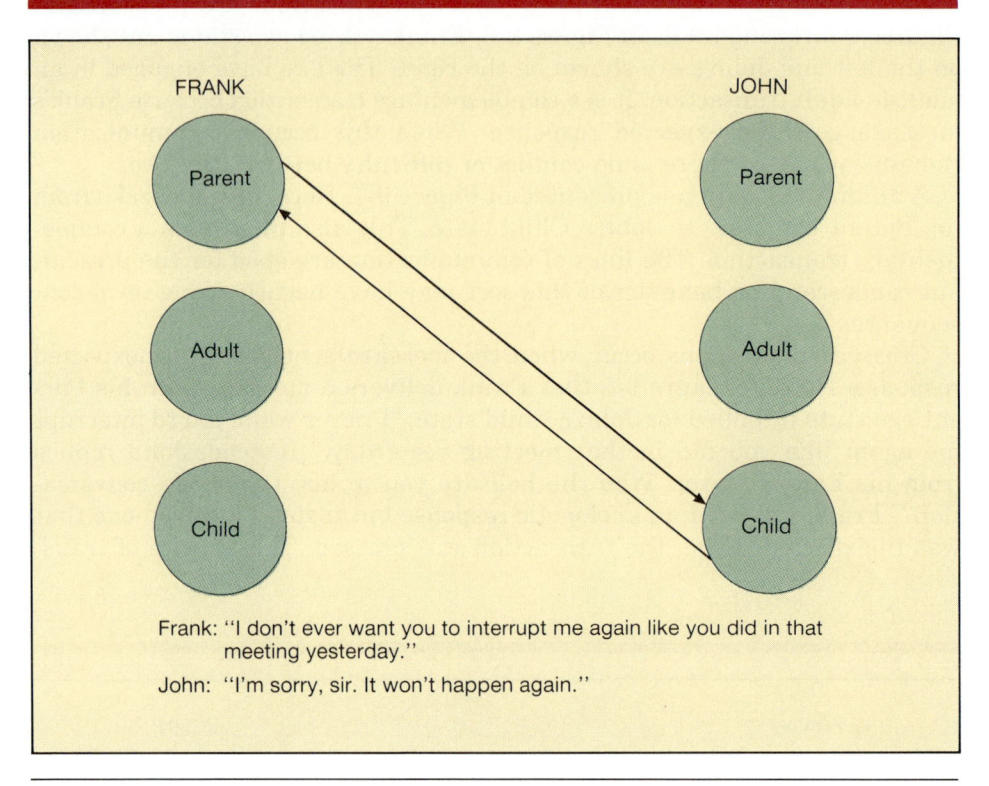

FIGURE 9-7 | A Complementary Transaction Involving Parent and Child Ego States

Frank: "I don't ever want you to interrupt me again like you did in that meeting yesterday."
John: "I'm sorry, sir. It won't happen again."

Source: Used with permission of Bristol-Myers Products, A Division of Bristol-Myers Company.

actions are generally unproductive and represent a breakdown in communication. While individuals should use all their ego states, the Adult should remain in charge. As previously mentioned, it is through this state that behavioral changes occur.

At Bristol-Meyers Products, a development program uses transactional analysis as the model. Since its inception, this program has reached more than 1000 managers, supervisors, professionals, and sales representatives. As a Bristol-Meyers HRM executive puts it, "The model is unique in that it teaches basic behavioral principles and does so in a down-to-earth, practical manner, using words that all people know and understand. It can be successfully employed at all levels in the organization." The program was developed because, "It was clear to me, as a human resource executive, that the poor handling of people (self and others) was the primary reason for the failure of managers." As individuals in a firm learn to analyze their own social interactions, better communication and greater organizational effectiveness can follow.

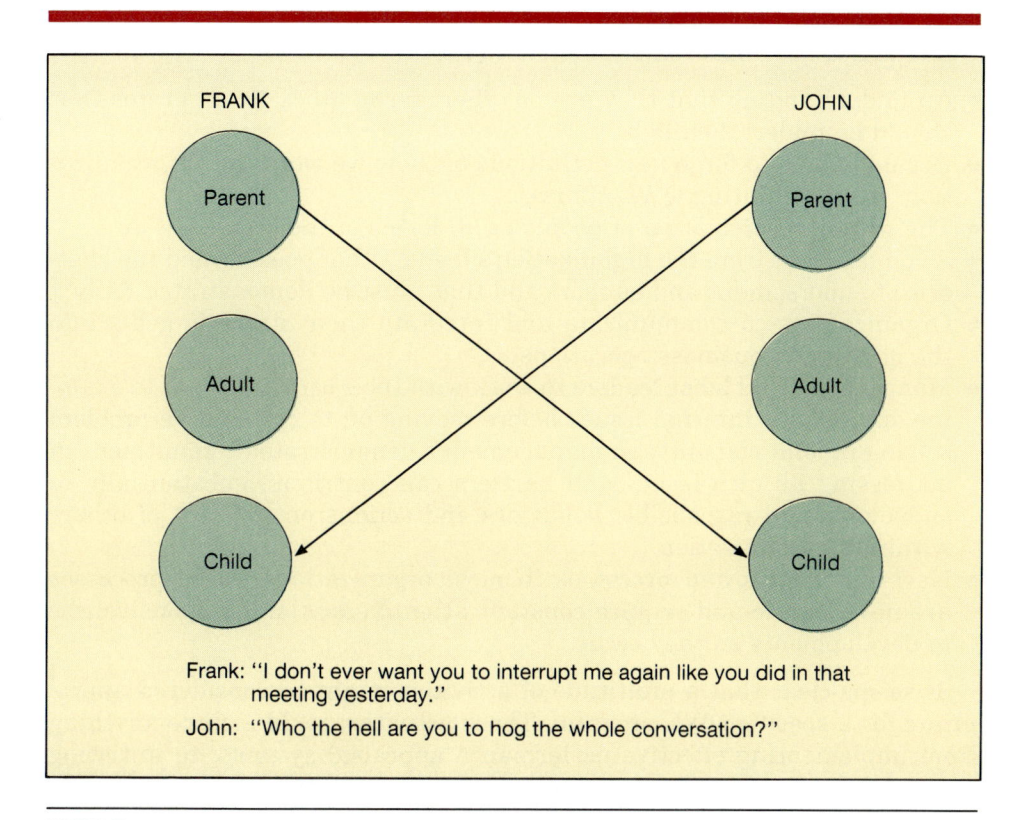

FIGURE 9-8 | An Unexpected Response Results in a Crossed Transaction

Source: Used with permission of Bristol-Myers Products, A Division of Bristol-Myers Company.

Quality of Work Life

During the past decade, a concept that has many implications for employee participation has received much attention. It is called **quality of work life (QWL)** and is the extent to which employees satisfy significant personal needs through their organizational experiences. The basic philosophy underlying the concept is that improvements in the quality of work life stem from efforts at every organizational level to enhance human dignity and growth.[27]

Any firm that wants to develop a QWL program must first determine the goals it wants to achieve with the program. Therefore citing a list of appropriate activities as with, for example, MBO programs is difficult. The goals and actions undertaken are the joint responsibility of management, the union, and other members of the organization.

---

[27] Lee M. Ozley and Judith S. Ball, "Quality of Work Life: Initiating Successful Efforts in Labor–Management Organizations," *Personnel Administrator*, 27 (May 1982), p. 27.

However, certain guidelines may be helpful in initiating QWL efforts. Generally, QWL improvement efforts call for:

- An understanding that they are not short-term, quick-fix programs that should be undertaken lightly.
- Organizations to forge new definitions of "how we work in this organization" when initiating QWL efforts.
- The willing participation of people at all levels of the organization.
- A commitment from the organization's leaders that goes beyond the rhetoric of endorsement and support and that must be demonstrated daily.
- Organizations to communicate and integrate their strategic goals into the day-to-day business operations.
- Management and labor leaders to work with their constituencies to examine and resolve internal issues before moving on to cooperative problem solving in joint committees; management's demonstrated commitment in addressing its own issues and barriers can contribute substantially to supportive and responsible behaviors and actions on the part of others within the organization.
- New approaches and processes in most organizations; these processes are never static and require constant attentiveness and responsiveness to developments as they occur.[28]

It seems clear that a multitude of activities might be considered appropriate for a specific QWL program. These activities could include anything from implementing effective performance appraisal systems, to initiating counseling programs, to developing a more open approach to internal communication.

Sensitivity Training

An OD technique designed to make us more aware of ourselves and our impact on others is referred to as **sensitivity training**. It is quite different from traditional forms of training, which stress the learning of a predetermined set of concepts.[29]

Sensitivity training features a group—often called a training group or T-group—in which there is no preestablished agenda or focus. The trainer's purpose is merely to serve as a facilitator in this unstructured environment. Participants are encouraged to learn about themselves and others in the group. Some objectives of sensitivity training are to increase:

1. Self-awareness and insight into the participant's behavior and its meaning in a social context.
2. Sensitivity to the behavior of others.
3. Awareness and understanding of the types of processes that facilitate or inhibit group functioning and the interactions between different groups.

---

[28] *Ibid.* p. 27.

[29] James L. Gibson and John M. Ivancevich, *Organizations: Behavior, Structure, Processes*, 4th ed. (Plano, Texas: Business Publications, 1982), pp. 580–581.

4. Diagnostic skills in social, interpersonal, and intergroup situations.
5. The participant's ability to intervene successfully in intergroup or intragroup situations so as to increase member satisfaction, effectiveness, and output.
6. The participant's ability to analyze continually his or her own interpersonal behavior in order to achieve more effective and satisfying interpersonal relationships.[30]

When sensitivity training begins, there is no agenda—and no leaders, no authority, and no power positions. Essentially, a vacuum exists until participants begin to talk. Through dialogue people begin to learn about themselves and others. Participants are encouraged to look at themselves as others see them. Then, if they want to change, they can attempt to do so.

Although the purpose of sensitivity training (to assist individuals to learn more about how they relate to other people) cannot be questioned, the technique has been roundly criticized. It is clear that sensitivity training often involves anxiety-provoking situations as stimulants for learning. In addition, some critics believe that it is one matter for participants to express true feelings in the psychological safety of the laboratory but quite another to face their coworkers back on the job.[31] Information learned in a sensitivity group may prove to be irrelevant or even damaging unless the participant returns to an organizational environment that supports the use of that knowledge.[32] Individuals may be encouraged to be more open and supportive in the T-group, but when they return to their jobs, they often have not really changed. In addition, participants often undergo severe emotional stress during training. And finally, the results are mixed concerning whether sensitivity training improves organizational effectiveness.[33]

■ ORGANIZATIONAL DEVELOPMENT: AN EXAMPLE

Ronald C. Pilenzo, president of the Society for Human Resource Management, tells of a major change he was involved in at International Multifoods Corporation. The company was confronted with the challenge of how to integrate women into its management ranks. The organization was very conservative and did not wish to create special opportunities (jobs) for women. It was seeking a way to (1) sensitize men holding managerial positions; (2) create an awareness in women employees of job opportunities and their individual responsibilities for self-determination and self-development; and (3) achieve affirmative action goals.

---

[30] John P. Campbell and Marvin D. Dunnette, "Effectiveness of T-Group Experiences in Managerial Training and Development," *Psychological Bulletin*, 70(2) (August 1968), pp. 23–104. Copyright © 1968 by the American Psychological Association. Reprinted by permission.

[31] Irwin L. Goldstein, *Training in Organizations: Needs Assessment, Development, and Evaluation*, Second Edition (Monterey, California: Brooks/Cole Publishing Company, 1986) p. 243.

[32] Frank E. Saal and Patrick A. Knight, *Industrial/Organizational Psychology: Science and Practice* (Pacific Grove, California: Brooks/Cole Publishing Company, 1988) p. 245–246.

[33] Huse and Cummings, p. 98.

After conducting extensive research on the subject, discussing the challenge with consultants and women who were experts in the field, and reviewing existing programs, Pilenzo made the following proposal to top management:

1. Design a program to fit the "organizational personality" of the company and its unique needs.
2. Offer the program on a voluntary basis to *all* women, regardless of position and rank, and on a mandatory basis to men holding managerial positions.
3. Obtain full top-management support and participation.
4. Design and install a skills inventory system to identify available skills of both men and women employees nationwide to support the program.

The program was accepted by top management. Over a two-year period, more than 700 women employees and 250 executives attended sessions designed for each group. The president of the company personally introduced the first four meetings for the men to emphasize the company's commitment and goals. During the course of the program, fifteen to twenty high-potential women candidates were identified for top management positions. Another group of women began self-development programs. The financial cost of the program was significantly less than comparable programs in other companies, primarily because of the use of existing company resources and available talent.

■ USE OF CONSULTANTS

Organization development efforts rely heavily on the use of qualified consultants who work with teams from the firm's management and work groups. These teams come from throughout the organization, from top management to the shop floor.[34] The consultant—a facilitator—assists both types of groups in identifying goals and solving problems that interfere with goal achievement. The consultant is also responsible for helping guide implementation of planned change.

A consultant may come from within the organization or from the outside. The role of the consultant is to utilize his or her specialized knowledge in making proposals for intervention in the organization's activities. They assist managers in bringing about change in areas such as communication, leadership styles, and motivational techniques.

Management frequently believes that an outside expert brings objectivity to a situation and obtains acceptance and trust from organizational members more easily. However, another popular approach is to utilize internal consultants (employees of the firm) as effective change agents. Proponents of this tactic believe that the internal consultant, who knows both the formal and informal nature of the organization, can often produce desired results at a lower cost.

---

[34] Fred E. Fiedler and Joseph E. Garcia, "Comparing Organization Development and Management Training," *Personnel Administrator*, 30 (March 1985), p. 35.

■ ORGANIZATION DEVELOPMENT PROGRAM EVALUATION

When an OD effort has been implemented, the following question must be asked: "Did anything happen as a result of this experience?" All too often the answer is: "We don't know." Evaluation of an OD effort is more difficult than determining whether an employee has learned to operate a particular piece of equipment. Nevertheless, management should evaluate the effort. The company has probably invested a considerable amount of time and money in the program and deserves to know whether it has produced tangible benefits.

One means of measuring program effectiveness is by assessing changes in meeting performance criteria.[35] Some of the factors to be measured might include (1) productivity, (2) absenteeism rate, (3) turnover rate, (4) accident rate, (5) costs, and (6) scrap. An improvement in these and other areas may mean that the OD yielded desired results. For instance, a lower turnover rate might mean that workers are more satisfied with their work and have chosen to remain with the firm. Lower costs per unit produced suggests that workers may be paying more attention to their work. Although such evaluative data are useful, they probably will not provide the entire answer.

An excellent means of determining the extent of change in employee attitudes is through the use of a survey questionnaire. This survey is administered to employees prior to OD efforts and after implementation of the change program. A measurable difference in total employee satisfaction may well suggest that the effort was effective.

Effectiveness should not be measured only when the program has been completed. Rather, questionnaires should be administered periodically over an extended period of time. Evaluation is a continuous process in which performance criteria are considered in order to measure the effect of the change effort. As early as the 1950s, OD was identified as a promising and effective approach to organizational change. This appraisal has proved accurate, with the successful utilization of OD by many organizations.[36]

---

[35] Gibson and Ivancevich, pp. 541–548.
[36] Fiedler and Garcia, p. 36.

SUMMARY

Corporate culture is the system of shared values, beliefs, and habits within an organization that interacts with the formal structure to produce behavioral norms. The organization's reward system identifies the types of behavior and attitudes that are important for success.

Corporate culture evolves from the examples of top management, stemming largely from what they do, not what they say. Other factors also interact to shape the culture of a firm. Three of them—communication, motivation, and leadership—have a special impact on a firm's psychological environment. Organizational characteristics, administrative processes, organizational structure, and management style help shape corporate culture.

Most behavioralists advocate an open and participative culture. Some contend that such a culture is best for all situations. The opposite of the open and participative culture is a closed and autocratic one. This culture's greater rigidity results from strict adherence to a formal chain of command, a narrower span of control, and stricter individual accountability.

The prevailing managerial approach in many organizations is highly structured. Consequently, most attempts to alter organizational culture have been directed at creating a culture that is more open and participative. Open and participative cultures often improve employee morale and satisfaction.

Despite the benefits of a participative approach, greater employee participation in decision making involves certain prerequisites and limitations. The requirements for greater participation in decision making are (1) sufficient time; (2) adequate ability and interest on the part of the participants; and (3) restrictions generated by the present structure and system.

Organization development (OD) applies behavioral science knowledge to an organization-wide effort to improve its effectiveness. Some common OD techniques include survey feedback, team building, quality circles, management by objectives, job enrichment, transactional analysis, quality of work life, and sensitivity training. Some of these techniques may be combined to provide a strategic approach to organization development. In survey feedback, information about the organization is collected and made available to employees so that they can diagnose problems and develop action plans to solve them. A conscious effort to develop effective work groups throughout the organization is known as team building. Quality circles are groups of employees who meet regularly with their supervisors to identify production problems and recommend actions for solutions. Management by objectives (MBO) is a philosophy of management that emphasizes joint setting of objectives by superior and subordinate and using these objectives as the primary basis for motivation, evaluation, and self-control. Job enrichment is the deliberate restructuring of a job to make it more challenging, meaningful, and interesting. Transactional analysis (TA) considers each individual's three ego states—the Parent, the Adult, and the Child—in helping people understand interpersonal relations. Quality of work life (QWL) is the extent to which employees satisfy significant personal needs through their organizational experiences. An OD technique designed to make us aware of ourselves and our impact on others is sensitivity training.

Organization development efforts rely heavily on the use of qualified consultants who work with groups of managers and workers from throughout the organization. The consultant is a facilitator who helps the groups identify goals and solve problems that interfere with goal achievement. The consultant may also be responsible for helping guide implementation of planned change.

One method of measuring program effectiveness is to assess changes in meeting performance criteria. Some of the factors measured might include (1) productivity, (2) absenteeism rate, (3) turnover rate, (4) accident rate, (5) costs, and (6) scrap. An improvement in these and other areas may mean that the OD effort has led to improvements. An excellent way to determine the extent of change in employee attitudes is through the use of a survey questionnaire.

Questions for Review

1. Define corporate culture. What factors determine corporate culture?
2. Does a participative culture improve productivity? Defend your answer.
3. What are the values of an open and participative culture?
4. What are the limitations of participation?
5. Define each of the following terms:
   (a) Organization development
   (b) Survey feedback
   (c) Team building
   (d) Quality circles
   (e) Job enrichment
   (f) Quality of work life
   (g) Transactional analysis
   (h) Sensitivity training
6. How can organization development programs be evaluated?
7. Explain the use of consultants in organization development.

Terms for Review

Corporate culture
Communication
Motivation
Leadership
Organizational structure
Organization development (OD)
Survey feedback

Team building
Quality circles
Management by objectives (MBO)
Job enrichment
Transactional analysis (TA)
Quality of work life (QWL)
Sensitivity training

INCIDENT 1 — Implementing MBO

When Bruce McDaniel retired because of ill health in 1989, he appointed his 26-year-old son, Jim, president of the family firm. The company, McDaniel Corporation of Marietta, Georgia, marketed a line of hospital beds. The company manufactured the metal frames for the beds but purchased hydraulic items, springs, and certain other parts. The company also sold hospital furniture items and maintained a crew to repair the McDaniel beds. Employment at the firm totaled about 500.

With an MBA degree from Georgia State University and two years experience with the company, Jim was eager to take over. He believed that his college training and work experience had prepared him well. One of the first things Jim wanted to do was to give decision-making authority to the managers. He remarked, "I felt this would let me pay attention to the big picture while the day-to-day problems were solved lower in the organization." He felt that one effective tool for helping him shift more authority downward in the organization would be an MBO program.

Bruce McDaniel had been president and owner of McDaniel Corporation for thirty years. During that time the firm had grown from a small hospital supply company with three employees to its present size. Bruce had been a hard worker, often putting in fifteen hours a day. Jim said that his dad was a "pleasant autocrat" because he insisted on making every important decision, but Bruce had such an affable personality that no one objected.

For a while, Jim tried to behave pretty much as his father had, giving managers firm decisions on matters they brought to him. But about a month after his father's retirement, Jim called a meeting to tell the managers that the firm was going to implement an MBO program. He made a brief presentation to them about how the system would work. He especially emphasized that they would have more responsibility in their areas and that he expected MBO principles to be applied down to the supervisory level.

Questions

1. Explain the process Jim should follow in implementing MBO. Is he on the right track?
2. Discuss any likely pitfalls.

INCIDENT 2 — Close to the Vest

For the past few years, sales at Glenco Manufacturing had been falling, reflecting an industry-wide decline. In fact, Glenco had actually been able to increase its share of the market slightly. Although forecasts indicated that demand for its products would improve in the future, Joe Goddard, the company president, believed that something needed to be done immediately to help the firm survive this temporary slump. As a first step he employed a consulting firm to determine whether reorganization might be helpful.

A team of five consultants arrived at the firm. They told Mr. Goddard that they first had to gain a thorough understanding of the current situation before they could make any recommendations. Mr. Goddard assured them that the company was open to them. They could ask any questions that they thought were necessary.

The grapevine was full of rumors virtually from the day the consulting group arrived. One employee was heard to say, "If they shut down the company, I don't know if I could take care of my family." Another worker said, "If they move me away from my friends, I'm going to quit."

When workers questioned their supervisors, they received no explanations. No one had told the supervisors what was going on, either. The climate began to change to one of fear. Rather than being concerned about their daily work, employees worried about what was going to happen to the company and their jobs. As a result, productivity dropped drastically.

A month after the consultants departed, an informational memorandum was circulated throughout the company. It stated that the consultants had recommended a slight modification in the top levels of the organization to achieve greater efficiency. No one would be terminated. Any reductions would be the result of normal attrition. By this time, however, some of the best workers had already found other jobs, and company operations were severely disrupted for several months.

Questions

1. Why did the employees tend to assume the worst about what was happening?
2. How could this difficulty have been avoided?

Experiencing Human Resource Management

This exercise provides students with further insight into management by objectives (MBO). MBO is a philosophy of management that emphasizes the setting of agreed-on objectives by superior and subordinate managers and using these objectives as the primary basis for motivation, evaluation, and self control. It facilitates achievement of results by directing efforts toward attainable goals. MBO is a management approach that encourages managers to anticipate and plan for the future. It deemphasizes guessing or making decisions based on hunches.

Patsy Olson is the controller for Multifoods International and three supervisors of various specialties report directly to her. Today she must meet with her supervisors in order to put in place management's latest directive—management by objective (MBO). As Patsy prepares for her meeting, she thinks, "I am sure that not every supervisor is in total agreement as to the appropriateness of MBO. I've got to tell them exactly how to apply MBO, as much in line with their management styles as possible. I have been in various management positions for the past 20 years, and I have seen management policies and practices come and go. Now I must make sure that each of the supervisors involved understand how to apply the new system. I wonder how Nita, Robert, and Doug will react."

Nita Dickey has been in various management positions for the past 15 years, and has seen management policies and practices come and go. She is ready to find out exactly how to implement management's latest miracle—MBO. Nita is sure that this is just another experiment in futility, but she will go along. After all, what is the harm of letting the people upstairs experiment as long as it is a short one.

Robert Zackery has been out of college for six years and he is eager to see how MBO actually works in practice. He is anxious to get this experiment under way. This could be just the way to make some sorely needed changes.

Doug Warner has a degree in industrial psychology and is very excited about MBO. He believes that the primary emphasis of an organization should be on the employee. This person is eager to get this organizational change under way. For some time Doug has been bothered by the lack of emphasis on the human element by some of the less progressive supervisors.

Once these supervisors get together, the result will probably be less than total agreement. If you like that kind of thing, volunteer. This exercise will require four of you, so raise your hands quickly to assure you can actively participate. Those of you who are not lucky enough to participate, observe carefully. Additional instructions will be provided by the instructor.

REFERENCES

Alber, Antone F. "Making Job Enrichment Pay Off." *Supervisory Management*, 27 (January 1982), pp. 30–33.

Aluise, J. J., et al. "Organizational Development in Academic Medicine: An Educational Approach." *Health Care Management Review*, 10 (Winter 1985), pp. 37–43.

Cowan, J. "Is Organization Development Out of Date?" *Training and Development Journal*, 39 (May 1985), pp. 18ff.

Cox, Martha Glenn, and Jane Covey Brown. "Quality of Worklife: Another Fad or Real Benefit?" *Personnel Administrator*, 27 (May 1982), pp. 99–153.

Davidson, Jeffrey P. "A Task-Focused Approach to Team Building." *Personnel*, 62 (March 1985), p. 16.

Drucker, P. F. "A Prescription for Entrepreneurial Management." *Industry Week* (April 29, 1985), pp. 33–34ff.

Ernest, R. C. "Corporate Culture and Effective Planning (Organizational Culture Grid)." *Personnel Administrator*, 30 (March 1985), pp. 49–50ff.

Franke, Arnold G., Edward J. Harrick, and Andrew J. Klein. "The Role of Personnel in Improving Productivity." *Personnel Administrator*, 27 (March 1982), pp. 83–88.

Gardner, M. P. "Creating a Corporate Culture for the Eighties." *Business Horizons*, 28 (January–February 1985), pp. 59–63.

Hellriegel, Don, John W. Slocum, and Richard W. Woodman. *Organizational Behavior*, 5th ed. (St. Paul, Minn.: West Publishing Company, 1989).

Herzberg, Frederick, and Alex Zautra. "Orthodox Job Enrichment: Measuring True Quality in Job Satisfaction." *Personnel*, 53 (September–October 1976), pp. 54–68.

Huse, Edgar F., and Thomas G. Cummings. *Organization Development and Change* (St. Paul, Minn.: West Publishing Company, 1985).

Jamieson, D. W. "Improving Organizations Is Not for Lone Rangers." *Training and Development Journal*, 39 (May 1985), p. 83.

Kanarick, Arnold. "The Far Side of Quality Circles." *Management Review*, 70 (October 1981), pp. 16–17.

Kanter, R. M. "Growth Through Cultural Change." *Management World*, 14 (April 1985), p. 21.

"Lessons from the Volvo Experience." *International Management*, 33 (February 1978), pp. 42–46.

Littlejohn, Robert F. "Team Management: A How-to Approach to Improved Productivity, Higher Morale, and Lasting Job Satisfaction." *Management Review*, 71 (January 1982), pp. 23–28.

Magnet, Myron. "The Decline and Fall of Business Ethics." *Fortune* (December 8, 1986), pp. 65ff.

Meares, Larry B. "A Model for Changing Organizational Culture." *Personnel*, 63 (July 1986), pp. 38–42.

Mohrman, Susan A., and Ian I. Mitroff. "Business Not as Usual." *Training and Development Journal*, 37 (June 1987), pp. 37–43.

Nave, James L. "Gauging Organizational Climate." *Management Solutions*, 31 (June 1986), pp. 14–18.

Niehoff, Marilee, and M. Jay Romans. "Needs Assessment as One Step Toward Enhancing Productivity." *Personnel Administrator*, 27 (May 1982), pp. 35–39.

Ozley, Lee M., and Judith S. Ball. "Quality of Work Life: Initiating Successful Efforts in Labor–Management Organizations." *Personnel Administrator*, 27 (May 1982), pp. 27–33.

Pascale, R. "The Paradox of Corporate Culture: Reconciling Ourselves to Socialization." *California Management Review*, 27 (Winter 1985), pp. 26–41.

Reynolds, Peter C. "Imposing A Corporate Culture." *Psychology Today*, 21 (March 1987), pp. 32–38.

Richardson, Peter R. "The Challenge of Strategic Change." *Canadian Business Review*, 13 (August 1986), pp. 29–32.

Sharplin, Arthur, *Strategic Management* (New York: McGraw-Hill, 1985).

Shrivastava, P. "Integrating Strategy Formulation with Organizational Culture." *Journal of Business Strategy*, 5 (Winter 1985), pp. 103–111.

Snyder, Robert J. "A Model for the Systematic Evaluation of Human Resource Development Programs." *Academy of Management Review*, 5 (July 1980), pp. 431–443.

"Three Faces of Organizational Change." *Training*, 22 (March 1985), pp. 108–109.

Wehrenberg, Stephen B. "The Vicious Circle of Training and Organizational Development." *Personnel Journal*, 65 (July 1986), pp. 94–100.

CHAPTER 10

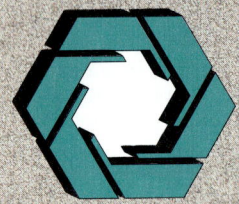

CAREER PLANNING AND DEVELOPMENT

Chapter Objectives

1. Define career planning and development and describe factors affecting career planning.
2. Explain the importance of individual career planning and how a thorough self-assessment is crucial to career planning.
3. Explain the nature of career planning, discuss career paths, and identify methods of organization career planning and development.
4. Describe career development and describe the avenues available for beginning a career in human resources.

Bob Allen and Thelma Gowen, both supervisors in the trust department of American Bank of New York, were in the employee lounge having a cup of coffee and discussing a point of mutual concern. Bob said, "I'm beginning to get frustrated. When I joined American four years ago, I really felt that I could make a career here. Now I'm not so sure. I spoke with the boss last week about where I might be in the next few years and all she kept saying was, 'There are all kinds of possibilities.' I need more than that. I'd like to know what specific opportunities might be available if I continue to do a good job. I'm not sure if I want to spend my career in the trust department. There may be better chances for advancement in other areas. This is a big bank."

Thelma replied, "I'm having the same trouble. She told me that 'the sky's the limit.' I'd also like to know where I might progress if I decide to stay with American. I wonder what 'the limit' means to her."

Obviously, American Bank has no career planning and development program. Bob is frustrated, and Thelma wants to know what career avenues are available to her. Lacking this knowledge, they may decide not to remain with the bank. Career planning and development are important to the company also—to ensure that people with the necessary skills and experience will be available when needed. According to an American Management Association study, promoting career development is the hallmark of a superior manager.[1]

In this chapter, we first discuss the concept of career planning and development. Next, we identify several factors that affect career planning and then discuss the nature of career planning. Then we address individual career planning and the

---

[1] Robert W. Goddard, "Building Careers for Your Employees," *Management World*, 14 (June 1985), p. 13.

reasons that organizations get involved in career planning. We then describe types of career planning that organizations conduct and follow that with a section on methods used in career planning and development. We devote the last part of the chapter to how a person might begin a career in human resources.

■ CAREER PLANNING AND DEVELOPMENT DEFINED

A **career** is a general course that a person chooses to pursue throughout his or her working life. **Career planning** is a process whereby an individual sets career goals and identifies the means to achieve them. The major focus of career planning should be on matching personal goals and opportunities that are realistically available. Career planning should not concentrate only on advancement opportunities. From a practical standpoint, there are not enough high level positions to make upward mobility a reality for everyone. A tight market became even tighter during the 1980s, as many organizations trimmed the number of management positions, especially middle-management positions. At some point, career planning needs to focus on achieving psychological successes that do not necessarily entail promotions.

Individual and organizational careers are not separate and distinct. A person whose individual career plan cannot be followed within the organization will probably leave the firm sooner or later. Thus organizations should assist employees in career planning so that both can satisfy their needs. A **career path** is a flexible line of progression through which an employee typically moves during employment with a company. Following an established career path, the employee can undertake career development with the firm's assistance. **Career development** is a formal approach taken by the organization to ensure that people with the proper qualifications and experience are available when needed.[2]

Career planning and development benefit both the individual and the organization. For example, a large bank estimated that it saved $1.95 million in one year through its career counseling program. Turnover dropped by 65 percent, performance improved by 85 percent, productivity increased by 25 percent, and opportunity for promotion increased by 75 percent.[3]

■ FACTORS AFFECTING CAREER PLANNING

Several factors affect a person's view of a career. The individual should recognize and consider the most important factors when planning a career. We describe two such factors, life stages and career anchors, in this section.

Life Stages

People change constantly and thus view their careers differently at various stages of their lives. Some of these changes result from the aging process

---

[2] Tom Jackson and Alan Vitberg, "Career Development, Part 3: Challenges for the Individual," *Personnel*, 64 (April 1987), p. 54.

[3] Milan Moravec, "A Cost-Effective Career Planning Program Requires a Strategy," *Personnel Administrator*, 27 (January 1982), p. 28.

and others from opportunities for growth and status. The basic life stages are shown in Figure 10-1.

The first stage is that of establishing identity. A person typically reaches this stage between the ages of ten and twenty. The individual explores career alternatives and begins to move into the adult world. Stage two involves growing and getting established in a career. This stage typically lasts from ages twenty to forty. During this stage, a person chooses an occupation and establishes a career path. The third stage, self-maintenance and self-adjustment, generally lasts to age fifty and beyond. At this point, a person either accepts life as it is or makes adjustments. Career change and divorce occur during this phase because people seriously question the quality of their lives. The final stage is that of decline. Diminishing physical and mental capabilities may accelerate this stage. A person may have lower aspirations and less motivation during the decline stage, resulting in additional career adjustments.

The majority of developmental activities are directed at new, younger workers, even though most individuals have career development needs throughout their working lives. Since passage of the last amendment to the Age Discrimination in Employment Act, there has been no mandatory retirement age and therefore, the maintenance and adjustment stage is likely to

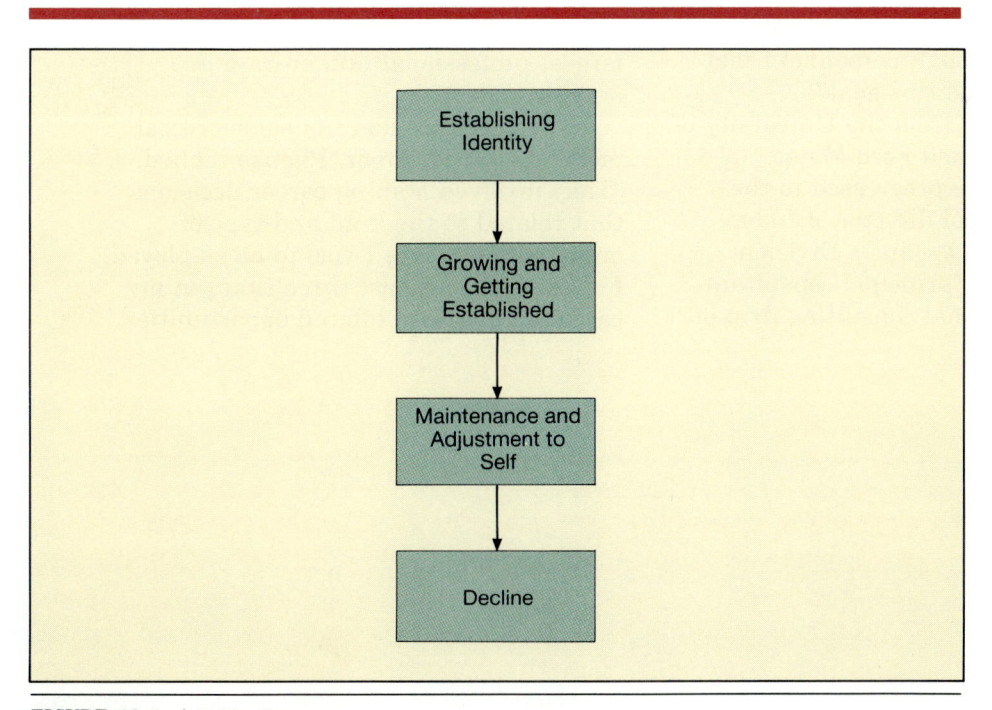

FIGURE 10-1 | Life Stages

Source: Adapted from James W. Walker, *Human Resource Planning*. (New York: McGraw-Hill Book Company, 1980). Used with permission of the McGraw-Hill Book Company.

Executive Insights

Ronald C. Pilenzo
President and Chief Operating Officer, Society for Human Resource Management

During the early 1950s when Ronald C. Pilenzo was trying to decide on a career, the human resource field was only beginning to emerge and make its presence felt. But, he says, "I wanted a career that offered wide scope and diversity, as opposed to a highly structured job that offered very narrow career ranges. Through personnel I feel that I have achieved this goal."

After graduation from the University of Detroit, Pilenzo joined Ford Motor Company, where he progressed to the position of personnel director of Industrial and Chemical Products Division. Later, he became a principal consultant with the international consulting firm of Raymond E. Danto, where he was responsible for all human resource and organization consulting. He subsequently joined Allied Supermarkets, Inc., as director, corporate recruiting, compensation, and manpower planning. In this position he was responsible for 18,000 employees in eleven major divisions covering forty-three states. Pilenzo next served as director, manpower and organization development, with Evans Products Company for five years before he joined International Multifoods as director, corporate compensation and management development, on the corporate human resource staff in 1975. In 1980, he was selected to become president and chief operating officer of the American Society for Personnel Administration (ASPA), the world's largest professional human resource organization.

When asked to identify some critical moments in his career, Pilenzo replied, "They involved making career decisions that related to the kind and type of organization where I was to be employed. For example, at least three times in my career I have been offered opportunities to create a professional organization where either one did not exist or one existed that was not performing satisfactorily." He accepted all three challenges, but says, "Interesting challenges present high-risk situations." He did not fail and has become one of the most respected professionals in his field.

When asked about the qualities needed for success, he replies, "Personnel executives need to be tough-minded, intelligent, and capable of working within and outside the human resource function, not in a vacuum. They must be individuals who can work comfortably in a changing environment that involves complex problems with no readily available solutions. The successful human resource executive will probably have a personality profile that is comparable to an operating executive."

Asked to comment regarding the earning potential of human resource executives, Pilenzo stated, "It is interesting to note that in the past five years, salaries for human resource executives have risen substantially faster than salaries for almost any other functional management group. It is not unusual today to find major corporations' top human resource executives earning salaries and bonuses in the six-figure range."

He also believes that company loyalty is not the same as in the past. He says, "In today's changing world, and with people's obviously shifting value systems, loyalty to an organization presents an interesting dilemma. The days when employees dedicated their entire lives to the organization are probably at an end. This does not mean that while people are employed in an organization, they should not give their best possible effort. What it does mean, however, is that people now place a different value on company loyalty. This means that younger people today generally consider loyalty to self above loyalty to company."

Finally, Pilenzo states, "It is no longer sufficient or desirable for organizations to employ human resource people who desire a career in human resources simply because they 'like people' and enjoy 'helping others.' In fact, people who see this as their primary role are usually unsuccessful as professional human resource managers."

be extended.[4] Consequently, future employees will probably need career development as much in later years as they do in the initial years of their working lives.

Career Anchors

All of us have different aspirations, backgrounds, and experiences. Our personalities are molded, to a certain extent, by the results of our interactions with our environments. Edgar Schein's research identified five different motives that account for the way people select and prepare for a career. He called them **career anchors**.[5]

1. *Managerial Competence.* The career goal of managers is to develop qualities of interpersonal, analytical, and emotional competence. People using this anchor want to manage people.
2. *Technical/Functional Competence.* The anchor for technicians is the continuous development of technical talent. These individuals do not seek managerial positions.
3. *Security.* The anchor for security-conscious individuals is to stabilize their career situations. They often see themselves tied to a particular organization or geographical location.
4. *Creativity.* Creative individuals are somewhat entrepreneurial in their attitude. They want to create or build something that is entirely their own.
5. *Autonomy and Independence.* The career anchor for independent people is a desire to be free from organizational constraints. They value autonomy and want to be their own boss and work at their own pace.

One of the implications of these career anchors is that companies must be flexible enough to provide alternative paths to satisfy people's varying needs.

■ CAREER PLANNING

The process by which individuals plan their life's work is referred to as career planning.[6] Through career planning, a person evaluates his or her own abilities and interests, considers alternative career opportunities, establishes career goals, and plans practical development activities.

In addition to a self-assessment, an individual should also make a corporate opportunity assessment, asking questions such as:

1. What are the prospects for promotion or transfer from my present job?
2. What percentage of employees reach a certain target level within this organization?

---

[4] James W. Walker, *Human Resource Planning* (New York: McGraw-Hill, 1980), pp. 331–332.

[5] Edgar Schein, "How 'Career Anchors' Hold Executives to Their Career Paths," *Personnel*, 52 (May–June 1975), pp. 11–24.

[6] James W. Walker, "Does Career Planning Rock the Boat?" *Human Resource Management*, 17 (Spring 1978), p. 2.

3. What are the pay ranges for various job levels?
4. Where is the fastest growth and therefore the best promotion opportunity in the company?
5. If I have reached a dead end, what are paths for moving down or laterally so that I can move up faster somewhere else?[7]

Career planning should begin with a person's placement in an entry-level job and initial orientation. Management will observe the employee's job performance and compare it with job standards. At this stage, management will note strengths and weaknesses, enabling them to assist the employee in making a tentative career decision. Naturally, this decision can be altered later as the process continues. This tentative career decision is based on a number of factors, including personal needs, abilities and aspirations, and the organization's needs. Management can then schedule human resource development programs that relate to the employee's specific needs. For instance, a person who wants a career in human resources may require some legal training.

Remember that career planning is an ongoing process. It takes into consideration the changes that occur in people and organizations. This type of flexibility is absolutely necessary in today's dynamic organizational environment.[8] Not only do the firm's requirements change, but individuals may choose to revise their career expectations. An employee might believe, for instance, that he or she could be more productive in human resources than in marketing or vice versa. Rather than lose a valued employee, the firm may attempt to accommodate the employee.

Individual Career Planning

Career planning begins with self-understanding, which helps a person to see which career anchor may be predominant. Then, the person is in a position to establish realistic goals and determine what to do to achieve these goals. This action also lets the person know whether his or her goals are realistic.

Learning about oneself is referred to as **self-assessment**. Anything that could affect one's performance in a future job should be considered.[9] Realistic self-assessment may help a person avoid mistakes that could affect his or her entire career progression. Often an individual accepts a job without considering whether it matches his or her interests and abilities. This approach often results in failure. A thorough self-assessment will go a long way toward helping match an individual's specific qualities and goals with the right job or profession.

---

[7] Marilyn A. Morgan, Douglas T. Hall, and Alison Martier, "Career Development Strategies in Industry: Where Are We and Where Should We Be?" *Personnel*, 56 (March/April 1979), p. 14.

[8] John E. McMahon and Joseph C. Yeager, "Manpower and Career Planning," in Robert L. Craid (ed.), *Training and Development Handbook* (New York: McGraw-Hill, 1976), pp. 11–18.

[9] Paul Frichtl, "Keep Score," *Industrial Distribution*, 75 (August 1986), p. 37.

Some useful tools include a strength/weakness balance sheet and a likes and dislikes survey. However, any reasonable approach that assists self-understanding is helpful.

Strength/Weakness Balance Sheet. A self-evaluation procedure, developed originally by Benjamin Franklin, that assists people in becoming aware of their strengths and weaknesses is called a **strength/weakness balance sheet**. Employees who understand their strengths can use them to maximum advantage. By recognizing their weaknesses, they avoid having to utilize those qualities or skills. Furthermore, by recognizing weaknesses, they are in a better position to overcome them. This attitude is summed up by the statement "If you have a weakness, understand it and make it work for you as a strength; if you have a strength, do not abuse it to the point where it becomes a weakness." The first step in self-assessment, then, is to recognize your strengths and weaknesses.

To use a strength/weakness balance sheet, the individual lists strengths and weaknesses as he or she perceives them. This is quite important because believing, for example, that a weakness exists can equate to a real weakness. Thus a person who believes that he or she will make a poor first impression when meeting someone will probably make a poor impression. The perception of a weakness becomes a self-fulfilling prophesy.

The mechanics for preparing the balance sheet are quite simple. To begin, draw a line down the middle of a sheet of paper. Label the left side "strengths" and the right side "weaknesses." Record all perceived strengths and weaknesses. You may find it difficult to write about yourself. Remember, however, that no one else need see the results. The primary consideration is complete honesty.

Figure 10-2 shows an example of a strength/weakness balance sheet. Obviously Wayne did a lot of soul-searching in making these evaluations. Typically, a person's weaknesses will outnumber strengths in the first few iterations. However, as the individual repeats the process, some items which first appeared to be weaknesses may eventually be recognized as strengths and should then be moved from one column to the other. A person should devote sufficient time to the project to obtain a fairly clear understanding of his or her strengths and weaknesses. Typically, the process should take a minimum of one week. The balance sheet will not provide all the answers regarding a person's strengths and weaknesses, but many people have gained a better understanding of themselves by completing it.

Likes and Dislikes Survey. An individual should also consider likes and dislikes as part of a self-assessment. A **likes and dislikes survey** assists individuals in recognizing restrictions they place on themselves. For instance, some people aren't willing to live in certain parts of the country and such feelings should be noted as a constraint. Some positions require a person to spend a considerable amount of time traveling. Thus an estimate of the amount of time a person is willing to travel would also be helpful. Recognition of such self-imposed restrictions may reduce future career problems.

Other limitations involve the type of firm an individual will consider working for. The size of the firm might also be important. Some like a

Strengths	Weaknesses
Work well with people.	Get very close to few people.
Like to be given a task and get it done in my own way.	Do not like constant supervision.
Good manager of people.	Don't make friends very easily with individuals classified as my superiors.
Hard worker.	
Lead by example.	Am extremely high-strung.
People respect me as being fair and impartial.	Often say things without realizing consequences.
Tremendous amount of energy.	Cannot stand to look busy when there is no work to be done.
Function well in an active environment.	Cannot stand to be inactive. Must be on the go constantly.
Relatively open-minded.	
Feel comfortable in dealing with high-level businesspersons.	Cannot stand to sit at a desk all the time.
Like to play politics. (This may be a weakness.)	Basically a rebel at heart but have portrayed myself as just the opposite. My conservatism has gotten me jobs that I emotionally do not want.
Get the job done when it is defined.	
Excellent at organizing other people's time. Can get the most out of people who are working for me.	Am sometimes nervous in an unfamiliar environment.
	Make very few true friends.
Have an outgoing personality—not shy.	Not a conformist but appear to be.
Take care of those who take care of me. (This could be a weakness.)	Interest level hits peaks and valleys.
	Many people look on me as being unstable. Perhaps I am. Believe not.
Have a great amount of empathy.	
Work extremely well through other people.	Divorced.
	Not a tremendous planner for short range. Long-range planning is better.
	Impatient—want to have things happen fast.
	Do not like details.
	Do not work well in an environment where I am the only party involved.

FIGURE 10-2 | Strength/Weakness Balance Sheet

Source: Wayne Sanders.

major organization whose products are well known. Others prefer a smaller organization, believing that the opportunities for advancement may be greater or the environment better suited to their tastes. All factors that could affect an individual's work performance should be listed in the likes and dislikes survey. An example of this type of survey is shown in Figure 10-3.

A self-assessment such as this one helps a person understand his or her basic motives, setting the stage for pursuing a management career or seeking further technical competence. A person with little desire for management responsibilities should probably not accept a promotion to supervisor or enter management training. People who know themselves can more easily make the decisions necessary for successful career planning. Many people get sidetracked because they choose careers based on haphazard plans or on the wishes of others rather than what they believe to be best for themselves.

Getting to know oneself is not a point-in-time occurrence. As individuals progress through life, priorities change. Individuals may think that they know themselves quite well at one stage of life and later begin to see themselves quite differently. Therefore self-assessment should be viewed as a continuous process. Career minded individuals must heed the Red Queen's admonition to Alice: "It takes all the running you can do, to keep in the same place."[10]

Likes	Dislikes
Like to travel.	Do not want to work for a large firm.
Would like to live in the East.	
Enjoy being my own boss.	Will not work in a large city.
Would like to live in a medium-size city.	Do not like to work behind a desk all day.
Enjoy watching football and baseball.	Do not like to wear suits all the time.
Enjoy playing racquetball.	

FIGURE 10-3 | Likes/Dislikes Survey

Source: Wayne Sanders.

---

[10] Lewis Carroll, *Through the Looking Glass* (New York, Norton, 1971), p. 127.

HRM In Action

"Fred, since you work in human resources, maybe you can explain why we hired Mary Moore," Sam Hakala asked of the human resource manager, Fred McCord. "What's the problem with Mary, Sam?" "Well, I went in to see Mary and asked her to develop a career plan for me. I wanted to know how long it will take me to advance up the corporate ladder. She obviously doesn't know much about career planning." "What did she do, Sam?" Fred repeated. "Well, instead of outlining a career plan, she said that I would need to first gain some self-insight. I've been here five years, and now she says I don't have enough self-insight, can you believe that? She wants me to do her job for her. In my opinion, someone should clean house in that department."

How would you respond?

Organizational Career Planning

Although the primary responsibility for career planning rests with the individual, organizations should actively assist in the process. From the organization's viewpoint, career planning involves a conscious attempt to maximize a person's potential contributions. Firms that promote career planning programs for their employees reap many benefits. As Hendy Stewart MacKenzie Burns, an internationally known Shell Oil Company executive, said, "Good managers are people who aren't worried about their own careers, but rather the careers of those who work for them. My advice: Don't worry about yourself. Take care of those who work for you, and you'll float to greatness on their achievements."[11]

The process of establishing career paths within a firm is referred to as **organizational career planning**. Firms should undertake organizational career planning programs only when they contribute to achieving basic organizational goals. Therefore the rationale and approach to career planning programs varies among firms. In most organizations, career planning programs are expected to achieve one or more of the following objectives:

- *More effective development of available talent*. Individuals are more likely to be committed to development that is part of a specific career plan. They can better understand the purpose of development.
- *Self-appraisal opportunities for employees considering new or nontraditional career paths*. Some excellent workers do not view the traditional upward mobility as an optimum career path. Other workers see themselves in deadend jobs and seek relief. Rather than lose these workers, a

---
[11] Goddard, p. 12.

firm can offer career planning to help them identify new and different career paths.
- *More efficient development of human resources within and among divisions and/or geographic locations.* If the traditional progression of workers was upward within a division, career paths should be developed that cut across divisions and geographic location.
- *A demonstration of a tangible commitment to EEO and affirmative action.* Adverse impact can occur at virtually any level in an organization. Firms that are totally committed to reducing adverse impact often cannot find qualified women and minorities to fill vacant positions. One means of overcoming this problem is an effective career planning and development program. Frequently, AAPs require companies to set up career development programs for women and minorities.
- *Satisfaction of employees' personal development needs.* Individuals who see their personal development needs being met tend to be more satisfied with their jobs and the organization.
- *Improvement of performance through on-the-job training experiences provided by horizontal and vertical career moves.* The job itself is the most important influence on career development. Each job can provide different challenges and experiences.
- *Increased employee loyalty and motivation, leading to decreased turnover.* Individuals who believe that the firm is interested in their career planning will be more likely to remain with the organization.
- *A method of determining training and development needs.* If a person desires a certain career path and does not presently have the proper qualifications, this lack identifies a training and development need.[12]

All these objectives may be desirable. But successful career planning depends on a firm's ability to satisfy those that it considers most crucial to employee development and the achievement of organizational goals.

As Figure 10-4 shows, a career planning program may prompt some employees to develop more realistic expectations. This ultimately leads to enhanced performance, improved retention, and better utilization of talent. Although certain benefits are associated with career planning, risks are also involved. Difficulties occur when the career planning program raises employee expectations to unrealistic levels. When this occurs, organizational disruption, diminished performance, and higher turnover may result. Therefore a career planning program should be based on developing realistic expectations.[13]

■ CAREER PATHS

Recall that a career path is a flexible line of progression through which an employee typically moves during employment with a company. Career paths usually have focused on upward mobility within a particular occupation.

---
[12] Moravec, p. 29.
[13] Walker, p. 3.

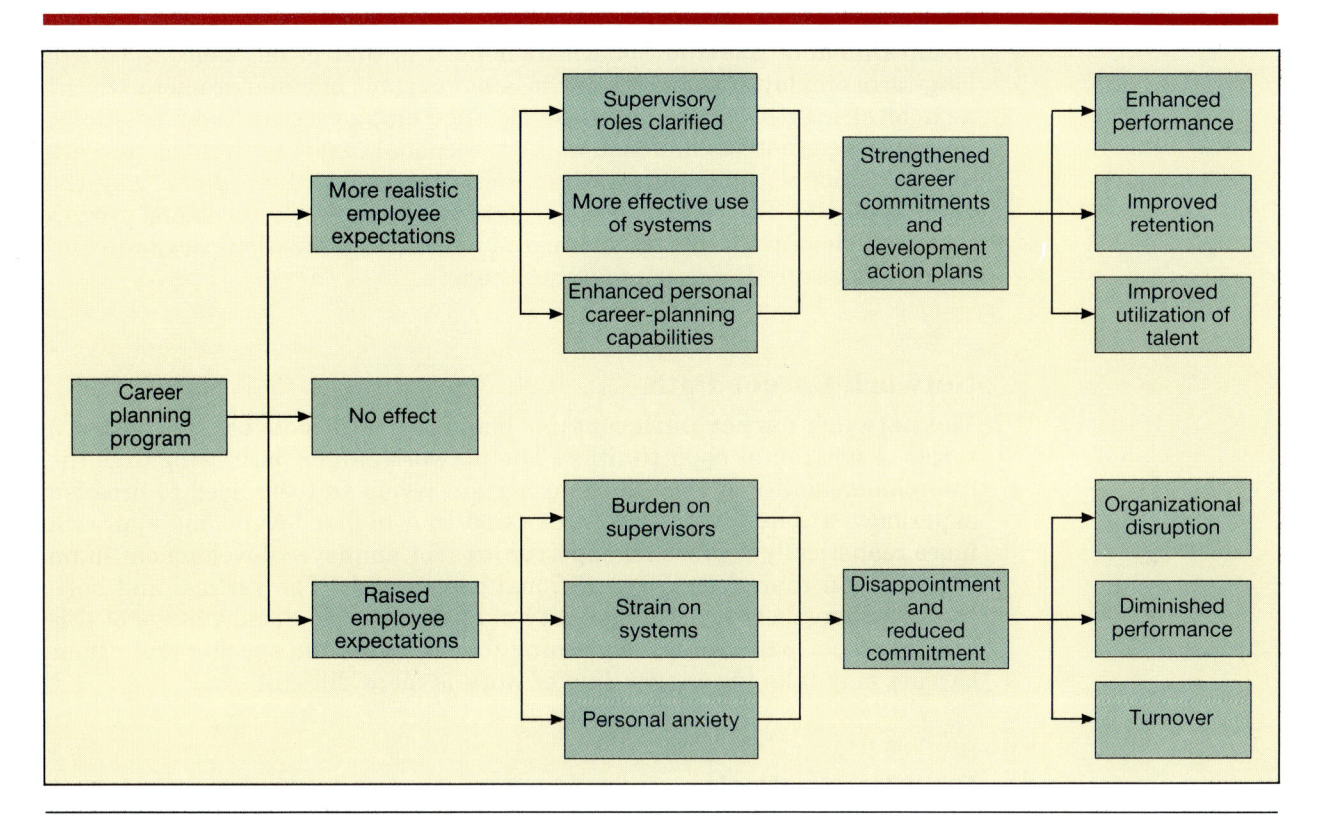

FIGURE 10-4 | The Effects of Career Planning

Source: James W. Walker, "Does Career Planning Rock the Boat?" *Human Resource Management*, 17 (Spring 1978), p. 3. Used with the permission of Human Resource Management, University of Michigan, Ann Arbor, Mich.

one of three types of career paths may be used: traditional, network, and dual.

Traditional Career Path

The **traditional career path** is one wherein an employee progresses vertically upward in the organization from one specific job to the next. The assumption is that each preceding job is essential preparation for the next higher level job. Therefore, an employee must move, step by step, from one job to the next to gain needed experience and preparation. This type of career path is most likely to be found in clerical and production operations.

One of the biggest advantages of the traditional career path is that it is straightforward. The path is clearly laid out, and the employee knows the specific sequence of jobs through which he or she must progress. However, it fails to recognize that other jobs may provide equivalent or better experience that could enable an employee to advance without performing certain jobs in the established sequence. Another potentially serious disadvantage of the traditional career path is that of blockage; that is, a long-term employee at one level who is not capable of being promoted to the next level may block the progress of other employees in lower positions. Perhaps the greatest challenge to the traditional career path is the new era of international competition, which has drastically changed the way the game is played. The certainties of yesterday's business methods and growth have vanished in many industries, and neither organizations nor individuals can be assured of ever regaining them.

Network Career Path

The **network career path** contains both a vertical sequence of jobs and a series of horizontal opportunities. The network career path recognizes the interchangeability of experience at certain levels and the need to broaden experience at one level before promotion to a higher level. This approach more realistically represents opportunities for employee development in an organization than does the traditional career path. The vertical and horizontal options lessen the probability of blockage. One disadvantage of this type of career path is that explaining to employees the specific route their careers may take for a given line of work is more difficult.

Dual Career Path

The dual career path was originally developed to deal with the problem of technically trained employees who had no desire to move into management—the normal procedure for upward mobility in an organization. The **dual career path** recognizes that technical specialists can—and should be allowed to—contribute their expertise to a company without having to become managers. Consequently, it provides an alternative progression for employees such as scientists and engineers. Individuals in these fields can increase their specialized knowledge, make contributions to their firms, and be rewarded without entering management. Whether on the management or technical side of the path, compensation would be comparable at each level.

The dual career path is becoming increasingly popular. In our high-tech world, specialized knowledge is often as important as managerial skill. Rather than creating poor managers out of competent technical specialists, the dual career path permits an organization to retain both highly skilled managers and highly skilled technical people.[14]

Career Path Information

Information regarding career options and opportunities must be available before individuals can begin to set realistic career objectives. One way to

---

[14] Donald L. Caruth, Robert M. Noe III, and R. Wayne Mondy, *Staffing the Contemporary Organization* (New York, Quorum Books, 1988), pp. 253–254.

provide it is to develop career path information for each job. This information can be developed from job descriptions, based on historical trends within the organization, or based on similarities to other jobs in the same job family.[15] A small sample of job titles with related career guidance information is shown in Table 10-1. Career path information is particularly useful because it:

1. Shows each employee how his or her job relates to other jobs.
2. Presents career alternatives.
3. Describes educational and experience requirements for a career change.
4. Points out the orientations of other jobs.[16]

■ PLATEAUING

A problem that many individuals who aspire to move upward in an organization are now experiencing is plateauing. **Plateauing** occurs when an employee's job functions and work content remain the same because of a lack of promotional opportunities within the firm.[17] Plateauing has become more common recently because many organizations are reducing the number of management positions, developing a "lean, mean" management team. International competition has also slowed the growth of firms that might otherwise have needed more management positions. In addition, women and minorities are now competing for positions that once were not available to them.

Between 1950 and 1976, many companies offered extraordinary opportunities for advancement. However, the picture today is quite different, as a large number of people with similar educational backgrounds compete for fewer promotions. In our society, promotion has always been an important measure of success. Thus plateauing will present new challenges for those involved with career planning and development.

Several approaches have been suggested to deal with this problem.[18] One possibility is to move individuals laterally within the organization. Although status or pay may remain unchanged, the employee is given the opportunity to develop new skills. Firms that want to encourage lateral movement may choose to pay a transfer bonus or utilize a skill-based pay system that rewards individuals for the type and number of skills they possess. Another approach, which we've already discussed, is job enrichment. It rewards without promoting an employee by increasing the challenge of the job, giving it more meaning and the employee a greater sense of accomplishment.

Exploratory career development is yet another way of dealing with plateauing. It gives an employee the opportunity to test ideas in another field

---

[15] Dennis J. Kravetz and Stephanie E. Derderian, "Developing a Career Guidance Program Through the Job Family Concept," *Personnel Administrator*, 29 (October 1980), p. 41.

[16] *Ibid.*, p. 42.

[17] Geraldine Spruell, "Say So Long to Promotions," *Training and Development Journal*, 39 (May 1985), pp. 70–74.

[18] Beverly Kaye and Kathryn McKee, "New Compensation Strategies for New Career Patterns," *Personnel Administrator*, 31 (March 1986), pp. 61–68.

TABLE 10-1 | Sample Job Titles and Related Career Guidance Information

Conventional Investigative Job Family

Job title	Division	Prerequisites – Supervisory	Prerequisites – Educational level	Prerequisites – Years of experience	Career Path – From	Career Path – To
Senior Staff Accountant	Accounting	No	B.A. or B.S.	3–4	Staff Accountant Supervisor—Accounts Receivable Provider Auditor	Cost Analysis Coordinator Credit and Collection Coordinator Supervising Senior Staff Accountant
Cost Production Supervisor	Accounting	Yes	Some college	2–3	Supervisor—Cash Receipts Staff Accountant—Payroll	Supervisor—Government Reporting Assistant Manager—Payroll Accounts Payable Cost Production Coordinator
Cost Analyst	Controller	Yes	B.A. or B.S.	4–5	Senior Financial Analyst Cost Analyst Senior Staff Accountant	Manager—Cost Management and Investments Manager—Budget Administration Manager—Corporate Reporting and Business Analysis
Reports Analyst	Accounting	No	Some college	1–2	Payroll Processor Statistical Clerk IV Report Specialist	Management Information Coordinator Staff Accountant—Payroll

Source: Reprinted from Dennis J. Kravetz and Stephanie E. Derderian, "Developing a Career Guidance Program Through the Job Family Concept," from the October 1980 issue of *Personnel Administrator*, copyright © 1980, The American Society for Personnel Administration, Alexandria, Virginia.

without committing to an actual move. Demotions have long been associated with failure, but limited promotional opportunities in the future may make them more legitimate career options. If the stigma of demotion can be removed, more employees—especially older workers—might choose to make such a move. In certain instances this approach might open up a clogged promotional path and, at the same time, permit a senior employee to escape unwanted stress without being thought a failure.

■ CAREER DEVELOPMENT

Career development includes any and all activities that prepare a person for progression along a designated career path. Thus career development usually involves both formal and informal means. Career development programs may be conducted in-house or by outside sources, such as professional organizations or colleges and universities.

In-house programs are usually planned and implemented by a training and development unit within the firm's human resource department. Line managers are also frequently utilized to conduct program segments. Outside the company, organizations such as the Society for Human Resource Management and the American Management Association are active in conducting conferences, seminars, and other types of career development programs.

Certain principles should be observed with regard to career development.[19] First, the job itself has the greatest influence on career development. When each day presents a different challenge, what is learned on the job may be far more important than formally planned development activities. Second, the type of developmental skills that will be needed is determined by specific job demands. The skills needed to become a first-line supervisor will likely differ from those needed to become a middle manager. Third, development will occur only when a person has not yet obtained the skills demanded by a particular job. If the purpose of a transfer is to further develop an employee—and the individual already possesses the necessary skills for the new job—little or no learning will take place. Finally, the time required to develop the necessary skills can be reduced by identifying a rational sequence of job assignments for a person.

Responsibility for Career Development

Many key individuals must work together if an organization is to have an effective career development program. Management must first make a commitment to support the program through policy decisions and allocating resources to the program. Human resource professionals are then responsible for implementing it by providing the necessary information, tools, and guidance—and program liaison with top management.

---

[19] Harry L. Wellbank, Douglas T. Hall, Marilyn A. Morgan, and W. Clay Hammer, "Planning Job Progression for Effective Career Development and Human Resources Management," *Personnel*, 55 (March–April 1978), p. 12.

The worker's immediate supervisor is responsible for providing support, advice, and feedback. Through the supervisor, a worker can find out how supportive of career development the organization actually is. Finally, individual employees are ultimately responsible for developing their own careers. "You can lead a horse to water but you can't make it drink" is an appropriate analogy for career development.

Unrealistic expectations on the part of participants are a major problem associated with a career development program. Employees often see the opportunity for promotion as the major outcome of their participation. If no positions are available, individuals often become disappointed and frustrated.

■ METHODS OF ORGANIZATION CAREER PLANNING AND DEVELOPMENT

Organizations can assist individuals in career planning and development in numerous ways. Some currently utilized methods, most of which are used in various combinations, are

- *Management by Objectives (MBO).* MBO provides an excellent means of assisting in career planning and development. Recall that the superior and subordinate jointly agree on job objectives that can be accomplished during a certain period of time. The resources made available to achieve these objectives may well include development programs. In addition, failure to achieve objectives may assist in planning for future developmental needs.
- *Career Counseling.* Persons either inside or outside the organization may counsel employees in career planning and development. Human resource professionals are often called on for assistance, as are psychologists and guidance counselors. Colleges and universities often provide services.
- *Company Material.* Some firms provide material specifically developed to assist their workers in career planning and development. Such material is tailored to the firm's special needs.
- *Performance Appraisal System.* The firm's performance appraisal system can also be a valuable tool in career planning. Noting and discussing an employee's weaknesses can uncover development needs. If overcoming a particular weakness seems difficult or even impossible, an alternate career path may be the solution.
- *Workshops.* Some organizations conduct workshops lasting two or three days for the purpose of helping workers develop careers within the company. Employees define and match their specific career objectives with the needs of the company.

Career Development Program: An Example

Realizing that highly skilled employees hold the key to corporate growth, Detroit Edison designed an Initial Professional Development Program (IPDP). The program helps build individual careers, and in so doing, ensures the development of employees to satisfy future human resource needs.

Detroit Edison's program is available to most entry-level professionals who possess a bachelor's degree and have less than three years experience related to their major field of study. If selected for the program, participants assume the primary responsibility for their professional growth and are expected to take advantage of various opportunities provided.

The IPDP takes place over a three-year period and involves a number of specific developmental activities (see Figure 10-5). The major activities include rotating work assignments and participation in company seminars. Work assignments involve the participants in stimulating and productive projects. Assistance is given by seasoned professionals who answer questions and provide guidance. Attendance at three formal seminars gives trainees the opportunity to expand skills and interact with employees from other functional areas of the company.

Additional development opportunities are provided in-house through courses covering such subjects as communication skills, power systems engineering, economic analysis, and problems and challenges faced by public utilities. Also, although not required, program participants are encouraged to take advantage of educational opportunities at local colleges and universities. Many employees have earned advanced degrees with the aid of Detroit Edison's educational assistance program.

■ BEGINNING A CAREER IN HUMAN RESOURCES

Individuals desiring a career in human resources may enter the field in one of two basic ways: They may go to work in another field and later transfer to human resources; or they may obtain an entry-level position in human resources. Surprisingly, the second approach is often the more difficult. In order to assist in solving this dilemma, we asked human resource practitioners in various firms the following questions:

1. Which entry-level position in your firm would be most helpful if a person desires to progress into human resources?
2. What types of education or experience are most desirable for these entry-level positions?
3. Which human resource entry-level position would best assist a person's career progression in your firm?

As you can see in Table 10-2, the responses to these questions weren't consistent. Some firms clearly stress work in other functional areas before an employee moves into human resources, whereas others believe in direct entry into the human resources area.

Entry-Level Positions in Other Fields

Executives in numerous firms believe that an employee should gain experience in another field before moving into human resources. They reason that potential human resource professionals need varied exposure in the

Three Year Schedule

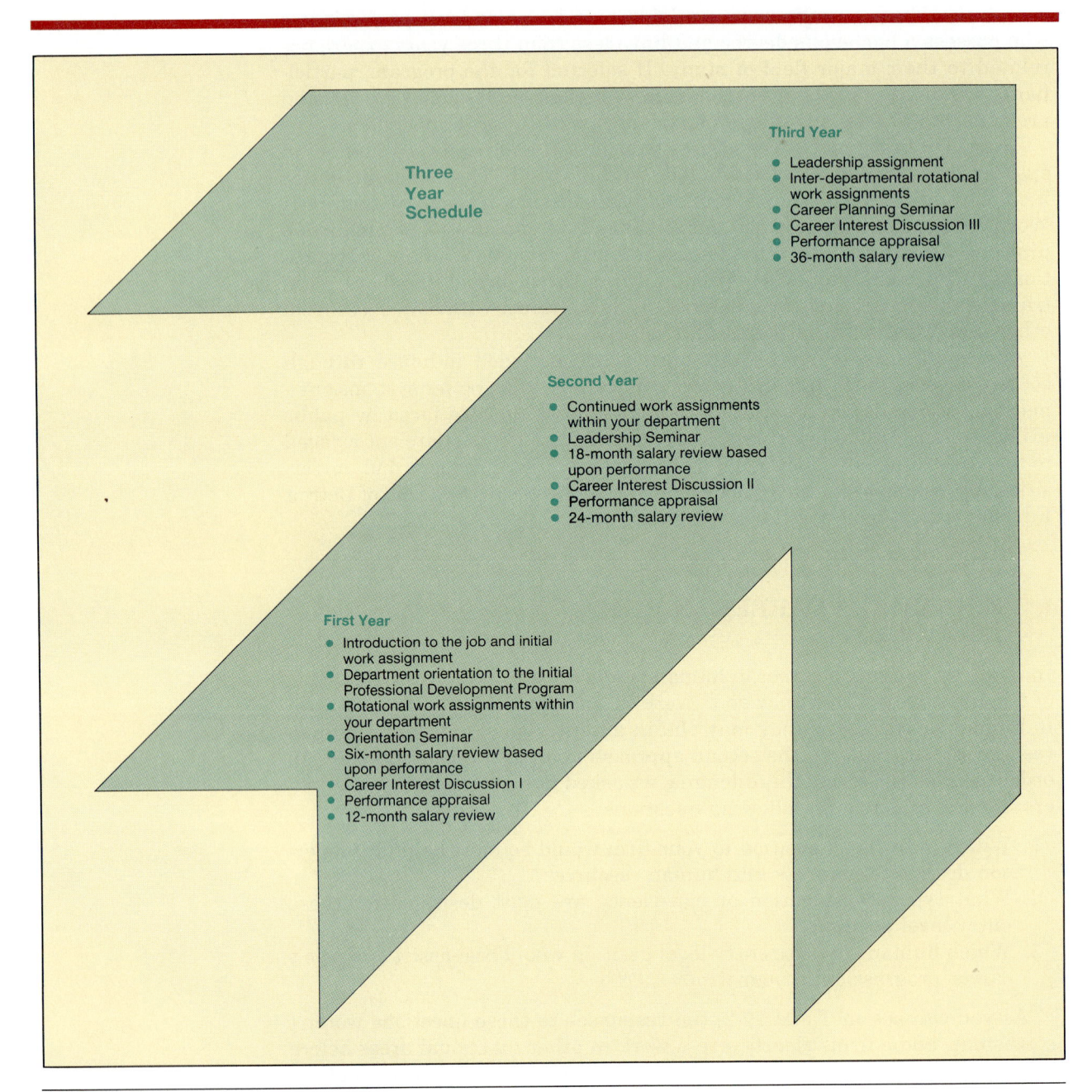

Third Year
- Leadership assignment
- Inter-departmental rotational work assignments
- Career Planning Seminar
- Career Interest Discussion III
- Performance appraisal
- 36-month salary review

Second Year
- Continued work assignments within your department
- Leadership Seminar
- 18-month salary review based upon performance
- Career Interest Discussion II
- Performance appraisal
- 24-month salary review

First Year
- Introduction to the job and initial work assignment
- Department orientation to the Initial Professional Development Program
- Rotational work assignments within your department
- Orientation Seminar
- Six-month salary review based upon performance
- Career Interest Discussion I
- Performance appraisal
- 12-month salary review

FIGURE 10-5 | Detroit Edison's Professional Development Program

Source: Used with the permission of Detroit Edison.

company to be effective in human resource positions. That is, they believe such exposure can increase the person's credibility in dealing with other managers. Trans World Airlines, for one, selects human resource specialists from among their experienced reservation sales agents.

Entry-Level Positions in Human Resources

Not all firms require broad-based experience for those entering human resources. In fact, the number of individuals entering the human resource field directly appears to be increasing. This trend may be the result, in part, of specialized knowledge currently expected of human resource professionals. Firms that need people who can be productive very quickly in human resources do not feel that basic training time is available.

Several firms believe that the compensation specialty provides excellent entry-level positions. For example, the Grumman Corporation identifies salary administration as the best entry-level position "because it affects almost every aspect of human resource work and company operations." Management of Teledyne, Inc., believes that "starting in wage and salary provides an individual with exposure to relationships of job classifications throughout the company," and that this background is helpful to the human resource practitioner.

The nature of the firm's business may also affect the best human resource entry-level position. Labor-intensive organizations—those that have high labor costs relative to total operating costs—appear to emphasize staffing and recruitment positions in which interviewing skills are important. For instance, Denny's, Inc., lists the "interviewer" as being the best human resource entry-level position. Walt Disney Productions also identifies the "human resource interviewer" position as one of the best.

Entry-Level Positions: An Overview

Practitioners do not agree as to the most appropriate entry-level position for individuals aspiring to a job in human resources. A position considered best by one firm may not be viewed the same way by another. The nature of the firm's business or management's human resource philosophy may account for these differences. Some firms stress the need for operating experience before entering human resources. Others believe that direct entry into human resources provides a more suitable beginning. People with ability who truly desire a position in human resources will likely be given the opportunity. But, as Ronald C. Pilenzo, president and chief operating officer for the Society for Human Resource Management, stated in Executive Insights earlier in the chapter, "It is no longer sufficient or desirable for organizations to employhuman resource people who desire a career in human resources simply because they 'like people' and enjoy 'helping others.' In fact, people who see this as their primary role are usually unsuccessful as professional human resource managers."

TABLE 10-2 | Careers in Human Resource Management

Company	Entry-Level Position	Education/Experience
A. B. Dick Company	*Assistant Hourly Employment Manager Shop Foreman Assistant Salary Administrator	Bachelor's degree for all positions
Bristol-Myers Products	Human Resource Assistant	Bachelor's degree with two or three years experience in general human resource work
Conoco, Inc.	*Human Resource Trainee Any position with Conoco	Bachelor's or master's degree in human resource administration, industrial relations, organizational development, business, or engineering
Denny's, Inc.	*Interviewer	Bachelor's degree in business or two years in human resource interviewing
	Wage and Salary Analyst	Bachelor's degree and one year experience in human resources, preferably with compensation experience
	Human Resource Administrator	Bachelor's degree and/or two years experience in human resources
GAF Corporation	*Production Supervisor Industrial Engineer Wage and Salary Analyst Safety Specialist	B.S.I.E., B.S.M.E., B.B.A. B.A. with relevant coursework B.S. with relevant coursework
General Cable Technologies	Assistant Plant Industrial Relations Manager Compensation Analyst	B.S. in industrial relations B.S. in industrial relations
Gerber Products Company	*Supervisor Trainee *Administrative Trainee	Four years of college Four years of college
Grumman Corporation	*Salary Analyst Employment Interviewer Career Development Analyst	Bachelor's degree in any of a variety of concentrations including psychology, business, and data processing
Hartmarx	Human Resource Assistant Compensation Assistant Employee Relations Assistant Human Resource Director (small plant or store)	Bachelor's or master's degree in business, human resource, or employee relations

*Indicates best entry-level position.

Company	Entry-Level Position	Education/Experience
International Paper Company	*Supervisor—Employee Relations Administrator—Industrial Relations Entry level specialist assigned to the Corporate Human Resources Department	B.S. or B.A. in human resource or industrial management B.S. or B.A. in industrial labor relations, or B.S. in industrial management
Manville Corporation	*Employee Relations Supervisor *Plant Supervisor *Benefits Clerk	Bachelor's degree and some plant experience desirable
Motorola, Inc.	*Employment Interviewer	B.S. or B.A.; no experience
Nabisco Brands, Inc.	*Human Resource Assistant (Field)	Bachelor's degree in such fields as business or psychology
Rockwell International Corporation	Supervisory Trainee (Field) Industrial Relations Trainee	M.B.A. in human resource or industrial relations
Shell Oil Company	Employee Relations Analyst	Bachelor's or master's degree in human resource or industrial relations preferred
Squibb Corporation	Human Resource Assistant (nonexempt recruiting)	Two or three years experience of human resource related activities preferred
Stokely-Van Camp, Inc.	Employee Relations–Management Trainee	Master's degree (preferably in human resources)
Teledyne, Inc.	*Wage and Salary Representative Labor Relations Representative	B.A. or human resource or financial administrative experience B.A. or general plant or human resource administrative experience
Trans World Airlines	Reservation Sales Agent	High school diploma, customer contact, and sales experience
USX	Labor Relations Trainee Employee Relations Trainee Line Operations Management Trainee	Law degree Master's degree, accreditation, experience Technical degree plus leadership
Walt Disney Productions	Human Resource Interviewer Human Resource Assistant Wage and Salary Analyst	People skills; B.A. and/or equivalent People skills; B.A. and/or equivalent Salaried experience and statistical orientation

SUMMARY

A career is a general course a person chooses to pursue throughout his or her working life. Career planning is a process whereby the individual sets career objectives and identifies the means to achieve them. Career paths are flexible lines of progression though which people typically move during their employment with a company. Career development is an organization's formal approach to ensuring that people with the proper qualifications and experience are available when needed.

People change constantly and thus view their careers differently at various stages of their lives. The first stage is that of establishing identity, typically between the ages of ten and twenty. During this stage, a person explores career alternatives and begins to move into the adult world. Stage two involves growing and getting established in a career, which typically lasts from ages twenty to forty. During this stage a person chooses an occupation and establishes a career path. The third stage, self-maintenance and self-adjustment, generally lasts to age fifty and beyond. A person either accepts life as it is or makes adjustments. The final stage is that of decline. Diminishing physical and mental capabilities may bring on this stage. A person may come to terms with lowered aspirations and motivations, resulting in career changes.

Edgar Schein's research identified five different motives that account for the way people select and prepare for a career, which he called career anchors: managerial competence, technical/functional competence, security, creativity, and autonomy and independence. One of the implications of these career anchors is that companies must be flexible enough to provide alternative paths to satisfy people's varying needs.

Learning about oneself is referred to as self-assessment. Two useful tools in this endeavor include preparing a strength/weakness balance sheet and a likes and dislikes survey.

The process by which individuals plan their life's work is referred to as career planning. It involves evaluating abilities and interests, considering alternative career opportunities, establishing career goals, and planning practical development activities. Career planning is a continuous process, which begins with a person's employment and initial orientation. Job performance is observed and compared with job standards. Strengths and weaknesses will be noted, enabling management to assist the employee in making a tentative career decision. This tentative career decision is based on a number of factors, including personal needs, abilities, and aspirations, as well as the needs of the organization. Management can then schedule training and development programs that relate to the employee's specific needs.

Depending on the organization and the nature of the jobs involved, one of three types of career paths may be used: traditional, network, and dual. In the traditional career path, an employee progresses vertically upward in the organization from one specific job to the next. The network career path contains both a vertical sequence of jobs and a series of horizontal opportunities. The dual career path recognizes that technical specialists can and should be allowed to continue to contribute without having to become managers. Plateauing is a career condition that occurs when job functions and work content remain the same because of a lack of promotional opportunities within the firm.

Organizations can assist individuals in numerous ways with their career planning and development. Some currently used methods, most of which are used in various combinations, are management by objectives (MBO), career counseling, company materials, performance appraisal system, and workshops.

For individuals desiring a career in human resources, there are two basic ways of entering the field: from another field or directly into an entry-level position in human resources. Practitioners don't agree as to the best way to obtain an entry-level human resource position. However, people with ability who truly desire to obtain a position in human resources will likely be given the opportunity.

Questions for Review

1. Define the following terms:
   (a) Career
   (b) Career planning
   (c) Career path
   (d) Career development
2. Identify and discuss the basic life stages that people pass through.
3. List and briefly define the five types of career anchors.
4. How should a strength/weakness balance sheet and a likes and dislikes analysis be prepared?
5. What kind of questions should a person involved in career planning attempt to answer?
6. Describe the stages in the organizational career planning process.
7. Why is it important for firms to engage in organizational career planning?
8. What are three types of career paths? Briefly describe each.
9. Define plateauing. How does plateauing impact human resource management?
10. Identify and describe some of the methods of organizational career planning.
11. What are the two basic means for entering the field of human resources? Why might a firm favor one means over the other?

Terms for Review

Career
Career planning
Career path
Career development
Career anchors
Self-assessment
Strength/weakness balance sheet

Likes and dislikes survey
Organizational career planning
Traditional career path
Network career path
Dual career path
Plateauing

INCIDENT 1 — In the Dark

"Could you come to my office for a minute, Bob?" asked Terry Geech, the plant manager. "Sure, be right there," said Bob Glemson. Bob was the plant's quality control director. He had been with the company for four years. After completing his degree in mechanical engineering, he worked as a production supervisor and then as maintenance supervisor, prior to moving to his present job. Bob thought he knew what the call was about.

"Your letter of resignation catches me by surprise," began Terry. "I know that Wilson Products will be getting a good person, but we sure need you here, too." "I thought about it a lot," said Bob, "but there just doesn't seem to be a future for me here." "Why do you say that?" asked Terry. "Well," replied Bob, "the next position above mine is yours. With you being only 39, I don't think it's likely that you'll be leaving soon." "The fact is that I am leaving soon," said Terry. "That's why it's even more of a shock to learn that you're resigning. I think I'll be moving to the corporate office in June of next year. Besides, the company has several plants that are larger than this one and we need good people in those plants from time to time, both in quality control and in general management." "Well, I heard about an opening in the Cincinnati plant last year," said Bob, "but by the time I checked, the job had already been filled. We never know about opportunities in the other plants until we read about the incumbent in the company paper."

"All this is beside the point now. What would it take to get you to change your mind?" asked Terry. "I don't think I will change my mind now," replied Bob, "I've given my word that I am going to join them."

Questions

1. Evaluate the career planning and development program at this company.
2. What actions might have prevented Bob's resignation?

INCIDENT 2 ■ Decisions, Decisions ■

A nervous Jerry Fox was ushered into the Levitt Corporation president's office by the secretary. In the office he encountered Allen Anderson, the human resource manager, and Mr. Gorman, the vice-president. Jerry was flattered when Mr. Gorman stood to shake his hand.

"I'll make this short and sweet," Mr. Gorman said. "You probably have heard that Allen plans to retire at the end of next year. In preparing for the staff changes, we would like to move you in as his assistant to get some cross training." Jerry responded, "Why me, Mr. Gorman? I'm a purchasing coordinator; I've never even worked in the human resource area."

"Well," replied Mr. Gorman, "we've been watching you carefully. I have personally reviewed your qualifications. From the company's standpoint, we know you can do the job. We need people who have been out in the company and can bring fresh perspectives to the human resource area." Mr. Gorman instructed Jerry to spend some time with Allen discussing the idea. Then he said he had to leave for another meeting. As he shook Jerry's hand, he said, "We would like to coordinate your transition from the purchasing department to make it as smooth as possible for everyone, and I know you're involved in some priority projects over there. Allen will get back with me on a time frame after you and he talk."

Jerry was 32 and he had been with Levitt for seven years. His business administration degree, from Arizona State, had included a heavy concentration in behavioral science courses, and he thought that probably was a factor in his selection. But he had worked only in purchasing. After three successful years as a buyer, he had been promoted to purchasing coordinator, with responsibility for supervising eight buyers and a small clerical staff.

He knew that he was respected throughout the company. This was especially true in the production department, which had a great deal of interaction with purchasing. The production manager made no secret of his high regard for Jerry. Jerry also had taken time to get to know members of the finance and research department. His purpose in pursuing all of these relationships, though, was to help him do his purchasing job better. He had no idea at all that he would be considered for a job in the human resource department.

Questions

1. How should Jerry respond to the new assignment? Discuss.
2. What are the main qualifications for a senior human resources job? Discuss Jerry's apparent qualifications for such a job.

EXPERIENCING HUMAN RESOURCE MANAGEMENT

Career planning and development is extremely important to many individuals. They want to know how they fit into the future of the organization. Employees who believe that they have a future with the company are often more productive than those who don't. This exercise is designed to assist in understanding what it takes for a certain human resource professional to climb the organizational ladder. This climb is partially dependent on the individual's self-perceptions and perceptions of past experiences with the company. This exercise provides one method of individual career planning for the human resource manager described in the scenario below.

The individual being evaluated is 35 years old and is at a career crossroads. Upon self-reflection and appraisal at a birthday party, the person realizes that while only moderate success in ten years with the organization has been achieved, few others in the organization of comparable age and experience have any more "book or common sense intelligence." In fact, the company is inundated with middle- and upper-level managers much older, and often less intelligent, who seem to spend an inordinate amount of time at the country club.

Assume that you are this person and have set your sights on an important human resource middle management position in the next five to seven years, and a top management position with your organization in the next ten to fifteen years. You have figured out that there are 20 factors that determine upward movement in your organization. You are now trying to decide which are most important for survival and success, and which are least important. This decision will determine whether you take the career crossroad to organizational survival and success, or the crossroad to career failure and stagnation.

You will each be given a list of 20 factors that are essential for an individual's survival and success in an organization. You will rank the importance of each factor for your survival and success in the organization. Write the number "1" beside the **most important factor**, the number "2" beside the **second most important factor**, and so on through the number "20," the **least important factor**.

Everyone in the class can participate in this exercise. Each student will complete Exhibit 1, the "Business Survival and Success Factors," as he or she believes the individual described in the scenario would. Your instructor will provide the participants with additional information necessary to complete the exercise.

REFERENCES

Archer, F. W. "Charting a Career Course." *Personnel Journal*, 63 (April 1984), pp. 60–64.

Austin, William M. "The Job Outlook in Brief." *Occupational Outlook Quarterly*, 30 (Spring 1986), pp. 2–31.

Baker, Herbert George, and Virginia M. Berry. "Processes and Advantages of Entry-Level Counseling." *Personnel Journal*, 66 (April 1987), pp. 111–121.

Bardwick, Judith M. "The Plateauing Trap, Part I: Getting Caught." *Personnel*, 63 (October 1986), pp. 46–52.

Evans, Paul. "New Directions in Career Management." *Personnel Management*, 18 (December 1986), pp. 26–30.

Foxman, Loretta D., and Walter L. Polsky. "Professional Answers to Career Questions." *Personnel Journal*, 64 (March 1985), pp. 14–16.

Gutteridge, Thomas, Lynn Slavenski, Peggy Hutcheson, and Dana Robinson. "What Steps Can HRD Practitioners Take to Develop Themselves Professionally?" *Training and Development Journal*, 40 (December 1986), pp. 22–27.

Jackson, Tom, and Alan Vitberg. "Career Development, Part 3: Challenges for the Individual." *Personnel*, 64 (April 1987), pp. 54–57.

Kleiman, Marcia P. "Retain Valuable Employees with Career Adaptation Counseling." *Personnel Journal*, 64 (September 1985), pp. 36–39.

McAfee, R. Bruce, and Paul J. Champagne. "Employee Development: Discovering Who Needs What." *Personnel Administrator*, 33 (February 1988), pp. 92–98.

Phillips, Jack J. "Four Practical Approaches to Supervisors Career Development." *Personnel*, 63 (March 1986), pp. 13–16.

Polsky, Walter L., and Loretta D. Foxman. "Professional Answers to Career Questions." *Personnel Journal*, 55 (September 1986), pp. 35–37.

Shore, Lynn McFarlane, and Arvid J. Bloom. "Developing Employees Through Coaching and Career Management." *Personnel*, 63 (August 1986), pp. 34–41.

Sims, Henry P., and James W. Dean, Jr. "Beyond Quality Circles: Self-Managing Teams." *Personnel*, 62 (January 1985), pp. 25–32.

CHAPTER 11　PERFORMANCE APPRAISAL

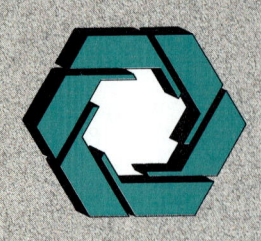

CHAPTER OBJECTIVES

1. Define performance appraisal, identify its basic objectives, and describe the performance appraisal process.
2. Identify who is usually responsible for performance appraisal, typical appraisal periods, and various methods used.
3. List the problems that have been associated with performance appraisal and describe the importance of the appraisal interview.
4. Explain the characteristics of an effective performance appraisal system and describe how assessment centers are used to assess an employee's management potential.

"Tim, we must increase our productivity," exclaimed Doug Parsley, vice-president of production for Black and Decker. "If we don't, the foreign competition is 'going to eat our lunch.' Worker productivity hasn't declined, but they seem to have little incentive to increase it."

"I agree with you Doug," said Tim Overbeck, vice-president for human resources. "We really don't have a good system for differentiating various performance levels. There is no incentive for a superior worker to do any more work than anyone else. We need a better system; one that rewards employees for what they do. Maybe that would give them a desire to work harder."

Doug Parsley was beginning to realize a need for identifying his top producers. All managers need to be able to recognize differences in job performance. Employees can then be rewarded on the basis of their contributions toward achieving organizational goals. The appraisal method used must be perceived as being fair and equitable, and it should also serve to identify employee development needs.

We begin this chapter by defining performance appraisal and describing its uses. We then present the performance appraisal process and responsibility for appraisal. We follow with a discussion of the performance appraisal period, methods, and problems. Next, we describe the characteristics of an effective appraisal system, legal implications, and the appraisal interview. We devote the final portion of the chapter to assessment centers and human resource development for multinational corporations. The overall purpose of this chapter is to emphasize the importance of performance appraisal as it relates to human resource management and its special implications for development of the firm's human resources.

■ PERFORMANCE APPRAISAL DEFINED

Nothing is more discouraging for a top producer in a work group than to receive the same pay increase as a marginal employee. A major incentive to do superior work is destroyed. Although the work of managers, other professionals, and operative employees is informally appraised continuously, formal, periodic evaluations are also desirable. **Performance appraisal (PA)** is a formal system of periodic review and evaluation of an individual's job performance.[1,2]

Developing an effective performance appraisal system is most difficult. A survey of 3,500 organizations revealed that managers' major human resource concern was the PA system used in their firms.[3] The evidence suggests that many managers are not pleased with their appraisal efforts. For example, a Conference Board study of more than 290 organizations found widespread dissatisfaction with appraisal systems. This attitude was prevalent despite the fact that over one half of the responding firms had developed new systems within the three years preceding the study.[4] Developing an effective performance appraisal system has been, and will continue to be, a high priority of human resource management.

■ USES OF PERFORMANCE APPRAISAL

The overall objective of performance appraisal systems is to evaluate and give feedback to employees that will improve employee, and thus the organization's, effectiveness. In addition, performance appraisal data are potentially useful in a variety of ways. A recent survey identified the areas in which businesses actually use appraisal information. The results are summarized in Table 11-1. They indicate that at least 50 percent of those who responded use the appraisal process in areas related to compensation (merit pay increases), communication (feedback), human resources planning (performance potential, succession planning), career planning, and internal employee administration.[5]

Human Resource Planning

In assessing a firm's human resources, data must be available that describe the promotability and potential of all employees, especially key executives.

---

[1] Thomas N. Baylie, Carl J. Kujawski, and Drew M. Young, "Appraisals of 'People' Resources," In Dale Yoder and Herbert G. Heneman, Jr. (eds.), *ASPA Handbook of Personnel and Industrial Relations, Staffing Policies and Strategies*, Vol. 1. (Washington, D.C.: The Bureau of National Affairs, 1974), pp. 4–168.

[2] R. Wayne Mondy, Robert M. Noe III, and Robert E. Edwards, "What the Staffing Function Entails," *Personnel*, 63 (April 1986), p. 55.

[3] Douglas B. Gehrman, "Beyond Today's Compensation and Performance Appraisal Systems," *Personnel Administrator*, 29 (March 1984), p. 21.

[4] William M. Fox, "Consentient Merit Rating: A Critical Incident Approach," *Personnel*, 58 (July–August 1981), p. 70.

[5] Charles J. Fombrun and Robert J. Laud, "Strategic Issues in Performance Appraisal: Theory and Practice," *Personnel*, 60 (November–December 1983), p. 26.

TABLE 11-1 | Uses of Performance Appraisal Systems

Rank	Function for which Appraisal Is Used	Percentage
1	Merit increases	91
2	Performance results/feedback/job counseling	90
3	Promotion	82
4	Termination or layoff	64
5	Performance potential	62
6	Succession planning	57
7	Career planning	52
8	Transfer	50
9	Human resource planning	38
10	Bonuses	32
11	Development and evaluation of training programs	29
12	Internal communications	25
13	Criteria for selection procedure validation	16
14	Expense control	7

Source: Adapted, by permission of the publisher, from "Strategic Issues in Performance Appraisal: Theory and Practice," by Charles J. Fombrun and Robert J. Laud, *Personnel* (November–December 1983), pp. 26, 28. Copyright © 1983 Charles J. Fombrun and Robert J. Laud. Published by American Management Association, New York. All rights reserved.

Management succession planning is a key concern for all firms, and PA yields essential data for this activity. A well-designed appraisal system provides a profile of the organization's human resource strengths and weaknesses.[6]

Recruitment and Selection

Performance evaluation ratings may be helpful in predicting the future performance of job applicants. For example, a significant number of successful managers may have received their training from certain schools or majored in particular fields. This type of knowledge could certainly influence a firm's approach to recruitment. Also, in validating selection tests, employee ratings may be used as the variable against which test scores are compared. In this instance, the selection test's validity would depend largely on the accuracy of appraisal results.

---

[6] Fombrun and Laud, p. 24.

EXECUTIVE INSIGHTS

Joyce Lawson
Consultant,
Human Resources
Management
Consulting

Human resource management has become increasingly complex, particularly in the past two decades. This complexity is reflected in the types of questions, concerns, and problems raised by management and employees, such as:

- Some of our businesses have job posting systems. Should we consider expanding open promotion systems to all businesses? What kinds of jobs should be included: hourly only, nonexempt and exempt salaried, some management, etc.? What are the key elements for a successful system?
- Turnover is increasing on job X. Why are employees leaving? Are there selection procedures we can use to identify those employees who will stay and those who will leave? Can a test publisher send something for us to use? What do the government's selection guidelines say about this?
- Companies with performance appraisal systems for professional employees usually have only *one* system. Our many businesses have developed their own, so we have *many* systems. Should we establish one system to be applied companywide? Are the various systems working? Can they work more effectively?
- The cost of transferring an employee has increased dramatically; the cost to the employee has increased as well. "Quality of life" issues are affecting employees' willingness to transfer. Are these factors influencing the company's ability to transfer required skills? Should we be doing anything more or different?

These questions, and many others like them, are often asked of Joyce Lawson, a consultant in human resource management, by operating business managers, human resource professionals, and corporate management. Her responses are based on twenty-five years of experience in virtually every aspect of human resource management, both with the General Electric Company and as an independent consultant. As a generalist, she advises businesses on such diverse procedures as reduction in force, performance appraisal systems, appeals procedures for employees, selection and promotion systems, and employee transfers. Lawson says, "In the past few years, the questions that have demanded most of my time are the ones related to appeals procedures or problem-solving procedures for professional employees, performance appraisals, and employee relocation."

She cites a particular instance from the early 1980s, when changes in the economy and the housing market made the transfer of employees a significant cost of doing business: "One large company had established a reputation for having one of the best transfer policies among its peers, and had introduced a new home-sale assistance program and a mortgage interest differential allowance to increase its assistance to transferring employees. Despite the new program, recruiters told us they were not getting their first choices for jobs and that employees were turning down transfer opportunities. We had to find out why. The finance and relocation people were as interested as the employee relations managers. So we went to recently transferred employees and asked them about their relocation experiences. What we found was that moving was a stressful experience, created by a volatile housing market, high mortgage rates, a perceived lack of adequate information about the transfer process, and a need for spouse employment assistance.

"So the finance and relocation people made improvements in the home-sale assistance program and mortgage interest differential allowance. Additionally, we assigned the coordinating responsibility for a transfer to the employee relations managers—many parties are involved and we had to ensure that they all work effectively. We established a checklist to help them do the coordinating job.

"We published an employee relocation information package spelling out what the company policy was all about, the important parts of the program, and what was expected of the employees. And we established guidelines for spouse employment assistance for operating divisions to follow. We did not leave it there; we surveyed employees after their transfer for a period of time to ensure that the company was on top of their experiences, good and bad," she concludes.

"The one thing," Lawson says, "we can be sure of in the human resource management business is that it never gets boring. As soon as one concern is resolved, another interesting question comes along, which cannot be answered without a lot of research. That is what makes this a fascinating, worthwhile profession."

Joyce Lawson has served as a member of various employer group committees and currently is a member of the board of the Society for Human Resource Management Foundation. The professional association that receives most of her attention is the International Association for Personnel Women; she has served as a member of the executive board for a number of years and is a past president. "This organization has offered great opportunities for women to develop as professionals in their chosen career and, as the organization grows, so do the members—personally and professionally. I feel I have contributed a lot, but I have received more through my participation," she relates.

Human Resource Development

A performance appraisal should point out an employee's specific needs for training, education, and development.[7] For instance, if Mary Jones receives a marginal evaluation on writing skills, additional training in written communication may be indicated. If the human resource manager finds that a number of first-line supervisors rate low in verbal skills, training sessions in spoken communication may be needed. By identifying these deficiencies, the human resource manager is able to develop HRD programs that permit individuals to build on their strengths and minimize their deficiencies. An appraisal system does not guarantee that employees will be properly trained and developed. However, the task of determining training and development needs is simplified when appraisal data are available.

Career Planning and Development

Career planning and development may be viewed from either an individual or organizational viewpoint. In either case, PA data are essential in assessing an employee's strengths and weaknesses and in determining potential. Managers may use such information to counsel subordinates and assist them in developing and implementing their career plans.

Compensation Programs

Performance appraisal results provide a basis for decisions regarding pay increases. Most managers believe that outstanding job performance should be rewarded tangibly with raises. They believe that "what you reward is what you get." This may be a basic problem with the compensation practice described at the beginning of the chapter by Doug Parsley, the production vice-president. He has discovered that a system is needed to encourage people to produce at their highest level of efficiency over the long run. He also realizes that the same rewards for poor performers and top producers will likely lead to marginal performance even from its previously productive employees. To encourage good performance, a firm should design and implement a fair performance appraisal system and then reward the most productive workers accordingly.

Internal Employee Relations

Performance appraisal data are also frequently used for decisions in several areas of internal employee relations, including promotion, demotion, termination, layoff, and transfer. For example, an employee's mastery of certain tasks may become apparent, as may areas in which development is required.

---

[7] Baylie, Kujawski, and Young, pp. 4–168.

An employee's performance in one job may be useful in determining his or her ability to perform another job on the same level, as is required in the consideration of transfers. Or when the performance level is unacceptable, demotion or termination may be indicated. When employees working under a labor agreement are involved, employee layoff is typically based on seniority. However, when management has more flexibility, an employee's performance record may be a more rational criterion.

Assessment of Employee Potential

Some organizations attempt to assess employee potential as they appraise job performance. It has been said that the best predictors of future behavior are past behaviors.[8] However, an employee's past performance in a job may not accurately indicate future performance in a higher level or different position. The best salesperson in the company may not have what it takes to become a successful district sales manager. The best computer programmer may, if promoted, be a disaster as a data processing manager. Overemphasizing technical skills and ignoring other equally important skills is a common error in promoting employees into management jobs. Recognition of this problem has led some firms to separate the appraisal of performance, which focuses on past behavior, from the assessment of potential, which is future oriented. These firms have established "assessment centers," which we discuss in a later section.

■ THE PERFORMANCE APPRAISAL PROCESS

Many of the external and internal environmental factors discussed in Chapter 2 can influence the appraisal process. Legislation, for example, requires that appraisal systems be nondiscriminatory. In the 1977 case of *Mistretta* v. *Sandia Corporation* (a subsidiary of Western Electric Company, Inc.), a Federal District Court judge ruled against the company, stating that "there is sufficient circumstantial evidence to indicate that age bias and age based policies appear throughout the performance rating process to the detriment of the protected age group.[9] The *Albermarle Paper* v. *Moody* case supported validation requirements for performance appraisals, as well as for selection tests. Organizations should avoid using any appraisal method that results in a disportionately negative impact on a protected class.[10] For example, are women consistently being rated lower than men? If so, their promotion potential would also be affected.

The labor union is another external factor that might affect a firm's appraisal process. Unions have traditionally stressed seniority as the basis

---

[8] L. L. Cummings and Donald P. Schwab, "Designing Appraisal Systems for Information Yield," *California Management Review*, 20 (Summer 1978), p. 22.

[9] James W. Walker and Daniel E. Lupton, "Performance Appraisal Programs and Age Discrimination Law," *Aging and Work*, 2 (Spring 1978), pp. 73–83.

[10] Roberta V. Romberg, "Performance Appraisal, 1: Risks and Rewards," *Personnel*, 63 (August 1986), p. 20.

for promotions and pay increases. They may vigorously oppose the use of a management designed performance appraisal system that would be used for these purposes.

Factors within the internal environment can also affect the performance appraisal process. For instance, the type of corporate culture can serve to assist or hinder the process. In today's highly complex organizations, employees must often rely on co-workers in performing their tasks. A closed, nontrusting culture may discourage the cooperation needed to successfully complete a job. In such an environment, performance may suffer even though an individual worker would like to do a good job. Recognizing the true contributions of an individual worker in such an environment may also be quite difficult.

Identification of specific goals is the starting point for the PA process (see Figure 11-1). An appraisal system may be unable to effectively serve all the purposes desired, so management should select those specific PA goals that it believes to be most important and can be realistically achieved. For example, some firms may want to stress employee development, whereas other organizations may want to focus on administrative decisions, such as pay adjustments. Too many performance appraisal systems are poorly designed because management hasn't established clear objectives. In these instances, managers haven't determined specifically what they want the system to accomplish, often anticipating too much from one system.[11]

After specific appraisal goals have been established, workers must understand what is expected from them in their jobs. It is helpful when their supervisors review with them the major duties determined through job analysis and contained in the job description. In fact, informing employees of what is expected of them may be a manager's most important employee-relation task.[12]

The supervisor then observes work performance, evaluates it against established job performance standards, and communicates the evaluation results to the worker. The performance evaluation discussion with the supervisor serves to reestablish job requirements in the employee's mind.

■ RESPONSIBILITY FOR APPRAISAL

In most organizations, the human resource department is responsible for designing and overseeing performance appraisal programs. Responsibility for actually conducting the appraisals varies from company to company. However, line management must directly participate in the program if it is to succeed. Several possibilities exist as to who will actually rate the employee, some of which we present next.

---

[11] Ed Yager, "A Critique of Performance Appraisal Systems," *Personnel Journal*, 60 (February 1981), p. 129.

[12] J. Kenneth Matejka and Richard J. Dunsing, "Great Expectations," *Management World*, 16 (January 1987), p. 16.

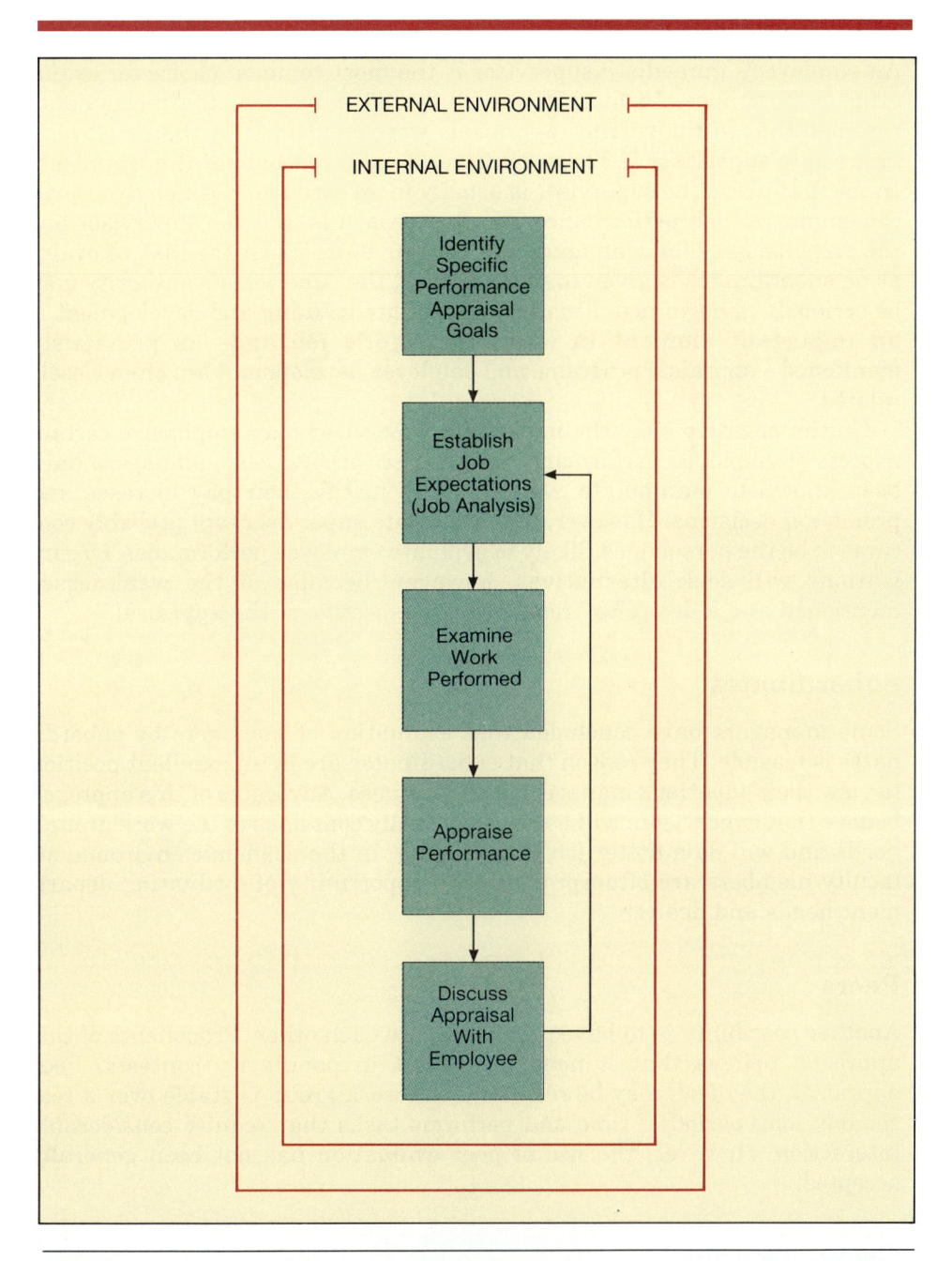

FIGURE 11-1 | The Performance Appraisal Process

Immediate Supervisor

An employee's immediate supervisor is the most common choice for evaluating performance. In fact, in one study, 96 percent of the respondents revealed that in their firms, appraisals were conducted by the employee's immediate supervisor.[13] There are several valid reasons for this approach. In the first place, the supervisor is usually in an excellent position to observe the employee's job performance. Another reason is that the supervisor has the responsibility for managing a particular unit. When the task of evaluating subordinates is given to someone else, the supervisor's authority may be seriously undermined. Finally, subordinate training and development is an important element in every manager's job and—as previously mentioned—appraisal programs and employee development are often closely related.

On the negative side, the immediate supervisor may emphasize certain aspects of employee performance and neglect others. Also, managers have been known to manipulate evaluations to justify their pay increase and promotion decisions. However, the immediate supervisor will probably continue to be the person most likely to evaluate employee performance. Organizations will seek alternatives, however, because of the weaknesses mentioned and a desire to broaden the perspective of the appraisal.

Subordinates

Some managers have concluded that evaluation of managers by subordinates is feasible. They reason that subordinates are in an excellent position to view their superior's managerial effectiveness. Advocates of this approach believe that supervisors will become especially conscious of the work group's needs and will do a better job of managing. In the academic environment, faculty members are often provided the opportunity of evaluating department heads and deans.

Peers

Another possibility is to have peers evaluate each other. Proponents of this approach believe that it need not result in popularity contests. Peer appraisal, they feel, may be reliable if the work group is stable over a reasonably long period of time and performs tasks that require considerable interaction. However, the use of peer evaluation has not been generally accepted.

Group Appraisal

Group appraisal involves the use of two or more managers who are familiar with the employee's performance to evaluate it as a team. For instance, if a person regularly works with the data processing manager and the financial manager, these two individuals might jointly make the evalua-

---

[13] Fombrun and Laud, p. 27.

tion. An advantage of this approach is that it injects a degree of objectivity by utilizing "outside parties." A disadvantage is that it diminishes the role of the immediate supervisor. Also, it may be difficult to get managers together for a group appraisal because of other demands on their time.

Self-Appraisal

If employees understand the objectives they are expected to achieve and the standards by which they are to be evaluated, they are—to a great extent—in the best position to appraise their own performance.[14] Also, because employee development is self-development, employees who appraise their own performance may become more highly motivated. Self-appraisal has great appeal to managers who are primarily concerned with employee participation and development.

Combinations

In seeking an answer to the question, "Who should evaluate?" you need to recognize that these approaches are not mutually exclusive. In fact many are used in combination. For example, in order to minimize subjectivity, a manager may be rated separately by a group of fellow workers, including the immediate superior, two or three higher level managers, two or three peers, and workers in lower positions. The combined use of several methods may provide greater insight into an individual's actual performance.

■ THE APPRAISAL PERIOD

Performance evaluations are usually prepared at specific intervals. In most organizations, they are made either annually or semiannually. Individuals are often evaluated just before the end of the probationary period. Evaluating new employees several times during their first year of employment is also a common practice. The following are the evaluation periods for three companies:

- The New York Times Company evaluates all its guild and nonunion employees annually. Craft unions are not included in this process.
- Cessna Aircraft Company appraises all monthly salaried employees and all weekly salaried supervisors approximately once a year.
- General Mills, Inc., evaluates all employees annually, except for operative, nonexempt employees, who are evaluated each six months.

The appraisal period may begin with the employee's hiring-in date, or all employees may be evaluated at the same time. Although both practices have advantages, staggered appraisals seem to have greater merit. There may not be sufficient time to evaluate each employee adequately if all

---

[14] Margaret A. Bogerty, "How to Prepare for Your Performance Review," *SAM Advanced Management Journal*, 47 (Autumn 1982), p. 12.

appraisals are conducted at the same time. The problem would be especially acute in large departments.

■ PERFORMANCE APPRAISAL METHODS

Managers may choose from among several appraisal methods. The type of performance appraisal system utilized depends on its purpose. If the major emphasis is on selecting people for promotion, training, and merit pay increases, some traditional method such as rating scales may be most appropriate. Collaborative methods, such as MBO, are designed to assist employees in developing and becoming more effective.[15]

Rating Scales

A widely used appraisal method, which rates employees according to defined factors, is called the **rating scales method**. Using this approach, judgments about performance are recorded on a scale.[16] The scale is divided into categories—normally 5–7 in number—which are often defined by adjectives such as *outstanding, average,* or *unsatisfactory*. While a global rating may be provided, the method generally allows for the use of more than one performance criterion. One reason for the popularity of the rating scales method is its simplicity, which permits many employees to be evaluated quickly.[17]

The factors chosen for evaluation are typically of two types: job-related and personal characteristics (see Figure 11-2).[18] Note that job-related factors include quantity and quality of work, whereas personal factors include such attributes as dependability, initiative, adaptability, and cooperation. The rater (evaluator) completes the form by indicating the degree of each factor that is most descriptive of the employee and his or her performance.

Some firms provide space for the rater to comment on the evaluation given for each factor. This practice may be especially encouraged, or even required, when the rater gives either the highest or lowest rating. For instance, if an employee is rated *unsatisfactory* on initiative, the rater might have to provide written justification for this low evaluation. The purpose of this type of requirement is to avoid arbitrary and hastily made judgments.

As you can see in Figure 11-2, each factor and each degree have been defined. In order to receive an *exceptional* rating for the factor *quality of work*, a person must consistently exceed the prescribed work requirements. The more precisely the various factors and degrees are defined, the better

---

[15] Robert L. Taylor and Robert A. Zawaki, "Trends in Performance Appraisal: Guidelines for Managers," *Personnel Administrator*, 29 (March 1984), p. 71.

[16] J. Peter Graves, "Let's Put Appraisal Back in Performance Appraisal: Part I," *Personnel Journal*, 61 (November 1982), p. 848.

[17] Stuart Murray, "A Comparison of Results-Oriented and Trait-Based Performance Appraisals," *Personnel Administrator*, 28 (June 1983), p. 100.

[18] Because the system depicted makes liberal use of personal factors that may not be job related, it has been described by a reviewer as "a good example of a poor method."

CHAPTER 11 Performance Appraisal

Employee's Name _____

Job Title _____

Department _____

Supervisor _____

Evaluation Period:
From _____ to _____

Instructions for Evaluation:
1. Consider only one factor at a time. Do not permit rating given for one factor to affect decision for others.
2. Consider performance for entire evaluation period. Avoid concentration on recent events or isolated incidents.
3. Remember that the average employee performs duties in a satisfactory manner. An above average or exceptional rating indicates that the employee has clearly distinguished himself or herself from the average employee.

EVALUATION FACTORS	Unsatisfactory. Does not meet requirements.	Below average. Needs improvement. Requirements occasionally not met.	Average. Consistently meets requirements.	Good. Frequently exceeds requirements.	Exceptional. Consistently exceeds requirements.
QUANTITY OF WORK: Consider the volume of work achieved. Is productivity at an acceptable level?					
QUALITY OF WORK: Consider accuracy, precision, neatness, and completeness in handling assigned duties.					
DEPENDABILITY: Consider degree to which employee can be relied on to meet work commitments.					
INITIATIVE: Consider self-reliance, resourcefulness, and willingness to accept responsibility.					
ADAPTABILITY: Consider ability to respond to changing requirements and conditions.					
COOPERATION: Consider ability to work for and with others. Are assignments, including overtime, willingly accepted?					

POTENTIAL FOR FUTURE GROWTH AND DEVELOPMENT:
☐ Now at or near maximum performance in present job.
☐ Now at or near maximum performance in this job, but has potential for improvement in another job, such as: _____

☐ Capable of progressing after further training and experience.
☐ No apparent limitations.

EMPLOYEE STATEMENT: I agree ☐ Disagree ☐ with this evaluation
Comments: _____

_____
Employee   Date _____

_____
Supervisor   Date _____

_____
Reviewing Manager   Date _____

FIGURE 11-2 | Rating Scales Method of Performance Appraisal

the rater can evaluate worker performance. Evaluation agreement throughout the organization is achieved when each rater interprets the factors and degrees in the same way.

Many rating scale performance appraisal forms also provide for an assessment of the employee's growth potential. The form shown in Figure 11-2 contains four categories relating to a person's potential for future growth and development. They range from "now at or near maximum performance in present job" to "no apparent limitations." Although there are drawbacks in attempting to evaluate both past performance and future potential at the same time, this practice is often followed.

The Use of Rating Scales at the Southland Corporation

At the Southland Corporation, immediate supervisors are required to conduct a written performance review of nonexempt and exempt employees at least annually. An example of the form used to appraise nonexempt employees is shown in Figure 11-3. The appraisal system involves seven steps:

- Select key job parts
- Describe employee performance
- Rate employee performance
- Determine overall efficiency
- Prepare for the performance appraisal discussion
- Present results and (an optional step) prepare a performance development plan
- Obtain necessary signatures

Key job parts are aspects of the job such as duties, responsibilities, and assignments that are so important that their performance affects overall success or failure. Key job parts are determined by job analysis for each job family. The rating supervisor selects those that are most relevant to the job of the employee being evaluated. Normally, 6–8 job parts are utilized. Again referring to Figure 11-3, note that the supervisor evaluates performance on a five-point scale. The factors used, however, are not nebulous personality traits, which are so often used. Rather, they are job-related factors. This approach not only conforms to requirements of the *Uniform Guidelines*, but also places the rating supervisor's task of evaluating performance on a solid foundation.

Critical Incidents

The **critical incident method** requires that written records be kept of highly favorable and highly unfavorable work actions. When such an action affects the department's effectiveness significantly—either positively or negatively—the manager writes it down. It is called a critical incident. At the end of the appraisal period, the rater uses these records along with other data to evaluate employee performance. With this method, the appraisal is more likely to cover the entire evaluation period and not, for example, focus on the last few weeks or months. However, if a supervisor has many employees to rate, the time required for recording behaviors may become excessive.

Essay

In the **essay method**, the rater simply writes a brief narrative describing the employee's performance. This method tends to focus on extreme behavior in the employee's work rather than routine day-to-day performance. Ratings of this type depend heavily on the evaluator's writing ability. As the evaluations are reviewed, a positive evaluation may be negatively received if the evaluator misspells words or cannot write a good paragraph. Some supervisors, because of their excellent writing ability, can make even a marginal worker sound like a top performer. Comparing evaluations might be difficult as no common criteria exist. However, some managers believe that the essay method is the best approach to employee evaluation.

Work Standards

The **work standards method** compares each employee's performance to a predetermined standard or expected level of output. Standards reflect the normal output of an average worker operating at a normal pace. Work standards may be applied to virtually all types of jobs, but they are most frequently used for production jobs. Several methods may be utilized in determining work standards, including time study and work sampling.

An obvious advantage of using standards as appraisal criteria is objectivity. However, in order for them to perceive that the standards are objective, employees should understand clearly how the standards were set. It follows that the rationale for any changes to the standards must also be carefully explained.

Ranking

In using the **ranking method**, the rater simply places all employees from a group in rank order of overall performance. For example, the best employee in the department is ranked highest, and the poorest is ranked lowest. A major difficulty occurs when individuals have performed at comparable levels.

Paired comparison is a variation of the ranking method in which the performance of each employee is compared with every other employee in the group. The comparison is often based on a single criterion, such as overall performance. The employee who receives the greatest number of favorable comparisons is ranked highest.

Some professionals in the field argue for use of a comparative approach—such as ranking—whenever human resource decisions are made. For exam-

Employee Name _____John Jacobs_____

Employee Title _____MIS Supply Clerk_____

Employee Social Security Number _____450-30-2641_____

Location _____

Period of Evaluation __2/88__ to __2/89__

Date of Last Review __2/88__

Supervisor's Name _____Harry Hines_____

Supervisor's Title _____MIS Supply Supervisor_____

Type of Review _____

Refer to the *Performance Appraisal System Reference Guide* before completing this form.

KEY JOB PARTS	PERFORMANCE DESCRIPTION	PERFORMANCE RATING*
1. Typing ■ Typing from handwritten draft ■ Typing information on forms ■ Statistical or financial typing ■ Typing from recorded dictation		N/A 1 2 3 4 5
2. Maintaining and ordering supplies ■ Checking supply levels ■ Ordering and picking up supplies	Employee needs to work with forms order and inventories more to gain more experience in this area. Make sure letters are prepared for checks taken from area.	N/A 1 2 ③ 4 5
3. Copying and recording information ■ Making routine entries in files, books, or on forms ■ Keeping tallies or lists	Employee does well making entries in check logs and on transmittals.	N/A 1 2 ③ 4 5
4. Making job-related decisions ■ Setting priorities for own work ■ Deciding the best way to complete an assignment ■ Reading and interpreting policies, rules, and procedures ■ Doing limited research (calling, looking things up in manuals, etc.) to resolve a problem or question ■ Conducting research or analyzing information	Employee has improved in limited research and writing Request for Assistance. Still needs to review all possibilities when researching missing reports.	N/A 1 2 ③ 4 5

*Ratings are defined in *Reference Guide* and range from "well below performance requirements (1)" to "well above performance requirements (5)."

FIGURE 11-3 | Performance Appraisal System for Nonexempt Employees

Source: Used with the permission of the Southland Corporation Personnel Research Department.

KEY JOB PARTS	PERFORMANCE DESCRIPTION	PERFORMANCE RATING*
5. Processing requests ■ Receiving and reviewing incoming correspondence, telephone calls, or other requests ■ Deciding what the problem or inquiry is ■ Preparing responses to inquiries ■ Persuading others to take action or change their opinions ■ Responding to telephone inquiries		N/A 1 2 3 4 5
6. Proofreading and checking work ■ Reviewing forms, reports, correspondence for completeness and accuracy ■ Checking material for errors in typing, spelling, punctuation, grammar, capitalization or word usage ■ Checking work done by others to make sure procedures and/or instructions have been followed	Employee does well in checking the completeness of production output. Has improved in locating one-page reports attached to multipage reports.	N/A 1 2 3 ④ 5
7. Performing routine calculations ■ Adding, subtracting, multiplying, or dividing ■ Computing wages, taxes, commissions, etc. ■ Determining rates, discounts, etc. by referring to tables		N/A 1 2 3 4 5
8. Sorting, filing, or retrieving information ■ Sorting information ■ Filing or retrieving information (in an existing filing system) ■ Developing new filing or cross-index systems ■ Searching for missing files, forms, orders, etc.		N/A 1 2 3 4 5
9. Preparing written reports ■ Writing reports which summarize available information ■ Writing short, routine reports ■ Writing long or complicated reports ■ Preparing financial statements or numerical or statistical reports ■ Composing or initiating correspondence	Prepares precise transmittals and Request for Assistance.	N/A 1 2 ③ 4 5

FIGURE 11-3 | *Continued*

Task	Rating	Comments
10. Performing receptionist duties ■ Answering and routing telephone calls ■ Taking and distributing messages ■ Greeting visitors	N/A 1 2 3 4 5	
11. Scheduling ■ Contacting individuals to schedule meetings ■ Making travel arrangements ■ Reserving meeting facilities	N/A 1 2 3 4 5	
12. Performing data entry and retrieval tasks ■ Operating a key punch, data entry terminal, or verifier ■ Look up information using CRT	N/A 1 2 3 4 5	
13. Performing accounting functions ■ Posting to ledgers ■ Receiving, counting, or paying out checks or cash ■ Balancing receipts ■ Debiting/crediting accounts	N/A 1 2 3 4 5	
14. Operating and maintaining office machines ■ Setting up and adjusting machines (such as an offset press) ■ Cleaning or performing simple repairs on office machines ■ Operating simple office machines such as copying machines	N/A 1 2 3 ④ 5	Continues to do a good job operating all machines in distribution. He is an excellent operator of the burster.
1'istributing material ■ Picking up or distributing materials ■ Preparing materials for mailing or shipping	N/A 1 2 3 ④ 5	Does well at preparing materials for mailing or shipping.
16. Performing supervisory duties ■ Making work assignments ■ Conducting employee evaluations ■ Coordinating activities of assigned employees ■ Resolving conflicts or problems among assigned employees	N/A 1 2 3 4 5	
17. Computer operations ■ Operating Central Processing Unit ■ Operating a high-speed printer (on-line to CPU) ■ Operating tape drives	N/A 1 2 3 4 5	

*Ratings are defined in *Reference Guide*

FIGURE 11-3 | *Continued*

CHAPTER 11 Performance Appraisal

KEY JOB PARTS	PERFORMANCE DESCRIPTION	PERFORMANCE RATING*
18. Word Processing ■ Operating a word processor using a terminal or printer ■ Inputting and manipulating statistical data ■ Inputting and formatting text		N/A 1 2 3 4 5
19. Operating a Personal Computer ■ Creating simple programs ■ Performing sort, math and merge functions		N/A 1 2 3 4 5
20. Computer Knowledge ■ Input Documents	Employee has a good knowledge of distribution area. Needs to expand his knowledge of Data Control—Input, UCC7, Schedule.	N/A 1 2 ③ 4 5
21. General ■ Quality Control ■ Unsupervised Work ■ Attendance	Employee is very dependable and has an excellent attitude. He is very responsible and needs very little supervision. Employee continues to improve.	N/A 1 2 3 ④ 5
22. Attitude		N/A 1 2 3 4 5

*Ratings are defined in *Reference Guide.*

OVERALL PERFORMANCE DESCRIPTION

Well below performance requirements. [1]	Below performance requirements. [2]	Meets performance requirements. [3]	Above performance requirements. ④	Well above performance requirements. [5]

Refer to the *Guide to Developing Goals* before completing this section.

PERFORMANCE GOALS/RESULTS DESIRED	ACTION SUPERVISOR WILL TAKE TO HELP EMPLOYEE ACHIEVE GOALS	ACTION EMPLOYEE WILL TAKE TO ACHIEVE GOALS	TARGET DATE
1. Work with forms orders and inventories to gain more experience in this area. 2. Ensure that checks are accounted for with letters. 3. Improve research techniques. 4. Expand knowledge of UCC7 and scheduling.			

FIGURE 11-3 | *Continued*

EMPLOYEE COMMENTS:

Employee Signature _____ Date __8/15/89__

NOTE: Your signature does not necessarily signify your agreement with the appraisal; it simply means that the appraisal was discussed with you.

Reviewer's Signature _____ Date __8/15/89__

Second Level Reviewer's Signature _____ Date __8/15/89__

FIGURE 11-3 | *Continued*

ple, they feel that employees are not promoted because they achieve their objectives but rather because they achieve them better than others in their work group. Such decisions do not involve a single individual, and therefore should be considered on a broader basis.[19]

Forced Distribution

In the **forced distribution method**, the rater is required to assign individuals in the work group to a limited number of categories similar to a normal frequency distribution. As an example, employees in the top 10 percent are placed in the highest group, the next 20 percent in the next group, the next 40 percent in the middle group, the next 20 percent in the next group, and the remaining 10 percent in the lowest category. This approach is based on the rather questionable assumption that all groups of employees will have the same distribution of excellent, average, and poor performers. If one department has all outstanding workers, the supervisor would likely be hard pressed to decide who should be placed in the lower categories.

Forced-Choice and Weighted Checklist Performance Reports

The **forced-choice performance report** requires that the appraiser choose from a series of statements about an individual those that are most or least descriptive of the employee. One difficulty with this method is that the descriptive statements may be virtually identical.

Using the **weighted checklist performance report**, the rater completes a form similar to the forced-choice performance report, but the various responses have been assigned different weights. The form includes questions related to the employee's behavior, and the evaluator answers each question either positively or negatively. The evaluator is not aware of each question's weight, however.

As with forced-choice performance reports, the weighted checklist is expensive to design. Both methods strive for objectivity, but the evaluator doesn't know which items contribute most to successful performance.

Behaviorally Anchored Rating Scales

The **behaviorally anchored rating scale (BARS) method** combines elements of the traditional rating scales and critical incidents methods. Using BARS, job behaviors derived from critical incidents—effective and ineffective behavior—are described more objectively. Individuals familiar with a particular job identify its major components. They then rank and validate

---
[19] Graves, p. 918.

specific behaviors for each of the components.[20] Because BARS typically requires considerable employee participation, it may be accepted more readily by both supervisors and subordinates. Behaviorally anchored rating scales are potentially more reliable than graphic rating scales and, therefore, more defensible from the legal point of view.[21]

In BARS, various performance levels are shown along a scale and described in terms of an employee's specific job behavior. Table 11-2 illustrates a portion of a BARS system that was developed to evaluate interviewers and claims deputies for the employment service of a state department of labor. Note that the factor *ability to absorb and interpret policies* is job related and carefully defined. Instead of using adjectives at each scale point, BARS uses behavioral anchors related to the criterion being measured. This modification clarifies the meaning of each point on the scale. For example, instead of dealing with *outstanding performance*, an actual example of such behavior is provided. This approach facilitates discussion of the rating because specific behaviors can be addressed.[22] This method was developed to overcome weaknesses in other evaluation methods. While reports on the effectiveness of BARS are mixed, it does not seem to be superior to other methods in overcoming rater errors or in achieving psychometric soundness.[23] A specific deficiency is that the behaviors used are activity oriented rather than results oriented. This poses a potential problem for supervisors, who have to rate employees who are performing the activity but not accomplishing the desired goals.[24]

Management By Objectives

As previously discussed, the MBO concept values and utilizes employee contributions. It is also an effective method of evaluating an employee's performance. In traditional approaches to performance appraisal, personal traits of employees are often used as criteria for evaluating performance. In addition, the role of the evaluating supervisor is similar to that of a judge. With MBO, the focus of the appraisal process shifts from the worker's personal attributes to job performance. The supervisor's role changes from that of an umpire to that of a counselor and facilitator. Also, the employee's function changes from that of passive bystander to that of active participant.

Individuals jointly establish objectives with their superiors, who then give them some latitude in how to achieve those objectives. At the end of the appraisal period, the employee and supervisor meet for an appraisal

---

[20] Roger J. Plachy, "Appraisal Scales that Measure Performance Outcomes and Job Results," *Personnel*, 60 (May–June 1983), p. 59.

[21] Ronald G. Wells, "Guidelines for Effective and Defensible Performance Appraisal Systems," *Personnel Journal*, 61 (October 1982), p. 777.

[22] Graves, pp. 848–849.

[23] Stephen J. Carroll and Craig E. Schneier, *Performance Appraisal and Review Systems: The Identification, Measurement, and Development of Performance in Organizations* (Glenview, Ill.: Scott, Foresman, 1982), p. 117.

[24] Plachy, p. 59.

TABLE 11-2 | BARS for Factor: "Ability to Absorb and Interpret Policies"

Interviewers and claims deputies must keep abreast of current changes and interpret and apply new information. Some can absorb and interpret new policy guides and procedures quickly with a minimum of explanation. Others seem unable to learn even after repeated explanations and practice. They have difficulty learning and following new policies. When making this rating, disregard job knowledge and experience and evaluate ability to learn on the job.

Very Positive	9	This interviewer could be expected to serve as an information source concerning new and changed policies for others in the office.
	8	Could be expected to be aware quickly of program changes and explain these changes to employers.
	7	Could be expected to reconcile conflicting policies and procedures correctly to meet immediate job needs.
	6	Could be expected to recognize the need for additional information to gain better understanding of policy changes.
Neutral	5	After receiving instruction on completing ESAR forms, this interviewer could be expected to complete the forms correctly.
	4	Could be expected to require some help and practice in mastering new policies and procedures.
	3	Could be expected to know that there is a problem, but might go down many blind alleys before realizing they are wrong.
	2	Could be expected to incorrectly interpret program guidelines, thereby referring an unqualified person.
Very Negative	1	Even after repeated explanations, this interviewer could be expected to be unable to learn new procedures.

Source: Adapted from Cheedle W. Millard, Fred Luthans, and Robert L. Ottemann, "A New Breakthrough for Performance Appraisal," *Business Horizons*, 19 (August 1976), p. 69. Copyright © 1976 by the Foundation for the School of Business at Indiana University. Reprinted by permission.

interview. They first review the extent to which the objectives have been achieved and second the actions needed to solve remaining problems. Under MBO, the supervisor keeps communication channels open throughout the appraisal period. The problem-solving discussion during the appraisal interview is merely another conversation designed to assist the worker in progressing according to plan. At this time, objectives are established for the next evaluation period and the process is repeated.

It should be obvious that not all leadership styles are compatible with the participative concept of MBO. It probably would not be successful in an organization run by highly autocratic managers. An attempt to implement an MBO appraisal system in such a setting would likely result in top management concluding that "MBO is okay in theory, but no good in practice." The theory *is* sound, but implementation problems often stem from the incompatibility of the theory with the organization's culture.

Actual Use of Various Appraisal Methods

A study of 1,000 industrial and 300 nonindustrial firms that comprise the *Fortune* 1300 revealed how these organizations use performance appraisal systems by job level.[25] Definitions of appraisal approaches used in the study were generally the same as those provided in this chapter. One exception was a second variation of management by objectives in which action plans are not established. For our purposes, we combined these systems into one: objectives-based approach—MBO.

As you can see in Table 11-3, a large number of firms (29 percent) do not use a formal system to evaluate hourly workers. This approach may reflect philosophical differences between union and management. None of the responding firms utilized MBO for this group of employees. However, a work standards approach is used for hourly workers and for the nonexempt group by 29 percent and 33 percent, respectively, of the firms.

In the remaining categories, some form of MBO dominates: exempt (73 percent); professional (75 percent); supervisory (75 percent); middle management (86 percent); and top management (82 percent). The use of essay, work standards, and behaviorally anchored ratings is also significant. Conspicuously missing from the listings are graphic rating scales, which appear only in the hourly and nonexempt categories. Multiple responses indicate that more than one appraisal system is used in some companies.

Another major study of performance appraisal systems provided results that are significantly different from those just discussed. This study of 200 randomly selected *Fortune* 500 and *Second* 500 firms revealed substantial changes in the use of appraisal systems over a five-year period.[26] The study—a replication of an earlier one—indicated that the use of collaborative systems (MBO and BARS) relative to other systems for evaluating managers declined from 57 percent in 1976 to 47 percent in 1981 (see Table 11-4). Based on results of this study, traditional methods are regaining their earlier popularity.

■ PROBLEMS IN PERFORMANCE APPRAISAL

Many performance appraisal methods have been severely criticized. The rating scales method seems to have received the greatest attention. In all

---

[25] Fombrun and Laud, p. 28.
[26] Taylor and Zawaki, pp. 71–80.

TABLE 11-3 | Rank Order of Performance Appraisal System Use by Job Level

	Percent*		Percent*
Hourly (N = 160)		**Nonexempt† (N = 237)**	
No system	29	Work standards approach	33
Work standards approach	29	Essay	30
Graphic rating scales	23	Behaviorally anchored ratings	28
Essay	14	Graphic rating scales	26
Behaviorally anchored ratings	14	Objectives-based approach—MBO	19
Exempt† (N = 247)		**Professional (nonmanagerial) (N = 234)**	
Objectives-based approach—MBO	73	Objectives-based approach—MBO	75
Essay	36	Essay	36
Work standards approach	32	Work standards approach	33
Behaviorally anchored ratings	24	Behaviorally anchored ratings	24
Supervisory (N = 235)		**Middle Management (N = 238)**	
Objectives-based approach—MBO	75	Objectives-based approach—MBO	86
Essay	36	Essay	37
Work standards approach	32	Work standards approach	27
Behaviorally anchored ratings	25	Behaviorally anchored ratings	24
Top Management (N = 217)			
Objectives-based approach—MBO	82		
Essay	33		
Work standards approach	24		
Behaviorally anchored ratings	18		

*Multiple responses to some questions result in percentages greater than 100. N = number of responses.

†The terms *exempt* and *nonexempt* refer to whether a job so classified is subject to provisions of the Fair Labor Standards Act. They are more fully discussed in chapter 12.

Source: Adapted, by permission of the publisher, from "Strategic Issues in Performance Appraisal: Theory and Practice," by Charles J. Fombrun and Robert J. Laud, *Personnel* (November–December 1983), p. 24. Copyright © 1983 by the Charles J. Fombrun and Robert J. Laud. Published by American Management Association, New York. All rights reserved.

fairness, many of the problems commonly mentioned are not inherent in the method but, rather, reflect improper usage. For example, raters may be inadequately trained, or the appraisal device actually used may not be job related.

Lack of Objectivity

A potential weakness of traditional performance appraisal methods is that they lack objectivity. In the rating scales method, for example, commonly used factors such as attitude, loyalty, and personality are difficult to meas-

TABLE 11-4 | Performance Appraisal Systems Used for Evaluating Managers 1976–1981

	Percent of Responding Firms Reporting System Type	
Year of Survey	Traditional	Collaborative
1976	43	57
1981	53	47

Source: Adapted from Robert L. Taylor and Robert A. Zawacki, "Trends in Performance Appraisal: Guidelines for Managers," from the March 1984 issue of *Personnel Administrator*. Copyright © 1984, The American Society for Personnel Administration, Alexandria, Virginia.

ure. In addition, these factors may have little to do with an employee's job performance.

Some subjectivity will always exist in appraisal methods. However, the use of job-related factors does increase objectivity. Employee appraisal-based primarily on personal characteristics may place the evaluator—and the company—in untenable positions with the employee and EEO guidelines. The firm would be hard pressed to show that these factors are job related.

Halo Error

Halo error occurs when the evaluator perceives one factor as having paramount importance and gives a good or bad overall rating to an employee based on this one factor. For example, David Edwards, accounting supervisor, placed a high value on "neatness," which was a factor used in the company's performance appraisal system. As David was evaluating the performance of his senior accounting clerk, Carl Curtis, he noted that Carl was not a very neat individual and gave him a low ranking on this factor. David also permitted, consciously or unconsciously, the low ranking on neatness to carry over to other factors, giving Carl undeserved low ratings on all factors. Of course, if Carl was very neat, the opposite could have occurred. Either way, the halo error does a disservice to the employee involved or the organization.

Leniency

Giving undeserved high ratings is referred to as **leniency**. Thomas M. Jordan, vice-president of human resources for Sea-Land Service, Inc., stated that one of the major problems encountered in his company's appraisal system is "getting managers to be objective and honest, especially where poor performance is involved." Often evaluations will be inflated if a supervisor is required to discuss them with employees. In many situations the evaluating supervisor simply gives the employee the benefit of the doubt. These actions are often motivated by a desire to avoid controversy over the appraisal. This practice is most prevalent where highly subjective factors are used as performance criteria.

Strictness

Being unduly critical of an employee's work performance is referred to as **strictness**. While leniency is usually more prevalent than strictness, some managers apply an evaluation more rigorously than the company standard. When one manager is overly strict on an entire unit, workers in that unit suffer with regard to pay raises and promotion. Strictness typically occurs when managers do not have an accurate definition of the various evaluation factors.

Central Tendency

Central tendency is a common error that occurs when employees are incorrectly rated near the average or middle of the scale. Some rating scale systems require the evaluator to justify in writing extremely high or extremely low ratings. In these instances, the rater may avoid possible controversy or criticism by giving only average ratings.

Recent Behavior Bias

Anyone who has observed the behavior of young children several weeks before Christmas can readily identify with the problem of recent behavior bias. All of a sudden, it seems, the wildest hellions in the neighborhood develop angelic personalities in anticipation of the rewards they expect to receive.

Individuals in the workforce are not children, but they are human. Almost every employee can tell the supervisor the month, day, and hour that he or she is scheduled for a performance review. Although their actions may not be conscious, employee behavior often improves, and productivity tends to rise several days or weeks before the scheduled evaluation. It is only natural to remember recent behavior more clearly than actions from the more distant past. However, performance appraisals generally cover a specified period of time and an individual's performance should be considered for the entire period.

Personal Bias

Supervisors doing performance appraisals may have biases related to their employees' personal characteristics such as race, religion, gender, or age.

While federal legislation protects such employees, discrimination continues to be an appraisal problem.

Discrimination in appraisal can be based on many factors in addition to those mentioned. For example, mild-mannered people may be appraised more harshly simply because they do not raise serious objections to the results. This type of behavior is in sharp contrast to the "hell raisers" who often confirm the adage, "the squeaking wheel gets the grease."

Judgmental Role of Evaluator

Supervisors conducting performance evaluations are at times accused of "playing God" with their employees. In some instances they control virtually every aspect of the process. Manipulation of evaluations by managers to justify their pay increase and promotion decisions is one example of how supervisors may abuse the system. They make decisions about the ratings and typically try to sell their version to the employees. The highly judgmental role of some evaluators often places employees on the defensive. Such relationships are hardly conducive to employee development, morale, and productivity.

■ CHARACTERISTICS OF AN EFFECTIVE APPRAISAL SYSTEM[27]

Validation studies of an appraisal system may be the most direct and certain approach to determining whether the system is satisfactory. However, such studies can be costly and time consuming. Also, many smaller firms will simply not have a sufficient number of positions to meet technical validation requirements.

It is unlikely that any appraisal system will be totally immune to legal challenge. However, systems that possess certain characteristics may be more legally defensible. And, at the same time, such systems can provide a more effective means for achieving performance appraisal goals.

Job-Related Criteria

The criteria used for appraising employee performance must be job related (valid). The *Uniform Guidelines* and court decisions are quite clear on this point. More specifically, job information should be determined through job analysis. Subjective factors, such as initiative, enthusiasm, loyalty, and cooperation, are obviously important. However, they virtually defy defini-

---

[27] Portions of this section were adapted from Ronald G. Wells, "Guidelines for Effective and Defensible Performance Appraisal Systems," *Personnel Journal*, 61 (October 1982), pp. 776–782.

HRM In Action

"Bill, you're the human resource manager and I have a human resource problem that I need your advice on," said Marvin Alexander, production supervisor for Service International. "Tom has worked for me for four years. He is likable and never misses a day of work. However, he is strictly mediocre at his job, despite numerous retraining attempts, conferences, and even incentives. I hear that the company is preparing for a reduction in force. As I was working on Tom's appraisal this morning, he stuck his head in the door, handed me three cigars, and said his wife had just had triplets. That sure puts pressure on me."

How would you respond?

---

tion and measurement. Unless factors such as these can be clearly shown to be job related, they should not be used in formal evaluations.

Performance Expectations

Managers must clearly explain performance expectations to their subordinates in advance of the appraisal period. Otherwise, it isn't reasonable to evaluate employees using yardsticks that they know nothing about.

The establishment of highly objective work standards is relatively simple in many areas such as manufacturing, assembly, and sales. However, for many other types of jobs this task is more difficult. Still, evaluation must take place and performance expectations, however elusive, should be defined in understandable terms.

Standardization

Employees in the same job category under the same supervisor should be appraised using the same evaluation instrument. In addition, the appraisals should cover similar periods of time. Feedback sessions and appraisal interviews should be regularly scheduled for all employees.

Another aspect of standardization is formal documentation. Records should include a description of employee responsibilities, expected performance results, and the way these data will be viewed in making appraisal decisions. However, smaller firms are not expected to maintain performance appraisal systems that are as formal as those used by large organizations.

The courts reason that objective criteria are not as important in firms with fewer than thirty employees because a smaller firm's top managers are more familiar with their employees' work.[28]

Qualified Appraisers

Responsibility for evaluating employee performance should be assigned to the individual, or individuals, who directly observe at least a representative sample of job performance. Usually, this person is the employee's immediate supervisor.

Situations that lessen the immediate supervisor's ability to appraise performance objectively include those found in matrix organizations. In that case, certain employees may be formally assigned to a supervisor but actually work under various project managers. Also, a supervisor who is in a new position may have insufficient knowledge of employee performance initially. In such instances, multiple raters may be used.

In order to ensure consistency, appraisers must be well trained. Training should emphasize that performance appraisal is a significant component of every manager's job. Training should also stress that a primary task of the supervisor is to ensure that subordinates understand what is expected of them.[29] In addition, training itself is an ongoing process. It responds to changes in the appraisal system and to the fact that supervisors, for various reasons, may deviate from established procedures. Training should cover how to rate employees and conduct appraisal interviews and include written instructions. These instructions should be rather detailed and stress the importance of making objective and unbiased ratings.

It has been suggested that nonsupervisory employees should also receive a set of the performance appraisal instructions. The major benefits cited for this approach include not only the provision of a performance management and planning tool, but also a legal safeguard to deal with potentially disgruntled employees.[30]

Open Communication

Most employees have a strong need to know how well they are performing. A good appraisal system provides highly desired feedback on a continuing basis. A worthwhile goal is to avoid surprises during the appraisal interview. Even though the interview presents an excellent opportunity for both parties to exchange ideas, it should not serve as a substitute for day-to-day communication.

---

[28] Barry J. Baroni, "The Legal Ramifications of Appraisal Systems," *Supervisory Management*, 27 (January 1982), pp. 41–42.

[29] Milan Moravec, "How Performance Appraisal Can Tie Communication to Productivity," *Personnel Administration*, 26 (January 1981), p. 52.

[30] Beverly L. Kaye and Shelley Krantz, "Preparing Employees: The Missing Link in Performance Appraisal Training," *Personnel*, 59 (May–June 1982), p. 24.

Employee Access to Results

> Now let's imagine you are in a bowling alley where drapes are hanging midway down the alley. You can't see the pins and you never know how many pins your ball knocked over. Your coach is standing behind you saying, "You're doing fine, just keep bowling." You keep rolling the balls and the coach keeps encouraging you. But, you don't know the score. You don't really know how well you are doing. At the end of the game, the scorekeeper informs you that you have set a new record—for low score. You are flabbergasted and disappointed. You're out. You are off the team. Tough luck.[31]

Obviously, this anecdote does not describe the best way to manage a bowling team or, for that matter, any other type of organization. Yet, in too many instances the same kind of mistakes are made when employees are not fully informed of the rules of the game and are not provided adequate feedback on their performance. Such a situation is uncomfortable at best and, at worst, totally demoralizing and defeating.

As a result of the Federal Privacy Act of 1974, employees of the federal government and federal contractors must be given access to their employment files, which may include performance appraisal data. While this requirement does not currently apply to all employees in the private sector, there are good reasons—aside from the threat of broader legislative coverage—for allowing such access. Most importantly, employees will not trust a system they don't understand. Secrecy will invariably breed suspicion and thereby thwart efforts to obtain employee participation.

For the many appraisal systems that are designed to improve performance, withholding appraisal results would be unthinkable. Employees simply could not perform better without having access to this information. Also, permitting employees to review appraisal results allows them to detect any errors that may have been made. Or the employee may simply disagree with the evaluation and may want to challenge it formally.

Due Process

In connection with a formal challenge, ensuring due process is vital. A formal procedure should be developed—if one doesn't exist—to permit employees to appeal appraisal results that they consider inaccurate or unfair. They must have a procedure for pursuing their grievances and having them addressed objectively.

A review of court cases makes it clear that perfect appraisals are not expected from employers. Nor is it anticipated that supervisory discretion should be removed from the process. However, the courts normally require the following:

1. *Either the absence of adverse impact on member of certain groups or validation of the process.* As with the selection process, an unvalidated

---

[31] Largent Parks, Jr., "Appraising Personnel Appraisals," *National Underwriters* (August 27, 1983), p. 13.

performance appraisal system has the potential to have a negative impact on members of certain groups.
2. *A review process that prevents one manager from directing or controlling a subordinate's career.* The performance appraisal should be reviewed and approved by someone or some group higher in the organization.
3. *The rater must have personal knowledge and contact with the employee's job performance.* This requirement may appear to be too obvious but there are instances where the rater does not have an adequate opportunity to observe employee performance. When this situation exists, the chances of a valid appraisal are virtually zero.
4. *The use of formal appraisal criteria that limit the manager's discretion.*[32] A system is needed that forces managers to base evaluations on certain preestablished criteria.

■ LEGAL IMPLICATIONS

An estimated 30 million workers had their performance formally appraised during a single year in the 1980s. Thus appraisals are widely used in industry and government. Yet, the process still contains many potential sources for error.[33] Mistakes in appraising performance can have serious repercussions in various areas of human resource management, such as the improper allocation of money for merit increases. In addition, mistakes can result in costly legal action brought against a firm. In settling cases, courts have held employers liable for back pay, court costs, and other costs related to training and promoting certain group members. The four most common forms of human resource actions that lead to Age Discrimination in Employment Act (ADEA) complaints are promotions, layoffs, retirements, and discharges. A study that analyzed 26 ADEA cases decided in federal courts where employee appraisal had been a determinative factor found that employers with formal appraisal systems were successful 73 percent of the time. However, employers who did not use a formal system were successful defendants only 40 percent of the time.[34]

The courts continue to emphasize the requirement for specifically relating performance appraisal factors to actual job content. In *Wade* v. *Mississippi Cooperative Extension Service*, the 5th Circuit Court ruled that in a performance appraisal system general characteristics such as "leadership, public acceptance, attitude toward people, appearance and grooming, personal conduct, outlook on life, ethical habits, resourcefulness, capacity for growth, mental alertness, loyalty to organization" are "susceptible to partiality and to the personal taste, whim, or fancy of the evaluator." The court also held that such characteristics are "patently subjective in form and

---

[32] Patricia Linenberger and Timothy J. Keaveny, "Performance Appraisal Standards Used by the Courts," *Personnel Administrator*, 26 (May 1981), p. 94.

[33] N. B. Winstanley, William H. Holley, and Hubert S. Field, "Will Your Performance Appraisal System Hold Up in Court?" *Personnel*, 59 (January–February 1982), pp. 59–64.

[34] Michael H. Schuster and Christopher S. Miller, "Performance Appraisal and the Age Discrimination in Employment Act," *Personnel Administrator*, 29 (March 1984), pp. 48–57.

obviously susceptible to completely subjective treatment" by those conducting the appraisals. The key point in this decision is that the trait rating systems are generally suspect because they have no job-content basis. The burden of proof for demonstrating the relationship between a performance appraisal system and actual job content rests entirely with the employer.[35] Despite the *Uniform Guidelines*, one survey indicated that fewer than 50 percent of the companies responding considered these guidelines when designing their performance appraisal systems.[36]

While it is unlikely that any appraisal system will be totally immune to legal challenge, systems that possess the characteristics previously discussed are apparently more legally defensible. At the same time, they can provide a more effective means for achieving performance appraisal goals.

■ THE APPRAISAL INTERVIEW

The Achilles' heel of the entire evaluation process is the appraisal interview itself.[37] In spite of the problems involved, supervisors usually conduct a formal appraisal interview at the end of an employee's appraisal period. This interview is essential if employee development is to be achieved.[38] However, effective performance appraisal systems require more than this single interview. Rather, the supervisor should continually discuss with the employee his or her responsibility for development and improvement and emphasize the manager's supportive role.[39]

A successful appraisal interview requires structure so that both the supervisor and the subordinate will view it as a problem-solving rather than a fault-finding session.[40] The supervisor should consider three basic purposes when planning an appraisal interview: discussing the employee's performance, assisting the employee in setting objectives, and suggesting means for achieving them.[41] For instance, the supervisor might rate a worker average on the factor "quality of production." In the interview, the supervisor should discuss what reasonable improvement during the next appraisal period means. In suggesting ways to achieve a higher level objective, the supervisor might recommend specific methods. The interview should be scheduled soon after the end of the appraisal period. Employees usually know when their interview should take place, and their anxiety tends to increase when it is delayed. Interviews with top performers are often pleasant experiences. However, many supervisors are reluctant to meet face-to-

---

[35] Donald L. Caruth, Robert M. Noe III, and R. Wayne Mondy, *Staffing the Contemporary Organization* (New York: Quorum Books, 1988), p. 58.

[36] Fombrun and Laud, p. 27.

[37] C. O. Colvin, "Everything You Always Wanted to Know about Appraisal Discrimination," *Personnel Journal*, 60 (October 1981), pp. 758–759.

[38] Elizabeth Sidney, "The Assessment Interview," *Management Decision*, 24 (January 1986), p. 33.

[39] John F. Kikoshi and Joseph A. Litterer, "Effective Communication in the Performance Appraisal Interview," *Public Personnel Management Journal*, 12 (Spring 1983), p. 33.

[40] Randall Brett and Alan J. Fredian, "Performance Appraisal: The System Is Not the Solution," *Personnel Administrator*, 26 (December 1981), p. 61.

[41] *Ibid.* p. 62.

face with poor performers. They tend to postpone these anxiety-provoking interviews.

The amount of time devoted to an appraisal interview varies considerably with company policy and the position of the evaluated employee. Although costs must be considered, there is merit in conducting separate interviews for discussing (1) employee performance and development, and (2) pay increases. Many managers have learned that as soon as pay is mentioned in an interview it tends to dominate the conversation. For this reason, a rather common practice is to defer pay discussions. A brief interview for this purpose should be held within one or two weeks after the appraisal interview.

Conducting an appraisal interview is often one of management's more difficult tasks. It requires tact and patience on the part of the supervisor. Praise should be provided when warranted, but it can have only limited value if not clearly deserved. Criticism is especially difficult to give. So-called constructive criticism is often not perceived that way by the employee. Yet, it is difficult for a manager at any level to avoid criticism when conducting appraisal interviews. The supervisor should realize that all individuals have some deficiencies that may not be changed easily, if at all. Continued criticism may lead to frustration and have a damaging effect on employee development. Again, this possibility should not allow undesirable employee behavior to go unnoticed. However, discussions of sensitive issues should focus on the deficiency, not the person. Threats to the employee's self-esteem should be minimized whenever possible.[42]

A serious error that a supervisor sometimes makes is to surprise the subordinate by bringing up some past mistake or problem. For example, if an incident had not been previously discussed, it would be most inappropriate for the supervisor to state, "Two months ago, you failed to properly coordinate your plans for implementing the new accounts receivable procedure." Good management practice and common sense dictate that such situations be dealt with when they occur and not be saved for the appraisal interview.

The entire performance appraisal process should be a positive experience for the employee. In practice, however, it often is not. Negative feelings can often be traced to the appraisal interview and the manner in which it was conducted by the supervisor. Ideally, employees will leave the interview with positive feelings about the supervisor, the company, the job, and themselves. The prospects for improved performance will be bleak if the employee's ego is deflated. Past behavior can't be changed, but future performance can. Specific plans for the employee's development should be clearly outlined and mutually agreed on. Cessna Aircraft Company has developed several hints for supervisors that have been helpful in conducting appraisal interviews (see Figure 11-4).

---

[42] Donald Caruth, Bill Middlebrook, and Frank Rachel, "Performance Appraisals: Much More Than a Once-a-Year Task," *Supervisory Management*, 27 (September 1982), p. 33.

1. Give the employee a few days notice of the discussion and its purpose. Encourage the employee to give some preparatory thought to his or her job performance and development plans. In some cases, have employees read their written performance evaluation prior to the meeting.

2. Prepare notes and use the completed performance appraisal form as a discussion guide so that each important topic will be covered. Be ready to answer questions employees may ask about why you appraised them as you did. Encourage your employees to ask questions.

3. Be ready to suggest specific developmental activities suitable to each employee's needs. When there are specific performance problems, remember to "attack the problem, not the person."

4. Establish a friendly, helpful and purposeful tone at the outset of the discussion. Recognize that it is not unusual for you and your employee to be nervous about the discussion and use suitable techniques to put you both more at ease.

5. Assure your employee that everyone on Cessna's management team is being evaluated so that opportunities for improvement and development will not be overlooked and each person's performance will be fully recognized.

6. Make sure that the session is truly a discussion. Encourage employees to talk about how they feel they are doing on the job, how they might improve, and what developmental activities they might undertake. Often an employee's viewpoints on these matters will be quite close to your own.

7. When your appraisal differs from the employee's, discuss these differences. Sometimes employees have hidden reasons for performing in a certain manner or using certain methods. This is an opportunity to find out if such reasons exist.

8. These discussions should contain both constructive compliments and constructive criticism. Be sure to discuss the employee's strengths as well as weaknesses. Your employees should have clear pictures of how you view their performance when the discussions are concluded.

9. Occasionally the appraisal interview will uncover strong emotions. This is one of the values of regular appraisals; they can bring out bothersome feelings so they can be dealt with honestly. The emotional dimension of managing is very important. Ignoring it can lead to poor performance. Deal with emotional issues when they arise because they block a person's ability to concentrate on other issues. Consult Personnel for help when especially strong emotions are uncovered.

10. Make certain that your employees fully understand your appraisal of their performance. Sometimes it helps to have an employee orally summarize the appraisal as he or she understands it. If there are any misunderstandings they can be cleared up on the spot. Ask questions to make sure you have been fully understood.

11. Discuss the future as well as the past. Plan with the employee specific changes in performance or specific developmental activities that will allow fuller use of potential. Ask what you can do to help.

12. End the discussion on a positive, future-improvement-oriented note. You and your employee are a team, working toward the development of everyone involved.

FIGURE 11-4 | Suggestions for Conducting Appraisal Interviews

Source: Used with the permission of Cessna Aircraft Company.

■ ASSESSMENT CENTERS

Many employee performance appraisal systems evaluate an individual's past performance and at the same time attempt to assess his or her potential for advancement. Other organizations have developed a separate approach for assessing potential. This process often takes place in what is appropriately referred to as an assessment center.

The **assessment center** method requires employees to perform activities similar to those they might encounter in an actual job. These situational activity exercises are based on a thorough job analysis.[43] The assessors usually observe the employees somewhere other than their normal workplace, over a certain period of time. The assessors selected are typically experienced managers who both participate in the exercises and evaluate performance. Assessment centers are used increasingly to (1) identify employees who have higher level management potential; (2) select first-line supervisors; and (3) determine employee developmental needs. Assessment centers are used by more than 1,000 organizations,[44] including small firms and large corporations, such as General Electric Company, J. C. Penney Company, Ford Motor Company, and AT&T. A typical schedule for G.E.'s supervisory assessment center (SAC) is shown in Table 11-5. The SAC program is used for selecting new employees and assessing the management potential of current employees. Note the number of exercises that are utilized in evaluating a participant's behavior.

An evaluation of the General Electric SAC process revealed that:

> The SAC was based on a job analysis of a supervisor's job and is considered to have content validity.[45] The SAC provides all candidates an equal opportunity to demonstrate their skills and does not discriminate against any employee group. For example, a study of more than 1,000 candidates from fourteen company locations showed that the success ratios were acceptable for caucasians, minorities, and women. Those individuals who scored highest in the SAC are the same individuals who have subsequently received the greatest number of job promotions. Thus one area of predictive validity of the SAC was demonstrated.

As many as half a dozen assessors may evaluate each participant, as at General Electric. The participant's position in the organization often determines the amount of time spent in the center. First-line supervisory candidates may only spend a day or two, whereas more time may be needed for those being considered for middle-management and executive jobs. After the session is over, the participants return to their jobs and the assessors prepare their evaluations. Interestingly, because the assessors are often not full-time members of the human resource development staff, they fre-

---

[43] Cabot L. Jaffee and Joseph T. Sefcik, Jr., "What Is an Assessment Center?" *Personnel Administrator*, 25 (February 1980), pp. 40–43.

[44] *General Electric Assessment Center Manual*, General Electric Company.

[45] Content validity is inherent in the assessment center process when the exercises developed are based on job analysis. This type of validity is acceptable according to the *Uniform Guidelines*.

TABLE 11-5 | Typical Schedule for General Electric Company's Supervisory Assessment Center

Day 1

Approximately four hours per candidate are required for the background interview and an in-basket exercise. The interview covers such traditional areas as work experience, educational background, and leadership experience. The in-basket exercise provides an opportunity for the individual to demonstrate how he or she would handle administrative problems including day-to-day "fire-fighting." All Day 1 activities are scheduled on an individual basis and are typically administered by persons in Employee Relations.

Day 2

An additional four hours are devoted to group and individual exercises. Group exercises related to reallocation of resources allow an individual's performance to be observed as the candidate solves problems in peer group situations. In the individual exercises each candidate assumes the role of a supervisor to handle four typical work-related problems. Six operating managers serve as the SAC staff for Day 2 activities. They observe and evaluate the performance of six candidates. The staff completes structured rating forms on each candidate's performance immediately following each exercise. After all exercises have been completed and the candidates dismissed, the staff conducts an overall evaluation of each individual's potential for a supervisory position. Over fifty pieces of data from each candidate's performance are reviewed along with information obtained from the interview. The staff then arrives at a consensus decision and a recommended course of action for each candidate.

Source: Used with permission of the General Electric Company.

quently gain further insight into how managers in their organization should function. And even though a primary purpose of assessment centers is to identify management potential, the J. C. Penney experience indicates that the "participants gain valuable insights into their own strengths, weaknesses, and interests." These insights permit management and the individual to make plans for the employee's development.

■ HUMAN RESOURCE DEVELOPMENT IN MULTINATIONAL CORPORATIONS

As we mentioned earlier, a key purpose of employee performance appraisal is human resource development. A firm's success and even survival depend on having competent and well-trained employees at every level of the organization. Performance appraisal systems serve the function of pointing out specific areas where training and development are needed. This role assumes even greater importance in the international arena. For example, human resource development needs are often quite different for multinational corporations. Career development is helped or hindered by the internal and external factors affecting the firm. The performance appraisal process should reflect the unique culture of the host country as well as the needs of the firm.

Human Resource Development

Only a few multinational corporations offer formal training programs to prepare people to live and work overseas. People who were regarded as superior employees have often failed because they were ill-equipped to cope with the complexities and dangers of intercultural management.[46] A review of placement decisions of some American multinational corporations found that they reported 30 percent of their placements to be mistakes—primarily because of the employees' failure to adjust properly to a new culture.[47] Companies that do offer training to expatriate employees generally provide training that is not comprehensive.[48] The duration of cross-cultural training programs tends to be relatively short, considering the amount of knowledge and skills that need to be taught. Also, spouses tend to be left out of whatever training is offered by the company. However, multinational corporations are beginning to study how different cultures communicate and work with each other.[49]

A major objective of intercultural training is to help people cope with unexpected events in a new culture. It is essential that the person chosen is suitable for cross-cultural work. The most senior person or the person with the most technical competence may not have such skills.[50] An individual overwhelmed by a new culture will be unable to perform effectively. Moreover, someone who is poorly prepared may inadvertently offend or alienate a foreign host and perhaps jeopardize existing long-term relations with a host country.[51] Training should be sufficient to permit the person selected (and spouse) to understand the new culture and adapt to their anticipated roles.[52]

---

[46] Michael Berger, "Building Bridges over the Cultural Rivers," *International Management*, 42 (July–August 1987), p. 61.

[47] P. Christopher Earley, "Intercultural Training for Managers: A Comparison of Documentary and Interpersonal Methods," *Academy of Management Journal*, 30 (4) (December 1987), p. 685.

[48] Mark E. Mendenhall, Edward Dunbar, and Gary R. Oddou, "Expatriate Selection, Training and Career-Pathing: A Review and Critique," *Human Resource Management*, 26 (Fall 1987), pp. 331–345.

[49] Berger, p. 61.

[50] Prabhu Guptara, "Searching the Organization for the Cross-Cultural Operators," *International Management*, 41 (August 1986), p. 40.

[51] Earley, p. 685.

[52] *Ibid*.

Career Development

Foreign assignments have often been thought of as providing career advancement opportunities. However, the relationship between expatriation and career development and advancement is often unclear. The impetus for overseas assignment seems to come more from meeting immediate human resource needs than creating an integrated career development strategy for future corporate executives.[53]

Whatever the case, without generous support during the overseas assignment, employees can become demoralized, frustrated, and anxious.[54] Despite a company's intention to provide career advancement opportunities, skilled managers assigned to foreign operations may ultimately perceive that their careers have suffered. Some managers have returned from foreign assignments to find no job available, or they have been given jobs that do not utilize the skills they obtained overseas. To solve this problem, a "godfather" system has been set up in companies such as Control Data Corporation.[55] Before someone leaves on assignment, a specific executive is appointed godfather to look after the person's interests while he or she is in a foreign country and to help the person achieve a smooth transition upon returning home. A repatriation plan is worked out, including the duration of the assignment and the job to which the appointee will return. Ordinarily the godfather is the person's future boss. During the overseas assignment, the individual is kept informed of major events occurring in the unit that he or she will be assigned to in the future. Not only is a logical career plan worked out, there is no feeling of being lost in the vast international shuffle of the company.

Some repatriated managers say that the overseas assignment is a haphazard, ill-planned affair that usually accompanies vertical advancement. Yet upon return, many have difficulty readjusting to domestic operations, have less self-esteem, and, on occasion, have to look for a new job. Human resource professionals who are unaware of the challenges facing the repatriated manager may unknowingly allow career obstacles to persist for the expatriate.

There is a need to assist the expatriate manager in career development. By putting in place policies and procedures toward that end, an organization can both more efficiently manage human resources globally and encourage more employees to accept foreign assignments. The fundamental nature of such a system must be comprehensive; that is, the emphasis should not be solely on predeparture activities. The ideal international career management program should assess (and give feedback on and preparation for) career and skill issues prior to departure, during the assignment, and subsequent to repatriation.[56]

---

[53] Mendenhall, Dunbar, and Oddou, p. 331.

[54] Phillip R. Harris, "Employees Abroad: Maintain the Corporate Connection," *Personnel Journal*, 65 (August 1986), p. 108.

[55] David M. Noer, "Integrating Foreign Service Employees to Home Organization: The Godfather Approach," *Personnel Journal*, 53 (January 1974), pp. 45–50.

[56] Mendenhall, Dunbar, and Oddou, p. 331.

Performance Appraisal

Failure to develop highly flexible standards for performance evaluations of the expatriate manager may result in the manager viewing his role as undefined and dysfunctional. Present performance evaluations focus on personality traits, communication skills, belief in mission, and organizational structure, but fail to focus on the overall performance of an expatriate manager after arrival in a host country.[57] The performance evaluation system may need to be completely rethought and rewritten with regard to individuals working for multinational corporations.

SUMMARY

Performance appraisal is a system that provides a periodic review and evaluation of an individual's job performance. The overriding purpose of performance appraisal is to improve the organization's effectiveness. Identification of specific objectives provides the starting point for the performance appraisal process. Because an appraisal system cannot serve all purposes, a firm should select those specific objectives it desires to achieve. Next, workers must understand what is expected of them on the job. Supervisors normally discuss with employees the major duties contained in their job descriptions.

Work performance is observed and periodically evaluated against previously established job performance standards. The results of the evaluation are then discussed with the workers. The performance evaluation interview serves to reestablish job requirements in the employee's mind. The process is dynamic and ongoing. The human resource department is responsible for designing and overseeing the performance appraisal process. The person who actually conducts performance appraisals varies from company to company. However, direct participation by line management is necessary for success. The actual rating of the employee may be done by the immediate supervisor (most commonly), subordinates, peers, group appraisal, self-appraisal, and combinations of these methods.

Performance appraisal methods include (1) rating scales, (2) critical incidents, (3) essay, (4) work standards, (5) ranking, (6) forced distribution, (7) forced-choice and weighted checklist performance reports, (8) behaviorally anchored rating scales, and (9) management by objectives. Problems associated with these performance appraisal methods include lack of objectivity, halo error, leniency, central tendency, recent behavior bias, personal bias, and the judgmental role of the evaluator ("playing God").

At the end of the appraisal period, the evaluator usually conducts a formal appraisal interview with the employee. The key to a successful inter-

---

[57] Gurudutt M. Baliga and James C. Baker, "Multinational Corporate Policies for Expatriate Managers: Selection, Training, Evaluation," *SAM Advanced Management Journal*, 50 (Autumn 1985), p. 36.

view is to structure it so that both the manager and subordinate will approach it as a problem-solving, rather than a fault-finding, session. This interview is essential for achieving employee development.

Certain appraisal system practices have successfully withstood legal challenges. Because improperly constituted systems can result in costly legal action against a firm, appraisal systems should be based on job content.

Many employee performance appraisal systems evaluate past performance and at the same time attempt to assess potential for advancement. Other organizations have developed a separate approach for assessing potential: the assessment center. The assessment center method requires employees to perform activities similar to those that they might confront in an actual job. Assessment centers are being used increasingly for (1) identifying employees who have higher level management potential; (2) selecting first-line supervisors; and (3) determining employees' developmental needs.

Human resource development requirements are somewhat different for multinational corporations. Training and development, career development, and performance appraisal needs must be carefully evaluated to ensure proper reentry into the domestic workforce.

Questions for Review

1. State and briefly discuss the basic purposes of performance appraisal.
2. What are the basic steps in the performance appraisal process?
3. Briefly describe the various alternatives for who should conduct performance appraisal.
4. Briefly describe each of the following methods of performance appraisal:
   a. Rating scales
   b. Critical incidents
   c. Essay
   d. Work standards
   e. Ranking
   f. Forced distribution
   g. Forced-choice and weighted checklists
   h. Behaviorally anchored rating scales
   i. Management by objectives
5. What are the various problems associated with performance appraisal? Briefly describe each.
6. Why should employee performance and development be discussed separately from pay increases?
7. Describe how an assessment center could be used as a means of performance appraisal.
8. What are the characteristics of an effective appraisal system?

Terms for Review

Performance appraisal (PA)
Group appraisal
Rating scales method
Critical incident method
Essay method
Work standards method
Ranking method
Paired comparison
Forced distribution method
Forced-choice performance report

Weighted checklist performance report
Behaviorally anchored rating scale (BARS) method
Halo error
Leniency
Strictness
Central tendency
Assessment center

INCIDENT 1 ■ Objectives? ■

It was performance appraisal time again and Alex Funderburk knew that he would receive a low evaluation. Janet Stevens, Alex's boss, opened the appraisal interview with this comment, "The sales department had a good increase this quarter. Also, departmental expenses are down considerably. But, we are nowhere near accomplishing the ambitious objectives you and I set last quarter." "I know," said Alex. "I thought we were going to make it, though. We would have, too, if we had received that big Simpson order, and if I could have gotten us on the computer a little earlier in the quarter."

"I agree with you, Alex," said Janet. "Do you think we were just too ambitious or do you think there was some way we could have made the Simpson sale and speeded up the computerization process?" "Yes," replied Alex, "we could have received the Simpson order this quarter. I just made a couple of concessions to Simpson and their purchasing manager tells me he can issue the order next week. The delay with the computer was caused by a thoughtless mistake I made. I won't let that happen again."

The discussion continued for about thirty minutes longer. Alex discovered that Janet was going to mark him very high in all areas despite his failure to accomplish the goals they had set.

Prior to the meeting, Janet had planned to suggest that the unattained goals for last period be set as the new objectives for the coming quarter. After she and Alex had discussed matters, however, they both decided to establish new, somewhat higher objectives. As he was about to leave the meeting, Alex said, "Janet, I feel good about these objectives, but I don't believe we have more than a 50 percent chance of accomplishing them." "I believe you can do it," replied Janet. "If you knew for sure, though, they wouldn't be high enough." "I see what you mean," said Alex, as he left the office.

Questions

1. What was wrong or right with Janet's appraisal of Alex's performance?
2. Should the new objectives be higher or lower than they are? Explain.

INCIDENT 2 — Performance Appraisal?

As the production supervisor for Sweeny Electronics, Mike Mahoney was generally well thought of by most of his subordinates. Mike was an easygoing individual who tried to help his employees anyway he could. If a worker needed a small loan until payday, he would dig into his pocket with no questions asked. Should an employee need some time off to attend to a personal problem, he would not dock the individual's pay; rather, he would take up the slack himself until the worker returned.

Everything had been going smoothly, at least until the last performance appraisal period. One of Mike's workers, Bill Overstreet had been experiencing a large number of personal problems for the past year. Bill's wife had been sick much of the time and her medical expenses were high. Bill's son had a speech impediment and the doctors had recommended a special clinic. Bill, who had already borrowed the limit the bank would loan, had become upset and despondent over his general circumstances.

When it was time for Bill's annual performance appraisal, Mike decided he was going to do as much as possible to help him. Although Bill could not be considered more than an average worker, Mike rated him outstanding in virtually every category. Because the firm's compensation system was tied heavily to the performance appraisal, Bill would be eligible for a merit increase of 10 percent in addition to a regular cost of living raise.

Mike explained to Bill why he was giving him such high ratings and Bill acknowledged that his performance had really been no better than average. Bill was very grateful and expressed this to Mike. As Bill left the office he was excitedly looking forward to telling his friends about what a wonderful boss he had. Seeing Bill smile as he left gave Mike a warm feeling.

Questions

1. From Sweeny Electronic's standpoint, what difficulties might Mike Mahoney's performance appraisal practices create?
2. What can Mike do now to diminish the negative impact of his evaluation of Bill?

Experiencing Human Resource Management

Performance appraisal (PA) is an essential aspect of human resource management. It is a formal system that provides a periodic review and evaluation of an individual's job performance. Developing an effective performance appraisal system is difficult. However, some managers do not take PA as seriously as they should. Such attitudes are counterproductive and frequently lower individual and group productivity.

Larry Beavers, supervisor of the electrical department, has a busy day scheduled, but he needs to squeeze in the last of his performance appraisals. They are due today, and he has only got one more signature to get. Upon arriving for work he thinks, "I hate doing performance appraisals. It is the worst part of a supervisor's job. But, it does allow me to point out deficiencies that the workers must be aware of if they are to improve their performance. The guy I'm appraising today has always exceeded his quotas, he is very helpful to the workers he likes, and is excellent on the new computerized production setup; but if he wants to advance he will need to change his behavior. He seems to have problems working with the females on the line, and doesn't seem to be very open minded. Also, on September 23rd he failed to secure his work area. This guy really has problems. Maybe our talk will do some good; either way I need to get this done. On the positive side, this is the last performance appraisal until next year."

Today is the day that Alex Martin gets his performance appraisal and he is excited about it. Before the meeting with Larry, his supervisor, he thinks, "I've been very good on the new computerized setup, and very helpful to my friends on the line, and this will help me get my promotion. I expect that the boss saved my performance appraisal for last to praise my performance and recommend me for that promotion that I've been deserving for some time. I've been passed over for promotion for too long, this has been a great year for me, and this will cap off a year of excellent performance."

When these two get together it will be a meeting of two quite different minds, and in all likelihood the meeting will be filled with disagreement and dissatisfaction, and maybe even hard feelings. This exercise will require two of you to actively participate. One person will play the supervisor conducting the performance appraisal and the other will be the evaluated employee. Only two can play; the rest of you observe carefully. Your instructor will provide the participants with additional information necessary to complete the exercise.

REFERENCES

Baird, Lloyd S., Richard W. Beatty, and Craig Eric Schneier. *The Performance Appraisal Sourcebook* (Amherst, Mass.: Human Resource Development Press, 1982).

Banks, C. G., and L. Roberson. "Performance Appraisers as Test Developers." *Academy of Management Review*, 10 (January 1985), pp. 128–142.

Brett, Randall, and Alan J. Fredian. "Performance Appraisal: The System Is Not the Solution." *Personnel Administrator*, 26 (December 1981), pp. 61–68.

Caruth, Donald L., Robert M. Noe III, and R. Wayne Mondy. *Staffing the Contemporary Organization* (Westport, Conn.: Quorum Books, 1988).

Dipboye, R. L. "Some Neglected Variables in Research on Discrimination in Appraisals." *Academy of Management Review*, 10 (January 1985), pp. 115–127.

Edwards, M. R., and J. R. Sproull. "Making Performance Appraisals Perform: The Use of Team Evaluation." *Personnel*, 62 (March 1985), pp. 28–32.

Gehrman, Douglas B. "Beyond Today's Compensation and Performance Appraisal Systems." *Personnel Administrator*, 29 (March 1984), pp. 21–27.

Gordon, R. F. "Does Your Performance Appraisal System Really Work?" *Supervisory Management*, 30 (February 1985), pp. 37–41.

Harris, Phillip R. "Employees Abroad: Maintain the Corporate Connection." *Personnel Journal*, 86 (August 1986), pp. 108–110.

Holley, William H., and Hubert S. Field. "Will Your Performance Appraisal System Hold Up in Court?" *Personnel*, 59 (January–February 1982), pp. 59–64.

Jacobs, R., and S. W. J. Kozlowski. "A Closer Look at Halo Error in Performance Ratings." *Academy of Management Journal*, 28 (March 1985), pp. 201–212.

Lanza, P. "Team Appraisals." *Personnel Journal*, 64 (March 1985), pp. 46–51.

Lee, C. "Increasing Performance Appraisal Effectiveness: Matching Task Types, Appraisal Process, and Rater Training." *Academy of Management Review*, 10 April 1985), pp. 322–331.

Matejka, J. Kenneth, and Richard J. Dunsing. "Great Expectations." *Management World,* 16 (January 1987), pp. 16–19.

Mendenhall, Mark E., Edward Dunbar, and Gary R. Oddou. "Expatriate Selection, Training and Career-Pathing: A Review and Critique." *Human Resource Management*, 26 (Fall 1987), pp. 331–345.

Mondy, R. Wayne, Robert M. Noe III, and Robert E. Edwards. "What the Staffing Function Entails." *Personnel*, 63 (April 1986), pp. 55–58.

Nathan, B. R., and R. A. Alexander. "The Role of Inferential Accuracy in Performance Rating." *Academy of Management Review*, 10 (January 1985), pp. 109–115.

Schuster, D. V. "Performance Recognition: The Power of Positive Feedback." *Training*, 22 (January 1985), pp. 69ff.

Schuster, Michael H., and Christopher S. Miller. "Performance Appraisal and the Age Discrimination in Employment Act." *Personnel Administrator*, 29 (March 1984), pp. 48–58.

Sidney, Elizabeth. "The Assessment Interview." *Management Decision*, 24 (January 1986), pp. 33–36.

Slattery, P. D. "Performance Appraisals Without Stress." *Personnel Journal*, 64 (February 1985), pp. 49–50ff.

Taylor, Robert L., and Robert A. Zawaki. "Trends in Performance Appraisal: Guidelines for Managers." *Personnel Administrator*, 29 (March 1984), pp. 71–76.

White R. N. "Corrective Action: A Treatment Plan for Problem Performers." *Personnel*, 62 (February 1985), pp. 7–9.

Woods, J. G., and T. Dillion. "The Performance Reveiw Approach to Improving Productivity." *Personnel*, 62 (March 1985), pp. 20–27.

PART THREE

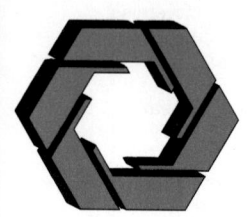

CASE

Parma Cycle Company: Training the Workforce

As the September 1988 date for the new plant opening drew near, Mary Higgins, director of employee development at Parma Cycle Company in Parma, Ohio, grew increasingly nervous. With only six months to train the workforce for the new Clarksdale, Mississippi, plant, Mary knew that there was little room for error.

Mary had already arranged to lease a building near the Clarksdale factory site, and some of the machinery for the new plant was being installed in that building for training purposes. Most of the machinery was similar to that being used at Parma, and Mary had selected trainers from among the supervisory staff at the Parma plant. One machine, however, a robotized frame assembler, was entirely new. The assembler was being purchased from a Japanese firm. Mary had sent two operators to train in the Japanese factory and they were both back.

In connection with all this activity, Mary had personally made two trips to Clarksdale. She had also retained a training consultant, a management professor from the University of Mississippi. The training consultant had agreed to help Mary plan the training program and to evaluate the program as it went along. It was at the consultant's suggestion that Mary decided to use a combination of vestibule training and classroom lectures in developing a trained workforce prior to factory start-up time. In the past, Parma Cycle had used on-the-job training almost exclusively. This approach wasn't feasible, she felt, at the new plant.

As Mary was thinking about how short the time was, the phone rang. It was the human resource director, Jesse Heard, telling her that he was ready for their meeting. When she got to his office she found him studying a training report she had prepared a few days earlier. "Mary," said Jesse, "It looks like you have things well under control for the Clarksdale plant. But I don't see anything here about training the workers who are going to be transferred down from this plant." "Well," said Mary, "they have all been working in bicycle manufacture for quite a while. I thought it might not be necessary to have any formal training for them." "That's true," said Jesse, "but most of them will be taking different jobs when they move to Clarksdale." "I'll get on it right away," said Mary.

"What are we going to do about supervisory training at the Clarksdale plant?" asked Jesse. Mary replied, "I think we'll use the same system we use here for the long haul. We'll bring our supervisors up through the ranks and have quarterly off-site seminars. To start, the supervisors who move down from Parma can help train the others." Jesse asked, "What do you think about bringing the supervisors hired in Clarksdale up here for a few days to help them learn how we do things?" "That's a good idea," said Mary. "We can pair them off with some of our better people at Parma."

"That won't help us with performance evaluations, Mary," said Jesse. "You know we're going to use a different system down there. We've decided to use management by objectives down to the supervisory level and a new three-item rating scale for the workers." "I know," answered Mary. "I'd planned classroom training on that beginning the month after start-up at the Clarksdale plant. I'm going to conduct those sessions myself. Because the performance scores will be used to allocate incentive bonuses, I want to make sure they are consistently assigned."

"Mary," said Jesse, "I'm really impressed with the way you are taking charge of our training effort for the Clarksdale plant. Just keep up the good work." "Thank you, Jesse," said Mary. "I'll get back to you next week on the training I recommend for the workers who will transfer down from Parma."

Questions

1. Describe how an untrained person hired in Clarksdale could become a competent machine operator by the time the new plant opens.
2. Do you think Mary needed the training consultant? Why or why not?
3. What do you think of Jesse's idea to have the supervisors for the new plant trained by those transferred from Ohio? Explain your answer.

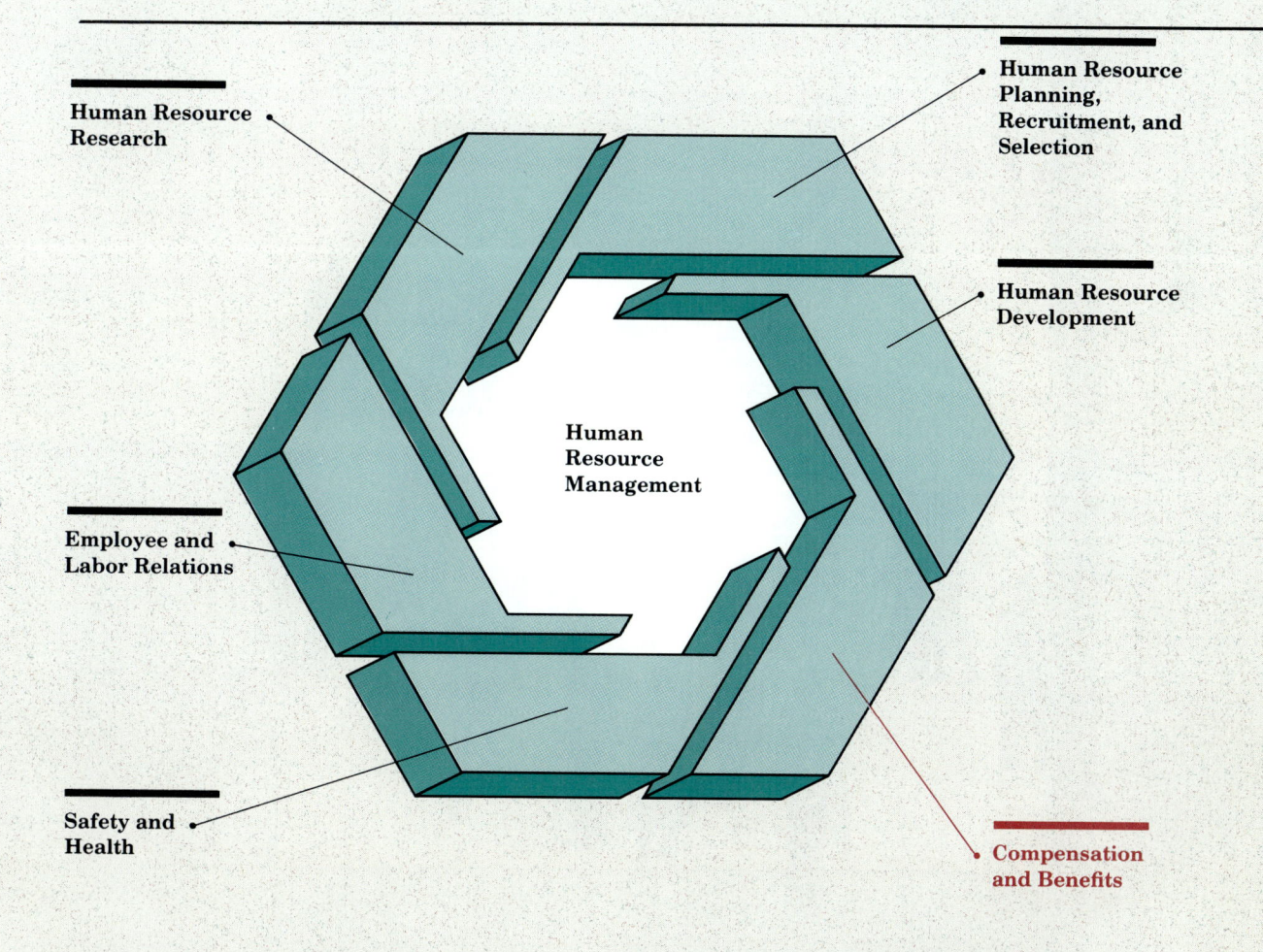

P·A·R·T F·O·U·R

COMPENSATION AND BENEFITS

- Human Resource Research
- Human Resource Planning, Recruitment, and Selection
- Human Resource Development
- Employee and Labor Relations
- Safety and Health
- Compensation and Benefits

Human Resource Management

CHAPTER 12   FINANCIAL COMPENSATION

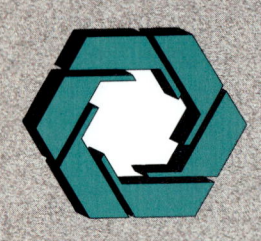

Chapter Objectives

1. Define compensation and explain the concept of compensation equity.
2. Describe the organization and the labor market as determinants of financial compensation.
3. Define job evaluation and describe the basic job evaluation methods.
4. Describe the employee as a determinant of financial compensation and explain the factors associated with job pricing.
5. Describe the compensation issues of comparable worth, pay secrecy, and pay compression.

■ Earl Lewis and his wife are full of excitement and anticipation as they leave their home for a shopping trip. Earl recently found a job after several weeks of unemployment, and the paycheck he received today will enable them to make a down payment on a much needed refrigerator.

■ Inez Scoggin's anxiety over scheduled minor surgery was somewhat relieved. Her supervisor has assured her that 90 percent of her medical and hospitalization costs will be covered by her firm's health insurance plan.

■ Trig Ekeland, executive director of the local YMCA, returns home dead tired from his job each evening no earlier than six o'clock. His salary is small compared with the salaries of many other local managers who have similar responsibilities. Yet, Trig is an exceptionally happy person who believes that his work with youth, civic leaders, and other members of the community is extremely important and worthwhile.

■ Joanne Abrahamson has been employed by a large manufacturing firm for eight years. Although her pay is not what she would like it to be, her job in the accounts payable department enables her to have contact with some of her best friends. She likes her supervisor and considers the overall working environment to be great. Joanne would not trade jobs with anyone she knows.

Compensation and benefits are obviously important to Earl Lewis and Inez Scoggin, as they are to most employees. However, for Trig and Joanne, other factors in a total compensation package assume even greater importance. These components include a pleasant work environment and job satisfaction. Because it has many elements, compensation administration is one of the most difficult and challenging areas confronting human resource professionals.

We begin this chapter with an overview of compensation and an explanation of compensation equity. Next, we discuss determinants of individual financial compensation. We then present the organization, the labor market, and the job as determinants of financial compensation. Next, we address job evaluation and the employee as determinants of financial compensation. We devote the final portion of the chapter to job pricing and other compensation issues. We leave a discussion of benefits, as well as nonfinancial factors, to Chapter 13.

■ COMPENSATION: AN OVERVIEW

Compensation refers to every type of reward that individuals receive in return for their labor. The components of a total compensation program are shown in Figure 12-1. **Direct financial compensation** consists of the pay that a person receives in the form of wages, salaries, bonuses, and commissions. Earl Lewis has just received direct financial compensation in the form of his paycheck. **Indirect financial compensation** (benefits) includes all financial rewards that are not included in direct compensation. Inez Scoggin will receive indirect financial compensation because her company pays 90 percent of all medical and hospital costs. As you can see in Figure 12-1, this form of compensation includes a wide variety of rewards that are normally received indirectly by the employee.

Nonfinancial compensation consists of the satisfaction that a person receives from the job itself or from the psychological and/or physical environment in which the person works. Trig Ekeland and Joanne Abrahamson are receiving important forms of nonfinancial compensation. Trig is extremely satisfied with the job he performs. This type of nonfinancial compensation consists of the satisfaction received from performing meaningful job-related tasks. Joanne's job permits her to have contacts with close friends. This form of nonfinancial compensation involves the psychological and/or physical environment in which the person works.

All such rewards comprise a total compensation program. People have different reasons for working, and the most appropriate compensation package depends on those reasons. When individuals are responsible for providing food, shelter, and clothing for their families, money may well be the most important reward. However, some people work many hours each day, receive little pay, and yet love their work. To a large degree, adequate compensation is in the mind of the receiver. It is often more than the financial compensation received in the form of a paycheck. An organization's viewpoint was summarized by Richard G. Jamison, director of compensation for Rockwell International, when he stated in Executive Insights, "Compensation has a direct and important impact on the bottom line of company results."

■ COMPENSATION EQUITY

Organizations must attract, motivate, and retain competent employees. In doing so, firms strive for equity in their compensation systems. **Equity** is workers' perceptions that they are being treated fairly. Compensation must

CHAPTER 12 Financial Compensation

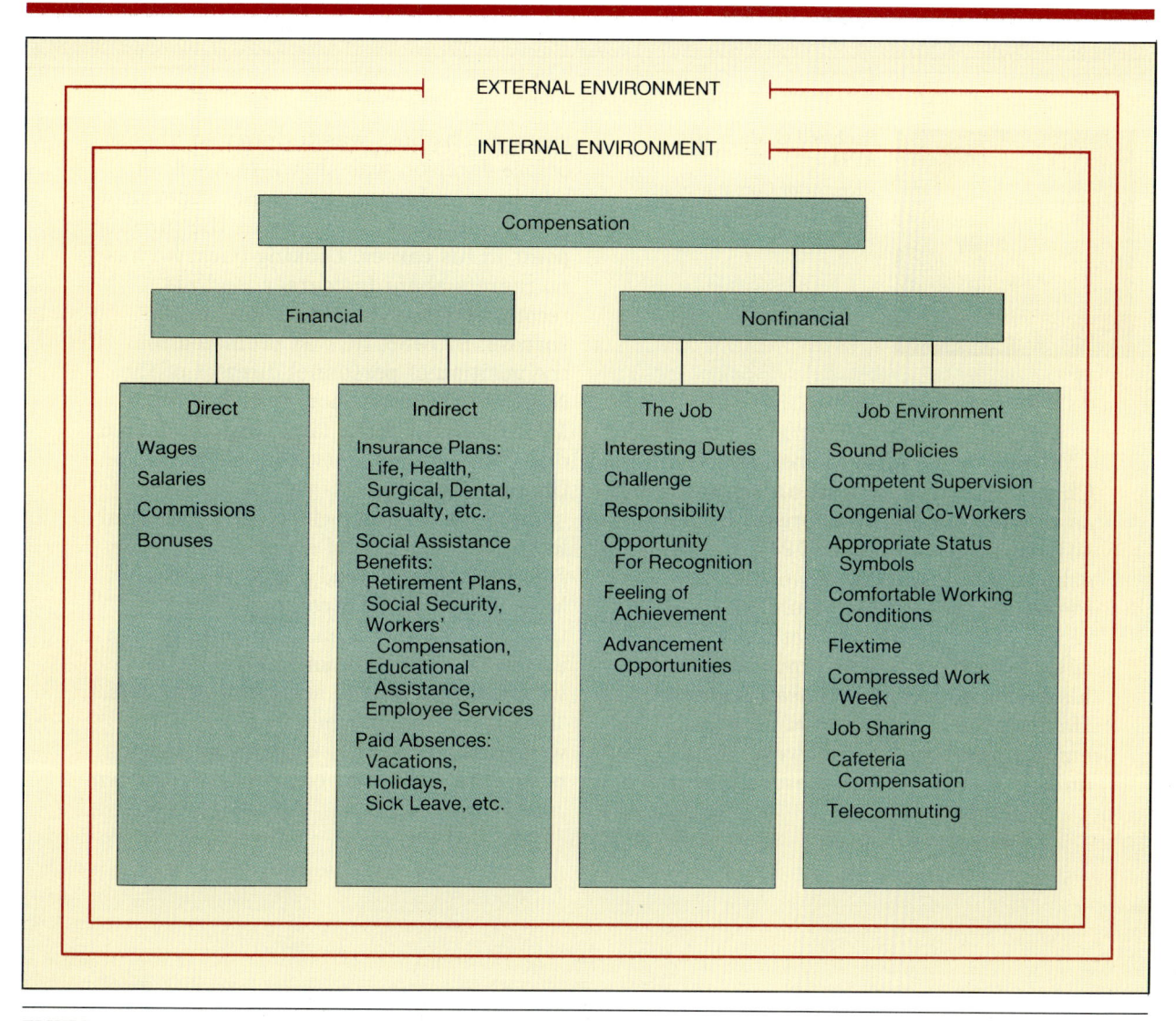

```
                    EXTERNAL ENVIRONMENT
                    INTERNAL ENVIRONMENT

                         Compensation
                    ┌─────────┴─────────┐
                 Financial          Nonfinancial
                ┌────┴────┐         ┌────┴────┐
              Direct   Indirect   The Job   Job Environment
```

Direct	Indirect	The Job	Job Environment
Wages	Insurance Plans: Life, Health, Surgical, Dental, Casualty, etc.	Interesting Duties	Sound Policies
Salaries		Challenge	Competent Supervision
Commissions	Social Assistance Benefits: Retirement Plans, Social Security, Workers' Compensation, Educational Assistance, Employee Services	Responsibility	Congenial Co-Workers
Bonuses		Opportunity For Recognition	Appropriate Status Symbols
		Feeling of Achievement	Comfortable Working Conditions
		Advancement Opportunities	Flextime
	Paid Absences: Vacations, Holidays, Sick Leave, etc.		Compressed Work Week
			Job Sharing
			Cafeteria Compensation
			Telecommuting

FIGURE 12-1 | Components of a Total Compensation Program

be fair to all parties concerned and be perceived as fair.[1] When chief executives are paid in excess of $26 million in one year[2] and receive huge bonuses along with "golden parachutes," serious questions arise as to what constitutes fairness within an organization.

External equity exists when a firm's employees are paid comparably to those who perform similar jobs in other firms. Compensation surveys enable organizations to determine the extent to which external equity is present.

---

[1] Thomas R. Horton, "80s Style Compensation," *Credit and Financial Management*, 89 (November 1987), p. 10.

[2] "Who Made the Most—and Why," *Business Week* (May 2, 1988), p. 51.

Executive Insights

Richard G. Jamison, APD

Director of Compensation, Rockwell International Corporation

Richard G. Jamison joined the Vick Chemical Division of Richardson-Merrell as a co-op student from Drexel University. Upon graduation in 1953, he was asked, "Would you mind working in Personnel for a while?" Jamison remembers that he was not terribly enthusiastic about this proposal because his major in college had been statistics. He accepted the position of assistant employment manager, however, and quickly discovered the reason for the request. His boss was terminated almost before Jamison was shown to his desk, and he soon became personnel supervisor for the entire plant. This was the turning point in his career. Looking back, he has no regrets about his career, and his record provides the evidence of his success. In 1956, he was promoted to the position of personnel director of the National Drug Division of Richardson-Merrell. Eight years later, he was named director of compensation and benefits for General Mills.

Jamison joined Rockwell International in 1974 as director of compensation, the position he holds today. In this capacity, he is responsible for compensation throughout the company, including executive compensation. In connection with this specialized area, Jamison says, "Executives know when they perform well. And, when they do, they expect to be rewarded. If your compensation system does this, fine. If not, you will lose your best people."

He believes that the field of compensation is extremely exciting and says, "It has a direct and important impact on the bottom line of company results." When asked about the difficulties a compensation manager might face, he said, "It's managing compensation practices in a multi-industry corporation where the economy is having an adverse affect on one business unit while another is growing. Although internal consistency is desirable, salaries cannot be overmanaged to the point of forcing all units to ignore the competitive demands of their particular business."

Jamison believes that human resources is broadening its scope and that to be a successful practitioner, a person needs a good understanding of the total operations of the business. "We need to avoid becoming so enthralled with our specialty that we lose sight of the total business picture," Jamison says.

Jamison is past president of the Pittsburgh Personnel Association, Philadelphia Chapter of ASPA, and the Twin Cities Personnel Association. He has held several leadership positions within ASPA, including regional vice-president, national treasurer, and national vice-president. He also served as treasurer of the Personnel Accreditation Institute and is the past chairman of the steering committee for the Conference Board Council on Compensation. He is a member of the American Compensation Association. In 1979, Jamison received the Distinguished Service Award at West Virginia University and, in 1984, was given the William W. Winter Memorial Publications Award. He has been elected to Who's Who in Finance and Industry each year since 1977.

Internal equity exists when employees are paid according to the relative value of their jobs within an organization. Job evaluation is a primary means for determining internal equity. **Employee equity** exists when individuals performing similar jobs for the same firm are paid according to factors unique to the employee. The most common factor is employee performance, as determined by performance appraisal.

Inequity in any category can be the source of severe morale problems. Regarding employee equity, for example, suppose that two workers in the same firm are performing similar jobs and one employee is far superior to the other in performance. If both workers receive equal raises, employee equity does not exist and the more productive employee is likely to be unhappy. Many workers are very concerned with pay equity, both internal and external.

■ DETERMINANTS OF INDIVIDUAL FINANCIAL COMPENSATION

As with the other aspects of human resource management, compensation decisions are affected by many factors. The primary determinants of compensation are shown in Figure 12-2. The organization, the labor market, the job, and the employee all have an impact on job pricing and the ultimate determination of an individual's financial compensation.

■ THE ORGANIZATION AS A DETERMINANT OF FINANCIAL COMPENSATION

Managers tend to view financial compensation as both an expense and an asset. It is an expense in the sense that it reflects the cost of labor. In service industries, for example, labor costs account for more than 50 percent of all expenses. However, financial compensation is an asset when it induces employees to put forth their best efforts and to remain in their jobs. Compensation programs have the potential to influence employee work behavior, encouraging workers to be more productive.[3] Improved performance, increased productivity, and lower turnover are sought by all managers, which accounts for the serious attention compensation receives from top management.

Corporate culture has a major influence on an individual's financial compensation. An organization often establishes—formally or informally—compensation policies that determine whether it will be a pay leader or a pay follower, or strive for an average position in the labor market. **Pay leaders** are those organizations that pay higher wages and salaries than competing firms. Such organizations expect to have lower per unit labor costs. They feel that they will be able to attract high-quality, productive

---

[3] George T. Milkovich and Jerry M. Newman, *Compensation*, 2nd ed. (Plano, Texas: Business Publication, 1987), p. 3.

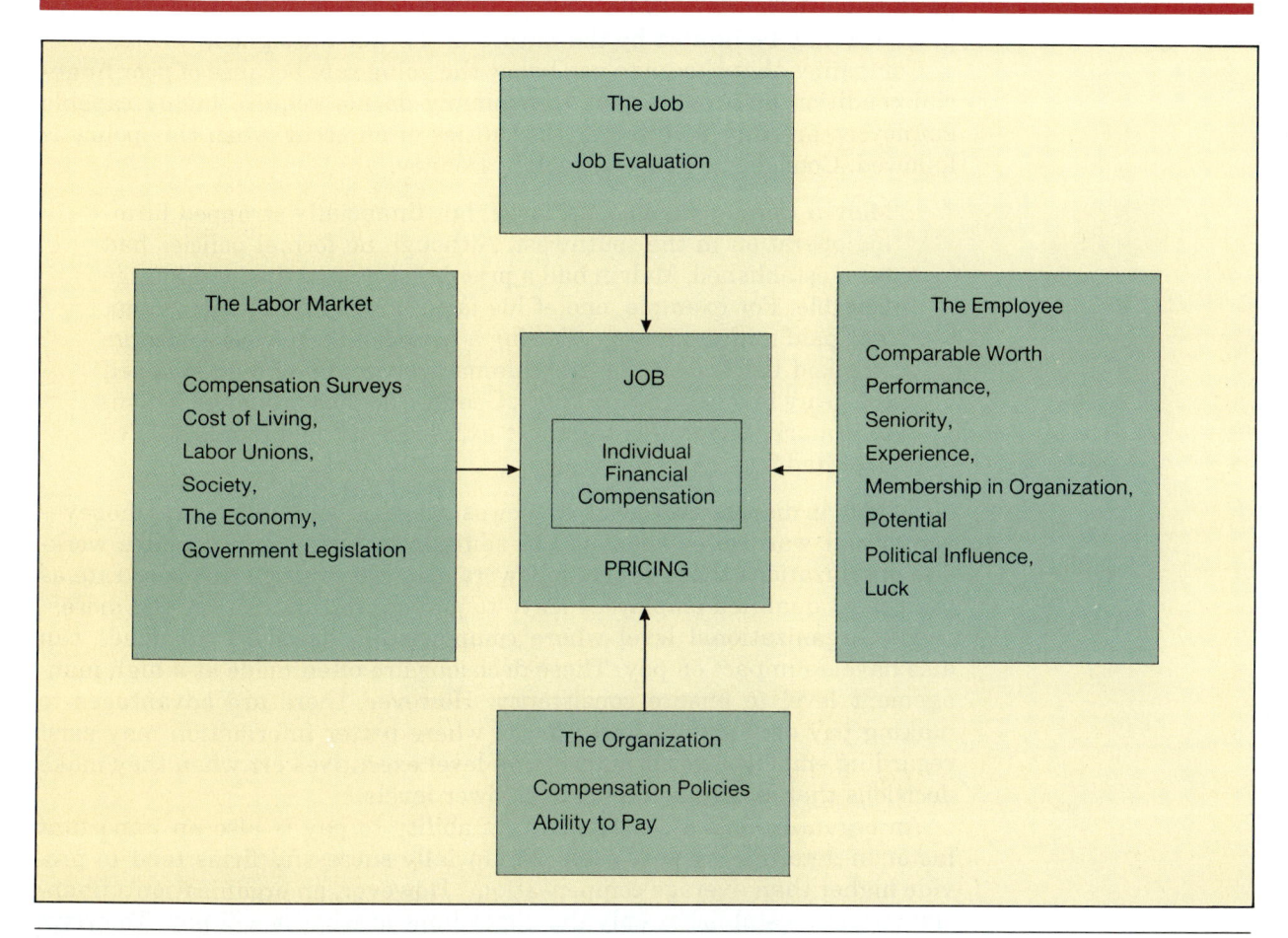

```
                    The Job
                  Job Evaluation

 The Labor Market                              The Employee

 Compensation Surveys         JOB              Comparable Worth
 Cost of Living,                               Performance,
 Labor Unions,              Individual         Seniority,
 Society,                   Financial          Experience,
 The Economy,              Compensation        Membership in Organization,
 Government Legislation                        Potential
                                               Political Influence,
                            PRICING            Luck

                        The Organization
                      Compensation Policies
                         Ability to Pay
```

FIGURE 12-2 | Primary Determinants of Individual Financial Compensation

employees. Higher paying firms usually attract more and better qualified applicants than do lower paying companies in the same industry.[4]

The **going rate** is the average pay that most employers provide for the same job in a particular area or industry. Many organizations have a policy that calls for paying the going rate. In such firms, management believes that it can employ qualified people and still remain competitive by not having to raise the price of goods or services. Employers with this policy may be overlooking the possibility of hiring more proficient workers. Yet, many firms have jobs that require only average employee qualifications. An assembly worker who tightens four bolts every minute and a half is an example. In this situation, an excellent employee may not be any more

---

[4] Gene Milbourn, Jr., "The Relationship of Money and Motivation," *Compensation Review*, 12 (Second Quarter 1980), p. 33.

productive than one with only average ability. Thus a person's productive potential may be limited by the nature of the work assigned.

Companies that choose to pay below the going rate because of poor financial condition or a belief that they simply do not require highly capable employees are **pay followers**. Difficulties often occur when this policy is followed. Consider the case of Melvin Denney.

> Melvin Denney managed a large, but financially strapped farming operation in the southwest. Although no formal policies had been established, Melvin had a practice of paying the lowest wage possible. For example, one of his farm hands, George McMillan, was paid minimum wage. During a period of three weeks, George wrecked the tractor, severely damaged a combine, and stripped the gears in a new pickup truck. George's actions prompted Melvin to remark, "George is the most expensive darned employee I've ever had."

As Melvin discovered, paying the lowest wage possible didn't save money—actually, it was quite expensive. In addition to hiring unproductive workers, organizations that are pay followers may have a high turnover rate as their most qualified employees leave to join organizations that pay more.

The organizational level where compensation decisions are made can also have an impact on pay. These decisions are often made at a high management level to ensure consistency. However, there are advantages to making pay decisions at lower levels where better information may exist regarding employee performance. Top-level executives err when they make decisions that should be handled at lower levels.

An organization's assessment of its ability to pay is also an important factor in determining pay levels. Financially successful firms tend to provide higher than average compensation.[5] However, an organization's financial strength establishes only the upper limit of what it will pay. To arrive at a specific pay level, management must consider other factors.

■ THE LABOR MARKET AS A DETERMINANT OF FINANCIAL COMPENSATION

Potential employees located within the geographical area from which employees are recruited comprise the **labor market**. Labor markets for some jobs extend far beyond the locality of a firm's operations. Human resource management of an aerospace firm in Seattle, for example, may be concerned about the labor market for engineers in Wichita or Orlando. Managerial and professional employees are often recruited from a wide geographical area. In fact, nationwide recruitment isn't unusual for certain skills.

Moreover, pay for jobs within these markets may vary considerably. Secretarial jobs, for example, may carry an average salary of $26,000 per year in a large, urban community but only $12,000 or less in a small, rural town.

---

[5] David W. Belcher and Thomas J. Atchison, *Compensation Administration*, 2nd ed. (Englewood Cliffs, N.J.: Prentice-Hall, 1987), p. 127.

CHAPTER 12 Financial Compensation

Compensation managers must be aware of these differences in order to compete successfully for employees. The going wage, or prevailing rate, is an important guide in determining pay. Many employees view it as the standard for judging the fairness of their firm's compensation practices.

Compensation Survey

Large organizations routinely conduct compensation surveys to determine prevailing pay rates within labor markets. These studies provide information for establishing both direct and indirect compensation. The decisions that must be made prior to conducting a compensation survey include determining (1) the geographic area of the survey, (2) the specific firms to contact, and (3) the jobs to include. The geographic area to be included in the survey is often determined from employment records. Data from this source may indicate maximum distance or time that employees are willing to travel to work. Also, the firms to be contacted in the survey are often from the same industry but may also include others—regardless of industry—that compete for the same skills. Because obtaining data on all jobs in the organization may not be feasible, the human resource department often surveys only key jobs. A **key job** is one that is well known in the company and industry and that can be easily defined.

The primary difficulty in conducting a compensation survey involves determining comparable jobs. Recall that organizing work and designing jobs can be done in many different ways. A job in one company may only roughly resemble a job with a similar title in another. For this reason, job titles have little value in compensation surveys. Instead, the analyst must use well-written job descriptions when requesting compensation data.

There are other ways to obtain compensation data in a given labor market. Some professional organizations periodically conduct surveys. The U.S. Bureau of Labor Statistics also makes yearly surveys and provides data by area, industry, and job type. In addition, a number of journals, such as *Compensation Review* and *Hospital Administration*, report compensation information periodically. Some organizations choose to use other sources, even though they are large enough to afford surveys. Several life insurance companies, for example, use compensation data provided by the Life Office Management Association. They may supplement these data with survey information supplied by Hay Associates, the Society for Human Resource Management, and American Management Association.

Cost of Living

The logic for using cost of living as a pay determinant is simple: When prices rise over a period of time and pay does not, "real pay" is actually lowered. A pay increase must be roughly equivalent to the increased cost of living if a person is to maintain a previous level of real wages. For instance, if someone earns $24,000 during a year in which the average rate of inflation is 5 percent, a $100 per month pay increase will be necessary merely to maintain that person's standard of living.

People living on fixed incomes (primarily the elderly and the poor) are especially hard hit by inflation. But they are not alone; most employees also suffer financially. Recognizing this problem, some organizations index pay increases to the inflation rate. Some firms will sacrifice "merit money" to provide across-the-board increases designed to offset the results of inflation.

Labor Unions

An excerpt from the Wagner Act prescribes the areas of mandatory collective bargaining between management and unions as "wages, hours, and other terms and conditions of employment." These broad bargaining areas obviously have great potential impact on compensation decisions. The union affects company compensation policies in three important areas: (1) the standards used in making compensation decisions, (2) wage differentials, and (3) payment methods.[6]

When a union uses comparable pay as a standard in making compensation demands, the employer must obtain accurate labor market data. When a union emphasizes cost of living, management may be persuaded to include a **cost-of-living allowance (COLA)**. This is an escalator clause in the labor agreement that automatically increases wages as U.S. Bureau of Labor Statistics cost of living index rises.

Unions may also attempt to create, preserve, or even destroy pay differentials between wages for craft workers and unskilled workers. The politics of a given situation will determine the direction taken. For instance, if the unskilled workers have the strongest membership, an attempt may be made to eliminate pay differentials.

Management may want to use incentive plans to encourage greater productivity. However, decisions to implement such plans may be scrapped if the union strongly opposes this approach. Employee acceptance of such a plan is essential for successful implementation, and union opposition may make it unworkable.

Society

Compensation paid to employees often affects a firm's pricing of its goods or services. For this reason, consumers may also be interested in compensation decisions. At times in the past, the government has responded to public opinion and stepped in to encourage business to hold down wages and prices. The process of "jawboning," initiated by President John F. Kennedy in the early 1960s, involved using the prestige of the presidency to informally pressure large companies and unions to hold the line.

Businesses in a given labor market are also concerned with the pay practices of competitors. For instance, when the management of a large

---

[6] Cyril C. Ling, *The Management of Personnel Relations* (Homewood, Ill.: Richard D. Irwin, 1965), pp. 146–151.

electronics firm announced plans to locate a branch plant in a relatively small community, it was confronted by local civic leaders. Their questions largely concerned the wage and salary rates that would be paid. Subtle pressure was applied to keep the company's wages in line with other wages in the community. The electronics firm agreed to begin operations with initial compensation at a lower level than it usually paid. But the firm's management made it clear that a series of pay increases would be given over a period of two years to maintain its own "pay leader" policy.

The Economy

The economy definitely affects financial compensation decisions. For example, a depressed economy generally increases the labor supply. This, in turn, serves to lower the going wage rate. In most cases, the cost of living will rise in an expanding economy. Because the cost of living is commonly used as a pay standard, the economy's health exerts a major impact on pay decisions. Labor unions, government, and society are all less likely to press for pay increases in a depressed economy, but attitudes change as conditions improve.

Legislation

Federal and state laws can also affect the amount of compensation a person receives. We next describe some of the more significant pieces of federal legislation in this area.

Davis–Bacon Act of 1931. The Davis–Bacon Act of 1931 was the first national law to deal with minimum wages. It requires federal construction contractors with projects valued in excess of $2,000 to pay at least the prevailing wages in the area. The Secretary of Labor has the authority to make this determination, and the prevailing wage is often the average local union rate. Davis–Bacon has come under fire, with critics claiming that it has resulted in construction cost overruns approaching 20 percent. Critics have also charged that the act is inflationary and obstructs minority hiring because of its limitation of one apprentice for every three full-time journeymen on a job.[7]

Social Security Act of 1935, as Amended. The Social Security Act established a federal payroll tax to fund unemployment and retirement benefits. The act also set up the Social Security Administration. Employers were required to share equally with employees the cost of old-age, survivors, and disability insurance. Employers were required to pay the full cost of unemployment insurance. Unemployment benefits are paid through agencies in each of the fifty states for a minimum period of twenty-six weeks.

---

[7] George Fowler, "Davis–Bacon Needs a Decent Burial," *Nation's Business*, 67 (March 1979), p. 57.

Walsh–Healy Act of 1936. The Walsh–Healy Act of 1936 requires companies with federal supply contracts exceeding $10,000 to pay prevailing wages. The act differs from the Fair Labor Standards Act in that overtime payment is required for hours worked over forty per week or eight per day.

Fair Labor Standards Act of 1938, as Amended. The most significant law affecting compensation is the Fair Labor Standards Act of 1938 (FLSA). It establishes a minimum wage, requires overtime pay, and provides standards for child labor. This act is administered by the Wage and Hour Division of the U.S. Department of Labor. The basic requirements of the act apply to employees engaged in interstate commerce.[8]

As of January 1986, the act provided for a minimum wage of not less than $3.35 an hour. It also required overtime payment at the rate of one and one-half times the employee's regular rate after forty hours of work in a 168-hour period. Although most organizations and employees are covered by the act, certain classes of employees are specifically exempt from overtime provisions. However, nonexempt employees, many of whom are paid salaries, must receive overtime pay.

Exempt employees are categorized as executive, administrative, and professional employees and outside salespersons. An executive employee is essentially a manager (such as a production manager) with broad authority over subordinates. An administrative employee, while not a manager, occupies an important staff position in an organization and might have a title such as systems analyst or assistant to the president. A professional employee performs work requiring advanced knowledge in a field of learning normally acquired through a prolonged course of specialized instruction. This type of employee might have a title such as company physician, legal counsel, or senior statistician. Outside salespeople sell tangible or intangible items away from the employer's place of business. Employees in jobs not conforming to these definitions are considered nonexempt.

During one year alone in the 1980s, the Wage and Hour Division received over 46,000 wage complaints and conducted more than 68,000 investigations. The agency recovered $745 million in unpaid overtime wages owed to 291,000 employees. An employer must be aware of the minimum wage level, maintain accurate payroll records, and accurately identify workers covered by the act.[9]

Equal Pay Act of 1963. The Equal Pay Act of 1963 (an amendment to the FLSA) has also influenced the field of compensation. In 1972, amendments expanded the act to cover employees in executive, administrative, professional, and outside sales force categories as well as employees in most state and local governments, hospitals, and schools. The purpose of this legislation is to prohibit discrimination in pay on the basis of sex. The act has

---

[8] *Employment Relations under the Fair Labor Standards Act* (Washington, D.C.: U.S. Department of Labor, Employment Standards Administration, Wage and Hour Division, WH Publication 1297; revised May 1980, reprinted August 1985).

[9] William S. Hubbartt, "The Ten Commandments of Salary Administration," *Administrative Management*, 43 (April 1982), p. 60.

teeth, as evidenced by the millions of dollars paid to women employees to compensate them for past discriminatory pay policies.

The act applies to all organizations and employees covered by the FLSA, including the exempt categories. The act requires equal pay for equal work for both men and women. Equal work is defined as work requiring equal skill, effort, and responsibility, which is performed under the same or similar working conditions. The act doesn't prohibit the establishment of different wage rates based on seniority or a merit system. Also permitted are pay systems that are based on the quantity or quality of production and differentials based on any factor other than sex. In recent years, the act's effect has been less significant because a violation of the Equal Pay Act may also be a violation of Title VII of the Civil Rights Act.

Employee Retirement Income Security Act of 1974. Passed in 1974, the Employee Retirement Income Security Act (ERISA) is one of the most complex pieces of federal compensation legislation ever to be passed. The purpose of the act is described as follows:

> It is hereby declared to be the policy of this Act to protect . . . the interests of participants in employee benefit plans and their beneficiaries . . . by establishing standards of conduct, responsibility and obligations for fiduciaries of employee benefit plans, and by providing for appropriate remedies, sanctions, and ready access to the federal courts.[10]

Note that the word protect is used here because the act does not force employers to create employee benefit plans. It does set standards in the areas of participation, vesting of benefits, and funding for existing and new plans. Numerous existing retirement plans have been altered in order to conform to this legislation.

Consolidated Omnibus Budget Reconciliation Act of 1985 (COBRA). COBRA requires employers to continue specified health insurance coverage at group rates for certain employees and their families following termination of employment. Traditionally, employers receive a tax deduction for expenses paid or incurred for any group health plan. The act doesn't allow such deductions unless each "qualified beneficiary" under the group health plan who would lose coverage as a result of a "qualifying event" is entitled to elect continuation coverage under the plan within the election period. A qualifying event is (1) termination of the covered employee (except in cases of gross misconduct), (2) reduction of hours of the covered employee, (3) the death of the covered employee, (4) the divorce or legal separation of the covered employee from his or her spouse, (5) eligibility of the covered employee for Medicare benefits, and (6) a child ceasing to be a dependent. The requirements of COBRA do not apply to a group health plan for any calendar year in which employers employed less than 20 employees on a typical business day.

---

[10] *U.S. Statutes at Large 88*, Part I, 93rd Congress, 2nd Session, 1974, p. 833.

■ THE JOB AS A DETERMINANT OF FINANCIAL COMPENSATION

The jobs people are given to do are a major determinant of the amount of financial compensation they will receive. Organizations pay for the value they attach to certain duties, responsibilities, and other job-related factors (such as working conditions). Management techniques utilized for determining a job's relative worth include job analysis, job descriptions, and job evaluation.

Job Analysis and Descriptions

Before an organization can determine the relative difficulty or value of its jobs, it must first define their content, which it normally does by analyzing jobs. Recall from Chapter 4 that job analysis is the systematic process of determining the skills and knowledge required for performing jobs. Recall, also, that the job description is the primary by-product of job analysis, consisting of a written document that describes job duties and responsibilities. Job descriptions are used for many different purposes, including job evaluation. Job descriptions are essential to all job evaluation methods, the success of which depends largely on their accuracy and clarity.

Job Evaluation

Job evaluation is that part of a compensation system in which a firm determines the relative value of one job in relation to another.[11] The basic purpose of a job evaluation is to eliminate internal pay inequities that exist because of illogical pay structures. For example, a pay inequity exists if the mailroom supervisor earns more money than the accounting supervisor.

More specifically, job evaluation has the potential to:

- Identify the organization's job structure.
- Bring equity and order to the relationships among jobs.
- Develop a hierarchy of job value that can be used to create a pay structure.
- Achieve a consensus among managers and employees regarding jobs and pay within the firm.[12]

The concept of internal pay equity previously discussed is closely related to the purposes of job evaluation. It refers to the relationship between the pay that employees believe they should receive and that which they actually receive. Although individuals may be concerned with external equity, they basically believe that their pay should be related to their contributions to the firm. They quickly become unhappy when they perceive that some-

---

[11] Richard I. Henderson, *Compensation Management*, 4th ed. (Reston, Va.: Reston Publishing Company, 1985), p. 231.

[12] Roger J. Plachy, "The Case for Effective Point-Factor Job Evaluation, Viewpoint I," *Personnel*, 64 (April 1987), p. 31.

one in the organization receives more pay for performing the same or lower level work.

At the Bendix Corporation, the precise method of implementing job evaluation programs is left to the discretion of individual business groups and divisions. However, corporate philosophy serves as a basic guide to these operating units. This philosophy includes the belief that the job evaluation process is the foundation of a sound compensation system. Thus the job evaluation process must satisfy the following requirements:

- Provide a consistent measure of job worth that can be easily understood by everyone concerned.
- Involve managers from its inception through its administration and subsequent revision.
- Protect employees from favoritism, bias, and resultant internal pay inequities.
- Measure the job and not the performance of the employees doing the job.
- Apply to broad job clusters within functional groups.

The human resource department is usually responsible for administering job evaluation programs. However, actual job evaluation is typically done by committee. The committee often consists of managers from different functional areas. A typical committee might include the human resource director as chairperson and the vice-presidents for finance, production, and marketing. However, the composition of the committee usually depends on the type and level of the jobs that are being evaluated. In all instances, it is important for the committee to keep personalities out of the evaluation process. As the Bendix approach indicates, it is the job that should be evaluated, not the person(s) performing the job.

Small- and medium-sized organizations often lack job evaluation expertise and may elect to use an outside consultant. When employing a qualified consultant, management should require that the consultant develop an internal job evaluation program and train company employees to administer it properly.

Organizations use four basic job evaluation methods: ranking, classification, factor comparison, and point.[13] A firm should choose one method and modify that method to its particular needs. The ranking and classification methods are nonquantitative, whereas the factor comparison and point methods are quantitative approaches.

Ranking Method. The simplest of the four job evaluation methods is the ranking method. In the **ranking method**, the raters examine the description of each job being evaluated and arrange the jobs in order according to their value to the company. The procedure is essentially the same as that discussed in Chapter 11 regarding the ranking method for performance appraisal. The only difference is that jobs, not people, are being evaluated.

---

[13] Milkovich and Newman, p. 109.

The first step in this method—as with all the methods—is conducting job analysis and writing job descriptions.

Classification Method. The **classification method** involves defining a number of classes or grades to describe a group of jobs. In evaluating jobs by the classification method, the raters compare the job description with the class description. The class description that most closely agrees with the job description determines the classification for that job. For example, in evaluating the job of word processing clerk, the description might include these duties:

1. Data enter letters from prepared drafts.
2. Address envelopes.
3. Deliver completed correspondence to unit supervisor.

Assuming that the remainder of the job description includes similar routine work, this job would most likely be placed in the lowest job class.

The best-known example of this method is the federal government's Civil Service System. This system has eighteen grades (GS-1 to GS-18). At the bottom of the scale (GS-1), the nature and typical duties of the job are very simple and routine. Jobs become progressively more difficult through GS-18, which involves high-level executive tasks. However, clearly defining grade descriptions for many diverse jobs is difficult. For this reason, the federal government has now implemented a Factor Evaluation System (FES). This system combines three methods of job evaluation: ranking, factor comparison, and point. However, the FES is not the only job evaluation plan used within the federal government. As with private industry, the government's approach is to select and adapt systems according to specific needs.[14]

Factor Comparison Method. The basic version of the factor comparison method was developed by Eugene Benge and is somewhat more complex than the two previously discussed qualitative methods. In the **factor comparison method** raters need not keep the entire job in mind as they evaluate, instead they make decisions on separate aspects, or factors, of the job. A basic underlying assumption is that there are five universal job factors:

- Mental requirements, which reflect mental traits such as intelligence, reasoning, and imagination.
- Skill, which pertains to facility in muscular coordination and training in the interpretation of sensory impressions.
- Physical requirements, which involve sitting, standing, walking, lifting, etc.
- Responsibilities, which cover areas such as raw materials, money, records, and supervision.

---

[14] *Ibid.*, p. 116.

CHAPTER 12   Financial Compensation

- Working conditions, which reflect the environmental influences of noise, illumination, ventilation, hazards, and hours.[15]

The committee first ranks the relative degree of difficulty of each of the five factors for the selected key jobs. Job descriptions serve as a basis for making these decisions. An example of this initial ranking (average of all raters on the committee) is shown in Table 12-1. Note that the jobs are first ranked according to mental requirements. The systems analyst job ranked highest, followed by programmer (2), console operator (3), and data entry clerk (4). The same ranking procedure was used for the other four factors.

The committee next allocates pay rates for each job to each factor. This allocation is based on the importance of the respective factor to the job. For example, allocating the systems analyst's average pay rate ($12.00 per hour) to each of the five factors is shown in Table 12-2. This step is probably the most difficult to explain satisfactorily to employees because the decision is highly subjective.

After assigning pay rates to each factor for each job, the committee places the results in a format similar to that shown in Table 12-3. This procedure results in a ranking of jobs within each factor on the basis of pay rates. (Rank order is shown in parentheses.)

By comparing the ranking of factor difficulty (DR) with the ranking of factor pay (PR), we can determine the committee's consistency. The two separate rankings are shown side-by-side in Table 12-4. Note that no differences exist. If there had been a ranking inconsistency, the jobs affected would not be used in the next step.

A job comparison scale consisting of the five universal factors is developed next (see Figure 12-3). This scale is used to rate other jobs in the group being evaluated. The raters compare each job, factor by factor, with those appearing on the job comparison scale. They then place them on the chart in an appropriate position. For example, assume that the committee is evaluating the job of programmer analyst (which was not used as a key job). It determines that this job has fewer mental requirements than that of systems analyst but more than those of programmer. The job would then be placed on this chart between these two jobs at a point agreed on by the committee. In this example, the committee evaluated the mental requirements factor at $3.80. The committee repeats this procedure for the remaining four factors and for all jobs to be evaluated.

The factor comparison method provides a systematic approach to job evaluation. However, at least two problems with it should be noted. The assumption that the five factors are universal has been questioned because certain factors may be more appropriate to some job groups than others. Also while the steps are not overly complicated, they are somewhat detailed and may be difficult to explain.

Point Method. In the **point method**, raters assign numerical values to specific job components and the sum of these values provides a quantitative

---
[15] John A. Patton, C. L. Littlefield, and Stanley A. Self, *Job Evaluation: Text and Cases*, 3rd ed. (Homewood, Ill.: Richard D. Irwin, 1964), p. 115.

TABLE 12-1 | Average Ranks of Factor Difficulty for Key Jobs

Job	Factor				
	Mental	Skill	Physical	Responsibility	Working Conditions*
Systems analyst	1	4	2	1	3
Data entry clerk	4	1	1	4	1
Programmer	2	3	3	2	4
Console operator	3	2	4	3	2

*The poorer the working conditions, the higher the rating. (The highest rating is 1.)

TABLE 12-2 | Allocation of Pay to Factors

Job: Systems analyst	Mental	$4.00
Average pay per hour: $12.00	Skill	2.00
	Physical	0.80
	Responsibility	4.00
	Working conditions	1.20

assessment of a job's relative worth.[16] Most job evaluation plans in use today are some variation of the point method.[17] Some 95 percent of the major corporations in the United States are thought to use this method to evaluate jobs.[18] Point method plans are also used by many small companies. Their use has been encouraged by associations such as the National Electrical Manufacturers' Association, the Life Office Management Association, and the Administrative Management Society.

The point method requires selection of job factors according to the nature of the specific group of jobs being evaluated. Normally, organizations develop a separate plan for each group of similar jobs (job clusters) in the company. Shop jobs, clerical jobs, and sales jobs are examples of job clusters. The procedure for establishing a point method is illustrated in Figure 12-4. After determining the group of jobs to be studied, analysts conduct job

---
[16] Donald L. Caruth, *Compensation Management for Banks* (Boston: Bankers Publishing Company), p. 65; (Columbus, Ohio: Charles E. Merrill, 1984), p. 93.

[17] Leonard R. Burgess, *Wage and Salary Administration* (Columbus, Ohio: Charles E. Merrill, 1984), p. 93.

[18] Edward E. Lawler III, "What's Wrong with Point-Factor Job Evaluation," *Personnel*, 64 (January 1987), p. 38.

TABLE 12-3 | Average Ranks of Pay Rates by Factor for Key Jobs

Job	Mental	Skill	Physical	Responsibility	Working conditions	Pay rate
Systems analyst	$4.00(1)	$2.00(4)	$0.80(2)	$4.00(1)	$1.20(3)	$12.00
Data entry clerk	1.50(4)	2.70(1)	1.00(1)	1.30(4)	1.40(1)	7.90
Programmer	3.40(2)	2.50(3)	0.70(3)	3.00(2)	1.00(4)	10.60
Console operator	2.30(3)	2.60(2)	0.60(4)	1.80(3)	1.30(2)	8.60

TABLE 12-4 | Comparison of Difficulty Ranking (DR) and Pay Ranking (PR) By Factor

	Factor									
	Mental		Skill		Physical		Responsibility		Working conditions	
Job	DR	PR	DR	PR	DR	PR	DR	PR	DR	PR
Systems analyst	1	1	4	4	2	2	1	1	3	3
Data entry clerk	4	4	1	1	1	1	4	4	1	1
Programmer	2	2	3	3	3	3	2	2	4	4
Console operator	3	3	2	2	4	4	3	3	2	2

analysis and write job descriptions. The job evaluation committee will later use these descriptions as the basis for making evaluation decisions.

Next, the analysts select and define the factors to be used in measuring job value. These factors become the standards used for the evaluation of jobs. They can best be identified by individuals who are thoroughly familiar with the content of the jobs under consideration. Education, experience, job knowledge, mental effort, physical effort, responsibility, and working conditions are examples of factors typically used. Each factor should be significant in helping to differentiate jobs. Factors that exist in equal amounts in all jobs obviously would not serve this purpose. As an example, in evaluating a company's clerical jobs, the factor working conditions would be of little value in differentiating jobs if all jobs in the cluster had approximately the same working conditions. The number of factors used varies, with the average being approximately eleven.[19]

The committee must establish factor weights according to their relative importance in the jobs to be evaluated. For example, if experience is con-

---
[19] See Belcher and Atchison for a detailed discussion of compensable factors.

	Mental	Skill	Physical	Responsibility	Working Conditions
$4.00	Systems Analyst (Programmer Analyst)			Systems Analyst	
3.80					
3.50	Programmer				
3.00		Data Entry Clerk		Programmer	
2.50		Console Operator Programmer			
2.00	Console Operator	Systems Analyst		Console Operator	
1.50	Data Entry Clerk			Data Entry Clerk	Data Entry Clerk Console Operator Systems Analyst
1.00			Data Entry Clerk Systems Analyst Programmer Console Operator		Programmer
.50					
.00					

FIGURE 12-3 | Job Comparison Scale

sidered quite important for a particular job cluster, this factor might be weighted as much as 35 percent. Physical effort (if used at all as a factor in an office cluster) would likely be low—perhaps less than 10 percent.

The next consideration is to determine the number of degrees for each job factor and define each degree. Degrees represent the number of distinct levels associated with a particular factor. The number of degrees needed for each factor depends on job requirements. If a particular cluster required virtually the same level of formal education (a high school diploma, for example), fewer degrees would be appropriate than if some jobs in the cluster required advanced degrees.

The committee then determines the total number of points to be used in the plan. The number may vary, but 500 or 1,000 points may work well. The use of a smaller number of points (for example, 50) would not likely provide the proper distinctions among jobs, whereas a larger number (such as 50,000) would be unnecessarily cumbersome. The total number of points in a plan indicates the maximum points that any job could receive.

CHAPTER 12   Financial Compensation   451

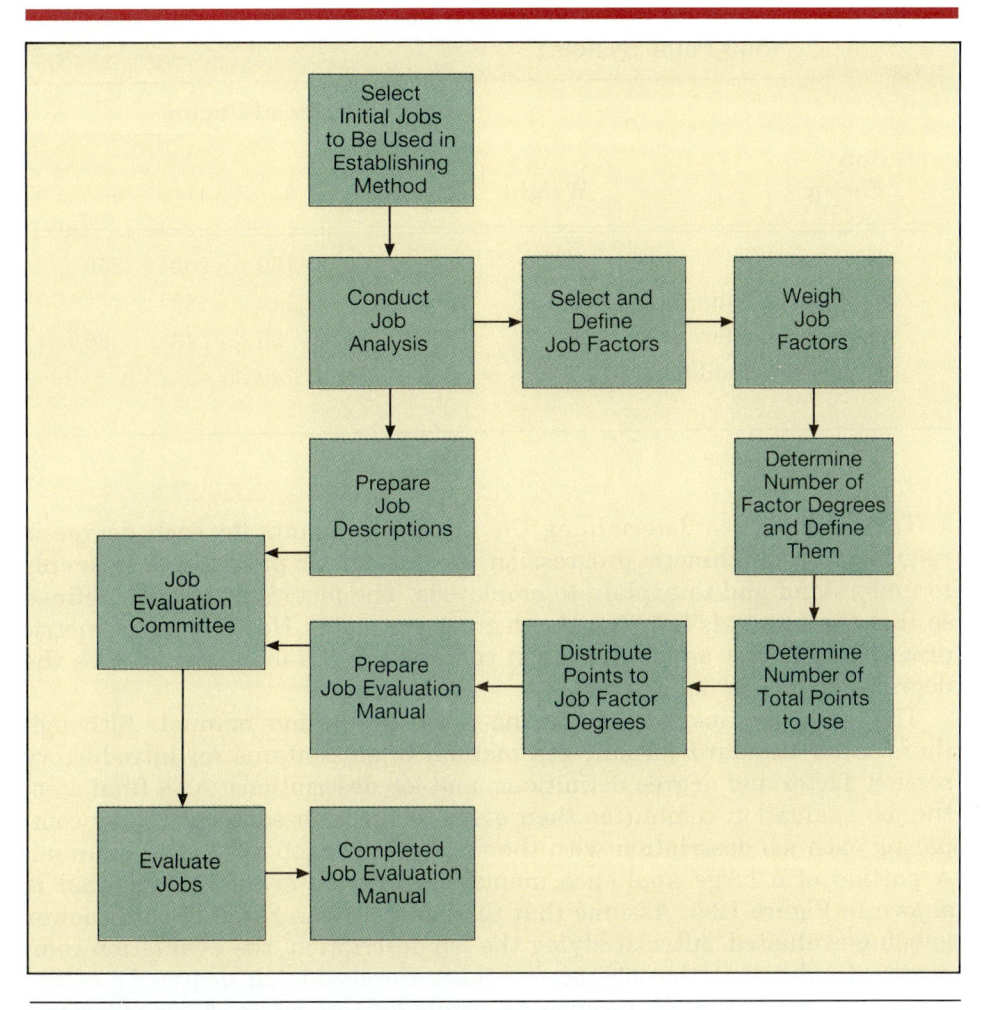

FIGURE 12-4 | Procedure For Establishing the Point Method of Job Evaluation

[Flowchart: Select Initial Jobs to Be Used in Establishing Method → Conduct Job Analysis → Select and Define Job Factors → Weigh Job Factors → Determine Number of Factor Degrees and Define Them → Determine Number of Total Points to Use → Distribute Points to Job Factor Degrees → Prepare Job Evaluation Manual → Job Evaluation Committee; Conduct Job Analysis → Prepare Job Descriptions → Job Evaluation Committee → Evaluate Jobs → Completed Job Evaluation Manual]

The next step is to distribute point values to job factor degrees (see Table 12-5). As you can see, factor 1 has five degrees, factor 2 has four, factor 3 has five, and factor 4 has three. Maximum points are easily calculated by multiplying the maximum points in the system by the assigned weights. For education, the maximum points would be 250 (50 percent weight multiplied by 500 points). Points for the minimum degree correspond to the percentage weight assigned to the factor (50 points). The degree interval may be calculated by subtracting the minimum number of points from the maximum number, and dividing by the number of degrees used minus 1. For example, the interval for factor 1 (education) is:

$$\text{Interval} = \frac{250 - 50}{5 - 1} = 50$$

TABLE 12-5 | Overview of the Point System (500-Point System)

Job Factor	Weight	\multicolumn{5}{c}{Degree of Factor}
		1	2	3	4	5
1. Education	50%	50	100	150	200	250
2. Responsibility	30%	30	70	110	150	
3. Physical effort	12%	12	24	36	48	60
4. Working conditions	8%	8	24	40		

This approach to determining the number of points for each degree is referred to as arithmetic progression. An arithmetic progression is simple to understand and to explain to employees. The factors have been defined so that the intervals between the degrees are equal. However, a geometric progression is just as valid when it conforms to the manner in which the degrees have been defined.[20]

The next step involves preparing a job evaluation manual. Although there is no standard format, the manual often contains an introductory section, factor and degree definitions, and job descriptions. As a final step, the job evaluation committee then evaluates jobs in each cluster by comparing each job description with the factors in the job evaluation manual. A portion of a large appliance manufacturer's job evaluation manual is shown in Figure 12-5. Assume that the job of human resource interviewer is being evaluated. After studying the job description, the evaluation committee decides that the job requirements closely match degree IV of the "factor contacts." The job receives 80 points for this factor. After determining the point values of all factors, the committee totals them to obtain the numerical value of the human resource interviewer job. The committee determines the values of all other jobs in each cluster in the same manner.

Point plans have been criticized for the amount of time and effort required to design them and for supporting traditional bureaucratic management.[21] However, a redeeming feature of the method is that, once developed, the plan may be used over a long period of time. The procedure for using an established point method is presented in Figure 12-6. As new jobs are created and the contents of old jobs substantially changed, job analysis must be conducted and job descriptions rewritten. The job evaluation committee evaluates the jobs and updates the manual. Only when job factors change, or for some reason the weights assigned become inappropriate, does the plan become obsolete.

---

[20] Other alternatives, such as geometric progession and irregular progression, exist. For a detailed discussion of methods of progression, see Patton et al., pp. 153–154.

[21] Lawler, pp. 39–40.

CHAPTER 12 Financial Compensation 453

> **FACTOR: CONTACTS**
>
> This factor considers the responsibility for working with other people to get results, either interdepartmental or outside the plant. In the lower degrees, it is largely a matter of giving or getting information or instructions. In the higher degrees, the factor involves dealing with or influencing other persons. In rating this factor, consider how the contacts are made, the duration of the contacts, and their purposes.
>
> Level (Degree)   Points
>
> IV   Usual purposes of the contacts are to discuss problems and possible solutions, to   80
> secure cooperation or coordination of efforts, and to get agreement and action; more than ordinary tact and persuasiveness required.
>
> III   Usual purposes of the contacts are to exchange information or settle specific problems   40
> encountered in the course of daily work.
>
> II   Contacts may be repetitive but usually are brief and with little or no continuity.   20
>
> I   Contacts normally extend to persons in the immediate work unit only.   10
>
> **FACTOR: COMPLEXITY OF DUTIES**
>
> This factor considers the complexity of duties in terms of the character of the tasks to be performed, the scope of independent action allowed, and the exercise of perception and judgment required.
>
> Level (Degree)   Points
>
> IV   Performs work where only general methods are available. Independent action and   60
> judgment are required regularly to analyze facts, evaluate situations, draw conclusions, make decisions, and take or recommend action.
>
> III   Performs duties working from standard procedures or generally understood methods.   80
> Some independent action and judgment are required to decide what to do, determine permissible variations from standard procedures, review facts in situations, and determine action to be taken, within limits prescribed.
>
> II   Standard procedure limits independent action and judgment to decisions not difficult to   40
> make since choices are limited. Duties require deciding when to ask for assistance.
>
> I   Little or no independent action or judgment. Duties are so standardized and simple as   20
> to involve little choice as to how to do them.

FIGURE 12-5 | Point Method of Job Evaluation (Example of Two Factors)

The **Hay guide chart-profile method** is a highly refined version of the point method that uses the factors of know-how, problem solving, accountability, and, where appropriate, working conditions. Point values are assigned to these factors to determine the final point profile for any job. The Hay method is an extremely popular approach to determining compensation. It is used by some 5,000 employers worldwide including 130 of the 500 largest U.S. corporations.[22] The popularity of the Hay method gives it an impor-

---
[22] Henderson, p. 222.

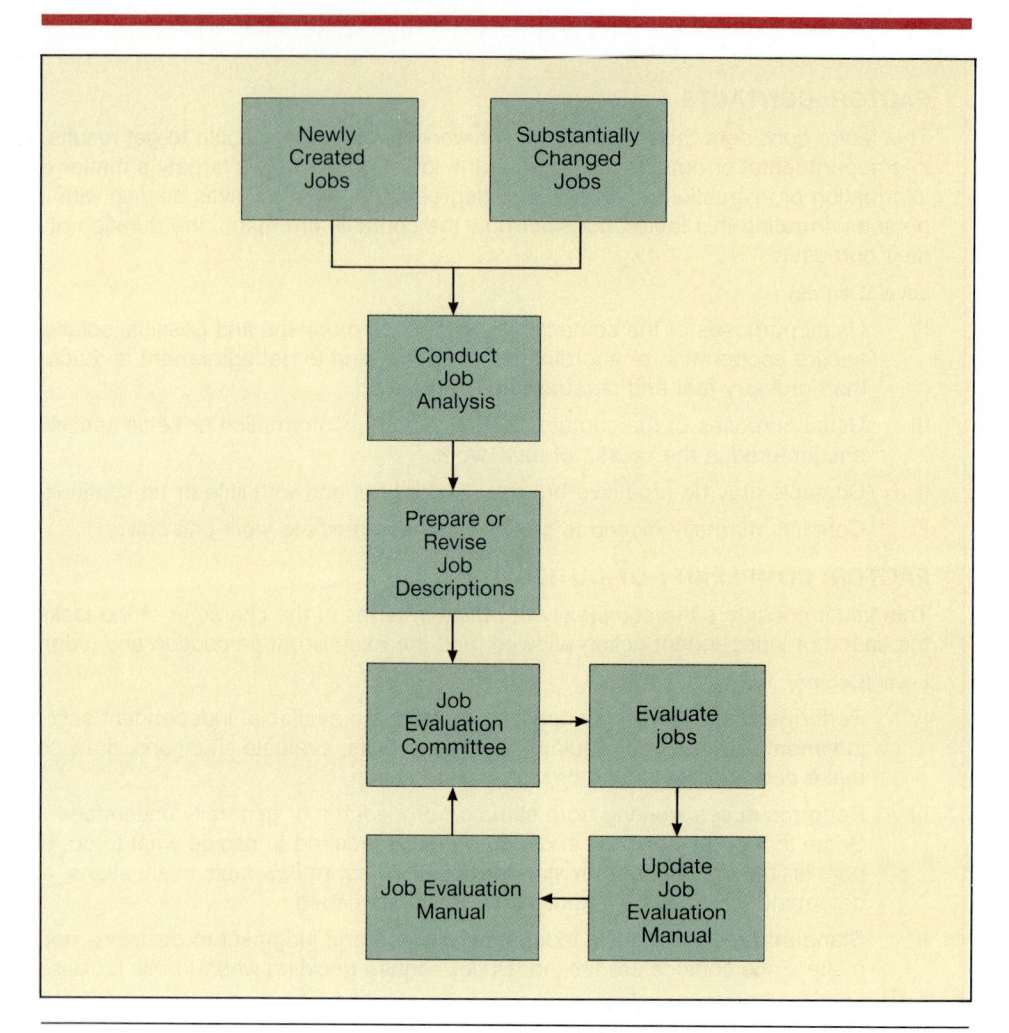

FIGURE 12-6 | Procedure for Using an Established Point Method of Job Evaluation

tant advantage: It facilitates job comparison between firms. Thus the plan serves to determine both internal and external equity.

■ THE EMPLOYEE AS A DETERMINANT OF FINANCIAL COMPENSATION

In addition to the organization, the labor market, and the job, factors related to the employee are also essential in determining pay equity. We discuss each of these factors in this section.

Performance

Nothing is more demoralizing to outstanding employees than to be paid the same as less productive workers. Therefore management generally prefers a pay system based on employee performance. Such an approach rewards individuals according to their productivity. Further, in such a system, pay serves as an incentive for employees to give their best efforts.

A prerequisite to a merit system is a sound performance appraisal program. If pay is to be related to performance, an organization must have a valid means of determining varying performance levels. Across-the-board dollar or percentage pay increases are still common, but this approach is slowly losing ground. Pay increases are to a greater extent now being based on achievement of performance goals.[23]

Seniority

The length of time an employee has been associated with the company, division, department, or job is referred to as seniority. Management prefers performance as the primary basis for compensation changes; labor unions tend to favor seniority, which they believe provides an objective and fair basis for pay increases. Many union leaders believe performance evaluation systems are too subjective and permit management to reward favorite employees arbitrarily.

An acceptable performance–seniority compromise might be to permit employees to receive pay increases to the midpoints of their pay grades on the basis of seniority. The rationale is that workers performing at an acceptable level should eventually receive the average wage or salary of their pay grades. However, progression beyond the midpoint should be based on performance. This practice would permit only the outstanding performers to reach the maximum rate for the grade and reflects the initial rationale for rate ranges.

Experience

Regardless of the nature of the task, very few factors have a more significant impact on performance than experience. "Experience has taught our best racquetball players how to really play the game," the director of a state university's recreational facility recently exclaimed. This statement, no doubt, was true. But, as someone else put it, "Experience has also taught our worst racquetball players how to play." The point is that, while experience is invaluable, not all experience is good experience. A person can play golf for ten years (without lessons from a pro, of course), have a hook that almost returns to the tee box, and be further away than ever from being a good golfer.

Although not always realized in business circles, the same is true of management experience. How much ahead of the game is the manager who has been a poor manager for two decades? Managers who comment, with considerable confidence and pleasure, that they have had twenty years of management experience may actually have much less because of the dupli-

---

[23] "Compensation Currents," *Compensation Review*, 17 (First Quarter 1985), p. 2.

cation involved. Nevertheless, experience is often indispensable and, in many cases, management does compensate employees on this basis. Sometimes the practice is justified because of the valuable insights that can only be acquired through experience on the job. Occasionally, however, experience may be rewarded even though it is irrelevant.

Membership in the Organization

Some components of individual financial compensation are given to employees without regard to the particular job they perform or their level of productivity. These rewards are provided to all employees simply because they are members of the organization. For example, an average performer occupying a job in pay grade 1 may receive the same number of vacation days, the same amount of group life insurance, and the same reimbursement for educational expenses as a superior employee working in a job classified in pay grade 10. In fact, the worker in pay grade 1 may get more vacation time if he or she has been with the firm longer. Rewards based on organizational membership are intended to maintain a high degree of stability in the workforce and to recognize loyalty.

Potential

Potential is useless if it is never realized. Yet, organizations do pay some individuals based on their potential. In order to attract talented young people to the firm, the overall compensation program must appeal to the person with no experience or any immediate ability to perform difficult tasks. Many young employees are paid well because they have the potential to become a first-line supervisor, manager of compensation, vice-president of marketing, or possibly even CEO.

College graduates typically do not have significant business experience for employment managers to examine. Lacking such a record, organizations turn elsewhere for factors to predict the success of the graduate. Grades in college are often considered. Although the relationship between grades and job performance is arguable, human resource recruiters and line managers often have no alternative but to emphasize a student's academic success. Of course, other factors might indicate potential, so questions asked of college prospects often include:

- What percentage of your school expenses did you pay?
- What class offices did you hold?
- To what professional student associations did you belong, such as Society for Human Resource Management, Society for Advancement of Management, Pi Sigma Epsilon, Delta Sigma Pi, or Alpha Kappa Psi? Did you hold offices in any of these organizations?
- Were you a member of a social sorority or fraternity? What leadership positions did you occupy?

These and many other questions may not relate directly to the job but are nevertheless asked as organizations attempt to identify individuals who can provide future leadership. The people sought are those with potential.

Political Influence

Political influence is a factor that obviously should not be used to determine financial compensation. However, to deny that it exists would be unrealistic. It is disheartening to hear someone say, "It's not what you know, it's who you know." Yet, there is an unfortunate element of truth in that statement. To varying degrees in business, government, and not-for-profit organizations, a person's "pull" or political influence may sway pay and promotion decisions. It may be natural for a manager to favor a friend or relative in granting a pay increase or promotion. Whether it is natural or not, if the person receiving the reward is not truly deserving, this fact will soon become known throughout the work group. This practice can have a devastating impact on employee morale. Employees want—and are demanding—equitable treatment. However, there is nothing equitable about a person receiving a promotion and/or pay increase based strictly on politics. The practice should be strictly avoided.

Luck

You've undoubtedly heard the expression, "It certainly helps to be in the right place at the right time." There is more than a little truth in this statement as it relates to a person's compensation. Positions are continually coming open in firms. Realistically, there is no way for managers to foresee many of the changes that occur. For instance, who could have known that the purchasing agent, Joe Flynch, an apparently healthy middle-aged man, would suddenly die of a heart attack? Although the company may have been grooming several managers for Joe's position, none may be capable of immediately assuming the increased responsibility. The most experienced person, Tommy Loy, has been with the company only six months. Tommy had been an assistant buyer for a competitor for four years. Because of his experience, Tommy receives the promotion and the increased financial compensation. Tommy Loy was in the right place at the right time.

When asked to explain their most important reasons for success and effectiveness as managers, two chief executives responded candidly. One said, "Success is being at the right place at the right time and being recognized as having the ability to make timely decisions. It also depends on having good rapport with people, a good operating background, and the knowledge of how to develop people." The other replied, "My present position was attained by being in the right place at the right time with a history of getting the job done." Both executives recognize the significance of luck combined with the ability to perform. Their experiences lend support to the idea that luck works primarily for the efficient.

■ JOB PRICING

The primary considerations in pricing jobs are the organization's policies, the labor market, and the job itself. If allowances are to be made for individual factors, they too must be considered. Recall that the process of job evaluation results in a job hierarchy. It might reveal, for example, that the job of senior accountant is more valuable than the job of computer operator, which in turn is more valuable than the job of senior invoice clerk. At this point, the relative value of these jobs to the company is known but their absolute value isn't. Placing a dollar value on the worth of a job is called **job pricing**. It takes place after the job has been evaluated and the relative value of each job in the organization has been determined. However, as shown in Figure 12-2, additional factors should be considered in determining the job's absolute value. Firms often use pay grades and pay ranges in the job pricing process.

Pay Grades

A **pay grade** is the grouping of similar jobs to simplify the job pricing process. It is much more convenient for organizations to price fifteen pay grades rather than 200 separate jobs. The simplicity of this approach is similar to a college or university's practice of grouping grades of 90 to 100 into an "A" category, grades of 80 to 89 into a "B", etc. A false implication of preciseness is also avoided. While job evaluation plans may be systematic, none is scientific.

Plotting jobs on a scatter diagram is often useful in determining the appropriate number of pay grades. In Figure 12-7, each dot on the scatter diagram represents one job as it relates to pay and evaluated points, which reflect its worth. By following this procedure, it is likely that a certain point spread will work satisfactorily (100 points used in this illustration). Each dot represents one job but may involve dozens of individuals who fill that one job. The large dot at the lower left represents the job of data entry clerk, which was evaluated at 75 points. The data entry clerk's hourly rate of $7.90 represents either the average wage currently being paid for the job or its market rate. This decision depends on how management wants to price its jobs.

A **wage curve** (or pay curve) is the fitting of plotted points in order to create a smooth progression between pay grades. The line that is drawn to minimize the distance between all dots and the line—a line of best fit—may be straight or curved. However, when the point system is used (normally considering only one job cluster), a straight line is the usual result, as in Figure 12-7. Two approaches used in drawing this wage line are the least squares line (a statistical version) and the less sophisticated "eyeball" approach. Some compensation specialists use the latter because it's simpler.

Pay Ranges

The next decision is whether all individuals performing the same job will receive equal pay or whether pay ranges will be used. A **pay range** includes a minimum and maximum pay rate with enough variance between the two to allow some significant pay difference. Pay ranges are generally preferred

CHAPTER 12　Financial Compensation

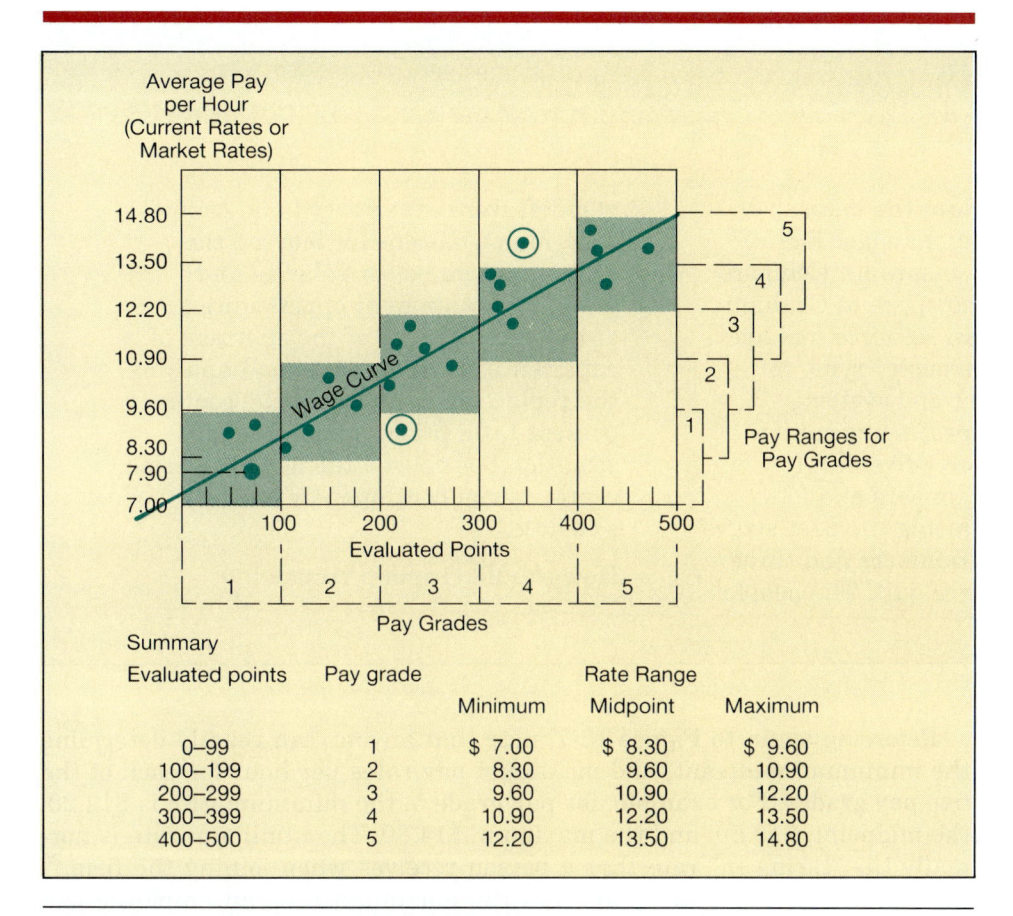

Summary				
Evaluated points	Pay grade	Rate Range		
		Minimum	Midpoint	Maximum
0–99	1	$ 7.00	$ 8.30	$ 9.60
100–199	2	8.30	9.60	10.90
200–299	3	9.60	10.90	12.20
300–399	4	10.90	12.20	13.50
400–500	5	12.20	13.50	14.80

FIGURE 12-7 Scatter Diagram of Evaluated Jobs Illustrating the Wage Curve, Pay Grades, and Rating Ranges

because they allow employees to be paid according to length of service and performance. Pay then serves as a positive incentive. When pay ranges are used, a method must be developed to advance individuals through the range. Although many organizations grant pay increases based on seniority, others hold the view that only outstanding performers should be allowed to advance to the top of their pay ranges. This philosophy also dictates that any discrepancy between where a person is in the pay range and where he or she could be—based on performance—should be corrected within a reasonable amount of time. This approach would necessitate larger pay increases for outstanding performers who are being paid at or near the bottom of their pay ranges.[24]

---

[24] Graef S. Crystal, "Outlook on Compensation and Benefits: To the Rescue of Pay for Performance," *Personnel*, 62 (January 1985), p. 9.

HRM In Action

Lynn Marlow, the data processing manager for National Insurance Company, was perplexed as she spoke to Graham Johnston, the human resource manager. Lynn said, "I have trouble trying to recruit programmers and systems analysts. The data processing center employs a total of forty-five people, including ten programmers and four systems analysts. During the past six months, seven programmers and three systems analysts have quit. The people who left were experienced and competent. Major reasons for leaving the company were better salaries and greater advancement opportunities elsewhere. Because of the shortage of experienced programmers and analysts, the replacements hired by the company possess little prior experience. This situation has caused the data processing center to run continuously behind schedule."

How should Graham respond?

Referring again to Figure 12-7, note that anyone can readily determine the minimum, midpoint, and maximum pay rates per hour for each of the five pay grades. For example, for pay grade 5, the minimum rate is $12.20, the midpoint, $13.50, and the maximum $14.80. The minimum rate is normally the "hiring in" rate that a person receives when joining the firm.[25] The maximum pay rate represents the maximum that an employee can receive for that job, regardless of how well the job is performed. A person at the top of a pay grade will have to be promoted to a job in a higher pay grade in order to receive a pay increase unless (1) an across-the-board adjustment is made, or (2) the job is reevaluated and placed in a higher pay grade. This situation has caused numerous managers anguish as they attempt to explain the pay system to an employee who is doing a tremendous job but is at the top of a pay grade. Consider this situation:

> Everyone in the department realized that Martha Wilson was the best secretary in the company. At times she appeared to do the job of three secretaries. Bill Merideth, Martha's supervisor, was especially impressed. Recently he had had a discussion with the human resource manager to see what could be done to get a raise for Martha. After Bill described the situation, the human resource manager's only reply was, "Sorry, Bill. Martha is already at the top of her pay grade. There is nothing you can do unless you can have her job upgraded or promote her to another position."

---

[25] Howard Risher, "Inflation and Salary Administration," *Personnel Administrator*, 26 (May 1981), p. 36.

CHAPTER 12   Financial Compensation

Situations such as Martha's present human resource managers with a perplexing problem. Many would be inclined to make an exception to the system and give Martha a salary increase. However, this action would violate a basic principle, which holds that every job in the organization has a maximum value, regardless of how well it is performed. In addition, making exceptions to the compensation plan could soon result in widespread pay inequities.

The rate ranges established should be large enough to provide an incentive to do a better job. At times, pay differentials may need to be greater to be meaningful, especially at higher levels. There may be logic in having the rate range become increasingly wide at each consecutive level (see Figure 12-8). Consider, for example, what a $50 per month salary increase would mean to a file clerk earning $600 per month (an 8.3 percent increase) and to a senior cost accountant earning $1,500 per month (a 3.3 percent increase). Assuming an inflation rate of 8 percent, the file clerk would be able to stay even, while the cost accountant would obviously fall behind.

Some workplace conditions do not favor pay ranges. For instance, in a situation where all or most jobs are routine, with little opportunity for

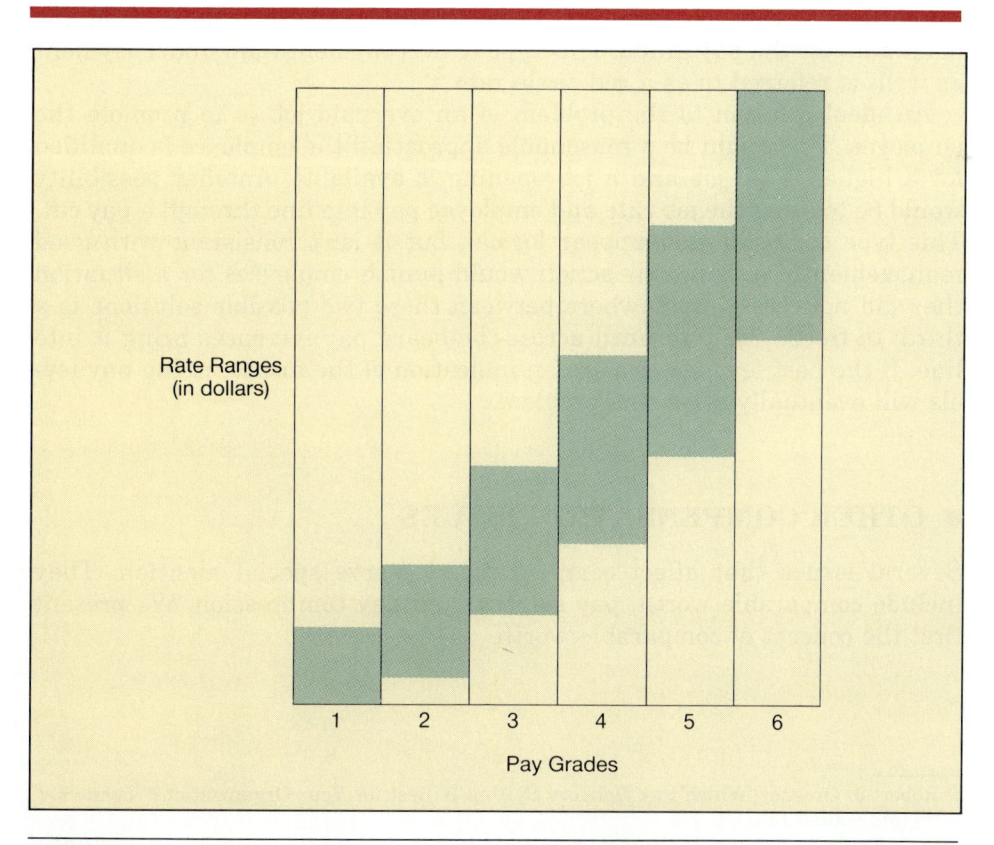

FIGURE 12-8 | Rate Ranges on Percentage Spreads

employees to vary their productivity, a single, or fixed, rate system may be more appropriate. When single rates are used, everyone working the same job receives the same pay, regardless of seniority or productivity.[26]

Adjusting Pay Rates

When pay ranges have been determined and jobs assigned to pay grades, it may become obvious that some jobs are overpaid and others underpaid. Underpaid jobs are normally brought to the minimum of the pay range as soon as possible. Referring again to Figure 12-7, you can see that a job evaluated at about 225 points and having a rate of $9.00 per hour is represented by a circled dot immediately below pay grade 3. The job was determined to be difficult enough to fall in pay grade 3 (200–299 points). However, employees working in the job are being paid 60 cents per hour less than the minimum for the pay grade ($9.60 per hour). Some jobs in pay grade 2 and even in pay grade 1 are paid more. Good management practice would be to correct this inequity as rapidly as possible by placing the job in the proper pay grade and increasing the pay of those who work that job.

Overpaid jobs present more of a problem. An overpaid job for pay grade 4 is illustrated in Figure 12-7 (note the circled dot above pay grade 4). Employees in this job earn $14.00 per hour, or 50 cents more than the maximum for the pay grade. This type of overpayment (and underpayment as well) is referred to as a red circle rate.[27]

An ideal solution to the problem of an overpaid job is to promote the employee. This might be a reasonable approach if the employee is qualified for a higher rated job and a job opening is available. Another possibility would be to bring the job rate and employee pay into line through a pay cut. This type of action may appear logical, but it isn't consistent with good management practice. This action would punish employees for a situation they did not create. Somewhere between these two possible solutions is a third: to freeze the rate until across-the-board pay increases bring it into line. If the past few decades are an indication of the future, rising pay levels will eventually solve this problem.

■ OTHER COMPENSATION ISSUES

Several issues that affect compensation deserve special mention. They include comparable worth, pay secrecy, and pay compression. We present first the concept of comparable worth.

---

[26] Robert J. Greene, "Which Pay Delivery System Is Best for Your Organization?" *Personnel*, 58 (May–June 1981), p. 52.

[27] J. D. Dunn and Frank M. Rachel, *Wage and Salary Administration: Total Compensation Systems* (New York: McGraw-Hill, 1971), p. 228.

Comparable Worth

The comparable worth theory extends the concept of the Equal Pay Act, and it has become an extremely important political and social issue.[28] The theory became somewhat heated after Clarence Pendleton, Chairman of the U.S. Commission on Civil Rights, stated that comparable worth amounts to "Looney Tunes," which would skew the free-market system.[29] The Equal Pay Act requires equal pay for equal work, but advocates of comparable worth prefer a broader interpretation: requiring equal pay for comparable worth. **Comparable worth** requires the value for dissimilar jobs (e.g., company nurse and welder) to be compared under some form of job evaluation and pay rates to be assigned according to their evaluated worth. Because of the widespread support for this theory, it isn't likely to fade quickly.[30]

The basic premise of comparable worth is that jobs traditionally held by women are paid less than those traditionally held by men, even though both types may make equal contributions to the organization's goals.[31] Specifically, for the first quarter of 1984, the median weekly earnings of full-time women employees was 65 percent of that of men.[32] Jobs that have historically been filled by women pay less, and when employers use market data for establishing pay rates, the pay differentials are perpetuated. Many business managers and business groups oppose comparable worth, but some human resource executives believe that pay systems based on the comparable worth concept are fairer than those that rely on market pricing.[33]

Opponents of comparable worth contend that the earnings gap reflects an overall statistic and does not compare the earnings of two people performing the same job. They state that the gender difference is explainable by the large number of young women who have recently entered the workforce at entry-level pay rates. They also point out that a substantial number of women are employed in low-paying industries. Another point frequently made is that women often voluntarily leave the workforce to raise a family, while men continue with the job and receive promotions and pay increases.

Comparable worth detractors often state that the real problem in pay gap is gender segregation in jobs rather than either the underpayment of

---

[28] John F. Sullivan, "Comparable Worth and the Statistical Audit of Pay Programs for Illegal Systematic Discrimination," *Personnel Administrator*, 30 (March 1985), p. 10.

[29] "Oaker, Pendleton Trade Barbs over Comparable Worth Argument," *Resource*, ASPA (May 1985), p. 1.

[30] Lawrence Z. Lorber, J. Robert Kirk, Stephen L. Samuels, and David J. Spellman III, *Sex and Salary: A Legal and Personnel Analysis of Comparable Worth* (Alexandria, Va.: The ASPA Foundation, 1985), p. 51.

[31] Doug Grider and Mike Shurden, "The Gathering Storm of Comparable Worth," *Business Horizons*, 30 (July–August 1987), pp. 81–82.

[32] "Twenty Questions on Comparable Worth," The Equal Employment Advisory Council, 1984. Reprinted in *Personnel Administrator*, 30 (April 1985), p. 65.

[33] Daniel Seligman, "Pay Equity Is a Bad Idea," *Fortune* (May 1984), p. 140.

jobs traditionally filled by women or the overpayment of jobs traditionally filled by men.[34] Furthermore, they note that existing law prohibits employers from paying women at a lower rate than a man for doing the same work. A more effective solution, they suggest, would be to continue to enforce equal opportunity and equal pay laws. In addition, women should be encouraged to enter nontraditional occupations and be provided with equal access to education, training programs, and employment. Also, efforts should be continued to promote a nondiscriminatory socialization process for children. These alternatives, rather than artificially raising the price of labor for special groups, will address the problem of gender discrimination.[35]

Perhaps the greatest fear of implementing comparable worth standards is the cost of replacing market forces of supply and demand with a government-imposed system of job evaluation. One source estimated that closing the earnings gap would cost $320 billion a year.[36]

The Washington state case is perhaps the best known example of comparable worth in action. In 1982, the state was sued by the American Federation of State, County, and Municipal Employees (AFSCME). The union charged that women employees of the state were being discriminated against. In fact, some jobs traditionally filled by women had been evaluated at a higher level under the state's job evaluation plan, but the pay rates were less than for jobs traditionally filled by men. The discrimination charge was upheld in U.S. District Court and the District Judge's order required the state immediately to bring all workers in the job categories filled predominantly with women up to their evaluated rates. The U.S. Court of Appeals for the Ninth Circuit overturned this decision, which otherwise could have cost the State of Washington $1 billion.[37] The issue will probably be decided finally by the U.S. Supreme Court.

In addition to Washington, a number of other states are obviously taking comparable worth seriously. For example, Minnesota has been giving average raises of $1,600 to more than 8000 employees in job categories filled predominantly with women.[38] At this time, at least 20 states have passed comparable worth legislation.[39] The goal of nondiscriminatory pay practices is one that every organization should seek to achieve for ethical and legal reasons, but whether comparable worth is an appropriate solution remains to be seen.

Pay Secrecy

Organizations tend to keep their pay rates secret for various reasons. If a firm's compensation plan is illogical, secrecy may indeed be appropriate

---

[34] Sullivan, p. 103.

[35] Julie M. Buchanan, "Comparable Worth: Where Is It Headed?" *Human Resources: Journal of the International Association for Personnel Women*, 2 (Summer 1985), p. 12.

[36] "Twenty Questions on Comparable Worth," p. 65.

[37] Carrie Dolan and Leonard M. Apcar, "Washington State Union to Fight Ruling that Hurts Equal Pay—Equal Jobs Drive," *The Wall Street Journal*, September 6, 1985, p. 6.

[38] Seligman, pp. 136–137.

[39] Grider and Shurden, p. 85.

because only a well designed system can stand careful scrutiny.[40] An open system would almost certainly require managers to explain its rationale for pay decisions to subordinates.

Secrecy has curious results, however. For example, managers who are unaware of pay rates in their firm tend to overestimate the pay of managers around them and to underestimate what higher level managers make. Such perceptions destroy much of the motivation intended in a differential pay system and indirectly contribute to turnover.[41]

Ideally, a firm will strive to develop a logical pay system, which reflects both internal and external equity. Employees in the process should participate to the greatest extent feasible. Compensation managers should take the lead in ensuring that employees understand the bases for their pay. Obviously, management cannot make all employees happy. The dissatisfaction and costs associated with a secret pay system, however, seem to make it a highly questionable practice.

Pay Compression

Organizations normally strive for both internal and external pay equity. In practice, however, this is often difficult or even impossible to accomplish. For example, in order to attract an engineer to a firm, an unusually high salary may have to be paid. Individuals possessing the skills needed to perform this job are in short supply relative to the demand for their services. Therefore these workers, and others in similar situations, are able to command high salaries (and in the process experience external pay equity).[42]

But how does the hiring of this type of employee affect internal equity? Other jobs within the firm may have greater value to the firm—as determined by job evaluation—but are now paid less than the engineers. In this instance, the firm sacrificed internal equity because it had little choice in the matter, assuming that it had to fill the engineer job.

Situations of this type may also result in a troublesome problem called pay compression. **Pay compression** occurs when workers perceive that the pay differential between their pay and that of employees in jobs above or below them is too small.[43] It can be created in several ways, including the hiring of new employees at pay rates comparable to those of current employees who may have been with the firm for several years. Making pay adjustments at the lower end of the job hierarchy without commensurate adjustments at the top is also a common cause of pay compression.

Pay compression may also result from granting pay increases on a flat cents-per-hour basis over a long period of time. Percentage increases, on

---

[40] Caruth, p. 244.

[41] Edward E. Lawler III, *Pay and Organizational Effectiveness: A Psychological View* (New York: McGraw-Hill, 1971) pp. 174–175, 196–197.

[42] Hubbartt, p. 24.

[43] Thomas J. Bergmann, Frederick S. Hills, and Laurel Priefert, "Pay Comparison: Causes, Results and Possible Solutions," *Compensation Review*, 15 (Second Quarter 1983), pp. 17–18.

the other hand, maintain relative differences in pay rates. The result of compression is dissatisfaction on the part of employees in higher level jobs. With the slope of the pay curve flattened, there is less financial incentive for employees to strive for promotion.[44]

SUMMARY

Compensation refers to the rewards that individuals receive in return for their labor. Direct financial compensation consists of the pay that a person receives in the form of wages, salary, bonuses, and commissions. Indirect financial compensation (benefits) includes all financial rewards that are not included in direct compensation. Nonfinancial compensation is the satisfaction a person receives directly from the job or from the psychological and/or physical job environment. All these types of compensation comprise a total compensation program.

Equity refers to the perception by workers that they are being treated fairly. External equity exists when employees performing jobs within a firm are paid at levels comparable to those paid for similar jobs in other firms. Internal equity exists when employees are paid according to the relative value of their jobs within the organization. Job evaluation is a primary means for determining internal equity. Employee equity exists when individuals performing similar jobs in the same firm are paid according to factors unique to the employee, such as productivity.

Many factors interact with and affect compensation. The organization, the labor market, the job, and the employee all have an impact on determining the individual's financial compensation.

Before a company can determine the relative difficulty or value of its jobs, it must first define their content. This is normally achieved through job analysis. Job evaluation is that part of a compensation system by which a firm determines the relative values of its jobs. The basic purpose of job evaluation is to eliminate internal pay inequities that exist because of illogical pay structures. Organizations use four basic job evaluation methods: ranking, classification, factor comparison, and point. The ranking and classification methods are qualitative, whereas the factor comparison and point methods are quantitative approaches.

In the ranking method, raters examine the description of each job being evaluated and arrange the jobs in order according to their value to the company. The classification method defines a number of classes, or grades, of jobs. The factor comparison method is based on the assumption that five universal job factors exist; Raters need not keep the entire job in mind as they evaluate, and they make decisions on separate aspects, or factors, of

---

[44] Bruce R. Ellig, "Pay Inequities: How Many Exist Within Your Organization?" *Compensation Review*, 12 (Third Quarter 1980), p. 42.

the job. In the point method, numerical values are assigned to specific job components and the sum of these values represents a job's relative worth.

Placing a dollar value on the worth of a job is called job pricing. Jobs are priced after they have been evaluated and the relative value of each job in the organization has been determined. A pay grade is the grouping of similar jobs to simplify the job pricing process. A pay range includes a minimum and maximum pay rate, with enough variance between the two to allow some significant pay difference. Pay ranges allow employees to be paid according to length of service and performance levels. When pay ranges are used, a method must be developed to advance individuals through the range.

Several issues that impact compensation deserve special mention, including comparable worth, pay secrecy, and pay compression. Comparable worth requires the value for dissimilar jobs (e.g., company nurse and welder) to be compared under some form of job evaluation and pay rates to be assigned according to their evaluated worth. The basic premise of comparable worth is that jobs traditionally held by women are paid less than those traditionally held by men, even though both types of jobs may contribute equally to achieving the organization's goals.

Organizations tend to keep their pay rates secret for various reasons. If a firm's compensation plan is illogical, secrecy may indeed be appropriate because only a well-designed system can stand careful scrutiny.

Pay compression occurs when workers perceive that the differential between their pay and that of employees in jobs above or below them is too small. It can be created in several ways, including hiring new employees at pay rates comparable to those of current employees who may have been with the firm for several years. Making pay adjustments at the lower end of the job hierarchy without commensurate adjustments at the top is a common cause of pay compression.

Questions for Review

1. Define each of the following terms:
   (a) Compensation
   (b) Direct financial compensation
   (c) Indirect financial compensation
   (d) Nonfinancial compensation
2. Distinguish among external equity, internal equity, and employee equity.
3. What are the primary determinants of financial compensation? Briefly describe each.
4. Distinguish among a pay follower, a pay leader, and a going-rate organization.
5. How has government legislation affected compensation?
6. Give the primary purpose of job evaluation.
7. Distinguish among the four basic methods of job evaluation: ranking, classification, factor comparison, and point.
8. What is the purpose of job pricing? Discuss briefly.
9. State the basic procedure for determining pay grades.
10. What is the purpose for establishing pay ranges?
11. Describe the various factors relating to the employee in determining pay and benefits.
12. Describe each of the following concepts:
    (a) Comparable worth
    (b) Pay secrecy
    (c) Pay compression

Terms for Review

Compensation
Direct financial compensation
Indirect financial compensation
Nonfinancial compensation
Equity
External equity
Internal equity
Employee equity
Pay leaders
Going rate
Pay followers
Labor market
Key job
Cost-of-living allowance (COLA)

Exempt employees
Job evaluation
Ranking method
Classification method
Factor comparison method
Point method
Hay guide chart-profile method
Job pricing
Pay grade
Wage curve
Pay range
Comparable worth
Pay compression

INCIDENT 1 ▪ It's Just Not Fair! ▪

During a Saturday afternoon golf game with his friend Randy Dean, Harry Neil discovered that his department had hired a recent university grad as a systems analyst—at a starting salary almost as high as Harry's. Although Harry was good natured, he was bewildered and upset. It had taken him five years to become senior systems analyst and attain his current salary level at Trimark Data Systems, Inc. He had been generally pleased with the company and thoroughly enjoyed his job.

The following Monday morning Harry confronted Dave Edwards, the human resource director, and asked if what he had heard was true. Dave apologetically admitted that it was and attempted to explain the company's situation: "Harry, the market for systems analysts is very tight and in order for the company to attract qualified prospects, we have to offer a premium starting salary. We desperately needed another analyst and this was the only way we could get one."

Harry asked Dave if his salary would be adjusted accordingly. Dave answered, "Your salary will be reevaluated at the regular time. You're doing a great job, though, and I'm sure the boss will recommend a raise." Harry thanked Dave for his time but left the office shaking his head and wondering about his future.

Questions

1. Do you think Dave's explanation was satisfactory? Discuss.
2. What action do you believe the company should have taken with regard to Harry?

INCIDENT 2 — Job Evaluation: Who or What?

David Rhine, compensation manager for Farrington Lingerie Company, was generally relaxed and good natured. Although he was a no-nonsense, competent executive, David was one of the most popular managers in the company. This Friday morning, however, David was not his usual self. As chairperson of the company's job evaluation committee, he had called a late morning meeting at which several jobs were to be considered for reevaluation. The jobs had already been rated and assigned to pay grade 3. But the office manager, Ben Butler, was upset that one was not rated higher. To press the issue, Ben had taken his case to two executives who were also members of the job evaluation committee. The two executives (production manager Bill Nelson and general marketing manager Betty Anderson) then requested that the job ratings be reviewed. Bill and Betty supported Ben's side of the dispute and David was not looking forward to the confrontation that was almost certain to occur.

The controversial job was that of receptionist. There was only one receptionist position in the company and it was held by Beth Smithers. Beth had been with the firm twelve years—longer than any of the committee members. She was extremely efficient, and virtually all the executives in the company, including the president, had noticed and commented on her outstanding work. Bill Nelson and Betty Anderson were particularly pleased with Beth because of the cordial manner in which she greeted and accommodated Farrington's customers and vendors, who frequently visited the plant. They felt that Beth projected a positive image of the company.

When the meeting began, Dave said, "Good morning. I know that you're busy so let's get the show on the road. We have several jobs to evaluate this morning and I suggest we begin . . ." Before he could finish his sentence, Bill interrupted. "I suggest we start with Beth." Betty nodded in agreement. When David regained his composure, he quietly but firmly asserted, "Bill, we are not here today to evaluate Beth. Her supervisor does that at performance appraisal time. We're meeting to evaluate jobs based on job content. In order to do this fairly with regard to other jobs in the company, we must leave personalities out of our evaluation." David then proceeded to pass out copies of the receptionist job description to Bill and Betty, who were most irritated.

Questions

1. Do you feel that David was justified in insisting that the job, not the person, be evaluated? Discuss.
2. Do you believe that there is a maximum rate of pay for every job in an organization, regardless of how well the job is being performed? Justify your position.
3. Assuming that Beth is earning the maximum of the range for her pay grade, in what ways can she obtain a salary increase?

Experiencing Human Resource Management

In the future, one of the key issues concerning pay will be comparable worth. If comparable worth becomes law, organizations will have to base salaries and wages on job evaluation scores. They will be determined by the requirements of the job itself—skills required, knowledge required, effort required, working conditions, and responsibilities—rather than the workings of the labor market. Then equal pay for different jobs of the same value will have to be determined, not by looking at the "going rate" in the marketplace, but rather at the job's difficulty, importance, and the training required to properly perform it. This exercise has been developed to impart an understanding and appreciation of the concept of comparable worth.

The concept of comparable worth is based on three premises:

1. That it is possible to compare different jobs and establish a "correct pay" relationship for them.
2. That the pay established by the supply and demand of the job market is often inequitable and discriminatory, especially with respect to pay for women.
3. That the government and the courts must intervene to ensure that pay relationships are corrected and made equitable.

Everyone will be given a copy of Exhibit 1, and based on these three premises determine the following:

1. Which of the following jobs would you consider "comparable"? (Select a job from the second list and write it beside the job on the first list to which you feel it "compares.")
2. What average monthly salary would you assign to each position? After 10 minutes everyone will sign their Exhibits and turn them in. Then, three participants with dissimilar comparisons will list their comparisons and salaries on the chalkboard and debriefing will begin.

REFERENCES

"Are Companies Alienating the Great Middle?" *Management Review*, 74 (May 1985), p. 5.

Baxter, D. "Why Does a Company Need Salary Ranges?" *Personnel Administrator*, 30 (April 1985), p. 12.

Belcher, David W., and Thomas J. Atchison. *Compensation Administration*, 2nd ed. (Englewood Cliffs, N.J.: Prentice-Hall, 1987).

Bookbinder, Stephen M., and Robert M. Seraphin. "Making Pay for Performance Work." *Personnel*, 64 (September 1987), p. 66.

Buchanan, Julie M. "Comparable Worth: Where Is It Headed?" *Human Resources: Journal of the International Association for Personnel Women*, 2 (Summer 1985), p. 12.

Burgess, Leonard R. *Wage and Salary Administration* (Columbus, Ohio: Charles E. Merrill, 1984).

Cissell, Michael J. "Designing Effective Reward Systems." *Compensation and Benefits Review*, 19 (November–December 1987), pp. 19–25.

"Compensation Currents." *Compensation Review*, 17 (First Quarter 1985), p. 2.

Crystal, Graef S. "Outlook on Compensation and Benefits: To the Rescue of Pay for Performance." *Personnel*, 62 (January 1985), p. 9.

Davis, K. R., Jr., et al. "What College Graduates Want in a Compensation Package." *Compensation Review*, 17 (1985), pp. 42–53.

Dunn, J. D., and Frank M. Rachel, *Wage and Salary Administration: Total Compensation Systems* (New York: McGraw-Hill, 1971).

Ellig, Bruce R. "Strategic Pay Planning." *Compensation and Benefits Review*, 19 (July–August 1987), p. 28.

Employment Relations under the Fair Labor Standards Act (Washington, D.C.: U.S. Department of Labor, Employment Standards Administration, Wage and Hour Division, WH Publication 1297; revised May 1980, reprinted August 1985).

Feuer, Dale. "Paying for Knowledge." *Training: The Magazine of Human Resources Development*, 21 (May 1987), p. 57–64.

Ginsburg, Sigmund G. "Motivating with Money." *American School and University*, 59 (July 1987), p. 11.

Grant, Dale B. "Total Compensation Management." *Compensation and Benefits Review*, 18 (September–October 1986), pp. 62–67.

Grider, Doug, and Mike Shurden. "The Gathering Storm of Comparable Worth." *Business Horizons*, 30 (July–August 1987), p. 81–82.

Henderson, Richard I. *Compensation Management*, 4th ed. (Reston, Va.: Reston Publishing Company, 1985), p. 231.

Hoffman, Carl C. "Are Multiple-Pay Systems Worth the Risk?" *Management Review*, 76 (July 1987), pp. 39–44.

Horton, Thomas R. "80s Style Compensation." *Credit and Financial Management*, 89 (November 1987), p. 10.

Hurwick, Mark R. "Strategic Compensation Designs that Link Pay to Performance." *Journal of Business Strategy*, 7 (Fall 1986), pp. 79–83.

Kien, J. M. "Keeping Up with the Jones's." *Pulp and Paper*, 59 (May 1985), p. 5.

Kuhne, R. J., and B. Toyne. "Who Manages the International Compensation and Benefits Program?" *Compensation Review*, 17 (1985), pp. 34–41.

"Latin America Poses Challenges to Executive Remuneration Plans." *Employee Benefit Plan Review*, 39 (January 1985), pp. 60–61.

Lawler, Edward E. III. "What's Wrong with Point-Factor Evaluation." *Personnel*, 64 (January 1987), p. 38.

Lorber, Lawrence Z., J. Robert Kirk, Stephen L. Samuels, and David J. Spellman III. "Sex and Salary: A Legal and Personnel Analysis of Comparable Worth." Alexandria, Va.: The ASPA Foundation (1985), p. 51.

Metzger, M. "Year End Compensation Accruals." *The CPA Journal*, 55 (April 1985), pp. 64–66.

Mickler, Mary Louise. "Merit Pay: Boon or Boondoggle?" *Clearing House*, 61 (November 1987), pp. 137–141.

Milkovich, George T., and Jerry M. Newman. *Compensation*, 2nd ed. (Plano, Texas: Business Publications, 1987), p. 3.

Morjaes, R. "Pay Policy: No Company Should Be Without One." *Accountancy*, 96 (March 1985), pp. 148–151.

Murphy, B. S. et al. "Pay Raises to Match Competing Bids Do Not Violate the Equal Pay Act." *Personnel Journal*, 64 (February 1985), p. 14.

Nasar, S. "Why Wages Won't Take Off." *Fortune* (April 1985), pp. 62–64.

"Outlook on Compensation and Benefits." *Personnel*, 62 (February 1985), pp. 72–74.

Plachy, Roger J. "The Case for Effective Point-Factor Job Evaluation, Viewpoint I." *Personnel*, 64 (April 1987), p. 31.

Schuster, Jay R. and Patricia K. Zingheim. "Merit Pay: Is It Hopeless in the Public Sector?" *Personnel Administrator*, 32 (October 1987), pp. 83–84.

Sears, D. "Make Employee Pay a Strategic Issue." *Compensation Review*, 17 (1985), pp. 55–60.

"Seniority Under Siege." *Fortune* (June 1987), pp. 10–11.

Stull, G. J. "Effective Compensation: Qualified Cash or Deferred Arrangements." *Taxes*, 63 (April 1985), pp. 267–277.

Sullivan, J. F. "Comparable Worth and the Statistical Audit of Pay Programs for Illegal Systematic Discrimination." *Personnel Administrator*, 30 (March 1985), pp. 102–111.

"Ten Terrific Employers (For Working Parents' Money)." *Money*, 14 (May 1985), p. 144.

"Twenty Questions on Comparable Worth." The Equal Employment Advisory Council, Reprinted in *Personnel Administrator*, 30 (April 1985), p. 65.

"Who Made the Most and Why." *Business Week* (May 2, 1988), p. 51.

"Women at Work." *Business Week* (January 28, 1985), p. 85.

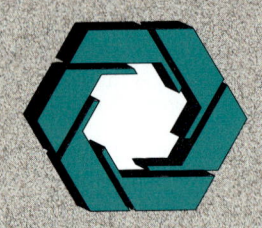

CHAPTER 13   BENEFITS AND OTHER COMPENSATION ISSUES

Chapter Objectives

1. Define benefits and describe their importance to the total compensation program.
2. Explain the various incentive compensation programs that are available.
3. Describe how compensation for managers, professionals, and sales representatives is determined.
4. Explain the many forms of nonfinancial compensation that employees are beginning to expect.
5. Describe factors that affect compensation in multinational corporations.

■ John Hicks—a college dropout—was a senior credit clerk at Ajax Manufacturing Company. A bright young man, John had been with Ajax for four years. He had received excellent performance ratings in each of several positions he had held with the firm. However, during his last appraisal interview, John's supervisor implied that promotion to a higher level job would require additional formal education. Because John appeared to be receptive to the idea, his supervisor suggested that he check with human resources to learn the details of Ajax's educational assistance policy.

■ Arnold Anderson, Bob Minnis, and Mason Kearby are all employed as shipping clerks for Mainstreet Furniture Company. Arnold and Bob are energetic young people who consistently work hard each day. Both earn about $6.50 per hour. Mason is a "good ole boy" who spends most of his time flipping quarters with dock workers and talking with anyone who will listen. Yesterday, work was piling up in the department and Arnold and Bob were working furiously to keep up. Mason was nowhere to be found. "Arnold," Bob said disgustedly, "the pay here just isn't fair. We do twice as much work as Mason yet he makes as much as we do." "I know," Arnold acknowledged, "but we all punch in and out at the same time."

■ Liz Nichols was a divorcée and the mother of three elementary school children. She worked as an illustrator for Busiform Company to support her family. Her normal working hours were from 8:00 A.M. to 5:00 P.M., Monday through Friday. The children's school began each weekday morning at 9:00 A.M. and ended at 3:30 P.M. Satisfactory arrangements had been made for the children after school. However,

continued on next page

> *continued from previous page*
>
> she faced an almost impossible task of transporting them to school in the morning and arriving at her job on time. The school's principal permitted the children to enter the building at 7:45 each morning to wait until classes began, but Liz was afraid that she couldn't count on this practice to continue indefinitely. When Busiform management announced implementation of a new system of flexible working hours, Liz was delighted.

Although these anecdotes may seem to have little in common, each relates to the broad area of compensation. John is investigating the possibility of continuing his education through his company's educational assistance program. Arnold and Bob are angry because a less productive worker makes as much money as they do. Liz believes that the new flexible working hours will solve her most difficult problem in caring for her children.

We begin the chapter with a discussion of benefits, both mandated and voluntary. Next, we present various types of incentive compensation systems, followed by a discussion of special pay considerations that are provided to managers, professionals, and sales representatives. Then we describe nonfinancial compensation that stems from the job itself and the job environment. In the final section we deal with the unique aspects of compensation in multinational corporations. The overall purpose of this chapter is to emphasize the significance of benefits in a total compensation system and provide an overview of other important issues associated with compensation programs.

■ BENEFITS (INDIRECT FINANCIAL COMPENSATION)

Most organizations recognize that they have a responsibility to their employees by providing insurance and other programs for their health, safety, security, and general welfare (see Figure 13-1). These programs are called **benefits** and include all financial rewards that generally are not paid directly to the employee. Benefits cost the firm money, but employees usually receive them indirectly. For example, an organization may spend $1,500 a year to pay the health insurance premiums for each nonexempt employee. The employee does not receive money but does obtain the benefit of health insurance coverage. This type of compensation has two distinct advantages: (1) it is generally nontaxable to the employee; and (2) in the case of insurance, the premium rates are much less for large groups of employees than for individual policies.

Generally speaking, benefits are provided to employees because of their membership in the organization. They are typically not related to employee productivity and therefore do not serve as motivation for improved performance. However, an attractive benefit package can assist in the recruitment and retention of a qualified workforce.

The cost of benefits is high and is growing rapidly, costing employers some $350 billion a year. In 1986, the average cost of benefits in all indus-

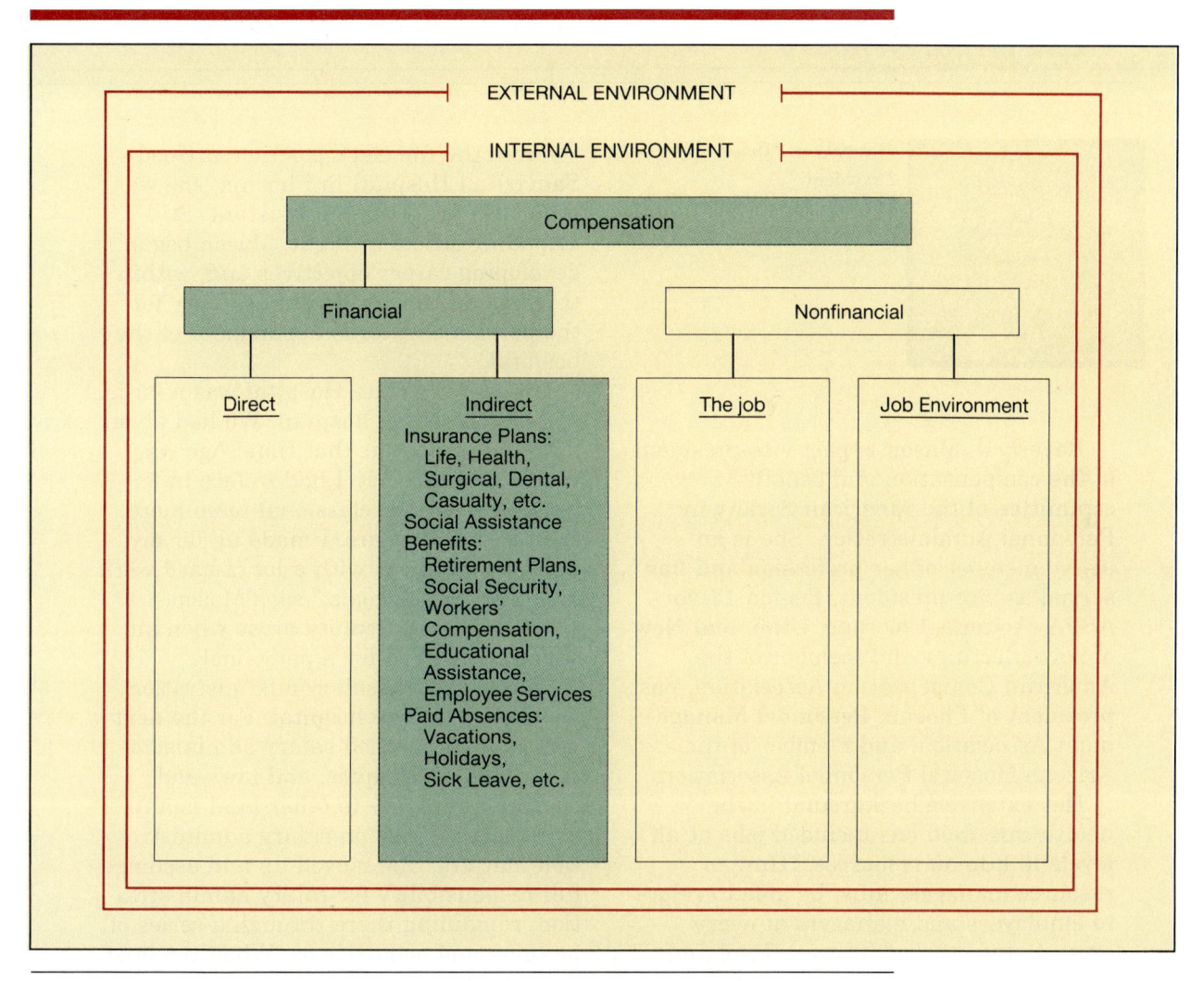

FIGURE 13-1 | Typical Benefits in a Total Compensation Program

tries, as a percentage of total financial costs, was over 38 percent. The average annual benefits costs per employee ranged from $13,450 in the rubber, leather, and plastic industries to $5,102 in department stores.[1] A typical worker who earns $24,800 per year receives approximately $9,424 more, indirectly, in the form of benefits. This proportion no doubt accounts for the much less frequent use of the term *fringe* benefits. In fact, the ben-

---

[1] Albert G. Holzinger, "The Real Costs of Benefits," *Nation's Business*, 76 (February 1988), p. 30.

Executive Insights

Beverly J. Mason
President,
Oakmark of Phoenix

Beverly J. Mason is past vice-president of the compensation and benefit committee of the American Society for Personnel Administration. She is an active member of her profession and has served as vice-president, Region 17, for ASPA (Arizona, Colorado, Utah, and New Mexico), lecturer and member of the American Compensation Association, past president of Phoenix Personnel Management Association, and member of the Arizona Hospital Personnel Association.

Her extensive background in the health care field has included jobs at all levels in human resources. "Human resource managers must be able to relate to employees and managers at every level. I have worked at every level and understand the problems and concerns of both employees and supervisors," says Mason. "If you can't communicate, you can't make it in our field."

While still in college, she began her career in human resources. "As a personnel file clerk at age 17, I wasn't giving too much thought to a career," says Mason. However, this job proved to be the beginning of a long and rewarding career.

From the file clerk position at Good Samaritan Hospital in Phoenix, she was promoted to personnel assistant. Still attending school at night, Mason began developing career objectives and, within three years, assumed responsibility for the personnel records department of the hospital.

"Good Samaritan Hospital was a large, 650-bed, teaching hospital. We had about 2,000 employees at that time. Age was the biggest obstacle I had to face in working with a professional team more than twice my years. I made up for my lack of experience with a lot of hard work and solid career goals," says Mason.

Her next opportunity arose when an opening occurred for a personnel technician in the salary administration department of the hospital. For the next year, she researched salary administration plans, techniques, and laws and became a resource to other local health care professionals on salary administration matters. She moved up and assumed full responsibility for salary administration, remaining there through a series of mergers and acquisitions. When the dust settled, she was corporate manager of salary administration for Samaritan Health Service. Samaritan is a large, nonprofit, health care corporation that owns and operates hospitals, clinics, and related services throughout Arizona and Utah.

Mason headed the salary administration department at Samaritan until July 1977. She recalls, "I learned a great deal from 1975 to 1977. The health care field was beginning to be treated as big business and management was expected to evolve with it. There was a lot of turmoil, a few unionizing attempts, and 'fallout' from the management ranks because they couldn't keep up. Human resource managers had their hands full with labor shortages, salary increases running 15 percent annually, and the community screaming about rising health care costs."

All the attention the health care field was getting was a boost to Mason's career. Valley National Bank sought her out to head its salary administration program in July 1977. "I was misquoted on the front page of our local paper concerning salary increases for county employees the morning the bank board of directors voted on bringing me in as an officer. I was serving on a special task force reviewing proposed salary increases for county employees; the subject was very controversial because their wages had been frozen. Although the bank directors voted me in, I think they were a little worried about my press following!" she reports.

She stayed at Valley for two years. She feels that this experience broadened her knowledge and provided insight into another specialized field. They never quite made her a banker, though, and on August 1, 1979, the senior vice-president for Samaritan lured her back to that company.

Mason's career took a slightly different turn in December 1980, when she was asked to assume responsibility for benefits in addition to her responsibilities for salary administration. "Samaritan had grown to over 7,000 employees, was self-insured, and self-administered almost all of its benefit plans. It was a real challenge for an individual who had limited exposure to benefits administration," she says. Mason spent three years designing and implementing benefit plans, conducting benefit fairs, and improving the overall understanding of employee benefits and their costs.

Her next career opportunity came in January 1984. The president of DynaCor, Inc., asked her to join his executive staff as corporate manager of human resources. Her people skills and ability to get things done were what they were looking for. DynaCor specializes in providing services to the health care market. They also own and operate long-term care facilities in Arizona and South Dakota. "This was a most challenging position. We went through the phases of rapid growth, cutbacks, and reorganization. I had to draw on my own experience as well as that of my fellow professionals." In 1985, she was promoted to vice-president, human resources.

Mason's latest career opportunity came in 1986. She was promoted to president of a joint venture between DynaCor and the Oakmark Corporation. Oakmark of Phoenix was formed to offer third-party administration and physician billing services to major employers, HMOs, and physicians throughout Maricopa County.

efits that employees receive today are significantly different from those of just ten years ago.[2]

Benefits Required by Law

Some organizations would probably provide mandated benefits regardless of legal requirements. However, most firms have no choice in the matter and must provide certain benefits to their employees. Some might say, "If it is required by law, then it is not a benefit." Nevertheless, the firm is contributing additional money on behalf of their employees. For this reason, these items are considered to be benefits. Legally required benefits include social security, unemployment compensation, and workers' compensation.

Social Security. The Social Security Act of 1935 created a system of retirement benefits. Subsequent amendments to the act added other forms of protection, such as disability insurance, survivors benefits, and, most recently, medicare. Today, approximately nine out of ten employees in the United States are covered by social security. Disability insurance protects employees against loss of earnings resulting from total disability. Survivors benefits are provided to certain members of an employee's family when he or she dies. These benefits are paid to the widow, widower, and unmarried children of the deceased employee. Unmarried children may be eligible for survivors benefits until they are eighteen years old. In some cases, students retain eligibility until they are nineteen. Medicare provides hospital and medical insurance protection for individuals sixty-five years of age and older and for those who have become disabled.

While employees must pay a portion of the cost, the employer makes an equal contribution for social security coverage. It is the employer's part that is considered a benefit. As Table 13-1 shows, in 1937 workers paid 1 percent of the first $3,000 they earned—a maximum of $30. At that time, only 40 percent of American workers were covered. During the first forty years of its existence, the maximum tax increased to $965.25. From 1977 to 1987, the maximum tax almost tripled and projections indicate steady increases in the future. Today, approximately 95 percent of the workers in this country pay into and may draw social security benefits.

The normal retirement age under social security will be increased after the turn of the century. Beginning with employees who reach age sixty-two in the year 2000, the retirement age will be increased gradually until 2009 when it reaches age sixty-six. After stabilizing at this age for a period of time, it will again increase slowly until 2027 when it reaches age sixty-seven. These changes will not affect medicare, with full eligibility under this program holding at age sixty-five.[3]

Unemployment Compensation. An individual laid off by an organization covered by the Social Security Act may receive unemployment compen-

---

[2] Robert E. Perkins, "The Employer's Role in Benefits Evolution," *Personnel*, 64 (February 1987), p. 66.

[3] "Compensation Currents," *Compensation Review*, 15 (Third Quarter 1983), p. 4.

TABLE 13-1 | Social Security Taxes, 1977–1990 and After

	Tax Rate for Employee and Employer (Each)				
Year	For cash benefits	For hospitalization insurance	Total	Maximum Taxable Wage	Maximum Tax
1937	— %	— %	1.00%	$ 3,000	$ 30.00
1977	—	—	5.85	16,500	965.25
1984	5.70	1.30	7.00	37,800	2,646.00
1985	5.70	1.35	7.05	39,600	2,791.80
1986	5.70	1.45	7.15	42,000	3,003.00
1987	5.70	1.45	7.15	43,800	3,131.70
1988	6.06	1.45	7.51	45,000	3,379.50
1989	6.06	1.45	7.51	48,000	3,604.80
1990 (and after)	6.20	1.45	7.65	*	*

*The maximum will rise automatically as earnings levels increase.

Sources: *Your Social Security* (Washington, D.C.: U.S. Government Printing Office), January 1986 and 1987 editions; *Social Security '88* (Madison, Conn.: Business and Legal Reports), p. 1.

sation for up to twenty-six weeks. While the federal government provides certain guidelines, unemployment compensation programs are administered by the states and the benefits vary by state. A payroll tax paid by employers funds the unemployment compensation program.

Workers' Compensation. Workers' compensation benefits provide a degree of financial protection for employees who incur expenses resulting from job-related accidents or illnesses. As with unemployment compensation, the various states administer individual programs, subject to federal regulations. Employers pay the entire cost of workers' compensation insurance. Their premium expense is directly tied to their past experience with job-related accidents and illnesses. This situation should encourage employers to actively pursue health and safety programs—topics discussed in Chapter 14.

Voluntary Benefits

Organizations voluntarily provide a seemingly endless number of benefits. These benefits may be classified as (1) payment for time not worked, (2) employee health and security benefits, (3) services to employees, and (4) premium pay. Generally speaking, such benefits are not legally required. They are provided voluntarily by some firms and as a result of union–management negotiations in others.

Payment for Time Not Worked. In providing payment for time not worked, employers recognize that employees need time away from the job.

For instance, paid vacations provide workers with an opportunity to rest and become rejuvenated, while also encouraging them to remain with the firm. Paid vacation time typically increases with seniority. For example, employees with six-months' service may receive one week of vacation; employees with one year of service, two weeks; ten-years' service, three weeks; and fifteen-years' service, four weeks.

A senior executive with a month of vacation and an annual salary of $96,000 would receive approximately $8,000 each year while not working. A junior employee earning $24,000 a year might receive two weeks of vacation time worth about $1,000.

Each year many firms allocate to each employee a certain number of days of sick leave, which they can use when ill. Employees who are too ill to report to work continue to receive their pay up to the maximum number of days accumulated. As with vacation pay, the number of sick leave days typically depends on seniority. However, some sick leave programs have been severely criticized. At times they have been abused by individuals calling in sick when all they really wanted was additional paid vacation. In order to counter this situation, some firms require a doctor's statement after a certain number of sick leave days have been taken.

Employees are also paid at other times, even though they aren't working. Holidays, coffee breaks, rest periods, jury duty service, voting time, clean-up time, and bereavement time are all in this category.

Employee Welfare. Benefits that provide for general employee welfare may be of several kinds. Health insurance typically includes hospital room and board costs, service charges, and surgical fees. This increasingly costly benefit is often paid in part, or totally, by the employer. Many plans provide for major medical benefits to cover extraordinary expenses. The use of "deductibles" is a common feature of major medical benefits. For example, the employee may have to pay the first $200 of medical bills before the insurance takes over payment. In order to control health care costs, a number of firms have increased the amount of deductibles and at times have even reduced the scope of insurance coverage.

In some firms, health insurance premiums alone amount to almost 10 percent of the total payroll. In an attempt to control medical costs, some 30 percent of the businesses that provide medical benefits now use some type of utilization review service. **Utilization review** is a process that scrutinizes medical diagnoses, hospitalization, surgery, and other medical treatment and care prescribed by doctors. The reviewer, often a registered nurse, explores alternatives to the treatment provided, such as outpatient treatment or admission on the day of surgery. The objective of this process is, of course, to hold the line on businesses' portion of the nearly $400 billion Americans spend annually on medical care.[4] Beverly J. Mason, who is spotlighted in the previous Executive Insights, once had the task of helping

---

[4] Ellen Paris, "Hold That Scalpel?" *Forbes* (May 6, 1985), pp. 35–36.

employees to understand the value of employee benefits and their significant costs to the firm.

Wellness is a concept that focuses on the prevention of illness and diseases. It is also an approach to health care that offers great promise in stemming the tide of increasing treatment costs. Heavy smoking, poor nutrition, and undue stress are lifestyle and personal habit patterns that wellness programs challenge. It is important that the challenge succeed because these patterns contribute to diseases that account for a large share of health care expenditures.

There is considerable evidence that wellness programs work. For example, New York Telephone estimates annual savings of more than $2 million in reduced absenteeism and lowered medical costs from its stop-smoking program. Kennecott Corporation has reduced its medical care costs by more than 50 percent for the 12,000 employees participating in its wellness program.[5] We discuss topics related to wellness, such as stress and physical fitness, in Chapter 14.

Group life insurance is a benefit commonly provided to protect the employee's family in the event of his or her death. The cost of group life insurance is low. Some plans call for the employee to pay part of the premium. Coverage may be a flat amount, say, $10,000 or be based on the employee's annual earnings. For example, a worker earning $20,000 per year may have $40,000 worth of group life coverage. Typically, members of group plans do not have to show evidence of insurability. This provision is especially important to older employees and those with physical problems. Many of these employees may find the cost of individual insurance to be prohibitive.

Private retirement plans provide income for employees who retire after reaching a certain age or having served the firm for a specific period of time. Pension plans are vitally important to employees because social security was not designed to provide complete retirement income. The Employee Retirement Income Security Act of 1974 (ERISA) was passed to strengthen existing and future retirement programs. The act also ensures that retired employees will receive deserved pensions.

In 1984, ten years after ERISA became law, a major amendment, the Retirement Equity Act (REACT), was enacted. The purpose of this act is to provide greater equity in private pension plans for covered workers and their spouses. Changes were made in some of ERISA's rules, which originally tended to penalize working women. These modifications increase the likelihood that women will actually receive benefits on the basis of their participation in the workforce or as a surviving spouse.[6] Key features of REACT include:

---

[5] Robert D. Kilpatrick, "Increasing the Wellness Effort," *Industry Week* (February 4, 1985), p. 14.

[6] Jack H. Schechter, "The Retirement Equity Act: Meeting Women's Pension Needs," *Compensation Review*, 17 (First Quarter 1985), pp. 13–21.

- Pension plans must pay benefits as a qualified joining-and-survivor annuity when a participant retires, unless the employee's spouse consigns the benefit election form in which some other option is chosen.
- The qualified joint-and-survivor annuity requirement now also applies to defined-contribution pension plans other than employee stock ownership plans (ESOPs).
- Pension and profit-sharing plans must pay a survivor benefit to the widow or widower of any vested participant who dies before retirement, not just those of active employees who are fifty-five and older.
- Plans are allowed to honor state law alimony awards and other support orders if the order meets uniform basic standards, which may include an order to pay a benefit to the ex-spouse, even if the covered employee has not retired.
- Employees who are absent from work because of pregnancy, childbirth, adoption, or infant care are protected against break-in–service penalties for up to a year.
- A nonvested employee who leaves the employer's service and then comes back within five years will be entitled to credit for that earlier service, even if it was for less than five years.
- The minimum age for plan participation and benefit accrual cannot be higher than twenty-one, and the minimum age for vesting service cannot be higher than eighteen.
- Service pensions and other subsidized retirement benefits—as well as optional payment forms—can only be dropped from a plan with respect to benefits that are earned after the plan is amended to make the change.
- Plans can cash out benefits worth up to $3,500 without the recipient's consent (the amount previously was $1,750).[7]

Another piece of legislation that has an important effect on retired employees is the Comprehensive Omnibus Budget Reconciliation Act (COBRA). This act became law in 1986 and requires, among other things, that most employers in the private sector make available to terminated or retired employees and their families continued health benefits for a period of time, usually eighteen months. The cost of these benefits, however, must be borne by the former employee.

It is not yet clear how many individuals will take advantage of the benefits provided by COBRA. In many instances, employees will utilize coverage from their next employer or their spouse's employer. In either case, the cost will almost always be less.[8]

Supplemental unemployment benefits (SUB) first appeared in auto industry labor agreements in 1955.[9] They are designed to provide additional income for employees receiving unemployment insurance benefits. These plans have spread to many other industries and are usually financed by the

---

[7] Judith F. Mazo, "Another Compliance Challenge for Employers: The Retirement Equity Act," *Personnel*, 62 (February 1985), p. 43.

[8] Joan C. Szabo, "The Bite of COBRA," *Nation's Business*, 74 (December 1986), p. 54.

[9] David W. Belcher, *Compensation Administration* (Englewood Cliffs, N.J.: Prentice-Hall, 1974), p. 315.

company. They tend to benefit newer employees because layoffs are normally determined by seniority. For this reason, employees with considerable seniority are often not enthusiastic about SUB.

Employee Services. Organizations offer a variety of benefits that can be termed employee services. These include company subsidized food services, financial assistance for employee operated credit unions, legal and income tax aid, club memberships, athletic and recreational programs, discounts on company products, moving expenses, parking spaces, and tuition rebates on educational expenses. Such benefits can greatly enhance the employment relationship.

Premium Pay. **Premium pay** is compensation paid to employees for working long periods of time or working under dangerous or undesirable conditions. As we mentioned in Chapter 12, payment for overtime is required for nonexempt employees who work beyond forty hours in a given week. However, some firms pay overtime for hours worked beyond eight in a given day and pay double time—or even more—for work on Sundays and holidays.

Additional pay provided to employees who work under extremely dangerous conditions is called **hazard pay**. A window washer on skyscrapers in New York City might well be given extra compensation because of dangerous working conditions. Military pilots receive extra money in the form of flight pay because of the hazards involved.

A **shift differential** is paid to employees for the inconvenience of working undesirable hours. This type of pay may be provided on the basis of additional cents per hour. For example, employees who work the second shift ("swing" shift) from 4:00 P.M. until midnight might receive $0.35 per hour above the base rate for that job. The third shift ("graveyard" shift) often warrants an even greater differential. For example, an extra $0.42 per hour may be paid for the same job. Shift differentials are sometimes based on a percentage of the employee's base rate.

A Comprehensive Voluntary Benefits Program

International Business Machines Corporation offers a comprehensive voluntary benefits program. The program is noncontributory; that is, the company bears the full cost of the benefits. The growth of the IBM benefits program is shown in Figure 13-2. Note that since its inception, the program has improved and has been enlarged to meet changing employee needs. Three of the most recent additions are particularly interesting: the adoption assistance plan, the retirement education assistance plan, and the elder care referral service (ECRS).

Under the adoption assistance plan, IBM reimburses employees for 80 percent of eligible charges up to a maximum of $1750 for each adoption. Eligible charges include:

- Adoption agency fees
- Placement fees
- Lawyers' fees and other required legal fees

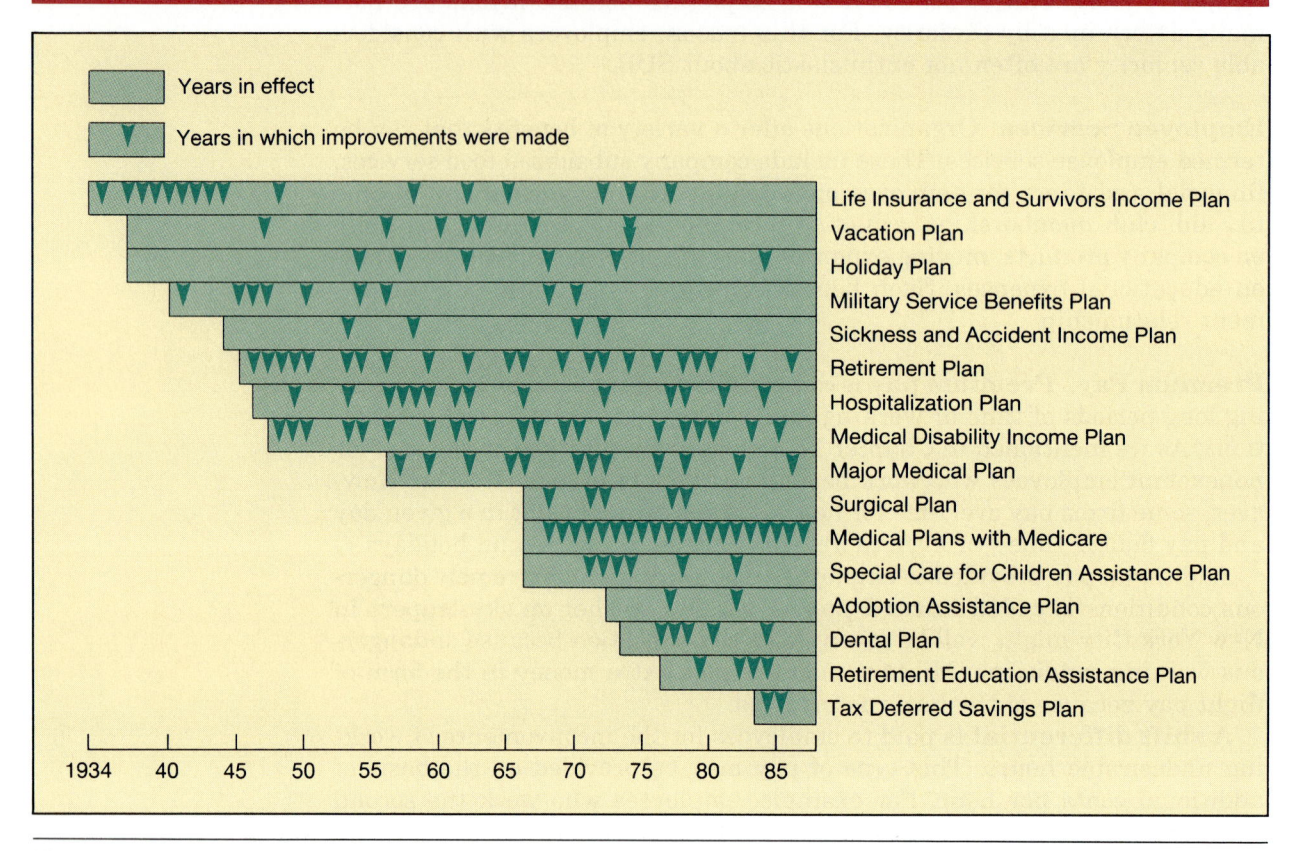

Figure 13-2 | IBM Benefits: Growth History

Source: Reprinted courtesy of International Business Machines Corporation.

- Maternity fees (child's natural mother)
- Temporary foster care charges (immediately preceding placement of the child with the adopting family)

The IBM retirement education assistance plan is designed to help employees and their spouses prepare for activities and personal fulfillment in their retirement years. Under this plan, IBM will reimburse tuition costs for retirement courses—up to $2500 per individual—upon evidence of course completion. This plan covers any course offered by nationally accredited colleges and postsecondary schools, as well as adult continuing-education courses conducted by state certified schools or educational organizations. Other courses that appear to meet the intent of the plan are also considered for reimbursement. An employee's eligibility in this plan begins five years before he/she is eligible to retire and continues until two years after the actual date of retirement.

The IBM Elder Care Referral Service is the first nationwide corporate program of its kind designed to provide consultation and referrals to employees seeking care and services for elderly relatives. This service was introduced in 1988 to respond to a growing need among IBM employees that relates to the fact that people over 65 now represent the fastest growing segment of our population. ECRS is a program designed to clarify employee concerns and identify resources to assist in the care of relatives aged 60 and over. The service is provided through a nationwide network of approximately 200 community-based consultation and referral organizations. These organizations provide personalized consultation, consumer information, and assistance in determining the type of elder care needed, along with referrals to the organizations best suited to provide such care. IBM will pay all costs for consultation and referrals, and employees or their older relatives are responsible for paying the fees to agencies furnishing the care. All regular IBM employees, retirees under the retirement plan, individuals receiving benefits under the medical disability income plan, spouses of these individuals, and surviving spouses who are eligible for IBM medical benefits may use the service.

New Benefits

Several new benefits have recently appeared on the scene in addition to those included in IBM's innovative plan. One such benefit is subsidized day-care centers where the firm provides facilities for young children of employees for a modest fee. Parents typically transport the children to and from the center. While there, the children engage in supervised play and receive meals. This benefit is an effective recruitment aid and helps to reduce absenteeism. The need for such programs is emphasized by the fact that during the 1980s, approximately half the American women with children under six years of age were in the workforce.[10] Although relatively few companies provide substantial child-care assistance, the number is growing rapidly. According to the U.S. Department of Health and Human Services, almost 600 firms provided this type of benefit in 1983, compared to only 100 five years earlier.[11]

In an attempt to conserve energy and relieve traffic congestion some firms have begun transporting workers to and from work. Participating employees pay a portion of the cost and ride in company vans or buses. Some employees find this service a very convenient, attractive alternative to driving in heavy traffic.

Massachusetts Mutual Life Insurance Company has initiated two new health care benefits.[12] One of these programs serves to detect and treat high blood pressure. Once each year, all employees are offered a physical examination. When a case of high blood pressure is detected, the employee is referred to his or her own physician for further diagnosis and treatment. The company pays all medical costs for this treatment. The company and employees believe that this program literally saves lives and, for this reason, it is a very popular benefit.

---

[10] "The New Corporate Goodies," *Dun's Review*, 18 (July 1981), p. 49.
[11] Carol Dilks, "Employers Who Help with the Kids," *Nation's Business*, 72 (February 1984), p. 59.
[12] "The New Corporate Goodies," p. 49.

The other program encourages employees to stop smoking. The company will reimburse any person on the payroll who consults a hypnotist for treatment. Although the program is new, about half the employees in the program have stopped smoking cigarettes.

Communicating Information about the Benefits Package

Employee benefits can help a firm recruit and retain a quality workforce. Management depends on an upward flow of information from employees in order to know when benefit changes are needed. In addition, because employee awareness of benefits is often severely limited, the program information must be communicated downward.[13] Regardless of the technical soundness of a benefits program, a firm simply cannot get its money's worth if its employees do not know what they are receiving. Workers may even become resentful if they aren't frequently reminded of the value of the company's benefits. Employees may resent having to pay a portion of some benefits but overlook the larger picture of what they receive and the substantially greater costs borne by their employer.[14]

The Employee Retirement Income Security Act provides still another reason for communicating information about a firm's benefits program. This act requires organizations with a pension or profit-sharing plan to provide employees with specific data at specified times. The act further mandates that the information be presented in an understandable manner and include:

- The kind of plan.
- Eligibility requirements.
- Amount of benefits due at specific times and payment options.
- Surviving dependents' benefits.
- How the pension trust is invested.
- Who is responsible for managing the plan.[15]

Naturally, organizations can go beyond what is legally required. In fact many firms, such as the Southland Corporation, did so even before ERISA's enactment. As shown in Figure 13-3, Southland's report provides each employee with a compensation and benefits profile. A summary of this type informs employees of their total compensation package and assists the firm in achieving its financial compensation and benefits objectives.

■ INCENTIVE COMPENSATION

One of the most significant U.S. economic problems in recent years has been the slowdown in the productivity growth rate. This problem, which

---

[13] Jeffrey C. Claypool and Joseph P. Cangemi, "The Annual Employee Earnings and Benefits Letter," *Personnel Journal*, 60 (July 1981), p. 49.

[14] Robert M. McCafferty, "Employee Benefits: Beyond the Fringe?" *Personnel Administrator*, 26 (May 1981), p. 30.

[15] Robert Krogman, "Is Your Company Getting the Most Out of Its Benefit Program?" *Personnel Administrator*, 25 (May 1980), pp. 45–46.

Prepared for:	John Doe 2828 N. Haskell Ave. Dallas, TX 75204	Hire Date: 01/05/82 Employee #: 987654321

COMPENSATION

Listed below is a schedule of compensation and benefits which Southland provided you either directly or indirectly for 1984:

Regular Earnings		$ 22,326.20
Profit Sharing Deferral	$1,665.90	
Earned Bonus		$ 2,679.14
F.I.C.A — Social Security		$ 1,662.83
Medical Expense Reimbursement		$ 282.71
Company Paid Medical Insurance Premium		$ 2,133.69
Profit Sharing Company Contribution		$ 883.01
Educational Reimbursement		$ 629.57
Vacation Days	10	
		$ 30,597.15

This Year 1985

Compensation:
Based on Your Present Annual Salary of	$ 25,260.00
and Including:	
Normal Bonus	$ 3,031.20
Your Estimated Compensation for 1985 Will Be	$28,291.20

Benefits

This benefits statement has been prepared for you based on information in Southland's records as of 02/19/85. Every effort has been made to assure the accuracy of the information reported, however, errors can occur. In all cases, actual benefits will be paid in accordance with the governing plan documents or insurance contracts. For more details on any of your benefits, refer to your plan booklets.

Benefits Package:
Protection for Today and Tomorrow . . .

Health Care

Hospital and Medical Benefits are provided for you by the Southland Corporation at no cost to you.

You have extended this benefit for 2 or more dependents at the cost of $14 per week. This premium is deducted from your check on a pre-tax basis.

Your medical plan reimburses 70% of all eligible hospital expenses after a $150 in-patient deductible (maximum $450 per year). With pre-admission certification the hospital deductible is waived and hospital room and board charges are paid at 80%. Your medical plan reimburses 70% of eligible non-hospital expenses after a $200 deductible per year. After your out-of-pocket expenses in 1985 have reached $3,000 (not including hospital deductible) you will be reimbursed 100% for eligible medical expenses for the remainder of the year. The lifetime maximum for reimbursement per covered individual is $1,000,000

Dental Benefits

Your medical plan reimburses 70% of eligible dental expenses. Dental expenses are subject to the annual deductible. The maximum reimbursement for 1985 for each insured individual is .... $ 1,000

FIGURE 13-3 | The Southland Corporation Individual Employee Compensation and Benefits Profile

Source: Used with the permission of the Southland Corporation.

Disability Benefits

Your disability benefits are based on your average weekly earnings at the time this statement was prepared and are subject to change.

	Monthly	Benefits Period Annual	Total

Disability benefits are provided for you after 90 days of employment at no cost. Benefits are based on 75% of your weekly earnings for the first 26 weeks of disability—65% thereafter during the remainder of the disability, before applicable deductions. Your benefits for the first 26 weeks would be $384.67
Per week, benefits thereafter would be $333.38
Per week, and could be payable for a total of 51 weeks.

Life Insurance Benefits

Your life insurance benefits are based on your average weekly earnings at the time this statement was prepared and are subject to change.

At no cost to you, The Southland Corporation has provided term life insurance to your beneficiary or estate in the amount of .... $ 13,335.62

You have elected to increase the amount of your term life insurance by selecting:
    Additional life insurance payable to your beneficiary as a lump sum in the amount of .... $ 40,006.86
    Survivors life insurance payable to your beneficiary as a lump sum in the amount of .... $ 40,006.86

The total life insurance benefit payable to your beneficiary in the event of your natural death is .... $ 80,013.72

Through the election of additional life insurance and survivor's life insurance, you have added:

    AD&D on yourself in the amount of .... $ 80,013.72
    Life insurance on your eligible spouse in the amount of $6,667.81
    Life insurance on each of your eligible dependent children in the amount of $3,333.90

The total life insurance benefit payable to your beneficiary in the event of your accidental death is $160,027.44

For more detailed information regarding other life insurance coverage, contact your division personnel manager or the group insurance department.

Employee Stock Ownership Plan

The employee stock ownership plan (ESOP) allows eligible employees to receive shares of the Southland Corporation common stock and participate in the growth of the company. If you were employed for one year or more on December, 31, 1984, you will receive share allocations. These shares will be allocated to an account in your behalf. For 1983, Southland contributed in excess of $3,000,000
This amount was used to purchase shares of stock on behalf of eligible employees. Your account is paid to you if you retire or leave the company, or to your beneficiary in the event of your death. ESOP participants will receive their individual statements at the annual profit sharing meeting.

FIGURE 13-3 | *Continued*

CHAPTER 13 Benefits and Other Compensations

Profit Sharing

The 1984 company contribution was in excess of $18,000,000

Your profit sharing account balance is payable to you at retirement. Payment may be made in a lump sum or on an installment schedule, whichever you select. Your account is payable to Jane Doe in the event of your death. Payment may be made in a lump sum or on an installment schedule, whichever your beneficiary elects. Your individual statement will be available to you at the annual profit sharing meeting.

The foundation of your retirement income will be your Southland profit sharing account along with social security. An individual retirement account (IRA) is another way to plan for your future and also provide tax advantages. IRA accounts are available through profit sharing. The Southland Credit Union, or other financial institutions. Consult with a savings/investment specialist to determine an approach that best suits your own savings ability and retirement goals.

Other Benefits

Social Security:

Southland matches your FICA payment for social security benefits. These benefits are provided to you by the United States government at age 65 or as early as age 62 at a reduced basis. Your spouse, age 65 or older, can receive additional social security payments equal to 40 to 50% of your benefit. In the event of your death or disability, benefits may be payable to your eligible dependents. For more detailed information, contact the Social Security Administration.

Credit Union:

You and your family members may join the credit union at any time after your employment. Secured and unsecured (signature) loans are available to credit union members at competitive rates. The credit union offers you the convenience of payroll deductions for savings, making loan payments and for the direct deposit of your paycheck for those with checking accounts. The credit union also offers you many savings plans including regular shares (savings), checking (share draft) accounts, certificate accounts, individual retirement accounts (IRA) and an insured money management star account.

Workers' Compensation and Unemployment Compensation:

The Southland Corporation pays the required cost of federal and state mandated benefits such as workers' compensation, unemployment compensation and disability benefits in some states.

Paid Time off for:

Vacation:
During 1984, you accrued 10 days of vacation time to be taken during 1985. This time may be adjusted if you were on a leave of absence during 1984.

Jury Duty:
Full pay for time served on jury duty.

Sick days:
Sick days vary by division as does eligibility.

Holidays:
Holidays vary by division as does eligibility.

Death in Family:
Full pay up to three days if there is a death in your immediate family.

In addition to all of the above, Southland provides numerous other valuable benefits which are significant and important to you:

Service Awards	Scholarships	Matching Gifts
Pre-Retirement Publications	Company Publications	Monthly Stock Investment
Leave of Absence	United States Auto Club	Holiday Gift Program
Discount Buying Service	Educational Reimbursement	Employee Assistance Program

apparently is being resolved, became especially severe during the mid-1980s.[16] While compensation is most often determined by how much time an employee spends at work, compensation programs that relate pay to productivity are referred to as **incentive compensation**. A primary purpose of an incentive plan is to encourage greater productivity from individuals and work groups. The assumption made by management is that money will motivate performance. Productive workers, such as Arnold Anderson and Bob Minnis (mentioned at the beginning of the chapter), probably would prefer to be paid on the basis of their output. In fact, they may not maintain their high performance level for long if they are not so paid. Money can serve as an important motivator for those who value it—and many individuals do. However, a clear relationship must exist between performance and pay if money is to serve as an effective motivator.

Output standards must be established before any type of incentive system can be introduced. This standard is a measure of work that an average, well-trained employee, working at a normal pace, should be able to accomplish in a given period of time. For example, a firm may determine that employees in a particular department should be able to produce five finished parts per hour. The standard then becomes five. Time study specialists in industrial engineering or methods departments are often responsible for establishing work standards. A more direct approach to balancing pay and performance is to pay incentive compensation, which can be offered on an individual, group, or companywide basis.

Individual Incentive Plans

Many individual incentive plans have been used in an attempt to improve worker productivity and a firm's profitability. Under an incentive plan, if Arnold Anderson produces more than Mason Kearby (another employee performing the same job), he would be paid more for producing more.

A predetermined amount of money is paid for each unit produced under a **straight piecework plan**. The piece rate is calculated by dividing the standard hourly output into the job's pay rate. For example, if the standard output is 0.04 hour per unit, or 25 units per hour, and the job's pay rate is $5 per hour, the piece rate would be $0.20. Thus an employee who produced at the rate of 280 units per day would earn $56 in an eight-hour day (280 units × 8 hours × $0.20). Most incentive plans in use today have a guaranteed base. In this example, it would be the $5 per hour rate.

The straight piecework plan is the most commonly used incentive system.[17] It is simple and employees can easily understand it. One possible weakness (which is minimized by the use of computers) is that any change in the overall pay scale necessitates computing new piece rates for every job. The standard hour plan was devised to overcome this problem.

---

[16] Edward M. Glaser, "Productivity Gains Through Worklife Improvement," *Personnel*, 57 (January–February 1980), p. 71.

[17] George T. Milkovich and Jerry M. Newman, *Compensation*, 2nd ed. (Plano, Texas: Business Publications, 1987), p. 314.

The **standard hour plan** is an individual incentive plan under which time allowances are calculated for each unit of output. Again, let's assume that 25 units per hour, or 0.04 hour per unit, is the standard output, $5 the hourly job rate, and eight hours the time worked per day. Under these assumptions, an employee would have an allowance of 0.04 hour per unit of output (instead of a piece rate of $0.20 per unit).

An employee producing at the rate of 280 units per day would receive an allowance of 0.04 hour per unit for all units produced in a day. Therefore, in an eight-hour day, this employee would earn 11.2 standard hours (280 units × 0.04 hour per unit). The pay for the day would be 11.2 standard hours × $5 per hour, or $56. The standard hour plan has the characteristics of the straight piecework plan. However, its advantage is that piece rates need not be recalculated for every pay rate change.

One potential problem with both the straight piecework plan and the standard hour plan is related to the output standard. Typically, industrial engineers establish the standard, which the workers may distrust. Employees may also view with considerable skepticism any change in the standard, although it may be justified in the eyes of management. Moreover, when individual output cannot be easily distinguished, group and companywide plans offer alternatives to individual incentive plans.

Group Incentive Plans

As we suggested earlier, paying individual incentives isn't always feasible. Work is often organized in such a manner that productivity results from group effort. It is then difficult, if not impossible, to determine each individual's contribution. In this event, if incentives are used, they must be provided to the group. For example, if the group produced 100 units over standard, each member would receive incentive compensation on a pro rata basis.

Group incentives have both advantages and disadvantages. For instance, in the assembly of electrical transformers, ten employees may be working on one phase of the operation. They must work together to successfully accomplish the overall task. If nine employees perform their tasks but one does not, the productivity of the entire group may suffer. However, the peer pressure exerted in such a situation can be so great that the affected individual will either conform to the group's standards or leave the group. Group incentive plans tend to foster teamwork and often encourage peers to serve as counselors and coaches for new members. Group members tend to lend a helping hand when it is needed.

Companywide Plans

In baseball, an outstanding pitcher or a great outfield isn't the standard by which the team is judged. The standard is the team's overall won–loss record. The criterion for success focuses on the team's performance, not the achievements of individuals. In business, companywide plans offer a feasi-

HRM In Action

"Did you realize that we spent over $70,000 on our incentive program last year?" said Barry Cline, production manager, to the human resource manager, Elisia Chaumont. "For a company our size, we sure spend a lot of money for what we get. Frankly, I think the employees are paid too much. What do you think about upping the standards a bit? It could save the company a lot of money."

How would you respond?

---

ble alternative to the incentive plans previously discussed. They may be based on the organization's productivity, cost savings, or profitability. To illustrate the concept of companywide plans, we discuss profit sharing, employee stock ownership, and the Scanlon plan.

Profit Sharing. **Profit sharing** is a compensation plan that results in the distribution of a predetermined percentage of the firm's profits to employees. Many firms use this type of plan to integrate the employee's interests with those of the company. Profit-sharing plans can aid in recruiting, motivating, and retaining employees, which usually enhances productivity.

There are several variations of profit-sharing plans, but the three basic forms are current, deferred, and combination.[18]

- Current plans provide payment to employees in cash or stock as soon as profits have been determined.
- Deferred plans involve placing company contributions in an irrevocable trust to be credited to the account of individual employees. The funds are normally invested in securities, and become available to the employee (or his or her survivors) at retirement, termination, or death.
- Combination plans permit employees to receive payment of part of their share of profits on a current basis, while payment of part of their share is deferred.

Normally, most full-time employees are included in a company's profit-sharing plan after a specified waiting period. Vesting determines the amount of "profit" an employee actually owns in his or her account and is often established on a graduated basis. For example, an employee may become 25 percent vested after being in the plan for two years; 50 percent vested after three years; 75 percent vested after four years; and 100 percent vested

---

[18] J. D. Dunn and Frank M. Rachel, *Salary Administration*: *Total Compensation Systems* (New York: McGraw-Hill, 1971), pp. 261–262.

after five years. This approach to vesting may tend to reduce turnover by encouraging employees to remain with the company.

Profit sharing tends to tie employees to the economic success of the firm. Reported results include increased efficiency and lower costs. However, in recent years the Employee Retirement Income Security Act and the introduction of employee thrift plans have slowed the growth of profit-sharing plans.[19] Also, variations in profits have had an impact. For example, if the company does not make sufficient profits for several years, employees may not benefit from the plan. This may be a special problem when employees have become accustomed to receiving added compensation from profit sharing and when the plan itself represents a major part of the firm's benefits program.

Employee Stock Ownership Plan. A companywide incentive plan whereby the company provides its employees with common stock is called an **employee stock ownership plan (ESOP)**. Currently, company contributions to ESOPs are tax deductible expenses.

Many of the benefits of profit-sharing plans have also been cited for ESOPs. Specifically, ESOP advocates have suggested that employees obtain a stake in the business and become more closely identified with the firm—a relationship that theoretically increases motivation. Finally, from a company viewpoint, when ESOPs borrow money to buy stock, tax benefits multiply for the sponsoring firm if the plan is used as a financing tool for anything from a stock buyout to a leveraged buyout.[20]

Although the potential advantages of ESOPs are impressive, critics point out the dangers of employees having all their eggs in one basket. Employees would be in a vulnerable position should their company fail.

Scanlon Plan. The **Scanlon Plan** is a gain-sharing plan designed to bind employees to the firm's performance. It is the most popular plan of its type.[21] Gain-sharing plans (also known as productivity incentives, team incentives, and performance sharing incentives) generally refer to incentive plans that involve many or all employees in a common effort to achieve a firm's productivity objectives.[22]

The Scanlon Plan was developed by Joseph Scanlon in 1937, and it continues to be a successful approach to group incentive, especially in smaller firms. Employees are financially rewarded for savings in labor costs that result from their suggestions. These suggestions are evaluated by employee–management committees. Savings are calculated as a ratio of payroll costs to the sales value of what that payroll produces. If the company is able to reduce payroll costs through increased operating efficiency, it shares the savings with its employees.

---

[19] David W. Belcher and Thomas J. Atchison, *Compensation Administration*, 2nd ed. (Englewood Cliffs, N.J.: Prentice Hall, 1987), p. 290.

[20] Laura Jereski, "Behind the ESOP Surge," *Forbes* (December 14, 1987), p. 140.

[21] Belcher and Atchison, p. 289.

[22] Barry W. Thomas and Madeline Hess Olsen, "Gain Sharing: The Design Guarantees Success," *Personnel Journal*, 67 (May 1988), p. 73.

In reflecting on his company's experience with the Scanlon plan, George Sherman (vice-president of human resources for Midland-Ross) stated: "American workers want and, in my judgement, are entitled to a piece of the action when, through their own efforts and ingenuity, they are able to help the company do better."[23]

■ COMPENSATION FOR MANAGERS

Managerial skill largely determines whether a firm succeeds. Thus providing adequate compensation for managers is vital. Because managerial effectiveness and the firm's welfare are so closely related, it isn't unusual for managers' compensation—especially for top executives—to be linked to the company's performance.

Determining Managerial Compensation

A survey of *Fortune* 200 companies indicated that these firms prefer to relate salary growth for the highest level executives to overall corporate performance. For the next management tier, they integrate overall corporate performance with market rates and internal considerations to come up with compensation factors. For lower level managers, they tend to determine salaries on the basis of market rates, internal pay relationships, and individual performance.[24]

In general, the higher the managerial position, the greater the flexibility managers have in designing their jobs. Management jobs are often difficult to define because of their complexity. And when they are defined, they are often described in terms of anticipated results rather than tasks or how the work is accomplished. Thus market pricing may be the best approach to use in determining managerial pay for several reasons. First, the jobs are very important to the organization and the people involved are highly skilled and difficult to replace. Second, the firm often has a considerable investment in developing managers. Third, even though the market may support a high-wage decision, managers comprise a relatively small percentage of the total workforce, and the overall impact on total labor costs will be small. Finally, because of their outside contacts, managers are likely to know the going market rates.[25]

In using market pricing, organizations utilize compensation survey data to determine pay levels for a representative group of jobs. These data may be obtained from such sources as the American Management Association and Sibson & Company, Inc. Some organizations also adapt point and factor comparison methods of job evaluation to determine the relative value of management jobs.

---

[23] "Scanlon Plan Puts Everyone on the Team," *Iron Age* (August 9, 1976), p. 18.

[24] James T. Brinks, ADP, "Executive Compensation: Crossroads of the '80s," *Personnel Administrator*, 26 (December 1981), p. 23.

[25] Belcher and Atchison, p. 377.

Types of Managerial Compensation

Managers typically prefer to receive the bulk of their compensation in the form of salary because it determines their standard of living. Salary also provides the basis for other forms of compensation. An executive might receive life insurance protection at the rate of two and a half times his or her salary. Moreover, bonuses are often related to salary. These payments supplement salary and may be paid on a current or deferred basis. Payment of bonuses reflects the managerial belief in their incentive value. According to one report, 92 percent of executives in manufacturing and 81 percent in banking receive bonuses that are tied to base salary.[26]

The stock option is another form of compensation that is designed to further integrate the interests of management with those of the organization. Although various types of plans exist, the typical **stock option plan** gives the manager the option to buy a specified amount of stock in the future at or below the current market price. This form of compensation is advantageous when stock prices are rising. However, there are potential disadvantages to stock option plans. A manager may feel uncomfortable investing money in the same organization in which he or she is building a career. As with profit sharing, this method of compensation is popular when a firm is successful. But during periods of decline when stock prices fall, the participants may become disenchanted.

Deferred compensation—pay that is held in trust for a manager until retirement—is often used to provide a delayed reward for executives. This permits them to receive income when it is taxed at a lower rate.

An interesting, although extreme, case of executive compensation occurred a number of years ago. A large electronics firm supposedly lured a brilliant executive away from a competitor by offering him virtually everything but the "kitchen sink." The following inducements apparently were offered: an annual salary of $120,000 (an increase of $30,000), an immediate payment of $250,000 or equivalent stock options, an option to buy 90,000 shares of company stock, and a loan at no interest for ten years of $5.4 million with which to exercise his stock option.[27]

That is obviously an extreme example of executive perks. **Perquisites (perks)** are any special benefits provided by a firm to a small group of key executives that are designed to give the executives something extra.[28] In addition to status, these rewards either are not considered as earned income or are taxed at a lower level than ordinary income.[29] Some of the more common perks are:

- Company provided car.
- Accessible, no cost, parking.
- Limousine service—the chauffeur may also serve as a bodyguard.

---

[26] Milkovich and Newman, p. 574.

[27] Reprinted with permission from *Electronics*, August 19, 1968, p. 47. Copyright © by McGraw-Hill, 1968. All rights reserved.

[28] Karen M. Evans, "The Power of Perquisites," *Personnel Administrator*, 29 (May 1984), p. 45.

[29] Since the late 1970s, the IRS has required firms to place a value on more perks and has recognized them as imputed income.

- Kidnap and ransom protection.
- Counseling service—including financial and legal services.
- Professional meetings and conferences.
- Spouse travel.
- Use of company plane and yacht.
- Home entertainment allowance.
- Special living accommodations away from home.
- Club memberships.
- Special dining rooms.
- Season tickets to entertainment events.
- Special relocation allowances.
- Use of company credit cards.
- Medical expense reimbursement—coverage for all medical costs.
- Reimbursement for children's college expenses.
- No- and low-interest loans.[30]

A **"golden parachute" contract** protects executives in the event that their firm is acquired by another. The executives, if negatively affected, may receive maximum agreed-to payouts under both short- and long-term incentive plans.[31]

Perquisites extend a firm's benefit program on an individual basis. For a reason not entirely clear, they seem to be more popular in smaller firms than in major organizations.[32]

Some people criticize the high level of executive pay and benefits. In fact, news stories about executives who receive huge pay increases command a great deal of attention. This is especially true when the economy is faring poorly. The answer to the question, "Are executives overpaid?" is difficult if not impossible to determine. One compensation expert, Robert Sibson, suggests that there may be some overpayment for mediocrity, but that there is at least an equivalent underpayment for high levels of business performance. He also believes that current executive pay levels show only a slight increase over previous years.[33]

■ COMPENSATION FOR PROFESSIONALS

People in professional jobs are initially compensated primarily for the knowledge they bring to the organization. Because of this, the administration of compensation programs for professionals is somewhat different than for managers. Many professional employees eventually become managers. For those who do not desire this form of career progression, some organizations have created a dual track of compensation. It provides a separate pay structure for professionals, which may overlap a portion of the managerial

---

[30] Richard I. Henderson, *Compensation Management: Rewarding Performance*, 4th ed. (Reston, Va.: Reston Publishing Company, 1985), pp. 655–656.

[31] Graef S. Crystal, "Outlook on Compensation and Benefits: To the Rescue of Pay for Performance," *Personnel*, 62 (January 1985), p. 8.

[32] Bruce R. Ellig, "Perquisites: The Intrinsic Form of Pay," *Personnel*, 58 (January–February 1981), pp. 23–31.

[33] "In Practice: Overpaying Execs," *Training and Development Journal*, 39 (April 1985), p. 10.

pay structure. This approach doesn't require professionals who are performing exceptionally well to accept management positions in order to increase their compensation. However, in other organizations, the only way to increase professionals' pay is to promote them into management. A serious organizational problem is created when a highly competent and effective professional is unable to perform satisfactorily as a manager.

Professional career curves, shown in Figure 13-4, have been developed especially for determining compensation for professional jobs. Career curves are based on the assumption that the more experience an individual has, the higher his or her earnings should be. However, as you can see, career curves may also reflect varying performance levels. In this particular field, a professional employee who has twenty-years' experience and performs at a level 10 percent above the average (average = 100) would presumably earn nearly $3,200 per month. On the other hand, a person with the same experience but performing only at the 80 percent level would presumably earn about $2,400 a month. Some type of performance appraisal system is obviously necessary in order to make these productivity distinctions.

■ SALES COMPENSATION

Because designing compensation programs for sales employees involves unique considerations, some executives assign this task to the sales staff rather than to human resources. Still, many general compensation practices apply to sales jobs. For example, job content, relative job worth, and job market value should be determined.

The straight salary approach is at one extreme in sales compensation. In this method, salespersons receive a fixed salary regardless of their sales levels. Organizations use straight salary primarily when they stress continued product service after the sale. For instance, many sales representatives who deal largely with the federal government are compensated in this manner.

At the other extreme, the person whose pay is totally determined as a percentage of sales is on straight commission. An example of a salesperson in this category might be door-to-door salespersons. A director of compensation has stated that "The only 'pure' nondeferred compensation plan is the 100 percent sales commission plan. This type of pay is probably the most effective one to motivate salespeople. Unfortunately, straight commission is inappropriate for most of the selling that is done today."

Between these extremes are endless part-salary, part-commission combinations. The possibilities increase when various types of bonuses are added to the basic compensation package. The emphasis given to either commission or salary depends on several factors, including the organization's philosophy toward service, the nature of the product, and the amount of time required to close a sale.

In addition to salary, commissions, and bonuses, salespersons often receive other forms of compensation that are intended to serve as added incentives. Sales contests that offer television sets, refrigerators, or expense-paid vacations to exotic locations are common.

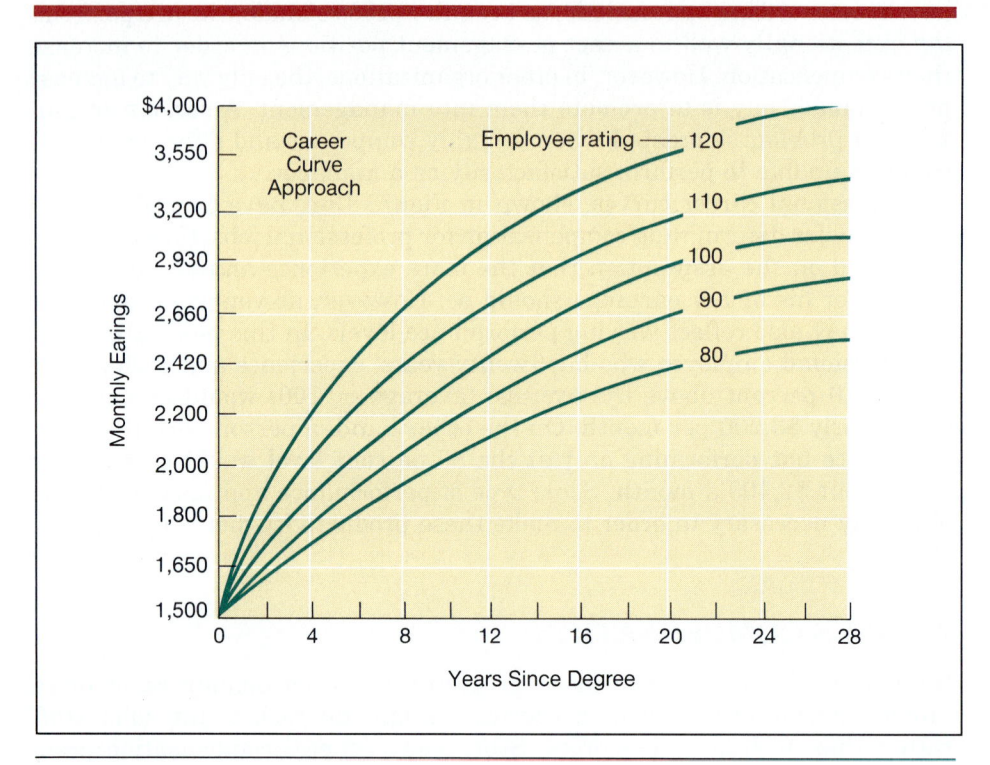

FIGURE 13-4 | Professional Career Curves

Source: Adapted, by permission of the publishers from *Compensation: A Complete Revision of Wages and Salaries* by Robert E. Sibson (New York: AMACOM, a division of American Management Associations). All rights reserved.

If any one feature sets sales compensation apart from other programs, it is the emphasis on incentives. The nature of sales work often simplifies the problem of determining individual output. Sales volume can usually be related to specific individuals, a situation that encourages payment of incentive compensation. Also, experience in sales compensation practices over the years has supported the concept of directly relating rewards to performance.

■ NONFINANCIAL COMPENSATION

In recent years, most Americans have been able to satisfy their basic physiological and safety needs, so their interests have tended to shift somewhat away from money as the primary form of compensation. As employees receive sufficient cash to provide for basic necessities (and then stereos, color TVs, VCRs, and PCs), they tend to desire rewards that will satisfy higher order needs. Specifically, social, ego, and self-actualization needs are becoming more important. These needs may be satisfied through the job itself and/or the job environment. Figure 13-5 shows the basic nonfinancial elements of the total compensation package.

The Job

A major human resource management objective is to satisfactorily match job requirements and employee abilities and aspirations. Although the task of job design is typically performed by other organizational units, human resource management has a distinct responsibility for recruiting, selecting, and placing individuals in those jobs. Also, a good case could be made for directly involving human resources in the task of job design. A "good" job has the potential for becoming an important part of nonfinancial compensation. Because of this, a number of organizations have become actively engaged in job enrichment, which we discussed in Chapter 9.

The job is a central issue in many theories of motivation, and it is also a vital component of a total compensation program. Employees may receive important rewards by performing meaningful jobs. This type of reward is intrinsic in nature, but management determines job content and therefore the job's compensation possibilities are largely controlled by the organization. The selection and placement processes are extremely important in this context. A job that is challenging to one person may be quite boring to another, and failure to recognize this fact often leads to serious problems.

The Job Environment

The job environment is also an important aspect of nonfinancial compensation. We discussed the significance of a warm, supportive corporate culture in Chapter 9. Many organizations have paid lip service to making jobs more rewarding. However, others have made concerted efforts to improve many of the factors that surround the job.

Sound Policies. Human resource policies and practices expressing management's sincerity in its employee relationships can serve as positive rewards. For example, fostering stable employment reflects a company's respect for its employees, as IBM has done. Over a period of four decades, despite severe recessions and dramatic technological changes, no IBM employee has ever been laid off because of economic necessity. If a firm's policies show respect—rather than disrespect, fear, doubt, or lack of confidence—the result can be rewarding to both the employees and the organization.

Competent Supervision. Nothing in the job environment can be so demoralizing to employees as an incompetent supervisor. Successful organizations offer continuing programs that emphasize supervisory and executive development. These programs ensure, insofar as possible, the continuity of sound leadership and management.

Congenial Co-Workers. Although a few individuals in this world may be quite self-sufficient and prefer to be left alone, this attitude is not preva-

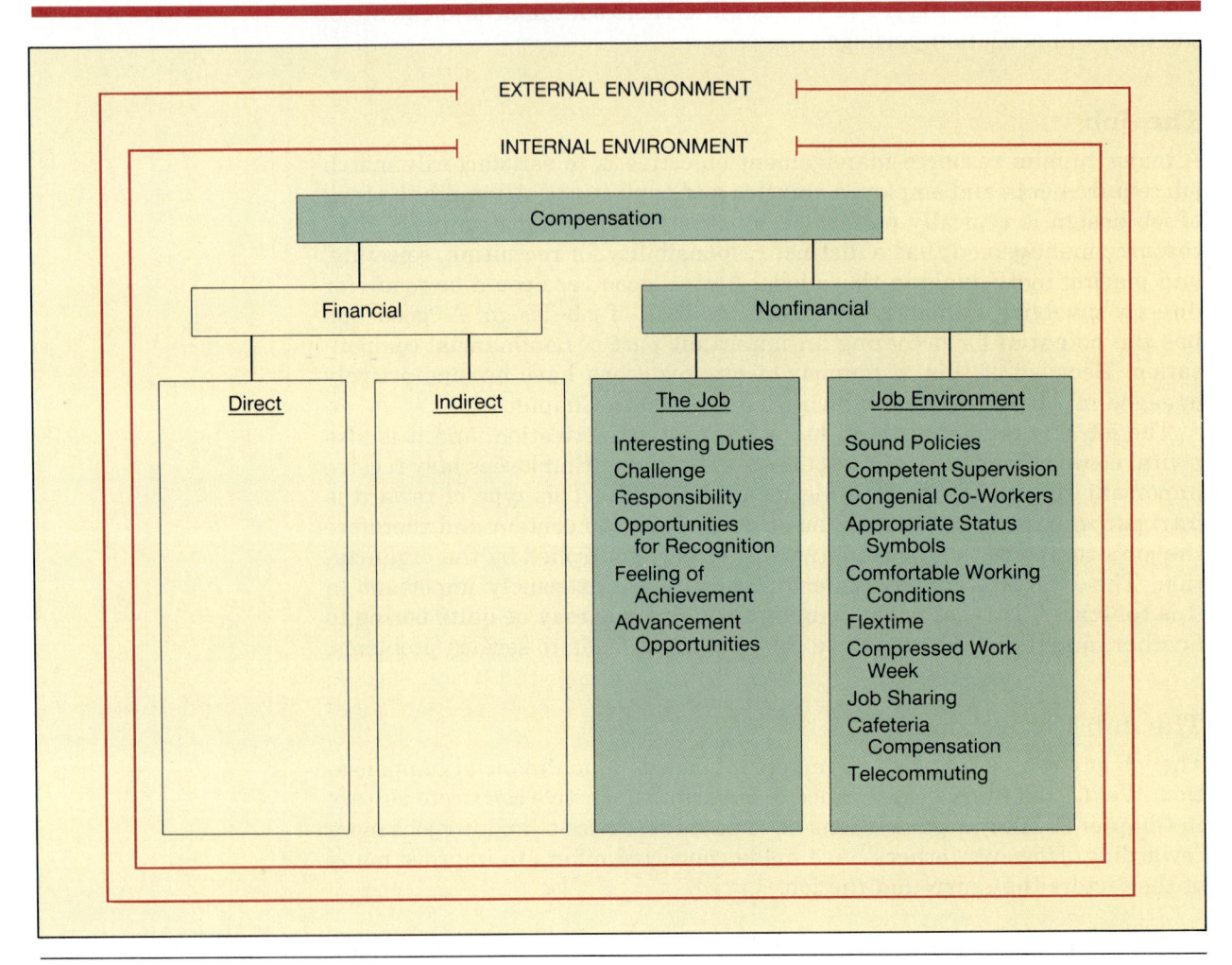

```
                        ┌─ EXTERNAL ENVIRONMENT ─┐
                        ┌─ INTERNAL ENVIRONMENT ─┐

                              Compensation

                Financial                    Nonfinancial

         Direct        Indirect        The Job           Job Environment

                                   Interesting Duties    Sound Policies
                                   Challenge             Competent Supervision
                                   Responsibility        Congenial Co-Workers
                                   Opportunities         Appropriate Status
                                     for Recognition       Symbols
                                   Feeling of            Comfortable Working
                                     Achievement           Conditions
                                   Advancement           Flextime
                                     Opportunities       Compressed Work
                                                           Week
                                                         Job Sharing
                                                         Cafeteria
                                                           Compensation
                                                         Telecommuting
```

FIGURE 13-5 | Nonfinancial Elements of a Total Compensation Program

lent. Most people possess, in varying degrees, a desire to be accepted by their work group. This acceptance helps them satisfy basic social needs. It is very important that management, in its staffing efforts, be concerned with developing compatible work groups.

Appropriate Status Symbols. At times, employees compare the size of their offices with those of peers or measure the distance from their offices to the CEO's. When such extreme behavior occurs, it is time to examine the firm's policy regarding status symbols. While these symbols may be appropriate in achieving certain purposes—such as providing incentives for employees to progress in the firm—management must take care not to overemphasize them. However, status symbols (such as office size, desk size and quality, other office furnishings, floor covering, office location, title, parking space, or make of company car) can serve as compensation because they often appeal to employees' ego needs. Some organizations tend to minimize the use of status symbols, but other firms use them liberally. A crucial point to remember in providing such rewards is to provide them equitably.

Comfortable Working Conditions. Good working conditions are taken for granted in many organizations today. However, a brief return to nonair-conditioned offices would quickly remind us of their importance. The view that working conditions can be a form of compensation is reinforced by pay plans that increase the financial reward for jobs that entail relatively poor working conditions.

Flextime. The practice of permitting employees to choose, with certain limitations, their own working hours is referred to as **flextime**. It was introduced in Germany in the late 1960s and has since spread throughout Europe and the United States. In a flextime system, employees work the same number of hours per day as they would on a standard schedule. However, they are permitted to work these hours within what is called a *band width*, which is the maximum length of the work day (see Figure 13-6). Core time is that part of the day when all employees must be present. Flexible time is the time period within which employees may vary their schedules.[34] A typical schedule permits employees to begin work between 6:00 A.M. and 9:00 A.M. and to complete their workday between 3:00 P.M. and 6:00 P.M.

Perhaps flextime's most important feature is that it allows employees to schedule their time to minimize conflicts between personal needs and job requirements. Remember in the incident at the beginning of the chapter this advantage would be quite attractive to individuals, such as Liz Nichols, who have scheduling problems. Liz now has the opportunity to arrive at work later, after taking her children to school.

With flextime, personal needs can be accommodated without employees being tempted to illegitimately use sick leave. Flextime also permits employees to work at hours when they feel they can function best. It caters to those who are early risers or those who prefer to work later in the day. The public also seems to reap benefits from flextime. Transportation services, recreational facilities, medical clinics, and other services can be better utilized as a result of reduced competition for service at conventional peak times.

Flextime is not suitable for all types of organizations. Its use may be severely limited in assembly-line operations and companies utilizing multiple shifts. However, flextime is feasible in many situations, benefitting both the employee and the employer. Clearly, the use of plans such as flextime are compatible with desires of employees (especially younger ones) to have greater control over their work situations.

---

[34] Tim Burt, "Making the Most of Time with Flexible Working Hours," *Personnel Executive*, 1 (March 1982), p. 37.

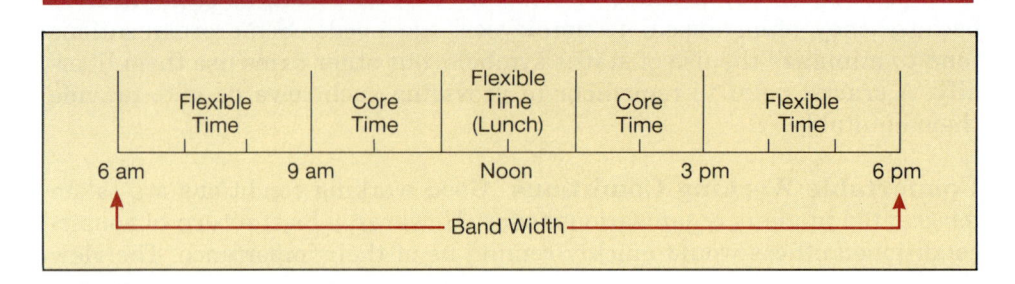

FIGURE 13-6 | Illustration of Flextime

The Compressed Workweek. Any arrangement of work hours that permits employees to fulfill their work obligation in fewer days than the typical five-day workweek is referred to as the **compressed workweek**. The most common compressed workweek is four ten-hour days. Working under this arrangement, employees have reported greater job satisfaction. In addition, the compressed workweek offers the potential for better use of leisure time for family life, personal business, and recreation.[35] Employers in some instances have cited advantages such as increased productivity and reduced turnover and absenteeism.

However, work scheduling and employee fatigue problems have been encountered. In some cases, these problems have resulted in lower product quality and reduced customer service. Some firms have even reverted to the conventional five-day week. It seems clear that, overall, acceptance of the compressed workweek is not as clear-cut as acceptance of flextime.

Job Sharing. A relatively new approach to work—job sharing— is attractive to people who want to work fewer than forty hours per week. In **job sharing**, two part-time people split the duties of one job in some agreed-on manner and are paid according to their contributions. From the employer's viewpoint, compensation is paid for only one job, but creativity is obtained from two employees. The total financial compensation cost may be greater because of the additional benefits provided; however, this expense may be offset by increased productivity. Job sharing may be especially attractive to individuals who have substantial family responsibilities and to older workers who wish to move gradually into retirement.

Flexible Compensation (Cafeteria Compensation). **Flexible compensation plans** permit employees to choose from among many alternatives in deciding how their financial compensation will be allocated. They are given considerable latitude in determining how much they will take in the form of salary, life insurance, pension contributions, and other benefits. Cafete-

---

[35] Simcha Ronen and Sophia B. Primps, "The Compressed Work Week as Organizational Change: Behavioral and Attitudinal Outcomes," *Academy of Management Review*, 6 (January 1981), p. 61.

ria plans permit flexibility in allowing each employee to determine the compensation package which best satisfies his or her particular needs.

The rationale behind cafeteria plans is that employees have individual needs and preferences. A sixty-year-old man would probably not desire maternity benefits in an insurance plan. At the same time, a twenty-five-year-old woman who regularly jogs three miles each day might not place a high value on a parking space near the firm's entrance. Some of the possible compensation vehicles utilized in a cafeteria approach are shown in Table 13-2.

Obviously, organizations cannot permit employees to select all their financial compensation vehicles. For one thing, benefits required by law must be provided. In addition, it is probably wise to require that each employee have core benefits, especially in areas such as retirement and medical insurance. Some guidelines would likely be helpful for most employees in the long run. However, the freedom to select highly desired benefits would seem to maximize the value of an individual's compensation. Involvement in the determination of tailored compensation plans should also effectively communicate the cost of benefits to employees.

TRW, Inc., has had a flexible compensation program since 1974. The program was inspired by a general belief that employees should have more flexibility and self-determination in shaping their compensation packages. The plan developed at TRW is based on the following principles:

- The core plan will be available to each employee at the company's expense.
- Plans that are better, but more costly than the current plan, will be developed and made available at the employee's expense.
- Plans that provide less coverage, and that are less costly than the current plan, will be developed and an employee given credit toward other benefits or given the difference in cash.
- The core plan will be reviewed annually and will be maintained at a competitive level.
- Additional choices will be added as experience is gained and as new elements of the total compensation package can be defined on a choice basis.

Choices in the current plan include health care, hospital, surgical, maternity, supplemental accident, and major medical benefits. Future possibilities for expanded areas of choice are additional vacation, retirement supplement, group auto and homeowners' insurance, and long-term disability compensation.

In spite of new legislative restrictions, the number of flexible compensation programs is increasing, primarily because such plans provide substantial advantages for both employer and employee.[36] For example, the employer can:

- Improve its competitive position in the marketplace by appealing to individual needs.

---

[36] Susan J. Velleman, "Flexible Benefit Packages that Satisfy Employees and the IRS," *Personnel*, 62 (March 1985), p. 33.

TABLE 13-2 | **Compensation Vehicles Utilized in a Cafeteria Compensation Approach**

Accidental death, dismemberment insurance
Birthdays (vacation)
Bonus eligibility
Business and professional membership
Cash profit sharing
Club memberships
Commissions
Company medical assistance
Company provided automobile
Company provided housing
Company provided or subsidized travel
Day-care centers
Deferred bonus
Deferred compensation plan
Dental and eye care insurance
Discount on company products
Education costs
Educational activities (time off)
Free checking account
Free or subsidized lunches
Group automobile insurance
Group homeowners' insurance
Group life insurance
Health maintenance organization fees
Home health care
Hospital-surgical-medical insurance
Incentive growth fund
Interest-free loans
Long-term disability benefit
Matching educational donations
Nurseries
Nursing-home care
Outside medical services
Personal accident insurance
Price discount plan
Recreation facilities
Resort facilities
Sabbatical leaves
Salary continuation
Savings plan
Scholarships for dependents
Severance pay
Sickness and accident insurance
Stock appreciation rights
Stock bonus plan
Stock purchase plan

- Provide a degree of cost control by shifting a portion of the costs to employees—but generally in ways that provide them with tax savings.
- Make employees more aware of the value of their compensation.
- Limit contributions to benefits programs without alienating employees.

Advantages to employees that may be highly valued include:

- Having greater control over a significant aspect of their employment.
- Being able to save money by paying a portion of benefit costs with tax-deferred dollars.

While flexible compensation programs add to the organization's administrative burden, advantages seem to greatly outweigh shortcomings. Therefore, systems of this type will likely become more common in the future.

Telecommuting. **Telecommuting** allows employees to work at home, or at least in a location away from the office. They perform their work over data lines tied to a computer as if they were at the office. In keeping with this concept and to combat the steady increase in employment costs, Control Data Corporation (CDC) developed a program it calls HOMEWORK. This innovative approach is a home-based training and employment program for persons seeking a nontraditional work environment.

Using a personal computer located in the employee's home and connected by telephone to CDC's computer network, both training and job duties are carried out without loss of efficiency and quality. An example of a HOMEWORK job is that of business application programmer. Initially, HOMEWORK was available only to a few severely disabled employees. It has now been expanded, and the program has great potential for many other employees. Additional HOMEWORK programs that have wide-ranging implications for other employers in both the private and public sectors are being developed by CDC. The following advantages have been cited for both employee and employer:

- Permits effective use of human resources.
- Eliminates the need for office space.
- Provides flexible working hours.
- Eliminates costs associated with travel to and from work.
- Enhances intellectual functioning.
- Helps establish strong bonds and company loyalty.
- Permits a higher level of self-care for severely disabled employees.
- Reduces costs of health care (CDC's costs decreased 50–75 percent for most of its participants).
- Increases employees' self-concept and confidence levels.
- Provides a means for reentering a traditional work environment.

As many as 100,000 people regularly work at home at least part-time, and more than 350 companies have some form of telecommuting program for their employees.[37] Some forecasters have predicted that 10 million Americans could be working at home within the next 15 years.[38]

---

[37] Karen A. Fortin and Shirley Dennis-Escottier, "Telecommuting Adds a New Dimension to Office in the Home," *The Woman CPA*, 48 (October 1986), p. 11.

[38] Carol-Ann Hamilton, "Telecommuting," *Personnel Journal*, 66 (April 1987), p. 91.

While telecommuting has many advantages, it also has some potential pitfalls. For example, ties between employees and their firms may be weakened, and successful programs will require a higher degree of trust between employees and their supervisors. However, one thing seems certain: The size of the workforce should increase with the ability of telecommuting to expand the utilization of handicapped workers and workers with small children.

■ COMPENSATION IN MULTINATIONAL CORPORATIONS

A major problem that confronts multinational corporations is how to provide equitable compensation systems for workers given overseas assignments. Typically, employees from the parent country receive a salary, an overseas premium of up to 50 percent, relocation allowances, and living expense allowances. Normally, individuals from the parent country receive higher pay than workers from the host country. These differentials tend to create resentment and reduce cooperation. Many Americans have found that their standard of living and social class is considerably better in foreign countries than it had been at home. The drop in living standards when they return may create some difficulties. An important incentive for U.S. citizens to accept assignments in foreign countries is the opportunity to exclude a portion of their income earned in the foreign country from U.S. income taxes. Internal Revenue Service regulations allow a U.S. citizen to exclude certain income earned while working in a foreign country, provided that the individual resides in the foreign country twelve months or longer. The IRS issued a decision in 1985 on the taxation of U.S. citizens working abroad. In 1988, the exclusion was $85,000 and reaches a top of $95,000 in 1990. To qualify for this exclusion, a taxpayer must have a tax home in a foreign country for 330 days of foreign presence.[39]

Successful management of employee benefits in a multinational corporation depends on various factors. Perhaps the most important one is a corporate policy statement that outlines specific instructions for the development, approval, and administration of all benefits plans. This policy statement should clearly establish that no benefits plan is to be implemented or changed by a foreign subsidiary without prior approval of the corporate benefits department. Employee benefits covered by the policy statement should include any payment of company funds to employees other than base salary, such as pensions, medical and life insurance, vacations, and severance pay.[40]

In drafting the policy statement, two general objectives must be kept in mind. First, the organization's overall welfare must be given primary consideration. Second, employee benefits must be competitive on the interna-

---

[39] Marion Gajek and Monica M. Sabo, "The Bottom Line: What HR Managers Need to Know About the New Expatriate Regulations," *Personnel Administrator*, 31 (February 1986), p. 87.

[40] Neil B. Krupp, "Managing Benefits in Multinational Organizations," *Personnel*, 63 (September 1986), p. 76.

tional level if a multinational corporation is to attract and retain the dynamic, aggressive kind of leadership that it requires to be successful.[41]

SUMMARY

Most organizations recognize a responsibility to their employees by providing programs covering their health, safety, security, and general welfare. These programs are called benefits and include all financial rewards that generally are not paid directly to the employee. Benefits cost the firm money, but employees usually receive them indirectly. This type of compensation has two distinct advantages. First, it is generally nontaxable to the employee. Second, in the case of insurance, the premium rates are much less for large groups of employees than for individual policies. Legally required benefits include social security, unemployment compensation, and workers' compensation.

A seemingly endless number of benefits are provided voluntarily by organizations. These benefits may be classified as (1) payment for time not worked, (2) employee health and security benefits, (3) services to employees, and (4) premium pay. Although they are provided voluntarily, some no doubt have resulted from union–management negotiations. Employee benefits can help a firm recruit and retain a quality workforce. Management depends on an upward flow of information from employees in order to know when benefit changes are needed. In addition, because employee awareness of benefits is often severely limited, information about benefits must also be communicated downward.

Compensation is most often determined by how much time an employee spends at work. Compensation programs that relate pay to productivity provide an incentive for greater individual and work group productivity. A predetermined amount of money is paid for each unit produced under a straight piecework plan. The standard hour plan is an individual incentive plan under which time allowances are calculated for each unit of output. However, work is often organized in such a manner that productivity results from group effort. Determining each individual's contribution is then difficult, if not impossible, and the group must be given the incentive—and the reward.

Companywide incentive plans include profit sharing, employee stock ownership plan (ESOP), and the Scanlon plan. The latter is the most popular plan of its type.

Managerial skill significantly affects a firm's success. Managerial effectiveness and the firm's welfare are closely related. Therefore it isn't unusual for a large portion of management compensation—especially for top executives—to be linked to the company's performance. Managers typically

---
[41] *Ibid.*

receive the bulk of their compensation as salary, which provides the basis for other forms of compensation.

The stock option is designed to integrate the interests of management and the organization. Deferred compensation—pay that is held in trust for a manager until retirement—is often used because of its tax advantages. Perquisites (perks) are any special benefits provided by a firm to a small group of key executives to give them something extra.

Professionals are initially compensated primarily for the knowledge they bring to the organization. Many professional employees eventually become managers. For those who don't want to move into management, some organizations have created a dual compensation track. The dual track provides a separate pay structure for professionals, which may overlap a portion of the managerial pay structure.

Compensation programs for sales employees involve unique considerations, but general compensation practices such as job content, relative job worth, and job market value still apply to sales jobs. The straight salary approach is at one extreme in sales compensation. At the other extreme is the straight commission. There are endless part-salary, part-commission combinations between these extremes.

As employees receive sufficient cash to provide for basic necessities, they tend to want rewards that will satisfy higher order needs. Specifically, social, ego, and self-actualization needs become more important. These needs may be satisfied by the job itself and/or the job environment.

Permitting employees to choose, within certain limits, their own working hours is known as flextime. Any arrangement that permits employees to work full-time but in fewer days than the typical five-day workweek is called a compressed workweek. In job sharing, two part-time people split the duties of one job in some agreed-on manner and are paid according to their contributions. Flexible compensation plans permit employees to choose from among many alternatives in allocating their financial compensation. Telecommuting permits employees to work at home and communicate via computer and telephone.

A major problem confronting multinational corporations is equitable compensation for workers given overseas assignments. Typically, employees from the parent country receive a salary, an overseas premium of up to 50 percent, relocation allowances, and living expense allowances. Many Americans find that their standard of living and social status has improved considerably over what it had been in the United States. The drop in living standards when they return may create some difficulties. An important incentive for U.S. citizens to accept overseas assignments is the opportunity to exclude a portion of their income earned in the foreign country from U.S. income taxes. Successful management of employee benefits depends primarily on a corporate policy statement that outlines specific instructions for the development, approval, and administration of all benefits plans.

Questions for Review

1. Define benefits. What are the general purposes of benefits?
2. Which benefits are required by law?
3. What are the basic categories of voluntary benefits? Give an example of each type.
4. Distinguish among premium pay, hazard pay, and shift differential pay.
5. What is meant by the term incentive compensation? When would an individual incentive plan, as opposed to a group incentive plan, be used?
6. Define the following terms:
   a. Straight piecework
   b. Standard hour plan
   c. Profit sharing
   d. Employee stock ownership plan
   e. Scanlon plan
7. What are major determinants of compensation for managers? List and define the primary types of managerial compensation.
8. Why are nonfinancial compensation considerations becoming so important?
9. Distinguish between flextime and compressed workweek.
10. What are some of the factors that affect compensation for individuals in multinational corporations?

Terms for Review

Benefits
Utilization review
Wellness
Premium pay
Hazard pay
Shift differentials
Incentive compensation
Straight piecework plan
Standard hour plan
Profit sharing
Employee stock ownership plan (ESOP)

Scanlon plan
Stock option plan
Deferred compensation
Perquisites (perks)
"Golden parachute" contract
Flextime
Compressed workweek
Job sharing
Flexible compensation plans
Telecommuting

INCIDENT 1 — A Double-Edged Sword

The decline in oil prices during the mid-1980s adversely affected many industries. Profits were down for all major oil companies and many of their suppliers. Few new orders were received by the producers of drilling fluids, for example, and many existing orders were canceled or scaled back. As a supplier of drilling fluids, Beta Chemical Company's sales plummeted. Beta, located in Lafayette, Louisiana, supplies companies such as Texaco, Shell, and Pennzoil, as well as independent oil drillers, often called "wildcatters."

Beta had implemented a comprehensive profit-sharing plan in the 1970s, after several years of rapidly increasing sales and profits. The decision was based largely on an attitude survey of the employees at Beta, which showed that they strongly preferred profit sharing over other benefits.

In the late 1980s, the compensation plan at Beta provided for base wages about 20 percent below wage levels for similar jobs in Lafayette. But half of company profits were paid out each quarter as a fixed percentage of employee wages. Distributed profits averaged more than 50 percent of base wages. This caused average total compensation at Beta to be 20 percent above that in the area. Because of the high pay, Beta remained a popular employer, able to take its pick from a long waiting list of applicants.

Benefits were kept to a minimum at Beta. There was no retirement plan and a very limited medical plan designed to cover catastrophic illnesses only. Employees considered this a good bargain, though, in light of the above-average compensation.

Profits were down markedly in 1987 and the profit-sharing bonus was less than half the historical average. Earnings declined further for the first two quarters of 1988. By mid-year, it was clear that the company would be in the red for the entire second half. A board meeting was called in late August to discuss the profit-sharing program. One director made it known that he felt the company should drop profit sharing. The human resource director, Vince Harwood, was asked to sit in at the board meeting and to make a presentation suggesting what the company should do about compensation.

Questions

1. Evaluate the compensation plan at Beta.
2. If you were Mr. Harwood, what would you recommend for the short term? For the long term?

INCIDENT 2 — A Benefits Package Designed for Whom?

Wayne McGraw greeted Robert Peters, his next interviewee, warmly. Robert had an excellent academic record and appeared to be just the kind of person Wayne's company, Beco Electric, was seeking. Wayne is the university recruiter for Beco and had already interviewed six graduating seniors at Centenary College.

Based on the application form, Robert appeared to be the most promising candidate to be interviewed that day. He was twenty-two years old, had a 3.6 overall grade point average and a 4.0 in his major field, industrial management. He was the vice-president of the Student Government Association and was activities chairman for Kappa Alpha Psi, a social fraternity. The reference letters in Robert's file revealed that he was both very active socially and a rather intense and serious student. One of the letters, from Robert's employer the previous summer, expressed satisfaction with Robert's work habits.

Wayne knew that discussion of pay could be an important part of the recruiting interview. But he did not know which aspects of Beco's compensation and benefits program would appeal most to Robert. The company has an excellent profit-sharing plan, although 80 percent of profit distributions are deferred and included in each employee's retirement account. Health benefits are also good. The company's medical and dental plan pays almost 100 percent of costs. A company cafeteria provides meals at about 70 percent of outside prices, although few managers take advantage of this. Employees get one week of paid vacation after the first year and two weeks after two years with the company. In addition, there are twelve paid holidays each year. Finally, the company encourages advanced education, paying for tuition and books in full and often allowing time off to attend classes during the day.

Questions

1. What aspects of Beco's compensation and benefits program are likely to appeal to Robert? Explain.
2. Is the total compensation package likely to be attractive to Robert? Explain.

Experiencing Human Resource Management

Due to a downward trend in business and resulting financial constraints over the last two years, Straight Manufacturing Company has been able to grant only cost-of-living increases to its employees. However, the firm has just signed a lucrative three-year contract with a major defense contractor. As a result, management has formed a salary review committee to award merit increases to deserving employees. Members of the salary review committee have only $13,500 of merit money and deciding who will receive merit increases will be difficult. Louis Convoy, Sharon Kubiak, J. Ward Archer, Ed Wilson, C. J. Sass, and John Passante have been recommended for raises.

Louis Convoy, Financial Analyst, has an undergraduate business degree, and is currently working on an M.B.A. His previous work experience has allowed him to develop several outstanding financial contacts.

Sharon Kubiak, HRM Administrative Assistant, began as a secretary and after three years with the organization was promoted to her present position. Because her first position was that of secretary, her current salary is not at the range commensurate with her new position and responsibilities.

J. Ward Archer, Assistant Plant Manager, worked three years as a production foreman after obtaining his undergraduate degree in business. He then received an M.B.A. degree from Harvard two years ago. He is viewed by many as a "successful fast tracker."

Ed Wilson, Production Foreman, has been with the organization for nine years, the last two of which has been as a production foreman. Last year he virtually single-handedly prevented a wildcat strike. To become a member of management as a production foreman, Ed took a pay cut in comparison to his union wages.

C. J. Sass, Director of Computer Services, has a doctoral degree in computer sciences and was hired away from a business college at a leading eastern university three years ago. Two and one-half years ago he introduced a corporate-wide Human Resource Information system that has refined the internal recruiting and promotion policies of the organization.

John Passante, District Sales Manager, has been with the organization for twelve and one-half years. In his tenth year with the organization, John was promoted to District Sales Manager, and has done a fine job in that position.

Six students will serve on the salary review committee. While the committee would like to award significant merit increases to all those who have been recommended, there are limited funds available for raises. The committee must make a decision as to how the merit funds will be distributed. Your instructor will provide the participants with additional information necessary to complete the exercise.

REFERENCES

Adair, Donald R. "Golden Parachutes Can Be More Than an Executive's Bailout." *Bottomline* (March 1987), p. 39.

Adamache, K. W. "Fringe Benefits: To Tax or Not to Tax?" *National Tax Journal*, 38 (March 1985), pp. 47–64.

Akerlof, G. A. "Gift Exchange and Efficiency-Wage Theory: Four Views." *The American Economic Review*, 74 (May 1984), pp. 79–83.

Aschkenasy, J. "Erlenborn Eyes Newly Proposed Taxation of Employee Benefits." *National Underwriter (Life and Health Insurance Edition)* (February 23, 1985), p. 2.

Bacas, H. "Passing the Buck on Benefits." *Nation's Business*, 73 (February 1985), pp. 18–21.

Belcher, David W., and Thomas J. Atchison. *Compensation Administration*, 2nd ed. (Englewood Cliffs, N.J.: Prentice Hall, 1987), p. 290.

"Benefits Important in Costs of Hiring Elderly (Senate Special Committee on Aging Study)." *Employee Benefit Plan Review*, 39 (March 1985), pp. 13–16.

"Benefits That Benefit." *Banking Journal*, 79 (February 1987), pp. 88–89.

Borman, Melissa A. "What Do Women Get?" *Across the Board*, 21 (March 1987), pp. 19–21.

Brooks, L. D. et al. "How Profitable Are Employee Stock Ownership Plans?" *Financial Executive*, 50 (May 1982), pp. 32–34.

Bushardt, S. C., and A. R. Fowler. "Compensation and Benefits: Today's Dilemma in Motivation." *Personnel Administrator*, 27 (April 1982), pp. 23–26.

Caruth, Donald L. *Compensation Management for Banks* (Boston: Bankers Publishing Company, 1986), pp. 152–177.

Cockrum, Robert B. "Has the Time Come for Employee Cafeteria Plans?" *Personnel Administrator*, 28 (July 1982), pp. 66–72.

"Communications as the Marketing of Benefits." *Benefits Plan Review*, 39 (March 1985), pp. 79ff.

Cooper, G. A. "An Actuary's View of Benefits in the Future." *Risk Management*, 32 (March 1985), pp. 34–36ff.

Crystal, Graef S. "Outlook on Compensation and Benefits: To the Rescue of Pay for Performance." *Personnel*, 62 (January 1985), p. 8.

"Defensive Design Has Held Basic Need for Employee Benefit Plans in 1985." *Journal of Accountancy*, 159 (March 1985), pp. 23ff.

"Executive Perks: What's Out, What's In." *Dun's Business Month*, 129 (February 1987), pp. 75–77.

Gohrich, Peter W. "Implementing a Flexible Benefit Plan." *Small Business Report*, 11 (November 1986), p. 29.

Harkavy, J., and H. R. Kahn. "Senator Packwood Speaks Out on Employee Benefits." *Risk Management*, 32 (March 1985), p. 7.

"Better Than Free." *Forbes* (June 15, 1987), p. 221.

Kenny, John B. "Competency Analysis for Trainers: A Model for Professionalization." *Training and Development Journal*, 36 (May 1982), pp. 142–148.

Kerr, J. R. "Diversification Strategies and Managerial Rewards: An Empirical Study." *Academy of Management Journal*, 28 (March 1985), pp. 155–179.

Lawyer, M. S., and J. G. Gourlay, Jr. "Having Capital Problems? ESOPs May Be the Answer." *ABA Banking Journal*, 74 (March 1982), pp. 117ff.

Levinson, Richard H., and John Bertke. "Executive Benefits." *Business Insurance* (June 9, 1986), pp. 18–19.

Mazo, Judith F. "Another Compliance Challenge for Employers: The Retirement Equity Act." *Personnel*, 62 (February 1985), p. 43.

Milkovich, George T., and Jerry M. Newman. *Compensation*, 2nd ed. (Plano, Texas: Business Publications, 1987).

"More Employer-Supported Childcare Assistance Needed." *Management Review*, 76 (August 1987), pp. 10–11.

"Neater Way to Flexible Pay." *Economist* (March 29, 1986), pp. 11–12.

Nestlebaum, Karen. "Golden Parachuters Ride for a Fall." *Management Review*, 75 (March 1986): pp. 38–41.

O'Dell, Carla, and Jerry McAdams. "The Revolution in Employee Rewards." *Management Review*, 76 (March 1987), pp. 30–31.

Olney, Peter B., Jr. "Meeting the Challenge of Comparable Worth: Part 2." *Compensation and Benefits Review*, 19 (May–June 1987), pp. 15–23.

Paris, Ellen. "Hold That Scalpel?" *Forbes* (May 6, 1985), pp. 35–36.

Perkins, Robert E. "The Employer's Role in Benefits Evolution." *Personnel*, 64 (February 1987), p. 66.

"Popularity Growing in Use of PAYSOPS." *Pension World*, 20 (June 1984), p. 14.

"Post-Retirement Benefits Facing Intense Scrutiny (Life and/or Medical Benefits)." *Employee Benefit Plan Review*, 39 (February 1985), pp. 22ff.

"Practice: Overpaying Execs." *Training and Development Journal*, 39 (April 1985), p. 10.

Schechter, Jack H. "The Retirement Equity Act: Meeting Women's Pension Needs." *Compensation Review*, 17 (First Quarter 1985), pp. 13–21.

Schuster, M., and G. Flortowski. "Wage Incentive Plans and the Fair Labor Standards Act." *Compensation Review*, 14 (1982), pp. 34–46.

Thomas, Edward G. "Update on Alternative Work Methods." *Management World*, 11 (January 1982), pp. 30–31.

Tinsley, LaVerne C. "Worker's Compensation: Key Legislation in 1981." *Monthly Labor Review*, 105 (February 1982), pp. 24–30.

"Travel as an Incentive." *Dun's Business Month*, 119 (April 1982), pp. 26–27.

Villeman, Susan J. "Flexible Benefit Packages That Satisfy Employees and the IRS." *Personnel*, 62 (March 1985), pp. 33–41.

Weiss, Barbara. "Child Care: The Employee Benefit of the Future." *Drug Topics* (February 17, 1986), pp. 11–13.

"Workers' Compensation: How It Works." *National Safety News*, 131 (July 1985), pp. 30–34.

Yoder, Dale, and Herbert G. Heneman, Jr. (eds.). *ASPA Handbook of Personnel and Industrial Relations: Motivations and Commitment*, vol. 2 (Washington, D.C.: The Bureau of National Affairs, 1975).

PART FOUR

CASE

Parma Cycle Company: The Pay Plan

At Parma Cycle Company in Parma, Ohio, wage rates for hourly workers were established by a three-year labor–management agreement. The agreement provided for cost-of-living adjustments (COLA) based on changes in the U.S. Consumer Price Index. Wage rates varied according to job class and by seniority within each class. For example, a machine operator with two to four years seniority earned $10.75 per hour. With four to eight years seniority the rate increased to $12.60 an hour. A company-paid health plan provided medical and dental tal care for employees. The company contributed 6.5 percent of wages to a retirement plan administered by the machinists union.

Salaried workers at Parma Cycle were paid straight salaries based on a forty-hour workweek. For first- and second-level managers and clerical workers, work beyond forty hours in any week was compensated on a pro rata basis. Above the second management level there was no additional compensation for work after forty hours per week. COLA adjustments were made semiannually for all salaried employees.

Only in the sales department at Parma was any kind of incentive compensation program in effect. The sales representatives were paid a commission averaging about 2 percent of sales in addition to straight salary. The sales manager assigned the sales representatives to particular territories; they were generally given a choice of territories according to seniority. Once a sales representative had become accustomed to a given territory, however, requests to change were usually turned down. As older sales representatives left the company some of the younger ones moved into the better sales areas. This caused some of the more senior sales representatives to insist upon changes in territory to increase their sales potential. This was done in a few cases but no consistent policy was developed.

Parma Cycle Company was building a new plant in Clarksdale, Mississippi, in 1988. The new plant was to employ about 530 people, two-thirds the number working at the main plant in Parma, Ohio. Of course, the workforce would be smaller than that at first. About two months before the new plant was scheduled to open, Jesse Heard, the human resource director, was asked to meet with the president to discuss the compensation policies that would be followed in Clarksdale. Jesse knew that Jim Burgess, the president, tended to take a personal hand in matters relating to pay, so he prepared thoroughly for their meeting.

Mr. Burgess had a reputation for getting right to the heart of the matter. "I'm worried about the pay differentials that we are going to have between this plant and the one in Clarksdale," he began. "As I see it, some of the people down there won't be paid half as much as similar workers here." "That's true," said Jesse. "That really is the main reason for the move to Clarksdale. Without the union and with the low wage rates in that area, we will be able to pay just what the market requires. Most of the helpers and trainees will be available, we think, at minimum wage." "How will the pay classifications down there compare to those up here?" asked Mr. Burgess. "Well," said Jesse, "up here we have 'workers' and 'machine operators' and the pay within classes is by seniority. Down there we plan to have helpers/trainees, grades 1 and 2, and machine operators, grades 1, 2, and 3. Seniority won't count. We will promote workers based on the recommendations of their supervisors and their performance evaluation scores."

"I liked the incentive plan when you told me about it before, Jesse," said Mr. Burgess. "Let's go over it again. As I understand it, we are going to take 30 percent of the cost savings and pay it out as semiannual bonuses." "Yes," said Jesse, "To some degree, we modeled the plan after that at Lincoln Electric. [Lincoln is a Cleveland maker of electric welding products.] An individual's bonus will be a certain percentage of the gross wages paid during that period. But we will multiply that by the person's performance evaluation score." "Will the standard costs be the same as the ones we have here at the Parma plant?" asked Mr. Burgess. "Yes, they will," answered Jesse.

Mr. Burgess continued, "The last time we talked I think you said that we would save money in Clarksdale on the benefits package too." "Yes," replied Jesse, "For one thing, the tradition in that area is for the company to pay a health insurance premium for a worker and for the worker to pay the portion applicable to any dependents. Also, we don't have a dental plan down there, just medical. Finally, I don't think that we will even have a retirement program for those workers, at least not for a few years." "I think I know the answer," said Mr. Burgess, "but what about the ones who transfer down from Parma?" "They'll have the same benefits they have here," replied Jesse. "We will continue to cover them under the same insurance plan and guarantee that their wages will keep pace with those of similar workers here at Parma."

Questions

1. What are the pros and cons of paying workers on the basis of seniority?
2. How do cost-of-living adjustments (COLA) work?
3. Is anything legally wrong with Parma's plan for paying salaried workers? Explain.
4. Are the pay and benefits differentials between the plants likely to create problems? Why? Why not?

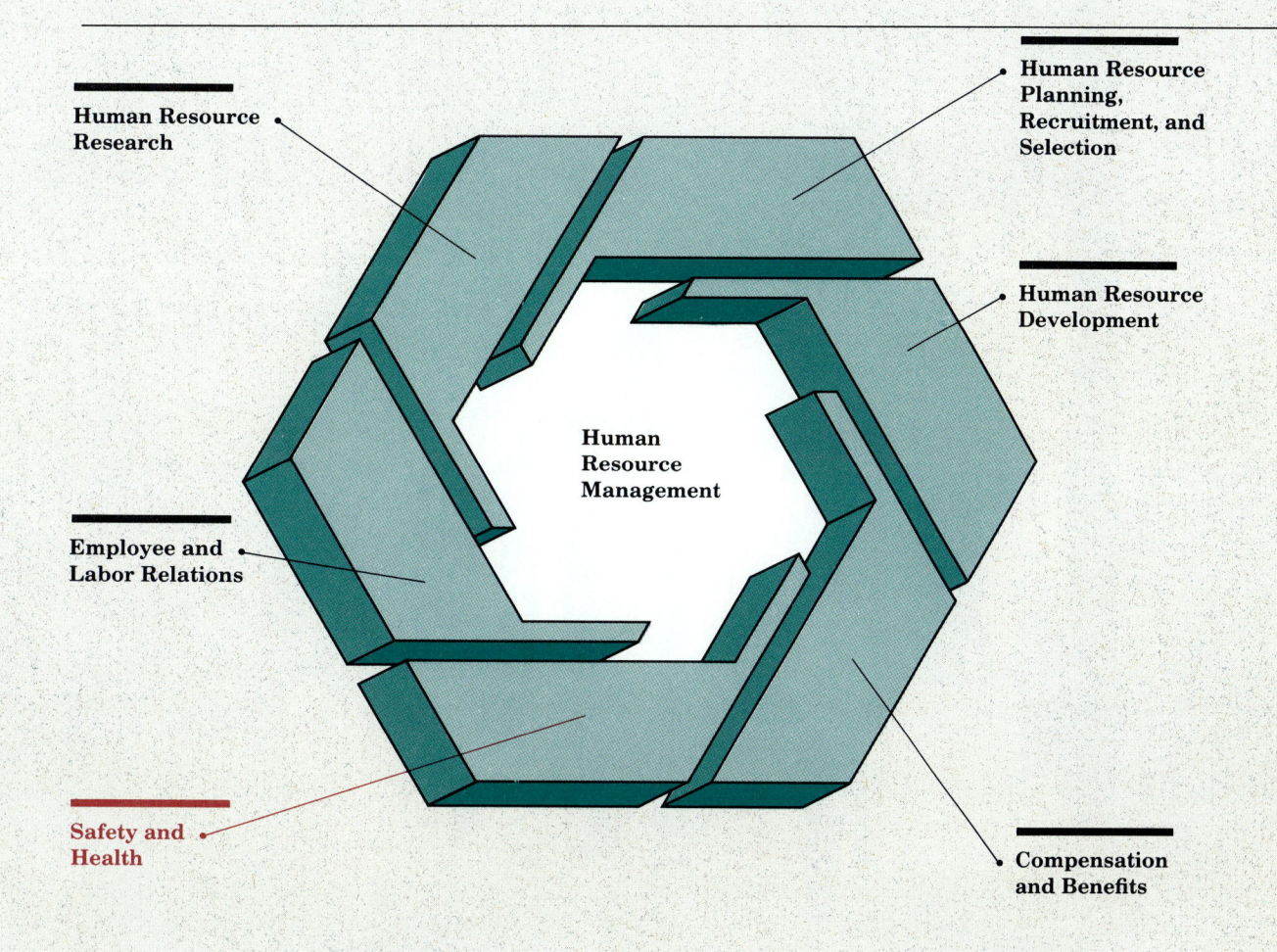

P·A·R·T F·I·V·E

SAFETY AND HEALTH

- Human Resource Research
- Human Resource Planning, Recruitment, and Selection
- Human Resource Development
- Human Resource Management
- Employee and Labor Relations
- Safety and Health
- Compensation and Benefits

CHAPTER 14

A SAFE AND HEALTHY WORK ENVIRONMENT

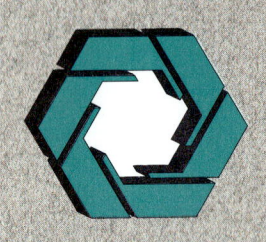

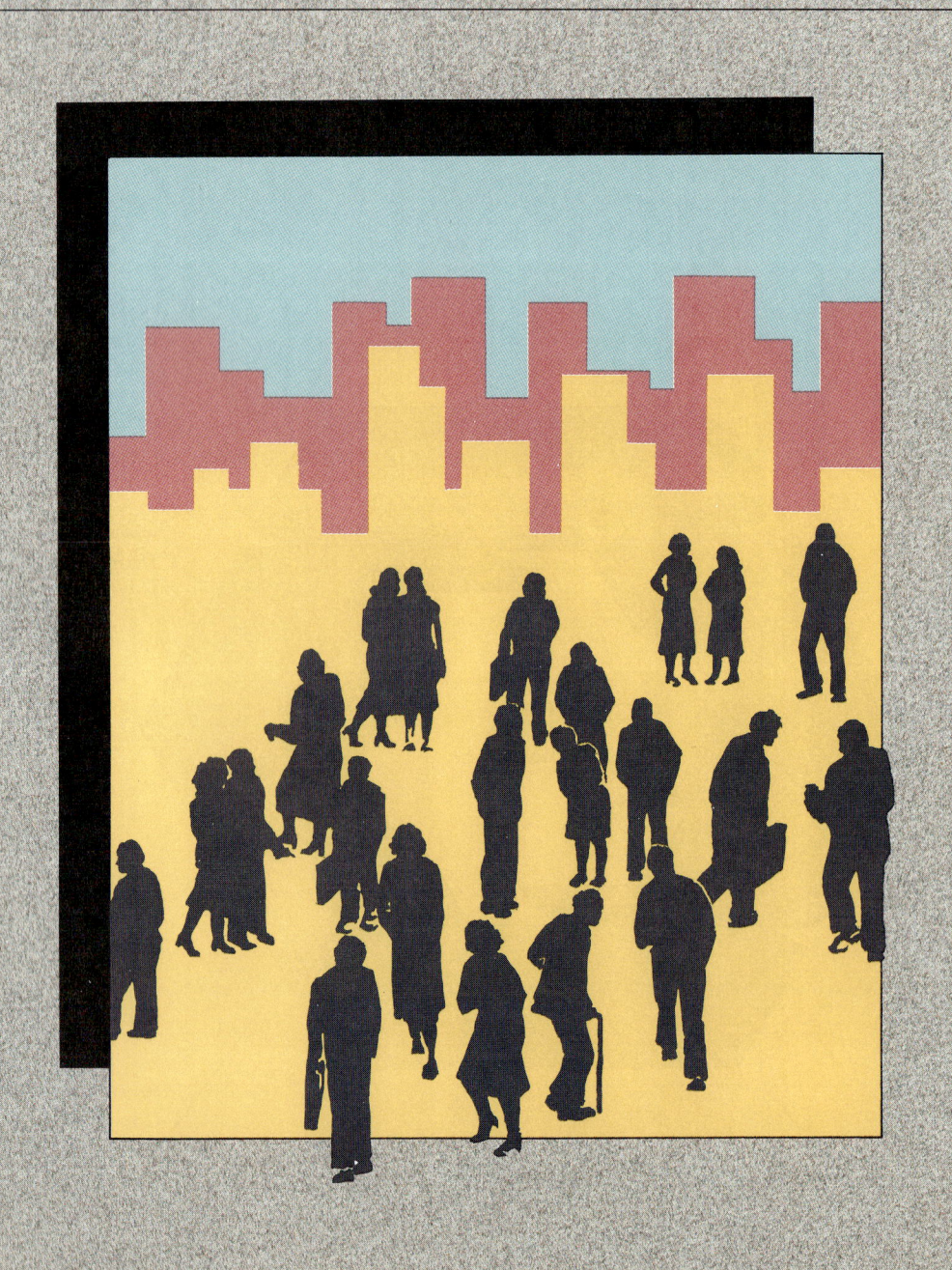

CHAPTER OBJECTIVES

1. Describe the Occupational Safety and Health Act, the importance of safety programs in business operations, and explain health and wellness programs.
2. State the nature of stress, the importance of stress management in business today, and describe why burnout is of major concern to management.
3. Describe physical fitness programs, alcohol abuse programs, drug abuse programs, and employee assistance programs.
4. Describe the possible impact of AIDS in the workplace.

■ Dionne Moore, safety engineer for Sather Manufacturing, was walking through the plant when she spotted a situation that immediately drew her attention. Someone had spilled a large quantity of oil on the floor and had not cleaned it up. Just at that moment, Ron Wade, one of the firm's employees, stepped on the oil. His feet went out from under him and the packages he was carrying scattered everywhere. Ron landed squarely on his back and for a moment did not move. He got up slowly but it appeared that he was not injured. Dionne was relieved, but became quite concerned when she realized the many possible consequences of the accident.

■ Bob Byrom, production foreman for King Electronics, is concerned about the health of one of his best workers, Cecil Weeks. For the past several months Cecil has been relatively ineffective on the job. He has been doing sloppy work and many of his co-workers have complained about his poor disposition. Recently, Bob observed Cecil at his locker during a work break take a bottle from a brown bag and drink from it. The odor on Cecil's breath suggested to Bob the cause of Cecil's changed work habits. Bob believes that Cecil may be an alcoholic. He wonders what should be done.

Dionne and Bob are each involved with but a few of the many critical areas related to employee safety and health. Dionne realizes that safety is a major concern in an organization and that she must constantly strive to minimize or eliminate accidents such as the one she just witnessed. Bob has just discovered that the poor performance of one of his employees may be caused by a drinking problem.

In our discussion, **safety** involves protecting employees from injuries caused by work-related accidents. **Health** refers to employees' freedom from physical or emotional illness. You may wonder why the human resource professional should be concerned with these aspects of work life. The answer becomes quite clear when you realize that safety and health problems can seriously affect productivity. Employee accidents and illnesses can dramatically lower a firm's effectiveness. Although line managers are primarily responsible for maintaining a safe and healthy work environment, human resources provides staff expertise to help them deal with these issues. In addition, the human resource manager is frequently responsible for coordinating and monitoring specific safety and health programs. In Executive Insights, Nina Woodard, vice-president of human resource management for First Interstate Bank of Casper, indicates that safety and health are two of her major concerns even though the bank's environment is relatively free from such problems.

We begin the chapter by discussing the impact of the Occupational Safety and Health Act on today's businesses and the topic of safety in the workplace generally. Next, we present topics related to health and wellness programs, stress management, and burnout. We then describe physical fitness programs, alcohol abuse programs, and drug abuse programs. We devote the final portion of the chapter to employee assistance programs and AIDS in the workplace. The overall purpose of this chapter is to provide an understanding of the importance of safety and health in organizations today.

■ THE OCCUPATIONAL SAFETY AND HEALTH ACT

For years, industrial safety has been a major problem that seemingly resisted solution. Prior to 1971, it was regulated primarily by the workers' compensation laws of the various states. When Congress passed the Occupational Safety and Health Act of 1970, it quickly became one of the most controversial laws affecting human resource management. There is little doubt that the act's intent is justified and that many businesses have long neglected safety and health. The act's basic requirements are summarized in Table 14-1.

The act's enforcement by the Occupational Safety and Health Administration (OSHA) dramatically altered management's role in the area of safety and health. Administrative changes have been made to make the agency more responsive to valid criticism and to overcome the negative image which it originally had. At the same time, OSHA continues to take its inspection and enforcement responsibilities quite seriously. When appropriate, it seeks criminal sanctions against corporations or individuals. In one instance, a corporate safety director was sentenced to three months in jail and fined $10,000 for lying to an OSHA inspector. The agency is definitely alive and well. During a single year in the 1980s, OSHA conducted more than 71,000 inspections. It detected almost 120,000 violations and levied fines totaling $9 million. Less than 3 percent of the violations were contested. While attempting to tighten its procedures, OSHA is also emphasizing the preventive effect of its inspections.[1] For example, all companies employing more than 10 workers are now required to maintain data regarding hazardous substances in the workplace. In addition, they must display warning labels when applicable. Although substantial benefits are antici-

---

[1] B. S. Murphy et al., "OSHA: Alive and Well," *Personnel Journal*, 65 (June 1986), pp. 32–35.

TABLE 14-1 | Job Safety and Health Protection

The Occupational Safety and Health Act of 1970 provides job safety and health protection for workers through the promotion of safe and healthful working conditions throughout the nation. Requirements of the act include the following.

Employers

Each employer must furnish to each of his employees a place of employment free from recognized hazards that are causing or are likely to cause death or serious harm to employees; and shall comply with occupational safety and health standards issued under the act.

Employees

Each employee shall comply with all occupational safety and health standards, rules, regulations, and orders issued under the act that apply to his or her own actions and conduct on the job. The Occupational Safety and Health Administration (OSHA) of the Department of Labor has the primary responsibility for administering the act. OSHA issues occupational safety and health standards, and its Compliance Safety and Health Officers conduct jobsite inspection to ensure compliance with the act.

Inspection

The act requires that a representative of the employer and a representative authorized by the employees be given an opportunity to accompany the OSHA inspector for the purpose of aiding the inspection. Where there is no authorized employee representative, the OSHA Compliance Officer must consult with a reasonable number of employees concerning safety and health conditions in the workplace.

Complaint

Employees or their representatives have the right to file a complaint with the nearest OSHA office requesting an inspection if they believe unsafe or unhealthful conditions exist in their workplace. OSHA will withhold, on request, names of employees complaining. The act provides that employees may not be discharged or discriminated against in any way for filing safety and health complaints or otherwise exercising their rights under the act. An employee who believes he or she has been discriminated against may file a complaint with the nearest OSHA office within thirty days of the alleged discrimination.

Citation

If upon inspection OSHA believes an employer has violated the act, a citation alleging such violations will be issued to the employer. Each citation will specify a time period within which the alleged violation must be corrected. The OSHA citation must be prominently displayed at or near the place of alleged violation for three days, or until it is corrected, whichever is later, to warn employees of dangers that may exist there.

Proposed Penalty

The act provides for mandatory penalties against employers of up to $1,000 for each serious violation and for optional penalties of up to $1,000 for each nonserious violation. Penalties of up to $1,000 per day may be proposed for failure to correct violations within the proposed time period. Also, any employer who willfully or repeatedly violates the act may be assessed penalties of up to $10,000 for each such violation. Criminal penalties are also provided for in the act. Any willful violation resulting in death of an employee, upon conviction, is punishable by a fine of not more than $10,000 or by imprisonment for not more than six months, or by both. Conviction of an employer after a first conviction doubles these maximum penalties.

Continued on next page

TABLE 14-1 | Continued

> **Voluntary Activity**
> While providing penalties for violations, the act also encourages efforts by labor and management, before an OSHA inspection, to reduce injuries and illnesses arising out of employment. The Department of Labor encourages employers and employees to reduce workplace hazards voluntarily and to develop and improve safety and health programs in all workplaces and industries. Such cooperative action would initially focus on the identification and elimination of hazards that could cause death, injury, or illness to employees and supervisors. There are many public and private organizations that can provide information and assistance in this effort, if requested.

Source: *OSHA Bulletin* (poster) (Washington, D.C.: U.S. Department of Labor).

pated, compliance with this new rule is estimated to cost industry $687 million in the first year.[2]

The agency is also concentrating on high-risk industries, such as meatpacking, where there is greater potential for reducing injuries and illnesses (see Table 14-2). Industries with lower accident and illness rates will not receive as much attention as before. Although it has emphasized safety in the past, OSHA has begun moving more into areas that affect health. Inspectors trained in these areas are now being employed.

Many of OSHA's rules have been simplified. For instance, instead of requiring that a fire extinguisher be a certain number of inches above the floor, the rule now states only that it has to be readily accessible. In addition, numerous inappropriate rules have been eliminated, a trend that is expected to continue. The agency's leaders are expected to maintain their enforcement pressure on businesses, but they appear to be taking a more positive and realistic approach than they did in the past.

■ SAFETY

Thousands of workers are killed or injured each year as a result of job-related accidents. The cost of these accidents is substantial—$33 billion in 1984 alone—as Table 14-3 shows. Unfortunately, the cost is often passed along to the consumer in the form of higher prices. Thus everyone is affected, directly or indirectly, by job-related accidents. Although many businesses had elaborate safety programs years before the Occupational Safety and Health Act was passed, a large number of firms didn't establish formal safety programs until it was enacted.

The Focus of Safety Programs

Safety programs may be designed to accomplish their purposes in two primary ways. The first approach is to create a psychological environment and

---
[2] Hazel Bradford, "OSHA Orders Benzene Curb," *Engineering News Record* (September 10, 1987), p. 10.

TABLE 14-2 | Industries with the Highest Injury and Illness Incidence Rates in 1984 and Percentage Changes from 1983

	1984		1983		
Industry	Rank	Incidence rate*	Rank	Incidence rate*	**Percent Change**
Meatpacking plants	1	33.4	1	31.4	6.4
Mobile homes	2	30.7	2	29.8	3.0
Structural wood members, n.e.c.[†]	3	24.8	3	28.5	−13.0
Prefabricated wood	4	26.6	7	22.1	20.4
Self-contained mobile homes	5	24.9	5	25.5	−2.4
Automatic merchandising machines	6	24.6	18	19.6	25.5
Vitreous plumbing fixtures	7	24.4	19	19.5	25.1
Hoist, cranes, and monorails	8	24.1	119	14.1	70.9
Cold finishing of steel shapes	9	22.9	29	18.8	21.8
Reclaimed rubber	10	22.8	22	19.3	18.1

*The incidence rates represent the number of injuries and illnesses per 100 full-time workers.
[†]The abbreviation n.e.c. stands for *not elsewhere classified*.

Source: *Occupational Injuries and Illnesses in the United States by Industry, 1984* (Washington, D.C.: U.S. Department of Labor, Bureau of Labor Statistics, May 1986), Bulletin 2259, p. 3.

attitudes that promote safety. Accidents can be reduced when employees consciously or subconsciously think about safety. This attitude must permeate the firm's operations, and a strong company policy emphasizing safety and health is crucial. For example, a major chemical firm's policy states: "It is the policy of the company that every employee be assigned to a safe and healthful place to work. We strongly desire accident prevention in all phases of our operations. Toward this end, the full cooperation of all employees will be required." As the policy infers, no one person is assigned the task of making the workplace safe. It is everyone's job from top management to the lowest level employee, and everyone should be encouraged to come up with solutions to safety problems. Although accident prevention requires a sustained effort by everyone, "everyone's responsibility often becomes no one's responsibility." Therefore, the firm's managers, who have the authority to direct that the safety effort be carried out, must take the lead. The unique

TABLE 14-3 | Job-Related Accidents Costs

Compensation paid to all workers in the nation who are under workers' compensation laws was approximately $16,145,000,000 in 1982 (latest figures reported by the Social Security Administration). Of this amount, $4,820,000,000 was for medical and hospital costs and $11,325,000,000 for wage compensation. These figures are not comparable to Council cost estimates due to differences in coverage of workers and types of cases.

TOTAL COST IN 1984 .... $33,000,000,000

Direct Costs $15,400,000,000

Includes wage losses of $6,800,000,000 insurance administrative costs amounting to about $4,300,000,000 and medical costs of $4,300,000,000.

Indirect Costs $15,400,000,000

Includes the money value of time lost by workers other than those with disabling injuries, who are directly or indirectly involved in accidents. Also included would be the time required to investigate accidents, write up accident reports, etc.

Fire Losses $2,200,000,000

Cost per Worker $320

This figure indicates the value of goods or services each worker must produce to offset the cost of work injuries. It is *not* the average cost of a work injury.

Source: *Accident Facts* (Chicago, Ill.: National Safety Council, 1985), p. 24.

role of management is made clear by the fact that OSHA places the responsibility for employee safety primarily on the employer.[3]

The second approach to safety program design is to develop and maintain a safe working environment. Here, the physical work environment is altered to prevent accidents. Even if Joe Smith, a machine operator, has been partying all night and can barely open his eyes, the safety devices on his machine will help keep him safe. It is in this area that OSHA has had its greatest influence. For instance, the agency's guidelines for power transmission apparatus are shown in Table 14-4. Through procedures such as these—and those developed by individual organizations—an attempt is made to create a physical environment where accidents cannot occur.

---

[3] Alton L. Thygerson, *Safety*, 2nd ed. (Englewood Cliffs, N.J.: Prentice-Hall, 1986), p. 258.

TABLE 14-4 | Office of Safety and Health Administration Guidelines for Power Transmission Apparatus

Power Transmission Apparatus

All belts, pulleys, shafts, flywheels, couplings, and other moving power transmission parts must be securely guarded.

A flywheel located so that any part is seven feet or less above a floor or platform must be guarded with an enclosure of sheet, perforated or expanded metal, or woven wire. It must also be fenced in with guard rails.

All exposed parts of horizontal shafting must be enclosed in a metal or wire cage on a frame of angle iron or iron pipe securely fastened to the floor or frame of the machine. If wire mesh forms the enclosure, it should be the type in which the wires are strongly fastened at every cross point, either by welding, soldering, or galvanizing.

Projecting shaft ends must be guarded by nonrotating caps or safety sleeves.

Pulleys or sheaves seven feet or less from the floor must be guarded with metal or wire mesh enclosures.

Horizontal, vertical, and inclined belt, rope, and chain drives must be enclosed in metal or wire mesh cages. The same applies to chains, sprockets, couplings, and gears.

Guards for horizontal overhead belts must run the entire length of the belt and follow the line of the pulley to the ceiling. This also applies to overhead rope and chain drives.

Source: *Essentials of Machine Guarding* (Washington, D.C.: U.S. Department of Labor, Office of Safety and Health Administration, July 1975), OSHA no. 2227, pp. 10, 12.

Developing Safety Programs

Organizational safety programs require planning for prevention of workplace accidents. Plans may be relatively simple, as for a small retail store, or more complex and highly sophisticated, as for a large automobile assembly plant. Regardless of the organization's size, top management's support is essential if safety programs are to be effective. The top executives in a firm should be aware of the tremendous economic losses that can result from accidents.

Some of the reasons for top management's support of a safety program are listed in Table 14-5. As you can see, the lost productivity of a single injured worker is not the only factor to consider. Every phase of human resource management is involved. For instance, the firm may have difficulty in recruitment if it gains a reputation for having hazardous working conditions. Employee relations may be seriously eroded if workers believe that management doesn't care enough about them to make their workplace

TABLE 14-5 | **Reasons for Management's Support of a Safety Program**

- *Personal loss.* Most individuals strongly prefer not to be injured. The physical pain and mental anguish associated with injuries is always unpleasant and may even be traumatic. Of much greater concern is the possibility of permanent disablement or even death.
- *Financial loss to injured employees.* Most employees are covered by company insurance plans or personal accident insurance. However, an injury may result in financial losses not covered by the insurance.
- *Lost productivity.* When an employee is injured, there will be a loss of productivity to the firm. In addition to obvious losses, there are often hidden costs. For example, a replacement may need additional training to replace the injured employee. Even when a person can be moved into the injured employee's position, efficiency may suffer.
- *Higher insurance premiums.* Workers' compensation insurance premiums are based on the employer's history of insurance claims. The potential for savings related to employee safety provides a degree of incentive to establish formal programs.
- *Possibility of fines and imprisonment.* Since the enactment of OSHA, a willful and repeated violation of its provisions may result in serious penalties.
- *Social responsibility.* Many executives feel responsible for the safety and health of their employees. A number of firms had excellent safety programs years before OSHA. They understand that safety is in the best interest of the firm.

safe. Compensation may also be affected if the firm must pay a premium to attract qualified applicants and retain valued employees. Maintaining a stable workforce may become very difficult if the workplace is perceived as hazardous.

Managers in unionized firms should recognize that a collective bargaining agreement—even if it contains both no-strike and grievance arbitration clauses—does not prohibit an employee walkout if objective evidence of abnormally dangerous working conditions exists. Managers in union-free firms should be aware that their employees' right to walk out when hazardous working conditions exist is also protected by the Labor Management Relations Act. Whether the firm is unionized or union-free, it is an unfair labor practice to interfere with workers' rights with regard to safe working conditions.[4]

Companies with effective safety programs work to involve virtually everyone in the firm. Line managers are normally responsible for controlling conditions that cause accidents. As part of this responsibility, they must set

---

[4] John J. Hoover, "Workers Have New Rights to Health and Safety," *Personnel Administrator*, 28 (April 1983), p. 47.

the proper safety example for other employees. If a supervisor fails to use safety devices when demonstrating use of the equipment, subordinates may feel that the devices aren't really necessary. The line manager's attitude can also affect a worker's attitude toward safety training. Comments such as, "Let's go to that boring safety meeting," aren't likely to elicit enthusiastic support from subordinates. The supervisor can show support for the safety program by conscientiously enforcing safety rules and cooperating with those who monitor the program.

In many companies, a staff person coordinates the overall safety program. Some major corporations have risk management departments, which anticipate losses associated with safety factors and prepare legal defenses in the event of lawsuits. Titles such as safety director and safety engineer are common. One of the safety director's primary tasks is to provide safety training for company employees. This involves educating line managers about the merits of safety and how to recognize and eliminate unsafe situations. Although the safety director operates essentially in an advisory capacity, a well-informed and assertive director may have considerable power in the organization.

Accident Investigation

At times accidents happen even in the most safety-conscious firms. Each accident, whether or not it results in an injury, should be carefully evaluated to ensure that it does not recur. The safety engineer and the line manager jointly investigate accidents. One of the responsibilities of any supervisor is to prevent accidents. To do so, the supervisor must learn—through active participation in the safety program—why accidents occur, how they occur, where they occur, and who is involved. Supervisors gain a great deal of knowledge about accident prevention by helping prepare accident reports.

Safety should also be emphasized during the training and orientation of new employees. The early months of employment are often critical because, as Table 14-6 shows, work injuries decrease substantially with length of service.[5] Note that the pattern is consistent for both men and women. This knowledge should lead supervisors to stress safety as they train new employees.

Evaluation of Safety Programs

Perhaps the best indicator that a safety program is succeeding is a reduction in the number and severity of accidents. Thus program evaluation involves more than counting the number of accidents; it must also consider their severity. Statistics such as frequency and severity rates are often used in program evaluation. The **frequency rate** is expressed by the fol-

---

[5] Norman Root and Michael Hoefer, "The First Work-Injury Data Available from New BLS Study," *Monthly Labor Review*, 102 (January 1979), p. 77.

TABLE 14-6 | Accident Rates by Length of Service

Length of Service	Men[*]	Women[*]
1 month	10.64	8.78
2–3 months	5.90	5.47
4–6 months	3.41	3.31
7–12 months	1.72	1.84
2–3 years	0.84	0.95
4–5 years	0.43	0.46
6–10 years	0.21	0.23
11–25 years	0.06	0.05
26–35 years	0.02	0.01

[*]Rates are expressed as the average percent per month of work injuries, by length of service, for 218,446 men and 52,136 women in ten states, 1976–1977.

Source: Norman Root and Michael Hoefer, "The First Work-Injury Data Available from New BLS Study," *Monthly Labor Review*, 102, (January 1979), p. 77. Reprinted by permission.

lowing formula, which yields the number of lost-time accidents per million person-hours worked:

$$\text{Frequency rate} = \frac{\text{Number of lost-time accidents} \times 1{,}000{,}000}{\text{Number of person-hours worked during the period}}$$

Although this formula is often used, OSHA has developed one that is conceptually different.[6] The agency's formula is:

$$\text{Incident rate} = \frac{\text{Number of injuries and/or illnesses}}{\text{Total hours worked by all employees during reference year}} \times 200{,}000 \text{ (Base for 100 full-time equivalent workers who are working 40 hours per week, 50 weeks per year.)}$$

where the constant represents the base for 100 full-time equivalent workers at 40 hours per week, 50 weeks per year. The major differences between this formula and the first one are that both injuries and illnesses are considered and that the base for reporting injury frequency rates is 100 full-time employees (as opposed to million person-hours).

The **severity rate** indicates the number of days lost because of accidents per million person-hours worked. It is expressed by the formula:

$$\text{Severity rate} = \frac{\text{Number of person-days lost} \times 1{,}000{,}000}{\text{Number of person-hours worked during period}}$$

---

[6] Lyne R. Schauer and Thomas S. Ryder, "New Approach to Occupational Safety and Health Statistics," *Monthly Labor Review*, 95 (March 1972), pp. 18–19.

In addition to program evaluation criteria, an effective reporting system is needed to ensure that accidents are recorded. When a new safety program is initiated, the number of accidents may decline significantly. However, some supervisors may be failing to report certain accidents to make the statistics for their units look better. Proper evaluation of a safety program depends on the accurate reporting and recording of data.

To be of value, the conclusions derived from an evaluation must be used to improve the safety program. Gathering data and permitting them to collect dust on the safety director's desk do not solve problems or prevent accidents. The results of the evaluation must be transmitted upward to top management and downward to line managers in order to generate improvements.

■ HEALTH AND WELLNESS PROGRAMS

The reason for a firm to be concerned about its employees' health becomes crystal clear when employee worth is calculated. For instance, how valuable is a highly qualified executive who has developed and implemented a new marketing program? Or what is the worth of a skilled engineer trained by the firm for five years? Consider, for example, the bright, forty-year-old executive who succumbs to alcoholism because of job stress; the machinist, who because of job boredom, turns to drugs to brighten the day; or the designer who pushes herself so hard that she dies of cardiac arrest while driving to work. Loss of an individual's productivity because of health problems definitely affects an organization's profitability.

Union support has also hastened the establishment of more effective health programs. Unions are placing industrial health issues high on their list of demands in collective bargaining. Rather than concentrating on pay, unions now seek gains in such areas as health care and recreational facilities.

Environmental factors play a major role in the development of physical and mental disorders. The traditional view that health is dependent on medical care and is simply the absence of disease is changing. Today, many individuals perceive that optimal health can be achieved through environmental safety, organizational changes, and different lifestyles. Infectious diseases, over which the individual has little control, are not the problem they once were. For example, from 1900 to 1970 the death rate from major infectious diseases dropped dramatically. Yet, the death rate from major chronic diseases such as heart disease, cancer, and stroke increased by more than 250 percent.[7] Although chronic lifestyle diseases are much more prevalent today, people have a great deal of control over certain of them. These are the health problems related to heavy smoking, undue stress, lack of exercise, obesity, and alcohol and drug abuse.[8]

---

[7] Cathy J. Brumback, "EAPs—Bringing Health and Productivity to the Workplace," *Business*, 37 (April–June 1987), p. 42.

[8] Robert H. Rosea, "The Picture of Health in the Work Place," *Training and Development Journal*, 38 (August 1984), p. 26.

EXECUTIVE INSIGHTS

Nina E. Woodard
Vice-President, Human Resource Management, First Interstate Bank of Casper, N.A.

Nina E. Woodard is a charter member of the Energy Capital Chapter of ASPA in Casper, Wyoming. She served as the chapter's past president, state director and Region 16 vice-president for 1984–1985. She was recently reelected chapter president. Woodard believes that human resource management issues are the cornerstone of future business successes. It is becoming increasingly important to make conscious and purposeful decisions relative to employment, compensation, training and development, health and safety, and employee relations. "Without proper direction in these areas," Woodard states, "a business will not be able to achieve consistent and profitable results. As the CEO and chief financial officer operate as the head of the business body, the human resources officer is the heart. This position is the center of the organization's circulatory system, pumping vital support to the body's farthest extremities to keep them functional and vibrant."

Effective utilization of the five basic management functions—planning, organizing, staffing, leading, and controlling—as life skills and an action orientation are Woodard's strengths. She applies them in her role as human resources manager and in other important aspects of her life. Woodard feels that the profession must be able to provide a framework that will accommodate change and that human resource professionals must be effective change agents.

Woodard's background includes participation in the American Banker's Association Personnel School and Graduate Personnel School. She was recently graduated from Pacific Coast Banking School in Washington State. In order to maintain her skills, she continually reads and is involved in extensive networking activities through SHRM and other professional organizations.

Her entrance into banking occurred quite by accident when she sought employment to help pass the time while her husband served in Vietnam. She spent several years working in various operational positions and eventually landed a position in the newly formed personnel department at what was then the First National Bank of Casper in 1975. Since then, she has taken advantage of every available opportunity to enhance and develop her expertise in human resources and has ascended to the top human resources management position at the bank.

During the 1985 national ASPA conference, Woodard sat for and passed the accreditation exam as a Senior Professional in Human Resources (SPHR). In the previous year, she was one of six women in the United States to be honored with a scholarship by the National Association of Bank Women.

Woodard has utilized volunteer leadership as a valuable tool to develop management skills. She lends her expertise to community and state activities, as well as applying it to her position at First Interstate. Woodard has served as an instructor at Casper Community College, conducting courses in both human resources and marketing management. She is an often sought-after speaker and presenter in the areas of management, motivation, and business. Originally from California and Iowa, the Woodards have lived in Casper since 1971.

A formal company wellness program involves more than merely dispensing aspirin and bandages. As with a safety program, it should reflect a company philosophy that emphasizes the value of its human assets. Many of the procedures used in establishing an effective safety program are also applicable to a company wellness program. A firm with the reputation of having a healthy work environment is in a stronger position to achieve many other human resource objectives. For instance, recruitment may be easier because more people want to work for the company. Employee and management relations may also improve when workers believe that the company has their best interests at heart.

A wellness program starts with initial applicant screening and continues throughout the worker's employment. It typically is concerned with potential health hazards such as certain fumes, dust, gases, liquids, and solids that have proven harmful to workers' health. A wellness program also may emphasize, for example, reducing the noise level in a plant because loss of hearing can result from excessive and prolonged exposure to noise. In recent years, a major health concern has been that of workers' exposure to hazardous substances such as asbestos. In addition to monitoring traditional health problems, many organizations have expanded the scope of their health concerns to include a number of problems and programs that are closely related to wellness, such as stress management.

■ STRESS MANAGEMENT

A notable trend within U.S. industry is an increasing concern for employees' emotional well-being. Managers are becoming more aware that long-term productivity depends largely on the dedication and commitment of the company's employees. Another reason is that employees increasingly hold their employers liable for emotional problems they claim are work related.[9] In fact, during the past few years, stress related mental disorders have become the fastest growing occupational disease. Stress claims now account for almost 14 percent of occupational disease claims, up from 5 percent less than a decade ago.[10] It is interesting to note that the three most used drugs in the United States are tranquilizers, hypertension drugs, and ulcer medication.[11] Regardless of the reason, programs dealing with stress and its related problems are becoming increasingly popular.

Stress is the body's reaction to any demand made on it. It is therefore a highly individual condition. Certain events may be quite stressful to one person but not to another. Moreover, the effect of stress is not always neg-

---

[9] Mitchell S. Novit, "Mental Distress: Possible Implications for the Future," *Personnel Administrator*, 27 (January 1982), p. 59.

[10] Randall Poe, "Does Your Job Make You Sick?" *Across the Board*, 24 (January 1987), p. 34.

[11] C. Wallis, "Stress: Can We Cope?" *Time* (June 6, 1983), p. 48.

ative. For example, mild stress actually improves productivity,[12] and it can be helpful in developing creative ideas. In fact, the only people without stress are dead.[13] Although everyone lives under a certain amount of stress, if it is severe enough and persists long enough, it can be harmful. In fact, stress can be as disruptive to an individual as any accident. It can result in poor attendance, excessive use of alcohol or other drugs, poor job performance, or even overall poor health.

There is increasing evidence that undue stress is related to the diseases that are leading causes of death—coronary heart disease, stroke, hypertension, cancer, emphysema, diabetes, and cirrhosis—and also to suicide.[14] Stress costs U.S. industry an estimated $20-$50 billion each year.[15] The cost to a single firm may be as much as 6 percent of total sales.[16]

Aside from humanitarian reasons, the economic factor is sufficient to gain management's interest in helping employees manage stress. A legal factor may provide still another reason. One manager filed suit against his company charging that his physical ailments, including a heart attack, were caused by the pressure of his job. The man won his case and the company was ordered to make a cash settlement.[17]

The National Institute for Occupational Safety and Health (NIOSH) is one organization that has studied stress as it relates to work. This organization's research indicates that some jobs are generally more stressful than others. The twelve most stressful jobs are listed in Table 14-7. The linkage is lack of employee control over their work.[18] People in these jobs may feel trapped and that they are treated more like machines than people. Some of the less stressful jobs are held by workers who have more control over their jobs, such as college professors and master craftpersons.

The fact that certain jobs are being identified as more stressful than others has important managerial implications. Managers are responsible for recognizing significantly deviant behavior and referring employees to health professionals for diagnosis and treatment. (Refer to Figure 14-1 for behavior that may indicate problems.) In addition, managers should monitor their employees' progress and provide them with the incentive to succeed. They should inform employees that there are rewards for lifestyle

---

[12] Michael Pesci, "Stress Management: Separating Myth from Reality," *Personnel Administrator*, 27 (January 1982), p. 59.

[13] Hans Selye, "Secret of Coping with Stress," *U. S. News and World Report* (March 21, 1977), p. 1.

[14] John M. Ivancevich and Michael T. Matteson, "Optimizing Human Resources: A Case for Preventive Health and Stress Management," *Organizational Dynamics*, 9 (Autumn 1980), pp. 5-8.

[15] Oliver L. Niehouse and Karen B. Massoni, "Stress—An Inevitable Part of Change," *Advanced Management Journal*, 44 (Spring 1979), p. 17.

[16] Randy Wiegel and Sheldon Pinsky, "Managing Stress: A Model for the Human Resource Staff," *Personnel Administrator*, 27 (February 1982), p. 56.

[17] Ivancevich and Matteson, p. 6.

[18] Niehouse and Massoni, p. 41.

TABLE 14-7 | Stressful Jobs

Where the Pressure Builds Up

12 Jobs with the most stress

1. Laborer
2. Secretary
3. Inspector
4. Clinical lab technician
5. Office manager
6. Supervisor
7. Manager/administrator
8. Waitress/waiter
9. Machine operator
10. Farm owner
11. Miner
12. Painter

Other high-stress jobs (in alphabetical order)

- Bank teller
- Clergy
- Computer programmer
- Dental assistant
- Electrician
- Firefighter
- Guard
- Hairdresser
- Health aide
- Health technician
- Machinist
- Meatcutter
- Mechanic
- Musician
- Nurses' aide
- Plumber
- Policeperson
- Practical nurse
- Public relations person
- Railroad switchperson
- Registered nurse
- Sales manager
- Sales representative
- Social worker
- Structural-metal worker
- Teachers' aide
- Telephone operator
- Warehouse worker

Source: From a ranking of 130 occupations by the federal government's National Institute for Occupational Safety and Health.

changes and that the advantages are greater than the costs involved.[19] Stress may result in many complex problems, but it can generally be handled successfully.[20] In the following section, we describe burnout, a condition that often results from organizational and individual failure to deal with stress effectively.

Burnout

Cheryl Weaver supervised fifty people in the administrative department of a large insurance firm. She was a competent and conscientious manager with a reputation for doing things right and on time. Until recently, Cheryl had been strongly considered as a candidate for the position of vice-president—administration.

---
[19] "Keeping a Wellness Program Well," *Training: The Magazine of Human Resources Development*, 24 (September 1987), p. 68.
[20] Pesci, p. 58.

- Reduced clarity of judgment and effectiveness
- Rigid behavior
- Medical problems
- Strained relationships with others due to irritability
- Increasing excessive absence
- Emerging addictive behaviors (e.g., drugs, alcohol, smoking)
- Expressions of inadequacy and low self-esteem
- Apathy or anger on the job

FIGURE 14-1 | Signs of Stress: What Managers Should Look For

Source: Michael Pesci, "Stress Management: Separating Myth from Reality," Reprinted from the January 1982 issue of *Personnel Administrator*. Copyright © 1982, The American Society for Personnel Administration, Alexandria, Virginia.

However, things have changed. Cheryl behaves differently. She can't seem to concentrate on her work and appears to be a victim of "battle fatigue." "Oh, Cheryl," a co-worker advised, "You'll make it. You've always been so strong." But Cheryl surprised her associate when she responded, "I don't want to be told I'll make it on my own. I already know I can't."

Cheryl doesn't know exactly what has caused her run-down condition. She senses that she is at her wits end and desperately needs assistance. Cheryl apparently is the victim of a stress related phenomenon known as burnout. **Burnout** is a state of fatigue or frustration, which stems from devotion to a cause, way of life, or relationship that did not provide the expected reward.[21] Burnout is often associated with a mid-life or mid-career crisis, but it can happen at different times to different people.[22]

Individuals in the helping professions, such as teachers and counselors, seem to be susceptible to burnout because of their jobs, whereas others may be vulnerable because of their upbringing, their expectations, or their personalities.[23] Burnout is frequently associated with people whose jobs require working closely with others under stressful and tension-filled conditions.[24] Although any employee may experience this condition, perhaps 10 percent of managers and executives are so affected.[25] The dangerous part of burnout is that it is contagious. A highly cynical and pessimistic burnout victim can quickly transform an entire group into burnouts. There-

---

[21] Herbert J. Freudenberger, *Burnout: The High Cost of High Achievement* (Garden City, N.Y.: Anchor Press, Doubleday and Company, 1980), p. 13.

[22] John G. Nelson, "Burnout—Business's Most Costly Expense," *Personnel Administrator*, 25 (August 1980), p. 82.

[23] Dick Friedman, "Job Burnout," *Working Woman*, 5 (July 1980), p. 34.

[24] Christina Meslack and Susan E. Jackson, "Burned-Out Cops and Their Families," *Psychology Today*, 12 (May 1979), p. 59.

[25] Beverly Norman, "Career Burnout," *Black Enterprise*, 12 (July 1981), p. 45.

fore, it is important that the problem be dealt with quickly. Once it has begun, it is difficult to stop.[26]

Some of the symptoms of burnout include: (1) chronic fatigue; (2) anger at those making demands; (3) self-criticism for putting up with demands; (4) cynicism, negativism, and irritability; (5) a sense of being besieged; and (6) hair-trigger display of emotions.[27] Other symptoms might include recurring health problems, such as ulcers, back pain, or frequent headaches. The burnout victim is often unable to maintain an even keel emotionally. Unwarranted hostility may occur in totally inappropriate situations.

Burnout is a problem that should be dealt with before it occurs. In order to do so, managers must be aware of potential sources of stress. These sources exist both within and outside the organization.

Sources of Stress[28]

Regardless of its origin, stress possesses the same devastating potential. Some factors are controllable to varying degrees; others aren't. In the following paragraphs we discuss some of the primary sources of stress.

The Family. Although a frequent source of happiness and security, the family can also be a significant stressor. As a result, nearly one half of all marriages end in divorce, which itself is quite stressful. When divorce leads to single parenthood, the difficulties may be compounded.

Children are one of life's great sources of happiness. Yet, consider the effect of an infant awakening parents in the middle of the night with a severe asthmatic attack! Anxiety levels rise significantly as the parents watch their child struggle for each breath. Academic or extreme social adjustment problems for a teenager can also create much anguish for the entire family.

A relatively recent phenomenon is the dual-career family. When both husband and wife have job and family responsibilities, traditional roles are altered. What happens when one partner is totally content with a job and the other is offered a sought-after promotion requiring transfer to a distant city? At best, these circumstances are beset with difficulties.

Financial Problems. Problems with finances may place an unbearable strain on the family. For some, these problems are persistent and never quite resolved. Nagging, unpaid bills and bill collectors can create great tension and play a role in divorce.

---

[26] Cary Cherniss, "Job Burnout: Growing Worry for Workers, Bosses," *U. S. News and World Report*, 88 (February 1980), p. 72.

[27] Harry Levinson, "When Executives Burn Out," *Harvard Business Review*, 59 (May–June 1981), p. 76.

[28] Certain portions of this section were adapted from unpublished working papers of Robert L. Smith, Professor and Head of Counseling and Guidance Department, East Texas State University, 1982.

Living Conditions. Stress levels may be higher for people who live in densely populated areas. These people face longer lines, endure more hectic traffic jams, and contend with higher levels of air and noise pollution. Urban life has many advantages, but the benefits are not without costs—often in the form of stress.

Life Changes. Life change events have been weighted according to the stress they produce. As Table 14-8 shows, the most stressful life event is the death of a spouse. One study determined that 70 percent of the persons who registered more than 300 life change units (LCUs) in a year had an illness during the following year. It was also noted that these people tended to have multiple illnesses.[29]

Corporate Culture. Generally speaking, corporate culture has a lot to do with stress. The CEO's leadership style often sets the tone. An autocratic CEO who permits little input from subordinates may create a stressful environment. However, a weak CEO may encourage subordinates to compete for power, resulting in internal conflicts. Certain firms have even been considered stressful because the CEO insists on superior performance.

Even in the healthiest corporate culture, stressful relationships among employees can occur. Employee personality types vary and, combined with differing values and belief systems, they may so impair communication that stress is inevitable. Also, competition encouraged by the organization's reward system for promotion, pay increases, and status may add to the problem.[30]

Role Ambiguity. **Role ambiguity** exists when an employee doesn't understand the content of the job. The employee may feel stress when he or she doesn't perform certain duties expected by the supervisor, even though the employee didn't know to do them. An employee may also feel pressure from above when he or she mistakenly, although innocently, attempts to perform tasks that are part of someone else's job. These situations often result from role ambiguity, a condition that can be quite threatening to an employee and produce feelings of insecurity.

Role Conflict. **Role conflict** occurs when an individual is placed in the position of having to pursue opposing goals. For example, a manager may be expected to increase production while having to decrease the size of the workforce.[31] Attaining both goals may be impossible and stress is likely to result. A nationwide survey identified the extent of such problems. It revealed

---

[29] E. K. Erich Gunderson and Richard H. Rahe (eds.), *Life Stress and Illness* (Springfield, Ill.: Charles C Thomas, 1974), p. 62.

[30] "Can You Cope with Stress?" *Duns Review*, 106 (November 1975), p. 90.

[31] Arthur P. Brief, "How to Manage Managerial Stress," *Personnel*, 57 (September–October 1980), p. 27.

TABLE 14-8 | Life Change Events

Type of Event		LCU Values
Family	Death of spouse	100
	Divorce	73
	Marital separation	65
	Death of close family member	63
	Marriage	50
	Marital reconciliation	45
	Major change in health of family	44
	Pregnancy	40
	Addition of new family member	39
	Major change in arguments with wife	35
	Son or daughter leaving home	29
	In-law troubles	29
	Wife starting or ending work	26
	Major change in family get-togethers	15
Personal	Detention in jail	63
	Major personal injury or illness	53
	Sexual difficulties	39
	Death of a close friend	37
	Outstanding personal achievement	28
	Start or end of formal schooling	26
	Major change in living conditions	25
	Major revision of personal habits	24
	Changing to a new school	20
	Change in residence	20
	Major change in recreation	19
	Major change in church activities	19
	Major change in social activities	18
	Major change in sleeping habits	16
	Major change in eating habits	15
	Vacation	13
	Christmas	12
	Minor violations of the law	11
Work	Being fired from work	47
	Retirement from work	45
	Major business adjustment	39
	Changing to different line of work	36
	Major change in work responsibilities	29
	Trouble with boss	23
	Major change in working conditions	20
Financial	Major change in financial state	38
	Mortgage or loan over $10,000	31
	Mortgage foreclosure	30
	Mortgage or loan less than $10,000	17

Source: Reprinted from E. K. Eric Gunderson and Richard H. Rahe (eds.), *Life Stress and Illness* (Springfield, Ill.: Charles C Thomas, 1974), by courtesy of the publisher.

that 35 percent of the respondents had complaints about role ambiguity, and 48 percent felt that they were victims of role conflict.[32]

Job Overload. When employees are given more work than they can reasonably handle, they become victims of **job overload**. A critical aspect of this problem is that the best performers in the firm are often the ones so affected. These individuals have proven that they can perform more so they are given even more to do. At its extreme, work overload becomes burnout.

Working Conditions. The physical characteristics of the workplace, including the machines and tools used, can create stress. Overcrowding, excessive noise, poor lighting, and poorly maintained work stations and equipment can all adversely affect employee morale and increase stress. Something as apparently benign as an antiquated duplicating machine that doesn't always work properly can create great stress when an important report must be assembled and sent to the CEO first thing in the morning.

It is important for managers to be aware of sources of stress. It is equally important that they implement programs to deal with stress effectively.

Coping with Stress

A number of programs and techniques may effectively prevent or relieve excessive stress. General organizational programs, while not specifically designed to cope with stress, may nevertheless play a major role. The programs and techniques listed in Table 14-9 are discussed in the chapters of this text as indicated. Their effective implementation will achieve these results:

- A corporate culture that holds anxiety and tension to an acceptable level is created. Employee inputs are sought and valued, employees are given greater control over their work, and communication is emphasized.
- Each person's role is defined, yet care is taken not to discourage risk-takers and those who want to assume greater responsibility.
- Individuals are given the training and development they need to successfully perform current and future jobs. Equal consideration is given to achieving personal and organizational goals. Individuals are trained to work as effective team members and to develop an awareness of how they and their work relate to others.
- Employees are assisted in planning for career progression.
- Employees participate in making decisions that affect them. They know what is going on in the firm, what their particular roles are, and how well they are performing their jobs.
- Employee needs, financial and nonfinancial, are met through an equitable reward system.

---

[32] Peter J. Frost, Vance F. Mitchell, and Walter R. Nord, *Organizational Reality: Reports from the Firing Line*, 2nd ed. (Glenview, Ill.: Scott, Foresman, 1982), p. 446.

TABLE 14-9 | Organizational Programs and Techniques That Can Be Effective in Coping with Stress

General Organizational Programs	Chapter
Job analysis	4
Human resource development	8
Effective communication, motivation and leadership styles (corporate culture)	9
Organization development	9
Career planning and development	10
Performance appraisal	11
Compensation	12, 13
Specific Techniques	
Hypnosis, transcendental meditation, biofeedback, and relaxation response	14
Specific Organizational Programs	
Physical fitness, alcohol and drug abuse, and employee assistance programs	14

Table 14-9 also identifies several specific techniques that individuals can utilize to deal with stress. These methods include hypnosis, biofeedback, transcendental meditation, and the relaxation response.

Hypnosis is an altered state of consciousness that is artificially induced and characterized by increased receptiveness to suggestions. A person in a hypnotic state may therefore respond to the hypnotist's suggestion to relax.[33] Hypnosis can help many people cope with stress. The serenity achieved through dissipation of anxieties and fears can restore an individual's confidence. A principal benefit of hypnotherapy is that peace of mind continues after the person awakens from a hypnotic state. This tranquility continues to grow, especially when the person has been trained in self-hypnosis.[34]

Biofeedback is a method that can be used to control involuntary bodily processes, such as blood pressure or heart rate.[35] For example, using equipment to provide a visual display of blood pressure, individuals may learn to lower their systolic blood pressure levels.

Transcendental meditation (TM) is a stress-reduction technique whereby a secret word or phrase (mantra) provided by a trained instructor is mentally repeated while an individual is comfortably seated. Repeating the mantra over and over helps prevent distracting thoughts. It has suc-

---

[33] Herbert Benson, *The Relaxation Response* (New York: William Morrow, 1975), p. 72.

[34] E. M. Cherman, *Stress and the Bottom Line: A Guide to Personal Well-Being and Corporate Health* (New York: AMACOM, a Division of American Management Associations, 1981), p. 273.

[35] Benson, pp. 55–56.

cessfully produced the following physiologic changes: decreased oxygen consumption, decreased carbon-dioxide elimination, and decreased breathing rate. Transcendental meditation results in a decreased metabolic rate and a restful state.[36]

The relaxation response is another technique for dealing with the stressful consequences of living in our modern society. This approach to dealing with stress was developed at Harvard's Thorndike Memorial Laboratory and Boston's Beth Israel Hospital. The technique has its roots in ancient religious, cultic, and lay practices such as Yoga. Use of this method was found to produce the same kind of physiologic changes as transcendental meditation. The feelings associated with this altered state of consciousness have been described as ecstatic, beautiful, and totally relaxing. Other individuals have felt a sense of well-being similar to that experienced after exercise, but without the fatigue.[37] Procedures for the relaxation response technique are shown in Figure 14-2.

Table 14-9 also lists organizational programs that are designed specifically to deal with stress and related problems. These include physical fitness, alcohol and drug abuse, and employee assistance programs.

■ PHYSICAL FITNESS PROGRAMS

Although few organizations have fully staffed facilities, about 50,000 U.S. business firms have exercise programs designed to help keep their workers physically fit.[38] From management's viewpoint, this effort makes a lot of sense. Loss of productivity resulting from coronary heart disease costs U.S. businesses approximately $32 billion annually.[39] The total cost to society is even higher because of lost tax revenue, health care costs, and the expense involved in finding and training replacements. Company-sponsored fitness programs often reduce absenteeism, accidents, and sick pay. Employees who are physically fit are more alert and productive, and their morale is higher.[40]

The Xerox Program

Xerox Corporation currently has nine in-house physical fitness centers at locations throughout the United States. The Xerox programs are designed to help employees avoid coronary heart disease and other degenerative disorders. A fitness program, carefully designed for each individual, helps people feel and look better. As an added benefit, it also enhances their self-

---

[36] *Ibid.*, pp. 60–62.

[37] *Ibid.*, pp. 112–114.

[38] Russell W. Driver and Ronald A. Ratliff, "Employer's Perceptions of Benefits Accrued from Physical Fitness Programs," *Personnel Administrator*, 27 (August 1982), p. 21.

[39] Robert Kreitner, "Employee Physical Fitness: Protecting an Investment in Human Resources," *Personnel Journal*, 55 (July 1976), p. 340.

[40] Kenneth H. Cooper, *The New Aerobics* (New York: A Bantam Book/Published by arrangement with M. Evans and Company, 1970), p. 13.

> 1. Sit quietly in a comfortable position.
> 2. Close your eyes.
> 3. Deeply relax all your muscles, beginning at your feet and progressing up to your face. Keep them relaxed.
> 4. Breathe through your nose. Become aware of your breathing. As you breathe out, say the word, "ONE," silently to yourself. For example, breathe IN . . . OUT, "ONE": IN . . . OUT, "ONE": etc. Breathe easily and naturally.
> 5. Continue for 10 to 20 minutes. You may open your eyes to check the time, but do not use an alarm. When you finish, sit quietly for several minutes, at first with your eyes closed and later with your eyes opened. Do not stand up for a few minutes.
> 6. Do not worry about whether you are successful in achieving a deep level of relaxation. Maintain a passive attitude and permit relaxation to occur at its own pace. When distracting thoughts occur, try to ignore them by not dwelling upon them and return to repeating "ONE." With practice, the response should come with little effort. Practice the technique once or twice daily, but not within two hours after any meal, since the digestive processes seem to interfere with the elicitation of the relaxation response.

FIGURE 14-2 | Procedures for the Relaxation Response

Source: "Procedures for the Relaxation Response," *The Relaxation Response* by Herbert Benson, M.D., with Miriam Z. Klipper. (New York, William Morrow and Company, 1975), pp. 114-115. Reprinted by permission of the publisher.

concept. Jim Post, program manager of executive fitness at Xerox, has stated: "We are concerned about the ever-increasing costs of medical and insurance premiums, but beyond that, we have an obligation to our people as people."

The Xerox executive fitness program emphasizes four areas: (1) cardiovascular fitness; (2) flexibility; (3) relaxation by means of biofeedback; and (4) weight conditioning. In the cardiovascular training program, the motorized treadmill is the primary tool. The bicycle ergometer is also used along with biofeedback training. Biofeedback, which we mentioned earlier, is a process whereby an individual monitors his or her own physiological states (such as pulse rate, skin temperature, blood pressure, muscular tension, and brain waves) through the use of bioinstruments. Electrodes placed over selected muscles during exercise indicate the level of muscular tension. By listening to an audio tone, individuals can actually measure and then relax the tension existing in a specific muscle.

Flexibility (the range of movement in a joint or joints) is achieved by using static methods. Static stretching holds muscles and connective tissues at their greatest length, thus helping to relax them. Joint flexibility helps prevent the aches and pains that are common with aging. Finally, relaxation, by means of biofeedback, is an important aspect of the exercise program. Appropriate exercise has been shown to have a greater effect on relaxation than the use of tranquilizers.

Xerox's weight conditioning program is used to strengthen major muscle groups and joints. The lifting of heavy weights, especially for middle-aged individuals, is carefully avoided; relatively light weights and frequent repetition are emphasized.

The Kimberly-Clark Program

At Kimberly-Clark Corporation, approximately 1,200 employees participate in a health management program. A staff of twenty-three full-time health care professionals administers this program, utilizing a $2.5 million facility. Prior to admission, employees undergo a physical and medical history exam. Each employee then receives an individualized health prescription. The program at Kimberly-Clark was begun after its top management made a commitment to reduce health care costs.[41]

The Future of Such Programs

The number of programs such as those at Xerox and Kimberly-Clark is expected to increase dramatically in the future. Firms now recognize that healthy workers contribute directly to the profitability of the organization. Summing up the rationale for fitness programs, one corporate president stated:

> Companies will continue to invest in the health and well-being of their employees, and not just to keep health care costs down. They are now starting to see that there is a direct productivity-related benefit to keeping people healthy. Also, people like to be in a situation where management says: Sure you can jog—there is a jogging track, and here is counseling for how to quit smoking, or whatever. So, the absorption by employers of more health care costs, mostly resulting from making available more health care benefits, is going to rise—not because it's a social requirement but because it makes good business sense.[42]

■ ALCOHOL ABUSE PROGRAMS

Alcoholism is a disease characterized by uncontrolled and compulsive drinking that interferes with normal living patterns. It is a significant problem and can both result from and cause excessive stress. Although our society

---

[41] Ivancevich and Matteson, p. 6.
[42] "Today's Trends Suggest Revolutionary Changes for Business in the Future," *Personnel Administrator*, 30 (February 1985), pp. 70–71.

attaches a stigma to the disease, in 1956 the American Medical Association described it as treatable.[43]

An individual may feel that drinking improves his or her ability to cope. However, alcohol rarely improves performance; it almost always impairs performance. As a person starts to drink excessively, the drinking itself results in greater stress. This increased stress is dealt with by more drinking, making a vicious circle.[44] Alcohol abuse affects people at every level of society, from top-level managers to the skid-row homeless. It is also one of the most difficult conditions to detect. Sometimes a person progresses to advanced stages of alcohol abuse before perceiving that he or she may actually be an alcoholic. By then, the person's career may be on the verge of destruction. Early signs of alcohol abuse are especially difficult to identify. Often the symptoms are nothing more than an increasing number of absences from work. Over a period of time, productivity may begin to decline, or accidents may occur more frequently.[45] A normally pleasant person can become highly disagreeable.

Some of the warning signs that supervisors look for with regard to alcohol abuse are shown in Table 14-10. Any one of these signs taken individually doesn't necessarily suggest the excessive use of alcohol. It is when they are observed as a pattern that alcohol problems may exist. However, no longer does alcohol abuse result in automatic termination. In fact, an increasing number of firms are establishing alcohol abuse programs and supervisors are now being trained to cope with this health problem.

■ DRUG ABUSE PROGRAMS

Cocaine, heroin, PCP, THC, crack and numerous other mind-altering substances have definitely found their way into the workplace. In fact, an estimated one out of seven employees is affected by significant drug or alcohol addiction.[46] Numerous firms have recognized that drug problems exist and have taken positive action to deal with them. One such formal program is illustrated in Figure 14-3. The program includes (1) safeguards that identify drug problems or prevent them from occurring, and (2) mechanisms that lead to discharge of drug abusers from the firm.

A major purpose of the program is to ensure that drug abusers are not hired. However, if a person becomes an abuser after employment, a supervisor may be forced to resort to discipline for work-related irregularities such as absenteeism and low productivity. All supervisors should be trained to look for signs of drug abuse. And if there is evidence it does exist, the employee should be required to report to the medical department where a bona fide attempt will be made to salvage the person. However, failure to

---

[43] W. David Gibson, "They're Bringing Problem Drinkers Out of the Closet," *Chemical Week* (November 15, 1978), p. 85.

[44] Derek Rutherford, "Alcoholic Solution," *The Accountant* (August 21, 1980), p. 310.

[45] Kenneth P. Camisa, "How Alcoholism Treatment Pays for Itself," *SAM Advanced Management Journal*, 47 (Winter 1982), p. 55.

[46] Thomas R. Horton, "Drugs in the Workplace," *Management Review*, 76 (February 1987), p. 5.

TABLE 14-10 | Warning Signs of Alcohol Abuse

Warning Signs

The New York City Affiliate, Inc., National Council on Alcoholism, considers the following work-related problems to be possible indications of alcohol abuse:

- Absenteeism
- Ineffectiveness on the job
- Tardiness (particularly mornings and after lunch)
- Careless and sloppy work
- Accidents on the job
- Unexplained absences from the workplace
- Inability to remember details and commitments
- Leaving work early
- Avoidance of co-workers and supervisors
- Unpredictable and inappropriate behavior
- Customers' complaints
- Co-workers' complaints
- Unreasonable resentment
- Overreaction to criticism
- Borrowing money from co-workers
- Grandiose, aggressive, belligerent behavior
- "Jekyll and Hyde" personality

Source: "They're Bringing Problem Drinkers Out of the Closet," *Chemical Week* 123 (November 15, 1978), p. 85. Reprinted by permission.

comply with the supervisor's direction should reasonably result in discharge.

The medical department works with employees or refers them to appropriate agencies for treatment. If an employee assistance program exists, it may be able to deal with the problem. In either event, there should be an ongoing educational program that constantly reminds employees of the dangers of drug abuse.

■ EMPLOYEE ASSISTANCE PROGRAMS

Chief executive officers are fond of saying, "Employees are our most important asset." Actions speak louder than words, however, and Thomas R. Horton, president and CEO of the American Management Associations, believes that the most useful approach in dealing with impaired workers is through an employee assistance program.[47] An **employee assistance program (EAP)** is a comprehensive approach that many organizations have taken to deal with burnout, alcohol and drug abuse, and other emotional

---
[47] *Ibid.*, p. 5.

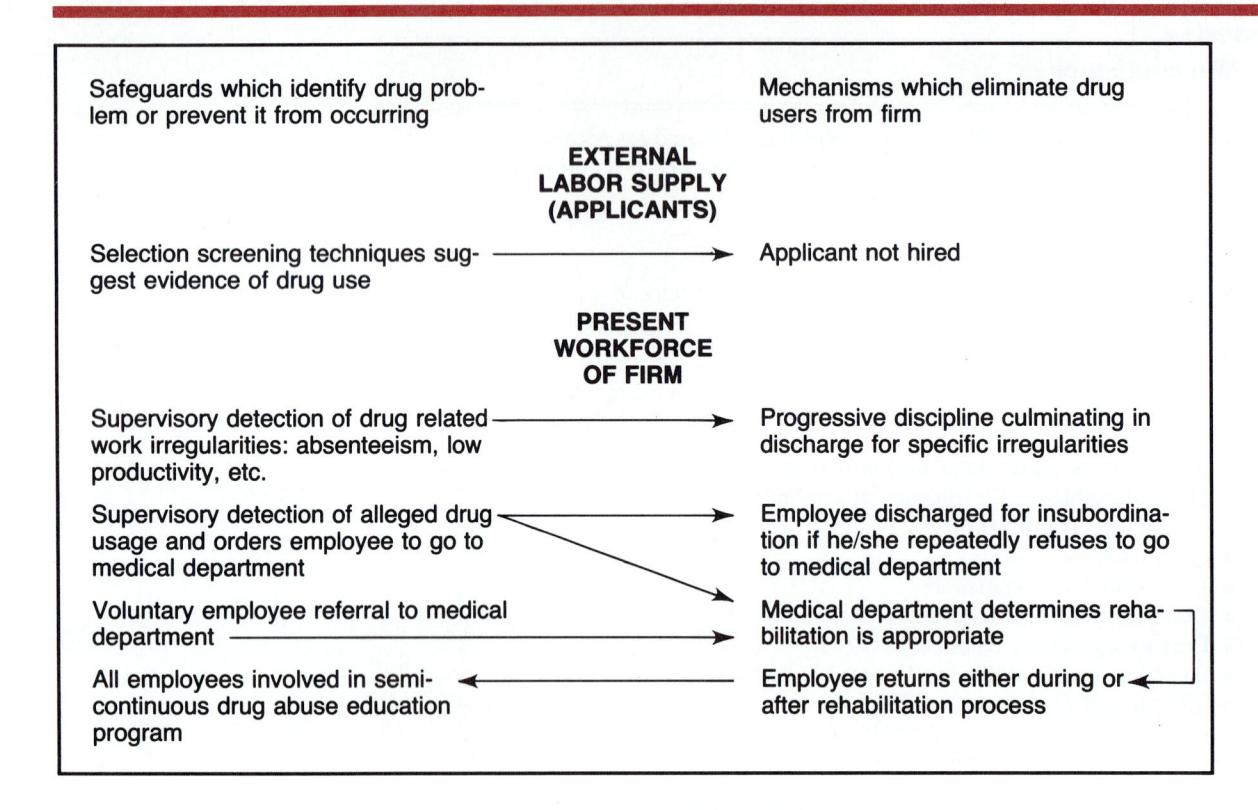

Safeguards which identify drug problem or prevent it from occurring	Mechanisms which eliminate drug users from firm
EXTERNAL LABOR SUPPLY (APPLICANTS)	
Selection screening techniques suggest evidence of drug use →	Applicant not hired
PRESENT WORKFORCE OF FIRM	
Supervisory detection of drug related work irregularities: absenteeism, low productivity, etc. →	Progressive discipline culminating in discharge for specific irregularities
Supervisory detection of alleged drug usage and orders employee to go to medical department →	Employee discharged for insubordination if he/she repeatedly refuses to go to medical department
Voluntary employee referral to medical department →	Medical department determines rehabilitation is appropriate
All employees involved in semi-continuous drug abuse education program ←	Employee returns either during or after rehabilitation process

FIGURE 14-3 | Safeguards and Mechanisms Used to Eliminate Employee Drug Use

Source: Ken Jennings, "The Problem of Employee Drug Use and Remedial Alternatives," *Personnel Journal* (November 1977). Copyright © 1977. Reprinted with permission.

disturbances. In an EAP, a firm either provides in-house professional counselors or refers employees to an appropriate community social service agency. Typically, most or all of the costs—up to a predetermined amount—are borne by the employer. The EAP concept includes a response to personal psychological problems that interfere with both an employee's well-being and overall productivity.[48] The purpose of EAPs is to provide emotionally troubled employees with the same consideration and assistance given employees having physical illnesses. There are at least 10,000 EAPs in the United States today, including 80 percent of the *Fortune* 500 firms.[49] They are being set up primarily to increase worker productivity and reduce costs. For example, an executive of a national benefits consulting firm states that

---

[48] Fred Dickman and William G. Emener, "Employee Assistance Programs: Basic Concepts, Attributes and an Evaluation," *Personnel Administrator*, 27 (August 1982), p. 55.

[49] Patricia Galagan, "Here's the Situation," *Training and Development Journal*, 41 (July 1987), p. 21.

HRM In Action

"I just don't know what to do about Robert Lewis," said production supervisor, Marty Fagetti, to Eli Richard, the human resource manager. "Lately I've noticed that Robert has missed work frequently. Even when he shows up, he is usually late. His eyes are always bloodshot, and he seems to move in slow motion. He also doesn't hang around with the "old gang" anymore. Again, today, he didn't show up for work. I just received a call from the police saying he was in the drunk tank and wanted us to be called."

What action would you suggest?

---

investments in EAPs are returned many times over in the form of increased productivity and decreased health care claims.[50]

L. C. Barry, employee relations director, American Coil Spring Company, describes the purpose of its program as follows:

> Its intent is to help employees whose personal problems are affecting their work. Frequently, drinking, drugs, impending divorce, finances, etc., will adversely affect a person's attendance, productivity, or relationship with fellow employees. Often they result in disciplinary action and ultimately termination. The intent of the EAP is to catch these problems early on and refer the employee to counseling before his or her job is in jeopardy.

The Kemper Group also has a successful EAP. At Kemper, the following principles guide administration of the program:

1. We believe that alcoholism, drug addiction, and emotional disturbances are illnesses and should be treated as such.
2. We believe the majority of employees who develop alcoholism, other drug addiction, or emotional illness can be helped to recover, and the company should offer appropriate assistance.
3. We believe the decision to seek diagnosis and accept treatment for any suspected illness is the responsibility of the employee. However, continued refusal of an employee to seek treatment when it appears that substandard performance may be caused by any illness is not tolerated. We believe that alcoholism, or drug addiction, or emotional illness should not be made an exception to this commonly accepted principle.
4. We believe that it is in the best interest of employees and the company that when alcoholism, other drug addiction, or emotional illness is present, it should be diagnosed and treated at the earliest possible date.

---

[50] Kay Wyrtzen, "Employee Assistance Programs," *Supervision*, 47 (May 1985), pp. 6–7.

5. We believe that the company's concern for individual alcohol consumption, drug use, and behavioral habits begins only when they result in unsatisfactory job performance, poor attendance, or behavior detrimental to the good reputation of the company.
6. We believe that confidential handling of the diagnosis and treatment of alcoholism, or other drug addiction, or emotional illness is essential.

In emphasizing the potential benefits of EAPs, one major firm's EAP brochure cites the program's advantages:

1. Early recognition and resolution of business and personal problems.
2. Retention of valuable employees.
3. Improved productivity and profits.
4. Reduced absenteeism.
5. Improved morale.[51]

Employee assistance programs are justified not only because they help improve the quality of life for employees, but also because they enhance an organization's performance. EAP advocates estimate savings of as much as one dollar and seventeen cents for every dollar spent. Improvements are claimed to be in the form of lower absenteeism, decreases in workers' compensation claims and accidents.[52]

To become even more effective, however, directors of EAPs need to reexamine the practice of waiting for supervisory referrals. Typically, problems are not dealt with until they have adversely affected job performance. Instead, EAPs should actively promote health improvement and disease prevention programs. Prevention of alcohol and drug abuse is more cost effective than treatment, which is the common EAP practice.[53]

In the future, companies may have to expand their EAPs to deal with the AIDS issue. In order to effectively address this concern, human resource professionals must understand the nature and impact of this disease on the workplace.

■ AIDS IN THE WORKPLACE

AIDS (acquired immune deficiency syndrome) is a disease that undermines the body's immune system, leaving the person susceptible to a wide range of fatal diseases. AIDS has become a worldwide epidemic, and it has been estimated that the number of people with this disease may total anywhere between 500,000 and three million within the next five years. Thirty-two thousand cases have been reported in the United States since 1981 and

---

[51] Hermine Zagat Levine, "Employee Assistance Programs," *Personnel*, 62 (April 1985), p. 14.

[52] "Employee Assistance Programs for Workers Boost Bottom Line," *Training and Development Journal*, 41 (June 1987), p. 20.

[53] Keith McClelland, "The Changing Nature of EAP Practice," *Personnel Administrator*, 30 (August 1985), p. 34.

more than half the victims have died. It has been predicted that 270,000 Americans will contract AIDS within the next five years.[54]

Although AIDS has become more feared than cancer, a relatively small percentage of firms have established formal policies to deal with it. One survey indicated that only 7.4 percent of organizations have such a policy.[55] It is apparent that some firms do not want to treat AIDS differently from other major illnesses. In one important respect, however, AIDS does differ significantly from all other diseases: It is always fatal. This fact no doubt accounts for both rational and irrational fears. Employees often refuse to work with someone they believe has the disease, despite assurance from medical experts that the disease cannot be transmitted through casual contact. This poses problems for managers because AIDS is generally considered a handicap and its victims are protected from discrimination in employment. At this time, it seems that the most aggressive action being taken by business firms regarding AIDS is in developing information programs that emphasize how to avoid contracting the dread disease.

Firms that do provide AIDS training sessions for their employees often use more than one technique. Among the methods used are seminars, workshops, discussion groups, articles in employee publications, videocassettes, literature in the company library, and health fairs.[56] Providing training sessions is a commendable first step. However, it is quite clear that business organizations, in concert with the federal government, must soon deal more directly with a disease that has the potential to kill more people than the Black Plague during the Middle Ages. If human resources is truly the heart of the organization, as Nina Woodard stated in Executive Insights, the chief human resource officer will be the catalyst in this effort.

---

[54] George E. Stevens, "Understanding AIDS," *Personnel Administrator*, 33 (August 1988), p. 84.

[55] Dale Feuer, "Workplace Issues: Testing, Training and Policy," *Training: The Magazine of Human Resources Development*, 24 (October 1987), p. 68.

[56] Hermine Zagat Levine, "AIDS in the Work Place," *Personnel*, 63 (March 1986), p. 57.

SUMMARY

Safety involves protecting employees from injuries caused by work-related accidents. Health refers to the employees' freedom from physical or emotional illness. For years, industrial safety has been a major problem that seemingly resisted solution. Prior to 1971, it was regulated primarily by the workers' compensation laws of the various states. When Congress passed the Occupational Safety and Health Act, it quickly became one of the most controversial laws affecting human resource management. It has dramatically altered management's role in the area of safety and health.

One approach to safety programs is to create a psychology of promoting safety. Another approach to safety programs is to develop and maintain a safe working environment. Evaluation of safety programs involves measuring both the frequency and severity of accidents.

Promoting employee health has led many firms to develop wellness programs. They start with initial applicant screening and continue throughout workers' employment. These programs typically are concerned with minimizing or eliminating a wide variety of potential health hazards such as certain fumes, dust, gases, liquids, and solids which are harmful to workers' health.

Stress is the body's reaction to any demand made on it. Everyone lives under some stress, which can be positive if not excessive but can be damaging when it is excessive. Burnout is a state of fatigue or frustration, which stems from devotion to a cause, way of life, or relationship that did not provide the expected reward. Burnout is often associated with a midlife or mid-career crisis, but it can happen at different times to different people. Symptoms of burnout include: (1) chronic fatigue; (2) anger at those making demands; (3) self-criticism for putting up with demands; (4) cynicism, negativism, and irritability; (5) a sense of being besieged; and (6) hair-trigger display of emotions. Stress can be managed and firms are helping employees deal with it in various ways.

Although few organizations have fully staffed facilities, about 50,000 U.S. business firms have exercise programs designed to help keep their workers physically fit. Company-sponsored fitness programs often reduce absenteeism, accidents, and sick pay. Employees who are physically fit are more alert and productive, and their morale is higher.

Alcoholism is a disease characterized by uncontrolled and compulsive drinking that interferes with normal living patterns. It is a significant problem and can both result from, and cause excessive stress. In 1956, the American Medical Association described it as treatable.

Cocaine, heroin, PCP, THC, crack, and numerous other mind-altering substances have found their way into the workplace. One out of seven employees is thought to be affected by significant drug or alcohol addiction. Numerous firms have recognized that drug problems exist and have taken positive action to deal with them.

An employee assistance program (EAP) is a comprehensive approach that many organizations have taken to deal with burnout, alcohol and drug abuse, and other emotional disturbances. In an EAP, a firm either provides in-house professional counselors or refers employees to an appropriate community social service agency. The EAP concept includes a response to personal psychological problems that interfere with both an employee's well-being and overall productivity. The purpose of EAPs is to provide emotionally troubled employees with the same consideration and assistance given employees having physical illnesses.

AIDS (acquired immune deficiency syndrome) is a disease that destroys the body's immune system, leaving the person susceptible to a wide range of fatal diseases. AIDS has become a worldwide epidemic, but so far, most business firms have not directly dealt with the AIDS problem. It is the human resource professional's responsibility to lead firms in taking more aggressive action in dealing with this dread disease.

Questions for Review

1. Distinguish between safety and health.
2. What are the primary ways in which safety programs are designed? Discuss.
3. What are some measurements that would suggest the success of a firm's safety program?
4. What are the purposes of health and wellness programs?
5. Why should a firm attempt to identify stressful jobs? What could an organization do to reduce the stress associated with a job?
6. Why should a firm be concerned with employee burnout?
7. What are some signs that a supervisor might look for in identifying alcohol abuse?
8. Explain why employee assistance programs are being established.
9. What concerns should a manager have regarding AIDS in the workplace?

Terms for Review

Safety
Health
Frequency rate
Severity rate
Stress
Burnout
Role ambiguity
Role conflict
Job overload

Hypnosis
Biofeedback
Transcendental meditation (TM)
Alcoholism
Employee assistance program (EAP)
AIDS (acquired immune deficiency syndrome)

INCIDENT 1 ■ To Test or Not to Test ■

John Barnes, human resource manager of Miller Chemical Company, had just read a report of a case filed in district court against a large neighboring company. One of that company's truck drivers had been involved in a accident in which two people were killed. The driver had been tested by the police and evidence of cocaine use was found.

John discussed the matter with the company president, Julienne Peacock, who was familiar with the case. "Ms. Peacock," he said, "I think we should adopt a policy of drug screening as a part of all pre-employment physicals." She replied, "I'm not sure that the testing requirement could be defended if we ever had a serious legal complaint. But the company could be in trouble if employee drug use led to negligence in some of these plant jobs." John asked, "What about the testing program for current employees? Should it be made a part of the annual physicals? Annual physicals aren't really mandatory now, but we can make them so."

Questions

1. What is the primary purpose of a testing program such as the one John wants to establish?
2. What would Miller Chemical do if an employee became a drug abuser after employment?

INCIDENT 2 ■ A Star Is Falling ■

"Just leave me alone and let me do my job," said Manuel Gomez. Dumbfounded, Bill Brown, Manuel's supervisor, decided to "count to ten" before responding to Manuel's fury. As he walked back to his office, Bill thought about how Manuel had changed over the past few months. He had been a hard worker and extremely cooperative when he came to work for Bill two years earlier. The company had sent Manuel to two training schools and had received glowing reports about his performance in each of them.

Until about a year ago, Manuel had a perfect attendance record and was virtually an ideal employee. At about that time, however, he began to have personal problems, which resulted in a divorce six months later. Manuel had requested a day off several times to take care of personal business. Bill had attempted to help in every way he could without getting directly involved in Manuel's personal affairs. But he was aware of the strain Manuel must have experienced as his marriage broke up and he and his wife engaged in the inevitable disputes over child custody, alimony payments, and property.

During the same time period, top management initiated a push for improving productivity. Bill found it necessary to put additional pressure on all his workers, including Manuel. He tried to be considerate but he had to become much more performance oriented, insisting on increased output from every worker. As time went on, Manuel began to show up late for work and actually missed two days without calling Bill in advance. Bill attributed Manuel's behavior to extreme stress. Because Manuel had been such a good worker for so long, Bill excused the tardiness and absences, only gently suggesting that Manuel should try to do better.

Sitting at his desk, Bill thought about what might have caused Manuel's outburst a few minutes earlier. Bill had simply suggested to

Manuel that he shut down the machine he was operating and clean up the surrounding area. This was a normal part of Manuel's job and something he had been careful to do in the past. Bill thought that the disorder around Manuel's machine might account for the increasing number of defects in the parts he was making. "This is a tough one. I think I'll talk to the boss about it," thought Bill.

Questions

1. What do you think is likely to be Manuel's problem? Discuss.
2. If you were Bill's boss, what would you recommend that he do?

EXPERIENCING HUMAN RESOURCE MANAGEMENT

At times, workers have personal problems that negatively influence their work and that may make the workplace unsafe. When this occurs, both managers and human resource professionals may be required to become involved to maintain a safe and healthy work environment. Dealing with personal problems is often difficult, and assisting employees in dealing with their personal problems can be even more taxing on managers. However, because of the possible adverse impact of a problem employee on workforce productivity, this situation must be addressed by individuals involved in human resource management. This exercise should provide a better understanding of how to handle a most difficult issue, that of resolving employee problems.

"I am going to do it, and I am going to do it today. This has gone on long enough!" thought Annette Dommert, the data processing manager. "I can't put it off any longer. I realize that Walter has been with the company for 14 years, and with this department for 11 of those years, but this drinking thing is out of hand. Lately the problem is affecting other members of the work group. His friends are covering up pretty well for him, but that is causing their productivity to go down. Evidently Walter is not going to be able to work things out, and the situation will only get worse. We are going to meet today and resolve this matter one way or the other; he's dry or he's out! I am not a villain, and I really want him to work things out but this is causing the department problems."

Walter Hollingsworth, a programmer in the data processing department, was concerned. He thought, "I heard from a friend in the boss' office that I am going to get chewed out about my drinking. I have always gotten my work done, but I guess I've let things slip lately. I know I can lick this problem. I'm going to straighten myself out, and when I meet with the boss I'll admit that I drink too much sometimes, everybody does; it has only recently affected my work. I'll do better in the future. I have been with the

continued on next page

> *continued from previous page*
>
> company for 14 years, and with this division for 11 of those years. One problem in all those years makes me a good risk. I can do it, and I deserve a chance. The boss should be compassionate."
>
> If you are a sensitive person, you could have a role in this exercise. Only two of you can actively participate, so volunteer quickly. One of you will play Annette and the other will play Walter. The rest of you observe carefully. Your instructor will provide the additional information necessary to participate.

REFERENCES

Aberth, John. "Worksite Wellness Programs: An Evaluation." *Management Review*, 75 (October 1986), pp. 51–53.

Axline, Larry L. "Identifying and Helping the Troubled Executive." *Personnel*, 61 (November 1987), pp. 10–18.

Barker, Frank H. "In Pursuit of a Healthier Work Force." *Journal of Business Strategy*, 8 (Fall 1987), pp. 17–21.

Booth, R. "What's New in Health and Safety Management." *Personnel Management*, 17 (April 1985), pp. 36–39.

Bradford, Hazel. "OSHA Orders Benzene Curb." *Engineering News Record* (September 10, 1987), p. 10.

Brumback, Cathy J. "EPAs—Bringing Health and Productivity to the Workplace." *Business*, 37 (April–June 1987), p. 12.

Cahan, V., and P. Dwyer. "Formaldehyde Limits: A Continuing Battle." *Chemical Week* (April 17, 1985), pp. 11ff.

Dickens, W. T. "Difference Between Risk Premiums in Union and Nonunion Wages and the Case for Occupational Safety Regulations." *American Economic Review*, 74 (May 1984), pp. 320–323.

Feinberg, Mortimer R. "Stifling Stress." *Restaurant Business Magazine* (March 20, 1986), p. 90.

"Four No-Smoking Approaches at Metropolitan." *Employee Benefit Plan Review* (October 1986), pp. 68–70.

Goldbeck, Willis B. "AIDS and the Workplace; Business Fights the Epidemic." *Futurist*, 22, (March–April 1988), pp. 18–19.

Good, Roger K. "What Bechtel Learned Creating an Employee Assistance Program." *Personnel Journal*, 63 (September 1984), p. 80.

Hanson, D. "Study Criticizes Federal Protection of Workers from Illness, Injury." *Chemical Engineering News* (April 29, 1985), pp. 14–15.

Hayes, James L. "Recognizing and Managing Employee Stress." *Credit and Financial Management*, 85 (November 1983), pp. 17–18.

Horton, Thomas R. "Drugs in the Workplace." *Public Management*, 69 (September 1987), pp. 2–4.

Howard, James S. "Employee Wellness: It's Good Business," *Dun & Bradstreet Reports*, 35 (May–June 1987), pp. 31–34.

Ivancevich, John M., Michael T. Matteson, and Cynthia Preston. "Occupational Stress, Type A Behavior, and Physical Well-Being." *Academy of Management*, 25 (September 1987), p. 68.

"Keeping Drugs Out of the Workplace." *Human Resources: Journal of the International Association for Personnel Women*, 2(3) (Summer 1985), pp. 8–9.

Kelley, Kevin P. "Effective Communication Is the Key to Getting Your Safety Message Accepted." *Occupational Hazards*, 19 (November 1987), p. 59.

Kuzola, Lad. "Fitness Pays Off; Wellness Programs Can Reduce Costs." *Industry Week* (August 5, 1985), p. 32.

Levine, Hermine Zagat. "Employee Assistance Programs." *Personnel*, 62 (April 1985), p. 14.

Lundblad, E. C. "Incentive Programs Reduce Accidents, Save Money." *National Safety News*, 131 (January 1985), pp. 35–37.

Lyons, Paul V. "EPAs: The Only Real Cure for Substance Abuse." *Management Review*, 76 (March 1987), p. 38.

Moffic, Robert P., Dennis J. Moffic, and Ralph B. Tower. "Auditing the Troubled Employee." *Internal Auditor*, 12 (August 1985), pp. 30–36.

Murphy, B. S., et al. "OSHA: Alive and Well." *Personnel Journal*, 65 (June 1986), pp. 32–35.

Murray, T. H. "The Lethal Paradox in Occupational Health Research." *Business and Society Review*, 53 (Spring 1985) pp. 20–24.

"NLRB Limits Union Access (Limitations on a Union's Ability to Gather Workplace Information That Could Affect Safety and Health of Workers)." *Engineering News-Record* (February 2, 1985), pp. 50–51.

"OSHA Ordered to Talk About Toxics." *Engineering News-Record* (June 6, 1985), p. 54.

"OSHA Sued for Failure to Shield Whistle Blowers (Worker Complaints)." *Engineering News-Record* (June 13, 1985), pp. 11–12.

Pesci, Michael. "Stress Management: Separating Myth from Reality." *Personnel Administrator*, 27 (January 1982), pp. 57–67.

Poe, Randall. "Does Your Job Make You Sick?" *Across the Board*, 24 (January 1987), p. 34.

"Right to Know: An Ongoing Battle Grows Hotter." *Chemical Week* (January 16, 1985), pp. 8–10.

Robinson, J. C. "Radical Inequality and the Probability of Occupation-Related Injury or Illness." *Milbank Memorial Fund Quarterly Health and Society*, 62 (Fall 1984), pp. 567–590.

Rosen, Robert H. "The Picture of Health in the Work Place." *Training and Development Journal*, 84 (August 1984), p. 26.

"Safety Last." *Economist* (February 16, 1985), p. 69.

Spencer, J. A. "Health Education Is Required!" *National Safety News* (January 1985), pp. 32–34.

Srachta, B. "Motivation, a Key to Fewer Accidents." *National Safety News* (January 1985), pp. 63–64.

Stackel, Leslie. "EPAs in the Work Place." *Employment Relations Today* (August 1987), pp. 289–294.

Stark, J. Norman, and M. C. D. Stark. "Employees' Right to Know." *Management Focus*, 31 (July 1986), pp. 27–29.

Thygerson, Alton L. *Safety*, 2nd ed. (Englewood Cliffs, N.J.: Prentice-Hall, 1986).

Wilkerson, Roderick. "Keep That Safety Committee Moving." *Supervision*, 40 (March 1978), p. 24.

"Workplace Hazards Seen Exacerbated by U.S. Policy." *Chemical Marketing Reporter* (January 28, 1985), pp. 63–64.

Wrich, James T. "EAPs: Ethical Considerations." *Personnel Administrator*, 30 (August 1985), pp. 12–13.

Yehay, Stephen C., and Garon E. Dodge. "Criminal Prosecutions for Occupational Injuries: An Issue of Growing Concern." *Employee Relations Law Journal*, 13 (August 1987), pp. 197–223.

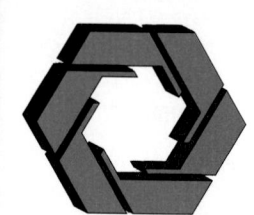

PART FIVE

CASE

Parma Cycle Company: Safety and Health at the New Plant

"I want the new plant to be a model of safety and health," said Mr. Burgess, the president of Parma Cycle Company in Parma, Ohio. "I do too," said Jesse Heard, the human resource director, "but you have to be aware that it's going to cost a lot." "Remember now, Jesse," the president replied, "we're putting the plant in Clarksdale, Mississippi, primarily to reduce costs. I believe that the main thing we can do for safety is to train our workers to be safety conscious. That doesn't cost much." "That's the main thing, I know," said Jesse, "but we'll also have to spend some money. There are several areas where safety can be improved by installing hand rails. Also, a good number of the machines will come in without chain and belt guards. We'll have to have those fabricated." "Well," said Mr. Burgess, "let's just try to meet the OSHA requirements on those kinds of things. I'd like to see a cost–benefit analysis of anything that goes beyond the OSHA standards." Mr. Burgess was referring to the U.S. Occupational Safety and Health Administration.

At about that time, Cliff Brubaker, the chief engineer at Parma, who had also been summoned to the meeting, came in. After a few niceties, Cliff asked, "Mr. Burgess, making sure that all the machinery and the machine layouts meet OSHA requirements made engineering the new plant a lot more difficult. We won't be able to use our floor space nearly as efficiently at Clarksdale as we do here at Parma. Also, the workflow is going to be less efficient because I had to separate machines to keep the area noise level below the maximum standard. Don't you think we could fudge a little on some of this? The Parma plant doesn't come close to meeting OSHA requirements and we have only had one fine since I've been here."

"I don't think you can trade off personal safety against a few dollars of cost savings," Jesse said. "You remember when Joe Blum lost his arm last year? The company came out okay on that because Joe didn't sue us. But what about Joe? How much was his arm worth?" "Don't get upset, Jesse," said Cliff. "I know what you mean and I really feel the same way. But we can go to extremes."

Mr. Burgess spoke up, "I don't think that meeting OSHA standards is going to extremes. Besides, if companies like Parma Cycle don't take some initiative in protecting workers, we're going to see even more enforcement efforts in the future. I want to make sure that you both understand my position. Everything in the plant at Clarksdale is to meet OSHA requirements for safety and health as a minimum. If the requirements can be exceeded with no additional cost, I want to opt for maximum safety. If you have to spend extra money to improve safety or health at the Clarksdale plant, I want to see a benefit–cost analysis on each item." "I think that that's clear enough," said Jesse. "Me to," said Cliff, "but I'll have to get back with you on a number of the modifications we had planned."

Questions

1. What do you think of Mr. Burgess' insistence on using OSHA standards as a goal?
2. Do you agree with Jesse that "you can't trade off worker safety against a few dollars of cost savings"?

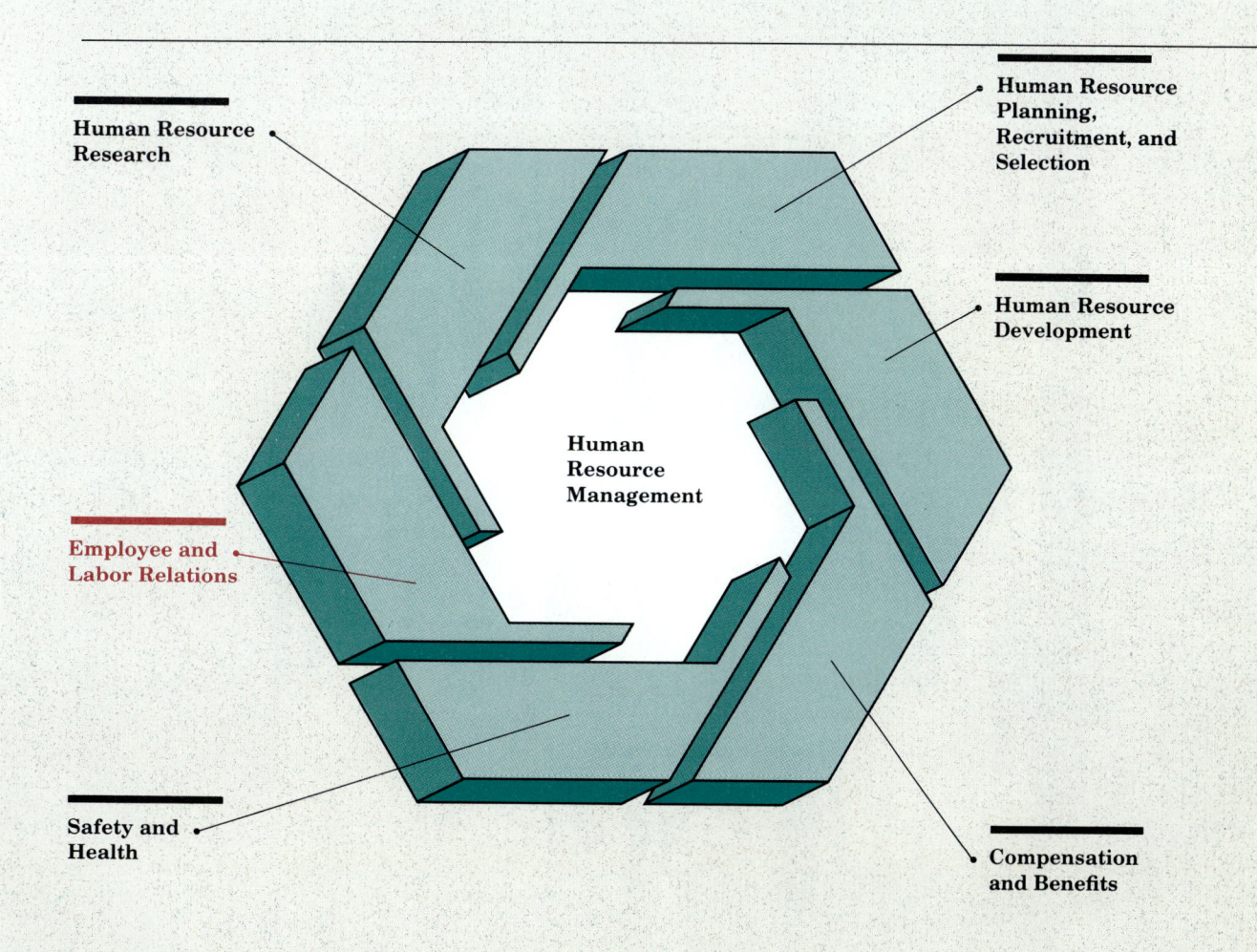

P·A·R·T S·I·X

EMPLOYEE AND LABOR RELATIONS

- Human Resource Research
- Human Resource Planning, Recruitment, and Selection
- Human Resource Development
- Employee and Labor Relations
- Human Resource Management
- Safety and Health
- Compensation and Benefits

CHAPTER 15   THE LABOR UNION

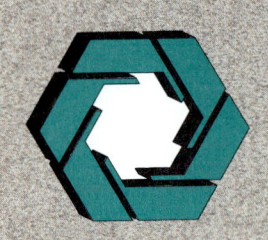

CHAPTER OBJECTIVES

1. Describe the history of the labor movement.
2. Explain the most significant union objectives, identify the reasons why employees join unions, and describe the basic structure of the union.
3. Explain what is involved in establishing the collective bargaining relationship and relate the future of unionism and collective bargaining in a global economy.
4. Explain the various strategies that a union may use to gain bargaining union recognition, explain signs of a troubled labor movement, and discuss why there is a growing legalistic approach to collective bargaining.

> Robert Sweeney, president of United Technologies, was disturbed and disappointed. He had just been informed by the NLRB that a majority of his employees had voted to have the union represent them. The past months had been difficult ones, with charges and countercharges being made by both management and labor. The vote had been close, with only a few votes tipping the scales in favor of labor.
>
> He looked at the human resource manager, Marthanne Bello, and said: "I don't know what to do. The union will demand so much we can't possibly be competitive."
>
> Marthanne replied: "Just because the union has won the right to be represented doesn't mean that we have to accept all their terms. I believe that a reasonable contract can be negotiated. I know many of those guys and I am sure that we can work out a contract that will be fair to both sides."

Robert Sweeney is not only troubled, but he is also misinformed as to the necessary impact of collective bargaining. Employees have decided to unionize, but that in no way mandates management acceptance of contractual terms which would adversely impact the health and profitability of the company. We begin this chapter with a history of the labor movement in the United States and the legislation relating to it. Next, we discuss the objectives of unions, the reasons why employees join unions, and the multilevel organizational structure of unions. Then we address the steps taken to establish a collective bargaining relationship and some union strategies used to obtain recognition. Finally, we review the issue of collective bargaining and unionism in a global economy, the signs of a troubled labor movement, and the growing legalistic approach to collective bargaining.

560 PART SIX Employee and Labor Relations

■ THE LABOR MOVEMENT BEFORE 1930

Unions are not a recent development in American history. The earliest unions originated toward the end of the eighteenth century about the time of the American Revolution. Although these early associations had few characteristics of present-day labor unions, they did bring workers in craft or guild-related occupations together to consider problems of mutual concern. These early unions were local in nature and usually existed for only a short time.[1]

Development of the labor movement has been neither simple nor straightforward. Instead, it has experienced as much failure as success. Employer opposition, the impact of the business cycle, the growth of American industry, court rulings, and legislation have exerted their influence in varying degrees at various times. As a result, the history of the labor movement has somewhat resembled the movement of a pendulum. At times, the pendulum has moved in favor of labor and, at other times, it has swung toward the advantage of management.

Prior to the 1930s, the trend definitely favored management. The courts strongly supported employers in their attempts to thwart the organized labor movement. This was first evidenced by the use of criminal and civil conspiracy doctrines derived from English common law. A **conspiracy**, generally defined, is the combination of two or more persons who band together to prejudice the rights of others or of society (e.g., by refusing to work or demanding higher wages). An important feature of the conspiracy doctrine is that an action by one person, though legal, may become illegal when carried out by a group.[2] In 1806, the year in which the conspiracy doctrine was first applied to labor unions, the courts began to influence the field of labor relations.[3] From 1806 to 1842, seventeen cases went to trial charging labor unions with conspiracies. These cases resulted in the demise of several unions and certainly discouraged other union activities. The conspiracy doctrine was softened considerably by the decision in the landmark case *Commonwealth* v. *Hunt* in 1842. In that case, Chief Justice Shaw of the Supreme Judicial Court of Massachusetts contended that labor organizations were legal. Thus in order for a union to be convicted under the conspiracy doctrine, it had to be shown that the union's objectives were unlawful or the means employed to gain a legal end were unlawful. To this day the courts continue to exert a profound influence on both the direction and character of labor relations.

Other tactics used by employers to stifle union growth were injunctions and yellow-dog contracts. An **injunction** is a prohibiting legal procedure that was used by employers to prevent certain union activities, such as strikes and unionization attempts. A **yellow-dog contract** was a written agreement between the employee and the company made at the time of

---

[1] *Brief History of the American Labor Movement* (Washington, D.C.: U.S. Department of Labor Statistics), Bulletin 1000 (1970), p. 1.

[2] Benjamin J. Taylor and Fred Witney, *Labor Relations Law*, 5th ed. (Englewood Cliffs, N.J.: Prentice-Hall, 1987), pp. 12–13.

[3] *Ibid.*, pp. 14–18.

employment, prohibiting a worker from joining a union or engaging in union activities. Each of these defensive tactics, used by management and supported by the courts, severely limited union growth.

In the latter half of the nineteenth century the American industrial system started to grow and prosper. Factory production began to displace handicraft forms of manufacturing. The Civil War gave the factory system a great boost. Goods were demanded in quantities that only mass production methods could supply. The railroads developed new networks of routes spanning the continent and knitting the country into an economic whole. Employment was high and unions sought to organize workers in both new and expanding enterprises. Most unions during this time were small and rather weak, and many did not survive the economic recession of the 1870s. Union membership rose to 300,000 by 1872 and then dropped to 50,000 by 1878.[4] This period also marked the rise of radical labor activity and increased industrial strife as unions struggled for recognition and survival.[5]

Out of the turbulence of the 1870s emerged the most substantial labor organization that had yet appeared in the United States. The Noble Order of the Knights of Labor was founded in 1869 as a secret society of the Philadelphia garment workers. After its secrecy was abandoned and workers in other areas were invited to join, it grew rapidly, reaching a membership of more than 700,000 by the mid-1880s. Internal conflict among the Knights' leadership in 1881 gave rise to the nucleus of a new organization that would soon replace it on the labor scene.[6] That organization was the American Federation of Labor (AFL).

Devoted to what is referred to as either "pure and simple unionism," or "business unionism," Samuel Gompers of the Cigarmakers Union, led some twenty-five labor groups representing the skilled trades to found the American Federation of Labor in 1886. Gompers was elected the first president of the AFL, a position he held, except for one year (1894–1895, when he adamantly opposed tangible support for the strikers of the Pullman group), until his death in 1924. He is probably the single most important individual in American trade union history. The AFL began with a membership of some 138,000 and doubled that number during the next twelve years.[7]

In 1890, Congress passed the Sherman Anti-Trust Act. This marked the entrance of the federal government into the statutory regulation of labor organizations. Although the primary stimulus for this act came from public concern over business's monopoly power, court interpretations soon applied its provisions to organized labor. Later, in 1914, Congress passed the Clayton Act (an amendment to the Sherman Act), which, according to Samuel Gompers, was the Magna Carta of Labor. The intent of this act was to remove labor from the purview of the Sherman Act. Again, judicial interpretation nullified that intent and left labor even more exposed to

---

[4] *Brief History*, p. 9.
[5] Foster Rhea Dulles, *Labor in America*, 3rd ed. (New York: Crowell, 1966), pp. 114–125.
[6] *Ibid.*, pp. 126–149.
[7] *Brief History*, pp. 15–16.

Executive Insights

Art Hobbs
Vice-President, Employee Relations,
E-Systems, Inc.

In 1970, Art Hobbs graduated from the University of Texas at Arlington with a degree in business management. Twelve years later he was named vice-president, employee relations/administration for E-Systems, Inc., Greenville Division. His meteoric rise in the field of human resource management is a tribute to his pursuit of excellence and the skillful execution of a professional career plan. His first job upon graduation was with Texas Power and Light Company as a field account manager. In this position, he was placed in various assignments of increasing responsibility in the area of field accounting. While with TP&L, Hobbs received training in all facets of district-level operations, including human resources, accounting, and marketing. That initial training continues to have a major impact on his career. In 1973 he joined Frito-Lay, Inc., as a training specialist and was quickly recognized for his overall grasp of the human resource function. Less than a year later, he was promoted to personnel manager for the Lubbock, Texas, and Denver, Colorado, operations. Early in 1978, Hobbs returned to the Dallas headquarters of Frito-Lay as employee relations manager and, later, as the manager of Management Institute. In this position he was responsible for developing and implementing a centralized "Institute" approach to management skills training.

When the position of director, employee relations opened up at E-Systems, Inc., Hobbs was asked to apply. He did so and was offered the position, which he accepted in late 1979. In that position he was accountable for all employee relations functions including staffing, compensation, benefits, administrative services, labor relations, EEO, and training/management development. One year later he was promoted to director of administration, and his responsibility was expanded to include security and public relations in addition to employee relations. In September 1982, Hobbs was named vice-president, employee relations/administration.

When asked to describe a major problem he had encountered in the area of human resources and how he ultimately resolved it, Hobbs replied, "For many years, the working relationship between organized labor and management at the Greenville Division of E-Systems was best described as adversarial. During previous contract negotiations, the adversary, or win–lose approach, had resulted in an extended strike, the results of which have lingered on to the present time. Day-to-day activity involving labor and management were characterized by one-upmanship and very little true problem solving was achieved. I developed a proactive labor relations program emphasizing problem prevention rather than reaction." Some specific elements of this program include:

- Building a responsible relationship with union representatives.
- Holding regular meetings with union officials to discuss issues and concerns before they become grievance problems.
- Increasing floor time for labor relations representatives.
- Striving for win–win solutions to problems.
- Orientation and training for supervisors on how to administer the day-to-day aspects of the labor agreement.
- Communicating with supervisors/managers on a regular basis regarding contract interpretation, grievance settlements, etc.
- Administering a new employee orientation program with a special section on how to resolve problems, questions, and concerns.

Hobbs notes that implementing this new proactive labor relations program, achieved several positive results. These include: fewer grievances and arbitrations, less time spent by company and union representatives on grievances, a new labor agreement negotiated with a no strike vote taken, and an improved working climate among supervisors and the bargaining unit.

While new challenges lie ahead, he takes great pride in his accomplishments in the field of human resources management. "My only regret," he says, "is that I did not recognize my interest in human resources while in college. But, there were not that many human resource courses available while I was in school. Today's graduates have a much better opportunity to be exposed to the advantages of a major in human resource management."

lawsuits.[8] Nonetheless, as a result of industrial activity related to World War I, the AFL grew to almost five million members by 1920.[9]

During the 1920s, labor faced legal restrictions on union activity and unfavorable court decisions. The one exception to such repressive policies was the passage and approval of the *Railway Labor Act of 1926*. This wasthe first time that the government declared without qualification the right of private employees to join unions and bargain collectively through representatives of their own choosing without interference from their employers. It also set up special machinery for the settlement of labor disputes. Although the act covered only employees in the railroad industry (a later amendment extended coverage to the airline industry), it foreshadowed the extension of similar rights to other classes of employees in the 1930s.

■ THE LABOR MOVEMENT AFTER 1930

The 1930s found the United States in the midst of the worst depression in its history. The unemployment rate rose as high as 25 percent.[10] The sentiment of the country began to favor organized labor as many people blamed business for the agony that accompanied the Great Depression. The pendulum began to swing away from management and toward labor. This swing was assisted by several acts and actions that supported the cause of unionism.

Anti-Injunction Act (Norris–LaGuardia Act)—1932

The Great Depression caused a substantial change in the public's thinking about the role of unions in society. Congress reflected this thinking in 1932 with the passage of the Norris–LaGuardia Act. It affirms that U.S. public policy sanctions collective bargaining and approves the formation and effective operation of labor unions.[11] While this act did not outlaw the use of injunctions, it severely restricted the federal courts' authority to issue them in labor disputes. It also made yellow-dog contracts unenforceable in the federal courts.[12]

National Labor Relations Act (Wagner Act)—1935

In 1933, Congress made an abortive attempt to stimulate economic recovery by passing the *National Industry Recovery Act* (NIRA). Declared unconstitutional by the U.S. Supreme Court in 1935, the NIRA did provide the

---

[8] E. Edward Herman, Alfred Kuhn, and Ronald L. Seeber, *Collective Bargaining and Labor Relations* (Englewood Cliffs, N.J.: Prentice-Hall, 1987), pp. 32–34.

[9] *Brief History*, p. 27.

[10] *Historical Statistics of the United States, Colonial Times to 1970, Bicentennial Edition*, Part I (Washington, D.C.: U.S. Bureau of the Census, 1975), p. 126.

[11] Taylor and Witney, pp. 78–81.

[12] *Ibid.*, pp. 81–85.

nucleus for legislation that followed it. Section 7a of the NIRA proclaimed the right of workers to organize and bargain collectively. Congress did not, however, provide procedures to enforce these rights.[13]

Undeterred by the Supreme Court decision and strongly supported by organized labor, Congress speedily enacted a comprehensive labor law, the National Labor Relations Act (Wagner Act). This act, approved by President Roosevelt on July 5, 1935, is one of the most significant labor–management relations statutes ever enacted. Drawing heavily on the experience of the Railway Labor Act of 1926 and Section 7a of the NIRA, the act declared legislative support, on a broad scale, of the right of employees to organize and engage in collective bargaining. The spirit of the Wagner Act is stated in Section 7, which defines the substantive rights of employees:

> Employees shall have the right to self-organization, to form, join, or assist labor organizations, to bargain collectively through representatives of their own choosing, and to engage in other concerted activities, for the purpose of collective bargaining or other mutual aid or protection.

The rights defined in Section 7 were protected against employer interference by Section 8, which detailed and prohibited five management practices deemed to be unfair to labor:

1. Interfering with or restraining or coercing employees in the exercise of their right to self-organization.
2. Dominating or interfering in the affairs of a union.
3. Discriminating in regard to hire or tenure or any condition of employment for the purpose of encouraging or discouraging union membership.
4. Discriminating against or discharging an employee who has filed charges or given testimony under the act.
5. Refusing to bargain with chosen representatives of employees.

The National Labor Relations Board (NLRB) was created by the National Labor Relations Act to administer and enforce the provisions of the act. The NLRB was given two principal functions: (1) to establish procedures for holding bargaining-unit elections and to monitor the election procedures; and (2) to investigate complaints and prevent unlawful acts involving unfair labor practices. However, current NLRB election procedures are often cumbersome because of technicalities employers can use to delay elections for years.[14] Much of the NLRB's work is delegated to thirty-three regional offices throughout the country.

In recent years, many labor leaders expressed their dismay with the composition of the NLRB. According to some, the Reagan administration made it easier for employers to beat unions by changing the way labor law is interpreted and enforced. William Wynn, president of the United Food

---

[13] *Ibid.*, pp. 150–151.

[14] Sandra Atchison and Aaron Bernstein, "A Silver Bullet for the Union Drive at Coors?" *Business Week* (July 11, 1988), pp. 61–62.

and Commercial Workers, stated, "There has been a total breakdown in the system of law and order established for labor–management relations."[15] Evidently, Wynn believes that the labor–management relations system of law and order is unfair in terms of its treatment of labor. If this is actually so, the probability of a continuation of these practices in the Bush administration appears quite likely.

Following passage of the Wagner Act, union membership increased from approximately 3 million to 15 million between 1935 and 1947.[16] The increase was most conspicuous in industries utilizing mass production methods. New unions in these industries were organized on an industrial basis rather than a craft basis, and members were primarily unskilled or semiskilled workers. An internal struggle developed within the AFL over the question of whether unions should be organized to include all workers in an industry or strictly on a craft or occupational basis. In 1935, ten AFL-affiliated unions and the officers of two other AFL unions formed a "Committee for Industrial Organization" to promote the organization of workers in mass production and unorganized industries. The controversy grew to the point that in 1938, the AFL expelled all but one of the Committee for Industrial Organization unions. In November 1938, the expelled unions held their first convention in Pittsburgh and reorganized as a federation of unions under the name of Congress of Industrial Organizations (CIO). The new federation included the nine unions expelled from the AFL and thirty-two other groups established to recruit workers in various industries. John L. Lewis, president of the United Mine Workers, was elected the first president of the CIO.[17]

The rivalry generated by the two large federations stimulated union organizing efforts in both groups. With the ensuing growth, the labor movement gained considerable influence in the United States. However, many individuals and groups began to feel that the Wagner Act favored labor too much. This shift in public sentiment was in part related to a rash of costly strikes following World War II. Whether justified or not, much of the blame for these disruptions fell on the unions.

Labor Management Relations Act (Taft–Hartley Act)—1947

In 1947, with public pressure mounting, Congress overrode President Truman's veto and passed the Labor Management Relations Act (Taft–Hartley Act). The Taft–Hartley Act extensively revised the National Labor Relations Act and became Title I of that law. A new period in the evolution of public policy regarding labor began. The pendulum had begun to swing toward a more balanced position between labor and management.

Some of the important changes introduced by the Taft–Hartley act included:

---

[15] *U.S. News & World Report* (September 10, 1984), pp. 62–65.

[16] *Brief History*, p. 65.

[17] *Ibid.*, pp. 29–33.

1. Modifying Section 7 to include the right of employees to refrain from union activity as well as engage in it.
2. Prohibiting the closed shop (the arrangement requiring that all workers be union members at the time they are hired) and narrowed the freedom of the parties to authorize the union shop (the employer may hire anyone he or she chooses, but all new workers must join the union after a stipulated period of time).
3. Broadening the employer's right of free speech.
4. Providing that employers need not recognize or bargain with unions formed by supervisory employees.
5. Giving employees the right to initiate decertification petitions.
6. Providing for government intervention in "national emergency strikes."

A further, significant change extended the concept of unfair labor practices to unions. Labor organizations were to refrain from:

1. Restraining or coercing employees in the exercise of their guaranteed collective bargaining rights.
2. Causing an employer to discriminate in any way against an employee in order to encourage or discourage union membership.
3. Refusing to bargain in good faith with an employer regarding wages, hours, and other terms and conditions of employment.
4. Engaging in certain types of strikes and boycotts.
5. Requiring employees covered by union-shop contracts to pay initiation fees or dues "in an amount which the Board finds excessive or discriminatory under all circumstances."
6. "Featherbedding," that is, requiring that an employer pay for services not performed.

One of the most controversial elements of the Taft–Hartley Act is its Section 14b, which permits states to enact right-to-work legislation. **Right-to-work laws** are laws that prohibit management and unions from entering into agreements requiring union membership as a condition of employment. Twenty-one states, located primarily in the South and West, have adopted such laws, which are a continuing source of irritation between labor and management.[18] Much of the impetus behind the right-to-work movement is provided by the National Right to Work Committee, based in Springfield, Virginia.

For about ten years after the passage of the Taft–Hartley Act, union membership expanded at about the same rate as nonagricultural employment. But all was not well within the organized labor movement. Since the creation of the CIO, the two federations had engaged in a bitter and costly rivalry. Both the CIO and the AFL recognized the increasing need for cooperation and reunification. In 1955, following two years of intensive negotiations between the two organizations, a merger agreement was ratified, the AFL–CIO became a reality and George Meany was elected presi-

---

[18] Right-to-work states include: Alabama, Arizona, Arkansas, Florida, Georgia, Idaho, Iowa, Kansas, Louisiana, Mississippi, Nebraska, Nevada, North Carolina, North Dakota, South Carolina, South Dakota, Tennessee, Texas, Utah, Virginia, and Wyoming.

dent. In the years following the merger, the labor movement faced some of its greatest challenges.

Labor–Management Reporting and Disclosure Act (Landrum–Griffin Act)—1959

Corruption had plagued organized labor since the early 1900s. Periodic revelations of graft, violence, extortion, racketeering, and other improper activities aroused public indignation and invited governmental investigation. Even though the number of unions involved was small, every disclosure undermined the public image of organized labor as a whole.[19] Corruption has been noted in the construction trades and the Laborers, Hotel and Restaurant, Carpenters, Painters, East Coast Longshoremen, and Boilermakers unions. The inability of the labor movement to deal with massive corruption and racketeering may be evidence of deep-seated union problems.[20] For example, the International Brotherhood of Teamsters recently faced a change of leadership because of its alleged ties to organized crime.[21]

Scrutiny of union activities is a focal point in today's labor environment, but it began to intensify right after World War II. Ultimately, inappropriate union activities led to the creation in 1957 of the Senate Select Committee on Improper Activities in the Labor or Management Field, headed by Senator McClellan of Arkansas. Between 1957 and 1959, the McClellan Committee held a series of nationally televised public hearings that shocked and alarmed the entire country. As evidence of improper activities mounted—primarily against the Teamsters and Longshoremen/Maritime—the AFL–CIO took action.

In 1957, the AFL–CIO expelled three unions (representing approximately 1.6 million members) for their practices. One of them, the Teamsters, was the largest union in the country.

In 1959, largely as a result of the recommendations of the McClellan Committee, Congress enacted the Labor–Management Reporting and Disclosure Act (Landrum–Griffin Act). This act marked a significant turning point in the involvement of the federal government in internal union affairs. The Landrum–Griffin Act spelled out a "Bill of Rights of Members of Labor Organizations" designed to protect certain rights of individuals in their relationships with unions. The Act requires extensive reporting on numerous internal union activities and contains severe penalties for violations. Employers are also required to file reports when they engage in activities or make expenditures that might undermine the collective bargaining process or interfere with protected employee rights. In addition, the act amended

---

[19] Dulles, pp. 382–383.

[20] Herman Benson, "Union Democracy," *Unions in Transition* (San Francisco: ICS Press, 1988), p. 343.

[21] Harris Cooingwood, "The Teamsters' Vacuum at the Top," *Business Week* (July 25, 1988), p. 41.

the Taft–Hartley Act by adding additional restrictions on picketing and secondary boycotts.[22]

In 1974, Congress extended coverage of the Taft–Hartley Act to private, not-for-profit hospitals. This amendment brought within the jurisdiction of the National Labor Relations Board some two million employees. Proprietary (profit-making) health care organizations were already under NLRB jurisdiction. The amendment does not cover government operated hospitals; it applies only to the private sector.

Even though the AFL–CIO merger was completed in 1955, internal conflict remained. The Teamsters expulsion was followed in 1968 by the disaffiliation of the second largest union in the country, the United Automobile Workers (UAW). This split was caused primarily by personality and philosophical clashes between Walter Reuther, president of the UAW, and Meany. Shortly thereafter the UAW and the Teamsters formed the Alliance of Labor Action [ALA] with the possible aim of developing a rival federation.[23] The ALA lasted only until the untimely death of Walter Reuther in a plane crash in 1970. The UAW reaffiliated with the AFL–CIO in July 1981. The Teamsters Union was allowed to reaffiliate in October 1987, when it brought its 1.6 million members back into the AFL–CIO.[24]

Despite the reaffiliation of the Teamsters with the AFL–CIO, union membership dropped from about one third of the nonfarm workforce in 1950 to 17 percent in 1987.[25] Moreover, unions have won fewer and fewer representation elections as collective bargaining agents. As you can see in Figure 15-1, unions won 57.1 percent of these elections held by the NLRB in 1968. By 1983, union victories had dropped to only 43.0 percent.[26]

■ THE PUBLIC SECTOR

Government (public-sector) employees are generally considered a class apart from private-sector workers. This is reflected in their exclusion from the coverage of general labor legislation.[27] However, like their counterparts in private industry, government employees have demonstrated a persistence in organizing in order to gain an effective voice in the terms and conditions of their employment.

For many years the federal government had no well-defined policy on labor–management relations regarding its own employees. In order to

---

[22] *Brief History*, pp. 58–61.

[23] *Ibid.*, p. 139.

[24] "The AFL–CIO: A Tougher Team with the Teamsters," *Business Week* (November 9, 1987), p. 110.

[25] Larry T. Adams, "Union Membership of Wage and Salary Employees in 1987," *Current Wage Developments* (Washington, D.C.: U.S. Department of Labor, Bureau of Labor Statistics, February 1988), p. 4.

[26] U.S. National Labor Relations Board, *Forty-Eighth Annual Report 1983* (Washington, D.C.: U.S. Government Printing Office, 1983), p. 13; U.S. National Labor Relations Board, *Forty-Sixth Annual Report 1981* (Washington, D.C.: U.S. Government Printing Office, 1981), pp. 18, 205–206.

[27] Examples include the Social Security Act, Fair Labor Standards Act, and the National Labor Relations Act, as amended.

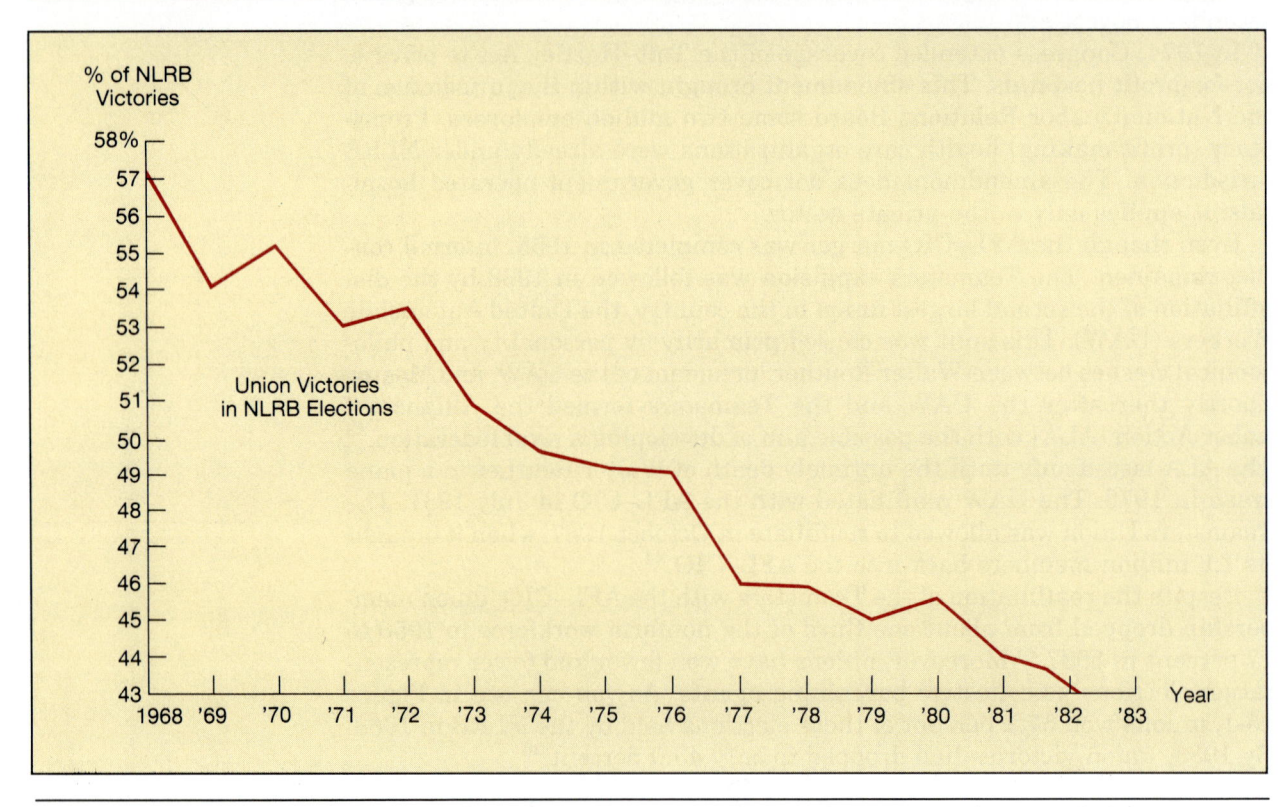

FIGURE 15-1 | Union Victories in NLRB Elections

Source: National Labor Relations Board.

address this situation, President Kennedy issued Executive Order 10988 in 1962. Section 1(a) of the Order stated:

> Employees of the federal government shall have, and shall be protected in the exercise of, the right, freely and without fear of penalty or reprisal, to form, join and assist any employee organization or to refrain from any such activity.

For the first time in the history of the federal civil service, a uniform, comprehensive policy of cooperation between employee organizations and management in the executive branch of government was established. Employees were permitted to organize and negotiate human resource policies and practices and matters affecting working conditions that were within the administrative discretion of the agency officials concerned. However, Public Law 84-330, passed in 1955, made it a felony to strike against the U.S. government.[28]

---

[28] Section 305 of the Labor Management Relations Act of 1947 also makes it unlawful for government employees to participate in any strike.

Executive Order 10988 established the basic framework for collective bargaining in federal government agencies. Subsequent EOs revised and improved this framework and brought about a new era of labor relations in the public sector.[29] In fact, the federal government transferred to and codified the provisions of those executive orders in Title VII of the Civil Service Reform Act of 1978. This act regulates most of the labor–management relations in the federal service. It establishes the Federal Labor Relations Authority (FLRA), which is modeled on the National Labor Relations Board. The intent of the FLRA is to bring the public sector model in line with that of the private sector. Requirements and mechanisms for recognition and elections, dealing with impasses, and handling grievances are covered in the act.

The U.S. Postal Service is not subject to Title VII of the Civil Service Reform Act of 1978. It was given independent government agency status by the Postal Reorganization Act of 1970. Postal employees were given collective bargaining rights comparable to those governing private industry. National Labor Relations Board rules and regulations controlling representation issues and elections are applicable to the postal service. Unfair labor practice provisions are also enforced by the NLRB. However, the right to strike is prohibited and union-shop arrangements are not permitted.

Labor Relations and Bargaining Patterns

There is no uniform pattern to state and local labor relations and bargaining rights. Some states have no policy at all, whereas a haphazard mixture of statutes, resolutions, ordinances, and civil service procedures exists in others. However, public-employer legislation passed by state and local government accelerated noticeably after the issuance of EO 10988 in 1962.[30] By 1984, forty-one states and the District of Columbia had collective bargaining statutes covering all or some categories of public employees. By 1980, thirty-eight states had passed some form of legislation that obligates state agencies and local governments to permit their public employees to join unions and to recognize bona fide labor organizations. Prior to 1960, less than a handful of states had such legislation. The diversity of state labor laws makes it difficult to generalize about the legal aspects of collective bargaining at the state and local levels.

Unilateral determination of the conditions of employment by public employers is increasingly being questioned. These decisions are being questioned not only by government workers, but also by the unions and associations that represent them. Placed in the middle between their employees and the general public, state and local governments are being forced to specify in clearer terms the collective bargaining rights of workers.[31]

---

[29] Executive Order 11491 (effective January 1, 1970); EO 11616 (effective November 1971); EO 11636 (effective December 1971); EO 11838 (effective May 1975).
[30] Herman, Kuhn, and Seeber, p. 407.
[31] Taylor and Witney, p. 649.

Employee Associations

Membership in public sector professional and state employee associations greatly exceeds private sector unionization.[32] The largest of the employee associations, the National Education Association, has become the largest "union" in the United States.[33] In the past, employee associations were concerned primarily with the professional aspects of employment and avoided any semblance of unionism. In recent years, this approach changed as public- and private-sector unions have actively organized both professional and government employees. Many employee associations now enthusiastically pursue collective bargaining relationships.

The greater public-sector penetration indicates that the process of unionization in the public sector differs from that in the private labor market. One factor that accounts for dramatic membership gains is clearly the role played by government employee associations, particularly at the state and local level. Challenged by established unions, the associations either merged with unions or transformed themselves into collective bargaining organizations. Many are becoming de facto unions, as with National Education Association. Another reason that huge membership gains were made so quickly was the encouragement union organizations received from public-sector management.[34]

■ UNION OBJECTIVES

As previously indicated, the labor movement has a long history in the United States. Although each union is a unique organization seeking its own objectives, several broad objectives characterize the labor movement as a whole:

1. To secure and, if possible, improve the living standards and economic status of its members.
2. To enhance and, if possible, guarantee individual security against threats and contingencies that might result from market fluctuations, technological change, or management decisions.
3. To influence power relations in the social system in ways that favor and do not threaten union gains and goals.
4. To advance the welfare of all who work for a living, whether union members or not.[35]
5. To create mechanisms to guard against the use of arbitrary and capricious policies and practices in the workplace.

The underlying philosophy of the labor movement is that of organizational democracy and an atmosphere of social dignity for working men and

---

[32] Leo Troy, "The Rise and Fall of American Trade Unions: The Labor Movement from FDR to RR," *Unions in Transition* (San Francisco: ICS Press, 1988) p. 85.

[33] Walter Galenson, "The Historical Role of American Trade Unionism," *Unions in Transition* (San Francisco: ICS Press, 1988), p. 68.

[34] Troy, p. 85.

[35] Edwin F. Beal and James P. Begin, *The Practice of Collective Bargaining*, 5th ed. (Homewood, Ill.: Richard D. Irwin, 1982), p. 91.

women. In order to accomplish these objectives, most unions recognize that they must strive for continued growth and power. Although growth and power are related, we will discuss them separately to identify the impact of both factors on unionization.

Growth

To maximize its effectiveness a union must strive for continual growth. Members pay dues, which are vital to promoting and achieving union objectives. Obviously, the more members the union enlists, the more dues they pay to support the union and the labor movement. Thus an overall goal of most unions is continued growth. But, as we previously mentioned, the percentage of union members in the workforce is declining. Most union leaders are concerned about this trend. Much of a union's ability to accomplish its objectives is derived from strength in numbers. For this reason, unions must continue to explore new sources of potential members. Unions are now directing much of their attention to organizing the service industries, professional employees, and government employees. Despite these efforts, nothing appears to be on the horizon to change this downward trend.[36] However, you shouldn't assume that employers will have a free hand to act in the future. Union membership is expected to decline in the future, accompanied by continual decline in labor's political and bargaining muscle.[37]

Power

According to a 1985 survey, "management continues to improve its power base in relation to organized labor."[38] Most observers agree that the power base of organized labor continues to erode. We define *power* here as the amount of external control that an organization is able to exert. As we mentioned previously, a union's power is influenced to a large extent by the size of its membership and the possibility of future growth. However, we also have to consider other factors when assessing the future power base of unions.

The importance of the jobs held by union members significantly affects union power. For instance, an entire plant may have to be shut down if unionized machinists performing critical jobs decide to strike. Thus a few strategically located union members may exert a disproportionate amount of power. A union's power can also be determined by the type of firm that is unionized. Unionization of truckers, steel workers, or farm workers can affect the entire country and subsequently enhance union's power base. Through control of key industries, a union's power may extend to firms that

---

[36] *New Management Magazine* (Los Angeles: University of Southern California, Winter 1986), pp. 19–22.

[37] *Ibid.*, pp. 20–22.

[38] R. Wayne Mondy and Shane R. Premeaux, "The Labor/Movement Power Relationship Revisited," *Personnel Administrator*, 30 (May 1985), p. 52.

are not unionized. For instance, in some geographic areas of the country the power of the trucking unions extends well beyond firms that the truckers serve. Firms that depend on deliveries by the trucking industry may yield to union pressures in order to continue receiving services.

By achieving power, a union is capable of exerting its force in the political arena. The political arm of the AFL–CIO is the **Committee on Political Education (COPE)**. Founded in 1955, its purpose is to support politicians who are friendly to the cause of organized labor. The union recommends and assists candidates who will best serve its interests. Union members also encourage their friends to support those candidates. The larger the voting membership, the greater is the union's influence with politicians. With "friends" in government, the union is in a much stronger position to maneuver against management.

As reduced union strength contributes to weaker unions at the bargaining table, labor leaders will strive to increase their political clout. Probably the most striking feature of labor's decline was reported by the Labor Department in 1985. According to this report, compensation gains for union workers slowed, rising only 2.6 percent compared to 4.6 percent for nonunion workers.[39] This slowdown in union gains, coupled with declining union membership and organizing activities, caused unions to compensate by increasing their political activity.[40] One example of union's increased emphasis on political activity is their unprecedented action in supporting a candidate for the presidential nomination. Union's political activity will parallel their changing philosophy toward a desire for "more government intervention" in the U.S. economy and society.[41]

As unions become more political, an internally explosive situation could be brewing because the goals of public- and private-sector unions have different overall goals. Over the long term, these goals may conflict. "This is because private-sector unions, with the help of government intervention, want to raise members' income. To the extent they are successful, their members become subject to higher taxes, which their fellow public-sector unions will want to push even higher."[42] Regardless of the internal impact of an increased emphasis on political activities, the inevitability of union political involvement is a reality.[43]

■ WHY EMPLOYEES JOIN UNIONS

Individuals join unions for many different reasons, and these reasons tend to change over time. They may involve job, personal, social, or political considerations. It would be impossible to discuss them all, but the following are some of the major reasons: dissatisfaction with management, need

---

[39] *New York Times* (January 29, 1986), p. D1.

[40] Troy, p. 104.

[41] Stan Crock, "The Duke Is Still Playing Hard-To-Get With Labor," *Business Week* (August 29, 1988), p. 39.

[42] "The Changing Situation of Workers and Their Unions," A Report by the AFL–CIO Committee on the Evolution of Work (Washington, D.C.: AFL–CIO, February, 1985).

[43] *New Management Magazine*, pp. 19–22.

for a social outlet, opportunity for leadership, forced unionization, and peer pressure.

Dissatisfaction with Management

Every job holds the potential for real dissatisfactions. Each individual has a boiling point that can trigger him or her to consider a union as a solution to real or perceived problems. Unions look for problems in organizations and then emphasize the advantages of union membership as a means of solving them. Remember that Art Hobbs, vice-president, employee relations for E-Systems, said, "For many years, the working relationship between organized labor and management at the Greenville Division of E-Systems was best described as adversarial." Some of the more common reasons for employee dissatisfaction are described in the following paragraphs.

Compensation. Employees want their compensation to be fair and equitable. Wages are important to them becuse they provide both the necessities and pleasures of life. If employees are dissatisfied with their wages, they may look to a union for assistance in improving their standard of living. However, the ability of the unions to make satisfactory gains in income has been severely hampered in the past few years. Of the contracts negotiated in 1987, the average wage increase ranged from only 2 to 4 percent, with the primary emphasis on other forms of compensation.[44]

An important psychological aspect of compensation involves the amount of pay an individual receives in relation to that of other workers performing similar work. If an employee perceives that management has shown favoritism by paying someone else more to perform the same or a lower level job, the employee will likely become dissatisfied. Union members know precisely the basis of their pay and how it compares with others. Therefore pay inequities, with seniority as the accepted criterion for fairness, are less likely to become a major problem area.

Two-Tier Wage System. The **two-tier wage system** is a wage structure that reflects lower pay rates for newly hired employees than those received by established employees performing similar jobs. One of the most controversial developments in collective bargaining is the two-tier wage system. Several industries (airlines, trucking, supermarkets, aerospace, and shipbuilding) are already operating under such contracts. Under this system, newly hired workers are paid less than employees already on the payroll. While the two-tier system basically provides unequal pay for equal work, the system does save organizations a great deal of money in labor costs, and at the same time provides more jobs. The system has been accepted by unions in lieu of wage cuts in companies hit hard by deregulation, foreign competition, and aggressive nonunion competitors.

There are two basic types of two-tier scales: temporary and permanent. In a temporary system, the new employees are hired for less than those

---

[44] Kurt Fernandez, "1987 Employer Bargaining Objectives," *Collective Bargaining Negotiations and Contracts* (Washington, D.C.: The Bureau of National Affairs, 1987).

hired earlier, but they can advance to parity over time. In a permanent system, the new hires will never achieve parity. There are also variations and modifications of these basic types of scales, and some companies have even instituted a third (lower) tier.

According to a 1987 survey, about 30 percent of those firms that did not currently have a two-tier wage system would aggressively bargain for that option. Nearly 100 percent of those who presently have such a compensation system would fight for its continuation.[45] Because of the possible impact of the two-tier wage system on reducing labor cost, it is quickly becoming part of the American labor scene. However, according to a recent survey, side effects that can be expected include employee resentment, quality problems, limited cooperation, decreased productivity, and decreased employee loyalty. These problems are compounded when such compensation systems are not properly implemented.[46] Therefore, management should cautiously implement two-tier wage systems, at all times emphasizing the long-term benefits to the union such as enhanced job security.

Job Security. For a young employee, job security is often less important than it is for an older worker. The young employee may feel that "If I lose this job, I can always get another." But, if employees see management consistently terminating older workers to make room for younger, more aggressive employees, they may begin to think about job security. If the firm doesn't provide its employees with a sense of job security, they may turn to a union. Employees are more concerned than ever before about job security with the decline in employment in such key industries as automobiles, rubber, and steel. This concern has recently been translated into legislation, with enactment by Congress of a plant closing bill in 1988 which requires employers to give advance notification prior to plant closings.

Management's Attitude. People like to feel that they are important. They do not like to be considered a commodity that can be bought and sold. Thus employees do not like to be subjected to arbitrary and capricious actions by management. In some firms, management's attitude is one of insensitivity to the needs of its employees. When this situation occurs, employees may perceive that they have little or no influence in job-related matters. Workers who feel that they are not really part of an organization are prime targets for unionization.

Management's attitude may be reflected in such small actions as how bulletin board notices are written. Memos addressed "To All Employees" instead of "To Our Employees" may indicate managers that are indifferent to employee needs. Such attitudes likely stem from top management. But they are noticed initially by employees in the actions of first-line supervisors. Workers may notice that supervisors are judging people entirely on what they can do, how much they can do, and when they can do it. Employ-

---

[45] Kurt Fernandez, "1987 Employer Bargaining Objectives," *Unions in Transition* (San Francisco: ICS Press, 1988), pp. 334–335.

[46] Shane R. Premeaux, R. Wayne Mondy, and Art L. Bethke, "The Two-Tier Wage System," *Personnel Administrator*, 31 (November 1986), pp. 92–100.

ees may begin to feel that they are treated more as machines than people. Supervisors may fail to give reasons for unusual assignments and may expect employees to dedicate their lives to the firm without providing adequate rewards. The prevailing philosophy may be: "If you don't like it here, leave." A management philosophy such as this, which does not consider the needs of employees as individuals, makes the firm ripe for unionization. Management must keep in mind that unions would never have gained a foothold if management had not abused its power.[47]

A Social Outlet

By nature, many people have strong social needs. They generally enjoy being around others who have similar interests and desires. Some employees join a union for no other reason than to take advantage of union-sponsored recreational and social activities that members and their families find fulfilling. Some unions now offer day-care centers and other services that appeal to working men and women and increase their sense of solidarity with other union members. People who develop close personal relationships, in either a unionized or union-free organization, will likely stand together in difficult times.

Providing Opportunity for Leadership

Some individuals aspire to leadership roles, but it isn't always easy for an operative employee to progress into management. However, employees with leadership aspirations can often satisfy them through the union. As with the firm, the union also has a hierarchy of leadership, and individual members have the opportunity to work their way up through its various levels. Employers often notice employees who are leaders in the union, and it is not uncommon for them to promote such employees into managerial ranks as supervisors.

Forced Unionization

It is generally illegal to require that an individual join a union prior to employment. However, in the twenty-nine states without right-to-work laws, it is legal for an employer to agree with the union that a new employee must join the union after a certain period of time (generally thirty days) or be terminated. This is referred to as a union-shop agreement. However, data are not available to indicate the number of employees who become union members because of these compulsory agreements.

Peer Pressure

Many individuals will join a union simply because they are urged to do so by other members of the work group. Friends and associates may con-

---
[47] *Ibid.*, p. 100.

stantly remind an employee that he or she is not a member of the union. This social pressure from peers is difficult to resist. Failure to join the union may result in rejection of the employee by other workers. In extreme cases, union members threaten nonmembers with physical violence and sometimes carry out these threats.

■ UNION STRUCTURE

The labor movement has developed a multilevel organizational structure over time. This complex of organizations ranges from local unions to the principal federation, the AFL–CIO. Each level has its own officers and ways of managing its affairs. Many national unions have intermediate levels between the national and the local levels. In this section, however, we describe only the three basic elements of union organization: (1) the local union; (2) the national union; and (3) the federation, or AFL–CIO.

The Local Union

The basic element in the structure of the American labor movement is the **local union** (or simply, the local). To the individual union member, it is the most important level in the structure of organized labor. Through the local, the individual deals with the employer on a day-to-day basis. There are approximately 65,000 locals in the United States, most of which are affiliated with one of the 170 or so national or international unions. The latter are generally organized along industry or craft lines[48] and ninety-four are affiliated with the AFL–CIO.

There are two basic kinds of local unions: craft and industrial. A **craft union**, such as the Carpenters and Joiners union, is typically composed of members of a particular trade or skill in a specific locality. Members usually acquire their job skills through an apprenticeship training program. An **industrial union** generally consists of all the workers in a particular plant or group of plants. The type of work they do and the level of skill they possess are not a condition for membership in the union. An example of an industrial union is the United Auto Workers.

The local union's functions are many and varied. Administering the collective bargaining agreement and representing workers in handling grievances are two quite important activities. Other functions include keeping the membership informed about labor issues, promoting increased membership, maintaining effective contact with the national union, and, when appropriate, negotiating with management at the local level.

The National (or International) Union

The most powerful level in the union structure is the national union. As we stated previously, most locals are affiliated with national unions. Some

---
[48] Daniel K. Benjamin, "Combination of Workmen: Trade Unions in the American Economy," *Unions in Transition* (San Francisco: ICS Press, 1988), p. 104.

national unions are called international because they have affiliated locals in Canada.

A **national union** is composed of local unions, which it charters. As such, it is the parent organization to local unions. The local union—not the individual worker—holds membership in the national union. The national union is supported financially by each local union, whose contribution is based on its membership size.

The national union is governed by a national constitution and a national convention of local unions, which usually meets every two to five years. The day-to-day operation of the national is conducted by elected officers, aided by an administrative staff. The national union is active in organizing workers within its jurisdiction, engaging in collective bargaining at the national level, and assisting its locals in their negotiations. In addition, the national union may provide numerous educational and research services for its locals, dispense strike funds, publish the union newspaper, provide legal counsel, and actively lobby at national and state levels.

AFL–CIO

The American Federation of Labor and Congress of Industrial Organizations (AFL–CIO) is the central trade union federation in the United States. It represents the interests of labor and its member national unions at the highest level. The federation does not engage in collective bargaining; however, it provides the means by which member unions can cooperate to pursue common objectives and attempt to resolve internal problems faced by organized labor. The federation is financed by its member national unions and is governed by a national convention, which meets every two years.

As shown in Figure 15-2, the structure of the AFL–CIO is complex. The federation has state bodies in all fifty states and Puerto Rico. In addition, national unions can affiliate with one or more of the trade and industrial departments. These departments seek to promote the interests of specific groups of workers who are in different unions but who have common interests. The federation's major activities include:

1. Improving the image of organized labor.
2. Extensive lobbying on behalf of labor interests.
3. Political education through COPE.
4. Resolving disputes between national unions.
5. Policing internal affairs of member unions.

The AFL–CIO is a loosely knit organization of more than 90 national unions. It has little formal power or control. The member national unions remain completely autonomous and decide their own policies and programs. Not all national unions are members of the federation. In fact, one of the largest unions, the Teamsters, was expelled in 1957 and did not rejoin the AFL–CIO until October 1987. In the late 1970s affiliated unions represented approximately seventeen million members, or about 78 percent

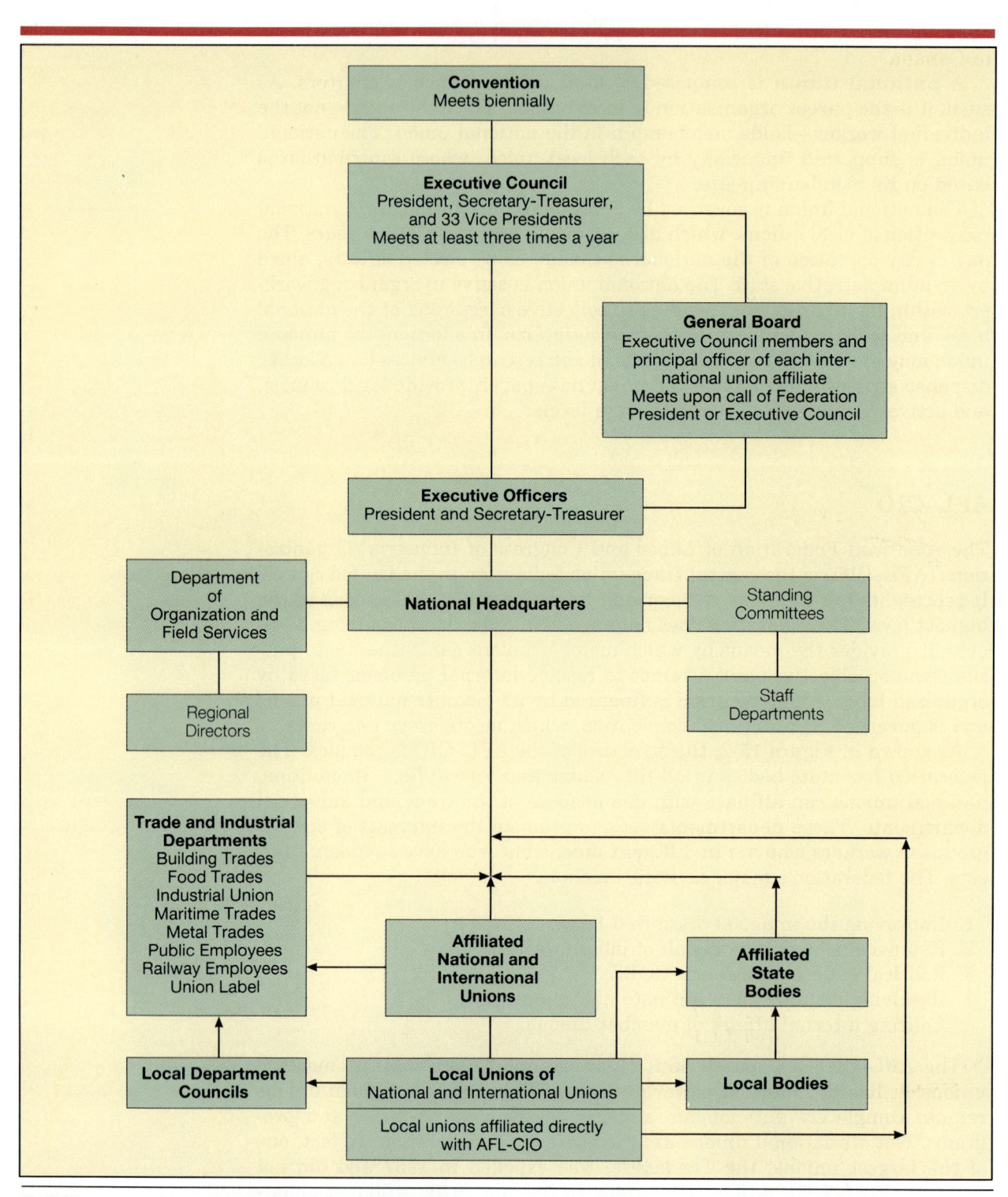

FIGURE 15-2 | The Structure of the AFL–CIO

Source: Bureau of Labor Statistics, *Directory of National Unions and Employee Associations*, 1980.

CHAPTER 15 The Labor Union 581

of all union members in the United States.[49] Currently, the AFL–CIO represents approximately fourteen million members.[50]

■ ESTABLISHING THE COLLECTIVE BARGAINING RELATIONSHIP

The primary law governing the relationship of companies and unions is the National Labor Relations Act, as amended.[51] Collective bargaining is one of the key parts of the act. Section 7 states that "employees shall have the right to self-organization, to form, join, or assist labor organizations, to bargain collectively through representatives of their own choosing, or to engage in other concerted activities for the purpose of collective bargaining...."

As defined by Section 8(d) of the act, **collective bargaining** is:

> The performance of the mutual obligation of the employer and the representative of the employees to meet at reasonable times and confer in good faith with respect to wages, hours, and other terms and conditions of employment, or the negotiation of an agreement, or any question arising thereunder, and the execution of a written contract incorporating any agreement reached if requested by either party, but such obligation does not compel either party to agree to a proposal or require the making of a concession.

The act further provides that the designated representative of the employees shall be the exclusive representative for *all* the employees in the unit for purposes of collective bargaining. A **bargaining unit** consists of a group of employees, not necessarily union members, recognized by an employer or certified by an administrative agency as appropriate for representation by a labor organization for purposes of collective bargaining. A unit may cover the employees in one plant of an employer, or it may cover employees in two or more plants of the same employer. Although the act requires the representative to be selected by the employees, it does not require any particular procedure to be used, so long as the choice clearly reflects the desire of the majority of the employees in the bargaining unit. The employee representative is normally chosen in a secret ballot election conducted by the NLRB. When a union desires to become the bargaining representative for a group of employees, several steps leading to certification have to be taken (see Figure 15-3). External and internal factors can affect the process. The primary external factors are legislation and the union; the prevailing corporate culture can affect the internal environment.

---

[49] *Directory of National Unions and Employee Associations* (Washington, D.C.: U.S. Department of Labor, Bureau of Labor Statistics), Bulletin 2079 (September 1980), p. 73.
[50] "Why Are Unions Running Scared?" *U.S. News & World Report* (September 10, 1984), pp. 62–65.
[51] Common usage is the Labor Management Act of 1947 (Taft–Hartley Act).

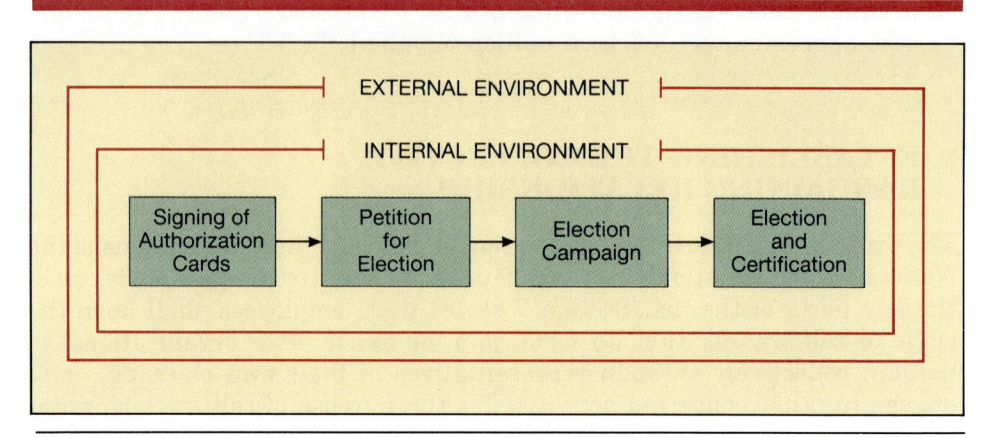

FIGURE 15-3 | The Steps That Lead to Forming a Bargaining Unit

Signing Authorization Cards

A prerequisite to forming a recognized bargaining unit is to determine whether there is sufficient interest on the part of employees. Evidence of this interest is expressed when at least 30 percent of the employees in a work group sign an authorization card. The **authorization card** is a document indicating that an employee wants to be represented by a labor organization in collective bargaining. Most union organizers will not proceed unless at least 50 percent of the workers in the group sign cards. An authorization card used by the International Association of Machinists and Aerospace Workers is shown in Figure 15-4.

Petition for Election

After the authorization cards have been signed, a petition for an election may be made to the appropriate regional office of the NLRB. When the petition is filed, the NLRB will conduct an investigation. The purpose of the investigation is to determine, among other things, the following:

1. Whether the Board has jurisdiction to conduct an election.
2. Whether there is a sufficient showing of employee interest to justify an election.
3. Whether a question of representation exists (for example, the employee representative has demanded recognition, which has been denied by the employer).
4. Whether the election will include appropriate employees in the bargaining unit (for instance, the Board is prohibited from including plant guards in the same unit with the other employees).
5. Whether the representative named in the petition is qualified (for example, a supervisor or any other management representative may not be an employee representative).

YES, I WANT THE IAM

I, the undersigned, an employee of

(Company) _____

hereby authorize the International Association of Machinists and Aerospace Workers (IAM) to act as my collective bargaining agent with the company for wages, hours and working conditions.

NAME (print) _____ DATE _____
ADDRESS (print) _____
CITY _____ STATE _____ ZIP _____
DEPT. _____ SHIFT _____ PHONE _____
Classification _____
SIGN HERE X _____

NOTE: This authorization to be SIGNED and DATED in EMPLOYEE's OWN HANDWRITING. YOUR RIGHT TO SIGN THIS CARD IS PROTECTED BY FEDERAL LAW.

FIGURE 15-4 | An Authorization Card

Source: The International Association of Machinists and Aerospace Workers.

6. Whether there are any barriers to an election in the form of existing contracts or prior elections held within the past twelve months.[52]

If these conditions have been met, the NLRB will ordinarily direct that an election be held within thirty days. Election details are left largely to the agency's regional director. Management is prohibited from making unusual concessions or promises that would encourage workers to vote against union recognition.

Campaign

When an election has been ordered, both union and management usually promote their causes actively. Unions will continue to encourage workers to join the union and management may begin a campaign to tell workers the benefits of remaining union-free. The supervisor's role during the campaign is crucial. Supervisors need to conduct themselves in a manner that

---

[52] *A Guide to Basic Law and Procedures under the National Labor Relations Act* (Washington, D.C.: U.S. Government Printing Office, October 1978), pp. 11–13.

avoids violating the law and committing unfair labor practices. Specifically, they should be aware of what can, and cannot, be done in the preelection campaign period. In many cases it is not so much what is said by the supervisor as how it is said.[53] Human resource professionals can give them a lot of help in these matters. Throughout the campaign, they should keep upper management informed about employee attitudes.

Theoretically, both union and management are permitted to tell their stories without interference from the other side. At times, the campaign becomes quite intense. An election will be set aside if it was marked by conduct that the NLRB considers to have interfered with the employee's freedom of choice. Examples of such conduct are:

- An employer or a union threatening loss of jobs or benefits to influence employees' votes or union activities.
- An employer or a union misstating important facts in the election campaign when the other party does not have a chance to reply.
- Either an employer or a union inciting racial or religious prejudice by inflammatory campaign appeals.
- An employer firing employees to discourage or encourage their union activities or a union causing an employer to take such an action.
- An employer or a union making campaign speeches to assembled groups of employees on company time within twenty-four hours of an election.

Election and Certification

The NLRB monitors the secret-ballot election on the date set. Its representatives are responsible, first, for making sure that only eligible employees vote and, second, for counting the votes. Following a valid election, the Board will issue a certification of the results to the participants. If a union has been chosen by a majority of the employees voting in the bargaining unit, it will receive a certificate showing that it is now the official bargaining representative of the employees in the unit. However, the right to represent employees does not mean, as was assumed by Robert Sweeney in the incident at the beginning of this chapter, the right to dictate terms to management that would adversely affect the organization. The bargaining process does not require either party to make concessions; it only compels them to bargain in good faith.

Union Strategies in Obtaining Bargaining Unit Recognition

Unions may use various strategies to obtain recognition by management. Unions generally try to make the first move because this places management in the position of having to react to union maneuvers. The search for groups of employees to organize involves a continuous effort by union lead-

---

[53] Art Bethke, R. Wayne Mondy, and Shane R. Premeaux, "Decertification: The Role of the First-Line Supervisor," *Supervisory Management*, 31 (February 1986), pp. 21–23.

ers. To begin a drive, unions often look for disaffection. Union organizers recognize that if management's house is in order, organizing employees will be extremely difficult. Some indications that employees are ripe for organizing include:

- A history of unjustified and arbitrary management treatment of employees.
- Compensation below the industry average.
- Lack of concern for employee welfare.

A union does not normally look at isolated conditions of employee unrest. Rather, it attempts to locate general patterns of employee dissatisfaction. Whatever the case, the union will probably not make a major attempt at organizing unless it believes that it has a good chance of success.

The union may take numerous approaches in getting authorization cards signed. One effective technique is to first identify workers who are not only dissatisfied, but who are also influential in the firm's informal organization. These individuals can assist in developing an effective organizing campaign. Information is obtained through the grapevine regarding who was hired, who was fired, and management mistakes in general. Such information is beneficial to union organizers as they approach company employees. Statements such as this are common: "I hear Bill Adams was fired today. I also understand that he is well liked. No way that would have happened if you had a union."

Ultimately, the union must abandon its secret activities. Sooner or later, management will discover the organizing attempt. At this point, union organizers may station themselves and other supporters at company entrances and pass out "throwsheets" or campaign literature proclaiming the benefits of joining the union and emphasizing management weaknesses. They will talk to anyone who will listen in their attempt to identify union sympathizers. Employees who sign an authorization card are then encouraged to convince their friends to sign also. The effort often mushrooms yielding a sufficient number of signed authorization cards before management has time to react.

Union efforts continue even after the election petition has been approved by the NLRB. Every attempt is made by the organizers to involve as many workers from the firm as possible. The outside organizers would like to take a back seat and let company employees convince their peers to join the union. Peer pressure typically has a much greater effect on convincing a person to join a union than outside influence does. Whenever possible, unions utilize peer pressure to encourage and expand unionization.

■ SIGNS OF A TROUBLED LABOR MOVEMENT

The labor movement appears to be in serious trouble, even though Lane Kirkland, president of the AFL–CIO asserts that "labor's obituary has been written at least once in every one of the 105 years of our existence...."[54]

---

[54] Seymour Martin Lipset, *Unions in Transition* (San Francisco: ICS Press, 1988), cover.

HRM In Action

Sandy Marshall, one of the workers in the plant, has just come to see the human resource manager, Lonnie Miller, for advice. Apparently a union organizer approached her yesterday and asked her to help with the union organizing effort. Lonnie knows that lately there have been growing tensions and a lot of talk about unions. He has even seen what appears to be authorization cards being passed about. Lonnie knows that if Sandy starts working for the union, she will have a lot of influence. She seems to be a natural leader, and Lonnie thinks she is supervisory material.

What advice would you give her?

However, the evidence (Figure 15-5) points to a steady decline in union membership, organizing success, number of unionized government workers, and bargaining gains. These areas are fundamental to union growth and survival. Membership is down to 17.0 percent of the workforce, and even the number of unionized government workers declined over a recent seven-year period. Share of representation elections won by unions is down to 43.7 percent, and those who are represented by a bargaining unit have felt a steady decline in average annual wage increases negotiated by unions. These are not encouraging signs for those who support unionism. Employers have gained the upper hand by employing sophisticated tactics to defeat organizing attempts. However, fading union strength will not enable management to deal with workers in a free and unrestricted manner. Some business leaders believe that they will get a union-free environment, but they may well inherit a legalistic system instead. Unionism seems to be declining, but legalized worker protection is a real and growing trend.

■ THE GROWING LEGALISTIC APPROACH

Recent emergence of an employee rights movement has the potential to "forge revolutionary changes in the workplace and the way companies manage people."[55] As nonunion sentiment intensifies, the courts and state legislatures are becoming the most effective champions of employee rights. As union membership declines so does union political and legal clout. However, according to Harvard labor law specialist Paul C. Weiler, employee rights will be protected by a legalistic system.[56] A web of legislation is

---
[55] John Hoerr et al., "Beyond Unions," *Business Week* (July 8, 1985), p. 72.
[56] Hoerr et al., p. 74.

CHAPTER 15 The Labor Union

Signs of Troubled Labor Movement

Members: Union Members as Share of Nonfarm Labor Force
- 1970: 27.3%
- 1975: 25.5%
- 1980: 21.9%
- 1984: 19.0%

Government Workers — Unionized Government Employees
- 1970: 4,008,000
- 1975: 5,751,000
- 1980: 5,641,000
- 1982 (latest): 5,510,000

Organizing: Share of Representation Elections Won by Unions
- 1981: 55.2%
- 1982: 48.2%
- 1983: 45.7%
- 1984 (latest): 43.7%

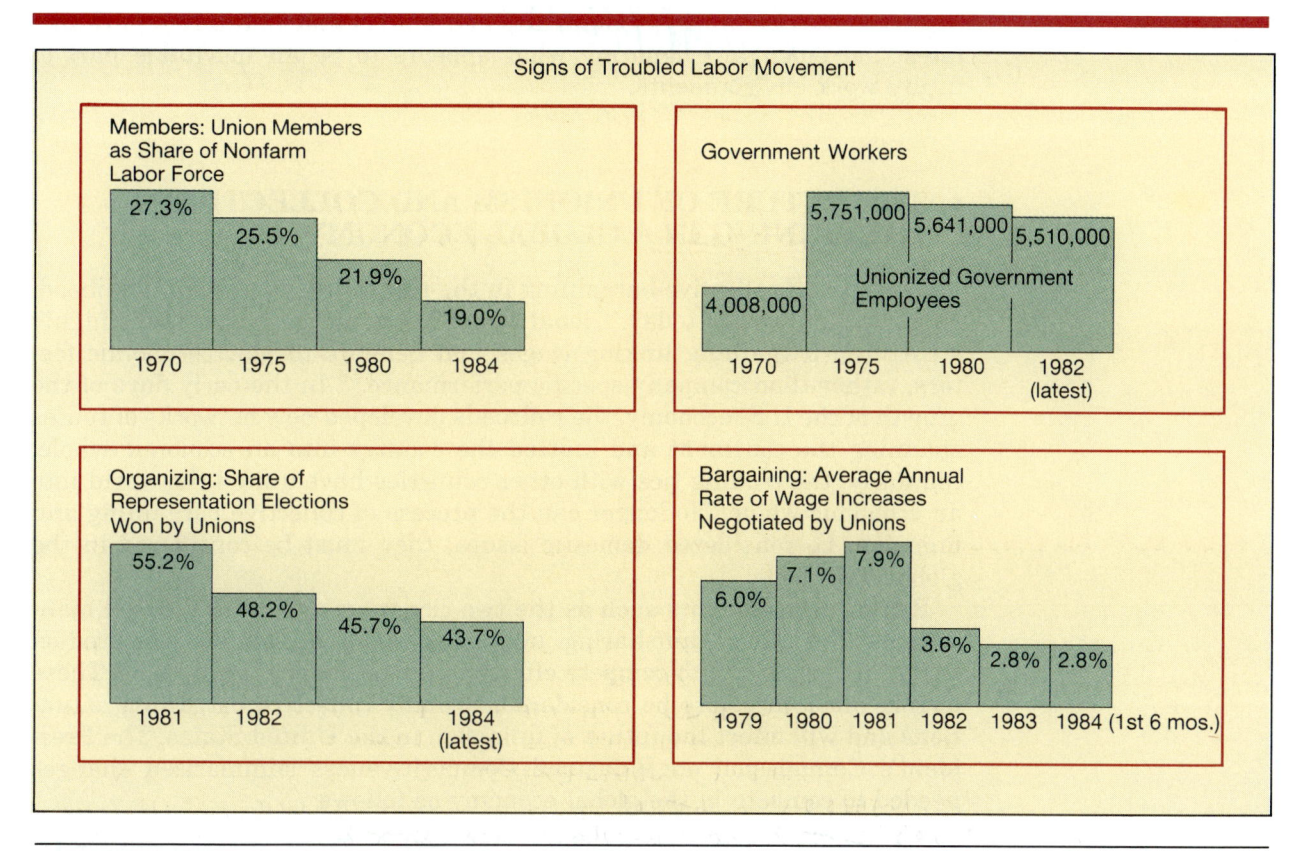

Bargaining: Average Annual Rate of Wage Increases Negotiated by Unions
- 1979: 6.0%
- 1980: 7.1%
- 1981: 7.9%
- 1982: 3.6%
- 1983: 2.8%
- 1984 (1st 6 mos.): 2.8%

FIGURE 15-5 | Signs of a Troubled Labor Movement

Source: U.S. Department of Labor. National Labor Relations Board, *Union Sourcebook*, 1984 Edition, by Leo Troy and Neil Sheflin (Box 226WOB, West Orange, N.J. 07052).

growing at the national, state, and local levels and in all aspects of the work environment. Legislation has been developed with regard to right-to-know laws, whistleblower protection, prohibition against a mandatory retirement age, notice requirements of plant shutdowns, severance pay for workers affected by plant shutdowns, employee privacy protection, enhanced standards for a safe and healthful workplace, protection against discrimination in hiring, promotion, and discharge, prohibitions against sex discrimination in pay, retirement security protection, national minimum wage, and limitations on company ability to discharge and discipline employees for union activity.

This growing network of legal protection may eventually replace collective bargaining. However, top AFL–CIO officials refuse to accept legislation as an acceptable substitute for bargaining or the suggestion that unions are in permanent decline. Regardless of the state of unionism, the employee rights movement will continue to expand, providing employees with more influence in their work.[57] Companies and unions that fail to recognize this latest movement are ignoring what appears to be an inevitable part of future work environments.

■ THE FUTURE OF UNIONISM AND COLLECTIVE BARGAINING IN A GLOBAL ECONOMY

Unionism and collective bargaining in the future will not, in all likelihood, be as we know them today. Global competition will no longer allow highly structured bargaining linking wages and benefits to macroeconomic factors, rather than company-specific performance.[58] In the early days of the growth of the U.S. economy, the railroads developed new networks of routes spanning the continent and knitted the country into an economic whole. Similarly, the trading ties with other countries have united the world into an economic whole. No longer can the process of collective bargaining and unionism be considered domestic issues; they must be considered in the global spectrum.

Recent developments such as the two-tier wage system, increased management flexibility, gainsharing, and employee identification with productivity, are necessary to compete effectively in a global environment. These factors must therefore be considered in many collective bargaining situations and will affect the future of unionism in the United States. The President's Commission on Industrial Competitiveness summarized changes needed to compete in the global economy as follows:

- Labor management cooperation is essential. The new cooperative relationships will maximize productivity by involving employees and their elected representatives in the decision-making process.
- Employee incentives must be strengthened to reward the efforts of individual employees and to emphasize the linkage between compensation and performance.
- Displaced workers must be handled in a more resourceful manner. Employers must be encouraged to strengthen their commitment to employee security and will be required to provide early notification of plant closings. All parties should work toward the goal of reemployment.
- Improved work skills must be developed by training employees to effectively compete in the job market. Specifically, employers should be encouraged to take a more systematic approach in their training activities.[59]

Obviously, times have changed and will continue to change, and labor and management must evolve to compete in the global economy. Neither labor or management should attempt to hold on to the practices of the past because today's global economy will not tolerate such entrenched behavior.

---

[57] Hoerr et al., p. 77.

[58] Alexander B. Trowbridge, "A Management Look at Labor Relations," *Unions in Transition* (San Francisco: ICS Press, 1988), p. 417.

[59] "Global Competition: The New Reality," *Vol. 2, Report of the President's Commission on Industrial Competitiveness*, (Washington, D.C.: U.S. Government Printing Office, 1985), pp. 137–160.

SUMMARY

The labor movement has not enjoyed simple and straightforward progress. Prior to the 1930s, attitudes definitely favored management. This was first evidenced by the use of criminal and civil conspiracy doctrines derived from English common law. Other tactics used by employers to stifle union growth were injunctions and yellow-dog contracts. In 1890, Congress passed the Sherman Anti-Trust Act. This marked the entrance of the federal government into the statutory regulation of labor organizations. Later, in 1914, Congress passed the Clayton Act (an amendment to the Sherman Act). The intent of this act was to remove labor from the purview of the Sherman Act. During the 1920s labor faced legal restrictions on union activity and unfavorable court decisions. The one exception to such repressive policies was enactment of the Railway Labor Act of 1926.

The pendulum began to swing away from management and toward labor after 1930. Congress passed the Norris–LaGuardia Act in 1932, affirming the use of collective bargaining and approving the formation of labor unions. In 1933 Congress made an abortive attempt to stimulate economic recovery by passing the National Industry Recovery Act (NIRA). Undeterred by a Supreme Court decision and strongly supported by organized labor, Congress speedily enacted a comprehensive labor law, the National Labor Relations Act (Wagner Act). Drawing heavily on the experience of the Railway Labor Act of 1926 and Section 7a of the NIRA, the act declared legislative support, on a broad scale, of the right of workers to organize and engage in collective bargaining. In 1947, with public pressure mounting, Congress overrode President Truman's veto and passed the Labor Management Relations Act (Taft–Hartley Act), which extensively revised the National Labor Relations Act. One of the most controversial elements of the Taft–Hartley Act permits states to enact right-to-work legislation. Right-to-work laws are laws that prohibit management and unions from agreements requiring union membership as a condition of employment. In 1959, Congress enacted the Labor–Management Reporting and Disclosure Act (Landrum–Griffin Act), which spelled out a "Bill of Rights of Members of Labor Organizations" designed to protect certain rights of individuals in their relationships with unions.

Government employees are generally considered a class apart from private-sector workers. This is reflected in their exclusion from the coverage of general labor legislation. However, like their counterparts in private industry, government employees have demonstrated a persistence in organizing in order to gain an effective voice in the terms and conditions of their employment. Membership in public-sector professional and state employee associations greatly exceeds private-sector unionization.

Most unions recognize that they must strive for continued growth and power. Members pay dues, which are essential for achieving union objectives. A union's power is influenced to a large extent by the size of its membership and the possibility of future growth. By achieving growth and power, a union is capable of exerting political force. The political arm of the AFL–CIO is the Committee on Political Education (COPE).

Individuals join unions for many different reasons, and these reasons tend to change over time. They may involve job, personal, social, or political considerations. Some of the major reasons are: dissatisfaction with management, need for a social outlet, opportunity for leadership, forced unionization, and peer pressure.

The labor movement has developed a multilevel organizational structure: (1) the local union; (2) the national union; and (3) the federation, or AFL–CIO. The basic element in the structure of the American labor movement is the local union, of which there are two basic kinds: craft and industrial. A national union is composed of local unions, which it charters. The American Federation of Labor and Congress of Industrial Organizations (AFL–CIO) is the main trade union federation in the United States.

The primary law governing the relationship of companies and unions is the National Labor Relations Act, as amended. A bargaining unit consists of a group of employees, not necessarily union members, recognized by an employer or certified by an administrative agency as appropriate for representation by a labor organization for purposes of collective bargaining. A prerequisite to forming a recognized bargaining unit is to determine whether there is sufficient interest on the part of employees. After authorization cards have been signed, a petition for an election may be made to the appropriate regional office of the NLRB. The NLRB monitors a secret-ballot election. Unions may use various strategies to obtain recognition by management. Unions generally try to make the first move because this places management in the position of having to react to union maneuvers.

Unionism and collective bargaining in the future will not, in all likelihood, be as we know it today. Global competition will no longer allow highly structured bargaining that links wages and benefits to macroeconomic factors rather than company-specific performance. Recent developments, such as the two-tier wage system, increased management flexibility, gainsharing, and employee identification with productivity, are necessary to compete effectively in a global environment.

Many signs point to serious trouble in the labor movement. Certain fundamental indicators of union growth and survival are declining. As antiunion sentiment grows, however, a legalistic approach to employee protection appears to be replacing collective bargaining.

Questions for Review

1. Describe the development of the labor movement in the United States.
2. List the unfair labor practices by management that were prohibited by the Wagner Act.
3. What union actions were prohibited by the Taft–Hartley Act?
4. In what way does unionization of the public sector differ from unionization of the private sector?
5. Why would unions strive for continued growth and power? Discuss.
6. What are the primary reasons for employees joining labor unions?

CHAPTER 15 The Labor Union

7. What steps must a union take in attempting to form a bargaining unit? Briefly describe each step.
8. Describe the ways unions might go about gaining bargaining unit recognition.
9. Describe the process of collective bargaining and unionism in a global economy.
10. Discuss the signs of a troubled labor movement.

Terms for Review

Conspiracy
Injunction
Yellow-dog contract
Right-to-work laws
Committee on Political Education (COPE)
Two-tier wage system

Local union
Craft union
Industrial union
National union
Collective bargaining
Bargaining unit
Authorization card

INCIDENT 1 ■ Work Rules ■

Jerry Sharplin eagerly drove his new company pickup onto the construction site. He had just been assigned by his employer, Lurgi-Knost Construction Company, to supervise a crew of sixteen equipment operators, oilers, and mechanics. This was the first unionized crew Jerry had supervised. As he approached his work area, he noticed one of the "cherry pickers" (a type of mobile crane with an extendable boom) standing idle with the operator beside it. Jerry pulled up beside the operator and said, "What's going on here?"

"Out of gas," the operator said.

"Well, go and get some," Jerry said.

The operator reached to get his thermos jug out of the tool box on the side of the crane and said, "The oiler's on break right now. He'll be back in a few minutes."

Jerry remembered that he had a five gallon can of gasoline in the back of his pickup. So he quickly got the gasoline, climbed on the cherrypicker, and started to pour it into the gas tank. As he did so, he heard the other machines shutting down in unison. He looked around and saw all the other operators climbing down from their equipment and standing to watch him pour the gasoline. A moment later, he saw the union steward approaching.

Questions

1. Why did all the operators shut down their machines?
2. If you were Jerry, what would you do now? Explain.

INCIDENT 2 ■ Union Appeal ■

In late 1982, a vigorous union organizing campaign was underway at Dodge Tube Company in Rochester, North Carolina. The management at Dodge was strongly anti-union and made no bones about it. Roger Verdon was a general foreman at Dodge, with the responsibility for four supervisors and about eighty machine operators and helpers. Roger had become increasingly incensed as the union's organizing attempts became more apparent.

At first, fliers and other promotional literature had been handed out at the plant gates. There had been an increasing number of complaints and Roger felt that many of them were caused by the union organizing activity. The workers in general had become more belligerent, Roger thought, and he saw indications of more and more secret communication. Workers who had previously been his friends seemed to have pulled away. While they were not unfriendly, they typically limited their conversation with him to office matters.

Roger felt that Dodge was a good employer and treated its people fairly. Discipline was administered by supervisors on the spot. Helpers were paid minimum wage, but few stayed in that position very long. Most helpers were either fired or promoted to machine operator within about six months. The machine operators were placed in pay grade 1, 2, or 3 at the discretion of the supervisor. Supervisors were encouraged to base pay grade assignments only on job proficiency. Most of the supervisors were required to participate in the company's management training program. The ones who were not college graduates were required to complete a correspondence course in management from the University of Maryland during their first six months as supervisors.

The company had an aggressive health and safety program. Workers in noisy areas were required to wear ear plugs and a worker who failed to do so was immediately fired. The same was true of safety glasses in areas involving grinding, drilling, or chipping. The workers in and around the tube cleaning area were required to wear respirators after an OSHA inspector cited the company for the amount of particulate matter in the air.

One day in early December, Roger observed what he considered to be the "last straw." He saw a worker from another part of the plant walking through his area handing out cards to the workers. Bob asked to see one of the cards and saw that it was a union authorization card. He decided to have a meeting with his supervisors.

Questions

1. What factors could have produced union organizing activity?
2. What can Roger do about it?

CHAPTER 15   The Labor Union

EXPERIENCING HUMAN RESOURCE MANAGEMENT

Unionization is often met with mixed feelings by all concerned. Management is usually opposed to such efforts. Beth Morrison, the production manager of the heavy motors division, knows that upper management does not care much for unions. They believe that this unionizing effort is not good for anybody involved with this company and that the union wants to turn our employees against us, and go about doing what they have done to so many firms—destroy their competitive edge. The firm must do everything possible to circumvent this union organizing effort, but it must do that in line with NLRB guidelines.

Beth thought "I've got to meet with Ray Miller, the supervisor over in section four today. He is a little too overeager. We don't want this union, but we also don't want the NLRB down on our necks. Indirect threats are OK, but direct threats can get us in trouble. The supervisor must understand the ground rules, and apply those rules to stop this union. Obviously, we don't want this union, but no supervisor can threaten loss of jobs or benefits, or fire anybody, at least until after the election. However, if they ask for your opinion, by all means discourage workers from unionizing."

If you are anti-union or pro-union, there is a role for two of you here. One of you will play the production manager and the other will play the supervisor. The rest of you observe carefully. Your instructor will provide the participants with additional information.

REFERENCES

Adams, Larry T. "Changing Employment Patterns of Organized Workers." *Monthly Labor Review*, 108(2) (February 1985), pp. 25–30.

Atchison, Sandra, and Aaron Bernstein. "A Silver Bullet for the Union Drive at Coors?" *Business Week* (July 11, 1988), pp. 61–62.

Benson, Herman. "Union Democracy." *Unions in Transition* (San Francisco: ICS Press, 1988).

Bethke, Art, R. Wayne Mondy, and Shane R. Premeaux. "Decertification: The Role of the First-Line Supervisor." *Supervisory Management*, 31 (February 1986), pp. 21–23.

———. "Beyond Unions." *Business Week* (July 8, 1985), p. 72.

Brown, T. P. "Appropriate Bargaining Units in Health-Care Institutions: The Disparity of Interests Test." *Employee Relations Law Journal*, 10 (Spring 1985), pp. 717–722.

Caruth, Don, and Harry N. Mills. "Working Toward Better Union Relations." *Supervisory Management*, 30 (February 1985), pp. 7–13.

———. "Collective Bargaining and Fifty Years of the CIO." *Labor Law Journal*, 36 (August 1985), pp. 659–664.

Craver, Charles B. "The Current and Future Status of Labor Organizations." *Labor Law Journal*, 36 (April 1985), pp. 210–225.

Deligman, Daniel. "Who Needs Unions?" *Fortune* (July 12, 1985), pp. 54–66.

Doyle, P. M. "Area Wage Surveys Shed Light on Decline in Unionization." *Monthly Labor Review*, 108 (September 1985), pp. 13–19.

Gennard, J. "What's New in Industrial Relations." *Personnel Management*, 17 (March 1985), pp. 19–21ff.

Hughes, M. J. "White-Collar Organizing—We're Not Giving Up." *Management Review*, 74 (March 1985), pp. 54–56.

Krajci, T. J. "Labor Relations in the Public Sector." *Personnel Administrator*, 30 (May 1985), pp. 43ff.

Lardaro, Leonard. "Authorization Card Reliability and the Impact of Actions by the NLRB: An Examination of Several Uses." *Labor Law Journal*, 35 (June 1984), pp. 344–351.

Mondy, R. Wayne, and Shane R. Premeaux. "The Labor/Management Power Relationship Revisited." *Personnel Administrator*, 30 (May 1985), pp. 52–57.

Porter, Andrew A., and Kent F. Murman. "A Survey of Employer Union-Avoidance Practices." *Personnel Administrator*, 28 (November 1983), pp. 66–71.

Premeaux, Shane R., R. Wayne Mondy, and Art L. Bethke. "The Two-Tier Wage System." *Personnel Administrator*, 31 (November 1986), pp. 92–100.

Saltzman, G. M. "Bargaining Laws as a Cause and Consequence of the Growth of Teacher Unionism." *Industrial Labor Relations Review*, 38 (April 1985), pp. 335–351.

Schwartz, Stanley J. "The National Labor Relations Board and the Duty of Fair Representation." *Labor Law Journal* (December 1983), pp. 781–789.

Tidwell, Gary L. "The Supervisor's Role in a Union Election." *Personnel Journal*, 62 (August 1983), pp. 640–645.

Troy, Leo. "The Rise and Fall of American Trade Unions: The Labor Movement from FDR to RR." *Unions in Transition* (San Francisco: ICS Press, 1988).

Voos, Paula B. "Does It Pay to Organize? Estimating Costs to Unions." *Monthly Labor Review*, 107 (June 1984), pp. 43–44.

———. "Why Are Unions Running Scared?" *U.S. News & World Report* (September 10, 1984), pp. 62–65.

———. "Why Unions Lose at Many Companies." *Nation's Business* (August 1982), pp. 50–51.

CHAPTER 16

COLLECTIVE BARGAINING

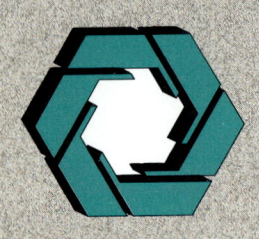

CHAPTER OBJECTIVES

1. Discuss the collective bargaining process, describe the role of the human resource manager in it, and explain the psychological aspects of collective bargaining.
2. Describe what both labor and management do as they prepare for negotiations.
3. Explain typical bargaining issues and the process of negotiating.
4. Identify and describe ways to overcome breakdowns in negotiations and describe what is involved in ratifying and administering the agreement.
5. Discuss the future of collective bargaining.

Barbara Washington, the chief union negotiator, was meeting with company representatives on a new contract. Both the union team and management had been preparing for this encounter for a long time. Barbara's deep concern was whether union members would support a strike vote if one were called. Sales for the industry were generally down because of imports. In fact, there had even been some layoffs at competing firms. The union members' attitude tended to be one of, "Get what you can for us, but don't rock the boat." She hoped, however, that skillful negotiating could win concessions from management.

In the first session, Barbara's team presented its demands to management. The team had determined that pay was to be the main issue, and a 20 percent increase spread over three years was demanded. Management countered by saying that since sales were down it could not afford to provide any pay raises. After much heated discussion, both sides agreed to reevaluate their positions and meet again in two days.

Barbara met with her negotiating team in private, and it decided to decrease the salary demand slightly. The team felt that the least they could accept was a 15 percent raise.

At the next meeting, Barbara presented the revised demands to management. They were not well received. Bill Thompson, the director of industrial relations, began by saying: "We cannot afford a pay increase in this contract, but we will make every attempt to ensure that no layoffs occur. Increasing wages at this time will virtually guarantee a reduction in force."

continued on next page

PART SIX   Employee and Labor Relations

> *continued from previous page*
>
> Barbara's confidence collapsed. She knew that there was no way that the general membership was willing to accept layoffs and that a strike vote would be virtually impossible to obtain. She asked for a recess to review the new proposal.

Barbara is experiencing the negotiating crunch that has existed for several years in the United States. The power pendulum has swung in favor of management, and this movement makes it very difficult for union negotiators to effectively bargain with management on certain issues, including pay increases.

We devote the first portion of this chapter to the collective bargaining process and the human resource manager's role in it. We then describe the psychological aspects of collective bargaining and preparing for negotiations. Next, we address bargaining issues, negotiating, and overcoming breakdowns in negotiations. We end the chapter with a discussion of ratifying and administration of the agreement. The overall purpose of this chapter is to identify and describe the many factors involved in the collective bargaining process.

■ THE COLLECTIVE BARGAINING PROCESS

The collective bargaining process is fundamental to management–labor relations in the United States. Extensive collective bargaining activity occurs each year. In 1988 alone, 3.4 million workers were covered by major collective bargaining agreements scheduled to expire or be reopened. This represents 39 percent of the 8.7 million employees under major agreements in private industry and state and local government.[1] Similar levels of collective bargaining activity occur each year. During the 1980s—and for the foreseeable future—management has had and is expected to have the power advantage in collective bargaining. In fact, according to the Bureau of National Affairs' (BNA's) Collective Bargaining Negotiations and Contracts service, 95 percent of employers are very confident about achieving their collective bargaining goals in the future.[2]

Even though collective bargaining is widely practiced, there is no precise format of what to do or how to do it. In fact, diversity is probably the most prominent characteristic of collective bargaining in the United States. The collective bargaining process, in general, is shown in Figure 16-1. As you can see, both external and internal environmental factors can influence the process. For instance, the form of the bargaining structure can affect the conduct of collective bargaining. The four major types of structure are: (1) one company dealing with a single union; (2) several companies dealing with a single union; (3) several unions dealing with a single company; and

---

[1] U.S. Bureau of Labor Statistics, *Collective Bargaining Activity in 1988* (Washington, D.C.: U.S. Government Printing Office).

[2] Kurt Fernandez, "1987 Employer Bargaining Objectives," *Collective Bargaining Negotiations and Contracts* (Washington, D.C.: The Bureau of National Affairs, 1987), p. 61.

CHAPTER 16   Collective Bargaining

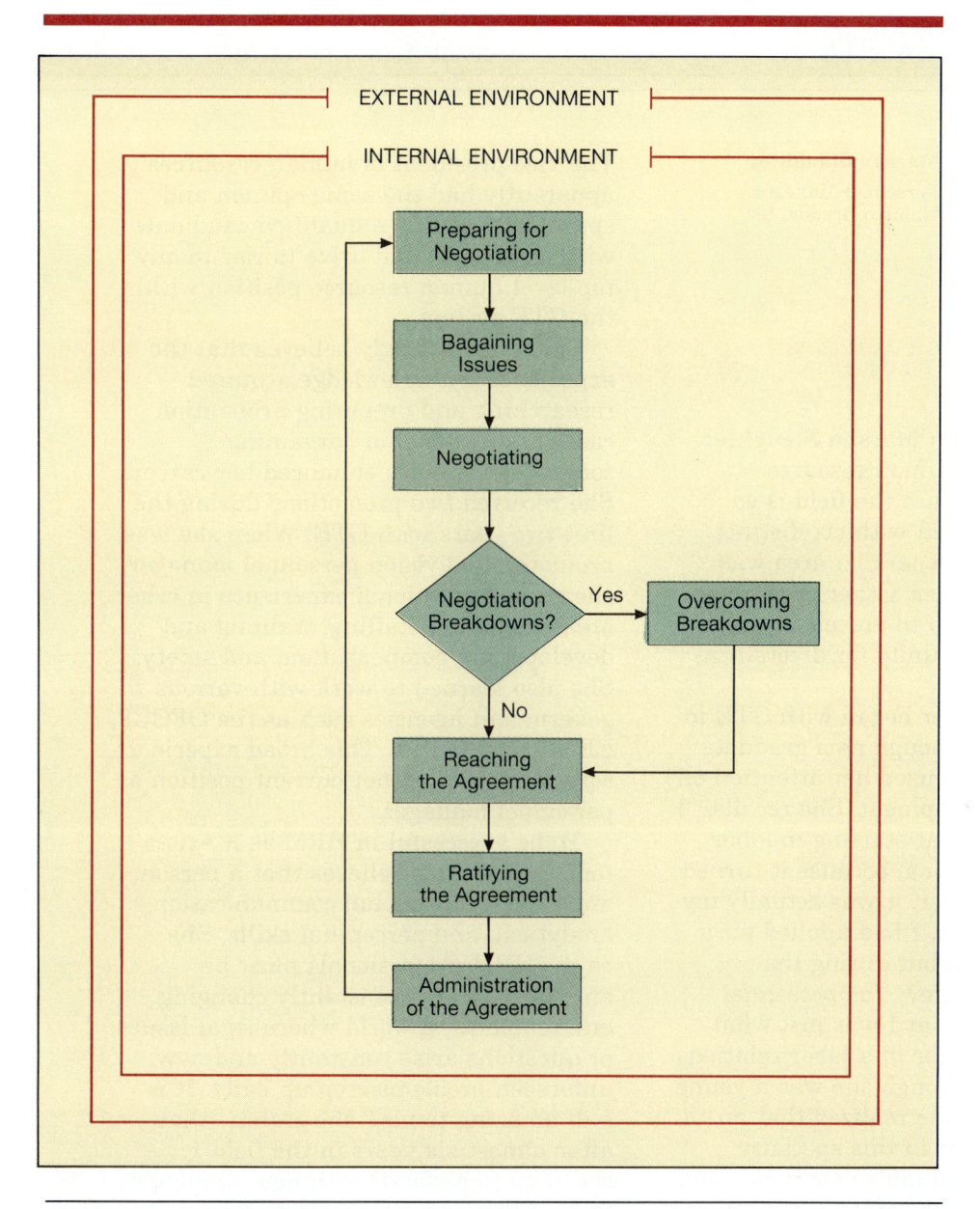

```
┌─────────────── EXTERNAL ENVIRONMENT ───────────────┐
│  ┌──────────── INTERNAL ENVIRONMENT ────────────┐  │
│  │                                              │  │
│  │         ┌──────────────────┐                 │  │
│  │    ┌──▶│   Preparing for  │                 │  │
│  │    │    │   Negotiation    │                 │  │
│  │    │    └────────┬─────────┘                 │  │
│  │    │             ▼                           │  │
│  │    │    ┌──────────────────┐                 │  │
│  │    │    │    Bargaining    │                 │  │
│  │    │    │      Issues      │                 │  │
│  │    │    └────────┬─────────┘                 │  │
│  │    │             ▼                           │  │
│  │    │    ┌──────────────────┐                 │  │
│  │    │    │   Negotiating    │                 │  │
│  │    │    └────────┬─────────┘                 │  │
│  │    │             ▼                           │  │
│  │    │        ╱─────────╲     Yes   ┌──────────┐
│  │    │       ╱ Negotiation╲────────▶│Overcoming│
│  │    │       ╲ Breakdowns?╱         │Breakdowns│
│  │    │        ╲─────────╱           └────┬─────┘
│  │    │             │ No                  │       │
│  │    │             ▼                     │       │
│  │    │    ┌──────────────────┐           │       │
│  │    │    │     Reaching     │◀──────────┘       │
│  │    │    │   the Agreement  │                   │
│  │    │    └────────┬─────────┘                   │
│  │    │             ▼                             │
│  │    │    ┌──────────────────┐                   │
│  │    │    │     Ratifying    │                   │
│  │    │    │   the Agreement  │                   │
│  │    │    └────────┬─────────┘                   │
│  │    │             ▼                             │
│  │    │    ┌──────────────────┐                   │
│  │    └────│  Administration  │                   │
│  │         │  of the Agreement│                   │
│  │         └──────────────────┘                   │
│  └────────────────────────────────────────────────┘
└──────────────────────────────────────────────────────┘
```

FIGURE 16-1 | The Collective Bargaining Process

(4) several companies dealing with several unions. Most contract bargaining is carried out under the first type of structure. The process can become quite complicated when several companies and unions are involved in the same negotiations.

Another environmental factor influencing collective bargaining is the type of union–management relationship that exists. When a group of workers decide they want union representation, changes occur in the organiza-

EXECUTIVE INSIGHTS

Marsha Slaughter
Personnel Manager,
Nabisco Brands, Inc.

A primary reason Marsha Slaughter chose a career in human resource management was that the field is so varied. A career field with six distinct specialities and a generalist area was very appealing to her. Other professions simply did not seem to present as much challenge or opportunity for diversification.

Slaughter's career began with GTE in labor relations, although as a graduate student she had focused her attention on training and development. She recalls, "I wish I could say that starting in labor relations was my idea, because it turned out so well. However, it was actually my employer's decision. I had applied for a generalist position but during the employment interview, the personnel manager decided that I was just what they were looking for in a labor relations assistant." Even though she was a young college graduate, she realized that an entry-level position in this specialty would provide invaluable experience and an excellent base for career advancement.

The vice-president of human resources apparently had the same opinion and specifically sought a qualified candidate with the ability and drive to rise to any top-level human resource position within the GTE system.

Slaughter strongly believes that the experience and knowledge acquired researching and preparing arbitration cases and serving on bargaining committees greatly enhanced her career. She received two promotions during the first two years with GTE. When she was promoted to division personnel manager, she gained additional experience in other areas including staffing, training and development, compensation, and safety. She also learned to work with various government agencies such as the OFCCP, EEOC, and OSHA. This broad experience serves her well in her current position as personnel manager.

To be successful in HRM as it exists today, Slaughter believes that a person must have exceptional communication, analytical, and perceptual skills. She says, "HRM professionals must be able to work in a constantly changing environment—a world where legal issues or questions arise constantly and new, unforseen problems crop up daily. It is still amazing to me," she states, "that after almost six years in the field I continue to be faced with new challenges. Since I have a tendency to become bored when I'm not challenged, this works to my advantage."

In college, Slaughter was exposed to many HRM topics. One course in particular required considerable research and presentation of papers on specific current topics. "At that time," she recalls, "none of us thought we would ever be facing issues such as AIDS in the workplace, transsexual employees, drug testing, or employment-at-will issues. On the other hand, the avant-garde concepts of that period, such as quality circles and employee participation teams, have now become rather commonplace."

One experience from college always stuck in Slaughter's mind. The East Texas State University ASPA chapter, which she served as president, often invited guest speakers to the campus. One such speaker seemed to concentrate on all the negative aspects of human resources as he perceived them. Slaughter relates, "This talk was so negative that he almost had me convinced I had made a mistake choosing HRM as a major. He told us that human resource managers always played the adversarial role with the operations people and were, therefore, highly unpopular. He also bemoaned the fact that HRM professionals had little real authority in comparison with line management which made it difficult to enforce human resource policies."

Slaughter believes that this individual was off base in his thinking and probably also in the way he approached line managers. Her response is, "I have had no real problem with lack of authority because I deal with each manager individually, using an approach that is effective with his or her personality type. I try to use influence rather than authority to accomplish my objectives. For example, when a manager's actions violate the labor agreement or state or federal laws and need to be corrected, I try to handle such situations with finesse—not with heavy-handed hand slapping."

Slaughter believes that HRM professionals should take every opportunity to help educate others who are not well versed in a given human resource areas. This approach, she feels, will result in other managers seeking advice and input prior to taking action involving HRM expertise. "Once you gain the respect of your peers for your competence and knowledge," she adds, "you will not need formal authority because you will have the most potent ability of all—the power to influence and persuade others. When you have developed a strong rapport with your peers, you will be thought of as one of the team, not as an adversary. In my opinion, that's the only way to become a truly effective human resource professional."

tion. In the absence of a union, management exercises virtually unlimited authority, except for the limitations imposed by the growing web of employee legal rights protection. As we noted in Chapter 15, these legal protections may well replace collective bargaining in the future.[3] However, for the present, when a union becomes the bargaining representative, management must change its style of decision making to include union bargaining agents. When employees take collective action, such as slowdowns and strikes, an adversarial relationship can be created, with varying degrees of conflict. Sloane and Witney list six types of union–management relations that may exist in an organization:

1. *Conflict.* Each challenges the other's actions and motivation; cooperation is nonexistent; uncompromising attitudes and union militancy are present.
2. *Armed truce.* Each views the other as antagonistic but tries to avoid head-on conflict; bargaining obligations and contract provisions are strictly interpreted.
3. *Power bargaining.* Management accepts the union; each side tries to gain advantage from the other.
4. *Accommodation.* Each tolerates the other in a live and let live atmosphere and attempts to reduce conflict without eliminating it.
5. *Cooperation.* Each side accepts the other and works together to resolve human resource and production problems as they occur.
6. *Collusion.* Both "cooperate" to the point of adversely affecting the legitimate interests of employees, other businesses in the industry, and the consuming public; this involves conniving to control markets, supplies, and prices illegally and/or unethically.[4]

The nature and quality of union–management relations vary over time. The first three types of relationships mentioned are generally unsatisfactory; collusion is unacceptable, and cooperation has been rare in the past. Typically, U.S. union–management relations appear to be some form of accommodation. In all likelihood, collective bargaining during the 1990s will be more cooperative, with joint economic survival being all important. Furthermore, a lessening of the adversarial relationships and cooperation in areas never possible in the past is a real future prospect.[5]

Depending on the type of relationship encountered, the collective bargaining process may be relatively simple or it may be a long, tense struggle for both parties. Veteran labor negotiator Robert J. Harding, a consulting firm executive, offers the following seven tips for successful collective bargaining:

---

[3] John Hoerr et al. "Beyond Unions," *Business Week* (July 8, 1985), p. 77.

[4] Arthur A. Slone and Fred Witney, *Labor Relations*, 4th ed. (Englewood Cliffs, N.J.: Prentice-Hall, 1981), pp. 28–35.

[5] Abby Brown, "An Interview with Fritz Ihrig," *Personnel Administrator*, 31 (April 1986), p. 60.

CHAPTER 16   Collective Bargaining   603

1. Don't underestimate the importance of the first preparatory, nonadversarial meeting between labor and management representatives; instead use this opportunity to set the ground rules for future sessions.
2. Carefully document each meeting because accurate, well-organized notes can be quite useful in initial, and subsequent, contract negotiations.
3. If the CEO is well regarded by employees, consider including that person in the sessions.
4. Within the bounds of law and propriety, develop a personal profile of each member of the committee who will take part in the collective bargaining process.
5. Accept negotiators as peers; never underestimate them.
6. Maintain strong communications with those individuals who best know the people most affected by the contract and the issues being discussed.
7. If negotiations break down, consider federal mediation.[6]

Regardless of the complexity of the bargaining issues, the ability to reach agreement is the key to any successful negotiation. Success requires good communication skills and an understanding of the seven negotiation tips.

As we stated previously, the first step in the collective bargaining process is preparing for negotiations. This step is often extensive and ongoing for both union and management. After the issues to be negotiated have been determined, the two sides confer to reach a mutually acceptable contract. Although breakdowns in negotiations can occur, both labor and management have at their disposal tools and arguments that can be used to convince the other side to accept their views. Eventually, however, management and the union reach an agreement that defines the rules of the game for the duration of the contract. The next step is for the union membership to ratify the agreement.

Note the feedback loop from administration of the agreement to preparing for negotiations in Figure 16-1. Collective bargaining is a continuous and dynamic process, and preparing for the next round of negotiations often begins virtually from the time a contract is ratified. The steps depicted for the collective bargaining process form the basic outline for the remainder of this chapter.

■ THE HUMAN RESOURCE MANAGER'S ROLE

When a firm is unionized, the human resource manager's role tends to change rather significantly. In a unionized environment, the human resource manager must deal primarily with a union organizational structure consisting of union stewards and business agents rather than with individual workers. The human resource manager is the one who must live with the consequences of the contract, and therefore he or she should be an integral part of the ultimate resolution of contractual issues. According to

---

[6] Abby Brown, "Labor Contract Negotiations: Behind the Scenes," *Labor Relations: Reports from the Firing Line* (Plano, Tex.: Business Publications, 1988), pp. 305–308.

veteran negotiator Fritz Ihrig, if the human resource manager is a strong and capable individual, that person should actually negotiate the contract.[7] Successful negotiators must have a thorough understanding of what is going on and an appreciation of the human element of the collective bargaining process.

Because the role of first-line supervisors is crucial, the human resource manager *must* maintain close contact with them before, during, and after collective bargaining. First-line supervisors administer the contract and know whether it is working well or there are problems with it. Through an active and involved role, the human resource manager can limit problems such as animosity, fighting, games, role-playing, and a "stick it to them" mentality. Human resource managers who assume their proper roles in the collective bargaining process can make that process more beneficial to all concerned.

■ PSYCHOLOGICAL ASPECTS OF COLLECTIVE BARGAINING

Prior to collective bargaining, both the management team and the union team have to prepare positions and accomplish certain other tasks. Vitally important also for those involved are the psychological aspects of collective bargaining. Psychologically, the collective bargaining process is often difficult because it is an adversarial situation and must be approached as such. It is "a situation that is fundamental to law, politics, business, and government, because out of the clash of ideas, points of view, and interests come agreement, consensus, and justice".[8]

In effect, those involved in the collective bargaining process will be matching wits with the competition will experience victory as well as defeat, and will ultimately resolve problems, resulting in a contract. The role of those who meet at the bargaining table "essentially involves the mobilization and management of aggression," in a manner that allows them to hammer out a collective bargaining agreement.[9] Because those involved must "mobilize and manage aggression" their personalities have a major impact on the negotiation process. The attitudes of those who will be negotiating have a direct effect on what can be accomplished and how quickly a mutually agreed-on contract can be finalized. Problems are compounded by differences in the experience and educational backgrounds of those involved in the negotiation process.[10] Finally, the longer, more involved, and intense the bargaining sessions the greater the psychological strain on all concerned. As psychological pressures intensify, the gap between labor and management can easily widen, further compounding the problems of achieving mutual accommodation.

---

[7] Brown, "An Interview with Fritz Ihrig," p. 60.

[8] Harry Levinson, "Stress at the Bargaining Table," *Labor Relations: Reports from the Firing Line* (Plano, Tex.: Business Publications, 1988), p. 310.

[9] *Ibid.*

[10] Gary N. Chaison and Mark S. Plovnick, "Is There a Collective Bargaining?" *California Management Review*, 28 (4) (1986), p. 116.

CHAPTER 16 Collective Bargaining

■ PREPARING FOR NEGOTIATIONS

Because of the complex issues facing labor and management today, the negotiating teams must carefully prepare for the bargaining sessions. Prior to meeting at the bargaining table, the negotiators should thoroughly know the culture, climate, history, present economic state, and wage and benefits structure of the organization and similar organizations.[11] Because the length of a typical labor agreement is three years, negotiators should develop the perspective of making the contract successful both now and in the future. This point of view should prevail for both management and labor, although it rarely does. During the term of an agreement, both sides probably discover contract provisions that need to be added, deleted, or modified. These items become proposals to be addressed in the next round of negotiations.

Bargaining issues can be divided into three categories: mandatory, permissive, and prohibited. **Mandatory bargaining issues** fall within the definition of wages, hours, and other terms and conditions of employment (see Table 16-1). These issues generally have an immediate and direct effect on workers' jobs. A refusal to bargain in these areas is grounds for an unfair labor practice charge. **Permissive bargaining issues** may be raised, but neither side may insist that they be bargained over. For example, the union may want to bargain over health benefits for retired workers or union participation in establishing company pricing policies, which management may choose not to bargain over. **Prohibited bargaining issues** such as the closed shop are statutorily outlawed.

The union must continuously gather information regarding membership dissatisfaction. The union steward is normally in the best position to collect such data. Because stewards are usually elected by their peers, they should be well-informed regarding union members' attitudes. The union steward constantly funnels information up through the union's chain of command where the data are compiled and analyzed. Union leadership attempts to uncover any areas of dissatisfaction because the general union membership must approve any agreement before it becomes final. It would be foolish for union leaders to demand management concessions and have the members reject their proposals. Because they must be elected, union leaders will lose their positions if the demands they make of management do not represent the desires of the general membership.

Management also spends long hours preparing for negotiations. The many interrelated tasks that management must accomplish are presented in Figure 16-2. In this example, the firm allows approximately six months to prepare for negotiations. All aspects of the current contracts are considered, including flaws that should be corrected. When preparing for negotiations, management should listen carefully to first-line supervisors. These individuals must administer the labor agreement on a day-to-day basis and must live with any error that management makes in negotiating the contract. An alert first-line supervisor is also able to inform upper management of the demands unions may plan to make during negotiations.

---

[11] Brown, "An Interview with Fritz Ihrig," p. 56.

TABLE 16-1 | Mandatory Bargaining Issues

- Wages
- Hours
- Discharge
- Arbitration
- Paid holidays
- Paid vacations
- Duration of agreement
- Grievance procedure
- Layoff plan
- Reinstatement of economic strikers
- Change of payment from hourly base to salary base
- Union security and checkoff of dues
- Work rules
- Merit wage increase
- Work schedule
- Lunch periods
- Rest periods
- Pension plan
- Retirement age
- Bonus payments
- Cancellation of seniority upon relocation of plant
- Discounts on company products
- Shift differentials
- Contract clause providing for supervisors keeping seniority in unit
- Procedures for income tax withholding
- Severance pay
- Nondiscriminatory hiring hall
- Plant rules
- Safety
- Prohibition against supervisor doing unit work
- Superseniority for union stewards
- Partial plant closing
- Hunting on employer's forest reserve where previously granted
- Plant closedown and relocation
- Change in operations resulting in reclassifying workers from incentive to straight time, or cut work force, or installation of cost saving machinery
- Price of meals provided by company
- Group insurance—health, accident, life
- Promotions
- Seniority
- Layoffs
- Transfers
- Work assignments and transfers
- No-strike clause
- Piece rates
- Stock purchase plan
- Workloads
- Change of employee status to independent contractors
- Motor carrier—union agreement providing that carriers use own equipment before leasing outside equipment
- Overtime pay
- Agency shop
- Sick leave
- Employer's insistence on clause giving arbitrator right to enforce award
- Management rights clause
- Plant closing
- Job posting procedures
- Plant reopening
- Employee physical examination
- Bargaining over "bar list"
- Truck rentals—minimum rental to be paid by carriers to employee-owned vehicles
- Arrangement for negotiation
- Change in insurance carrier and benefits
- Profit sharing plan
- Company houses
- Subcontracting
- Production ceiling imposed by union
- Most favored nation clause

Source: Reed Richardson, "Positive Collective Bargaining," Chapter 7.5 of *ASPA Handbook of Personnel and Industrial Relations*, pp. 7–120, 121. Copyright © 1979 by The Bureau of National Affairs, Inc., Washington, D.C. Reprinted by permission.

CHAPTER 16 Collective Bargaining

	September	October	November	December	January	February	March	April	May

(2) Analysis of Past grievances

(1) *Develop plan for negotiations

(11) Review the existing contract

(3) Compare contract with other contracts

(12) *Refine bargaining strategy

(4) Wage and benefit sureys*

(5) Compensation costs and personnel data*

(13) *Set bargaining guidelines

(6) *Designate bargaining team

(7) *Designate coordinating committee

(8) Coordination with other employers

(9) Contingency planning

(10) Communication programs

(14) Finalize proposals

*from Wages Committee

NEGOTIATIONS BEGIN — NEGOTIATIONS — CONTRACT EXPIRATION DATE

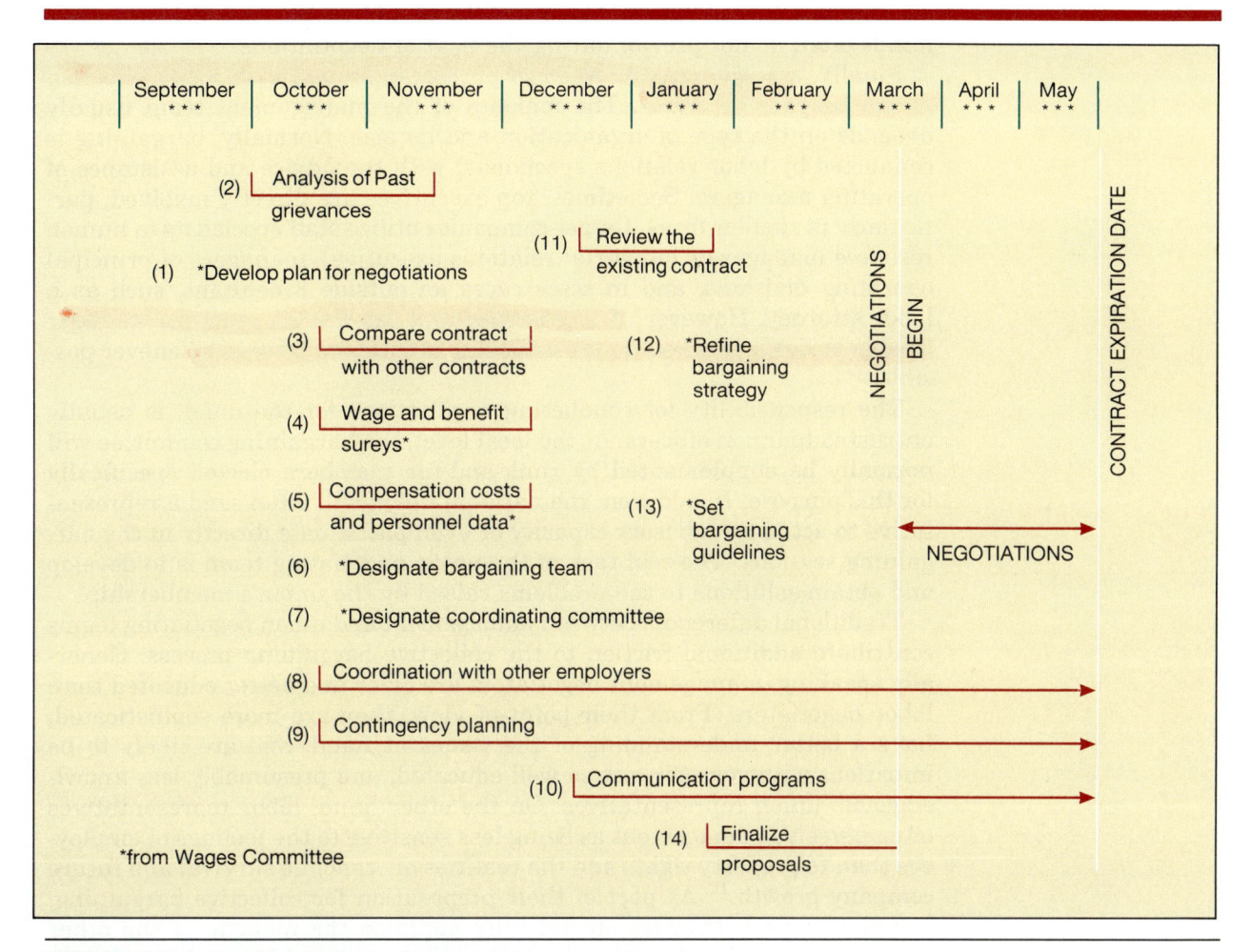

FIGURE 16-2 | An Example of Company Preparations for Negotiations

Source: Adapted from Ronald L. Miller, "Preparations for Negotiations," *Personnel Journal*, Copyright © January 1978. Reprinted with permission.

Management also attempts periodically to obtain information regarding employee attitudes. Surveys are often administered to workers to determine their feelings toward their jobs and job environment. When union and management representatives sit down at the bargaining table, both sides like to know as much as possible about employee attitudes.

Another part of preparation for negotiations involves identifying various positions that both union and management will take as the negotiations progress. Each usually takes an initial extreme position, representing the conditions union or management would prefer. The two sides will likely determine absolute limits to their offers or demands before a breakdown in negotiations occurs. They also will likely prepare fallback positions based on combinations of issues. Preparations should be detailed because clear minds often do not prevail during the heat of negotiations.

Finally, a major consideration in preparing for negotiations is selection of the bargaining teams. The makeup of the management team usually depends on the type of organization and its size. Normally, bargaining is conducted by labor relations specialists, with the advice and assistance of operating managers. Sometimes, top executives are directly involved, particularly in smaller firms. Larger companies utilize staff specialists (a human resource manager or industrial relations executive), managers of principal operating divisions, and in some cases an outside consultant, such as a labor attorney. However, it is essential that the human resource manager become actively involved in the collective bargaining process whenever possible.

The responsibility for conducting negotiations for the union is usually entrusted to union officers. At the local level, the bargaining committee will normally be supplemented by rank-and-file members elected specifically for this purpose. In addition, the national union will often send a representative to act in an advisory capacity or even participate directly in the bargaining sessions. The real task of the union negotiating team is to develop and obtain solutions to the problems raised by the union's membership.

Traditional differences between management and union negotiating teams contribute additional friction to the collective bargaining process. Generally speaking, management negotiators are older and better educated than labor negotiators. From their point of view, they are more sophisticated, have a better understanding of the issues at hand, and are likely to be impatient with younger, not so well educated, and presumably less knowledgeable union representatives. On the other hand, labor representatives often perceive management as being less sensitive to the feelings of employees than to property rights and the realities of economic survival and future company growth.[12] As part of their preparation for collective bargaining, negotiators on both sides should fully appraise the makeup of the other team in terms of their strengths and weaknesses and bring this information to bear in the negotiations.

■ BARGAINING ISSUES

The document that emerges from the collective bargaining process is called a labor agreement or contract. It regulates the relationship between employer and employees for a specified period of time. Each agreement is unique and there is no standard or universal model. Despite many dissimilarities, certain topics are included in virtually all labor agreements. These include recognition, management rights, union security, compensation and benefits, grievance procedure, employee security, and job-related factors.

---

[12] Levinson, p. 312.

Recognition

This section usually appears at the beginning of the labor agreement. Its purpose is to identify the union that is recognized as the bargaining representative and to describe the bargaining unit, that is, the employees for whom the union speaks. A typical recognition section might read:

> The XYZ Company recognizes the ABC Union as the sole and exclusive representative of the bargaining unit employees for the purpose of collective bargaining with regard to wages, hours, and other conditions of employment.

Management Rights

A section that is often, but not always, written into the labor agreement spells out the rights of management. If no management's rights section is included, management may reason that it retains control of all topics not described as bargainable in the contract. The precise content of the management rights section will vary by industry, company, and union. When included, management rights generally involve:

1. Freedom to select the business objectives of the company.
2. Freedom to determine the uses to which the material assets of the enterprise will be devoted.
3. Power to discipline for cause.[13]

In a brochure it publishes for all its first-line supervisors, AT&T describes management's rights when dealing with the union, including the following:

> You should remember that management has all such rights except those restricted by law or by contract with the union. You either make these decisions or carry them out through contact with your people. Some examples of these decisions and actions are:

- To determine what work is to be done and where, when, and how it is to be done.
- To determine the number of employees who will do the work.
- To supervise and instruct employees in doing the work.
- To correct employees whose work performance or personal conduct fails to meet reasonable standards. This includes administering discipline.
- To recommend hiring, dismissing, upgrading, or downgrading of employees.
- To recommend employees for promotion to management.[14]

---

[13] Edwin F. Beal and James P. Begin, *The Practice of Collective Bargaining*, 6th ed. (Homewood, Ill.: Richard D. Irwin, 1982), pp. 295–298.

[14] *Management/Employee/Union Relations* (Dallas: Southwestern Bell Telephone Company, December 1971), p. 3.

Union Security

Union security is typically one of the first items negotiated in a collective bargaining agreement. The objective of union security provisions is to ensure that the union continues to exist and perform its function. A strong union security provision makes it easier for the union to enroll and retain members. We describe some basic forms of union security clauses in the following paragraphs.

Closed Shop. A **closed shop** is an arrangement whereby union membership is a prerequisite to employment. Such provisions are generally illegal in the United States.

Union Shop. As we mentioned in Chapter 15, a **union shop** is a requirement that all employees become members of the union after a specified period of employment (the legal minimum is thirty days) or after a union shop provision has been negotiated. Employees must remain members of the union as a condition of employment. The union shop is generally legal in the United States, except in states that have right-to-work laws.

Maintenance of Membership. Employees who are members of the union at the time the labor agreement is signed, or who later voluntarily join, must continue their memberships until the termination of the agreement, as a condition of employment. This form of recognition is also prohibited in most states that have right-to-work laws.

Agency Shop. An **agency shop** provision does not require employees to join the union; however, the labor agreement requires, as a condition of employment, that each nonunion member of the bargaining unit must "pay the union the equivalent of membership dues as a kind of tax, or service charge, in return for the union acting as the bargaining agent."[15] The agency shop is outlawed in most states that have right-to-work laws.

Exclusive Bargaining Shop. Thirteen of the twenty-one states having right-to-work laws allow only exclusive bargaining shop provisions. Under this form of recognition, the company is legally bound to deal with the union that has achieved recognition, but employees are not obligated to join or maintain membership in the union or to financially contribute to it.

Open Shop. An open shop describes the absence of union security rather than its presence. The **open shop**, strictly defined, is employment that is open on equal terms to union members and nonmembers alike. Under this arrangement, no employee is required to join or financially contribute to the union.

Dues Checkoff. Another type of security that unions attempt to achieve is the checkoff of dues. A checkoff agreement may be used in addition to

---
[15] Beal and Begin, p. 286.

CHAPTER 16   Collective Bargaining   611

any of the previously mentioned "shop" agreements. Under the **checkoff of dues** provision, the company agrees to withhold union dues from members' paychecks and to forward the money directly to the union. Because of provisions in the Taft–Hartley Act, each union member must voluntarily sign a statement authorizing this deduction. Dues checkoff is important to the union because it eliminates much of the expense, time, and hassle of collecting dues from each member every pay period or once a month.

Compensation and Benefits

This section typically constitutes a large portion of most labor agreements. The importance of compensation and benefits is illustrated in a 1987 survey of union members. Those surveyed ranked pay, pensions, and benefits as the second, third, and fifth most important compensation-related items.[16] Virtually any item that can affect compensation and benefits may be included in labor agreements. Some of the items frequently covered are:

- *Wage rate schedule*. The base rates to be paid each year of the contract for each job are included in this section. At times, unions are able to obtain a cost-of-living allowance (COLA) or escalator clause in the contract in order to protect the purchasing power of employees' earnings. These clauses are generally related to the Consumer Price Index (CPI) prepared by the Bureau of Labor Statistics.
- *Overtime and premium pay*. Provisions covering hours of work, overtime, and premium pay, such as shift differentials, are included in this section.
- *Jury pay*. Some firms pay an employee's entire salary when he or she is serving jury duty. Others pay the difference between jury pay and the compensation that would have been earned. The procedure covering jury pay is typically stated in the contract.
- *Layoff or severance pay*. The amount that employees in various jobs and/or seniority levels will be paid if they are laid off or terminated is presented in this section.
- *Holidays*. The holidays to be recognized and the amount of pay that a worker will receive if he or she has to work on a holiday are specified. In addition, the pay procedure for times when a holiday falls on a worker's normal day off is provided.
- *Vacation*. This section spells out the amount of vacation that a person may take, based on seniority. Any restrictions as to when the vacation may be taken are also stated.

Grievance Procedure

A portion of most labor agreements is devoted to a grievance procedure. It contains the means whereby employees can voice dissatisfaction with and appeal specific management actions. Also included in this section are the

---
[16] Shane R. Premeaux, R. Wayne Mondy, and Art L. Bethke, "Decertification: Fulfilling Unions' Destiny?" *Personnel Journal*, 32 (June 1987), p. 148.

procedures for disciplinary action by management and the termination procedure that must be followed. We devote a portion of Chapter 18 to disciplinary action and the grievance process.

Employee Security

This section of the labor agreement establishes the procedures that cover job security for individual employees. According to a 1987 survey, employee security was the prime concern of union members.[17] Seniority and grievance handling procedures are the key topics related to employee security. Seniority is determined by the amount of time that an employee has worked in various capacities with the firm. Seniority may be companywide, by division, by department, or by job. Agreement on seniority is important because the person with the most seniority, as defined in the labor agreement, is typically the last to be laid off and the first to be recalled. The seniority system also provides a basis for promotion decisions. When qualifications are met, employees with the greatest seniority will likely be considered first for promotion to higher level jobs.

Job-Related Factors

Many of the rules governing employee actions on the job are included here. Some of the more important factors are company work rules, work standards, and rules related to safety. This section varies, depending on the nature of the industry and the product manufactured. Work rules are vitally important to both employers and employees. In fact, 84 percent of the employers surveyed in 1987 planned to seek to relax restrictive work rules in future contracts.[18]

■ NEGOTIATING THE AGREEMENT

There is no way to ensure speedy and mutually acceptable results from negotiations. At best, the parties can attempt to create an atmosphere that will lend itself to steady progress and productive results. For example, the two negotiating teams usually meet at an agreed-on neutral site, such as a hotel. It is generally important that a favorable relationship be established early in order to avoid "eleventh hour" bargaining.[19] It is equally important that union and management negotiators strive to develop and maintain clear and open lines of communication. Collective bargaining is a problem-solving activity, so good communication is essential to its success. Negoti-

---

[17] *Ibid.*

[18] Fernandez, p. 63.

[19] Eleventh-hour bargaining refers to last-minute settlement attempts just prior to the expiration date of an existing agreement. Failure to reach agreement in this manner frequently results in a strike.

ations should be conducted in the privacy of the conference room, not in the news media. If the negotiators feel that publicity is necessary, joint releases to the media may avoid unnecessary conflict.

The negotiating phase of collective bargaining begins with each side presenting its initial demands. Because a collective bargaining settlement can be expensive for a firm, the cost of various proposals should be estimated as accurately as possible. Some changes can be quite expensive, others cost little if anything, but the cost of the various proposals being considered must always be carefully deliberated. The term negotiating suggests a certain amount of give and take, the purpose of which is to lower the other side's expectations. The union will bargain to upgrade their members' economic and working conditions. The company will negotiate to maintain or enhance profitability. One of the most costly components of any collective bargaining agreement is a wage increase provision. An example of the negotiation of a wage increase is shown in Figure 16-3.

In this example, labor initially demands a $0.40 per hour increase. Management counters with an offer of only $0.10 per hour. Both labor and management—as expected—reject each other's demand. Plan B calls for labor to lower its demand to a $0.30 per hour increase. Management counters with an offer of $0.20. The positions in Plan B are feasible to both sides, as both groups are in the bargaining zone. Wages within the bargaining zone are those that management and labor can both accept, in this case an increase of between $0.20 and $0.30 per hour. The exact amount will be determined by the power of the bargaining unit and the skills of the negotiators.

The realities of negotiations are not for the weak of heart and at times are similar to a high-stakes poker game. A certain amount of bluffing and raising of the ante takes place in many negotiations. The ultimate bluff for the union would be when a negotiator says, "If our demands are not met, we are prepared to strike." Management's version of this bluff would be to threaten a lockout. We will discuss each of these tactics later, but utilizing them is a form of power politics. The party with the greater leverage can expect to extract the most concessions. In recent years, management has gained negotiating power, with 84 percent of union members surveyed believing that management now has the upper hand in labor negotiations.[20]

Even though one party in the negotiating process may appear to possess the greater power, negotiators often take care to keep the other side from losing face. They recognize that the balance of power may switch rapidly. By the time the next round of negotiations occurs, the pendulum may be swinging back in favor of the other side. Even when management appears to have the upper hand, it may make minor concessions that will allow the labor leader to claim gains for the union. Management may demand that workers pay for grease rags that are lost (assuming that the loss of these rags has become excessive). In order to obtain labor's agreement to this demand, management may agree to provide new uniforms for the workers

---

[20] R. Wayne Mondy and Shane R. Premeaux, "The Labor/Management Power Relationship Revisited," *Personnel Administrator*, 30 (May 1985), p. 55.

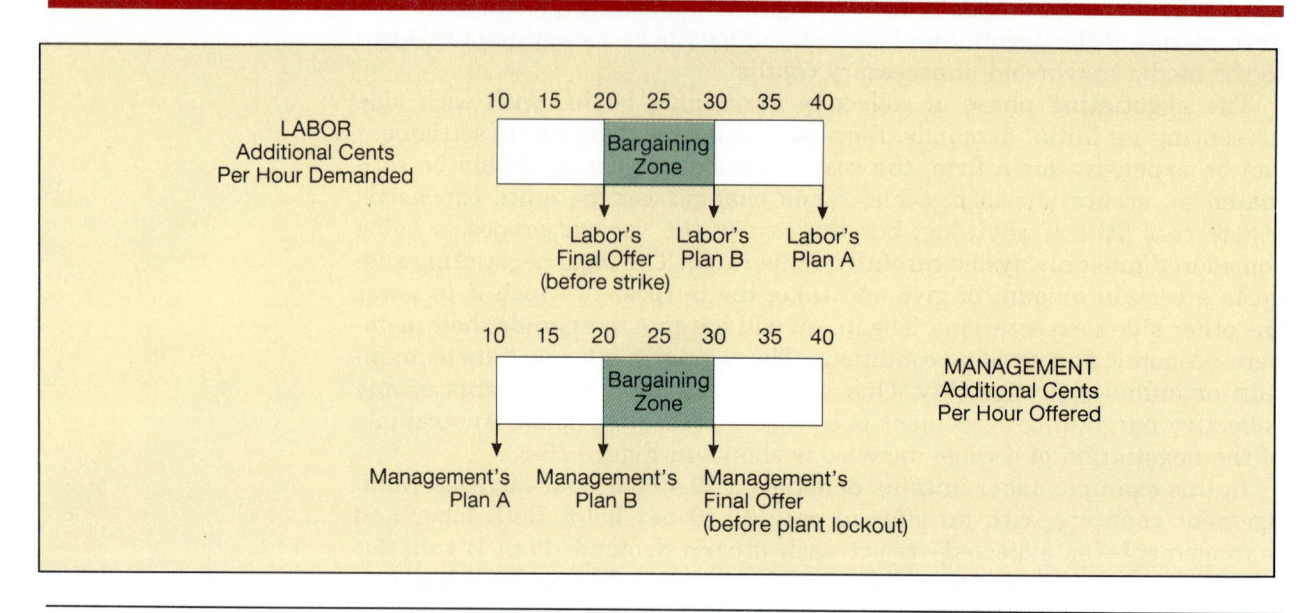

FIGURE 16-3 | An Example of Negotiating a Wage Increase

if the cost of these uniforms would be less than the cost of lost rags. Thus labor leaders, although forced to concede to management's demand, could show the workers that they have obtained a concession from management.

As we mentioned previously, each side usually does not expect to obtain all the demands presented in its first proposal. However, management must remember that a concession may be difficult to reverse in future negotiations. For instance, if management agreed to provide dental benefits, withdrawing these benefits in the next round of negotiations would be difficult. Labor, on the other hand, can lose a demand and continue to bring it up in the future. Demands that the union does not expect to receive when they are first made are known as **beachhead demands**.

■ BREAKDOWNS IN NEGOTIATIONS

At times negotiations break down, even though both labor and management may sincerely want to arrive at an equitable contract settlement. Several means of removing roadblocks may be used in order to get negotiations moving again. Breakdowns in negotiations can be overcome through third-party intervention, union strategies, and management strategies.

Third-Party Intervention

Often an outside person can intervene to provide assistance when an agreement cannot be reached and a breakdown occurs—that is, when the two sides reach an impasse. The reasons behind each party's position may be quite rational. Or the breakdown may be related to emotional disputes that tend to become distorted during the heat of negotiations. Regardless of the cause, something must be done to continue the negotiations. The two basic types of third-party intervention are mediation and arbitration.

Mediation. In **mediation**, a neutral third party enters a labor dispute when a bargaining impasse has occurred. The objective of mediation is to persuade the parties to resume negotiations and reach a settlement. A mediator has no power to force a settlement but can help in the search for solutions, make recommendations, and work to open blocked channels of communication. Successful mediation depends to a substantial degree on the tact, diplomacy, patience, and perseverance of the mediator. The mediator's fresh insights are used to get discussions going again.

Arbitration. In **arbitration**, a dispute is submitted to an impartial third party for a binding decision. Arbitration is very much a part of many human resource managers' jobs. Remember that Marsha Slaughter, in her Executive Insight, stated that "the experience and knowledge acquired researching and preparing arbitration cases and serving on bargaining committees greatly enhanced her career." There are two principal types of union–management disputes: rights disputes and interests disputes. Those that involve disputes over the interpretation and application of the various provisions of an existing contract are referred to as rights arbitration. This type of arbitration is used in settling grievances. Grievance arbitration is common in the United States and is discussed in Chapter 18. The other type of arbitration, interest arbitration, involves disputes over the terms of proposed collective bargaining agreements. In the private sector, the use of interest arbitration as an alternative procedure for impasse resolution is not a common practice. Unions and employers rarely agree to submit the basic terms of a contract (such as wages, hours, and working conditions) to a neutral party for disposition. They prefer to rely on collective bargaining and the threat of economic pressure (such as strikes and lockouts) to decide these issues.[21]

In the public sector, most governmental jurisdictions prohibit their employees from striking. As a result, interest arbitration is used to a greater extent than in the private sector. Although there is no uniform application of this method, fourteen states have legislation permitting the use of interest arbitration to settle unresolved issues for public employees. In a number of states, compulsory arbitration of interest items is required at various jurisdictional levels.[22] A procedure used in the public sector is final-offer arbitration, which has two basic forms: package selection and issue-by-issue selection. In package selection, the arbitrator must select one party's entire offer on all issues in dispute. In issue-by-issue selection, the

---

[21] Raymond A. Smardon, "Arbitration Is No Bargain," *Nation's Business* (October 1974), pp. 80–83.
[22] Benjamin J. Taylor and Fred Witney, *Labor Relations Law*, 4th ed. (Englewood Cliffs, N.J.: Prentice-Hall, 1983), pp. 652–653.

arbitrator examines each issue separately and chooses one or the other party's final offer on each issue.[23]

Sources of Mediators and Arbitrators

The principal organization involved in mediation efforts, other than some state and local agencies, is the Federal Mediation and Conciliation Service (FMCS). The FMCS was established as an independent agency by the Taft–Hartley Act in 1947. Either or both parties involved in negotiations can seek the assistance of the FMCS, or the agency can offer its help if it feels that the situation warrants. Federal law requires that the party wishing to change a contract must give notice of this intention to the other party sixty days prior to the expiration of a contract. If no agreement has been reached thirty days prior to the expiration date, the FMCS must be notified.

In arbitration, the disputants are free to select any person as their arbitrator, so long as they agree on the selection. Most commonly, however, they make a request for an arbitrator to either the American Arbitration Association (AAA) or the FMCS. The AAA is a nonprofit organization with offices in many cities. Both the AAA and the FMCS maintain lists of arbitrators. Only people who can show, through references, experience in labor–management relations, and acceptance by both labor and management as neutrals are selected for inclusion on these lists.[24]

Union Strategies for Overcoming Negotiation Breakdowns

There are times when a union believes that it must exert extreme pressure to get management to agree to its bargaining demands. Strikes and boycotts are the primary means that the union may use to overcome breakdowns in negotiations.

Strikes. When union members refuse to work in order to exert pressure on management in negotiations, their action is referred to as a **strike**. A strike halts production, resulting in lost customers and revenue, which the union hopes will force management to submit to its terms.

The timing of a strike is important in determining its effectiveness. An excellent time is when business is thriving and the demand for the firm's goods or services is expanding. However, the union might be hard-pressed to obtain major concessions from a strike if the firm's sales are down and it has built up a large inventory. In this instance, the company would not be severely damaged.

Contrary to many opinions, unions prefer to use the strike only as a last resort. In recent years, many union members have been even more reluc-

---

[23] Robert E. Allen and Timothy J. Keaveny, *Contemporary Labor Relations* (Reading, Mass.: Addison-Wesley, 1983), pp. 558–559.

[24] Donald Austin Woolf, "Arbitration in One Easy Lesson: A Review of Criteria Used in Arbitration Awards," *Personnel*, 55 (September–October 1978), p. 76.

tant to strike because of the fear of being replaced. A 1989 Supreme Court ruled that when a union goes on strike and the company hires replacements, they do not have to lay off these individuals at the end of the strike. Strikes are extremely expensive not only for the employer, but also for the union and its members. A union's treasury is often depleted by payment of strike benefits to its members. In addition, members suffer because they aren't receiving their normal pay. Although strike benefits help, union members certainly cannot maintain a normal standard of living on them because they are minimal. Sometimes during negotiations (especially at the beginning) the union may want to strengthen its negotiating position by taking a strike vote. Members often give overwhelming approval to a strike. This vote does not necessarily mean that there will be a strike, only that the union leaders now have the authority to call one if negotiations reach an impasse. A favorable strike vote can add a sense of urgency to efforts to reach an agreement.[25]

Successful passage of a strike vote has additional implications for union members. Virtually every national union's constitution contains a clause requiring the members to support and participate in a strike if one is called. If a union member fails to comply with this requirement, he or she can be fined. Thus union members place themselves in jeopardy if they cross a picket line without the consent of the union. Fines may be as high as 100 percent of wages for as long as union pickets remain outside the company. However, the Supreme Court has ruled that an employee on strike may resign from the union during a strike and avoid being punished by the union. More subtle measures, such as sickouts and work slowdowns, have been used successfully by union members in order to avoid the impact of a strike on the membership and still bring pressure on the company to meet union demands.

Boycotts. The boycott is another of labor's weapons to get management to agree to its demands. A **boycott** involves an agreement by union members to refuse to use or buy the firm's products. A boycott exerts economic pressure on management, and the effect often lasts much longer than that of a strike. Once shoppers change buying habits, their behavior will likely continue long after the boycott has ended. At times, significant pressures can be exerted on a business when union members, their families, and friends refuse to purchase the firm's products and encourage the public not to patronize the firm. This approach is especially effective when the products are sold at retail outlets and are easily identifiable by brand name. For instance, the decade-old boycott against Adolph Coors Company, which ended in the summer of 1987, was effective because the product, beer, was directly associated with the company.[26] The practice of a union attempting to encourage third parties (such as suppliers and customers) to stop doing business with the firm is known as a **secondary boycott**. This type of boycott was declared illegal by the Taft–Hartley Act.

---

[25] Beal and Begin, pp. 221–222.
[26] Sandra Atchison and Aaron Bernstein, "A Silver Bullet for the Union Drive at Coors?" *Business Week* (July 11, 1988), p. 61.

Management's Strategies for Overcoming Negotiation Breakdowns

Management may also use various strategies to encourage unions to come back to the bargaining table. One form of action that is somewhat analogous to a strike is called a lockout. In a **lockout**, management keeps employees out of the workplace and may run the operation with management personnel and/or temporary replacements. Unable to work, the employees do not get paid. Although the lockout is used rather infrequently, the fear of a lockout may bring labor back to the bargaining table. A lockout is particularly effective when management is dealing with a weak union, when the union treasury is depleted, or when the business has excessive inventories.

Another course of action that a company can take if the union strikes is to operate the firm by placing management and nonunion workers in the striking workers' jobs. The type of industry involved has considerable effect on the impact of this maneuver. If the firm is not labor intensive and if maintenance demands are not high, as at a petroleum refinery or a chemical plant, this practice may be quite effective. When it is utilized, management will likely attempt to show how production actually increases with the use of nonunion employees. For example, unionized employees at Southwestern Bell Telephone Company went on strike and the company continued to provide virtually uninterrupted service to consumers. At times management personnel will actually live in the plant and have food and other necessities delivered to them.

Another way management can continue operating a firm during a strike is by hiring replacements for the strikers. Hiring replacements on either a temporary or a permanent basis is legal when the employees are engaged in an economic strike, that is, one that is part of a collective bargaining dispute. However, a company that takes these courses of action risks inviting violence and creating bitterness among its employees which may adversely affect the firm's performance long after the strike has ended.

■ RATIFYING THE AGREEMENT

Most collective bargaining leads to an agreement without a breakdown in negotiations or disruptive actions. Typically, agreement is reached before the current contract expires. After the negotiators have reached a tentative agreement on all contract terms, they prepare a written agreement covering those terms, complete with the effective and termination dates. The approval process for management is often easier than for labor. The president or CEO has usually been briefed regularly on the progress of negotiations. Any difficulty that might have stood in the way of obtaining approval has likely already been resolved with top management by the negotiators.

However, the approval process is more complex for the union. Until a majority of members voting in a ratification election approve it, the proposed agreement is not final. At times, union members reject the proposal and a new round of negotiations must begin. In recent years, approximately 10 percent of all tentative agreements have been rejected when presented to the union membership. Many of these rejections might not have occurred if union negotiators had been better informed of the desires of the membership.

■ ADMINISTERING THE AGREEMENT

Negotiating, as it relates to the total collective bargaining process, may be likened to the tip of an iceberg. It is the visible phase, the part that makes the news. The larger and perhaps more important part of collective bargaining is administration of the agreement, which is seldom viewed by the public.[27] The agreement establishes the union–management relationship for the duration of the contract. Usually, neither party can change the contract's language until the expiration date, except by mutual consent. However, the main problem encountered in contract administration is uniform interpretation and application of the contract's terms. Administering the contract is a day-to-day activity. Ideally, the aim of both management and the union is to make the agreement work to the benefit of all concerned. Often, this is not an easy task.

Management is primarily responsible for explaining and implementing the agreement. This process should begin with meetings or training sessions not only to point out significant features but also to provide a clause-by-clause analysis of the contract. First-line supervisors in particular need to know their responsibilities and what to do when disagreements arise. Additionally, supervisors and middle managers should be encouraged to notify top management of any contract modifications or new provisions required for the next round of negotiations.

The human resource manager plays a key role in the day-to-day administration of the contract. He or she gives advice on matters of discipline, works to resolve grievances, and helps first-line supervisors establish good working relationships within the terms of the agreement. As we mentioned previously, when a firm is unionized, the HRM function tends to change rather significantly, and it may even be divided into separate human resources and industrial relations departments. The Bendix Corporation provides an excellent example of this separation of activities. The company has both a vice-president of human resources and a vice-president of industrial relations (see Figures 16-4 and 16-5). In situations such as this, the vice-president of human resources may perform all human resource management tasks with the exception of industrial relations. The vice-president of industrial relations would likely deal with all union-related matters. As one vice-president of industrial relations stated:

> My first challenge is, wherever possible, to keep the company union-free and the control of its operations in the hands of corporate management at all levels. Where unions represent our employees, the problem becomes one of negotiating collective bargaining agreements which our company can live with, adminis-

---

[27] Harold W. Davey, *Contemporary Collective Bargaining*, 3rd ed. (Englewood Cliffs, N.J.: Prentice-Hall, 1972), p. 141.

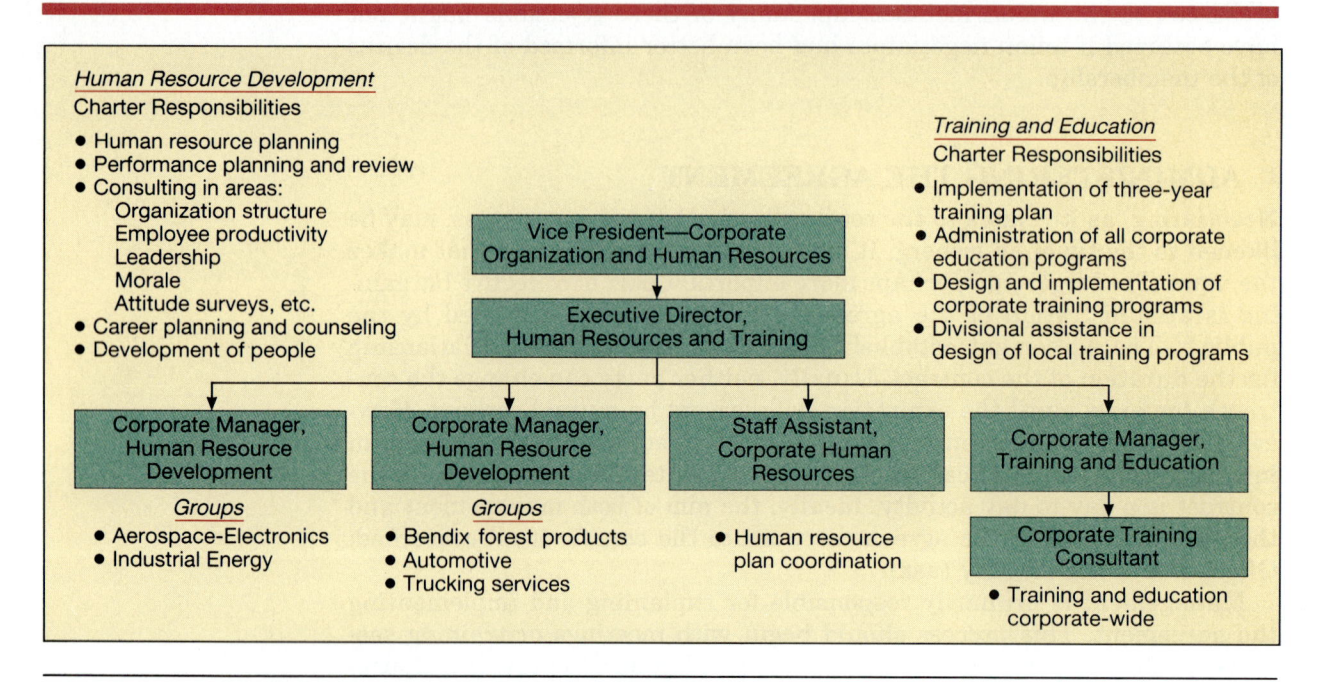

FIGURE 16-4 | The Organization of the Human Resource Department at Bendix Corporation

Human Resource Development
Charter Responsibilities

- Human resource planning
- Performance planning and review
- Consulting in areas:
  - Organization structure
  - Employee productivity
  - Leadership
  - Morale
  - Attitude surveys, etc.
- Career planning and counseling
- Development of people

Training and Education
Charter Responsibilities

- Implementation of three-year training plan
- Administration of all corporate education programs
- Design and implementation of corporate training programs
- Divisional assistance in design of local training programs

Vice President—Corporate Organization and Human Resources
↓
Executive Director, Human Resources and Training

- Corporate Manager, Human Resource Development
  Groups
  - Aerospace-Electronics
  - Industrial Energy
- Corporate Manager, Human Resource Development
  Groups
  - Bendix forest products
  - Automotive
  - Trucking services
- Staff Assistant, Corporate Human Resources
  - Human resource plan coordination
- Corporate Manager, Training and Education
  ↓
  Corporate Training Consultant
  - Training and education corporate-wide

Source: Bendix Corporation.

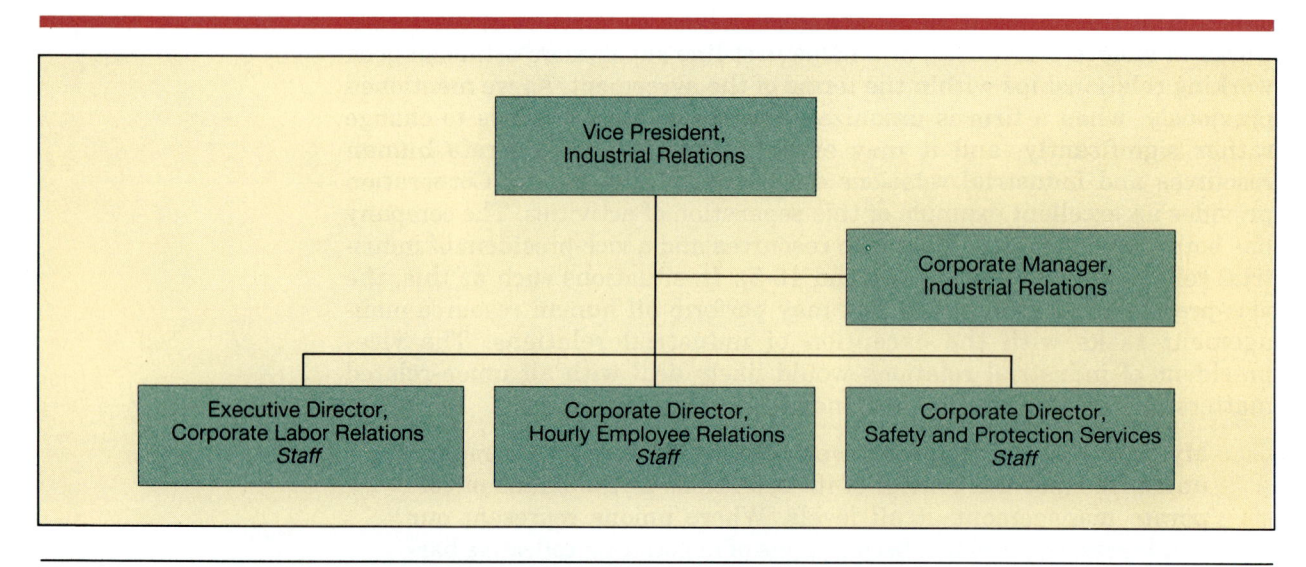

FIGURE 16-5 | The Corporate Industrial Relations Department at Bendix Corporation by Functional Responsibility

Vice President, Industrial Relations

- Corporate Manager, Industrial Relations
- Executive Director, Corporate Labor Relations *Staff*
- Corporate Director, Hourly Employee Relations *Staff*
- Corporate Director, Safety and Protection Services *Staff*

Source: Bendix Corporation.

HRM In Action

"I think I might have messed up this morning," said the maintenance supervisor, Carlos Chavez, to Doug Williams, the industrial relations manager. "One of the workers in my section wasn't doing the job exactly to specs and I blew up and told him to hit the road. Five minutes later the union steward was in the office reading me the riot act. She said something like situations such as this are covered in our contract and that I was violating it. I had never spoken to the worker before about that particular offense and the steward said the contract called for both oral and written warnings before termination."

How would you respond?

tering these labor agreements with the company's interests paramount (consistent with good employee relations), and trying to solve all grievances arising under the labor agreement short of their going to arbitration, without giving away the store.

■ THE FUTURE OF COLLECTIVE BARGAINING

The collective bargaining process and the labor movement both have changed in recent years. They no doubt will change further in the years ahead in response to forces of varying magnitude and conflicting perspectives.

Industrial and Occupational Change

Of the many environmental conditions that shape an organization's labor–management relations, none is more pervasive or dominant than the market for the firm's goods or services and its own labor market.[28] In the 1980s, the trend was toward increased competition within product markets. This trend has a strong international dimension, reflecting the growing interdependence of world markets and will, in all likelihood, continue into the 1990s. Competition fosters innovation, opens up new market opportunities, and creates new jobs. Firms in mature markets, however, with fewer prospects for growth and expansion, cannot offer a wide variety of job opportunities. In such situations, employers and employees alike need to concern themselves with career transitions, job losses, and organizational restructuring.

---
[28] Thomas A. Kochan and Thomas A. Barocci, *Human Resource Management and Labor Relations* (Boston: Little, Brown, 1985), pp. 528–529.

Historically, unions have had their greatest success in the manufacturing, mining, transportation, and construction industries. With the relative decline in importance of these industries and the relative growth in importance of service industries, union membership has declined. Major increases in employment have taken place in wholesale and retail trades; finance and insurance; general service industries; and federal, state, and local government. However, with the exception of government, these industries have had low union membership in the past.[29]

The pattern of employment by occupation has also changed markedly over time. Major changes in white-collar occupations include increases in the number of professional and clerical employees. In blue-collar occupations, the proportion of operative employees increased through 1950; then a long-term decline in the use of laborers and an increase in service occupations occurred.[30] It is also interesting to note that between 1955 and 1984 a larger proportion of industrial workers were assigned to nonproduction jobs.[31] The shift toward more professional, services, and white-collar occupations implies that future employees may well have different expectations of their work. Not only may labor need to rethink its organizing strategy, but management also needs to sharpen its managerial skills in negotiating and team building.

In addition, the composition of the labor force will change dramatically in the future. New entrants in the labor force from 1985 to the year 2000 are expected to be 15 percent U.S. born white men, 42 percent U.S. born white women, 7 percent U.S. born nonwhite men, 13 percent U.S. born nonwhite women, 13 percent immigrant men, and 10 percent immigrant women.[32] Union leadership will need to redefine organizing strategies to attract those who will account for future growth in the U.S. employment sector.

Multinational Corporations and Foreign Competition

Unions often point to multinational corporations as an important cause of U.S. economic problems, especially unemployment. Many companies have located part or all of their operations outside the United States to take advantage of lower labor and material costs and favorable tax laws. Investment funds have been diverted to foreign operations, costing the U.S. economy jobs.[33] However, Japanese and European firms have invested significantly in U.S. marketing and manufacturing, which has created new jobs here in the United States. As these firms hire American workers, some interesting collective bargaining situations will likely be created.

---

[29] David A. Dilts and Clarence R. Deitsch, *Labor Relations*, (New York: Macmillan, 1983), p. 363.

[30] John A. Fossum, *Labor Relations*, 3rd ed. (Plano, Tex.: Business Publications, 1985), pp. 472–473.

[31] *Ibid.*, pp. 475–477.

[32] Bruce Nussbaum, "Needed: Human Capital," *Business Week* (September 19, 1988), p. 103.

[33] Dilts and Deitsch, pp. 364–365.

Foreign competition has had major impacts on employment in several U.S. industries already. The shoe, apparel, auto, steel, and rubber industries have lost jobs, and their remaining employees have also felt the effects at the bargaining table in terms of wage and work-rule concessions.[34]

Obviously, unionism and collective bargaining in the future will not be as they are today. Global competition will no longer allow highly structured bargaining linking wages and benefits to macroeconomic factors, rather than company-specific performance.[35] No longer can the process of collective bargaining and unionism be considered domestic issues; they must be considered in global terms. Labor and management must evolve to compete effectively in the global economy. Neither labor or management can expect to hold on to the practices of the past because today's global economy will not tolerate such entrenched behavior.

■ TECHNOLOGY AND PRODUCTIVITY

Several events have occurred in a relatively short period of time to complicate labor relations and the collective bargaining process. One of the most dramatic developments is the science of robotics. The microprocessor and the silicon chip gave robots greater capabilities than had previously been envisioned.[36] Now in their second generation, robots have senses of vision and touch. Utilization of robots in manufacturing has increased dramatically in the last decade, with the number currently in use approaching 120,000.[37]

Technology may have an even greater impact on future work environment. It appears that the new machines will continue to reduce the number of jobs available in the years ahead and will alter the nature of the work performed.[38] The increased use of robots is often supported because of the growing concern for quality control and competitiveness in international markets. Without doubt, this technology increases productivity. Union leaders, however, have recently bargained for advance notice of robot installation and for retraining rights so that workers can learn new skills for long-term employment.

Of much concern in the United States is the relatively slow rate of growth in productivity compared to that for other industrialized nations. According to a 1986 U.S. Department of Commerce report, the rate of growth in productivity in the United States is less than that in Japan, Canada, the United Kingdom, France, and the Federal Republic of Germany. Although the gap has begun to narrow, the major challenge facing U.S. management during the 1990s is to achieve productivity growth to ensure that the United States remains as it has always been, the most productive nation in the

---

[34] Fossum, pp. 364–365.

[35] Alexander B. Trowbridge, "A Management Look at Labor Relations," *Unions in Transition* (San Francisco: ICS Press, 1988), p. 417.

[36] Michael R. Carrell and Christina Heavrin, *Collective Bargaining and Labor Relations* (Columbus, Ohio: Charles E. Merrill, 1985), pp. 411–412.

[37] Allen and Keaveny, pp. 634–635.

[38] *Ibid.*

world. To do so, U.S. management and labor need to find ways to improve cooperation and productivity. Such improvements could benefit both management and labor through increased profits and better job security.

Concession Bargaining

Beginning in 1980, a new bargaining process referred to as concession, giveback, or nontraditional bargaining emerged. Many industries were suffering economic hardship—because of deregulation in some cases and foreign competition in others—reflected in high rates of unemployment and business failures. Employees in a number of industries approved deferral of pay increases, reduced benefits, and work-rule changes. Some of the industries in which workers made concessions were railroads, retailing, auto, rubber, airlines, and meat packing. In return for employee concessions, employers generally agree to demands such as:

- Increased job security.
- Profit-sharing plans.
- Participation in some areas of decision making.
- Equality of sacrifice.[39]
- Financial support.
- Retraining of displaced workers.
- Employee ownership.
- Quality of worklife plans.[40]

These programs require management and union cooperation to solve the problems of the organization and provide mutual benefits. The essence of successful and continued concession bargaining is the development of mutual trust and respect by both parties.

Conclusions

The outlook for organized labor isn't very bright. Union membership as a percentage of the total labor force is dropping; its traditional blue-collar industrial base is melting away. Domestic manufacturers are moving operations overseas, and foreign firms are flooding the U.S. market with goods. Productivity increases in this country are lagging behind those of most of the industrialized nations, and new technology is taking away jobs. Workers have given up pay raises and benefits to keep their jobs. A new wage system of unequal pay for equal work is being negotiated in a growing number of companies. Such reverses for organized labor have generated changes in unions' strategy, tactics, and leadership.

Maybe now is the time for labor and management to move away from adversarial toward cooperative union–management relationships. Neither has to give up anything—they just need to pool their strengths. Harvard

---

[39] Carrell and Heavrin, pp. 420–422.
[40] Chaison and Plovnick, p. 118.

professor D. Quinn Mills knows the turmoil that gave birth to the modern union movement.[41] However, he sees little trust between management and labor, and envisions a real adversarial system. In the past, collective bargaining was practiced primarily as rule-making, which is self-defeating for both parties. Management now needs fewer rules for, and willing cooperation from, the workforce. Unions need company management that is sensitive to the needs of the workers. Mondy and Premeaux came to a similar conclusion when they observed, "Now is the time for management to lessen its adversarial relationship with union members and build cooperation between union and management . . . [to] build for the future."[42]

But Ben Fisher, for thirty years a major negotiator for the United Steelworkers of America, notes that "although there is general agreement that job security is at the heart of current bargaining concerns, it is not always admitted that long-run job security first requires that there be jobs."[43] He believes that if the workplace is not competitive, there is no hope for the people involved. The overriding issue for the U.S. economy is jobs, and successful businesses create jobs. American workers need jobs—good and secure jobs in order to improve their real standard of living. If management does not recognize the depth of labor's difficulties, it is likely to compound the problem. Labor relations must target issues that are crucial to workers, as well as management.

SUMMARY

Collective bargaining is fundamental to management–labor relations in the United States. Labor and management go through periods in which one has the power to dictate the majority of terms to the other party. During the 1980s—and for the foreseeable future—management had—and is expected to have—the power advantage in collective bargaining.

Its structure can affect how collective bargaining is conducted. The four major types of structure are: (1) one company dealing with a single union; (2) several companies dealing with a single union; (3) several unions dealing with a single company; and (4) several companies dealing with several unions. Another environmental factor influencing collective bargaining is the current union–management relationship. It may allow the collective bargaining process to be relatively simple, or it may cause a long, tense struggle.

When a firm is unionized, the role of human resource management tends to change rather significantly. In major corporations in which the large majority of the operative employees belong to unions, the HRM function

---

[41] See D. Quinn Mills, "Reforming the U.S. System of Collective Bargaining," *Monthly Labor Review* (March 1983), pp. 18–22.
[42] Mondy and Premeaux, "The Labor/Management Power Relationship Revisited," p. 55.
[43] See Ben Fischer, "Labor's Dilemma: Adapting to Post-Recession Unionism," *Industry Week* (August 6, 1984), pp. 41–44.

may even be divided into separate human resources and industrial relations departments. The human resource manager must maintain contact with first-line managers before, during, and after collective bargaining. These supervisors administer the contract and know whether it is working.

There are three collective bargaining categories: mandatory, permissive, and prohibited. Mandatory bargaining issues fall within the definition of wages, hours, and other terms and conditions of employment. Permissive bargaining issues may be raised, but neither side may insist that they be bargained over. Prohibited bargaining issues are those issues that are statutorily outlawed and thus illegal.

The document produced by the collective bargaining process is called a labor agreement or contract. It regulates the relationship between the employer and the employees for a specified period of time. Each agreement is unique, and there is no standard or universal model. Despite many dissimilarities, certain topics are included in virtually all labor agreements: recognition, management rights, union security, compensation and benefits, grievance procedure, employee security, and job-related factors.

Union security is typically one of the first items negotiated in a collective bargaining agreement. This section could specify a closed shop, a union shop, an exclusive bargaining shop, or an open shop. Under a checkoff of dues provision, the company agrees to withhold union dues from members' checks and to forward the money directly to the union.

At times negotiations break down, even though both labor and management may sincerely want to arrive at an equitable contract settlement. Several means of removing roadblocks may be used in order to get negotiations moving again, including third-party intervention, union strategies, and management strategies.

The two basic types of third-party intervention are mediation and arbitration. Strikes and boycotts are the primary means that the union may use to overcome a breakdown in negotiations. When union members refuse to work in order to exert pressure on management in negotiations, their action is referred to as a strike. A boycott involves an agreement by union members to refuse to use or buy the firm's products.

Management may also use various strategies to encourage unions to resume negotiations. In a lockout, management keeps employees out of the workplace and may run the operation with management personnel and/or temporary replacements. Management can continue operations during a strike by utilizing management personnel and hiring nonunion replacements for the strikers.

Unions often point to multinational corporations as an important cause of U.S. economic problems, especially unemployment. Foreign competition has had a major impact on employment in several U.S. industries already. The shoe, apparel, auto, steel, and rubber industries have lost jobs, and their remaining employees have also felt the effects at the bargaining table in terms of wage and work-rule concessions. Developments such as increased management flexibility, gainsharing, and employee identification with productivity are necessary to compete effectively in a global environment. These factors must therefore be considered in many collective bargaining situations and will affect the future of unionism in the United States.

Questions for Review

1. Describe the basic steps involved in the collective bargaining process.
2. Distinguish among mandatory, permissive, and prohibited bargaining issues.
3. Why is it said that "at times negotiations are similar to a high-stakes poker game"?
4. Define each of the following:
   (a) Closed shop
   (b) Union shop
   (c) Agency shop
   (d) Maintenance of membership
   (e) Checkoff of dues
5. What are the primary means by which breakdowns in negotiations may be overcome? Briefly describe each.
6. What is the human resource manager's role in the collective bargaining process?
7. What is involved in the administration of a labor agreement?
8. What appears to be the future of collective bargaining?

Terms for Review

Mandatory bargaining issues
Permissive bargaining issues
Prohibited bargaining issues
Closed shop
Union shop
Agency shop
Open shop
Checkoff of dues

Beachhead demands
Mediation
Arbitration
Strike
Boycott
Secondary boycott
Lockout

INCIDENT 1 • Maybe I Will, Maybe I Won't •

Only yesterday, Bill Brown had been offered a job as an operator trainee with Gem Manufacturing. He had recently graduated from Milford High School in a small town in the Midwest. Bill had no college aspirations, so upon graduation, he moved to Chicago to look for a job.

Bill's immediate supervisor spent only a short time with him and then turned him over to Gaylord Rader, an experienced operator, for training. After they had talked for a short time, Gaylord asked, "Have you given any thought to joining our union? You'll like all of our members."

Naturally, Bill had not. Moreover, he had never associated with union members, and his parents had never been members either. At Milford High his teachers had never really talked about unions. The fact that this union operated as an open shop meant nothing to Bill. Bill replied, "I don't know. Maybe. Maybe not."

The day progressed much the same with seemingly everyone asking virtually the same question. They were all friendly, but there seemed to be a barrier that separated Bill from the other workers. One worker looked Bill right in the eyes and said, "You're going to join, aren't you?" Bill still did not know, but he was beginning to lean in that direction.

After the buzzer rang to end the shift, Bill went to the washroom. Just as he entered, David Clements, the union steward, also walked in. After they exchanged greetings, David said, "I hear that you're not sure about wanting to join our union. You and everyone else reaps the benefits of the work we've done in the past. It just wouldn't be fair, do you think, to be rewarded for what others have done. Tell you what, why don't you join us down at the union hall tonight for our beer bust. We'll discuss it more then."

Bill nodded in the affirmative and finished cleaning up. "That might be fun," he thought.

Questions

1. Why does Bill have the option of joining or not joining the union?
2. How are the other workers likely to react toward Bill if he chooses not to join? Discuss.

INCIDENT 2 ■ What's Causing the Turnover? ■

Alonzo Alexander, human resource manager for Hyatt Manufacturing, had a problem that he did not know how to handle. His firm was unionized and the relationship between management and the union had generally been good. The firm also had a strong affirmative action program, which required Alonzo to recruit women for jobs which had traditionally been filled by men. Hyatt had made major strides in implementing this program throughout the firm, with the notable exception of the machine department. There were only two women among the 33 operators in that department, both of whom had been hired within the past two months.

Alonzo had continued to locate numerous women applicants for the machine operator jobs. Some had trained at the local trade school and were obviously well qualified. A reasonable percentage of the women were hired but they never stayed long. Reviewing records of exit interviews with women who had quit the machine department, Alonzo categorized the main reasons given for leaving as follows: to take a better job (10 responses); pay not high enough (5); personal and family obligations (3); personal relationships on the job (12); and supervision (2).

When Alonzo interviewed co-workers of women who had quit, he felt that he got little cooperation. Typical comments were, "They just had their feelings on their shirtsleeves." "They were treated like any other worker; if they couldn't hack it maybe they didn't belong here." At one point the union steward complained that the continued questioning of workers could be considered harrassment.

Questions

1. What action would you suggest that Alonzo take? Discuss.
2. How might the union be involved in helping Alonzo solve the problem?

EXPERIENCING HUMAN RESOURCE MANAGEMENT

A major part of the human resource manager's job is to advise managers at all levels regarding human resource matters. The human resource manager's knowledge and experience are often required in dealing with union matters, especially in handling situations that have an impact on future unionization. This exercise provides additional insight into the importance of properly handling employee problems in a unionized environment.

The human resource manager, Gregory Menchew, works very closely with all the managers and employees in an attempt to settle problems before they become critical. Today, one of the union stewards, Eugene Wilson, called for an appointment and said he had a complaint. The manager agreed to talk to Eugene, but prior to that conversation wants to talk to the supervisor, Larry Bradley. That way Gregory can get both sides of the story. The manager really hopes this is not a major problem, since it appears that the company is moving toward union decertification, and problems now might derail the decertification effort.

Larry Bradley has been with the company for twelve years, the last four as a supervisor. He is a very safety-conscious supervisor with a reputation for strictly enforcing the rules. In Larry's opinion, because of this safety-consciousness, there has not been a lost-time accident in the division since Larry became the supervisor. There is a rule in the plant, well known to everyone, that every intersection is a "4-way stop" for fork-lift trucks. According to the labor–management agreement, even minor safety violations justify a three-day suspension and a written warning. Larry saw a fork-lift truck, with Charlie Fox at the wheel, come around a corner at high speed and not stop at an intersection. Virtually no one except Charlie Fox and Larry were at the plant, but Larry suspended Charlie for three days, and placed a written warning in his personnel folder.

Eugene Wilson was elected union steward last year. There have been few grievances since the election, and therefore Eugene has done little as union steward. A couple of workers have brought complaints, but management was correct in each case and workers were told so. Eugene likes being the union steward, but believes that it might be tough to be reelected unless he can make a "show." Charlie Fox was improperly suspended for three days. Eugene has found his reelection platform.

Three individuals will participate in this exercise: one to serve as the human resource manager, one to serve as the supervisor, and another to play the role of union steward. Your instructor will provide the participants with additional information necessary to complete the exercise.

REFERENCES

Barbush, Jack. "Do We Really Want Labor on the Ropes? We're Entering a New Era of Industrial Relations and That's Cause for Concern." *Harvard Business Review*, 63 (July–August 1985), pp. 10–16.

Berstein, J. "The Evolution of the Use of Management Consultants in Labor Relations: A Labor Perspective." *Labor Law Journal*, 36 (May 1985), pp. 292–299.

Bethke, Art L., R. Wayne Mondy, and Shane R. Premeaux. "Decertification: The Role of the First Line Supervisor." *Supervisory Management*, 31 (February 1986), pp. 21–23.

Cappilli, P. "Theory Construction in Industrial Relations and Some Implications for Research." *Industrial Relations*, 24 (Winter 1985), pp. 90–102.

DeMoss, R. C. "Double Breasting—An Intriguing Approach to Business Revitalization." *Employee Relations Today*, 12 (Winter 1985), pp. 55–62.

Fischer, Ben. "Labor's Dilemma: Adopting to Post-Recession Unionism." *Industry Week* (August 6, 1984), pp. 41–44.

Flare, Steven. "Pay Cuts Before the Job Even Starts." *Fortune* (January 9, 1984), pp. 75–77.

Freedman, Audrey, and William E. Fulmer. "Last Rites for Pattern Bargaining." *Harvard Business Review*, 60 (March–April), pp. 39–42ff.

Greenberg, Murray, and Philip Harris. "The Arbitrator's Employment Status as a Factor in the Decision-Making Process." *Human Resource Management*, 20 (Winter 1981), pp. 26–29.

Harking, P. J. "Labor Relations: The Fickle Nature of Employment Agreements." *Personnel Journal*, 64 (May 1985), pp. 76ff.

Hoerr, J. "Pleading Labor's Case at Japan's U.S. Plants." *Business Week* (May 13, 1985), pp. 30–31.

Iteina, J. M. "The Frustrations of Labor, the Revolt of Workers." *Personnel Administrator*, 30 (May 1985), pp. 22ff.

Klein, Stuart M., and Kenneth W. Rose. "Formal Policies and Procedures Can Forestall Unionization." *Personnel Journal*, 61 (April 1982), pp. 275–281.

Kochan, T. A. et al. "U.S. Industrial Relations in Transition." *Monthly Labor Review*, 108 (May 1985), pp. 28–29.

Kohl, J. P., and D. B. Stephens. "On Strike: Legal Development in Labor-Management Relations." *Cornell Hotel/Restaurant Administration Quarterly*, 25 (February 1985), pp. 71–75.

Leonard, J. F. "Striking Harmony with Unions." *Training and Development Journal*, 39 (March 1985), pp. 72–74.

Mills, D. Quinn. "Reforming the U.S. System of Collective Bargaining." *Monthly Labor Review* (March 1983), pp. 18–22.

Mondy, R. Wayne, and Shane R. Premeaux. "Management/Union Perception of Recent Layoffs." *Personnel Administrator*, 29 (November 1984), pp. 37–46.

———, "The Labor/Management Power Relationship Revisited." *Personnel Administrator*, 30 (May 1985), pp. 51–55.

"Nissan: Rising Sun over Industrial Relations." *Economist* (April 27, 1985), pp. 69–70.

Premeaux, Shane R., R. Wayne Mondy, and Art L. Bethke. "Decertification: Fulfilling Unions' Destiny?" *Personnel Journal*, 32 (June 1987), pp. 144–148.

Reisman, B., and L. Compa. "The Case for Adversarial Unions." *Harvard Business Review*, 63 (May–June 1985), pp. 22–24ff.

Rohan, T. M. "Employee Relations: Do Something Outrageous!" *Industry Week* (January 7, 1985), pp. 49–50.

Ross, Irwin. "Employers Win Big in the Move to Two-Tier Contracts." *Fortune* (April 29, 1985), pp. 82–84ff.

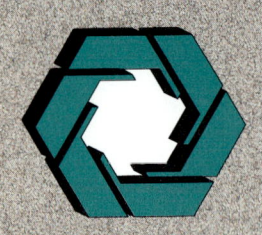

CHAPTER 17 UNION-FREE ORGANIZATIONS

CHAPTER OBJECTIVES

1. Explain why employees choose not to join a union and describe both the costs and benefits of unionization.
2. List and describe the various strategies and tactics a firm might use to maintain its union-free status.
3. Explain union decertification and describe the role of the human resource manager in a union-free organization.

■ Wayne Sanders recently joined Royal Airlines as a reservation agent in Dallas. Prior to this job he had been employed by Muse Airline of New York. When that airline went out of business recently, he was offered a job with Royal. The pay wasn't as good, and he seemed to be working harder, but he needed the job.

During his first week on the job, he was carrying on a conversation with several workers on his shift. "I don't see why we don't have a union here. Who's going to represent us when managment puts the screws on?" Wayne's conversation was quickly cut off by one of the other workers, who replied, "We don't believe in unions at Royal. Management has done a good job. If you believe you need a union to represent you, maybe you don't need to work here." Wayne nodded his head to indicate his understanding and did not mention his feelings about wanting a union again.

■ In an unrelated incident, Brad Carpet, general manager for Royal, was visibly upset. He had just been walking through the Royal terminal and accidentally heard one of the supervisors severely reprimanding an employee in front of co-workers. Brad called the supervisor aside and said, "We're a union-free organization and hope to remain this way. What you just did was one of the fastest ways to create a feeling among our employees that they need a union."

These incidents describe some employee and management attitudes in union-free firms. Wayne Sanders had just discovered that many of his fellow employees feel they do not need to be represented by a union. On the other hand, Brad Carpet is quite concerned that the actions of one of his supervisors may create an atmosphere where employees believe they do need a union. Employees of union-free firms comprise a major part of the labor force in the United States. Remaining union-free is the obvious choice of management. However, continuation of a union-free environment can be threatened by many work-related factors of which management must be acutely aware.

We begin this chapter with a discussion of the reasons that employees avoid joining unions. We then present a cost/benefit analysis of unionization. Next, we describe strategies and tactics for maintaining union-free status. We devote the final portion of the chapter to union decertification and the role of the human resource manager in a union-free organization.

■ WHY EMPLOYEES AVOID JOINING UNIONS

Most employees in the United States do not belong to unions. Basically, employees avoid unions when the human resources system deals directly and effectively with employees and their needs.[1] Maintaining a union-free organization requires maintaining an environment in which labor cannot successfully organize. The old saying that "management gets what it deserves" is never more true than when a union successfully organizes a group of employees.[2] After the union arrives and successfully organizes, management usually recognizes the avoidable mistakes that led to unionization. However, a well-conceived and implemented employee relations system could substantially reduce the likelihood of unionization. Employees don't join unions for various reasons, some of which are shown in Figure 17-1.

In the first place, it costs money to be a union member. Typically, there is an initiation fee followed by dues that must be paid regularly. From time to time, there may also be special assessments. Although dues typically do not amount to more than two percent of before-tax pay, many individuals would rather use this money in other ways. A worker who makes $24,000 annually would pay dues of approximately $40 per month, in addition to the initiation fee and any special assessments.

Also, many employees think that unions are unnecessary. They believe that they shouldn't have to depend on a third party to help satisfy their job-related needs. These individuals feel that their value to the organization should be judged on an individual basis. If their performance is superior, the rewards should be appropriate and direct. Joining a union, they believe, is an admission that others control their destiny, limiting opportunities to maximize rewards.

In addition, just as there may be peer pressure in some firms to encourage employees to join the union, in other instances there may be as much pressure against union affiliation. Even if an individual might desire to join a union, the informal work group may be powerful enough to stop the individual from joining. As Wayne Sanders discovered in the incident at the beginning of the chapter, the prevailing attitude of his co-workers to maintain a union-free status created extreme peer pressure on him to conform.

Reprisals for union activities are illegal in the United States. Even so, some employees would feel insecure about their jobs if they engaged in

---

[1] Alexander B. Trowbridge, "A Management Look at Labor Relations," *Unions in Transition* (San Francisco: ICS Press, 1988), p. 415.

[2] John P. Bucalo, Jr., "Successful Employee Relations," *Personnel Administrator*, 31 (April 1986), p. 63.

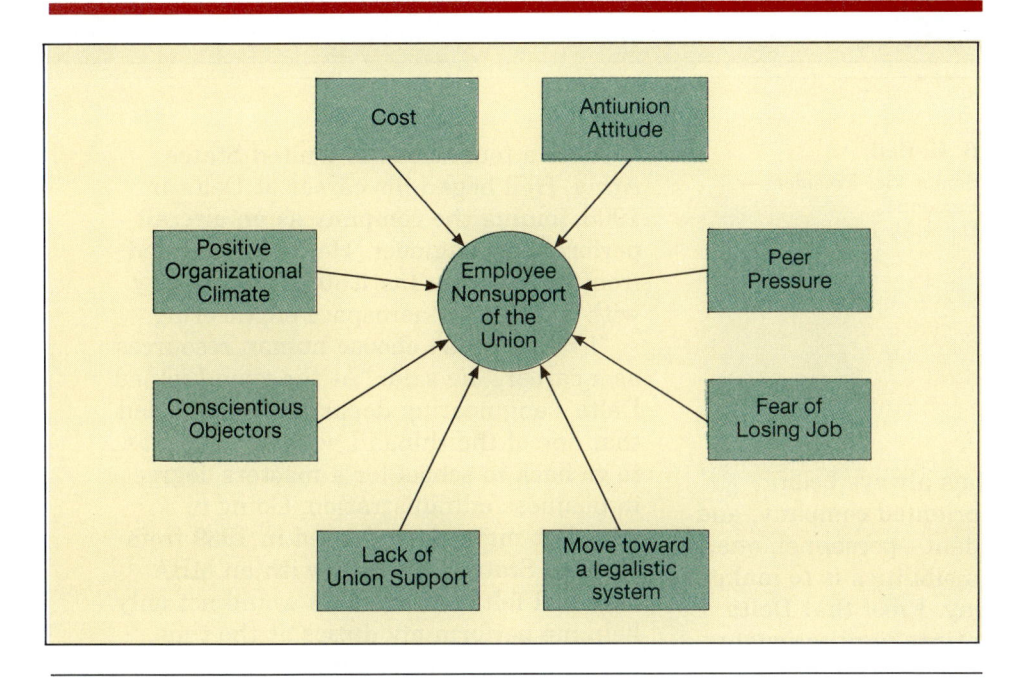

FIGURE 17-1 | Why Employees Don't Join Unions

Center: Employee Nonsupport of the Union

Surrounding factors: Cost, Antiunion Attitude, Peer Pressure, Fear of Losing Job, Move toward a legalistic system, Lack of Union Support, Conscientious Objectors, Positive Organizational Climate

---

union activities. Perhaps they have seen workers who supported a union receive what they perceive as unfair treatment from their employers. A worker who can be easily replaced may decide not to take a chance on losing his or her job by supporting union activities.

Establishing a union is much like starting a business. The cost of starting and maintaining a union must be evaluated in relation to the revenue and other benefits to be gained. Under certain circumstances a union may decide to expend little or no effort to create a new bargaining unit. For instance, a union would tend to favor organizing a unit of five hundred skilled workers rather than a group of fifty semiskilled employees. Although the union might like to help the fifty employees, the cost of organizing and supporting their demands might be excessive.

Unions also recognize that there are certain industries, firms, and locations in the country with a tradition of resisting unions. For instance, in the Sunbelt states unions commonly experience organizing difficulties. Also, a union may believe that additional attempts to unionize an organization, such as IBM Corporation, are a waste of money, because previous efforts proved fruitless. According to the *Daily Labor Report*, a "union's campaign to organize IBM is a task likened to putting a man on the moon."[3]

---

[3] "Unions Launch Campaign to Organize IBM; Task Likened to Putting 'Man on the Moon'," *Daily Labor Record* (Washington, D.C.: The Bureau of National Affairs, January 22, 1987), p. A-1.

Executive Insights

R. H. Heil
Senior Vice-President—Personnel,
Delta Air Lines, Inc.

Delta Air Lines has always been known as a people-oriented company, and as senior vice-president—personnel, one of Russ Heil's responsibilities is to make sure it stays that way. Proof that Delta takes personnel relations very seriously can be seen by the fact that Delta was rated as one of the top three work environments in America by the author of "The One Hundred Best Companies in America to Work For." In 1982, Delta employees presented their company with a rather unique Christmas present—a $30 million B-767 aircraft.

After a tour with the United States Army, Heil began his career at Delta in 1966, joining the company as an aircraft performance engineer. He had graduated from the Georgia Institute of Technology with a degree in aerospace engineering.

"I really didn't choose human resources as a career," he said. "At the time I joined Delta's engineering department, I decided that one of the things I wanted to do was to go back to school for a masters degree in business administration. Going to school at night, I graduated in 1969 from Georgia State University with an MBA degree. I felt that an MBA would not only help me perform my duties at the time, but also would better prepare me for whatever opportunities and challenges were presented in the future."

After receiving his MBA, Heil worked for several years for the head of Delta's operations division, where he became involved in many general policy matters as well as technical projects. Then in

1972, when Delta announced its merger with Northeast Airlines, his career took a major turn. He was asked to join the personnel division to help with many facets of the merger. He has been in human resources since, moving through various positions of increasing responsibility until being promoted to his current position in 1984.

At Delta, Heil sees the role of personnel as simply to make sure that Delta people are treated fairly and with respect, no matter where they work in the company. "I think it is extremely important," he said, "that the human resource implications be considered when major operational decisions are made. Here, the human resource function is accorded much greater weight in the decision-making process than perhaps in many firms. The human resource function is a separate division having status equal to other divisions of the company. In fact, most major operating decisions are not made until the human resource aspects have been considered, and the human resource division has made its input concerning those decisions. We work very hard to avoid decisions that have a detrimental impact on the people of Delta. Our people are, without question, our most valued asset."

When asked what he sees as the biggest challenge he faces as head of the human resource division, he responded, "My biggest challenge is to ensure that Delta maintains the feeling of family that has characterized the growth and development of the company for over 60 years. We work very hard to preserve that feeling, even though we now number almost 53,000 employees. At Delta the individual is recognized as an individual. Each individual can be heard, and the company can respond to the individual's needs. We don't want our people to feel that they have become lost in the bigness of the company."

Some employees have religious or moral beliefs that preclude them from joining organizations. Because unions are organizations, such employees refuse to work for a firm where union membership is required.

As we discussed in Chapter 15, the growing web of employee legal protection may well replace union representation in the future. According to Harvard labor law specialist Paul C. Weiler, employee rights in the future will be protected by a legalistic rather than a collective bargaining system.[4]

Finally, there may be factors within the company that keep employees from joining a union. The corporate culture (discussed in Chapter 9) may be one that encourages open communication and employee participation. Workers may have excellent relationships with their supervisors. Trust may exist to the point that workers may feel that they do not need a third party to represent them in their dealings with management. When this attitude is present, the employees identify strongly with the objectives of the company and are likely to resist organizing efforts.

COSTS AND BENEFITS OF UNIONIZATION

Valid reasons exist for management's acceptance or rejection of unionization, as shown in Figure 17-2. We discuss the rationales for both philosophies next.

Acceptance of Unionization Attempts

There may be times when resisting unionizing attempts is not advantageous. In such situations, management must set aside personal feelings and make decisions that are in the firm's best interest. For example, in certain areas of the United States, the maritime and construction unions often provide a ready source of labor from their hiring halls. A firm operating in one of these industries in an area which is strongly unionized may find it advantageous to accept unionization in order to obtain qualified workers.

In addition, there are situations in which union–management relationships are quite good and well established. In such instances, it may be prudent to keep that union. Otherwise, a more demanding union may take its place. Thus management rationalizes that it can work within the present system, whereas the future, with a different union, may be uncertain.

Management may also desire unionization of competing firms. If a competitor attempts to enter the industry by paying lower nonunion wages, the established firms will likely desire unionization of the new firm. Costs to all firms producing similar products remain relatively constant when all are unionized. An additional factor determining whether a firm should resist unionization attempts involves a realistic appraisal of whether it can remain union-free. In some cases, the firm would have little hope of staying union-free. For example, a maritime company located in New York City

---
[4] John Hoerr et al., "Beyond Unions," *Business Week* (July 8, 1985), p. 74.

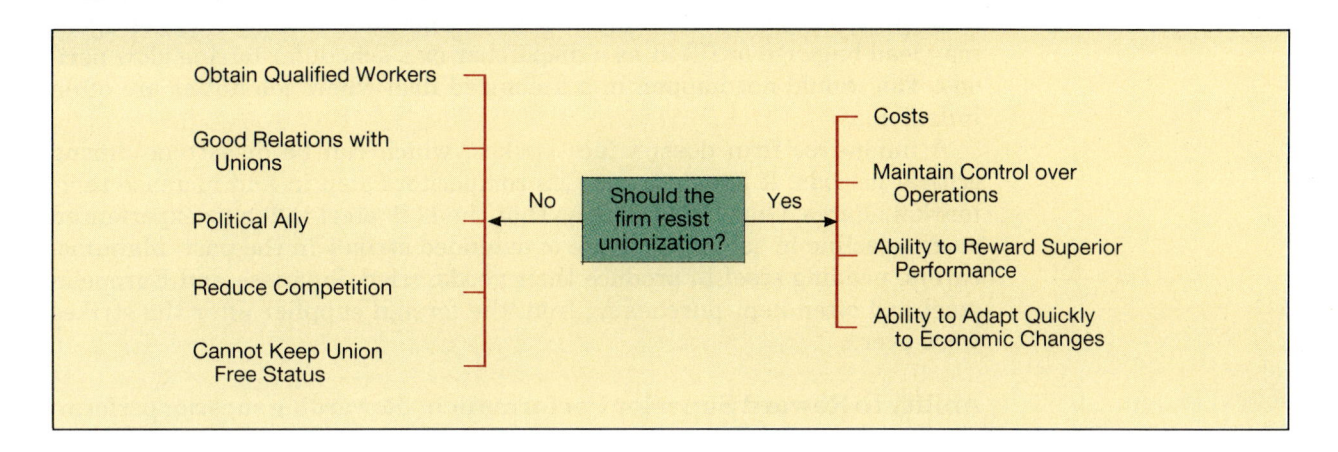

FIGURE 17-2 | Should the Organization Resist Unionization?

No (reasons): Obtain Qualified Workers; Good Relations with Unions; Political Ally; Reduce Competition; Cannot Keep Union Free Status

Yes (reasons): Costs; Maintain Control over Operations; Ability to Reward Superior Performance; Ability to Adapt Quickly to Economic Changes

would have little chance of remaining union-free. In such cases it would probably be in the firm's best interest to begin developing a strategy for working with a union.

Resistance to Unionization Attempts

Although there may be valid reasons for a firm to accept unionization, a large majority of executives would prefer that their companies remain union-free. In fact, that is a major goal for many organizations. We describe some of the reasons for remaining union-free next.

Costs. The compensation paid to union members is generally higher than that for nonunion workers. However, firms realize that they must remain conpetitive in order to survive. Delta Air Lines, a union-free organization, has had considerable success in comparison to its unionized competitors because of employees' desire for jobs and security.

In general, unionization increases labor costs.[5] Factors that contribute to these costs include: "the high cost of complex, payroll-padding work rules; work stoppages, strikes and slowdowns; lengthy negotiations and the grind of arbitration cases; and layoff by seniority."[6] The type of working relationship between labor and management will have a considerable impact on costs.

Maintaining Control over Operations. Management typically wants to operate without restrictive union work rules and other provisions that could

---
[5] Jerry Eisen, "Don't Be Complacent about Union Organizing," *Personnel Administrator*, 30 (August 1985), p. 122.

[6] Wiley I. Beavers, "Employee Relations Without a Union." In Dale Yoder and Herbert G. Heneman, Jr. (eds.), *ASPA Handbook of Personnel and Industrial Relations: Employee and Labor Relations*, Vol. III (Washington, D.C.: The Bureau of National Affairs, 1976), p. 7-82.

reduce its authority. When a firm is unionized, management relinquishes some of its control. For example, with a union-free airline, a ticket agent may load baggage or fill in as a dispatcher or a scheduler during slow periods. This would not happen in a unionized firm where job duties are often inflexible.

A union-free firm doesn't face strikes, which can be disastrous during critical periods. It avoids having its competitors step in and increase their market shares. One of the reasons that the U.S. steel industry experienced such a decline in sales is because of extended strikes in the past. Manufacturers, needing steel to produce their goods, tried Japanese and European steel and often kept purchasing from the foreign supplier after the strikes were over.

Ability to Reward Superior Performance. Rewarding superior performance in a union-free organization is often much easier. A study involving twenty-six nonunion firms revealed that "company executives believe they achieve higher productivity than they would if they were organized."[7] In union-free organizations, promotions and salary increases may be based solely on performance instead of seniority. In a unionized organization, the compensation paid each worker is specified by the agreement, not based on performance.

Ability to Adapt Quickly. Most organizations experience fluctuations in demand for their products. Some firms undergo severe business downturns before the cycle reverses. Union-free firms are typically able to respond more easily to changing conditions. If wages must be reduced to remain competitive, the union-free firm can generally adjust them rapidly. The unionized firm is bound by the labor agreement and cannot lower wages unless the union agrees to a contract change. When the automobile industry was in severe difficulty because foreign products were less expensive and of better quality, management could not quickly lower wages to be competitive. Any wage concessions had to be negotiated. Often these negotiations were unsuccessful, partially resulting in the severe slump in the sale of U.S. made automobiles throughout most of the 1980s.

When worker must be laid off as a result of declining demand, management in a union-free firm is able to lay off marginally productive employees. The seniority system determines who will be laid off in a unionized company, further diminishing management's ability to raise productivity.

■ STRATEGIES AND TACTICS FOR REMAINING UNION-FREE

Some managers believe that the presence of a union is evidence of management's failure to treat employees fairly.[8] The factors that the AFL–CIO

---

[7] Fred K. Foulkes, "How Top Nonunion Companies Manage Employees," *Harvard Business Review*, 59 (September–October 1981), p. 90.

[8] Beavers, p. 7-83.

believes will significantly reduce chances of unionizing are listed in Table 17-1. According to a 1986 report published in *Unions in Transition*, certain similar characteristics help organizations remain union-free: competitive pay and strong benefits, a team environment, open communication, a pleasant work environment, and the avoidance of layoffs.[9]

If a firm's goal is to remain union-free, it must establish its strategy long before a union organizing attempt begins. The development of long-term strategies and effective tactics for the purpose of remaining union-free is crucial because the employees' decision to consider forming a union is usually not made overnight. Negative attitudes regarding the company are typically formed over a period of time and well in advance of any attempt at unionization.

If a firm desires to remain union-free, it must borrow some of the union's philosophy. Basically, management must be able to offer workers equal or better conditions than they could expect with a union. Weakness in any critical area may be an open invitation to a union.[10] As shown in Figure 17-3, all aspects of an organization's operations are involved in maintaining its union-free status.

Effective First-Line Supervisors

Extremely important to an organization's ability to remain union-free is the overall effectiveness of its management, particularly its first-line super-

TABLE 17-1 | AFL–CIO: Factors That Reduce the Chances for Union Organizing

1. A conviction by employees that the boss is not taking advantage of them.
2. Employees who have pride in their work.
3. Good performance records kept by the company. Employees feel more secure on their jobs when they know their efforts are recognized and appreciated.
4. No claims of highhanded treatment. Employees respect firm but fair discipline.
5. No claim of favoritism that's not earned through work performance.
6. Supervisors who have good relationships with subordinates. The AFL–CIO maintains that this relationship of supervisors with people under them—above all—stifles organizing attempts.

Source: "What to Do When the Union Knocks," *Nation's Business*, 54 (November 1966); p. 107. Copyright © 1977 by *Nation's Business*. Reprinted by permission.

[9] Trowbridge, pp. 415–416.
[10] *Ibid.*, p. 417.

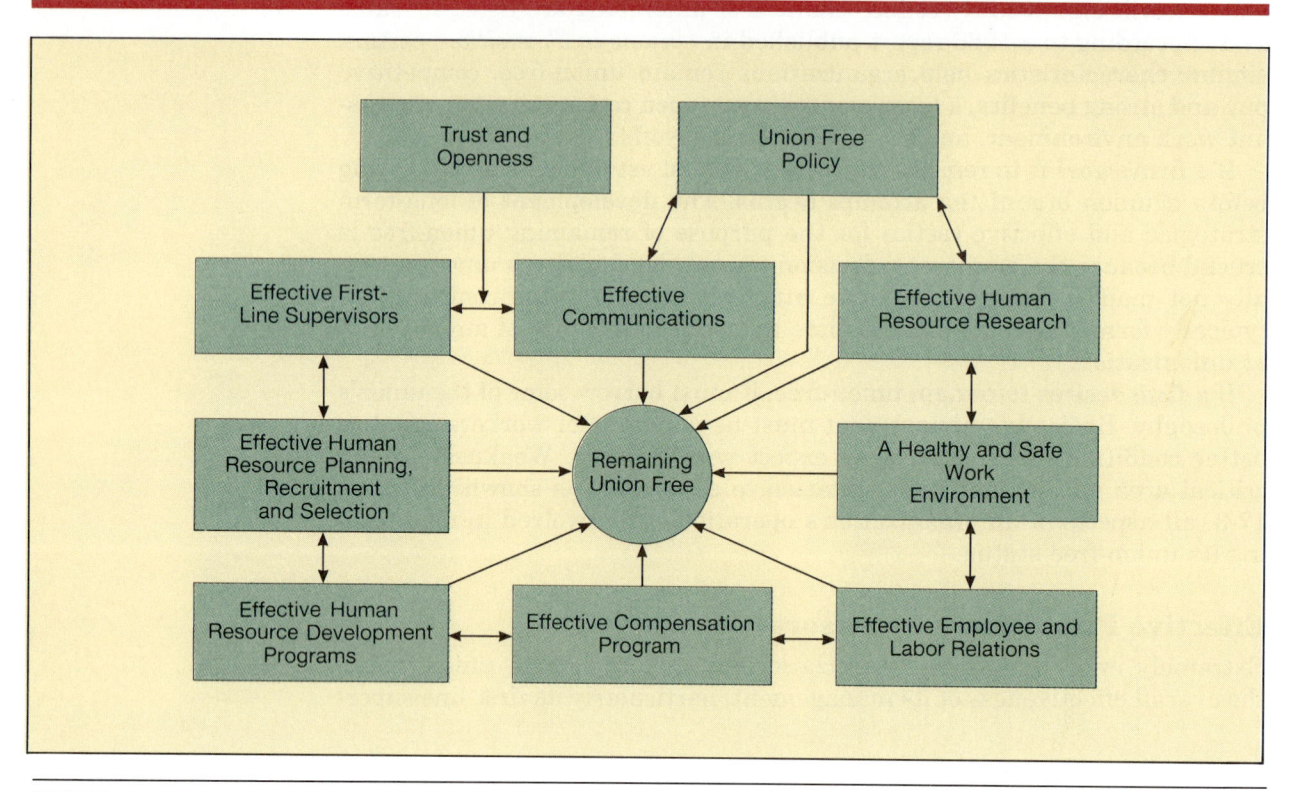

FIGURE 17-3 | Factors Involved in Maintaining a Union-Free Status

visors. These supervisors represent the first line of defense against unionization. Their supervisory ability often determines whether unionization will be successful. The supervisor assigns work, evaluates each individual's performance, and provides praise and punishment. The manner in which he or she communicates with the employee in these, and other matters, can affect the individual's attitude toward the firm. Even though the first-line supervisor is the lowest level of management, in the workplace this individual usually has more influence over employees than any other manager.

The supervisor also must communicate information about the firm to employees. Information regarding profits, sales, how the firm's products compare to competitors', and the like are important. The grapevine may reveal that sales are declining, which would likely disturb many workers. If the supervisor explains that sales are down across the industry, but are expected to return to normal in the next quarter, employees might be less anxious.

In order for a supervisor to be able to communicate effectively with employees, he or she must possess timely and accurate information. If an employee is aware of company plans before the supervisor, the supervisor loses credibility. For instance, if top management changes a company policy regarding safety hats in a particular area and the supervisor is not told of the change, the supervisor might continue to tell employees to adhere to the old policy. Any disciplinary action resulting from such a situation would embarrass the supervisor.

The supervisor must also be adept at interpreting the signals of nonverbal communication. A well-trained supervisor can identify symptoms of unrest among employees. For instance, increasing signs of resentment, where there were none before, may indicate union activity. The recent creation of informal groups may also indicate unrest. The supervisor might notice that workers may stop talking or change the subject when he or she approaches. A competent supervisor will notice these signs and report them immediately to upper level management. There may be patterns of similar activities in other departments, suggesting an attempt at unionization. This knowledge can assist management in developing appropriate strategies and tactics.

One of the fastest ways to convert a nonunion person into a union advocate is to allow favoritism. To the worker, favoritism is equivalent to discrimination. The supervisor must establish an atmosphere in which the worker believes that he or she can receive fair treatment and equitable rewards.

Union-Free Policy

The fact that the organization's goal is to remain union-free should be clearly and forcefully communicated to all its members. Such a policy statement might read as follows:

> Our success as a company is founded on the skill and efforts of our employees. Our policy is to deal with employees as effectively as possible, respecting and recognizing each of them as individuals.
>
> In our opinion, unionization would interfere with the individual treatment, respect and recognition the company offers. Consequently, we believe a union-free environment is in the employees' best interest, the company's best interest, and the interest of the people served by the corporation.[11]

This type of policy evolves into a philosophy that affects everyone in the organization. All employees, from the lowest paid worker to top management, must understand it. No major human resource-related decision should be made without asking, "How will this affect our union-free status?" In Executive Insights, Russ Heil, senior vice-president—personnel for Delta Airlines, states, "We work very hard to avoid decisions that have an adverse impact on the people of Delta. Our people are, without question, our most valued asset." It is likely that this type of attitude has been a major factor in Delta's ability to remain union-free.

The union-free policy should be repeatedly communicated to every worker. Workers must be told why the company advocates the policy and how it

---

[11] James F. Rand, "Preventive-Maintenance Techniques for Staying Union-Free," *Personnel Journal*, 59 (June 1980), p. 497.

HRM In Action

As Allen Fender, human resource director for Service Industries, rounded the corner in the mixing department he heard the supervisor, Judy Morgan, reprimanding one of her employees in front of five other workers. It was obvious that the worker was very embarrassed and wanted to get back to work but Judy continued to press the issue. Service had recently been experiencing some worker unrest, and there were rumblings of a unionization attempt.

What actions should Allen take?

---

affects them. This involves much more than sending a memo each year to all employees stating that the company's goal is to remain union-free. Every means of effective communication may be needed to convince employees that the organization intends to remain union-free.

Effective Communication

One of the most important actions an organization that wants to remain union-free can take is to establish credible and effective communication. Employees must be given the information they need to perform their jobs and provided feedback on their performance. Management should openly share information with workers concerning activities taking place within the organization. In addition, management must listen to expressions of employee needs and their perceptions of management policies and practices.

In order to sustain employee cooperation in the pursuit of organizational goals and remain union-free, management must consider the needs of employees. Employees want and need to know:

- Their standing in relation to the official, formal authority structure.
- Their standing in relation to the informal organization with respect to individual status, power, acceptance, and so on.
- Events that have a bearing on their own, and the company's, future economic security.
- Operational information that will enable them to develop pride in the job.

One approach taken to encourage open communication is the open-door policy. The **open-door policy** gives employees the right to take any grievance to the person next in the chain of command if the problem cannot be resolved by the immediate supervisor. Delta Air Lines is well known for its open-door policy, which enables employees to air any grievances. An effective open-door policy represents an attitude of openness and trust among people within the organization. It is counterproductive to state that an open-door policy exists and then punish an employee for bypassing his or her immediate supervisor. The employee must not fear that talking to the manager next in line will be detrimental to his or her career. Although it might seem that an open-door policy would result in wasted time for upper and middle managers, in most instances this has not proven to be the case. The mere knowledge that an employee can move up the chain of command with a complaint without fear of retribution often encourages the immediate supervisor and the employee to work out their differences.

Trust and Openness

Openness and trust on the part of managers and employees alike are important to remain union-free. The old expression, "actions speak louder than words," is certainly valid for an organization that desires to remain union-free. Credibility, based on trust, must exist between labor and management, and this trust develops only over time. If employees perceive that the manager is being open and receptive to ideas, feedback is encouraged. Managers need this feedback to do their jobs effectively. However, if managers give the impression that their directives should never be questioned, communication will be stifled and credibility lost.

One of the major factors in the success of Japanese businesses is said to be that managers trust not only their workers, but also their peers and superiors. As a result, a simpler organizational structure than that generally used in the United States is possible. More levels of management result in higher overhead costs and more time-consuming decision making. Japanese firms assume that workers at all levels are competent and trustworthy. As a result, they do not have to employ highly paid executives to review the work of other highly paid executives.[12]

Effective Human Resource Planning, Recruitment, and Selection

A firm's ability to remain union-free relates closely to its human resource planning, recruitment, and selection practices. For instance, if a firm used only word of mouth from current employees as a recruiting source, a very homogeneous workforce of friends and relatives could develop. Such a workforce would likely have strong interpersonal relationships. However, should management take action against any worker, the work group might perceive this as an action against them all. For this reason, and others discussed in Chapter 6, the human resource manager recruits from a wide variety of sources.

The method of human resource planning used can have a major impact on the organization's susceptibility to unionization. If it is constantly hir-

---

[12] "Trust: The New Ingredient of Management," *Business Week* (July 6, 1981), p. 104.

ing and terminating employees in reaction to fluctuating demand for its products, the firm may face unionization. However, a firm can often maintain stable employment with adequate planning.

Effective Human Resource Development Programs

Many employees want the opportunity to grow and advance within the organization. Employees can often attain these goals through training and development. A philosophy that is genuinely supportive of HRD would extend from top management to the lowest level employee. As we discussed in Chapter 8, the success of any companywide training and development program depends on the support and interest shown by top management. Management support is crucial because its attitudes will filter down and influence employees at other levels of the organization.

One important requirement of human resource development is that employees have a genuine desire for self-improvement. Some employees are content in their present positions, while others desire to develop their potential. More employees will wish to improve their skills if they are able to see a relationship between increased training and higher pay and other rewards. An organization takes a giant step toward remaining union-free when it provides avenues for advancement in skill and status. The seniority system often denies union employees these opportunities.

Supervisors also need training to prepare them to deal with organizing attempts. If the union knows that supervisors have been thoroughly trained in the tactics of dealing with unionizing efforts, it may decide against organizing attempts. This type of training will also assist in preventing costly mistakes that could lead to charges of unfair labor practices during an organizing campaign. Training is necessary because the supervisor's actions can actually bind the employer. Ignorance on the part of the supervisor is no excuse for inappropriate behavior.

Effective Compensation Programs

The financial compensation that employees receive is the most tangible measure they have of their worth to the organization. If an individual's pay is substantially below that provided for similar work in the area, the employee will soon become dissatisfied. Compensation must remain relatively competitive if the organization expects to remain union-free.[13]

The compensation program should be intelligently planned and communicated to all employees. They must understand what they are being compensated for, and how the system works. If employees perceive the system as being unfair, they are ripe for unionizing activities.

The same approach should be followed with regard to benefits. The organization need not have the best benefits in a geographic area or an industry to protect its union-free status. However, the benefits package must be

---

[13] Rand, p. 498.

competitive. Employees must know what benefits they are actually receiving. Too often, management doesn't adequately inform employees about their benefits. When such a situation exists, the organization is wasting financial resources, and jeopardizing its union-free status.

A Healthy and Safe Work Environment

An organization that gains a reputation for failing to maintain a safe and healthy work environment leaves itself wide open for unionization. For years unions have campaigned successfully by convincing workers that the union will provide them with a safer work environment. In fact, labor organizations were leading advocates of the Occupational Safety and Health Act and continue to support this type of legislation.

Effective Employee Relations

Virtually no organization is free from employee disagreements and dissatisfaction. Therefore, a means of resolving employee complaints, whether actual or perceived, should be available. The **grievance procedure** is a formal process that permits employees to complain about matters affecting them. Most labor–management agreements contain formal grievance procedures, and union members regard handling grievances as one of the most important functions of a labor union. Until the early 1980s, grievance procedures were not so common in union-free organizations. However, since that time many nonunion firms have started grievance procedure programs. When employees do not have ways to voice their complaints and have them resolved, even small gripes may grow into major problems.

The grievance procedure is a way of keeping problems from becoming serious. Total commitment to such a policy needs to start with top management and be instilled in every manager. Supervisors should develop an attitude of wanting to resolve problems before they become formal complaints.[14] Employees who believe that management is concerned with resolving problems lack a major reason for needing a union.

A means of resolving grievances in union-free organizations is through the use of ombudspersons. This approach has been used for some time in Europe, and the practice is becoming more popular in the United States. An **ombudsperson** is a complaint officer with access to top management, who hears employees' complaints, investigates them, and sometimes recommends appropriate action. Because of their access to top management, ombudspersons can often resolve problems swiftly. In many cases, they simply help employees locate people who can solve their problems. Sometimes, ombudspersons recommend specific action to managers. The Singer Company uses an ombudsperson system. In a company newsletter, Harry

---

[14] George W. Bohlander and Harold C. White, "Building Bridges: Nonunion Employee Grievance Systems," *Personnel*, 65 (July 1988), p. 62.

P. Hancock, Jr., senior director, employee relations program, described its ombudsperson program, which is shown in Figure 17-4.

In recent years the ombudsperson has assumed the additional duties of helping uncover scandals within organizations. Large defense contractors,

---

In A Less Than Perfect Universe . . .

See the Ombudsperson

An employee is fired for cause, disciplined or perceives himself or herself a victim of discrimination. To reverse the decision or remedy the situation, the employee tries normal channels—but remains dissatisfied with the results.

In many organizations, the story would end here. At Singer, because of the Corporate Ombudsperson program started in 1976, the story can have another chapter or two. And, although the story may not necessarily have a happy ending, employees are guaranteed that they won't be subjected to harassment or retribution for contacting the Ombudsperson.

A concept borrowed from Scandinavia, the Ombudsperson function entails an impartial investigation of and assistance in equitably settling complaints. At Singer this corporate-wide function is the responsibility of Harry P. Hancock, Jr., senior director, employee relations programs. "Because the program is informal rather than formal and the range of cases is varied," explains Mr. Hancock, "there is really no single modus operandi. I handle each case as it presents itself."

The range of cases include grievances about performance appraisals, involuntary discharge, sexual harrassment, sexual discrimination, denial of promotion, formal reprimand and conflict with or unfair treatment by a supervisor.

For the purpose of illustrating the thoroughness of the Ombudsperson proceedings, Mr. Hancock describes how he might deal with a discharge-for-cause case brought to his attention by an employee who had exhausted all normal channels and remained dissatisfied.

"In the investigation and evaluation," he explains, "we rely heavily on the division personnel staff. Our objective is to make sure that:

- The rule or policy allegedly broken by the employee has been published, posted or otherwise made known to employees.

- The employee has been warned about any earlier infractions and given counseling.
- The employee has been given a reasonable length of time to improve performance.
- The proposed disciplinary action is appropriate to the infraction.
- Other employees charged with similar infractions have been treated in a similar manner."

If it is determined that the employee has been unfairly discharged, the case is discussed with the immediate supervisor who initiated the action. If the decision is not reversed or amended at this level—which it usually is—then the discussion is brought to successively higher levels. On the other hand, if it is judged that the decision was appropriate, the employee is so advised and the case is closed.

Most problems are resolved, of course, through Singer's normal channels. Resolving a problem via normal channels includes an initial discussion with the immediate supervisor. If the issue is not settled at that level, then the matter is taken to higher levels, in the specific unit. Equal Opportunity coordinators, industrial relations personnel and other employee relations specialists may become involved.

In cases of terminations of employees with more than ten years of continuous service, standard procedure requires that those terminations be approved by members of the Management Committee.

If employees, after having gone through normal channels, still believe that they have received unfair treatment then they can bring the matter to the attention of the Ombudsperson.

FIGURE 17-4 | Description of an Ombudsperson Program

Source: Used with permission of The Singer Company.

CHAPTER 17　Union-Free Organizations

such as McDonnell Douglas and General Electric, have used ombudspersons to respond to questions raised regarding product design safety or defense contract billings. Workers who believe that a problem exists can now bypass the supervisor and talk to the ombudsperson.[15]

Effective Human Resource Research

Human resource research can reveal changes in attitudes within the organization that could lead to unionization. One purpose of human resource research is the early identification of employee dissatisfaction. Corrective action should be taken before workers feel a need for a union to solve their problems. Ignored problems often encourage unionization.

Research may reveal symptoms of worker unrest. For instance, statistics that reveal an increase in the turnover rate may indicate growing employee dissatisfaction. Good exit interviews, as part of the research effort, can assist management in identifying the problems causing higher turnover before they become critical.[16]

Another indicator of employee dissatisfaction is the number of customer complaints received. For example, research that reveals increasing customer complaints because of lower quality might point to certain employees who have problems that need resolving. Accident frequency, maintenance costs, and theft are other indicators of employee dissatisfaction.[17]

■ UNION DECERTIFICATION

Until 1947, once a union was certified, it was certified forever.[18] However, the Taft–Hartley Act made it possible for employees to decertify a union. This action results in a union losing its right to act as the exclusive bargaining representative of a group of employees. **Decertification** is essentially the reverse of the process that employees must follow to be recognized as an official bargaining unit. In recent years, many decertification elections have been held.

The 1980s have not been a good decade for America's labor unions. Organized labor lost 2.7 million members between 1980 and 1984 alone, and many observers expect this trend to continue. In addition, because this decline occurred while the nation's workforce increased, the proportion of those employed who were union members declined even more dramatically. According to the *Union Sourcebook*, organized labor's share of the workforce is expected to decline to the point where it represents only 13 percent

---

[15] Michael Brody, "Listen to Your Whistleblower," *Fortune*, 24 (November 1986), pp. 77–78.
[16] Wanda R. Embrey, R. Wayne Mondy, and Robert M. Noe, "Exit Interview: A Tool for Personnel Development," *Personnel Administrator*, 24 (May 1979), p. 48.
[17] Beavers, pp. 7-69–7-70.
[18] 93 Daily Congressional Record 3954 (23 April 1947).

of all nonfarm workers by the year 2000.[19] The two primary reasons for this decline are decertification and the U.S. economy's continuing shift to service industries.

In light of this significant reduction in union ranks, the outcome of certification and decertification elections are of increasing concern to unions. Unions have won about half the certification elections each year since 1981. However, during the same period, unions lost three fourths of the decertification elections. More than 600 bargaining units decertified their unions in each of the last three years.[20]

Some union leaders are concerned that the trend may even be spreading to larger firms. Should this occur, the foundation of the U.S. labor movement would be threatened. Not only would the total number of union members decline, but unions' hold on major domestic industries would be substantially reduced.[21] Decertification elections have been won in such well-known firms as Holiday Inn, Goodyear, Dow Chemical, Sears, American Airlines, and the Washington Post. However, smaller firms appear to be achieving the greatest won–lost decertification record. Perhaps this is because it is easier for management to reestablish trust with employees in smaller firms.

Decertification Procedure

The rules established by the NLRB spell out the conditions for filing a decertification petition. At least 30 percent of the bargaining unit members must petition for an election. As might be expected, this task by itself may be difficult because union supporters are likely to strongly oppose the move. Although the petitioners' names are supposed to remain confidential, many union members are fearful that their signatures on the petition will be discovered.

Timing of the NLRB's receipt of the decertification petition is also critical. The petition must be submitted between sixty and ninety days prior to the expiration of the current contract. When all these conditions have been met, the NLRB regional director will schedule a decertification election by secret ballot.

The NLRB carefully monitors the events leading up to the election. Current employees must initiate the request for the election. If the NLRB determines that management initiated the action, it probably won't certify the election. After the petition has been accepted, however, management can support the decertification election attempt. If a majority of the votes cast are against the union, the employees will be free from that union. Strong union supporters are all likely to vote. Thus if a substantial number of employees are indifferent to the union and choose not to vote, decertification may not occur.

---

[19] Leo Troy and Niel Shevlin, *Union Sourcebook, IRDIS*, West Orange, N.J.; 1985–2000: Richard B. Freeman of Harvard University, BW.

[20] Woodruff Imberman, "How to Win a Decertification Election," *Management Review*, 66 (September 1977), p. 38.

[21] *Ibid.*

Management and Decertification

When management senses employee discontent with the union, it often does not know how to react. Many times, management decides to do nothing, reasoning that it is best not to get involved or that it may even be illegal to do so. But if it does want to get involved, management can use a variety of legal tactics. Basically, if management really wants the union decertified, it must learn how to be active rather than passive.

Meetings with union members to discuss the benefits of becoming union-free have proven beneficial. In fact, they are often cited as being the most effective campaign tactic. These meetings may be with individual employees, small groups, or even entire units. Management explains the benefits and answers employees' questions.

Management may also provide workers with legal assistance in preparing for decertification. Because the workers probably have never been through a decertification election, this type of assistance may prove invaluable. For example, the NLRB may not permit an election if the paperwork has not been properly completed. Management must always remember that it cannot initiate the decertification action; that is the workers' responsibility.

The most effective means of accomplishing decertification is to improve the corporate culture so that workers no longer feel the need to have a union. This cannot be done overnight, as mutual trust and confidence must be developed between workers and the employer.

If decertification is to succeed, management must eliminate the problems that initially led to unionization. Although many executives believe that pay and benefits are the primary reasons for union membership, these factors are probably not the real cause.[22] Failure to treat employees as individuals is often the primary reason for unionization. The real problems often stem from practices such as failing to listen to employees' opinions, dealing with workers unfairly and dishonestly, and treating employees as numbers and not as people. Many organizational attitudes and actions indicate to employees how the firm feels toward them, including:

- Poor housekeeping.
- Poor supervision.
- Inadequate wage differentials among various skill levels.
- Inadequate preventive maintenance.
- Arbitrary company policies.
- Unfair promotional policies.
- An ineffective complaint and discipline procedure.[23]

Such problems may have led initially to unionization. Even if an organization desires to become union-free, it cannot become so immediately. Unsatisfactory conditions must be eliminated, and this takes time.

---

[22] *Ibid.*

[23] *Ibid.*

■ THE ROLE OF THE HUMAN RESOURCE MANAGER

The human resource manager in a union-free firm has a somewhat different role than his or her counterpart in a unionized company. The tasks of the human resource manager in a unionized firm often revolve around contract negotiations and grievance handling. The human resource manager in a union-free firm must work toward creating an atmosphere in which workers will not feel the need for union representation. Human resource managers serve as the catalyst for developing and maintaining nonunion attitudes.

In the mid-1960s, many senior labor relations professionals gave primary attention to stabilizing collective bargaining relationships. At that time, the most important force for change was the rise of laws and governmental regulations mandating nondiscrimination and affirmative action in employment. Affirmative action brought about rational human resource policies and practices, which resulted in management focusing on better employment relationships. The Conference Board survey on labor–management relations showed that preventing the spread of unionism and developing effective employee relations systems are more important to managers today than achieving sound collective bargaining results.[24] These changes in priority, along with the current emphasis on remaining or becoming union-free, have increased HRM responsibilities. They, in turn, gave human resource managers greater corporate power and importance throughout the 1980s.[25]

The desire for union-free operations, and the greater emphasis on employee oriented policies, has created a management perspective that emphasizes the individual employee over adversary labor relations. The union-free approach is basically a human resource system that bypasses the union and deals directly with the individual worker—and his or her needs. This human resource system matches compensation and benefits with worker performance, properly designs the organization and the workplace to enhance productivity and worker satisfaction, and involves employees in solving workplace problems and making decisions.[26]

Remaining union-free requires a strong commitment by management at all levels and open communication, and trust. In many ways, the commitment necessary to maintain a union-free environment requires a much more demanding effort by the human resources professional. Some organizations may not maintain that commitment and therefore will become vulnerable to organizing efforts. The old maxim is still true: "Unions don't organize employees, managers do"—through mistakes, neglect, and (unfortunately) plain greed.[27] The human resource manager, therefore, must ensure that an employee relations system is created whereby employees

---

[24] Trowbridge, p. 414.
[25] *Ibid.*
[26] David C. Metz, "12 Key Factors in Staying Union Free—A Checklist for Employers," 30 CUE, Washington, D.C.
[27] Trowbridge, p. 417.

CHAPTER 17   Union-Free Organizations

are treated in a positive manner, allowing each individual to maintain his or her self-esteem and advance individually as the organization advances.

SUMMARY

Most employees in the United States don't belong to unions. Their reasons for not joining are many and varied. It costs money to be a union member, many employees think that unions are unnecessary, and peer pressure against union affiliation may be exerted. Reprisals against employees for union activities are illegal in the United States. Even so, some employees would feel insecure about their jobs if they engaged in union activities. Certain employees have religious or moral beliefs that preclude them from joining organizations, including unions.

Under certain circumstances a union may decide to expend little or no effort to establish a new bargaining unit. Unions also recognize that there are certain industries, firms, and locations in the country with an anti-union tradition. Moreover, the growing web of employee legal protection may well substitute for union representation in the future.

Valid reasons exist for management's acceptance or rejection of a union. There may be times when resistance to organizing attempts isn't advantageous. In addition, there are situations where the relationship between management and the union is quite good and well established. Management may also desire unionization of competing organizations.

Although there may be valid reasons for a firm to accept unionization, a large percentage of executives prefer that their companies remain union-free. In fact, that is a major goal for many organizations. Some reasons for remaining union-free are costs, maintaining control over operations, ability to reward superior performance, and ability to adapt quickly to changing conditions.

To remain union-free, an organization must establish its strategy and tactics long before a union organizing attempt begins. This approach is crucial because the employee's decision to consider forming a union is usually not made overnight. Extremely important to remaining union-free is overall management effectiveness, particularly that of first-line supervisors. The fact that the organization's goal is to remain union-free should be clearly communicated to everyone in the organization. One of the most important considerations of remaining union-free is the establishment of credible communication. Openness and trust on the part of managers and employees are essential. Ability to remain union-free relates closely to the organization's human resource planning, recruitment, and selection practices. Lack of opportunity to grow and advance, inadequate or inequitable financial compensation, a reputation for having an unsafe and unhealthy work environment leave an organization wide open to unionization. A means of resolving employee complaints, whether actual or perceived, should be available. Human resource research can reveal changes in attitudes within the organization that could lead to unionization.

Decertification means that a union has lost its right to act as the exclusive bargaining representative of a group of employees. The process is essentially the reverse of what a union must go through to be recognized as an official bargaining unit. In light of significant reductions in union ranks, the outcome of certification and decertification elections is of increasing concern to unions.

Rules established by the NLRB specify the procedures for filing a decertification petitition and holding a decertification election. When all of the conditions have been met, the NLRB regional director will schedule a decertification election by secret ballot. The NLRB carefully monitors the events leading up to the election.

The most effective means to accomplish decertification is to improve the corporate culture so that workers no longer feel the need to have a union. This takes time because mutual trust and confidence must develop. If decertification is to succeed, management must eliminate the problems that initially led to unionization.

The human resource manager in a union-free firm has a somewhat different role from his or her counterpart in a unionized company. The tasks of the human resource manager in a unionized firm often revolve around contract negotiations and grievance handling. The human resource manager in a union-free firm must work toward creating an atmosphere in which workers will not feel the need for union representation. Human resource managers serve as the catalyst for developing and maintaining nonunion attitudes.

Questions for Review

1. What are the most important reasons for employees not joining unions? Discuss each of them.
2. There are reasons both for and against a firm resisting unionization attempts. What are they?
3. Briefly describe the factors involved in maintaining a union-free status.
4. What role does the first-line supervisor play in helping a firm remain union-free?
5. Describe the process of decertification.
6. How might the role of a human resource manager change if he or she moves from a unionized firm to a union-free firm? Discuss.

Terms for Review

Open-door policy
Grievance procedure

Ombudsperson
Decertification

CHAPTER 17 Union-Free Organizations

INCIDENT 1 ▪ Being Fair ▪

Ed Davis is a supervisor at the Paxma Manufacturing Company, a manufacturer of a special kind of filler material for packaging. Ed was transferred to his present job from another plant. He accepted the transfer because he felt it would provide a better opportunity for promotion. Ed's new section includes fifteen workers whose jobs are essentially identical. The workload of Paxma often fluctuates, requiring extensive use of overtime. This overtime is very popular among the workers and Ed's predecessor had distributed it on a simple rotation basis.

When Ed took over, he felt that overtime should be a reward for excellent performance. He also felt that certain workers needed the overtime more than others. Ed did not discuss this with the workers but simply began to assign the overtime as he saw fit.

Everything seemed to be going well until the day Ed was called to the office of Mary Donnelly, the human resource manager. After a brief greeting Mary said, "Ed, I hear through the grapevine that there's a good deal of dissension in your crew. Some of the workers feel they're not being given their fair share of overtime." Ed replied, "I assign everybody their share. It's just not always an equal share." "That may be true, Ed," said Mary, "but at least a couple of the workers believe that most of the overtime has been going to the three new people you've hired." "Who told you that?" asked Ed. "I don't think that should be important," Mary answered, "but you need to think about whether there's any substance to the impression your workers have." "You may be right," said Ed. "I suppose I could unconsciously have favored the people I selected."

Questions

1. Was the human resource manager correct in getting involved in the line function of assigning overtime? Explain.
2. What would you do if you were Ed?

INCIDENT 2 ▪ Open the Door! ▪

Barney Cline, the new human resource manager for Ampex Utilities, was just getting settled in his new office. He had recently moved from another firm to take over his new job. Barney had been selected over several in-house candidates and numerous other applicants because of his record of getting things done. He had a good reputation for working through people to get the job accomplished.

Just then his phone rang. The person on the other end of the line said, "Mr. Cline, could I set up an appointment to talk with you?" "Certainly," Barney said, "when do you want to get together?" "How about after work? It might be bad if certain people saw me speaking to anyone in management."

Barney was a bit puzzled, but he set up an appointment for 5:30 P.M., when nearly everyone would be gone. At the designated time there was a knock on his door; it was Mark Johnson, a senior maintenance worker who had been with the firm for more than ten years.

After the initial welcome, Mark began by saying, "Mr. Cline, several of the workers asked me to talk to you. The grapevine has it that you're a fair person. The company says it has an open-door policy. We're afraid to use it. Roy Edwards, one of the best maintenance men in our section, tried it several months ago. They hassled him so much that he quit only last week. We just don't know what to do to get any problems settled. There have been talks of organizing a union. We really don't want that, but something has to give."

Barney thanked Mark for his honesty and promised not to reveal the conversation. In the weeks following the conversation with Mark, Barney was able to verify that the situation existed as Mark had described it. There was considerable mistrust between managers and the operative employees.

Questions

1. What are the basic causes of the problems confronting Ampex Utilities?
2. How should Barney attempt to resolve this problem?

Experiencing Human Resource Management

Union organizing attempts are a real challenge to human resource managers and first-line supervisors. During a recent conference on maintaining union-free status, the point was stressed that supervisors are the key to preventing companies from being organized. Therefore, those in human resource management should maintain direct and continual contact with supervisors. This exercise is designed to give participants an opportunity to experience what goes on when a union is being considered.

Two committees, one employee group and one manager group, will discuss the prospects of unionization. Each committee must come up with a recommendation for or against unionization and state their reasons for their recommendation. The spokesperson for the employee group is Bob Jones and the group members are Gerald Young, Julie Faire, and Tony Wells. Bob Jones is a very outspoken union advocate and he has always believed this company should have a union. He believes wages are lower here than at unionized firms in the area and sees too much "brother-in-lawing" going on around here. Besides, he was denied a raise recently and was told that the boss just did not "feel" he deserved one.

This is Gerald Young's first job, but his father is the union steward of another company. He often said, "What you guys need over there is a good union." Last month when production standards were raised, Gerald's piece-rate bonus was wiped out. His dad says they do not pull that in a unionized firm.

Julie Faire has been working here for several years, and the company has always been good to her. She had some family problems last year and her boss let her off for several days. Could a union be better than her understanding boss?

Tony Wells is an old hand here, and has seen lots of things come and go over the years. Tony's experience has been that if employees have enough guts to go to their supervisors directly they can usually get satisfaction. It seems that too many people today are looking for a "free lunch."

continued on next page

> *continued from previous page*
>
> The spokesperson for the supervisor group, Charlie Neal, is very anti-union. Charlie is really fed up with all this union talk and believes that these people do not seem to know when they are well off. Charlie has been with the company for nearly twenty years and does not intend to put up with a union now. He believes the company should "get tough." Charlie has a pretty good idea of who is leading the unionizers. If the other supervisors will listen, it will be easy enough to find reasons to get rid of the troublemakers.
>
> Beverly Woods has been a supervisor for only a few years, but previously she was a supervisor in a unionized company. Beverly has a healthy respect for unions and some feeling for how they get their power. It seems that this is a great opportunity for the supervisors to get together with the employees and solve the employee's legitimate complaints. She believes this would be all it would take to convince employees that they do not need a union.
>
> According to what is determined in the conference, there may be an agreement proposed that will prevent unionizing, or will create a delaying action such as a joint committee. There may be hard lines drawn leading to a showdown, or even an immediate call for a union election. The groups will decide, and the spokespersons will report their decisions. Your instructor will provide the participants with additional information necessary to complete the exercise.

REFERENCES

Adams, C. T. "Changing Employment Patterns of Organized Workers." *Monthly Labor Review*, 108 (February 1985), pp. 25–31.

Angle, Harold L., and James L. Perry. "Dual Commitment and Labor–Management Relationship Climates." *Academy of Management Journal*, 29 (March 1986), pp. 31–47.

Barbash, Jack. "Do We Really Want Labor on the Ropes?" *Harvard Business Review*, 63 (July–August 1985), pp. 10–16.

Bleiberg, R. M. "Organized Labor's Future: More Today May Be Less, But There's a Lot Up for Grabs." *Barrons* (February 25, 1985), p. 9.

Bohlander, George W., and Harold C. White. "Building Bridges: Nonunion Employee Grievance Systems." *Personnel*, 65 (July 1988), pp. 62–67.

Bucalo, John P., Jr. "Successful Employee Relations." *Personnel Administrator*, 31 (April 1986), p. 64.

Clark, K. B. "Unionization and Firm Performance: The Impact on Profits, Growth, and Productivity." *American Economic Review*, 74 (December 1984), pp. 893–919.

Diaz, Edmund M., John W. Minton, and David M. Saunders. "A Fair Nonunion Grievance Procedure." *Personnel*, 64 (April 1987), pp. 13–18.

Eisen, Jerry. "Don't Be Complacent about Union Organizing." *Personnel Administrator*, 30 (August 1985), p. 122.

Foulkes, Fred K. "How Top Nonunion Companies Manage Employees." *Harvard Business Review*, 59 (September–October 1981), pp. 90–96.

———. "Decertification: Is the Current Trend a Threat to Collective Bargaining?" *California Management Review*, 24 (Fall 1981), pp. 14–22.

Harrison, Edward L., Douglas Johnson, and Frank M. Rachel. "The Role of the Supervisor in Representation Election." *Personnel Administrator*, 26 (September 1981), pp. 67–71.

Hoerr, John. "Beyond Unions." *Business Week* (July 8, 1985), pp. 72–77.

Hoover, John J. "Union Organization Attempts: Management's Response." *Personnel Journal*, 61 (March 1982), pp. 214–219.

Hughes, Charles L. *Making Unions Unnecessary* (New York: Executive Enterprises, 1976).

Lewis, Ephraim. "BW/Harris Poll: Confidence in Unions Is Crumbling." *Business Week* (July 8, 1985), p. 76.

Markham, S., and D. Scott. "Controlling Absenteeism: Union and Nonunion Differences." *Personnel Administrator*, 30 (February 1985), pp. 87–88ff.

McCollum, J. K., and Norris, D. R. "Nonunion Grievance Machinery in Southern Industry." *Personnel Administrator*, 29 (November 1984), pp. 106–112.

McCracken, P. W. "Giving Unions Their Due." *Across the Board*, 21 (November 1984), pp. 59–60.

Mooney, Marta. "Let's Use Job Security as a Productivity Builder." *Personnel Administrator*, 29 (January 1984), pp. 38–44.

Mulcahy, Robert W., and Jon E. Anderson. "The Bargaining Battleground Called Comparable Worth." *Public Personnel Management*, 15 (Fall 1986), pp. 233–245.

Pfeffer, Jeffrey, and Jerry Ross. "Union-Nonunion Effects on Wage and Status Attainment." *Industrial Relations*, 19 (Spring 1980), pp. 140–150.

Premeaux, Shane R., R. Wayne Mondy, and Art L. Bethke. "The Two-Tier Wage System." *Personnel Administrator*, 31 (November 1986), pp. 92–100.

Rand, James F. "Preventive-Maintenance Techniques for Staying Union-Free." *Personnel Journal*, 59 (June 1980), pp. 497–499.

Sappir, Mark Z. "The Employer's Obligation Not to Bargain When the Issue of Decertification Is Present." *Personnel Administrator*, 27 (February 1982), pp. 41–45.

Swann, James P., Jr. "Formal Grievance Procedures in Nonunion Plants." *Personnel Administrator*, 26 (August 1981), pp. 66–70.

Tidwell, G. L. "The Meaning of the No-Strike Clause." *Personnel Administrator*, 29 (November 1984), pp. 51–53ff.

Voos, P. B. "Trends in Union Organizing Expenditures." *Industrial Labor Relations Review*, 38 (October 1984), pp. 52–63.

CHAPTER 18

INTERNAL EMPLOYEE RELATIONS

CHAPTER OBJECTIVES

1. Distinguish between discipline and disciplinary action, identify and describe the steps involved in the disciplinary process, and describe the steps involved in progressive discipline.
2. Explain how grievance handling is typically conducted under a collective bargaining agreement and in union-free firms.
3. State how termination conditions may differ when operative employees, executives, managers, or professionals are involved and explain the concept of employment at will.
4. Explain the role of internal employee relations with regard to resignations, demotions, layoffs, transfers, promotions, and retirements.
5. Discuss the legal implications of internal employee relations and how multinational corporations cope with internal employee relations.

■ Bob Halmes, the production supervisor for American Manufacturing, was mad at the world when he arrived at work. The automobile mechanic had not repaired his car on time the day before, so he had been forced to take a taxi to work this morning. No one was safe around Bob today, and it was not the time for Phillip Martin, a member of Local 264, to report for work late. Without hesitation, Bob said: "You know our company can't tolerate this type of behavior. I don't want to see you around here anymore. You're fired." Just as quickly, Phillip replied, "You're way off base. Our contract calls for three warnings for tardiness. My steward will hear about this."

■ Bill Morton, a ten-year employee at Ketro Productions, arrived at the office of the human resource manager to turn in his letter of resignation. He was obviously upset at his supervisor. When the human resource manager, Robert Noll, asked what was wrong, Bill replied: "Yesterday, I made a mistake and set my machine up wrong. It was the first time in years that I've done that. My boss chewed me out in front of my friends. I wouldn't take that from the president, much less a two-bit supervisor!"

These scenarios represent only two of the many situations that human resource managers confront when dealing with internal employee relations. Bob Halmes has just been reminded that his power to fire Phillip Morton has limits. The resignation of Bill Martin might have been avoided if his supervisor had not shown poor judgment and disciplined him in front of his friends.

In this chapter, we first define internal employee relations. Next, we discuss the reasons for disciplinary action, the disciplinary action process, approaches to disciplinary action, and the administration of disciplinary action. We then describe grievance handling under a collective bargaining agreement and for nonunion employees. Next, we review termination, employment at will, resignation, demotion, layoff, transfer, promotion, and retirement. We devote the last portion of the chapter to legal implications of internal employee relations and internal employee relations in multinational corporations.

■ INTERNAL EMPLOYEE RELATIONS DEFINED

The status of most workers is not permanently fixed in an organization. Employees constantly move upward, laterally, downward, and out of the organization. In order to ensure that workers with the proper skills and experience are available at all levels, constant and concerted efforts are required to maintain good internal employee relations. A well-conceived and implemented employee relations program is very beneficial to both the organization and its employees. **Internal employee relations** consists of those human resource management activities associated with the movement of employees within the organization and include the actions of promotion, transfer, demotion, resignation, discharge, layoff, and retirement. Discipline and disciplinary action are also crucial aspects of internal employee relations.

Increasingly, management is patterning employee relations systems on models provided by such leaders as IBM and the Hewlett-Packard Company, which have been committed to good employee relations from their founding. These employee relations systems go beyond providing competitive salaries and benefits, involving workers in decision making, and treating employees fairly. Such systems also deal with matters such as establishing an employee grievance procedure and a no-layoff policy. The trend toward more responsible internal employee relations systems seems to spreading among industry leaders, which could usher in an era dedicated to sound and equitable employee relations.

■ DISCIPLINARY ACTION

Discipline is the state of employee self-control and orderly conduct and indicates the extent of genuine teamwork within an organization. **Disciplinary action** invokes a penalty against an employee who fails to meet established standards. Effective disciplinary action addresses the employee's wrongful behavior, not the employee as a person.[1] Incorrectly administered disciplinary action is destructive to both the employee and the organization. Thus disciplinary action should not be applied haphazardly.

A necessary, but often trying, aspect of internal employee relations is the application of disciplinary action. Disciplinary action is not usually an action of first resort. Normally, there are more positive ways of convincing employees to adhere to company policies that are necessary to accomplish organi-

---

[1] Keith Davis, *Human Behavior at Work* (New York: McGraw-Hill, 1977), p. 261.

zational goals. However, managers must administer disciplinary action when company policies are violated. Disciplinary policies afford the organization the greatest opportunity to accomplish organizational goals, thereby benefiting both employees and the corporation. Not only is there a need for such policies, but a process should also exist to assist employees in appealing disciplinary actions arising from their violation. Because disciplinary action involves interaction between human beings, the process is sometimes biased and emotional, and therefore such actions are not always justified. Unjustified action is unfair to the employee involved, is counterproductive, and has contributed to the loss of union-free status by some firms. It has also resulted in wildcat strikes, walkouts, and slowdowns in unionized firms. Even if employees don't react overtly to unjustified disciplinary actions, morale will likely decline, negatively affecting the firm.

Despite management's desire to solve employee problems in a positive manner, at times this is not possible. A major purpose of disciplinary action is to ensure that employee behavior is consistent with the firm's rules. Rules are established to further the organization's objectives. When a rule is violated, the effectiveness of the organization is diminished to some degree, depending on the severity of the infraction. For instance, if a worker is late to work once, the effect on the firm may be minimal. Consistently being late is another matter because it negatively affects both the productivity of the worker and the morale of other employees. Supervisors must realize that disciplinary action can be a positive force for the company when it is applied responsibly and equitably. The firm benefits from developing and implementing effective disciplinary policies. Without a healthy state of discipline, or the threat of disciplinary action, the firm's effectiveness may be severely limited.

Disciplinary action can also help the employee become more productive, thereby benefiting the employee in the long-run. For example, if a worker is disciplined because of failure to monitor the quality of his or her output—and quality improves after the disciplinary action—it has been useful in the worker's development. Because of improved performance, the individual may receive a promotion or pay increase. The employee is reminded of what is expected and fulfills these requirements better. Effective disciplinary action can thus encourage the individual to improve his or her performance, ultimately resulting in gain for that individual.

■ THE DISCIPLINARY ACTION PROCESS

The disciplinary action process is dynamic and ongoing. Because one person's actions can affect others in a work group, the proper application of disciplinary action fosters acceptable behavior by other group members. Conversely, unjustified or improperly administered disciplinary action can have a detrimental effect on other group members.

The disciplinary action process is shown in Figure 18-1. The external environment affects every area of human resource management, including disciplinary policies and actions. Changes in the external environment, such as technological innovations, may render a rule inappropriate—they

Executive Insights

Barbara Sullivan
President, Sullivan and Associates

Barbara Sullivan, president of Sullivan and Associates in Los Angeles, was well on the road to becoming a social worker when she met her first human resource professional who inspired her to change her career goal. "Barbara, can you run the College Placement Service Office?" "Sure," was the answer of the naive second year graduate student at Tuskegee Institute in Alabama. Thus began a career in human resources. While serving an internship in public personnel services at Tuskegee Institute, Sullivan was assigned to the Student Placement Office for her field project. When the director of the office became ill, she was given the responsibility of coordinating the recruitment program. She talked to the various recruiters who came to interview on campus about the work they performed. As a result of that experience, and after graduation from college, Sullivan sought employment in the human resource field in Los Angeles.

However, she was surprised to discover that her master's degree in guidance and counseling and her related human resource experience did not eliminate the "need more experience" response from prospective employers. She wanted to be a recruiter, but in 1967, companies were not hiring many black women recruiters. After searching three months for a job, Sullivan finally accepted the only human resource-related position offered to her. She became an employment counselor for an employment agency. After working there for one year, she felt that her agency interviewing experience qualified her to apply for an interviewer's position in the human resource department of Cedars Sinai Medical Center, where she was hired. While employed there, she held the positions of employment manager, EEO coordinator, and employee counselor/trainer.

Sullivan was hired next as human resource director for a new medical facility, West Adams Community Hospital, where she organized and managed the human resource function. At West Adams, she and her department of two employees were responsible for staffing, policy development, training, compensation, and benefits for more than four hundred employees. She also found herself responsible for fighting a union organizing drive, which prepared her for the same situation later in her career.

Sullivan's career goals led her to seek a broader challenge to further her human resource knowledge and experience. "I felt

I was at the top at West Adams, yet I needed to learn more to sharpen my skills." She next joined Children's Hospital as assistant personnel director where she was mentored by two competent women skilled in human resources and organizational development. "After three years at Children's Hospital, I knew I was professional-ready," states Sullivan, "and needed to move to the next challenge." She found it by responding to an advertisement in the Los Angeles Times for a personnel director for the City Attorney's Office, City of Los Angeles.

Sullivan says, "The human resource function, more than any other area, provides the opportunity and exposure for developing executive skills. The combination of people (staffing), project, and financial tasks embodied in the daily duties of a human resource generalist are readily transferable to the executive suite." She is currently proving this as she and her partner, Elaine Wegener (president of the personnel consulting firm PACT), continue to build the highly praised temporary and permanent placement agency, Quest.

Olympic fever hit L.A. in the early 1980s and it also attracted Barbara. She took a leave from Quest and helped establish four staffing centers. The citywide centers processed and placed more than 70,000 workers for the 1984 Olympic Games. She was promoted several times during her employment. After the Olympic Games, Barbara began another business venture: a wholesale hosiery distribution company. In this business, she and her two partners have developed more than 1,000 distributors.

Barbara's current consulting practice, Sullivan and Associates, oversees a placement program for employees who have been laid off as a result of reductions in staff or plant closures. The firm also designs and implements marketing and sales programs for a major client, Encore Temps, Inc., as well as assisting it in identifying, staffing, and opening new branches. The firm also designs staffing, training, and human resource programs for other clients in the Los Angeles area.

"Because we are human resource professionals, we conduct our offices as extensions of our clients' human resource operations," states Sullivan. She feels that there is a definite need for the services that agencies such as hers provide. She envisions developing a more cooperative spirit in the future between consulting firms and companies, as service to the companies evolves professionally.

Barbara serves on several boards and advisory groups, including the United Negro fund, African American Museum of Art, and International Association for Personnel Women.

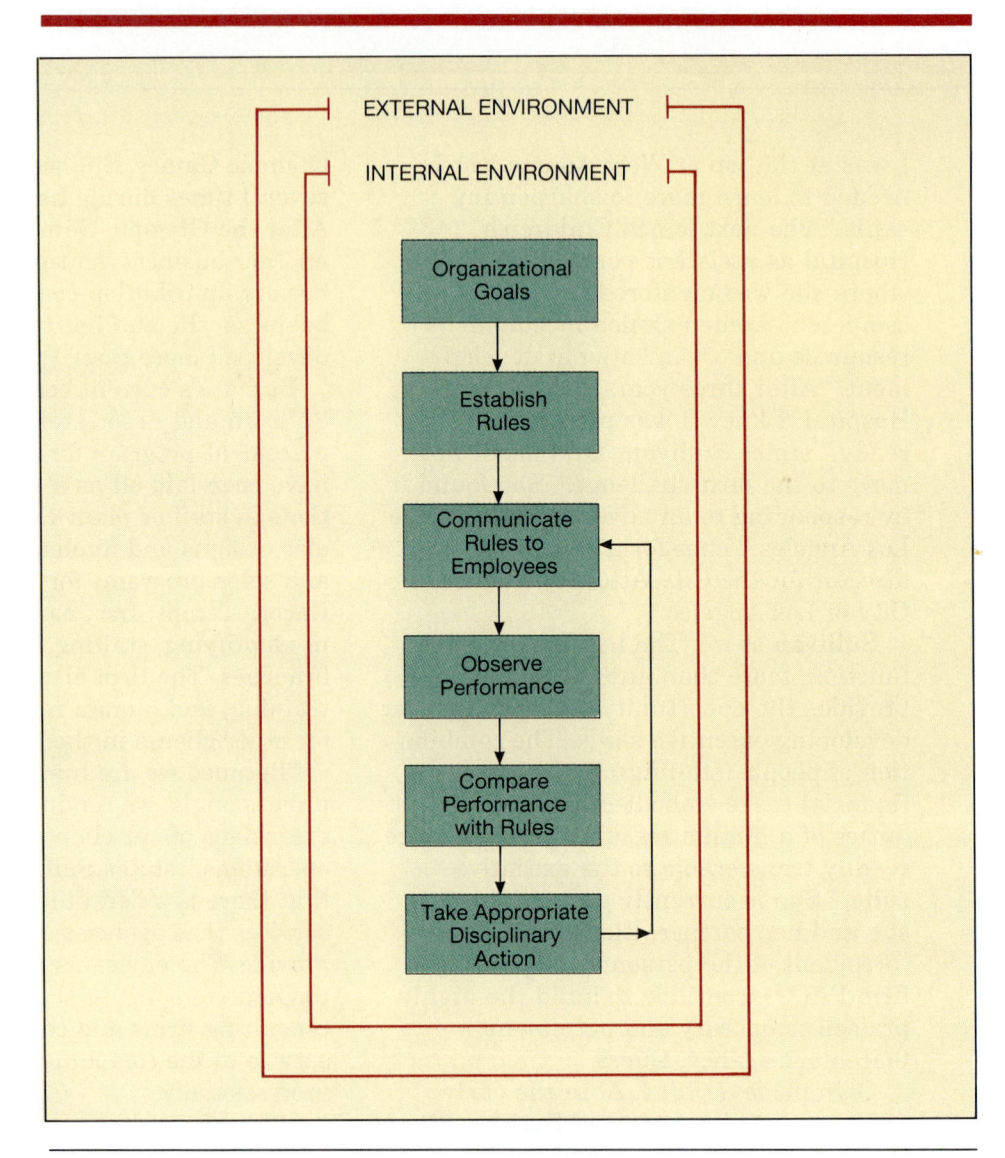

FIGURE 18-1 | The Disciplinary Action Process

may necessitate new rules. Laws and government regulations that affect company policies and rules are also constantly changing. For instance, OSHA has caused many firms to establish safety rules.

Unions are another external factor. Specific punishment for rule violations are subject to negotiation and inclusion in the agreement. For instance, the union may negotiate three written warnings for tardiness before a worker is suspended instead of the two warnings a present contract might require.

Changes in the internal environment of the firm can also alter the disciplinary process. Through organizational development, the firm may alter

CHAPTER 18   Internal Employee Relations   667

its culture. This change may result in first-line supervisors handling disciplinary action more positively. Organization policies can also have an impact on the disciplinary action process. For instance, a policy of treating employees as mature human beings would significantly affect the process.

The disciplinary action process deals largely with infractions of rules. Rules are specific guides to behavior on the job. The do's and don'ts associated with accomplishing tasks may be highly inflexible. For example, company rules may prohibit smoking in certain areas and require that hard hats be worn in hazardous areas for safety reasons.

After management has established rules, they must be communicated to employees. Individuals cannot obey a rule if they do not know it exists. So long as employee behavior doesn't vary from acceptable practices, there's no need for disciplinary action. But when an employee's behavior violates a rule, corrective action may be necessary. The purpose of this action is to alter the types of behavior that can have a negative impact on achievement of organizational objectives—not merely to chastise the violator.

Note that the process shown in Figure 18-1 includes feedback from the point of taking appropriate disciplinary action to communicating rules to employees. When appropriate disciplinary action is taken, employees should realize that certain behaviors are unacceptable and should not be repeated. However, if appropriate disciplinary action is not taken, employees may view the behavior as acceptable and repeat it.

■ APPROACHES TO DISCIPLINARY ACTION

Several concepts regarding the administration of disciplinary action have been developed. We discuss three of these concepts next: the hot stove rule, progressive disciplinary action, and disciplinary action without punishment.

The Hot Stove Rule

One approach to administering disciplinary action is referred to as the hot stove rule. According to this approach, disciplinary action should have the following consequences, which are analogous to touching a hot stove:

1. *Burns immediately.* If disciplinary action is to be taken, it must occur immediately so that the individual will understand the reason for it. With the passage of time, people have the tendency to convince themselves that they are not at fault, which tends to partially nullify later disciplinary effects.
2. *Provides warning.* It is also extremely important to provide advance warning that punishment will follow unacceptable behavior. As individuals move closer to a hot stove, they are warned by its heat that they will be burned if they touch it and thus have the opportunity to avoid the burn if they so choose.
3. *Gives consistent punishment.* Disciplinary action should also be consistent in that everyone who performs the same act will be punished accordingly. As with a hot stove, each person who touches it with the

same degree of pressure, and for the same period of time, is burned to the same extent.
4. *Burns impersonally*. Disciplinary action should be impersonal. The hot stove burns anyone who touches it—without favoritism.

Although the hot stove approach has some merit, it also has weaknesses. If the circumstances surrounding all disciplinary situations were the same, there would be no problem with this approach. However, situations are often quite different, and many variables may be present in each individual disciplinary case. For instance, does the organization penalize a loyal, twenty-year employee the same as an individual who has been with the firm less than six weeks? Thus a supervisor often finds that he or she cannot be completely consistent and impersonal in taking disciplinary action. Because situations do vary, the progressive disciplinary action philosophy may be more realistic—and more beneficial to both the employee and the organization.

Progressive Disciplinary Action

Progressive disciplinary action is intended to ensure that the minimum penalty appropriate to the offense is imposed. Its use involves answering a series of questions about the severity of the offense. The manager must ask a series of questions—in sequence—to determine the proper disciplinary action as illustrated in Figure 18-2. After the manager has determined that disciplinary action is appropriate, the appropriate question is: "Does the violation warrant more than an oral warning?" If the improper behavior is minor and has not previously occurred, perhaps only an oral warning will be sufficient. Also, an individual may receive several oral warnings before a "yes" answer applies. The manager follows the same procedure for each level of offense in the progressive disciplinary process. The manager does not consider termination until each lower level question is answered "yes." However, major violations, such as hitting a supervisor or another worker, may justify immediate termination of the employee.

In order to assist managers in recognizing the proper level of disciplinary action, some firms have formalized the procedure. One approach is to establish progressive disciplinary action guidelines, as shown in Table 18-1. In this example, a worker who is absent without authorization will receive an oral warning the first time it happens and a written warning the second time; the third time, the employee will be terminated. Fighting on the job is an offense that normally results in immediate termination. However, specific guidelines for various offenses should be developed to meet the needs of the industry and the organization. For example, smoking in an unauthorized area may be grounds for immediate dismissal in an explosives factory. On the other hand, the same violation may be less serious in a plant producing concrete products. Basically, the penalty should be appropriate to address the severity of the violation, and no greater.

CHAPTER 18 Internal Employee Relations

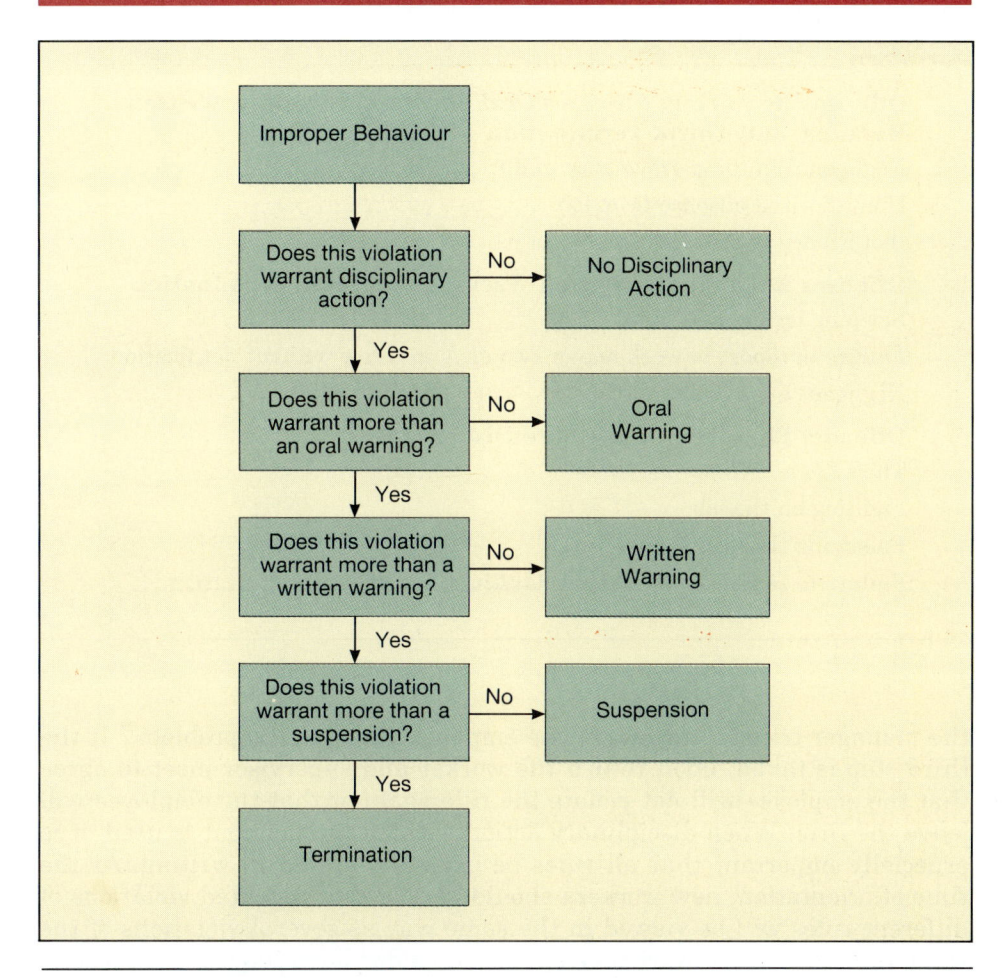

FIGURE 18-2 | The Progressive Disciplinary Approach

Disciplinary Action Without Punishment

Disciplinary action without punishment gives a worker time off with pay to think about whether he or she really wants to follow the rules and continue working for the company.[2] When an employee violates a rule, the manager issues an "oral reminder." Repetition brings a "written reminder." The third violation results in the worker having to take one, two, or three days off (with pay) to think about the situation. During the first two steps

---
[2] Laurie Baum, "Punishing Workers with a Day Off," *Business Week* (June 16, 1986), p. 80.

TABLE 18-1 | Suggested Guidelines for Disciplinary Action

Offenses Requiring, First, an Oral Warning, Second, a Written Warning, and Third, Termination
Negligence in the performance of duties
Unauthorized absence from job
Inefficiency in the performance of job

Offenses Requiring a Written Warning and Then Termination
Sleeping on the job
Failure to report to work one or two days in a row without notification
Negligent use of property

Offenses Requiring Immediate Discharge
Theft
Fighting on the job
Falsifying time cards
Failure to report to work three days in a row without notification

---

the manager tries to encourage the employee to solve the problem.[3] If the third step is taken, upon return the worker and supervisor meet to agree that the employee will not violate the rule again or that the employee will leave the firm. When disciplinary action without punishment is used, it is especially important that all rules be explicitly stated in writing. At the time of orientation, new workers should be told that repeated violations of different rules will be viewed in the same way as several violations of the same rule. This keeps workers from taking undue advantage of the process.

■ ADMINISTRATION OF DISCIPLINARY ACTION

As you might expect, disciplinary actions are not pleasant supervisory tasks. Many managers find them to be quite difficult. Reasons for managers wanting to avoid disciplinary action include:

1. *Lack of training*. The supervisor may not have the knowledge and skill necessary to handle disciplinary problems.
2. *Fear*. The supervisor may be concerned that top management will not support a disciplinary action.
3. *The only one*. The supervisor may feel that "No one else is disciplining employees, so why should I?"
4. *Guilt*. The supervisor may think: "How can I discipline someone if I've done the same thing?"

---

[3] David N. Campbell, R. L. Fleming, and Richard C. Grote, "Discipline Without Punishment—At Last," *Harvard Business Review*, 63 (July–August 1985), p. 168.

5. *Loss of friendship.* The supervisor may believe that disciplinary action will damage friendship with an employee or the employee's associates.
6. *Time loss.* The supervisor may begrudge the valuable time that the interview takes.
7. *Loss of temper.* The supervisor may be afraid of losing his or her temper when talking to an employee about a rule violation.
8. *Rationalization.* The supervisor may reason that "The employee knows it was the wrong thing to do, so why do we need to talk about it?"[4]

These reasons apply to all forms of disciplinary action—from an oral warning to termination. However, we should mention some additional reasons regarding termination. Supervisors often avoid this form of disciplinary action, even when it is in the company's best interest. This reluctance often stems from breakdowns in other areas of the human resource management function. For instance, if a supervisor has consistently rated an employee high on annual performance appraisals, the supervisor's position for terminating a worker for poor performance would be weak. It is embarrassing to decide to fire a worker and then be asked why you rated this individual so high on the previous evaluation. It could be that the employee's productivity has actually dropped substantially. It could also be that the employee's productivity has always been low but that the supervisor has been reluctant to give the individual a low rating.

Another problem related to reluctance to fire employees for cause is poor record keeping. Without adequate documentation, the supervisor may have trouble justifying to upper level management that a person should be terminated. Rather than run the risk of a decision being overturned, the supervisor retains the ineffective worker.

Finally, some supervisors believe that even attempting to terminate women and minorities is useless. However, the statutes and subsequent court decisions have never meant to protect nonproductive workers. Anyone whose performance is consistently below standard can, and should, be terminated after the supervisor has made reasonable attempts to salvage the employee.

A supervisor may be perfectly justified in administering disciplinary action, but there is usually a proper time and place for doing so. For example, disciplining a worker in the presence of others may embarrass the individual and actually defeat the purpose of the action. Even when they are wrong, employees resent disciplinary action administered in public. The incident at the beginning of the chapter in which Bill Martin quit his job because he was disciplined before his peers provides an excellent illustration. By disciplining employees in private, supervisors allow them to save face with their peers.

In addition, many supervisors may be too lenient early in the disciplinary action process and too strict later. This lack of consistency doesn't give the worker a clear understanding of the penalty associated with the inappropriate action. As Robert F. Garrett, manager of labor relations for

---

[4] Wallace Wohlking, "Effective Discipline in Employee Relations," *Personnel Journal*, 54 (September 1975), p. 489.

Georgia-Pacific Corporation, stated: "A supervisor will often endure an unacceptable situation for an extended period of time. Then, when the supervisor finally does take action, he or she is apt to overreact and come down excessively hard." However, consistency does not necessarily mean that the same penalty must be applied to two different workers for the same offense. For instance, employers would be consistent if they always considered the worker's past record and length of service. For a serious violation, a long-term employee might only receive a suspension, while a worker with only a few months' service might be terminated for the same act. This type of action could reasonably be viewed as being consistent.

In order to assist management in administering discipline properly, a *Code on Discipline Procedure* has been prepared by the Advisory, Conciliation and Arbitration Service. The purpose of the code is to give practical guidance on how to formulate disciplinary rules and procedures and use them effectively. The code recommends the actions shown in Table 18-2. As you can see, it stresses communication of rules, telling the employee of the complaint, conducting a full investigation, and giving the employee an opportunity to tell his or her side of the story.

■ GRIEVANCE HANDLING UNDER A COLLECTIVE BARGAINING AGREEMENT

If employees in an organization are represented by a union, workers who believe that they have been disciplined or dealt with unjustly can appeal

TABLE 18-2 | Recommended Disciplinary Procedures

- All employees should be given a copy of the employer's rules on disciplinary procedures. The procedures should specify which employees they cover and what disciplinary actions may be taken, and should allow matters to be dealt with quickly.
- Employees should be told of complaints against them and given an opportunity to state their case. They should have the right to be accompanied by a trade union representative or fellow employee of their choice.
- Disciplinary action should not be taken until the case has been fully investigated. Immediate superiors should not have the power to dismiss without reference to senior management, and, except for gross misconduct, no employee should be dismissed for a first breach of discipline.
- Employees should be given an explanation for any penalty imposed, and they should have a right of appeal, with specified procedures to be followed.
- When disciplinary action other than summary dismissal is needed, supervisors should give a formal oral warning in the case of minor offenses, or a written warning in more serious cases.

Source: "Code on Discipline Procedure," *Industrial Management*, 7 (August 1977), p. 7. Used with permission.

HRM In Action

As Billy Bowen, a first-line supervisor for Kwik Corporation, entered the office of Sandra Findley, human resource director, he was obviously disturbed and wanted help. Billy started the conversation by saying, "Allen Smith, one of my employees, violated a serious company policy today by failing to wear his safety glasses on a very dangerous job. The company policy states that any employee who does not follow the stated policy will receive a written reprimand on the first offense and will be terminated on the second violation. Allen has already received one reprimand and has just committed his second violation. However, he has been one of my best workers for over five years, and letting him go could have a really negative impact on productivity.

What advice should Sandra provide?

---

through the grievance and arbitration procedures of the collective bargaining agreement. The grievance procedure has been described as "one of the truly great accomplishments of the American industrial relations movement. For all its defects...it constitutes a social invention of great importance."[5] The grievance system encourages and facilitates the settlement of disputes between labor and management. A grievance procedure permits employees to express complaints without jeopardizing their jobs. It also assists management in seeking out the underlying causes and solutions to grievances.

The Grievance Procedure

Virtually all labor agreements include some form of grievance procedure. A **grievance** can be broadly defined as an employee's dissatisfaction or feeling of personal injustice relating to his or her employment. A grievance under a collective bargaining agreement is normally well defined. It is usually restricted to violations of the terms and conditions of the agreement. Other conditions that may give rise to a grievance are:

- A violation of law.
- A violation of the intent of the parties as stipulated during contract negotiations.
- A violation of company rules.

---

[5] Neil W. Chamberlain, *The Labor Sector* (New York: McGraw-Hill, 1955), p. 240.

- A change in working conditions or past company practices.
- A violation of health and/or safety standards.[6]

Grievance procedures have many common features. However, variations may reflect differences in organizational or decision-making structures or the size of a plant or company. Some general principles based on widespread practice can serve as useful guidelines for effective grievance administration:

- Grievances should be adjusted promptly.
- Procedures and forms used for airing grievances must be easy to utilize and well understood by employees and their supervisors.
- Direct and timely avenues of appeal from rulings of line supervision must exist.[7]

The multiple-step grievance procedure shown in Figure 18-3 is the most common type. In the first step, the employee usually presents the grievance orally and informally to the immediate supervisor in the presence of the union steward. This step offers the greatest potential for improved labor relations and a large majority of grievances are settled here. The procedure ends if the grievance can be resolved at this first step. If it remains unresolved, the next step involves a meeting between the plant manager or human resource manager and higher union officials, such as the grievance committee or the business agent or manager. Prior to this meeting the grievance is written out, dated, and signed by the employee and the union steward. The written grievance states the events as the employee perceives them, cites the contract provision that allegedly has been violated, and indicates the settlement desired. If the grievance is not settled at this meeting, it is appealed to the third step. This step typically involves the firm's top labor representative (such as the vice-president of industrial relations) and high-level union officials. At times, depending on the severity of the grievance, the president may represent the firm. A grievance that remains unresolved at the conclusion of the third step may go to arbitration, if provided for in the agreement and the union decides to persevere.

Labor-relations problems can escalate when the supervisor is not equipped to handle grievances at the first step. Although the first step is usually handled informally by the union steward, the aggrieved party, and the supervisor, the supervisor must be prepared. The supervisor should obtain as many facts as possible before the meeting because the union steward is likely to have done his or her homework.

The supervisor needs to recognize that the grievance may not reflect the real problem. For instance, the employee might be mad at the company for modifying its pay policies, even though the change was agreed to by the union. In order to voice discontent, the worker might file a grievance for an unrelated, minor violation of the contract. The idea of hidden causes of

---

[6] K. L. Sovereign and Mario Bognanno, "Positive Contract Administration." In Dale Yoder and Herbert G. Heneman, Jr. (eds.), *ASPA Handbook of Personnel and Industrial Relations: Employee and Labor Relations*, Vol. III (Washington, D.C.: The Bureau of National Affairs, 1976), pp. 7-161–7-162.

[7] *Ibid.*, p. 7-164.

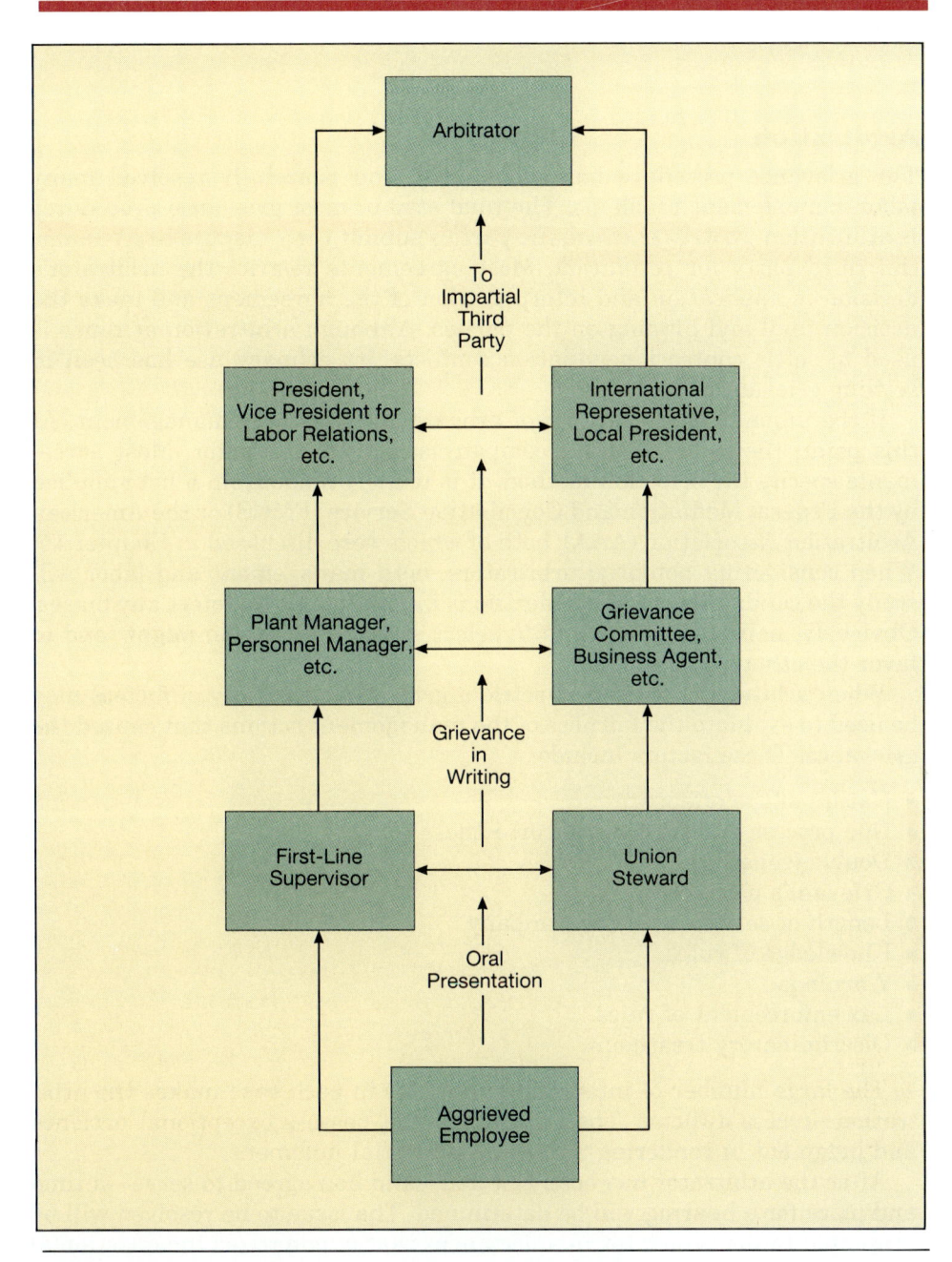

FIGURE 18-3 | A Multiple-Step Grievance Procedure

Source: Robert W. Eckles et al., *Essentials of Management for First-Line Supervision* (New York: John Wiley & Sons, 1974), p. 529. Reprinted by permission of John Wiley & Sons, Inc.

grievances has been referred to as the "iceberg theory"[8] and must always be explored.

Arbitration

The grievance procedure has successfully and peacefully resolved many labor–management problems. The final step in most grievance procedures is arbitration. In **arbitration**, the parties submit their dispute to an impartial third party for resolution. Most agreements restrict the arbitrator's decision to application and interpretation of the agreement and make the decision final and binding on the parties. Although arbitration at times is used to settle contract negotiation conflicts, its primary use has been in settling grievances.

If the union decides in favor of arbitration, it notifies management. At this point, the union and the company select an arbitrator. Most agreements specify the selection method. It is usually made from a list supplied by the Federal Mediation and Conciliation Service (FMCS) or the American Arbitration Association (AAA), both of which were discussed in Chapter 16. When considering potential arbitrators, both management and labor will study the candidates' previous decisions in an attempt to detect any biases. Obviously, neither party wants to select an arbitrator who might tend to favor the other's position.

When arbitration is used to settle a grievance, a variety of factors may be used to evaluate the fairness of the management actions that caused the grievance. These factors include:

- Nature of the offense.
- Due process and procedural correctness.
- Double jeopardy.
- Grievant's past record.
- Length of service with the company.
- Knowledge of rules.
- Warnings.
- Lax enforcement of rules.
- Discriminatory treatment.

The large number of interacting variables in each case makes the arbitration process difficult. The arbitrator must possess exceptional patience and judgment in rendering a fair and impartial judgment.

After the arbitrator has been selected—and has agreed to serve—a time and place for a hearing will be determined. The issue to be resolved will be presented to the arbitrator in a document that summarizes the question(s) to be decided. It will also point out any contract restrictions that prohibit the arbitrator from making an award that would change the terms of the contract.

At the hearing, each side presents its case. Arbitration is an adversary proceeding, so a case may be lost because of poor preparation and presen-

---
[8] *Ibid.*, p. 7-159.

tation. The arbitrator may conduct the hearing much like a courtroom proceeding. Witnesses, cross-examination, transcripts, and legal counsel may all be used. The parties may also submit, or be asked by the arbitrator to submit, formal written statements. After the hearing, the arbitrator studies the material submitted and testimony given and reaches a decision within thirty to sixty days. The decision is usually accompanied by a written opinion giving reasons for the decision.

The courts will generally enforce an arbitrator's decision unless: (1) the arbitrator's decision is shown to be unreasonable or capricious in that it did not address the issues; (2) the arbitrator exceeded his or her authority; or (3) the award or decision violated a federal or state law.

Proof That Disciplinary Action Was Needed

Any disciplinary action administered may ultimately be taken to arbitration, when such a remedy exists. Employers have learned that they must prepare records that will constitute proof before an arbitrator.

The supervisor should document any employee behavior suggesting that disciplinary action may ultimately be required. The burden of proof is on the employer, so the supervisor should record information regarding events, circumstances, places, and witnesses. It is not sufficient for the employer to allege that the employee is incompetent; the arbitrator will demand clear proof.

Written warnings offer substantial proof of disciplinary action and the reasons for it. Although the format of a written warning may vary, the following information should be included:

1. Statement of facts concerning the offense.
2. Identification of the rule that was violated.
3. Statement of what resulted or could have resulted because of the violation.
4. Identification of any previous similar violations by the same individual.
5. Statement of possible future consequences should the violation occur again.
6. Signature and date.

An example of a written warning is shown in Figure 18-4. In this instance, the worker has already received an oral reprimand. The individual is also warned that continued tardiness could lead to termination. It is important to document oral reprimands because they may be the first step in disciplinary action leading ultimately to arbitration.

Weaknesses of Arbitration

Arbitration has achieved a certain degree of success in resolving grievances. However, it is not without weaknesses. Some practitioners claim that arbitration is losing its effectiveness because of the length of time

> DATE: August 1, 1989
> TO: Shane Boudreaux
> FROM: Wayne Sanders
> SUBJECT: Written Warning
>
> We are quite concerned because today you were thirty minutes late to work and offered no justification for this. According to our records, a similar offense occurred on July 25, 1989. At that time you were informed that failure to report to work on time is unacceptable. I am therefore notifying you in writing that you must report to work on time. It will be necessary to terminate your employment if this happens again.
>
> Please sign this form to indicate that you have read and understand this warning. Signing is not an indication of agreement.
>
> _____
> Name
>
> _____
> Date

FIGURE 18-4 | An Example of a Written Warning

between the first step of the grievance procedure and final settlement. Often, 100–250 days may elapse before a decision is made.[9] The reason for the initial filing of the grievance may actually be forgotten before it is finally settled.

Others object to the cost of arbitration, which has been rising at an alarming rate. The cost of settling even a simple arbitration case can be quite high, even though it is typically shared by labor and management. Forcing every grievance to arbitration could be used as a tactic to place either management or the union in a difficult financial position.

■ GRIEVANCE HANDLING IN UNION-FREE ORGANIZATIONS

As we mentioned in Chapter 17, until the early 1980s few union-free firms had formalized grievance procedures. In fact, a 1977 study by Scott found that only 11 percent of union-free firms (91 of 793) had any kind of griev-

---

[9] Lawrence Stessin, "Expedited Arbitration: Less Grief Over Grievances," *Harvard Business Review*, 55 (January–February 1977), p. 129.

ance procedure.[10] Today this is not the case, as more and more firms establish formal grievance procedures.

While the step-by-step procedure for handling union grievances is common practice, the means of resolving complaints in union-free firms varies. A well-designed grievance procedure ensures that the worker has ample opportunity to make complaints without fear of reprisal. If the system is to work, employees must be well informed about the program and convinced that management wants them to use it. Most employees are hesitant to formalize their complaints and must be constantly urged to avail themselves of the process.[11] The fact that a manager says, "Our workers must be happy because I have received no complaints," does not necessarily mean that employees have no grievances. In a closed, threatening corporate culture, workers may be reluctant to voice their dissatisfaction to management.

Typically, an employee initiates a complaint with his or her immediate supervisor. However, if the complaint involves the supervisor, the individual is permitted to bypass the immediate supervisor and proceed to the employee-relations specialist or the manager at the next higher level. The grievance ultimately may be taken to the organization's top executive for a final decision.

■ TERMINATION

Termination is the most severe penalty that an organization can impose on its employees. Therefore, it should be the most carefully considered disciplinary action. The experience of being terminated is traumatic for employees regardless of their position in the organization. Feelings of failure, fear, disappointment, and anger can occur. It is also a difficult time for the person making the termination decision. Knowing that termination may affect not only the employee but an entire family increases the trauma. Not knowing how the terminated employee will react also may create considerable anxiety for the manager who must do the firing. Regardless of the similarities in the termination of employees at various levels, distinct differences exist with regard to nonmanagerial/nonprofessional employees, executives, managers, and professionals. Termination is an extremely serious form of discipline, and must therefore always be carefully considered and appropriate.

Termination of Nonmanagerial/Nonprofessional Employees

Individuals in this category are neither managers nor professionally trained individuals, such as engineers or accountants. They generally include employ-

---

[10] William G. Scott, *The Management of Conflict: Appeal System in Organizations* (Homewood, Ill.: Richard D. Irwin, 1977), pp. 56–80.

[11] James P. Swann, Jr., "Formal Grievance Procedures in Non-Union Plants," *Personnel Administrator*, 26 (August 1981), p. 67.

ees such as steel workers, secretaries, truck drivers, and waiters. If the firm is unionized, the termination procedure is typically well defined in the labor–management agreement. For example, drinking on the job might be identified as a reason for immediate termination. Excessive absences, on the other hand, may require three written warnings by the supervisor before termination action can be taken.

When the firm is union-free, these workers could be terminated at any time for any reason. A history of unjustified terminations within a firm, however, may provide an opportunity for unionization. In many union-free organizations, violations justifying termination are included in the firm's employee handbook. At times, especially in smaller organizations, the termination process is informal, with the first-line supervisor advising employees as to what actions warrant termination. Regardless of the size of the organization, employees should be informed by a representative of management of the actions that warrant termination.

Termination of Executives

Executive termination must be viewed from a different perspective. Executives usually have no formal appeal procedure. The decision to terminate an executive has probably been approved by the chief executive officer in the organization. In addition, the reasons for termination may not be as clear as for lower level employees. Some of the reasons include:

1. *Economic.* At times, business conditions may force a reduction in the number of executives.
2. *Reorganization.* In order to improve efficiency, a firm may reorganize, resulting in the elimination of some executive positions.
3. *Philosophical differences.* A difference in philosophy of conducting business may develop between an executive and other key company officials. In order to maintain consistency in management philosophy, the executive may be replaced.
4. *Decline in productivity.* The executive may have been capable of performing satisfactorily in the past, but, for various reasons, he or she can no longer perform the job as required.

This list does not include factors related to illegal activities or actions taken that are not in the best interests of the firm. Under those circumstances, the firm has no moral obligation to the terminated executive.

While an organization may derive positive benefits from terminating executives, they also present a potentially hazardous situation for the organization. Many corporations are concerned about developing a negative public image that reflects insensitivity to the needs of their employees. They fear that such a reputation would impede their efforts to recruit high-quality managers. Also, terminated executives have, at times, made public statements detrimental to the reputation of the firm.

Termination of Middle and Lower Level Managers and Professionals

In the past, the most vulnerable and perhaps the most neglected group of employees with regard to termination has been middle and lower level managers and professionals, who are generally not union members and thus not protected by a labor–management agreement. They also may not have the political clout that a terminated executive may have. Termination may have been based on something as simple as the attitude or feelings of an immediate superior on a given day. Some firms have begun to provide outplacement services for these individuals.

Outplacement

Many organizations have established a systematic means of assisting terminated employees in locating jobs. In **outplacement**, a terminated employee is given assistance in finding employment elsewhere. Through outplacement, the firm tries to soften the impact of termination, particularly for an employee who has been with the firm for a long time. Often an outside consultant is employed to aid the terminated employee in finding appropriate employment elsewhere. The reason for termination will likely determine the amount of effort devoted to outplacement assistance. If the individual was terminated because of a reduction in the workforce, more effort is likely than if the individual made a serious error in judgment that harmed the company.

The use of outplacement began at the executive level but has recently been used at other organizational levels. In executive termination, the use of outside consultants probably is superior to the use of in-house staff members. The released executive may not trust insiders and may be more open with an outsider. When executive outplacement is used, outplacement consultants provide the executive with a variety of services. Consultants may initially assist the executive in performing a thorough self-assessment to determine his or her future career interests. The consultant will also instruct the executive in proper interviewing techniques. Because the executive may not have had an interview in many years, the consultant can help the individual prepare for reentry into the job market. The outplacement consultant also may assist the executive in identifying firms that could best use his or her capabilities. At organizational levels lower than upper middle management, the outplacement consultant is often the human resource manager. Much the same services may be provided to other terminated individuals.

■ EMPLOYMENT AT WILL

Approximately two of every three U.S. workers' jobs depend almost entirely on the continued goodwill of their employers. Individuals falling into this category are known as "at-will employees." Generally, the U.S. legal system presumes that the jobs of such employees may be terminated at the will of the employer and that these employees have a similar right to leave their jobs at any time.[12] **Employment at will** is an unwritten contract that is created when an employee agrees to work for an employer, but there is no agreement as to how long the parties expect the employment to last. Because of a century-old common law precedent in the United States, employment of indefinite duration can, in general, be terminated at the whim of either party.

With the exception of a few states, the employment-at-will rule is the current standard everywhere in the country. However, a trend appears to be developing that could afford workers greater job security. Many courts have decided that terminations of at-will employees are unlawful if they are contrary to general notions of acceptable "public policy" or if they are done in "bad faith."[13]

Although the concept of employment at will remains strong, judges, legislators, and employees are increasingly willing to challenge rigid notions of unlimited employer discretion. In addition, court decisions are eroding employment-at-will doctrine in 30 states. New Jersey, California, and Michigan are among the most influential states that have established new limitations on the power of employers to dismiss workers.[14]

However, employers can do certain things to protect themselves against litigation for wrongful discharge based on a breach of implied employment contract. For example, statements in documents such as employment applications and policy manuals that suggest job security or permanent employment should be avoided[15] if employers want to minimize charges of wrongful discharge. Companies such as Sears Roebuck & Company have long been determined in protecting their right to terminate at will. Each job applicant signs a statement that he or she can be terminated at any time "with or without cause," which has helped Sears win court cases. According to Mark A. Jacoby, head of the employment law practice at Weil, Gotshal & Manges in New York: "To minimize liability, corporations have to treat each dismissal as though it were under a 'just cause' provision of a contract." As companies are devising better defenses, one new reality confronting managers is that more than ever, firing decisions are likely to be second-guessed.[16]

■ RESIGNATION

Even when an organization is totally committed to making its environment a good place to work, workers will still resign. Some employees cannot see

---

[12] Lawrence Z. Lorber, J. Robert Kirk, Kenneth H. Kirschner, and Charlene R. Handorf, *Fear of Firing: A Legal and Personal Analysis of Employment at Will* (Alexandria, Va.: The ASPA Foundation, 1984), p. 1.

[13] *Ibid.*, p. 1.

[14] John Hoerr et al., "Beyond Unions," *Business Week* (July 8, 1985), p. 75.

[15] Lorber et al., p. 20.

[16] Hoerr et al., pp. 73, 75–77.

promotional opportunities, or at least not enough, for themselves and will move on. A certain amount of turnover is healthy for an organization and is often necessary to afford employees the opportunity to fulfill career objectives. But when turnover becomes excessive, something must be done. The most qualified employees are often the ones who resign because they are more mobile. On the other hand, marginally qualified workers seemingly never leave. If excessive numbers of a firm's highly qualified and competent workers are leaving, means must be found to reverse the trend.

Analyzing Voluntary Resignations

A frequently given reason for resignation is to obtain a better salary and/or benefits. However, most firms conduct salary surveys or otherwise keep in touch with what competitors are paying. Research has shown that when workers mention pay as a reason for resigning, they often have other, deeper reasons for deciding to leave. The cause may be a department manager with whom no one can work or a corporate culture that is stifling creative employees. Management should identify the causes and correct them as quickly as possible.

When a firm wants to determine the real reasons that individuals decide to leave, it can use the exit interview and/or the postexit questionnaire. The exit interview typically is the last major contact the employee has with the company. The exit interview encourages the employee to tell the reasons for resigning openly and freely. A human resource professional usually conducts this interview. An employee is not as likely to respond as freely during an interview with the supervisor, reasoning that he or she may need a letter of recommendation from the supervisor in the future. The typical exit interview involves the following:

- Establishment of rapport.
- Purpose of the interview.
- Attitudes regarding the old job.
- Exploration of reasons for leaving.
- Comparing the old and new jobs.
- Changes recommended.
- Conclusion.[17]

Specific topics that might be covered by the interviewer during the exit interview are listed in Figure 18-5. Note that the interviewer is focusing on job-related factors and is probing for the real reasons that the person is leaving. Over a period of time, properly conducted exit interviews can provide considerable insight into why employees are leaving. Patterns are often identified that uncover weaknesses in the firm's human resource management system. Knowledge of the problem permits corrective action to be taken.

The postexit questionnaire is sent to former employees several weeks after they leave the organization. Usually, they have already started work

---

[17] Wanda R. Embrey, R. Wayne Mondy, and Robert M. Noe, "Exit Interview: A Tool for Personnel Development," *Personnel Administrator*, 24 (May 1979), p. 46.

> 1. Let's begin by your outlining briefly some of the duties of your job.
> 2. Of the duties you just outlined, tell me three or four that are crucial to the performance of your job.
> 3. Tell me about some of the duties you liked the most and what you liked about performing those duties.
> 4. Now, tell me about some of the duties you liked least and what you did not like about performing those duties.
> 5. Suppose you describe the amount of variety in your job.
> 6. Let's talk a little bit now about the amount of work assigned to you. For example, was the amount assigned not enough at times, perhaps too much at times, or was it fairly stable and even overall?
> 7. Suppose you give me an example of an incident that occurred on your job that was especially satisfying to you. What about an incident that was a little less satisfying.
> 8. Let's talk now about the extent to which you feel you were given the opportunity to use your educational background, skills, and abilities on your job.
> 9. Tell me how you would assess the quality of training on your job.
> 10. Suppose you describe the promotional opportunities open to you in your job.

FIGURE 18-5 | Questions Related to General Job Factors

Source: Wanda R. Embrey, R. Wayne Mondy, and Robert M. Noe, "Exit Interview: A Tool for Personnel Development." Reprinted from the May 1979 issue of *Personnel Administrator*, copyright © 1979, The American Society for Personnel Administration, Alexandria, Virginia.

at their new company. The questionnaire is structured to draw out the real reason that the employee left. Ample blank space is also provided so that former employees can express their feelings about, and perceptions of, the job and the organization. One strength of this approach is that the individuals are no longer with the firm and may respond more freely to the questions. A weakness is that the interviewer is not present to interpret and probe for the real reasons for leaving.

Advance Notice of Resignation

Most firms would like to have at least two-week's notice of resignation from departing workers. However, a month's notice may be desired from professional and managerial employees who are leaving. When notice is desired by the firm, the policy should be clearly communicated to all employees. If they want departing employees to give advance notice, companies have certain obligations. For instances, suppose that a worker gives notice—then is terminated immediately. Word of this action will spread rapidly to other employees. Should they decide to resign, they will likely not give any advance notice.

However, permitting a resigned worker to remain on the job once a resignation has been submitted may create some problems. If bad feelings exist between the employee and the supervisor, or the company, the departing worker may be a disruptive force. On a selective basis, the firm may wish to pay the employee for the notice time and ask him or her to leave immediately. However, this action should not often be necessary.

■ DEMOTION AS AN ALTERNATIVE TO TERMINATION

Termination frequently is the solution used when a person isn't able to perform his or her job. At times, however, demotions are used as an alternative to discharge, especially when a long-term employee is involved. The worker may have performed satisfactorily for many years, but his or her productivity may then begin to decline for a variety of reasons. Perhaps the worker is just not physically capable of performing the job any longer. Or the individual may no longer be willing to work the long hours that the job requires. **Demotion** is the process of moving a worker to a lower level of duties and responsibilities, which typically involves a reduction in pay. Emotions often run high when an individual is demoted. The demoted person may feel betrayed, loss of respect from peers, embarrassment, anger, and disappointment. The employee's productivity may also decrease further. For these reasons, demotion should be used very cautiously.

One means of reducing the trauma associated with a demotion is to establish a probationary period in which a promoted worker is permitted to try out the new job. Should the person not work out, the individual will not view moving back to the old job so negatively.

If demotion is chosen over termination, efforts must be made to preserve the self-esteem of the individual. The person may be asked how he or she would like to handle the demotion announcement. A positive image of the worker's value to the company should be projected.

The handling of demotions in a unionized organization is usually spelled out clearly in the labor–management agreement. Should a decision be made to demote a worker for unsatisfactory performance, the union should be notified of this intent and given the specific reasons for the demotion. Often the demotion will be challenged and carried through the formal grievance procedure. Documentation is necessary for the demotion to be upheld. Even with the problems associated with demotion for cause, it is often easier to demote than to terminate an employee. In addition, demotion is often less devastating to the employee. For the organization, however, the opposite may be true if the demotion creates lingering ill-will and an embittered employee.

■ LAYOFF

The economic well-being of many companies rises and falls in cycles. At times a firm's goods or services may be in great demand; at other times demand falls. Often when demand is low, the firm has no other choice but to lay off workers. Although being laid off is not the same thing as being fired, it has the same short-term effect: The worker is unemployed.

Being laid off can be worse psychologically than being terminated. With termination, the relationship with the firm is severed, and the former employee has no choice but to look for another job. This is not the case with a layoff because the worker still has some ties to the firm. In many cases, the laid-off worker does not even have a general idea of when he or she will be recalled. In the meantime, the worker's financial resources dwindle. The longer the layoff, the more frustrating it becomes. Lifestyles may change and tension increases.

Whether the firm is union-free or unionized, well-thought-out layoff/recall procedures should be developed. Workers should understand when they are hired how the system will work in the event of a layoff. When the firm is unionized, the layoff procedures are usually stated clearly in the labor–management agreement. Seniority usually is the basis for layoffs, with the least senior employees laid off first. The agreement also likely has a clearly spelled out *bumping* procedure. When senior-level positions are eliminated, the people occupying them have the right to bump workers from lower level positions, assuming that they have the proper qualifications for the lower level job. When bumping occurs, the composition of the workforce is altered.

Procedures for recalling laid-off employees are also usually spelled out in labor–management agreements. Again, seniority is typically the basis for worker recall, with the most senior employees being recalled first.

The trend in many union-free companies such as IBM and Hewlett-Packard is to establish no-layoff policies.[18] However, regardless of a union-free firm's current stand on the issue of layoffs, it should establish layoff procedures prior to facing one. In union free-firms also, seniority should be an integral part of any layoff procedure. But, frequently, other factors should be considered. Productivity of the employee is typically an important consideration. When productivity is a factor, management must be careful to see to it that productivity, not favoritism, is the actual basis. Workers generally have an accurate perception of their own productivity level and that of their fellow employees. Therefore, it is important to accurately define both seniority and productivity considerations well in advance of any layoffs.

■ TRANSFERS

The lateral movement of a worker within an organization is called a **transfer**. A transfer may be initiated by the firm or by an employee. They do not, and should not, infer that a person is being promoted or demoted.

Transfers serve several purposes. First, firms often find it necessary to reorganize. Offices and departments are created and abolished in response to the company's needs. In order to fill positions created by reorganization,

---
[18] Hoerr et al., p. 76.

employee moves not entailing promotion may be necessary. The same is true when an office or department is closed. Rather than terminate valued employees, management may transfer them to other areas within the organization.

A second reason for transfers is to make positions available in the primary promotion channels. Firms are typically organized into a hierarchical structure resembling a pyramid. Each succeeding promotion is more difficult to obtain because fewer positions exist. At times, very productive but unpromotable workers may clog promotion channels. Other qualified workers in the organization may find their opportunities for promotion blocked. When this happens, a firm's most capable future managers may seek employment elsewhere. In order to keep promotion channels open, the firm may decide to transfer employees who are unpromotable but productive at their present levels.

Another reason for transfers is to satisfy employees' personal desires. The reasons for wanting a transfer are numerous. An individual may need to work closer to home to care for aging parents. Or the worker may dislike the long commuting trips to and from work. Factors such as these may be of such importance that employees may resign if a requested transfer is not approved. Rather than risk losing a valued employee, the firm may agree to the transfer.

Transfers may also be an effective means of dealing with personality clashes. Some people just cannot get along with each other. Because each of the individuals may be a valued employee, transfer may be an appropriate solution to the problem. But human resource managers must be cautious regarding the "grass is greener on the other side of the fence" syndrome. When some workers encounter a temporary setback, they immediately ask for a transfer—before they even attempt to work through the problem.

Before any worker's request for transfer is approved, it should be analyzed in terms of the best interests of both the firm and the individual. Disruptions may occur when the worker is transferred if, for example, a qualified worker isn't available to step into the position being vacated.

Management should establish clear policies regarding transfers. Such policies let workers know in advance when a transfer request to be approved is likely and what its ramifications will be. For instance, if the transfer is for personal reasons, some firms do not pay moving costs. Whether the organization will or will not pay should be clearly spelled out.

■ PROMOTION

A **promotion** is the movement of a person to a higher level position in the organization. The term *promotion* is one of the most emotionally charged words in the field of human resource management. An individual who receives a promotion normally receives additional financial rewards and the ego boost associated with achievement and accomplishment. Most employees feel positively about being promoted. But for every individual who gains a promotion, there are probably others who were not selected. If these individuals wanted the promotion badly enough, they may slack off or even resign. If the consensus is that the wrong person was promoted, considerable resentment may result.

Promotions in the future may not be as available as in the past. For one thing, many firms are reducing the number of levels in their hierarchies. As the number of middle management positions declines, fewer promotional opportunities will be available. The effect of these changes is that more people will be striving for fewer promotion opportunities. Consequently, organizations must look for ways other than promotion to reward employees. One alternative is the dual-track system that we described in Chapter 10, whereby highly technical individuals can continue to receive financial rewards without progressing into management.

■ RETIREMENT

Most long-term employees leave an organization by retiring. Retirement plans may be based on a certain age or after a certain number of years, or both. Upon retirement, former employees usually receive a pension each month for the remainder of their lives.

In the past there were far too many instances of retirement-plan failure. Many workers who retired believing that they would receive lifelong pensions were devastated to find that retirement programs had been insufficiently funded by their employers. In 1974, the Employee Retirement Income Security Act (ERISA) was passed for the purpose of protecting employees participating in company-sponsored retirement plans.

Early Retirement

Sometimes employees will retire before reaching the organization's age or length of service requirement. Often, retirement pay is reduced for each year that the retirement date is advanced. From an organization's viewpoint, early employee retirement has both positive and negative aspects.

From a positive viewpoint, a long-term worker may have begun performing below expectations. Rather than fire this worker, the company may offer early retirement. Also, even though an older worker is still performing adequately, this individual may be blocking a promotion channel for highly qualified workers. Further, if an extended layoff is expected, a product line is being discontinued, or a plant is being closed, early retirement may be a responsible solution to the problem of surplus employees.

From a negative viewpoint, valued employees may take advantage of the early retirement option and leave the organization. In addition, early retirement is often more expensive to the company than normal retirement. And, early retirement decisions are often made on short notice, resulting in some disruption of operations.

Retirement Planning

Strong emotions often accompany anticipation of retirement. Questions such as, "Do I have enough money?" "What will I do?" "Will I be able to adjust?"

and many more often haunt the individual as retirement approaches. Just as a well-planned orientation program eases the transition of a new hire into the organization, a company-sponsored retirement planning program eases the transition of long-term employees from work to leisure.

Often a firm devotes time, staff, and money to provide useful information to workers approaching retirement. Typically, such information relates to finances, housing, relocation, family relations, attitude adjustment, and legal affairs.[19]

Some firms have taken retirement planning a step further. At times firms consider both the social and psychological implications of the retirement and change process. Adaptation to retirement living is the focus of this form of planning. Individuals who have already retired are brought to meetings to speak, and to answer questions regarding retirement life. Managing the change in lifestyle is often a topic for discussion,[20] which is helpful to all those considering retirement. Retirement is a major event in an individual's life, and employers can often help to make the transition much smoother.

■ LEGAL IMPLICATIONS OF INTERNAL EMPLOYEE RELATIONS

Many people believe that equal employment opportunity legislation primarily affects individuals entering the company for the first time. Nothing could be further from the truth. Virtually all phases of internal employee relations are affected. Of special concern to the EEOC are decisions relating to promotion. The Household Finance Corporation paid more than $125,000 to white-collar women employees who charged that they were denied promotion because of their gender. Under terms of a consent decree, the company also agreed to hire women for 20 percent of the branch representative openings (subject to availability) until women comprised 20 percent of such representatives. It also was required to hire 20 percent of its new employees from specified minority groups for clerical, credit, and branch representative jobs, until the total of such employees reached 65 percent of their population proportion in the labor area. Household Finance Corporation also agreed to train women and minority employees to help them qualify for better jobs where they are underrepresented.[21]

One of the largest payments ever made was under an agreement signed by AT&T with the EEOC and the Department of Labor. It provided for payment of approximately $15 million to employees allegedly discriminated against. The agreement also called for additional affirmative action and for

---

[19] Marilyn Merikangas, "Retirement Planning with a Difference," *Personnel Journal*, 62 (May 1983), p. 420.
[20] *Ibid.*
[21] *U.S.* v. *Household Finance Corporation*, 4 EPD para. 7680 (N.D. Ill., 1972)—Consent decree.

an estimated $50 million in yearly payments for promotion and wage adjustments to minority and women employees.[22]

Termination of workers when they reach a certain age is a major concern in enforcement of the Age Discrimination Act. In *EEOC* v. *Liggett and Myers*, the commission alleged that age was a factor in the discharge of approximately 10 percent of the employees during a reduction in force. The court ruled against the company, and back-pay recovery is estimated at $20 million. In *Hagman and EEOC* v. *United Airlines*, a jury awarded $18.2 million to 112 pilots who had been forced to retire at age sixty. In *EEOC* v. *Home Insurance Company*, an age discrimination case was won on behalf of 143 employees who had been forced to retire at age sixty-two; back-pay recovery is estimated at $6–8 million.

In 1986, the Age Discrimination in Employment Act was further amended by removing the upper age ceiling for mandatory retirement. Employers who attempt to systematically retire workers for factors other than performance are coming under increased scrutiny by EEOC. The problem in many cases is that prior to termination, high performance evaluations were often given to the employees involved. These evaluations provide the terminated employees with the data they need to develop valid cases contending that the reason for termination was age, not declining performance.

Some firms have tried to open avenues for promotion of younger workers by offering early voluntary retirement. A potential problem with this option is whether the retirement is truly voluntary. Exerting excessive pressure on employees to retire when they really do not want to is beginning to receive considerable EEOC attention.

The thrust of EEO legislation is that women and minorities should not receive unequal treatment, and internal employee relations should reflect this principle. For instance, are blacks being fired at a higher rate than whites? Are women not receiving promotional opportunities? The same questions may be asked about demotions and layoffs. As more and women and minorities enter the workforce, EEO administration will likely focus increasingly on internal employee relations.

■ INTERNAL EMPLOYEE RELATIONS IN MULTINATIONAL CORPORATIONS

As evidenced by the preceding discussion, internal employee relations in the United States are subject to laws, government regulations, union–management agreements, court decisions, and the corporate culture of a firm. Firms operating in the United States must develop their internal employee relations system within these constraints.

For the multinational corporation, the factors affecting internal employee relations in its home country often have to be altered to meet the norms of the host country. For instance, in Japan there are often limitations on layoffs, terminations, and demotions. Obviously, foreign firms operating there

---

[22] U.S. Equal Employment Opportunity Commission, *Affirmative Action and Equal Employment: A Guidebook for Employers*, Vol. 1 (Washington, D.C.: U.S. Government Printing Office, January 1974), p. 10.

will probably not adhere to Japanese norms such as lifetime employment but will have to accommodate many others. Even firms that have very effective approaches to domestic internal employee relations may need to revise their system to account for host country variations.

SUMMARY

A necessary, but often difficult aspect of internal employee relations is disciplinary action. A major purpose of disciplinary action is to ensure that employee behavior is consistent with the firm's policies, rules, and regulations. Disciplinary action invokes a penalty against an employee who fails to meet company standards of behavior.

The disciplinary action process is dynamic and ongoing. Rules are established to facilitate the accomplishment of organizational objectives. These rules must be communicated to employees because they can't obey a rule if they don't know it exists. So long as employee behavior does not vary from acceptable practices, disciplinary action is not needed. But when an employee's behavior violates a rule, corrective action should be taken. The purpose of this action is to alter behavior that can have a negative impact on the organization. When the progressive disciplinary action approach is followed, an attempt is made to make the penalty appropriate to the violation (or accumulated violations).

If the employees in an organization are represented by a union, workers who believe that they have been disciplined or dealt with unjustly can appeal through the grievance procedure of the collective bargaining agreement. A grievance procedure permits employees to express complaints without jeopardizing their jobs. In arbitration, the parties submit a dispute to an impartial third party for resolution, if it cannot otherwise be settled.

Termination is the most severe penalty that an organization can impose on an employee. The procedure used to terminate operative employees—and for them to appeal the decision—is usually well defined. However, executives do not have a formal appeals procedure. In the past, the most vulnerable and perhaps the most neglected groups of employees with regard to termination have been middle and lower level managers and professionals, who generally are not union members and thus not protected by a labor agreement.

Employment at will is created when an employee agrees to work for an employer but there is no agreement as to how long the parties expect the employment to last. In the United States, employment of indefinite duration can, in general, be terminated at the whim of either party.

Internal employee relations also pertain to resignation, demotion, layoff, transfer, promotion, and retirement. Even in the best organizations, some workers will still resign. Two techniques—the exit interview and the post exit questionnaire—may be used to help determine the real reasons that an individual has decided to leave the organization.

At times, demotion of an employee may be a better alternative than termination. Demotion involves moving a worker to a lower level of duties and responsibilities, and typically, less pay.

At times, a firm has no choice but to lay off employees. Although being laid off does not have the same negative connotation as being fired, it has the same short-term effect: The worker is unemployed.

A person can move laterally within the organization by transfer. A transfer may be initiated by the firm or by the employee. Transfers do not, and should not, infer a promotion.

The means by which long-term employees usually leave an organization is through retirement. Retirement may be based on a certain age, a certain number of years' service, or both.

Most people believe that equal employment opportunity legislation primarily affects individuals entering the company for the first time. Nothing could be further from the truth. Virtually all phases of internal employee relations are affected. Of special concern to the EEOC are decisions relating to promotion. A multinational corporation headquartered in the United States often must alter their approach to internal employee relations to meet the norms of the host country.

Questions for Review

1. Distinguish between discipline and disciplinary action.
2. In progressive disciplinary action, what steps are involved before employee termination?
3. What are the steps that should typically be followed in handling a grievance under a collective bargaining agreement?
4. Why is arbitration often used in the settlement of grievances in a unionized firm?
5. How would grievances typically be handled in a union-free firm? Describe briefly.
6. Termination is a traumatic experience for most employees. How does termination often differ with regard to nonmanagerial/nonprofessional employees, executives, managers, and professionals?
7. What is meant by the phrase employment at will?
8. Briefly describe the techniques available to determine the real reasons that an individual decides to leave an organization.
9. Distinguish between demotions, transfers, and promotions.
10. What are some legal implications of internal employee relations?

Terms for Review

Internal employee relations
Discipline
Disciplinary action
Progressive disciplinary action
Disciplinary action without punishment
Grievance
Arbitration
Outplacement
Employment at will
Demotion
Transfer
Promotion

INCIDENT 1 ■ Step Over the Line ■

Quality Business Forms, Inc., has a policy stating that an employee should not be absent more than four days during a ninety-day work period without medical verification. If an employee does not have medical reasons for excessive absences, he or she may be subject to disciplinary action.

Ed Thompson has been employed by Quality for more than twenty-one years. In the past three years he has had an abnormal number of absences, which his supervisor chose to ignore because of Ed's long tenure with the company. When Ed's supervisor was transferred and another individual in the department, Alice Randall, assumed the supervisory position, she immediately advised Ed that his absenteeism was excessive and that it would have to cease or disciplinary action would be taken. Ed claimed that he had been injured on the job five years previously and that his absences were a result of that injury. Randall reviewed Ed's health records, which contained no report of such an injury.

Ed's attendance improved during the first six months under Randall's supervision but began to deteriorate during the latter part of the year. Ed, warned again about absenteeism, came back with his previous excuse. At this point, Randall contacted the human resource manager for assistance in dealing with Ed. She was told that further disciplinary steps should be taken along with a complete physical evaluation by the corporate medical doctor.

The physical exam was conducted immediately and no physical abnormalities were found.

The doctor gave Ed this information verbally, but Ed refused to accept the findings. He was then counseled by the human resource manager, his supervisor, and his department manager. Ed listened very intently to what was being said and took notes. He was told that the next step in the disciplinary procedure would be dismissal if his absenteeism continued. He said he understood and he would work when he felt good and would not work when he did not feel good.

Thirty days later Ed and his supervisor were called in to the human resource office at 7:00 A.M., and Ed was terminated. Ed was shocked at actually being fired, since it was necessary for the president of the company to approve the termination of an employee with a long service record. A discrimination charge was filed but was dropped when no grounds could be established. A workers' compensation claim was received but could not be substantiated. And, finally, an unemployment claim was submitted, but it was dismissed.

Questions

1. Do you agree with the standards developed by the firm with regard to absenteeism?
2. What responsibilities rest with an employer with regard to when a long-term employee should be terminated?

INCIDENT 2 ■ Something Is Not Right ■

As Norman Blankenship came into the office at Consolidated Coal Company's Rowland mine, near Clear Creek, West Virginia, he told the mine dispatcher not to tell anyone of his presence. Norman was the general superintendent of the Rowland operation. He had been with Consolidated for more than 23 years, having started out as a coal digger.

Norman had heard that one of his section bosses, Tom Serinsky, had been sleeping on the job. Tom had been hired two months earlier and assigned to the Rowland mine by the regional human resource office. He went to work as section boss, working the midnight to 8:00 A.M. shift. Because of his age and experience, he was the senior person in the mine on his shift.

Norman took one of the battery-operated jeeps used to transport workers and supplies in and out of the mine and proceeded to the area where Tom was assigned. Upon arriving, he saw Tom lying on an emergency stretcher. Norman stopped his jeep a few yards away from where Tom was sleeping and approached him. "Hey, you asleep?" Norman asked. Tom awakened with a start and said, "No, I wasn't sleeping."

Norman waited a moment for Tom to collect his senses and then said, "I could tell that you were sleeping. But that's beside the point. You weren't at your work station. You know that I have no choice but to fire you." After Tom had left, Norman called his mine foreman, who had accompanied him to the dispatcher's office, and asked him to complete the remainder of Tom's shift.

The next morning, Norman had the mine human resource officer officially terminate Tom. As part of the standard procedure, the mine human resource officer notified the regional director that Tom had been fired and gave the reasons for firing him. The regional human resource director asked the mine human resource officer to put Norman on the line. When he did so, Norman was told, "You know that Tom is the brother-in-law of our regional vice-president, Bill Frederick?" "No, I didn't know that," replied Norman, "but it doesn't matter. The rules are clear, I wouldn't care if he was the regional vice-president's son."

The next day, the regional human resource director showed up at the mine just as Norman was getting ready to make a routine tour of the mine. "I guess you know what I'm here for," said the human resource director. "Yeah, you're here to take away my authority," replied Norman. "No, I'm just here to investigate," said the human resource director.

When Norman returned to the mine office after his tour, the human resource director had finished his interviews. He told Norman, "I think we're going to have to put Tom back to work. If we decided to do that, can you let him work for you?" "No, absolutely not," said Norman. "In fact, if he works here, I go." A week later, Norman learned that Tom had gone back to work as section boss at another Consolidated coal mine in the region.

Questions

1. What would you do now if you were Norman?
2. Do you believe that the human resource director handled the matter in an ethical manner? Explain.

EXPERIENCING HUMAN RESOURCE MANAGEMENT

Isadore Lamansky is the manager of the machine tooling operations at Lone Star Industries and has five supervisors who report to him. One of his employees is Susie Canton, a supervisor in maintenance. As Isadore comes to work this morning, his thoughts focus on Susie: "Today is the day that I must talk to Susie. I sure hate to do it. I know she is going to take it the wrong way. Ever since Susie was promoted to Unit Supervisor she has had trouble maintaining discipline. She tries too hard to keep the men in line because she thinks they are continually trying to push her, and she lets the women get away with murder. Well I guess I'll get this over with, that's what I get paid for."

The grapevine is strong at Lone Star Industries and it didn't take long for Susie to hear rumors. She thinks, "The word is that old Isadore is going to come down on me. He recommended someone else for my job because he doesn't like women in charge. The reason it is so hard to maintain discipline is the fact that the men I supervise intentionally push me to see what I'll do. The women support me, they are proud of me; the men just want me gone. He is probably going to dredge up some minor stuff to reprimand me about; we need more women in charge, and the boss will have to accept that I'm here for good!"

Who is right, and who is wrong? Can there be a reasonable solution to the problems that exist? This exercise will require two of you to participate. We need one person to play Susie and another person to play the manager. All others observe carefully. Ask the instructor for additional information if you are participating.

REFERENCES

Barkhaus, Robert S., and Meek, Carol L. "A Practical View of Outplacement Counseling." *Personnel Administrator*, 27 (March 1982), pp. 77–81.

Baum, Laurie. "Punishing Workers with a Day Off." *Business Week* (June 16, 1986), p. 80.

Baxter, John D. "Mid-Manager Morale Sinks to a Low Level." *Iron Age* (April 19, 1985), pp. 61–67.

Bearak, Joel A. "Termination Made Easier: Is Outplacement Really the Answer?" *Personnel Administrator*, 27 (April 1982), pp. 63–71.

Beitner, E. I. "Justice and Dignity: A New Approach to Discipline." *Labor Law Journal*, 35 (August 1984), pp. 500–505.

Benefield, Clifford J. "Problem Performers: The Third-Party Solution." *Personnel Journal*, 64 (August 1985), pp. 96–101.

Bradshaw, David A., and Linda Van Winkle Deacon. "Wrongful Discharge: The Tip of the Iceberg?" *Personnel Administrator*, 30 (November 1985), pp. 74–76.

Bryant, Alan W. "Replacing Punitive Discipline with a Positive Approach." *Personnel Journal*, 29 (February 1984), pp. 79–87.

Cameron, D. "The When, Why, and How of Discipline." *Personnel Journal*, 63 (July 1984), pp. 37–39.

Campbell, David N., R. L. Fleming, and Richard C. Grote. "Discipline Without Punishment—At Last; Why and How You Should Implement a Nonpunitive Approach to Discipline." *Harvard Business Review*, 63 (July 1985), pp. 162–170.

Carrell, Michael R., and Frank E. Kuzmits. "Amended ADEA's Effects on HR Strategies Remain Dubious." *Personnel Journal*, 66 (May 1987), pp. 111–119.

Cohen, S. L., and Prestor, J. "Solving the Promotion Puzzle." *Management World*, 14 (February 1985), pp. 16–18.
Discenza, Richard, and Howard L. Smith, "Is Employee Discipline Obsolete?" *Personnel Administrator*, 30 (June 1985), pp. 175–186.
Engel, Paul G. "Preserving the Right to Fire." *Industry Week* (March 18, 1985), pp. 39–40.
Franzem, Joseph J. "Easing the Pain." *Personnel Administrator*, 32 (February 1987), pp. 48–56.
Gilberg, Kenneth R. "Employee Terminations: Risky Business." *Personnel Administrator*, 32 (March 1987), pp. 40–44.
Gould, Richard. "Are You Firing Talented Managers?" *Management Review*, 76 (March 1987), pp. 49–52.
Greer, Charles R., and Chalmer E. Labig, Jr. "Employee Reactions to Disciplinary Action." *Human Relations*, 40 (August 1987), pp. 507–523.
Hoban, Richard. "The Outplacement Option: Everybody Wins!" *Personnel Administrator*, 32 (June 1987), pp. 184–190.
Holloway, William W. "Coping with Employee Turnover in the Age of High Technology." *Personnel Administrator*, 30 (May 1985), pp. 108–115.
Kleiman, Lawrence S., and Kimberly J. Clark. "Users' Satisfaction with Job Posting." *Personnel Journal*, 29 (September 1984), pp. 104–108.
Krajci, Thomas J. "Outplacement en Masse: A Marketing Approach." *Personnel Administrator*, 32 (May 1987), pp. 90–95.
Lo Bosco, M. "Consensus on Nonunion Grievance Procedures." *Personnel*, 62 (January 1985), pp. 61–64.
Lorber, Lawrence Z., J. Robert Kirk, Kenneth H. Kirschner, and Charlene R. Handorf. *Fear of Firing* (Alexandria, Va.: The ASPA Foundation, 1984).
MacRury, King. "Between a Rock and a Hard Place: What Do You Do When a Longtime Employee Begins to Gum up the Works?" *Inc.*, 8 (July 1986), pp. 101–103.
Madson, Roger B., and Barbara Knudson-Fields. "Productive Progressive Discipline Procedures." *Management Solutions*, 32 (May 1987), pp. 17–25.
McClellan, Keith. "The Changing Nature of EAP Practice." *Personnel Administrator*, 30 (August 1985), pp. 29–37.
McConnell, Patrick L. "Is Your Discipline Process the Victim of Red Tape?" *Personnel Journal*, 65 (March 1986), pp. 64–72.
Milbourn, Gene, Jr. "The Case Against Employee Punishment." *Management Solutions*, 31 (November 1986), pp. 40–44.

Miller, Richard E. "Outplacement Myths Unlock the Mystery of Its Ineffectiveness." *Personnel Journal*, 66 (January 1987), pp. 26–30.
Montana, Patrick J. "Preretirement Planning: How Corporations Help." *Personnel Administrator*, 31 (June 1986), pp. 121–128.
Moore, Perry. "The Problems and Prospects of Cutback Management." *Personnel Journal*, 30 (January 1985), pp. 91–95.
O'Brien, F. P., and D. A. Drost. "Non-Union Grievance Procedures: Not Just an Anti-Union Strategy." *Personnel*, 64 (September–October 1984), pp. 61–69.
Olson, F. C. "How Peer Review Works at Control Data." *Harvard Business Review*, 62 (November–December 1984), pp. 58–59.
―――. "Outplacement Helps Ease Termination for Employee and Employer." *Savings Institution*, 105 (December 1984), p. 127.
Raelin, Joseph A. "Job Security for Professionals." *Personnel*, 64 (July 1987), pp. 40–48.
Rasco, Ed. "The Floggings Will Continue Until Morale Improves." *Management World*, 16 (January 1987), pp. 33–35.
Richey, Jerome. "Signed Waivers with Pay Protect Discharge Process." *Personnel Journal*, 66 (May 1987), pp. 130–132.
Scelsi, Paul. "Middle Manager Woes." *Management World*, 16 (April–May 1987), pp. 20–22.
Shore, Harvey. "SMR Forum: Employee Assistance Programs—Reaping the Benefits." *Sloan Management Review*, 25 (Spring 1984), pp. 69–73.
Silverhorn, Colin P. "Planning for a Smaller Organization: A Guide for HR Managers." *Personnel*, 64 (March 1987), pp. 60–67.
Trisler, S. "Grievance Procedures: Refining the Open-Door Policy." *Employment Relations Today*, 11 (Autumn 1984), pp. 323–327.
Veglahn, Peter A. "The Five Steps in Practicing Effective Discipline." *Management Solutions*, 32 (November 1987), pp. 24–29.
Vernon-Gerstenfeld, Susan, and Edmund Burke. "Affirmative Action in Nine Large Companies: A Field Study." *Personnel Journal*, 62 (April 1985), pp. 54–60.
Watts, Patti. "Preretirement Planning: Making the Golden Years Rosy." *Personnel*, 64 (March 1987), pp. 32–39.
Wynbrandt, James, and Jack J. Leedy. "Managing Corporate Retirement Policy." *Management Review*, 76 (June 1987), pp. 47–51.

P·A·R·T S·I·X

CASE

Parma Cycle Company: The Union Organizing Effort

The Clarksdale, Mississippi, plant of Parma Cycle Company had been open for only six months in March 1989, when the first efforts at unionization became apparent. A known union organizer was in town and prounion leaflets began to appear around the factory. As the human resource director at Clarksdale, Edward Deal had been expecting this to occur. He knew that the workers who had been brought down from the main plant in Parma, Ohio, had a strong union tradition. He also knew that the wage and benefits package at Clarksdale was far less liberal than that at the Parma plant. So far, this hadn't created a major problem. Most of the workers recruited from the Clarksdale area felt that they were well paid in comparison to others in that area.

In the plant that same day, Janice Snively was thinking about whether she should talk to the human resource director. Janice had been hired by Parma two weeks prior to start-up. She had previously worked as a maintenance supervisor at a garment factory about sixty miles from Clarksdale. She had taken a slight pay cut in order to take what she thought would be a better job in the long run and to be nearer her family, who lived in Clarksdale.

Janice's crew of ten machine operators and two parts handlers was among the best in the plant. Janice had made friends with each of them and they obviously respected her. She felt that one reason she was a good leader was her willingness to "get her hands dirty." Because of her experience in maintenance she was able to repair the machines herself when they broke down. When an operator was absent, she would simply take over that machine in order to keep the work flowing.

Lately she had noticed a change. The workers seemed to be shutting her out. In a couple of instances, when several of her crew were congregated at one table in the lunch room, the conversation stopped as she approached and then awkwardly began again. The change of topic was obvious. For the first time, too, she began to hear complaints from the employees. For example, the operator of the cut-off machine, which cuts certain frame members to size, complained of the speed with which the machine operated. "I have less than one second to move the cutoff piece before the tubing feeds through to start another cut. I'll be lucky not to lose an arm," he said. There had been a number of similar complaints, many of them related to safety, some to working conditions, and a number of workers had asked about when their next raise was coming.

Janice thought that handling these kinds of problems was part of the supervisor's job, so she wasn't too concerned. Because of something that had happened this morning, though, Janice decided it was time to talk to the human resource director.

Janice walked in as Ed was thinking about the advantages and disadvantages of having a union. "Ed," she said, "I want you to look at this. One of the workers gave it to me and asked if it is true. I didn't know how to answer." Janice handed Ed a mimeographed sheet (reproduced below). After studying the sheet for a moment Ed said, "It's basically true, but I wish it weren't."

697

DID YOU KNOW?

- Parma's workers in Ohio do not pay for their dependent's medical insurance. You do!

- Parma's employees in Ohio have dental insurance. You don't!

- Employees in Ohio have ten paid holidays. You have only eight.

- Trainees at the Ohio plant get $7.50 per hour. At Clarksdale, they get minimum wage.

- Senior machine operators in Ohio get $12.60 an hour. Here, they get $8.90 or less.

Questions

1. What do you think caused the unionizing attempt at Parma Cycle's Clarksdale plant?
2. What sequence of events is likely to occur before the Clarksdale plant becomes unionized?
3. Assuming that Parma Cycle wishes to prevent unionization of the Clarksdale plant, what might the union and management legally do before and after a union representation election is ordered by the NLRB?

P·A·R·T S·E·V·E·N

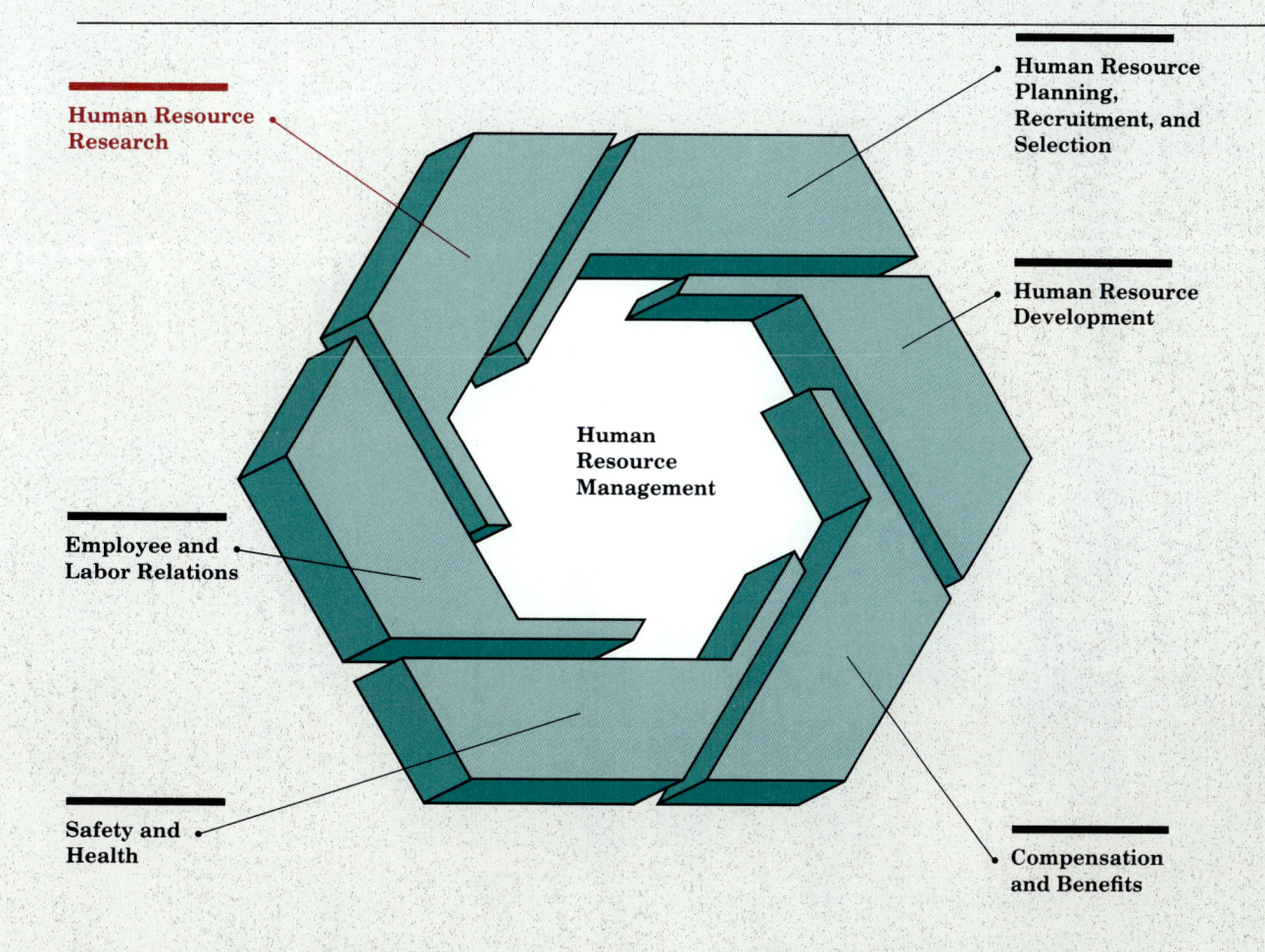

HUMAN RESOURCE RESEARCH

Human Resource Research

Human Resource Planning, Recruitment, and Selection

Human Resource Development

Compensation and Benefits

Safety and Health

Employee and Labor Relations

Human Resource Management

CHAPTER 19 HUMAN RESOURCE RESEARCH

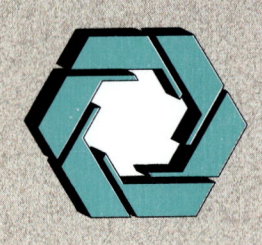

CHAPTER OBJECTIVES

1. Explain why human resource research must consider the productivity challenge.
2. Explain the importance of research to human resource management, identify the basic methods of inquiry for research, and describe the steps in the research process.
3. Describe how quantitative methods may be used in human resource research, how the human resource function may be evaluated, and how technological advances can affect human resource management.

> Annette Dommert, human resource manager for Saint Joseph Medical Center in Decatur, Illinois, was disturbed as she studied the list of workers who had resigned during the past month. For the sixth month in a row, the number of terminations had increased. To compound the problem, the terminations were in critical areas such as X-ray and laboratory. Quite a few RNs had also turned in their resignations. Annette had conducted exit interviews with many of the workers who had quit, and most had responded that they were leaving for "more money." However, Annette was well aware of the salary schedules of the other hospitals in the area. Saint Joseph's pay level was well in line overall and even higher in a few categories.
>
> Annette knew that a continued exodus of qualified workers would have a serious impact on patient care at Saint Joseph. She decided to propose a confidential questionnaire to be administered to all employees in the hospital in an attempt to identify reasons for the excessive turnover.

Employee attitudes revealed through human resource research can be of tremendous benefit to managers such as Annette Dommert as they attempt to determine the real reasons for high turnover rates and other indicators of employee dissatisfaction. Without this information, a situation may continue to erode until the quality of goods and services seriously erodes.

We begin this chapter by presenting the productivity challenge. Next, we discuss the benefits of human resource research and methods of inquiry in human resource research. We then describe the research process and quantitative methods in human resource research. We end the chapter with sections on evaluating the human resource function and technological advances that affect human resource management.

■ THE PRODUCTIVITY CHALLENGE

A major focus of human resource management is to find ways to increase a firm's productivity. **Productivity** is a measure of the relationship between inputs (labor, capital, natural resources, and energy) and the quality and quantity of outputs (goods and services). Historically, the United States has had the highest level of productivity of any major industrialized country, but that lead has been declining in recent years. Productivity is affected not only by the capability and motivation of workers but also by technology, capital investment, capacity utilization, scale of production, and many other factors.

How does productivity in the United States compare with that in other countries? Figure 19-1 shows the relative levels of productivity in terms of output per employed person in the major industrialized countries for more than two decades. Note that although the United States has a commanding lead over most of these other countries, its lead is narrowing relatively. In the 1980s, U.S. business and government leaders were concerned about the rate of growth in productivity, which was less than that for other industrial nations. Table 19-1 shows the rates of change for the countries included in Figure 19-1. Table 19-1 does not show productivity levels, but rather the rates of growth in productivity. Productivity in the United States grew more slowly than in any of the other countries. However, this difference narrowed during the second period shown. This condition resulted in part because the United States started from a higher base. For example, in 1960, when Japanese productivity was less than one fourth that in the United States, an increase in productivity by the same absolute amount for both countries would have yielded a percentage increase four times as high for Japan. Still, the major challenge facing U.S. management now and during the 1990s is to achieve productivity growth levels that will retain our position as the most productive major industrial nation in the world. Remember, productivity includes a measure of both the quality and the quantity of output, so productivity levels actually determine competitive position.

Several authorities—such as John Naisbitt, author of *Megatrends*, and Thomas Peters and Robert Waterman, authors of *In Search of Excellence*—have noted the shift in the United States from an industrial to a service and information economy. For example, it is harder to calculate the output of a systems analyst or a financial adviser than that of a person who works on an automobile assembly line. Nevertheless, improvements in productivity are a central focus of management. Human resource research has an important role to play in measuring and analyzing productivity and productivity trends and helping to find solutions to productivity problems.

■ BENEFITS OF HUMAN RESOURCE RESEARCH

The human resource manager's job, as we discussed in Chapter 1, is vastly different from only a few years ago. In order to contend with mounting responsibilities, the human resource manager has discovered that information derived from research is constantly required. **Human resource**

CHAPTER 19   Human Resource Research   703

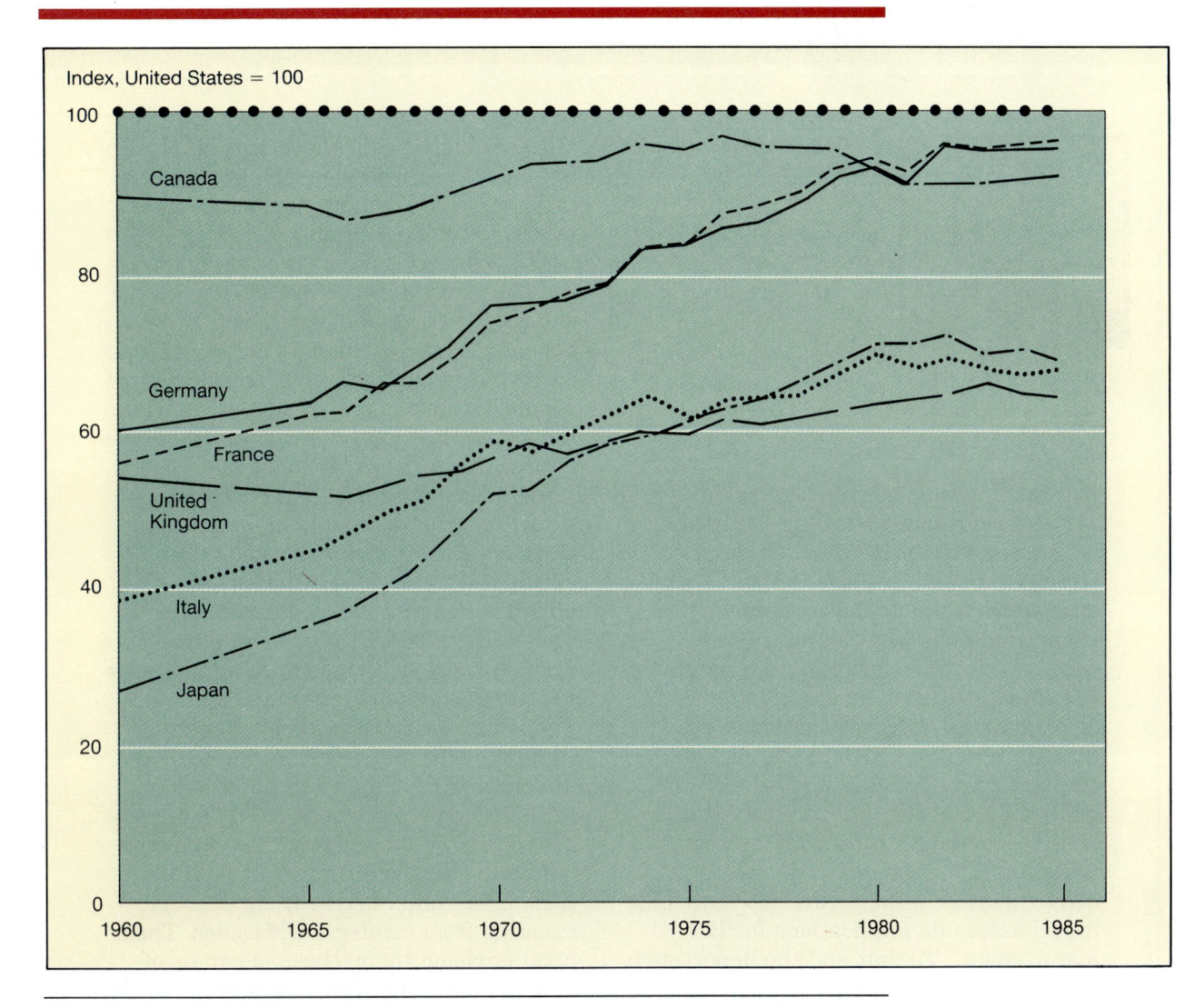

FIGURE 19-1 | Relative Levels in Real Gross Domestic Product per Employed Person

Source: U.S. Bureau of Labor Statistics.

research is the systematic study of a firm's human resources for the purpose of maximizing personal and organizational goal achievement.

Applications of human resource research are numerous and are increasing rapidly. The potential benefits of sound human resource research also are numerous. Management has begun to realize the full significance of the human component on an organization's ability to achieve its goals. This enlightenment, however belated, has occurred at a time when the competitive nature of business makes it increasingly difficult to obtain and retain qualified individuals.

EXECUTIVE INSIGHTS

Paul A. Banas, Ph.D.
Manager, Employee Development, Corporate Strategic Research and Planning, Ford Motor Company

Paul A. Banas has demonstrated the value of continuous learning, adaptability, persistence, and vision. Under his direction, human resource research has evolved from a function concerned with traditional employee relations issues, such as selection, performance appraisal, employee attitudes, and motivation, to one concerned with broader strategic human resources (HR) issues, such as employee development, employee involvement, leadership, organization culture, communication, and strategic planning. The orientation of his department is to the future—to anticipate it and assess its implications for HR management. To that end the department investigates leading-edge HR concepts and applications and proposes changes in HR policy, strategy, and programs that are consistent with the company's mission, values, guiding principles, and strategic business plan.

Dr. Banas points out that all the company's strategic business issues have one thing in common: Their resolution depends on the capacities (breadth), competencies (depth), and commitment of people. Given the role of the HR function, the HR professional has a significant role to play in the company's sucess.

Banas believes that the HR professional must understand the language of business and its strategic issues. In effect, HR professionals must think like businessmen and -women and be able to relate HR strategy to business strategy. They must demonstrate their competence in strategic and operational HR planning. They must complement their analytical thinking with systems thinking and understand the application of systems thinking to improvement of HR processes. They must be familiar with leading-edge HR technology and computer applications. They must derive their strategic research from strategic HR issues. They must envision themselves as equals of managers in other functional areas in the decision-making process and behave accordingly. They must engage in continuous life-long learning. Banas recognizes that this vision is a tall order but one that he knows is obtainable. According to Banas, "By keeping this vision before us at all times we have the power to create our own future."

Dr. Banas originally intended to pursue a career in the physical sciences, graduating with a bachelor's degree in chemistry. In fact, he prides himself on his published research on rocket fuels. However, on his way to becoming a famous chemist, he was side-tracked by a tour of duty in the U.S. Navy, which significantly changed his career goals.

During his service in the Navy, he was assigned to a rocket and explosives producing plant as the safety officer. He was responsible for investigating industrial accidents to determine their probable causes and prevention. Inevitably, he discovered, they resulted from inappropriate human behavior. As a result of his efforts to learn about changing human behavior in order to prevent accidents, he became so intrigued by psychology that he applied for and was accepted for graduate study at the University of Minnesota, where he earned his Ph.D. in industrial/organizational psychology.

After receiving his doctorate, Dr. Banas worked as a research psychologist for the U.S. Personnel Research Office in Washington, D.C. Subsequently, he became a research scientist and consultant for Human Sciences Research in McLean, Virginia, from which he left to join the corporate personnel research staff at the Ford Motor Company.

Dr. Banas has published more than 25 articles and numerous internal research papers. He is active in several professional organiations, including the Society of Industrial/Organizational Psychology, the Academy of Management, the Strategic Planning and Management Forum, the Society for Human Resource Management, and the Industrial Relations Research Association. He has served as a reviewer for *Personnel Psychology*, *The Journal of Applied Psychology*, and *Human Resources Planning*. For several years he has served on the board of directors of the Ball Foundation and the Michigan Quality of Worklife Council. In addition, he has maintained contact with the academic world through his teaching of courses in organization behavior, industrial psychology, management, leadership, and survey research.

TABLE 19-1 | Rates of Growth in Productivity

Country	Real Gross Domestic Product per Employed Person	
	1965–1977	1980–1985
United States	1.04	1.6
Canada	1.48	1.7
France	3.72	2.3
Germany	3.60	1.9
Japan	6.08	5.2
United Kingdom	2.44	2.8

Note: Figures are average annual percent change.
Source: U.S. Department of Commerce.

Specific applications of human resource research depend to a large extent on a firm's needs. As Table 19-2 shows, the type of research presently being conducted overlaps, but differences do exist. These variations reflect the size, goals, and specific problems of particular organizations.

Effective Management

Laws, government regulations, and judicial decisions have called into question many past human resource management practices. Managers must now be prepared to prove that their employment decisions are based on valid requirements. However, as Walter Tornow, vice-president and executive consultant for Control Data Corporation, states, "On the whole, government regulations have had a positive effect because they cause organizations to examine and document their practices in ways that heretofore were not deemed necessary for some."

Another reason for the increased need for human resource research relates to rapid changes in the composition of the workforce. Research is required to determine how the goals of these new workforce members can be integrated with those of the firm.

Largely because of increased educational opportunities, managers and nonmanagers alike have become more sophisticated in their employment expectations. To respond appropriately, managers may need to modify their approaches to HRM. Although a highly autocratic manager may have been successful in the past, a similar style today may quickly lead to resentment and lower productivity. Also, the organizational structure may need to be modified. The means of identifying appropriate managerial styles and organizational structure will continue to be a major task of human resource research.

The nature of work itself has also been changing rapidly. This has caused firms to continuously strive to upgrade their workforces. One of management's most difficult tasks is to get employees to accept change resulting

TABLE 19-2 | Uses of Human Resource Research

Company	Research Area
Atlantic Richfield Company	■ Selection test validation Assessment center validation Survey research
Fleming Companies, Inc.	■ Specific emphasis on turnover, turnover reasons, turnover costs Identification of high potential employees for accelerated development Impact of union contracts on compensation Improving performance appraisal
Control Data Corporation	■ Staffing, compensation, interviewing, performance appraisal, management training, surveys of employee attitudes, productivity enhancement, employee development, selection
Ashland Oil, Inc.	■ Selection at both the exempt and nonexempt levels and also in the early identification of people with potential to become high-level managers
Ford Motor Company	■ Selection, opinion surveys, career progress, performance appraisal, quality motivation, management potential, organization

from new technology. The use of robotics in automobile assembly plants has created a tremendous need for retraining. The new General Motors Saturn plant in Springhill, Tennessee, required many new employee skills. It isn't easy for a person to accept the fact that his or her skill is no longer needed and that person must learn a new skill. Research may indicate ways in which people may learn to accept change more readily, and thereby continue to be productive members of the workforce.

Human Resource Planning, Recruitment, and Selection

Plans must be made to recruit, select, and retain productive employees. Each organization has a distinct personality, as does an individual. Thus organizations must seek to find the best match between their needs and those of their employees. Research can help explain why an individual may be an excellent worker in one firm and a poor worker in another, even though the jobs seem to be similar.

Recruitment research is directed toward determining how individuals with high potential can be encouraged to apply for jobs with the firm. Firms need to determine the most likely sources of qualified candidates for their jobs. It does little good to know the qualities that prospective employees should possess and not know where and how to recruit them.

The objective of employee selection research is to identify prospective employees with the greatest potential for success. As you might expect, the definition of a successful employee varies from organization to organization. This research often attempts to identify factors such as background and experience, education, and test scores associated with differentiating successful from less successful applicants.[1] Complicating these efforts are variations in the profiles of successful workers by geographic location and gender. For instance, in one study, a profile of successful men and women was developed for a firm. Although there were as many successful women as men, the profiles based upon biographical data were essentially different.[2]

Human Resource Development

Research is also quite important in the area of human resource development. Studies may identify the employees who can benefit from training. For instance, a high error rate associated with certain employees might indicate the need for additional training.

Also, research into the usefulness of the training program may be needed. Are workers better prepared to do their jobs after training, or is the training an exercise in futility? Training and development is expensive and its costs must be justified.

In addition, the type of training and development that is needed may be identified through human resource research. The productivity of different departments may suggest that certain managers benefit from leadership and communication training. Finally, an analysis of employee performance may suggest additional areas of training and development that are needed.

Compensation

Both actual and perceived inequities in the firm's compensation system can create problems. Managers must be able to identify actual inequities and correct them, as well as provide information to employees to help overcome misperceptions. In order to maintain a fair pay policy, many firms conduct extensive compensation surveys. In addition, in-house surveys are often conducted to determine employee attitudes regarding pay. Compensation

---

[1] R. Wayne Mondy and Frank N. Edens, "An Empirical Test of the Decision to Participate Model," *Journal of Management*, 2(2) (Fall 1977), pp. 11–16.

[2] "Job Longevity Differs by Sex," *Convenience Store News* (May 2, 1975), p. 1.

research is widely used to identify potential problems before they get out of hand. For instance, if the supply and demand for skilled employees in the labor force is constantly changing, an organization's compensation program can rapidly become outdated and must therefore be closely monitored.

Employee and Labor Relations

Research in the area of employee and labor relations focuses primarily on areas that affect individual job performance. Some of this research may be needed to identify factors that will permit the firm to remain union-free. Research may show that internal factors, such as working conditions, may have a detrimental effect on employee productivity and job satisfaction. This type of information can prompt actions that would help an organization remain union-free. When problems are left unsolved, the worker may believe that the only remedy to the situation is to join the union. Continually monitoring factors that affect employee and labor relations will probably always prove beneficial to both the employee and the organization.

Safety and Health

The primary task of research in health and safety relates to identification of potential problem areas. For instance, research may be conducted to determine the locations and causes of accidents. It also can be used to identify characteristics of workers having higher accident probabilities. Accident patterns may be identified and changes recommended to prevent their occurrence. Health and safety concerns increased during the 1980s and will probably be even more important in the future. Therefore, human resource managers must make every attempt to identify health and safety problems and solve them as quickly as possible.

■ METHODS OF INQUIRY IN HUMAN RESOURCE RESEARCH

The type of problem and the particular needs of the organization determine, to a large extent, the method of inquiry that will be used. Specific research methods that are particularly useful include the case study, the survey feedback method, and the experiment.

The Case Study

The **case study** is an investigation into the underlying causes of specific problems in a plant, a department, or a work group. The results of the research apply only to that particular set of problems and cannot be generalized. Typical problems that the case study method might be used to investigate include:

- An excessively high turnover rate at a particular plant.
- A high absenteeism rate in a specific department.
- A high accident rate at a certain building site.
- Low morale in a particular department.
- The low number of minority group members in a certain plant.
- The underlying reasons for a wildcat strike at a particular location.

Naturally, there are many more situations in which the case study method may be appropriate. Although the results can't be generalized, the results of such studies may suggest possible new management approaches. The human resource management example later in this chapter provides an illustration of a case study provided by an outside consultant for a regional medical center. In other situations, the firm's human resource manager will conduct the research.

The Survey Feedback Method

A major function of human resource research is to determine periodically the attitudes of employees toward their jobs, pay, and supervision. Typically, this is done by means of survey questionnaires. Responses to questions may also reveal ways by which to improve productivity. Recall that Annette Dommert, in the case at the beginning of the chapter, is proposing a confidential questionnaire to be administered to all employees in the hospital. In the **survey feedback method**, anonymous questionnaires are used to systematically collect and measure employee attitudes. The Ford Motor Company uses the survey method to obtain the opinions of its salaried workers every other year. The results are published in Ford's in-house publication, *The American Road*.

Surveys may be either the objective multiple-choice type or the scaled-answer type, which asks for degrees of agreement or disagreement (see Figure 19-2). Objective analysis of survey results often requires a more detailed study. Possible bases for comparison of survey results might be by:

1. Section or department.
2. Age.
3. Gender.
4. Seniority.
5. Job level or degree of responsibility.
6. Changes in attitudes from previous surveys.
7. Comparison with other divisions, departments, or work groups.
8. Comparison with a standardized score if a validated instrument is being used.

The data become more meaningful to management when analyzed by various subgroups. A major point to consider is that survey responses often identify symptoms rather than causes. For instance, even if the compensation and benefits program is quite competitive, a low evaluation in this area (symptom) may reflect—not an inadequate compensation system—but general dissatisfaction with management style. When surveys are administered, the researcher should avoid concentrating on isolated responses.

Why did you decide to do what you are now doing?

a. Desire to aid or assist others
b. Influenced by another person or situation
c. Always wanted to be in this vocation
d. Lack of opportunity or interest in other vocational fields
e. Opportunities provided by this vocation
f. Personal satisfaction from doing this work

What do you like least about your job?

a. Nothing
b. Pay
c. Supervisor relations
d. Problems with fellow workers
e. Facilities
f. Paper work and reports

Considering all aspects of your job, evaluate your compensation with regard to your contributions to the needs of the organization. Circle the number that best describes how you feel.

Pay Too Low		Pay Low		Pay Average		Pay Above Average		Pay Too High	
1	2	3	4	5	6	7	8	9	10

What are your feelings about overtime work requirements? Circle the number that best indicates how you feel.

Unnecessary				Necessary on Occasion			Necessary		
1	2	3	4	5	6	7	8	9	10

FIGURE 19-2 | Examples of Multiple-Choice and Scaled Response Survey Questions

Instead, the data should be viewed from a broader perspective, which may uncover a pattern or general trend. Collectively, the responses will likely reflect this trend if there are difficulties in the organization.

When surveys are used to identify employee attitudes and opinions, confidentiality of responses must be ensured.[3] Employees must believe that their specific responses will not be communicated to management. For this reason, outside consultants are often employed to administer the question-

---

[3] R. Wayne Mondy and Wallace F. Nelson, "Job Satisfaction Among Radiologic Technologies," *Applied Radiology*, 7(4) (July–August 1978), p. 66.

naire. Even if the human resource professionals are completely ethical, employees may still perceive them as a tool of management. Rightly or wrongly, employees may always wonder whether the human resource department will succumb to management pressure to reveal specific employee responses.

Confidentiality means more than merely omitting a worker's name on the questionnaire. Even in a large firm, numerous sections consist of only a small number of employees. Or in a large department, a characteristic of a particular worker may make identification easy. For instance, a department might have only one woman in it. Protection of such a person's confidentiality is crucial to obtaining accurate results. The researcher must constantly be alert to these situations and be prepared to consolidate groups when necessary to preserve anonymity.

Survey results must be communicated back to the affected groups. Employees need to see what their collective responses were. And if surveys are to be taken seriously, management must act on the results.

When survey results are communicated to management, it is often best for each department or section head to be contacted individually. For instance, if the survey suggests that problems exist in the marketing department, the department head will likely be more receptive to criticism if his or her peers are not listening. Just as workers do not like to be disciplined in the presence of their co-workers, managers do not like to receive survey results in the presence of others. Better results are typically obtained when the data are discussed with each person or group separately.

At times, surveying every employee is not feasible because of time or cost restraints. **Sampling** is the process by which only a portion of the total group is studied, from which conclusions are drawn for the entire group. For example, let's assume that the total number of workers in a firm is 5,000. The time, effort, and cost necessary to survey all 5,000 workers may be prohibitive. If so, the researcher will probably decide to survey a smaller sample group. For example, a sample size of 500 workers may be deemed representative of the entire group. Conclusions are based on the responses from the employees comprising the sample and then applied to the entire group of 5,000 employees.

The Experiment

A method of inquiry that involves the manipulation of certain variables while others are held constant is referred to as an **experiment**. This method utilizes both a control group and an experimental group. The control group continues to operate as usual, whereas selected variables are manipulated for the experimental group. For instance, a manager may want to determine the effect that a new training program will have on productivity. The control group would continue to perform tasks in the conventional manner. The experimental group would receive the training. The assumption is that any change in productivity in the experimental group results from the training. On the surface, the experiment would appear to be an excellent means of inquiry. Actually, isolating the many interrelated variables affecting people and their performance can be extremely difficult.

CHAPTER 19   Human Resource Research

■ THE RESEARCH PROCESS

A systematic approach to human resource research is needed. The most fruitful research is accomplished by following a logical process, such as that shown in Figure 19-3.

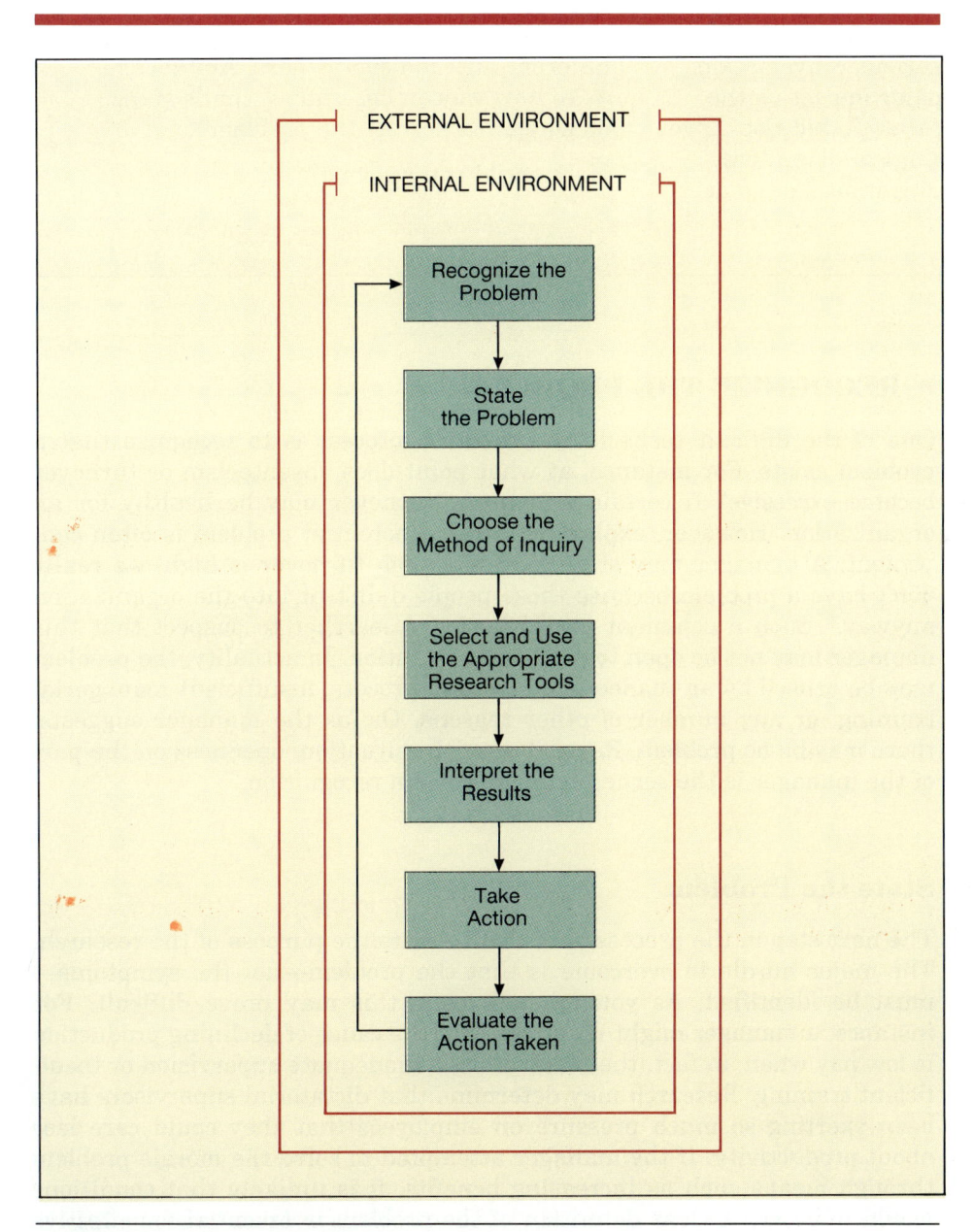

FIGURE 19-3 | The Human Resource Research Process

HRM In Action

Bob Stephens, president of Queens Manufacturing Company, and Mary Bushnell, the company's human resource director, were engaged in a serious conversation that could have a major impact on the future of the firm. "Mary," said Bob, "I've been hearing rumblings of discontent throughout the organization. For some reason that I can't figure out, people at Queens just don't appear to be as happy as they have been in the past. And it isn't just isolated instances. There is a different attitude everywhere. Any ideas as to how we can determine what's going on so we can correct the problem?"

How would you respond?

■ RECOGNIZE THE PROBLEM

One of the difficult tasks in the research process is to recognize that a problem exists. For instance, at what point does absenteeism or turnover become excessive? A certain amount of turnover may be healthy for an organization. However, explaining away a potential problem is often convenient. A manager may state, "Even though turnover is high, we really don't have a problem because those people didn't fit into the organization anyway." Such a comment would lead a researcher to suspect that this manager may not be open to problem recognition. In actuality, the problem may be caused by an inadequate selection process, insufficient managerial training, or any number of other reasons. Or, as the manager suggests, there may be no problem. Regardless of the situation, openness on the part of the manager is the cornerstone of problem recognition.

State the Problem

The next step in the process is to clearly state the purpose of the research. The major hurdle to overcome is that the problem—not the symptoms—must be identified. As you might expect, this may prove difficult. For instance, a manager might maintain that the cause of declining production is low pay when, in fact, the real reason is inadequate supervision or insufficient training. Research may determine that dictatorial supervisors have been exerting so much pressure on employees that they could care less about productivity. If the manager attempted to solve the morale problem through means such as increasing benefits, it is unlikely that conditions would improve. A clear definition of the problem is essential for effective research.

Choose the Method of Inquiry

The method of inquiry chosen depends to a large extent on the nature of the research. The methods of inquiry previously described—the case study, the survey, and the experiment—are all valuable. However, most human resource research involves either the case method or the survey.

Select and Use the Appropriate Research Tools

Numerous quantitative tools are available for use by the human resource researcher. We do not suggest that all managers be experts in mathematics and statistical theory in order to take advantage of their use. However, managers do need to know:

- Availability of quantitative tools.
- Circumstances under which these tools should be used.
- Strengths and weaknesses of each method.
- How to interpret the results.

The selection of a tool depends on the particular purpose for which the research is being conducted.

Interpret the Results

The person closest to the problem should participate in interpreting the results. When outsiders alone attempt to do this, they often arrive at strange conclusions. For instance, the survey may suggest that major dissatisfaction exists in the engineering department. A person not close to the situation might mistakenly identify the problem as one of inadequate supervision. Actually, the engineers may have voiced their dissatisfaction with the condition of their facilities.

Take Action

The most difficult phase of the research process is to take action based on research findings. They may have identified areas where changes need to be made. The human research manager now becomes the catalyst to convince line management that a change is necessary. Many times, this task is quite difficult. Telling a manager that his or her managerial style is causing excessive turnover can be uncomfortable. However, the benefits of research are realized only when action is being taken to resolve the problem that has been identified.

Evaluate the Action Taken

No research effort is complete until the action has been evaluated. Evaluation requires an objective assessment of whether the action has solved the problem and if so, how. Recall that Figure 19-3 shows a feedback loop from evaluation to problem recognition. Determining whether the problem has been adequately solved will assist in future research attempts. Revisions may be needed or the entire research effort may need to be rethought, but the information gained through a well-conceived research project almost always proves useful.

■ QUANTITATIVE METHODS IN HUMAN RESOURCE RESEARCH

Numerous quantitative methods are available to those who conduct human resource research. Most of these tools are available on both mainframe and personal computers. We describe only some of the most commonly used methods.

Correlation Analysis

Many times a researcher would like to know the relative strength of the relationships between variables. **Correlation analysis** measures the degree of association that exists between two or more variables. For instance, is there a relationship between job satisfaction and employee absenteeism? Figure 19-4 shows a high *negative* relationship between job satisfaction and employee absenteeism: As job satisfaction goes down, absenteeism goes up. Figure 19-5 shows a high *positive* correlation between the level of employee education and productivity: The higher the education level is, the greater the productivity. Note that these correlations are based on data from one firm. They might not hold for another firm and thus cannot be universally applied. The benefits of correlation analysis are considerable, but it must be used with caution. A correlation can be deceptive when the relationship does not reflect cause and effect. A high but meaningless correlation may exist. Human resource managers should be alert to this potential problem and not make decisions based on erroneous interpretations.

Regression Analysis

We described regression analysis in Chapter 5 as a technique that has proven useful in human resource planning. It has also proven beneficial in human resource research. As we previously stated, the purpose of regression analysis is to utilize the relation between two or more quantitative variables so that one variable can be predicted from the other, or others. For instance, a manager might like to determine whether employee productivity can be estimated from educational attainment (refer to Figure 19-5). In regression analysis terminology, the productivity level is referred to as the dependent variable. The education level used to estimate the level of productivity is called the independent variable. In this example, there is only one independent variable, so the process is referred to as simple lin-

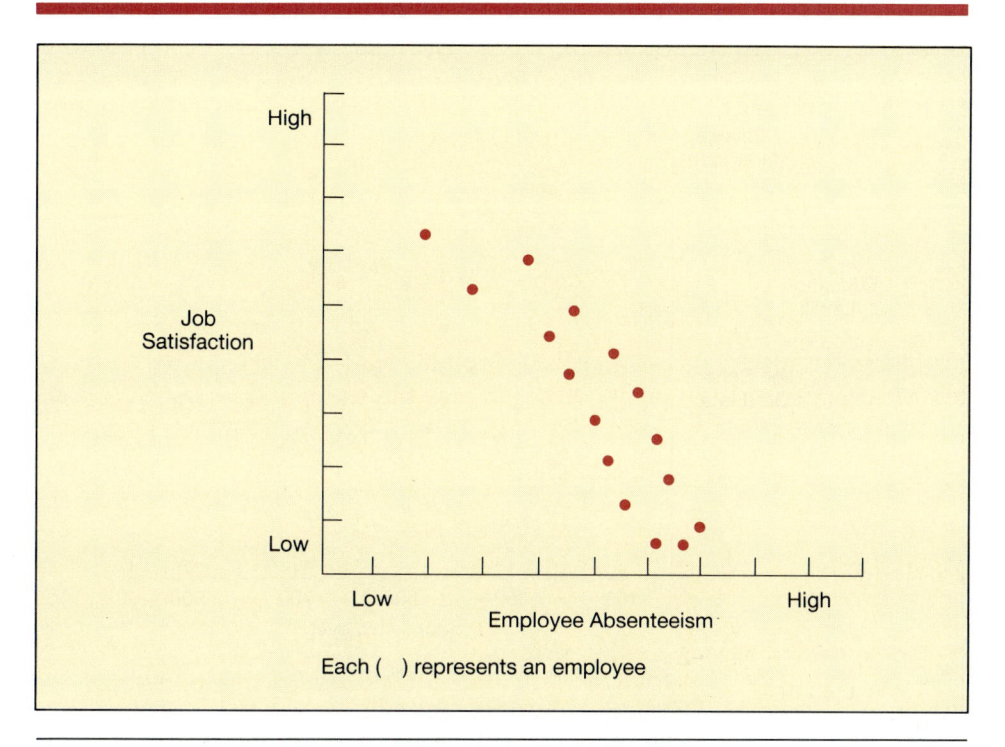

FIGURE 19-4 | The Negative Correlation Between Job Satisfaction and Employee Absenteeism at a Particular Firm

ear regression. The use of two or more independent variables is termed multiple regression.

When regression analysis is used in human resource research, some possible dependent variables might be:

- Satisfaction level of employees.
- Length of employment of employees.
- Productivity level of employees.
- Accident rate of employees.

Employment data that might be used as the independent variable include:

- Background and biographical data.
- Work history with the firm.
- Personal goals and aspirations.
- Test scores.

The researcher might attempt to determine through regression analysis which of the independent variables aid in differentiating productive and less productive workers. The regression model developed using these variables may help the manager to identify prospective employees who are likely to become successful workers, thereby improving selection decisions.

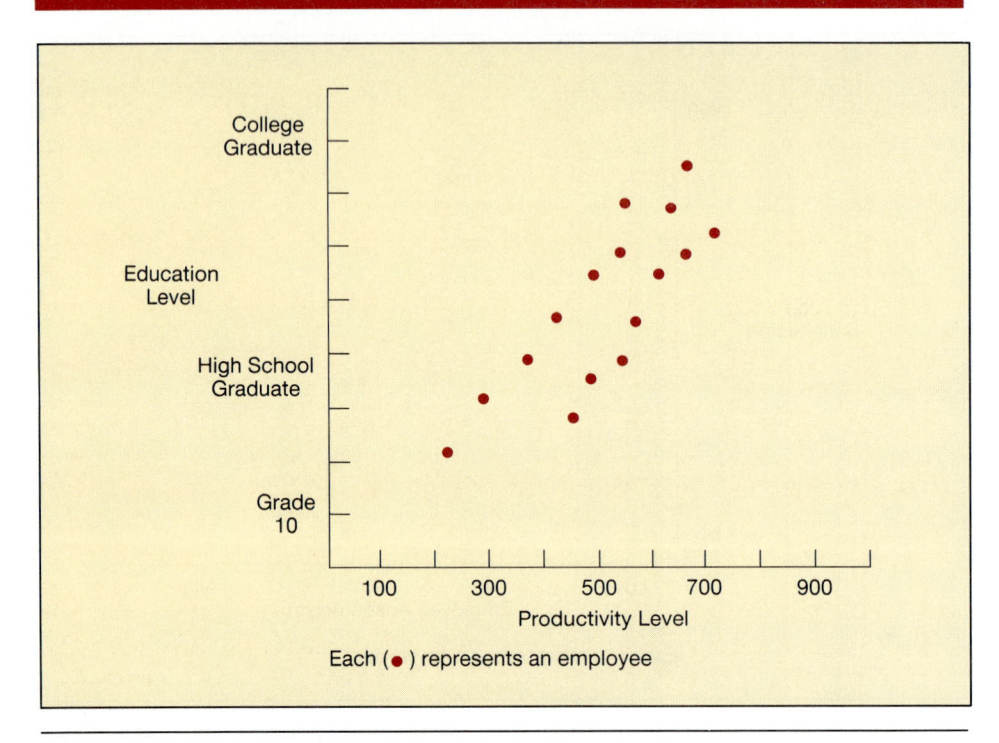

FIGURE 19-5 | The Positive Correlation Between Education Level and Level of Productivity at a Particular Firm

The model's accuracy must be validated through other statistical means. But if the model proves appropriate, it may useful in the selection process.

■ DISCRIMINANT ANALYSIS

The purpose of discriminant analysis is to identify factors that differentiate between two or more groups in a population. When two-group discriminant analysis is used, an attempt might be made to identify factors that differentiate:

- Satisfied from less satisfied employees.
- Long-term from short-term employees.
- Productive from less productive employees.
- Accident-prone from less accident-prone employees.

Only the imagination of the researcher limits the factors that can be used. Some of the potential factors that the researcher might use to differentiate two groups include:

- Background and biographical data.
- Work history with the firm.

- Personal goals and aspirations.
- Test scores.

For instance, suppose the researcher was attempting to determine whether certain background or biographical factors differentiated satisfied and less satisfied workers. As with regression analysis, the level of satisfaction becomes the dependent variable. However, unlike regression, individuals in the two groups are identified as either satisfied or less satisfied. Through the use of discriminant analysis, independent variables capable of distinguishing between the two selected groups are identified. The mechanics of discriminant analysis also permit the researcher to determine the reliability of the model developed.

Time Series Analysis

A technique that has proven quite helpful in making projections is time series analysis. Time series analysis is a variation of regression analysis in which the independent variable is expressed in units of time. As in regression analysis, both a dependent variable and an independent variable are required. However, the independent variable is now associated with time and the dependent variable is associated with demand. When the number of employees required in a company is closely associated with demand for the firm's product, time series analysis may prove useful in forecasting the organization's human resource needs. Using the same general mathematical procedure as in regression analysis, a time series equation can be derived and estimates of future demand calculated.

■ HUMAN RESOURCE RESEARCH: AN ILLUSTRATION

We present an actual example in order to illustrate how human resource research may be used in an organization. At the firm's request, it will not be identified. The techniques used and the benefits achieved are factual. The organization, a regional medical center in the southwest, had experienced rapid growth and the accompanying growing pains. The human resource director and the hospital administrator recognized that problems were developing and called in an outside consultant. He was to work with them in identifying and solving those problems before they became critical.

The consultant first talked with numerous employees to get a general view of the situation. Hesitancy of employees to talk about certain subjects and their apparent nervousness during the informal interviews suggested the existence of problems.

The next phase of the research project involved developing a survey tailored specifically to the hospital. Sample questions, which are shown in Figure 19-6, were developed. As you can see, topics ranged from managerial style to compensation. Administration of the questionnaire to all hospital employees was a critical step, and maintaining each participant's confidentiality was crucial. The hospital administrator's role was to notify

What do you like most about your job?
a. Helping or providing service for others
b. Learning opportunities
c. Personal satisfaction
d. Being around people
e. The work you perform at this hospital at this job
f. Nothing
g. Other (Specify)
h. Other (Specify)

What do you like least about your job?
a. Nothing
b. Pay
c. Supervisor relations
d. Problems with fellow workers
e. Facilities
f. Paper work and reports
g. Patient related problems
h. Doctor related problems
i. Other (Specify)
j. Other (Specify)

How would you describe your overall working environment? Circle the number that best describes how you feel.

Extremely Frustrating		Frustrating		Acceptable		Above Average		Excellent Work	
1	2	3	4	5	6	7	8	9	10

What do you think of strikes in the health care field? Circle the number which indicates how you feel.

Strongly Favor		Favor		Neutral		Opposed		Strongly Opposed	
1	2	3	4	5	6	7	8	9	10

What do you think about the system of giving pay increases at this hospital? Circle the number that best describes how you feel.

Very Bad		Poor		Satisfied		Good		Excellent	
1	2	3	4	5	6	7	8	9	10

Considering all aspects of your job, evaluate your compensation with regard to your contributions to the needs of the hospital. Circle the number that best describes how you feel.

Pay Too Low		Pay Low		Pay Average		Pay Above Average		Pay Too High	
1	2	3	4	5	6	7	8	9	10

FIGURE 19-6 | Sample Survey Questions

the employees of the survey. From that point on, the employees would have no further contact with any member of the administration regarding the survey.

Groups of employees met with the consultant in the room where the survey was to be administered. He first explained the survey's purpose and then assured the employees of confidentiality. Employees were told that summary results only would be provided to the administration. At this point it became even more obvious that problems did exist. Many employees wanted to know in detail the relationship between the consultant and the administration. Continuous assurances of confidentiality had to be given. Because of the nature of hospital work, the researcher had to administer the questionnaire over a forty-eight-hour period. To further ensure confidentiality, the respondents were told that they should put their completed questionnaires in blank envelopes so they could not be identified. Some employees even chose to mail their responses to the consultant rather than risk having the questionnaire get lost at the hospital.

The next phase entailed analyzing the results. Data from each employee were entered into a computer. The data were analyzed for the entire hospital and for each of its departments.

Statistics for the entire hospital proved inconclusive. However, when the survey results were evaluated by departments, some obvious problems began to surface. Employees in certain departments appeared to be much more discontented than workers in other departments. For instance, the levels of satisfaction in the radiology and lab departments appeared to be consistently below the satisfaction level of the hospital in general. Although not as negative, job satisfaction among nurses and aides was also below the hospital average. Figure 19-7 shows the summary of responses by department regarding overall working environment.

At this point, however, only symptoms had been uncovered. The next phase entailed identification of specific problems. The results of the survey were presented to each department head individually. They reviewed the results, discussed what the symptoms revealed, and participated in the identification of problems.

The analysis of the radiology department provides an excellent illustration of the difference between the identification of symptoms and identification of problems. The hospital had experienced rapid growth during the past few years, and, while other departments had increased staff to handle the increased workload, the radiology department had not. This placed considerable pressure on the employees in the department. A mistake made in this department could have serious consequences for patients. Also, questioning of workers revealed that the salary level of this department had not kept pace with radiology departments in nearby hospitals. The combination of these two factors—a department under pressure and an unrealistic salary level—resulted in considerable job dissatisfaction. The cause of the dissatisfaction had now been determined. The same procedure was used in the other departments where employees had expressed low job satisfaction.

The consultant was now able to provide the hospital administrator with not only the survey results, but also some sound recommendations. Sugges-

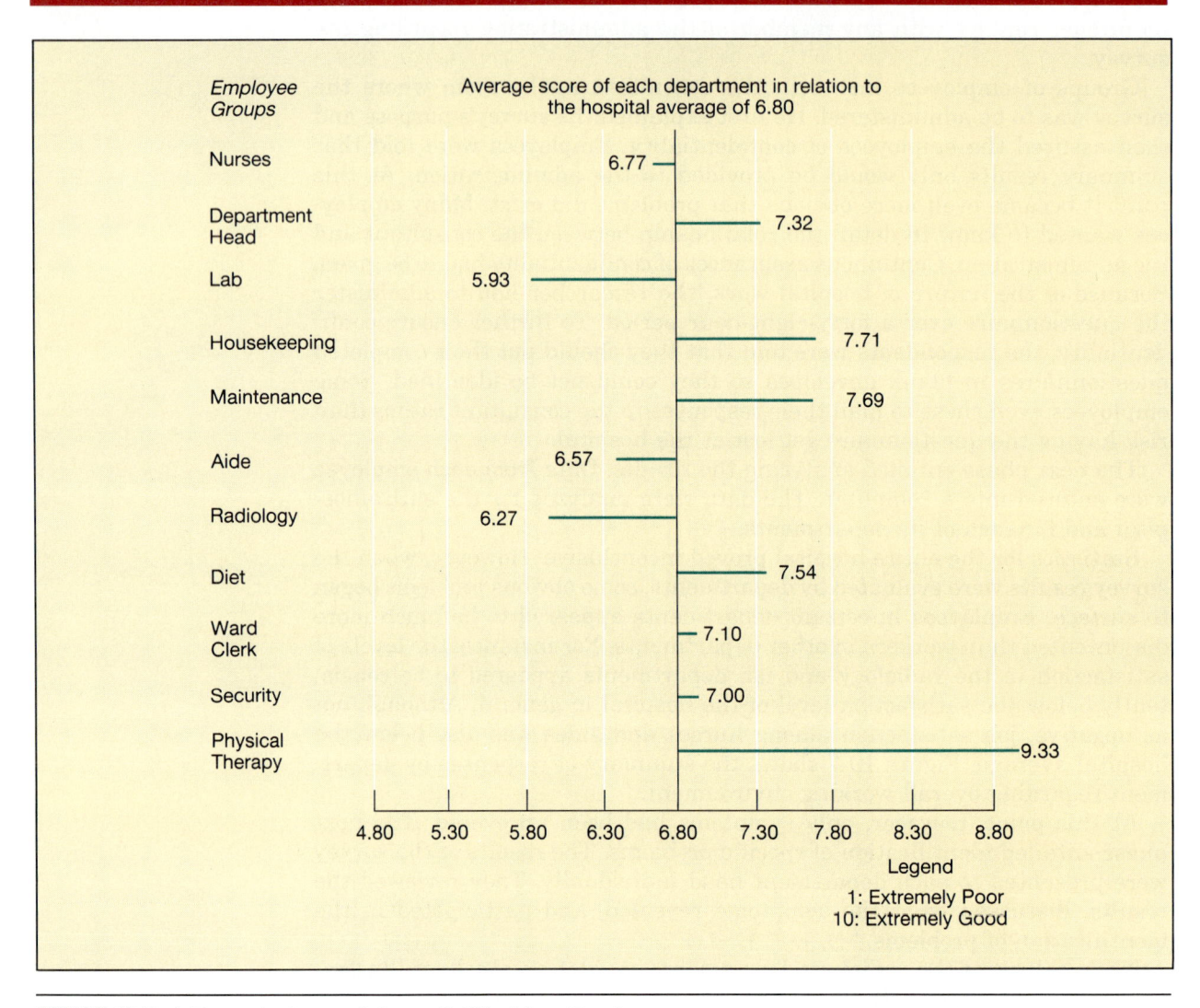

FIGURE 19-7 | Descriptions of Overall Working Environment

Employee Groups	Average score of each department in relation to the hospital average of 6.80
Nurses	6.77
Department Head	7.32
Lab	5.93
Housekeeping	7.71
Maintenance	7.69
Aide	6.57
Radiology	6.27
Diet	7.54
Ward Clerk	7.10
Security	7.00
Physical Therapy	9.33

Legend
1: Extremely Poor
10: Extremely Good

tions for improvement were made for each department, as well as for the entire hospital. They included:

1. Implementation of a management training program emphasizing communication skills, leadership, motivation, and other human relation techniques.
2. Reevaluation of the hospital's compensation program, including reacquainting employees with their benefits package, clarifying the method of granting pay increases, and evaluating new benefits.

The timing of the research and resulting implementation of the recommendations later proved to be crucial. Within a year, a major attempt at unionizing the hospital was made, but it failed. The research study, which identified human resource problems and proposed solutions, was credited with being the major factor in preparing the hospital for its successful efforts to remain union-free.[4]

■ EVALUATING THE HUMAN RESOURCE MANAGEMENT FUNCTION

The success of any organization depends not only on the formulation and execution of well-thought-out plans, but also on the continuous evaluation of progress toward accomplishment of specified objectives. For an organization as a whole, evaluation may be performed in terms of profitability ratios, sales increases, market penetration, and a host of other factors. For individual functional units within the organization, such as the human resource department, evaluation may be more difficult because of the absence of absolute measures that indicate whether the unit is fulfilling its mission. Yet the need for evaluation is just as important in these areas as it is in others.

How should an organization go about evaluating its human resource management function? Are there particular measures or indicators that reveal how well this function is meeting its responsibilities and supporting the organization's efforts to reach its objectives? Two basic methods may be used to evaluate human resource management activities: checklists and quantitative measures.

The checklist approach poses a number of questions that can be answered either "yes" or "no." This method is concerned with whether important activities have been recognized and, if so, whether they are being performed. Essentially, the checklist is an evaluation in terms of what should be done and the extent to which it is being done. Some typical human resource checklist questions are shown in Table 19-3. The more "yes" answers there are, the better the evaluation; "no" answers indicate areas or activities where follow-up or additional work is needed to increase HRM's effectiveness. Organizations deciding to use this evaluation approach will, undoubtedly, come up with many other questions to ask. The checklist method is purely an internal evaluation device. It is not a vehicle for comparing one company with another.

The second method for evaluating the performance of human resource activities is a quantitative one. It relies on the accumulation of various types of numerical data and the calculation of certain ratios from them. Numerical data is useful primarily as an indicator of activity levels and trends. Ratios show results that in themselves are important but that also reveal, when maintained over a period of time, trends that may be even more important.

In some instances, quantitative measures may be used for external comparisons with other organizations. However, since very few performance

---
[4] R. Wayne Mondy and Wallace F. Nelson, "Job Satisfaction Among Radiologic Technologies," *Applied Radiology*, 7(4) (July–August 1978), pp. 65–67. Copyright © Barrington Publications, Inc., 825 S. Barrington Avenue, Los Angeles, California 90049. Reprinted by permission.

TABLE 19-3 | Typical Human Resource Checklist Questions

- Are all legally mandated reports submitted to requiring agencies on time?
- Have formalized procedures and methods been developed for conducting job analysis?
- Are human resource requirements forecasts made at least annually?
- Is the recruiting process effectively integrated with human resource planning?
- Does the application form conform to applicable legal and affirmative action standards?
- Are all employees appraised at least annually?
- Are skills inventories maintained on all employees?
- Are career opportunities communicated clearly to all employees?

standards exist for the HRM function, external comparisons should always be interpreted with care. For example, the area in which the amount of external comparative data is probably greatest is employee turnover. While it may be tempting to evaluate an organization's turnover in terms of the "industry average" or by size of workforce, such comparisons may be meaningless. There is just too much variation in the factors that affect a specific organization's turnover, such as the nature of the local labor market, the number of long-time employees, the ability of the firm to pay competitive rates, the company's reputation as an employer, and so on.

One measure that can truly be considered a standard is the four-fifths or 80–20 rule, which measures the selection rate of women and minorities against other employees. Generally, as we have previously discussed, this ratio should approximate 80 percent. But even so, there are exceptions to this standard because of the specific situations that organizations face.

In short, although quantitative data may be useful for external comparisons with similar companies, they are probably most helpful in establishing internal baselines and showing the direction of movement from those baselines.[5] Some examples of quantitative measures for human resource management are listed in Table 19-4.

■ TECHNOLOGICAL ADVANCES AFFECTING HUMAN RESOURCE MANAGEMENT

Technological advances in computer hardware and software occur virtually every day. These developments have the potential of improving human

---

[5] Donald L. Caruth, Robert M. Noe III, and R. Wayne Mondy, *Staffing the Contemporary Organization* (New York: Quorum Books, 1988), pp. 283–299.

TABLE 19-4 | Examples of Quantitative Human Resource Management Measures

- Women and minorities selection ratio
- Women and minorities promotion ratio
- Women and minorities termination ratio
- Minority and women hiring percentage
- Minority and women workforce percentage
- Requirements forecast compared to actual human resource needs
- Availability forecast compared to actual availability of human resources
- Average recruiting cost per applicant
- Average recruiting cost per employee hired
- Percentage of positions filled internally
- Average testing cost per applicant
- Percentage of required appraisals actually completed
- Percentage of employees rated in highest performance category
- Percentage of appraisals appealed
- Turnover percentage
- New hire retention percentage
- Percentage of new hires lost

resource management and raising employee productivity. It's impossible to foresee all the new uses for each technological breakthrough. The only certainty is that managers must be aware of these innovations and alert to their capabilities. Failure to keep up with developments in this rapidly changing area can threaten a firm's competitive position and possibly even its survival. We next discuss some of the more important developments and trends that have the potential for significantly changing human resource management.

Teleconferencing

Partly because of the high cost of business travel, in terms of both time and money, teleconferencing is becoming increasingly popular. **Teleconferencing** is a method of conducting or participating in multiparty discussions by telephone or videophone. Teleconferencing may become a major means of not only improving managerial communication and productivity, but also of lowering their cost. Such systems could allow human resource managers to resolve many problems without ever meeting in person with other parties, thus saving both time and money.

Voice Mail

Voice mail is spoken messages transmitted electronically and stored for delivery to the recipient at a later time. When a voice mail system is used, an individual gains access by dialing a special number and providing a password and user-identification number. The user may then listen to any new messages, replay old messages, eliminate messages, and/or record messages for others. Managers can place confidential information in the system and know that the message will be received in the exact manner that it was sent. Voice mail could prove useful when human resource managers are dealing with sensitive matters, such as layoffs, and want to avoid phone communications, which could be overheard.

Word Processing

A computer application that permits an operator to create and edit written material is referred to as **word processing**. Probably the most popular application of microcomputers is in this area. Word processing allows simplified editing of virtually all forms of manuscripts and correspondence. For example, inserting a new paragraph at the beginning of a ten-page manuscript no longer requires retyping the entire document as it once did. Managers have found that they, too, can use word processing. The manager merely types out the memo, edits it on the screen, and with a few commands, prints it out. Word processing has become one of today's most significant communication enhancement tools. Word processing also allows human resource managers to develop sensitive documents, such as workforce reduction plans or performance appraisal reports, without risking a breech of security.

Spreadsheet Programs

Spreadsheet programs provide a column–row matrix on which numbers or words can be entered and stored, and calculations performed on that data. The major advantage of a spreadsheet program resides with its ability to answer "what if" questions quickly and accurately. Spreadsheet analysis is particularly beneficial in activities such as human resource planning.

Decision Support Systems

Often computer departments are backed up with demands for urgently needed information. To overcome this problem, many managers have acquired their own microcomputers and software. An alternative is a **decision support system (DSS)**, an information system that allows users to interact directly with a mainframe computer to quickly process and retrieve information. Normally DSSs are sophisticated database systems capable of retrieving, displaying, and processing a wide variety of information. Graphics, simulation, modeling, and quantitative analysis are also typically available through decision support systems. Obviously, DSSs can be very useful in human resource planning.

Database Management

Information subsystems are commonly developed for accounting, office management, manufacturing, marketing, and human resources. Often the data and programs in these subsystems are considered to be separate and distinct, resulting in a tremendous amount of redundant data and programming. For example, the accounting system would normally contain names and social security numbers of all employees—and so would the human resource files. The purpose of **database management** is to reduce such redundancies insofar as possible. The term thus refers to the integration of information subsystems in order to reduce the duplication of information, effort, and cost.

Computer Graphics

"A picture is worth a thousand words." Managers already can use computer programs to produce various kinds of graphs and charts in both black and white and color. Through computer graphics, visual relationships among several pieces of data can be seen immediately. Human resource managers continually process data that could be graphically presented, thereby illustrating the message much more effectively than simple text could.

Data Communication

The sending of data produced by a computer over some form of communication medium, such as phone lines, is referred to as **data communication**. This form of communication is becoming increasingly important in the business world. Human resource managers can transmit documents over phone lines and eliminate wasted time and possible misunderstandings and thereby facilitate decision making. For example, prior to a teleconference it is often useful to transmit information so that everyone involved can become familiar with the exact nature of the discussion before the conference begins.

Telecommuting

As previously mentioned in Chapter 13, many firms have turned to telecommuting as a way of meeting particular human resource needs. When workers are able to remain at home or at least away from the office and perform their work over telephone lines tied to a computer, as if they were at the office, the procedure is called **telecommuting**. Telecommuting is not for everyone, but certain people such as writers, reservation agents, researchers, and computer programmers can easily adapt to this style of work. Telecommuters often have more productive time since they do not drive to and from work. Also, handicapped people who cannot easily get to an office find telecommuting an excellent alternative.

Although the concept of telecommuting has many positive aspects, managers often have difficulty in coping with it in practice. The question they often ask is, "How do I supervise a person that I never see?" And some workers dislike telecommuting because they miss the friendly association with co-workers. Pacific Bell has a systematic procedure for selecting the types of jobs and the types of people who would benefit from telecommuting. In spite of the potential difficulties associated with telecommuting, between 300,000 and 600,000 Americans are telecommuting.[6] Expectations are that four to five million employees will be telecommuting by the mid 1990s, and by the year 2000, 20 percent of the United States labor force will work at home.[7] Subsequently, human resource professionals must be prepared to deal with this alternative type of work.

Voice Recognition

The traditional way for a person to communicate with computers has been by means of punch cards, tape, disk, or keyboard—translated into computer language by programs. A new development is computer voice recognition. Programs have been designed to accept voice input to control their operations. The manager cannot yet carry on a full-fledged conversation with a computer, but there is no reason to doubt that this capability will be available in the future.

A major use of voice recognition that has progressed past the developmental phase is in the area of word processing. Rather than have a worker keyboard in textual material, the user speaks directly to the computer, and the words appear on the screen. Many managers resist entering data themselves through a keyboard, but their resistance is expected to diminish when their actual words appear instantly on the screen. People who have become very skilled at dictating should find the changeover relatively simple. This technology could be very beneficial to human resource managers when the inevitable paperwork that accompanies human resource management must be prepared.

Program Generators

Program generators are programs that have been designed to write other programs. Still in its infancy, the program generator is expected to have a

---

[6] William H. Wagel, "Telecommuting Arrives in the Public Sector," *Personnel*, 65 (October 1988), p. 14.

[7] Robert O. Metzger and Mary Ann Von Glinow, "Off Site Workers: At Home and Abroad," *California Management Review*, 30 (Spring 1988), p. 102.

major impact on management information support systems in the future. Often a data processing department gets bogged down with the demands placed on it by users. A report that is needed today may not be available for weeks because the programmer does not have the time to complete the job. It is expected that when program generators become generally available, managers will receive much faster turnaround of information at less cost. Data processing departments will likely require fewer programmers to accomplish the same tasks. As program generation becomes more advanced, it could prove quite useful in specialized and ever-changing areas, such as human resource planning and job analysis.

SUMMARY

Human resource research is aimed at maximizing personal and organizational goal achievement. Human resource research should be systematic, with specific applications depending to a large extent on a firm's particular needs. From time to time, all aspects of the HRM functions have needs for research.

The type of problem confronting the human resource manager determines, to a large extent, the method of inquiry that will be used. When called on to uncover the underlying reasons for a particular occurrence, the human resource manager often uses the case method. The survey feedback method is used to determine employee attitudes. A method of inquiry that involves the manipulation of certain variables while others are held constant is referred to as an experiment.

The seven basic steps in the research process are (1) recognizing the problem, (2) stating the problem, (3) choosing the method of inquiry, (4) selecting and using the appropriate research tool, (5) interpreting the results, (6) taking action, and (7) evaluating the action taken.

Numerous quantitative tools are available for use by human resource managers. The purpose of correlation analysis is to measure the degree of association between two or more variables. The purpose of regression analysis is to determine the relationship between two or more variables so that one variable can be predicted from the others. The purpose of discriminant analysis is to identify factors that differentiate two or more groups in a population. Time series analysis permits projections to be made over time.

Two basic methods may be used to evaluate how human resource management activities: checklists and quantitative measures. The checklist approach poses a number of questions that can be answered either "yes" or "no." This method is concerned with whether important activities have been recognized and, if so, whether they are being performed. The quantitative method relies on accumulating numerical data and calculating various ratios from this data for comparative purposes.

Technological advances in computer hardware and software occur virtually every day. These developments have the potential for improving human resource management and raising employee productivity. Teleconferencing is a method of conducting or participating in multiparty discussions by telephone or videophone. Voice mail is electronic transmission and storage of spoken messages for delivery to the recipient at a later time. A computer application that permits an operator to create and edit written material is referred to as word processing. Spreadsheet programs provide a column–row matrix on which numbers or words can be entered and stored and calculations performed on the data. A decision support system (DSS) is an information system that allows users to interact directly with a mainframe computer to quickly process and retrieve information. The purpose of database management is to reduce data and programming redundancies as much as possible; the term thus refers to the integration of the various information subsystems in order to minimize duplication. The sending of data produced by a computer over some form of communication medium, such as telephone lines, is referred to as data communication. When workers are able to remain at home and perform their work over telephone lines tied to a computer, as if they were at the office, the procedure is called telecommuting. Computer programs have now been designed that accept voice input to control their operations. Program generators are programs that have been designed to write other programs.

Questions for Review

1. Describe the general methods of inquiry available for use by the human resource researcher.
2. Why would the experiment rarely be used as a means of inquiry in human resource management?
3. Identify the basic steps of the research process.
4. Why has management begun to realize that organizations can benefit from effective human resource research?
5. Briefly define each of the following quantitative tools as they may be used in human resources:
   (a) Correlation analysis
   (b) Regression analysis
   (c) Discriminant analysis
   (d) Time series analysis
6. Explain how the human resource management function may be evaluated.
7. Identify and define the technological advances affecting human resource management that were discussed in the text.

Terms for Review

Productivity
Human resource research
Case study
Survey feedback method
Sampling
Experiment
Correlation analysis
Teleconferencing
Voice mail
Word processing
Decision support system (DSS)
Database management
Data communication
Telecommuting
Program generators

INCIDENT 1 — Best Not to Know

Mike Manton was president of Sadler Federal Bank, a Muncie, Indiana, mortgage lender. The company had about 100 employees and assets totaling $250 million in 1989. Mike had managed the company since the mid-1950s. He became the principal owner in 1984, when he put together a group of investors to convert Sadler from a saver-owned savings and loan company to a federal bank. Mike had always taken pride in knowing every employee by name, both before and after the management-led buyout. He often remarked that his company was "just one big, happy family."

In 1988, however, Mike had sensed growing dissatisfaction. Turnover increased and the workers just didn't seem as happy anymore. When Mike mentioned it to his office manager, Jeffery Wilson, Jeffery agreed that there had been a change. "I don't know what has caused it," said Jeffery, "but I do know that things are getting worse." Jeffery suggested a professionally conducted attitude survey to identify the problem. Mike agreed, and the survey was conducted with the assistance of a professor from Indiana University. Employees were encouraged to give honest answers and were given the usual assurances of anonymity. They were told that the company management would receive only generalized summaries of the survey results.

Mike found the results shocking. It was evident that a large number of his people were dissatisfied with various aspects of their jobs. Some thought the pay was too low. Others felt that supervision was inadequate or arbitrary. Many objected to harsh working conditions. A few even mentioned the "high and mighty" attitude of the "big boss." Mike told Jeffery, "I simply cannot believe that the people I trusted could be so unappreciative of the jobs Sadler had provided them over the years."

He called in his vice-presidents, three of whom were co-owners, to discuss the results of the survey. After describing the survey results, he remarked, "We've always provided good jobs for our people and respected their rights. But if I knew who the strongest dissenters were, I don't think we would want them around. If they aren't happy with this company, they can leave."

Questions

1. If you were one of the vice-presidents, how would you handle the situation?
2. Discuss Mike's attitude concerning the survey results.

INCIDENT 2 — So What's the Problem?

Isabelle Anderson is plant manager for Hall Manufacturing Company in Alexandria, Louisiana, a company that produces a line of relatively inexpensive painted wood furniture. Six months ago, Isabelle became concerned about the turnover rate among workers in the painting department. Manufacturing plant turnover rates in that part of the South generally averages about 30 percent and this was true at Hall. The painting department, however, had experienced a turnover of nearly 200 percent in each of the last two years. Because of the limited number of skilled workers in the area, Hall had an extensive training program for new painters, and Isabelle knew that the high turnover rate was very costly.

Isabelle conducted exit interviews with many of the departing painters. Some of them said that they were leaving for more money, others for better benefits, and most cited some kind of "personal reasons" for quitting. Isabelle checked and found that Hall's wages and fringe benefits were competitive with, if not better than, those of other manufacturers in the area. She then called in Nelson Able, the painting supervisor, to discuss the problem. Nelson's response was, "You know how this younger generation is. They work to get enough money to live on for a few weeks and then quit. I don't worry about it. Our old timers can take up the slack." "But Nelson," Isabelle replied, "we have to worry about the turnover rates. It's really costing the company a lot of money. I'm going to ask Joe Swan to administer a survey to get to the bottom of this." Nelson replied, "Do whatever you think is right. I don't see any problem."

Questions

1. Do you agree that a survey of employees is the best way to identify the problem? Explain.
2. If you determine that a survey is needed, what kind of survey would you conduct and how would you analyze the results?

EXPERIENCING HUMAN RESOURCE MANAGEMENT

After studying this text, students should have a much better appreciation of what type of work human resource managers are involved in. In this exercise, participants will attempt to develop a profile of the attributes a human resource manager should possess. Knowledge gained throughout the semester should be used in identifying necessary attributes.

Participants will have a copy of Exhibits 1, 2, and 3. The attributes listed in Exhibit 1 may be more or less important for a human resource manager. Participants will order this list by assigning the letter "A" to the five attributes that you think are the most important for a human resource manager to have. Assign a "B" to the five attributes you think second most important; "C" to the five attributes third most important; and "D" to the five attributes that you feel are least important. Definitions of each of these attributes are listed in Exhibit 2. You will have 10 minutes for this activity.

After doing your individual rankings of these attributes, all students, except 6 individuals, will be placed into either Group 1 or Group 2. The six individuals not assigned to Groups 1 or 2 will make up the Review Committee; these individuals will sit together and reach a consensus on the attribute rankings. Groups 1 and 2 will also review the individual rankings of each of its members, discuss them, and then agree on a group ranking for the attributes listed. Exhibit 3, a Group Summary Sheet, is provided for this purpose. You will have 15 minutes for this activity.

After the completion of this exercise, the debriefing will begin by asking both groups, "What are the top five qualities needed by human resource professionals? Why?"

continued on next page

> *continued from previous page*
>
> Then, ask members of the Review Committee, "Which group identified the most appropriate top five qualities needed by human resource professionals? Why?"
>
> Next, ask both groups, "What were the least important qualities needed by human resource professionals? Why?"
>
> Then, ask members of the Review Committee, "Which group identified the most appropriate least important qualities needed by human resource professionals? Why?"
>
> The result of this exercise should be a realistic profile of what attributes a human resource manager should possess to be effective.

REFERENCES

Barrett, G. V. "The Concept of Dynamic Criteria: A Critical Reanalysis." *Personnel Psychology*, 38 (Spring 1985), pp. 41–56.

Bownas, D. A. "A Quantitative Approach to Evaluating Training Curriculum Content Sampling Adequacy." *Personnel Psychology*, 38 (Spring 1985), pp. 117–131.

Cosgrove, Charles V. "How to Report Productivity: Linking Measurements to Bottom-Line Financial Results." *National Productivity Review*, 6 (Winter 1986), pp. 63–71.

Faley, R. H. "Age Discrimination and Synthesis of the Legal Literature with Implications for Future Research." *Personnel Psychology*, 37 (Summer 1984), pp. 327–350.

Gow, Jack F. "Human Resources Managers Must Remember the Bottom Line." *Personnel Journal*, 64 (April 1985), pp. 30–33.

Hackman, J. Richard, and Greg R. Oldham. "Motivation Through the Design of Work: Test of a Theory." *Organizational Behavior and Human Performance*, 16 (August 1976), pp. 250–279.

Hill, Charles W. L., Michael A. Hitt, and Robert E. Hoskisson. "Declining U.S. Competitiveness: Reflections on a Crisis." *Academy of Management Executive*, 2 (February 1988), pp. 51–59.

Jones, R. R. "1984 Was a Good Year for R&D Salaries." *Research & Development*, 27 (March 1985), pp. 67–70.

Keller, R. T. "A Cross-National Validation Study Toward the Development of a Selection Battery for R&D Professional Employees." *Trans Engineering Management*, 31 (November 1984), pp. 162–165.

Layton, William G., and Eric J. Johnson. "Break the Mold: Strategies for Productivity." *Personnel Journal*, 66 (May 1987), pp. 74–78.

Likert, Rensis. *The Human Organization* (New York: McGraw-Hill, 1967).

Martin, David C., and Kathryn M. Bartol. "Managing Turnover Strategically." *Personnel Administrator*, 30 (November 1985), pp. 63–73.

Mondy, R. Wayne, and Harry N. Mills. "Choice Not Chance in Nurse Selection." *Supervisor Nurse*, 9 (November 1978), pp. 35–39.

Portwood, James D., and Robert W. Eichinger. "The Challenge of Human Resource Management: Adding Value." *Human Resource Planning*, 8 (December 1985), pp. 209–228.

Pucik, V. "White Collar HRM: A Comparison of the U.S. and Japanese Automobile Industries." *The Columbia Journal of World Business*, 19 (Fall 1984), pp. 87–94.

Rollins, Thomas, and Jerrold R. Bratkovich. "Productivity's People Factor." *Personnel Administrator*, 33 (February 1988), pp. 50–63.

Tung, Rosaline L. "Strategic Management of Human Resources in the Multinational Enterprise." *Human Resource Management*, 23 (Summer 1984), pp. 129–141.

Williams, D. R. "Employment in Recession and Recovery: A Demographic Flow Analysis." *Monthly Labor Review*, 108 (March 1985), pp. 35–42.

Zarandona, J. L., and M.A. Camuso. "A Study of Exit Interviews: Does the Last Word Count?" *Personnel*, 62 (March 1985), pp. 47–48.

PART SEVEN

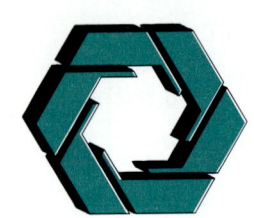

CASE

Parma Cycle Company: Looking Ahead

Edward Deal was jubilant. He had just received notification from the National Labor Relations Board that the union representation election at Parma Cycle's Clarksdale, Mississippi, plant had gone against the union. The margin was small, only 53 percent to 47 percent, but Ed considered it a significant victory. As human resource director at Clarksdale, he had done everything within his power to prevent the plant from becoming unionized. For example, wages and benefits at Clarksdale had started far below those at the Parma, Ohio, plant. At Edward's insistence, the package had been made competitive in the labor market. His recommendation for this had not been approved until top management was convinced that a unionizing effort was underway at Clarksdale.

With the new wage and benefits package, Parma Cycle became the highest paying employer in the Clarksdale area. From Ed's vantage point, morale seemed to be quite high in the plant. Jobs with Parma were much sought after. An average day saw twenty or thirty new job applicants. In fact, the rush of job applicants had forced Edward to post a sign reading "No Jobs Available."

There were still a couple of things that concerned Edward, though. First, the representation election had been extremely close. Twenty-five more votes would have swung it in the union's favor. Ed thus felt a certain insecurity about the prospects for future unionizing attempts at the plant. He knew that the company would have to live up to workers' expectations in order to keep the union out. He was also concerned about the qualifications of the workers he had hired. During the recruiting process, all that Ed had been able to offer to new trainees was minimum wage. The average wage for beginning workers at Parma's Clarksdale plant had been only $5.20 an hour. Consequently, only very young, mostly unskilled workers had applied. They had been trained to some degree but were certainly no match for the workforce at Parma's Ohio plant.

He decided to call Jesse Heard, his old boss and the human resource director at the Parma, Ohio, plant. After a friendly greeting, Ed got right to the point. "Jesse," he said, "I thought we were surely going to lose the representation election and I'd have been thrilled to get even a 1 percent victory margin. But, let's not kid ourselves. If we don't do a super job of keeping our workers satisfied, the union will get those extra 25 votes next time." "You're right," replied Jesse, "and even if you do, the result might be the same in the long run." "Why is that?" asked Ed. Jesse answered, "There has been a good deal of pressure by the union up here for us to recognize a bargaining unit at Clarksdale. I don't know how long top management will have the will to resist." "You really know how to let the air out of a fella's balloon," said Ed. "I don't mean to do that," Jesse replied, "but I do think we need to take a realistic view."

"Speaking of being realistic," continued Ed, "let's face it. We started the plant in Clarksdale to reduce labor costs and we hired a full complement of employees here at very low rates compared to those we are paying now. We have raised wages and we still have

734

the same workers. The only way we can really have lower costs now is for the workers here to produce more than those at Parma." "I see what you mean," said Jesse, "I'll be down for a visit in a couple of months. I don't know if I can help in any way, but we can sure talk about it."

A few weeks later Ed decided that it was time to find out a little more about his workforce. He called Jules Cagney, a professor of human resources at Memphis State University (Tennessee) and asked him to recommend a research design. "Professor Cagney," said Edward, "I am not as concerned about keeping the union out as I am about treating our people fairly and maintaining a high level of motivation. I mainly want to know what their attitudes and concerns are so that we can design the human resource program around that." "I'll do some thinking about that," said Cagney, "and be back in touch with you within a day or two."

Questions

1. What kind of study should Cagney recommend? Explain.
2. What are the trends in human resources that Ed should consider in designing or redesigning the human resource program at Clarksdale?

GLOSSARY

Adverse impact: A concept established by the *Uniform Guidelines*; occurs if women and minorities are not hired at the rate of at least 80 percent of the best-achieving group.

Advertising: A way of communicating the firm's employment needs to the public through media such as radio, newspaper, or industry publications.

Affirmative action program (AAP): A program that an organization develops to employ women and minorities in proportion to their representation in the firm's labor market.

Agency shop: A labor agreement provision requiring, as a condition of employment, that each nonunion member of the bargaining unit pay the union the equivalent of membership dues as a service charge for the union acting as the bargaining agent.

AIDS (acquired immune deficiency syndrome): A disease that undermines the body's immune system, leaving the person susceptible to a wide range of fatal diseases.

Aiming: The ability to move the hands quickly and accurately from one spot to another, which is important in jobs such as electronics parts assembly.

Alcoholism: A treatable disease characterized by uncontrolled and compulsive drinking that interferes with normal living patterns.

Apprenticeship training: A combination of classroom and on-the-job training.

Arbitration: A process in which a dispute is submitted to an impartial third party for a binding decision.

Assessment center: An appraisal approach that requires employees to participate in a series of activities similar to those they might be expected to do in an actual job.

Authorization card: A document indicating that an employee wants to be represented by a labor organization in collective bargaining.

Availability forecast: Determining whether the firm will be able to secure employees with the necessary skills and the sources of these individuals.

Bargaining unit: A group of employees, not necessarily union members, recognized by an employer or certified by an administrative agency as appropriate for representation by a labor organization for purposes of collective bargaining.

Beachhead demands: Demands that the union does not expect management to meet when they are first made.

Behavior modeling: A training method that utilizes videotapes prepared specifically to illustrate how managers function in various situations for the purpose of developing interpersonal skills.

Behaviorally Anchored Rating Scale (BARS) method: A performance appraisal method that combines elements of the traditional rating scales and critical incidents methods.

Benefits: All financial rewards that generally are not paid directly to the employee.

Biofeedback: A method of learning to control involuntary bodily processes, such as blood pressure or heart rate.

Board interview: A meeting in which one candidate is interviewed by several interviewers.

Bottom-up approach: A forecasting method beginning with the lower organizational units and progressing upward through the organization to ultimately provide an aggregate forecast of employment needs.

Boycott: Refusal by union members to use or buy their firm's products.

Burnout: A state of fatigue or frustration stemming from devotion to a cause, way of life, or relationship that did not provide the expected reward.

Business games: Simulations that represent actual business situations.

Career: A general course of action a person chooses to pursue throughout his or her working life.

Career anchors: Research conducted by Edgar Schein that identified five different motives to account for the way people select and prepare for a career.

Career development: A formal approach taken by the organization to ensure that people with the proper qualifications and experience are available when needed.

Career paths: Flexible lines of progression through which employees typically move during their employment with a company.

Career planning: A process whereby an individual sets career goals and identifies the means to achieve them.

Case study: A training method that utilizes simulated business problems for trainees to solve; a research method that attempts to uncover the underlying reasons for occurrence of a problem in a specific area such as a plant, a department, or a section.

Checkoff of dues: An agreement where the company agrees to withhold union dues from members' checks and to forward the money directly to the union.

Classification method: A job evaluation method by which classes or grades are defined to describe a group of jobs.

Closed shop: An arrangement whereby union membership is a prerequisite to employment.

Coaching: An on-the-job approach to management development in which the manager is given an opportunity to teach on a one-to-one basis.

Cognitive aptitude tests: Tests to measure an individual's ability to learn, as well as to perform a job.

Collective bargaining: The performance of the mutual obligation of the employer and the representative of the employees to meet at reasonable times and confer in good faith with respect to wages, hours, and other terms and conditions of employment, or the negotiation of an agreement, or any question arising thereunder, and the execution of a written contract incorporating any agreement reached if requested by either party, but such obligation does not compel either party to agree to a proposal or require the making of a concession.

Committee on Political Education (COPE): The political arm of the AFL–CIO.

Communication: The transfer of information, ideas, understanding, or feelings between people.

Comparable worth (CW): Determination of the values of dissimilar jobs (such as company nurse and welder), by comparison, under some form of job evaluation and assignment of pay rates according to the jobs' evaluated worth.

Compensation: Every type of reward that individuals receive in return for their labor.

Compressed work week: Any arrangement of work hours that permits an employee to fulfill a work obligation in fewer days than the typical five-day workweek.

Computer-based training: A teaching method that takes advantage of the speed, memory, and data manipulation capabilities of the computer for greater flexibility.

Concurrent validity: A validation method in which test scores and criterion data are obtained at essentially the same time.

Conspiracy: The combination of two or more persons who band together to prejudice the rights of others or of society (such as by refusing to work or demanding higher wages).

Construct validity: A test validation method to determine whether a test measures certain traits or qualities that have been identified as important in performing the job.

Content validity: A test validation method whereby a person performs certain tasks that are actual samples of the kind of work the job requires or completes a paper-and-pencil test that measures relevant job knowledge.

Corporate culture: The system of shared values, beliefs, and habits within an organization that interacts with the formal structure to produce behavioral norms.

Correlation analysis: A method of measuring the degree of association between two or more variables.

Cost-of-living allowance (COLA): An escalator clause in a labor agreement that automatically increases wages as the U.S. Bureau of Labor Statistics cost of living index rises.

Craft unions: Bargaining units, such as the Carpenters and Joiners, that are typically composed of members of a particular trade or skill in a locality.

Criterion-related validity: A test validation method that compares the scores on selection tests to some aspect of job performance as determined, for example, by performance appraisal.

Critical incident method: A performance appraisal technique that requires a written record of highly favorable and highly unfavorable employee work behavior.

Cut-off score: The score below which an applicant will not be considered further for employment.

Cyclical variations: Reasonably predictable movements about a trend line that occur over a period of more than a year.

Data communication: Sending data produced by a computer over some form of communication medium, such as telephone lines.

Database management: Integration of information subsystems in order to reduce duplication of information, effort, and cost.

Decertification: Election by a group of employees to withdraw a union's right to act as their exclusive bargaining representative.

Decision support system: An information system that allows users to interact directly with a mainframe computer to quickly process and retrieve information.

Deferred compensation: Pay that is held in trust for a manager until retirement.

Demotion: The process of moving a worker to a lower level of duties and responsibilities, which typically involves a pay cut.

Development: Individual growth not related to a specific present or future job.

Direct financial compensation: Pay that a person receives in the form of wages, salary, bonuses, and commissions.

Disciplinary action: Invoking a penalty against an employee who fails to meet organizational standards or comply with organizational rules.

Discipline: The state of employee self-control and orderly conduct.

Disciplinary action without punishment: A process whereby a worker is given time off with pay to think about whether he or she really wants to follow the rules and continue working for the company.

Dual career path: A method of rewarding technical specialists and professionals who can, and should be allowed to, continue to contribute significantly to a company without having to become managers.

Education: Activities conducted to improve the overall competence of an individual in a specific direction and beyond the current job.

Employee assistance program (EAP): One comprehensive approach that many organizations have taken to deal with burnout, alcohol and drug abuse, and other emotional disturbances.

Employee equity: Payment of individuals performing similar jobs for the same firm commensurate with factors unique to each employee.

Employee requisition: A document that specifies job title, department, and the date by which an open job should be filled.

Employee stock ownership plan (ESOP): A companywide incentive plan whereby the company provides its employees with common stock.

Employment agency: An organization that assists firms in recruiting employees and also aids individuals in their attempts to locate jobs.

Employment at will: An unwritten contract that is created when an employee agrees to work for an employer with no agreement as to how long the parties expect the employment to last.

Employment interview: A goal-oriented conversation in which the interviewer and applicant exchange information.

Equity: The perception by workers that they are being treated fairly.

Equivalent forms method: Verification of selection test reliability by correlating the results of tests that are similar but not identical.

Essay method: A performance appraisal method whereby the rater simply writes a brief narrative describing the employee's performance.

Ethics: The discipline dealing with what is good and bad, or right and wrong, or with moral duty and obligation.

Executive orders: Directives issued by the president, which have the force and effect of laws enacted by the Congress.

Executive search firms: Organizations that are retained by a company to search for the most qualified executive available for a specific position.

Executives: Top-level managers, who report directly to the corporation's chief executive officer or the head of a major division.

Exempt employees: Employees who are categorized as executive, administrative, or professional employees and outside salespersons.

Experiment: A method of inquiry that involves the manipulation of certain variables while others are held constant.

External environment: The factors that affect a firm's human resources from outside the organization's boundaries.

External equity: Payment of employees at rates comparable to those paid for similar jobs elsewhere.

Factor comparison method: A job evaluation method in which (1) raters need not keep the entire job in mind as they evaluate and (2) raters make decisions on separate aspects, or factors, of the job; the method is based on the assumption that there are five universal job factors.

Finger dexterity: The ability to make precise, coordinated finger movements, such as those performed by an electronics assembler or a watchmaker.

Flexible compensation plans: A method that permits employees to choose from among many alternatives how their financial compensation will be allocated.

Flextime: The practice of permitting employees to choose, with certain limitations, their own working hours.

Forced-choice performance report: A performance appraisal technique in which the rater is given a series of statements about an individual and indicates which items are most or least descriptive of the employee.

Forced distribution method: An appraisal approach in which the rater is required to assign individuals in the work group to a limited number of categories similar to a normal frequency distribution.

Frequency rate: A formula used to calculate the number of lost-time accidents per million person-hours worked.

Functional job analysis (FJA): A comprehensive approach to formulating job descriptions that concentrates on the interactions among the work, the worker, and the work organization.

Generalists: Persons who perform tasks in a wide variety of human resource-related areas.

Going rate: The average pay that most employers provide for the same job in a particular area or industry.

"Golden parachute" contract: An executive perquisite provided for the purpose of protecting executives in the event their firm is acquired by another.

Grievance: An employee's dissatisfaction or feeling of personal injustice relating to his or her employment.

Grievance procedure: A formal, systematic process that permits employees to complain about matters affecting them and their work.

Group appraisal: The use as a team of two or more managers who are familiar with an employee's performance to appraise it.

Group interview: A meeting in which several job applicants interact in the presence of one or more company representatives.

Guidelines oriented job analysis (GOJA): A method that responds to the growing amount of legislation affecting employment decisions by utilizing a step-by-step procedure to describe the work of a particular job classification.

Halo error: Perception by an evaluator that one factor is of paramount importance and gives a good or bad overall rating to an employee based on that one factor.

Hay guide chart-profile method: A highly refined version of the point method of job evaluation that uses the factors of know-how, problem solving, accountability, and where appropriate, working conditions.

Hazard pay: Additional pay provided to employees who work under extremely dangerous conditions.

Health: An employee's freedom from physical or emotional illness.

Human resource development (HRD): A planned, continuous effort by management to improve employee competency levels and organizational performance through training, education, and development programs.

Human resource information system (HRIS): Any organized approach to obtaining relevant and timely information on which to base human resource decisions.

Human resource management (HRM): Utilization of the firm's human resources to achieve organizational objectives.

Human resource managers: Individuals who normally act in an advisory (staff) capacity when working with other (line) managers regarding human resource matters.

Human resource planning: The process of systematically reviewing human resource requirements to ensure that the required number of employees, with the required skills, are available when they are needed.

Human resource research: The systematic study of a firm's human resources for the purpose of maximizing personal and organizational goal achievement.

Hypnosis: An altered state of consciousness that is artificially induced and characterized by increased receptiveness to suggestions.

In-basket training: A simulation in which the participant is given and asked to establish priorities for handling a number of business papers, such as memoranda, reports, and telephone messages, that would typically cross a manager's desk.

Incentive compensation: Directly relating pay to productivity.

Indirect financial compensation: All financial rewards that are not included in direct compensation.

Industrial unions: Bargaining units that generally consist of all the workers in a particular plant or group of plants.

Injunction: A prohibitive legal procedure used by employers to prevent certain union activities such as strikes and unionization attempts.

Internal employee relations: Those human resource management activities associated with promotion, transfer, demotion, resignation, discharge, layoffs, and retirement.

Internal environment: The factors that affect a firm's human resources from inside the organization's boundaries.

Internal equity: Payment of employees according to the relative values of their jobs within an organization.

Internship: A special form of recruitment that involves placing students in temporary jobs with no obligation either by the company to permanently hire the student or by the student to accept a permanent position with the firm.

Job: A group of tasks that must be performed if an organization is to achieve its goals.

Job analysis: The systematic process of determining the skills and knowledge required for performing specific jobs in the organization.

Job analysis schedule (JAS): A systematic method of studying jobs and occupations developed by the U.S. Department of Labor.

Job bidding: A technique that permits individuals in the organization who believe that they possess the required qualifications to apply for a posted job.

Job description: A document that provides information regarding the tasks, duties, and responsibilities of the job.

Job design: The process of determining the specific tasks to be performed, the methods used in performing these tasks, and how the job relates to other work in the organization.

Job enlargement: A change in the scope of a job so as to provide greater variety to the worker.

Job enrichment: Restructuring the content and level of responsibility of a job to make it more challenging, meaningful, and interesting to the worker.

Job evaluation: That part of a compensation system in which management determines the relative values of various jobs.

Job knowledge questions: Questions that assess the knowledge required for performing a job, which a person must possess prior to filling the job.

Job knowledge tests: Tests designed to measure a candidate's knowledge of the duties of the position for which he or she is applying.

Job overload: A condition that exists when employees are given more work than they can reasonably handle.

Job posting: A procedure for communicating to company employees the fact that job openings exist.

Job pricing: Placing a dollar value on the worth of a job.

Job rotation: A training method that involves moving employees from one job to another for the purpose of giving them broader experience.

Job-sample simulation questions: Situations in which an applicant may be required to actually perform a sample task from the job.

Job sharing: The filling of a job by two part-time people who split the duties of one full-time job in some agreed-on manner and are paid according to their contributions.

Job specification: The minimum acceptable qualifications that a person should possess in order to perform a particular job.

Key job: A job that is well known in the company and industry and can be easily defined.

Labor market: The geographical area from which employees are recruited for a particular job.

Leadership: Influencing others to do what the leader wants them to do.

Leased employees: Individuals provided by an outside firm at a fixed hourly rate, similar to a rental fee, often for extended periods.

Leniency: Giving undeserved high performance appraisal ratings.

Likes and dislikes survey: A procedure that helps individuals recognize restrictions they place on themselves.

Local union: The basic element in the structure of the U.S. labor movement.

Lockout: A management decision to keep employees out of the workplace and operate with management personnel and/or temporary replacements.

Long-run trend: Projecting demand for a firm's goods or services, typically five years or more into the future.

Management by objectives (MBO): A philosophy of management that emphasizes the setting of agreed-on objectives by superior and subordinate managers and the use of these objectives as the primary basis of motivation, evaluation, and control efforts.

Management development: Learning experiences provided by an organization for the purpose of upgrading skills and knowledge required in current and future managerial positions.

Management inventory: Detailed data regarding each manager to be used in identifying individuals possessing the potential to move into higher level positions.

Management position description questionnaire (MPDQ): A form of job analysis designed for management positions that uses a checklist method to analyze jobs.

Mandatory bargaining issues: Those issues that fall within the definition of wages, hours, and other terms and conditions of employment.

Manual dexterity: The coordinated movements of both hands and arms, such as those required by large assembly jobs.

Media: Special methods of communicating ideas and concepts in training and development.

Mediation: A process whereby a neutral third party enters and attempts to resolve a labor dispute when a bargaining impasse has occurred.

Mission: The organization's continuing purpose or reason for being.

Motivation: The willingness to put forth effort in the pursuit of organizational goals.

Multinational corporation (MNC): An organization that conducts a large part of its business outside the country in which it is headquartered and has a significant percentage of its physical facilities and employees in other countries.

National union: An organization composed of local unions, which it charters.

Network career path: A method of job progression that contains both vertical and horizontal opportunities.

Nonfinancial compensation: The satisfaction that a person receives by performing meaningful job tasks or from the psychological and/or physical environment in which the job is performed.

Norm: The distribution of many scores obtained by people similar to the applicants being tested.

Objectivity: The condition that is achieved when all individuals scoring a given test obtain the same results.

GLOSSARY

Occupational Measurement System (OMS): A method of job analysis that enables organizations to collect, store, and analyze information pertinent to human resources by means of an electronic database.

Ombudsperson: A complaint officer with access to top management, who hears employees' complaints, investigates them, and sometimes recommends appropriate action.

On-the-job training (OJT): An informal approach to training in which the person learns job tasks by actually performing them.

Open-door policy: A company policy whereby employees have the right to take any grievance to the person next in the chain of command if a satisfactory solution cannot be obtained from their immediate supervisor.

Open shop: Employment that is open on equal terms to union members and nonmembers alike.

Operative employees: All workers in a firm except managers and professionals such as engineers or accountants.

Organization development (OD): An organization-wide application of behavioral science knowledge to the planned development and reinforcement of a firm's strategies, structures, and processes for improving its effectiveness.

Organizational career planning: The process of establishing career paths within a firm.

Organizational structure: The purposeful way in which the human resources of the firm are related or arranged.

Orientation: The guided adjustment of new employees to the company, the job, and the work group.

Outplacement: A process whereby a terminated employee is given assistance in finding employment elsewhere.

Paired comparison: A variation of the ranking method of performance appraisal that involves comparing the performance of each employee with that of every other employee in the group.

Pay compression: A situation which occurs when workers perceive that the pay differential between their pay and that of employees in jobs above or below them is too small.

Pay followers: Companies that choose to pay below the going rate because of a poor financial condition or a belief that they simply do not require highly capable employees.

Pay grade: The grouping of similar jobs to simplify the job pricing process.

Pay leaders: Those organizations that pay higher wages and salaries than competing firms.

Pay range: A minimum and maximum pay rate for a job, with enough variance between the two to allow some significant pay difference.

Payroll-based stock ownership plan (PAYSOP): A special type of ESOP in which stock of a firm is placed in a trust.

Performance appraisal: A formal system of periodic review and evaluation of an individual's job performance.

Permissive bargaining issues: Issues that may be raised, but neither side may insist that they be bargained over.

Perquisites (perks): Special benefits provided by a firm to key executives to give them something extra.

Plateauing: A career condition that occurs when job functions and work content remain the same because of a lack of promotional opportunities within the firm.

Point method: An approach to job evaluation in which numerical values are assigned to specific job components and the sum of these values provides a quantitative assessment of a job's relative worth.

Policy: A predetermined guide established to provide direction in decision making.

Position: The tasks and responsibilities performed by one person; there is a position for every individual in an organization.

Position analysis questionnaire (PAQ): A structured job analysis questionnaire that uses a checklist approach to identify job elements.

Predictive validity: A validation method that involves administering a test and later obtaining the criterion information.

Predictor variables: Factors known to have had an impact on employment levels.

Premium pay: Compensation paid to employees for working long periods of time or working under dangerous or undesirable conditions.

Productivity: A measure of the relationship between inputs (labor, capital, natural resources, and energy) and the quality and quantity of outputs (goods and services).

Profession: A vocation characterized by the existence of a common body of knowledge and a procedure for certifying its practitioners.

Profit sharing: A compensation plan that distributes a predetermined percentage of the firm's profits to employees.

Program generators: Computer programs that have been designed to write other programs.

Programmed instruction: A teaching method that requires no intervention by an instructor.

Progressive disciplinary action: An approach to disciplinary action designed to ensure that the minimum penalty appropriate to the offense is imposed, which involves answering a series of questions about the severity of the offense.

Prohibited bargaining issues: Those issues that are statutorily outlawed from collective bargaining.

Promotion: The movement of a person to a higher level position in the company.

Promotion from within: The policy of filling vacancies above entry-level positions with present employees.

Psychomotor abilities tests: Aptitude tests that measure strength, coordination, and dexterity.

Quality circles: Groups of employees who meet regularly with their supervisors to identify production problems and recommend actions for solutions.

Quality of work life (QWL): The extent to which employees satisfy signficant personal needs through their organizational experiences.

Random variations: Changes for which there are no patterns.

Ranking method: A job evaluation method in which the raters examine the description of each job being evaluated and arrange the jobs in order according to their value to the company; a performance appraisal method in which the rater places all employees in a given group in rank order on the basis of their overall performance.

Rating scales method: A widely used performance appraisal method that rates employees according to defined factors.

Realistic job preview (RJP): A method of conveying job information to an applicant in an unbiased manner, including both positive and negative factors.

Recruitment: The process of attracting individuals on a timely basis, in sufficient numbers and with appropriate qualifications, and encouraging them to apply for jobs with an organization.

Recruitment methods: The specific means by which potential employees are attracted to an organization.

Recruitment sources: Where qualified individuals are located.

Reference checks: Means of providing additional insight into the information provided by an applicant and to verify the accuracy of the information provided.

Regression analysis: A quantitative technique used to predict one item (known as the dependent variable) through knowledge of other items (known as the independent variables).

Reliability: The extent to which a selection test provides consistent results.

Requirements forecast: An estimate of the numbers and kinds of employees the organization will need at future dates in order for it to realize its stated objectives.

Right-to-work laws: Laws that prohibit management and unions from agreements requiring union membership as a condition of employment.

Role ambiguity: A condition that exists when employees lack clear information about the content of their jobs.

Role conflict: A condition that occurs when an individual is expected to achieve opposing goals.

Role playing: A training method in which training participants "act out" job techniques needed in specific situations without the benefit of either a script or rehearsal.

Safety: Protecting employees from injuries caused by work-related accidents.

Sampling: The process by which only a portion of the total number of individuals are studied, from which conclusions are drawn for the entire group.

Scanlon plan: A gain-sharing plan designed to bind employees to the firm's performance.

Seasonal variations: Reasonably predictable changes that occur over a period of a year.

Selection: The process of choosing from a group of applicants those individuals best suited for a particular position.

GLOSSARY

Selection ratio: The number of people hired for a particular job compared to the total number of individuals in the applicant pool.

Self-assessment: The process of learning about oneself.

Sensitivity training: An organizational development technique that is designed to make people aware of themselves and their impact on others.

Severity rate: A formula that is used to calculate the number of days lost because of accidents per million person-hours worked.

Shareholders: The owners of a corporation.

Shift differentials: Additional money paid to reward employees for the inconvenience of working undesirable hours.

Simulation: A technique for experimenting with a real-world situation by means of a mathematical model that represents the actual situation.

Simulators: Training devices of varying degrees of complexity that duplicate the real world.

Situational questions: Questions that pose a hypothetical job situation to determine what the applicant would do in such a situation.

Skills inventory: Information maintained on nonmanagerial employees as to their availability and preparedness to move into higher level positions or laterally.

Social responsibility: The implied, enforced, or felt obligation of managers, acting in their official capacities, to serve or protect the interests of groups other than themselves.

Special events: A recruitment method that involves an effort on the part of a single employer, or group of employers, to attract a larger number of applicants for interviews.

Specialist: An individual who may be a human resource executive, a human resource manager, or a nonmanager who is typically concerned with only one of the six functional areas of human resource management.

Split-halves method: A method of determining the reliability of a test by dividing the results into two parts and then correlating the results of the two parts.

Standard hour plan: An individual incentive plan under which time allowances are calculated for each unit of output.

Standardization: The degree of uniformity of the procedures and conditions related to administering tests.

Stock option plan: The opportunity for a manager to buy a specified amount of stock in the company in the future at or below the current market price.

Straight piecework plan: A predetermined amount of money is paid for each unit produced.

Strategic planning: The determination of overall organizational purposes and goals and how they are to be achieved.

Strength/weakness balance sheet: A self-evaluation procedure developed originally by Ben Franklin that helps people to become aware of their strengths and weaknesses.

Stress: The body's reaction to any demand made on it.

Stress interview: A form of interview that intentionally creates anxiety to determine how an applicant will react in certain types of situations.

Strictness: Being unduly critical of an employee's work performance.

Strike: An action by union members who refuse to work in order to exert pressure on management in negotiations.

Structured interview: Consistently asking each applicant for a particular job the same series of job-related questions.

Survey feedback: A survey method and research technique that systematically collects information about organizations and employee attitudes and makes the data available in aggregated form to employees and management so that problems can be diagnosed and plans developed to solve them.

Team building: A conscious effort to develop effective work groups throughout the organization.

Telecommuting: A procedure whereby workers are able to remain at home or otherwise away from the office and perform their work, as if they were at the office, over telephone lines tied to a computer.

Teleconferencing: A method of conducting or participating in multiparty discussions by telephone or videophone.

Teletraining: A method of training people efficiently and effectively, utilizing teleconferencing.

Test-retest method: Determining selection test reliability by giving the test twice to the same group of individuals and correlating the two sets of scores.

Traditional career path: A vertical line of career progression from one specific job to the next.

Training: Those activities that serve to improve an individual's performance on a currently held job or one related to it.

Transactional analysis (TA): An organizational development method that considers the three ego states of the Parent, the Adult, and the Child in helping people understand interpersonal relations and thus assists in improving an organization's effectiveness.

Transcendental meditation: A stress-reduction technique whereby an individual mentally repeats a secret word or phrase (mantra), provided by a trained instructor, while comfortably seated.

Transfer: The lateral movement of a worker within an organization.

Two-tier wage system: A wage structure that pays newly hired employees less than established employees for performing the same or similar jobs.

Union: A group of employees who have joined together for the purpose of dealing collectively with their employer.

Union shop: A requirement that all employees become members of the union after a specified period of employment (the legal minimum is thirty days) or after a union shop provision has been negotiated.

Unstructured interview: A meeting with a job applicant during which the interviewer asks probing, open-ended questions.

Utility analysis: Determination of the ratio of benefits to costs for any selection technique.

Utilization review: A process that scrutinizes medical diagnoses, hospitalization, surgery, and other medical treatment and care prescribed by doctors.

Validity: The extent to which a test measures what it purports to measure.

Vestibule training: Training that takes place away from the production area on equipment that closely resembles the actual equipment used on the job.

Vocational interest tests: A method of determining the occupation in which a person has the greatest interest and from which the person is most likely to receive satisfaction.

Voice mail: Spoken messages transmitted electronically and stored for delivery to the recipient at a later time.

Wage curve (or pay curve): The fitting of a curve to plotted points in order to create a smooth progression between pay grades.

Weighted Application Blank (WAB): One technique for identifying factors that differentiate successful and less successful employees.

Weighted checklist performance report: A performance appraisal technique whereby the rater completes a form similar to the forced-choice performance report but in which the various responses have been assigned different weights.

Wellness: A concept that focuses on the prevention of illness and disease.

Word processing: A computer application that permits an operator to create and edit written material.

Work-sample tests: Identification of a task or set of tasks that are representative of the job and use of these tasks for selection testing.

Work standards method: A performance appraisal method that compares each employee's performance to a predetermined standard or an expected level of output.

Worker requirements questions: Questions that seek to determine the applicant's willingness to conform to the requirements of the job.

Wrist-finger speed: The ability to make rapid wrist and finger movements, such as those required in inspector-packers and assembly operations jobs.

Yellow-dog contract: A written agreement between the employee and the company made at the time of employment, prohibiting a worker from joining a union or engaging in union activities.

Zero-base forecasting: A method for estimating future employment needs using the organization's current level of employment as the starting point.

INDEX

A. B. Dick Company, 372
Aburdene, Patricia, 271*n*
Academic achievement, coverage of, in employment interview, 234
Accidents in workplace, 520. *See also* Safety
 costs of, 521
 frequency rate, 529–530
 by length of service, 530
 investigation of, 529
 severity rate, 530
Accountability objective, 203
Acquired Immune Deficiency Syndrome (AIDS), 231, 548
Acuff, Hall A., 242*n*
Adams, Larry T., 10*n*, 50*n*, 569*n*
Administrative Management Society, 448
Administrative processes, 320
Adoption assistance plan, 483–484
Advance notice, of resignation, 684–685
Adverse impact, 86–89
Advertising
 and equal opportunity, 197
 as recruitment method, 185–187
Affirmative action, 80, 93, 95–99
 and last-hired, first-fired seniority, 84
 and recruitment, 195–198
AFL-CIO. *See* American Federation of Labor and Congress of Industrial Organizations
Age discrimination,
 in appraisals, 412
 in hiring practices, 75, 78, 213
 and terminations, 690
Age Discrimination in Employment Act (1967), 75, 78, 213, 412, 690
Agency shop, 610
AIDS, 231, 548
Aiming, 230
Albermarle Paper Company v. *Moody*, 81, 222, 387
Alcohol abuse, warning signs of, 544
Alcohol abuse programs, 543
Alcoholism, 543
Allen, Robert E., 615*n*, 623*n*
Allen, Steve, 56
Alliance of Labor Action (ALA), 569
Alpha Kappa Psi, 456
American Airlines, 650
American Arbitration Association (AAA), 616, 676
American Association of University Women, 198

American Compensation Association, 19, 23
American Federation of Labor (AFL), 561, 567
American Federation of Labor and Congress of Industrial Organizations (AFL-CIO), 579, 581
 Committee on Political Education as political arm of, 573–574
 formation of, 567, 569
 structure of, 580
American Federation of State, County, and Municipal Employees (AFSCME), 464
American Management Association, 279, 367, 439, 495
American Society for Personnel Administration, 19, 20, 24, 193, 279, 367, 439, 456
American Society for Training and Development, 19, 22–23
American Tobacco Company v. *Patterson*, 84
Anti-Injunction Act (1932), 564
Antinepotism rule, 180, 215
Apcar, Leonard M., 464*n*
Applicant pool, 217
Appraisal interview, 413–414, 416
Appraisal methods, 403–404
 characteristics of effective, 408–411
Appraisers, qualified, 409–410
Apprenticeship training, 291
Arbitration, 615, 676–678
Arbitrators, sources of, 615–616
Arrest record, hiring discrimination based on, 214
Arvey, Richard D., 258*n*
Asbestos, worker exposure to, 532
Ash, Ronald A., 113*n*
Ashland Oil, Inc., 706
Assessment centers, 278, 414–415
Atchison, Sandra, 565*n*, 617*n*
Atchison, Thomas J., 438*n*, 449*n*, 493*n*, 494*n*
Atlantic Richfield Company, 706
AT&T, 132, 415
Audiovisual aids, 296, 297
Authority, workers' attitudes toward, and leadership style, 319
Authorization card (union), 582
Availability forecast, 154

Bacas, Harry, 46*n*
Background investigation, 241
Bahl, Frederick W., 53

Baird, Lloyd, 276*n*, 278*n*, 283*n*, 284*n*
Baker, H. Kent, 264*n*
Baker, James C., 246*n*, 419*n*
Bakke, Allen, 83–84
Baliga, Gurudutt M., 246*n*, 419*n*
Ball, Judith S., 339*n*, 340*n*
Banas, Paul A., Ph.D., 704–705
Bank of America, 267
Bargaining issues, 608–612
Bargaining unit, 581
Barocci, Thomas A., 621*n*
Baron, James N., 119*n*
Baroni, Barry J., 409*n*
Barry, L. C., 236, 546–547
BARS, 404
Baum, Laurie, 669*n*
Baylie, Thomas N., 382*n*, 383*n*
Beachhead demands, 613
Beal, Edwin F., 572*n*, 609*n*, 610*n*, 616*n*
Beavers, Wiley, 21, 23*n*, 639*n*, 640*n*, 650*n*
Begin, James P., 572*n*, 609*n*, 610*n*, 616*n*
Behavior, interpretation of, in employment interview, 258
Behavioral change, 299
Behaviorally anchored rating scales (BARS), 401–403
Behavioral norms, 56
Behavior bias, 407
Behavior modeling, 282–283
Behavior sample, as problem in employment interview, 257
Belcher, David W., 438*n*, 449*n*, 482*n*, 493*n*, 494*n*
Belenky, Ann Holt, 128*n*
Bell, Chip R., 275, 275*n*
Bello, Marthanne, 559
Bemis, Stephen E., 128*n*
Bendix Corporation, 445
Benefits. *See* Employee benefits
Benge, Eugene, 446
Bennett, Keith W., 315*n*
Benson, Herbert, 540*n*
Benson, Herman, 568*n*
Berger, Michael, 418*n*
Bergmann, Thomas J., 465*n*
Bernstein, Aaron, 565*n*, 617*n*
Berra, Robert L., 40, 42–43
Bethke, Art, 50*n*, 79*n*, 141*n*, 577*n*, 584*n*, 611*n*, 651*n*
BFOQ (Bona fide occupational qualification), 90, 98, 197, 212
Bidding procedures, 180
Bilby, William T., 119*n*
Biofeedback, 540, 542
Blanchard, Kenneth H., 283*n*

Board interview, 236
Bogerty, Margaret A., 391n
Bognanno, Mario, 673n
Bohlander, George W., 647n
Bona fide occupational qualifications (BFOQ), 90, 98, 197, 212
Boone, Mary E., 298n
Bottom-up approach to forecasting, 151
Bowman, Joel P., 255n
Boycotts, 617
Bradford, Hazel, 521n
Branchaw, Bernadine P., 255n
Bredwell, Jo, 186n
Brett, Randall, 413n
Brief, Arthur P., 538n
Brinks, James T., 494n
Bristol-Myers Products, 337, 338, 339, 372
Broadwell, Martin M., 296n
Brody, Michael, 649n
Brown, Abby, 603n, 604n
Brown, Bill, 5
Brown, Charles, 208, 210–211
Brumback, Cathy J., 531n
Bucalo, John P., Jr., 634n
Buchanan, Julie M., 464n
Buford, James A., Jr., 227n
Bumping procedure, 686
Burgess, Leonard R., 448n
Burnout, 534–535
Burns, Hendy Stewart MacKenzie, 361
Burt, Tim, 501n
Business games, 281–282
Business unionism, 561
Byrnes, Thomas A., 193n

Cafeteria compensation, 503–505
Camisa, Kenneth P., 543n
Campbell, David N., 669n
Campbell, John P., 341n
Campion, James E., 258n
Campion, Michael A., 235n
Cangemi, Joseph P., 486n
Career
  definition of, 352
  in human resources, 369, 371–374
Career anchors, 356
Career counseling, 368
Career development, 352, 367–369, 387. *See also* Career planning; Management development
  in multinational corporations, 418–419
Career orientation, in employment interview, 234–235
Career paths, 352, 362, 364
  dual, 364–365
  information on, 365, 366
  network, 364
  traditional, 364
Career planning, 9, 352, 356–357. *See also* Career development
  effects of, 363
  factors in, 352–353, 356
  individual, 357–360
  organizational, 361–362
Carpenters and Joiners Union, 578
Carrell, Michael R., 75n, 623n, 624n
Carroll, Stephen J., 403n
Caruth, Donald L., 48n, 127n, 365n, 412n, 414n, 465n, 724n
Case study, 282, 295
  in human resource research, 709–710
Central tendency, 256, 407
CEO, leadership style of, 536, 538
Cessna Aircraft Company, 184, 391, 414
Chaison, Gary N., 604n, 624n
Chamberlain, Neil W., 673n

Champion International Corporation, 17, 21
Change sequence, 264–265
Checkoff of dues provision, 610
Cherman, E. M., 540n
Cherniss, Cary, 535n
Chevron Corporation, 278, 286, 288, 289
Chief human resource officer, changing world of, 13–15
Child care, hiring discrimination based on, 82, 214
Child-care services, 44
Cigarmakers Union, 561
Citizenship, discrimination on basis of, 92–93, 212
City of Richmond v. *J. A. Croson Co.*, 85
Civil Rights Act (1964), Title VII of, 73, 74, 75, 78, 84, 129
Civil Rights Act (1866), 74–75, 86
Civil Rights Act (1871), 74–75
Civil Service Commission, 82
Civil Service Reform Act (1978), 570, 571
Civil service system, 82, 217, 570, 571
Classification method of job evaluation, 446
Classroom lecture, 285
Claypool, Jeffrey C., 486n
Closed shop, 610
Coaching, 281
Cognitive aptitude tests, 229
Collective bargaining, 440, 581–585, 598–599, 602–603
  bargaining issues, 608–612
  breakdown in negotiations, 614–618
  future of, 621–625
  campaign, 583–584
  definition of, 581
  election and certification, 584
  in global economy, 588
  growing legalistic approach in, 586–588
  human resource manager's role in, 603–604
  petition for election, 582–583
  preparing for negotiations, 604–608
  psychological aspects of, 604
  signing authorization cards, 582
  union strategies in obtaining bargaining unit recognition, 584–585
Collective bargaining agreement
  administering, 618–620
  and dangerous working conditions, 528
  grievance handling under, 672–678
  negotiating, 612–613
  ratifying, 618
Colleges, recruitment from, 183–184
Colvin, C. O., 413n
Committee for Industrial Organization, 566
Committee on Political Education (COPE) (AFL-CIO), 573–574
Commonwealth v. *Hunt*, 560
Communication, 315
  and corporate culture, 315
  in union-free firm, 644–645
Community colleges, as recruitment source, 183
Companywide plans, 491–494
Comparable worth, 463–464
Compensation, 10, 112, 387. *See also* Managerial compensation
  as bargaining issue, 610–611
  cafeteria, 503–505
  deferred, 495
  definition of, 432
  direct financial, 432
  factors in determining, 436–457

flexible, 503–505
and human resource research, 708
incentive, 486, 490–494
indirect financial, 432
for managers, 494–496
in multinational corporations, 506–507
nonfinancial, 432, 499–506
for professionals, 497
as reason for joining union, 575
sales, 497–498
in union-free firm, 646–647
Compensation equity, 432–433, 436
Compensation Review, 23, 439
Compensation survey, 439
Competition
  and external environment, 51
  in multinational environment, 61–62
Competitors, recruitment of, 184
Comprehensive Omnibus Budget Reconciliation Act (COBRA), 482
Compressed workweek, 502
Computer, choosing, 164
Computer-based training, 285
Computer graphics, 726–727
Conarroe, Richard R., 184n
Concession bargaining, 624
Concurrent validity, 227
Condon, Susan Goff, 47n
Conference method, as instructional approach, 282
Confidence, building, 266–267
Congress of Industrial Organizations (CIO), 566
Conoco, Inc., 372
Consolidated Omnibus Budget Reconciliation Act (COBRA) (1985), 443
Conspiracy, 560
Construct validity, 228
Consultants, use of, in organization development, 342
Content validity, 227–228, 415n
Contingency search firms, 193
Contrast effects, in employment interview, 256
Control Data Corporation (CDC), 419, 505, 706
Conviction record, hiring discrimination based on, 214
Cooingwood, Harris, 568n
Cook, James R., 298n, 300n
Cooper, Kenneth H., 541n
Corning Glass, 132
Corporate culture
  and administrative processes, 320
  definition of, 313–314
  effect of, on compensation, 436
  factors that determine, 315
  and internal environment, 55–56
  motivation, 315, 318–321
  and organizational characteristics, 320
  and organizational structure, 320–321
  organization development, 323–341
  participative culture, 322–323
  as source of stress, 536, 538
  types of, 321–322
  use of consultants, 342
Correlation analysis, 716
Cost-benefit analysis, and implementation of HRD program, 275
Cost-of-living allowance (COLA), 439–440, 611
Craft union, 578. *See also* Unions
Credit record, hiring discrimination based on, 213
Criterion-related validity, 227

INDEX

Critical incident method of performance appraisal, 394
Crock, Stan, 574n
Cronin, Richard J., 192n
Crossed transactions, 337
Crowley, Mary, 76
Crystal, Graef S., 459n, 496n
Crystal, John C., 108n
Cultural sensitivity, 246
Cummings, L. L., 387n
Cummings, Thomas G., 323n, 324n, 341n
Curtis, David, 8
Customers
 and external environment, 51–52
 in multinational environment, 62
Cut-off scores, 228
Cyclical variations, 150

Database management, 726
Data communication, 727
Davey, Harold W., 619n
Davidson, Jeffrey, P., 327n
Davis, Keith, 663n
Davis, Ronald H., 254n
Davis-Bacon Act (1931), 441
Dawson, John G., 222n
Day-care centers, subsidized, 485
Day-care referral services, 44
Deal, Terrence E., 314n
Deale, Charles W. L., 177–178n,
Decision support systems, 726
Decker, Robert L., 232n, 257n
Deems, Richard S., 108n
Deferred compensation, 495
Deitsch, Clarence R., 622n
Delta Airlines, 643
Delta Sigma Pi, 456
Demotion, 685
Dennis-Escottier, Shirley, 506n
Denny's, Inc., 371, 372
Denova, Charles, 255n
Derderian, Stephanie E., 365n
DeSanto, John F., 151n
Detroit Edison, 369
Development, 270. See also Career development; Management development; Organization development
Dickman, Fred, 546n
Dictionary of Occupational Titles (DOT), 119
Dilks, Carol, 485n
Dilts, David A., 622n
Dipboye, Robert L., 256n
Direct financial compensation, 432
Directive interview, 235
Disciplinary action, 662–663
 administration of, 670–672
 approaches to, 667–670
 and arbitration, 677
 hot stove rule, 667–668
 process of, 663, 666–667
 progressive, 668
 suggested guidelines for, 670
 without punishment, 668–670
Discriminant analysis, 718
Discrimination
 age, 75, 78, 213
 on basis of national origin, 92–93, 212
 on basis of physical handicaps, 212
 on basis of pregnancy, 78–79, 213
 against minorities, 85, 100, 197
 and promotion opportunity, 82, 84
 racial, 74, 80–81, 213
 religious, 90–91, 212
 reverse, 82–84, 86
 sex, 82, 83, 84–85, 91–93, 212

Displaced workers, 588
Dolan, Carrie, 464n
Dommert, Annette, 701
Dopyera, John, 298n
Dothard v. *Rawlingson*, 83
Dow Chemical, 650
Drake Beam Morin, Inc., 191
Dress and appearance, as hiring standard, 215
Driver, Russell W., 541n
Drug abuse programs, 544–545
Drug testing, 231
Dual career paths, 364–365, 536
Due process, 411
Dulles, Foster Rhea, 561n, 568n
Dunbar, Edward, 246n, 418n
Dunbar, Mendenhall, 419n
Dunn, J. D., 462n, 492n
Dunnette, Marvin D., 341n
Dunsing, Richard J., 389n

Eadie, William F., 233n
Earley, P. Christopher, 418n
Earlier retirement, reversal of trend toward, 45
Economic factors, and job design, 131
Economy, effect of, on compensation decisions, 441
Edens, Frank N., 11n, 708n
Education, 270
Education requirements, as hiring standard to avoid, 215
Edwards, Bob, 191, 270
Edwards, Robert E., 8n, 108n, 147n, 268–269, 382n
EEOC v. *Home Insurance Company*, 690
EEOC v. *Liggett and Myers*, 690
Eibirt, Henry, 12n
Eichinger, Robert W., 8n
Eisen, Jerry, 639n
Elco Industries, 315
Elder Care Referral Service, 483, 484–485
Eleventh-hour bargaining, 612n
Ellig, Bruce R., 466n, 496n
Embrey, Wanda R., 649n, 683n
Emener, William G., 545n
Employee
 access to results, 410–411
 assessment of, 386–387
 as determinant of financial compensation, 454–457
Employee assistance programs, 545–548
Employee benefits, 10, 474–475
 as bargaining issue, 610–611
 communicating information about, 486
 companywide plans, 491–494
 comprehensive voluntary program of, 483–485
 group incentive plans, 491
 new, 485–486
 as required by law, 478–479
 voluntary, 479–480
Employee equity, 436
Employee experience, and compensation, 455–456
Employee information, 160
Employee leasing, 178
Employee morale, 322–323
Employee participation, 267, 270
Employee performance, and compensation, 454–455
Employee Polygraph Protection Act, 241
Employee potential, and compensation, 456–457
Employee recording, in job analysis, 115
Employee recruitment, 112

Employee referrals, 193–194
Employee relations, 10
 in union-free firm, 647–649
 and workplace safety, 527
Employee requisition, 174
Employee Retirement Income Security (ERISA) (1974), 443, 481, 486, 493, 688
Employee rights movement, 586–588
Employee security, as bargaining issue, 611–612
Employee selection, 112
Employee services, 483
Employee stock ownership plan (ESOP), 482, 493–494
Employee welfare, 480–483
Employment agencies, 187, 197–198
Employment application, 219–222
Employment at will, 681–682
Employment interview, 231–232
 content of, 233–235
 legal implications of, 232–233
 methods of, 236–239
 objectives of, 233
 potential problems in, 254–258
 types of, 235–236
Enitame, J. O., 61n
Entry-level positions, 371–374
 training methods for, 290
Environmental factors, 39–41
 affecting selection process, 212–218
 external environment, 41–53
 internal environment, 53–56
 and multinational corporations, 56–63
 role of in development of physical and mental disorders, 531
Equal employment opportunity, 74
 and affirmative action, 80, 93, 95–99
 and Equal Employment Opportunity Commission, 75, 86–88
 executive order 11246, 79–80
 guidelines on discrimination due to national origin, 92–93
 guidelines on discrimination due to religion, 93
 implications for multinational corporations, 99–100
 interpretative guidelines on sexual harassment, 91–92
 laws affecting, 74–76, 78–79
 and recruitment, 195–198, 219
 Supreme Court decisions on, 80–86
 Uniform Guidelines for Employee Selection Procedures, 88–90
Equal Employment Opportunity Commission (EEOC), 75, 86–88
Equal opportunity clause, in government contracts, 92
Equal Pay Act (1963), 129, 442–443, 463
Equity, 432
 employee, 436
 external, 433, 435
 internal, 436
Equivalent forms method, 226
Essay method of performance appraisal, 394
Ethics, and human resource management, 23–25
Evaluation, of human resource management function, 722–724
Evaluator, judgmental role of, 407–408
Evans, Karen M., 495n
Everly, George S., Jr., 264n
Exception reports, 162
Exclusive bargaining shop, 610
Executive, 15. See also Management; Managers

termination of, 680
Executive Order 10988, 569, 570
Executive Order 11246, 79–80
Executive search firms, 192–193
Exempt employees, 442
Experiment, in human resource research, 712
External environment, 41
 and competition, 51
 and customers, 51–52
 labor force, 41–49
 legal considerations, 49
 of recruitment, 178–179
 and shareholders, 50–51
 and society, 49–50
 and technology, 53
 and unions, 50
External equity, 433, 435
External sources, of recruitment, 157, 181–185
External supply, 157
Exxon, 283

Factor comparison method of job evaluation, 446
Fair Labor Standards Act (1938), 129, 442
Family, as source of stress, 536
Fashman, Zachary D., 222n
Fear, Richard A., 190n, 232n
Federal Department Stores, 283
Federal Labor Relations Authority (FLRA), 571–572
Federal Mediation and Conciliation Service (FMCS), 615, 616, 676
Federal Privacy Act (1974), 411
Federation of Business and Professional Women's Talent Bank, 198
Field, Hubert S., 118n
Felton, Barbara, 235n
Fernandez, Kurt, 575n, 576n, 598n
Ferris, Gerald R., 239n, 245n
Feuer, Dale, 231n, 548n
Fiedler, Fred E., 342n, 343n
Field, Hubert S., 412n
Final-offer arbitration, 615
Fine, Sidney A., 126n
Finger dexterity, 229–230
Firefighters Local Union 1984 v. *Carl W. Stotts*, 84
Fireman's Fund Insurance Company, 47
First impression bias, 254
First-line supervisors, in union-free firm, 641–643
First National Bank, 335
Fisher, Ben, 625
Flanholtz, Eric G., 12n, 53n
Fleming, R. L., 669n
Fleming Companies, Inc., 706
Flexibility, 542
Flexible compensation plans, 503–505
Flextime, 501–502
Flippo, Edwin B., 49n, 147n
Florida Power Corporation, 274–275
Flynn, Brian H., 62n
Foltz, Roy G., 190n, 330n
Fombrun, Charles J., 382n, 389n, 404n, 412n
Forced-choice performance report, 401
Forced distribution method of performance appraisal, 400–401
Ford Motor Company, 415, 706
Forecasting, 163
 human resource availability, 153–157
 human resource requirements, 153
 techniques of, 150–153
 terminology of, 149–150

Forster, Max H., 296n
Fortin, Karen A., 506n
Fossum, John A., 622n
Foulkes, Fred K., 640n, 649n
Fowler, George, 441n
Fox, William M., 382n
Frantzreb, Richard B., 151n
Fredian, Alan J., 413n
Frequency rate, of accidents, 529–530
Freudenberger, Herbert J., 534n
Frichtl, Paul, 357n
Friedman, Dick, 535n
Frost, Peter J., 538n

GAF Corporation, 372
Gainsharing, 588
Gajek, Marion, 506n
Galagan, Patricia, 546n
Galenson, Walter, 572n
Garcia, J. Robert, 180n, 343n
Garnishment record, hiring discrimination based on, 215
Garrett, Robert F., 671
Gates Learjet, 236
Gatewood, Robert D., 118n
Gaylord, Sara R., 235n
Gehrman, Douglas B., 145n, 147n, 382n
Gender, hiring discrimination based on, 82, 83, 91–92, 212
General Cable Technologies, 372
General Electric, 290, 415, 649
Generalist, 15
General learning concepts, 277
General Mills, Inc., 391
Geometric progression, 452n
Gerber Products Company, 372
Gest, Ted, 75n
Gibson, James L., 340n, 343n
Gibson, W. David, 543n
Glaser, Edward M., 490n
Glickstein, Gloria, 191n, 194n
Global economy, collective bargaining in, 588
Goals, lack of, as problem in employment interview, 254
Goddard, Robert W., 351n, 361n
Godfrey, Gayla, 74, 76–77
Godkewitsch, Michael, 271n
Going rate, 437
"Golden parachute" contract, 496
Goldstein, Irwin L., 341n
Gompers, Samuel, 561
Goodale, James G., 232n
Goodpaster, Kenneth E., 50n
Goodyear, 650
Gordon, Jack, 280n, 281n, 285n, 300n
Governmental civil service systems, 217
Government contracts, equal opportunity clause in, 94
Gow, Jack F., 12n
Graves, J. Peter, 392n, 400n, 403n
Greene, Robert J., 462n
Greenlaw, Paul S., 256n
Gribben, Susan, 238n
Grider, Doug, 463n, 464n
Grievance, 673
Grievance arbitration, 615
Grievance handling, 647, 673–674
 as bargaining issue, 611
 in non-union organizations, 678–679
 under collective bargaining agreement, 672–678
Griggs v. *Duke Power Company*, 80–81, 84, 222
Grote, Richard C., 669n
Group appraisal, 390
Group incentive plans, 491

Group interview, 236
Gruber, Katherine, 20n, 21n, 22n
Grumman Corporation, 371, 372
Guest, Robert H., 131n
Guidelines oriented job analysis (GOJA), 128
Gunderson, E. K. Erich, 536n, 537n
Guptara, Prabhu, 245n, 418n
Gyllenhammar, Pehr, 335, 336

Hackman, J. Richard, 131, 131n
Hafer, John C., 244n
Hagman and EEOC v. *United Airlines*, 690
Hall, Douglas T., 357n, 367n
Halo error, 256, 405–406
Hamilton, Carol-Ann, 506n
Hammer, W. Clay, 367n
Hancock, Harry P., Jr., 647–648
Handicapped workers, 47
Handorf, Charlene R., 682n
Harassment
 on basis of national origin, 90
 sexual, 84–85, 91–93
Hargis, Kenneth, 299n
Harris, Phillip R., 57n, 245n, 418n
Harris, Thomas A., 336n
Hartmarx, 372
Harvey, James L., 5n, 8n
Hay Associates, 439
Hay guide chart-profile method of compensation, 453–454
Hazard pay, 483
Health, 10, 519. *See also* Wellness programs
 and environmental factors, 531
 and human resource research, 709
 programs for, 531–532
Health care benefits, 485
Heavrin, Christina, 623n, 624n
Height and weight requirements, and hiring discrimination, 83, 213
Heil, R. H. (Russ), 636–637, 643
Hellman, John S., 13n, 14n
Hellriegel, Don, 324n
Henderson, Richard I., 444n, 453n, 496n
Heneman, Herbert G., Jr., 75n, 296n
Heneman, Herbert S., 126n
Herman, E. Edward, 561n, 571n
Herzberg, Frederick, 132, 322
Hewlett-Packard, 44, 271, 662, 686
High schools, recruitment from, 181, 183
Hills, Frederick S., 465n
Hiring policies
 discrimination in, 212–215
 restricted, 158
Hitt, Michael A., 327n
Hixon, Allen L., 245n
Hobbs, Art, 562–563, 575
Hoefer, Michael, 529n
Hoerr, John, 586n, 587n, 588n, 598n, 638n, 682n, 686n
Hofstede, Geert, 57n
Holiday Inn, 650
Holidays, 10
Holley, William H., 412n
Holley, William L., 227n
Holmberg, Stephen R., 264n
Holzinger, Albert G., 475n
HOMEWORK, 505
Honeywell, Inc., 208
Hoover, John J., 528n
Hornstein, Harvey A., 324n
Horton, Thomas R., 433n, 544n, 545, 545n
Hospital Administration, 439
Host country nationals (HCNs), 58, 59

INDEX

Hoth, C. C., 244n
Hot stove rule, 667–668
Hoyman, Michelle, 89n
Hubbartt, William S., 442n, 465n
Huber, Vandra L., 208n
Human resource assistant, 203
Human resource availability forecasting, 153–157, 160
Human resource development (HRD), 8–10, 264–265, 383, 386
  definition and scope, 270–271
  determining needs, 276–278
  establishing objectives, 278–279
  evaluating, 298–300
  factors influencing, 273–276
  and human resource research, 708
  implementing programs, 296, 298
  management development, 279–285
  methods of, 279, 280, 293–295
  in multinational corporations, 415, 417–419
  objectives in, 299–300
  process of, 271–272
  selecting media, 295–296
  supervisory management training programs, 286, 288–290
  in union-free firm, 646
Human resource development manager, 274, 275
Human resource development specialists, 275–276
Human resource forecasting. *See* Forecasting
Human resource function, 17, 18, 19, 20, 21
Human resource gaps, 160–161
Human resource information systems (HRIS), 162–165
Human resource management (HRM)
  careers in, 372–373
  definition of, 4
  environmental factors affecting, 39–41
  and ethics, 23–25
  evaluation of, 722–724
  evolution of, 12–13
  external environment, 41
  functions of, 8–12
  professionalization of, 17, 19
  technological advances affecting, 724–728
Human resource manager
  changing world of chief, 13–15
  and collective bargaining, 603–604
  definition of, 5, 8
  distinguishing among executives, generalists, and specialists, 15
  specialist functions of, 13
  in union-free firm, 11, 652–653
Human resource needs forecast, 160
Human resource planning (HRP), 8, 147–149, 382–383
  example of, 158–162
  forecasting availability, 153–157
  forecasting requirements, 153
  human resource forecasting techniques, 150–153
  human resource information systems, 162–165
  and human resource research, 707–708
  surplus employees, 157–158
  terminology of forecasting, 149–150
  in union-free firm, 645–646
Human resource program, monitoring results of, 161–162
Human resource requirements forecasting, 153
Human resource research (HRR), 11, 701

benefits of, 703, 706–709
definition of, 706
illustration of, 719–722
methods of inquiry in, 709–712
productivity challenge, 701–703
quantitative methods in, 715–719
recognizing the problem, 713–715
research process, 712
in union-free firm, 649
uses of, 706
Human Resources: Journal of the International Association for Personnel Women, 23
Hunt, Gary T., 233n
Hunter, John E., 223n, 245n
Huse, Edgar F., 323n, 324n, 341n
Hypnosis, 540

IBM, 44, 285–286, 287, 635, 662, 686
Ihrig, Fritz, 603
Imberman, Woodruff, 651n
Immediate supervisor, responsibility of, for performance appraisal, 389–390
Immigrants from developing areas, in labor force, 47–48
Immigration Reform and Control Act (1986), 79
In-basket training, 283
Incentive compensation, 486, 490–494
Incentive plans, 440, 490–491
Indirect financial compensation, 432
Individual career planning, 357–360
Individual incentive plans, 490–491
Industrial union, 578. *See also* Unions
Information Science Incorporated (InSci), 164
Ingle, Sud, 329n, 330n
Injunction, 560
Internal employee relations, 387
  definition of, 662
  and disciplinary action, 662–663, 666–672
  legal implications of, 689–690
  in multinational corporations, 690–691
Internal environment, 53
  and corporate culture, 55–56
  and mission, 54–55
  and policies, 55
  of recruitment, 179–180
Internal equity, 436
Internal recruitment, 179, 180–181
Internal sources of supply, 154
International Association for Personnel Women, 19, 23
International Association of Quality Circles, 330
International Motor Company, 324
International Paper Company, 373
International Personnel Management Association, 19, 23
International union, 578–579. *See also* Unions
Internships, 191–192, 283
Interpersonal competence, in employment interview, 234
Interview, *See also* Employment interview
  group, 236
  in job analysis, 115
Interviewer
  bias of, in employment interview, 256–257
  characteristics of, 238
  domination of, in employment interview, 255
  lack of training, as problem in employment interview, 257

Interview planning, 238
Irregular progession, 452n
Ivancevich, John M., 340n, 343n, 533n, 542n
Iverstine, Joe, 60n, 62n

Jackson, Douglas N., 217n, 232n
Jackson, Susan E., 535n
Jackson, Tom, 352n
Jaffee, Cabot L., 414n
Jamison, Richard G., 432, 434–435
Jansonius, John V., 178n
Jawboning, 440
Jay, Anthony, 314n
Jennings, Ken, 546n
Jennings, Margarette C., 126n
Jereski, Laura, 493n
Job, 108
  as aspect of nonfinancial compensation, 499
  as determinant of financial compensation, 444–454
Job analysis, 108–109, 209, 452
  and compensation, 444
  conducting, 115, 118
  date of, 119–120
  Department of Labor job analysis schedule, 121, 126
  guidelines oriented job analysis, 128
  job description, 118–120
  job design, 131–133
  job specification, 120–121
  and the law, 129
  management position description questionnaire, 27–28
  methods of, 113–115
  occupational measurement system, 128–129
  position analysis questionnaire, 127
  reasons for conducting, 109, 112–113
  types of data collected through, 114
Job analysis information, 113
Job analysis questionnaire, 116–117
Job analysis schedule, 121, 126
Job applicants
  acceptance of, 243
  rejection of, 243–244
Job bidding, 180
Job description, 109, 118–120, 122, 444, 452
Job design, 131–133
Job enlargement, 133
Job enrichment, 132–133, 335–336
Job environment, 499–506
Job evaluation, 444–445
  classification method, 446
  comparable worth, 463–464
  factor comparison method, 446
  job pricing, 457–462
  pay secrecy, 464–465
  point method, 447–452
  ranking method, 445–446
Job fairs, 190
Job identification, 118–119
Job knowledge questions, 236
Job knowledge tests, 230
Job overload, as source of stress, 538
Job performance, 56
Job posting, 180–181
Job pricing, 457–462
Job procedures, 239
Job-related accidents, 526
Job-related criteria, 408–409
Job-related factors, 612
Job rotation, 284
Job safety and health protection, 524
Job-sample simulation questions, 236

INDEX

Job security, 576
Job sharing, 46, 502–503
Job specification, 109, 112, 120–121
Job standards, 113
Job summary, 120
Job Training Partnership Act (JTPA), 292–293
Johnson, Lyndon B., 78
Jordan, Thomas M., 406

Kandola, R. S., 230n
Kasper, John, 315
Kay, Jane, 5
Kaye, Beverly, 367n, 410n
Keaveny, Timothy J., 411n, 615n, 623n
Kelly Services, Inc., 47
Kemper Group, 547
Kennecott Corporation, 481
Kennedy, Allan A., 314n
Kennedy, John F., 440, 569
Key job, 439
Kikoshi, John F., 413n
Kilmann, Ralph H., 314n
Kilpatrick, Robert D., 481n
Kimberly-Clark Corporation, 542
Kinard, Jerry, 60n, 62n
Kirk, J. Robert, 463n
Kirk, Robert, 682n
Kirkland, Lane, 585
Kirschner, Kenneth H., 682n
Knecht, G. Bruce, 240n
Knight, Patrick A., 341n
Kochan, Thomas A., 621n
Kohl, John P., 256n
Korn/Ferry International, 192
Krantz, Shelley, 410n
Kravetz, Dennis J., 365n
Kreitner, Robert, 541n
Krislov, Joseph, 60n
Krogman, Robert, 486n
Krupp, Neil B., 507n
Kuhn, Alfred, 561n, 571n
Kuhnle, Robert, 283n
Kujawski, Carl J., 382n, 383n
Kurbis, Ernie A., 151n
Kuzmits, Frank E., 75n

Labor, Department of
  job analysis schedule, 121, 126
  and voluntary reduction of workplace hazards, 525
Labor force
  breakdown of new entrants, 41–42
  as determinant of compensation, 438–443
  and external environment, 41–49
  immigrants from developing areas in, 47–48
  leased employees, 47
  for multinational corporations, 58–59
  older workers in, 45–46
  part-time workers in, 46–47
  persons with disabilities in, 47
  projected size of U.S., in 1995, 41
  temporary employees in, 47
  women in, 44
  young persons with limited education or skills in, 48–49
Labor-intensive organizations, 371
Labor-management relations, 10–11
Labor Management Relations Act (1947), 528, 566–567
Labor-Management Reporting and Disclosure Act (1959), 567–569
Labor movement
  history of, 559–569
  signs of troubled, 585–586

Labor unions, 440. *See also* Unions
Laird, Dugan, 276n, 278n, 283n, 284n, 292n
Lamb, Sue Ries, 235n
Landrum-Griffin Act (1959), 567–569
Latham, Gary, 232n, 276n, 278n
Laud, Robert J., 382n, 389n, 404n, 412n
Lawler, Edward E., III, 448n, 452n, 465n
Lawrence, Daniel G., 222n
Lawrie, John, 154n
Lawson, Joyce, 384–385
Layoffs, 158, 685–686
Leadership, 318–320
League of United Latin American Citizens, 198
Learning, 299
Leased employees, 47
Lecture, 295
Lee, Chris, 271n, 275n
Legal considerations
  and external environment, 49
  of internal employee relations, 689–690
  of interviewing, 232–233
  for multinational corporations, 57
  and recruitment practices, 179, 195–198
  and selection process, 209
Legislation
  and employee compensation, 129, 442–443, 463
  equal employment opportunity, 74–76, 78–79
  and job analysis, 129
Leniency, problem of, in performance appraisal, 406
Levesque, Joseph D., 209n, 238n
Levine, Edward L., 113n
Levine, Hermine Zagat, 547n, 548n
Levinson, Harry, 535n, 604n, 608n
Lewis, John L., 566
Lie detector tests, 241
Life changes, as source of stress, 536, 537
Life Office Management Association, 439, 448
Life stages, and career planning, 352–353, 356
Likert, Jane Gibson, 265n
Likert, Rensis, 265n
Likes and dislikes survey, 358, 360
Lill, David J., 336n
Lincoln Electric Company, 320
Linder, Jane C., 313n
Line manager, in safety program, 528–529
Linenberger, Patricia, 411n
Ling, Cyril C., 440n
Lionel, Dan, 184n, 186n
Lipset, Seymour Martin, 585n
Litterer, Joseph A., 413n
Littlefield, C. L., 447n, 452n
Living conditions, as source of stress, 536
Local union, 578. *See also* Unions
Lockout, 617
Lockwood, Howard C., 75n
London, Manual, 239n
Lone Star Industries, 273
Longnecker, Justin G., 267n
Longshoremen/Maritime, 568
Long-term trend, 149–150
LoPresto, Robert, 193n
Lorber, Lawrence Z., 463n, 682n
Lotus Development Corporation, 44
Lubliner, Murray J., 174n
Lunborg, Louis, 267
Lupton, Daniel E., 387n
Lynley, Judy, 11

Macher, Ken, 286n
MacKenzie, Fred T., 324n
Magnus, Margaret, 175n, 177n, 184n, 194n, 304n
Management
  attitude of, as reason for joining union, 576–577
  dissatisfaction with, as reason for joining union, 574–577
  effective, and human resource research, 707
  preparation of, for negotiations, 608–609
  strategies of, for overcoming negotiation breakdowns, 617–618
  and union decertification, 651
Management Analysis Center, Inc., 314
Management and skills inventories, 180
Management by objectives (MBO), 330–335, 368, 403, 404
Management development, 279–286
  behavior modeling, 282–283
  business games, 281–282
  case study, 282
  classroom lectures, 285–286
  coaching, 281
  computer-based training, 285
  conference method, 282
  at IBM, 285–286, 287
  in-basket training, 283
  internships, 283
  job rotation, 284
  programmed instruction, 284–285
  role playing, 283–284
  supervisory training programs, 286, 288–290
Management inventories, 154–155
Management Position Description Questionnaire (MPDQ), 27–28
Management rights, as bargaining issue, 609
Management skills/development, 280
Management style, 321
Management teams, effective, 327, 328
Manager
  leadership factors related to, 318–319
  termination of, 681
Managerial compensation, 494–496. *See also* Compensation
  classification method, 446
  factor comparison method, 446–447
  job analysis, 444
  job evaluation, 444–445
  point method, 447–454
  ranking method, 445–446
Mandatory bargaining issues, 605, 606
Manpower, Inc., 47
Manual dexterity, 230
Manville Corporation, 373
Marital status, hiring discrimination based on, 212
Marks, Susan 187, 188
Marriott Corporation, 45
Martier, Alison, 357n
Martin v. Wilks, 86
Maslow, A., 322
Mason, Beverly J., 476–477, 480
Massachusetts Mutual Life Insurance Company, 485
Massoni, Karen B., 533n
Matejka, J. Kenneth, 389n
Mathis, Robert L., 327n
Matteson, Michael T., 533n, 542n
Matthews, John B., Jr., 50n
Mazo, Judith F., 482n
McCafferty, Robert M., 486n
McClellan, Senator, 568

INDEX

McClellan Committee, 568
McClelland, David, 60
McClelland, Keith, 548n
McCormick, E. J., 114n, 126n
McDonald's, 45
McDonnell Douglas, 649
McGregor, Douglas, 322, 327
McKee, Kathryn, 5, 6–7, 367n
McKenzie, Robert C., 223n
McMachon, John E., 357n
McManus, George J., 270n
McMillan, John D., 13n
Meany, George, 567
Media, audiovisual, 296, 297
Mediation, 614–615
Mediators, sources of, 615–616
Medical insurance, 10
Mendenhall, Mark E., 246n, 418n
Merikangas, Marilyn, 689n
Meritor v. *Savings Bank* v. *Vinson*, 84–85, 92
Meslack, Christina, 535n
Metzger, Robert O., 727n
Middlebrook, Bill, 414n
Middlemist, Dennis, 327n
Mid-life crisis, 534–535
Milbourn, Gene, Jr., 437n
Milkovich, George T., 436n, 445n, 446n, 490n, 495n
Millard, C. W., 302n
Miller, Christopher S., 412n
Miller v. *Bank of America*, 92
Mills, D. Quinn, 624–625
Mills, Harry N., 157n
Mindel, R. M., 230n
Minorities
  discrimination against, 85
  improving recruitment of, 100
  utilization of, 197
Minority Business Enterprises, 85
Mission, and internal environment, 54–55
Mistretta v. *Sandia Corporation*, 387
Mitchell, Vance F., 538n
Mondy, R. Wayne, 8n, 11n, 49n, 50n, 108n, 127n, 147n, 157n, 174n, 365n, 382n, 412n, 576n, 577n, 584n, 611n, 613n, 625, 649n, 651n, 683n, 708n, 710n, 722n, 724n
Monsanto Company, 18, 132, 333–335
Moravec, Milan, 352n, 362n, 410n
Morgan, Marilyn A., 357n, 367n
Motivation, 315, 318–321
Motorola, Inc., 373
Muldrow, Tressie W., 223n
Mullins, Terry W., 254n
Multinational corporations
  career development in, 418–419
  compensation in, 506–507
  competition in, 61–62
  environmental factors affecting, 56–63
  equal employment opportunity for, 99
  and foreign competition, 622–623
  human resource development in, 417–419
  employee relations in, 690–691
  labor force for, 58–59
  legal considerations for, 57
  performance appraisal in, 419
  and shareholders, 61
  and society, 59–60
  staffing in, 245–247
  and unions, 60–61
Murphy, B. S., 520n
Murray, Stuart, 392n
Multiple regression, 152–153
Myers, David C., 126n
Myers, Donald W., 108n, 129n

Nabisco Brands, Inc., 373
Nadler, Leonard, 270n
Naisbitt, John, 271n, 703
National Association for the Advancement of Colored People, 198
National Council of Negro Women, 198
National Education Association, 571–572
National Electrical Manufacturers' Association, 448
National Institute for Occupational Safety and Health (NIOSH), 533
National Labor Relations Act (1935), 178, 564–566, 581–585
National Labor Relations Board (NLRB), 565, 650–651
National origin
  guidelines on discrimination due to, 92–93
  hiring discrimination based on, 92–93, 212
National union, 578–579. *See also* Unions
National Urban League, 198
Neale, Margaret A., 208n
Negotiation breakdowns, strategies for, 616–618
Nelson, John G., 535n
Nelson, Wallace F., 710n, 722n
Nemec, Margaret M., 187n
Network career path, 364
Newman, Jerry M., 436n, 445n, 446n, 490n, 495n
New York Life Insurance Company, 46–47
New York Telephone, 481
New York Times Company, 391
Niehouse, Oliver L., 533n
Noble Order of the Knights of Labor, 561
Noe, Robert E., 174n
Noe, Robert M., III, 8n, 108n, 127n, 147n, 365n, 382n, 412n, 649n, 683n, 724n
Noer, David M., 419n
Noise level, reduction of, 532
Nondirective interview, 235
Nonfinancial compensation, 432, 499–506
Nonmanagerial/nonprofessional employees, termination of, 679–680
Nonmonetary rewards, 10
Nonverbal communication, in employment interview, 257–258
Nord, Walter R., 538n
Norman, Beverly, 535n
Norris, Dwight R., 227n
Norris-LaGuardia Act (1932), 564
Northcraft, Gregory B., 208n
Novit, Mitchell S., 532n
Nussbaum, Bruce, 622n
Nyweide, Jeffrey O., 147n

Oberman, Steve M., 217n, 232n
Objectivity, in performance appraisal, 404–405
O'Brien, Fabius, 45n
Observation, in job analysis, 115
Occupational experience, in employment interview, 234
Occupational measurement system, 128–129
Occupational Safety and Health Act, 10n, 129, 520–521, 524
Occupational Safety and Health Administration (OSHA), 520–521, 666
Oddou, Gary R., 246n, 418n, 419n
Office of Federal Contract Compliance Programs (OFCCP), 78, 80

Office of Safety and Health Administration, guidelines for power transmission apparatus, 527
Older workers, in labor force, 45–46
Oldham, Greg R., 131, 131n
Olsen, Madeline Hess, 493n
Olson, Howard C., 126n
Ombudsperson, 647–649
On-demand reports, 162
On-the-job training (OJT), 291
Open communication, 267, 410
Open-door policy, 644
Open shop, 610
Operational level accreditation for professionals in human resources (PHR), 33–34
Operative employees, 9
  training of, 290–293
Organization analysis, 276
Organization development, 9
  and job enrichment, 335–336
  and management by objectives, 330–335
  methods of, 368–369
  purpose of, 9
  and quality circles, 327, 329–330
  and quality of work life, 339–340
  and sensitivity training, 340–341
  and survey feedback, 324–326
  and team building, 327
  and transactional analysis, 336–338
Organizational career planning, 361–362
  methods of, 368–369
Organizational change, 263
  change sequence, 264–265
  reasons for resisting change, 265–266
  reducing resistance to change, 266–267
Organizational characteristics, and corporate culture, 320
Organizational development, 341–343
Organizational goals, 160
Organizational hierarchy, 217
Organizational structure, 320–321
Orientation, 300
  emphasis on safety in, 529
  purposes of, 300–302
  reorientation, 304
  stages in effective, 302
  training supervisor, 302, 304
O'Sullivan, Devin, 297n
Ouchi, William, 13, 314n
Outplacement, 681
Output standards, 490
Overtime, 176–177
Ozley, Lee M., 339n, 340n

Paid vacations, 10
Paired comparison, 400
Pan American World Airways, 184
Panza, Carol M., 298n, 300n
Pardue, William B., 5
Parent country nationals (PCNs), 58, 59
Paris, Ellen, 480n
Parkel, James, 147
Parks, Largent, Jr., 410n
Parma Cycle Company, 259–260
Parry, Juanita F., 23n
Participative culture, 322–323
Participative management, 331
Part-time workers, 46–47
Pascale, Richard, 322n
Patterned interview, 235, 237
Patterson v. *McClean Credit Union*, 86
Patton, John A., 447n, 452n
Paunonen, Sampo, 217n, 232n
Pay compression, 465–466
Pay followers, 438

INDEX

Pay grades, 458
Pay leaders, 436
Payment for time not worked, 479–480
Pay ranges, 458–462
Pay rates, adjusting, 462
Pay secrecy, 464–465
Pearlman, Kenneth, 245n
Peer pressure, as reason for joining union, 577–578
Peers, responsibility of, for performance appraisal, 390
Pendleton, Clarence, 463
Penney, J. C., Company, 48, 415
Pension plans, 481–482
Performance appraisal, 9
   definition of, 381–382
   legal implications, 412
   methods of, 391–403
   in multinational corporations, 419
   period of, 391
   problems in, 404–408
   process of, 387–389
   responsibility for, 389–391
   uses of, 382–383
Performance criteria, assessing changes in meeting, 343
Performance expectations, 409
Perkins, Robert E., 478n
Perks, 495–496
Permissive bargaining issues, 605
Perquisites, 495–496
Personal analysis, 276, 278
Personal bias, 407
Personality tests, 231
Personal qualities, in employment interview, 234
Personnel Accreditation Institute (PAI), 19, 20–22, 33–36
Personnel Administrator, 20
Persons with disabilities, in labor force, 47
Pesci, Michael, 532n, 533n
Peters, Thomas, 314n, 703
Phillips v. Martin Marietta Corporation, 82
Physical examination, 242
Physical fitness programs, 541–543
Physical handicap, hiring discrimination based on, 212
Physical requirements, hiring discrimination based on, 83, 213
Pilenzo, Ronald C., 341, 354–355, 374
Pinsky, Sheldon, 533n
Pinto, P. R., 127n
Pi Sigma Epsilon, 456
Pitone, Louise, 298n
Plachy, Roger J., 401n, 403n, 444n
Plateauing, 365, 367–368
Plous, F. K., Jr., 335n
Plovnick, Mark S., 604n, 624n
Poe, Randall, 532n
Point method, 447–452
Polaroid, 132
Policies, and internal environment, 55
Policy level accreditation
   for senior professional in human resources (SPHR)—generalist, 35–36
   for senior professional in human resources (SPHR)—specialist, 34–35
Political influence, on compensation, 457
Polygraph tests, 241
Portwood, James D., 8n
Position Analysis Questionnaire (PAQ), 127
Post, Jim, 542

Postal Reorganization Act (1970), 571
Powell, Gary N., 196
Predictive validity, 227
Predictor variables, 152–153
Pregnancy, hiring discrimination based on, 78–79, 213
Pregnancy Discrimination Act, 78–79
Preliminary interview, 218–219
Premature judgments, in employment interview, 254
Premeaux, Shane R., 50n, 576n, 577n, 584n, 611n, 613n, 625n, 651n
Premium pay, 483
President's Commission on Industrial Competitiveness, 588
Priefert, Laurel, 465n
Primps, Sophia B., 502n
Privacy Act (1974), 240
Private employment agencies, 187
Probationary period, 218
Productivity, 588, 623
   as challenge, 701–703
   and incentive compensation, 486, 490–494
Profession, characteristics of, 17
Professional accreditation, 33–36
Professional associations, as referral source, 193
Professional career curves, 497
Professional in human resources, 33–34
Professionalization, of human resource management, 17, 19
Professionals, compensation for, 497
Profitability, 56
Profit sharing, 482, 492–493
Program generators, 728
Programmed instruction, 284–285, 295
Progressive disciplinary action, 668
Prohibited bargaining issues, 605
Promotion, 687–688
   and discrimination, 82, 84, 412
   from within, 179–180
Psychological tests, 228–231, 246
Psychomotor abilities tests, 229–230
Public employment agencies, 187
Public Law 84-330, 570
Public Personnel Management, 23
Public sector
   arbitration in, 615
   employee associations in, 571–572
   and Executive Order 10988, 569–570
   labor relations and bargaining patterns in, 571
   and Public Law 84-330, 570
Punishment
   disciplinary action without, 668–670
   as motivation, 315, 318
Pursell, Elliott D., 235n

Quality circles, 327, 328, 329–330
Quality of work life (QWL), 339–340
Quantitative methods, in human resource research, 715–719
Questionnaires, in job analysis, 113–115
Questions, in employment interview, 255–256, 258
Quigley, John L., 12

Race, hiring discrimination based on, 74, 80–81, 213
Rachel, Frank, 414n, 462n, 492n
Rahe, Richard H., 536n, 537n
Railway Labor Act (1926), 561, 563, 565
Ramer, Donald C. Z., 191n, 194n
Rand, James F. 643n, 646n
Randall, John S., 284n
Randle, Yvonne, 12n, 53n

Random variations, 150
Ranking method
   in job evaluation, 445–446
   in performance appraisal, 392–394, 400
Rating scales, in performance appraisal, 392–394
Ratliff, Ronald A., 541n
Realistic job previews, 239
Recognition, as bargaining issue, 608
Recruiters, 187, 189–190
Recruitment, 8, 174–175, 383
   alternatives to, 175–178
   external environment of, 178–179
   external sources of, 181–185
   and human resource research, 707–708
   internal environment of, 179–180
   methods of, 174, 180–181, 185–187, 189–194
   role of legal considerations in, 179
   sources, 174
   under the law, 195–198
Reduced hours, 158
Reed-Mendenhall, Diana, 302n
Reference checks, 240–241
Regression analysis, 152–153, 717–718
Rehabilitation Act (1973), 78, 242
Reinhart, Carlene, 285n
Relatives, employment of, 180, 215
Religion
   guidelines on discrimination due to, 90–91
   hiring discrimination based on, 90–91, 212
Reorientation, 304
Resignation, 682–685
Resistance, reducing, to change, 264
Restricted hiring policies, 158
Results, monitoring, 161–162
Resume databases, 194
Retirement, 688
   early, 158, 688
   planning for, 688–689
Retirement benefits
   employee stock ownership plans, 493–495
   IBM program for, 484–485
   pension plans, 481–482
   profit sharing, 482, 492–493
   Social Security, 441, 478
Retirement education assistance plan, 483, 484
Retirement Equity Act (REACT), 481–482
Reverse discrimination, 82–84, 86
Rewards, as motivation, 315
Reynolds, Peter C., 315n
Rickard, Scott T., 241n
Right-to-work laws, 567, 577, 610
Risher, Howard, 460n
Robertson, David E., 89n
Robertson, I. T., 230n
Robinson, Jerold F., 45n
Robinson, Ronda, 89n
Robotics, 623
Rockwell International Corporation, 373
Role ambiguity, 538
Role conflict, 538
Role playing, 278, 283–284, 295
Romberg, Roberta V., 387n
Ronen, Simcha, 502n
Root, Norman, 529n
Rose, John T., 336n
Rosea, Robert H., 531n
Rosenbaum, Bernard L., 282n
Ross, James F., 232n
Routine reports, 162
Rowland, Kendrith M., 147n, 239n, 245n
Ruch, Floyd L., 226n, 229n

INDEX

Russ, Charles F., Jr., 145n, 147n
Rutherford, Derek, 543n
Ryder, Thomas S., 530n

Saal, Frank E., 341n
Sabo, Monica M., 506n
Sabo, Richard, 320
Sackmann, Sonja, 12n, 53n
Safety, 10, 519
  and human resource research, 709
Safety programs, 521
  accident investigation, 529
  coordination of, 529
  developing, 527–529
  evaluation of, 529–531
  focus of, 521, 525–526
  management support of, 528
  voluntary activity in, 525–526
Safe work environment, in union-free firm, 647
Salary. *See* Compensation
Sales compensation, 497–498
Salsburg, Barbara L., 222n
Sampling, 712
Samuels, Stephen L., 463n
Sanders, Wayne, 634
Sargent, Alice S., 283n
Scanlon, Joseph, 493
Scanlon Plan, 493
Schanie, Charles F., 227n
Schares, Gail, 61n
Schauer, Lyne R., 530n
Schechter, Jack H., 481n
Scheiber, Milton R., 273
Schein, Edgar, 356n
Schmidt, Frank L., 223n, 245n
Schneier, Craig E., 276n, 278n, 283n, 284n, 403n
Schreier, James W., 186n
Schulman, Susan, 298n
Schultz, Duane P., 226n
Schuster, Michael H., 412n
Schwab, Donald P., 387n
Schwartz, Howard M., 314
Scott, William G., 679n
Sea-Land Service, Inc., 406
Sears, 650
Seasonal variations, 150
Secondary boycott, 617
Seeber, Ronald L., 561n, 571n
Sefcik, Joseph T., Jr., 414n
Selection, 8, 208–209, 383
  acceptance of job applicants, 243
  administration of selection tests, 222–223
  background investigation, 241
  cut-off scores, 228
  effect of legal considerations on, 81, 209
  employment interview, 231–232
  environmental factors affecting, 209, 212–218
  hiring criteria to avoid, 212–215
  and human resource research, 707–708
  methods of interviewing, 236–239
  in multinational environment, 245–247
  physical examination, 242
  polygraph tests, 241
  preliminary interview, 218–219
  reference checks, 240–241
  rejection of job applicants, 243–244
  selection decision, 209, 241–242
  types of psychological tests, 228–231
  types of validation studies, 227–228
  and utility analysis, 244–245
Selection ratio, 217
Selection tests
  administration of, 222–223

advantages of, 223
characteristics of properly designed, 224–227
disadvantages of, 223–224
norms on, 225
objectivity of, 224
reliability of, 225–226
standardization of, 224
validity of, 226–227
Self, Stanley A., 447n, 452n
Self-appraisal, 390–391
Self-assessment, 357
Self-employed workers, recruitment of, 185
Seligman, Daniel, 463n, 464n
Selye, Hans, 532n
Senate Select Committee on Improper Activities in the Labor or Management Field, 568
Seniority, 611–612
  and compensation, 455
Senior Professional in human resources
  Generalist, 35–36
  Specialist, 34–35
Sensitivity training, 295, 340–341
Severity rate, 530
Sex discrimination, 82, 83, 91–92, 212
Sexual harassment, 84–85
  interpretative guidelines on, 91–93
Shareholder activism, 51
Shareholders
  and external environment, 50–51
  and multinational corporations, 61
Sharplin, Arthur, 49n, 56n, 147n, 313n
Shaw, Robert J., 327n
Shell Oil Company, 373
Sherman, Jay L., 239n
Sherman Anti-Trust Act, 561
Shevlin, Niel, 650n
Shift differential, 483
Shurden, Mike, 463n, 464n
Sibson, Robert, 496
Sibson & Company, Inc., 495
Sick leave, 10
Sidney, Elizabeth, 413n
Sigrist, Charles J., 177n, 178n
Silverthorne, Colin P., 149n
Simulation, 153, 292
Situational questions, 236
Skills inventory, 155–156
Slaughter, Marsha, 615
Slocum, John W., 324n
Smardon, Raymond A., 615n
Smart, Bradford D., 219n, 240n
Smith, Robert L., 536n
Social needs, as reason for joining union, 577
Social responsibility, 49
Social Security, 478
Social Security Act (1935), 441, 478
Society
  and compensation, 440–441
  and external environment, 49–50
  and multinational corporations, 59–60
Society for Advancement of Management, 456
Society for Human Resource Management, 20
Soder, Dee Ann, 128n
Southland Corporation, 394, 395–399, 486, 487–489
Sovereign, K. L., 673n
Special events, as recruitment method, 190–191
Specialist, 15
Spellman, David J. III, 463n
Split-halves method, 226

Spouse, background of, as hiring standard, 214
Spreadsheet programs, 726
Spruell, Geraldine, 365n
Squibb Corporation, 373
Staffing, in multinational environment, 245–247
Standard hour plan, 491
Standardization, in testing, 409
Standard Oil Company of California, 373
Stanton, Edwin S., 174n
Static stretching, 542
Stereotyping, 196, 256–257
Stessin, Lawrence, 678n
Stevens, George E., 78n, 548n
Stock option plan, 495
Stokely-Van Camp, Inc., 373
Stone, C. Harold, 226n, 229n
Stoops, Rick, 186n
Straight piecework plan, 490
Strategic planning, 147
Strength/weakness balance sheet, 358, 359
Stress, 537
  burnout, 533–535
  coping with, 539–540
  management of, 532–533
  sources of, 536–538
Stress interview, 237
Stress tests, 246
Strictness, in performance appraisal, 406–407
Strikes, 616–617
  in public sector, 570
Structured interview, 235
Subcontracting, 177
Subordinates
  characteristics of, and leadership style, 319
  responsibility of, for performance appraisal, 390
Sullivan, Barbara, 664–665
Sullivan, Frederick L., 85n
Sullivan, John F., 463n, 464n
Summers, Scott L., 147n
Supervisor
  in appraisal interview, 413–414
  in disciplinary actions, 670–672
  training programs for, 286, 288–290, 302, 304
  in union-free firm, 641–643
Supplemental unemployment benefits, 482–483
Supreme Court decisions, on equal employment opportunity, 80–86
Surplus employees, 157–158
Survey feedback, 324–326
  in human resource research, 710–712
Swann, James P. Jr., 679n
Sweeney, Robert, 559, 584
Szabo, Joan C., 482n

Taft-Hartley Act (1947), 566–567, 610, 615, 617, 649–650
Task analysis, 276, 278
Tauber, Mark S., 301n
Taylor, Benjamin J., 560n, 564n, 571n, 615n
Taylor, G. Stephen, 45n
Taylor, Robert L., 392n, 404n
Team building, 327, 329
Teamsters Union, 568, 569, 579
Technology, 623
  and external environment, 53
  and human resource management, 724–728
  impact of, on job design, 131

in multinational environment, 62–63
Telecommuting, 505–506, 727
Teleconferencing, 298, 724–725
Teledyne, Inc., 371, 373
Teletraining, 298
Temporary employees, 47, 177
Termination, 679
  demotion as alternative to, 685
  of executives, 680
  of managers and professionals, 681
  of nonmanagerial/nonprofessional employees, 679–680
Test-retest method of determining selection test reliability, 226
Texas Instruments, 132, 180
T-group, 340
Third country nationals (TCNs), 58, 59
Third-party intervention, in labor negotiations, 614–615
Thomas, Barry W., 493n
Thompson, Julie, 243
Thygerson, Alton L., 526n
Time series analysis, 718–719
Title VII. See Civil Rights Act (1964)
Tornow, Walter, 108, 110, 127n, 707
Townsend, David, 60n, 62n
Traditional career paths, 364
Training group, 340
Training and development, 270
  for entry-level professional employees, 290
  for operative employees, 290–293
  for management, 279–286
  ratings of effectiveness of alternative, 294
  for supervisors, 286, 288–290, 302, 304
Transactional analysis, 336–338
Transcendental meditation (TM), 540
Transfers, 686–687
Trans World Airlines, 371, 373
Tregoe, Benjamin B., 270n
Trowbridge, Alexander B., 11n, 12n, 588n, 623n, 634n, 641n, 652n
Troy, Leo, 571n, 572n, 574n, 650n
Trust, building, 266–267
TRW, Inc., 503
Two-tier wage system, 575–576, 588

Unemployed, recruitment of, 185
Unemployment compensation, 478–479
  supplemental, 482–483
Unemployment rate, 178–179
Uniform Guidelines for Employee Selection Procedures, 88–90, 97
Union(s)
  effect of, on job design, 131–132
  employer attempt to slow growth of, 560
  and external environment, 50
  growth of membership, 561, 566
  and multinational corporations, 60–61
  objectives of, 572–574
  preparation of, for negotiations, 608–609
  reasons for avoiding joining, 634–635, 638
  reasons for joining, 574–578
  and safe workplace, 528
  strategies of, for overcoming negotiation breakdowns, 616–617
  structure of, 578–581
  support of, for health and wellness program, 531

Union activities, reprisals for, 634–635
Union Carbide, 283
Union decertification, 649–651
Union-free organizations
  grievance handling in, 678–679
  policy in, 643–644
  strategies and tactics for remaining, 640–649
Unionism, future of, 588
Unionization, costs and benefits of, 638–640
Unionization attempts
  acceptance of, 638–639
  resistance to, 639–640
Union security, as bargaining issue, 610
Union shop, 610
United Automobile Workers (UAW), 569
United Mine Workers, 566
United States Tobacco Company, 547
U.S. Employment Service, 187
U.S. Postal Service, 571
Universities, recruitment from, 183–184
University of California Regents v. *Bakke*, 83–84
Unsolicited applicants, 194
Unstructured interview, 235
Upper management, management style of, 321
USX, 373
Utility analysis, 244–245
Utilization review, 480

Vacation pay, 479–480
Validation studies, 227–228
Values, of participation, 322–323
Van Maldegiam, Norman E., 192n, 193n
Velleman, Susan J., 505n
Vestibule training, 292
Veterans Administration, U.S., 198
Vickers v. *Veterans Administration*, 78
Vitberg, Alan, 352n
Vocational interest tests, 230–231
Vocational schools, recruitment from, 181, 183
Vogel, David, 51n
Voice mail, 725
Voice recognition, 728
Volvo, A. B., 335
Von Glinow, Mary Ann, 727n

Wade v. *Mississippi Cooperative Extension Service*, 412
Wage curve, 458
Wagel, William H., 727n
Wagner Act (1935), 440, 564–566
Wakefield, J. Alvin, 193n
Walgreen's Drugs, 46
Walker, James W., 356n, 362n, 387n
Wallis, C., 532n
Walsh-Healy Act (1936), 442
Walt Disney Productions, 371, 373
Walters, Claire O., 13n
Wanous, John P., 239n
Wards Cove Packing Co., Inc. v. *Atonio*, 85–86
Washington Post, 650
Washington v. *Davis*, 82
Waterman, Robert, 703
Waterman, Robert H., Jr., 314n
Weber, Austin, 192n
Weber v. *Kaiser Aluminum and Chemical Corporation*, 82–83
Wehrenberg, Stephen, 283n, 324n

Weight and height requirements, and hiring discrimination, 83, 213
Weighted application blank, 219, 222
Weighted checklist performance report, 401
Weiler, Paul C., 586–587, 638
Weiss, Alan, 218n, 236n
Wellbank, Harry L., 367n
Wellness programs, 481, 531–532
  and AIDS training sessions, 548
  alcohol abuse, 543
  burnout, 533–541
  drug abuse, 544–545
  employee assistance, 545–548
  physical fitness, 541–543
  stress management, 532–533
Wells, Ronald G., 401n, 408n
Westinghouse, 283
Wexley, Kenneth, 276n, 278n
Weyerhaeuser, 132
White, Harold C., 647n
Wiegel, Randy, 533n
Williams, Barbara, 56
Williams, Loi Dene, 302n
Williams, Sandra, 5
Winstanley, N. B., 412n
Witney, Fred, 560n, 564n, 571n, 615n
Wohlking, Wallace, 671n
Women. See also Sex discrimination; Sexual harassment
  and child care, 44, 82, 214
  improving recruitment of, 100
  in labor force, 44, 197
  and pregnancy discrimination, 78–79, 213
Woodard, Nina E., 520, 522–523
Woodman, Richard W., 324n
Woolf, Donald Austin, 616n
Word processing, 725–726
Worker requirements questions, 236
Worker's compensation, 479
Work experience requirements, as hiring standard, 214
Working conditions, 538
Work measurement studies, 113
Workplace
  accidents in. See Accidents in workplace
  AIDS in, 548
Work-sample tests, 230
Work standards method of performance appraisal, 400
Wright, Peter, 60n, 62n
Wrist-finger speed, 230
Wynn, William, 565
Wyrtzen, Kay, 546n

Xerox Corporation, 541–542

Yager, Ed, 389n
Yeager, Joseph C., 357n
Yellow-dog contract, 560, 564
Yoder, Dale, 75n, 126n, 296n
Young, Drew M., 316–317, 382n, 383n
Young persons with limited education or skills, in labor force, 48–49

Zawaki, Robert A., 392n, 404n
Zeira, Yoram, 59n
Zenger, John H., 299n
Zero-base forecasting, 150–151
Zimmerman, John W., 270n